Hoosier Faiths

Whiting
Hammond
East Chicago
Gary
Merrillville
Lake
Porter
Valparaiso
Michigan City
LaPorte
LaPorte
Notre Dame
South Bend
St. Joseph
Mishawaka
Elkhart
Goshen
Elkhart
LaGrange
Steuben
Angola
Ligonier
Noble
DeKalb
Donaldson
Marshall
Starke
Kosciusko
Winona Lake
Whitley
Allen
Ft. Wayne
Jasper
Pulaski
Fulton
North Manchester
Newton
Rensselaer
Miami
Wabash
Huntington
Huntington
Wells
Adams
Berne
White
Cass
Logansport
Peru
Carroll
Marion
Grant
Blackford
Upland
Jay
Benton
Warren
Kokomo
Howard
Lafayette
Tippecanoe
Clinton
Tipton
Delaware
Muncie
Randolph
Fountain
Montgomery
Crawfordsville
Boone
Cicero
Madison
Anderson
Chesterfield
Henry
New
Castle
Wayne
Richmond
Parke
Hendricks
Plainfield
Putnam
Greencastle
Marion
Indianapolis
Hancock
Spiceland
Fayette
Union
St. Mary
of the
Woods
Vigo
Terre
Haute
Clay
Owen
White
Morgan
River
Johnson
Franklin
Shelby
Rush
Franklin
Sullivan
Greene
Fork
West
Monroe
Bloomington
Brown
Bartholomew
Columbus
Hope
Decatur
Oldenburg
Ripley
Dearborn
Jennings
Ohio
Rising Sun
Knox
Vincennes
Daviess
Martin
Bedford
Lawrence
Fork
White
Jackson
River
Jefferson
Madison
Scott
Hanover
Switzerland
River
Pike
Dubois
Orange
Paoli
East
Fork
Washington
Salem
Clark
Ohio
Princeton
Oakland City
Gibson
Ferdinand
Crawford
Floyd
New Albany
Harrison
Posey
New Harmony
Vanderburgh
Evansville
Newburgh
Warrick
Spencer
St.Meinrad
Perry
Wabash
River
Ohio
River
Ohio
River

0   20   40
miles

L. C. Rudolph

Hoosier Faiths

A History of
Indiana Churches &
Religious Groups

Indiana University Press   *Bloomington • Indianapolis*

All photographs by Kim Charles Ferrill; Collection
P290; Copyright Indiana Historical Society, 1994.
Map of Indiana by John Hollingsworth.
Preparation and publication of this book were
assisted by a grant from Lilly Endowment, Inc.

The paper used in this publication meets the minimum requirements of
American National Standard for Information Sciences—Permanence of
Paper for Printed Library Materials, ANSI Z39.48-1984.

(∞) ™

Manufactured in the United States of America

Library of Congress Cataloging-in-Publication Data

Rudolph, L. C.
    Hoosier faiths : a history of Indiana's churches and religious
        groups / L. C. Rudolph.
            p.   cm.
        Includes bibliographical references and index.
        ISBN 0-253-32882-9 (alk. paper)
        1. Christian sects—Indiana. 2. Indiana—Church history.
    3. Indiana—Religion. I. Title.
    BR555.I6R83   1995
    280'.09772—dc20   94-43452

        1   2   3   4   5   00   99   98   97   96   95

Contents

This book describes Indiana's major religious groups. The descriptions tell where and how the groups began, more carefully if they are not well known. They include many stories by and about church members.

Readers are likely to come to the book with some appreciation of the state's religious profile. Over two million Hoosiers attend services during a typical week. They gather at some ten thousand locations. According to expert estimate, they contributed over two billion dollars to religious causes in a recent year.[1]

Many readers are probably aware of some of the more obvious landmarks of Indiana's religion, perhaps (1) that Catholics have internationally recognized centers at such places as Notre Dame, Saint Meinrad, Ferdinand, Saint Mary of the Woods, and Oldenburg; (2) that Northern Indiana has Mennonites, Amish, and bearded sorts of Brethren; (3) that twenty-nine of the state's colleges have past or continuing links to churches; (4) that most of the state's 823 private elementary and secondary schools are operated by churches and that churches are the largest providers of day care centers for children; (5) that there were important religious dimensions to the communal experiments now memorialized at New Harmony.[2]

Readers will have recognized the familiar church buildings typical of the 4,644 "mainline" congregations of the Catholics, Methodists, Christians, Baptists, Lutherans, Presbyterians, United Church of Christ, and Episcopalians widely established across the state. They will also have seen about the same number of newer buildings typical of a younger echelon of churches. This book is intended to offer them an enriched understanding of both.[3]

Each major group has a section. There is no intention to make these essays either equal in length or in direct proportion to the size of the group's membership. Narratives end as a conversation or lecture might, when the basic identity of the group seems to be established and when some of its characteristic stories have been told. Many especially interesting groups are not in the book. Indiana has lively practitioners of Baha'ism, Buddhism, Hare Krishna, Scientology, Transcendental Meditation, the Unification Movement, Unity, and The Way. The communities of Swami Chetananada (Rudrananda Ashram in Bloomington) and Doug Easterday (Daystar Christian Ministry at Martinsville) grew strong in Indiana before moving away. Padanaram in Martin County is a very substantial enterprise which embodies the communal vision of Daniel Wright. There was not enough time or room to do them justice.

Readers who approach the book by subject or by religious group name should be sure to use the index as well as the table of contents. Alexander Campbell will be featured in the pages on Christians but he will also be found debating Robert Owen in the pages on New Harmony. An alert scholar considering the impact of Methodism on the religious life of the state will want to remember how the Methodist emphasis on perfect holiness affected Wesleyans, Free Methodists, Nazarenes, and many Pentecostals. A student of Catholicism should note the prominence of that church in the discussions of ethnic minorities and of charismatic movements.

This project and book grew out of an interest of Dr. Grover L. Hartman and his colleagues in the Indiana Religious History Association. It was initiated by Dr. Robert W. Lynn and his colleagues at Lilly Endowment. At their joint suggestion I undertook the task.

Since a substantial literature search was essential, I suggested production of a bibliography as a first step. That bibliography was separately published as *Religion in Indiana* by L. C. Rudolph and Judith E. Endelman (Indiana University Press, 1986, 232 p.). Persons who wish to write a history of an Indiana church or to search out publications or archival materials on religion in Indiana for any reason are likely to find it a useful place to begin. Descriptions and pictures of many of Indiana's historic churches appear in *Where God's People Meet* by Joseph M. White.

Dozens of librarians and historians have helped in this work. They have contributed beyond any reasonable expectation. They have supplied me with the best of their historical resources without drowning me in the mass of them. They have read my manuscript drafts and redrafts. I am very deeply grateful to them all.

Preface

NOTES

1. An estimate of 10,000 locations for Indiana church services seems safely conservative. Eighty-nine church bodies responding to *Churches and Church Membership in the United States 1990* (Atlanta, Ga.: Glenmary Research Center, 1992, 456 p.) reported a total of 7,134 churches in Indiana. That total omits some very substantial non-reporting Indiana communions such as the African Methodist Episcopal Church, the Church of God in Christ, the Jehovah's Witnesses, the National Baptist Conventions, and the United Pentecostal Church. It also omits many smaller non-reporting denominations and the very large number of independent and unaffiliated congregations that appear only in the directories of local newspapers or function with no public registry whatever.

The estimate of an average weekly attendance of two million seems conservative as well. Gallup polls report that weekly church attendance has remained at a constant 40 to 42 percent of the national population between 1969 and 1987. See *Presbyterian Outlook* (21 March 1988): 5, citing *Emerging Trends* for January 1988. National Science Foundation researchers conducted their "Middletown III" survey in Muncie in 1978. Of their adult respondents 33 percent of women and 28 percent of men said they were regular attenders of religious services (four times a month or more); 10 percent of women and 8 percent of men said they were intermittent attenders (one to three times a month); 35 percent of women and 35 percent of men said they were occasional attenders (less often than once a month). Twenty-two percent of women and 29 percent of men said they never attended. See Theodore Caplow et al., *All Faithful People: Change and Continuity in Middletown's Religion* (Minneapolis, Minn.: University of Minnesota Press, 1983), 73, 75, 306–7.

The estimate of contributions is based on a survey of Hoosiers over age eighteen conducted for the Indiana Donor's Alliance by the Public Opinion Laboratory of Indiana University–Purdue University at Indianapolis in March of 1988. Approximately two-thirds of its respondents stated that they attended church either "once or twice a month" or "nearly every week." The poll indicated that "Hoosiers gave about $2,200,000,000 last year to religious organizations and about $300,000,000 to other groups they viewed as worthy of their support." See "The Baseline of Voluntarism and Giving in Indiana: Report of a Telephone Survey of a Sample of Residents Prepared for the Indiana Donor's Alliance," Brian Vargus and Jennie Lengacher, principal investigators, with the assistance of Holly Duke (Indianapolis, Ind.: The Public Opinion Laboratory, Indiana University–Purdue University, Indianapolis, September 1988, 50 p.).

2. The twenty-nine colleges in order of their founding are Hanover (Presbyterian), Wabash (Presbyterian), Franklin (Baptist), Notre Dame (Catholic), DePauw (Methodist), Saint Mary of the Woods (Catholic), Saint Mary (Catholic), Taylor (Methodist), Earlham (Friends), University of Evansville (Methodist), Butler (Christian), Valparaiso (Lutheran), Saint Meinrad (Catholic), Oakland City (General Baptist), Saint Joseph (Catholic), Manchester (Brethren), Saint Francis (Catholic), Goshen (Mennonite), Huntington (United Brethren), University of Indianapolis (Methodist), Summit Christian (Missionary), Anderson (Church of God), Indiana Wesleyan (Wesleyan), Marian (Catholic), Grace (Grace Brethren), Ancilla (Catholic), Bethel (Missionary), Calumet (Catholic), Holy Cross (Catholic). A great many other colleges were founded by churches but have left no continuing institution.

3. The number 4,644 is a calculation from *Churches and Church Membership in the United States 1990*, 18–19, for the eight denominations named. To illustrate the diversity in the immediate vicinity of one small city, the church directory of the Bloomington *Herald-Times* for 24 June 1989 listed ninety-four congregations within these eight denominations but ninety-two congregations outside them, at least fifty of the latter estimated to be pentecostal in practice.

Glaciers shaped the land that would become Indiana. They left level and fertile soil in the north. Their meltwater sculptured the south into less fertile hills and valleys. Almost all of Indiana's 36,291 square miles were covered with great hardwood trees, with bushy undergrowth, and all too often with water.

Prehistoric peoples, including builders of huge earthen mounds for social and religious functions, seem to have left the area before 1600. Later Indian groups immigrated—Miamis who moved southeast from Wisconsin and Illinois into northeastern Indiana in the 1600s; Potawatomis who were pushed westward from the Lake Huron area in the early 1700s; Delawares who became a force in Indiana about the middle of the 1700s; Wea, Piankeshaw, and Shawnee groups variously linked to these larger tribes. Their religion was a rich blend of accommodation to spirit forces perceived in every part of the universe. The Indians were overrun by Europeans and the impact of their religion on Indiana was largely lost.

France and Britain contended for empire in the western world, in North America, and so in Indiana. In the early 1700s Catholic missionaries were in this "New France" accompanying French explorers. They established congregations of Indian converts and ministered to clusters of French families at trading posts later to be named Lafayette, Fort Wayne, and Vincennes. Their missionary enterprise was crippled and very nearly destroyed when French power in North America was broken by defeat in the French and Indian War in 1763 and when the mission-minded Jesuit order was suppressed in France in 1764. French contributions of leadership and support to Catholicism in Indiana were destined to become very great indeed but had to be delayed for a time until they could be directed through American Catholic channels beginning in the 1800s.

Indiana was crucially shaped by decisions of the British colonies on America's eastern seaboard and the entity called the United States into which they combined in 1787. The original colonies gave up their chartered claims to western lands in return for a promise of the nation that those lands would be allowed to become new and equal states. Possession of western lands was very exciting and unifying for the infant republic. Decisions about oversight and development of those western lands remained high on the national agenda. Midwestern settlers became champions of the American union which they counted as their own.

Indiana's religious heritage from the new United States was infinite variety. That variety was the most obvious characteristic of religion in the developing nation. It rep-resented radical change. The arrangement long traditional among European peoples was one established church cooperating with the government to be responsible for ministering to all the people within a country or territory. The admission that Catholics, Lutherans, Reformed, and Church of England should be allowed to exist at the same time, even in carefully separated territories, had come after great suffering and loss of life in the 1600s. The notion that two or more religious loyalties could be tolerated side by side, intermingled, legal everywhere within the same governmental unit, was nearly inconceivable. Only some radical free church groups, later called "left-wing," claimed that such unrestricted belief and expression should be their right wherever they were. These were voluntary groups without much status or power.

Religion in America was territorial too at first. There were colonies with churches of England of the congregational type established over large areas in New England, and colonies with churches of England of the episcopal type established over large areas of the South. No other religions were officially tolerated there. But in America the European system of territorial regulation of religion simply broke down. There were too many religions, too many governmental units, too many free church advocates, and too many bidders for competent settlers whatever their faith, to maintain any official assortment by religion. No church establishment was written into the new national constitution. On the contrary, when the Bill of Rights was added to the Constitution in 1791, the First Amendment said "Congress shall make no law respecting an establishment of religion, or prohibiting the free exercise thereof."

Religious liberty and pluralism now had a base in national law but the full product of that decision came slowly. There were still the state laws by which certain churches were officially privileged and there were pat-

Introduction

terns of local custom and settlement which modified slowly. Life in an older colony dominated by one religious persuasion might go on for a long time much as before. However, European state churches in America kept separating themselves from European control. Free churches were rejoicing and multiplying. Reluctantly or not, all moved toward a new and technically equivalent status as "denominations." In such a western territory as Indiana, recipient of settlers across the whole range of religious belief and practice, there was no religious unity from the beginning and denominations had no restraints. Side by side they sought voluntary members sufficiently loyal to commit time and money to each group's support. They could not count on isolation or dominance. They had to adjust to the strenuous demands of a new environment and to each other.

It was citizens and prospective citizens of the United States who were poised to pour into the Ohio Valley as soon after the American Revolution as the power of the British and the Indians could be reduced. They seemed to come from everywhere. One could find population clusters from Europe, from New England, and from the Middle Colonies, especially Pennsylvania. But most of all they entered Indiana in the early years from Kentucky, Tennessee, Virginia, and North Carolina. Even if they came from Ohio, they were likely to have made a stop there on their way from the South.

The new shape of American religion was denominationalism. That was what hit Indiana—denominations engaged in flat-out, wide-open competition. All vestiges of unity or of orderly assignment of religious territories on the pattern of Europe or of the seaboard colonies had passed away. The older religious groups appeared on Indiana soil. The founding of new ones seemed a natural expression of religious liberty. Denominational disciplines and techniques already tested on the frontiers of Pennsylvania, Ohio, or Kentucky were now aimed broadside at frontier Indiana. Local congregations were commonly overseen by lay officers (elders, deacons, class leaders, stewards) and served periodically by itinerant preachers.

For all denominations the booming population was a challenge. In the early decades of the 1800s Indiana's birth rate ranked among the highest in the world. Immigrants kept pouring in. For much of the first fifty years most members of this new population lived in widely separated neighborhoods in the woods. Their trips to trading centers or to revival grounds were seasonal, they were difficult, and they were infrequent. Preachers who hoped to enlist and serve these people must travel to meet them in their thousands of neighborhoods and preach to them in

their groves, cabins, or log meetinghouses. There were few formally ordained clergy to do this. Missionary agencies from outside could send only a handful of workers when there was work for hundreds. In a time of scattered population served by few roads and fewer bridges, the traveling preacher moving among the neighborhoods became a heroic figure. Young men with native ability but little formal education aspired to the role. Following their conversion in a revival they often felt called to preach and put their gifts to test at once among their friends. From such motivated volunteers out of their own ranks, Indiana's major Protestant churches—Methodists, Baptists, Christians, United Brethren—raised up their corps of ministers. Some of them accomplished real miracles of self-education to make themselves into pastors, educators, editors, and expert revivalists.

Yale president and church historian Ezra Stiles had surveyed the colonial scene in 1783 and said he thought the future of Christianity in America would lie about equally with Congregationalists, Presbyterians, and Episcopalians. His prediction was wrong. By 1850 it was the Methodists and Baptists who had surged into the nation's religious leadership. Fresh immigrations from the European continent were nourishing increased congregations of Catholics, Lutherans, and Jews. The Christians and Mormons, denominations not even formed in the days of Ezra Stiles, had taken their places among America's top ten.

Indiana's religious heritage from the new United States included an eagerness to discover and reproduce biblical religious models. Thomas Jefferson said "As to tradition, if we are Protestants we reject all tradition, and rely on the scripture alone, for that is the essence and common principle of all the Protestant churches." That was increasingly the position of the American denominations. Each chose to or was forced to focus less on history and tradition and more on appeal to the Scriptures. Each sought to justify its own interpretations and practices as more closely conforming to those of the early church as pictured in the New Testament than those of its rivals. The left-wing free churches especially sought a source of unquestioned authority to undercut any claims of Catholics or right-wing Protestants to priority over them. They found it in the Bible, long affirmed by Christians as the Word of God. Disallowing every other authority by asserting "no creed but the Bible," they evaluated every religious manifestation in terms of their own reconstruction of the primitive church. Catholics, Lutherans, Episcopalians, Congregationalists, Presbyterians, Baptists, Quakers, and Methodists were forced to enter argument on these terms whether they liked it or not, especially if they expected to be heard beyond the enclaves of their own kind. All this was further reinforced by the sense of beginning again in a new land, the very place to cast off all earlier accretions and restore the church in its New Testament purity. Each denomination built its American model on its perceptions of the primitive church, somewhat conditioned both by past history and fascinations of the moment, and advanced it as a blueprint plain in the Word of God.

Indiana's religious heritage from the new United States also included evangelism by revivals. At least since the days of Jonathan Edwards, Gilbert Tennent, and George Whitefield in the American colonies during the first half of the 1700s, revivals were being described and expected. Revivals were times of religious fervor when an unusual number of conversions took place. Conversions were specific occasions of reorientation in which persons were moved on the basis of direct personal experience to know and confess Jesus Christ as their Savior from sin and Lord of their lives. Revivals which were once regarded as miraculous and unpredictable outpourings of God's grace became cultivated, then scheduled, and then nearly routinized. Faced with a national population as much as 90 percent unchurched, most of the voluntary churches found revivalism a useful tool for attracting and evangelizing the population. The most able preacher evangelists filled their schedules with big meetings. Revivalism entered the very character of the denominations. It reduced theological issues to simple chains of texts. It reduced religious decisions to choices between sharp and contrasting alternatives demanding immediate action. Revivalism established a pattern of common worship which made each Sunday service, each church meeting, even each funeral an occasion for evangelistic preaching and appeal for decision. Kentucky, Tennessee, and most of the rural South experienced the "Great Revival" between 1800 and 1805, just as Indiana was beginning to draw its first wave of white settlement from that region. From the beginning "revival" and "big meeting" were well used words in the Hoosier religious vocabulary. They were pivotal events in many a Hoosier religious biography.

The work of Indiana's early preachers included study, frequent preaching, education of members at many levels, supervision of congregations, celebration of sacraments, sick and family visitation, conduct of weddings and funerals, and leadership in community events. Churches were expected to be moral forces in their communities because of their ecclesiastical procedures against moral offenders and even more because of their persistent standard raising through word and practice. Frontier life could be crude and violent. Whiskey was a kind of omnipresent currency. On the Ohio in 1824 it cost twelve and one-half cents for a gallon which could get a dozen men drunk. Energetic young people made up a majority of the population. At any gathering—muster, dance, election, shooting match, race, revival—their enthusiastic interaction might degenerate into brawling. Town planners, even some less than pious ones, often supported church organization to make their place more attractive to sober settlers and so give it stability.

Even though they were nearly all Christians and engaged in a similar ministry, Indiana's religious leaders of the nineteenth century had to be prepared to argue their denomination's positions. They spent much time and energy defending their differences against their competitors, differences over baptism or church government or missionary method or worship practice. Each group was sure it was right and should prevail. Publishers issued at least thirty books which were transcriptions of religious debates involving Indiana participants. These were debates of the kind that extended over several days and produced thick volumes designed for public instruction and oratorical ammunition. Hundreds of such debates were conducted without being published and untold thousands of sermons devoted to one point or another of denominational teaching. Religious activity in Indiana was frequently conducted as a contest, recorded as a contest, and written into history as a contest. Each group deplored the denominational bickering of all the others; nobody liked the noise unless he was making it. This lively combination of oratorical scrapping and revival was ideally suited to catch the attention of Hoosiers. Generations were thus motivated to study the Bible and to focus their wits on religious subjects. The drive to survive or to dominate became energy for evangelism. Earnest dialogue and heated exchange were efficient tools for teaching. The character of the state and its people was shaped in the process.

The growth in church membership was remarkable. By 1906 the state population had multiplied to an estimated 2,710,898. The churches had grown even faster. Their membership of 938,405 was equal to more than 34 percent of the state's increased population. New immigration and ethnic patterns were plain. Catholics, with 205,705 members, were almost as numerous as Methodists. Missouri Synod Lutherans, with 34,105, were the state's seventh largest denomination.

Significant changes were under way among Protestants. Evangelism of the rural frontier had established thousands of churches under control of conservative lay officers fond of their own local traditions. By the latter half of the 1800s many of these congregations, especially those which had become town or city churches, were confronting their officers with a series of revolutionary proposals. People wanted such things as (1) Sunday schools with a semi-independent structure of officers linked to regional and state conventions and heavily scheduled with occasions for celebration; (2) church extension or home mission programs, often linked with Sunday school expansion and promoted by a paid executive; (3) women's organizations led by their own female officers and engaged in support of mission enterprises foreign and domestic outside control of the local officers; (4) youth organizations and camps operated under their own officers and sponsors; (5) musical instruments and musical organizations in the churches; (6) colleges and seminaries to train leadership including paid professional ministers. Most of these proposals were resisted at first and then slowly adopted. People became enthusiastic about these new programs and kept the churches growing.

Adaptation to Indiana's new maturity brought the churches health and prosperity. Adaptation also caused concern. Churches which welcomed change were often the ones to forego emotional religious experience including datable conversions, to abandon old revival practices including camp meetings, and to cease pursuit of the experience of a second blessing of perfect holiness. They were less strict about rules on dress and drinking and dancing. They were more hospitable to the insights of evolutionary science and of biblical criticism. They were less inclined to debate about doctrines and more inclined to interchurch cooperation. They were sometimes rich and certainly looked comfortable in the midst of the rising urban world.

A cohort of reformers arose who did not want the church so comfortable with the world. They said adaptation could be dangerous innovation. Indiana's denominational variety was thus further enriched as these reformers formed new fellowships for preserving old ways, fellowships such as Wesleyans, Free Methodists, Church of God, Christian and Missionary Alliance, Nazarenes, and Churches of Christ. Pentecostals added a new dimension to the old ways by encouraging each prospective member to seek a personal infilling with the Holy Spirit and to speak in tongues. Independent congregations announced their conservative position by describing themselves as "old-fashioned" or "Bible-believing" or "fundamental." Congregations of these younger churches on

the town perimeters grew even more vigorously than their older siblings in the town centers. Several built their national headquarters in Indiana at Marion (Wesleyans), Winona Lake (Free Methodists and Grace Brethren), Anderson (Church of God), Fort Wayne (Missionary Church), Huntington (United Brethren), and Indianapolis (Pentecostal Assemblies of the World).

Indiana's larger cities provided many instances of religious vitality. Revivalists conducted city campaigns. Persons moving from rural churches transferred their energy to city churches. Concentrations of wealth and population were bases of support for large congregations impressively housed and equipped. Religious institutions and foundations arose. The urban poor found their churches to be not only places for worship and study but also their own centers for racial or ethnic identity and for united efforts in support of social justice. The homeless and destitute knocked at the doors of church agencies and found help. Yet Christianity, reared in the cities of the ancient world, accommodated less well to Indiana's cities. Pioneer neighborhoods in the Hoosier woods, some so poor that they were little more than scattered slums, had been evangelized in the nineteenth century by circuit riders recruited from revival converts and from Sunday schools. Twentieth century urban concentrations seemed more forbidding. Church agencies ministered there but with less optimism and less evidence of progress. When the researchers of Indiana University–Purdue University at Indianapolis reviewed the data from their telephone survey in March of 1988, the thing which struck them first was that the rate of church attendance was very significantly lower in Indiana's ten most populous counties.

Religion in Indiana is not easy to quantify. Membership and attendance figures are imprecise. Now familiar estimates of pioneer membership as low as 10 percent of the population may fail to take into account the tendency of one enrolled adult member to represent the affiliation of a large family or the general mindset of the pioneer population in favor of evangelical Protestantism which gave the revivals their opportunity. No national religious census has been taken since 1936. Later statistics have been gathered by councils of churches but these reports are also inexact and the reporting categories hardly comparable. Several denominations and almost all independent congregations will not report their data to a council of churches. National polls for the most recent years have indicated consistently that nearly 70 percent of Americans are members of churches or synagogues and about 40 percent of Americans attend church or synagogue in a typical week.

The real impact of religion in Indiana is even more difficult to weigh. Negative evaluators may maintain that nothing of importance occurs in the churches or as a result of the teaching done there. If 93 percent of respondents tell Gallup they believe in God or a universal spirit, that is not necessarily a significant declaration. Some evaluators grant that religion has instrumental impact wherever they can document and measure some direct effect of it on politics, economics, esthetics, intellectual life, or social behavior. Active participants in religious life are likely to agree that faith has important consequences in such areas. But they usually go on to affirm that their religious faith does not find its true nature or full value in being instrumental to something else. It deals with ultimate concerns and eternal effects quite beyond the scale of ordinary measurement.[1]

NOTES

1. This introduction includes themes developed by Sidney E. Mead in "Denominationalism: The Shape of Protestantism in America," *Church History* 24 (December 1954): 291–320; the Stiles citation is from p. 294 and the Jefferson quotation from p. 293. The ideal of restoration of the primitive church is further treated in a collection of essays entitled *The American Quest for the Primitive Church* (Urbana, Ill.: University of Illinois Press, 1988, 257 p.) and in *Illusions of Innocence: Protestant Primitivism in America, 1630–1875* by Richard T. Hughes and C. Leonard Allen (Chicago: University of Chicago Press, 1988, 296 p.). The price and potency of whiskey on the Ohio in 1824 is cited from p. 61 of the *Diary of William Owen, from November 10, 1824, to April 20, 1825*, ed. Joel Hiatt (Indianapolis, Ind.: Bobbs-Merrill, 1906, 134 p.).

Hoosier Faiths

INDIANS

At least thirteen thousand years ago descendants of Asian peoples moved across a land bridge from Siberia to the Americas. As they migrated south and east they developed hundreds of additional tribes or bands, languages, cultures, and religious outlooks. These "Indians" related the cycles of their lives to the vast natural resources; their religious practices were linked in part to their union with the rhythms of nature and the movements of wild game. There were sanctioned procedures for those being born, coming of age, marrying, seeking healing, mourning, or dying. They often made war and made peace among themselves; their religions offered rituals and symbols to reinforce their conflicts and their friendships. Particular persons and events so shaped tribal history that they entered the sacred memory and practice of the peoples.[1]

Prehistoric inhabitants of Indiana may have hunted large animals now extinct—bison, mammoth, mastodon. Along the Ohio, Wabash, and White rivers they found freshwater mussels a reliable source of food, building up deep mounds of the emptied shells spread over several acres. On these well-drained elevations they made encampments. Among the shells they left some remains of plants and animals, some artifacts of their own manufacture, and some burial sites of their dead. Other camps and burial sites less well marked than the shell middens left similar identifiable remains—interred bones of persons and dogs, bone and stone tools, pipes, fire-marked clay or rock or wood. Artifacts were buried with some of the dead, artifacts so varied in nature and number that no religious pattern has been clearly inferred.[2]

Mound Builders

Between 1000 B.C. and A.D. 1500 some Indian people in Indiana built large earthen mounds, by far the most dramatic manifestations of the state's prehistoric culture. There were hundreds of these earthworks; a survey in 1873 indicated over two hundred in Knox County alone and twelve within the city limits of Vincennes. These mounds have been the basis of many false tales suggesting they were evidence of the existence in Indiana of some exotic old-world culture, perhaps derived from Atlantis or the Egyptians or the Lost Tribes of Israel or ancient astronauts.[3]

These mounds have also been the focus of scientific investigations. With the encouragement and support of Eli Lilly, president of Indiana Historical Society, Angel Mounds site was brought under state ownership and protection. It was so designated because a family named Angel once owned the land. With an interpretive center and with reconstruction of houses, stockade, and temple it became Angel Mounds State Memorial located on the Ohio River a few miles east of Evansville. Here was a three-terraced, flat-topped mound about 650 feet by 300 feet and 44 feet high; there were smaller mounds as well. Investigation revealed that from about A.D. 1200 to about A.D. 1500 Angel site had an established community life of considerable sophistication for at least one thousand persons—log stockade, substantial houses, plaza, crop cultivation, satellite settlements, social stratification. One mound seemed clearly related to religious functions. While no historical documents existed for this Indiana community, there were instructive parallels between the structure at Angel site and those of kindred mound building cultures in the South which did persist long enough to be described by European explorers. These descriptions spoke of a rectangular temple built on a mound, facing east, inhabited by effigies and particularly by one important human effigy or idol, devoted to sun worship and to vigils and rituals honoring the remains of revered persons such as chiefs.[4]

Bodies were buried in some of Indiana's mounds along with artifacts of varied rarity. This practice seemed to indicate a socially defined population, a funeral ceremonialism, and a concept of preparation for an afterlife. But Indiana's mounds were not only burial places. Some of these ambitious constructions seemed to have been designed for religious ceremonies related to astronomical events. Complex earthworks corresponded to complex astronomical alignments even more detailed than the basic ones marking the positions of the sun at the time of the summer and winter solstices.[5]

Indiana Tribes

European explorers and settlers in Indiana saw no mound builders. These were gone from Indiana before 1600. The Indians known to European explorers had migrated to the area much later; no link has been established between them and the prehistoric peoples. The Miamis moved from Wisconsin and Illinois into Indiana late in the 1600s. Some of their associates were known as the Piankashaw, Wea, Eel River, and Mississinewa tribes.[6] The Potawatomis were pressing into Indiana from the Lake Huron area beginning in the early 1700s; the Miamis were able to stop the advancing Potawatomis and hold them north of the Eel River.[7]

So the Potawatomis became the primary tribe in extreme northern Indiana while the Miamis predominated in central and southern areas. The Delaware tribes were under pressure from advancing white settlers in Pennsylvania and Ohio. The Miamis allowed the Delawares to move westward into east-central Indiana by 1770, particularly on the upper waters of the West Fork of White River. The Shawnees who had earlier lived in the South were often associated with the Delawares. In Indiana the Delawares welcomed the Shawnees to live among them

once more.[8] In spite of this seeming congestion, all of the tribes taken together probably had fewer than ten thousand members in Indiana. They cultivated corn, beans, peas, melons, pumpkins, squash, and tobacco. These they augmented with wild fruit, nuts, edible wild plants, and especially fish and wild game.[9]

Impact of Europeans

All these Indian people arriving in Indiana had already been impacted by Europeans. Soldiers, traders, and government agents usually preceded and always outnumbered the missionaries. The driving force was trade. As soon as the white traders introduced guns and ammunition, all the tribes must have these from the traders in order to survive. Indian populations were small and declining but revenge was important; inter-tribal raiding, war, and violence were common. As soon as the white traders offered metal tools, metal utensils, woven cloth, and prized trinkets, the native crafts began to fade. From then on the tune was called by the dominant white culture, enforced by the power of the white armies and the Indian dependence on treaty annuities.[10]

What the white traders wanted were Indian hunters and trappers who would harvest animal pelts and these in such copious quantities that endless extension of trapping and hunting territories was required. What the white government agents wanted were Indian warriors who would make alliances and become troops in the wars to determine political control of the region. Even after fur had lost much of its value, Indians were courted to be fighters. Indians allied with the French against the British and lost. They allied with the British against the Americans and lost. When the French gave up their claim to Indiana in 1763 and the British conceded defeat in 1783 and 1815, the Indians were not parties to those treaties. No agents were authorized to act for the whole population of them. The Miamis were the best organized with a principal chief and with an annual grand council of chiefs at Kekionga (later Fort Wayne). But no chief had authority to act in a way that would bind all the members of even one tribe or band. In the view of Europeans the territory now really belonged to the government of the white Americans and its citizens. To American settlers the land itself appeared largely unused and so was vacant to be occupied.

The religion of the Indians was also impacted by Europeans. That religion was as decentralized and as varied as Indian life and government. All the Indians of Indiana were members of the Algonquian language group, but they spoke several tongues and required interpreters for intertribal councils. Descriptions of their religions were generally written long after tribes had been exposed to borrowings from each other and from European cultures. They often spoke of one or more superior spirit persons or powers who were creators and caretakers of the people. All living things, plant and animal, were considered as beings and agents of divinity having supernatural powers. Dreams or visions or trances cultivated by extreme stimulation or privation or exhaustion were occasions for messages from such supernatural beings (a Bear, a Wolf, a Tree, an Old Man), messages with overt direction for future conduct. Great spirits and their subordinate agents warranted prayers of gratitude or supplication by Indian individuals and groups if there were to be good crops and successful hunts. There was often a superior evil spirit as well, accompanied by a host of evil spirits bringing unhappiness and misfortune to the people and continuing to afflict the wicked after death. Ghosts of the deceased made visitations on the living, especially at night. Propitiation of all the spirits was a continuing concern, tobacco being a customary offering. Each living person and each band or tribe had some level of spiritual power, often focused or symbolized in an object or collection of objects related to accounts of their origins or of their personal mystic experiences. Some persons exhibited so much spiritual power that they functioned as local shamans to help fellow tribe members to order their religious practice or as healers and prophets of even wider reputation. Evil power might also be concentrated in some persons who were recognized as witches deserving death.[11]

There was a dynamic growth and flexibility in Indian religion everywhere, not least in the hands of Algonquian language orators and story tellers. Thus a Shawnee chief at Fort Wayne in 1803 easily incorporated the Europeans in his account of creation. The Master of Life first made the Shawnee from his brain and all other Indian peoples descended from the Shawnee, he said. Then the French and English were created from the Master's breast, the Dutch from his feet, and the Americans from his hands. These latter inferior creations were made white and placed beyond the "stinking lake" which was the Atlantic. Two years later the creation of the Americans appeared in the account of the Shawnee prophet Tenskwatawa as a growth "from the scum of the great Water when it was troubled by the Evil Spirit," a froth "driven into the Woods by a strong east wind."[12]

Trade for European technology soon ruined the Indian economy. American government officials made Fort Wayne the official center of Indian trade for the Ohio Valley in 1802 and consolidated their predominance over the British traders during the next decade. By then the beaver, so useful in trade with the French and the British, were nearly extinct. The heavy concentrations of mink and muskrat were far to the north. Some deer hides were available to trade with the Americans but the main fur in trade at the Fort Wayne agency was the more lowly raccoon. White hunters and squatters as well as Indian commercial hunters and trappers were destroying the wild game at such a rate that Indians found little to eat or to trade. Indians now needed European goods to survive and desired even more than they needed.[13]

Exploitation of the Indian weakness for alcohol, a problem since the importation of British rum, now created a devastating appetite and disease as traders dealt in American corn whiskey. Many Indians would travel great distances to find whiskey; they would sell, exchange, or promise anything to get it.[14] The Indians wanted goods and credit. The government of the United States would give goods, credit, and annuities for large cessions of land. So the Indians sold the land. Gradually they shifted the focus of their economy to the places where the government land payments and annuities were delivered and divided—Fort Wayne, Logansport, Vincennes. This dependency was a depressing sight. William Henry Harrison, governor of Indiana Territory with headquarters at Vincennes, said in summer of 1801 that he could tell at a glance whether an Indian belonged to a distant tribe or to a tribe near Vincennes. The distant ones were "well Clothed healthy and vigorous" while local ones were "half naked, filthy and enfeebled with Intoxication."

> I have had much difficulty with the small tribes in this immediate Neighbourhood—viz.—the Peankashaws, Weas & Eel river Indians, these three tribes form a body of the greatest Scoundrels in the world—they are dayly in this town in considerable numbers and are frequently intoxicated to the number of thirty or forty at once—they then commit the greatest disorders—drawing their knives and stabing every one they meet with—breaking open the Houses of the Citizens killing their Hogs and cattle and breaking down their fences. But in all their frolicks they generally suffer most severely themselves they kill each other without mercy.[15]

Baptist preacher Isaac McCoy moved to the Vincennes area in 1803 and served for a while as the town's jailor.

> McCoy's sympathy for the Indians was apparently the result of his almost daily witness of their degradation and sufferings as they were encamped about the post of Vincennes. Bullied by the whites and victimized by their own craving for alcoholic liquors, the natives were an easy prey for the motley group of shopkeepers and

traders of the town. The Indians who visited the fort were systematically stripped of their annuities, their furs, and even their weapons and clothing, being left in a pitiable and helpless condition. It was the miserable friendlessness of the natives that prompted McCoy's proposal to undertake missionary work among them.[16]

"Civilizing" the Indians

White Americans who cared about preserving the Indians knew that the old bases for Indian life were fast being removed by white trade and encroachment. Most of them wished that the Indians would become like respectable white citizens so that one farm would be enough land to support an Indian family and produce some surplus with which to trade. An Indian's best hope, as they saw it, was to become a sober farmer and a Christian. George Washington and his secretary of war Henry Knox wanted "to introduce among the Indian tribes a love for exclusive property" and "to send missionaries with implements of husbandry."[17] Thomas Jefferson offered the same kind of advice to William Henry Harrison, pioneer governor of Indiana Territory.

> Our system is to live in perpetual peace with the Indians, to cultivate an affectionate attachment from them, by every thing just & liberal which we can [do] for them within the bounds of reason, and by giving them effectual protection against wrongs from our own people. The decrease of game rendering their subsistence by hunting insufficient, we wish to draw them to agriculture, to spinning & weaving . . . When they withdraw themselves to the culture of a small piece of land, they will percieve how useless to them are their extensive forests, and will be willing to pare them off from time to time in exchange for necessaries for their farms & families . . . They will in time either incorporate with us as citizens of the US. or remove beyond the Mississippi. The former is certainly the termination of their history most happy for themselves.[18]

The government's trading house established for the Ohio Valley trade at Fort Wayne in 1802 was soon offering the Indians "spelling books, Bibles, corn mills, plowshares, garden seeds, and other items reflective of plans to 'civilize' the natives." Jefferson's policy had a hard edge; Indian leaders who resisted civilization could be allowed to go heavily into debt at the trading post and so be motivated to sell out and move west.[19]

William Henry Harrison certainly could be no easy optimist about peaceful integration of Indian and white populations or even of the Indian populations with each other. His proclamation on 9 May 1801 forbade whites to settle, hunt, or survey on Indian lands but the boundary lines were not run or marked so he had little success. His three proclamations between 1801 and 1803 restricted and finally forbade whiskey selling to Indians; these proclamations also had limited effect. He told the secretary of war in July of 1801 that there were perhaps six hundred Indian warriors on the Wabash and six thousand gallons of whiskey was being supplied to them annually. He himself plied the Indians with whiskey when it suited his purpose. He said it was "too evident that a great many of the Inhabitants of the Fronteers consider the murdering of Indians in the highest degree meritorious."[20]

He thought the real owners of the land being ceded by the Treaty of Fort Wayne in 1809 were the Miamis and the Weas, but said he went well beyond what he considered mere justice to make the Delawares, Potawatomis, and Kickapoos parties to the treaty as well in order to avoid wars of vengeance among the tribes themselves.[21] He reported with approval to Jefferson's secretary of war Henry Dearborn in 1801 that the Delawares were "making another attempt to become agriculturalists."

> They are forming settlements upon the White river a branch of the Wabash under the conduct of two Missionaries of the Society of "The United Brethren for propogating the gospel amongst the Heathens" otherwise Meravians. To assist them in this plan the Chiefs desire that one half of their next annuity may be laid out in impliments of agriculture, and in the purchase of some domestic animals as Cows and Hogs. The Kaskaskeas & Peankashaws request the same thing and the Patawatimies wish a few corse hoes may be sent with their goods.[22]

Harrison was a very active agent in securing title to Indian lands, acquiring the southern third of Indiana and nearly all of Illinois in treaties negotiated with various tribes between 1803 and 1809.

> This does not mean that the United States seized the land and then brutally drove the Indians away homeless—an American myth that has little foundation in fact. In return for lands ceded to the government, Harrison pledged the protection of the United States to the tribe or tribes involved, and typically agreed to pay cash or annuities, or both, supposed to be equal to the current value of the land. There were also agreements with some of the tribes whereby, in addition to paying for vacated lands and providing new territory for the Indians to settle on, the United States agreed to erect schools, hospitals, churches, gristmills, sawmills, and the like; to provide teachers, physicians, millers, blacksmiths; to furnish food, blankets, tobacco, farm implements, weapons, horses, and other domestic animals.[23]

Harrison was also an advocate of the government's continuing policy of "civilizing" the aborigines.[24]

Civilization and religious conversion of the Indians often mingled in the imagery of this national policy. The combination of missionary and Indian agent seemed perfectly reasonable to Isaac McCoy as he began planning his Indian work at Vincennes in 1818.

> Oue benevolent measures would not be liable to be thwarted by an ill-natured Agent, and every movement in the Agency might be rendered subservient to their Civilization. The Indians might be persuaded to accept of such articles as part of their annuities, as incline them to Civilization such as Cattle, hogs, etc . . . And knowing that he could obtain stock, and implements of husbandry, he [the Indian] would hardly fail to become a farmer, a Citizen of the U.S. A Christian.[25]

As the House Committee on Indian Affairs said when recommending a federal "civilization fund" of $10,000 annually in 1819: "Put into the hands of their children the primer and the hoe, and they will naturally, in time, take hold of the plow; and as their minds become enlightened and expand, the Bible will be their book, and they will grow up in habits of morality and industry, leave the chase to those of minds less cultured, and become useful members of society."[26] The government had no machinery of its own for dispensing the civilization fund so churches often received it to send missionaries on the dual errand of making Indians into Christians and good citizens, understood as one and the same mission. Proper religion would help Americanize the aborigines. Missionaries who received little or no government assistance, such as the Moravians in Indi-ana, still had to invest a major portion of their labor in teaching the basics of civilization if the Indians were to survive. Religion was an integral part of the curriculum at most government and church schools for Indians.

Many Indian chiefs in Indiana came to terms with the national policy of civilizing the Indians. Little Turtle was a principal chief of the Miamis. His warriors and his leadership were central in the Indian confederation which defeated the white armies led by generals Josiah Harmar in 1790 and Arthur St. Clair in 1791. But after the Battle of Fallen Timbers against general Anthony Wayne in August of 1795, Little Turtle was among the signers of the Treaty of Greenville ceding all of southern Ohio, a strip of southeastern Indiana, plus Clark's Grant and the key points of Vincennes, Ouiatanon (Lafayette), and the Wabash-Maumee portage. Along with Five Medals of the Potawatomis and several other chiefs, Little Turtle visited President Jefferson in 1802.

On their way to Washington in June of that year, the chiefs also visited some Quakers of Baltimore Yearly Meeting—the Committee of Friends on Indian Affairs. It was here that Little Turtle made an eloquent appeal for prohibition of trade in liquor which "may justly be called Poison" and which "has destroyed a great part of your Red Brethren."[27] Those Quakers sent a gift of agricultural tools to the Indians at Fort Wayne in 1803—"6 sets of Plough Irons, and their appurtenances, such as clevises, &c; 10 leather collars, 10 pair of Haims, 10 Pair of iron chains, & 10 Backbands, 50 Axes, 6 Mattocks, 6 iron wedges, 6 Maul rings and 50 Hoes."[28] The letter of thanks came from Chief Little Turtle and Chief Five Medals "and others."

> Brothers, you will see from what has been said that our prospects are bad at present though we hope the Great Spirit will change the minds of our people & tell them that it will be better for them to cultivate the earth than to drink whiskey. Brothers, We hope the Great Spirit will permit some of you to come and see us when you will be able to know whether you can do anything for us or not.[29]

The Baltimore Quakers sent more tools. They sent a delegation of Quaker visitors to Fort Wayne in 1804 which recommended total abstinence from alcohol and total involvement in agriculture. Chief White Loon of the Mississinewas was one of the respondents. He spoke of the evils of destroying game for the fur alone and of the exchange of those furs for whiskey. He claimed the conversion of Indian hunting grounds to pastures and fields of corn was now begun and said "We are disposed to go on as we have begun, until our habits and manners, as well as the face of our country shall be changed, and look like those of the white people."[30] The Quakers also sent farmers to show the Indians how to farm. In several instances in Indiana the federal government contracted with religious agencies to carry out treaty provisions to provide the Indians with schools, churches, and agricultural services. Indiana was the scene of one especially ambitious experiment when Quaker demonstration farmer William Kirk came to Fort Wayne in 1806 with a federal grant of $6,000, a very substantial investment of President Jefferson in his policy of Indian settlement. Baptist missionary Isaac McCoy received federal contracts in support of his Indian work at Fort Wayne and at Carey Mission just north of the Indiana border in Michigan, as did Catholic missionaries for their substantial work among the Potawatomis.[31]

In a way the story of Indian religion in Indiana was a tragedy. The joint efforts of the government agencies and denominational missionaries to settle, civilize, and convert the Indians were generally failures. That task was greater than anyone realized at the time and the forces committed to accomplish it were feeble. Schools for Indian children had hard going. Work standards and punctuality were hard to teach. Indian parents sometimes felt the missionaries were under obligation to them for sending the children to school. The policy of the government and the missionaries for the Indians was to civilize and convert but the attitude shown toward the Indians by the advancing frontier farmers was a mixture of hatred and fear. They wanted the Indians removed. The Indians responded with a corresponding hatred and fear. Indian communities never became established in the Hoosier agricultural economy to become bases for stable missionary churches in the way their sponsors intended.

Very few Indian men were enthusiastic farmers. Little Turtle and Five Medals wrote to the Quakers in 1803, "We are sorry to say that the minds of our people are not so much inclined towards the cultivation of the earth as we could wish them." Little Turtle told the visiting Quaker delegation in spring of 1804, "I as well as some other of My brother chiefs have been endeavouring to turn the minds of our people towards the Cultivation of the Earth but I am sorry to say we have yet not been able to effect any thing."[32] In November of 1810 Harrison told the legislature of Indiana Territory of the government's intent to spare the Indians from "utter extirpation" by encouraging them in agriculture now that the wild game was gone.

> But a most formidable opposition has been raised to it by the warriors, who will never agree to abandon their old habits until driven to it by absolute necessity. As long as a deer is to be found in their forests they will continue to hunt . . . Is one of the fairest portions of the globe to remain in a state of nature, the haunt of a few wretched savages, when it seems destined by the Creator to give support to a large population, and to be the seat of civilization, of science, and of true religion?[33]

For the Shawnees in Indiana, farming was not nearly so highly esteemed as hunting. When some Delaware warriors on the White River learned that the Quaker William Kirk had arrived to teach them to farm, they said: "This man tires his horse in vain. He would better stay at home and work for himself as he pleases. We do not need anyone to teach us how to work. If we want to work we know how to do it according to our own way and as it pleases us."[34] The Delaware chiefs were willing to agree that civilized agriculture was desirable in order to get government advocates to keep silent about it. However the Delaware men had little intention of doing the "women's work" of dirt farming. Their tribal memory also reached back to 1782 when white militia had mas-

sacred ninety Indians who had become Christians and farmers at Gnadenhütten mission in eastern Ohio.[35] The government program of instructing Indians through demonstration farms broke down in a bitter power struggle among the white agents at Fort Wayne which wasted the funds allotted for the work of William Kirk and produced minimal results.[36]

By 1823 Baptist missionary Isaac McCoy had concluded there was no hope for enclaves of Indians surrounded by whites in the East. He published his convictions in his *Remarks on the Practicability of Indian Reform, Embracing Their Colonization* and threw all his energy into his plan for a new Indian homeland west of the Mississippi.[37] Over the protests of priests Louis Deseille and Benjamin Petit, the Catholic congregations of the Potawatomis were also broken up and sent west.

Tenskwatawa the Prophet

Indiana's revitalization of tribal religion also ended tragically. In spring of 1805 in a Shawnee village on the upper White River, a minor shaman experienced an overwhelming transportation to the spirit world which revolutionized his life and empowered him for a special role as a divine messenger. He took the new name Tenskwatawa or Open Door, and was also known as The Prophet. His new message attacked and rejected all things associated with white people, particularly the Americans—e.g., no white trade, no white food, no white intermarriage, no white clothing, no white domestic animals. Most strenuously of all, he campaigned against the use of whiskey.[38] He did not preach great alteration of his tribe's basic religion so he had the appeal of a restorer of the good old Indian ways. He did delineate sharp distinctions between sin and salvation, between the rewards of paradise and the torments of hell. And he changed some details of tribal religious practice which had the effect of elevating his new sacred objects and rituals over traditional ones in the hands of other shamans or of individual tribe members.

There was in him not only the profile of an Indian shaman but also the technique of an American revival preacher. He demanded transformation of individual and tribal character. He embodied the rising tribal insight that the Indian people had been overrun and ruined by American white people. His revival both inspired and expressed the Indian cry for revenge and justice.

> The Prophet assured his followers that the Master of Life had revealed the true character of the Americans to him in a vision. According to Tenskwatawa, in the vision the Long Knives [Americans] had taken the form of a great

ugly crab that had crawled from the sea, its claws full of mud and seaweed. Meanwhile, the Master of Life had spoken, saying, "Behold this crab. It comes from Boston and brings with it part of the land in that vicinity. If you Indians will do everything which I have told you, I will overturn the land, so that all the white people will be covered and you alone shall inhabit the land."[39]

Since Tenskwatawa himself judged which practices of Indians or whites were abominations, heard the confessions of violators, and determined which persons were witches requiring destruction, he became a person of great power. Under his influence the Delawares tortured and burned the three Indians who had associated themselves with the Moravian missionaries on the White River. That ended the Moravian mission in 1806.

Tenskwatawa's teammate, and sometimes his sibling rival, was his older brother. Tecumseh was something of a prophet himself but was primarily a charismatic Shawnee war chief destined to become the hero and most visible leader of the revitalization movement after 1809. He saw clearly that scattered bands and tribes of Indians dependent on whites for subsistence would never be able to withstand white pressure for land acquisition. It was he who ranged the West from the Great Lakes to Florida and from the Ohio River to the Missouri enlisting an Indian federation to stop any further land cessions by any Indians and eventually to drive the Americans back into the sea. He especially sought angry young war chiefs like himself who had not personally signed the treaties alienating the land. Tecumseh told Harrison that he and his followers intended to kill all the chiefs who had been parties to the Treaty of Fort Wayne which ceded more than two million acres of Indiana land in 1809.[40]

Only a few of the Miamis were interested in the campaign of Tecumseh and Tenskwatawa; most of the Shawnees did not assist. Support came mostly from the northern portion of the Ohio Valley—Potawatomis, Kickapoos, Wyandots, and Delawares.[41]

> In the Delaware Indian world of anxiety, insecurity, and frustration, at a time of a strong nativistic trend, the Prophet was a religious revivalist who gave the Indians something to cling to. His preachings were more in keeping with native cosmology than the theology of the Moravians and Baptists, and the Indians followed him blindly.[42]

Potawatomi chief Main Poc, a religious leader himself, became a convert and invited the restorationists to set up their village on the central Wabash near the mouth of the Tippecanoe. From 1808 this was the place to which Tecumseh and the chiefs who were his colleagues sent their recruits. This was the place where Tenskwatawa systematically instructed and inspired them, receiving their pledges of loyalty. Population at this Prophetstown was fluid, estimates for summer of 1810 ranging from 650 to nearly 3,000. This was a center of Indian religious excitement for all the West.[43]

After years of correspondence and councils involving these Shawnee brothers, William Henry Harrison moved on Prophetstown with an army of about a thousand in November of 1811. Tecumseh was away in the South on a whirlwind trip among the tribes to complete his Indian federation. When Harrison came to the gates of Prophetstown, Tenskwatawa proposed a delay for a conference but then approved a plan for a surprise Indian attack designed to eliminate Harrison and his forces in their overnight encampment. Losses in this Battle of Tippecanoe were heavy on both sides but Prophetstown was destroyed. So was the influence of Tenskwatawa, since his promises of Indian invincibility were broken. Tecumseh died at the Battle of Thames, north of Lake Erie, in October of 1813, faithful to his alliance with the British against the Americans. Many histories and stories have recorded him as an ideal Indian and a hero.[44] Tenskwatawa knew many lean years at the mercy of Indian agents of the British during his exile in Canada. Then he accepted an invitation by Governor Lewis Cass of Michigan to return to the United States in 1825 and help gather all the scattered Shawnees for removal to Kansas. He died in obscurity in Kansas in 1836. Histories and stories done by white people with no sympathy for his religion or his opposition to white immigrants have generally portrayed Tenskwatawa as a charlatan and scoundrel; Indian people have generally agreed.[45]

Within the lifetime of Tenskwatawa the official policy of the United States government toward Indians had changed. By the time of the presidency of Andrew Jackson and the federal Indian Removal Act of 1830, the interest of the government and its agents shifted from civilizing Indians in locations east of the Mississippi. Indiana's white population had increased from about 4,875 in 1800 to 344,031 in 1830. The government Indian policy of civilization and assimilation was plainly failing. Whites continued to overrun the land. Indian practice generally was to "catch fish, and plant patches of corn; dance, paint, hunt, get drunk, when they can get liquor, fight, and often starve."[46] The new policy was to apply pressure to extinguish Indian land claims by purchase and to remove the Indians to the vast western lands of Jefferson's Louisiana Purchase.[47]

The story of religion among the Indians of Indiana was a tragedy. It was also a tapestry of fascinating and heroic figures. There were the pre-Columbian builders of massive complexes of mounds. There were the later chiefs and their tribes who were forced to add to the complexities of their own cultures some responsible adjustment to relentless pressures from Europe. There were Tenskwatawa, Tecumseh, and their colleagues, convinced they must champion Algonquian traditions and resist both invasion and proselytism by whites. There were the white missionaries moved to offer the Indians opportunity for civilization and conversion which they believed to be the only hope for their salvation. And there came to be a substantial number of Indian Christians. Some who were removed to the West moved as congregations of Christians. When the troops of general John Tipton finally came to evict the Indian leader and lay preacher Menominee and his band of Potawatomis from Indiana in 1838, they confined many of the Indians in the most convenient enclosure—the Catholic church in their village. From there they sent them on the so-called trail of death to Kansas.

Earliest Catholic missionaries to the Potawatomis had been Jesuits; beginning in 1830 the renewed sequence of missionaries was Stephen Badin (1830–1835), Louis Deseille (1834–1837), and Benjamin Petit (1837–1839). Petit said the Potawatomis at his mission points eagerly enlisted each other for the Christian faith and taught each other the prayers and the catechism. At the end of 1837 he wrote "There are now a thousand to twelve hundred Christians, and what a fervor, what a wonderful and touching simplicity." In May of 1838 he said "Ah, I shall do everything possible to keep from abandoning them! If they leave, I want to go with them at least as far as the Jesuit missions on the Mississippi." It was Petit who accompanied the Potawatomis as pastor on their forced march west in 1838.[48]

A great many Indians remained in Indiana. When the Potawatimis ceded their remaining land in Indiana in 1832, there were some 110 specific land reservations created in Indiana for particular Indian persons or bands.[49] It became government policy to keep reducing or eliminating these reservations by purchase and by exchange for western land but several Indian families, particularly those with white blood and a history of government cooperation, were able to retain control of some of their Indiana land and to exempt themselves from removal to the West. Potawatomi Chief Leopold Pokagon was a friend of Baptist missionary Isaac McCoy but in his personal religion a persistent and devoted Catholic, instrumental in restoring the ministry of priests at South Bend. He eventually used the proceeds from the sale of his reservation to establish a home and a Catholic parish just beyond the border of Indiana in Michigan.[50]

The Miamis were granted about twenty Indiana reserves. They suffered terribly during removal from their lands and from the ravages of whiskey. Their agent in Kansas said that only 275 remained there by 1854. However some individual Miamis and their families remained, survived, and thrived in Indiana. The list of Miamis exempt from emigration in 1846 "included 55 members of the Meshingomesia family, 22 from the Slocum family, 28 of the Godfroys, and 43 Richardville-Lafontaine members."[51] Chief Meshingomesia of the Mississinewa band became a Baptist, joining other members of his family as builders and patrons of a meetinghouse and school. Miami Chief Jean Baptiste Richardville and his son-in-law Francis Lafontaine who succeeded him were Catholics. Richardville was once reputed to be the richest man in Indiana; his children and grandchildren received an excellent education and took respected places among their white contemporaries. William Wells was a white child captive of the Miamis who married Little Turtle's daughter. Their son graduated from West Point; their three daughters were educated in private schools and married a doctor, an army captain, and a judge. Frances Slocum was a white child captive who became the wife of a successor of Little Turtle as Miami war chief. Her two sons-in-law became Baptist preachers.[52] Historians of the Miamis have noted that about half of the Miami candidates for removal either remained in Indiana or returned there, an accepted and respected stratum of Hoosier society. Tracing Indian heritage became a matter of interest not only because of government payments due or because of genealogical pride in Indian origin but also because of loyalty to and affection for ancient cultural traditions including religion.[53]

NOTES

1. Generalization about Indian religion is a hazardous enterprise. Narratives of early white missionaries and pioneers are likely to describe Indian practices as excesses of savagery. On the other hand, some twentieth-century writers offer an idealized image of a unified Indian world of beautiful ecological simplicity. Archaeologists and anthropologists are loath to generalize at all; they prefer to report only what they have discovered about one particular practice of some members of one particular tribe at one particular time. Evidence seems to suggest an ever-dynamic kaleidoscope of Indian cultures and religions, each with its full share of personal tensions and social complexities. Some Indians of Indiana were religious statesmen; some practiced liturgies leading to murder and

even to cannibalism. See *The American Indian and the Problem of History*, ed. Calvin Martin (New York: Oxford University Press, 1987), 64–66; Calvin Martin, "Epilogue: The Indian and the Ecology Movement," in Calvin Martin, *Keepers of the Game: Indian-Animal Relationships and the Fur Trade* (Berkeley, Calif.: University of California Press, 1978), 157–88; Jerry E. Clark, *The Shawnee* (Lexington, Ky.: University Press of Kentucky, 1977), 29; James A. Clifton, *The Prairie People: Continuity and Change in Potawatomi Indian Culture 1665–1965* (Lawrence, Kans.: Regents Press of Kansas, 1977), 174; Harvey Lewis Carter, *The Life and Times of Little Turtle, First Sagamore of the Wabash* (Urbana, Ill.: University of Illinois Press, 1987), 14.

2. James H. Kellar, "Indiana's Prehistory," in John D. Barnhart and Dorothy L. Riker, *Indiana to 1816: The Colonial Period* (Indianapolis, Ind.: Indiana Historical Bureau and Indiana Historical Society, 1971), 13–56; James H. Kellar, *An Introduction to the Prehistory of Indiana* (Indianapolis, Ind.: Indiana Historical Society, 1983), 22–35.

3. Eli Lilly, *Prehistoric Antiquities of Indiana* (Indianapolis, Ind.: Indiana Historical Society, 1937), 76–80; Robert Silverberg, *Mound Builders of Ancient America: The Archaeology of a Myth* (Greenwich, Conn.: New York Graphic Society, 1968, 369 p.); Kellar, *Introduction to the Prehistory*, 14, 36.

4. James H. Madison, *Eli Lilly: Archaeologist* (Bloomington, Ind.: Glenn A. Black Laboratory of Archaeology, 1988, 21 p.); Glenn A. Black, *Angel Site*, 2 vols. (Indianapolis, Ind.: Indiana Historical Society, 1967), 1:273–82; Kellar, *Introduction to the Prehistory*, 16–22.

5. Donald R. Cochran, "Adena and Hopewell Cosmology: New Evidence from East Central Indiana," in *Native American Cultures in Indiana*, ed. Ronald Hicks (Muncie, Ind.: Minnetrista Cultural Center and Ball State University, 1992), 26–40; Karen Dalman, "Earthworks," *Outdoor Indiana* 54 (April 1989): 12–15.

6. Bert Anson, *The Miami Indians* (Norman, Okla.: University of Oklahoma Press, 1970), 13; C. A. Weslager, *The Delaware Indians* (New Brunswick, N.J.: Rutgers University Press, 1972), 332–33; W. Vernon Kinietz, *The Indians of the Western Great Lakes 1615–1760* (Ann Arbor, Mich.: University of Michigan Press, 1940), 162.

7. R. David Edmunds, *The Potawatomis* (Norman, Okla.: University of Oklahoma Press, 1978), 15; Otho Winger, *The Potawatomi Indians* (Elgin, Ill.: Elgin Press, 1939), 66; Clifton, *Prairie People*, 158–61.

8. Lawrence H. Gipson, *The Moravian Indian Mission on White River* (Indianapolis, Ind.: Indiana Historical Bureau, 1938), 17; Clark, *Shawnee*, 63, 68; Weslager, *Delaware*, 332–33.

9. Edmunds, *Potawatomis*, 15; Clark, *Shawnee*, 57; Anson, *Miami*, 20–21.

10. Robert F. Berkhofer, *Salvation and the Savage* (Lexington, Ky.: University of Kentucky Press, 1965), 105; Clark, *Shawnee*, 42, 72–73.

11. James H. Howard, *Shawnee! The Ceremonialism of a Native Indian Tribe and Its Cultural Background* (Athens, Ohio: Ohio University Press, 1981, 454 p.); *Native North American Spirituality of the Eastern Woodlands*, ed. Elisabeth Tooker (New York: Paulist Press, 1979, 302 p.); Edmunds, *Potawatomis*, 19–21; Anson, *Miami*, 22–26; Weslager, *Delaware*, 493–99; Clark, *Shawnee*, 48–50.

12. R. David Edmunds, *The Shawnee Prophet* (Lincoln, Nebr.: University of Nebraska Press, 1983), 38; Clark, *Shawnee*, 52–53.

13. Clark, *Shawnee*, 88–89.

14. Weslager, *Delaware*, 106–7, 340–41.

15. *Messages and Letters of William Henry Harrison, 1800–1811* (Indianapolis, Ind.: Indiana Historical Commission, 1922), 27–29.

16. John F. Cady, "Isaac McCoy's Mission to the Indians of Indiana and Michigan," *Indiana History Bulletin* 16 (February 1939): 105.

17. Joseph A. Parsons, "Civilizing the Indians of the Old Northwest, 1800–1810," *Indiana Magazine of History* 56 (September 1960): 197.

18. Parsons, "Civilizing the Indians," 195–96.

19. Clark, *Shawnee*, 89; Parsons, "Civilizing the Indians," 196.

20. Harrison, *Messages and Letters*, 24–30; Gipson, *Moravian Indian Mission*, 18–19.

21. Harrison, *Messages and Letters*, 488–89.

22. Harrison, *Messages and Letters*, 30.

23. Weslager, *Delaware*, 350.

24. "Civilization" is a slippery term in this context. Nineteenth century white Americans were prone to view Indians as uncivilized savages, even the ones that engaged in trade, adopted firearms, used metal utensils, wore European clothing, drank beverage alcohol, or practiced Christian religion. So long as the tribesmen did not speak English and labor as yeoman farmers, they were counted somewhere short of civilization. See R. David Edmunds, "George Winter: Mirror of Acculturation," in *Indians and a Changing Frontier: The Art of George Winter* (Indianapolis, Ind.: Indiana Historical Society, 1993), 23–39.

25. Lela Barnes, "Isaac McCoy and the Treaty of 1821," *Kansas Historical Quarterly* 5 (May 1936): 125.

26. Henry Warner Bowden, *American Indians and Christian Missions* (Chicago: University of Chicago Press, 1981), 167.

27. *A Brief Account of the Proceedings of the Committee, Appointed by the Yearly Meeting of Friends, Held in Baltimore, for Promoting the Improvement and Civilization of the Indian Natives* (London: Phillips and Fardon, 1806), 18.

28. "An Early Contribution from the Friends to the Indians," *Indiana Magazine of History* 6 (June 1910): 87–88.

29. Joseph E. Walker, "Plowshares and Pruning Hooks for the Miami and Potawatomi: The Journal of Gerard T. Hopkins, 1804," *Ohio History* 88 (Autumn 1979): 366.

30. John S. Tyson, *Life of Elisha Tyson* (Baltimore, Md.: B. Lundy, 1825), 75–76.

31. Parsons, "Civilizing the Indians," 207–13. These missionary enterprises are further discussed in the relevant denominational sections of this book.

32. Walker, "Plowshares and Pruning Hooks," 366, 393–94.

33. Harrison, *Messages and Letters*, 492–93.

34. Gipson, *Moravian Indian Mission*, 450.

35. Gipson, *Moravian Indian Mission*, 9–10, 256; Weslager, *Delaware*, 342.

36. Parsons, "Civilizing the Indians," 207–13; Carter, *Life and Times of Little Turtle*, 161–64, 197–210.

37. Isaac McCoy, *Remarks on the Practicability of Indian Reform, Embracing Their Colonization* (Boston: Lincoln and Edmands, 1827, 47 p.).

38. Gregory Evans Dowd, *A Spirited Resistance: The North American Indian Struggle for Unity, 1745–1815* (Baltimore, Md.: Johns Hopkins University Press, 1992), 123–47. For fuller detail on laws and regulations based on Tenskwatawa's visions, see Edmunds, *Shawnee Prophet*, 33–40, and Howard, *Shawnee*, 197–211.

39. Edmunds, *Shawnee Prophet*, 38.

40. Howard, *Shawnee*, 18, 210–11; Harrison, *Messages and Letters*, 459–63.

41. Clark, *Shawnee*, 34.

42. Weslager, *Delaware*, 343.

43. Edmunds, *Potawatomis*, 166–67, 170.

44. R. David Edmunds, *Tecumseh and the Quest for Indian Leadership* (Boston: Little, Brown and Company, 1984), 187–225; Howard, *Shawnee*, 197–211.

45. Edmunds, *Shawnee Prophet*, 184–190; Howard, *Shawnee*, 198.

46. Edmunds, *Potawatomis*, 240.

47. Irving McKee, *The Trail of Death: Letters of Benjamin Marie Petit* (Indianapolis, Ind.: Indiana Historical Society, 1941), 17–20; Edmunds, *Potawatomis*, 240–72.

48. McKee, *Trail of Death*, 34, 52, 66, 87–88; Winger, *Potawatomi*, 43–53.

49. Leon M. Gordon, "The Red Man's Retreat from Northern Indiana," *Indiana Magazine of History* 46 (March 1950): 51.

50. James A. Clifton, *The Pokagons, 1683–1983: Catholic Potawatomi Indians of the St. Joseph River Valley* (New York: University Press of America, 1984), 67–76; Winger, *Potawatomi*, 141–49.

51. Gordon, *Red Man's Retreat*, 51–52, 60; Anson, *Miami*, 226.

52. Otho Winger, *The Last of the Miamis* (North Manchester, Ind.: The Author, 1935), 11–16, 26–27, 33–34; Anson, *Miami*, 126, 189, 209–12.

53. Anson, *Miami*, 226, 266, 269–303; Winger, *Last of the Miamis*, 12.

About Methodists and Catholics

The most substantial units of Indiana's religious past and present are the Methodists and the Catholics. In 1990 these two made up 40 percent of the state's reported religious adherents. Together their adherents equaled 20 percent of the state's total population. Their churches and institutions have become prevalent religious landmarks in Indiana towns.[1]

Neither the Methodists nor the Catholics were decisively shaped in Indiana. Their identity and their institutional ways were established before Indiana was opened to them. They moved into Indiana in strength in the 1800s and flourished. At the time their growth and even their survival often appeared to them to be a hard struggle. On the grander scale of history they looked like armies that were not to be denied. Indiana was in their line of march.

NOTES

1. Churches and Church Membership in the United States 1990. An Enumeration by Region, State and County Based on Data Reported by 133 Church Groupings, *ed. Martin B. Bradley and others (Atlanta, Ga.: Glenmary Research Center, 1992). This enumeration reports a number of "members" and a number of "adherents." The adherents are defined as "all members, including full members, their children and the estimated number of other regular participants who are not considered as communicant, confirmed or full members." In Hoosier Faiths all citations of religious statistics for 1990 not otherwise located are from this compilation. Citations for 1980 without other documentation are from* Churches and Church Membership in the United States 1980. An Enumeration Based on Data Reported by 111 Church Bodies, *ed. Bernard Quinn and others (Atlanta, Ga.: Glenmary Research Center, 1982). Citations of statistics for 1906, 1916, 1926, or 1936 without further attribution are from the published federal census reports of religious bodies for those years.*

EARLY METHODISTS

Though the Catholics came to Indiana first, it was the growth of the Methodists which dominated the history of religion in Indiana in the first half of the 1800s. American Methodists were just entering an era of spectacular expansion as white settlers began to occupy Indiana about 1800. They had weathered the American Revolution, during which they were often under suspicion because of John Wesley's pro-British stand. They had managed to keep growing right through the revolutionary period. Francis Asbury had been confirmed in his leadership of the American Methodists, being named superintendent or bishop at the Christmas Conference at Baltimore in 1784. His combination of a local ministry by local preachers and class leaders and exhorters, with an itinerant ministry by full time traveling preachers, all designed to produce continuous revival, had been tested in the West.

Methodist Routes West

From the Appalachian watershed in the back country South a magnificent river system fed westward toward the Ohio. Along these rivers and along the traces marked through the mountain gaps pressed the southern pioneers into Tennessee and Kentucky and across the Ohio into Indiana. Methodist strategists had known the settlers along these southern routes for a long time. Holston circuit was formed among them in 1783, a year before the Methodist Episcopal Church was officially organized for America in 1784. Circuits were added endlessly in Methodist fashion:

Nolichucky, Greenbriar, French Broad, New River, Kentucky.[1] Bishop Francis Asbury crossed the southern Appalachians to visit the new circuits on his annual horseback round of four to six thousand miles directing Methodist developments. "Over the Alps" he called it.[2] He anguished over one of the descents which was steep like the roof of a house for nearly a mile so that he rode, he walked, he sweated, he trembled, and his old knees failed. "O, my jaws and teeth!" he wrote. "O, the rocks, hills, ruts, and stumps! My bones, my bones!"[3]

Another major route west to Indiana was based in the headwaters of the Ohio River in western Pennsylvania. Access was either overland or along stream valleys by way of the Potomac to Fort Cumberland, then up Wills Creek and over the watershed to Casselman Creek and down the Youghiogheny River to the Monongahela. Thomas Cresap and Christopher Gist marked the mountain traces for this route as Daniel Boone had done for the Wilderness Road. When the Monongahela joined the Allegheny at Fort Pitt to form the Ohio, travelers had that mighty river as an unequaled natural route to the shores and the rivers of Indiana. Settlers on this route were also on Methodist ground. Redstone circuit first extended over an immense area on both sides of the Monongahela when founded in 1784. Expansion added circuits named Ohio, Clarksburg, Pittsburg, Washington, Little Kanawha, Muskingum, West Wheeling, Hockhocking, and Guyandotte. All were on the visitation agenda and under the eye of Bishop Asbury.[4]

Thus Methodism had crossed the Appalachian watershed and moved with the white pioneers along the same west-flowing rivers which brought most of the early settlers to Indiana. Some of them were Methodists on the move; some met Methodists on the way. A few were authorized Methodist local preachers or class leaders or exhorters, those members whose religious leadership had been recognized or former traveling preachers whose family obligations had required them to settle. Such persons need not and often did not wait for the appearance of a traveling preacher to begin a Methodist organization. They gathered their neighbors and began a local unit to be linked in a traveling preacher's circuit as soon as one appeared. It was effective church extension. Methodism in the nation increased twenty-fold (1,939 percent) from 1800 to 1850 while the general population was increasing four and one-third times (437 percent). In 1800 Methodists comprised about 1.2 percent of the total population; in 1850 they made up 5.4 percent. And church attendance in this era was usually at least twice as large as the membership.[5]

Western Conference

The year 1800 was one to remember for the Methodists. General Conference at Baltimore was the scene of a great revival among those in attendance and as the preachers returned to their circuits the whole church was responding to the new impulses.[6] Bishops Francis Asbury and Richard Whatcoat crossed the Cumberland Gap and traveled the Wilderness Road in September of that year, along with young William McKendree. They were on their way to Kentucky for the first session of the Western Conference established by the Methodists in 1796 to encompass all the lands west of the Appalachian Mountains. There was really only one district in it so far, so it was variously called Western Conference, Kentucky Conference, or Kentucky District.[7] McKendree was the newly appointed presiding elder for its nine circuits and fourteen preachers. Eight years later he preached a sermon of such power at General Conference that he was chosen to be Asbury's associate and put on the national circuit as newly elected bishop.

> Methodism made the Old Northwest her homeland. Almost every town and village, even crossroads, from Pittsburgh to Prairie du Chien, had its little Methodist church. The man who had originally put the whole thing together was William McKendree. In 1800 he had come full of vigor across the Cumberland Gap to take charge of the Western District. His election in 1808 did not

change his way of life or his commitment to the work in the west. No man more completely personified the westward movement of Methodism, at least west to the Mississippi.[8]

The year 1800 was one to remember for Indiana too. Indiana Territory was established. Land was soon for sale at Vincennes for two dollars per acre. Settlers poured in. Revivals in Kentucky spread their influence north; James McGready of Great Revival fame preached in Indiana. Methodist local preachers and exhorters were at work among the new settlers. Francis Asbury came to Indiana only once. Standing barely within its borders at Lawrenceburg in 1808, he considered the new territory and made an entry in his journal. "In this wild there may be twenty thousand souls already. I feel for them."[9] William McKendree had wide national responsibilities as bishop and could not remain in the state for very long at a time. But the burgeoning Methodist Church and the strategies of these two bishops were soon represented in Indiana by a remarkable corps of workers. What the Methodists had done so successfully in multiplying the Holston circuit and the Redstone circuit west of the Appalachians, they now repeated in the Old Northwest, particularly in three areas of early settlement in early Indiana.

Early Methodists on the Ohio

Virginia awarded 150,000 acres of land on the Indiana side of the Ohio River to George Rogers Clark and the veterans of his campaign during the Revolution, that grant confirmed by the United States in 1784. The census of 1800 reported 919 settlers already in Clark's grant. The earliest local Methodist gatherings there were probably unrecorded. First reliably recorded Methodist preaching in Indiana was in 1801 at a settlement called Springville in Clark's grant; local preachers Samuel Parker and Edward Talbot crossed the Ohio River from Kentucky and conducted a two-day meeting. Then in the summer of 1802 Andrew Mitchell brought presiding elder William McKendree across the Ohio in a canoe to form official Methodist classes at Charlestown and New Chapple. Benjamin Lakin crossed the river to this Indiana portion of his Salt River circuit in 1803, preaching at a location in the woods near Charlestown and at the Robertson neighborhood five miles north.[10] A junior preacher on the Salt River and Shelby circuit was a brash nineteen-year-old named Peter Cartwright. His *Autobiography* states:

> It is probable that the first introduction of Methodism in the State of Indiana was in 1802 or 1803. In the fall of

1804 Clark's Grant, or the Illinois Grant, as it was called, which was opposite and north of Louisville, was then included in the Salt River and Shelbyville Circuits, and Brother Benjamin Lakin and myself crossed the Ohio River, and preached at Brother Robertson's and Prather's. In this grant we had two classes, and splendid revivals of religion: and if my recollection serves me correctly, this Illinois Grant was formed into a Circuit in 1807–8, and Moses Ashworth was appointed to travel it; it was called Silver Creek Circuit. This was the first regular circuit ever formed in the State of Indiana, and composed of one hundred and eighty-eight members.[11]

Early Methodists on the Whitewater

Following the successful campaign of General Anthony Wayne and the battle of Fallen Timbers in 1794, the Treaty of Greenville opened up half of Ohio and a narrow triangle in the southeast corner of what is now Indiana to white settlement. By 1805 this portion of Indiana along the Whitewater River had a substantial "Kentucky" settlement just south of present day Richmond and a "Carolina" settlement just above the present city of Brookville. The whole area was being settled fast. Methodists James Cole and Enoch Smith and Benjamin McCarty of the Carolina group began meeting with some others and petitioned John Sale, presiding elder of the Ohio district, to send them a regular traveling preacher. In March of 1806 John Sale sent Joseph Oglesby to form a new circuit west of the Great Miami. Oglesby quickly established a four-week preaching round named Whitewater Circuit including Indiana area between Lawrenceburg and Richmond.[12]

Early Methodists on the Wabash

The largest cluster of European population in early Indiana was in the Vincennes area with 1,538 in the vicinity according to the census of 1800. Vincennes Circuit first appeared in the Methodist minutes for 1809 with William Winans listed as preacher. He conducted a night service at the fort on the Wabash for government officers, a few English and French settlers, and two or three Indians. William Henry Harrison held the candle so the young preacher could read his text and hymn.[13] Peter Cartwright, having now progressed from a preaching recruit to be ordained a deacon in the traveling ministry by Francis Asbury in 1806, strenuously trained by William McKendree, and ordained a traveling elder by McKendree in 1808, also played a pioneering role in Methodist extension around Vincennes. His own account of his public rout of the Shakers at Busseron, not far from Vincennes, concluded:

> And perhaps this victory may be considered among the first-fruits of Methodism in that part of this new country. This was in 1808. At this meeting I collected, as well as I could, the names and places where it was supposed they wanted Methodist preaching. I made out and returned a kind of plan for a circuit, carried it to Conference, and they were temporarily supplied by the presiding elder in 1809 and 1810. In 1811 the circuit was called St. Vincennes, and was attached to the Cumberland District, and Thomas Stilwell appointed the preacher in charge.[14]

Later in that narrative he said:

> The next circuit formed in the State of Indiana was called Vincennes Circuit, which I formed in 1808, at the time I fought the memorable battle with the Shakers, in the Busroe Settlement, elsewhere named in this narrative. This circuit was temporarily supplied probably till 1811; it then had 125 members, and Thomas Stilwell was its first regular preacher; it belonged to the Green River District.[15]

In 1812 Cartwright had official oversight of Methodists in western Indiana, having been appointed by Francis Asbury to be presiding elder of Wabash District which included Vincennes Circuit.[16]

Building Indiana Conference

From these three early population centers the structural units of Methodism multiplied in classic fashion, especially with the rapid expansion of population after 1815. Circuit riders of the 1820s and 1830s like Allen Wiley, Calvin Ruter, James Armstrong, James Havens, and Joseph Tarkington were soon producing the record of service which would elevate them to the rank of presiding elder.[17] The newer circuits were generally the longer ones.

> Indianapolis Circuit, in 1825, comprised the following preaching-places: In the county of Marion: Indianapolis, Headley's, M'Laughlin's, and Lamaster's; in the county of Madison: Pendleton, Shetterley's and Smith's; in Hamilton County: Danville [sic], Wilson's, and Claypool's; in Hendricks County and in the county of Morgan: Matlock's, Barlow's, Booker's, Martinsville, Culton's, and Ladd's; at Hough's, in Johnson County, and Ray's and Rector's in Shelby County.[18]

John Strange, a mature preacher with thirteen years of experience in Ohio and a national reputation for pulpit eloquence, elected Indiana as his work place in 1824. For the remaining eight years of his life he set the Hoosier woods ablaze with his oratory.[19] "Brush College" was his alma mater, he said,

> more ancient, though less pretentious, than Yale, or Harvard, or Princeton. Here I graduated, and I love her still. Her academic groves are the boundless forests and prairies of these western wilds; her Pierian springs are the gushing fountains from rocks and mountain fastnesses; her Arcadian groves and Orphic songs are the wild woods, and the birds of every color and every song, relieved now and then with the bass hootings of the night owl and the weird treble of the whip-poor-will; her curriculum is the philosophy of nature and the mysteries of redemption; her library is the word of God; the discipline and hymn book, supplemented with trees and brooks and stones, all of which are full of wisdom and sermons and speeches; and her parchments of literary honors are the horse and saddle-bags.[20]

By 1832 that pioneer preacher and presiding elder John Strange was worn out and dying. Indiana Conference took up a collection that year to help purchase a house and lot for him in Indianapolis. He had refused all previous offers of gifts of property since "his avowed purpose was, never to stop while he could put his leg over the back of the horse, so as to get in the saddle."[21] That meeting at New Albany in 1832 was the official beginning of Indiana Conference, now for the first time separated, named "Indiana," and coterminous with the state boundaries with just a strip of southern Michigan included. Presiding elders were already administering districts named Madison, Charlestown, Indianapolis, and Vincennes. Most of the northern third of the state was still in a "missionary district"; James Armstrong was supervising pioneer Methodist efforts in such emergent areas as Fort Wayne, South Bend, and the Upper Wabash. There were sixty-five traveling preachers in the conference serving 20,035 members, the Methodists having already far surpassed the Baptists as the most numerous religious denomination in the state.[22]

Calvin W. Ruter, pastor at Indianapolis, was elected conference secretary. Presiding elders Allen Wiley, James Havens, William Shanks, James Thompson, and James Armstrong had all been raised from the ranks of Indiana's horseback preachers by the decision of the Methodist hierarchy based upon approval by the people. They were among the best recognized and respected leaders in the state, having repeatedly addressed thousands in each year's cycle of visitation of congregations, quarterly meetings, and conferences. At New Albany they moved with efficiency and confidence under the gavel of presiding bishop Joshua Soule as they led their colleagues to write

the by-laws, to handle all the business affairs of the new conference, and to examine and assign all the preachers and the applicants to become preachers. On the very first day of the first meeting of Indiana Conference, Ruter, Wiley, and Armstrong were named a committee to consider establishing a Methodist literary institution for the state. Two days later the committee reported generally in favor of such a Methodist school with Wiley, Armstrong, Havens, Thompson, and Shanks commissioned to collect information for the building program.[23] To ease the minds of those who feared a formally educated clergy, the committee report said:

> We are aware that when a Conference Seminary is named, some of our preachers and many of our people suppose we are about to establish a manufactory in which preachers are to be made. But nothing is farther from our views, for we are fully of Mr. Bernge's opinion who, when comparing ministers to pens, observes "that although the Seminaries have been trying to make pens for some hundreds of years, they will not write well till God nibs them."[24]

Formation of the new Indiana Conference consolidated and organized the great Methodist strength already present in the state. It also pointed forward to an era of conspicuous progress. By 1843, the eve of the division of the state into two conferences, there were 216 traveling preachers and 488 local preachers serving a Methodist membership of 67,219. By 1860 membership had reached 96,965, organized in four conferences.[25]

Pioneer Methodist Preaching

Preaching is what made the Methodists grow—preaching that was regular, frequent, and exciting. The system was engineered to produce charismatic preachers. When those home-grown young men were enlisted for leadership, there were requirements for entry and more requirements for continuation and a course of study on which to be examined. But the crucial requirement was genuine religious faith very powerfully conveyed. The preacher must have "rousement," must be able to produce shaking or moving or to "start a fire on ice."[26] When the most renowned men preached at quarterly meetings or conferences or camp meetings, there was conscious ranking of their efforts and boosting of local champions. The members of Whitewater Circuit counted their circuit rider John Strange the equal of any preacher and "were all anxious, that our circuit preacher should preach as well as the presiding elder; but he could not do it." Presiding elder Samuel Parker preached so powerfully on Psalms

89:15 that Strange "had the good sense to make short metre of his performance, and let the people go home full of the glorious truths which they had heard from Parker." Visiting bishops were often upstaged at conference by selected local and regional preachers; members liked to see their champions "beat the bishop."[27] That seems never to have happened to Matthew Simpson who became a bishop after serving as president of Indiana Asbury (later DePauw University). Simpson liked to wear plain homespun, appearing to be the merest youth, and then take his hearers by storm with incomparable preaching. Hoosiers counted him the prince of orators. "His logic is all on fire," one lawyer said.[28]

The excitement was not merely noise, though Methodist preaching involved noise aplenty. Successful preachers were praised as "pathetic," following a description of the dangers of hell with heartfelt pleading for the souls of the people. Preachers "told their experience" and applied the miracle of their deliverance to the all too evident needs of the hearers. They wept. They sang, often sweeping dramatically from sermon to song to prayer to exhortation. Their voices gripped the people by disclosing levels of feeling barely suppressible. When suppression could no longer hold the mounting feelings of the preacher or the people or their mutual stimulation, the meeting might spontaneously "break out" into shouts of praise or song or bodily exercises or prayer. This predictable and yet unpredictable breaking out was precisely what most of the preachers and hearers wanted. Instructions for a camp meeting often made plain that non-religious talk and activities were unwelcome. Getting excited and getting religion and getting conversions and getting lives changed were what the meeting was all about. Diversions were only diverting and were the devil's tools.[29]

Early Methodist preaching was generally successful; the morale of Methodist preachers was generally high. They reviewed the rising membership statistics and concluded "The Lord of Hosts is with us."[30] At least seventy-five Hoosier Methodist preachers became subjects of biographies or autobiographies. In these they appeared as heroic figures, champions in the Lord's battles against ranges and phalanxes of opponents, empowered to be winners of many converts as "seals" of their ministerial calling. They saw themselves as heroes and thousands of their neighbors so regarded them.

Enlisting Methodist Preachers

This role model of the heroic traveling preacher had great weight for gifted young men on the frontier. Such a one involved in seeking out his own salvation might find clear certification of his saved status in a fruitful ministry. Lack of formal education need not be a limitation. The fellowship of preachers was indeed one of competition for excellence in performance, but for eager recruits it was also an excellent teaching and support group; congregations knew how to provide encouragement and were sympathetic toward beginners.

Some pessimists said it was dangerous for Methodists to keep reducing the size of the circuits as population increased; soon there would not be enough preachers to staff so many charges. In fact, shortage of ministers was no major problem for Indiana Methodists in the early years. Gifted and articulate young men kept receiving a "call to preach," a call often nearly simultaneous with their conversion, or at least reported so in retrospect.[31] It was not difficult to receive a license from the presiding elder to test one's gifts locally as an exhorter or a local preacher. That openness to untrained young men at the bottom of the organization of preachers was a democratic element in Methodism. It was also possible to arrange with the presiding elder to be a temporary traveling preacher riding a circuit with a senior minister. A presiding elder might well take the initiative to suggest such an experiment to test a candidate's acceptability to the people.

With proper sponsorship, certainly that of the presiding elder of his district, a young man could be "admitted on trial" as a full time traveling preacher in the conference. With a good record alongside a senior preacher, the neophyte might be "continued on trial," might be ordained a deacon and so authorized to administer the sacraments, might be ordained an elder as the mark of his maturity in the conference of traveling preachers, and might eventually be appointed by the bishop as a presiding elder in charge of a district. This last was a very prestigious and demanding position.[32] A presiding elder was responsible directly to the bishop for the oversight of the district, and was expected to preach with great power, with or without notice, wherever he appeared. Allen Wiley considered the system and his own career.

> Although I am a warm friend to all literature and science, yet I ask what are colleges and theological institutions compared with this course of training ministers? I answer, they are poor, time-wasting, mind-cramping, heart-freezing, zeal-destroying, soul-neglecting things, of which it should be said to every man called of God to preach the Gospel, let the dead bury their dead, but go thou and preach the Gospel, but with the science of heaven, and "with the Holy Ghost sent down from heaven."[33]

Allen Wiley: Mentor of Indiana Methodism

Allen Wiley of Indiana provided what is probably the best available record of the life and concerns of early Methodism in the Old Northwest. Not so flamboyant as the writings of Peter Cartwright, Wiley's history offered a more quiet and steady account by a man who knew the full range of early Methodism in Indiana and who invested his life in it with great impact.[34]

Born in Virginia, 15 January 1789, Wiley was living with his parents just north of Harrison on the Whitewater River in Indiana by 1804. Along the way he had one brief period of schooling under William Houston near Lexington, Kentucky. In Indiana he had only a few winter sessions with local schoolmasters. The religious persons he knew were mostly Baptists. In 1808 he married Margaret Eades, daughter of a local Baptist layman who had secured Baptist preaching for the neighborhood. In the house of his father-in-law he first experienced the regular practice of religious devotion in a family setting. This experience was heightened for Wiley by the conduct of the Eades family when his father-in-law died in the fall of 1808. He resolved that he, too, would become religious but made little progress because he lacked assurance and discipline in his search. The growing impact of Methodist preaching tipped the scale. Methodist circuit rider Joseph Oglesby was a "new thing" on the Whitewater, and Allen Wiley found him very impressive. Oglesby excited the emotions of young Wiley though Wiley was "not religious" at the time. Thomas Hellums, one of Indiana's weeping Methodist preachers, rode Whitewater Circuit and touched Wiley with his deep piety. At a two day meeting at Benjamin McCarty's house, preacher Benjamin Lakin said "I feel an impression that there is some young man, or young woman, in this house, who will be tramping in hell before this time next year." Wiley said "I felt as awful as death, judgment, and eternity, could make me."[35] One of the preaching points on the circuit developed at the home of Richard Manwaring. At Manwaring's, early in 1809, the twenty-year-old seeker Allen Wiley heard Moses Crume preach. Then he volunteered to pilot this Methodist preacher seven miles on the road to his next appointment. "During our travel, we had much grave conversation on the subject of religion," Wiley said. "At parting, I proposed to purchase the small *Scriptural Catechism* published by the church, and which he carried for sale. He, however, declined selling, but gave me one; and this very small book laid the foundation of my present theological knowledge."[36]

The emotional excitement of Methodist meetings was slow to find favor with Wiley. In the winter of 1807 at McCarty's house, a Methodist service was so full of grieving and leaping and shouting that Wiley thought the exercises were "the veriest enthusiasm and wildfire." He looked at Margaret Eades, his Baptist bride to be, and thought how he would never for all the world want her caught up in such extremism.[37] At the first camp meeting ever held in Whitewater, about five miles above Harrison in 1808, Wiley was among those who went forward publicly asking the prayers of the church and the instructions given by the ministers to penitents, but he had no experience of regenerating grace.[38] Even after admission to probationary church membership in 1810

> I viewed the altar exercises in a cool, stoical manner until my heart became hard, and my mind skeptical, to such a degree, that my soul was as miserable as it could well be out of hell. In the midst of my dreadful distress, Crume came to me, and asked me how I felt? I told him of my misery, and he invited me to come into the altar, and hear the mourners weep and pray, and join in prayer with and for them. With much reluctance, I consented, and the snare of the devil was broken in five minutes, and his poor prisoner released from his misery. Here I learned that a neglect of duty, and cold criticisms on the work of God's grace, were not good for the soul.[39]

It was as a seeker that he "had much grave conversation on the subject of religion" with Moses Crume; that he "resolved to become religious and began to read the Bible" and kneeled down to pray in an unsuccessful attempt to begin regular family prayer following his father-in-law's death; that he borrowed and read the Methodist *Discipline* under the guidance of Crume; that he joined the Methodist Church as a probationer "with much fear and trembling" on 18 April 1810 at age twenty-two; that he was baptized by pouring by Moses Crume, along with his two oldest children, about one year after he joined the church.[40] He wrote of himself:

> When he joined the Methodists, he well knew that this course would subject him to much reproach, which, however, was the very thing he needed, as it cut him off from the world, and brought him in closer intercourse with the people of God. Sometime in the summer after he joined the church, at a love feast, under the concluding prayer, he trusts, God forgave his sins, and made him measurably a new creature; but he did not receive that bright and strong evidence of his gracious state that many do; but his assurance was a gradual work, and continues to increase to the present day. When he trav-

els from Brookville down to Harrison or elsewhere, and sees the old house yet standing, in which he was blessed of God, he feels mournful, yet glad—mournful to see the old house decaying, but glad that the Lord converted him in it. It is the same house in which Moses Crume received him in church more than thirty-five years ago, and where, he trusts, his name was registered in the Lamb's book of life.[41]

Now he had his testimony. Almost at once he "began to feel impressions that he would be called to preach." This was not a new idea but a possibility he had mentioned occasionally to his friends even before his conversion. His friends and Moses Crume were persuaded he would be a preacher. Crume gave him a written permit to exhort in 1811 which was renewed by the local quarterly conference in 1812.[42] In July of 1813 he was licensed as a local preacher, by his own report probably the first person who was both converted and licensed to preach in Indiana. Only full time traveling preachers could be members of conference. Wiley did not have money or education. He did have a wife and five children under age eight "settled in the wild woods, two miles from where any person lived." However, he was so well and favorably known among Methodists that Russel Bigelow urged him to travel the Lawrenceburg Circuit as junior preacher "through the winter" of 1816–17. Wiley agreed to the three months of temporary duty on the circuit if his wife would consent, thinking she would not. At Bigelow's urging, Margaret Wiley consented.

Wiley and Bigelow were an effective team and there was "a gracious budding in almost all parts of the circuit." Wiley agreed to keep traveling until the end of the conference year, then to become a traveling preacher on trial taking regular full-time circuit assignments. He found that the people would respond to his preaching and that he could conduct camp meeting revivals; 1,189 members were added on his charges during the first four years of his ministry. He was ordained a deacon in the traveling ministry by Bishop McKendree in 1818 and an elder by Bishop Roberts in 1820. The "temporary duty" became thirty-one years of itinerancy.[43]

In 1818 a round of his Whitewater Circuit brought Wiley home to his family only "two days and two pieces of days in the winter and four days in the summer"; there were "thirty-two or three regular sermons in twenty-nine days beside some extra ones." His total pay on Whitewater Circuit, as a married man with seven children, was $76 for the year 1821–22. For 1824–25 on Madison Circuit his claim for his large family according to the *Dis-*

cipline would have been $328. But the collections for the two preachers on the circuit were $130 of which Wiley received $84, mostly in produce.[44]

Indiana was to be his parish. Twenty-seven of his thirty appointments were entirely within the state—eleven years a circuit rider when bridges or roads were few, fourteen years a presiding elder with one of his early districts stretching from the Ohio River to the Great Lakes and including twenty of the rising county seat towns, five years a stationed preacher in principal towns with nearby preaching points added. When he joined the Methodist Church in 1810, the whole membership in Indiana's three circuits was not over eight hundred or nine hundred; in the year of his death the two Methodist conferences in the state reported 60,599 members served by 241 traveling preachers and 572 local preachers.[45] A contemporary non-Methodist lawyer claimed that Allen Wiley had himself done more to improve the manners and morals of Indiana than any other citizen in it.[46]

Allen Wiley's Writings

Realizing that no other person knew the history of Methodism in the state so well as he, Wiley prepared and submitted his "Introduction and Progress of Methodism in Southeastern Indiana" in thirty-seven installments for publication in the *Western Christian Advocate* between 15 August 1845 and 11 December 1846.[47] Realizing that there was no adequate manual for the conduct of preachers serving in the Methodist itinerant system in the Midwest, he prepared a series of twenty articles on the subject for the *Western Christian Advocate* in 1834 and 1835 and revised them in 1845 for publication as a book entitled *A Help to the Performance of Ministerial Duties*. In these books he spoke with equal candor about the state, about its people, about Methodist preachers individually and collectively, and about those parts of the Indiana Methodist enterprise which particularly exercised his mind.[48]

Wiley advocated early division of large circuits so the preachers would have more time for pastoral work and promotion of benevolent causes among the people. He wanted the circuits named for towns with post offices so that people who heard the names would know where the circuits were. The people must be visited personally by the preachers. He had no sympathy with those who protested that smaller circuits would cause a shortage of preachers or result in a lack of support, being sure that the Lord would raise up an ample number of Methodist preachers and that the Methodist people who were provided more pastoral leadership would pay more for pastoral support.[49]

> Some seem to think the traveling preachers can never do their duty unless they are always on horseback, in the pulpit, or the class-room. All these three places are very appropriate for them, but they can never do half their work there in this day. When the country was sparsely settled, and the rides long, the people did not expect more than preaching and class meeting, but now they do expect more, and they will backslide unless the preachers visit them; and if we may judge from the way some of them talk, they backslide purposely because the preachers do not do their duty as pastors. Brethren, you should do your duty, and leave the people without excuse.[50]

While off their horses the preachers were to lead the people in support of Sunday schools, missionary societies, tract societies, Bible societies, temperance societies, and educational institutions—Methodist ones, of course.[51] Preachers must also visit the sick personally, and that with skill and insight. "It is a melancholy fact, that many who are the most ready to visit the sick, are not calculated to do them that kind of good which they most need." On sick calls there was to be sensitive conversation about things that really matter. It was a time for prayer and "if the preacher has a voice for singing, a suitable hymn, sung with pious gravity, will usually be attended with good."[52]

So long as the charges were large and scattered, circuit riders had to stay in the saddle and had to accomplish their pastoral work by careful appointment and oversight of class leaders coupled with quality time spent with the classes by the traveling preacher himself. On each round the preacher was "to become truly acquainted with the spiritual state of the members of society . . . by a close examination of each one." Preachers who neglected their classes would not be useful very long.[53]

> I am aware many preachers preach so long and so loud that they are not well able to meet class after they are done preaching. But one criminal act can never be an excuse for another. A violation of the solemn promise not to speak too long nor too loud, is not a justifiable excuse for neglecting class meetings, which are indispensable to a growth in grace among our people.[54]

Wiley on Revivals and Camp Meetings

About revivals and camp meetings Wiley was somewhat ambivalent, precisely because of his own life experience. "There is no man in Indiana who has had the same amount of experience in this matter as myself," he said. As an enthusiast for Methodist growth, he was well aware that perhaps half the members in the Methodist church were the fruit of camp meetings. He loved camp meetings and filled his history with accounts of their "glorious work." He himself shared leadership in the first camp meeting in the vicinity of Madison which left "most of the young men in the town converted and in the church, and many old ones, too." From Madison the revival "spread in different directions."[55] He devised ways to make the camps less of a burden on the host community. By his plan and announcement for a camp meeting near Brookville in 1818, those attending were to "come with their wagons, and grain, and hay, and feed troughs, and watering buckets, for we did not intend to feed man, woman, or child, horse, ox or ass." Those accustomed to attend camp meetings to "sponge" went hungry and went home. That is the way he handled a camp meeting in 1826 near Charlestown too. Those who professed to be converted at the meeting were given individual notes of admission to present to their local class leaders back home, which almost all of them did. By 1822 he stopped reporting camp meeting converts until they had appeared on the local class rolls.[56]

But even well-regulated camp meetings could not endure because they were constantly invaded.

> Since the country has become more densely populated, there are more persons who go to such meetings merely for recreation, than in former days; in consequence of which, hucksters find it a more profitable business to attend these meetings than formerly; hence they increase in numbers and daring. I have myself seen as many as fourteen huckster wagons at one camp meeting, and perhaps one-fourth as many boys, and lads, and young men, and even middle-aged, and old men about them, as were on the camp ground to attend religious service. Many of these young, and even middle-aged persons, never came on the camp ground, unless it was to interrupt the quiet of the meeting. While they are about these wagons, they learn to run, jump, wrestle, play, yell, swear, talk vulgar, and in some instances, gamble on the Lord's day. Perhaps, in some instances, there is more mischief done to the morals of the youth of the land about these wagons, than there is religious good effected on the camp ground. Now, although the preachers and their people are not to blame for the evil done, yet in view of the fact that we see the mischief is done, in consequence of the coming together of such crowds of heedless sinners, we and other denominations will have to give up our popular meetings in the woods. I will ask any man

who has any judgment and conscience if this is fair? Does our going to a grove to worship God, give a set of rude, covetous persons a right to annoy us, and demoralize our children, and the children of the community in general?[57]

He noted that some states passed legislation to protect camp meetings from vendors of cakes, melons, beer, cider, and whiskey. Indiana actually passed such a law but bungled its implementation so badly that the law itself was dropped, an event viewed as a victory by the hucksters.[58]

There was something else Wiley found disquieting about big revival successes, indoors or out. "It is a melancholy fact, that a prosperous year is almost always succeeded by a year of declension." When Methodist preachers Robert Finley and Walter Griffith hit southeastern Indiana the same year as the Mississippi valley earthquakes, Whitewater Circuit gained 280 members and Lawrenceburg Circuit 183 members in the reports for fall of 1813. However, "the high pressure movements of this year were succeeded with a sad reaction the next year, and it was some years before the church was as healthy and vigorous as she had been."[59] He was also much concerned that alongside the increasing Methodist membership in the West were perhaps half as many persons that were once Methodists but were no longer Methodists or members of any church.

> Such persons are really and permanently injured in their character and moral feelings, and in their future and eternal destiny. The church is, also, injured in her character and influence; for thinking men will conclude, that there must be some defect in her economy or administration, or she would take better care of the persons who join her. He must be dull indeed, who does not know that for the same persons to join and leave the church frequently tends to make her common and contemptible in the eyes of the public. I have viewed these things till, with an aching heart I have been tempted to think, in some cases, what is called a revival is a matter to be deplored; and I have earnestly inquired in my own mind, is there no remedy for evils which succeed and sometimes seem to grow out of, a good thing? I believe there is; but it can only be found in the combined prudence and piety of that class of preachers called revivalists and their successors.[60]

Prudence demanded that wherever proselytes in a revival exceeded the number of sound converts and members the preachers had better beware of "a distressing and calamitous flight." Those in charge of the meetings had better "cease their strong efforts to proselyte" and give themselves to strenuous instruction and discipline of the converts with emphasis on visitation and pastoral care.[61]

Wiley on Methodist Family Life

Wiley wanted the Methodists of Indiana to be pardoned and regenerated persons. They were not intended to be living in uncertainty or discomfort about their spiritual condition, a situation he thought likely to result from some medium level of unfaithfulness well short of entire wickedness or backsliding.

> We are fully persuaded that you can not long retain your religious enjoyment unless you aim at such a degree of grace as will result in your entire sanctification; for when Christ died for us, it was to redeem us from all iniquity and to purify us unto himself, a peculiar people, zealous of good works. We would most earnestly urge you to read and study much on the doctrine of holiness or entire sanctification. After having ourselves read most that has been written on this subject, we would take the liberty to recommend the writings of Mr. Wesley and Mr. Fletcher on this subject in preference to all others, as they state, and defend, and enforce the doctrine with a clearness and energy unequaled by any writers before or since their day.[62]

He wanted them to be a reading and intelligent people, not indiscriminate but selective readers, especially readers of the ample materials available from the Methodist Book Concern at New York and Cincinnati.[63] He wanted them in regular attendance at class meetings.

> Many join our Church as seekers of salvation who, if not attentive to this means of grace, soon lose their desires, and are in danger of living unconverted all their days; but if they attend the meetings named, they have the subject of religion so often and earnestly pressed upon them, that they are likely never to rest till converted to God; and he must be but a poor judge of fallen human nature, and have but a poor knowledge of Satan's devices, who thinks he can retain his piety with any less available means than were used by him in his attainment of so great a blessing. We therefore hope you will not regard attendance on class meeting as an unpleasant task, but as a great and gracious privilege, and that we shall not be under the necessity of dismembering any of you for willful neglect.[64]

Wiley wanted his people involved in regular family devotions with Scripture reading and prayer but also with regular singing and catechizing in the homes. He wanted them to be strenuous keepers of the Sabbath and abstainers from alcohol, this latter requirement for the membership having been temporarily lost in the transfer of Methodism from England to America. According to him, Methodists were to stand to sing and kneel to pray. And they were to be generous in support of ministers, missions, and "the benevolent institutions of the Church, which are intended to ameliorate the condition of suffering humanity."[65]

There were also churches to build. Wiley himself was attached to the old Methodist way of meeting in private homes rather than build churches.

> I can have more true religious enjoyment in standing behind a split-bottomed chair, on a week day, in a private house, and preaching to twenty-five or thirty simple hearted people, who fear and love God (if they will not chew and spit tobacco over the floor and furniture), than in preaching to hundreds in the best church this side of heaven. And then, after preaching, to meet the class, as they are seated in the good brother's house, which is for the time being God's own house and heaven's gate, is most delightful, and is the very next thing to heaven itself.[66]

But he knew in his administrative heart that Methodists must compete in building churches. At Madison the congregation held for too long onto their "little old meetin'- house, which had well nigh ruined them by causing them to lose from their congregation many valuable citizens who would now have been members of our church."[67]

Wiley's Evaluation of Methodist Preachers

Wiley held that democracy within the "Methodist economy" was to be carefully circumscribed. The episcopal machinery was to be responsive to the needs of the people and in some degree to their wants. Young men who found "approval with the people" were the candidates to be invited to test their gifts as exhorters and preachers.[68] The conference at every quarterly meeting of circuit personnel began with the query "are there any complaints?" Preachers who incurred many complaints in such meetings or in reports of the people directly to the presiding elder were not returned a second year to the same circuit. Wiley said, "If the practice were general to change all dull men often, and let them know that the people wish it to be so, it would rouse them to more effort, or drive them from the field where others would work better."[69] He wanted nobody to question the right of the duly elected bishop to appoint the presiding elders or the right of the bishop,

assisted by the presiding elders, to station the preachers. In the same way he wanted to keep inviolate the authority of the individual preacher to appoint and direct or remove class leaders, to receive or decline to receive members, and to renew or decline to renew tickets for admission to the love feast. He was sure that open election by the membership at any of these levels would loose such a competition and "electioneering spirit" as would destroy the peace and harmony of the church.[70]

Wiley was quick to defend the Hoosier Methodist preachers, as a group, against charges of ignorance and lack of theological training. Nobody could come close to them for success.[71] Yet he himself looked at the individual Methodist preachers of his generation with a very sharp eye and described them with a very sharp tongue. Traveling preachers should be more careful about licensing local men to preach or exhort, he said. "Were the preachers conscientious, as they should be, the quarterly conference would not have to spend so much time in examining the characters of so many drones, as is now the case, and the presiding elders would not have to write and sign so many useless licenses as they now do."[72] Wiley said Peter Cartwright had a redundancy of wit "and uses it more freely than a grave minister of the Gospel should. I suppose that nothing but death will cure him of this habit."[73] Samuel H. Thompson knew so many stories that the heads of his sermons were all tales, a style not advocated by Wiley because "I doubt the verity of ninety-nine out of the hundred of the anecdotes."[74] John Somerville had some acquirements but was regarded as having more talents than he really possessed. He was especially given to freakish allegorization of biblical texts; "I hope he has outlived them."[75] James T. Wells "was a good man and very conscientious, but his conscience was of that troublesome kind which was a great inconvenience to himself and all persons with whom he had much connection or intercourse."[76] Several preachers partially made up for their lack of training with zeal, such as George Randel who was reported to be "the best preacher he had ever heard, to be so ignorant as he was."[77] Hardest to use or to forgive were those preachers reported as feeble, without energy or zeal, not warm, not very animated, or tame.[78]

If Wiley felt constrained to accept some ignorant preachers, he did not intend for them to stay ignorant. Circuit rider Joseph Tarkington said: "The outfit of the itinerant, at that day, in addition to horse, saddle, and bridle, was a pair of saddle-bags, Bible, hymn-book, thread and needles for repairs, and a package of tallow candles. I always carried candles to read by, and many cabins were thus lit up that had not seen the light of candles hitherto."[79] The first three chapters of Wiley's manual for preachers set a very high standard of independent study. Seven hours of sleep were to be enough for a traveling preacher.

> On an average he will need two hours to ride to his appointments, and two more to hold meeting; fifteen minutes in the morning, and the same in the evening, to attend family worship, where he may stay, will make half an hour; twenty minutes, three times each day, for private devotion, will make an hour; thirty minutes, three times per diem, for eating, will be one hour and a half; and to the foregoing may be added two hours employed in profitable conversation with the children and others, where he may be; all of which will make sixteen hours out of twenty-four, leaving eight to be employed in mental culture, which will be as much time as most constitutions can endure close mental application, without endangering the health of the body. I have allowed two hours for riding, which, however, in fair weather, I consider the best time for learning grammar, or logic, or any similar study, or in preparation for the pulpit; and if thus employed may be added to the eight, which will make ten to be used in every twenty-four, in gaining a good store of general knowledge. Now, we behold the young man, with eight hours or more on his hands for valuable use, or the most criminal abuse.[80]

In the use of all this available time, the preacher was to demonstrate that he was a Methodist by using such a method as would not waste the time or his energies.

> At least two hours in each day ought to be spent in a close attention to Biblical studies; and more, if it be found necessary, to enable the young preacher to bring out of his treasury things new and old. Two hours may be employed, beside the time in riding, for the study of grammar, till that science be acquired. Two hours may be spent in reading doctrinal, and two in historical and scientific works.[81]

Wiley himself showed the way. Having begun his ministry with the most modest of elementary educations, he acquired sufficient liberal education and mastery of English to excel in preaching and writing. He served on the board of trustees for both Indiana University (1834–38) and Indiana Asbury University (DePauw). To the mastery of English he added competence in Hebrew, Latin, and Greek; he was offered appointment to the faculty of Indiana University to teach classical languages.[82]

Methodist itinerants rarely ended their traveling easily. The successful professionals kept going so long as they could throw a leg over the saddle. They viewed retirement, superannuation they called it, as worse than death.

They were given to repeated farewell trips around the circuit and emotional last sermons at camp meetings and conferences. Even Allen Wiley made a painful exit. After four years as presiding elder of Connersville district, named Brookville in 1843, he was stationed at Centenary Church in New Albany in 1846. To this forward-looking city congregation he may have seemed an old man at age fifty-seven. His wife was so limited by rheumatism that she could not walk across the room. A portion of the congregation let the bishop know that they wanted a new minister. Equally vexing to him was the "decrease in our numbers for several years past."[83] The Methodist church in Indiana had actually declined by about ten thousand members from 1843 to the year of Wiley's superannuation in 1847. "We fear preachers and people have been too languid in their prayers and less ardent in their zeal than they should be," Wiley said. "We should aim at nothing less than the conversion of the whole world, and for this we should pray day and night, and frequently join fasting with our prayers."[84] He died in July of 1848, a few months too early to hear that the trend had reversed. Indiana Methodism surged forward again. By 1860 there were 96,965 Methodist members, organized in four conferences.[85] They were to double again by the century's end.

NOTES

1. Frederick A. Norwood, *The Story of American Methodism* (Nashville, Tenn.: Abingdon Press, 1974), 147–48.

2. L. C. Rudolph, *Francis Asbury* (Nashville, Tenn.: Abingdon Press, 1966), 73.

3. *The Journal and Letters of Francis Asbury*, ed. Elmer T. Clark, J. Manning Potts, and Jacob S. Payton, 3 vols. (Nashville, Tenn.: Abingdon Press, 1958), 2:518, 631, 713.

4. Norwood, *Story of American Methodism*, 149–50.

5. Norwood, *Story of American Methodism*, 154; Winthrop S. Hudson, *Religion in America* (New York: Charles Scribner's Sons, 1965), 129–30.

6. Sydney E. Ahlstrom, *A Religious History of the American People* (New Haven, Conn.: Yale University Press, 1972), 436.

7. Herbert L. Heller, *Indiana Conference of the Methodist Church 1832–1956* (Greencastle, Ind.: Historical Society of the Indiana Conference, 1957), 22.

8. Norwood, *Story of American Methodism*, 152.

9. Asbury, *Journal and Letters*, 2:577.

10. William Warren Sweet, *Circuit-Rider Days in Indiana* (Indianapolis, Ind.: W. K. Stewart Co., 1916), 2, 4–5.

11. *Autobiography of Peter Cartwright, the Backwoods Preacher*, ed. W. P. Strickland (New York: Carlton and Porter, 1857), 167.

12. Allen Wiley, "Methodism in Southeastern Indiana (for the *Western Christian Advocate*)," *Indiana Magazine of History* 23 (March–December 1927): 4–9, 21–25; Sweet, *Circuit-Rider Days*, 5–9.

13. Fernandez C. Holliday, *Indiana Methodism* (Cincinnati, Ohio: Hitchcock and Walden, 1873), 28–29.

14. Cartwright, *Autobiography*, 55.

15. Cartwright, *Autobiography*, 167.

16. Cartwright, *Autobiography*, 78, 96, 126.

17. Sweet, *Circuit-Rider Days*, 39–45.

18. Holliday, *Indiana Methodism*, 69; Vincennes and Madison circuits are described and charted in Heller, *Indiana Conference*, 28–32.

19. Wiley, "Methodism," 432–42; John C. Smith, *Reminiscences of Early Methodism in Indiana* (Indianapolis, Ind.: J. M. Olcott, 1879), 23–51.

20. Smith, *Reminiscences*, 38–39.

21. Sweet, *Circuit-Rider Days*, 53; Wiley, "Methodism," 414–15.

22. Holliday, *Indiana Methodism*, 146; but note variant figures and the actual list of fifty-three appointments of preachers made for 1832 in Sweet, *Circuit-Rider Days*, 51–52, 108–10.

23. Sweet, *Circuit-Rider Days*, 91, 101–2, 120.

24. Sweet, *Circuit-Rider Days*, 102.

25. Holliday, *Indiana Methodism*, 146–47.

26. Thomas A. Kuster, "Frontier Homily: The Preaching of Indiana Methodist Circuit Riders" (Master's thesis, Indiana University, 1962), 72, 114–42; Theodore D. Welker, *Conflicts and Triumphs of an Itinerant: Rev. John Kiger, D.D.* (Cincinnati, Ohio: Cranston and Stowe, 1891), 51.

27. Wiley, "Methodism," 166.

28. George Richard Crooks, *The Life of Bishop Matthew Simpson of the Methodist Episcopal Church* (New York: Harper and Brothers, 1891), 200.

29. Kuster, "Frontier Homily," 124–25, 139; Wiley, "Methodism," 160–61.

30. Wiley, "Methodism," 159.

31. Kuster, "Frontier Homily," 64, 66.

32. Fernandez C. Holliday, *Life and Times of Rev. Allen Wiley . . . Also, Including His Original Letters, Entitled, "A Help to the Performance of Ministerial Duties."* (Cincinnati, Ohio: Swormstedt and A. Poe, 1853), 273–86.

33. Holliday, *Life and Times*, 286.

34. William Warren Sweet, Elizabeth Nottingham, Thomas Kuster, Fernandez C. Holliday, and almost all historians of Indiana Methodism are much indebted to the works of Allen Wiley.

35. Wiley, "Methodism," 24–38; Holliday, *Indiana Methodism*, 19–21.

36. Wiley, "Methodism," 43.

37. Wiley, "Methodism," 20, 38.

38. Wiley, "Methodism," 40, 42.

39. Wiley, "Methodism," 52.

40. Wiley, "Methodism," 43–45.

41. Wiley, "Methodism," 45.

42. Wiley, "Methodism," 45.

43. Wiley, "Methodism," 198–99; *Indiana Magazine of History* 23 (March 1927): 1–2.

44. Wiley, "Methodism," 211, 261–62, 286.

45. Holliday, *Life and Times*, 56, 102–3, 146.

46. *Indiana Magazine of History* 23 (March 1927): 2.

47. Citations here are from the republication in the four issues of *Indiana Magazine of History*, volume 23, for 1927.

48. Holliday, *Life and Times*, 76, 153–55; Citations here are from the book as it appears in part two of Holliday, *Life and Times*, 151–291.

49. Holliday, *Life and Times*, 60; Wiley, "Methodism," 317, 395, 402–3.

50. Wiley, "Methodism," 330.

51. Holliday, *Life and Times*, 121; Welker, *Conflict and Triumphs*, 213–17.

52. Holliday, *Life and Times*, 183, 185.

53. Holliday, *Life and Times*, 181–82.

54. Holliday, *Life and Times*, 182.

55. Wiley, "Methodism," 179, 183, 203–4.

56. Wiley, "Methodism," 212–13, 261, 299–300.

57. Wiley, "Methodism," 179–80.

58. Wiley, "Methodism," 180–81.

59. Wiley, "Methodism," 59–62, 160, 271.

60. Wiley, "Methodism," 151.

61. Wiley, "Methodism," 151–52.

62. Holliday, *Life and Times*, 112–13.

63. Holliday, *Life and Times*, 116; Kuster, "Frontier Homily," 72.

64. Holliday, *Life and Times*, 115.

65. Holliday, *Life and Times*, 114–16, 166; Sweet, *Circuit-Rider Days*, 147.

66. Wiley, "Methodism," 175.

67. Wiley's admonitions were widely heard. At the request of the Indiana Conference in 1847, he wrote the "pastoral address" to all Indiana Methodists. It was ordered published in the *Western Christian Advocate* and preachers were asked to read it to all their congregations. Holliday, *Life and Times*, 111–17; Wiley, "Methodism," 173–76, 420.

68. Holliday, *Life and Times*, 271–72.

69. Wiley, "Methodism," 423.

70. Holliday, *Life and Times*, 210, 219–30, 273, 275.

71. Holliday, *Life and Times*, 131–35.

72. Holliday, *Life and Times*, 272.

73. Wiley, "Methodism," 188.

74. Wiley, "Methodism," 146.

75. Wiley, "Methodism," 168–69.

76. Wiley, "Methodism," 206.

77. Wiley, "Methodism," 299.

78. Wiley, "Methodism," 49, 179, 304–5, 314, 405.

79. Holliday, *Indiana Methodism*, 259.

80. Holliday, *Life and Times*, 171.

81. Holliday, *Life and Times*, 173.

82. Holliday, *Life and Times*, 104.

83. Holliday, *Life and Times*, 85, 117.

84. Holliday, *Life and Times*, 117.

85. Holliday, *Indiana Methodism*, 147.

EARLY CATHOLICS

Methodists did dominate the religious history of Indiana in the first half of the 1800s. Nevertheless, it was the Catholics who had all the chronological priority, having been represented in the area long before the substantial influx of English-speaking settlers. French Catholics sought routes to link the St. Lawrence River and the Great Lakes to the Mississippi before Indiana had a name. They crossed its unmarked boundaries (1) by way of the Fox and the Wisconsin rivers; (2) by way of the Chicago and the Illinois rivers; (3) by way of the St. Joseph and the Kankakee rivers; and (4) by way of the Maumee and the Wabash rivers.[1]

Very early the missionaries evangelized this region under the jurisdiction of Quebec. Father Hennepin, in company with La Salle and Tonti, went over the St. Joseph-Kankakee portage. Father Claude Allouez had a chapel at Fort St. Joseph as early as 1680. Father Aveneau who died at Quebec in 1711, was among the Pottawatomis. Charlevoix, writing in 1721, states that the two villages of the Miamis and the Pottawatomis on the St. Joseph were mostly Christian, but for a long time were without a pastor. As a result, he continued, it would be difficult to bring them back to the exercises of their religion. Certainly the Indians in northern Indiana were attended, more or less regularly, by missionaries down to the fall of the French power; but the suppression of the Jesuits left them without a shepherd.[2]

In the early 1700s a few French families clustered at trading posts at Ouiatanon on the upper Wabash (Lafayette), at the point where the St. Marys and the St. Joseph rivers form the Maumee (Fort Wayne), and on the lower Wabash (Vincennes). They too received occasional ministry from Catholic missionary visitors. Vincennes received the most consistent ministry, although even it had spotty oversight at best. Catholic parish records there began in 1749 and a log church was erected in 1785.[3]

It should be remembered that from the departure of Father Devernai [as a result of the suppression of the Jesuits in 1763] until Father Gibault's visit in 1770 no priest was seen at Vincennes. Between 1770 and 1779 there were seven visits of a month or two; and from 1779 until 1784 no priest was in the town. Thus those that were more than 40 years of age had passed their childhood with an opportunity to attend Mass and be instructed by the priest during only a total period of one year.[4]

Bishop Benedict Joseph Flaget

Early Indiana Catholics were under the jurisdiction of bishops in Quebec and in Baltimore. Then, in 1810, Benedict Joseph Flaget was named bishop of the new Diocese of Bardstown, Kentucky, with Indiana a part of his charge. Flaget was the former pastor of Saint Francis Xavier Church at Vincennes and former schoolmaster for the Vincennes settlement, sure to be a friend of Catholic missions in Indiana. On his tours as bishop he would visit a few Catholic families just across the river from Louisville and a few scattered west in Indiana along the Buffalo Trace. At Vincennes he was welcomed at least seven times between 1810 and 1834 as episcopal visitor among the parishioners whom he had served as priest from 1792 to 1795. He did the best he could for them, and for the scattering of Catholic missionaries among the French and Indians of Indiana. But he always had too few priests. In 1815 Father Nerinckx said "Michigan has one priest. Indiana has no priest. Illinois has two priests."[5]

Lack of priests was the chief handicap of the successors of Flaget, bishops in the new Diocese of Vincennes (Diocese of Indianapolis after 1898) formed in 1834. Bruté, Hailandiere, Bazin, St. Palais, Chatard, Chartrand were their names. French clergy generally put a conservative continental imprint on the ecclesiastical organization and devotional practices of American Catholicism.[6]

Bishop Simon William Gabriel Bruté de Rémur

Simon William Gabriel Bruté de Rémur, spiritual director for a seminary in Maryland, was consecrated as the first bishop of Vincennes. He was "a voice crying in the wilderness," he said. After the party of clergy that installed him as bishop had gone home he was left essentially as pastor at Vincennes, spending Christmas of 1834 with no other ordained person for company. Simon Lalumiere, a native of Vincennes and the first Indiana priest ordained by the bishop of Bardstown, now at work among the missions of Daviess County, was the only priest permanently attached to the diocese. Joseph Ferneding was on loan from Bishop Flaget of Kentucky to remain in charge of several missions among the Germans in Dearborn, Franklin, and Ripley counties along the Ohio some 150 miles away. Ignatius St. Cyr was on loan from Bishop Rosati of St. Louis for one year and was stationed at Chicago, 225 miles away. Stephen Theodore Badin and Louis Deseille were under appointment from Bishop Fenwick of Cincinnati as missionaries among the Indians in northern Indiana, extending their ministry as well to Catholics in South Bend, Fort Wayne, Logansport, and along the line of the proposed Wabash and Erie Canal. Bruté's parish at Vincennes was so run down that only one man came to communion during the first month of his ministry there. Total income for the parish was no more than three hundred dollars per year, and most of that was paid in produce. By spring Vincennes parish life was rejuvenated. Sixty persons received their first communion at Easter; ninety were confirmed the following Sunday.[7]

Late in April Bruté and his only priest Lalumiere set out to survey the area of the new bishop's responsibility.

Lalumiere visited the east side of the diocese—Columbus, Shelbyville, Abington, Fort Wayne, Logansport, Peru, Lagro, Huntington. Bruté took a horseback ride of 550 miles into Illinois to Paris, Danville, Georgetown, and Chicago before turning east to Michigan City, La-Porte, the Indian missions of Louis Deseille near South Bend and on the Tippecanoe, and along the course of the Wabash back to Vincennes. It was a well reported survey.[8] Bruté intended to let the Catholic world know about his needs. His diocese comprised the whole of Indiana and about one-third of Illinois, "about 55,000 square miles or more," he said. The population was about 403,000 in 1830. Bruté thought there were at least 25,000 Catholics among them at the beginning of his episcopate, many drifting into religious indifference or losing their faith for want of priests. After his survey he said "I have resolved and I do the more so now to go to get priests from the old countries since I can get none here."[9] That was to be the pattern for the early bishops. Back to Europe they went, appealing everywhere on behalf of an exciting new frontier and on behalf of Indiana Catholics living and dying in the wilderness without the benefits of their church and its ministry.

Bruté was receiving support from the Leopoldine Society, a mission society organized in Vienna in 1828, so he sent them a report of his first tour of his diocese in 1835 and visited Austria on his European tour of 1835–36.[10] He was befriended by the Empress of Austria and Prince Metternich; he visited Rome to receive the Pope's benediction. In his native city of Rennes in the province of Brittany he explained his need for everything but particularly for a priest who could be his vicar-general and coadjutor and associate in the whole of his work. The bishop of Rennes designated Celestine de la Hailandiere who accepted the duty. Both lifted up the cause of the Diocese of Vincennes in the churches and seminaries of France until their departure for Indiana in July of 1836.[11]

Among others in Rennes, they were followed by Father Corbe and Benjamin Petit, a fine young lawyer, who renounced his worldly career, asking as a particular favor to be sent to the Indians so soon as he would be prepared for the priesthood; in Paris and Lyons, Michael Edgar Gordon Shawe, formerly of the British army, but then a student of St. Sulpice; Father Julian Benoit, now [1883] Vicar-General of Fort Wayne; Father Maurice De St. Palais, who was also at a later time to become Bishop of Vincennes. They took along with them at the same time, large sums of money and great stores of all kinds to furnish the different missions, in charge of which priests were to be appointed.[12]

Bishop Celestine de la Hailandiere

Hailandiere was back in Europe recruiting help for Vincennes in 1839 when he received word of Bruté's death and was consecrated his successor.

> He sent ahead quite a number of clerical students and several priests, under the lead of Father Aug. Martin, a clergyman of the Diocese of Rennes, widely known there at the time for his abilities, and who relinquished the post of chaplain of the Royal College of Rennes . . . With them he also sent large stores of sacerdotal vestments, sacred vessels, books, etc., which he had procured all over France by visiting friends of Bishop Bruté and his own. He had worked very hard indeed to procure all this. Great as was the quantity procured on the first voyage, it could not be compared to what was then brought along. He soon followed, bringing along with him large sums of money which he had obtained from various sources, but chiefly by pleading the needs of his mission before the Councils of the Society for the Propagation of the Faith in Paris and Lyons, and they promised a continuance of help for several years, giving it afterward steadily and largely.[13]

Immediate aid from Europe was important but even more important was planting Catholic institutions which could raise up Indiana's Catholic leadership on its own midwestern soil. Hailandiere convinced the newly established Society of the Holy Cross to send a delegation of brothers from France to Indiana under direction of Edward Sorin to found schools for boys. The efforts of this society, later allied with those of the Sisters of the Holy Cross, developed that most prominent complex of Indiana's Catholic institutions centered at Notre Dame and St. Mary at South Bend.[14] Hailandiere persuaded the Sisters of Providence at Ruillé-sur-Loir to send six sisters led by Mother Theodore Guerin and Sister Mary Joseph le Fer to develop education for girls, orphan asylums, and hospitals. They were the founders of St. Mary of the Woods near Terre Haute.[15]

Bishop James M. Maurice de Long d'Aussac de St. Palais

James M. Maurice de Long d'Aussac de St. Palais, bishop of Vincennes 1849–77, visited Europe three times. St. Palais named Joseph Kundek his vicar-general for the diocese and encouraged Kundek's efforts to secure priests for the German Catholic settlers he was colonizing at Jasper, Ferdinand, Celestine, and Troy. Kundek went to German-speaking Switzerland in 1852 where he told the story of America's need to the Benedictine Abbey of Einsiedeln. These Benedictines sent a delegation to America to investigate. The eventual result was a mission house established in Indiana in 1854 and named Saint Meinrad after the hermit monk long venerated at Einsiedeln. Following expansion and consolidation of the Indiana mission under leadership of the monk Martin Marty, Saint Meinrad was raised to the status of an abbey in 1870.[16] At Oldenburg in Franklin County, Indiana, St. Palais commended the enterprise of Mother Theresa and her Sisters of St. Francis. She had been invited there from Vienna in 1850 by local priest Francis Joseph Rudolf to be co-founder of a sisterhood to minister to his predominantly German parishes. St. Palais supported the request of the Benedictine fathers at St. Meinrad that the Benedictine sisters at St. Walburg, a Convent at Covington, Kentucky, establish a convent at Ferdinand to take charge of Catholic schools. Thus Indiana began sharing to some degree in the nation's remarkable increase of nuns, an increase from fewer than forty to more than forty thousand religious sisters during the nineteenth century giving the Catholic Church nearly four times as many nuns as priests by the century's close.[17]

Catholic Revivals

Indiana's call for help from abroad came at a time of renewed Catholic piety in Europe. Vigorous members of religious orders were open to a call to frontier missions overseas. Many were excited about investing their lives in ministry to the savages and to Catholics losing their faith in the American wilds. Revivals called "parish missions" had long been effective in renewing the faithful in Europe. Among the scattered immigrants and their children settling in America there were thousands of nominal Catholics barely on the fringes of the faith. Priests were scarce and parishes often feeble. It was a situation that cried for revival and Americans were attuned to revival. The first Catholic revivalists came from Europe. Later they came to be trained in the United States. They were generally ordained monks such as Redemptorists, Jesuits, Paulists, Vincentians, Franciscans, Passionists, or Benedictines.

A local priest would invite such a preacher or team of preachers to visit for about a week to lead a parish mission. Some of the preachers became specialists engaged full-time in this itinerant revival ministry. Some revivalists prepared manuals detailing every step in the conduct of a proper parish mission. They were masters of emotional motivation. The preachers spoke plainly and specifically about the shape of sin. They said that Catholics persisting in mortal sin were snuffing out the grace implanted by their baptism. They said many were in immediate danger of hell. They exhorted all hearers to nothing less than a conversion—repentance, a new heart, a new direction, a new kind of life. The repentant were urged to a searching time in the confessional leading to absolution and satisfaction. Then came the joyous celebration of communion. A good parish mission was to leave the individual members inspired for a new level of life, the parish church lifted up as a center of religious activity, and the pastor heartened for his labors. People renewed in their religion would be receiving the sacraments regularly. The pace of the whole range of personal pious practices would be quickened.[18]

The Jesuit Francis Xavier Weninger was one of the early Catholic revivalists to come to America. He arrived from Austria in 1848 and conducted his first mission in the United States in December of that year. It was held at Oldenburg, Indiana, at the invitation of the pastor Francis Joseph Rudolf.

> There was a marvelous response. Some people came from as great a distance as twenty miles, which meant rising at 2 o'clock in the morning, in order to be in time for the first sermon. Every Catholic who attended the mission went to confession. Over 1000 persons received Holy Communion, including over 300 married men. Father Rudolph [sic] asserts that, although three sermons were given daily in addition to the short communion address, not a single instruction passed but that the missioner drew from his hearers tears of repentance for their sins, and tears of joy because of the consolation of the grace of conversion. He makes mention of three particularly powerful sermons; the first was a solemn apology before the Blessed Sacrament for the sins that had been committed, the second was a still more solemn renewal of baptismal vows, and the third the touching farewell sermon.[19]

The next year Fort Wayne was on his expanding mission itinerary. About 280 missions were conducted in the Midwest between 1850 and 1860; Weninger himself did at least 170 of them. His instruction manual for such meetings grew to exceed two hundred pages. From his base at Saint Francis Xavier College at Cincinnati he conducted some eight hundred parish missions across the United States in a career extending over thirty-seven years. For nearly a century these revivals called "parish missions" or "retreats" or "exercises" were a staple of Catholic community life in Indiana. They were the most visible form of the persistent evangelical dimension of American Catholicism.[20]

Catholic Institutions

Catholic foundations began their work in Indiana in extreme simplicity and poverty. The survivors endured fires, crippling indebtedness, and dissension both internal and external. Members of the religious foundations were assigned to teach and to operate institutions with no more academic or technical or professional qualifications than the poorly prepared non-Catholics of the same era and generally with even less pay. Superiors were thrust into demanding leadership roles. Many responded admirably, combining ability with devotion and self denial to produce results quite beyond ordinary expectation. From the ranks of these orders and from their centers in Indiana, hundreds of religious workers poured into Catholic institutions. Before the end of the nineteenth century, Indiana, a major debtor to Catholic missionary assistance from Europe, was also a sender of Catholic educators and missionaries to the world.

Nor were the larger foundations mentioned above by any means to be the whole of the flowering of the state's Catholic institutions. Each parish wished to build a church worthy of the whole range of ministries and sacraments which centered there. An impressive church building was a testimony of the devotion of the people to their faith and to their ethnic pride. Most Catholics wanted to maintain parochial schools. When Mary Salesia Godecker summarized the schools and faculties in Indianapolis diocese in 1925 she said:

> We find the Sisters of St. Francis, Oldenburg, employed in forty-one schools and the diocesan Orphanage for boys; the Sisters of St. Benedict, Ferdinand, are engaged in thirty-three schools; the Sisters of Providence conduct thirty schools and the diocesan Orphanage for girls; the Sisters of Mercy are in charge of one school; the Ursuline Sisters are engaged in six schools; the Sisters of St. Joseph conduct two schools; the Brothers of the Sacred Heart conduct one school, and the remainder are conducted by lay teachers.[21]

And for Fort Wayne, the other diocese in the state:

> Sisters of Perpetual Adoration (in 18 schools), Sisters of Notre Dame (13), Sisters of the Holy Cross (13), Sisters of St. Joseph (11), Sisters of Providence (8), Poor Handmaids of Jesus Christ (7), Sisters of St. Agnes (6), Sisters of St. Francis of St. Kunigunda (6), Sisters of St. Francis of the Sacred Heart (5), Sisters of the Most Precious Blood (4), Sisters of the Holy Family of Nazareth (3), Sisters of Divine Charity (2), Sisters of St. Francis (2), Felician Sisters (2), Sisters of Mercy (1), Sisters of SS. Cyril and Methodius (1).[22]

Twenty-three of the Catholic schools in Indiana that year were public schools, staffed by qualified Catholic sisters with public school funds.[23] For the remaining 208, and for all Catholic schools to a large extent, support had to come from tuition and from church member contributions and from fund raising events. Tuition charges and annual expense per pupil had to be kept very low; this usually meant that the teaching was to be done by religious orders. Further foundations were established to care for the sick, the poor, and the orphans. Contemplatives devoted themselves to prayer on the world's behalf.

When Bruté became first bishop of Vincennes in 1834, he and Lalumiere were the only 2 priests in Indiana. There were 22 priests at the end of Bruté's episcopate in 1838, 35 priests when St. Palais became bishop in 1849, and 127 priests when St. Palais died in 1877.[24] St. Palais ordained 4 priests at the theological seminary at St. Meinrad in June of 1867, the first ordination of secular priests there. After considerable fuss about having to pay $75 per semester for board and tuition for his seminarians at St. Meinrad, the bishop ordained a class of eight to the priesthood there in September of 1868.[25]

Sources of Catholic Growth

If the number of priests grew fast, the number of Catholics grew faster. Bruté thought there were at least twenty-five thousand Catholics in his diocese in 1834. By 1838 he thought both the general population and the number of Catholics had about doubled so that he had at least fifty thousand to serve. He guessed, erroneously, that the Methodists formed one-fifth of the total population, the Baptists one-fifth, the Presbyterians one-fifth, the Catholics one-fifteenth, the Quakers one-twenty-fifth, the Lutherans one-fiftieth, the Episcopalians one-fiftieth, and those professing no creed one-third. He said there had been absolute progress in increasing the number of Catholic clergy but no progress relative to the increase in infidelity or even of Protestantism.[26] Even after the diocese of Chicago was created in November of 1843 and all Illinois territory was removed from the diocese of Vincennes, Indiana's estimated Catholic population was about fifty thousand again by 1850.

Part of the Catholic growth came by natural increase among the Catholic families settled in Indiana. There were also some Catholics among the immigrants from New York, Ohio, Kentucky, Tennessee, and the Carolinas. But the immigration from Europe was the most impressive source of Catholic growth. Even in the 1830s, when Bruté was finding his way as first bishop of the Diocese

of Vincennes, Indiana was aflame with transportation fever. There were great plans for roads and railroads and canals. The projects that actually got finished were often built by laborers from Europe. Stephen Theodore Badin wrote from northern Indiana to Bishop Purcell of Cincinnati: "I must go soon to Fort Wayne, thence visit the Forks of the Wabash where many Irish and German Catholics have been expecting me, who are employed in digging a canal, and are desirous of building a chapel."[27]

European laborers came to dig the canals and to occupy the lands made convenient for settlement by the new transportation. Auguste Martin wrote from Logansport in 1841 that most of his parishioners were Irish canal workers. Many of them had moved on to a new construction project in Illinois but most of the 125 Catholic families remaining were Irish. Indiana did not receive as many foreign immigrants as its neighboring states. Its best land was no longer as cheap as that in Illinois or Iowa and it had no metropolis like Cincinnati, St. Louis, or Chicago to attract immigrants from abroad. Nevertheless, many did come. In 1850 some 52.8 percent of Indiana's foreign-born were German and 23 percent were Irish. From 1850 to 1860 the foreign-born portion of the state's population grew from 5.6 percent to 8.8 percent. The state's population grew 36 percent in that decade but the number of foreign settlers and the membership of the Catholic Church in Indiana more than doubled.[28]

Growth in Southern Indiana

In southern Indiana the most progressive Catholic settlements were among the Germans in the river counties and the eastern counties. Evansville had 8,374 foreigners in a total population of 20,552 by 1860; about four-fifths of the citizens of greater Evansville were German immigrants or descendants of such. Spencer, Perry, and Dubois counties developed substantial rural immigrant communities, predominantly German. The river cities of Vincennes, New Albany, Jeffersonville, and Madison received sizable Catholic populations in spite of nativist pressure by the Know-Nothing movement. In the Whitewater valley north and northeast of Madison, Catholic life flourished. Irish laborers came in to construct the Whitewater Canal. Germans established their farms and mills with a convenient produce outlet through Lawrenceburg or Cincinnati. Missionary pastors Joseph Ferneding and Francis Joseph Rudolf were busy founding and serving new parishes, assisted by the Franciscans at Oldenburg. By 1860, eight southeastern counties had twenty-seven

Catholic churches, about as many as the whole northern half of the state. The number of foreign-born inhabitants in these Whitewater counties rose to average one to every five native Americans. The first Know-Nothing lodge in Indiana was established in Lawrenceburg in February of 1854. Newspaper editors in Aurora, Brookville, and Rushville viewed the "rise of Romanism" with alarm.[29]

Growth in Northern Indiana

Northern Indiana long remained missionary territory for Catholics. Indianapolis was a very special case with its improving transportation, its industrialization, and its influx of immigrants. Foreign-born population there rose from 1,927 in 1850 to 6,395 in 1860 with Irish and Germans predominant. Each had a thriving parish in the city by 1860. Anti-Catholic papers and speeches rallied only limited followings and did little to hamper the Catholic growth. Lafayette had a church for English-speaking Catholics and a church for German-speaking Catholics before 1860. So did Fort Wayne. Each of the rising Wabash towns formed its Catholic parish—Logansport, Peru, Lagro, and Huntington. The number of Catholic churches in northern Indiana nearly doubled between 1850 and 1857, again because of heavy immigration and improved transportation. However, many lacked resident pastors and depended on occasional missionary visits.[30]

In 1857 forty-two counties of northern Indiana were set off as the diocese of Fort Wayne.[31] With the new bishop John Henry Luers busy providing more priests, as many new parishes were formed during the years 1858 to 1860 as had been founded from 1850 to 1857. The northern border counties were inundated with immigrants in the 1850s, the foreign-born especially notable in the lake counties and in the St. Joseph–Kankakee region. The network of railroads kept bringing in the Irish and the Germans. So the Diocese of Fort Wayne began rather late and rather small—perhaps sixteen thousand Catholics scattered over its twenty thousand square miles in the beginning. Compared to the seventy-six Catholic churches in southern Indiana in 1857, northern Indiana had but twenty-seven. But the immigration rate favored the north. Sixty years later Catholic strength in the north exceeded that in the south and Catholic membership in the state had finally surpassed the Methodists. Northern Indiana's Diocese of Fort Wayne itself was destined to be divided to provide dioceses of Lafayette and Gary.[32]

The bishop of Fort Wayne had powerful allies in the institutions of the Congregation of Holy Cross. Notre Dame became a focal point for Catholic service. Members of orders located there ministered to and educated the Catholics in northern Indiana counties. Holy Cross priests staffed missions in the most important northern Indiana towns. Bishop Luers held retreats for his clergy at the University of Notre Dame, followed by synods to regulate the affairs of the diocese. He was entrusted by Rome with the task of drawing up a constitution and rules for the Sisters of the Holy Cross in America, since 1855 relocated at St. Mary adjacent to the University of Notre Dame. These institutions gave stability to the Catholic church in Indiana and gave cogent answers to its critics.[33]

Ministry to Indians

Indiana's Catholic bishops wanted to maintain their ministry to the Indians also, but that had to be conducted in the midst of the miseries of Indian displacement and removal. The specific plan of the French from about 1725 had been to create a large Indian center and Catholic mission on the lower Wabash. Thus a very small military garrison supplemented by a large concentration of friendly Indians could prevent penetration of the area by the British. But neither the Indians nor the French were ever allowed enough stability at Vincennes to develop such an establishment.[34] The white population kept driving the Indians into the northern part of the state. There they were a long way from the seat of the bishop of Bardstown, who expressed his frustration in 1828:

> Finally, it is untrue to say that I have no Indians in my diocese; many nations of these poor barbarians live in Indiana and Illinois, two states that come under my jurisdiction. But I have such a scarcity of priests for the Catholics near me that it is impossible to occupy that mission which is so totally different from that which I conduct. The repugnance so unconquerable that the savages have for civilization, their intellectual faculties degraded and stupefied, their hate and vengeance implacable, their drunkenness so constant and disgusting, their laziness insurmountable, their wandering and vagabonded life more necessary today because the presence of the white man drives away the game . . . make the work of the missionary less fruitful.[35]

A ministry to Indians was renewed at the request of a considerable Catholic remnant among the Potawatomis when Stephen Badin became their resident missionary in 1830. The Baptist Indian mission in northern Indiana and in Michigan, led by Isaac McCoy, had already decided in favor of a new location beyond the Mississippi and was leaving the area. Badin opened a school for the Indians and by 1832 had been awarded federal support of $1,000 per year to operate three mission schools among the Potawatomis in northern Indiana and southern Michigan. Badin did not know the Indian language and, at age sixty-two, considered himself too old to learn it. Through interpreters he was able to develop the life of parish and school. He especially wanted an orphan asylum for northern Indiana with Catholic sisters in charge. He offered three hundred acres of land he had bought as an endowment for the orphanage, got a state charter, and enlisted two Sisters of Charity to take charge of the institution. If the orphanage actually went into operation, it was the first in the state. By 1835 neither the orphanage nor the sisters were there and that year Badin gave his three hundred acres to Bruté, the new bishop of Vincennes. Within ten years Badin saw the beginning of the University of Notre Dame on the site he had provided.[36]

Dominican priest Louis Deseille succeeded Badin as resident missionary among the Potawatomis in 1833. In a treaty of 1832 these Indians had relinquished their title and interests to all lands in Indiana except for a few reservations principally around Lake Maxinkuckee and Twin Lakes in Marshall County and by the Tippecanoe River. When Bishop Bruté made his first tour of his diocese in 1835, he visited Deseille at South Bend. Together they visited the Indian mission at Chicako's Village on the Tippecanoe where Deseille had baptized about 120 persons. Deseille was learning the Indian language but still felt more comfortable speaking through his interpreter, a Canadian woman seventy years of age.[37] Bruté reported:

> We slept on the benches of the Chapel, and some of the straw from the floor, wrapped up in our great coats after the manner of the good Father. Our food was boiled corn, fish, venison, and wild turkey, minced together in one dish, and some cranberries broken and mixed with sugar, they get from trees. Our drink was water. Coffee was not to be had although this was the principle [sic] village. In the afternoon Vespers were sung in Ottawa, and as I should have mentioned before, by the aid of printed books. Many used them as they are very quick in learning to read, and have retentive memories. Some knew the whole contents of their Prayer books. They contain all the usual daily prayers, and exercises for Confession and Communion, a pretty long Catechism and a larger number of Canticles, with many of the principal Hymns and Anthems of the Church. Among others they have the "Pange Lingua" and the Psalms for Vespers translated in Ottawa.[38]

Deseille died in 1837. Benjamin Petit succeeded him as missionary that year, his first assignment as an ordained priest. He divided his time between the white settlers and the Indians with Notre Dame as a focal point. Many of the Indian reservations had been ceded to the United States in 1836. Mass removal of Menominee's band, the last major group sent westward, occurred in 1838. This Indian group wanted Petit to accompany them to the West and Petit wanted to go. Bishop Bruté finally gave permission in September when the forced migration was already under way. Petit accompanied the Indians to the Osage River in Missouri, sending back some description of the tragic journey. Fatigued and ill, Petit returned to St. Louis where he died 16 February 1839. There were other removals of Indians in 1841, 1847, and 1848. The Potawatomis who migrated, those who stayed to merge with the white population, and those who returned from the West to Indiana were persons of concern to the Catholic Church.[39]

Synods and Councils

In the tradition of American Catholics of the 1800s, some of Indiana's bishops convened their clergy as deliberative bodies to formulate regulations for certain areas of the life of the church. Hailandiere convened twenty-five of his clergy as the first synod of the Diocese of Vincennes in 1844. A series of such synods of the Diocese of Vincennes were held under Bishop Francis Silas Chatard in 1878, 1880, 1886, and 1891. Bishop Joseph Dwenger of the Diocese of Fort Wayne held synods in 1874, 1882, 1886, 1888, and 1892; Bishop Herman Alerding added one in 1903. Indiana was also participant in and subject to the legislation of provincial councils of Cincinnati in 1855, 1858, 1861, 1882, and 1889, since both Vincennes and Fort Wayne were suffragan sees within the ecclesiastical province headed by the Archbishop of Cincinnati.

This spate of synods and councils in the latter part of the 1800s was a response to the growth in Catholic population and the increasing complexity in Catholic life. Decisions had to be made without delay concerning liturgical and devotional practices, mixed marriages, property rights (with implications for organized labor), secret societies (also with implications for organized labor), clergy rights and discipline, parish governance, and the operation of parish schools. Legislation by provincial councils was then confirmed by the Holy See at Rome, sometimes with minor changes. The synods of the Diocese of Vincennes led by Bishop Francis Chatard reflected his hard line on most of these issues. His background among the

Baltimore gentry and his entire pre-episcopal career in Rome during the dramatic years of the 1860s and 1870s had programmed him in a very conservative direction.[40]

The American Catholic ideal of a school at every parish also owed much of its impetus to the enthusiasm of midwestern German Catholics who wished to preserve their German language and culture as well as religious instruction. Bishop Martin Spalding of Louisville and Archbishop John Purcell of Cincinnati were national champions of parochial schools.

> The Irish were heavily concentrated in New England and they were not very ardent in their support of parochial schools. In contrast to New England, the midwestern states of Ohio, Illinois, Indiana, Missouri, and Wisconsin were very supportive of Catholic schools. This was no doubt due to the early leadership and commitment of Bishop John Purcell as well as the high concentration of Germans in these states.[41]

This parochial school ideal was reflected in the provincial councils of Cincinnati in 1855, 1858, and 1861. It was extended nationally when the Third Plenary Council of Baltimore in 1884 mandated the opening and maintaining of a school at every Catholic parish.[42] The practice of legislating in regional councils was destined to fall into disuse as Catholic centralization increased, culminating in the Code of Canon Law of 1918. Bishops and clergy came to be seen as authorized field agents of the central authorities rather than as deliberators or legislators as they had been at least occasionally in the 1800s.

Anti-Catholicism

Catholics took some abuse in Indiana. The German Catholics were plainly different from the English-speaking and southern-oriented majority. For a generation they preferred their German language. Their religious services differed from the Protestant norm and seemed to reflect affiliation with a foreign power. Their religious leaders dressed differently, did not marry, and were not selected or hired by their congregations. The very number of Catholic immigrants appeared threatening. They kept snapping up the jobs and taking over the small businesses and buying up the land. They opened academies which attracted the daughters of Protestants but they tolerated no intermarriage unless the Protestant spouse converted. Sensing the isolation of their ethnic enclaves, they made that separation a virtue, finding unity in strict loyalty to their customs and leaders over against the unsympathetic environment. The non-German neighbors might call them derogatory names but they could note with pride

how a German could excel as a woodworker or make an Indiana farmstead blossom, or build a proper church with bells.

The fear among non-Catholics found expression. Presbyterian Charles Beecher at Fort Wayne told the American Home Missionary Society that Catholics were only a little less dangerous than Methodists. Eastern missionaries to Indiana often appealed for help to prevent Catholic domination of the state or to found schools to prevent Protestant children from being captured by Catholic academies. Founding schools was something Yankee missionaries liked to do anyway, and fear of Catholics enlisted Protestant supporters. Articles critical of Catholics might appear in any of a score of Protestant periodicals in the Old Northwest. Anti-Catholic pamphlets circulated including the *Awful Disclosures* of Maria Monk, a product of exploitation by the commercial press and by anti-Catholic charlatans.[43]

In May of 1842 criminal action was brought against Evansville priest Roman Weinzoepfel. He was charged with sexual assault on Mrs. Martin Schmoll who had come to the church to make her confession. The trials, the mob activity, the partisan newspaper accounts, the circulation of reports of the trial in pamphlet form, and the sentencing of Weinzoepfel in March of 1844 to five years in the penitentiary at Jeffersonville all incensed the population and heightened Catholic-Protestant tensions in Indiana. Continuing investigation convinced reasonable people that Weinzoepfel had been victimized and was in fact innocent. Governor Whitcomb received petitions on behalf of Weinzoepfel from both Protestants and Catholics and responded by issuing a pardon for him in February of 1845.[44]

Frederick W. Wood supplied Indiana-related ammunition against Catholics. He had come as a twenty-nine-year-old Catholic missionary from Germany in 1859, eager to learn English and "to convert Protestant America to the Roman Catholic faith." Archbishop Purcell at Cincinnati connected Wood with Bishop Luers of the Diocese of Fort Wayne who assigned him to Avilla in Noble County. He held later appointments at Mishawaka and Goshen. His uneasiness with the Catholic doctrine of the real presence in the Eucharist and his continuing criticism of his religious colleagues led to his withdrawal from the Catholic church on 4 July 1866. He became a Methodist; Bishop Simpson helped him locate as a professor. Wood's book *Six Years a Priest and a Decade a Protestant* embodied his disenchantment with Catholicism and provided a mine of evidence for those eager to document the Catholic menace. After many citations of the "danger to America from Roman Catholicism," Wood concluded that "the great contest between Romanism and Protestantism in America has commenced."[45]

> I see, how protestantism, is unanimously battling with Roman Catholicism. I see, how the Presbyterian infantry is attacking them; how the Methodist cavalry is pursuing them; how the Episcopalians and Lutherans are receiving them with their big cannons: "Bomb," "Bomb"; and how our Baptist brethren are lying in ambuscade, to draw them all, that should escape, into their baptismal river.[46]

Genuine differences between Catholics and Protestants were underscored and often recast as unpleasant stereotypes or sinister plots. Here, as in much of nineteenth century denominationalism in Indiana, the mood was triumphal. Religious error was to be vanquished by truth. Catholics grew so fast and so solidly that hope of full triumph over them was not very realistic. Protestant controversialists felt that the world must at least be warned and the Catholic schemes be exposed or restrained.

Catholics shared in the expression of intolerance. The polemic of Protestant periodicals was answered in kind from Cincinnati, in English by the *Catholic Telegraph* from 1831 and in German by *Wahrheitsfreund* from 1837. Official statements from the Vatican or from the Catholic hierarchy were not reassuring to Protestants and could be cited as a basis for fear. Catholic documents and catechisms which seemed to leave little room for dissent were even further shorn of subtlety in parochial school instruction or in local accusations of who was going to hell or at least, in their ignorance, to a very long term in purgatory. When the new church bell was raised at Jasper the priest was reported to have said that within two years there would not be a Protestant family within hearing; the bell could be heard for five miles.[47]

Perhaps the remarkable thing was that there was so little overt conflict. Territorial separation on the European pattern was impossible but contacts were structured and limited. Community economics played a role. If there were two undertakers, one could bury Protestants and one could bury Catholics. But not every town could afford a dual set of business or public institutions. The mortuary or the grain mill or the blacksmith shop or the dry goods store might be willing and even anxious to extend courtesies to both. Even if the schools were separate, the governmental agencies of township, county, and state must serve all equally. In the general fabric of community life a unity and respect were built at most locations in the state which even the hatred later engendered by the Ku Klux Klan was not able to destroy. Side

by side, the Methodists and Catholics became the state's major religious tenants.

NOTES

1. William McNamara, *The Catholic Church on the Northern Indiana Frontier* (Washington, D.C.: Catholic University of America, 1931), 1.

2. McNamara, *Catholic Church*, 2.

3. Thomas Timothy McAvoy, *The Catholic Church in Indiana, 1789–1834* (New York: Columbia University Press, 1940), 35, 66.

4. John Joseph Doyle, *The Catholic Church in Indiana, 1686–1814* (Indianapolis, Ind.: Criterion Press, 1976), 91. Thomas T. McAvoy, John Joseph Doyle, and Fintan Walker offer the best treatments of Indiana's Catholics in the French period. Pierre Gibault has had special attention as the priest who assisted George Rogers Clark in the taking of Vincennes.

5. Joseph Henry VanderBurgh Somes, *Old Vincennes* (New York: Graphic Books, 1962), 179; McAvoy, *Catholic Church*, 65–69, 122, 124–28, 131; Doyle, *Catholic Church*, 105; McNamara, *Catholic Church*, 13.

6. Jay P. Dolan, *The American Catholic Experience* (Garden City, N.Y.: Doubleday, 1985), 112–23.

7. Herman Joseph Alerding, *A History of the Catholic Church in the Diocese of Vincennes* (Indianapolis, Ind.: Carlon and Hollenbeck, 1883), 128–29, 375–76; Charles Blanchard, *History of the Catholic Church in Indiana*, 2 vols. (Logansport, Ind.: A. W. Bowen, 1898), 1:56; McNamara, *Catholic Church*, 53, 55; McAvoy, *Catholic Church*, 173–78, 182–90, 195, 199, 204.

8. See McAvoy, *Catholic Church*, 200, for location of five accounts of this journey.

9. McNamara, *Catholic Church*, 53, 55, 59; Alerding, *History*, 136, 146.

10. By the end of 1860 the Leopoldine Society of Austria had sent the Diocese of Vincennes 68,800 florins when a florin was valued at slightly less than fifty cents. Benjamin J. Blieb, *Austrian Aid to American Catholics 1830–1860* (Milwaukee, Wis.: The Author, 1944), 26–27. Between 1834 and 1870 the Society for the Propagation of the Faith, primarily French, gave the diocese $238,000. Theodore Roemer, *Ten Decades of Alms* (St. Louis, Mo.: B. Herder Book Co., 1942), 84-85.11.

11. Alerding, *History*, 124, 147–48, 165.

12. Alerding, *History*, 167.

13. Alerding, *History*, 169.

14. Mary Carol Schroeder, *The Catholic Church in the Diocese of Vincennes, 1847–1877* (Washington, D.C.: Catholic University of America Press, 1946), 28–29.

15. Tony Catta, *Father Dujarie: Pastor of Ruillé-sur-Loir, Canon of Le Mans, Founder of the Communities of the Sisters of Providence, and the Brothers of Saint Joseph, Now the Brothers of Holy Cross, 1767–1838* (Milwaukee, Wis.: Catholic Life Publications, 1960, 309 p.); Blanchard, *History*, 1:65; Alerding, *History*, 169–71.

16. Albert Kleber, *History of St. Meinrad Archabbey 1854–1954* (Saint Meinrad, Ind.: Grail, 1954), 17–219; Joseph M. White, *The Diocesan Seminary in the United States: A History from the 1780s to the Present* (Notre Dame, Ind.: University of Notre Dame Press, 1989), 117–19; Blanchard, *History*, 1:76, 79; Alerding, *History*, 206.

17. Mary Ewens, "The Leadership of Nuns in Immigrant Catholicism," in *The American Catholic Religious Life: Selected Historical Essays*, ed. Joseph M. White (New York: Garland Publishing, 1988), 101; Alerding, *History*, 587–93, 597–600.

18. Jay P. Dolan, *Catholic Revivalism: The American Experience 1830–1900* (Notre Dame, Ind.: University of Notre Dame Press, 1978, 248 p.).

19. *Central Blatt and Social Justice* 20 (July-August 1927): 136.

20. Dolan, *Catholic Revivalism*, 38, 78–79, 86, 88, 95–96, 105, 186-203; *Central Blatt and Social Justice* 20 (1927): 88–89, 135–37, 178–80.

21. Mary Salesia Godecker, *History of Catholic Education in Indiana: A Survey of the Schools 1702–1925* (Saint Meinrad, Ind.: Abbey Press, 1926), 67.

22. Godecker, *History*, 68–69.

23. Godecker, *History*, 66.

24. Blanchard, *History*, 1:61, 75, 80; McNamara, *Catholic Church*, 60.

25. Kleber, *History*, 180, 182.

26. McNamara, *Catholic Church*, 53, 59–60.

27. McNamara, *Catholic Church*, 61.

28. James H. Madison, *The Indiana Way* (Bloomington, Ind.: Indiana University Press, 1986), 326; McNamara, *Catholic Church*, 77; Schroeder, *Catholic Church*, 71–73.

29. Schroeder, *Catholic Church*, 79, 82–99.

30. Schroeder, *Catholic Church*, 99–105, 109–111.

31. The counties are named in Herman Joseph Alerding, *The Diocese of Fort Wayne*, 2 vols. (Fort Wayne, Ind.: Archer Printing Co., 1907–1941), 1:34.

32. Schroeder, *Catholic Church*, 138, 140; Alerding, *Diocese of Fort Wayne*, 1:34.

33. Edward Sorin, *Chronicles of Notre Dame du Lac*, trans. John M. Toohey, ed. James T. Connelly (Notre Dame, Ind.: University of Notre Dame Press, 1992), 335; McNamara, *Catholic Church*, 81; Schroeder, *Catholic Church*, 114; Alerding, *Diocese of Fort Wayne*, 1:35–66, 448.

34. Jacob Piatt Dunn, *The Mission to the Ouabache* (Indianapolis, Ind.: Bowen-Merrill, 1902), 254–330; Somes, *Old Vincennes*, passim.

35. McNamara, *Catholic Church*, 10.

36. McNamara, *Catholic Church*, 20, 25–34; Blanchard, *History*, 1:143.

37. McNamara, *Catholic Church*, 44, 63, 65, 70.

38. McNamara, *Catholic Church*, 66.

39. McNamara, *Catholic Church*, 70–75, 78–80.

40. Joseph M. White, Notre Dame, Ind., letter to L. C. Rudolph, Bloomington, Ind., 18 February 1985; John Henry Lamott, *History of the Archdiocese of Cincinnati, 1821–1921* (New York: Frederick Pustet Co., 1921), 214–22; Robert Emmett Curran, *Corrigan and the Shaping of Conservative Catholicism in America 1878–1902* (New York: Arno Press, 1978), 19, 104, 119, 316–17; Alerding, *History*, 173, 183–85.

41. Dolan, *American Catholic Experience*, 282.

42. James Aloysius Burns and Bernard J. Kohlbrenner, *A History of Catholic Education in the United States* (New York: Benziger Brothers, 1937), 138–46; Dolan, *American Catholic Experience*, 112–23.

43. Wesley Norton, *Religious Newspapers in the Old Northwest to 1861: A History, Bibliography, and Record of Opinion* (Athens, Ohio: Ohio University Press, 1977), 45–66, 161–78; Ray Allen Billington, *The Protestant Crusade 1800–1860: A Study of the Origins of American Nativism* (New York: Macmillan, 1938), 99–108.

44. William F. Timmermeyer, "The Rev. Roman Weinzaepfel [sic]: An Incident in American Nativism, 1841–1847" (Master's thesis, Catholic University of America, 1947, 148 p.); L. C. Rudolph and Judith Endelman, *Religion in Indiana: A Guide to Historical Resources* (Bloomington, Ind.: Indiana University Press, 1986), entries 516, 2199, 2218, 2692, 2693; Alerding, *History*, 505–44.

45. Frederick W. Wood, *Six Years a Priest and a Decade a Protestant* (Cleveland, Ohio: Crocker's Publishing House, 1876), 8, 257–73.

46. Wood, *Six Years a Priest*, 273.

47. Calvin Butler, Boonville, Ind., letter to Milton Badger, American Home Missionary Society, New York, 24 May 1847.

About Baptists and Christians

Baptists and Christians recognized no authority for truth beyond the Bible as the word of God and no authority for direction beyond the prayerful group decision of the local congregation. Frontier settlers liked this kind of independence and individualism and the assurance that they could personally use the Bible as a direct guide to reconstitute the pure apostolic church at any time or place. These two church families made this appeal directly and with great impact on Indiana's frontier.

BAPTISTS

Baptists were an important element in the population of early Indiana. There were some Baptists among the immigrants from the Northeast. More significantly, the major population stream flowing along the rivers from the back country South was heavy with Baptist influence. Squire Boone, trail blazer alongside his brother Daniel, was a Baptist preacher. In Kentucky the Baptist churches increased in number from 106 to 219 during the years 1800 to 1803 and their membership more than tripled. By 1820 Kentucky Baptists had 491 churches and almost 32,000 members; from that time they were never challenged as the state's largest denomination. It would have seemed logical for Baptists to have a similar priority in Indiana. Certainly Indiana's deep woods and scattered population were not new things for them. It was their normal procedure on the frontier to gather as a small group wherever they found themselves, to read and study and sing and pray, and to invite one or more ordained Baptist ministers (called elders) from neighboring churches to share in completing the organization and in constituting a church. That is the way they did it on Silver Creek near Charlestown in 1798. "John Fislar, Sophia Fisher, John Plattet, and Cattern Pettet" signed the minute of constitution under leadership of Isaac Edwards, a Baptist preacher. This was the first Protestant church in Indiana, mother Baptist church to many more.[1]

The McCoy Family

An uneducated wheelwright family from Pennsylvania named McCoy was to loom large in the history of Indiana Baptists. They got religion while living briefly in Kentucky during the Great Revival and then gradually migrated to Indiana. By 1802 William McCoy was visiting regularly from Kentucky to preach at Silver Creek church. In 1810 he shared in the ordination of his son Isaac, first of three of his sons to become Baptist ministers in Indiana. Isaac had a call to be pastor of Maria Creek church near Vincennes which had been organized with thirteen members in 1809. There is a record that the Silver Creek church agreed in 1815 to purchase a copy of the report of the newly formed Baptist Board of Foreign Missions in far-off Philadelphia. At Maria Creek, pastor Isaac McCoy was thinking that missions in America warranted attention as much as foreign missions. In his western wilderness he conceived a grand plan for home missions, never knowing that some church people in New England already had the idea and had a home missions enterprise in operation He applied to the Baptist Board, now no longer simply "foreign," in Philadelphia to go as a missionary to white settlers around St. Louis but when somebody else got that appointment he fastened his own attention on missions for the American Indians. In 1817 the Baptist Board gave him a missionary appointment for one year, the charge ambiguous and without enthusiasm. His church at Maria Creek bade him farewell and offered to give his mission support. Whatever the Board's intentions, McCoy's interest was now wholly focused on the Indians.[2]

Isaac McCoy's Indian Missions

He felt he dared not delay in getting some Indian work established lest the Board use that delay as an excuse to cancel the mission effort. Moving on the feeblest of arrangements and permissions, after his first commission from the Board had already expired, he purchased a small tract of land on Raccoon Creek in Parke County in 1818 and moved his wife and seven children into two log cabins in the woods there. They were ninety miles from their friends around Vincennes and at the very borders of white settlement so he could interface with the Indians. All the Indians McCoy ever met, and he eventually contacted all major tribes in Indiana, were terribly debauched and always being displaced. His descriptions of them were empirical and candid, a great disappointment to any readers of his accounts who have wished either to idealize Indians or to despise them. He felt that European displacement of the Indians was wrong; his repeated theme was "they are being destroyed." At the recommendation of friends and of Dr. Turner who was the government Indian agent there, the McCoys moved their mission and school to the primitive trading and military post at Fort Wayne in 1820. Now they were 270 miles north of their friends at Maria Creek. In 1822 they moved another hundred miles north of Fort Wayne to Carey Mission which they built far beyond white settlement in the forest near the present site of Niles, Michigan. Finally, they moved on with the Indians west of the Mississippi.[3]

McCoy was always sick. He was always traveling and moving materials through the wilderness under impossible conditions. The uprooted Indian youths attending his school stayed in his house and ate at his table and lived as members of his family, somewhere between six and sixty Indian children depending on the current strength of the school. He and Mrs. McCoy learned by hard experience that missionary candidates to work among Indiana's Indians were painfully few and the benevolent impulse of even those few was short lived in the face of actual mission life. The McCoys had little help during their Indiana years and sometimes none. At the same time they were very sensitive to the need for good public relations with all Indians and with all official or unofficial visitors to the mission schools. When the time came for Mrs. McCoy to give birth to another child in 1821, she took her three younger children and set out alone on 25 June for a trip by open canoe between three and four hundred miles down the Wabash through the wilderness to Vincennes. On 14 September she arrived back at Fort Wayne, having made the return trip of 270 miles overland accompanied by the three children and the new baby, to cheer her husband who had felt terribly lonely and overworked tending a household of forty-seven Indian youths in her absence.[4]

The Baptist Board could never understand why things were so expensive at Fort Wayne; supplies had to be hauled there in wagons over one hundred miles of bad road so that corn which might cost twenty-five cents per bushel elsewhere cost a dollar and a half there. The Board was so impoverished it could never provide timely notice of appointment or make timely payment or give any assurance of support beyond the immediate temporary grant. McCoy himself was so desperately impoverished with his huge household-school that he felt driven to develop a network of mission support in both money and produce. This support network consisted of small grants from the Baptist Board and limited Board approval for solicitation of mission funds among Baptists; of contributions from individual friends and donors; of gifts from individual churches; and most of all of government contracts in fulfillment of Indian treaties providing for education and services to particular tribes. His competitors for the government contracts and persons interested in continuing free trade of whiskey for Indian cash annuity payments were among those who saw McCoy as their opponent. They charged him with violation of their rights and with succeeding too well in raising support on behalf of his plans.[5] He accepted no financial aid from the Baptist Board after 1824 unless the gifts had been specifically designated for Indian work, though he always accounted in detail to the Board for all support received from any source for his mission work in Indiana and Michigan.[6]

By 1824 Isaac McCoy was convinced there was no hope for clusters of Indian people encysted among the advancing white settlers. That year he submitted to the Baptist Mission Board meeting at Washington his plan for a large, separate, and fully protected Indian state west of the Mississippi. With the Board's approval and a delegation of Baptist supporters, he presented the plan to the Secretary of War, John C. Calhoun, who joined its advocates. This grand plan and his own place in it animated his missionary life and his lobbying career for the rest of his days.[7] When the early Baptists of Indiana thought of "missions," one part of their mental image was likely to be Isaac McCoy and his efforts on behalf of the Indians. Neither missions nor Indians were always favorably regarded.

Efforts at Baptist Union

In theory the Baptists who came to Indiana were "united." In America there had been Regular Baptists, an orderly and organized sort with linkage to the Particular Baptists of England. They generally incorporated into their articles of faith the Philadelphia Confession, a very substantial statement which was adapted from the Westminster Confession familiar to English-speaking Calvinists worldwide. Throughout the 1700s the Philadelphia Association of Baptist Churches was linking Regular Baptist churches in Massachusetts, Connecticut, New York, New Jersey, Pennsylvania, Delaware, Maryland, and Virginia. Emissaries from the Philadelphia Association were organizing or reorganizing Baptist churches in their own stable image throughout the colonies.[8]

At the same time there were Separate Baptists, zealous revivalists orderly in business and discipline but informal, highly emotional, and spontaneous in their worship services. They were less concerned with a meticulous statement of faith than with preaching the need for an experience of radical conversion and a new birth. And they were a bit wary of Calvinism, having known some cooled Calvinists in their earliest days in New England and being so committed to revivalism that they wanted no doctrine which might seem to impede free personal decision. These Separate Baptists had developed from the revival in New England called the Great Awakening. Two converted Congregationalists named Shubal Stearns and Daniel Marshall had moved south and established Sandy Creek Baptist Church in North Carolina in 1755 from which place and from which date the whole world was to continue feeling the impact of fired-up Baptists. Because Regular Baptists and Separate Baptists needed to support their mutual right to exist in the face of established churches in the American colonies, they managed to "unite" in the struggle for civil and religious liberty in Virginia in 1787 and in other states shortly afterward.[9]

In Kentucky, on Indiana's doorstep, it took three tries to get some of the Regulars and some of the Separates into an agreement in 1801. For this agreement they eased the Regulars' stout expression of Calvinism and agreed:

> We, the committees of the Elkhorn and South Kentucky Associations, do agree to unite on the following plan. 1st. That the Scriptures of the Old and New-Testaments are the infallible word of God, and the only rule of faith and practice. 2nd. That there is only one true Godhead or divine essence, there are Father, Son, and Holy Ghost. 3rd. That by nature we are fallen and depraved creatures. 4th. That salvation, regeneration, sanctification, and justification, are by the life, death, resurrection, and ascension of Jesus Christ. 5th. That the saints will finally persevere through grace to glory. 6th. That believers' baptism by immersion is necessary to receiving the Lord's supper. 7th. That the salvation of the righteous, and punishment of the wicked will be eternal. 8th. That

it is our duty to be tender and affectionate to each other, and study the happiness of the children of God in general; to be engaged singly to promote the honour of God. 9th. And that the preaching Christ tasted death for every man shall be no bar to communion. 10th. And that each may keep up their associational and church government as to them may seem best. 11th. That a free correspondence and communion be kept up between the churches thus united.[10]

In fact, that union was not well cemented in Kentucky; it crossed the Ohio into Indiana very uneasily. Little Pigeon Baptist Association was the only one in Indiana to take the name United Baptists. The integration attempted by that union became a target for the advocates of so many differences within the Baptist family in Indiana that instead of unity there came a half century of searching, fifty years of controversy and argument and decision and redecision about who the Baptists really were.

Hardshell Baptists

In Indiana there were "Hardshells," a universally applied if unofficial nickname for those otherwise called Old Regular Baptists or Primitive Baptists or Anti-Means Baptists. They had little interest in pointing up the puny free will of man; what they wanted was no compromise in their assertion of the complete free initiative and direct action of God in his dealings with humankind. Some of their biblical texts were Genesis 45:8; 50:20; Psalm 139:1–4; Job 14:5; 23:13; Isaiah 14:24–27; 45:7; 46:10; Matthew 10:29–30; Acts 2:23; 4:27–28; Romans 8:28–39; Ephesians 1:4,11; 2:8,10; II Thessalonians 2:13; I Peter 1:2. They saw in the Bible a living God who decides and abides by his decisions; who plans and carries his plan through; who is able to know beforehand what will come to pass; who overlooks nothing and from whose will and power no creature, not even the smallest or most stubborn, can escape. All their doctrines were essentially orthodox Christian ones but the people on the midwestern frontier were belligerently democratic and so concerned with issues of free will that the Hardshells spent most of their energy advancing and defending their doctrine of predestination. They insisted that God in his grace has elected a particular number of sinners to be saved so he is never surprised at who comes to repentance nor is he ever thwarted in his election and its fulfillment. In their preaching, books, pamphlets, periodicals, debates, and in the conversations of their private lives, this was their major theme according to their autobiographies.

Indiana's Hardshell Baptists particularly protested against the position in article nine in the Baptist union agreement, "that the preaching [that] Christ tasted death for every man shall be no bar to communion." It was plain to them that not all humans were in fact being saved. If Christ tasted death for them all, then plainly his mission was a failure—an unbearable conclusion. They claimed that Christ died for the elect, such election being an indescribably great gift and inheritance which no power in earth or heaven could ever take away. Teaching anything else was imparting false doctrine which must indeed be a bar to communion. Hardshells practiced "close communion," allowing full fellowship and participation in the Lord's Supper only with those whose election had been recognized by narration of an acceptable religious experience and by baptism by immersion by a Baptist elder in the context of a Hardshell fellowship. Hardshell elder Lemuel Potter of Cynthiana, Indiana, hammered home the logic of "close communion" in four lectures delivered at Owensville, Indiana, on 12–14 April 1886. The *General Baptist Messenger* published at Owensville had dared to suggest that a Baptist deacon might be forgiven for the sin of offering the elements of the Lord's Supper to a visiting Methodist preacher sitting in the congregation.[11]

Narration of a religious experience prior to admission to membership had a particular cast among Hardshells. The candidate took care to offer nothing on his own behalf. There was an almost ritual renunciation of all earlier attempts to obtain salvation by ceasing to be bad or turning to be good or getting religion in an emotional experience of conversion. Wilson Thompson tells of a group of candidates applying for church membership in May of 1801 or 1802 being asked "You speak of being very great sinners; have you now become good, or are you the same sinners still?" The answer was prompt, "We are still great sinners, and in ourselves we are no better." The moderator put the vote and every hand went up at once to receive them; elder Davies commented later on "how beautifully them young people passed from law to gospel." It was after such heartfelt recognition of unworthiness that God granted these youth their experience.[12] Thompson, destined to be a Hardshell leader in Indiana, finally moved out of his self effort for salvation which had led to anguish so deep he could not even pray. To have prayed for his own salvation would have been to ask God to do an unjust act. This much of a prayer he did manage. "Lord thou knowest that I am an unholy rebel against thee; I have sinned greatly; am all corrupt and lost; but thou art just in all thy judgments, and I am justly condemned by thy righteous law." After this admission of God's justice in condemning him, he did receive God's gift of a religious experience, all brightness and beauty and assurance. "My burden was gone; the stream of justice that had been pursuing my life was withdrawn, and yet I was the same sinner as before!"[13] John F. Johnson tells how he lay on his bed at night tossing and sleepless in his search for assurance. His wife asked if he thought God would be just in condemning him. Johnson answered that he did not see how God could be just and not condemn him. After that answer his wife said that things might soon be different for him. She had "passed through a similar scene not long before." His happy experience came.[14]

To Baptists of this Hardshell and grace oriented sort, the common emphasis among frontier revivalists on the role of personal initiative and personal decision and mere acceptance of the gospel in effecting a sinner's salvation looked like blasphemy against the almighty God whose Spirit they held to be the only really effective agent in salvation. With whatever power they possessed, they would oppose this Arminianism.[15] Their power was considerable. Indiana's Presbyterians were not reliable defenders of predestination; New School Presbyterians were busy circumventing the doctrine and Old School Presbyterians generally maintained a dignified silence even in the face of Methodist attacks. But southern Indiana had a corps of Hardshell Baptist preachers who intended to answer any attack on the doctrine and even to seek out the opposition. Best known to later historians were Wilson Thompson (1788–1866) and Daniel Parker (1781–1844). Of quite comparable impact on the state were John F. Johnson (1800–1881), Joel Hume (1807–1891), Lemuel Potter (1841–1897), and James H. Oliphant (1846–1925).

Wilson Thompson

Wilson Thompson was born in Kentucky, learned the fallacy of his own working for salvation, and felt his darkness lifted by a direct gift of God in "Regular Old School Primitive Baptist" fashion. He began preaching about 1810 with an education so poor he "could not read a chapter nor a hymn intelligently" but continued unrelenting study of the Bible. "It has been a peculiarity through my whole life, that when any point of doctrine would fasten itself upon my mind, I would become insensible to all other things, until my mind was in some way relieved from its intense pursuit," he said. "It would take volumes to detail all the different exercises of mind through which I passed."[16] He matured as a revivalist and controversialist while preaching in Kentucky and Missouri; then he moved to Ohio about 1816 and applied his intensity there as well as in various excursions into eastern Indiana.

Thompson became acquainted with Isaac McCoy and seriously considered McCoy's invitation to join him in the work of Indian missions. However he reported a direct intervention from God which turned him violently antimission instead. From that time he stoutly opposed such humanly devised "means" of evangelism and reform as missionary societies, Bible societies, education societies, temperance societies, and Sunday schools. When the Miami Baptist Association and the White Water Baptist Association exploded into doctrinal and anti-mission controversy in the 1830s, Thompson was a chief agent. In 1821 he had published his views in a book entitled *Simple Truth* and in 1825 he published *Triumphs of Truth* to expand his views and to demolish objectors to the first book.[17] When the fight over Little Blue River church property threw the anti-mission and anti-means issues among Baptists into Indiana's Rush Circuit Court in 1846, Thompson himself was put on the witness stand and his books were largely featured. In the court proceedings the attorney for the Means party specifically named Thompson as the man who had produced the widespread division among Baptists, a jealous leader who "wanted to rule with a rod of iron, and without a rival."[18] It was reported that he "had great influence over the masses and in the associations, and always carried his point." In 1834 Thompson felt that the Lord was ordering him out of Ohio so he moved to Indiana, six miles northwest of Connersville. He was a Hoosier for more than thirty years. In April of 1866, participating in meetings for Antioch and Ross Run churches in Wabash County, Indiana, he preached a good predestinarian sermon on I John 5:1, 2 and then took to bed and died in his son's house in the midst of his family. The family gathered around his deathbed and sang "Time Like a Fleeting Shadow Flies," number 941 in the popular hymnbook Thompson himself had published.[19]

Daniel Parker

Wilson Thompson impacted eastern Indiana. Hardshell Baptist Daniel Parker hit the state from the western side. Parker had been a Baptist preacher in Tennessee, being in his early thirties and pastor of four churches when Luther Rice and the newly formed Baptist Board asked the churches and associations there to support missions.

At the first sight I was taken in, like the young man whose passion of love is so taken with the beauty, and fine dress of the damsel, that he forgets to consider the real merit, or virtue of the person. But in a short time I was brought to a reflection, and as I came to understand the plan, and try it by the word of God, I was constrained to fear it was a speculative plan, of mans [sic] invention, and not the Lord's work . . . My recourse was to a throne of grace, until I believe the Lord brought me to see that the mission system was the work of Satan, in opposition to the kingdom of Christ.[20]

The Concord Association in Tennessee was badly battered by anti-mission conflict after Parker "drew the sword against the error" and "was able to defeat the system." He was a veteran debater and controversialist by the time he moved from the South to Lamotte Church in Illinois in 1817. Isaac McCoy soon came to the churches in that area of the Indiana-Illinois border seeking support for missions. "This," reported Parker, "began the war on the Wabash."[21] Parker was relentless, especially in his attacks on McCoy's former church at Maria Creek which was the strong mother church of much of the Wabash Association and a leader of the supporters of missions. As the "war" progressed, Wabash Association, embracing most of two counties in Illinois along with Knox and Gibson counties in Indiana turned solidly antimission. Only Wabash, Maria Creek, Little Flock, Busseron, Union, Veals Creek, and Boggs Creek churches chose to remain friends of missions and withdrew in 1824 to form Union Association.[22]

Parker allowed no peace to any continuing supporters of Baptist missions. He laid out his objections in a pamphlet published in 1820.

The Baptist Board, he charged, was usurping the authority of Christ and openly violating the Scriptures in calling, training, and undertaking to direct the work of God's ministers. The attempt to supplant by human instrumentalities the direct agency of God in begetting his own children Parker sarcastically likened to an outsider aiding a neighbor family to secure a much-desired heir. The whole enterprise was, he contended, a source of downright moral evil. He attacked Isaac McCoy on the ground that it was no concern of religion that the Indians be educated and colonized.[23]

In 1824 he published from Vincennes *The Author's Defence, by Explanations and Matters of Fact. Remarks on Church Discipline, and Reflections of the Church of Christ, with the Utility and Benefits of Associations*. From 1829 to 1831 he issued his monthly newspaper called the *Christian Advocate*. Most of all, he stumped the neighboring

Baptist associations and churches, overwhelming any opponents in debate and playing effectively upon the local bias and prejudices of his hearers. He was popular enough and powerful enough to be elected a member of the Senate of Illinois from 1822 to 1826.[24]

Hosts of Indiana Baptists were ready to join Parker in his opposition to denominational agencies, missions, Sunday schools, benevolent societies, and educated ministers. The calls for support for Baptist missions following 1814 came to a proud and provincial people on the western frontier. These were repeated calls by agents and missionaries who in their zeal for missions were not always sensitive to local power structures and culture. To the westerners they seemed to take a stance as a cultural and moral elite. The missionaries wanted to raise funds and preached up the cause of the "lost heathen." For some frontier Baptists the theories of Parker and the Hardshells conveniently undercut the whole annoying benevolent enterprise.

However, the peculiar theology of Parker finally proved an embarrassment. In 1810, while still in Tennessee, Parker had heard an aged Baptist preacher advance a "two seed" theory which Parker himself at the time rejected as heresy. In the course of his own anti-mission efforts he became convinced that the theory was true and published it as his own in a pamphlet about 1824. It was a radical dualism claiming an independent eternal uncreated existence of both the devil and God. God *created* all but the devil *begat* a part of mankind; those begotten of the devil were his children and to their father they would and ought to go. So the non-elect are the devil's children in origin of their souls; there is no Gospel and no means of salvation for them. The elect are God's children in origin of their souls; they are the subjects of the Gospel and none shall be lost.[25] No missions or means or benevolent societies or Sunday schools can change either destiny. Thus God is absolved of blame for arbitrary predestination and Hardshell Baptists holding this view were absolved of any obligation to support any missions or means unless the charge was laid on them personally and directly by the Spirit of God.

This "Two-Seed-in-the-Spirit" doctrine was often recognized as a classical dualistic heresy even by the Hardshell Baptists. Wilson Thompson never embraced "two-seedism"; many Hardshell groups repudiated it as early as the 1820s. Lemuel Potter still found the teaching prevalent and felt compelled to issue a pamphlet against it in 1880.[26] It was certainly recognized as a classical heresy by the opponents of Hardshell Baptists in their perennial debates. The opponents would try to tar all Hardshell Baptists with the brush of Parker's "two seed" teaching.[27] The charge was only occasionally deserved.

All Parkerites were essentially "hardshells," but not all "hardshells" were Parkerite. Many associations in Indiana and Illinois, both those that exist or have died out, were at one time or another Parkerite. As early as 1824 the "two seed" Eel River Association in western Indiana, to which Otter Creek later belonged, organized and included several churches which had split off from other associations. Both Blue River Association (established 1816) and Lost River Association (established 1825) in southwestern Indiana came under Parker's influence about this time. In 1827 the Danville Association in Indiana became "two seed" as well as Sugar Creek Association in 1832, Bethlehem Association in Johnson County, Indiana, in 1842, and the Enon Association to the west of Indianapolis. In 1844 both the Paint Creek and Vermillion Associations in west Indiana also became Parkerite. Today the Blue River and Little Zion Associations are all that remain of these but they long ago rejected Parkerism and now simply call themselves primitive.[28]

Parker took his "two seed" doctrine to Texas in 1832. When he learned that Texas law prohibited establishment of churches other than Catholic, he returned to Illinois to organize the Pilgrim Church of Predestinarian Baptists. Then he emigrated to Texas in 1833 with the whole newly established congregation. His impact on Indiana was still heavy.

Even after Parker left the state, several Indiana associations embraced his views. A new sect called Old School Predestinarian Baptists appeared in 1842 under the guidance of R. M. Newport of Paris, Illinois, and H. T. Craig of Morgantown, Indiana, who edited a paper called the *Western Predestinarian Baptist*. Craig belonged to the Bethlehem Association which had become Parkerite the same year. The publication soon strangled to death, however, over the question of the origin of the devil. According to Nowlin there were 9,932 Parkerites remaining in the United States in 1893. Even without a later census it is certain that the number of believers declined steadily thereafter, a process which is continuing to this day.[29]

John F. Johnson

John F. Johnson (1800–1881) was of old Regular Baptist stock and married the granddaughter of an "Old School Baptist" preacher near his residence in western Virginia. In 1829 he and his wife and infant son migrated to Indiana, again in close proximity to zealous Baptists among his wife's family who were members of the Lebanon church of Henry County.[30] At the age of thirty Johnson came under painful conviction of his unworthiness before God. He was released from the weight of his sin by God's grace.

> Soon as it was light enough I arose, took the bible, opened and read, but it was a new book to me. The seals appeared to be opened, and it spoke in the sweetest accents. The promises were to me, and every line was fraught with consolation, and I could not conjecture why it was so, but wondered why I had never seen it so before. I read it till perhaps half an hour by sun, when my wife asked me to drive up the cows. I went, and while driving them through a beautiful sugar grove, I saw my Savior; not with my natural eyes, for my head was down and he was above, it seemed, at an angle of about forty-five degrees, the loveliest object that mortal ever beheld, and I raised my head, expecting to see him with my natural eyes; but no. Yet the most beautiful scenery met my eyes that I had ever beheld. That beautiful grove through which the sun was brightly shining with all his morning glory, seeming to gild every leaf with a supernatural luster. Had all the leaves been hung with the richest jewels they could not have been more beautiful. The very heavens seemed to declare the glory of God and the firmament to show his handiwork. Overwhelmed and overcome with the sublime and majestic scene, I fell upon my knees and poured out my petitions to my great Deliverer.[31]

Johnson said that "all was bright" for a week or ten days. He felt his mind was carried back into eternity where he saw the way of salvation complete in Jesus, exactly suited to his case, God's own work which could never be undone. He and his wife went to the regular fourth Sunday meeting, related their experience to the church, and were baptized in June of 1830. He was quick to assert that all this was God's gracious doing, not dependent on any merit of his own.

> I think the glorious view of my dear Savior had engrossed my whole attention and diverted my mind entirely from my sinful self, causing me to think my sins were all gone and I should be troubled with them no more. But after continuing for a while in that happy state of mind I was made to look back at my depraved nature, and there I saw to my sad surprise that I was still in my nature a polluted sinner.[32]

Johnson was a farmer and a doctor of medicine with plenty of practice tending the "chills, fevers and other maladies" of the new country, but after his conversion he felt a compelling call to preach. The congregation and of-

ficers of Lebanon Baptist Church became aware of his wrestling with the call. Before he had so much as attempted to utter a prayer in public, they licensed him to preach wherever he had opportunity "to the ends of the earth." There were five preachers in the congregation but Johnson was immediately in demand, preaching one to three times per week and traveling widely on horseback. When he felt that his preaching was crowding his practice of medicine he simply quit being a doctor.[33]

> We had settled in a new and heavily timbered country. In clearing out the farm and raising produce and stock for the support of the family, we were closely engaged. My labor was my principal dependence. I do not think that the churches helped me to the amount of ten dollars in the first five years of my labors, nor did I wish or expect it, for they, too, were in a new country, and had to encounter many hardships. I think that in those five years I was out on my professional work very nearly, if not quite, one-half of the laboring time; but we got along surprisingly. My sons were getting up so as to be considerable help. Joseph A. commenced plowing before he was eight years old, and the two next at about the same age. The land, though, was quite level, clear of rock, and very productive. After a few years we got our farm cleared of timber, and made our money principally by raising and selling hogs. I commenced in Indiana with a capital of two hundred and seventy dollars, and when we left that country for Kentucky, sold property to the amount of twelve thousand dollars; have always had enough to live upon, and such as was better than I deserved, and have no doubt but that I always shall have enough, hoping that I have the "promise of the life that now is, and of that which is to come."[34]

In agreement with the convictions of senior members of his wife's family, Johnson became strenuously antimission and anti-means. "New School Baptists" he called the supporters of the Indiana Baptist General Association, of missionary societies, and of every kind of organized benevolence. Such people were only thieves of the Baptist name; fighting them was no breach of Christian charity but a preacher's primary duty. They were "silly dupes" trying to redeem their brethren though David says in Psalm 49:7 none of them can by any "means" do it. They were "sons of Belial" pretending that the Lord's storehouse was to be filled with their ill-gotten filthy lucre. If they were allowed to have their way the land would be "drenched with the blood of the saints" and a religious aristocracy would be built "intolerant as Mahomedanism and cruel as Paganism." These missionaries begot illegitimate children among the Indians. Their "bladder-headed" supporters pretended to find support in the Scriptures but he demolished their proof texts.[35]

> As soon might we expect to find a frozen ocean in Africa, a boiling one in Greenland, grapes on thorns, figs on thistles, those hypocrites in heaven, or christians in final torment, as to think of finding the marks of the church of Christ in those dens of fashionable religion of our day. Turn to the apostolic church and ask, Who were their Reverends, Right Reverends, double D.'s, &c.? Who constituted their Missionary Board? Who its officers? Who their treasurers? Where were their funds kept? Where were their Theological Seminaries located, and who of their gospel preachers were prepared for the ministry there? Where their Sunday Schools, and who their teachers? Where, when and who was it that conducted their Judas pockets round their assemblies, to gratify that "covetousness which is idolatry," so plainly discovered in those money-whining mendicants? They talk about covetousness to those from whom they beg! Why it is as plain as open day that the term applies accurately to themselves. Covetousness consists in eagerness for gain, or craving what belongs to others. "Thou shalt not covet anything that is thy neighbor's." It is vanity for them to think of finding scriptural authority for their doctrines or practice. If they wish to read their genealogy, let them search their mother's records. There they may find it, and precedents too, plenteously.[36]

With great impatience he found:

> The world is constantly ringing with an incessant ding-dong of works; sinners, dead in sin, called upon to repent, believe, obey, pray, pay their money and use their means for the support of the Sunday Schools, Theological Seminaries, Tract Societies, Temperance Societies, Missionary Societies, and a host of other things are brought forward to purchase the blessings and procure the salvation of sinners.[37]

And he opposed it everywhere. His mailing address changed from Luray in Henry County to Muncie in Delaware County but his influence was wide. He put his violently Hardshell language into a series of articles published in Gilbert Beebe's periodical *Signs of the Times* and then gathered the articles into a booklet for even wider circulation. He himself circulated ceaselessly among the Hardshell churches and associations, having "daily appointments for weeks and even for months." At age seventy-six he commented "I feel well assured that I have traveled a distance that would reach more than three and perhaps four times around the globe on which we live."[38]

Joel Hume

Southwestern Indiana long remained a center of Hardshell Baptist activity. A visitor to the Salem Primitive Baptist Association in 1873 reported the association large and prosperous; "there was not a Missionary Baptist church in Posey County at that time." Several Hardshell elders were named as leaders partly responsible for that county's happy situation but preeminence was given to Joel Hume, "a great man, eloquent in his address, and regarded as a leader among our people."[39] Hume was a folk hero, death to the unwary debater who dared to underestimate his native ability and his tactics. When the Campbellites of Posey County wanted a debate to clarify issues with the local Hardshells, they knew Joel Hume was the man to stand for the Baptists. Hume agreed to the debate propositions:

> 1st. Is the doctrine of total hereditary depravity taught in King James' version of the Bible. (Hume will affirm.)
>
> 2nd. Is the doctrine of universal conditional salvation taught in the same book. (Hume denies.)
>
> 3rd. Do the scriptures teach the doctrine of immersion, in order to the forgiveness of sins. (Hume denies.)[40]

The Christians brought Elder Benjamin Franklin, a denominational heavyweight from Cincinnati, as Hume's opponent. The debate was scheduled at Mt. Vernon "commencing Nov. 14th and ending Nov. 17th, 1853: containing four hour-speeches and twelve half-hour-speeches on each side."[41] Franklin played to his partisans in the audience by repeatedly attacking predestination in a general way because it was not fair for anybody to be condemned for not doing what he could not do. He referred to Hume's "strong lungs . . . stentorian sound . . . profuse perspiration," like a steam boiler swelled to bursting.[42] Hume just as artfully played to the sympathies of his country constituents, hammering away with a great battery of biblical texts and implying that Franklin had come to play the role of educated big bug among the ignorant Hoosiers.[43]

> The gentleman has just found out, what every one here knew before he came—and what is it? It is that we are so ignorant, that we do not understand good language. Well, we acknowledge the fact, and we are truly sorry that our situation in childhood was such as to deprive us almost entirely of education, Being a poor orphan, without any means to educate myself, consequently, I never ciphered to the single rule of three, or studied English Grammar a moment in my life; but thank God, I can

read the Bible, and by its holy contents is this discussion to be tested. There is one thing that I exceedingly regret, and that is, that the friends of this learned gentleman have so imposed upon him, as to bring him so far to discuss a theological subject with such an ignoramus. I really think there is due him an apology, and should be certain to make it. But we pass.[44]

Hume accused Franklin of tinkering with the language of the King James version of the Scriptures, the agreed-upon umpire on all biblical questions, and commented that "even down here in the swamps of Indiana, where ignorance stalks abroad at noon day," that would be detected.[45] He taunted his adversary who was so favorably situated in the big city of Cincinnati but now seemed to be able to bring nothing against the doctrine of depravity which country people had not already heard and rejected. He scorned Franklin's positive view of human initiative and ability. Salvation is defined as regeneration. It is bringing new being into existence. No sinner does that. Only God does.[46] He hit Franklin with an especially strenuous statement of God's priority.

> But my worthy friend is not yet satisfied with the second of Acts. He tells us that he has at home eight different translations of the Bible, and they all agree with his views on the second chapter of Acts. He also has told us that his views are right according to the Greek lexicons. Well, this may be true or it may not; there are but few here who know any thing about Greek, and we seriously doubt our friend's knowledge of it. But be this as it may, we have shown you the plain common sense view of the subject, and we have given you several examples by which you are able to determine for yourselves whether Mr. Franklin or ourself is right upon the subject. It matters not with us if our friend had sixteen translations, and twenty-four Greek lexicons, backed up by all the logic he can raise, even Mr. Hedge's, not excepted, and after all he will never make this audience believe the doctrine of baptism in order to the forgiveness of sins. But the gentleman was made to wonder if it could be possible that we would take the position that sins were pardoned before repentance, and even challenged us to admit the position. Well, for the gentleman's special accommodation, and because we verily believe the doctrine, we now affirm that the pardon of the sins of God's people precedes their repentance.[47]

Such debates were never "won." The one between Hume and Franklin was published and circulated. So was Hume's debate with General Baptist Benoni Stinson at Owensville, Indiana, ten years later. Five propositions

concerning general or particular atonement, free will or predestination, were before those two mature campaigners.

> In the opening of each new subject the affirmant shall occupy one hour, and the respondent the same length of time. Each subsequently shall alternately occupy half an hour until the subject is disposed of . . . No proposition shall be discussed for more than one day nor less than a half day, unless by agreement of the debaters . . . The debate shall open precisely at 10 o'clock and close at 4.[48]

Hume brought a battery of at least seventy-five predestinarian Scripture texts. The stature of Hume was recognized by Stinson.

> I am aware of the strength of my opponent. He is a man who has frequently engaged in public debates. I am aware of his strength as a debater, and of his great influence as a minister in his own denomination. There is one consolation, however, that, up to the present time, all my acquaintance with Elder Hume has continued to confirm me in the first conviction I had of him, that he is conscientiously a Christian, and by deportment a gentleman. From such a source I may expect strong opposition, though I shall look for it in a gentlemanly and Christian manner.[49]

Hume responded with civil comments about Stinson. Then they debated for five days.

Lemuel Potter

In 1875 the Hardshell forces of Posey County were greatly augmented when Lemuel Potter was elected pastor of Bethlehem Church. He moved to Posey County in 1880 and by 1883 was pastor of four churches within the county's bounds. In 1885 he debated Cumberland Presbyterian preacher H. Clay Yates for six days at Owensville opposing foreign missions before "a very large and enthusiastic crowd of people." The published form of the debate ran to 669 pages. After the debate Potter gathered a Hardshell congregation in Owensville. He developed preaching points at Griffin and Wadesville in Posey County as well. Debates were nothing new for Potter. He claimed little interest in them, saying only "I will debate when my brethren think in their sober judgment that the cause of our people needs defending." In fact he was provocative, a fact already clear in his account of his first debate, as a young man, with a Campbellite. By his own report he had thirty such "public discussions."[50]

Potter had gotten his rudimentary education in southern Illinois and among the Primitive Baptists there had undergone his long and painful conversion followed by an even more wrenching decision to preach.[51]

> The first effort I ever made was Saturday before the second Sunday in January, 1865 . . . It was not long after I commenced preaching until I had four regular appointments . . . Baptist ministers, as a rule, were farmers, living upon their own farms, making their own livings, and each one of them pastoring from one to four churches, and sometimes five. The idea of the brethren giving a preacher a living, or any part of a living, at that time, was entirely unknown among the Old School Baptists in southern Illinois.[52]

Once he "very timidly, and with great diffidence broached the subject" of ministerial support while in the company of "two or three old brethren" in the church. One replied "If you want money for preaching you had better go to the Missionaries, where they hire their preachers." Instead Potter stood faithfully with the Primitive Baptists, briefly in Wisconsin but chiefly in southern Illinois with "calls and invitations more than half a dozen men could fill."[53] The issue of ministerial support kept concerning him, not only for himself.

> I have had a great many invitations to come to different neighborhoods to preach, with the promise from the one who invited me that they would help me pay expenses there and back if I would come. To help pay expenses is very good, but to pay all expenses and let the minister get home as well off as he left home is still better. In that respect, however, I have fared very well, and feel I have no complaint to enter, and what I say upon the subject of assisting the ministry is not for my own sake, so much as for the sake of other men in the ministry, who try to serve the churches, while, perhaps, the churches neglect their duty toward them. I think very little of a man hiring himself out to preach the gospel, but I also think very little of the idea of a set of people, who are blessed with an abundance of this world's goods, expecting a poor minister to come and preach to them at his own expense.[54]

His reputation as a Campbellite-killer kept growing after his debate with Dick Flower at Grayville, Illinois, in the summer of 1868.

> I thought then and do now [1894], that so far as arguments are concerned, neither of us did anything very great in that debate, however, the people seemed to concede the victory to me. I have thought many times that it was not so much because of my skill in arguing my points, and defending them, as the manner of my oppo

nent's treatment of me. However, I have studied the doctrine of the Campbellite people a great deal since then, and have had a great many debates with them, and I think I know as well what they teach as they do themselves, so far as their fundamental principles are concerned. I have had opportunities of learning their doctrine having had about nineteen public discussions with them.[55]

This was the mature defender of the Hardshell Baptist faith from opponents outside and from eccentric doctrines within who came to Indiana in 1880, his pattern well established as a controversialist and a traveler. He was no friend of Daniel Parker's "two-seedism" and published his pamphlet attacking it the year he moved to Indiana. He was even less a friend of Missionary Baptists. His ammunition against them was gathered in the record of his debate of four days and two nights with W. P. Throgmorton in July of 1887 and published in St. Louis in 350 pages of fine print the following year. Some critics said he attacked everybody and always got up with his arms full of clubs but he answered "I never did preach a congregation away." His newspaper was the *Church Advocate*, issued until one year before his death when he merged it with the *Monitor* of Elder R. W. Thompson. His autobiography, done after fourteen years of residence in Indiana, made a splendid register of his encounters with and victories over all who differed in any degree with Hardshell Baptists.[56]

Prominent as they were in controversy and debate, Joel Hume and his younger contemporary Lemuel Potter viewed their work primarily as pastoral. They were pastors of particular churches. Their wide travels were considered to be under direct leading of God's Spirit for the upbuilding of the whole of "our people." In his summary of his labors and travels Potter reported "I have, in all my labors, baptized about four hundred people, and married, perhaps, one hundred and twenty-five couples, and preached at least two hundred and fifty funerals."[57] Some critics asked the Hardshell preachers why they even bothered to preach if the salvation or damnation of the hearers was already predestined. Their answer was that God told them to preach and sent them to preach so they obeyed. And there was a further duty to build up the professing fellowship of the elect. Preaching is no good for the making of saints, said Potter, but one of its major objects is "for the perfecting of the saints . . . for the edifying of the body of Christ."[58]

> The perfecting of the saints is to give them all the instruction in righteousness, that they may be thoroughly furnished unto all good works. It always directs their

minds to the crucified Savior, as suitably adapted to their case, and that freely supplies all their wants. It reminds them of all his ordinances, and their obligations to observe them; it teaches them to deny ungodliness and worldly lusts, and live soberly, righteously and godly in this present world. When they see that there is no worthiness in themselves, and that Jesus has bestowed all His worthiness on them, freely, without any consideration on their part, and they are made to view Him as altogether lovely, and that His ways are perfectly just and right, and that there is a beauty in holiness, as well as joys that the world is utterly incapable of giving, and they are led to an implicit confidence in Him and His word, they are then willing and able to conform to His will, in obeying all the injunctions of His gospel . . . To edify is to build up in knowledge and piety. In this edification the saints mutually hold sweet communion with one another, their company becomes pleasant, and their fellowship is strengthened.[59]

James H. Oliphant

In their pastoral labors Hume and Potter circulated in the White River Association where they influenced a young Hardshell preacher destined to equal or eclipse them both. James H. Oliphant (1846–1925) was one of fourteen children of a pious Baptist couple who settled on a Monroe County farm about 1839. There were Old School Baptist preachers in his father's lineage and the Carmichael family members on his mother's side were Hardshells too. They had all been neighbors in North Carolina. Baptist preachers visited often at the family home, especially E. D. Thomas of Danville Association, but Oliphant showed no early inclination to become a Baptist preacher. In 1868 he became seriously interested in religion; both he and his wife passed through the struggle of conversion and "became satisfied" with a "solemn composure of mind." Soon he was interested in the plight of the Hardshell churches which were often weak and without pastors. Some "progressives" among the Hardshells had introduced innovations such as protracted meetings and the result had been further division in association ranks with loss of Hardshell ministers and members.

Oliphant resisted a call to preach because his wife and her family, former Methodists, were "utterly unreconciled to it." He lamented his own unworthiness and incompetency. But in February of 1870 he opened a public meeting at the home of Brother William Sparks near Stanford with a "poor little prayer." By the end of that year he had been called to the care of four churches and served that number of churches continuously for forty-

one years.[60] In January of 1872 he was ordained at the hands of three Baptist elders and three deacons.

Elders James Strickland, Joel Hume, Lemuel Potter, E. D. Thomas and others were frequent visitors among our churches, and defended with great ability the doctrine of the sovereignty of God in election, special atonement, effectual calling of the Holy Spirit, and perseverance of the saints. The Lord blessed our labors in defending these sentiments, and our churches grew in numbers and were blessed with peace and union.[61]

The growth and peace and union were spotty and temporary but the ministry of Oliphant was unwavering. He was an advocate of the old paths. "Here is the secret of pastoring a church," he said. "Teach it that everything new in religion is fake, and when elders get to be progressive, and want to modernize our people, avoid them, and encourage the members to be content with the things taught in the word."[62]

"The Gospel Light," a paper started by Elder H. A. Todd, in 1902, caused deep trouble among our people by introducing Fuller sentiments and reproaching our people in many ways. In 1904, S. B. Luckett, of Crawfordsville, wrote "A Candid Review of the Gospel Light," and soon after this pamphlet appeared "The Light" was discontinued, and "The Primitive Baptist" took the task of supplying its patrons. S. B. Luckett has been a distinguished writer, but he never excelled this little pamphlet. Elders Todd and Hackman went at once to the Missionaries. There were nearly a dozen of our elders that left us and went to the Missionaries. They tried first to modernize our people, and, failing to do so, they left us. It seems that there have ever been men among us who sought to make our people more acceptable to the world. The first move of this kind that ever came under my notice was in 1861–1865. A dozen preachers in southern Indiana went into Arminian practices, such as protracted meetings, mourner's benches, and Sunday schools. Division resulted, in which White River association was nearly evenly divided. I have seen this same move repeated several times since. It is the same spirit, a desire to conform more and more to the world. I have no doubt but that on and on through time men will rise up among us to repeat this move, and I think there will ever be men to oppose these efforts, and preserve our people from ruin by these "would be" reformers.[63]

Yet he was an activist, visiting "our people" in their gatherings not only in a continuing round of Indiana but also in Ohio, in Kentucky, in Missouri, in North Carolina, and even in West Virginia, Maryland, and Washington, D.C., from whence some of "our people" had arranged for a special railroad car for his trip to see the ocean. In Page County, Virginia, he found them taking up a public collection by passing baskets around! He was sorry to see this novelty but adjusted to it after the local brethren discussed it with him. He was moderator for the first national meeting of Primitive Baptists, held at Fulton, Kentucky, in 1900 with fourteen states represented. Those present solemnly read and approved the old London Confession section by section but Oliphant did not want such a novel assembly adopted as any regular practice. By the time he wrote his autobiography he had conducted more than one thousand funerals, including the funeral of Lemuel Potter who was borne to his grave at Poseyville by six Primitive Baptist elders. Oliphant's text for the sermon for the "immense audience" assembled to pay tribute was inevitable: "I have fought the good fight."[64]

Oliphant was recognized everywhere as a champion of predestination. People would accost him on the street or on public conveyances to discuss the subject. Though his formal education was very limited, he also chose to contend for the faith with his pen. When Lemuel Potter came to Oliphant's home church in Greene County in 1878 to debate a Methodist preacher for six days, Oliphant used the occasion to consolidate his own theological convictions.

> One of the questions was, "Falling from Grace." I wrote my first book, "Final Perseverance of the Saints," soon after this debate. Our people patronized it well—over six thousand were disposed of. The debate resulted in good to our people. Congregations were built up, and many additions were made to the church after that debate. I feel sure this was one debate that resulted in good.[65]

The next book was much larger, *Principles and Practices of the Regular Baptists Stated and Defended* in 444 pages. He did a book entitled *Regeneration* and one entitled *Justification* and one entitled *Thoughts on the Will*. In what can only be called a novel direction, he did a book in a popular style for young people called *Practical Suggestions for the Common People*. His public exchange of correspondence on predestination with Elder S. H. Durand appeared in periodicals and then in book form. The first edition of his *Hymnbook* sold 3,000 copies and several printings followed. Over a period of twenty years he supplied much copy to the papers of six Hardshell editors: (1) Elder Lemuel Potter and his *Church Advocate*; (2) Elder R. W. Thompson and his *Monitor*; (3) Elder Hassell and his *Gospel Messenger*; (4) Elder S. F. Cayce and his *Primitive Baptist*; (5) Elder Waters of Washington, D.C., and his *Zion's Advocate*; and (6) Elder Walter Cash of

St. Joseph, Missouri and his *Messenger of Peace*. His *Autobiography* at age 79 was brief. "All of this together has required much travel and labor, also much patience, and I suppose I may say much patience on the part of the churches and of other elders to bear with me," he said. "I attach no value to it all in respect to merit. 'Jesus only' is my hope. I feel no desire to repeat life."[66]

The people of southern Indiana were not very generous with Oliphant. He defended Hardshell practice against outsiders.

> A Presbyterian minister once asked me how it was that I had a home and things with no salary, and no system to raise money from the people. I told him that we believed that if a man loved the church and the members, and preached to them for their good, that good people would notice it, and would want him to keep at it, and would fix it so that he could keep at it. I told him that I believed this and had given my life to the churches on this principle, and I could sincerely recommend it as a safe course to pursue.[67]

He himself was ambivalent.

> I have had the care of a family all the way, and children never cease to be a burden to their parents, though they have homes of their own. I left home often in tears and left my wife in tears; but the brethren have generally been kind and aided me to pay my debts and buy my groceries. While some have been neglectful, shamefully so, there have been true brethren that came to my relief. My father-in-law was opposed to my becoming a minister. He thought that I would fail to support my family. But he was convinced that he was wrong before he died. I have always paid my debts, and always had plenty to eat and wear. I am out of debt and have a home.[68]

Then in a darker mood he detailed the struggles of his whole family in the face of poverty and concluded: "I think now I ought to have pursued a different course in regard to the matter. I ought to have taught the churches their duty and insisted on their doing it by me. I owed it to myself and family, and the interest of the churches required it." After twenty years of ministry, at age 44, he moved with his large family from Buena Vista in Monroe County to the vicinity of Crawfordsville where they were "favored with a little better success in worldly things" and "more favored in the way of assistance."[69]

Hardshell Decline

If the Hardshell Baptists were discourageable, they had plenty of grounds for depression. Joel Hume looked out on the large crowd gathered at Mt. Vernon for his debate with the Campbellite Benjamin Franklin at 9:30 A.M. on 15 November 1853 and conceded that three-fourths of the audience had already decided to agree with Franklin that the eternal salvation of sinners depended on something done by themselves while he was bound in good conscience to take an entirely different view.[70] The Missionary Baptist W. P. Throgmorton in his second speech for Wednesday, 13 July 1887, in the debate of four days and two nights with Lemuel Potter, painfully reminded Potter that the separating of the Hardshells from the larger body of Baptists was "like a fly taking wings and leaving an elephant."[71]

James Oliphant kept running into the assertion that the Primitive Baptists would pass away "when the ministers now living are dead." When a Campbellite preacher read him an article denouncing the Hardshells and claiming that education and science would soon wipe them out, Oliphant pointed out that at the Flood and at Sodom and with Elijah in the cave only a few were right and the many were wrong. In fact, he could not think of a time when the majority was right. He told that Campbellite preacher, "You better come over to us." In spite of continuing divisions which weakened the churches and in spite of a shortage of able young preachers to assure future leadership, his faith affirmed that "the truth is with us, and it will not die or cease from the world. As we see the truth rejected by a sin-loving world, and note the strength of the opposition, we can plainly see that if our people live as a denomination the Lord must sustain us." But he did get discouraged. Once he decided to quit preaching and confided this decision to a Methodist; the Methodist "said he expected my liver was bad, and that I needed something to stimulate my liver."[72] Oliphant preached on.

Part of the problem was the rigidity of the Hardshells against any stimulus if it pointed toward any change from traditional practice. They could differ and divide over the exact nature of their tradition but they could usually unite against any program or practice which could be labeled novelty or advancement. Even more serious was their conflict with the frontier mindset toward free will. Enoch Parr of Washington County was a thinking plain man who joined the Sharon Baptist Church in 1816, in time to participate in a typical rending of a Hoosier Baptist congregation.[73]

> About this time 1830 the Bible sosiety Sunday school union and some other societys was in use and a Society called the forenmision society used for the purpose of raising funds to school the Indians and fit out men to preach to the hethan. Against all these societys the association in their 16th item protested. this caused an other divison. So now we ware in three parties. The Regulars. The Misionarys and the Campbellites. The regulars oppose the raising money for any purpose but the most necessary. The misionarys ware for raising money for spreading the gospel. The Reform baptist or Campbellites objected to any article of faith—took the scripture for their creed.[74]

The parties which pleased him least were the Hardshells which "border upon Calvinism" and "taught me nothing."

> The Misionaries called the Regulars parkerites and as Regulars was made to mean almost any thing the regulars they divided into many parts all claiming to be the regulars without much reguard to their articles of faith. And as the regulars objected to almost any teaching but that of the Holy Ghost to quallfy a man to be a preacher. Some of the ignorant uninformed men profesed to be taught or qualified by the Holy Ghost to preach and some preached one thing and some another all profesing to have been taught by the Spirit. But the general doctrine was something like this. That Christ come into world to save the church. That the church stood full in Adam. That all adams posterity would be saved by relationship with Christ and was the elect. That if any was lost for whom Christ died then so much of the blood of Christ would be shed in vain. And as all agreed that there would be many lost some held there was two seed and some held two fold and some the elect and nonelect and as all profesed to be taught by the Spirit the scripture was not much used to support the varius notions of the saved and lost But according to my view such praching was better calculated to scatter the flock than to gather. But the common saying was that Gods people was Gods wheather many or few let them go. But that there is two orders of men made by the same or brought forth by the same creater. The one order the Special care and protection of God and the other order the vessels of his rath fited or intended for distruction. I deny. It is contrary to the declaration of Independence.[75]

Benoni Stinson and the General Baptists

General Baptists were not happy with the attempt to unite the Baptists either. Benoni Stinson (1798–1869) was their founder. Stinson was concerned about the Calvinistic cast of the Baptists in America. It seemed to him that whenever Baptists of a free will or Arminian persuasion agreed to join with the Regular Baptists to become United Baptists, all of them were soon Regular Baptists of a Calvinistic sort, affirming the orthodoxy of predestination. He believed that under the guise of union and of allowing the profession of Arminianism as "no bar to fellowship," the Regular Baptists had simply absorbed the Arminian Baptists in Virginia and North Carolina and now were about to do the same in his native state of Kentucky. By the time he was twenty-three he had been licensed and then ordained a minister by the United Baptists in Kentucky, an uneasy minister because he felt that "the doctrine of Free Salvation to all men" was not generally believed by his fellow United Baptist preachers. In 1822 he moved with his wife and infant child to Vanderburgh County in Indiana. A lively revival was going on and a Baptist church called New Hope was organized. Stinson was among the messengers sent from the new church with a petition to join the Wabash Association.[76]

There could hardly have been a more unhappy choice of an association for Benoni Stinson. He ran squarely into the territory of the most adamant of the Hardshells of Indiana. Wabash Association was under the influence of Daniel Parker and so Hardshell it made the United Baptists of Kentucky seem mild. "When I got there," Stinson said, "the Calvinists preached their hard doctrine, and hurt my feelings, and I thought wounded the cause of God. We, however, joined the Association, hoping for the better." Hope was renewed when Wabash Association ordered the formation of a new association. New Hope church was to belong to this new body and Stinson was a member of the organizing convention. But the new Salem Association was in Posey County, also under the influence of Daniel Parker, and second to none in Hardshell zeal. Stinson was not even allowed to insert the standard article "that the preaching that Christ tasted death for every man should be no bar to fellowship." He felt that if he ever preached the free will doctrine he really believed among these colleagues he would be tried for heresy. So he led a group of about thirty-three members from New Hope church in fall of 1823 to "establish an arm" of the church called Liberty. He was chosen pastor of this new congregation which was constituted on the principles of free salvation to all men. Said Stinson: "I then felt like the Calvinistic yoke was off my neck, and I was determined never to wear it any more, even if I lived and died in this church, connected with no other. But the Lord soon prospered my way."[77]

By 1824 the efforts of Stinson and his followers had led to the founding of the General Baptist denomination, born and bred in Indiana and without direct linkage to British Baptists of the same name. In October of that year ministers Benoni Stinson, Jesse Lane, and Daniel Jacobs with churches named Liberty, Union, Black River, and Providence enrolling 201 members formed Liberty Association of General Baptists. Always they had as an article of faith "We believe that Jesus Christ, by the grace of God, tasted death for every man; yet none can partake of his divine benefits, only by repentance toward God and faith in the Lord Jesus Christ." Stinson, not long ago the sickly eighth child of a divided home and possessed of scant education, became a hearty traveling preacher, moderator, and theologian for the group.[78] Their biblical texts were the ones which pictured human beings as free, able to choose, and responsible for their choices: Matthew 23:27, John 3:16, Revelation 3:20, and all passages which struck the theme of "whosoever will." All their doctrines were essentially orthodox Christian ones but the frontier was so concerned with the argument over predestination and Benoni Stinson was so bruised by this argument in his personal experience that the General Baptists spent much of their energy advancing and defending their strenuous position on free will.

Stinson himself became a symbolic champion of the doctrine. As the General Baptists saw it, the church father Augustine (354–430) had fastened a doctrine of "fatalism" onto Christianity by the force of his own person and John Calvin (1509–1564) had further expanded this error into a theological system. The pollution introduced by these two traditional teachers could be simply removed by recognizing that divine government works like human government. God does not foreordain or compel any act of the governed. He graciously sets forth the law for life and salvation; then he rewards obedience and punishes transgression. At first the General Baptists kept the traditional Baptist article of faith asserting God's dependability which said "that the saints will finally persevere through grace to glory." By 1844 this "once in grace always in grace" doctrine had come to seem incongruous so the emphasis was shifted to encourage human dependability and the article to read "We believe that he that shall endure to the end the same shall be saved."[79]

Stinson quickly saw his doctrinal kinship with Methodists and Cumberland Presbyterians. The three groups could and did sing, pray, preach, and hold social meetings together. Even though they differed over the practice of infant baptism, they could and did collaborate in protracted meetings, revivals, and camp meetings. Stinson did not see how sharing in the Lord's Supper could be denied these colleagues in evangelism. At the fifth meeting of the Association of General Baptists in 1828 they made it official: "*Agreed*, That we hold communion with all that are qualified according to the Scriptures, and are in good standing in their own churches, and believe Jesus Christ to be the true God and head of the church." To the emphasis on free will and free salvation had now been added the practice of free or open communion. Cumberland Presbyterian and Methodist and General Baptist pulpits were widely opened to each other.[80]

The General Baptists experienced continuing moderate growth. There were new associations gathered in Kentucky and Illinois and Missouri but the denomination's heartland long remained in the area of its birth, in Liberty and Union and Flat Creek associations in a few counties in the extreme southwestern corner of Indiana. This was also Hardshell Baptist territory. What they got from the Hardshells was not fellowship or intercommunion; they got opposition and debates like that five-day one at Owensville in Gibson County between Stinson and Joel Hume published in 1863.[81]

General Baptists toyed with the idea of merger with freewill Baptists in New England and with freewill Baptists in the South and with New Light Christians but inertia and aversion to outside influence blocked these efforts. When an executive of the Freewill Baptist Home Mission Board up north had the temerity to levy a monetary assessment for mission support on Indiana's Liberty Association of General Baptists just because it seemed that union of the two was imminent, that union effort promptly failed. By the 1870s there was little evidence that the General Baptists were going to accept or receive denominational service agencies by merger. Almost reluctantly they began forming agencies for themselves—a General Association of General Baptists to act for the whole body, a church newspaper, an educational institution, a board of home missions or church extension.[82]

When Dr. H. Pagan of Velpen sent a gift of five dollars for foreign missions to a meeting of Liberty Association in 1888 a group of the brethren retired to the grove and organized a General Baptist Foreign Mission Society, pledging some additional contributions toward that work. By March of 1889 they had augmented the doctor's gift and were able to send $101.43 to buy a share in the enterprise of an English missionary couple in India. All agencies of the church persisted in painful poverty, supported by a handful of visionary leaders in the name of a constituency not very zealous for benevolent agencies or for education.[83]

Agitation for a "seminary of learning" for General Baptists began in 1838. Oakland City College opened in Indiana in April of 1891, finally brought to birth by an "educational board" of the denomination but more im-

mediately by a Free Will Baptist minister born and educated in the East who chose to invest the last years of his career as its organizing president and much of his personal fortune to underwrite its beginnings. Through this ministry of A. D. Williams, continued by a cluster of friends and alumni of the school, the General Baptists fulfilled to some degree their aim to provide a college and theological school "within the reach of all energetic young men and women" in a section of the state where opportunities for higher education were very rare.

The limitation of the General Baptists lay in the same area as their original strength. In their strenuous advocacy of free will they seemed a one issue denomination. The uniqueness of that issue kept fading. Their natural opponents, the Hardshell Baptists, became scarce even in southwestern Indiana and nearly nonexistent elsewhere in the state. Thoroughgoing Calvinists among Regular Baptists or Presbyterians were few and were an insufficient foil for any energetic campaign of correction. To keep their place as heroic defenders of free will against predestination, General Baptists had to keep stating both sides of the argument themselves. Champions for predestination no longer appeared. Meanwhile the efficient forces of the Methodists and the Campbellites and the Cumberland Presbyterians and the Missionary Baptists were seeking no evidence of election as a basis for admission to fellowship; they were second to none in their appeals to free will. The General Baptists, slow to unite in or to share in programs for service or growth, were substantial and persistent but they were eclipsed.

Separate Baptists

When most Separate Baptists in the Carolinas and in Virginia and in Kentucky joined with Regular Baptists to become United Baptists in the late 1700s, some Separate Baptists declined to join. They took particular pride in their historic linkage with Shubal Stearns and Daniel Marshall and those pioneer Separate Baptists dating from 1755 at Sandy Creek, North Carolina. They gladly claimed this Separate Baptist heritage of informal and spontaneous worship and wanted no unification which might compromise it. They resisted any traditional creeds and understandings of election which might inhibit the operation of revivalism and free will. And the very word "separate" came to have special status with them through denominational affection and through connection with the Bible verse which said "Wherefore come out from among them, and be ye separate, saith the Lord" (II Corinthians 6:17).

By 1815 these continuing Separate Baptists were in Indiana. They formed a congregation named Indian Creek in Clark County and sent off James Long and Andrew Johnson as the congregation's first messengers to the Kentucky Association of Separate Baptists. In 1830 three congregations in Switzerland and Decatur counties organized Sand Creek Association as Indiana's mother association of Separate Baptists. Then three new associations were formed on Hoosier soil but their growth remained limited. Biographies of early ministers of White River Association record that four of its Separate Baptist preachers "went to the Christian Church." Abe Kiphant was "not quite as active in the ministry as some of his coworkers"; W. T. Griner "being a shoemaker by trade . . . does not devote a great deal of time to his church"; and William Robertson "like many others, did not use all his opportunities for winning souls" or "did not use his talent as greatly as he might."[84]

More zealous farmer-preachers in the denomination, who opted to do less farming and more preaching, were faced with the familiar problem of family support. Associations recommended that churches "adopt the *ad valorem* system of taxation for the support of the ministry" or "raise a fund sufficient for the same and pay her ministers a sufficiency for their support," or exhort members "to pay annually not less than fifty cents each nor more than twenty-five dollars, according to wealth." In fact, Separate Baptist preachers could not count on getting paid at all. An attempt to increase denominational potential by uniting with Freewill Baptists came to nothing. Like the General Baptists, the Separate Baptists were making advocacy of revivalism and free will their central theme at a time when many others in Indiana were doing the same more effectively. They preserved their tradition as footwashing Baptists and their loyalty to their Separate Baptist identity, and they remained small.[85]

Landmarkism

Thus Hoosiers knew several varieties of Baptists from the early days of Indiana's white settlement and knew them as strenuous advocates of their theological views. In addition, congregations of Baptists could always be gathered under local leadership and continued as independents without any wider denominational association. Indiana Baptists further varied across their own denominational lines in their theories of Baptist origins and history. There were opinions that Baptists could first be recognized among the English Puritans in the seventeenth century, or among the European Anabaptists in the sixteenth century, or in Judea in the first century among those who became followers of Jesus in the days of John the Baptist.

This last view, long known in some form to Baptist historians, was refined and elevated to an essential article of ecclesiology in the 1850s in the teaching and publishing of James R. Graves of Tennessee and his colleagues. Their "Old Landmarkism" asserted that individual Baptist churches were the only true churches since each one bearing the proper marks could trace its line of faith and practice from the New Testament church to the present through an unbroken apostolic succession of witnesses and martyrs gathered into true churches which were Baptist in fact, no matter what names the groups bore in their own time. Therefore the ordinances, missions, preaching, and all ecclesiastical acts of non-Baptists and of non–Landmark Baptists could be rejected as outside the blessed church and members of such "societies" could be regarded as second rate Christians if Christians at all. For those Hoosier Baptists inclined toward close communion and toward unquestionable local control over all phases of church life and mission, the logic of this validation of the absolute priority of individual Baptist congregations had great appeal.[86]

Reforming Baptists

Most volatile among the contemporary clusters of Baptists in early Indiana were those who later came to accept the leadership of that "Baptist" Alexander Campbell. Indiana's Baptists and Alexander Campbell were working out their religious identity in those same early decades of the 1800s. When Thomas Campbell and his son Alexander had become disturbed by denominational divisions in both their native Ireland and America and had agreed to break from their Presbyterian tradition, they formed a small congregation known as Brush Run church not far from Washington, Pennsylvania, and brought it into fellowship with the Redstone Baptist Association in Pennsylvania. It was not an easy relationship. Alexander Campbell was not very sanguine about the usefulness of any of the American denominations, making capital out of condemning their unlovely wrangling and expecting that they would all be eliminated by the force of his truth. He did select the Baptists as the most promising of a bad lot and focused his ministry for a few years on them. He saw no hope whatever for "Paido-Baptist" or "Pedobaptist" churches like Methodists, Presbyterians, Lutherans, or Episcopalians which baptized children but some faint hope for the reform of Baptists.

Amongst the Baptists it is to be hoped there are but few clergy; and would to God there were none! The grand and distinguishing views of the Baptists must be grossly perverted before they could tolerate one such creature . . . But some few Baptists, tickled by the love of novelty, and lured by the false majesty of Presbyterianism, exhibited in a classified priesthood, of ordinaries, co-ordinates, subordinates, priests, and Levites; ruling elders, licentiates, Reverends and Doctors of Divinity, have compromised the distinguishing features of their own grand peculiarities, and palmed upon themselves a species of demagogues, who, while they have all the airs, hauteur, and arrogance of some Paido-Baptist priests, have neither their erudition, nor their talents, nor their policy. They can neither wear the gown decently, nor conceal the cloven hoof.[87]

There is one vast difference, one essential and all-important difference betwixt the Baptists and Paido-Baptist views and societies. The Baptist views of the church of Jesus Christ are constitutionally correct; the Paido-Baptist views are unconstitutional. To make myself more intelligible—there are to be found in the Baptist system such views of the Christian church, as, if carried out to their legitimate issue, will place them on Apostolic grounds; but the legitimate issue of the views found in all the numerous sects of Paido-Baptists, would, if carried out, place them in the bosom of the Roman Pontiff. Yes, the one system would place the church upon the foundation of the Apostles and Prophets, Jesus Christ himself the chief corner-stone. The other system would place it upon St. Peter as the rock. The Baptist system is capable of being reformed or brought back again to the constitution of the kingdom of Heaven; the Paido-Baptist cannot. It must be destroyed. The one system carries in its bosom the means of its purification; the other, the fire that must consume it. The foundation of the former needs but to have the rubbish cleared away; the foundation of the later must be totally razed.[88]

Some Baptists in Indiana had already opted for the kind of reformation Campbell advocated. Like him they deplored denominational organizations, names, creeds, and the divisions which seemed to come with them. The ten churches organized in the Washington County area by John Wright and his family and named the Blue River Association of Free Will Baptists decided to dissolve their association, to drop the Baptist name and form of government, and henceforth to be Christians gathered in Churches of Christ. "They earnestly worked for the reformation of the churches and by 1821 there was scarcely a Baptist church in that region."[89] These were Baptists become Campbellites before the first issue of Campbell's *Christian Baptist* ever came into print. When

this publication did come into being, beginning in 1823, it came very forcefully upon the Baptists in Indiana.

It came, for example, to the Baptist congregation at Maria Creek fifteen miles north of Vincennes, founded in 1809 and the church which was Isaac McCoy's first pastorate. A history of that congregation says "About 1827 the *Christian Baptist* began to be read by Abner Davis and David Walford. This led to a division." After much unpleasantness, a large part of the membership withdrew to form the Bruceville Christian Church. The history continues "The following preachers who labored among the Baptists became preachers of primitive Christianity: Abner Davis, David Walford, Brice Fields, Albert T. Law, Maurice R. Trimble, and John B. Hayworth."[90]

It came, also, to Silver Creek Baptist Church, first in the state. Influenced by readers and followers of Campbell's *Christian Baptist*, the majority of its 230 members voted in 1829 to remove the Articles of Faith from the congregation's constitution. A minority withdrew and prepared a remonstrance denouncing the Campbellite invasion and declaring their intention to retain the Baptist Confession of Faith and the name Silver Creek Baptist Church. Deprived of the building, that minority withdrew to the shade of a natural basin nearby and were dubbed "the sink-hole elect." The majority kept the meeting house and named themselves the Silver Creek Christian Church. Under leadership of John T. and Absalom Littell, and beginning with the Baptist congregation in New Albany, the fourteen churches of the Silver Creek Baptist Association became Campbellite one by one. In 1837 it was Absalom Littell who finally signed the official minute which recorded the dissolution of the Silver Creek Association in order "to dispense with all forms and usages belonging to authoritative bodies." Littell is recognized as a Christian Church pioneer.[91]

In his more iconoclastic early period, the years 1823 to 1829 in which he issued the *Christian Baptist*, Alexander Campbell said much which earned him favor with that substantial portion of Hoosier Baptists opposing missions, benevolent societies, and salaried preachers. Volume one, number one, began with an essay entitled "The Christian Religion," delineating the pure and primitive church.

Their devotion did not diversify itself into the endless forms of modern times. They had no monthly concerts for prayer; no solemn convocations, no great fasts, nor preparation, nor thanksgiving days. Their churches were not fractured into missionary societies, Bible societies, Education societies: nor did they dream of organizing such in the world. The head of a believing household was not, in those days, a president, or manager of a board of foreign missions; his wife, the president of some female Education Society; his eldest Son, the recording secretary of some domestic Bible Society; his eldest daughter, the corresponding secretary of a mite society; his servant maid the vice president of a rag society; and his little daughter, a tutoress of a sunday school. They knew nothing of the hobbies of modern times. In their church capacity alone they moved. They neither transformed themselves into any other kind of association; nor did they fracture and sever themselves into divers societies. They viewed the church of Jesus Christ as the scheme of Heaven to ameliorate the world; as members of it, they considered themselves bound to do all they could for the glory of God and the good of men. They dare not transfer to a missionary Society, or Bible Society, or education Society, a cent or a prayer; lest in so doing they should rob the church of its glory, and exalt the inventions of men, above the wisdom of God.[92]

Volume one also contained a scalding series of five articles entitled "The Clergy."[93]

Behold the arrogance of their claims, the peerless haughtiness of their pretensions! They have said, and of them many still say; they have an exclusive right, an official right, to affix the proper interpretation to the scriptures; to expound them in public assemblies; insomuch, that it would be presumption in a layman, to attempt to exercise any of these functions which they have assumed. They must "christen" the new born infant; they must catechise and confirm the tender stripling; they must celebrate the rites of matrimony; they must dispense all ordinances in religion; they must attend the corpse to its grave, preach a funeral sermon, and consecrate the very ground on which it is laid.[94]

Who is called to believe any thing without evidence!! Does God command any man to believe without evidence! No, most assuredly. When, then, I hear a modern preacher either with, or without a Diploma in his pocket saying, that he is an ambassador of Christ, sent of God to preach the Gospel, moved by the Holy Ghost to take upon him the work of the ministry; I ask him to work a miracle, or afford some Divine attestation of his being such a character. If he cannot do this, I mark him down as a knave, or an enthusiast; consequently an imposter, either intentionally, or unintentionally.[95]

After satirizing the education of clergy at length Campbell concluded the series:

Money I think may be considered not merely as the bond of union in popular establishments; but it is really the rock on which the popular churches are built. Before church union is proposed the grand point to ascertain is,

are we able to support a church. Before we give a call let us see, says the prudent saint, what we can "make up." A meeting is called, the question is put—"how much will you give?" It goes round, each man writes his name or makes his mark. A handsome sum is subscribed. A petition is some times presented to the legislature for an act of incorporation, to confirm their union, and to empower them to raise by the civil law, or the arm of power, the stipulated sum. All is now secure. The church is founded upon this rock. It goes into operation. The parson comes. Their social prayers, praises, sacraments, sermons and fasts commence, every thing is put into requisition: but what is the *primum mobile*? What the moving cause? Money. As proof of this, let the congregation decrease by emigration or death; the money fails, the parson takes a missionary tour; he obtains a louder call; he removes; money failed is the cause; and when this current freezes, social prayers, praises, "sacraments," sermons, and congregational fasts all cease. Money, the foundation is destroyed; and down comes the superstructure raised upon it. Reader is not this fact? And dare you say that money is not the basis of the modern religious establishments? It begins with money, it goes on with money; it ends when money fails. Money buys Aesop's fables for the destined priest, money consecrates him to office, and a monied contract unites him and his parish. The church of Jesus Christ is founded upon another basis, nourished by other means, is not dissolved by such causes, and will survive all the mines of Peru, all the gold of Ophir. The modern clergy say they do not preach for money. Very well. Let the people pay them none and they will have as much of their preaching still. Besides there will be no suspicion of their veracity.[96]

It was a theme to be well worked and often repeated. Baptists who might have been reluctant to adopt a predestinarian argument against employing trained and ordained clergy to conduct a missionary program could find here an alternate rationale forcefully stated.

Even after Alexander Campbell became alienated from the Baptists, after his *Christian Baptist* was replaced with his somewhat more irenic *Millennial Harbinger* in 1830, and after the wholesale separation of Campbellite and Baptist congregations nationwide in the early 1830s, Baptists were still primary candidates for Campbellite evangelism.[97] Baptizing sinners was paralleled by "capsizing" Baptists. It was difficult to assess the number of Baptists feeding into the beginnings of the Christian Church in Indiana but not difficult to see that the number was large indeed. Christian Church historians Commodore Cauble and Henry K. Shaw named many of the Baptist churches making the change of allegiance. Cauble said "It will be impossible to mention all of the churches in Indiana that came to the New Testament position in the early days."[98]

Continued Development of the General Association

Among Indiana's maze of denominations and among this welter of Baptist constituencies, the main body of Regular Baptists (including the United Baptists and variously referred to later as Missionary, Northern, or American Baptists) made its way. Historical accounts of Hoosier Baptists have spoken much of advance in spite of challenges. Often the main body of Baptists looked like walking wounded. Between the more positive and aggressive enterprise of the Campbellites and the more negative and obstructive program of the Hardshells "the intermediate Regular Baptists, most of whom were eventually to become supporters of missions, drew fire from both sides, and had no choice but to pursue a cautious and apologetic policy."[99]

They kept growing because many incoming settlers were Baptist by persuasion and remained so. They kept growing because the independence and local autonomy and democratic principle of the Baptists appealed to the strong democratic notions and neighborhood orientation of the frontier folk. The Baptist farmer-preacher was typically raised up out of revival experience and regular hearing of the preaching of others. When he felt ready, or before if his neighbors were urgent, he could begin preaching. His calling tested, he could be ordained to serve a congregation, or gather a new congregation and be ordained as its pastor. He and his congregation members were much the same in circumstances and knew each other well. They kept growing because nearly all Regular Baptist pastors and people and their frontier constituents were heavily committed to revivals. Success in conducting revivals, the fruit of preaching as they saw it, was the primary validation of the minister's call and ordination.

Thus James M. Smith (b. 1819) of Shelby County entitled his autobiography *A Work on Revivals*, delineating the success of his ministry largely in terms of the impact of the scores of revivals he conducted and the hundreds of members added.[100] When Matthew McClain (b. 1806) of Scott County was old and blind, describing his life and labors orally for transcription by his son, he took pride in his efforts as a champion of education and of Sunday schools in the face of much opposition and prejudice, but the real excitement in this life story focuses on his revival preaching.[101] Taking the Bible as their guide and corrective, such pastors and churches kept extending the faith

as the state's population expanded. Their genius was that they could flourish on their own initiative. Such a farmer-preacher among the Missionary Baptists as Joshua Griffith (1823–1904), who served as ordained minister to Baptist churches in Switzerland and Jefferson counties from the time he was eighteen years of age in 1841 until he was eighty-one, put a Baptist pastoral stamp on a whole region.

> Usually the country churches at that time had services only once, or at most twice, monthly affording the minister opportunity for serving two or more churches. In this way, my father acquired a wide acquaintance since he served almost every church in Long Run Association. Nor were his activities limited to Baptists. There was scarcely a family of any creed within a radius of several miles that he did not at some time visit or for whom he did not perform an act of sympathy . . . The marriage record in Switzerland County alone shows in the neighborhood of 1700 weddings at which he officiated. Beside these there were many from adjoining counties as well as from Kentucky who came to him to be married. There were fifty-two people named McKay for whom he performed the ceremony.[102]

The *U.S. Baptist Annual Register* for 1833 illustrated the growth of the Baptists. It listed 21 Baptist associations in Indiana, over half named for rivers or creeks. Where there had been 29 churches in 1812 there were now 299 churches with 11,344 members served by 152 ordained ministers and 49 licentiates. But most of the churches were small and generally held services once each month. The more active ministers often served four churches each and received scant support from any of them. There was little interest in formal education for clergy; such education could be expensive and only make a preacher less acceptable to his congregations. Baptist historian Israel George Blake commented that over half of these associations of 1833 went anti-mission and many of them simply died out. Some were proud in their local freedom and averse to annoying outsiders, especially to paid and educated and equally proud Yankees collecting support for missions and Sunday schools and benevolent societies.[103]

The churches were generally members of an association in which Baptist principles and practice were to be discussed, but the actions and decisions of this association were merely advisory. There was a tendency to change from quarterly meetings of the association for program planning or serious deliberation to one annual meeting made the occasion for a great outdoor revival. In theory advice could be exchanged at that annual meeting about doctrine, discipline, and organization. However, unwillingness to take risks, and poor transportation, and bickering among the churches long prevented much oversight or antidote to localism.104

Baptist representatives for missionary and benevolent causes who came from outside the local congregation were handicapped in their visits to Indiana. They could collaborate with the already convinced but those who chose isolation would only be incensed at their coming. Gradually the churches in some associations in central and southern Indiana (White Lick, 1841; Indianapolis, 1843; Little Pigeon, 1843; Curry's Prairie, 1848; Coffee Creek, 1849; Sand Creek, 1850; Flat Rock, 1852; Long Run, 1852) cooperated to begin deliberate home mission efforts beyond the local churches but still within their own association's bounds. Baptists from New York and New England now migrating to northern Indiana were not anti-mission in sentiment and were outside the region of greatest anti-mission strength in the state. They welcomed the activity of outside missionaries among them and cooperated in a whole range of benevolent enterprises. Some associations and substantial town churches adopted the principle that it was the duty of the church to support the ministry.105

Most of all, the Baptists recovered from the limitations of mere localism because a few courageous individuals kept lifting up a missionary vision before the rest. Jesse Lynch Holman of Dearborn County, a judge of the Indiana Supreme Court and of federal district court as well as an active Baptist preacher and Sunday school teacher, was so highly respected in the state that his bold championship of the whole range of missionary and benevolent causes could hardly be ignored.106 Deacon John McCoy of Clark County repeatedly stood for Sunday schools, tract societies, and missionary societies when these faced not only Baptist lethargy but strenuous opposition. His survival of the Indian wars following the massacre at Pigeon Roost did not rate an entry in his diary, but of his "two sore conflicting warfares, Campbelism and Parkerism" he wrote on 11 February 1858:

> With humble gratitude to God I hail one more birthday in my short pilgrimage here on earth. I am now seventy-six years old—have been a professor of religion about thirty-five years, have experienced some sore trials in the world, but the hardest with false Brethren in the church. Have contended against Cambelism and Parkerism some times almost alone, but I have thought God blessed my feeble efforts. Yet very little have I done for my Blessed Master, who has done so much for me.107

But a new thing had appeared in 1833—the General Association of Baptists in the State of Indiana. What some had thought was a meeting to settle some differences between the Flat Rock and Indianapolis associations was made the occasion for forming this Indiana Baptist convention. Judge Jesse L. Holman, that supporter of the American Sunday School Union and of the Indiana Bible Society and of the Indian missions of Isaac McCoy, was the prime mover. He helped write the constitution and was named moderator of its board of trustees. The aim was "to unite the Baptists of Indiana in some uniform plan for promoting the prosperity of the Redeemer's kingdom within the bounds of the state by a more general spread of the gospel." Only seventeen churches were represented; the number of committed leaders was small. But now there was a central agency which could send out letters to the churches, negotiate with national missionary agencies offering help, and function as a clearing house for both correspondence and contributions. The new state association was an organization requiring extraordinary patience, having neither staff nor money and a constituency not anxious to furnish either. Those anti-mission wars kept raging. The association's average annual income for the first five years was less than three hundred dollars. In 1843-1844 income totaled eighty-seven dollars; Judge Holman and several other supporters had died.108

Another part of the new vision was a Baptist college for Indiana. It began as the Indiana Manual Labor Institute in 1834, its handful of founders and thirty-five trustees pretty well exhausting the supply of Indiana's Baptist champions of higher education, missions, the General Association, Sunday schools, tract and Bible distribution, and temperance. By 1844 it had a president and was chartered as Franklin College, continuing to share the General Association's desperate poverty.109 In fact it seemed never to take a secure breath in its early life but the ideal of some formal education for Baptist ministers would now be perpetually raised by the president and faculty of the college and by its friends or agents.

So when James M. Smith was a young man about twenty-two living in Union Township of Shelby County in a "wicked community" with over twenty still-houses, Joshua Currier, a friend of missions and temperance who came from the East and was pastor at Greensburg, held meetings there at Little Blue River Baptist Church beginning about 1841.110

> The revival changed the community entirely. Horse-racing, dancing, card-playing, drinking whisky, and gambling of all kinds were nearly altogether given up . . .

The people, from this time forward, went to church, and the church greatly prospered under the pastoral labors and preaching of Elder Joshua Currier. For five years or more, men who were drunkards to a great degree, and gamblers and desperately wicked, gave up their evil practices and made sober men and women and active Christians. The old log church was taken down, and a good frame church-house was built, and the people turned their attention to meeting and worshiping God. The change was so wonderful they began to prosper in the world and every thing.[111]

From there revival extended to other communities. Eighty members were added to Little Blue River Church. Of the seven new members who became Baptist preachers, James M. Smith, Matthew Phares, David J. Huston, and William Golding attended Franklin College. Smith's parishioners opposed his going to college, saying he could preach well enough without going to school but with great effort he studied at Franklin about a year.[112]

It done me good. I got a tolerable good knowledge of grammar and arithmetic, and other branches that I studied. Learned how to write composition, which I never had done before, and by being criticised and taught the rules of language and proper spelling, pronounciation, declamation and reading. It was the most paying thing of the kind I could have ever done for myself and others. For I know if I had not got that year's schooling and training that I got at Franklin, I never could have got along in the ministry and succeeded, as I trust I have, for it laid a foundation for me to study the Scriptures, and all that was necessary to aid me in the work of preaching the gospel. It helped me so I could go among men of learning and not be embarrassed, as I believe I would have been had I not went to the school as I did, and it would have been better for me and the cause of religion if I had went longer to school, but I had a family to support, and the church seemed to want my preaching. Means were hard to get to go on, so I did go but a little over a year to school, but I often thanked God for what I did learn at that school.[113]

Like his mentor Joshua Currier and his friends at Franklin, Smith became an expert at revivals and a champion of missions, of Sunday schools, of temperance, and of Baptist agencies of every kind. He and his kind offered a new model of home grown Baptist clergy with national and international vision, a model never lost but still slow to prevail.

State association secretary Timothy Cressy thought the tide had turned in 1850. He was a native of Connecticut, graduate of Amherst and of Newton Seminary, lately pastor of Indianapolis church for six years.

It is well known that it has been but a few years since Campbellism, Parkerism, anti-nomianism, and anti-missionisms were terrible havoc among our churches. But the doom of these is manifestly sealed, and the advocates of others are seeing the evil of their ways, while our denomination, as a whole, is settling down firmly upon the great principles of God's word, and assuming that stability, energy, and dignity of mature manhood, which are the necessary results of a severe training in the school of adversity. From the very nature of things the denomination can never again experience the vicissitudes of past years.[114]

That year Cressy died and the vicissitudes were back. Soon an argument broke out between missions agencies and several consistent leaders of the state association died. Under the pressures of the Civil War, 95 percent of the Baptist churches failed to support home missions. During the war the association changed its name to Indiana Baptist Convention and in 1867 Baptist work in the state was reorganized.[115] From that time there was a fairly consistent increase in support for a program to establish Baptist Sunday schools and Baptist churches in Indiana towns which lacked them. Baptist genius for local growth came to be balanced by a stimulating leadership at state level. Women's work played a significant role from about 1870, especially in foreign mission support.

Census takers in 1906 counted 60,203 Northern Baptists in Indiana. These finally organized Regular Baptists were prepared to parallel the even more organized Southern Baptists as the twin pillars of Indiana's Baptist strength for the twentieth century.

NOTES

1. Israel George Blake, *Finding a Way Through the Wilderness: The Indiana Baptist Convention, 1833–1983* (Indianapolis, Ind.: Central Publishing Co., 1983), 11–12; John Frank Cady, *The Origin and Development of the Missionary Baptist Church in Indiana* (Franklin, Ind.: Franklin College, 1942), 14–18.

2. Elizabeth Hayward, *John M'Coy: His Life and His Diaries* (New York: American Historical Company, 1948), 24, 42, 44; Benjamin F. Keith, *History of Maria Creek Church* (Vincennes, Ind.: A. V. Crotts, 1889), 6, 12–13.

3. Isaac McCoy, *History of Baptist Indian Missions* (1840; reprint, with a new introduction by Robert F. Berkhofer, Jr., New York: Johnson Reprint Corp., 1970), 29–35, 46–47; Isaac McCoy, *Remarks on the Practicability of Indian Reform*, 2d ed. (New York: Gray and Bunce, 1829, 72 p.).

4. McCoy, *History*, 109–10.

5. For a bitter tract against McCoy, see Timothy S. Smith, *Missionary Abominations Unmasked; or, A view of Carey Mission* (South Bend, Ind.: Beacon Office, 1883, 16 p.). Two balanced treatments of his work are George A. Schultz, *An Indian Canaan.*

Isaac McCoy and the Vision of an Indian State (Norman, Okla.: University of Oklahoma Press, 1972, 230 p.). and John Frank Cady, "Isaac McCoy's Mission to the Indians of Indiana and Michigan," *Indiana History Bulletin* 16 (February 1939): 100–13.

6. Walter Newton Wyeth, *Isaac McCoy: Early Indian Missions* (Philadelphia: W. N. Wyeth, 1895), 97; McCoy, *History*, 152–53.

7. Wyeth, *Isaac McCoy*, 91; Hayward, *John McCoy*, 64.

8. *Encyclopedia of Religion in the South*, ed. Samuel S. Hill (Macon, Ga.: Mercer University Press, 1984), 86–87.

9. *Encyclopedia of Religion in the South*, 685.

10. William Warren Sweet, *Religion on the American Frontier, the Baptists, 1783–1830. A Collection of Source Material* (New York: Henry Holt and Company, 1931), 23–24.

11. Lemuel Potter, *A Synopsis of Four Lectures on the Communion* (Evansville, Ind.: Courier Company, 1886, 64 p.).

12. Wilson Thompson, *The Autobiography of Elder Wilson Thompson* (Cincinnati, Ohio: Moore, Wilstach & Baldwin, 1867), 24–29.

13. Thompson, *Autobiography*, 45–47.

14. John F. Johnson, *A Compilation of J. F. Johnson's Writings* (Lawrenceburgh, Ky.: n.p., 1876), 545.

15. Some erroneously wrote it "Armenianism" and almost certainly said it that way. See Thompson, *Autobiography*, 12, 21, 301–7.

16. Thompson, *Autobiography*, 10, 72, 95–99, 186.

17. Anthony Howard Dunlevy, *History of the Miami Baptist Association* (Cincinnati, Ohio: Geo. S. Blanchard, 1869), 64–66; Thompson, *Autobiography*, 273–79, 307–19, 341–76.

18. George C. Clark, *Means vs. Anti-means; or, The Trial of the Baptist Church Case in the Rush Circuit Court* (Rushville, Ind.: The Republican Co., 1895), 15, 17, 24–30, 36–38, 63–67. The issues recurred in Indiana courts. In 1893 an Anti-Means party focused dramatically on the shift toward Arminianism among Baptists and won a case for their own priority before the Indiana Supreme Court. See Robert C. Pedigo, *Mount Tabor Church Trial* (Fort Branch, Ind.: Lemuel Potter, 1893, 28 p.).

19. Dunlevy, *History*, 64; Thompson, *Autobiography*, 482–94.

20. Daniel Parker, *The Author's Defence* (Vincennes, Ind.: E. Stout, 1824), 3–4.

21. Parker, *Author's Defence*, 5; Cady, *Origin and Development*, 50; other sources assign other dates for Parker's move to Illinois but 1817 seems most likely.

22. Terry E. Miller, "Otter Creek Church of Indiana: Lonely Bastion of Daniel Parker's 'Two-Seedism,'" *Foundations*, Rochester, N.Y. 18 (1975): 361.

23. Cady, *Origin and Development*, 51.

24. Dunlevy, *History*, 79; Miller, "Otter Creek Church," 361, 363; Cady, *Origin and Development*, 50–53.

25. William Pinckney Throgmorton, *The Throgmorton-Potter Debate* (St. Louis, Mo.: Nixon-Jones Printing Co., 1888), 36–37; Miller, "Otter Creek Church," 361–62.

26. Lemuel Potter, *Labors and Travels of Elder Lemuel Potter* (Evansville, Ind.: Keller Printing Company, 1894), 262–67; Miller, "Otter Creek Church," 364; Cady, *Origin and Development*, 53.

27. Joel Hume, *A Debate on the Doctrine of Atonement, between Rev. Joel Hume of Posey County, Ind., of the Regular Baptist Church, and Rev. Benoni Stinson of Vanderburgh County, Indiana, of the General Baptist Church* (Cincinnati, Ohio: E. Morgan & Co., 1863), 68–70; Throgmorton, *The Throgmorton-Potter Debate*, 35–37, 44, 68–70 and passim.

28. Miller, "Otter Creek Church," 363.

29. Miller, "Otter Creek Church," 364.

30. Johnson, *Compilation*, 139–40, 543.

31. Johnson, *Compilation*, 546.

32. Johnson, *Compilation*, 546–47.

33. Johnson, *Compilation*, 543, 547–55.

34. Johnson, *Compilation*, 555–56.

35. Johnson, *Compilation*, 9, 21, 47–53, 111–12, 141.

36. Johnson, *Compilation*, 53.

37. Johnson, *Compilation*, 112.

38. Potter, *Labors and Travels*, 262–67; Johnson, *Compilation*, 94, 148, 556.

39. James Harvey Oliphant, *The Autobiography of J. H. Oliphant of Crawfordsville, Ind.* (St. Joseph, Mo.: Messenger of Peace, 1923), 15, 19.

40. Joel Hume, *A Debate on Total Hereditary Depravity* (Mt. Vernon, Ind.: Larkin Dusouchet & Co., 1854), 4.

41. Hume, *Debate on Total Hereditary Depravity*, title page.

42. Hume, *Debate on Total Hereditary Depravity*, 33, 131, 231.

43. Hume, *Debate on Total Hereditary Depravity*, 13–20, 106–9, 144–45.

44. Hume, *Debate on Total Hereditary Depravity*, 39–40.

45. Hume, *Debate on Total Hereditary Depravity*, 67–68.

46. Hume, *Debate on Total Hereditary Depravity*, 71, 100–1.

47. Hume, *Debate on Total Hereditary Depravity*, 190–91.

48. Hume, *Debate on the Doctrine of Atonement*, xv.

49. Hume, *Debate on the Doctrine of Atonement*, 2.

50. H. Clay Yates, *Joint Discussion on Foreign Missions, between the Rev. H. Clay Yates and Elder Lemuel Potter* (Nashville, Tenn.: Cumberland Presbyterian Publishing House, 1886, 669 p.).

51. Potter, *Labors and Travels*, 14–34.

52. Potter, *Labors and Travels*, 22, 25, 35.

53. Potter, *Labors and Travels*, 36, 39.

54. Potter, *Labors and Travels*, 43.

55. Potter, *Labors and Travels*, 67–68.

56. Potter, *Labors and Travels*, 54–66, 75–91, 123, 262–67; Oliphant, *Autobiography*, 39.

57. Potter, *Labors and Travels*, 239.

58. Potter, *Labors and Travels*, 270, quoting Ephesians 4:12.

59. Potter, *Labors and Travels*, 271.

60. Oliphant, *Autobiography*, 6, 9, 11–12.

61. Oliphant, *Autobiography*, 15.

62. Oliphant, *Autobiography*, 18.

63. Oliphant, *Autobiography*, 31–32.

64. Oliphant, *Autobiography*, 20, 24, 27, 30, 32, 37, 40, 47.

65. Oliphant, *Autobiography*, 20; James Harvey Oliphant, *The Doctrine of the Final Perseverance of the Saints* (Indianapolis, Ind.: Baker & Randolph, 1878, 158 p.).

66. Oliphant, *Autobiography*, 39–40.

67. Oliphant, *Autobiography*, 46.

68. Oliphant, *Autobiography*, 45–46.

69. Oliphant, *Autobiography*, 65, 66, 68.

70. Hume, *Debate on Total Hereditary Depravity*, 95–96.

71. Throgmorton, *Throgmorton-Potter Debate*, 89.

72. Oliphant, *Autobiography*, 30, 34, 71, 76, 80.

73. Enoch Parr, "Memoir of Enoch Parr, 1808–1851," *Indiana Magazine of History* 22 (December 1926): 378, 401.

74. Parr, "Memoir," 402.

75. Parr, "Memoir," 403–4.

76. Alvin Dighton Williams, *Benoni Stinson and the General Baptists* (reprinted by General Baptist Historical Society. Evansville, Ind.: Unigraphic, 1975), 15–16, 39–40.

77. Williams, *Benoni Stinson*, 17, 39–41; Cady, *Origin and Development*, 52, 56.

78. Williams, *Benoni Stinson*, 32–33, 37–38, 42, 46–59.

79. Williams, *Benoni Stinson*, 9–15, 42, 52, 121.

80. Williams, *Benoni Stinson*, 62–64.

81. Williams, *Benoni Stinson*, 152–54; Hume, *Debate on the Doctrine of Atonement*, passim.

82. Williams, *Benoni Stinson*, 155–60, 182–99, 206–25.

83. Williams, *Benoni Stinson*, 227–29.

84. Morgan Scott, *History of the Separate Baptist Church* (Indianapolis, Ind.: Hollenbeck Press, 1901), 212, 230, 247, 251–52.

85. Scott, *History*, 239, 254, 258.

86. H. Leon McBeth, *The Baptist Heritage* (Nashville, Tenn.: Broadman Press, 1987), 447–61; Hugh Wamble, "Landmarkism: Doctrinaire Ecclesiology among Baptists," *Church History* 33 (December 1964): 429–47.

87. *Christian Baptist*, 2:49–50.

88. *Christian Baptist*, 2:51.

89. Madison Evans, *Biographical Sketches of the Pioneer Preachers of Indiana* (Philadelphia: J. Challen and Sons, 1862), 32.

90. Commodore Wesley Cauble, *Disciples of Christ in Indiana: Achievements of a Century* (Indianapolis, Ind.: Meigs Publishing Company, 1930), 64–65.

91. Cauble, *Disciples of Christ*, 27, 29; Blake, *Finding a Way*, 24–26.

92. *Christian Baptist*, 1:20.

93. *Christian Baptist*, 1:61–71, 91–96, 109–12, 133–39, 157–61.

94. *Christian Baptist*, 1:61–62.

95. *Christian Baptist*, 1:65–66.

96. *Christian Baptist*, 1:160–61.

97. Lester G. McAllister and William E. Tucker, *Journey in Faith: A History of the Christian Church (Disciples of Christ)* (St. Louis, Mo.: Bethany Press, 1975), 127–28, 136–46.

98. Henry K. Shaw, *Hoosier Disciples: A Comprehensive History of the Christian Churches (Disciples of Christ) in Indiana* (St. Louis, Mo.: Bethany Press, 1966), 55–60; Cauble, *Disciples of Christ*, 58–65.

99. Cady, *Origin and Development*, 69. While there may have been some variations, generally the Baptists who favored missions also favored the General Association of Baptists in the State of Indiana, Sunday schools, Bible societies, tract societies, temperance societies, education societies, educational standards for ministers, and regularly contracted pay for ministers. Those who opposed missions opposed all of these.

100. James M. Smith, *A Work on Revivals* (Indianapolis, Ind.: Printed for the Author, 1881, 298 p.).

101. William Thomas McClain, *Life and Labors of the Rev. Matthew McClain* (Indianapolis, Ind.: John G. Doughty, 1876, 232 p.).

102. Ella Porter Griffith, "Joshua Griffith: Pioneer Preacher," *Indiana Magazine of History* 36 (March 1940): 39–40.

103. Sweet, *Religion*, 58–76; Blake, *Finding a Way*, 29–30.

104. Blake, *Finding a Way*, 14–15.

105. Cady, *Origin and Development*, 158–62.

106. Israel George Blake, *The Holmans of Veraestau* (Oxford, Ohio: The Mississippi Valley Press, 1943), 9–42.

107. Hayward, *John M'Coy*, 410, 446–47.

108. Blake, *Finding a Way*, 28, 31–44, 53.

109. John Frank Cady, *The Centennial History of Franklin College* (Franklin, Ind.: n.p., 1934), 22, 47.

110. Smith, *Work on Revivals*, 32–34.

111. Smith, *Work on Revivals*, 24–25.

112. Smith, *Work on Revivals*, 20, 24, 26–28, 40.

113. Smith, *Work on Revivals*, 42.

114. Blake, *Finding a Way*, 57.

115. Blake, *Finding a Way*, 57, 65, 72.

About Christians

Alexander Campbell preferred that his colleagues in restoring the ancient order of things be called "Disciples" and organized into "Churches of Christ" or "Churches of God." Thomas Campbell, Walter Scott, Barton W. Stone, and some groups which came to be linked with Stone preferred the name "Christians." In the course of history every possible combination of the names seems to have been used by units of the fellowship, often without meaning to signify anything distinctive by the choice or combination.

Currently the name "Christian Church (Disciples of Christ)" is the official title for the more liberal, ecumenical, and mainline denomination which reported 89,932 adherents in Indiana in 1990. The name "Churches of Christ" generally designates the most conservative congregations which use no instrumental music in worship; the 1990 survey indicated 39,953 adherents for them in Indiana. A center group is the largest segment of the fellowship in Indiana and was itself the third largest denomination in the state in 1990 with an estimated 160,099 adherents; this third group is variously designated as (1) "Christian Churches and Churches of Christ," (2) "North American Christian Convention," or (3) "Independent Christian Churches."

The designation "Campbellite" was at first a term of opprobrium used by opponents of the movement but, like the word "Hoosier," has largely outlived and transformed the earlier unfavorable usage. When the term "Campbellite" is used here it is only one more effort to find a useful referent for this whole family of churches and it has no negative connotation.

CHRISTIANS

Alexander Campbell was the chief organizer of the movement whose members claimed the name Christians. However Indiana had at least four kinds of believers who wanted only the name Christians even before they overtly accepted a place in Campbell's movement for reformation. These groups wanted to avoid any denominational name or organization or creed. They wanted to take the Bible alone for their guide and authority. They were ready to cast off the burden of church history and dogma and restore the church on a New Testament model. Indiana was just opening for white settlement. They entered it possessed of opportunities equal to those of any of the traditional religious groups—religious liberty, a largely unchurched population, and an attractive platform of union on the basis of the Scriptures alone.

New Light Christians

The New Light name[1] was often given to Americans who urged intense personal piety and heartfelt experience of religion as more basic than traditional church orthodoxies. Indiana's New Light Christians rejected sectarian names with gusto. They felt commissioned to call all people to "come out of Babylon," out of captivity to confessions of faith, to church government, to church authority, and even to any burden of regularized structure for the local church. The invitation was to freedom and liberty; to enjoy such freedom and liberty together was to experience unity.

A little of this emphasis came west from the work of Abner Jones of Vermont, a Baptist preacher who chose to call the congregations he organized Christian churches. He and a Baptist colleague named Elias Smith established a Christian church at Portsmouth, New Hampshire, in 1802 and then their non-denominational fellowship widened. Everywhere they took the name Christian and acknowledged the Bible only as their creed. Smith issued the *Herald of Gospel Liberty* beginning in September of 1808. He was well aware of kindred movements in the West. The first issue of the *Herald* carried a reprint of the *Last Will and Testament of the Springfield Presbytery* with some comment on these Christian activities among Presbyterians in Kentucky.[2]

More of the impact on Indiana was energized in 1811 when this Jones-Smith movement in New England joined with the followers of James O'Kelly centered in the South and surging with Methodist revivalism. O'Kelly was a circuit rider who walked out of the Methodist General Conference at Baltimore in 1792 and eventually took a few thousand followers out of the Methodist Church with him. He resented what he considered the unchecked power of Bishop Francis Asbury and the authority of the Methodist *Discipline*. He waved his New Testament at the Conference and said "Put away all other books and forms and let this be the only criterion and that will satisfy me." This Okellian or Republican Methodist Church grew stout in Virginia and North Carolina; it moved with the heavy flow of southern population into Kentucky and Indiana.

At the suggestion of Rice Haggard they chose the name Christians and in Indiana were sometimes called "old" Christians.[3]

Most of all there was the influence of the schism of the New Lights or Stoneites from the Presbyterians in Kentucky which was to give its popular nickname of New Lights to this whole wing of the movement. Just as Indiana was being opened for white settlement in the early 1800s, an enthusiastic revival broke out in Kentucky. This was the "Great Revival" brought out of North Carolina with the preaching of James McGready, heightened in massive camp meetings like the one at Cane Ridge, Kentucky, in August of 1801, and harnessed by the Methodists and their collaborators as energy for the evangelism of the American West. The so-called Great Awakening of the century preceding "was a backyard bonfire in comparison with the religious conflagration lighted by the Revival of 1800."[4] Every denomination was affected. Five young Presbyterian preachers were among the participants in this Kentucky revival. They wanted their Presbyterian denomination to renounce the doctrine that God calls particular individuals personally to new life and to embrace the doctrine that God offers salvation generally to any and all persons who will repent and seek the new birth.

> The distinguishing doctrine preached by us was, that God loved the world—the whole world, and sent his Son to save them, on condition that they believed in him—that the gospel was the means of salvation—but that this means would never be effectual to this end, until believed and obeyed by us—that God required us to believe in his Son, and had given us sufficient evidence in his Word to produce faith in us, if attended to by us—that sinners were capable of understanding and believing this testimony, and of acting upon it by coming to the Saviour and obeying him, and from him obtaining salvation and the Holy Spirit. We urged upon the sinner to believe now, and receive salvation—that in vain they looked for the Spirit to be given them, while they remained in unbelief—they must believe before the Spirit or salvation would be given them—that God was as willing to save them now, as he ever was, or ever would be—that no previous qualification was required, or necessary in order to believe in Jesus, and come to him—that if they were sinners, this was their divine warrant to believe in him, and to come to him for salvation—that Jesus died for all, and that all things were now ready. When we began first to preach these things, the people appeared as just awakened from the sleep of ages—they seemed to see for the first time that they were

responsible beings, and that a refusal to use the means appointed, was a damning sin.[5]

Anticipating suspension, these Presbyterians withdrew from their denomination, renounced all creeds and church authorities, and issued a *Last Will and Testament of Springfield Presbytery* as a partial and informal statement of their position. Rice Haggard from the O'Kelly group of Christians in the East had come to be a participant in this western group and convinced the Kentuckians also to take the name Christians. Rather quickly two of the five preachers became Shakers, two returned to the Presbyterians, and only Barton W. Stone was left of the original five. He certainly was not left alone. As Stone said, the movement was spreading like fire in dry stubble. The Presbyterian congregations which had sided with the New Light preachers were aflame with revival; new converts and churches and preachers were constantly being added.[6]

Barton W. Stone (1772–1844)

Barton W. Stone did not generate the Kentucky New Light movement nor was he central in the earliest leadership of it. There was the disgrace of being deserted by his colleagues, especially the apostasy to the Shakers. He had neither time nor money enough to give the work his undivided attention and it had little visible administrative structure for his use to steer the movement. When he had energy beyond the immediate demands of his family and farming and teaching and revival preaching, he was prone to spend it on painstaking essays on the divinity of Christ, on the substitutionary atonement, and on the Trinity—all doctrines which made him very uncomfortable but which he could not let alone. There were repeated urgings from friends that he give up these "speculations," and he tried to do that.[7] He said his *Christian Messenger* was intended to present reports of the "progress and triumph of truth" because "such intelligence is worth more than volumes of dull theology, and vain speculations."[8] After an 1833 controversy in print with Thomas Campbell about the atonement, Stone reported:

> Some of our weak brethren are afraid that the passing remarks of Bro. Thomas Campbell and myself will ultimate in a controversy, and injury to the cause in which we profess to be engaged. We have been solicited by them to desist, and by others of stronger minds, lest that which is lame be turned out of the way. As a Bishop must not be self-willed, I have yielded to their wishes.[9]

As the New Light ranks in Kentucky kept growing and migrating over the West, Stone's stature kept increasing as one persistent evangelist and writer and teacher in those New Light ranks. In 1826 he began issuing his monthly paper called the *Christian Messenger* which provided a mailing address and a useful medium of expression for the fellowship. Indiana's Christian preachers of eastern rootage read the *Messenger*. They wrote to ask the advice of Editor Stone. They sent him news of their conference sessions and evangelistic successes to be reported in the paper. They recognized and to some extent acceded to the popular designation of their whole Christian movement as New Light. Conversely, Stone's western Christian church or New Light movement was considered a constituent unit of the loosely organized United States General Convention made up of the scattered Christian church movements and instituted at Portsmouth, New Hampshire, in 1819.

Indiana's Christians visited Stone in Kentucky to seek his counsel. They often invited him to come to Indiana to preach, for example at an evangelistic meeting at Bloomington in 1826 out of which a Christian church was organized. They made him welcome when he visited his daughter and grandchildren at Rockville. Old and nearly deaf, he was an honored senior among the fifty preachers attending the first state meeting of the Christian churches at Indianapolis in June of 1839. His five speeches were mostly exhortations to the young preachers; the Methodist meetinghouse was filled to hear his Sunday morning sermon. The brethren passed a resounding resolution inviting him to move to Indiana and locate his *Christian Messenger* among his Indiana friends. On this same trip he preached at Logansport and again at Bloomington.[10] Stone's theology was always being battered by critics. James Mathes of Indiana defended him:

> Perhaps no man of modern times was ever more misrepresented, calumniated and abused than he; and surely none ever exhibited more christian meekness, prudence and moderation than Eld. B. W. Stone. His bitterest enemies were compelled to acknowledge the superiority of his christian character, and moral deportment.[11]

Many witnesses spoke of Stone's generous spirit, of his humility, of his sweet temper, and of his passion for unity among Christians—characteristics which came to make him the beloved symbol of the New Light Christian fellowship and positioned him to be an effective agent in that near-miraculous merger of the New Light Christians with the Disciples or Reformers of Alexander Campbell

in 1832. Stone's support of that merger with the followers of Campbell required a heaping measure of grace. Campbell came west to debate for seven days with William L. Maccalla at Washington, Kentucky, in October of 1823. He brought with him ten copies of the first three numbers of his *Christian Baptist*. From that time forward he and his publications put the western New Light Christians into a kind of permanent eclipse. Campbell came to Kentucky oftener, stayed longer, and found there a more gratifying response than in any other field.[12] Stone and Campbell met personally and peaceably at Georgetown, Kentucky, in 1824. Stone said "I heard him often in public and in private." He carefully studied Campbell's doings and his flurry of publications with only occasional rebuttals. In his paper he said Campbell had "the arm of a Samson and the courage of a David tearing away the long established foundations of partyism, human authoritative creeds and confessions." He saw Campbell as a mighty power attacking every substitute for the Bible and its simplicity, making human edifices begin to totter and their builders tremble.[13]

> I will not say, there are no faults in brother Campbell; but there are fewer, perhaps, in him, than any man I know on earth; and over these few my love would throw a veil, and hide them from view forever. I am constrained, and willingly constrained to acknowledge him the greatest promoter of this reformation of any man living. The Lord reward him . . . It is not wonderful that the prejudices of the old Christian church should be great against us, and that they should so unkindly upbraid me especially, and my brethren in Kentucky, for uniting with the Reformers. But what else could we do, the Bible being our directory? Should we command them to leave the foundation on which we stood—the Bible alone—when they had come upon the same? By what authority could we command? Or should we have left this foundation to them, and have built another? Or should we have remained, and fought them for sole possession? They held the name Christian as sacred as we did—they were equally averse from making opinions the test of fellowship—and equally solicitous for the salvation of souls. This union, irrespective of reproach, I view as the noblest act of my life.[14]

These New Light Christians did not leave clear enough evidence of their prominence among the earliest churches in the Indiana forests. They were poor record keepers. Their "conferences" were often little more than informal huddles of a few elders and evangelists in connection with their seasonal camp meetings which were dedicated to the more urgent business of evangelization.

Such conferences were occasions to share information, to ordain new preachers, and to arrange the camp meeting appointments for the months ahead. Some participants felt it was a matter of principle to compile no church statistics and take no minutes of meetings lest encouragement be given to some kind of denominational structure or authority beyond the local churches, the very kind of "Babylon" from which they were dedicating their lives to set everybody free.[15]

Clement Nance, who came from the O'Kelly branch of Christians to become a colleague of Barton W. Stone, was one of Indiana's pioneers. He was for six years an associate judge in Floyd County but at the same time he was always a Christian preacher. He organized a church near New Albany in 1805 and served as clerk of the conference of Christian churches which developed. In 1827 Nance said "I expect that the state of Indiana will, in a short time, be filled with Churches or Congregations, who will own no other Lord but Jesus, and submit to no other creed but the Bible."[16] The size of the statewide fellowship did grow impressive—five Christian churches and four ministers by 1812; a cluster of Christian churches in Switzerland and Jefferson counties formed by Daniel Roberts of Maine before 1830; reports of early conferences held in Harrison and Monroe and Wabash counties; actual statistics for Indiana in 1826 listing the names of twenty-five ordained and four unordained ministers serving twelve hundred members.[17]

Even more impressive was the stature of the New Light Christian leadership raised up in the first generation in Indiana. In 1815 John McClung organized White River Church at Kent in Jefferson County and brought Love H. Jameson and Beverly Vawter into the ministry. Vawter organized seventeen churches in his area; Jameson gave much of his mature life to ministry in Indiana's major towns, including Indianapolis. James Mathes and Elijah Goodwin were to become editors of Indiana's *Christian Record* which shaped the movement in the state for over thirty years. Michael and Job Combs established congregations in Montgomery, Putnam, and Hendricks counties. Elijah Martindale and John Longley evangelized in Rush, Hamilton, Tippecanoe, and Delaware counties and shared in the conversion of Benjamin Franklin who was probably second only to Alexander Campbell in his editorial impact on the national Christian fellowship. John O'Kane evangelized much of east-central Indiana, was the first Christian church preacher to gather and establish a congregation in Indianapolis, and canvassed the state to raise the first $75,000 in funds necessary to open North Western Christian University (later Butler).

All these, and many more of the Hoosier leaders, began and long continued their ministries as New Light Christian preachers. These were among the premier debaters and evangelists who occupied the state and raised up the next generation of leadership.

Alexander Campbell's colleague and earliest biographer said it was the preachers of this Christian Connection who showed the early followers of Campbell the necessity for and the means for efficient evangelism.

> There had indeed been an almost entire neglect of evangelization on the part of the few churches which were originally connected with Mr. Campbell in his reformatory efforts. They had not a single itinerant preacher, and, although they made great progress in biblical knowledge, they gained comparatively few converts. The churches of the Christian Connection, on the other hand . . . made, through an efficient itineracy, large accessions everywhere, and increased with surprising rapidity. They were characterized by a simplicity of belief and manners and a liberality of spirit highly captivating, and possessed, in general, a striking and praiseworthy readiness to receive additional light from the Bible. They gained over, consequently, from the religious community many of the pious and peace-loving who groaned under the evils of sectarianism, while the earnest exhortations of zealous preachers and their direct personal appeals to sinners obtained large accessions from the world.[18]

For New Light Christians in Indiana, revivals and protracted meetings made up a permanent agenda. Even the Jones-Smith branch of Christians from New England, not originally revivalist, adopted this pattern when they moved west. As for the Okellian and Stoneite branches, they were born in revival and lived to extend it. There would be no way to tell the story of the foundation and growth of Indiana's Christian churches apart from them.[19]

Brethren Become Christians

The Brethren were sometimes called Tunkers, Dunkers, or Dunkards because of their style of baptism by immersion.[20] This whole pious brotherhood relocated from Germany to Pennsylvania in the early 1700s and then kept moving with the migrations of land seekers south and west. A Dunker minister named Joseph Stutzman settled in what was to become Clark County, Indiana, in 1802; most of his large family from North Carolina joined him. Dunkers named Hostetler, Leatherman, Snider, Hardman, Kern, Ribelin, and Sears moved in from Kentucky. Tensions arose between the parent association back east and some of the Dunkers in the Ohio Valley who were influenced by western independence and revival practices. About 1820 there arose an independent association of perhaps fifteen hundred Brethren among the congregations in Kentucky, Ohio, and Indiana. Joseph Hostetler, a young and charismatic preacher in Washington, Orange, and Lawrence counties, became a leader in it.[21]

At his ordination in 1821 Joseph Hostetler had been given a small Bible by his uncle Adam along with the advice "Preach and practice only what you find in this Holy Book." Along with the Scriptures he began reading the works of Alexander Campbell, those available being the published version of Campbell's debate with Maccalla and the first three volumes of his monthly paper called the *Christian Baptist*. After these had heightened his consciousness, he concluded that the religious denominations around him were very different from what he found in his Bible. Hostetler wrote to Campbell from Washington County 12 December 1825, introducing himself deferentially as no scholar—"a poor, illiterate man, who never has had the opportunity of receiving education, though he has always desired it"—belonging "to a church called German Baptists, sometimes Dunkards, whose government is the New Testament only." He expressed his appreciation for and his general agreement with Campbell saying "I . . . find myself edified, my views enlarged, and my faith strengthened." However, he wondered why such an advocate of primitive Christianity as Campbell was not practicing footwashing and not sharing the kiss of charity and not keeping the Lord's Supper only at night and not baptizing by immersion three times "forwards" rather than once "transversely." All these were things the Brethren were doing, based on their reading of biblical precedent. Campbell published Hostetler's letter in full in the *Christian Baptist* along with a long and careful and courteous response.[22]

By spring of 1826 Hostetler was preaching to a gathering of about one thousand at Orleans on the subject of primitive Christianity, championing the adoption of the name Christians and the abolishment of creeds. Faced with some opposition among Brethren preachers and threat of discipline by the association, he visited all the churches that would have any voice in his trial. In those churches he conducted an evangelistic campaign coupled with a personal campaign to bring the Brethren to Campbell's understanding and program of reformation. The campaign was successful; Hostetler and his supporters were poised to lead their whole fellowship with its fifteen churches into a new union.[23]

Free Will Baptists Become Christians

John Wright moved from Kentucky into Indiana in 1807. He and his wife were immersed in the Ohio River in the summer of 1808 and joined the Free Will Baptists, also known as the Depending Baptists or the Dependent Baptists. In January of 1810 he moved to a new wilderness tract in the Blue River area four miles south of the later location of Salem. He was followed there by his father Amos, his uncle Philbert, his younger brother Peter, and other brothers as well. Some of the family members had Dunker connections in North Carolina. John and Amos and Peter became active Baptist preachers. In 1810 they organized a congregation of Free Will Baptists in their neighborhood. Soon they had organized ten churches in their area and formed them into the Blue River Association of Free Will Baptists. But John Wright had a vision of churches based on the Bible alone, free of all historic names or creeds or divisions. Even the name Baptist was too much. In 1819 he offered a resolution in the church at Blue River in favor of dropping the name Baptist. He was willing to have individual members be called Friends, Disciples, or Christians. However, he found no biblical precedent for calling a church Christian and advocated naming any congregation the Church of Christ or Church of God. This change was soon accepted by all their congregations. The Blue River Association of Free Will Baptists was dissolved in favor of an informal annual meeting of Christians.[24]

John Wright promoted wider union on this "Bible only" basis. When he learned that southern Indiana's Brethren or Dunkers were coming to conclusions comparable to those of his own group, he recommended sending a letter proposing a union of the two bodies. He and his brother Peter presented the letter at the 1827 meeting of the Association of the Brethren. This was the very meeting at which Joseph Hostetler was preaching the sermon which he had predicted would be the "funeral discourse" for the Dunker Association. It was. The Dunkers agreed to take the name Christians and unite with the former Free Will Baptists on the basis of the Bible alone.[25]

Wright also recommended correspondence with Indiana's New Light Christians and was himself authorized to conduct it. That correspondence was probably with the Eastern Conference of the Christian Church in Indiana of which Beverly Vawter was clerk. The result was a unity conference held in 1828 near Edinburgh in which John Wright and Joseph Hostetler were leaders for the union of Free Will Baptists with Dunkers and Beverly Vawter was leader for the New Light Christians. The conference brought an agreement of the parties to be governed by the teaching and methods of the primitive evangelists as indicated in the Acts of the Apostles. They would all drop denominational names and creeds and cooperate in a loose organization called the Southern Indiana Association or the Southern District. New Light Elder J. Hatchitt described the conference for Barton W. Stone:

> The Bros. Wrights, whose names you will see in the minutes, have been formerly denominated "Depending Baptists"; but lately have laid that name aside, and now call themselves "the Church of Christ." I judge there are six or eight Elders among them, and many churches. When we met in conference together, we could find nothing to separate us asunder.—In fine, we saw as nearly eye to eye as any company of Elders who have assembled in modern times—and then there was such a sweet spirit of love. I shall never forget this meeting. We abounded in brotherly love. We were almost as cautious of wounding one anothers feelings as if we had been in our father's own country. The preachers while preaching were often bathed in tears. They wept profusely over sinners, and over the deplorable state of the world, while those preachers who were hearers shed the sympathetic tear with the speaker . . . Babylon must fall,—she is falling. The Lord's people will come out of her, and are comming out of her. In this state, we are not doing that main business that you are doing in Kentucky; but we are not asleep.[26]

Madison Evans reported that "only one church in all the vicinity refused to enter into the coalition, and it soon died of chronic sectarianism."[27]

John Wright was to play the role of mediator once more. About the time his colleagues among the Dunkers and Free Will Baptists and New Light Christians of southern Indiana were coming into their loose consolidation as Christians of the Southern District in 1828, a majority of their neighbors in the Silver Creek Association of Regular Baptists in the New Albany area were being won over to the support of Alexander Campbell's reformation movement. By 1837 they had rejected the association's earlier name, its articles of faith, and all its forms of government in favor of an informal annual meeting for mutual encouragement and a stand on the Bible alone. However the two groups were uneasy with each other, the Southern District group whispered to be "Arians" because of some unorthodox positions taken by eastern Christians or by Barton W. Stone and the Silver Creek group suspiciously labeled "Campbellites." Wright

dared to bring the two groups into dialogue and claimed to have brought them into actual union.

> Through the influence of himself, his brother Peter, Abram Kern, and others, on the part of what was called the Annual Meeting of the Southern District, which was composed of those who had been Baptists, Dunkers and Newlights; and through the efforts of Mordecai Cole and the Littells, on the part of the Silver Creek Association, a permanent union was formed between these two large and influential bodies of believers. In consequence of this glorious movement, more than three thousand struck hands in one day—not in person, but through their legal representatives, all agreeing to stand together on the one foundation and to forget all minor differences in their devotion to the great interests of the Redeemer's kingdom.[28]

The result gave him much satisfaction.

> So it was in southern Indiana: formerly we had "Regular baptist, separate baptists, German or Dunkard baptists, free will baptists, christian connexion, or as they were called, new lights." These societies in some respect were like the Jews and Samaritans of old: but the old gospel was preached among these warring sects, with great power, and success: and much of the partyism that had existed, was removed, and most of these party names were done away, by a union in Christ upon the bible alone. Formerly we all had in our respective churches, much that was purely human; but now in the church of God we have no need of the "mourning bench," the "anxious-seat," or any other institution of man's device: but in the church is the place where the solemn feast of the Lord's body is celebrated, and sincere worship is offered to the Father in spirit and in truth. The church is the place where saints are edified by the "apostles teaching, the fellowship, the breaking of bread and the prayers"; while from her sounds out the word of life, saying to the sinful sons of Adam, who have long wandered from God, "Here is room!" "All things are ready—come!" "Sinners and sectaries, will you give heed to the heavenly invitation, and come?" Your Father calls you.[29]

Thus about ten churches from the Free Will Baptists plus about fifteen churches from the Dunkers plus about fourteen churches from the Silver Creek Regular Baptist Association plus nearly all the New Light Christian churches in southeastern Indiana were loosely united in a positive orientation toward the advancing Campbellite reformation. Their incorporation in it would be gradual but nearly complete.[30]

The Campbells

At the same time that Barton W. Stone was participating in the New Light revolution in Kentucky and Indiana, another revolution was brewing in North Ireland with even larger implications for the Ohio Valley. This revolution was in the family of a Presbyterian named Thomas Campbell. The Campbells were not even aware of the American groups taking only the name Christians with which their future would be entwined.[31]

The Reverend Thomas Campbell was a minister for the Old Light Anti-Burgher Seceder Presbyterians. Those compound names for his denomination were mostly the result of a historic struggle of some Scots to select their own ministers and to maintain their independence over against any kind of state church. It was a designation a good deal more precise than Thomas was eager to maintain. But when he tried to effect a reunion of at least the Burghers and Anti-Burghers in Ireland, he quickly discovered how stubbornly persistent such divisions could be.[32]

Thomas was well educated. A Seceder named John Kinley had gotten the young man a teaching job in a good school in County Down. Thomas was so impressive and effective there that Kinley offered to finance his education for the ministry. That meant three years in Scotland at the University of Glasgow (1783–1786). There his teachers fired his mind with respect for facts and inductive reasoning and the "Common Sense" philosophy for which Thomas Reid of the Glasgow faculty was famous. Logic professor George Jardine and his colleagues were strong on the merits of the scientific philosophers John Locke and Francis Bacon. Next came seminary training with that noted professor and orthodox Calvinist the Reverend Archibald Bruce at Whitburn in Scotland. Thomas Campbell became so aptly orthodox that in later years he convinced a Baptist association of his orthodoxy by writing a whole essay on the Trinity without once using the word Trinity. Seminary completed, he was soon living at Rich Hill in County Armagh, working very hard as a Seceder pastor and proprietor of his own academy.[33]

While serving as a Presbyterian, Thomas was intrigued with some groups of independent Christians active in Scotland and Ireland. John Glas and his son-in-law Robert Sandeman founded few churches but Sandeman's writings were widely read. These Sandemanians were acid critics of existing churches. They distinguished sharply between the Old and the New Testaments, believed that faith is simple assent to the New Testament testimony concerning Christ, and aimed to restore New Testament practices within a congregational pattern including weekly observance of the Lord's Supper. Of a gentler spirit but more energetic were the Haldanes. James Alexander Haldane and his brother Robert were wealthy laymen in the Church of Scotland. They spent much of their time and money promoting evangelical revival in Scotland—importing the famous evangelist Rowland Hill from England, supporting Sunday schools and missions, enlisting young lay preachers as leaders of congregations and revivals. In 1799 they withdrew from the Church of Scotland. James Alexander Haldane wrote a book describing the model of an independent congregational church with ordinances and practices to be drawn from the Scriptures alone. Haldanians observed the Lord's Supper every week. There was a congregation of these Independents at Rich Hill where the Campbells lived. Thomas was a friend of the Independent pastor, sometimes attended evening services with that congregation, got acquainted there with notable visitors like James Alexander Haldane and Rowland Hill, and was much impressed with the toleration shown by the Independents for the opinions of every earnest Bible reader.[34]

Alexander was the eldest of Thomas Campbell's seven living children—gifted, extroverted, ambitious, and charged with a hyperactivity barely kept under discipline. He seemed to receive in compounded form all the influences at work upon his father. He boarded with a local merchant at Market Hill in order to attend a good elementary school. He spent two or three years in the academy operated by his uncles Archibald and Enos at Newry. His father, a professional educator, then took his son's education in hand. That meant Greek and Latin and university preparation. Since there seemed little prospect that Alexander would ever have enough money to actually enter university, Thomas himself led Alexander right on into college level work. Under his father's direction he studied John Locke's *Letters Concerning Toleration* and his *Essay Concerning Human Understanding*. His father's Seceder theological education was part of his heritage too; throughout his career Alexander seemed always to be easily at home in Bible, theology, and church history. When he declared early in his American ministry "we regard Arianism, semi-Arianism, and Socinianism, as poor, miserable, blind, and naked nonsense and absurdity," he appeared to know what it was he was condemning. Having gotten a vision of the nature of education and an excitement to possess it, "books were his constant delight, and self-education became with him a passion." He also shared with his father an unhappiness with the denominational dissension in North Ireland and a fascination with the thought and practice of the evangelical Independents.[35]

Then by a seeming miracle involving smallpox and shipwreck, Alexander got to spend most of a year at university. Alexander had told his father that it was his intention to go to the United States when he came of age. His father needed a break from his heavy labor in both parish and school. So it was arranged that Thomas would sail for America and scout out the land. Alexander, a precocious young man at nineteen, would remain at Rich Hill in charge of the academy and of the family awaiting word from Thomas. On the first of January of 1808 Thomas sent a letter back from Pennsylvania urging the family to sail for America. The letter arrived in March. Before they could leave some of the family caught smallpox. It was 1 October when they finally sailed from Londonderry but instead of a long trip to Philadelphia they had a short trip to shipwreck on the coast of Scotland. Meanwhile Alexander had confirmed his decision for the gospel ministry in the course of the shipwreck. Faced with the threat of stormy months ahead, the family decided to winter in Glasgow and give Alexander a chance to spend at least some time where Thomas had been educated.[36]

Alexander was enrolled at the University of Glasgow from late fall of 1808 until the end of the term in June of 1809. As in his father's days, Glasgow was in the forefront of institutions teaching the new science of Bacon and Locke and Newton, so all of Alexander's respect for scientific fact and inductive reasoning was reinforced. George Jardine was still Glasgow's mentor in logic. Alexander's notebook also recorded his respect for "the Aristotelian method of dispute" which develops a "versatility of speech . . . a command of words . . . a fluency and easeness of speech." In his "Essay First on Genius" he seemed to reflect his own inner drive when he copied a quotation from Quintilian, "Give me the boy whom praise Excites, whom glory assists & who weaps when conquered." He maintained a staggering academic regimen in addition to which he himself taught several classes for young people in the city.[37]

Equally influential was his extracurricular connection with Greville Ewing and the Glasgow congregation of the Haldanians. When the large Campbell family arrived in Glasgow as a kind of respected refugees, it was Greville Ewing who found them a proper house and got them acquainted in the city. It was Greville Ewing who introduced Alexander to the professors of the university to arrange his matriculation and invited him frequently to dinner or to tea or to student gatherings for discussion at his home. It was Greville Ewing whose Sunday evening sermons to a thousand or two in the circus building pleased Alexander much better than those of the Seceder pastor to his large congregation on Sunday morning. All the things he had previously admired in the Independents were now reinforced personally by Ewing and this Haldanian fellowship. Ewing was teaching from the writings of Robert Sandeman and James Alexander Haldane. He was advocating such specifics as independence of the local congregation; rejection of titles and privileges for clergy; the right and duty of laymen to teach and rule in the church; faith understood as simple belief of the scriptural testimony; and weekly observance of the Lord's Supper.[38]

When time came for his semi-annual communion with the Seceder Presbyterians, Alexander met the elders and received his metal token confirming his preparation. But he waited until the last table to be served and when the elements were passed he did not partake. Without public announcement, he was moving toward his decision to serve as an evangelist without pay, like the Haldane brothers, in an independent congregational movement to restore churches on a New Testament model. On 4 August 1809 the Campbell family finally sailed for America.[39]

Thomas Campbell had found the Associate Synod of North America meeting at Philadelphia when he stepped off the boat there on 13 May 1807. These Seceders accepted his credentials, received him into synod membership, gave him fifty dollars, and sent him off to preach in the Presbytery of Chartiers in southwest Pennsylvania. It was an immediate welcome and a happy settlement which did not last six months. Thomas preached some of his present convictions: that faith was not a matter of experience or assurance; that creeds and confessions which went beyond New Testament expression were not acceptable; that lay elders should exhort; that attending services of other communions should be allowed. His case was painstakingly dealt with on the docket of the presbytery and synod from October of 1807 until May of 1809. By then Thomas had paid back the fifty dollars, declined the authority of both presbytery and synod, and withdrawn from the Seceders.[40]

That did not put an end to his preaching. The area around Washington, Pennsylvania, had many Scotch-Irish settlers who had come to know him as a preacher. He held services in their houses. At the home of Abraham Altars he and some of his followers met in early summer of 1809 to clarify their principles. Thomas spoke at length of the evils of church divisions and of the beauty of a unity in which everything in religion not expressly found in the Bible would be abandoned. And he offered the motto "Where the Scriptures speak, we speak; where the Scriptures are silent, we are silent." On 17 August 1809 the congregation organized as the "Christian Association of Washington." On 7 September they approved the *Declaration and Address* which they had asked Thomas to write as a statement of their principles and objectives. In closely spaced print it ran to three pages of "Declaration" about the organization of the Christian Association, eighteen pages of "Address" expanding the argument about Christian unity, thirty pages of "Address" answering some possible criticisms, and three pages of "Postscript" suggesting two steps to be taken immediately.[41]

When Thomas Campbell was finally reunited with his family along a western Pennsylvania road on 19 October 1809, he and his son Alexander had a lot to tell each other. Two and one half years ago they had parted as established Seceder Presbyterians. Now Alexander had his spiritual pilgrimage to relate, how he had become a committed candidate for the ministry outside any known church. And Thomas, now leader of a radically independent little cluster of believers not yet a church, had a substantial statement of his present convictions ready for issue from a Pennsylvania print shop. Their common background and mutual experience had brought them out at much the same place. Alexander was ready to make propagation of these principles his life work. His schoolmaster father directed him first to six more months of strenuous study of the Scriptures. Not much seemed to be happening. Publication of the *Declaration and Address* in 1809 was pretty much a non-event. So far as it was an invitation to all denominations to lay down their non-biblical differences and unite, it was an invitation ignored. In 1810 Thomas approached the Presbyterians one time more but his application for membership of his Christian Association of Washington in the Presbyterian Synod of Pittsburgh was rebuffed.[42]

The new factor was the leadership of Alexander. He preached his first sermon in a private house on 15 July 1810. Within twelve months he had preached 106 more. A few days after the Presbyterian Synod rebuffed the application of the Christian Association in 1810, it was Alexander who was ready to answer the synod's criticisms with a public address. In 1811 he married a local girl named Margaret Brown; soon afterward her father gave the couple financial independence in the form of a large house and farm on Buffalo Creek. Alexander named it Bethany and developed it into a center for the new movement. When the Christian Association organized itself as Brush Run Church on 4 May 1811, Alexander was licensed to preach and on 1 January 1812 Brush Run Church ordained him. When Alexander's first child was born, he restudied the whole subject of baptism. As a result Thomas and Alexander and their wives and three others were immersed in Buffalo Creek on 13 June 1812. By the time Brush Run Church became a member of Redstone Baptist Association in September of 1815, Alexander was its most visible leader and an increasingly popular preacher among Baptist congregations. This popularity was occasionally jarred, as when he was asked to preach before Redstone Association in 1816 and delivered his "Sermon on the Law." The sermon outlined his dispensational view of Scriptures and declared Christians more free of the Old Testament than many Baptists claimed or cared to be.[43]

> All arguments and motives drawn from the law or Old Testament, to urge the disciples of Christ to baptize their infants; to pay tithes to their teachers; to observe holy days or religious fasts, as preparatory to the observance of the Lord's Supper; to sanctify the seventh day; to enter into national covenants; to establish any form of religion by civil law—and all reasons or motives borrowed from the Jewish law, to excite the disciples of Christ to a compliance with or an imitation of Jewish customs, are inconclusive, repugnant to Christianity, and fall ineffectual to the ground; not being enjoined or countenanced by the authority of Jesus Christ.[44]

A whole new era began in the early 1820s. Campbell debated the Presbyterian John Walker at Mt. Pleasant, Ohio, and the Presbyterian William L. Maccalla at Washington, Kentucky.[45] He found that he could be very powerful in debate, soliciting wide support by his presence on the platform both by expression of his views on the subject under discussion and by expansion on his whole program of reform for the churches. From the time of his visit to Kentucky to debate Maccalla in October of 1823, he was typically talking before a group of hearers and was himself the primary "discourser" wherever he went. He was prepared to do instant teaching on a wide range of subjects and always to reveal his vision of the church and his plea for union. He welcomed "discussions" to set straight any who resisted. In his maturity even a Presbyterian called him "perfectly self-possessed" and "perfectly at ease in the pulpit."

> He speaks like a "master of assemblies," who has entire confidence in the mastery of his subject and his powers, and who expects to carry conviction to the minds of his hearers, without any of those adventitious aids on which

ordinary men find it necessary to rely. On both evenings when I heard him, he held the great congregation, for an hour and a half, in that profound stillness which shows that his listeners are not aware of the lapse of time.[46]

Then there was publication. The Walker debate was issued in a first edition of 1,000 copies and quickly thereafter in a second edition of 3,000 copies. By the time of the Maccalla debate in fall of 1823, Campbell had his own printing establishment at Bethany and issued the book of 420 pages from there. During the infancy of this press, its first seven years up to 4 July 1830, Campbell issued from it some forty-six thousand volumes of his own works.[47] From there it grew and was the primary tool of his ministry for forty years. Debating and publishing soon made him a national figure. He said:

This is, we are convinced, one of the best means of propagating the truth and of exposing error in doctrine or practice. We now reap the benefit of the public debates of former times, and we have witnessed the beneficial results of those in our own time. And we are fully persuaded that a week's debating is worth a year's preaching, such as we generally have, for the purpose of disseminating truth and putting error out of countenance . . . and the man that cannot govern his own spirit in the midst of opposition and contradiction is a poor Christian indeed.[48]

It was the debating and publishing which made Campbell visible in Indiana. First it was his monthly paper called the *Christian Baptist*. During the days of its publication (August 1823 through December 1829), Campbell was an angry young man. Religious institutions had made little response to the invitations to reform and reunion in the *Declaration and Address* and in the personal presentations which he and his father had offered. If mainstream church people even knew of the proposed reformation, they were hardly moved to reply. Now Campbell chose to blast them out in Sandemanian style or in the style of the inescapable debater by "exposing error" and "reproving unrighteousness." The *Christian Baptist* castigated creeds, confessions of faith, synods, associations, Bible and missionary societies, religious experiences and testimonies, mourning benches and anxious seats, religious ranks and titles, preaching on isolated texts, clergy and the training programs which produced them, and every variation from the paradigm of New Testament practice as Alexander discerned it. No church organization was spared.

After seven years of this he changed the name of the paper from the *Christian Baptist* to the *Millennial Harbinger*. The paper in its new form was larger—now forty-eight pages per month for two dollars per year in ad-

vance plus postage. Its tone was less radical and more magisterial, seeking "amiability in the manner and firmness in the purpose" in order to "conciliate the passions, while we besiege the understanding." But the program was still demolition. The first sentence of volume one, number one of the *Harbinger* said: "This work shall be devoted to the destruction of Sectarianism [Campbell's name for all existing religious denominations], Infidelity, and Antichristian doctrine and practice."[49] Listed with the subjects to be attended to were:

1. The incompatibility of any sectarian establishment, now known on earth, with the genius of the glorious age to come. 2. The inadequacy of all the present systems of education, literary and moral, to develope the powers of the human mind, and to prepare man for rational and social happiness. 3. The disentanglement of the Holy Scriptures from the perplexities of the commentators and system-makers of the dark ages.[50]

The darkness of the dark ages had extended until delivery came "about the commencement of the present century" when the true gospel was "disinterred from the rubbish."[51]

Human happiness is our end and aim in all our editorial labors. But as in the scheme of Heaven wickedness must be punished, and the wicked afflicted; so in the most benevolent designs those who oppose the way of righteousness must be chastised, were it only by the exposure of their schemes. We still flatter ourselves that we shall have less occasion for the invective, and more room for the developement of the renovating truth. It is always, however, difficult to remove the rubbish without raising the dust . . . If it were lawful, or if it were benevolent, to make a truce with error, then opposition to it would be both unjust and unkind. If error were innocent and harmless, then we might permit it to find its own quietus or to immortalize itself. But so long as it is confessed that error is more or less injurious to the welfare of society, individually and collectively considered, then no man can be considered benevolent who does not set his face against it. In proportion as a person is intelligent and benevolent, he will be controversial, if error exist around him. Hence the Prince of Peace never sheathed the sword of the Spirit while he lived. He drew it on the banks of the Jordan and threw the scabbard away.[52]

Response from Indiana

Hoosiers enjoyed Alexander's dramatic name calling. He sounded a lot like the local New Light Christians calling the believers "out of Babylon." Here was a plucky fighter putting down bothersome authority figures. He called any ecclesiastical court a "monster horrific, shapeless, huge, whose light is extinct."

> By an ecclesiastical court, we mean those meetings of clergy, either stated or occasional, for the purpose of either enacting new ecclesiastical canons or of executing old ones.—Whether they admit into their confederacy a lay representation, or whether they appropriate every function to themselves, to the exclusion of the laity, is with us no conscientious scruple. Whether the assembly is composed of none but priests and Levites, or of one-half, one-third, or one-tenth laymen, it is alike anti-scriptural, anti-christian, and dangerous to the community, civil and religious. Nor does it materially affect either the character or nature of such a combination whether it be called Presbyterian, Episcopalian, or Congregational. Whether such an alliance of the priests and the nobles of the kirk be called a session, a presbytery, a synod, a general assembly, a convention, a conference, an association, or annual meeting, its tendency and result are the same. Whenever and wherever such a meeting either legislates, decrees, rules, directs or controls, or assumes the character of a representative body in religious concerns, it essentially becomes "the man of sin and the son of perdition."[53]

Here was a champion of the common man ready to stand with the martyrs.

> When opposed by the interested, by those whom the corruptions of christianity feed with bread and gratify with honor, I will call to mind the history of all the benefactors of men, and draw both comfort and strength from the remembrance that no man ever achieved any great good to mankind who did not wrest it with violence through ranks of opponents—who did not fight for it with courage and perseverance, and who did not, in the conflict, sacrifice either his good name or his life. John the Harbinger of the Messiah, lost his head. The Apostles were slaughtered. The Saviour was crucified. The ancient confessors were slain. The reformers all have been excommunicated. I know that we shall do little good if we are not persecuted. If I am not traduced, slandered, and misrepresented, I shall be a most unworthy advocate of that cause which has always provoked the resentment of those who have fattened upon the ignorance and superstition of the mass, and have been honored by the stupidity and sottishness of those who cannot think and will not learn. But we have not a few friends and associates in this cause. There are many with whom it shall be my honor to live and labor, and my happiness to suffer and die.[54]

Without so much as a visit from Campbell, subscriptions came in from Indiana. In the issues from December of 1825 through December of 1829, Campbell listed his new agents for the *Christian Baptist*. Indiana ranked fourth in the number of agents among the twenty states and foreign countries listed, tied with Tennessee with seventeen. Only Kentucky (30), Virginia (29), and Ohio (19)—states personally cultivated by Campbell—had more agents than Indiana. The other northern states ranked far below Indiana and Ohio. Campbell's reports of money received for volumes six and seven of the *Christian Baptist* followed much the same pattern, this time with Indiana ranking sixth in a field of twenty-four.[55] For the sake of those who were making wild guesses about his income from his paper, Campbell published his detailed monthly receipts in some issues of the *Millennial Harbinger* during its first two years, 1830 and 1831. These reports indicate the names of early clusters of Indiana subscribers at Bloomington, Hanover, Covington, Bruceville, Rushville, Vernon, Greencastle, Plum Orchard, Columbus, New Albany, Charlestown, Bedford, Connersville, Spring Hill, Salem, Rising Sun, Milton, Madison, Vincennes, Knoxville, Fairfield, Mount Pleasant, Lafayette, Economy, and New Providence. Campbell always thought that a single copy of his paper found many readers. Certainly the copies were handed around in Indiana. Few who began reading wanted to miss a round in this lively fight.

In the first volume of the *Millennial Harbinger*, for 1830, Campbell recognized the ongoing separation of his followers from the Baptists by inviting separate news and statistics from his "Reformers" for publication.

> We solicit from all the advocates of reform, news of the following character:—1st. The number of churches and public advocates for the sufficiency of the Holy Scriptures without human creeds, for the ancient gospel and order of things, in their counties and neighboring districts of country. 2d. The time when these churches declared their independence; their number and their progress. 3rd. The success attending the labors of the public advocates in converting men to God. We wish to be able to give correct information on the progress of the Restoration every month, that the disciples of Christ who continue stedfast in the Apostles' doctrine may know the passing events and history of the Reformation.[56]

News soon came from Indiana. At Hanover in Shelby County the *Harbinger* had caused a Baptist preacher to "overhaul his reckoning" and convert "a respectable church of Regular Baptists."[57] Instead of a plague of the cholera which they had feared, a congregation of Reformers in Jefferson County received seventeen "willing converts" within fifteen days.[58] James Challen immersed thirty-seven at Rising Sun and organized a congregation which moved at once to build a meetinghouse.[59]

Word came that John O'Kane was being harassed by the "old" Christians for switching to the Reformers but was being supported by "a few churches" while evangelizing east-central Indiana; in his missionary year he had witnessed the confessions of more than three hundred, many of them "formerly respectable members of the Methodist and Presbyterian churches."[60] John T. Littell of New Providence in Clark County sent in the account of his progression from service as a Baptist preacher to the position of a cautious Reformer in an association which had baptized 196 in the past year.[61] John B. New was a frequent correspondent. He reported from Vernon on 22 January 1834.

> The church in this place was built upon the foundation of the Apostles and Prophets, on the first Saturday in November, 1831, of thirteen members; and being surrounded by the united opposition of Baptists, Methodists, and Presbyterians, we girded on the gospel armor as well as we could in order to combat it. Our number was but eighteen until the first Friday in October last when we held a seven days' meeting. Brethren John O'Kane, Joseph Fassett, Chauncy Butler, and Jesse Maurity [Mavity] were with us, at which time forty-five were added to the church, thirty-five by immersion, the others having been before immersed. I have immersed six since. Our number is sixty-nine.[62]

One hundred seventy were immersed in the vicinity of Patriot within two months in 1836.[63] Of the fifty-six immersed by B. F. Hall and Newton Short at Jeffersonville in spring of 1841, "Fifteen were from the Methodists, one from the Presbyterians, one from the Lutherans. One Baptist also united."[64] When Samuel K. Hoshour immersed "three worthy heads of families" in a stream at Centreville early in 1839, an observer said "if these people will go into the water in the cold month of January, what may we not expect when warm weather comes?" The observer was right. In spring the Centreville congregation was back at the stream with ninety-five more.[65] During a "most animated meeting" of fourteen days at Bethany Church near Washington, fifty-nine were added, fifty-five going eight miles each way to be immersed in the White River in January.[66] Two ladies confessed their faith in Christ at Bruceville on a December Sunday in 1846. Elder J. W. Wolfe reported, "On Monday morning we cut a tomb in the icy stream, and buried them with their blessed Lord in baptism."[67] B. F. Hall immersed thirty-six persons in a pond in about fifteen minutes and offered that schedule as an answer to any Pedobaptists who claimed that the Apostles could not possibly have immersed three thousand on the day of Pentecost.[68]

By 1839 the burgeoning fellowship plainly needed a name. Campbell offered a series of articles in the *Harbinger* entitled "Our Name."[69] He had not yet fired all his ammunition on behalf of "Disciples," the name he preferred, when a union of forces finally wore down his resistance to the name "Christians" for the whole group. None too graciously he apologized to Barton W. Stone for pain inflicted in the course of the discussion and agreed to allow the name Christians but not to be bound to use it himself.

Indiana "State Meeting" and the "Cooperations"

Eighteen thirty-nine was also the year the Christians in Indiana held a "State Meeting" from 7–11 June at Indianapolis. This was an innovation; no other state had done it. F. W. Emmons sent the *Harbinger* a report of the meeting saying "There were present about fifty public speakers." The participants recommended more evangelists; more education—specifically at "Indiana State University at Bloomington"; and acceptance of the invitation of Crawfordsville to come there for another State Meeting the following year. Emmons emerged from the 1839 meeting with a list of 115 churches with 7,701 members; another reporter named Hayward soon added more churches to the list and thought that Indiana must have fifteen thousand members. Because he kept getting inquiries, Hayward also compiled and sent for publication a list of fifty-eight of "the most prominent preachers." This was Indiana's army of specialists in protracted meetings.[70] Campbell expressed appreciation for the report of Emmons to the *Harbinger* and added: "An annual meeting in some central point of each state in the union, conducted on similar principles, exhibiting the statistics of the churches united in the primitive faith and manners, would in many ways greatly promote the prosperity of the cause. Co-operation and combination of effort is the great secret of success."[71] The wonder was not that the statistics were so primitive and lacking in agreement nor that the State Meetings were to be anemic and precarious for years to come. The wonder was that the brethren at Indianapolis would issue an invitation for such a meeting, that fifty preachers would attend, that recommendations would actually be made from that meeting to the churches, and that Campbell would bless and encourage the event.

The excitement that Campbell had offered to early Hoosiers went far beyond his strenuous attacks on all existing denominations, exhilarating as these were. Even more captivating was his positive paradigm for restoration of the apostolic church of the New Testament and his plea for union on the basis of "the ancient order of things." Rejecting any other model as authoritative, he drew from the Book of the Acts of the Apostles and from the New Testament epistles a picture of a true church which was a local congregation of Bible readers and believers governed by elders selected from their own ranks. Nothing they did was to be directed by any ecclesiastical person or body beyond the local church. Everything they did that was related to salvation or to the government of congregational life was to be directed by a biblical "thus saith the Lord" and so based on a New Testament command or precedent. Affection for this model was very contagious. It made zealous Bible students of ordinary men and women. It encouraged local leadership and instilled in both officers and members the sure confidence that these congregations were the very churches of Jesus Christ and at the same time very much their own.[72]

Yet here in 1839 was a State Meeting which was a long way from a local congregation. Its name was not in the New Testament and it had no "thus saith the Lord." The Indianapolis preacher who issued the invitation called it a "general co-operation meeting." It was a large scale and conspicuous example among a whole complex of "co-operations" through which the individual New Testament type congregations had come to combine their energies to achieve mutual goals. Typically they chose to merge their pledges and offerings to support an evangelist for some designated area. Walter Scott, a founding father of the fellowship alongside Campbell, was supported in his pathbreaking program of evangelism in Ohio by such a voluntary plan of support involving the combined offerings of the churches. In Indiana John O'Kane accomplished his early wonders in Rush, Fayette, Decatur, and Marion counties as an evangelist employed by five churches in Rush County.[73]

Elijah Goodwin was a New Light preacher at Mount Vernon who read the *Millennial Harbinger* and became convinced that "our whole converting machinery was wrong." He brought his congregation over into Campbell's reformation and yearned to preach his new convictions. "We called a co-operation meeting," he said. The cooperating churches were to send messengers with completed lists of those willing to support an evangelist showing the amount of their subscriptions. Because the subscriptions "seemed to be sufficient," Goodwin went on his evangelistic circuit for the year 1840–41. For the year ending 1842, working for such a cooperation, Goodwin reported riding 2,925 miles and preaching 450 sermons. He apologized for having baptized only 108 that year on profession of their faith in Christ. For those who might be stimulated by an example of such a working cooperation, Goodwin sent for publication in the *Christian Record* the minutes of his Posey County cooperation meeting for 1843, complete with a list of supporting churches and how much each promised.[74]

Soon after the *Christian Baptist* was succeeded by the *Millennial Harbinger* both Alexander Campbell and Walter Scott had become advocates of such cooperations for reformation and salvation of the world. Campbell's mind was already stretching the concept from local to global dimensions.

> But some christians are so squeamish about the mode of doing this, that, fearing they may not do it in the best manner, they will not do it at all . . . But what, says another, has the church in *propria forma*, the church in its true character, to do for the salvation of the world! I answer, Every thing but what Jesus Christ, the Holy Spirit, and the Apostles have done.[75]

> The churches in every county, have from scripture and reason, all authority to bring their combined energies upon their own vicinity first, and when all is done at home, they may, and ought to co-operate with their weaker neighbors in the same state, and so on increasing the circle of their co-operations, as they fill up the interior, with all light and goodness, until the knowledge of the glory of the Lord cover the whole earth.[76]

That is the way the cooperation plan was to go. The individual congregations kept being offered opportunities and even urgings to share in cooperations ranging from an association of a few neighboring churches to counties, districts, the state, and even the national level with international commitments. Campbell found this cooperation pattern clearly in the New Testament. He came to speak of "the church" as the universal body in whose mission of salvation and service any cooperation not forbidden in Scriptures was allowable and encouraged.

By 1849 the Christians of Indiana were excited about the joint venture of founding a college, first ever to be established by the initiative of a State Meeting of Christians. Elijah Goodwin was commissioned in 1848 to visit the state's churches to discover if they wanted a college and, if so, where it should be located. The answer was that the Christians of the region should have a college and should build it at Indianapolis. On his long tour Goodwin learned a lot about the condition of the churches.

> In various parts of the State, I find small congregations of disciples who have been brought into existence by strange evangelists, and are now left without any regular preaching or teaching. They have not talent among themselves sufficient to make their meetings interesting and instructive, and therefore they are poorly attended. They are not able to sustain competent evangelists among them, and hence, if nothing is done to aid them speedily, they must soon cease to be. I find other churches that are able to do considerable for the cause, who are doing nothing for the want of some general system of co-operation. And I find another class of churches that are still more able, but are doing nothing for the advancement of Messiah's kingdom, because they have resident brethren among them who preach for them without charge. Now, while contemplating this state of things, I often ask myself, Can we not adopt some scriptural measure which will bring out the talents and means of the brotherhood, and distribute them more equally over the State? and by means of which the poor and destitute may "have the Gospel preached unto them." This, it seems to me, is absolutely necessary in order that the cause we plead may be established where the Gospel has never been preached by our brethren.[77]

He sent the eleven articles of his proposed "Constitution of the Indiana Christian Evangelizing Society" to James Mathes at the *Christian Record* and to Benjamin Franklin at the *Western Reformer* for publication in these Christian papers of Indiana. It was a "general system of co-operation," not this time an association of congregations but a society of all the individuals who would pay a dollar per year in support of the proclamation of the Gospel. Larger contributors might be life members or directors or life directors.[78]

This new cooperative plan was substantially adopted at the State Meeting held 6 October 1849 and established as the Indiana Christian Home Missionary Society. Later that same month in Cincinnati, a healthy delegation from Indiana took leadership in the first General Convendion of the Christian Churches which established a similar national society for mission supporters called the American Christian Missionary Society. Though not present at the first Convention, Alexander Campbell was perennially elected president of the Missionary Society and gave it his full support. The 1849 State Meeting at Indianapolis also organized a State Bible Society auxiliary and approved the Cincinnati-based programs of the Christian Tract Society and the Sunday School Library project. Thus the range of cooperations grew full.[79]

Resistance to Organization

A large body of the Christian membership in Indiana held back from this development of cooperations. When Editor James Mathes published Elijah Goodwin's proposed constitution for a state missionary society, he him- self noted that it lacked "any positive direct authority in the New Testament." But he agreed that something had to be done.

> With a membership of some Fifty-Thousand strong in Indiana, and possessing, as our brethren do, a very fair pro- portion of the wealth of our flourishing state, we are fully able to sustain the gospel in every town, village and neighborhood in the state. But with all these advantages, we are comparitively [sic] asleep . . . Only for a moment imagine Fifty thousand brethren and sisters, composing some three or four hundred churches, all devoted to the cause of God, both in person and property; co-operating together, and "striving together for the faith of the gospel." Their well sustained evangelists, flying abroad as on the wings of the wind, seeking the weary wanderers, and carrying the "glad tidings" to the destitute, in every nook and corner of the whole country—while as the fruits of their labor, thousands are persuaded to receive and obey the truth, and thus "bringing their glory and honor into the church of God": I say imagine, if you can, this state of things, and you have an idea of what the brotherhood in Indiana might do, if they would. Many efforts have been made, through the "State Meetings," "District Meetings," County "Cooperation Meetings," and single congregations, to wake up the brethren upon this deeply interesting subject; and our periodicals too, have called long and loud for reformation in this matter, but the churches sleep on![80]

Such an argument, based on urgent need and expediency rather than based on a "thus saith the Lord" from the Scriptures, brought an immediate rejoinder from Joseph Fasset of Columbus who would countenance "no society organized separate from the church to effect the conversion of the world." To go ahead with this state missionary society would concentrate power in the State Meeting to set up qualifications for elders.

> Then will be seen schisms, divisions, sects, heresies, hatred, envy, and all the attending evils which divisions engender. Farewell, then, to that peace, love, harmony, and prosperity, which have hitherto characterized the present reformation . . . I see no reason why we should be discouraged and desert the ship in which we have sailed so pleasantly for so many years.[81]

In fact Editor Mathes had so many misgivings and found so much opposition that he backed away entirely from supporting the plan for a state missionary society. In the *Christian Record* for April of 1849 he said he would simply stand for the "old scriptural plan." It took the spirited support of his editorial colleagues Elijah Goodwin and Benjamin Franklin to convince Mathes and sustain the new plan. Elijah Goodwin said Indiana had no "old scriptural plan," no good old system operating to which continued loyalty might be a virtue. What Indiana had was a desperate situation in which the unsupported evangelists of the first generation had impoverished themselves and their families in order to multiply converts and churches, in which prospective evangelists of the new generation were slow to commit themselves to full time work with no prospect of support, and in which the state was burdened by small Christian churches in poor health as well as important areas in which there were no Christian churches at all. He said systematic support must come.[82]

Not everybody agreed. Sometimes those members unconvinced of the need for organizational innovations went warily to cooperation meetings and were won over to the new plans. Sometimes they went to cooperation meetings where they remained unconvinced and were careful to oppose the formation of any continuing structure beyond the local congregation. A motion to adjourn the very first State Meeting in 1839 to reconvene in 1840 was opposed and declared out of order since there was no continuing organization to take such action. At the 1844 State Meeting a committee was appointed on Saturday to draft a letter to the churches; the committee reported on Monday "that to send a letter to the Churches as contemplated was not advisable."[83]

The attempt in 1851 to organize the Christian congregations of the Tenth Judicial District for missionary support in connection with the State Meeting was systematically opposed by messengers and elders from some of the churches. They argued their case in the *Christian Record*.[84]

> All lawful means for the distribution of the gospel or religious intelligence, can be employed by individuals, can be employed by the churches, without the organization of separate societies or organizations, composed of church members. This can be done without a state meeting, a district meeting, a missionary society constitution, or any other constitution except the Bible.[85]

They attended the district meeting in August of 1851 and amended each motion as it was presented to remove wording in support of any missionary structures beyond the local congregation.[86]

Mostly the opponents did not attend cooperation meetings at all, local, state, or national. Nor did they join missionary societies. They were well pleased with Campbell's early imagery of the self-governing local congregation of Bible readers as the true and only church agency in the ancient order of things. Among them Campbell's early attacks on paid denominational clergy could easily support a local aversion to raising full time support for any preacher. When a spokesperson for ten northeastern Indiana counties reported not one evangelist sustained by the churches in that area and appealed to the new Society to send one, the response was candid and negative.

> The churches have not heartily co-operated with the Society, and therefore but little has been done. A few individuals associated themselves together, at the State Meeting, in 1849, taking the name of the "I.C.H.M. Society," fully expecting the support and countenance of the brethren every where, in a work so purely philanthropic, as that of sending the gospel to the destitute. But in this, they were greatly mistaken. In the first place, the brethren in many places, were opposed to the State Meeting itself, that brought forth the Missionary Society, believing it to be an organization dangerous to the independence of the churches . . . Other objections were urged against the Society, too tedious to mention here . . . Under this state of things, the agent of the Society could collect but very little money for the Society. It was looked upon as a very uncertain enterprise.[87]

It was a difference in principle never resolved. By the middle of the nineteenth century one wing of the Christian reformation championed the radical independence of individual congregations, holding fast to that congregational model of the Bible's "ancient order of things" so winsomely advocated by Campbell in his early years. In all matters of faith, salvation, and church practice every congregation would demand a "thus saith the Lord" or an exact New Testament precedent. They would speak where the Scriptures speak and be silent where the Scriptures are silent. Another wing of the Christian reformation held faithfully to the principle of cooperation which was the mark of Campbell in his later years. Their impetus was the great hunger of the Campbells and of Barton W. Stone for Christian union. Their basis for union was also the Bible, especially a view of a New Testament church understood as a universal church engaged in a total mission of salvation. That mission was worthy of the most effective means so long as those means were not contrary to biblical injunction or precedent. Expedience needed no apology. By the end of the century these differences, seriously compounded by social and economic factors, had divided the fellowship.

Alexander Campbell as Editor

It has been a common assertion that Christian churches do not have bishops. Instead, they have editors. Alexander Campbell was the primary model for the role of Christian church editor. He once commented that as a traveling editor he was something like a nonresident bishop or a Baptist preacher with several congregations—pluralists, something like bigamists, "a species of nondescripts, oddities, and incongruities."[88] He had other roles. He was a successful farmer said to have died the richest man in West Virginia, delegate to a Virginia constitutional assembly, president of Bethany College, and president of the American Christian Missionary Society.[89] He was a nationally celebrated preacher and lecturer, in these capacities a public figure and symbol of his religious fellowship. But it was chiefly as editor and publisher that he exercised a bishop's functions. He was an interpreter of the Scriptures and teacher of a whole range of biblical, doctrinal, and practical theology, applying the truths of orthodoxy as he knew it to thousands of particular instances among the churches.

Campbell's mail was voluminous; he had his own post office at Bethany and was its postmaster. He disseminated information of the ecclesiastical world to his constituents and relayed the incoming news from local Christian churches to the wider fellowship, often with commentary. He was a defender against heresies and a wielder of discipline against false teachers who proved obstinate or dangerous. Particular rascals might expect to be disclosed by name in his magazine. The lack of middle level supervisors left the small churches vulnerable.

> No cause has been more injured by a set of travelling impostors, than the cause we humbly plead. We frequently receive letters inquiring into the character and pretensions of certain persons passing themselves off for Reformers. Much injury has been done already by these hypocrites and pretended advocates of the primitive institutions . . . The last year's success and prosperity of the cause seems to have greatly increased these impudent pretenders; and unless precautionary measures are adopted to preserve the public and the brethren from imposition, we may expect them to increase in the ratio of the conquests of the truth.[90]

Campbell always bore the burden of the churches on his heart and shoulders. The preface of each of his periodical volumes was a statement of the need for one volume more. In 1841 he said "though I have been scribbling for a quarter of a century, I have not more than about half written myself out." After twenty-nine years as

editor he said "we have not fully delivered ourselves on sundry matters in our horizon. New questions have arisen, and others may arise." In 312 months he issued 312 monthly numbers, "not having been one day confined to a bed of sickness during the last forty-five years." But the big thing was the continuing need of the churches. "The cause of a thorough evangelical reformation, according to the Holy Scriptures, is yet in its infancy," he said. "It needs to be watched over, cherished, and protected with all paternal care and tenderness."[91]

Those who learned from Alexander Campbell accrued a substantial body of reference materials over the years, a long shelf of works serving as a repository of his teaching. As early as 1830, a Baptist taunted him with the classic query: if the principles of your reformation are so clear in the Scriptures as you claim, why must you issue so much explanation?[92] But his pen was always busy. There was his *Family Testament*, a revised version of the New Testament with "one hundred and sixty pages of Prefaces, Critical Notes, and Tables Literary, Geographical, Historical, Chronological, Miscellaneous; together with the Maps of the Holy Land and the countries visited by the Apostle to the Gentiles; explanations of Words and Phrases alluding to ancient manners and customs; as well as the leading Terms and Sentences, subjects of sectarian controversy."[93] In this Bible the word was always "immersion" instead of "baptism" so that "John the Baptist" became "John the Immerser," a change which drove one Baptist editor to the prayerful decision to burn his copy of the book. This was by no means the only change. The revision found wide acceptance and Campbell counted his Bible the "most valuable service we have rendered this generation."[94]

There was his theological summary called the *Christian System* (368 pages). Campbell knew that Christians sang only a few familiar hymns but his *Christian Hymn Book* kept increasing until it contained 1,324 approved hymns because he viewed the hymns as a kind of substitute for a confession of faith and book of doctrine so that the people were to be instructed in the "marrow and fatness of the gospel" by reading them. He recognized Indiana as a major user of his hymnbook.[95]

Books publishing his debates with Presbyterians were progressively larger—with John Walker in 1820 (292 pages), with William Maccalla in 1823 (420 pages), and with Nathan L. Rice in 1843 (912 pages). There was the published version of his debate in 1829 with the rationalist Robert Owen (465 pages) and his debate in 1837 with Cincinnati's Catholic bishop John B. Purcell (360 pages). In Indiana James Mathes looked at the 912 pages of the

Campbell-Rice transcript and said "it seems to us that this debate will supersecede [sic] the necessity of any more public debates upon those topics."[96] Campbell also grew weary of going over the same controversial ground in debates with "every stripling and peevish old man in the community." When the debates had been held and published, let the people find their answers by reading them.[97]

It was Campbell's conviction that all persons should read the Bible with confidence and that they should read it afresh as if it had just been delivered to their hands from heaven unencumbered by opinions of professional clergy. The ordinary person with a Bible must be assured that he could read it, understand it, respond to it, live by it, and teach it to others. However, Campbell gave his readers some brief directions for reading the Bible in the first volume of the *Christian Baptist* saying that anybody going through the New Testament three times using his plan "will understand much more of the Christian religion than a learned divine would teach you in seven years."[98] He liked to call the Scriptures the "living oracles"; when he came to publish a book on the interpretation of the Scriptures (404 pages) it was so much a description of the church which he saw in the Bible that the title on its spine was *Christianity Restored*. The *Christian Preacher's Companion* (153 pages) established the "gospel facts" through quotations from early opponents of the gospel. His *Christian Baptism* (444 pages) included a chapter with a catechism of 114 questions and answers on the subject of baptism "for the most uneducated portion of the reading community" (1851 edition, 422 pages). Many of his sermons, addresses, and essays were separately published or gathered in anthologies.

Most of all, there was the ever expanding row of the volumes of his periodicals which he and his followers regarded less as ephemeral magazines than as valuable books appearing in parts. The *Christian Baptist* produced 2,010 pages in its volumes for seven years.[99] The *Millennial Harbinger* outlived Campbell only briefly; its forty years added forty volumes more. These were the cumulation of his teaching on every theme of theological thought and ecclesiastical practice, embodied in his essays and his answers to specific queries. They were also a register of his interactions with the ongoing life of the churches and so a kind of recorded minutes of his superintendency. The cumulation and circulation always pleased him. His preface for 1842 said "At the close of the present volume we shall have issued more than a million of monthly numbers." When he read the volumes of the *Christian Baptist* to prepare a selection from it for

reprinting, he found he did not really wish to change a thing.[100] Of the joint impact of the *Christian Baptist* and the *Millennial Harbinger* he said:

> Their influence and effects have wholly transcended our most sanguine expectations.—Hundreds of thousands, in our own America, have been directly or indirectly emancipated from such sinister and unhappy influences.—And every year the cause advances at home and abroad, on this side and beyond the Atlantic and Pacific oceans. It is the Lord's doings and marvelous in our eyes.[101]

Alexander Campbell was not a champion of pure democracy in church government. Not all opinions or votes were to be equal in the decisions of congregational living. As he saw it, the Baptists were all too prone to the error that any or every issue should be put to congregational vote and decided by majority.

> There never was a community that got along peaceably and profitably for any length of time that presumed to settle all matters of discipline by a public vote in a public assembly. Such societies as have advocated this wild democracy have either broken themselves to pieces, or greatly dishonored and injured the profession. No family, church, or state could be long kept in order, in harmony, and love under such an economy.[102]

Following the biblical pattern, elders were to be chosen. Then these elders, as the congregation's presbytery or senate, were to govern and they were to be obeyed. The power of faithful editors was not defined, but among the elders and preachers Campbell knew himself to be at least a first among equals.

Alexander Campbell was not the only person combining the roles of editor and publisher and debater and shepherd for the Christian churches. As the membership multiplied, very similar leaders arose in every region. There was no agency to define their relationship to Campbell or to the churches or to each other. Each one first earned recognition as a valued leader among some cluster of congregations and then issued a periodical to test that leadership more widely. It was no disgrace if the attempt proved temporary. Any creditable issue of a periodical was a contribution and the subscribers decided who should continue.

Some of Indiana's editorial offerings were short lived. An Indiana physician named Nathaniel Field offered the *Christian Review* in 1830, followed by his *Journal of Christianity*, followed by his *Israelite*. Field became a zealous abolitionist and adventist; eventually his home congregation at Jeffersonville divided over his interests and he wrote himself out of the fellowship of Christian churches entirely. John O'Kane published the *Christian Casket* briefly from Connersville in 1833. Daniel Cox announced his launching of the *Primitive Christian* from Vincennes in 1843, and in 1845, and again in 1848. P. T. Russell began advocating the Christian church cause in northern Indiana in 1846 with his *Investigator* issued from LaPorte and then from Mishawaka. Elder-musician Silas W. Leonard of Jeffersonville said in December of 1848 that he had commenced publishing the *Christian Vocalist*. Aaron Walker published the *Christian Foundation* at Kokomo from 1880 to 1884.[103] None of these found a continuing constituency. But Indiana was also home base for successful preacher-editors who saw themselves as Alexander's independent colleagues and were recognized as such.

Indiana Editors James M. Mathes (1808–1892) and Elijah Goodwin (1807–1879)

The first of Indiana's editorial giants was James Madison Mathes (1808–1892). His great grandparents were Presbyterians in North Ireland and Virginia. His grandparents became Baptists in Virginia and Kentucky. His parents crossed the Ohio from Kentucky about 1816 to flee the influences of slavery and to seek out Indiana's rich lands. Migrating north with stops in Washington and Jackson counties, they joined other Kentuckians settled in central Indiana in 1821, a year before the land was cleared for sale at two dollars per acre. New Light preachers came to the settlement in 1823. By 1828 they had renounced Calvinism and the Baptists and joined the congregation of New Light Christians at nearby Union Meeting House. As those New Light Christians merged into the "current reformation" of the Campbells, the whole Mathes family—Jeremiah and Florence and their eleven children—became members of the resulting Christian church. Florence became so firm in her new convictions that she persuaded Elder Michael Combs to immerse her again, her genuine "baptism for the remission of sins" as she finally came to understand it. James Madison Mathes was the second of the eleven children, the eldest of six sons. He began his teen years in the three-sided camp on the Mathes land on the West Fork of White River near the later site of Gosport. His *Autobiography* tells of his adventures there in the Indiana woods infested with timber rattlesnakes and of his athletic contests with youth of the Delaware Indians gathered and preparing to move to Arkansas Territory.[104]

Mathes believed his own conversion and baptism were focal points in the local history of the reformation movement. From the beginning of his ministry Alexander Campbell had opposed any emphasis on emotional experience as evidence of conversion and any use of such tools of emotional focus as the "anxious seat" or the "mourners' bench." Repentance based on acknowledgment of Jesus as the Son of God, baptism by immersion, and living the Christian life—for Campbell these were enough. Campbell had enunciated his belief in baptism for the remission of sins in his debate with Maccalla in 1823, a debate published and widely circulated. Campbell's views and teachings were under discussion in Indiana; his *Christian Baptist* was circulating. Walter Scott was lifting up the same views in preaching and practice in Ohio in 1827. By the account of Mathes himself, preachers like John Secrest from Ohio and D. R. Eckles from Kentucky were stirring up new thoughts in Mathes and in the other hearers at Indiana's Union Meeting House. By 1 September 1827 Mathes had Campbell's version of the Bible and a few numbers of his *Christian Baptist* in hand.[105] But Mathes still maintained that he himself came to conclusions identical to Campbell's in the summer of 1827 with no influence beyond the Bible.

> My plan was, to forget as far as possible all I had ever learned about religion, and take up the Bible, as though I now saw it for the first time, and endeavor, without prejudice or prepossession to learn what I could from its teachings. In my reading I became satisfied that the Bible was true, and that there was a living reality in the christian religion. I also discovered that the preaching I had heard from Baptists, Methodists and New Lights, was a very different thing from the preaching of the Apostles of Christ, who preached under the guidance of the Holy Spirit. This was to me, an important discovery. I read the Acts of the Apostles, and found that when mourners asked the Inspired teachers of Christianity in the beginning, what they must do to be saved, they were not invited to the "anxious seat." Indeed I could not find that they ever used the "anxious seat," or "mourning bench" on any occasion. I read with great care the 2nd chap. of Acts. Here I found three thousand sin convicted Jews, crying out in deep anguish of Spirit, and saying, "Men and brethren, what shall we do?" This was my case precisely, and I read the answer with much interest. "Repent and be baptised every one of you, in the name of Jesus Christ for the remission of sins, and you shall receive the gift of the Holy Spirit." (Ver. 38) Light now broke in upon my understanding. And I saw what had been the trouble with me and the religious teachers of all denominations—ignorance. I examined all the parallel passages, and become fully satisfied upon the whole subject. I "gladly received the word," and would have obeyed the gospel immediately if I had enjoyed the privilege. From

that moment the burden was removed from my mind, and I rejoiced greatly.[106]

Having persuaded the New Light elder John Henderson to baptize him "for the remission of sins, as the three thousand on the day of Pentecost were," he was immersed in Lime Stone Creek on the second Lord's day of October 1827.

> I was the first person in Indiana, so far as I know, that was baptized "for the remission of sins," and my Sister Eliza the second. I united with the Christian Body, at the Old Union Meeting house, Owen County Ind. and immediately became an active member. I would read the scriptures when called upon in the social meeting, pray and exhort. I read and studied the holy scriptures, day and night, fully intending, as soon as I was qualified, and had a little more age and experience, to go to preaching the "unsearchable riches of Christ."[107]

In March of 1829 Mathes married Sophia Glover, second daughter among the ten children of a neighboring farmer and shoemaker. They settled on eighty acres of deep woods in Morgan County, nearly a mile from any other inhabitant. Mathes was an accomplished axman.

> The first money I earned after marriage was by cutting and splitting one thousand rails ten feet long, for old Grand Father Ditamore, for which I received the round sum of three dollars! thirty three and one third cents per hundred! My children will no doubt smile at this, but I assure them that I considered myself quite fortunate in getting the job, as money was very scarce, and the price of labor very low. I made the whole thousand in five days, walking about a mile each morning after breakfast, and returning about sun down. I made the rails on the ground where Gosport now stands, while it was all in the woods. I laid out the money in buying two sugar kettles, for the purpose of sugar making by boiling the water derived by tapping the sugar maple, at the proper season.[108]

However, the incessant cutting of heavy timber and the strenuous log rollings with too little assistance destroyed his health.

Mathes deeply appreciated the early education he had received. His family had taken pains to teach him reading and spelling and had cheered his public recitation of memorized speeches. His father was an able reader and debater who had committed large sections of the Bible to memory.[109] The family of Presbyterian missionary Isaac Reed established a Sunday school in the settlement about 1824.

> To this little Sunday School I repared [sic] every Sunday morning, to recite lessons from the Holy Scriptures and other good books. I had a very retentive memory and therefore excelled all the pupils in my recitations. I committed to memory most of the New Testament, and select portions of the Old, during the first year. They were very anxious to have me commit the "Catechisms," and as my Parents made no objections to it, I undertook the "shorter Catechism," and succeeded; in a short time I could repeat the whole of it, and answer every question in it. This was the first school I ever attended, and it exerted a powerful influence over my life in that critical period, when my character was just forming. And I have always regarded it as providential, that I attended this little Sunday School. It kindled in my bosom the most ardent desire to obtain a good education, and no circumstance or misfortune could ever extinguish this thirst for knowledge in my mind. I desired to be good and wise, and to this end I never ceased to labor.[110]

Scott W. Young from Kentucky taught a day school in the neighborhood; Mathes attended every day he could get free from farm work, the scattered intervals totaling perhaps two years. His copy of the "English Reader" he bought with the proceeds of his collection of ten pounds of dried ginseng. "It was my own book," he said, "and I made my own of it. I read and re-read it, over and over again, until I well nigh committed it all to memory."[111] With so much education, he elected in 1831 to support his family by teaching school.

Wherever he went, following his baptism, he preached. When the citizens of Putnam County would not enroll their children in his school lest he make Campbellites of them, he said: "If you don't employ me, I shall have more time to study the scriptures and talk about the gospel, and you may rest assured that I will put in my time to the best advantage, and by the help of the Lord, I intend to make myself felt in Indiana."[112] His vocational preference kept shifting toward preaching. He brought his family and the people near his home fully into Alexander Campbell's reformation movement. In 1831 he brought in the whole Old Union congregation "with the loss of perhaps only one out of a membership of some 200." That same year he attended "a protracted, co-operation meeting at Crawfordsville." There he heard able preaching and met established preachers and "took part in the preaching" himself at their invitation. Now he began making preaching appointments away from home, "in the country" and in 1833 for the first time in Bloomington. In 1835 he was called by a large cooperation meeting at Old Union to do the work of an evangelist. For this he was "solemnly set apart to the work, by fasting, prayer, and the laying on of hands."[113]

As a full time preacher from 1835 to 1839 he "traveled and preached incessantly, and baptised a multitude of people, and organized a great many churches." Pay was never discussed. He received during the four years a total of about $120 in trade. And he built his confidence as an evangelist. Having been challenged by the Methodist circuit preacher Lorenzo Dow Smith at a village on the National Road ten miles west of Greencastle, Mathes found him rather easy to discredit. In Campbellite fashion, the debate was accompanied by a protracted meeting with many visiting preachers during which a Christian church was organized including nearly every Methodist in the place. Mathes learned that he could preach and that he could debate but he kept seeking improvement. In 1837 he did team preaching for two months with Joseph Fassett of Columbus, an educated easterner who had been one of Indiana's most able Baptist preachers and who had brought most of the Flat Rock Baptist Association along with him into the Christian church. Mathes counted this internship with Fassett "one of the most important events of my public life."[114]

Still he yearned for education. In 1838, at age thirty and accompanied by a wife in poor health and four small children, he moved to Bloomington to attend Indiana University.

> It was a strong faculty of good men. I immediately commenced the study of Greek language with Prof. Morrison. Algebra and the elementary principles of Mathematical science with Prof. Amen. While I recited Latin lessons also to Prof. Amen, out of regular hours. Dr. Wylie also spent an hour each day, with me alone, after his regular class was dismissed, in explaining and simplyfying the principles of the Greek Grammar. This extra instruction was excellingly valuable to me. The second year, I continued the study of Greek, and in addition to that, I went into the Presidents department, and studied and recited every day with the seignor Class, wrote down Dr. Wylie's Lectures on the Evidences of Christianity, Rhetoric, Elocution, and Metaphysics . . . My progress in all my studies was very rapid, and satisfactory to my teachers and myself. In Feb. 1839, I was chosen as one of the Anaversy speakers, to represent the Athenian Society.[115]

President Andrew Wylie was at this time so disenchanted with the Presbyterians and so friendly toward the position of Mathes that Mathes believed Wylie would join the Christian church. Mathes was an irregular student at the University for about three and one half years. At the same time he was a Christian preacher of considerable stature and well known locally. While attending college he preached every Sunday either in Bloomington or at some other church in the neighborhood. "We had a great many additions to the church in Bloomington during my stay," he said. Local church members aided him while he attended school; David Batterton and others helped him pay off his education debts when his study ended.[116]

In spring of 1841 Mathes moved back to Owen County and began a whirlwind of activity for the Christian church. Everybody wanted him. James Scott of the Methodist Church wanted him to debate. They did that for three days at Martinsville. In the concurrent protracted meeting the Christians immersed two of the debate moderators and largely increased the church at Martinsville. Mathes later published portions of the arguments. He was in great demand for protracted meetings.[117]

> During the latter part of 1842 and the first part of 1843, I traveled very extensively and preached day and night often three times a day for weeks together. There was a very general awakening among the people and sectarianism was tottering upon its throne. During the time above referred to, making one year of time, I immersed with my own hands six hundred and thirty five persons, upon the profession of their faith in the One Lord, and received some two hundred immersed persons into the church mostly from the Baptists, besides many more that were immersed by other brethren, at meetings where I was principal laborer.[118]

Mathes held meetings in the Putnam County court house, trying to get a foothold for the Christians in the Methodist stronghold at Greencastle. Universalist preacher Erasmus Manford interrupted one meeting to challenge Mathes to a debate. Manford had lately arrived from the East and become editor of the *Christian Teacher* at Terre Haute. Such an interruption and challenge was regular Universalist procedure and Manford was a respected challenger. The debate at the court house took four days before "an immense concourse of people." The Universalists failed to organize at Greencastle but the Christian church expanded.[119]

On 4 July 1843, at a high point of his local popularity, Mathes published the first issue of his *Christian Record*. Its prospectus appeared without comment in Alexander Campbell's *Millennial Harbinger*.

> A monthly periodical, of twenty four octavo pages, devoted to the cause of Bible Christianity, and to the destruction of heresy . . . The work will be put up in neatly printed covers, in a style not inferior to any work of the kind in the West; at the low price of One Dollar in advance. It will be published in Bloomington, Indiana so soon as a sufficient number of subscribers may be obtained.[120]

Demolition of denominations was high on the agenda. Along with news from the churches would be essays on the doctrine of Christ contrasted with the doctrines and commandments of men. There would be reviews of publications and documents standing in the way of Christian union and the conversion of the world. And there would be such news of debates as would be likely to result in good. In the preface to the first issue Mathes noted:

> We have in Indiana alone, more than twenty thousand brethren and sisters, who have taken the word of God alone, as the rule of their faith and manners; and comparatively, very few of them read any of our periodicals; perhaps not more than one, in a hundred! We have but one paper in the State, ("The Israelite") which, although it is ably edited by our beloved and intelligent brother Field; is not taken by many in "Central" or "Northern," Indiana. In the judgment of many intelligent brethren, a work, such as we propose publishing, is much needed in "Central Indiana."[121]

Since he had already been a public teacher of Christianity for eight years, had already met the attacks of the opposition, and had already baptized some two thousand Hoosiers, he felt he knew what the churches and people of Indiana wanted.[122]

Five hundred subscribers were enough to get him started.[123] He rode horseback twenty miles from his farm near Gosport twice a month to get the paper printed and mailed. In September of 1843 he moved back to Bloomington so he could work on the paper more conveniently on weekdays; he preached on Sundays at Clear Creek, Bloomington, Richland, and Republican. The fifth issue Mathes published with his own printing office and printer in Bloomington. It was the press of Dr. Nathaniel Field of Jeffersonville whose *Israelite* had announced the time for the second advent of the Lord as September of 1843 and now suffered some lack of credibility with subscribers. The printer was Charles G. Berry of Washington whose personal shift from Democrat to Whig had cost his job with a Democratic paper. Subscriptions rose to about one thousand in the first year and may eventually have reached five thousand.[124] On 4 July 1845 he announced an increase from twenty-four to thirty-two pages per month, still for one dollar per year.

Mathes and his wife seemed always sick and near death but he managed to live through many anniversaries. Forty years after launching the *Christian Record*, at his seventy-fifth birthday celebration in 1883, he could say: "Our grand plea has become popular with all the intelligent and unprejudiced men and women in the land, and from a few thousand then, the Christian brotherhood now numbers near one hundred thousand members in Indiana alone."[125] He himself had been the most visible spokesman for Indiana's Christian churches and the volumes of the *Christian Record* were the primary historical record of this era of great growth of the Christian fellowship in Indiana.

Mathes had the verve characteristic of an early Campbellite editor. In his view it was only natural and right that all other religious groups should fade as the whole population recognized the truth and entered the union of the Christian reformation. In the *Record* Mathes kept his readers supplied with ammunition on the linguistic shadings of all the Greek words in the Bible connected with baptism. He repeated proofs against those Pedobaptists who questioned whether three thousand could actually have been immersed in eight hours at Jerusalem on the day of Pentecost even if the Romans would have allowed three thousand Jews to be dipped in their baths or their cisterns maintained for drinking water. He was patient, if not entirely convincing, toward a persistent minority in the congregations who said that any church on the New Testament model would certainly be practicing footwashing and exchanging the kiss of peace. The former Dunker Joseph Hostetler unkindly remarked that a Campbellite who would substitute a handshake for the kiss of peace might just substitute sprinkling for immersion too.[126]

On the pages of the *Record* Mathes did refutations in installments of such symbolic representatives of the "sects" as the Universalist Erasmus Manford, the Methodists Williamson Terrell and A. Wright, the Lutheran E. Rudisill, and the Baptist T. R. Cressy.[127] He published "The Bible a Sufficient Creed," two sermons delivered by Charles Beecher at the dedication of Second Presbyterian Church of Fort Wayne and wrote a series of articles to taunt Beecher to follow the implications of these sermons by coming out of Presbyterianism into the Christian reformation.[128] He reported and commented on scores of debates in which he and other Christian preachers engaged in Indiana. He noted the speeches and publications of a variety of contemporaries, along with caustic comment. Less space was devoted to "the pretended infallibility of 'His holiness of Rome'" or "the pitiful 'Revelations' of that stupid Impostor, Jo. Smith of Nauvoo."[129] Readers sent him an endless chain of requests for interpretations of particular Bible texts plus some teasing queries such as "How could the Jerusalem church members make the weekly contribution if they already had all things in common?"[130] Particular cases of church discipline were offered for his review. He gave studied opinions on points of order: who should be admitted to the Lord's Supper; who needed to be immersed or immersed again; which issues ought to be decided by the elders and which by congregational vote.[131]

Rascals were exposed. The pages of the *Record* named James M'Vay as excluded from the fellowship at Plainfield and "now going upon his own responsibility"; Joseph Sextine as "palming himself on the brethren as a Christian and an object of charity" and as one who "becomes all things to all men, to get money"; G. W. Gage as a preacher-impostor from Texas who made off with a horse, a bridle, a watch, and a widow from Mt. Pleasant in Martin County; James Mainard, also known as James Free, as a man moving west from Terre Haute leaving a trail of creditors and deserted wives behind him; and George W. Wallace at Farmersburg as an impostor both as a doctor and a preacher and apt to solicit or borrow money on all sides.[132]

Mathes asked contributors to send "short, pithy articles, on practical subjects" and not "long, dry speculative articles." The *Record* was a paper which invited and nearly demanded reading. Only in later years, when a certain number of pages were designated to be filled each month by faculty members of North Western Christian University, did there come to be articles like "The History of Carbon" by John Young.[133]

A further contribution of Mathes was his personal overview and oversight of the Christian churches in Indiana. At any gathering of Indiana's church leaders he might appear to preach or debate or give counsel, and certainly to seek out new subscribers or to collect subscription payments due. Congregations everywhere wanted him to visit. Much as he loved to preach and much as his New Light Christian conscience impelled him to make converts by his personal efforts in evangelism, he knew he had a wider role.

> We have received a great many letters inviting us to attend protracted meetings, in almost every part of the country. And some brethren really seem to think hard of me because I do not visit them . . . Some well meaning persons say, "you had better quit publishing the Christian Record and spend all your time in preaching as formerly, we think you could do more good." To which I answer, that such persons are honestly mistaken. It is true, I could effect more in the way of proselyting, in the bounds of my labors, for there is something in the voice and energy of the living speaker, to move his hearers to immediate action; which it is perhaps, impossible to throw into his written compositions; but the circle of one man's labors must necessarily be very limited. A few

thousand persons only see and hear him during his short life, and even these soon forget what he has said. But not so with a written discourse; when published in the Christian Record, it is read by many thousand persons, who never would hear the voice of the writer. We can thus preach the gospel, to thousands every month, whose faces we shall never see, till we meet in the king's own country. And then it is not forgotten, or if it should be, there it is upon record, and can be referred to at any time. And if a written discourse does not produce such an immediate result, as one spoken, it is more durable. Again it is admitted upon all hands that the press is the most powerful engine known among men, for the rapid and correct diffusion of thought.[134]

But he did find time to travel widely among the churches. He made deliberate "tours," often titling accounts of them in the *Record* by the section of the state visited—to Vincennes and Washington (July 1843); to the North West (June 1844); to the South Part of the State (August 1844); Tour of Nineteen Days [including Kentucky] (December 1844); to Eastern Indiana (March 1845); to Northern Indiana (May 1846); to Southern Indiana (March 1851); to Southern Indiana (September 1851); Notes by the Way . . . to Northern Indiana (August 1855).[135] He took part in state meetings, district meetings, county meetings, local cooperation meetings, local protracted meetings, missionary society meetings, and Bible society meetings. He saw the strategic importance of establishing strong churches in the rising Indiana towns.

> My health is extremely poor at present, and has been the greater part of this season, so that I am not able to ride and preach much, if I had nothing else to do. Several points in Indiana, I am anxious to visit soon, as Crawfordsville, Frankfort, Martinsville, Edingburgh, Madison, Charlestown, Jeffersonville, New Albany, Terre Haute, Shaker Prairie, and many other points.[136]

His accounts of all these visits in the *Record* named the Christian church leaders in every place and spoke with affection of them, giving descriptions and statistics of local church life in a way well designed to stimulate Christian leaders everywhere and make them aware of the larger fellowship of which they were a part. Letters of response from readers of the tour accounts were then published as "News from the Churches" resulting in a happy compounding of the results of the editor's visitation. Generally the accounts of visits by Mathes were full of celebration and appreciation and approval. However, he could apply the bishop's rod. That division in the

North Salem church in Hendricks County in 1846 was disgraceful and was allowing "sectarian bigots" to rejoice while hardening sinners and the infidel in their stubborn unbelief.[137] In eastern Indiana in 1845 he found that the Christian churches had grown large and the members rich but only George Campbell and John B. New were employed as full time preachers in the whole area. He smelled apathy.[138] In his visits and in the *Record*, Mathes was an advocate of quality in congregational life. The old rural Baptist pattern of holding church services with preaching once a month would not do. Christians were to meet at the Lord's house on the first day of every week for "breaking the loaf" and "commemorating the Lord's death."[139]

> There is perhaps a greater lack among us upon this very subject than any other. It seems almost impossible to get the brethren generally to see and feel the importance of meeting regularly and punctually upon the first day of the week, "to break bread." Why is it so? Do we really disregard the command of the Lord, "Do this in memory of me?" But it is lamentably true, that in some congregations where there are some two hundred nominal members, that not more than twenty can be induced to attend the weekly meetings of the disciples! When the Preacher is to hold forth, there is then a general turnout! Does not this prove that such professors love the Preacher more than they love the Lord?[140]
>
> The standard of christian morality, piety, and devotion, is at present too low to bring the christian character up to the ancient model of christianity. To profess love and veneration for the Bible, and opposition to creeds, confessions of faith, and books of discipline of human origin, is not enough to constitute the christian.[141]

Christians were to support their full time preachers locally. A. B. Eperson asked Mathes in 1851, "Did the Christian Church ever oppose paying preachers? If so, why is she in favor of it now?" Mathes rehearsed the historical objections of Barton W. Stone and of Alexander Campbell and of other pioneer preachers against the "hireling system." He acknowledged that there were some doing occasional preaching whose talents and qualifications certainly warranted no salary. Such backward persons might be prone to oppose payment for anyone else. They might also cater to selfish members who were glad to call their own stinginess a virtue. But church people who opposed fair pay for preachers as a matter of principle needed to recognize that their zeal had carried them too far. They were opposing the Scriptures. "In their eagerness to escape from Babylon, they ran past Jerusalem."[142] Correct procedure was simple enough, he said. Individual churches or unions of churches agree to sustain the work of a preacher as their evangelist. They make a calculation of what it will require to support this preacher and his family for a specific period. Then they "make up the amount" and pay him. And they should be generous.[143]

> But sometimes it is objected to giving preachers a fair and just compensation for their labors, that it would spoil them! It would make them proud, and lift them above their business; and we want an humble ministry; we must therefore keep them poor! Why brethren, have you so little confidence in your public servants that you think they could not bear a comfortable living without becoming proud! How do you bear it? And why do you think the preachers would become proud, if they were even to become rich? Have you ever seen any of them tried? Did you ever know any of them to be made rich by their brethren? You have known many to become poor.[144]

Mathes also became a champion of cooperations at every level. Congregations should send representatives to attend such meetings and they should report to cooperations at local, county, district, and state levels such information as (1) the number of members and names of officers; (2) the order of the church in public worship and discipline; and (3) what was being done by the congregation for the spread of the gospel and what the congregation now brought in contributions or in secured pledges to support this cause for the coming year.[145] The calls to cooperation meetings, the urgings to participate, the minutes of the meetings, and the reports on mission projects undertaken made up a substantial fraction of copy in the *Record*.

There was too much for Mathes to do. He had done well financially in Bloomington being owner of a new two-story brick house, a farm of two hundred acres, and the *Christian Record* enterprise. To this he added the local newspaper "that I might enjoy a monopoly of the printing business in the place." Faced with so much opportunity, he decided in 1847 to invite Elijah Goodwin to move from Mount Vernon to Bloomington to be his associate. Goodwin was just one year older than Mathes. Like Mathes, he had been a New Light Christian youth with a burning zeal to preach. Like Mathes, he claimed to have come very near to Campbellite conclusions before studying Campbell. When he finally did read the *Millennial Harbinger* in 1837 and 1838 he, like Mathes, brought his New Light congregations with him into Alexander

Campbell's reformation. Like Mathes, he was a veteran evangelist who had baptized hundreds of converts and formed many new churches. He had much less education than Mathes, a few months of winter school in Daviess County plus two months in "an excellent grammar school in Gibson County," but by self discipline and self education he had become an excellent communicator. When the *Christian Record* was very young, in the January issue for 1845, Mathes had printed his public request that preacher Goodwin continue to send contributions for the paper because his "essays are read with much pleasure by the brethren generally." From the time of their partnership in 1847, the names of Mathes and Goodwin were everywhere in the records of the pioneer church in Indiana. For Christian church priority and ministerial support and evangelization and cooperations and education and mission organization, what Mathes said Goodwin would also be saying a few decibels more forcefully. What they did they often did together. One would be president of the meeting and the other secretary. When Mrs. Mathes died, Goodwin preached her funeral; when Goodwin died, Mathes compiled and published his memoirs.[146]

The idea in 1847 was that Mathes and Goodwin would be joint owners of the *Record*. The injection of Goodwin's gifts and vast energy was to mean both expansion of subscriptions and acceptance of many more of those preaching invitations from across the state. Mathes said "My partner, and my fellow-laborer, Eld. E. Goodwin, who is a very healthy and strong man, will alternate with me and visit many congregations . . . We expect (between us) to spend the time of one Evangelist, and will visit many congregations, and attend all the annual, co-operation, district, and other protracted meetings that we possibly can."[147] That hope was short lived. Mathes and his family were generally ill. It was Goodwin who did a lot of traveling and preaching for which he received little pay since "some supposed that we were actually making money very rapidly and were getting rich, and that we ought to preach everywhere we could just for the good of the cause and for the happiness of doing good." In a year and a half they had issued a volume and a half of the *Record* jointly but saw that the income from the paper was not enough to support two families. Goodwin went on the road with the State Meeting's commission to canvass the state's Christian churches about founding a college; he found consensus to locate the new college at Indianapolis.[148]

Meanwhile Mathes was yielding to pressure from agents of the State Meeting to move the *Record* to Indi-

anapolis. Ovid Butler wrote Mathes a glowing welcome to the capital city in June of 1851. He said the state brotherhood had hoped for years that the *Record* would locate there. Indianapolis was an important transportation and communication center. There the paper could easily collaborate with North Western Christian University and with the fellowship's Bible and Missionary Societies. Butler reminded Goodwin of the reformation's continuing mission to "subvert existing organizations and establish in their place the ancient order of the first Christian congregations." With the *Record* at Indianapolis, Mathes might be assuming leadership of tens of thousands on the battlefield of this moral revolution.[149]

Mathes established the *Record* in modest Indianapolis quarters.

> We have taken the room over the "Ladies' Fancy Store," north side of Washington, and between Illinois and Meridian Streets, nearly opposite the Palmer House. Entrance from the street. All those who take the Christian Record from the office will please call and get their papers. The office will generally be open from 7 o'clock A.M., till 5 o'clock P.M. But if at any time, we should be found absent, call at Bramwell's store, two doors west.[150]

Nevertheless, his vision was large. His was now "a well established journal" with "a very respectable list of subscribers." He thought Indiana had more reformation brothers and sisters than any other state in the Union. Illinois, Michigan, and Wisconsin had no papers to "plead the cause of the Bible alone." He felt his knowledge of the society and of the region was unmatched. "We hope the time is at hand when the religious news of the whole country west of the Alleghanies, will be concentrated in the Christian Record."[151]

It was not to be. The paper remained important but it remained modest. Mathes lost a lot of money in Indianapolis, chiefly in a bad bookstore partnership with John T. Cox. Overwork and business pressures further weakened his health. His wife, twenty years an invalid and fast failing, "greatly desired to go to the high rolling country near Bedford." To Bedford they went, moving to a little farm on Leatherwood some three miles east of town. Since the New Albany and Chicago Railroad ran through Bedford and offered good mail service, Mathes thought he could edit the *Record* from his farm there with the printing and mailing contracted elsewhere. Four years of attempting to manage this left him in frustration and poverty. Indianapolis was the rising center of Christian church activity and the board members of North Western Christian University wanted the *Record* to be issued from the capital again. Elijah Goodwin at Indianapolis finally took over the *Record* from Mathes and edited it seven more years in varied format but on the old principles. Mathes twice resurrected the *Record* at Bedford, from 1867 to 1875 and from 1882 to 1884.[152]

When Madison Evans made his selection of twenty-two "pioneer preachers of Indiana" in 1862, Mathes at age fifty-four and Goodwin at age fifty-five were already assured of their places in this top rank of Christian church leadership.[153] Mathes was cited as evangelist—"for thirty years past he has proselyted from two to three hundred per annum, making a total of five or six thousand." As a debater his mind was "well stored with the munitions of intellectual warfare." He had published his *Works of Barton W. Stone* in 408 pages. His *Letters to Bishop Morris*, including his "reasons for not being a Methodist," was very popular. He had served many congregations as preacher; he was pastor at Indianapolis and New Albany and Bedford.[154] As for Goodwin, he was a veteran of a six hundred-mile preaching circuit, capable of riding 3,472 miles and preaching 382 sermons in the year ending in October 1845. He had served as an agent and officer of North Western Christian University, had engaged in ten debates, and had served as pastor at Madison, Bloomington, and Indianapolis. The third edition of his book of sermons entitled *The Family Companion* had been issued in 1856.[155]

In 1862 Mathes and Goodwin still had a decade or two to preach and debate and add to their published works. Mathes, who was a warm advocate of Indiana University and a warmer advocate of North Western Christian University, would further make his educational mark as an organizer, president, and professor of biblical literature at the Bedford Male and Female College.[156] But by that year they had already become symbols and central service persons for Indiana's Christian churches, recognized as regional editors and planners and unofficial overseers in the style of Alexander Campbell. They were second to Campbell in historical priority and in national prominence but in no way second to him in daily operations in Indiana. Mathes reprinted Campbell's reports of his visit to Europe from the *Millennial Harbinger* in 1847 and 1848 because "comparatively few of our readers take that paper."[157]

Benjamin Franklin (1812–1878)

Madison Evans did not even include Benjamin Franklin among his twenty-two biographical sketches of Indiana's pioneer Christian church preachers. Perhaps Evans felt

Franklin was too young to name among the pioneers; he was but fifty when Evans published his compilation in 1862. In addition, Franklin had moved from Wayne County in Indiana to Cincinnati in 1850 and may have temporarily forfeited his claim to be a Hoosier.[158] He resided in Indiana for the first fifteen years and the last fourteen years of his preaching career but in Cincinnati for the fourteen years in the middle. Nevertheless, Franklin may have had more stature among the Christian churches of America and among the Christian churches of Indiana in 1862 than any of the pioneers Evans selected. In fact, that very year David Walk told a large gathering of the national Christian brotherhood in Cincinnati, "Probably next to Alexander Campbell, Bro. Franklin is more extensively known than any other man connected with the Reformation of the Nineteenth century."[159] It was a visibility earned as an evangelist and editor and publisher and debater and shepherd for the Christian churches after the manner of Campbell.

Franklin can hardly be said to have ever left Indiana. He was primarily an evangelist so he was rarely at home. Wherever his residence, he was likely to be in meetings in Indiana or soon scheduled to be there. Up to 1850 there were those years of preaching tours in eastern Indiana and western Ohio. "I feel for Indiana," Franklin wrote to Mathes in 1857. "Fifteen years of my poor but hard labor was in your glorious and enterprising Indiana. Many hundreds there, I had the happiness to introduce into the kingdom of God . . . They are near and dear to me yet, and my anxiety for their prosperity and happiness has not in the least abated."[160] In the same year that he moved to Cincinnati, he returned to Indiana to preach at Madison and to "fly across the land" by train to Indianapolis to meet with the commissioners of North Western Christian University, an institution for which he claimed to have been the first advocate in print.[161]

In June of the next year Franklin was back in New Albany reviewing two recent books on baptism; preaching at Slate's Run and Silver Creek and other places in the Clark County area; and preaching at Madison and Bloomington. In August he was back attending a district meeting of church leaders at Cambridge City; winning thirty additions to Rush County churches; preaching at Madison; preaching at Edinburgh; preaching at Rushville; preaching at Little Blue River; preaching at Fayetteville; preaching at Ben Davis Creek; preaching at Smelser's Mill; and preaching "in a grove." In 1853 he debated total hereditary depravity with Primitive Baptist preacher Joel Hume for four days at Mount Vernon. He responded to gloomy articles in the *Christian Record* picturing the lack of church growth in Indiana and warning that the Christian cause was "sick and dying." He resolved to shake off the lethargy of his regular ministry to two congregations in the Cincinnati area and to do even more evangelism by touring and by issuing a new periodical. During his years of evangelistic touring, right through the Civil War, Indiana was always high on his agenda. Hoosiers read his papers, enjoyed his preaching, and sought his leadership.[162]

Benjamin Franklin certainly had his religious rootage as an Indiana pioneer. He came to the forests of Henry County with his uncle Calvin Franklin in 1832. They were searching out the land; Benjamin's parents, Joseph and Isabella, and his seven younger siblings followed from Ohio in spring of 1833. Joseph was a farmer-miller-carpenter-shoemaker and he selected his land with a mill site on Deer Creek. Benjamin had earned a new ax by clearing right-of-way for the National Road in the fall of 1832. After he became twenty-one on 1 February 1833, he bought eighty acres of land, built a log cabin, married the thirteenth child of the neighboring Personett family, and established himself as a carpenter-miller with a fast growing family. His parents Joseph and Isabella were pious persons, Methodist Protestants now living in a neighborhood with strong New Light influence. A New Light preacher named Samuel Rogers came there from Ohio in 1834; he opened a school which five of the Franklin boys attended. Soon he began preaching at the schoolhouse and in private homes. Rogers had been baptized and ordained personally by Barton W. Stone and was already a veteran of thousands of miles of circuit riding in behalf of New Light revivals; he had also heard Alexander Campbell personally and had rejoiced in the insights of Campbell's publications. "Stone had given me the book," he said, "but Campbell taught me how to read it in its connection." At his services Rogers taught that baptism was essential to enjoyment of the forgiveness of sins.[163]

Another New Light preacher named Elijah Martindale came to the vicinity in 1835. After preaching at the home of the Stewarts, good friends of the Franklins, Martindale established a congregation which he visited once a month for many years. Martindale had married into a New Light family in Wayne County in October of 1815, left the Baptists and United Brethren to join the New Lights, and made his "first effort" as a preacher at Jacksonburg in 1820. By the time he extended his ministry to the Franklins, Martindale had combined his New Light zeal for evangelism with the teachings of the Campbell reformation and brought most of his converts into that reformation with him. "I had almost embraced the doctrine of baptism as a link in the chain of pardon before I ever heard of A. Campbell," he said, "but when I became acquainted with the writings of Campbell, Stone and others I was helped much in understanding the Scripture on this point and some others." Yet he was always expressing concern that the New Lights in seeking union with others might cool their revival enthusiasm at the risk of stoicism, might end up with meetings too cold and dry, might run too far through the temperate zone in order to meet the others and join them in the frigid zone. Martindale and Rogers held the house meeting in the winter of 1835–36 at which John Rogers and the brothers Benjamin and Daniel Franklin professed their faith. Martindale was the preacher that night; Rogers had been the chief influence on the young men and it was he who led the group with lanterns and torches to immerse the converts in the cold waters of Deer Creek.[164] In retrospect Rogers said,

> I have ever felt, in looking back over those times and considering that work, that, if I had done no more for my Master than to be instrumental in giving to the world Benjamin Franklin, I would have no reason to be ashamed . . . We may have scores of men among us more learned, in the popular sense, and more refined and elegant in manners and address; but it is my judgment that we have not a man among us who can preach the gospel with less admixture of philosophy and speculation, and with greater force, than Ben Franklin.[165]

Benjamin Franklin was rough and ignorant; that did not deter him. Now that he was a convinced believer, he wanted to make the gospel convincing to everybody else as well. He memorized much of the Bible. "Religion was his theme morning noon and night," said one of the young men who quickly became involved in his orbit. He began preaching at once—exhorting at the regular meetings of the church, accepting invitations to speak in school houses or private dwellings, taking his turn among other preachers at larger meetings. This east-central section of Indiana had the heaviest concentration of Christians in the state.[166]

An early example and tutor for Franklin was John Longley, a New Light preacher won from the Calvinism of the Baptists and personally trained up in the Kentucky revivals by Barton W. Stone. His lifetime statistics would include three wives, twenty-five children, and over eight thousand converts. Now in Rush County in Indiana, Longley benefited in his evangelistic meetings from the energy of young Ben Franklin, encouraged him because of his obvious potential, and offered Franklin some discipline. Longley kept count of the times Franklin said "my dear friends and brethering" during one sermon and reported to Franklin the total of 150.[167] Even more impressive as a preaching model for Franklin was John O'Kane, one of the best in the West and conveniently near at the time of Franklin's conversion. O'Kane was a preacher from Virginia and from the eastern wing of the Christian movement, brought by reading the publications of Barton W. Stone and by personal correspondence with Stone into the Christian church of the West which by then had united with the Campbellite reformers. So in a grove meeting at Milton in 1836 and repeatedly thereafter, Franklin had the example of a preacher of overwhelming power formulating the gospel exactly the way Franklin believed it.[168]

Hoosiers wanted to hear O'Kane. In spite of his roughness, Hoosiers soon wanted to hear Franklin. They liked his nimbleness of mind, his vitality, his plain directness, his force in preaching. There was in him no hesitation, no lack of confidence, no doubt that he was now offering the only correct formulation of the faith. He saw no way that another person could read the Bible honestly and arrive at conclusions different from his. He enjoyed being combative; in putting down opponents he was spicy, testy, stinging, acid, but never dull. All of the New Light drive for evangelism seemed concentrated in him. He was never really fulfilled unless engaged in protracted evangelistic meetings and if he was under agreement as minister to a particular church or churches, he was always requesting time off to conduct meetings elsewhere.[169] He was intoxicated with the grandeur of the reformation in which he shared. As a young man his excitement was fired anew every time he met with the leading preachers of the movement and every time they acknowledged him as one rising among the ranks of the leaders. He educated himself while engaged in his ministry, beginning with the most basic school textbooks. But the lessons he learned best were those from the substantial corpus of the publications of Campbell, Stone, and Scott. For him the church was always and only the local congregation as Campbell had early discerned it.

> The greatest peculiarity of christianity is to be found in its simplicity. Church organization is not a subject that will require years study [sic] and the utmost stretch of intelligence to comprehend it. It is not an intricate contrivance, but the most simple, clear and beautiful arrangement ever made for mortal man![170]

Franklin's fire for evangelism made him unhappy until every one of those individual churches could be built up in strength and commitment to be effective in winning converts.

> One of the most unwise things that has occurred amongst the disciples of Christ, is the constituting of so many little weak churches. It can be of no use to establish a new church, until there are numbers, talent, zeal, piety and means sufficient to keep up the established worship of God . . . It requires but little learning, talent, or piety, to struggle over six or eight states, baptize large numbers and organize little churches of fifteen or twenty persons, appoint A. and B. Elders, and C. and D. Deacons, without a weeks acquaintance with them, and leave perhaps to see them no more in the flesh. What a heartless and unreasonable work this has been! No greater injury could be inflicted on the cause of God than for teachers of religion to go through the land, making disciples and leaving them to perish without any oversight.[171]

He said such little churches were difficult to help if they had no members qualified to be elders, no means to build a respectable meeting house, and no base to support a preacher except "some brother who is able to preach for them without money and without price." They had no real defense against "some renegado of a preacher . . . with a tolerable gift of gab" who might circulate imposing on such weak places.[172]

Franklin's personal rise to prominence was extraordinary; he tolerated no obstacle. When he left secular business for full time preaching in 1840, his sale of his interest in a grist mill resulted in a troublesome debt rather than an asset. Six weeks after he left the mill for the ministry, his wife gave birth to twins so there was a family of six children for these young parents to support.[173] He was preaching most every day but had little or no pay. Some of Franklin's scalding comments were always reserved for church people who closed their eyes and purses to the needs of the preachers they invited to preach. He answered an inquiry about tithing:

> We do not know of any scripture which specifies any special amount, but this we are well satisfied of, that there are two classes that are not New Testament folks. One of the classes consists of preachers, and the other class consists of private members. The preachers are constantly coveting the goods of this world, and contriving to get all they possibly can, and ever threatening to "leave the field" if they do not get the desired amount. They pray as little as they can pass along with, preach as little as they can get off with, and hardly ever visit the sick, and are always complaining of their hard times. These are not in any way related to New Testament preachers. The class of private members alluded to, always contrive to give as little for the support of the gospel and every other good object as

they can possibly get along with, and do as little of every thing else that is good as will pass at all in the eyes of the world, and talk of an "abundant entrance into the ever- lasting kingdom of our Lord and Saviour Jesus Christ." These are not in any way related to the ancient New Tes- tament Christians.[174]

We have many times noticed this class of men. They hold on to the old fashioned buckskin purse, about fif- teen inches long and tied with a leather string about the mouth, which surrounds it not less that six to ten times, and tied in a hard knot every time. They never notice that the hat or basket, as the case may be, is coming till it is before their face, they are so absorbed in their devo- tions. They then startle up, under considerable alarm and excitement, and run the hand into a half dozen pockets before they hit the right one. The poor deacon stands waiting till half the audience is attracted to know what he is stopping so long for. At length the purse is untied, and after much fumbling and mumbling, a five cent piece is fished out, deposited in the hat, and the deacon relieved.[175]

For the Franklins there was a stay of less than two years serving congregations at and near New Lisbon, followed by a stay of less than two years serving congregations at or near Bethel, followed by a move to the Wayne County seat of Centreville in 1844.[176] Here, out of a background of poverty and poor education and in the midst of a house- hold of seven children, Franklin became an editor. In the new periodical Franklin said he had a "tolerable" list of subscribers and that he would preach just as much as ever in addition to getting out the paper. His *Reformer* took the name of a recently collapsed Christian paper in Ohio. It was a sixteen-page monthly pamphlet without cover, of- fered for fifty cents per year. Critics said there were already too many church papers but the *Reformer* survived. When Franklin enlarged it to sixty-four pages with cover for a dollar a year, Hoosier editor Mathes said "he cannot afford it." But Franklin afforded it by preaching as much as ever and by employing his family to run the print shop in their house and by adding subscribers. The paper became the *Western Reformer* and the location became Milton. It made a precarious merger with the *Gospel Proclamation* and then moved off to Cincinnati when Franklin was invited to locate in that new center of Campbellite activity in 1850. The geographical center of the fellowship was shifting from Bethany in Virginia to the Midwest. Franklin was part of the aggressive western leadership rising alongside Alexander Campbell.[177]

For a time Franklin was the most popular of the Christian church evangelistic preachers in the Midwest.

Though he was under contract as preacher for two Cincinnati area congregations, he held protracted meet- ings everywhere. For a time he was also the most popular Christian church editor in the Midwest, surviving in turn the rise and termination of the *Reformer*, the *Western Re- former*, the *Proclamation and Reformer*, the *Christian Age*, and the projected publication program of the American Christian Publication Society—all with much of his own following intact. His magazines offered much the same departments as the *Millennial Harbinger* of Campbell or the *Christian Record* of Mathes and Goodwin but the style was always Franklin's. His writing had the same punch as his preaching. Those who heard him gladly read his papers with the same appreciation. He taunted the de- nominational leaders by name, for example, fifteen letters to that Methodist "Campbellite killer" named Williamson Terrell who claimed he needed only two discourses in any community to finish off Campbellism.[178] He issued a specific challenge to Universalists:

> At any suitable time and place, we will undertake to prove that the Universalists differ from the bible in the following particulars: They believe in a different God—a different Devil—a different Hell—a different Heaven—a different Savior—a different Salvation—a different Sinner—a different Saint—a different Sin—a different Righteousness—a different Gospel—a different Judg- ment—a different second coming of Christ and a different Resurrection of the Dead![179]

He dashed off a whole series of simple dialogues "for those whose hearts sicken within them, at the thoughts [sic] of an article of any considerable length." One of these was reprinted in 1856 as a pamphlet entitled *Sincerity Seeking the Way to Heaven*. On his pilgrimage the young man named Sincerity exposes the utter inadequacy of the Romanist, of the Calvinist, of the Anti-Means Baptist, of the Universalist, of the Skeptic, and especially of Mr. Hon- esty who is a presiding elder of the Methodist church. Then Sincerity meets Priscilla of the Church of Christ who rescues him from his anxiety and confusion. On the morning of next Lord's day Sincerity appears in the Chris- tian assembly, hears the word, and confesses the Savior. "In a few minutes after, he and the preacher stood side by side in the water, some three feet deep . . ." Back in the af- ternoon at three o'clock "when the disciples met together to break bread," Sincerity accepts the invitation to unite with the congregation, is stoutly admonished about fol- lowing Christ, and receives the hand of fellowship from the believers. The pamphlet was issued with an "Appen- dix" citing Scripture proofs appropriate to the conversion, with a piece called "Scrap Doctors" putting down other groups who only got part of the correct way, and an "Address to the Reader" pointing out that he now had no possible ground for hesitation and should enter the joys of the Bible-governed life with promise of salvation. Fifteen thousand copies of the pamphlet *Sincerity* sold by 1880. A Methodist physician at White Oak in Greene County was reported converted and immersed because a copy was placed in his hands.[180]

Eighteen fifty-six was a year of focus for Franklin's career. That year he established the monthly *American Christian Review* under his own control, destined to become a weekly and a publishing company which was Franklin's voice for the remaining twenty-two years of his life and the continuing voice of a large segment of the Christian church after he was gone. That year he resigned as preacher for the two Cincinnati area congregations to become a full time traveling evangelist whose lifetime ministry would include immersing some eight thousand of his more than ten thousand converts and setting off religious awakenings wherever he went, even among the students at Alexander Campbell's own Bethany College.[181] It was his happiest year, he said.

> This year we have performed more labor than we have in any previous year of our life—had better success, everything considered, both in the pulpit and with the pen . . . We have issued four thousand copies of the *Review*; put about three thousand copies into circulation, and the balance are going every day. We have put many thousands of tracts also into circulation—more, so far as we know, than has ever been put in circulation among the brethren in one year before, and have preached more than a sermon for each day in the year.[182]

But then at the end of 1857 he said that year had been his happiest one.[183] The popular preacher with the popular journal had become a rider of steam boats and steam trains as a kind of visiting inspector. A biographer said:

> He was again in the eye of the brotherhood. His reputation as a well-informed Bible student and his powerful mastery of the pulpit arts drew many requests for his evangelistic services. Moreover, in a day when travelogs by roving editors were fairly common, Franklin's friends followed his romantic itineraries over wide areas. While the purpose of these tours was to preach the gospel, a more utilitarian object was to secure subscribers and to feel the pulse of the brotherhood on a wide variety of subjects.[184]

Then things began to change. The Franklin who had been so happily in love with the Christian fellowship kept discovering things in it to disappoint him. Former supporters resented his caustic attacks and became his critics. There had been some forecasts of Franklin's alienation. The leading men of the Christian fellowship had acknowledged him as useful and certainly irrepressible. But even in their complimentary expressions in print they kept reminding him of his clodhopping origins and of his truculent nature. Franklin took Walter Scott to task for counting the Christians among the Protestant sects and for seeming to describe some kind of Protestant union short of Campbellite terms. Soon afterward Scott wrote of Franklin's *Western Reformer:*

> The Editor, Benjamin Franklin, was a poor man, and withal but ill educated; but by virtue of his natural endowments and great devotion to God, he has risen to be one of the most interesting writers in the Reformation. He is very eloquent in speaking. His character is, we believe, without spot. Should he still devote himself to study, and prosecute improvement in the faith of our great Master, he will doubtless finally excel in all good and commendable attainments.[185]

His undoubted friend and editorial colleague James Mathes included a caveat in endorsing Franklin's paper: "Brother Franklin is one of our strongest preachers, who, notwithstanding his editorial duties, does a great deal of missionary labor. He is a bold, safe, and energetic writer. And sometimes when provoked a good deal, he is sarcastic and severe in his reviews and strictures."[186]

The staff at the established Christian center at Bethany in Virginia eyed Franklin coolly. Bruised by Franklin's violent defense of Cincinnati's American Christian Publication Society and by Franklin's counsel "Let Bethany not envy Cincinnati, nor Cincinnati envy Bethany," co-editor W. K. Pendleton of the *Millennial Harbinger* published six pages of heated reply.[187]

> The whole aim of nearly all that has been said in the "Christian Age" by Elder Franklin is directed against me personally. It is an attack, the most persistent, ungenerous and unfair, against "Prof. Pendleton." Why this should be, I cannot divine. I never injured Elder Franklin, that I know of, in all my life. My acquaintance with him is so slight, that I do not suppose I would recollect him, were I to meet him face to face. We have never had any correspondence, friendly or otherwise;— we have had no collision hitherto on any subject. His duties and mine are in no sort of rivalry or collision; and yet he seems determined, by all the ingenuity and *ad captandum* tact, that he can, in any sort of consistency with the bare semblance of truth, command, to injure my influence and misrepresent my personal character.[188]

As part of this Publication Society controversy, Alexander Campbell himself became so angry that he threatened to demolish Franklin. "If Elder Franklin thinks he can make any capital for himself or the Christian Age, by his assaults on me, I think he has a right to do it, and he must have it. As the matter now is, I court investigation. I am sorry, truly sorry, that I have such documents, and that I am constrained to use them."[189]

Franklin was extremely sensitive to suggestions that there were too many church papers. He reported such suggestions, including some from Campbell himself, and answered them. Editors depend entirely on paying subscribers, he said. So it is the people who decide by their support how many papers there will be and exactly which ones will survive. Readers are "the safest and best tribunal on earth for this purpose."[190] He was not awed by any editors who claimed priority because they were more erudite.

> It takes good sense and learning both to make a truly great man. But what is most contemptible is to see any one always making an ado about learning, who is in possession of neither learning nor good sense. Learning is surely a great advantage, but still fails to give some men the preeminence they seem to desire. The probability is, that such if they had some way to see themselves, as others see them, would discover that knowing how to read and spell, talk about nouns and verbs, and even pronounce a few Greek and Latin sentences, falls vastly short of being learned. That man who disceminates the most Bible knowledge and impresses the most of the mind and spirit of our holy religion upon the world is not only the most learned in religion and the nature of man, but is the most useful in the world. And whoever sets him aside for merely a little litterary taste and a few prettily pronounced words and wise looks, greatly injures the cause of Christ.[191]

Franklin had been uneasy from the first in the urban center of Cincinnati. He and his family in their poverty contrasted painfully with the comparative education and elegance of the household of his colleague and sponsor D. S. Burnet.[192] Burnet was the most influential Christian in Cincinnati. Even after his poverty was relieved, Franklin had maintained much of his base beyond the city among the people in the towns and rural places of Ohio and Kentucky and Indiana, people who sought his services for debates or protracted meetings and who treasured his *Review*. With him they shared a vision of the church as independent local congregation. Alexander Campbell had delineated it that way in the days of the *Christian Baptist*.

An individual church or congregation of Christ's disciples is the only ecclesiastical body recognized in the New Testament. Such a society is "the highest court of Christ" on earth . . . To manage the business of the church in all ages, it pleased the Head of the Church to appoint Bishops and Deacons . . . And in all those appointments the bishops and deacons were chosen from among those who believed; and they had previously assembled themselves, like others, to eat the supper. Besides this, they were numerous in every church . . . Now in selecting Bishops and Deacons, a church, or a number of people calling themselves a church, may choose to depart from this uniform practice of the Apostolic churches, i.e. they may hire a school or college man . . . and for their practice in so doing it is certain that they can plead neither Scripture precedent nor precept. In such a case, then, we have great and manifold reasons to suspect the character of the church, as well as that of the minister.[193]

They wanted such churches served and extended by an army of nonresident evangelists like Franklin, always rehearsing the uncompromising Campbellite plea. "No officer in the Kingdom of God, has any authority over the churches or preachers, except the officers of the individual congregations. The New Testament knows no jurisdiction of any office beyond the individual congregation, except where an evangelist is building up and establishing new congregations."[194] In the congregations they wanted a deepening of the simple piety and a reinforcement of the plain mannerisms with which their reformation had begun.

That did not seem to Franklin and his friends to be the way things were going. New preachers were entering the Christian ranks who knew little of the old evangelists and their ways. After a tour in Indiana to "look out through the country and see the shape of things," Franklin said:

> Old men are neglected . . . Aged men, such as God, under all dispensations, has required his people to honor and respect, are now sneered at as "common," "old fashed," "fogies," that may do to speak "in the country," but not in towns and cities! Young and vain men are flattered and inflated with conceit, if not real foppery and dandyism encouraged. But in all such cases, the ruin of the cause, and frequently both the ruin of the old preacher and the young is wrought. Several cases within our horizon furnish sad comments, demonstrative of all this.[195]

In response to two discourses claiming that preachers of the future must know geology, astronomy, history, and other disciplines and deploring preachers who were "behind the times" and "old fogy," Franklin said "We have no patience with this mere butterfly twaddle, toploftical aircastle, highfalutin and empty thing."[196]

Preachers old and new were leaving off traveling and settling down in the role of "pastor." Some allowed themselves to be called "Reverend" as the preachers of some other religious groups were doing. Colleges advertised themselves as training grounds for "educated pastors" and with support from Bethany there came to be talk of founding a graduate theological school to train Christian preachers. Franklin could see that the goal of all this was a supply of educated and resident pastors rather than an army of charismatic and itinerant evangelists like himself. Franklin wrote "We belong to the class who have no use for a theological school." He was for education but "educating a man is one thing, and making a preacher of him is another."[197]

> The man who teaches young men to preach, is not to be housed in a theological school . . . He must go out into the field and work with the young men, and show them how to work, not only by example show them how the work is done, but at the same time give them examples of piety, devotion, zeal, energy, industry and self-sacrifice . . . As soon as these young men leave the college, let them enter the field, if they can do so, under the direction of some experienced preacher, in whom they have confidence, read the Bible and history, write and study, five hours every morning; preaching from one to two discourses each day, and they will soon make preachers, and preachers too, worth something when they are made.[198]

For Franklin the role of "pastor" was unscriptural; this pastoral practice was displacing the rule of local elders and disrupting the New Testament plan.[199] He believed it to be a root cause of the lamentable decline of the churches. He growled about preachers who "are content to preach on Saturday night and twice on Lord's day at their regular appointments, and about once a year hold a protracted meeting of a week or ten days at each preaching-place. A man who does no more than this ought to reduce his pay to half price and dig the other half of his living out of the ground."[200]

> The command is to go, go and keep going, while God shall give us life . . . A little preaching on the Lord's day will not do the work. The Word should be preached every day and every night, as far as possible. We can not confine our labors to cities, towns, and villages, expecting preaching to be brought to us, as work to a tailor, hatter or shoemaker; but we must go out into the country, among the people, and be one of them, as messengers sent from heaven to take them to God. We are not to con-fine ourselves to the fine meeting-house, but, when we can do no better, go to the court-house, the town or city hall, the old seminary, the school-house, or the private dwelling, and preach to the people. We must not wait for the large assembly, but preach to the few, the small, humble and unpromising congregation; We must not merely pretend to preach, while we are only complaining of them, telling how bad they are; whining over them, and murmuring—showing contempt to them and all their arrangements—but preach to them in the name of the Lord, remembering that in every human form you see, there is a living spirit, upon which Jesus looked when he died, and which is worth more than the great globe on which he walks. No matter how lowly, how humble, how poor and uncomely all their temporal arrangements, you will find, on acquaintance, some who will love the Lord, turn from their sins, and become jewels in the Lord's, and also in the preacher's crown of rejoicing.[201]

Prosperous Christians were building more expensive churches. Central Christian Church in Cincinnati built a French gothic sanctuary to seat two thousand. It had a nave 34 feet wide, 125 feet long, and 103 feet high with a stained glass window said to be the largest in America. There was a choir and an organ in a gallery directly behind the pulpit. The whole cost of $140,000 was raised by dedication date. The dedication sermon by pastor W. T. Moore was based on the words of Jesus on the cross, "It Is Finished." The church published a pamphlet entitled "A Brief Account of the Origin, Progress, Faith and Practice of the Central Christian Church."[202] To Franklin it represented an awful complex—a rich church, an extravagant building, a pastor, an organ, a "creed" in addition to the Bible. "This church is progressing backward!" he cried. "Its first officer, 'the pastor,' as a separate and distinct officer from the overseers and deacons, is wholly unknown to the Scriptures. As a distinct office, what is now styled 'the pastorate' originated not with Christ or his apostles but with the Man of Sin."[203]

> We can not let this worldly show, this carnal display, this appeal to the lust of the flesh and the pride of life, pass without letting the brethren and all other abroad, where our columns are read and where we shall never see the people in this world, know how we look upon this temple and the description of it . . . They have utterly disregarded the views of the great body of the brotherhood, and, with the clear knowledge that an overwhelming majority was against them, they defiantly flourish this display before our faces![204]

It was the wealthy who were most subject to "worldly allurements" such as dancing, fairs, parties, and plays.

For Franklin it was not enough to say of these "they do no harm." One had to ask "do they do any good."[205] Indianapolis lawyer Ovid Butler had great influence within North Western Christian University and the American Christian Missionary Society, influence he made vocal in favor of the abolition of slavery and in support of the federal Union. Franklin attacked Butler and these "political" causes, implying that Hoosiers listened to Butler because he was wealthy. Franklin, with excellent credentials among the poor and simple, intended to show no deference to the rich.[206]

Organs began entering the Christian churches in the 1850s, often through the Sunday schools. Some members had introduced small cabinet organs or melodeons into their homes and appreciated their support of singing. Queries about them inevitably came to Franklin. He certainly knew the answer that Alexander Campbell once gave:

> The argument drawn from the Psalms in favor of instrumental music, is exceedingly apposite to the Roman Catholic, English Protestant, and Scotch Presbyterian churches, and even to the Methodist communities. Their churches having all the world in them—that is, all the fleshly progeny of all the communicants, and being founded on the Jewish pattern of things—baptism being given to all born into the world of these politico-ecclesiastic communities—I wonder not, then, that an organ, a fiddle, or a Jews-harp, should be requisite to stir up their carnal hearts, and work into ecstasy their animal souls, else "hosannahs languish on their tongues, and their devotions die." And that all persons who have no spiritual discernment, taste, or relish for their spiritual meditations, consolations and sympathies of renewed hearts, should call for such aid, is but natural. Pure water from the flinty rock has no attractions for the mere toper or wine-bibber. A little alcohol, or genuine Cogniac brandy, or good old Madeira, is essential to the beverage to make it truly refreshing. So to those who have no real devotion or spirituality in them, and whose animal nature flags under the oppression of church service, I think with Mr. G., that instrumental music would be not only a desideratum, but an essential prerequisite to fire up their souls to even animal devotion. But I presume, to all spiritually-minded Christians, such aids would be as a cow bell in a concert.[207]

Franklin continued Campbell's sarcastic mode. There might be appropriate occasions for instruments, he said,

> (1) Where a church never had or have lost the Spirit of Christ . . . (2) If a church has a preacher who never had, or has lost the Spirit of Christ, who has become a dry,

prosing and lifeless speaker . . . (3) If a church only intends being a fashionable society, a mere place of amusement and secular entertainment, and abandoning all idea of religion and worship . . . (4) If a church has in it a large number of dishonest and corrupt men . . . (5) If a church has given up all idea of trying to convert the world.[208]

The editorial staff of Campbell's *Millennial Harbinger* soon made peace with organs in churches.

> There are many things established and right, in the practical affairs of the church in this 19th century, that were not introduced in the days nor by the authority of the apostles—questions of mere expediency, that involve neither moral nor spiritual principle or teaching . . . We have no evidence that in apostolic days, the disciples owned houses, such as we call churches, at all.[209]

Mathes tiptoed the conservative side of the line. He said he was opposed to the use of the organ in worship but did not intend to divide any church over the issue. "I suffer no organ to drive me from my place in the church of Christ, nor from my duty as a disciple of Christ."[210] Bedford congregation got its organ and division in 1880 and Anderson introduced the instrument in 1882. Franklin said in 1867 that not ten congregations in the brotherhood were using the instrument but by 1885 the number had multiplied.[211]

For Franklin the use of an organ in Christian worship was never an option or a matter of expediency. Indeed the congregational singing might be bad enough to "scare even the rats from worship," but Franklin felt there were other ways to remedy that.[212] In Christian worship, what was not plain in the New Testament by illustration or direction was not permissible. There were plenty of musical instruments in the days of Jesus and plenty of precedent for their use in Old Testament practice but Franklin saw no record that Jesus or the apostles ever assisted worship with organ, melodeon, or violin. He said that modern Christians who introduced use of a musical instrument by majority vote of a congregation were violating the consciences of all those faithful worshipers who wished to stand with the first Christians. Such innovators he counted guilty of division, aggression, corruption, and apostasy. He said the pope of Rome was the one who had brought the organ from the theater into church worship. Even as a traveling evangelist, Franklin would not preach or worship where an organ was unless it was silenced for the time he was there. One congregation led singing with a flute. He tolerated it briefly and then decreed, "Hereafter we will dispense with the whistle." When the congregation at Bloomington introduced an organ in November of 1877, Franklin came to town the following spring to support a new congregation meeting in the courthouse.[213]

The "sects" or denominations did not fade away as scheduled. They did not even decrease but kept on growing alongside the Christians, regarding them as one more religious group to be integrated, refuted, or at least endured. Every town and village wrote its continuing history of conflicts and tensions. Christian agent Corbly Martin reported from Sweet Home in northern Indiana: "the Methodistic opposition has run to such an extravagant height, that it is truly becoming a pretty good auxiliary."

> In proselyting we are careful to bring them in only by breaking their hearts with the truth. We tell all men that we want not our peace disturbed by the ingress of any but such as are resolved to consecrate themselves wholly to the Lord. We say to them, "It will do neither you nor us any good, but a deal of harm, to baptize you, unless you have faith and repentance sufficient to break up the foundations of your love and practice of sin." Herein we are remarkably particular, because we cannot see how we are to save sinners by enlarging the congregation of the Lord with "a mass of ignorance and corruption"; and yet (do you believe it?) it is daily trumpeted in every corner of the land, that we preach water baptism alone for remission. "All they want of you is, to get you between two banks and give you a cold dipping!" All the slang and billingsgate of all the "Christian Advocates," ("falsely so called,") eastern and western, are reiterated throughout the length and breadth of our land, and employed against us. This I take as an indication that they are mortally afraid of us poor insignificant little farmers in our "Kentucky Jeans."[214]

D. Hodson at Russiaville said.

> We had the use of the Methodist church: our audiences were large and very attentive to hear the news of salvation and deliverance from sin. Our Methodist neighbors are getting alarmed at this point, and called us Water-Christians! No wonder, we have immersed the flower of their church at that point. They stated in my presence that the Presiding Elder would be there and teach the people the true mode of Baptism, and expose this water salvation![215]

At Saint Louis in Bartholomew County the Methodist circuit preacher locked the meeting house door against the Christian invader, took his whole congregation away with him to a Methodist meeting at Hope, and returned to join his flock in singing a Methodist song as the Campbellite preacher rode out of town.[216] After reporting that the Christian church in Indianapolis had added nearly two hundred members in the first three months of 1866 and had the second largest meeting house in the city, O. A. Burgess concluded:

> It is not to be wondered at that our religious neighbors love peace so much, and think discussions disturb the peace of mind that Christians ought to enjoy. They court peace and follow after peace; but they ought to know that the wisdom which cometh down from above is first pure, then peaceable. Let them not cry peace, peace; for there is no peace. We are sworn to eternal war against all forms of wickedness, whether the assumptions of the devil over the world, or the assumptions of the clergy over the Bible and the consciences of men.[217]

However, an increasing body of Christian church members and preachers in Indiana communities chose to have less war and more peace. They preferred to share in community religious observances, in pulpit exchanges, and in local ministerial associations. In the name of Christian charity or of desire for union, and in view of their profession of faith and manner of life, non-immersed persons in the denominations were being treated as fellow believers and even being admitted to communion with Christian congregations at the Lord's Table. In his early maturity and the fourteenth year of his editorship, Alexander Campbell had taken a guarded but positive stance toward the "pious unimmersed."

> Should I see a sectarian Baptist or a Pedobaptist more spiritually-minded, more generally conformed to the requisitions of the Messiah, than one who precisely acquiesces with me in the theory or practice of immersion as I teach, doubtless the former rather than the latter, would have my cordial approbation and love as a Christian. So I judge, and so I feel. It is the image of Christ the Christian looks for and loves; and this does not consist in being exact in a few items, but in general devotion to the whole truth as far as known . . . There is no occasion, then, for making immersion, on a profession of faith, absolutely essential to a Christian—though it may be greatly essential to his sanctification and comfort. My right hand and my right eye are greatly essential to my usefulness and happiness, but not to my life; and as I could not be a perfect man without them, so I cannot be a perfect Christian without a right understanding and a cordial reception of immersion in its true and scriptural meaning and design. But he that thence infers that none are Christians but the immersed, as greatly errs as he who affirms that none are alive but those of clear and full vision.[218]

For Campbell and for the continuing editorial staff of the *Millennial Harbinger* and for editors Mathes and Goodwin of the *Christian Record* and for an increasing number of the churches, this meant that particular classes of persons were neither invited nor rejected at communion services of Christians. Isaac Errett said it: "Spread the table in the name of the Lord, for the Lord's people, and allow all to come who will, each on his own responsibility." Editor Robert Richardson agreed. "Who will say that Luther was not a Christian," asked editor W. K. Pendleton. "Will Bro. Franklin say so?"[219] Even a Baptist debater once pointed out to Franklin the implication of his saying that, no matter what change of heart, there was no salvation without the water: "See in what an awful dilemma my opponent involves nine-tenths of the professedly Christian world."[220] Franklin said all this ecumenical equivocation was "a shrinking from our principles, yielding to popular feeling and a pseudo philosophy; mistaken, sophistical and sickly charity."[221] "Where is the use of parleying over the question of communing with unimmersed persons? Did the first Christians commune with unimmersed persons? It is admitted they did not. Shall we, then, deliberately do what they did not do?"[222]

Most troublesome of all, the churches were being torn over the issues of slavery and war. Franklin was an editor so every position he held was a public position; his interrogators left him no room for ambiguity. The unambiguous positions of Franklin had little chance of pleasing his contemporaries. At a time when public opinion was inflamed with the fever of war, Franklin was a pacifist who felt that neither he nor any other Christian should ever go to war for any cause.[223] He was a resident of the North and a loyal citizen of the Union who personally disapproved of the institution of slavery. That was enough to put off many of his supporters in the South. Yet his sharpest conflict was with Northerners afflicted with what he called "one-ideaism."

> A man addicted to one-ideaism can no more cover it than can a leopard change his spots. If he attempts to pray, he will commence with something else as a stepping-stone, regularly and unmistakably paving his way to his favorite idea. When it is put forth, and he is delivered of it, he is relieved for the time being, especially if he finds that some one is annoyed by it. If you call on him for an exhortation, a sermon, or if he writes, he may wind round and round, trace backward and forward, but it will, in spite of himself, in all his efforts to conceal it, be manifest to all, that he takes no interest in all he is saying, only as it subserves his purpose, in paving the way to the one idea, the centre around which the whole man revolves, and to which his whole existence is, for the time being, subservient. If that one idea is not dragged in, the man is not relieved, his burden is still upon his soul, and he is in

travail waiting to be delivered. You will see this class of men at conventions and meetings, both political and religious, without the most distant idea of promoting the objects of the convention or meeting, and with no higher aim than introducing their idea to notice, making the meeting an engine and men met under other obligations, and with the ostensible object of the meeting fully known to them, instruments to carry the pet idea on the high road to fortune.[224]

The "one idea" which especially irritated Franklin was the abolition of slavery. Since the master-slave relation was not overtly condemned in the Scriptures and since he believed that controversies over slavery and preservation of the Union were political matters, he felt these were not concerns of the churches. Like Alexander Campbell, he wanted silence on these subjects in the churches and church agencies. The churches, as spiritual institutions, should be left unscathed by political conflicts so they could press forward with their primary work of evangelism.[225]

When the war came Franklin quickly lost one thousand southern subscribers, mostly in middle Tennessee, just because he was located in the North. Christians in the North resented his failure to side with them against slavery and the South. In Indiana this resentment came first from such pioneer abolitionists as those associated with Ovid Butler at North Western Christian University at Indianapolis or with John Boggs who began his efforts in Bartholomew County. As the war developed the resentment against Franklin widened to include Elijah Martindale, Elijah Goodwin, Love H. Jameson, and the bulk of Christian members and clergy loyal to the North. The editor of the *Indianapolis Daily Journal* called Franklin a secessionist, Franklin's *American Christian Review* a secessionist publication, and Franklin's position "the meanest kind of treason—cowardly, insidious treason." Republicans for Lincoln counted Franklin unpatriotic. Democrats against Lincoln sounded him out but found he was no political friend of theirs. "We want no Republican churches nor Democrat churches, but Christian churches," he said. "There is no South nor North in our gospel." So he wanted to keep the pages of the *Review* free of discussion of slavery and the war at a time when the people of the nation seemed to care about little else. He had offered eight columns on slavery entitled "Where Is the Safe Ground" but that brought no peace. As the major northern cooperations and missionary society meetings yielded to pressure to produce strenuous "war resolutions" to endorse the Union and condemn the South, he felt more isolated from the leaders of the Christian fellowship and more angry.[226]

Remarkably, Franklin had remained in demand as an evangelistic preacher in both North and South right through the war years. No less remarkably, the circulation of the *Review* began to rebuild during the war period as "thousands of old friends returned to its support."[227] Mail to some sections of the South reopened in 1862. In recovering subscriptions there, Franklin reasserted his statement of the spirituality of the church.

> Our paper knows nothing but Jesus, and Him crucified—teaches nothing but the religion of Christ; maintains and defends nothing but the things of the kingdom of God and the name of Jesus, and is adapted to all sections and parts of the world where they love our Lord Jesus Christ, and His religion. We have determined to maintain one sheet free from all worldly issues, and make an effort to save all men.[228]

Franklin admired Tolbert Fanning, conservative Christian editor of the *Gospel Advocate* and founder of Franklin College near Nashville, Tennessee. This had become an especially warm friendship after Franklin visited the Fannings in spring of 1854. He was irritated with Fanning and David Lipscomb when they reestablished their *Gospel Advocate* in 1866 with an overt appeal to sectionalism. They said: "The fact that we had not a single paper known to us that Southern people could read without having their feelings wounded by political insinuations and slurs, had more to do with calling the *Advocate* into existence, than all other circumstances combined."[229] Fanning and Lipscomb could espouse the spirituality of the church and deplore any political or social statements by churches with considerable applause in the South. Their constituents had borne the sufferings of the South in defeat and were affronted by the war resolutions and loyalty oaths imposed by Northerners. They offered a southern paper for southern readers. Franklin, with the same religious stand and the same definition of the church, had a less automatic constituency. Slowly he linked with his southern colleagues again. Their common resistance to what they saw as innovations in church organization and manners and their shared anger at political actions by church bodies moved them together. They did speak the same language. Like Franklin, Lipscomb was a pacifist on principle with a reputation for "an excess of frankness." Both felt that those who had pressed the conflict had somehow abandoned God and the Bible.[230]

Five hundred new subscriptions for Franklin's *Review* arrived in the first two months of 1863. There were fifteen hundred new subscribers in the first three months of 1864 to bring the list to a new high of more than six thousand. Franklin was finding his people again. Some of these subscriptions were regained from the South but most were coming from Illinois and Indiana with Ohio, Kentucky, Missouri, and Iowa not far behind.[231]

By the end of 1866 Franklin came out against missionary societies in general and the national American Christian Missionary Society in particular. This was the Franklin long known as a champion of cooperations, the Franklin who had smashed such early Indiana opponents as lawyer Jeremiah Smith of Winchester, and physician Nathaniel Field of Jeffersonville with proofs of biblical precedent and logical rationale for organized missionary enterprises.[232] Whatever Mathes and Goodwin and Burnet said on behalf of organized missions, Franklin had been saying with more telling force. Out of the fire in his bones for evangelism, he had stoutly supported Indiana's pioneer plan for a state missionary society as delineated by Elijah Goodwin in 1849 and the national society founded later that year. Something had to be done, he said. He had been a regular platform speaker for Christian missionary societies and secretary pro tem for the national society in 1857. Out of his love for the teaching of the Christian fellowship and the joy of his career in it, he had reveled in the missionary meetings and in the contacts he had with the leading preachers there. In all this missionary enterprise he had been very inspirable and very inspiring for nearly twenty years.[233]

Now he switched. He said the missionary societies were not working very well; they raised little money and sent out few evangelists. In the missionary societies an organization and leadership had arisen interested in questions wider than evangelistic preaching. The organizational directions in which these leaders seemed to be taking the churches were the very directions Franklin had gone on record to oppose. He said he had written more than anybody on behalf of these societies which were to be confined exclusively to mission work but now had been forced to conclude they could not be confined. By their very nature they were "nothing but annoyances, opening the way for amendments, modifications, or changes of some sort, distracting our meetings, and were not only useless but injurious."[234]

> What, then, is the difference about? It is about a certain kind of co-operation, or associated effort; not in spreading the gospel, or evangelizing, but of raising money, forming an ecclesiasticism and grasping power; usurping authority to tax the people, negotiate union with "other denominations," employ "pastors" for churches, keep out impostors, heretics, etc., without spreading the gospel at

all. These and other matters caused the difference and form the ground of trouble.[235]

The current leadership did not cast Franklin off lightly. They respected his missionary record and his present power. Editor W. K. Pendleton of the *Millennial Harbinger* at Bethany responded with a mixture of surprise, anger, and holy sorrow. It was an error, he said, to hold that everything for which there was not a "thus saith the Lord" must be rejected.

> For ourself we have a short creed on the subject. We believe it is the divinely imposed duty of the church to seek to spread the gospel to every creature; to do this she must send out preachers; to do this she must raise money; to do this she must have concerted, that is, organized, action—and to do this is to cooperate. This is the ground we stand upon, and which we are pledged to defend. As God shall help us, we will do it.[236]

When Franklin proposed what he thought was a more democratic and decentralized plan for missions in which the individual churches would more closely control their contributions, the national fellowship in convention adopted his plan. But that "Louisville Plan" failed too, its system inoperative at the local church and district level.[237] Franklin was not sorry it was gone. "The Conventions themselves are the wrongs," he said, "and we can not cure the evil by attending and trying to mend them. There is but one cure for them, and that is to abolish them."[238]

Serving as watchdog against so many perceived errors and incursions gave Franklin a very negative image. In addition to the whole range of opponents in the denominational and pagan world, he now stood against the majority of his own Christian fellowship as well. Alexander Campbell was dead and schism was apparent. Franklin said:

> There are two elements in our midst, entirely alien to each other, at war, as much as flesh and spirit, in Paul's description. Some are clearly drifting into one current, and some into the other. The different things in which they manifest themselves, at one time in this and then in that, are not the cause, but only the occasion for manifestation. These two elements have existed fifteen years or more, but their growth has been continuous, and is increasing of late. In one half-hour's conversation the one or the other can be detected. The symptoms are discernible to any person of moderate spiritual discernment.[239]

What was happening to the Christian colleges so displeased him that he doubted if any college should ever be endowed and take the risk of future violation of the founder's purpose.[240] His patience grew shorter and his language more bitter.

The main body of Christians, especially some younger progressives, grew weary of him. They called him an "old fogy," a "legalist," a "croaker," an "alarmist," the "prince of wails," a "millstone around the neck of the reformation." They spoke of "tyranny of opinion," of "unwritten creeds," and of "iron bedsteads."[241] In his article entitled "Franklinian Stupidity," Carl Crabb said that people like Franklin "seem to be wholly incapable of appreciating anything that rises above the first plain, plodding ideas of Bro. Campbell and his co-laborers forty years ago." He asked "Who cannot see the difference between this cramped, cribbed, and confined discipleship and that more liberal theology now advocated by our more advanced scribes?"[242] Franklin's opponents felt his *Review* no longer represented the thinking of the larger fellowship so they established a stock company with $20,000 capital in 1865 and employed Isaac Errett to edit a new church paper called the *Christian Standard*. The *Standard* and Franklin's *Review* became regular combatants.[243]

But Franklin did not fade away. He had moved back to Indiana in spring of 1864, still publishing his *Review* from Cincinnati. Even if he had less acceptance now among the wealthy in the city churches and fewer invitations from the leading ministers, he was invited and reinvited to conduct meetings in the towns and rural places where he added hundreds of converts. From his home at Anderson the "Hoosier preacher," as his biographer calls him, saturated Indiana and Kentucky with extemporaneous sermons which he called "nothing short or pretty."[244] The two volumes of his sermons which he reduced to writing and published were printed again and again.[245] In 1873 he said he had so many calls for his preaching that he could "not go to one place out of ten" in response to invitations. These included invitations to go preaching in Ohio, Illinois, and Tennessee. The *Review* remained his editorial voice; he was still writing copy for it on the morning of 22 October 1878, the day he died. Evident in all this was a substantial body of people who counted Franklin a hero and savior of their movement to restore the ancient order of things. Franklin came to regard himself, and to be regarded by them, as their spokesman for opposition to the leadership, opposition to the present state of things, and opposition to the way things were going. They filled his mailbox with their fears of the doings of the progressives. To them he was nearly apostolic, "Old Ben." And his paper they called the "Old Reliable."[246]

Daniel Sommer (1850–1940)

When Benjamin Franklin died in 1878, there seemed to be no shortage of capable men to succeed him. Among these were W. B. F. Treat and Alfred Ellmore of Indiana, both powerful preachers and writers devoted to Franklin and his views.

> Who was the person Ben Franklin had in mind to be his successor as editor of the *Review*? There could be little question that Franklin, well-meaning though he was, had unconsciously encouraged a jealous spirit among his admirers. As a means of encouraging young men, Franklin held out to them the possibility that they might succeed him as the editor of his paper. Several young men, each one thinking of himself as fit to wear Franklin's mantle, found themselves jealous of each other, and that jealousy split the forces of those who opposed innovations in the North.[247]

Publisher George W. Rice declared that John F. Rowe was Franklin's real preference and installed Rowe as editor of the *Review*. Rowe had been writing for the *Review* since 1867; Franklin had often spoken highly of him and had taken pains to provide him visibility in Indiana. Rowe's eight-year tenure as editor of the *Review* was stormy and satisfied few. W. B. F. Treat succeeded Rowe in 1886 but only for a few months.[248]

Near the end of that year the *Review* got a new owner and editor. W. H. Krutsinger of Ellettsville said: "There is no more *American Christian Review*. The paper that Franklin founded and run until his death is a thing of the past. The best thing you can now do is to take and read the *Gospel Advocate*."[249] But Krutsinger's obituary for the *Review* was premature. Daniel Sommer was the new owner, a man destined to make the *Review* a northern counterpart to the South's *Gospel Advocate* as a continuing voice for Christian conservatives. He would emerge as a man of great influence in Indiana and would eventually bring his paper to Indianapolis.

Sommer was the child of a widowed seamstress in Maryland; he was a child of deep poverty, required to earn his way by doing manual work for hire from the age of nine. He matured into a giant who could hoist an anvil with one hand which most men could barely lift with two and with an ax could equal the output of two normal woodsmen. For his education there were only brief patches of schooling between the ages of eight and twelve plus one term in Louisa Harwood's Sunday school which wakened his religious interest. John Dallas Everett, one of his employers, taught him the principles of Alexander Campbell's reformation. Having been immersed by the Christians in August of 1869, he wanted to preach.[250] His counselors suggested some training at Bethany College.

> After reaching college I soon found I should have gone to a common school. Probably no young man ever went to college for the purpose of taking a course of study who was more ignorant than I was when I reached Bethany . . . What I had learned in earlier life concerning arithmetic I had forgotten almost entirely, and the same was true with reference to grammar. So when I reached Bethany College I did not know the difference between the object and subject of a verb. Declensions and conjugations had all left me, and I was nearly as innocent of the construction of words and sentences as though I had never looked at the pages of a grammar.[251]

Sommer compensated for lack of funds and lack of educational background with an overplus of conviction and ambition. However, his Bethany experience was mixed at best. Elocution professor Robert Kidd was a mentor and hero to him but others were less appreciated.

> Early in my life at Bethany I saw there was a difference between disciples and disciples. It became evident that some disciples were of the primitive or apostolic type, while others were of the modern or plastic type. Those constituting the former class I saw had stability, while those constituting the latter class had flexibility. The former disciples held that the world should bend to the church; the latter disciples held that the church should bend to the world.[252]

He was overtly critical of the college scene, of his fellow students, of president W. K. Pendleton and the faculty, of his financial sponsors in Baltimore, and of Bethany's local Christian congregation.[253]

In spring of 1871 Sommer met Franklin.

> Elder Benjamin Franklin, founder and editor of the American Christian Review, was preaching at Wellsburg, seven miles from Bethany, and I obtained permission to leave college a few days and go out to hear him . . . Grand old man! I only had the privilege of hearing him preach three times; but I heard him talk in conversation, and learned that in the Gospel he was certainly a master. I was most favorably impressed with him, and he seemed not to forget me.[254]

Sommer soon chose the Hoosier Franklin as the model for his ministry. They were colleagues in the search for the ancient order of things. They opposed innovations. They were sharp critics of many present tendencies of the Christian churches.

Operating from churches in Pennsylvania and Ohio, Sommer proceeded to earn a reputation as a successful evangelist like Franklin. He sent in some short articles which Franklin printed in the *Review*. In their correspondence Franklin did his usual thing of speculating about his successor as editor of the *Review*. He thought Sommer looked like a candidate.[255] He said in May of 1878, "I wish to open the way for you to write yourself into the confidence of the friends of truth, so that when I am gone they will look to you to defend the faith."[256] Sommer thought that meant he had been selected to make his mark in the fellowship and to take Franklin's place. He prepared a series of articles opposing theological schools, entitled it "Educating Preachers," and submitted the series for publication.

> From Satan's first contact with our race, till now, the one, great, fundamental offense of religious man has been his unsatisfied feeling with the God-given in religion. Of this feeling, colleges for ministerial education are an outgrowth. By whomsoever founded, or defended, they are a human device—a pride-fostering and church-impoverishing device.[257]

Before the articles could be published Franklin had died, and in spite of Sommer's inquiries the editorship went to another.[258]

Sommer was not easily dissuaded. In his ministerial poverty he joined L. F. Bittle to launch a monthly paper named the *Octograph*, named to show its apostolic faithfulness to the eight writers of the New Testament. By 1885 he had established his own press at Richwood, Ohio, where his three sons did much of the printing and his wife Kate did much of the publication. Then in 1886 he heard that the *American Christian Review* was faltering. He wrote to Edwin Allen in Cincinnati: "My Dear Sir:— Is the American Christian Review for sale? If so, on what terms? If it does not change hands, the editor of a certain rival paper will kill it with the club of outside ownership!"[259] After an all-night negotiating session, Sommer bought the *Review* without a down payment, for twelve promissory notes of $1,000 each and no security except a chattel mortgage on the paper itself. Word was circulated that a "prominent evangelist" was buying the *Review*. The first issue of the paper showing Sommer as "proprietor and publisher" was the one for 23 December 1886. It carried a large picture of Franklin on the front and announced Sommer as the new owner. Sommer said the name "American" was too localized and the name "Christian" was too sacred to be used in connection with a human enterprise, so he merged his papers as the *Oc-tographic Review*. Now Sommer was really Franklin's successor.[260]

Six months before he died, Franklin had advised Sommer to succeed by occupying "the most radical ground." Sommer should "take hold of some formidable men and publications and handle them with a master hand. Take hold of departures whenever you see them. In one word, defend the truth."[261] Franklin's final position as defender of the restoration of the ancient order of things and champion of the militant conservatives was just the beginning point for Sommer. Franklin and many others had long doubted that the Christian fellowship could ever suffer division so long as there was no body of creedal material to define differences and no ecclesiastical structure to vote or enforce a division. Sommer spoke for those who felt that the practices of modern Christians had already forced a separation. He used his popularity as a preacher and his periodical to precipitate and guarantee division. His "Arraignment of the New Digressives among Disciples of Christ" offered a round hundred complaints against beliefs and practices more or less common among churches of Christ.[262] He thought much of the trouble was the fault of the rich.

> As time advanced such of those churches as assembled in large towns and cities gradually became proud, or, at least sufficiently worldly-minded to desire popularity, and in order to attain that unscriptural end they adopted certain popular arrangements such as the hired pastor, the church choir, instrumental music, man-made societies to advance the gospel, and human devices to raise money. In so doing they divided the brotherhood of disciples.[263]

But Sommer never hesitated to list the ways in which Alexander Campbell himself had gone astray.

> My own estimate of Campbell is that he was always honest, dignified, eloquent. But he was a rhetorician rather than a logician, and his popularity caused him to forget much that he had written. Readers of his writings should have accepted truth he offered but rejected his errors. But as they did not all do this, we have two or three orders of "disciples" . . . Differences between Alexander Campbell and Daniel Sommer are so numerous and serious that I have but one prospect of ever imitating him in one particular. I have been informed that he spoke much of his time leaning on his cane. And if I ever need to use a cane in the pulpit, I may imitate him in that particular. But, since I reflect on the past, I recollect that nearly fifty years ago I had an attack of sciatic rheumatism—and then I used a cane! And that was the nearest to him that I ever was, I suppose. Though I don't suppose he ever addressed an audience of more than five

thousand people on one occasion. And I did that, as many supposed, at Sand Creek in Shelby County, Illinois, when the Sand Creek Declaration was offered. And that was the declaration in which lines of demarcation were drawn, as never before, between Churches of Christ and the so called "Christian Church." That demarcation assisted many to understand they should not follow those who were not careful to follow the Savior in name and organization; doctrine and practice, worship and work.[264]

That appearance at the Sand Creek Meeting House in Illinois in August of 1889 was symbolic of his program and mission. Christians had been holding a "homecoming" at Sand Creek annually since 1873. In his later years Ben Franklin had faithful followers in this area; they had written him to express their "hearty indorsement of the very noble, true and unwavering position you have ever maintained." Now that Franklin was gone they invited Sommer to the 1889 meeting as their editorial spokesman. It was an anniversary occasion designed for a "Declaration" and "Address" after the style of the *Declaration and Address* of Thomas Campbell eighty years before. Some local elders drafted the "Declaration" on Saturday the 17th; Sommer said two years later that Peter P. Warren wrote the document. Sommer was invited to approve and read the "Declaration" and to deliver the "Address" on Sunday the 18th. His invitation was to "make a thorough exposition of Modern Schoolism" even if it took two hours. He preached for an hour and forty minutes in the morning, collected $12,000 to save the *Review* by paying its debts, and added a further one hour sermon after the homecoming dinner.[265]

All parts of the program were rehearsals of the scriptural and historical bases of the conservative restoration movement. Even more pointedly, they were rehearsals of charges of violations of the ancient order by contemporary Christians: missionary societies, instrumental music in worship, the one-man pastor system, modern methods of raising money. Sommer contrasted the sensible, humble, and loyal disciples recognizable by their primitive simplicity with the fashion-conscious and proud class living mostly in towns and cities. The force of Sommer's rhetoric did not invite dissent; there were probably no dissenters present anyway.[266] The conclusion of the 940-word "Declaration" pronounced the division.[267]

It is, therefore, with the view, if possible, of counteracting the usages and practices that have crept into the churches, that this effort . . . is made. And, now, in closing up this address and declaration, we state that we are impelled from a sense of duty to say, that all such as are guilty of teaching, or allowing and practicing the many

innovations and corruptions to which we have referred, that after being admonished and having had sufficient time for reflection, if they do not turn away from such abominations, that we can not and will not regard them as brethren.[268]

Nothing would probably have come of the Sand Creek meeting itself except for Daniel Sommer. But Sommer had a conviction that division was inevitable, he had a sizable constituency of the same mind, and he had the *Review*. Now he had an event and a written text to lift up. By 1892 supporters of the Sand Creek Declaration were urged to insert a clause in every church property deed to prohibit instruments of music and other innovations.[269] One reported form of it provided that introduction of "inventions, devices of uninspired men, choirs, concerts, festivals, voting, or anything not plainly taught in the New Testament" should result in forfeiture, the property passing to "one or more Disciples who oppose all said innovations."[270]

In spring of 1892 Sommer visited Indiana "preaching on Lord's days and lecturing against infidelity during the week." He was encouraged by good prospects for the conservatives at North Salem, Bedford, Orleans, Williams, Springville, and Owensburg.[271] In May he observed:

In the early part of our history as disciples it is a fact that discourses on "Oneness in Christ" were very common. But who preaches on that subject now? In view of the mischievous work of those who advocate humanisms in the worship and work of the church that subject is seldom discussed. It is among the themes of the past . . . What then shall we do? Simply move onward. The Sand Creek Declaration is being adopted, and those who will not do right are purged out as old leaven. In the course of a few years the Church of Christ will stand entirely separated from the Christian Church. Then there will be no more fellowship between them than there now is between the Church of Christ and any other branch of sectarianism. Hallelujah![272]

Eventually every Christian congregation and periodical would be driven to recognize the division. The *Christian Standard* felt compelled to condemn Sommerism and Sand Creekism and to call for disfellowship of Sommer by the churches.[273] Alfred Ellmore, a Hoosier writer for the conservative *Christian Leader* in Cincinnati, named four possible courses a conservative could take. The only really viable one for him seemed to be "separate and have peace."

This leaven of unrighteousness has been twenty-five years in gathering its mass of corruption. And like the man of sin, whom it serves, it has come in the garb of righteousness, hence the deception . . . Like Catholicism and Mormonism, and every other ism, it is growing, and will continue to grow, as an eating cancer, and unless we cut it out the body will be ruined.[274]

Daniel Sommer always felt that his *Octographic Review* belonged in Indiana. In May of the first year of its publication he said:

> For years we have thought of Indianapolis as the city above all others from which the publication that would work a revolution should be issued. On this subject we have not changed our mind. Indiana was the home of the *Review's* founder, and doubtless is the state in which his influence was most largely felt. Indianapolis is the city in which about 15 lines of Rail Road concenter. Besides, it is perhaps more nearly than any other city in the center of our great brotherhood.[275]

In August of the same year he added:

> Something over four weeks ago we left home for this state (Ind.) and we must confess that the more we see of it the better we like it. The utter absence of aristocracy is delightful to a plain man. People seem to estimate each other at the point of character and regardless of wealth or grammar . . . Brethren of Indiana, we still think favorably of Indianapolis as the future home of the *Review*. It is a central place with excellent facilities. The Lord willing we shall get there, and hope all the people will say, "Amen."[276]

His services remained in great demand among Hoosiers and in 1894 the *Review* came to Indiana to stay. As Sommer later remembered, "The Sommers 'hit the rails' for Indianapolis—some in a huge boxcar with household and *Review* necessities plus the family horse,—others in a passenger coach. On arrival we boarded a trolly car for Northwest Indianapolis, where a large house had already been selected for us."[277]

At Indianapolis he supplemented the *Review* by publishing five novelettes, much in the Socratic style of his mentor Benjamin Franklin. In these a heroic plain person typically routed all religious professionals and demonstrated the superior claims of the Christian churches.[278] He appeared prominently as an expert witness in church property cases in the courts at Indianapolis, Salem, and Winchester. His impact was undeniable. Two years after Sommer moved to Indiana, E. B. Scofield of the Indiana Christian Missionary Society was concerned about the future of Christian churches in southern Indiana. One separation had already taken place. Scofield said Sommer's "loyal brethren" were "engaged in a campaign to stampede as many churches as possible, and close them to all aggressive and constructive enterprises." The

Christian Standard for 12 September and 5 December 1896 gave more details of the activities of "antis" in southern Indiana.[279] A later liberal historian confirmed the leadership of Sommer.

> The most serious schism in the Christian Churches occurred in southern Indiana, beginning in late 1895. It seemed to center in Lawrence and Owen counties. The congregations in this area, for the most part, were extremely conservative, independent, and uncooperative. Their leaders objected to Sunday schools, missionary societies, the Christian Endeavor movement, salaried (professional) pastors, and most of all to the use of instrumental music in church worship. The "ruling elders" in these congregations had faith only in the Bible, the *Firm Foundation*, the *Christian Leader*, the *Octographic Review*, and in their own ability to determine truth in religion. They held to the view that those who became members of a missionary or aid society, a Sunday school, or an Endeavor society were heretics and should be rejected by the church. One congregation excluded twenty-six members for belonging to Christian Endeavor, and a like number of "sisters" were excluded from another church for belonging to an aid society. Communication between these brethren and those in churches cooperating with Disciple institutions and agencies began to cease in the middle 1880's and almost came to an end by 1890. When a congregation took this extremist position it was usually indicated by stating that it had accepted the "Sand Creek" platform. In Indiana, the Sand Creek platform, Daniel Sommer, and the *Octographic Review* were almost synonymous terms. They meant schism.[280]

In one other area Sommer extended the position of Franklin. Out of his alienation from the continuing leadership at Bethany and his disappointment with the histories of colleges founded by the Christian fellowship, Franklin had done some heavy grumbling about church related schools.

> We did not and could not foresee that colleges could be made a power for evil as well as for good; that all depends on whose hands they are in; that infidels could be made professors; that worldly-minded men could become professors; that men who are not sound in the faith, have not the love of the truth, could get control of colleges, and that they could be turned upon the Bible and made engines to batter down the very thing they were intended to build up to maintain, defend and perpetuate, and made instruments to pull it down. We did not foresee, and could not, that men could get the control of colleges and vast sums of money, and conceive the idea that it is sectarian to be under the control of Chris-

tians and teach the Bible in those colleges; that a college of the Bible could be perverted from its purpose and turned away from its genuine friends.[281]

Franklin finally concluded that all schools should be "as purely secular as a bookstore," that religious instruction should be done entirely through the local church or by free enterprise of individuals, and that endowments were dangerous.[282]

Sommer absorbed some of this mindset against Bible colleges from Franklin. It correlated well with his own uneasiness as a student at Bethany and that of his sons Fred and Frank at Milligan College in Tennessee. The aversion was aggravated when his fellow conservatives in the South and in the border states kept establishing Bible colleges after the model of the Nashville Bible School. They were doing aggressive fund raising north of the Ohio as well and this incurred Sommer's wrath.[283]

> David Lipscomb as a plain and humble man, did not know what evils he introduced by what he did in advocating a so-called "Bible School." In the North we contended: "Let the State teach in secular domains, and let the Church teach in regard to faith." And I have mentioned two places (Bloomington, Ind., and Wichita, Kansas) where this contention is becoming established without even an extra building beside the meeting house in which the church worships. This plan is scriptural, and therefore is economical and safe. And, besides all this, we may safely say that a long and unpleasant controversy might have been avoided, by adopting it all over the brotherhood.[284]

Sommer accused Bible colleges of fostering pride, of developing a sense of "clergy" among college trained preachers which inferred that a man ought not to preach without a college education, and of being the main breeding ground for digressions from the ancient order. His energy was long consumed in contending against "using the Lord's money to establish religio-secular schools and giving them a sacred name as though they were divine institutions."[285]

After years of debating school administrators, of offending his friends, and of defending himself against charges of being an enemy of education, Sommer concluded that the southern brethren had become sufficiently sensitized to guard themselves against this error. In summary he said, "The controversy required of me from five to ten years' writing and preaching to save the churches of Christ north of the Ohio River from being deceived by the 'college craze,' which was common in the Southland."[286] Indiana developed no Bible college for the conservative churches of Christ.

Alexander Campbell and Indiana

Alexander Campbell was the primary teacher for Indiana's Christians. It was he who shaped the model of the faith which they treasured and who worded their plea to the world for union on the basis of the New Testament. His teaching and his answers to queries and his response to the events of four decades of church life set the tone and much of the content for Indiana's Christian periodicals. Hoosiers admired his achievements and venerated his person. Nevertheless there was often tension between Campbell and his Hoosier constituents. "Exuberantly fertile" was his favorite phrase for Indiana. It could have described the religious environment as well as the natural climate and soil. Campbell was working very hard. Especially after the founding of Bethany College in 1840, he had his hands full. He wanted patience and support; Indiana tended to be impatient and independent. Along with those marvelous reports of growth from Indiana's Christian evangelists came annoying evidences of non-conformity. Indiana seemed prone to break out, to run ahead of Campbell's plan in oblique directions.

First of all, the Hoosiers felt neglected. Alexander Campbell did not come to Indiana very often. He said in the *Harbinger* in 1834 that he had received a hundred calls to visit. "If we had the wings of an eagle, and the strength of Samson, we could not answer these queries." But Hoosiers felt Campbell should pay as much attention to Indiana as he did to the more cultivated society of Kentucky and Virginia. In 1838 he was moved to say "as soon as I can."[287] James Mathes tried especially hard but unsuccessfully to get him to Indianapolis for the first state meeting in 1839. "The desire of the brethren is, that brother A. Campbell would attend the meeting. Can you come? Will you come, brother Campbell?"[288]

When visiting Kentucky in 1840 Campbell repeated an earlier fleeting contact with the convenient river towns of New Albany and Madison but the interior of Indiana was still unvisited. In June of 1841, B. K. Smith of Indianapolis was still pleading "Can you not come? Do try." In 1846 Campbell reported that he had actually thought of touring Indiana on his way to the Illinois state meeting but had decided not to take the chance of contracting malaria.[289] By 1848 there was discussion in Indiana about founding a college. Love H. Jameson of Indianapolis voiced the discontent: "Indiana has been neglected by our brethren from abroad; why I know not, but it is a fact, that a man with half an eye can see; and as an Indianian in every sense of the word, when by our own unassisted efforts we have been able to help ourselves, I go in decidedly for Indiana and nothing else."[290]

It was the college that got Alexander Campbell's attention. Campbell was president of Bethany College and was wearing himself out in an effort to get it supported and endowed as the chief college for the Christian fellowship. Indiana's support for Bethany had been less than heroic. Campbell's published chart of contributions to Bethany for 1843–44 showed Virginia with pledges of $11,362.75 and Kentucky with $10,499.00 in pledges. For the same period Indiana had pledged $257.50 and had paid $2.00.[291] Then in spring of 1850 Campbell received a letter from Ovid Butler of Indianapolis. Part of it was about a visit to Indiana.

> There are some, and indeed, many of us, who cannot avoid the conviction, that in religion as in politics, the south claims and receives the principal attention of our leading brethren . . . We are anxious that you should visit the interior of this State, and especially Indianapolis, but we fear that further importunities would prove as unavailing as the past has [sic] been.[292]

The energizer came in the section of Butler's letter which said:

> At the last session of the Legislature of this State, the brethren procured a charter for "The North-Western Christian University," to be located at Indianapolis. I send you a copy of the charter in a separate envelop, and hope you will bestow some attention upon it, and notice the subject in the Harbinger, in such terms as you may think it deserves.[293]

Within the year Campbell found room in his schedule to make a long tour of the interior of Indiana even though "in autumn, Indiana has been celebrated for fevers, and in winter, for impassible roads."[294] In the meantime he vented his rage on the college plan. He hated the emphasis on regional loyalty to the Northwest. He resented what appeared to be pretension in the name "University." He asserted the priority of Bethany College on every count and his intention to press the logic of that priority on the Hoosiers.

> One good institution, well organized, well furnished with an able cohort of teachers, well patronized by the brethren and the public, is better than ten such as we are likely to have got up and spirited into life by such arguments and efforts, that tend much more to schism, rivalry, and false ambition, than to union, harmony, and successful action. I hope the brethren will hasten leisurely, and hear all the premises and arguments before they act in such a way as to create half-a-dozen of ill-

begotten, mishappen, club-footed, imbecile schools, under the name and title of Colleges and Universities.[295]

In many respects Alexander Campbell's tour of Indiana in 1850 was a triumph. He was in the state from 5 to 26 November and declared it exuberantly fertile four times. He crisscrossed the central portion of the state where Christian churches had already matured and grown strong. He went to Madison, Columbus, Bedford, Edinburgh, Rushville, Connersville, Metamora, and Brookville. At Martinsville cries of Hoosier babies defeated his efforts to speak but almost everywhere he was met by large crowds and large appreciation. His reputation grew during his engagements at Indianapolis until on Sunday, 8 November, he preached for two hours "to the largest concourse that could assemble in any house in the State" including the Governor and most members of the state constitutional convention. Next day he accepted an invitation to visit the convention and lead its members in prayer. During his three visits to Bloomington he renewed his acquaintance with President Wylie and preached twice on the weekend "in the spacious hall of the University of Indiana, in the presence of a very large, attentive, and deeply interested auditory, embracing its students and faculty."[296]

Campbell did not trim his message to avoid controversy. As part of his discourse at the University on Saturday he explained at length why use of the "Lord's Prayer" was not "in accordance with the genius and character of the present dispensation of that kingdom."

> Who, then, enlightened in the Christian Religion, can pray, "thy kingdom come?" I want no other proof of the darkness that yet covers much of Protestant Christendom, than the papal ceremonious hebdomidal [sic] abuse of "the Lord's prayer," as it is named in many hundred synagogues in this so-called "Bible enlightened land."[297]

And at the University on Sunday he offered "a discourse of more than an hour and three-fourths" on Paul's allegory in Galatians 4 contrasting the children of the bond woman Hagar with the children of the free woman Sarah.

> "The bond woman and her son," representing all sectarian churches—Rome, England and Scotland—with their national, animal and sensual hierarchies, and all their children scattered up and down in these thirty United States. "The child of the free woman," represented all that are born supernaturally, as Isaac was, by faith in God's promise, and who are free from guilt, and the slavery of pedobaptism or national birthrights, in all its modern or antique forms.[298]

What Alexander Campbell saw and reported in Indiana was immense potential. The state had it. Indianapolis had it. The Christian churches had it.

> Our Indiana brethren have much in their power. They are second only to the Methodists in number, wealth, and influence; and with the good and plain cause they have to argue, ought certainly, in a few years, to possess the largest moral and evangelical influence of any people in the State. The staple is, indeed, good. They are intelligent, liberal, hospitable, and remunerate their effective ministry with commendable zeal and liberality. They would not allow me to be at any expense, from the day that I put foot upon the soil till the day I left it.[299]

But even his investment of the month of November in visiting Indiana and his positive appraisal of the Indiana visit in print were not enough to relieve the tension between him and the Hoosiers. Even as Campbell gave primary loyalty to the support of Bethany College, the Christians in Indiana put their plans for North Western Christian University first. When Campbell was at the home of Ovid Butler during his 1850 visit, he was sure he heard a promise that Indiana leaders would combine their campaign to build North Western Christian University with a campaign to endow a chair of ancient languages at Bethany. In spite of his later protestations, Indiana's Christian fellowship denied that any official promise had ever been made and devoted its funding efforts to its own North Western Christian University. Comment and explanation dragged on through the decade, all of it leaving Campbell unsatisfied. This Indianapolis school was a "monument to free soil jealousy," he said.[300]

The relationship with Indiana kept getting mixed with the abolition of slavery. Campbell believed that slavery was not good and not economically sound. However, it did exist and it was not forbidden in the Scriptures. Masters and slaves within the churches should regulate their relation by the precepts of the Bible. Christian slaves of unchristian masters deserved Christian support to assure good treatment. In a candid expression Campbell once said "Much as I may sympathize with a black man, I love the white man more." He believed the institution of slavery was a matter of political opinion rather than a matter of faith so the churches and church agencies should avoid taking stands.[301] Abolitionists upset Campbell.

> I regard every Northern abolitionist Christian professor, who, in the spirit of the party, seeks to promulge his notions at the South in any way or manner productive of discontent or insubordination on the part of the slave, or in any way or manner outraging the feelings of the moral

or Christian master, as not only indiscreet and highly unchristian, but also in direct conflict with the objects sought to be accomplished by the truly benevolent and intelligent abolitionist.[302]

Indiana had zealous abolitionists, especially a cluster of them around Ovid Butler, a primary organizer and supporter of North Western Christian University. When Campbell made it painstakingly clear that Christians should "be subject to the higher powers" as commanded by Romans 13:1, and obey the Fugitive Slave Law as he and Governor Wright of Indiana agreed they should, Butler had to speak.[303] First he was appreciative of Campbell's recent visit.

> Let me say, that your notes of your tour of forty days through Indiana, &c., published in the January and February numbers of the Harbinger, are highly acceptable to the Indiana brethren. They are much gratified that you were so well pleased with the trip, and have expressed so favorable an opinion of the country and of the brethren. They hope, and I cannot avoid the expression of a personal wish, that this trip may be but the precursor of others, which shall tend to perpetuate and strengthen the bonds of Christian union and fellowship, and to stimulate to efforts which shall result in the increased progress and prosperity of the good cause, and in great good to our fellow-citizens.[304]

Then he stated his conscience on the Fugitive Slave Law.

> There is neither revolution nor rebellion—neither treason, felony, or breach of the peace, in a passive resistance to, or in an open, quiet, firm, and even stern disobedience of, the requirements of the Fugitive Slave Law. This indicates my position. As a lawyer and a citizen, I entertain a clear conviction that the law is unconstitutional, both in its principle and in its provisions. But the moral of obedience to its requirements depends not upon the question of its constitutionality. I have stronger and higher objections to the law. As a man, and as a Disciple of Jesus, I am constrained to regard its provisions as violations of the principle of humanity, and as controverting the statutes and institutes of the Lord Christ.[305]

The tension was further heightened when North Western Christian University admitted a handful of students who had been expelled from Bethany for agitating the subject of slavery. Alexander Campbell wrote angrily of the event.[306] The faculty of North Western Christian University sent an ill-tempered letter to Bethany asking for grounds for Bethany's dismissal of the students. They included a barb for Campbell: "We can appreciate, to some degree, the labors of its [Bethany College's] President, and we fully sympathize with him in the great purpose of those labors. We believe he has made an impression upon the world, which the trembling hand of age will not have strength enough to deepen, although it may avail, to some extent, to dim and mar its beauty." The Bethany faculty responded in kind.[307] Peace came but slowly between Bethany and the college at Indianapolis. When editor W. K. Pendleton listed the colleges of the Christian churches in the *Harbinger* in 1859, Indiana warranted special treatment. "There is, too, at Indianapolis, a *Northwestern* Christian University," he said, "but we fear it is too much tinctured with the fanatical sectarianism of politico-religious abolitionism to be of any service to the Christian church or cause."[308] Even the Hoosier moderates were quick to defend their school against such a charge. Unrepentant Christian abolitionists like George Campbell, John B. New, Love H. Jameson, and Alanson Wilcox were helping to establish Indiana's Republican Party.[309]

Alexander Campbell had a college but Hoosiers chose to set up and support their own. Alexander Campbell had a periodical but Hoosiers generally published and subscribed to their own. Alexander Campbell also had a *Hymn Book* which he preferred to have the whole Christian fellowship use.[310] He kept upgrading his *Hymn Book* by weeding out "sectarianism and speculating philosophy" and by increasing its size. He wavered a bit on whether to go so far as to print a suggested tune name alongside each hymn; some patrons liked a tune suggestion and some did not. Then a Hoosier took up the idea that people could sing better if the hymnbook actually included music! Elder and singing master Silas W. Leonard issued the *Christian Psalmist* in 1847.[311] Indiana editors James Mathes and Benjamin Franklin were promoters and sellers of the work. Alexander Campbell was not appreciative. He charged publishers of such books with violating his copyright on the hymns, with desecrating the hymnals by using them as school books, and with converting churches into singing schools.

> Touching these new things, I think the time has come that we should have a common or general understanding. The time for individual enterprize amongst us is either past or fast passing away. True, I have no faith in making new or old hymn books, with music on every alternate page, or on every page, for church or family service. I hold that learning to sing the praises of God, or learning the music, and praising God, are two dis-tinct operations of the human mind, and never can be properly associated. Fill your churches, brethren, with organs—with singing choirs—and your pews with "Christian hymns and appropriate music," and you will

become as cold and fashionable as Bostonians and New Englanders, and may sing farewell to revivals, and Christian warmth, and Christian ardor, and every thing that looks like living, zealous, active, and soul-redeeming Christianity.[312]

Silas Leonard would not be overpowered. He answered from Jeffersonville that he had asked permission of Campbell to set his *Hymn Book* to music but when Campbell declined he had used the hymnbook of Walter Scott with full permission. He said he would fully state and answer all of Campbell's arguments in the *Christian Vocalist* which he was now publishing. He challenged Campbell to bring him to trial in the congregation to which he belonged.[313]

> Brother A. C. thinks the time for individual enterprize has passed or is fast passing away among us, that note books should not have sacred words in them, and vice versa of hymn books, and that we ought to have but one hymn book, that is the h.b. his will be: (when?) from all of which positions I dissent, and beg leave in the spirit of love, and in the love of improvement to express my views thereon in a series of essays; commencing in March proximo. To the many Editors, preachers, teachers and colporteurs who have sold my books, to the 13000 singers in 18 of the United States and the Canadas who have bought them, do I give my thanks, and promise by the will and help of him to whom all praise is due, to make the books still more worthy of patronage.[314]

The *Christian Psalmist* was issued with round notes, with "buckwheat notes," and with numerical notes for wide use among Hoosiers.[315]

By the time of Alexander Campbell's death another Hoosier singing master was also moving beyond the limitations of the old *Hymn Book*. Knowles Shaw of Rush County stirred emotions across the nation with his sermons and songs, received some eleven thousand persons into Christian churches, and published five religious songbooks. He was composer of the gospel favorite "Bringing in the Sheaves."[316]

After very brief stopover visits in 1855 and 1857, Alexander Campbell made another long tour of Indiana in 1860. It was less a Campbellite campaign than the celebration of a fond farewell. At age seventy-two Campbell had bad health and a poor memory. He was accompanied by Isaac Errett and by his wife. Errett was a symbol of the cooperative mainstream of the Christian churches—corresponding secretary of the American Christian Missionary Society, and just selected for the position of co-editor of the *Harbinger* and financial agent for Bethany College. The college building at Bethany had burned on 10 December 1857; fundraising for Bethany was a major reason for the tour. Everybody wanted to see and hear Campbell one more time so they scheduled him for seventy-two discourses at thirty-two locations scattered from Lafayette to New Albany and Vincennes to Richmond. Travel was mostly by rail. Errett wrote the account of the trip with only mild condescension about Indiana's mud and poor congregational singing. The visitors declared Indianapolis to be a "favorable center of radiation" from which "much light should be spread abroad." Campbell visited North Western Christian University to give an extemporaneous address on "Literature, Science, Art, Morality, Politics and Religion" to the students of the Threskomathean Society. It was "quite discursive" Errett said, but "abounded in capital suggestions, good hits, and wise counsels" and deserved a larger audience than was present.[317]

Campbell was not able to keep the Civil War out of his family; his son Alexander was a Confederate officer while his nephew Archibald was a fiery Unionist and advocate of separate statehood for West Virginia. He was not able to keep the Civil War out of his churches; they espoused their regional loyalties and divided as surely as other American denominations. He was not able to keep the Civil War out of his college; while he was visiting in Indiana early in 1861 he was much disturbed to receive word that the southern majority among the students at Bethany had raised the Confederate flag over the school. As the war was cutting back Bethany's student body and carrying off the faculty, Campbell's health was failing so badly that he had to be eased out of personal leadership of the college and the broader fellowship.[318] R. L. Howe wrote from Indiana to cheer Campbell with the assurance that the work among Hoosiers was getting on fine without him.

> You have grown gray in the service of our blessed Master, and soon, no doubt will leave the dreary scenes of earth to enjoy that rest which remaineth for the Lord's people.—As words of encouragement, my dear and aged brother, I love to tell you, that in all my travels I meet hundreds who are rejoicing in the triumphs of truth, because of your arduous labors in writing and orally proclaiming the gospel, and now are calling you "blessed" on account of your work's sake. As still further for your cheer, I would add that the work of spreading the gospel, of preaching among the destitute, is being thoroughly inaugurated in our great and growing State.[319]

In the last mail alone Howe had word of 171 additions to Indiana's Christian churches, 133 by baptism. In the last month he had raised almost four hundred dollars in cash to assist in further evangelism.

Christian Branches

When Campbell died in 1866 the successors in his reformation in Indiana were busy sharing in the nationwide process of assorting themselves into two fellowships. The more conservative ones espoused the stringent program of the younger Alexander Campbell in his *Christian Baptist* days—complete displacement of all denominations by the greater unity of a restored New Testament church, an ancient order of things socially simple and governed by a plurality of elders in a structure entirely local. They abhorred organized administrative structures for the churches but did accept continuing leadership from such conservative editors as Benjamin Franklin and Daniel Sommer. The more progressive ones espoused the model of the mature Alexander Campbell—local congregations linked and interlinked in cooperative agencies developed piecemeal to conduct every useful enterprise for the whole Church.

Campbell's death was announced in the first issue of what was to be the unifying national voice of the progressives, the *Christian Standard* edited by Isaac Errett. Later progressive historians spoke of its significance: "More than to any other journal and person, it was to the *Christian Standard* and Isaac Errett that the Disciples were indebted for being saved from becoming a fissiparous sect of jangling legalists."[320] This larger segment of the Christians soon ceased to respond to every protest from the conservatives and proceeded to service its membership as convenient through societies and agencies and periodicals at Bethany, Cincinnati, St. Louis, and Chicago.[321] For these progressives the systematic organization of church women and young people released a tremendous energy for Sunday schools and church extension and missions.

> There developed an intense loyalty to the new Sunday school enterprise. The Sunday school provided an outlet for religious enthusiasm and became a center for experimentation in progressive faith. Because it was not thought to be the church, it did not come under the restrictions and limitations of the elder-deacon dominated church body. It was free to function in the area of religion and morality in a manner consistent with the advancing thought of the times. The development of women's work, especially as it was expressed in the Christian Woman's Board of Missions, was another facet by which religious faith was made functional to a heretofore restricted group. The "sisters" came into their own in the middle 1870's and in due time assumed more than

their share of ecclesiastical responsibilities. The Sunday school and the C. W. B. M. upset the old power structure of the local church and became a leavening influence which contributed to saving local congregations from self-imposed senility.[322]

Marcia Bassett Goodwin made Indianapolis an early publication and service center for Christian women and their mission work; the first issue of her *Christian Monitor* was issued there in the year of Campbell's death. When the national Christian Woman's Board of Missions was organized in 1874, headquarters were established in Indianapolis because most of the officers lived there. One Sunday in 1883 Zerelda Wallace interrupted service at Central Christian Church in Indianapolis to declare that she would not commune that day or any day in the future when fermented wine was used; she was first president of Indiana's branch of the Woman's Christian Temperance Union and a prominent national figure in temperance work. The Sunday school effort among Indiana's Christian churches was organized and improved and staffed until it "created more interest, developed greater enthusiasm, and reached more people than any movement the Disciples had ever before embraced in Indiana." By 1872 Indiana's Christian churches claimed 550 Sunday schools with 6,000 teachers and 65,000 scholars.[323]

When the American Christian Missionary Society took a census of the Christian churches in 1880, a substantial fraction of the conservative congregations simply did not report. They were not happy to be compared with denominational churches for any purpose; they had no sympathy with the Missionary Society; and some remembered the biblical account (II Samuel 24) of God's displeasure with King David for numbering his people. Even in this flawed count of 1880, Indiana reported 78,950 members in 675 congregations served by 580 preachers, clustered with Illinois and Kentucky at the very top of the list of states in Christian church strength.[324]

The statistical inexactness continued. S. N. D. North of the Federal Bureau of Census was puzzled when he looked at the forms being returned from Christian churches for the national religious census of 1906. The conservatives had no headquarters at which to inquire so North wrote to editor David Lipscomb of the *Gospel Advocate* asking help in understanding Campbellite divisions and in counting the two groups. Lipscomb laid out the differences between "Christian Churches" and "Churches of Christ" as he saw them. North then assigned J. W. Shepherd to do the census for the Churches of Christ. In spite of his efforts, Shepherd remained disappointed that so many of the conservative groups

continued to refuse to fill in and return the census forms, perhaps one reason that in this 1906 counting the national membership of the Christian Churches (982,701) outnumbered the membership of the Churches of Christ (159,658) nationally about six to one. The great strength of the conservative Churches of Christ was in the South— Tennessee (41,411), Texas (34,006), Kentucky (12,451), Arkansas (11,006). But Indiana was fifth with 10,259, more than twice the conservative membership reported for any other state north of the Ohio River.[325]

> The state, as a whole, was probably in advance of most other northern areas in the cause of primitive Christianity. An annual meeting with the Stony Point church in Clark County August 25 and 26, 1900, was attended by more than nine hundred people, largely from the extreme southern section. Daniel Sommer's removal from Ohio to Indianapolis in 1894 and the subsequent circulation of the *Octographic Review* proved a strong deterrent to the advancement of digression, especially in many of the rural and small town churches . . . The absence of Christian schools in the North and a brotherhood that was strongly negative on them . . . [resulted in] failure to produce as large a volume of capable preachers and elders. Primitive Christianity's conquests, then, were slower in the North, and when they did come, it was because southern Christians moved to the industrial areas to find employment.[326]

A continuing discussion about names for the branches of the fellowship forecast the eventual identification of three Christian groups. James H. Garrison's *Christian-Evangelist* became the voice of those welcoming contemporary biblical studies and sharing leadership in ecumenical efforts with other Protestant churches; they liked Alexander Campbell's name "Disciples of Christ." After the death of Isaac Errett in 1888, the *Christian Standard* came to be the organ of conservatives who used instrumental music in worship and favored limited cooperation among churches but resisted critical study of the Scriptures; they liked the name "Christian Churches." After the Sand Creek church property controversy in 1903, those conservatives refraining from instrumental music and most urgent about restoring a primitive New Testament church according to their vision of it accepted and preferred the name "Churches of Christ."[327]

NOTES

1. This people generally chose to be called "Christians." In Indiana they were also referred to as the Christian Connection, "old" Christians, Christ-yans, New Lights, Marshallites, and Stoneites.

Following the example of Christian Church historian Henry K. Shaw, I assign the name New Light Christians to all parts of the group. Henry K. Shaw, *Hoosier Disciples: A Comprehensive History of the Christian Churches (Disciples of Christ) in Indiana* (St. Louis, Mo.: Bethany Press, 1966), 36.

2. Charles C. Ware, *Barton W. Stone* (St. Louis, Mo.: Bethany Press, 1932), 154; Shaw, *Hoosier Disciples*, 28.

3. Frederick A. Norwood, *The Story of American Methodism* (Nashville, Tenn.: Abingdon Press, 1974), 128; James O'Kelly, *The Author's Apology for Protesting against the Methodist Episcopal Government*, cited in *History of American Methodism*, ed. Emory Stevens Bucke et al., 3 vols. (New York: Abingdon Press, 1964), 1:446; Lester G. McAllister and William E. Tucker, *Journey in Faith: A History of the Christian Church (Disciples of Christ)* (St. Louis, Mo.: Bethany Press, 1975), 80–81; Shaw, *Hoosier Disciples*, 27–28, 30, 33.

4. Ralph H. Gabriel, *The Course of American Democratic Thought*, 2d ed. (New York: Ronald Press Company, 1956), 35.

5. Barton W. Stone, *The Biography of Eld. Barton Warren Stone, Written by Himself* (Cincinnati, Ohio: Published for the Author by J. A. and U. P. James, 1847), 44–45.

6. Barton W. Stone, *History of the Christian Church in the West* (Lexington, Ky.: The College of the Bible, 1956), 49, reprint of a series of nine articles in the *Christian Messenger* from February through October of 1827; *Christian Messenger*, 1:75; Stone, *Biography*, 50–55, 61.

7. Robert Richardson, *Memoirs of Alexander Campbell*, 2 vols. (Philadelphia: J. B. Lippincott and Co., 1870), 2:200–4; Ware, *Barton W. Stone*, 210, 309–10; Stone, *History*, 46.

8. *Christian Messenger*, 6:30.

9. *Christian Messenger*, 7:293.

10. Shaw, *Hoosier Disciples*, 31, 62, 93; Stone, *Biography*, 80, 302–5; Ware, *Barton W. Stone*, 191, 307, 317; *Christian Record*, 2:38; *Heretic Detector*, 1839:181, 268–69.

11. *Christian Record*, 9:163–64.

12. William Garrett West, *Barton Warren Stone: Early American Advocate of Christian Unity* (Nashville, Tenn.: Disciples of Christ Historical Society, 1954), 209; D. Newell Williams, "Barton W. Stone's Calvinist Piety," *Encounter* 42 (Autumn 1981): 409–17; Ware, *Barton W. Stone*, 237, 285; Richardson, *Memoirs*, 2:88.

13. *Christian Messenger*, 1:204.

14. Stone, *Biography*, 76, 79.

15. Ware, *Barton W. Stone*, 218–19.

16. *Christian Messenger*, 2:16.

17. Shaw, *Hoosier Disciples*, 35–36.

18. Richardson, *Memoirs*, 2:199–200.

19. Richard T. Hughes described a pivotal role for Barton W. Stone and the New Light Christians in "The Apocalyptic Origins of the Churches of Christ and the Triumph of Modernism," *Religion and American Culture* 2 (Summer 1992): 181–214. Hughes found in Stone a persistent, primitivistic, counter-cultural, and anti-modern characteristic which differed from Campbell and survived in the fellowship following the Stone-Campbell merger of 1832. He argued that it was this Stoneite characteristic which combined with the stringent sectarianism of the youthful Alexander Campbell to become a basis for the exclusiveness of the conservative Churches of Christ. He understood Tolbert Fanning (1810–1874) and David Lipscomb (1813–1917) as important later leaders of the Churches of Christ in the middle South who embodied this exclusive primitivism. He also saw them opening an era in which their fellowship moved from the influence of Stone to adopt a more world-affirming view, the rational and progressive primitivism of Alexander Campbell which was fully attuned to modernity.

20. See their denominational section in this book for discussion of this continuing group in northern Indiana.

21. David B. Eller, "Hoosier Brethren and the Origins of the Restoration Movement," *Indiana Magazine of History* 76 (March 1980): 5–7; Madison Evans, *Biographical Sketches of the Pioneer Preachers of Indiana* (Philadelphia: J. Challen and Sons, 1862), 62–63.

22. *Christian Baptist*, 3:179.

23. Evans, *Biographical Sketches*, 63–65.

24. Eller, "Hoosier Brethren," 16; Evans, *Biographical Sketches*, 32.

25. Eller, "Hoosier Brethren," 13; Evans, *Biographical Sketches*, 66.

26. *Christian Messenger*, 2:260.

27. Commodore Wesley Cauble, *Disciples of Christ in Indiana: Achievements of a Century* (Indianapolis, Ind.: Meigs Publishing Company, 1930), 34, 37; H. Clay Trusty, "Formation of the Christian Church in Indiana," *Indiana Magazine of History* 6 (March 1910): 20–23; Eller, "Hoosier Brethren," 14; Shaw, *Hoosier Disciples*, 79–82; Evans, *Biographical Sketches*, 33.

28. Evans, *Biographical Sketches*, 34.

29. *Christian Record*, 3:119.

30. Trusty, "Formation," 23; Eller, "Hoosier Brethren," 19. For further information on the Silver Creek group, see the treatment of "Reforming Baptists" in the Baptist section of this book.

31. Winfred Ernest Garrison and Alfred T. DeGroot, *The Disciples of Christ: A History*, rev. ed. (St. Louis, Mo.: Bethany Press, 1958), 124.

32. McAllister and Tucker, *Journey in Faith*, 96; Garrison and DeGroot, *Disciples*, 127.

33. C. Leonard Allen, "Baconianism and the Bible in the Disciples of Christ," *Church History* 55 (March 1986): 65–80; McAllister and Tucker, *Journey in Faith*, 97–98, 122; Richardson, *Memoirs*, 1:46–47.

34. McAllister and Tucker, *Journey in Faith*, 94–95, 100; Garrison and DeGroot, *Disciples*, 51–52; Richardson, *Memoirs*, 1:60.

35. *Christian Baptist*, 1:189; Richardson, *Memoirs*, 1:76.

36. Richardson, *Memoirs*, 1:88, 101–2, 107, 114, 148; McAllister and Tucker, *Journey in Faith*, 102.

37. Alexander Campbell, *Alexander Campbell at Glasgow University 1808–1809*, transcribed with an introduction by Lester G. McAllister (Nashville, Tenn.: Disciples of Christ Historical Society, 1971), 3, 16, 74; Richardson, *Memoirs*, 1:130–39.

38. Richardson, *Memoirs*, 1:130, 187–88; Garrison and DeGroot, *Disciples*, 142–43.

39. Richardson, *Memoirs*, 1:189–90; Garrison and DeGroot, *Disciples*, 143.

40. Garrison and DeGroot, *Disciples*, 129–39.

41. Garrison and DeGroot, *Disciples*, 139–40.

42. Garrison and DeGroot, *Disciples*, 153–55; McAllister and Tucker, *Journey in Faith*, 116.

43. McAllister and Tucker, *Journey in Faith*, 116–17, 120–21; Garrison and DeGroot, *Disciples*, 154–55, 165–67.

44. Richardson, *Memoirs*, 1:478; see also *Christian Baptist*, 1:145–51.

45. From this point the name "Campbell" may be assumed to refer to Alexander Campbell.

46. *Millennial Harbinger*, 1850:273.

47. Richardson, *Memoirs*, 2:51.

48. Richardson, *Memoirs*, 2:90.

49. *Millennial Harbinger*, 1830:1, 44.

50. *Millennial Harbinger*, 1830:1.

51. *Millennial Harbinger*, 1830:4–5.

52. *Millennial Harbinger*, 1831:2, 41.

53. *Christian Baptist*, 1:277.

54. *Millennial Harbinger*, 1830:8.

55. Robert M. Hall, "The *Christian Baptist* 1823–1830" (Master's thesis, Butler University, 1947), 49–50.

56. *Millennial Harbinger*, 1830:429.

57. *Millennial Harbinger*, 1832:414–16.

58. *Millennial Harbinger*, 1832:609.

59. *Millennial Harbinger*, 1833:89.

60. *Millennial Harbinger*, 1833:138, 617.

61. *Millennial Harbinger*, 1833:575.

62. *Millennial Harbinger*, 1835:96.

63. *Millennial Harbinger*, 1836:430.

64. *Millennial Harbinger*, 1841:333.

65. *Millennial Harbinger*, 1839:238, 469.

66. *Millennial Harbinger*, 1851:177, 239–40.

67. *Christian Record*, 3:314.

68. *Millennial Harbinger*, 1839:426.

69. *Millennial Harbinger*, 1839:337–39, 401–3; 1840:17–29.

70. *Millennial Harbinger*, 1839:353–57, 551–52.

71. *Millennial Harbinger*, 1839:353.

72. Richardson, *Memoirs*, 2:96–97.

73. Shaw, *Hoosier Disciples*, 84, 90; Richardson, *Memoirs*, 2:174; Evans, *Biographical Sketches*, 333.

74. Elijah Goodwin, *Life of Elijah Goodwin, the Pioneer Preacher*, comp. James M. Mathes (St. Louis, Mo.: John Burns, 1880), 134, 157, 180; *Christian Record*, 1:91–93.

75. *Millennial Harbinger*, 32:248.

76. *Millennial Harbinger*, 31:437.

77. Goodwin, *Life*, 212–13.

78. Goodwin, *Life*, 212–16.

79. Goodwin, *Life*, 216; Shaw, *Hoosier Disciples*, 126–28.

80. *Christian Record*, 6:195–96.

81. *Christian Record*, 6:300–1.

82. *Christian Record*, 6:314–15, 369–75.

83. *Christian Record*, 2:90; 4:172–73.

84. *Christian Record*, 9:54–59, 135–37, 239–43, 292–97.

85. *Christian Record*, 9:56.

86. *Christian Record*, 9:88–91.

87. *Christian Record*, 9:29–30.

88. *Millennial Harbinger*, 39:3.

89. David Edwin Harrell, *Quest for a Christian America: The Disciples of Christ and American Society to 1866* (Nashville, Tenn.: Disciples of Christ Historical Society, 1966), 63; William E. Wallace, comp., *Daniel Sommer, 1850–1940. A Biography* (N.p., 1969), 265–66; Richardson, *Memoirs*, 2:304–18.

90. *Millennial Harbinger*, 33:239–40.

91. *Millennial Harbinger*, 41:230; 52:4; 48:715; 46:1.

92. *Millennial Harbinger*, 30:267, 290.

93. *Millennial Harbinger*, 33:5.

94. Richardson, *Memoirs*, 2:144–50; *Millennial Harbinger*, 34:576; 55:265–66, 462.

95. *Psalms, Hymns, and Spiritual Songs*, 5th ed. (N.p., 1862), 6; *Millennial Harbinger*, 55:51.

96. *Christian Record*, 2:129.

97. *Millennial Harbinger*, 35:432; 36:3–5.

98. *Christian Baptist*, 1:120–22; Richardson, *Memoirs*, 2:95–98.

99. *Christian Record*, 5:319.

100. *Millennial Harbinger*, 31:91–93.

101. *Millennial Harbinger*, 59:5.

102. *Millennial Harbinger*, 40:217.

103. Enos E. Dowling, "A Revival of the *Christian Record*, 1867–1875" (Master's thesis, Butler University, 1943), 78–79; *Christian Record*, 3:56–57, 380; 5:22, 24, 382; 9:151–52; Shaw, *Hoosier Disciples*, 107.

104. Enos E. Dowling, "James Madison Mathes, 1808–1892, Pioneer Indiana Preacher: Being an Edition of His Autobiography, with Notes, together with Material to Complete the Autobiography from 1867 to 1892" (Bachelor of Divinity thesis, Butler University, 1937), 19–21, 37–46, 55.

105. Dowling, "James Madison Mathes," 60–62, 66–67; Evans, *Biographical Sketches*, 284.

106. Dowling, "James Madison Mathes," 63–64.

107. Dowling, "James Madison Mathes," 71–72.

108. Dowling, "James Madison Mathes," 78.

109. Dowling, "James Madison Mathes," 9–10, 12, 29.

110. Dowling, "James Madison Mathes," 48–49.

111. Dowling, "James Madison Mathes," 52, 55.

112. Dowling, "James Madison Mathes," 82.

113. Dowling, "James Madison Mathes," 83–84.

114. Dowling, "James Madison Mathes," 85–100.

115. Dowling, "James Madison Mathes," 104–5.

116. Dowling, "James Madison Mathes," 107–9, 115.

117. Dowling, "James Madison Mathes," 117–20; Raymond L. Muncy, *Filling the Ancient Measure: A History of the Cloverdale, Indiana, Church of Christ 1841–1991* (Cloverdale, Ind.: Church of Christ, 1991), 21–31.

118. Dowling, "James Madison Mathes," 120.

119. Dowling, "James Madison Mathes," 122–25.

120. *Millennial Harbinger*, 43:238.

121. *Christian Record*, 1:3.

122. *Millennial Harbinger*, 43:238; *Christian Record*, 1:3.

123. Dowling, "James Madison Mathes," 147 suggests "some 500" initial subscribers; *Christian Record*, 3:4 says "about 800."

124. Dowling, "James Madison Mathes," 143, 147–48.

125. Dowling, "James Madison Mathes," 372.

126. *Christian Record*, 1:101–4, 182–88, 199–202, 220–22, 253–57, 261, 264–70; 4:207.

127. *Christian Record*, 15:65–69ff.; 3:7–9ff.; 6:277ff.

128. *Christian Record*, 4:236–45, 257–69; 6:108–9ff.

129. *Christian Record*, 2:3.

130. *Christian Record*, 3:76.

131. *Christian Record*, 1:259–60; 4:214–15; 6:111–12; 11:171.

132. *Christian Record*, 3:29; 5:189; 14:308–9; 9:181–82; 11:182–83; 16:101–10.

133. *Christian Record*, 1:4; 16:53–64.

134. *Christian Record*, 5:74.

135. *Christian Record*, 1:35ff.; 2:37ff., 60ff., 83ff., 180ff., 278ff.; 4:51ff., 72ff.; 8:145ff., 345ff; 12:289ff.

136. *Christian Record*, 5:75.

137. *Christian Record*, 4:76.

138. *Christian Record*, 2:280.

139. *Christian Record*, 1:226–27.

140. *Christian Record*, 2:268.

141. *Christian Record*, 2:4.

142. *Christian Record*, 9:122–23.

143. *Christian Record*, 2:246.

144. *Christian Record*, 2:245.

145. *Christian Record*, 4:156–57.

146. Dowling, "James Madison Mathes," 158–59; Goodwin, *Life*, 22, 26, 60–62, 64–65, 93–94, 133–44; *Christian Record*, 2:166.

147. *Christian Record*, 5:23, 75.

148. Goodwin, *Life*, 203–10; Dowling, "James Madison Mathes," 161.

149. *Christian Record*, 9:19–20; Dowling, "James Madison Mathes," 161–62.

150. *Christian Record*, 9:60.

151. *Christian Record*, 9:1–2, 18–19, 189, 312.

152. Dowling, "James Madison Mathes," 177–79, 189; Dowling, "Revival," 34; *Christian Record*, 14:8, 286.

153. Madison Evans, *Biographical Sketches of the Pioneer Preachers of Indiana* (Philadelphia: J. Challen and Sons, 1862, 422 p.). There are biographies and portraits of John Longley, John Wright, Absalom Littell, Joseph Hostetler, John B. New, Beverly Vawter, John P. Thompson, Michael Combs, Elijah Goodwin, Joseph Wilson, William Wilson, Love H. Jameson, James M. Mathes, R. T. Brown, George Campbell, John O'Kane, Thomas Lockhart, Jacob Wright, B. K. Smith, Benjamin F. Reeve, Joseph W. Wolfe, and Thomas J. Edmondson.

154. Evans, *Biographical Sketches*, 290, 293, 297.

155. Evans, *Biographical Sketches*, 170, 174–75, 177–79; *Christian Record*, 14:351.

156. *Christian Record*, 1:218–19; 2:68; 9:173–75; Dowling, "James Madison Mathes," 196–98.

157. *Christian Record*, 5:75.

158. Earl Irvin West, *Elder Ben Franklin: Eye of the Storm* (Indianapolis, Ind.: Religious Book Service, 1983), 79.

159. *American Christian Review*, 1862:2.

160. *Christian Record*, 15:211.

161. West, *Elder Ben Franklin*, 85–86.

162. West, *Elder Ben Franklin*, 99, 100–4, 201–10; *Christian Record*, 9:118–19; 13:165–68.

163. Joseph Franklin and J. A. Headington, *The Life and Times of Benjamin Franklin* (St. Louis, Mo.: Christian Board of Publication, 1879), 7, 46–47, 49; West, *Elder Ben Franklin*, 2–3, 16.

164. Elijah Martindale, *Autobiography and Sermons of Elder Elijah Martindale. Also Pioneer History of the Boyd Family*, by Belle Stanford (Indianapolis, Ind.: Carlon and Hollenbeck, 1892), 10, 25–29, 38–39, 41; West, *Elder Ben Franklin*, 7. Biographers offer dates for Franklin's profession and baptism ranging from 1834 to 1836. The first person account by Elijah Martindale fits well with Earl West's indication of a "cold winter night in February 1836" (West, *Elder Ben Franklin*, v). Rowe and Rice (*Biographical Sketch and Writings of Elder Benjamin Franklin*, written and compiled by John F. Rowe and G. W. Rice, Cincinnati, Ohio: G. W. Rice, 1881) date the conversion in 1834 on page 17 but their account on pages 20–21 fits better with the date of 1836. Franklin's own recollection in *Western Reformer*, 6:124, would seem to indicate late 1835 and so could refer to the winter of 1835–36.

165. Samuel Rogers, *Autobiography of Elder Samuel Rogers* (Cincinnati, Ohio: Standard Publishing Company, 1880), 149.

166. Franklin, *Biographical Sketch*, 18–20; West, *Elder Ben Franklin*, 9.

167. West, *Elder Ben Franklin*, 10; Franklin, *Life and Times*, 61; Franklin, *Biographical Sketch*, 20.

168. West, *Elder Ben Franklin*, 14.

169. Franklin, *Life and Times*, 65.

170. *Western Reformer*, 7:290.

171. *Reformer*, 4:182–83.

172. *Reformer*, 4:183–84.

173. Franklin, *Life and Times*, 63–64; Franklin, *Biographical Sketch*, 14, 20–21.

174. *Western Reformer*, 7:246–47.

175. Ottis L. Castleberry, *They Heard Him Gladly. A Critical Study of Benjamin Franklin's Preaching* (Rosemead, Calif.: Old Paths Publishing Company, 1963), 27.

176. Franklin, *Life and Times*, 66–68; Franklin, *Biographical Sketch*, 22–23.

177. Franklin, *Life and Times*, 103, 106; West, *Elder Ben Franklin*, 54, 61–65, 77; *Christian Record*, 6:352.

178. *Western Reformer*, 5:247–48 to 6:562–71; 7:353–61.

179. Erasmus Manford, *An Oral Debate . . . Between Erasmus Manford . . . and Benjamin Franklin* (Indianapolis, Ind.: Indiana State Journal Steam-Press, 1848), 4.

180. Benjamin Franklin, *Christian Experience; or, Sincerity Seeking the Way to Heaven* (Cincinnati, Ohio: Standard Publishing Company, n.d., 30 p.); *Western Reformer*, 5:4; *Christian Record*, 18:209; Franklin, *Life and Times*, 14.

181. James H. Bartholomew, "Benjamin Franklin: a Study of His Evangelistic Power" (Dissertation, Butler University, 1950), 2; Benjamin Franklin, *The Gospel Preacher: A Book of Twenty-one Sermons*, 2 vols. (Cincinnati, Ohio: G. W. Rice, 1877), 2:6; West, *Elder Ben Franklin*, 106; Franklin, *Life and Times*, 417, 450; *Millennial Harbinger*, 60:291–92; *American Christian Review*, 1857:382.

182. *American Christian Review*, 1856:380.

183. *American Christian Review*, 1857:382.

184. West, *Elder Ben Franklin*, 111.

185. *Protestant Unionist* (17 March 1847): 58.

186. *Christian Record*, 15:91.

187. *Millennial Harbinger*, 1854:625–31.

188. *Millennial Harbinger*, 1854:626.

189. *Millennial Harbinger*, 1854:599–600.

190. *Western Reformer*, 6:372–74; 7:5, 694.

191. *Western Reformer*, 7:695–96.

192. Franklin, *Life and Times*, 186–96; West, *Elder Ben Franklin*, 79–81.

193. *Christian Baptist*, 1:278; 2:26, 29.

194. Franklin, *Biographical Sketch*, 39.

195. *American Christian Review*, 1856:7.

196. *American Christian Review*, 1863:98.

197. *Millennial Harbinger*, 1865:364–66.

198. *Millennial Harbinger*, 1865:367.

199. Franklin, *Biographical Sketch*, 34.

200. Franklin, *Life and Times*, 106.

201. *American Christian Review*, 1856:55–56.

202. Earl Irvin West, *The Search for the Ancient Order*, 3 vols. (Indianapolis, Ind.: Religious Book Service, 1949–86), 2:140–43; West, *Elder Ben Franklin*, 291–92.

203. *American Christian Review*, 1872:100.

204. *American Christian Review*, 1872:60.

205. *Western Reformer*, 6:697–702.

206. West, *Elder Ben Franklin*, 178, 290.

207. *Millennial Harbinger*, 1851:581–82.

208. *American Christian Review*, 1860:19.

209. *Millennial Harbinger*, 1864:127–28.

210. *Evangelist*, 1881:197.

211. West, *Search*, 2:226–28.

212. West, *Search*, 1:311.

213. *American Christian Review*, 1863:187; 1870:188; 1878:180; Franklin, *Gospel Preacher*, 2:419–20; Franklin, *Life and Times*, 264: West, *Elder Ben Franklin*, 333.

214. *Millennial Harbinger*, 1841:524–25.

215. *Millennial Harbinger*, 1859:297.

216. *Western Reformer*, 7:535–39.

217. *Millennial Harbinger*, 1866:240.

218. *Millennial Harbinger*, 1837:412, 414.

219. *Christian Record*, 9:372–75; West, *Search*, 1:348; *Millennial Harbinger*, 1862:229.

220. Benjamin Franklin, *Debate on Some Distinctive Differences between the Reformers and Baptists. Conducted by Rev. Benjamin Franklin and Elder T. J. Fisher* (Louisville, Ky.: G. W. Robertson & Co., at the Kentucky Baptist Book Concern, 1858), 61.

221. *American Christian Review*, 1862:3.

222. *Millennial Harbinger*, 1862:120.

223. Franklin, *Life and Times*, 109; Franklin, *Biographical Sketch*, 46; West, *Elder Ben Franklin*, 172–74; *Western Reformer*, 5:222–24, 310–13.

224. Franklin, *Life and Times*, 284–85.

225. West, *Elder Ben Franklin*, 128–49.

226. West, *Elder Ben Franklin*, 141–42, 176–79, 194, 196, 213–14, 219; *Indianapolis Daily Journal*, 1 November 1861, 2; *American Christian Review*, 1856:35–39.

227. Franklin, *Life and Times*, 421.

228. *American Christian Review*, 1862:2.

229. *Gospel Advocate*, 1866:273.

230. West, *Elder Ben Franklin*, 171, 220, 236, 301, 306; West, *Search*, 2:9, 11, 14, 20.

231. West, *Elder Ben Franklin*, 195.

232. West, *Elder Ben Franklin*, 75–76, 223; West, *Search*, 2:46–49, 64; Franklin, *Life and Times*, 331–32; *American Christian Review*, 1867:148; *Western Reformer*, 7:490–91.

233. *Millennial Harbinger*, 1857:471; Franklin, *Life and Times*, 348–49; *Western Reformer*, 7:728–33.

234. *Millennial Harbinger*, 1867:9–20, 144–48, 241–44, 415–22, 552–58; Franklin, *Life and Times*, 303–8, 346–51; West, *Elder Ben Franklin*, 223–24.

235. *American Christian Review*, 1875:28.

236. West, *Elder Ben Franklin*, 225.

237. West, *Elder Ben Franklin*, 224–25, 230–33.

238. *American Christian Review*, 1875:52.

239. *Millennial Harbinger*, 1870:356.

240. West, *Elder Ben Franklin*, 296–97.

241. West, *Elder Ben Franklin*, 190, 222, 241; West, *Search*, 2:28–44, 134–36; Franklin, *Biographical Sketch*, 43.

242. *American Christian Review*, 1872:105.

243. Franklin, *Life and Times*, 318; Franklin, *Biographical Sketch*, 44; West, *Elder Ben Franklin*, 229–30.

244. West, *Elder Ben Franklin*, 244, 247, 293.

245. Volume one of *The Gospel Preacher* appeared in its thirty-third issue in 1947 and volume two was reprinted for at least the twentieth time in 1954. Castleberry, *They Heard Him Gladly*, 5.

246. *American Christian Review*, 1873:4; Franklin, *Life and Times*, 318, 426; Castleberry, *They Heard Him Gladly*, 33; Franklin, *Biographical Sketch*, 44.

247. West, *Search*, 2:311.

248. West, *Search*, 2:161, 227, 247–48, 307, 314, 455; West, *Elder Ben Franklin*, 301, 329, 333.

249. *Octographic Review*, 26 May 1887, 1.

250. Matthew C. Morrison, "Daniel Sommer's Seventy Years of Religious Controversy" (Ph.D. diss., Indiana University, 1972), 136; Wallace, *Daniel Sommer*, 76; West, *Search*, 2:293–95.

251. Wallace, *Daniel Sommer*, 76.

252. Wallace, *Daniel Sommer*, 91.

253. Wallace, *Daniel Sommer*, 83–85, 90–97.

254. Wallace, *Daniel Sommer*, 97.

255. West, *Search*, 2:299, 312.

256. *Octographic Review*, 7 September 1897, 1.

257. *American Christian Review*, 1879:17.

258. James Stephen Wolfgang, "A Life of Humble Fear: A Biography of Daniel Sommer, 1850–1940" (Master's thesis, Butler University, 1975), 66–69.

259. Wallace, *Daniel Sommer*, 159–60.

260. West, *Search*, 2:300–301, 317; Wallace, *Daniel Sommer*, 159–61; Wolfgang, "Life," 72.

261. *American Christian Review*, 1887:65.

262. West, *Search*, 1:330; 2:221–22; Wallace, *Daniel Sommer*, 8.

263. *Octographic Review*, 5 October 1897, 1.

264. Wallace, *Daniel Sommer*, 260, 267.

265. *American Christian Review*, 1872:149; Morrison, "Daniel Sommer's," 135–37, 158–59; *Octographic Review*, 11 September 1894, 1; Wolfgang, "Life," 84.

266. Morrison, "Daniel Sommer's," 141–57.

267. Historians have pointed out that the "origin" of the conservative fellowship now known as Churches of Christ was not at Sand Creek, Illinois, in August of 1889. "Church of Christ" as a congregational name was a favorite with the New Lights of Barton W. Stone in the 1830s and had been in continuous use. The strength of the rising conservatives after the Civil War was concentrated in the mid-South where the *Gospel Advocate* published by David Lipscomb at Nashville was their voice. The *Gospel Advocate* gave no attention to the Sand Creek "Address and Declaration" for three years and then roundly condemned it. However the "Address and Declaration" continued a very important tradition of conservative dissent among Campbellites in the Midwest, and Sommer was a highly visible leader for one segment of the Churches of Christ. Richard T. Hughes, "Twenty-Five Years of Restoration Scholarship: The Churches of Christ. Part I," *Restoration Quarterly* 25 (Fourth Quarter 1982): 250–56.

268. *Octographic Review*, 5 September 1889, 8.

269. Shaw, *Hoosier Disciples*, 274; West, *Search*, 2:434; Wolfgang, "Life," 89; *Christian Standard*, 1896:1,179.

270. *Christian Standard*, 1892:648.

271. *Octographic Review*, 3 May 1892, 1, 8.

272. *Octographic Review*, 24 May 1892, 1.

273. Morrison, "Daniel Sommer's," 164–65; West, *Search*, 2:430–38; *Christian Standard*, 1892:520–21, 540–41, 624–25.

274. *Christian Leader*, 17 December 1889, 4.

275. *Octographic Review*, 5 May 1887, 1.

276. *Octographic Review*, 25 August 1887, 1.

277. *American Christian Review*, April-May-June 1965, 4.

278. Morrison, "Daniel Sommer's," 147–250.

279. Wolfgang, "Life," 102–3; Shaw, *Hoosier Disciples*, 274; *Christian Standard*, 1896:725.

280. Shaw, *Hoosier Disciples*, 272–73.

281. *American Christian Review*, 1875:140.

282. Franklin, *Life and Times*, 395; West, *Elder Ben Franklin*, 296–98.

283. Wolfgang, "Life," 108, 113; West, *Search*, 2:385.

284. Wallace, *Daniel Sommer*, 222–23.

285. Wolfgang, "Life," 111; *Octographic Review*, 4 August 1903, 1.

286. *American Christian Review*, 15 July 1941, 9.

287. *Millennial Harbinger*, 1834:192; 1838:476.

288. *Millennial Harbinger*, 1838:284.

289. *Millennial Harbinger*, 1835:331; 1840:30–31; 1842:39; 1846:63.

290. *Western Reformer*, 6:365–66.

291. *Millennial Harbinger*, 1844:314.

292. *Millennial Harbinger*, 1850:330–31.

293. *Millennial Harbinger*, 1850:330.

294. *Millennial Harbinger*, 1850:333.

295. *Millennial Harbinger*, 1850:335.

296. Bruce Bigelow, "The Disciples of Christ in Antebellum Indiana: Geographical Indicator of the Border South," *Journal of Cultural Geography* 7 (Fall/Winter 1986): 49–58; *Millennial Harbinger*, 1851:15, 22. Campbell's full account of the tour is in *Millennial Harbinger*, 1851:13–22, 76–82.

297. *Millennial Harbinger*, 1851:21.

298. *Millennial Harbinger*, 1851:22.

299. *Millennial Harbinger*, 1851:81–82.

300. *Millennial Harbinger*, 1851:52, 235, 587; 1854:42, 465–69, 693–95; 1855:218.

301. *Millennial Harbinger*, 1845:193–96, 234; McAllister and Tucker, *Journey in Faith*, 191.

302. *Millennial Harbinger*, 1845:195.

303. *Millennial Harbinger*, 1851:27–35, 105–8; McAllister and Tucker, *Journey in Faith*, 197–99.

304. *Millennial Harbinger*, 1851:430.

305. *Millennial Harbinger*, 1851:432.

306. *Millennial Harbinger*, 1856:54–60, 111–17, 226–29.

307. *Millennial Harbinger*, 1856:226–29.

308. *Millennial Harbinger*, 1859:713.

309. *Millennial Harbinger*, 1860:50–52, 169–74; Harrell, *Quest*, 114.

310. *Millennial Harbinger*, 1848:710.

311. *Christian Record*, 4:316, 349; 5:24–25.

312. *Millennial Harbinger*, 1848:711.

313. *Christian Record*, 9:152.

314. *Western Reformer*, 7:139–40.

315. Shaw, *Hoosier Disciples*, 189.

316. William Baxter, *Life of Knowles Shaw, the Singing Evangelist* (Cincinnati, Ohio: Central Book Concern, 1879), 153, 184; McAllister and Tucker, *Journey in Faith*, 225.

317. *Millennial Harbinger*, 1861:162–68, 195–201; Shaw, *Hoosier Disciples*, 183–88.

318. Louis Cochran, *The Fool of God* (New York: Duell, Sloan and Pearce, 1958), 406; McAllister and Tucker, *Journey in Faith*, 207–8; Harrell, *Quest*, 133–38; Dowling, "James Madison Mathes," 196; Richardson, *Memoirs*, 2:644.

319. *Millennial Harbinger*, 1864:285–86.

320. Garrison and DeGroot, *Disciples*, 358.

321. West, *Search*, 2:102–12, 248–49.

322. Shaw, *Hoosier Disciples*, 193–94.

323. McAllister and Tucker, *Journey in Faith*, 222–23, 261–62, 291; Shaw, *Hoosier Disciples*, 204–5, 221–22; D. Newell Williams, ed., *A Case Study of Mainstream Protestantism: The Disciples' Relation to American Culture, 1880–1989* (Grand Rapids, Mich.: William B. Eerdmans, 1991, 578 p.).

324. West, *Search*, 2:166–67.

325. West, *Search*, 3:22–25.

326. West, *Search*, 3:186, 190.

327. McAllister and Tucker, *Journey in Faith*, 31, 221–22, 366–71; West, *Search*, 3:25–26.

About Placed Protestants

Presbyterians, Lutherans, Reformed, Episcopalians, and Congregationalists came to Indiana. In some earlier time and place each had been a privileged and perhaps an established church. They brought with them their confessions of faith, written standards of theology and polity, and stout historical identities.

Preachers for these groups were few in number during Indiana's pioneer years. They were likely to have been trained in colleges or even in theological seminaries. They were accustomed to some deference to their learning and to their ministerial office. They found deference a scarce commodity on the Indiana frontier. A preacher who could not earn his own living, "set a fire on ice" with impromptu preaching, and debate a Baptist or Campbellite was likely to be counted inconsequential by the general population. Appeals to educational credentials were likely to be dismissed as "biggity" pretensions which only increased the problem. Claims of church priority based on long and honorable tradition or on large membership in other parts of the world were likely to be dismissed as priestcraft or improper alliance of church and state.

The early Presbyterian, Lutheran, Reformed, and Episcopal clergy were often circulating through the neighborhoods of a few counties searching out settlers of their own religious persuasion. They found a few who were hungry for the familiar ministry of their tradition and eager to restore it. A settlement of Germans who were Lutheran, or Reformed, or that combination of Lutheran and Reformed called Evangelical, might reproduce a unit of old world culture with the church and minister included. Only occasionally were there enough of these placed Protestants at one location in rural Indiana to establish a church and support a pastor. Parent church bodies in Europe or in the eastern states might send mission aid, but they expected this to end after a time. The preachers often expressed the hope that more people of "their kind" would soon be coming to Indiana. They reported their heartbreak when people of "their kind" left their Indiana churches desolate by moving further west.

As towns and cities grew, these churches flourished. There were certain benefits to their lack of conformity to rural frontier standards. Town planners saw in them some element of quality which could attract a good grade of citizens. Their traditions were full of education and they were always opening schools. Their institutional structure and doctrine of the church were a support to them and a testimony to their neighbors. They never became established in Indiana in the territorial sense of their past history or in the sense of numerical predominance like the Methodists. However, well before the end of the 1800s, each came to a position of leadership and respect in the religious life of the state.

PRESBYTERIANS

Presbyterians claimed kinship with the whole Christian church in every age but had special roots in that renewal called the Reformation of the sixteenth century. Some pioneer teachers in this "Reformed" wing of the renewal were Huldreich Zwingli (1484–1531), John Calvin (1509–1564), Theodore Beza (1519–1605), Heinrich Bullinger (1504–1575), and John Knox (1514?–1572). Reformed strength developed mainly in a central band of Europe between the Lutheran north and the Catholic south—in France, Switzerland, Germany, the Netherlands, England, and Scotland.[1] Along with adopting the Scriptures as the primary standard of faith and practice, each of the national units kept formulating confessions of faith in its own vernacular language to express its religious convictions. English speakers among the Reformed particularly valued their Westminster Confession of Faith, Larger and Shorter Catechisms, and Directory for Worship. English Puritans and Scottish Presbyterians, convened by Parliament as the Westminster Assembly, prepared these documents between 1643 and 1649. The Puritan constituency in England became so splintered that the Westminster documents could not long maintain status there. It was the Scots who rallied to these Westminster standards, making them a touchstone of correct doctrine and the ammunition for battles over orthodoxy within and around the Reformed family for the next three hundred years.

Two unusual kinds of Presbyterians made their early impact on Indiana life and their particular contribution to the character of the denomination in the state. They were the psalm-singing Presbyterians and the Cumberland Presbyterians.

Psalm-singing Presbyterians

It was not unusual for early Presbyterians to sing psalms, but these particular fellowships limited the music of worship exclusively to their own metric versions of the biblical psalms without the assistance of musical instruments and continued to do so much longer than Presbyterians of other sorts. All early Presbyterians were likely to honor the Westminster Confession of Faith as a doctrinal guide secondary to the Scriptures and to teach the Shorter and Larger Catechisms based on that confession, but these groups were especially zealous in their maintenance of these doctrinal standards for members as well as ministers. All early Presbyterians were notable for long sermons, long services, and strenuous keeping of Sunday as the Sabbath, but these groups maintained their reputation for these characteristics most persistently. "Neglecting the ordinances," which was failure to attend church, was a serious offense which could result in exclusion from communion. Attending services of another denomination was long counted "occasional hearing" or "promiscuous hearing" which could also bring citation. All early Presbyterians were expected to lead a life befitting their profession of Christian faith under the oversight of their elected elders, but the officers and members of these congregations tended to settle in ethnic clusters in which they could advocate and occasionally enforce right belief and conduct among themselves. All early Presbyterians called prospective participants in the sacrament of the Lord's Supper to serious preparation and self-examination, but these groups practiced "close communion," raising sharply the question of worthiness even for their own members. These psalm-singers intended to be and were recognized as a people under discipline.

Some of them were called "Covenanters" or Reformed Presbyterians. They had endured generations of terrible conflict for the right of their Presbyterian form of Protestantism to exist in Scotland. They survived in their "societies" by a series of religious and military covenants among themselves and with the Puritans in England. William and Mary came to reign in Scotland and England in 1689, ending most of the actual killing of Protestants in Scotland. By 1690 Scotland had secured the establishment of its own Presbyterian state church. That was not enough for the Covenanters; what a king could grant a king could take away. Unless the sovereigns would make guarantees and own the strenuous covenants by which their societies had survived, Covenanters would have none of the new state church. They would continue to focus their religion in their own structure of societies. In 1743 their number finally included two ministers whom they considered properly ordained. With these ministers and some elders they organized a "Reformed Presbytery." Now this presbytery could ordain more ministers and the Covenanters' church could move with Scottish people of that persuasion as they colonized in North Ireland and in America.[2]

There were also the "Seceders" or Associate Presbyterians. They were within that state church settlement provided for Scotland in 1690 but came to feel they could not stay in it. In the continuing clergy of that state church they felt they saw too much of ignorance, error, and corruption. The sovereigns and the British Parliament renewed a system by which a favored wealthy patron could in effect own the local church, appointing and controlling the pastor through financial leverage with or without agreement of the congregation. Protest was overt and organized from 1722, with Ebenezer Erskine as one prominent leader. In 1736 the protestors had enough ministers to form a separated presbytery, an "Associate Presbytery" they called it. Now this presbytery could ordain more ministers and the Seceder church could move with Scottish people of that persuasion as they colonized in North Ireland and in America.[3]

In the short run the Covenanters and Seceders divided even further. They struggled to decide what degree of cooperation they could give to civil governments anywhere which did not explicitly recognize God in their constitutions or did not guarantee the identity or independence of their particular fellowship in language they approved. They became Old Lights and New Lights (sometimes called Old Side and New Side) or Burghers and Anti-Burghers. These divisions concerned their right or duty to vote, to sit on a jury, or to hold public office in any government not properly restricted from arrogant interference in religion. In America this wariness toward civic participation never seemed to limit their military obligation to the nation and they were known as stout patriots. In the long run the old issues did cool and the tendency among the psalm-singers was toward union. Most of the Covenanters and Seceders merged in 1782 to form the Associate Reformed Presbyterian Church. In 1858 this Associate Reformed Presbyterian Church merged with a continuing Seceder group to form the United Presbyterian Church in North America. A century later this substantial denominational body united with the largest mainline body of American Presbyterians to form the United Presbyterian Church in the U.S.A. In Indiana 5,305 bearers of the psalm-singers' tradition in twenty-one congregations served by twenty-one ministers entered the 1958 union.[4]

The earliest of these psalm-singing Presbyterians to come to Indiana were still far away from union. They were intensely loyal to their own clusters of Scottish families, to the particular history and written standards which gave them their identity, and to their familiar forms of worship. During the first sixty-five years of Indiana's settlement, their unique practices made them highly visible at a few places where they were concentrated. Some Seceders in Kentucky sent a letter to the General Synod of the Associate Church in Scotland about 1796 pleading for ministers. In reply the Seceders in Scotland ordained Robert Armstrong and Andrew Fulton and sent them off to Kentucky to constitute themselves into a presbytery to minister to whatever churches they could organize. The whole American West was their field. Because of their aversion to slavery and their interest in the new land opening for their settlement across the Ohio River, the Seceders kept moving northward from Kentucky. A group located in the vicinity of Madison was organized as Carmel Church in 1812. Missionary Andrew Fulton followed these constituents north and became their first pastor in 1815.[5]

There was at that time, we ought to say, no bounds to his field. His parishioners lived five miles beyond Madison, having to travel a distance of 14 miles to church through dense forests, north to Big Creek 20 miles, south to Clark 15 miles. This made the pastor's work very laborious as well as the people's, for they rode on horseback, carrying their children before and behind them; and frequently many of them walked 8 or 10 miles, heard two long sermons and returned sometimes when the stars were shining as they reached home.[6]

Psalm-singing Burgher and Anti-Burgher Seceders settling near Princeton were unsuccessful in their first attempt to relocate a Seceder preacher from Tennessee to the Indiana woods in 1809, but a young Covenanter named John Kell was willing to move in from the South to be their missionary. So Princeton's psalm-singers began with a society led by this Reformed Presbyterian preacher in 1810 and in 1820 built the town's first house of worship. Princeton was such a favored destination for migrating psalm-singing Presbyterians from the Chester District of South Carolina that the town and its environs became their strongest center in Indiana. For a century the place took on a distinct if highly varied Presbyterian complexion. Decades later the arrival of the railroad shops finally changed the community's tone.[7]

At one time during the seventies, we find eight Presbyterian groups in Princeton: one Presbyterian, two United Presbyterian, three Reformed Presbyterian, one Cumberland Presbyterian, and one German Evangelical. Altogether eleven different denominations of the Presbyterian Church existed in Princeton while yet a town of less than 2500 population. Nowhere else, probably, has there ever been such variety of interpretation of the same standards.[8]

Bloomington was another concentration point for psalm-singing Presbyterians. Most of them came to Monroe County from South Carolina also.

Here, in South Carolina, was one of these Scotch-Irish settlements to which the Scotch-Irish Presbyterians of this county are ancestrally related. In the southeastern part of what is now Chester county, South Carolina, on the waters of Little Rocky Creek, about fifteen miles southeast of the town of Chester, and only a few miles from the Fairfield county line—here, a hundred years ago, was one of the most numerous settlements of Irish Presbyterians in America. They were not United Presbyterians in those days—in the latter part of the eighteenth and the first of the nineteenth century. They were, on the contrary, much divided, and their divisions existed over what we to-day would consider the most fruitless, not to say trifling, subjects of controversy. Some were "Associate Presbyterians," some were "Burghers" and some were "Anti-Burghers." But they were all strict, strait-laced, rigid, stiff-backed, blue Presbyterians . . . A group of the Scotch-Irish Presbyterians came to Monroe County from another source, but were of identical stock. I refer to some families that came from western Pennsylvania and eastern Ohio about 1855, the time at which Rev. John Bryan came to Bloomington as the minister of the Associate Church.[9]

Covenanters arrived in 1820, organized a church in 1821, installed James Faris as pastor in 1827, and soon welcomed a whole colony of new additions from Rocky Creek. When elder Dorrance Woodburn and his family of twelve took one group of South Carolina immigrants into their home on 31 December 1830, they had forty Presbyterians living under one roof. Seceders organized in Bloomington in fall of 1834; their minister from 1855 to 1861 was John Bryan, father of William Lowe Bryan who became president of Indiana University. Strongest of all, the Associate Reformed Presbyterians arrived, organized their church by 1833, and kept receiving members from South Carolina at a lively rate.[10] The psalm-singers were interested in Bloomington in part because of the promise of its college; they came to be well represented in its student body, faculty, and administration. Theophilus Adam Wylie was professor of "mixed mathematics" (physics, chemistry, geology, and natural history) for some forty-six years. He was concurrently pastor of Bloomington's New Side Covenanter Church for thirty years. His daughter was one of the first women enrolled at Indiana University.[11]

During the War of 1812 some young men from the Old Zion congregation of Associate Reformed Presbyterians near Lexington, Kentucky, were sent from the Army along the Ohio River with a message to naval commander Oliver Perry on Lake Erie. After Perry sent his famous message "we have met the enemy and they are ours," the young psalm-singers were released from military service. They wanted to conserve their mustering out pay so they sold the horses they had been given and walked home from Lake Erie to Lexington. On that trip they saw the attractive land of Indiana Territory. So when Indiana's "New Purchase" opened for settlement about 1820, a cluster of Old Zion members at Lexington were ready to go pioneering again. They established New Zion congregation in Indiana's Decatur County in 1825, taking the name of the local village of Springhill after 1873. Continued accessions from the South added psalm-singing churches nearby at Milroy (1828), Shiloh (1832), Richland (1837), Glenwood (1847), and Rushville (1879). Richland Academy was opened with a stock subscription of $2,000 and flourished from 1858 to 1868; ten young men entered the ministry and two young women became missionaries from the Richland Church. The psalm-singers of Decatur and Rush counties had strong links with Monmouth College in Illinois; pastor T. H. McMichael of Springhill congregation became president of Monmouth.[12]

The psalm-singing Presbyterians had reason to grow weary of critics. Their neighbors and their children did not hesitate to chide them for being excessively traditional and ingrown. One son of the Princeton group left them to become an ordained minister in the mainline Presbyterian church. He told the United Presbyterian centennial gathering in 1911: "Rev. John McMaster preached long sermons, and I would get tired and sleepy, and I was not the only one thus affected. I remember often looking across the church and seeing men of mature years sound asleep, with their mouths open. I determined, when I was twelve years of age, that when I became a preacher I would try to always preach short sermons."[13] Rush County historian J. B. Blount acknowledged in 1888 that the United Presbyterians he knew at Milroy, Shiloh, Richland, Glenwood, and Rushville included "some of the most intelligent professional men of the county, and men zealous for every public improvement." Yet he was plainly exasperated that this "order" was so "extremely zealous and devoted to all the principles which give it distinction from other religious orders." Blount said one of the denomination's most striking features was its adherence to the primitive custom of psalm-singing. "There is an assiduity in this that amounts to almost dogmatism. Yet this good people would part with their lives sooner than yield up this fundamental factor of their public worship . . . They are a missionary and a Sunday School people, yet not characterized by an aggressiveness that would assure rapid growth."[14]

At Bloomington, Professor Theophilus Adam Wylie, just entering his thirty years as minister to the local Covenanters, recorded in his diary for 12 August 1838 his reaction to a neighboring Seceder communion service. There was the explanation of the psalm and the sermon which occupied the morning.

> After an intermission of a few minutes the exercises were continued by a Mr. Henderson. He began to exhort on the duty of self-examination, which amounts to the same thing as debarring . . . His general remarks, observations on the particular sins to which they were to direct their

attention,—the performance of this duty occupied about two hours and a half. It was the most tedious piece of work that I ever listened to. All that he said during this time I am sure might have been said to a much better purpose in half an hour. After that I left. I am sure that my feelings were not such as they ought to have been . . . I might have mentioned that Mr. Henderson debarred all who would sing any human compositions in worship, or would learn to sing by using verses of hymns.[15]

Indiana University professor James Albert Woodburn commented to the Monroe County Historical Society in 1908 on the steps by which six distinct and often rival Presbyterian churches in Bloomington had finally been consolidated into three—the three David Starr Jordan once described as "Reformed Presbyterians, United Presbyterians, and Presbyterians neither united nor reformed." In his presentation Woodburn showed tremendous appreciation for his own psalm-singing heritage.[16] But he had to say, "These divisions and contentions continued to exist long years after the causes that gave rise to them, and in America, too, where the conditions were such that the causes of division never could have existed."[17]

As a guest speaker for their centennial celebration in 1933, the United Presbyterians at Bloomington invited Anton Theophilus Boisen. He was the grandson of Theophilus Adam Wylie and had been reared as a semi-orphan in his grandfather's house and congregation. Now he was an honor graduate of Union Theological Seminary in New York, a student of social ethics and clinical medicine with Richard Cabot of Andover and Harvard, and a pioneer in clinical pastoral education affiliated with Chicago Theological Seminary.[18] It must have been highly visible to Boisen that the psalm-singers had come a long way. The centennial committee chairman was university president William Lowe Bryan and there was broad community participation. Even representatives of the town's continuing congregation of Covenanters attended the banquet. The program offered much instrumental music on both piano and violin. Boisen must also have been aware that the cluster of psalm-singers at Princeton had united almost fifty years before and had installed a large church organ before 1895. Springhill, the mother church of the Decatur and Rush County psalm-singers, had begun using an organ in its new church building in the early 1890s and before 1915 was styling itself with great openness as "Springhill Community Church."[19]

> To all who mourn and need comfort—to all who are weary and need rest—to all who are friendless and want friendship—to all who are homeless and want sheltering love—to all who pray and to all who do not,

but ought—to all who sin and need a saviour, and to whomsoever will—this church opens wide the door and makes a free place, and in the name of Jesus Christ the Lord, says "Welcome."[20]

Whatever he knew, Boisen chose to give his church fathers at Bloomington a shot of sociology sharp as a serpent's tooth.

> I would point out the fact that in the Psalm-singing Presbyterian churches in Bloomington the family and clan influence has been very strong. In President Andrew Wylie's letter to his uncle, Samuel B. Wylie, regarding my grandfather's appointment to Indiana University in 1837, he speaks of the New Side Reformed Presbyterian Church as "a small body which may possibly grow thru accessions from the south." You will probably agree that this judgment is correct. The Psalm-singing Presbyterian churches have seldom received any new members outside of those who have come into them thru birth or immigration. These churches have been racial churches. They have been held together by family and clan loyalty.[21]

He remarked on their conservatism, which he said was really an attempt to "maintain their group integrity on the basis of loyalty to something in the past and thus to resist the onslaughts of the surrounding culture," and their "tendency to overemphasize externalities and trivialities even to the point of splitting up over them."[22]

Boisen continued to write and publish about Bloomington churches. Words of appreciation for his own Scottish forebears seemed sincere but scarce.[23] Frequently, and at length, he laid them low with sociological analysis.

> There was a very conservative group consisting of the four psalm-singing Presbyterian churches. These were characterized by great loyalty to family and clan, by their emphasis upon Old Testament morality, and by their requirement of an educated ministry. Their services were long, their sermons doctrinal and dry, and church attendance was compulsory on the part of all members of the family. Family "worship" was held every day, often morning and evening. There was among them no appeal to the emotions and no attempt to win converts. Their growth came through birth and immigration.[24]

Invoking the evolutionary typology of Richard Niebuhr's *Social Sources of Denominationalism,* Boisen pronounced the psalm-singers nearly ossified.[25]

> And the Presbyterians? Their period of spontaneity and creativity lay in the time of John Knox three hundred years ago. They are merely a little further along in the process which characterizes any vital religious move-ment. In their psalm-singing offshoots we already see the terminal stages of institutional religion.[26]

So the psalm-singers, some of whom still felt wistful for the fine old stabilities and troubled about the speed with which the old ways were fading, were at the same time under attack for not changing fast enough.

One of Indiana's psalm-singing congregations kept its separate identity through all the mergers and survived years of decline. They were the Covenanters or Reformed Presbyterians established in 1821 at Bloomington. Roy Blackwood was their eleventh pastor, serving for the years 1954–61. Blackwood was a veteran of the Second World War who followed his college studies in chemistry with three years at the Reformed Presbyterian Theological Seminary in Pittsburgh and a doctorate in church history from the University of Edinburgh. He came to feel it was his pastoral calling to make Indiana a Covenanter mission field. He and the colleagues he enlisted kept gathering Hoosiers into small groups for intensive Bible study. Most of these Bible students had no Covenanter background but at several locations they chose to organize within that fellowship. As a result there were seven congregations of Reformed Presbyterians in Indiana in 1993. They were at Bloomington, Columbus, Evansville, Indianapolis (2), Kokomo, and West Lafayette.[27]

Cumberland Presbyterians

The Cumberland Presbyterians were similar to the psalm-singers in number and in impact on the state but they were at the opposite end of the spectrum of the Presbyterian family. The Cumberlands were revivalists—born in revival, successful at revival, extended by revival, committed to revival. Their origins were in the Great Revival of 1800 in Kentucky. Reaction to that famous outbreak polarized the area's Presbyterians. Some conservative Presbyterian ministers within Transylvania Presbytery and the Synod of Kentucky drew back, offended by the revival's disorder and emotional excesses. To be sure they had prayed for a religious awakening, but this was ridiculous. To them the revivalists who kept keying up the people did not sound like orthodox Calvinists and sometimes seemed to imply that persons who sought orthodoxy and quiet might not really be converted at all. Meanwhile the calls for preachers to service the religious awakening could hardly be denied.

> And although the few who remained friends to the revival labored in the work of the ministry night and day, yet the cries of the people for more preaching were

incessant; and those cries soon became so general that they were heard from many parts of an extensive frontier. The ministers in return could only pity and pray for them; the congregations being so numerous, and in such a scattered situation, that they could not by any possible endeavor supply them.[28]

Kentucky's Cumberland Presbytery became a center for champions of revivals. A majority of its members felt impelled to provide the preachers the people were crying for. They believed that the Lord who was providing the revival harvest was also providing the reapers, so it became their policy to approve the ablest of the enthusiastic young converts as exhorters, then licentiates, and then fully ordained presbytery members. They made a few changes in the regular Presbyterian examination procedures. Exceptions to requirements for classical education, once rarely granted, became frequent. Some candidates who could not integrate a doctrine of predestination with the general urgency to repent which they were expressing in their revival preaching were ordained after accepting the Westminster Confession of Faith "only insofar as they deemed it agreeable to the Word of God." Growth came quickly. By fall of 1805 Cumberland Presbytery had twenty ordained ministers and almost that many licentiates in addition. The Presbytery was cited for these changes as irregularities. In a painful procedure, partly illegal on the part of Kentucky Synod, the presbytery was dissolved and its members scattered.[29]

But Cumberland Presbytery did not die. Some of its members continued as an unofficial "council" trying to negotiate reunion with the parent body. When that attempt failed, three ministers organized an independent Cumberland Presbytery on 4 February 1810.

> We, Samuel McAdow, Finis Ewing, and Samuel King, regularly ordained ministers in the Presbyterian Church, against whom no charge, either of immorality or heresy, has ever been exhibited before any of the church judicatures, having waited in vain more than four years, in the meantime petitioning the General Assembly for a redress of grievances and a restoration of our violated rights, have and do hereby agree and determine to constitute into a Presbytery, known by the name of the Cumberland Presbytery, on the following conditions, to wit: all candidates for the ministry who may hereafter be licensed by this Presbytery, and all licentiates or probationers who may hereafter be Ordained by this Presbytery, shall be required, before such licensure and ordination, to receive and adopt the Confession and Discipline of the Presbyterian Church, except the idea of fatality, that seems to be taught under the mysterious doctrine of predestination. It is to be understood, how-

ever, that such as can clearly receive the Confession without an exception shall not be required to make any. Moreover, all licentiates, before they are set apart to the whole work of the ministry (or ordained), shall be required to undergo an examination on English grammar, geography, astronomy, natural and moral philosophy, and church history.[30]

Cumberland Presbyterians did not like to be confused with the New Lights or with any of their contemporaries who wanted no creed. They were confession writers; in 1814 they adopted and distributed their own amended form of the Presbyterian standards. Finis Ewing and Hugh Kirkpatrick agreed to print the Cumberland Confession of Faith "at eighty-seven and one-half cents per volume, upon good writing paper, neatly bound and lettered."[31] They did not like to be called Arminians, though that distinction was not easily made.

> These were the men who, in the infancy of the church, espoused the system of divine truth as taught by Cumberland Presbyterians, that system which is now preached by all successful evangelists, and is believed by a very large proportion of the evangelical churches: that Jesus died in the same sense for all men; that salvation is offered all on the same terms, "repentance towards God and faith in our Lord Jesus Christ"; "that whosoever believeth on him shall not perish," and "hath everlasting life and shall not come into condemnation; but is passed from death to life." Though this system was opposed by extremists on both sides, Calvinists and Arminians uniting in saying there was no ground between them on which to stand; yet these men rallied on this medium theology, and felt that they stood upon a rock.[32]

They did not like to be regarded as thieves of members from established Presbyterian churches, claiming that 90 percent of their membership had been won from "Satan's dominions" and that thousands of their camp meeting converts were enriching the ranks of other church denominations.[33] They certainly did not like to be labeled as enemies of education.

> Some fear lest the Presbytery should take too much liberty in licensing and ordaining unlearned men. If by this you mean you are afraid the Presbytery (in some instances) will dispense with the dead languages, your fears are well grounded. But if you are afraid we will license and ordain without a good English education, we hope your fears are without foundation. And while we thus candidly declare our intention to receive men as candidates, without a knowledge of languages, who are men of good talents, and who appear to be evidently called of God (believing as we do, that there are thou-

sands in the Presbyterian Church of such description, who would make more able, respectable, and more useful ministers of Jesus Christ than many who say they have been brought up at the feet of Gamaliel), we would nevertheless recommend it to all parents who have sons who promise fair for the ministry, to have them taught the Greek language, especially the Greek Testament. Some of us, brethren, intend to do ourselves what we here recommend, and thereby more fully convince you of our sincerity.[34]

Conversion of sinners and extension of the church were consuming interests of the Cumberlands from the start. They had been separated from the parent church because of their zeal to produce preachers to staff the revivals. In the chaotic days from 1806 to 1810 when their presbytery was dissolved and they existed only as an informal council, they kept right on sending out missionary riders. The first minutes of that new and independent Cumberland Presbytery for 1810 mentioned four circuits in operation. Cumberlands seemed to have utter confidence in their calling to go on adding circuit to circuit until they conquered the world for Jesus Christ. They did not wish to be slow about it. In 1813 their thirteen ministers were divided among three presbyteries to form Cumberland Synod. By 1829 their 120 ministers in eighteen presbyteries were formed in four synods in their new General Assembly.[35]

Out in the woods of Pike County in Indiana lived a widow named Elizabeth Lindsey. Back in Kentucky she had been a member of one of the first Cumberland Presbyterian churches organized by the independent Cumberland Presbytery and she missed its ministry terribly. She sent letters from her home at White Oak Springs, some four miles from Petersburg, to Cumberland preachers William Harris and Alexander Chapman. They were members of Kentucky's Logan Presbytery which also had responsibility for the evangelization of Illinois, Indiana, and Ohio. These preachers came to Pike County; out of the Cumberland camp ground at White Oak Springs came a church. In 1812 Mrs. Lindsey married Ashbury Alexander and moved to Dubois County. To "Alexander Camping Ground" there in Dubois County she invited Cumberland circuit riders including David Lowry; her husband became an elder in Shiloh Church which grew out of the camp ground.[36]

This [Mrs. Lindsey's initial work] was the beginning of Cumberland Presbyterianism in Indiana. In 1817 other ministers came and held meetings at Mt. Zion, in Gibson county, and in the following year meetings were held at Jesse McAlister's, and in the vicinity of Mechanicsville, in Vanderburgh county. The custom of holding annual camp-meetings soon became prevalent, and these were established at Mt. Zion, McAlister's, afterwards Knight's, Shiloh, commonly known as Alexander's camp-ground, in Dubois county, Milburn's, near Patoka, White Oak Springs, near Petersburgh, Cool Spring, at Washington, Lester's, ten miles above Washington, Osburn's, in Sullivan county, and Mt. Pleasant, in Gibson county. Churches were organized at all of these places, and probably in the order in which they have been named. Vincennes was probably the tenth organization in the State, but no camp-meetings were held there until some years afterwards, when a camp-ground was established on the farm of the widow Snyder, near the road leading to Washington.

The names of the honored men who inaugurated the work in this State were William Harris, Alexander Chapman, John and William Barnett, Finis Ewing, Dr. James Johnson, John M. Berry, Aaron Shelby, David Lowry, Henry Delaney, Hiram A. Hunter, William Lynn, Thomas Porter, William C. Long, and Alexander Downey. The first six of these made only occasional visits, usually at the time of camp-meetings, but the others came more frequently. The first regular circuit preacher was Rev. David Lowry, now Dr. Lowry, of Pierce City, Mo. Part of his field was in Indiana and a part in Kentucky. He preached in Vanderburgh, Gibson, Pike, Dubois, Daviess and Knox counties. After him came Messrs. Hunter, Downey and Lynn, in the order named. Messrs. Hunter and Downey enlarged the circuit, adding several counties along the White and Wabash rivers, extending it within six miles of Terre Haute. Afterwards Mr. Downey extended it to the vicinity of Delphi, in Carroll county. The men who "rode the circuit," or visited the country occasionally, were constant and untiring in their labors. They preached almost daily.[37]

Indiana Presbytery of the Cumberland Presbyterian Church, encompassing the whole state, was established in 1825 and held its first meeting at Portersville in Dubois County on 18 April 1826. It was Cumberland Presbyterian policy to establish a new presbytery as soon as at least four ordained ministers resided in the area to constitute it. Aaron Shelby, Alexander Downey, William Lynn, and Hiram A. Hunter had been designated to organize Indiana Presbytery and were present in 1826 along with elder commissioners from churches at Washington, Shiloh, Patoka, and Petersburg. Indicating the continuing vigor of the young church, this Indiana Presbytery had six licentiates and ten candidates for the ministry on the rolls at its opening and added four more candidates during the second day of its first meeting.[38]

The same synod meeting of 1825 which authorized the formation of Indiana Presbytery testified to its confidence in traditional Cumberland procedure: "The Heaven directed and highly approved method of promoting the word of God, by encamping on the ground four days and four nights in succession which was introduced in the glorious revival of 1800 has been continued and owned of heaven."[39] The primary business of every early meeting of Indiana Presbytery was the examination of candidates for the ministry and the assignment of members to their districts for evangelism for the coming six months.

> It was customary for our young men to attend all the camp-meetings within their reach, wherever their work might be. Camp-meetings were then regarded as the most efficient means of saving souls and building up the church. This plan of operation was moreover important, as it afforded the older ministers an opportunity to witness the ministrations of the young men, and thus be prepared to form opinions as to their probable usefulness and the propriety of their advancement . . . The ordained ministers assisted them only during the summer and fall at the camp-meetings; but many of those were most delightful seasons that can never be forgotten. And many protracted meetings held by the young men were productive of fruit that will enhance the joy of their souls when they shall meet them around the Throne of God . . . In summer and fall we held camp-meetings, assisted by the young men under the care of Presbytery, and in the winter and spring protracted meetings, which were often as successful as our camp-meetings.[40]

Indiana Presbytery reported 242 conversions and 71 baptisms in 1826; 312 conversions and 68 baptisms in 1827; 301 conversions and 114 baptisms in 1828. For the first statistical summary, in April of 1831, Indiana Presbytery reported twenty-four congregations and one thousand members.[41]

Although Indiana was one of the early recipients of Cumberland attention and the work of evangelism began briskly, the state never became a Cumberland Presbyterian stronghold. A Cumberland historian said "In Indiana hopes aroused by the promising start were not realized." Cumberland congregations were often formed out of camp grounds. The resulting churches, small and rural, found it difficult to reorient their ministry to the rising towns and cities.[42] As early as October of 1833, Indiana Presbytery saw that the age of itinerary was passing: "Whereas, the discipline of our church contemplates a mutual obligation between pastors and people; therefore, Resolved, That each organized church under the care of this Presbytery be recommended to select from among the ministry a man whom they will engage to support, and report to the next Presbytery, by a representative,

what minister they will support, and what they will give him annually."[43] General Assembly also took a strong stand for the pastoral system in 1836 and never ceased to press that standard on the churches.

> (1) Since many ministers, because of poverty or family obligations, could not become itinerant preachers, they were almost useless as ministers. Congregations should support them and put them to work as pastors. (2) The system would enable the minister to read and study and to prepare better sermons. (3) A pastor could devote much of his time to promoting piety and education of young people and to home visiting, personal conversations, and prayer with individuals and families. (4) A pastor, as a presbyter, would help in the governing of the local church. (5) Pastors were necessary to build up and maintain churches organized by missionaries. (6) The ministry was a profession and ministers should be able to work at their profession and get paid; the ministry should not be regarded as a public charity.[44]

But exhortation did not accomplish this change in southern Indiana where most of the Cumberlands of the state were located. There was a wariness of centralized direction or control. The 1834 General Assembly asked for advice about establishing a theological school. Should there be several regional schools or one institution under control of the Assembly? Indiana Presbytery responded with a resolution stating that "one school would be safer than many, and at this time none would be better than any." Many of the churches reached a low plateau of operation under direction of a handful of loyal officers and contented themselves with supply preachers. Few felt they were strong enough to take on the obligation of actually calling a pastor. Though there were many short term contracts year by year for some portion of a preacher's time, Indiana Presbytery did not have its first installed pastor within its bounds until 1844. In 1859 it had only two or three, and there was no increase during the next twenty years. The number of Indiana's Cumberland Presbyterian communicants more than doubled between 1830 and 1860, but Cumberlands in eight other states were eclipsing that rate of growth.[45]

Early Cumberland strength was notable in Dubois County. Shiloh Church encompassed the county with "wings" of its congregation at Portersville and Ireland. Hiram A. Hunter served the Shiloh Church from his residence at Portersville in the 1820s, circuit riding over all of Indiana Presbytery at the same time. Other prominent ministers at Shiloh were Alexander Downey and A. J. Strain, the latter a pioneer organizer of the county's public school system. Very heavy German immigration eventually displaced most of the county's Cumberlands in favor of Catholics and Lutherans. In 1831 there was enough Cumberland strength to extend into central Indiana and establish Wabash Presbytery. Its congregations at Martinsville, at Logansport, and at Hopewell Church near Flora came to have about two hundred members; the other seven numbered well under one hundred. Morgan Presbytery was organized at the residence of Thomas Coplin in Orange County 5 April 1844. Bloomfield was its only congregation outside Dubois County with a membership exceeding one hundred. A Cumberland minister who had spent most of his life in Morgan Presbytery said in 1876 "the churches in our Presbytery were few and feeble."[46]

Five southern counties remained the real centers of Cumberland strength in Indiana. Gibson County had Cumberland churches at Bethel, Fort Branch, Mt. Zion, Oakland City, Patoka, and Princeton. John E. Jenkins became pastor of Princeton's Cumberland Presbyterian Church in 1857 and served there over thirty years. "During the last half of the nineteenth century he was, beyond all question, the best known minister in Gibson county." Even the local psalm-singers welcomed his comments at their eighty-fifth anniversary observance.[47] Knox County had Hermon Church, a few miles southeast of Vincennes. Under the ministry of three brothers named Hall, this became for a time the second largest Cumberland congregation in the state. Pike County had Cumberland churches at Bethlehem, White River, and Petersburg. The Gladish and Lindsey families were Cumberland pioneers both in the county and in the state. James Ritchey, enlisted from Shiloh Church in Dubois County, was minister at Petersburg from 1835 to 1843. Ritchey superintended construction of the first houses of worship occupied by both the Princeton and Petersburg congregations, said to be the first brick church buildings erected by Cumberlands in the State of Indiana and certainly symbols of Cumberland status in these counties. Warrick County had modest churches at Boonville, Chandler, and Newburgh.[48]

At Newburgh pastors Benjamin Hall and Azel Freeman teamed up with the Cumberland benefactor A. M. Phelps as the founders and operators of Delaney Academy. From 1843 to 1867 the academy offered educational opportunity to Cumberland youths preparing for the ministry and to many other candidates for the professions. Of his eight years as principal, Azel Freeman wrote:

The course of studies pursued in the Academy was greatly varied at different times. Besides Arithmetic, English Grammar, Geography, History of the United States, and all the studies usually pursued in the common schools, there were frequently classes in English Composition and Rhetoric; in Natural Philosophy, Chemistry, Botany, Physiology, Zoology, Geology and Astronomy; in Mental and Moral Philosophy and Logic. In Latin there were classes not only in the Grammar and Latin Reader, but also in Caesar, Sallust, Virgil's Aeneid and Cicero's Orations. In Greek there were classes in Homer's Iliad. In Mathematics the course of study became at times equal to that in most colleges. There were classes in Elementary and Higher Algebra, in Geometry, Plane and Spherical Trigonometry, Surveying, Analytical Geometry, and Differential and Integral Calculus. There was much attention given to English Composition and Elocution; and there was an excellent Literary Society meeting once every week for Debate and the cultivation of Oratory. Delaney Academy trained many teachers for the common schools. I well remember that at one time, when Mr. Stilwell was my assistant teacher, we had in training twenty-six young ladies and gentlemen who had been teaching in the common schools, and were attending the Academy to perfect themselves as teachers. The Academy thus became practically a Normal School, and it furnished to the common schools some of the most efficient teachers of Southern Indiana. Many who are prominent members of the legal and medical profession were educated in part at this school.[49]

There was a direct linkage between the leaders of Delaney Academy at Newburgh and the founding of the Cumberlands' Lincoln College at Lincoln, Illinois. Indiana Presbytery took the initiative in 1862 to urge the Cumberland fellowship to establish "a first-class college in the North-West." The proposal to locate the college at Newburgh was outbid by Lincoln, Illinois. However, Delaney alumnus James Ritchey was the chief agent for raising Indiana Presbytery's share of the $50,000 needed to establish the college in Illinois and Azel Freeman, recently principal of Delaney Academy, opened the new school as president in November of 1866.[50]

Evansville Church, in Vanderburgh County, became the most prominent Cumberland congregation in Indiana. Its success reflected consolidation with an earlier rural church in Knight Township, persistent leadership and fund raising by a local society of Cumberland women, timely assistance from the Cumberland Board of Missions under its new policy of getting churches established in cities, addition of members from frequent revivals, and the labors of a series of able ministers. The General Assembly of the entire denomination met six times at Evansville, including the assembly of 1865 in which the Cumberland denomination managed to survive the Civil War without schism. Evansville's pastor from 1871 to 1890 was W. J. Darby; he was a person of national stature among Cumberlands. His church operated three Sunday schools with a total enrollment of over four hundred; eventually he became corresponding secretary for the Educational Society for the whole denomination. At Darby's suggestion the Woman's Board of Missions for the Cumberland denomination was formed; its headquarters, most of its officers, and the focus of its administrative activities were for many years at Evansville. The Cumberlands' first Board of Ministerial Relief for aid to destitute ministers was chartered in Indiana and headquartered in Evansville. With Darby's advice and assistance, Emmeline Thornton of Petersburg gave money for a home for needy Cumberland ministers and their families. This fifteen-room "Thornton Home" and its ten acres of land were located in Evansville. So was the headquarters of the Cumberland Presbyterian Christian Endeavor Societies, because Darby promoted Christian Endeavor and organized one of the earliest Christian Endeavor societies west of the Alleghenies. During Darby's tenure, Evansville also sought to be the location of the Cumberland Publishing House but lost that bid to Nashville, Tennessee.[51]

Talk of church union was lively at the turn of the century, particularly talk of union of the Cumberland Presbyterians with the Presbyterian Church in the U.S.A. The parent body was doing revision of its doctrinal standards at points crucial for Cumberlands. Darby, now working at General Assembly level, was zealous for the merger. His hand was plain in resolutions sent from presbyteries in Illinois and Indiana calling for actions leading to union. When the voting came in 1905, sixty Cumberland presbyteries voted for union and fifty-one against it. Not even Darby could marshal all Indiana Cumberlands to vote in favor. Morgan Presbytery, smallest of Indiana's three, voted negative. Evansville had the strength in numbers and conviction to maintain a continuing Cumberland congregation and for several years provided there a continuing institutional base for missions and for ministerial relief for the portion of the Cumberland body which declined merger. Nearly all of Indiana's 4,850 Cumberlands served by thirty-nine ministers in fifty-four churches did finally enter the union, a very substantial contribution to the flavor and heritage of the whole body of Hoosier Presbyterians. Denominational agencies of the continuing Cumberland Presbyterian Church were renewed in the South, particularly in Tennessee.[52]

Presbyterian Church in the U.S.A.

If the psalm singers and the Cumberlands are called "unusual" Presbyterians in Indiana's early history, the "usual" ones would be members of the Presbyterian Church in the United States of America. This was the largest Presbyterian body. English-speaking Presbyterians came early to the American colonies. There were English Presbyterians among the first colonizers in New England and in Virginia. In the comparative toleration of the middle colonies they were gathering congregations all through the 1600s. Francis Makemie came to Maryland from the Presbytery of Laggan in Ireland in 1683. His itinerant leadership resulted in the organization of America's first presbytery at Philadelphia in 1706. Three of the seven ministers attending had come from Ireland, one from Scotland, and three from New England.[53] Growth was steady, especially by immigration from North Ireland; there was a General Synod with four presbyteries by 1716. When the first Congress of the United States of America under its new constitution was meeting in New York in May of 1789, the first General Assembly of the Presbyterian Church in the United States under its new constitution was meeting in Philadelphia. That year there were sixteen presbyteries.[54] It was an auspicious beginning.

> In 1800 the Presbyterian Church was the most influential single denomination in the country. It had a learned ministry; a sizable membership that was distributed, though not uniformly, over the country as a whole; an efficient central government supplied by the new General Assembly; prestige from its unquestioned patriotism; and—together with many of the other churches—renewed spiritual vigor from the recent revival. The church was growing rapidly. By 1800 there were twenty-six presbyteries, as compared with sixteen some ten years before. In 1789, the year of the first Assembly, there had been 419 churches, as compared with 511 in 1803. The greatest task facing the church for many years to come was the evangelization of the frontier. The new General Assembly soon directed all congregations to make annual collections for home missions and to forward them to the Assembly. The church was determined to try to do its part to win America for Christ.[55]

But the West was really too big for the Presbyterians and their traditional standards of decency and order. As a denomination with a monumental legacy of doctrine and discipline, they were committed to sustained teaching and a well educated ministry. Such ministers could hardly be generated on the scene in the earliest years of a new frontier. Individual Presbyterian settlers or groups of settlers might appeal for qualified ministers and offer to assist them. But for a long time most of the preachers had to be educated elsewhere and commissioned elsewhere and sent. So the history of frontier Presbyterian development read like a history of missions.[56]

Presbyterians formed a missionary organization in 1802 and made heroic efforts to send a trained ministry westward to preach, conduct schools, establish colleges, and train up a new generation of ministers born on the frontier. But the mission strategists never had enough money or enough men for the huge territory—less than twenty-five hundred dollars per year from 1802 to 1811 for the whole Assembly. Midwestern settlers with an Appalachian background of a generation or two were not patient scholars of the Presbyterian curriculum. Frontier descendants of the Scotch-Irish immigrants were likely to have become Methodists or Baptists if they were committed to religion at all. At least a portion of Presbyterian leadership had championed the eastern revivals but the raucous and omnipresent western revivals following 1800 disconcerted and divided the Presbyterian clergy. Within the fellowship there was a perennial theological tension. An "Old School" group wanted all parts of the Presbyterian standards of doctrine and polity to be conservatively interpreted as matters of faith and kept safe from innovations; their views were best articulated at Princeton Seminary which was founded in 1812. A "New School" group wanted cooperation with the Congregationalists in a whole range of evangelical enterprises and favored some new understandings of Presbyterian doctrine and polity to suit the times. Voices for this view came from Yale Divinity School (1822) and Auburn Seminary (1821).[57] Carrying all this load, the Presbyterian Church in the United States of America entered Indiana rather feebly.

The first two Presbyterian preachers directed to visit Indiana did not go. Archibald Cameron and James Vance made excuses for failing their assignment when Transylvania Presbytery met at Hardin's Creek, Kentucky, on 5 October 1803. The Presbytery meeting in April of 1805 again had "a petition from a number of inhabitants of Knox County, Indiana Territory, praying for supplies." This time Thomas Cleland accepted the appointment and traveled in spring on "an uninhabited route" by way of "a small wilderness trace" to preach at the council house at Vincennes and "in a settlement twenty miles up the Wabash."[58] His was the first clear record of Presbyterian preaching in Indiana; there were certainly other Presbyterian horseback riders who crossed over from Kentucky.

In the years 1804, 5 and 6, short missionary excursions were made in the vicinity of Vincennes, by the Rev.

Messrs. Samuel Rannels, Samuel B. Robinson, James McGready and Thomas Cleland, members of the Transylvania Presbytery, Ky. The immediate fruits of those labors were the gathering and organization . . . of the first Presbyterian church in Indiana, which was consequently called after the name of the territory.[59]

There were horseback riders sent to Indiana by the General Assembly's Committee of Missions too. Committee policy in those years was to stretch its money as far as possible by paying little and making short term appointments, generally one to six months. Critics said it took the appointees half the term of their commission to get to the field and return. So they had time for only one ride through the assigned area before going back home to comment on the great need.[60]

Up to 1815 the General Assembly had commissioned eleven missionaries to Indiana for periods of from one to four months. They were Samuel Scott (1806–07), James Dickey (1807), Stephen Bovelle (1811), James McGready (1811–16), William Robinson (1813–14), Thomas Williamson (1805), Samuel Holt (1806), Thomas Cleland (1806), Daniel Gray (1815), Joseph Anderson (1815), and James Welch (1815).[61]

In 1814 the territorial legislature ordered its tax listers to conduct a census of Indiana Territory. The number of free inhabitants had grown to 63,897.[62] That same year Samuel J. Mills toured the West for the Massachusetts Missionary Society and reported the number of Presbyterian preachers. In all of Indiana Territory he found only one. That one was Samuel Scott who had come as a General Assembly missionary and was serving three preaching places constituting "Indiana Church" near Vincennes. Mills had the word of William Robinson that he was planning to move from Ohio and locate at Madison as a teacher. He had a report that a congregation of about thirty was about to settle a clergyman "between the forks of White River"; that was John McElroy Dickey who came from Kentucky as a young licentiate with no commission except an invitation from that handful of people in Daviess County.[63] Mills drew the picture of the Presbyterian enterprise in this Indiana Territory on the threshold of statehood: "It is probable, then, that there are three Presbyterian clergymen now in the Territory. But what are they for the supply of so many thousands? They are obliged to provide principally for their own support, by keeping school through the week, or by manual labor. They have, therefore, very little time to itinerate."[64] He named towns which seemed to offer good prospects for Presbyterian congregations but "there are people here who for five years past have not seen the face of a Presbyterian clergyman." John McElroy Dickey presented the same view.

> For several years those who were laboring in Indiana, seemed almost to labor in vain. Frequently I was ready to conclude that I was a curse instead of a blessing to the people among whom I labored. Sometimes I thought I was of no use, only to make the hearts of some of the pious who had been long destitute, glad to see something like a Presbyterian preacher. But few were added by emigration, until our brethren in the East began to feel for us, and the prayers of the East and the West met in ascending to the throne of God.[65]

General Assembly and its missionaries soon received a powerful new partner. Samuel J. Mills and the Massachusetts Missionary Society which was his patron had been harbingers of a new era. Faced with need for ministers for the West, the Presbyterians and Congregationalists had entered a Plan of Union in 1801. Congregational ministers could serve Presbyterian churches, or Presbyterian ministers could serve Congregational churches, wherever that was convenient. There were generous provisions for representation in the church governing bodies of each denomination and for sharing church discipline. This plan was perfectly timed to serve the opening of Indiana to white settlement. The effect was to make the college and seminary graduates of the eastern Congregational and "Presbygational" schools available for destitute Indiana. There was an impressive number of these graduates because revivals had recently stirred their educational institutions. They were sent out with Presbyterian and Congregationalist money through new mission societies.[66]

First there was a proliferation of these societies. Indiana received missionaries from the Connecticut Missionary Society, from the Young Men's Missionary Society of New York City, and from others as well. Then came consolidation. Several societies in the State of New York combined in 1822 to form the United Domestic Missionary Society. By 1826 this body had 127 missionaries, four of whom were in Indiana. That year the United Domestic Missionary Society combined with the Connecticut Missionary Society, the Massachusetts Missionary Society, and others to form the American Home Missionary Society. This new agency grew mightily. In 1836 its receipts were over $100,000. That year 191 of its 755 missionaries were in the West and 24 were serving in Indiana.[67] The American Home Missionary Society (AHMS) did not intend to spend its funds for part time preachers or mere horseback riders. It would make substantial grants to open new fields—perhaps $200 at first toward an annual salary of $400 for a missionary and family—expecting

that the local people would soon assume full support for a full time pastor besides having become contributors to missionary expansion themselves. In Indiana such full support for full time Presbyterian preachers never came easily. The churches were quick to seek mission help and slow to leave it.[68] "There is not a church in Indiana of the Presbyterian or Congregational order that did not spring from missionary efforts," said Joseph S. Clark.[69]

Since so few of Indiana's earliest settlers were from New England or from New York State, these eastern missionaries founded few Congregational churches but many Presbyterian churches under the Plan of Union. Isaac Reed was a notable example. He attended Middlebury College in Vermont, was taken under care of Long Island Presbytery in New York as a candidate for the ministry, was licensed by Fairfield Congregational Association in Connecticut, was ordained by Transylvania Presbytery in Kentucky, served under commissions from various eastern societies including the Connecticut Missionary Society and the American Home Missionary Society, and founded more churches than any eastern missionary to Indiana—all of them Presbyterian churches.[70] John McElroy Dickey described the improving situation for Presbyterians when he published his history:

> From this brief view it is manifest that the church of Indiana is deeply indebted to the Christian benevolence of distant societies. Of these the Connecticut Missionary Society seems to have the first claim. Her missionaries have been found among the first heralds of the Cross in these western wilds, and for whole years together have they prosecuted their arduous labors, amid perils and privations innumerable. And, with a perseverance that never tires, is her hand stretched out still for our encouragement and support. To the Board of missions under the General Assembly are we much indebted. Frequently has the solitary exile from Christian privileges been cheered by the transient visit of their missionary. It is to be lamented, however, that from the brevity of the commissions given by that body, and the extensive field of operations which they embrace, the good effected has been by no means proportionate to the time and treasure expended. Recently the Domestic Missionary Society of New York, which has now become the American Home Missionary Society, has extended its benevolent efforts even unto us. Several of its missionaries are already stationed within the bounds of Indiana.[71]

Dickey knew the Presbyterians could not possibly provide enough college-trained clergy to match the opportunities in Indiana, but he was pleased at the growth from one preacher and one church with forty or fifty members in 1810 to about fifteen preachers and fifty churches with two thousand members in 1828. The work appeared to be properly ordered and governed in the presbyteries of Salem (1824), Wabash (1825), and Madison (1825) all within the new Synod of Indiana formed in 1826.[72] He could hardly have forecast that the Presbyterian Church in the United States of America was about to cripple itself with a schism of thirty years at the very time its pioneer work in Indiana cried for unity. Within a decade the new synod, its presbyteries, and nearly every congregation in the state would be dismembered.

Old School and New School

The split produced the Presbyterian Church, Old School, and the Presbyterian Church, New School. One reason for the division was a difference of opinion which had existed among American Presbyterians from the beginning. Leonard J. Trinterud has demonstrated the cleavage between the English and the Scotch-Irish Presbyterians.[73] That conflict was sharpened as conservative Presbyterians became suspicious of the doctrinal formulations of certain New England theologians, especially those of Nathaniel William Taylor at Yale. The critical doctrines concerned sin, human ability, and salvation. The conservatives counted this New England theology especially dangerous precisely at the time when the American Home Missionary Society was busy supplying the church with young ministers who thought this theology was the latest and best.[74]

Princeton became the center for the Scotch-Irish group which was strong for a classically orthodox understanding of and strict subscription to the Westminster Confession. Many of the Scotch-Irish pastors who trained young ministers in their frontier homes and "log colleges" took this Old School position, as did the Indiana Theological Seminary at Hanover. On the other hand the English Presbyterians of the New School persuasion were often trained at Yale, Andover, Union, Auburn, or Lane. Generally, the New England men were hotly opposed to slavery and favorable to missions under the voluntary or nondenominational societies. The Old School men hedged on the issue of slavery in the interest of peace with the southern wing of the church and favored missions directly under the control of the General Assembly. No lines were exact. In general, it was the conservative, Scotch and Scotch-Irish, anti-abolition, rigidly Presbyterian Old School against the theologically experimental, English and New English, antislavery, loosely Presbyterian New School.

A special point of irritation for the conservatives was seeing the independent American Home Missionary Society send out young men whom they feared to be of questionable orthodoxy and do it in part with Presbyterian money. When the Old School party had a majority at the national General Assembly of 1837, they acted on the basis of their fears. They cut off four whole synods of the church—509 ministers, 599 churches and some 60,000 members—without warning and without formal trial. The synods exscinded were Western Reserve, Utica, Geneva, and Genesee—all organized under the Plan of Union and all heavily New School. Their exclusion would guarantee control of the remaining body by the Old School. Now the whole church across the nation had to divide in terms of allegiance either to the Old School Assembly or to the New School Assembly that was promptly formed.

In a way the Presbyterians of Indiana were passive victims of this divisive action far off to the east. Hoosier Presbyterians were not divided Old School or New School on the issue of slavery; almost all of them were against it. They needed every missionary they could get from both the General Assembly and the American Home Missionary Society and could not afford to be caught in some war between them. When the split seemed imminent, many Hoosiers asked for a united Western Missionary Society to continue receiving aid from both agencies and asked that their presbyteries be spared division.[75]

When a missionary was supported in Indiana by the American Home Missionary Society that did not necessarily mean that he was a champion of the "new divinity" or even that he was a New School man. John Finley Crowe of Hanover became an Old School partisan but he and his academy had been aided in the crucial beginning years of 1828–30 by an American Home Missionary Society commission. Even W. W. Martin, solidly Old School, reported the revival at his Livonia church through the pages of the New School *Indiana Religious Intelligencer*. Further, he served with Isaac Reed and John Dickey as an officer of the Indiana Missionary Society to locate missionaries of the American Home Missionary Society when they arrived in Indiana. The Synod of Indiana did not seek division. Its proceedings reflected the sorrow of the divided years. New School records spoke of the Old School as "friends of reform" and of the Assemblies of 1837 and 1838 which excluded them as "Reformed Assemblies." The Synod of Indiana, Old School, carefully stated that while it adhered to the Old School Assembly it did not count approval of the acts of the Assemblies of 1837 and 1838 as tests of membership.

But in other instances Indiana became an Old School–New School combat theater. For example, Indianapolis Presbytery had six minister members when it was formed in 1831. David Monfort, John R. Moreland, and William Sickels were solidly Old School. Jeremiah Hill, Samuel G. Lowry, and William W. Woods were missionaries of the American Home Missionary Society and two more missionaries of that society appeared ready to present their credentials for admission. The Old School group feared loss of control. Enlisting the support of elder delegates from vacant churches inclined to oppose any suspected novelty, the Old School members outmaneuvered and intimidated their New School colleagues until most of them left the scene.[76] One of the displaced New School ministers said:

> Such are the strenuous measures pursued by our presbytery at present that I am fearful that I shall be obliged to leave the Churches to which I now minister before long. All the ministers but myself in this Presbytery who ranked among the New School have left the bounds. The consequence is that there are two or three churches near here that are dwindling to nothing. They are discouraged. A fearful responsibility rests somewhere.[77]

Everywhere the tragedy had to be played to its conclusion. The Old School told its story through the *Western Presbyterian Herald*; a New School organ was the *Watchman of the Valley*. Hanover College and the Indiana Theological Seminary were Old School; the New School supported Wabash College and Lane Seminary. Indiana's settlers from the South or from Pennsylvania inclined to be Old School, but so much of the founding of churches had been done by eastern societies favoring the New School that the two bodies were nearly equal in size. A few cities like Madison, Indianapolis, and New Albany were large enough to support both Old School and New School congregations without serious damage to congregational life. Not so in most places. The most painful part of the disintegration of the denomination was the tearing apart of particular congregations. Churches with a handful of members divided doggedly and endured the tension over who got the church property, who got the church records, and who got the church name.

The Old School forces took the initiative. Generally they were able to point to disturbing thoughts, independent attitudes, or arrogance among New School appointees. They could rouse suspicion against a New School minister in the mind of an elder or a group already disaffected within a congregation. Philip S. Cleland of Jeffersonville said: "There is one man in the congregation who pretends to be an 'Old School' man and says he wishes an old school minister. He was also one of the founders of the church and feels he has a kind of right to govern as he pleases."[78] Eliphalet Kent reported from Greenwood: "Division has marred the beauty of Zion. New Providence Church, embracing formerly 40 members is reduced to about 20 and instead of being as formerly an energetic and prosperous Church, she has become measurably enfeebled and inactive by discouragement."[79] Bedford offered a demonstration of Old School tactics. Solomon Kittredge, the pastor, was a New Hampshire boy and a graduate of Andover Seminary. He came to Indiana as a missionary of the American Home Missionary Society in 1832. After a brief period of understudy with Benjamin Cressy at Salem, Kittredge went to Bedford, and there he stayed. His was a vital church filled to overflowing with young people. A new meetinghouse was under construction, temporarily delayed for lack of funds. In 1839 came the invasion:

> An Old School brother . . . was determined on rending my church in twain . . . A young minister was sent here to declare the Bedford Church vacant and to supply them a part of his time. Books and pamphlets and papers of a party character were put in circulation among my people. After these and other preparatory steps of a like character had been taken, a sacramental meeting . . . was appointed in the Bedford Church without consulting either the Session, the members of the Church, or myself . . . Father Martin (as he is called here, being one of the oldest ministers in this section of the country) . . . made a public statement respecting the New School heresy and the necessary measures that had been taken to cleanse the Church, and at the close took the names of all those who wished to "remain Presbyterian." . . . I made no direct opposition to the efforts the Old School brethren were making, said as little as possible on the subject of New and Old School but endeavoured to keep the minds of my people on things of higher importance. Seldom have I suffered greater distress in mind than during this season of trial . . . Only six of the members of my Church gave their names to the Old School.[80]

Neither group folded or failed; they coexisted. The state became overlaid with a multiplication and duplication of Old School and New School presbyteries and synods without comparable growth in real strength. Indiana had seven presbyteries in one synod just before the division; by 1851 fifteen presbyteries and four synods had been constituted with part or the whole of their jurisdiction within the state. In 1850 the Old School and New School Presbyterians in Indiana reported exactly the same number of ministers; the New School had a small majority of churches, while the Old School had a small majority of members. Together the two branches accounted for 216 churches, 134 ministers, and 10,418 members, just over 1 percent of the state's reported population of 988,416 for that year.[81]

Time began to heal the breach. While the Old School Synod of Northern Indiana was meeting at Logansport in October of 1845, the New School synod was also meeting there. It was the Old School synod which sent a committee suggesting a joint synodical prayer meeting. The union meeting was held. In 1849 the Presbytery of Salem, Old School, could say very frankly that the Old School Presbyterian church of Salem was about dead and it would be better if the local members would join the New School Presbyterians. Thirty years after Indianapolis Presbytery had divided with somber talk of heresy and subversion, the Indianapolis Presbytery, Old School, "hailed with unusual pleasure" the fraternal delegates from two New School presbyteries. They looked to a "harmonious and honorable blending of the two branches." In 1869 the presbytery vote for reunion was fifteen ayes to one nay. Ransom Hawley, the man who refrained from voting to divide the church back in 1838, was elected moderator of the reunited Presbytery of Indianapolis.[82]

Those thirty years of separation in Indiana only proved how useless the division had been. The New School did not go radical after all, and the Congregationalists, far from plotting to poison the Presbyterians with liberalism, abrogated the Plan of Union themselves in 1852. Old School and New School Presbyterians developed nearly duplicate structures for administration and benevolent work. The records of the two church bodies were so similar that only an alert reader could tell if he was studying an Old School or a New School volume. The time until the reunion of the two denominations in 1870 seemed very long to most Indiana Presbyterians and some communities did not wait.[83]

Presbyterian Preachers and the Indiana Frontier

During Indiana's pioneer years Presbyterian preachers differed conspicuously from the surrounding culture. Whether they were Old School from Princeton or Pennsylvania or the South; whether they were educated at the older colleges back east, or at Hanover (1827) or Wabash (1832) colleges newly instituted in Indiana, or in the manses of their pastor-mentors anywhere—in any case they conformed poorly to Indiana's frontier norms. They were trained more or less according to the standards of Europe or of the eastern seaboard. They were examined according to a procedure shared and recognized by Presbyterians everywhere. And they were received as members of a presbytery which was a fellowship including ruling elders but dominated by ministers, a governmental unit, a veritable trade union of educated clergy. There was only a very small band of them in the state of Indiana. They seemed always to be subscribing to eastern journals or going to school or talking about their schools or teaching schools. They were doing these things in a state where reading and schooling were so little regarded that two-thirds of the children did not attend school at all and the illiteracy rate in southern counties like Jackson, Martin, Clay, and Dubois was nearly 50 percent. Indiana rated lowest among the free states in literacy and the means of popular education.[84]

Presbyterian preachers thought a normal ministry was a settled ministry in which the church members contracted to give and actually gave adequate financial support to a formally trained minister who lived in their manse with his family and who shepherded his people as a closely knit and responsive community. They viewed their frontier situation as horseback ministers serving their handful of constituents scattered over a county or two as only temporary. Hoosier settlers, on the other hand, were slow to commit themselves to full membership or support. They had become more accustomed to preachers enlisted directly from the membership without delay or expense, preachers who managed to appear by their own arrangement wherever meetings were appointed and who were counted all the more admirable if they proved they were no hirelings by serving with never a mention of pay.

Presbyterians tended to preach a developed Calvinism, shaped by the historic constitutional documents of their church and by notes they had compiled during their formal schooling. They preferred to preach organized sermons in a controlled setting. Unless converted to western ways, they were likely to write out their sermons and read them to the people, "tying all their knots high in the air." However the bulk of Indiana's pioneers wanted revivals or protracted meetings with plenty of action and conversions. They wanted extemporaneous preaching in their own vernacular with illustrations raw and homely and the assumption of the superiority of the common pious man, especially the western man.[85]

Presbyterian preachers were enthusiastic about taking up collections for societies supporting Sunday schools, missions, Bible distribution, education, temperance, and many other specific efforts dedicated to the relief of suffering and the improvement of morality. They championed some combination of these causes in whatever places they worked. However a large body of Indiana's early settlers were still in the throes of deciding whether Sunday schools or missionary societies should be tolerated at all. As for all the organizations aimed at reform and improvement, Hoosiers often sensed in these some eastern agenda of organizing to expose and remedy the ignorance and poor morals of the West. They did not much care to be criticized, improved, or reformed, especially if it meant sending in scarce cash.[86]

Early Presbyterian commentators were critical of the conditions they found in Indiana. First reports from eastern missionaries almost always registered shock. They viewed citizens without Bibles, and too ignorant to read them in any case, as a particularly terrifying form of destitution. Isaac Reed gave away tracts to Hoosiers until he learned he must first ask bluntly whether they could read.[87] John U. Parsons said his neighborhood in Jefferson County practiced "total abstinence—from literature" and was headquarters for "ignorance and her squalid brood [of] . . . croaking jealousies . . . bloated bigotry . . . crocodile malice." He nicknamed the place "Purgatory." Ashbel Wells could count forty habitual drunkards at New Albany in the 1820s. Drunken gangs fighting in the streets forced the citizens to defend their homes with firearms. Mrs. E. O. Hovey, bride of the young Yankee minister at Coal Creek, discovered her own instant mission in the form of three totally illiterate women living within half a mile of her new home "who are mothers of large families and disposed to let their children grow up in the same way."[88]

The preachers they found on the scene rarely pleased the Presbyterians.

Some of our towns and villages contain cultivation and refinement, with the means of grace ably administered; but in most places there is an alarming destitution of intelligent, discriminating preaching. We say "intelligent and discriminating," for with the Catholics, the Cambellites, the Universalists, and the sects the burden of whose proclamation is invective against an educated ministry, there is no lack of preaching any where. This fact, however, increases rather than diminishes the obligation of intelligent Christians to render us assistance. "If the light be darkness, how great is that darkness!"[89]

Baptists were charged with "substituting mere declamation and noise for argument" and labeled consumers and sometimes dispensers of whiskey.[90] Moody Chase said there were ten preachers in Orange County when he arrived, but he wondered whether the people were any better prepared to promote benevolent institutions be-

cause of their influence. There were five Methodist preachers residing in Orleans alone but "notwithstanding this great number . . . when I came here there was no preaching oftener than once in 3 or 4 weeks and no prayer meeting or Sabbath school or Bible Class in the place."[91] A bitter attack against the Methodist preachers in northern Indiana came from Noah Cook.

The greatest obstacle there to the cause of vital piety . . . is Methodism. About the middle of the winter there appeared much seriousness among the people there and while I was considering whence help could be obtained to commence and continue a series of meetings, the Methodists commenced what they call a protracted meeting. This continued a few days and nearly broke down their society. About two weeks since another person of the same denomination commenced a meeting there for the purpose of retrieving the bad effects of the preceding one . . . An intelligent person, whether an humble Christian or a confirmed infidel, would tell you that the effect if not the design of the meeting was or is a satire upon the Christian religion and an attempt to bring it into disrepute. I know that many look upon the Methodists as coadjutors in the cause of Christ. But I cannot so view them and were it my dying testimony I should declare that they do much more hurt than good. A vast majority of the infidels that I have ever seen are of those who have once joined the Methodists and then left them under the notion of falling from grace—the Methodists saying that they have fallen from it but they saying if this is it (grace noise and groaning) then there is no such thing as real grace and consequently there is no such thing as grace religion.[92]

Presbyterian preachers leveled heavy fire at the culture and religion of pioneer Indiana. Quite as often they were targets themselves. They got even worse than they gave. With one voice the missionaries testify to Indiana's early prejudice against Presbyterians. The image of the Presbyterian preacher as the outlander, the latecomer, and the "educated big bug" was operative in Indiana from the beginning. Frontier culture could be cruelly intolerant of those who seemed to differ or to judge its ways.[93] Baptists and Methodists and New Lights had become well established with a clear priority in time, in numbers, and in evangelistic vigor. They had provided lay preachers when the Presbyterians had provided none. Campbellites were specialists at annoying Presbyterians; because of their aversion to creeds they found the minuscule distinctions between Old School Presbyterians and New School Presbyterians particularly amusing.

Opponents of organized support for missions, education, and social reform focused their displeasure on

Presbyterians. They often charged Presbyterians with coercion and with improper alliance of church and state. At Crawfordsville a Baptist church passed a resolution prohibiting any of its members from becoming subscribers to a temperance society and a Baptist minister near there declared himself ready to oppose any of the "benevolent institutions" of the day.[94] Jeremiah Hill reported that there were about thirty preachers in Owen and Greene counties "all of them nearly to a man opposed to Missionary operations, especially to the movements of Presbyterians."[95] Organizers of a Sunday school in Indianapolis were charged with receiving salaries for their services and exploiting the children through the price of books. It was also charged that the teachers got a commission for every scholar enrolled because the rolls were sent to England where every scholar named became a subject of the King of Great Britain.[96] At Jeffersonville a local physician and Baptist preacher not only violently opposed a temperance society but also any Sunday school, Bible society, tract society, or missionary education society on the grounds of "union of church and state" and infringement of the people's liberties. James Crawford reported from Jefferson County that religious sects were numerous "and all harmoniously unite in decrying education as a requisite to a public teacher and in abusing the learned clergy who take wages for their services."[97]

Even Presbyterian congregations might be wary of linkage with easterners and eastern societies. Consider the plight of Archibald Craig, whose house burned and whose family expenses mounted. His congregation was happy with his work but felt it could not raise its subscription. Nor, as a matter of principle, would it allow him to apply for mission aid. "I must pay for periodicals, support benevolent institutions, settle with the postmaster and stationer, pay taxes, discharge the bills of a schoolmaster, tailor, shoemaker etc., etc., out of $170—one half paid in produce and part of the other half paid in nothing at all in order that my people may convince this world that I do not preach for money."[98]

Presbyterian bashing often took the form of attacks on the doctrine of predestination. Presbyterians had no monopoly on the position. Catholics, Lutherans, Reformed, Congregationalists, and Baptists shared the predestinarian heritage. Presbyterian preachers in Indiana were not nearly so enthusiastic to advocate the doctrine as were the Hardshell Baptists and rarely debated the issue. New School Presbyterians were especially prone to find ways to avoid voicing any predestinarian "absurdities." But the Presbyterian confessional statements concerning predestination were not amended until the

end of the nineteenth century when union with the Cumberland Presbyterians was imminent. During Indiana's pioneer days every preacher in the Presbyterian Church in the U.S.A. had a copy of the Westminster Confession of Faith in his study and had made some level of affirmation of its system of doctrine. This Calvinist creed was written by the Assembly, called by the English Parliament, which met at Westminster Abbey 1643–47. Chapter three read:

> By the decree of God, for the manifestation of his glory, some men and angels (I Timothy 5:21; Matthew 25:41) are predestinated unto everlasting life, and others fore-ordained to everlasting death (Romans 9:22–23; Ephesians 1:5–6; Proverbs 16:4). These angels and men, thus predestinated and fore-ordained, are particularly and unchangeably designed; and their number is so certain and definite that it cannot be either increased or diminished (II Timothy 2:19; John 13:18) . . . The doctrine of this high mystery of predestination is to be handled with special prudence and care (Romans 9:20; Romans 11:33; Deuteronomy 29:29), that men attending the will of God revealed in his work, and yielding obedience thereunto, may, from the certainty of their effectual vocation, be assured of their eternal election (II Peter 1:10). So shall this doctrine afford matter of praise, reverence, and admiration of God (Ephesians 1:6; Romans 11:33); and of humility, diligence, and abundant consolation to all that sincerely obey the gospel (Romans 9:5,6,20; Romans 8:33; Luke 10:20).[99]

Rejection of predestination became a universal camp meeting ritual. Baynard Hall reported one of its forms at a camp meeting at Bloomington in 1824 in the capable hands of Methodist elder James Armstrong. The hour was Sunday morning and the subject was a rousing attack on Calvin, Calvinists, and Calvinism—"no subject is better for popularity at a camp meeting." First there was the story of Calvin and Servetus, featuring Servetus as Christian confessor and martyr and Calvin as diabolical persecutor. The whole was done with a voice choir of congregational participation.

> Judging from the frequency of the deep groans, loud amens, and noisy hallelujahs of the congregation during the narrative, had Calvin suddenly thrust in among us his hatchet face and goat's beard, he would have been hissed and pelted, nay possibly, been lynched and soused in the Branch; while the excellent Servetus would have been toted on our shoulders, and feasted in the tents on fried ham, cold chicken fixins and horse sorrel pies!
>
> Here is a specimen of Mr. S.'s mode of exciting triumphant exclamation, amens, groans, &c., against Calvin and his followers.—"Dear sisters, don't you love the

tender little darling babes that hang on your parental bosoms? (amen!)—Yes! I know you do—(amen! amen!)—Yes I Know, I Know it—(Amen, amen! hallelujah!) Now don't it make your parental hearts throb with anguish to think those dear infantile darlings might some day be out burning brush and fall into the flames and be burned to death! (deep groans.)—Yes it does, it does! But oh! sisters, oh! mothers! how can you think your babes mightn't get religion and die and be burned for ever and ever? (the Lord forbid—amen—groans.) But, oho! only think—only think oh! would you ever a had them darling infantile sucklings born, if you had a known they were to be burned in a brush heap! (No, no!—groans—shrieks) What! what what! if you had foreknown they must have gone to hell!—(hoho! hoho!—amen!) And does any body think He is such a tyrant as to make spotless, innocent babies just to damn them? (No! in a voice of thunder.)—No! sisters! no! no! mothers! No! no! no! sinners no!! he ain't such a tyrant! let John Calvin burn, torture and roast, but He never foreordained babies, as Calvin says, to damnation! (damnation—echoed by hundreds.)—Hallelujah! 'tis a free salvation! Glory! a free salvation!—(Here Mr. S. battered the rail of the pulpit with his fists, and kicked the bottom with his feet—many screamed—some cried amen!—others groaned and hissed—and more than a dozen females of two opposite colours arose and clapped their hands as if engaged in starching, &c. &c.) No ho! 'tis a free, a free, a free salvation!—away with Calvin! 'tis for all; all! ALL. Yes! shout it out! clap on! rejoice! rejoice! oho-oho! sinners, sinners, sinners, oh-ho-oho!" &c. &c.[100]

Many Presbyterian missionaries sent apologies to their sending agency for making frequent experimental relocations within the state. Their usefulness was being limited, they said, or they felt conditions must really be better somewhere else.

> You seem to regret my frequent changes of location and say that "nothing more discourages the efforts of the Society than the frequent changes of ministers." No one is more sensible of the evil tendency of such changes, than I am; or more deeply deplores the necessity of having to make them; yet such is the heterogeneous character of society, and the fluctuating state of things here in this "far West" that changes of this kind are often unavoidable however undesirable.[101]

Moody Chase said of his relocation from Paoli:

> The greater part of the town and vicinity are Quakers. Another part Methodists another infidels. And a very few—some four or five families—Presbyterians. I could not keep a S. School in operation. And some of our people had heard that I was a New School man and

under the H.M.S. away off to the East there. And it seemed to me that it was not best to fish where there were so few fish and they among so many rocks.[102]

Some were pushed out of Indiana because of combinations of mud, sickness, poverty, unappreciative constituents, and their own inflexibility. Some were pulled out of Indiana by excitement about greater possibilities in Illinois, Michigan, Missouri, Iowa, Oregon, and California.

Replacements for Indiana had to be of the right sort. Agent Henry Little sent the American Home Missionary Society a list of six places in Indiana which needed ministers. "Each of these places needs a man easy to describe but hard to find."[103] Society officers learned early that its missionary operations in southern states were more expensive and less fruitful that those in the Northwest. Among the states of the Northwest, Indiana was the most "southern" and proved the hardest field. Observant Indiana missionaries pointed out that Indiana was not getting its numerical share of the missionaries commissioned.

> I intend *Deo Volente* to write some things about Indiana shortly in order to remind you that "there is such a state as Indiana" and that while it has almost double the population of Illinois it is receiving but little more than half the aid, and has only about the same number of ministers. Illinois is supposed to have 375,000 inhabitants and Indiana 700,000. Illinois has 70 ministers and Indiana 76. In 1833 three years before Illinois had 38 ministers and Indiana 72 ministers. Why is this?[104]

Henry Little said it made no sense to send mission aid only to the newer frontiers; that would be like trying to clear a farm by cutting a tree here and there. The call was also to continue the work in Ohio and Indiana and "possess the land."[105]

Centers of Growth and Ministry

In spite of all the complaining about how tough conditions were and about how little they were accomplishing, dozens and finally scores of Presbyterian preachers stood fast with their congregations to make a contribution to Indiana's religious life. Standing out from the culture might make them targets; standing out from the culture might also make them standard raisers. There was little inclination to modify ministerial requirements. Indiana was mostly woods in 1831 but Salem's Benjamin Cressy told the students at Hanover:

> How absurd to suppose that it is either pleasing to God or profitable to men that the weak minded and ignorant

should fill the sacred office . . . He who would be a profound student in the Bible,—a workman that needeth not to be ashamed should have a knowledge of the original languages in which the scriptures were written: for how shall he satisfy his own mind amid the clashing of sectarian views, unless he be able himself to go to the fountain head? Destitute of an acquaintance with the Laws, customs, usages and sentiments of those nations where the Bible was written, how shall the minister employ in his service those rules of correct interpretation which are so essential in acquiring a critical knowledge of the scriptures? He whose great work is to combat the prejudices of men and mould the heart to the spirit of the gospel should be intimately acquainted with the laws of the mind. A thorough knowledge of mental philosophy will enable the minister "to touch skilfully the springs of thought" and to trace back and analyze the premises from which so many false inferences are deduced. No science affords such an extensive range for investigation as that of theology. It embraces almost every department of science and literature. And the more extensively acquainted with these various branches of knowledge the minister is, the more capable he is of comprehending the Bible. To enter even upon the threshold of theological science requires a vigorous mind, disciplined by habits of fixed attention.[106]

No Presbyterians rose to such great prominence as to eclipse all the rest. But in town after town after town the church came to be represented by a congregation with a persistent and competent ministry. Examples of the Old School style were John R. Moreland at Indianapolis, David Monfort at Franklin and Hopewell, and William Robinson at Madison. William W. Martin personified Old School opinion at Livonia for twenty-four years. There he operated his famous academy and reared his ten children—the three boys to be ministers and five of the daughters to be wives of ministers. Most significant of all, the Old School had John Finley Crowe, John Matthews, and their colleagues at Hanover College and Indiana Theological Seminary.[107] Crowe reminded Hoosier Presbyterians of the contribution of Hanover College in 1858.

Its collegiate [post-academy] existence commenced in 1833—twenty-five years ago. During that time, out of 223 graduates, 126 are Presbyterian ministers and students of theology—a proportion over one-half; while 36 are teachers, 10 of whom have been Professors in Colleges, and many of the rest Principals of prominent Seminaries. In this estimate we have included the present graduating class. One hundred and thirty others of its students have entered the ministry without graduating; making 226 of its alumni and students, who are and have been laborers in different parts of the Lord's vineyard—some in foreign lands, but principally in the "Great West," distributed through seventeen states and two territories. We believe that no other College in the United States can point to such a list.[108]

James H. Johnston commented in 1865 that of 124 active Old School Presbyterian ministers in Indiana, 44 had been students at Hanover College.[109]

For the New School Presbyterians the men and the money of the American Home Missionary Society kept coming. The society sent some men born and educated in the East, like the "polished preacher" Benjamin C. Cressy to Salem and the successful minister to youth Solomon Kittredge to Bedford. They sent some western-born seminarians back west with a commission. Such a one was Philip S. Cleland of Kentucky who, after studying at Andover Seminary, returned to serve over twenty-five years in Indiana. They commissioned some resident Indiana preachers to spend part of their time in missionary itineration. So Isaac Reed and John McElroy Dickey invested much effort in such missionary labor to the benefit of both their family budgets and Presbyterianism in the state.

When the State of Indiana was young, James H. Johnston, native of New York and pastor at Madison, was stated clerk of Indiana Synod and executive secretary of the Indiana Missionary Society. Missionaries arriving in Indiana reported to him for placement and he evaluated their work in the field for the Society. After eighteen years at Madison, Johnston accepted a missionary commission for himself and moved north to the Crawfordsville area in 1843.[110] That upper Wabash valley was an area of particular interest to the American Home Missionary Society and many a Yankee missionary suffered the shakes of the ague there before the mosquito pools could be drained.

James Chute of Massachusetts was their pioneer preacher at Fort Wayne. That was a tough place. Much of the population was composed of Indians, traders, speculators, and canal laborers. Chute preached to everybody in the county who would hear him, including the men on the canal. He preached in all the neighborhoods for the sake of those not accustomed to inconveniencing themselves by traveling to meetings. He pushed the temperance cause by law and persuasion until the sale of liquor to the Indians was prohibited, the issue of whiskey as a standard provision to canal workers was halted, and the temperance society gained ground to the point that consumption of whiskey dropped to one-eighth of what it had been two years earlier. When eighty people died in a single quarter, he ministered to the sick. Still the church grew very slowly. Chute kept explaining why the cost of living was so high and applying for more mission aid.

Besides serving his seven regular preaching points in his home county, he was always pleading the cause of his neighbors to the American Home Missionary Society. Huntington, Wabash, and Peru were among the rising county seat towns he worried about. Construction of a church building was begun at Fort Wayne in 1835 but Chute did not live to occupy its pulpit. He died that year of the "bilious fever."[111]

Missionary Martin M. Post of Vermont moved to the raw new settlement of Logansport at Christmas time in 1829 and there he stayed. The Presbyterian Church was the first on the scene, although only two persons in the area had ever been Presbyterian members. Post said: "I came here without experience in the duties of my calling, and with little practical knowledge of men, and none of Western life. Against strong withholding motives, induced decisively by a conviction of the superior claims of the new States on any little service my life could render, I sought my way, alone, to Indiana."[112]

The woods around Logansport were still full of Indians, regularly made drunk and fleeced by enterprising white men. Post promoted the range of good causes within his area. He superintended the first Sunday school in 1830, visited all families in the county to supply copies of the Bible in 1831, distributed tracts, established the first temperance society in 1831, and encouraged its growth to 250 members by 1837. For many years at least half of Post's ministry was out of town. Gradually those isolated settlers formed country congregations which, under his encouragement, had built churches by 1860. He had frequently gone to Miamisport which flourished until it merged with Peru. He went to Marion, South Bend, La-Porte, Michigan City, Valparaiso, and many other places. As he explored, Post sent letters to the American Home Missionary Society urging the importance of and the claims of the whole Wabash country. Canals, state roads, and the natural fertility were bound to make this an important area. He reported that there was not a handful of Presbyterians in most of these places, but that the citizens in general would support a minister if one came.[113]

Post and Johnston were but two members of a band of young Society missionaries in the upper Wabash valley deliberately planning and conducting Presbyterian evangelization in northern Indiana. Others were James A. Carnahan, James Crawford, Edmund O. Hovey, Samuel G. Lowry, Caleb Mills, James Thompson, and John Thompson—each a candidate for a biography in his own right. From them came the dream and the reality of Wabash Manual Labor College and Teachers' Seminary, founded at Crawfordsville in 1832 specifically for pre-

paring young Hoosiers for the ministry and for teaching. Caleb Mills, graduate of Dartmouth and Andover, was invited to come west as its first teacher and acting president—and concurrently part time missionary for a church six miles west of town to guarantee that he would receive at least some salary. He and missionary minister Hovey, native of New Hampshire and graduate of Dartmouth and Andover, were the heart of the faculty for the new college, serving side by side there for more than forty years. Elihu W. Baldwin, a New Yorker with degrees from Yale and Andover, moved west to become first president of Wabash in 1835.[114]

The American Home Missionary Society came to see the advantages of appointing regional representatives. "State agents . . . are the most economical appointments we can make," said the Society's New York executive Absalom Peters. A good agent could increase collection of missionary funds even in his own western territory far more than the cost of his salary, garner subscriptions for the Society's *Home Missionary*, multiply Sunday schools and promote a whole range of benevolent causes, require churches and ministers applying for Society aid to be more honest about their pledges and their prospects, assure some continuity of pastoral care by attracting missionaries to his area and pointing them toward strategic vacancies, evaluate the performance of missionaries at work, and provide aid to missionary families during times of crisis. James H. Johnston was given a one year appointment to such an agency with a salary of five hundred dollars as early as 1832.[115]

A whole new level of efficiency was achieved when New School preacher Henry Little of Madison accepted the "western agency" for Indiana and Ohio in 1840. His leadership came at a crucial time, just after the painful damage of the Old School-New School division and just in time for the impressive development of northern Indiana. Little left his wife and four children "among friends" at Madison and traveled constantly. First he went east to General Assembly to confer with Society executives, to see New York and New England again, "and get hold of some of the springs of action." He addressed the students at Andover about the need for missionaries in the West. In the East he collected money for the West; in the West he collected for missions "in small as well as large churches in each presbytery."[116]

Western steamboat captains knew Henry Little so well that he traveled "very cheap" on the river. The long inland trips were more expensive and exhausting. At Michigan City he wrote: "There are now mud-holes between me & my home that would scare anybody but a back woods man in the West, but as I have never yet been permanently stuck in a mud-hole, I hope to go through the whole of them & get home safe next week." After a horseback ride of 325 miles, delayed at a broken canal lock near Fort Wayne, he said the mosquitoes were "beyond all the books have said about them." He thought Ohio River mosquitoes were like wolves which only attack at night; northern Indiana mosquitoes bit night and day. There were accidents. "I was thrown out of a buggy last Saturday upon a rough down hill side of a McAdamized road & badly bruised in seven places but as my tongue was not hurt I told the usual story on the Sabbath."

In the churches Little presented his cause with such force and good humor that ministers and members always welcomed him, saving up their mission gifts in anticipation of his coming. During his first year as agent somebody at Greencastle gave him a horse for the mission cause; he was able to sell the horse for seventy dollars. In the years that followed he accepted many other gifts in kind and enough horses for a veritable Presbyterian cavalry.[117]

Just at the beginning of Little's agency the Society office in New York first advertised in the *New York Evangelist*, the *Boston Recorder*, the *New York Observer*, and the *Home Missionary* that it was willing to begin forwarding boxes or barrels of clothing, books, and useful articles packed by eastern churches for needy missionaries in the West. That was in August of 1841. By November of that year 169 boxes were accumulated at Detroit and the Society was into the missionary box business. Just before Christmas of 1841, Little sent thanks for Indiana's share. "Six boxes have come to hand and we shall be able to make many a heart glad by their distribution."[118] It was a lot of work to arrange for systematic distribution and acknowledgment of all the boxes which followed, but Henry Little personally saw the joy they brought.[119]

When times were hard Little cut his own pay one hundred dollars for the year and commented that missionaries were receiving little from their people but bread and meat. James H. Shields and his family of Greencastle received some clothing in that first distribution of boxes in fall of 1841 and were grateful. It was mostly bedclothes; what they needed even more desperately was wearing apparel. In 1842 there was a great revival in Greencastle. Fifty-seven were added to the Presbyterian church alone. Pastor Shields's wife and children could not even attend the meetings for want of shoes and clothing. By 1845 Shields was ministering in Owen County where riding in bad weather without a good coat brought back his fever for two or three weeks. Two boxes of clothing came. "When we received the boxes we all knelt down around them and with full hearts sent up our thanks to God."[120] Samuel G. Lowry at Rockville heard about the boxes.

> I observe a notice on the cover of the "Home Missionary" for this month respecting boxes for the West. I will venture to state frankly my own case and leave it to you to act as you think best. We have 8 children. The first 4, sons, 20–18–16–14 years of age. The oldest 3 I have had at College. The 2nd has just graduated. The next 3 are daughters, 12–10-and 8 years old. The next is a son near two years old. Besides these I have a widdow [sic] sister with three children that I have to provide for. She has two sons 8 and 5 years and a daughter 6 years old. I shall not say what kind of clothing I want. There is no kind that can come amiss in such a family."[121]

As Little began his work as agent in 1841 he said the New School in Indiana had only a few more than three thousand members while the Old School had nearly twice as many. "So the New School is left with a lot of small splintered congregations needing help."[122] The conservative Old School stance against any Yankee innovations was always appealing to Indiana's constituency. But the combination of the Wabash valley missionary group and the American Home Missionary Society effort as personified by Henry Little contributed Presbyterian growth and New School strength especially north of the National Road. In 1845 Henry Ward Beecher was New School Presbyterian preacher at Indianapolis and his brother Charles was New School missionary at Fort Wayne. Charles said he could count seventeen Old School congregations in northern Indiana compared to twenty-four for the New School.[123] In 1850 eleven of the counties in which Presbyterians were more than 75 percent New School were north of the National Road while only four such counties were in southern Indiana. Of the ten counties in which Presbyterians were between 51 and 75 percent New School, six were north of the National Road while only three were south of it.[124]

In the earliest years of Indiana's statehood, Presbyterian leaders on its frontiers found illiteracy, drunkenness, and preachers without formal education. Against these conditions they saw themselves as crusaders for the survival of a proper kind of church as well as crusaders for the very survival of the state and nation. In this situation they aimed to be reformers even at the cost of public resentment. So their effort went into home missions in order to provide their kind of preaching everywhere.

Schooling was also their passion. They wanted Bible classes and Bible distribution to be developed in every place. They established hundreds of Sunday schools, not only at their churches but also at points far beyond their parish perimeters. These Sunday schools were designed to teach illiterate persons to read, to read the Bible, and to enjoy all the excitements of using the school's lending library.[125] They operated all sorts of private weekday schools wherever there was space in their houses and churches. It was Caleb Mills, a minister and professor among the New School Presbyterians, who conducted an effective one-man campaign on behalf of public schools in Indiana. He embarrassed the Indiana legislatures of 1846-51 with his printed documentation of the sorry state of Indiana minds and finally enlisted many state forces in producing a system of common schools.[126]

Presbyterian "academies" could accept any literate scholar and offer him education up to college level. Presbyterians operated or shared in operating academies at Charlestown, Crawfordsville, Dunlapsville, Evansville, Fort Wayne, Franklin, Greensburg, Lebanon, Livonia, Logansport, New Albany, Newburgh, Orland, Paoli, Peru, Petersburg, Princeton, Richland, Richmond, Salem, Waveland, and additional places where their identity has been lost.[127] The academies at Hanover and Wabash developed into colleges. Presbyterians were also prominent in the early faculty and administration of Indiana University at Bloomington. However that university's Board of Trustees denied the persistent charge of Presbyterian monopoly in a statement issued 8 December 1830 noting that only five of fifteen trustees were Presbyterian and no sectarian domination existed.[128]

In the course of all this preaching and teaching and waiting for improvement, Presbyterian missionaries developed some understanding of Indiana. They kept supplying their colleagues in the East with advice about ministry to Hoosiers. Said James A. Carnahan at Lafayette:

> They want a man that can preach in the house or out of the house, on a stump or on a barrel, in a cabin or in a barn. One who if the people cannot hear him can speak a little louder and if that will not answer, who can hollow—who must and will be heard. One who can sit on a stool and lie on the chaff or in a log cabin without chinking and his wife if he has one must partake the same spirit.[129]

Henry Little asked if the Society could furnish the West with first rate ministers who could talk "right on" and talk to the point. Circulating tracts and books would not be enough. "If any man, whether politician, schoolmaster, or preacher will do good at the West he must keep in mind that we are a talking not a reading people.

If any Martin Luther is to arise and 'right up things' here he must see their faces and by his public appeals create an appetite for his books."[130] Charles Beecher at Fort Wayne said, "The population are in the woods . . . Can you not commission and send out a young man, unmarried, zealous, pious, who can ride like a Methodist circuit rider, live with any body and eat any how, any time and any thing? Such a man will in one year secure near half the means of a next years support. Such a man is a missionary."[131] President White at Wabash kept being embarrassed by letters from the East asking for a specific list of places in northern Indiana looking for a minister with indication of what support each congregation would pledge. Somehow the East must be made to understand that new areas of the West had neither churches nor salaries nor places to go.

> Now there are very few points where ministers are wanted. In fact there are strictly speaking neither points nor wants; both the places are to be looked up and the desire to be created. The need is great, pressing, immense, infinite. Points ought to be settled on immediately all over the country and can be. Moreover in most parts there are no churches and congregations large enough to pledge any considerable support; and if they were, they would not pledge any thing until the man was among them going from cabin to cabin winding himself into their hearts and laying down the truth at the threshold of their consciences like a zealous indefatigable honest man.[132]

Things were changing by the 1850s. Presbyterians had become acclimated to Indiana as a field of service. They were less the critics of culture and the subjects of attack now; they were more the accepted leaders of substantial church enterprises. Survival in a hostile environment, once a primary matter for Presbyterians, was hardly an issue any more. Indiana had well over two hundred Presbyterian congregations, many in town centers where they included not only those few families who were traditionally Presbyterian but also all those middle class Hoosier farmers and merchants and professional persons enlisted through preaching and teaching during the years of "missionating." In nineteenth century fashion, congregational attendance might be double the number of members. Those present heard sermons carefully prepared, sang from the new hymnbooks instead of lining out psalms, and took pride in the organs installed in their brick churches. Each church was the home for at least one Sunday school, for adult Bible study classes, for at least one weekly prayer meeting, and probably for an auxiliary missionary society, temperance society, tract society, Bible society, or education society.

Organized women's work had long been familiar. Missionary Ashbel Wells at New Albany reported in 1828 that the Female Bible Society of his church would soon complete the work of supplying every destitute family in the county with the word of God. They did it—probably the first county so supplied in the state. Peter Crocker wrote from Richmond in 1838, "We have recently formed a maternal association and sewing society which promises good and we have the pleasing prospect of being able in the course of the year to contribute something to the American Home Missionary Society." The Greencastle Presbyterian Church women were successively the Female Aid Society, Soldiers Aid Society, Willing Workers, Hatchet Sisters, and Ladies Aid.[133]

A certain mood of caution settled over the reforming zeal of most of the clergy. Moral reform and education and temperance and the abolition of slavery were certainly advocated. Indiana's synods and presbyteries were consistent in endorsing all these at some safe distance from the parishes. A few radicals kept speaking out in their own churches even on abolition, the most disruptive of all reform subjects. Sand Creek Presbyterian Church at Kingston in Decatur County withdrew from the denomination and joined the Free Presbyterians in order to dramatize their stand against slavery. Said their minister Benjamin Nyce from his pulpit on the Sunday after the Fugitive Slave Law was adopted in 1850: "To law framed of such iniquity I owe no allegiance. Humanity, Christianity, manhood revolt against it. For myself I say it solemnly, I will shelter, I will help, and I will defend the fugitive with all my humble means and power. I will act with any body of decent and serious men . . . in any mode not involving the use of deadly weapons, to nullify and defeat the operation of this law."[134]

Philip S. Cleland, John Finley Crowe, Daniel Smith, and Charles Beecher also refused to be quiet or moderate on the subject of slavery. But most sought to avoid anything disruptive for the sake of their ongoing church work. A Presbyterian historian commented:

In the earlier years, from 1826 until the late 1840s, missionaries acted directly to confront what they perceived as prevailing evils in society. Their pastoral duties seemed inseparable from interest in reform. They were rarely deterred when their assaults on illiteracy, drunkenness, or other transgressions stirred public opposition. But in the last decade before the Civil War, these missionaries or their successors often sought to evade controversy, even when an issue at hand, like slavery, was also perceived as a prevailing social evil . . . Certain developments in the temperance crusade and most aspects of the antislavery movement made the task of shepherding congregations difficult, or so the missionaries believed. They were convinced that politics and exciting secular events, like war, had power to devastate the peace and growth of their congregations. Facing the threat of this disruption, they remembered that they were called first and foremost to administer the gospel through their churches. They began mentally to separate churchly duties from the work of social reform. Their predecessors in the mission field had not been able to make such a separation.[135]

And by the 1850s the field had changed. Indiana's population of about a million, excited about developing industries and transportation connections, was less withdrawn and less inclined to regard eastern influences as alien. There was a public school law; even if the "school system" was new and feeble there was some hope for general literacy. Baptists, Methodists, and Christians now had their advocates of Sunday schools and were active in development of Sunday school publications and libraries. The strongest congregations of these large and popular denominations wanted and got educated pastors. They urged systematic support of missions. And each of these major denominations now had a college in Indiana. The literary quality of a published sermon or of a speech at a major public occasion no longer correlated with denomination. With the institutions of their Reformed tradition now on a firm footing in the state, and with invitations for friendly interaction coming from so many like-minded colleagues across denominational lines, Presbyterians gave increasing attention to cooperative undertakings among the churches.

NOTES

1. "Reformed" refers to a heritage in this particular wing of the sixteenth century reformation. "Presbyterian" refers to the usual form of government of these churches at every level by elected elders or "presbyters." So it is appropriate to speak of all these fellowships interchangeably as Reformed or Presbyterian. However, one popular usage prefers to employ the term Reformed broadly for this whole international family of churches. And the term Presbyterian more often appears in the names of that church family's denominations with origins among English speakers such as those in Scotland and the United States.

2. James Brown Scouller, *History of the United Presbyterian Church of North America*, American Church History Series, vol. 11 (New York: Charles Scribner's Sons, 1911), 150.

3. James A. Woodburn, *The Scotch-Irish Presbyterians in Monroe County, Indiana*, Indiana Historical Society Publications, vol. 4, no. 8 (Indianapolis, Ind.: Edward J. Hecker, 1910), 462–65. For a delineation of the whole psalm-singer heritage see Ray A. King, *A*

History of the Associate Reformed Presbyterian Church (Charlotte, N.C.: Board of Christian Education of the Associate Reformed Presbyterian Church, 1966, 132 p.).

4. *Minutes of the General Assembly of the United Presbyterian Church of North America*, Part 1 (1958): 1,000–1, 1,010–13.

5. H. P. Jackson, *A History of Carmel Congregation of the United Presbyterian Church, near Hanover, Jefferson County, Indiana* (Madison, Ind.: Courier Company, 1882, 28 p.); Scouller, *History*, 176–78.

6. Jackson, *History*, 6–7.

7. *Centennial Celebration of the United Presbyterian Church, Princeton, Indiana*, comp. Gilbert R. Stormont (Terre Haute, Ind.: Moore-Langen Printing Co., 1911), 13–16, 68–69, 77–83, 101.

8. Robert Archer Woods, "Presbyterianism in Princeton Indiana, from 1810 to 1930," *Indiana Magazine of History* 26 (June 1930): 94.

9. Woodburn, *Scotch-Irish Presbyterians*, 450–51. Woodburn's account lists the names of many psalm-singing families which migrated to Bloomington.

10. Woodburn, *Scotch-Irish Presbyterians*, 469–70, 475–80.

11. Anton T. Boisen, *Out of the Depths* (New York: Harper and Brothers, 1960), 18–20.

12. John E. Meek, *A History of Springhill, 1825–1975* (Rushville, Ind.: Wilkinson Printing, 1975), 1–3, 7; John W. Meloy, "A History of the Indiana Presbytery of the United Presbyterian Church," *Indiana Magazine of History* 31 (March 1935): 27–29.

13. *Centennial Celebration*, 89.

14. J. B. Blount, "Religious History," in *History of Rush County, Indiana* (Chicago: Brant and Fuller, 1888), 534.

15. James A. Woodburn, "United Presbyterian Beginnings," *Indiana Magazine of History* 30 (March 1934): 20.

16. Woodburn, *Scotch-Irish Presbyterians*, 441–42, 519–22; Woodburn, "United Presbyterian Beginnings," 28.

17. Woodburn, *Scotch-Irish Presbyterians*, 468.

18. Glenn H. Asquith, Jr., "Anton T. Boisen and the Study of 'Living Human Documents'," *Journal of Presbyterian History* 60 (Fall 1982): 244, 247–51, 256–57.

19. Woodburn, "United Presbyterian Beginnings," 17; *Centennial Celebration*, 51, 91–98, 111; Meek, *History*, 7.

20. *History of Decatur County, Indiana*, ed. Lewis A. Harding (Indianapolis, Ind.: B. F. Bowen and Company, 1915), 256.

21. *Bloomington United Presbyterian Church Centennial* (Bloomington, Ind.: United Presbyterian Church, 1934), 19.

22. *Bloomington United Presbyterian Church Centennial*, 19–20.

23. Anton T. Boisen, "Divided Protestantism in a Midwest County: A Study in the Natural History of Organized Religion," *Journal of Religion* 20 (October 1940): 372.

24. Boisen, "Divided Protestantism," 363.

25. H. Richard Niebuhr, *Social Sources of Denominationalism* (New York: Henry Holt and Co., 1929).

26. Boisen, "Divided Protestantism," 370. It is ironic that a modern biographer of Boisen says his essential genius may have lain in the way he combined his own psalm-singing Calvinist heritage with his clinical insight into human experience. See Asquith, "Anton T. Boisen," 260–62.

27. Keith R. Magill, "A Brief History of the Reformed Presbyterian Church of North America in Central Indiana" (Unpublished paper, Indianapolis, Ind., March 1980, 79 p.).

28. *A Circular Letter Addressed to the Societies and Brethren of the Presbyterian Church Recently under the Care of the Council by the Late Cumberland Presbytery, in which There Is a Correct Statement of the Origin, Progress, and Termination, of the Difference, between the Synod of Kentucky and the Former Presbytery of Cumberland* (Russellville, Ky.: Printed by Matthew Duncan, at the office of the "Farmer's Friend," 1810, 14 p.). Reprinted in Robert V. Foster, *A Sketch of the History of the Cumberland Presbyterian Church*, American Church History Series, vol. 11 (New York: Charles Scribner's Sons, 1911), 273.

29. R. Douglas Brackenridge, *Voice in the Wilderness* (San Antonio, Texas: Trinity University Press, 1968), 4; Louis B. Weeks, *Kentucky Presbyterians* (Atlanta, Ga.: John Knox Press, 1983), 48–49.

30. Foster, *Sketch*, 282.

31. Ben M. Barrus, Milton L. Baughn, and Thomas H. Campbell, *A People Called Cumberland Presbyterians* (Memphis, Tenn.: Frontier Press, 1972), 106.

32. W. J. Darby, and J. E. Jenkins, *Cumberland Presbyterianism in Southern Indiana* (Indianapolis, Ind.: Indiana Presbytery, 1876), 80. See also Barrus, Baughn, and Campbell, *People*, 326.

33. Darby and Jenkins, *Cumberland*, 25, 36, 112; Foster, *Sketch*, 289.

34. Foster, *Sketch*, 284.

35. Barrus, Baughn, and Campbell, *People*, 116–17; Brackenridge, *Voice*, 9.

36. Beulah B. Gray, *The Saga of Three Churches: A History of Presbyterianism in Petersburg 1821–1953* (N.p., 1953?), 106–8; Darby and Jenkins, *Cumberland*, 18, 71.

37. Darby and Jenkins, *Cumberland*, 18–19; see also 70–71.

38. Barrus, Baughn, and Campbell, *People*, 110; Darby and Jenkins, *Cumberland*, 20–21.

39. Barrus, Baughn, and Campbell, *People*, 110.

40. Darby and Jenkins, *Cumberland*, 66, 67, 77.

41. Darby and Jenkins, *Cumberland*, 21–23.

42. Barrus, Baughn, and Campbell, *People*, 128–31.

43. Darby and Jenkins, *Cumberland*, 23.

44. Barrus, Baughn, and Campbell, *People*, 208.

45. Barrus, Baughn, and Campbell, *People*, 131, 176–77, 200, 209. Indiana's 5,902 Cumberland Presbyterians in 1899 compared with 41,512 in Tennessee; 29,905 in Texas; 26,443 in Missouri; 16,197 in Kentucky; 14,892 in Illinois; 11,139 in Arkansas; 7,093 in Pennsylvania; and 6,477 in Alabama.

46. *Minutes of the General Assembly of the Cumberland Presbyterian Church* (1906), 602–12; Darby and Jenkins, *Cumberland*, 28, 55, 69, 85–86, 100.

47. *Centennial Celebration*, 107–12; Woods, "Presbyterianism in Princeton," 123.

48. Darby and Jenkins, *Cumberland*, 14, 41, 46, 63–64; Gray, *Saga*, 108, 111–14.

49. Darby and Jenkins, *Cumberland*, 106–7.

50. Darby and Jenkins, *Cumberland*, 104–9; Barrus, Baughn, and Campbell, *People*, 231–32.

51. Darby and Jenkins, *Cumberland*, 42–43; Barrus, Baughn, and Campbell, *People*, 128, 156–59, 174, 210–12, 248, 325, 380, 433, 491; Gray, *Saga*, 121–22, 131–32.

52. Barrus, Baughn, and Campbell, *People*, 324–25, 346, 380–81, 386–87; *Minutes of the General Assembly of the Cumberland Presbyterian Church* (1906), 60a–61a.

53. Lefferts A. Loetscher, *A Brief History of the Presbyterians* (Philadelphia: Westminster Press, 1958), 49–53.

54. James H. Smylie, *American Presbyterians: A Pictorial History* (Philadelphia: Presbyterian Historical Society, 1985), 49.

55. Loetscher, *Brief History*, 67–68.

56. Sydney E. Ahlstrom, *A Religious History of the American People* (New Haven, Conn.: Yale University Press, 1972), 444.

57. Leonard J. Trinterud, *The Forming of an American Tradition* (Philadelphia: Westminster Press, 1949), 268–69, 271; L. C. Rudolph, *Hoosier Zion: The Presbyterians in Early Indiana* (New Haven, Conn.: Yale University Press, 1963), 1–36; Loetscher, *Brief History*, 73; Smylie, *American Presbyterians*, 57; Ahlstrom, *Religious History*, 419, 462–63.

58. "Minutes of Transylvania Presbytery," 2:3, 70, 75, 103–11; Hanford A. Edson, *Contributions to the Early History of the Presbyterian Church in Indiana* (Cincinnati, Ohio: Winona Publishing Co., 1898), 36–40; Edward P. Humphrey and Thomas H. Cleland, comps., *Memoirs of the Rev. Thomas Cleland, D.D., Comp. from His Private Papers* (Cincinnati, Ohio: Moore, Wilstach, Keys and Co., 1859), 87–89, 103.

59. John M. Dickey, *A Brief History of the Presbyterian Church in the State of Indiana* (Madison, Ind.: C. P. J. Arion, 1828), 11–12.

60. Rudolph, *Hoosier Zion*, 40–42.

61. Rudolph, *Hoosier Zion*, 41.

62. Charles Kettleborough, *Constitution Making in Indiana*, 3 vols. (Indianapolis, Ind.: Indiana Historical Commission, 1916–1930), 1:65–69.

63. Samuel J. Mills, and Daniel Smith, *Report of a Missionary Tour through that Part of the United States which Lies West of the Allegany Mountains* (Andover, Mass.: Flagg and Gould, 1815), 15–16; Rudolph, *Hoosier Zion*, 74–76; Edson, *Contributions*, 61–80.

64. Mills and Smith, *Report*, 16.

65. *Home Missionary* 10 (1837): 31–32.

66. Rudolph, *Hoosier Zion*, 44–45. For a list of Indiana's earliest Presbyterian ministers with indication of their source, see Dickey, *Brief History*, 11–18.

67. Colin B. Goodykoontz, *Home Missions on the American Frontier, with Particular Reference to the American Home Missionary Society* (Caldwell, Idaho: Caxton Printers, 1939), 179–80.

68. Rudolph, *Hoosier Zion*, 62–63. As a reference aid to a file of 5,046 missionary letters see L. C. Rudolph, Ware William Wimberly, and Thomas W. Clayton, *Indiana Letters: Abstracts of Letters from Missionaries on the Indiana Frontier to the American Home Missionary Society, 1824–1893*, 3 vols. (Ann Arbor, Mich.: University Microfilms International, 1979).

69. Joseph S. Clark to Milton Badger, AHMS, New York, 29 April 1844.

70. Rudolph, *Hoosier Zion*, 46, 108–9; Edson, *Contributions*, 107–16.

71. Dickey, *Brief History*, 18.

72. Dickey, *Brief History*, 19–25; Rudolph, *Hoosier Zion*, 133–34.

73. Trinterud, *Forming*, 261–64, and *passim*.

74. Ahlstrom, *Religious History*, 403–22, 462–66.

75. Rudolph, *Hoosier Zion*, 120.

76. Rudolph, *Hoosier Zion*, 122–28.

77. Eliphalet Kent, Greenwood, to Absalom Peters, AHMS, New York, 27 November 1835.

78. Philip S. Cleland, Jeffersonville, to Absalom Peters, AHMS, New York, 3 October 1837.

79. Eliphalet Kent, Greenwood, to Absalom Peters, AHMS, New York, 6 April 1839.

80. Solomon Kittredge, Bedford, to Milton Badger, AHMS, New York, 12 November 1839.

81. Rudolph, *Hoosier Zion*, 101–3, 135. Addition of the psalm-singing and Cumberland Presbyterians would have brought the total Presbyterian membership in 1850 to about 2 percent of Indiana's population, a level fairly consistently maintained until 1980.

82. "Minutes of Northern Indiana Synod, Old School," 1:346–49; "Minutes of Salem Presbytery, Old School," 3:133; *History of Indianapolis Presbytery* (Indianapolis, Ind.: The Church at Work Publishing Co., 1887), 11–13.

83. Rudolph, *Hoosier Zion*, 132–33, 147–48.

84. Rudolph, *Hoosier Zion*, 16–19; Charles W. Moores, *Caleb Mills and the Indiana School System*, Indiana Historical Society Publications, vol. 3, no. 6 (Indianapolis, Ind.: Wood-Weaver Printing, 1905), 385–87; Emma Lou Thornbrough, *Indiana in the Civil War Era 1850–1880* (Indianapolis, Ind.: Indiana Historical Bureau and Indiana Historical Society, 1965), 461–64.

85. Rudolph, *Hoosier Zion*, 63–68.

86. For a treatment of reform activity in Indiana by missionaries of the American Home Missionary Society see Ware William Wimberly, "Missionary Reforms in Indiana, 1826–1860. Education, Temperance, Antislavery" (Ph.D. diss., Indiana University, 1977, 310 p.).

87. Isaac Reed, *The Christian Traveller* (New York: J. and J. Harper, 1828), 26, 34, 223, 225.

88. John U. Parsons, China, to Absalom Peters, AHMS, New York, 20 February 1833; Ashbel Wells, New Albany, to Absalom Peters, AHMS, New York, 26 June 1829, 5 January 1830, 16 November 1830; Mary Hovey, Coal Creek, to Martha White, Oswego, New York, 12 May 1832.

89. *Home Missionary* 17 (1844): 74.

90. Rudolph, *Hoosier Zion*, 23.

91. Moody Chase, Orleans, to Absalom Peters, AHMS, New York, 4 February 1833, 9 April 1833.

92. Noah Cook, Elkhart and Goshen, to Milton Badger, AHMS, New York, 1 April 1842, 18 June 1842.

93. Rudolph, *Hoosier Zion*, 17–19.

94. Claibourn Young, Boone County, to Absalom Peters, AHMS, New York, 14 February 1831.

95. Jeremiah Hill, Spencer, to Absalom Peters, AHMS, New York, 22 February 1831.

96. *Centennial Memorial, First Presbyterian Church, Indianapolis, Ind.* (Greenfield, Ind.: William Mitchell Printing Co., 1925), 210.

97. Michael A. Remley, Jeffersonville, to Absalom Peters, AHMS, New York, 14 March 1831; James Crawford, Jefferson County, to Absalom Peters, AHMS, New York, 31 January 1827.

98. Archibald Craig, Franklin County, to Absalom Peters, AHMS, New York, 2 February 1831.

99. *The Constitution of the Presbyterian Church, in the United States of America: Containing the Confession of Faith, the Catechisms, the Form of Government, the Book of Discipline, the Directory for the Worship of God, and General Rules for Judicatories: as Ratified by the General Assembly of 1821, and Amended by the General Assemblies of 1826, and 1833* (Philadelphia: Henry Perkins, 1850), 21, 24.

100. Baynard Hall, *The New Purchase; or, Seven and a Half Years in the Far West*, by Robert Carlton, Esq. (pseud.) Indiana Centennial Edition (Princeton, N.J.: Princeton University Press, 1916), 375–76. The printed key to Hall's pseudonyms identifies "Mr. S" as William Armstrong. "Mr. S" is almost certainly James Armstrong who was in the area and was presiding elder for Indiana District about this time.

101. Michael A. Remley, Columbus, to Absalom Peters, AHMS, New York, 28 November 1833.

102. Moody Chase, Orleans, to Absalom Peters, AHMS, New York, 11 August 1834.

103. Henry Little, Michigan City, to Milton Badger, AHMS, New York, 23 June 1847.

104. Moses H. Wilder, Bath, to Milton Badger, AHMS, New York, 21 November 1836.

105. Henry Little, Cincinnati, to Milton Badger, AHMS, New York, 1 April 1844.

106. Benjamin C. Cressy, *A Discourse on Ministerial Qualifications* (Madison, Ind.: Arion & Lodge, 1831), 9.

107. Rudolph, *Hoosier Zion*, 67–68, 73–75, 104, 122, 127, 140–43; Edson, *Contributions*, 56–60.

108. John Finley Crowe, *An Appeal to the Churches of the Synods of Indiana, in Behalf of Hanover College* (South Hanover, Ind.: n.p., 1858), 4–5.

109. James H. Johnston, *A Ministry of Forty Years in Indiana* (Indianapolis, Ind.: Holloway, Douglass, 1865), 23.

110. Edson, *Contributions*, 202–3; James H. Johnston, Crawfordsville, to Milton Badger, AHMS, New York, 18 September 1844, 30 October 1844.

111. George R. Mather, *Frontier Faith: The Story of the Pioneer Congregations of Fort Wayne, Indiana, 1820–1860* (Fort Wayne, Ind.: Allen County–Fort Wayne Historical Society, 1992), 27–32; Rudolph, *Hoosier Zion*, 82–83.

112. Martin M. Post, *A Retrospect after Thirty Years' Ministry at Logansport, Indiana* (Logansport, Ind.: Bringhurst, 1860), 8.

113. Rudolph, *Hoosier Zion*, 79–81.

114. Wimberly, "Missionary Reforms," 155–66; James Insley Osborne and Theodore Gregory Gronert, *Wabash College: The First Hundred Years, 1832–1932* (Crawfordsville, Ind.: R. E. Banta, 1932, 395 p.).

115. Annotation by Absalom Peters on letter of James H. Johnston, Madison, to B. H. Price, AHMS, New York, 12 December 1832.

116. Henry Little, Madison, to Milton Badger and Charles Hall, AHMS, New York, 30 March 1840, 30 July 1840, 10 May 1841.

117. Henry Little to Milton Badger, AHMS, New York: Michigan City, 23 June 1847; Miami Canal, 27 May 1846; Madison, 30 August 1849, 16 December 1841.

118. Henry Little, Madison, to Milton Badger, AHMS, New York, 16 December 1841.

119. Letters from Indiana missionaries made at least 235 references to boxes sent as part of this program, often references to large multiple shipments to missionaries gathered for a presbytery or synod meeting. Contents varied from well-used garments to a nine-volume set of Newton's *Works*. Material worth at least $20,000 in contemporary value came to Indiana and was targeted to missionary families needing help. See Necia Ann Musser, "Home Missions on the Michigan Frontier," 2 vols. (Ph.D. diss., University of Michigan, 1967), 1:77–80; L. C. Rudolph, "The Deacon's Pants," paper presented at spring workshop of Indiana Historical Society at Madison, Indiana, 9 May 1981, 13 p.

120. Henry Little, Madison, to Milton Badger, AHMS, New York, 9 March 1842; James H. Shields, Greencastle and Mill Grove, to Milton Badger, AHMS, New York, 14 February 1842, 29 November 1842, 14 January 1845.

121. Samuel G. Lowry, Rockville, to Charles Hall, AHMS, New York, 15 August 1842.

122. Henry Little, Madison, to Charles Hall, AHMS, New York, 1 February 1841.

123. Wimberly, "Missionary Reforms," 112–20; Mather, *Frontier Faith*, 163–78; Charles Beecher, Fort Wayne, to Milton Badger, AHMS, New York, 28 March 1845.

124. Bruce Bigelow and Gregory Rose, "The Geography of New School Presbyterians of Indiana in 1850: A Puzzling Map." *Proceedings of the Indiana Academy of the Social Sciences, 1985,* 3d ser., 20:85–90.

125. Wimberly, "Missionary Reforms," 85–139; Rudolph, *Hoosier Zion*, 162–66; *The Daisydingle Sunday-School* (Philadelphia: American Sunday School Union, 1849, 64 p.); David Marion McCord, "Sunday School and Public School. An Exploration of Their Relationship with Special Reference to Indiana, 1790–1860" (Ph.D. diss., Purdue University, 1976, 206 p.).

126. Moores, *Caleb Mills*, 359–638; Rudolph, *Hoosier Zion*, 168–71.

127. John Hardin Thomas, "The Academies of Indiana," *Indiana Magazine of History* 10 (December 1914): 331–58; Wimberly, "Missionary Reforms," 144–53; Rudolph, *Hoosier Zion*, 174–76.

128. Rudolph, *Hoosier Zion*, 178–82.

129. James A. Carnahan, Lafayette, to Absalom Peters, AHMS, New York, 14 September 1831.

130. Henry Little, Madison, to AHMS, New York, 1 February 1841, 30 December 1842.

131. Charles Beecher, Fort Wayne, to Milton Badger, AHMS, New York, 1 August 1845.

132. Charles White, Crawfordsville, to Milton Badger, AHMS, New York, 17 April 1845.

133. Ashbel Wells, New Albany, to Absalom Peters, AHMS, New York, 18 November 1828, 5 January 1830; Peter Crocker, Richmond, to Charles Hall, AHMS, New York, 15 January 1838; *Centennial of the Presbyterian Church, Greencastle, Indiana* (1925), 8.

134. Greensburg *Daily News*, 4 February 1914; Marion C. Miller, "The Antislavery Movement in Indiana" (Ph.D. diss., University of Michigan, 1938, 290 p.).

135. Wimberly, "Missionary Reforms," 284–86.

LUTHERANS

Lutherans were an international Christian fellowship named for Martin Luther (1483–1546), the most notable pioneer in the Reformation of the sixteenth century. In that century they defined the biblical faith they were laboring to restore in a series of doctrinal standards which they continued to hold with great respect and affection: Luther's catechisms, the Augsburg Confession, the Schmalcald Articles, the Formula of Concord. Theirs became the established church in many of the principalities of Germany and Scandinavia. In America there were Lutherans in the colonies of New York and Delaware. There were scattered Lutheran communities in the southern colonies from Maryland to Georgia. Their primary strength was in Pennsylvania.[1]

> The position of the Lutheran church in America rests upon a birthright. It is not an immigrant church that needed to be naturalized after it was transplanted from some European land. It is as old as the American nation and much older than the American republic. The Lutheran church in America is an integral and potent part of American Christianity. The people in the Lutheran churches of the land are a constituent and typical element of the American nation . . . The church and the nation were born at the same time, grew up side by side, and developed by similar stages of progress.[2]

So there were Lutherans in the early American colonies, but not very many. And they were not neatly organized. In the areas of Europe where they had been the established church, the state had provided much of the structure for Lutheran administration and support. In America they were established nowhere. In the colonies which had established English churches, Lutherans had to seek their place as a tolerated minority. In the colonies without established churches, Lutherans had to learn to work as one of many denominations in a free and plural setting. Variety was their characteristic from the beginning.

Lutheran minister Henry Melchior Muhlenberg had thought of going from Germany to be a missionary to India. Professor Francke at Halle convinced him to go to the struggling Lutherans of Pennsylvania instead. Muhlenberg became pastor for three churches in the Philadelphia area in 1742, but he was always visiting and encouraging Lutherans in all the colonies. He got the scattered Lutherans motivated to organize congregations, and found schools, and appeal for more church leaders from Germany, and adopt a Lutheran form of worship service. In 1748 he took a major step toward independent organization of Lutherans in the new land. He presided over a meeting of five other ministers and lay delegates from ten congregations to organize a synod which later became the Synod or the Ministerium of Pennsylvania. Lutheran immigrants kept arriving and multiplying. By 1771 Muhlenberg reported eighty-one congregations in Pennsylvania and adjacent colonies over which he exercised some oversight.[3]

Muhlenberg and his synod were one important part of America's Lutheran constituency, giving the church visibility and cohesion to survive the chaos of the war for national independence. But the Lutherans were still far from unified. Less than half of the Lutheran congregations in the colonies had joined this original synod. Many did not join because they were wary of any organization which might limit their new liberty. More chose the convenience of affiliating with other new synods being organized after the war in their own regions such as New York in 1786, North Carolina in 1803, Ohio in 1818, and Tennessee in 1820.[4] Each synod was independent.

In October of 1820 representatives of four synods (Pennsylvania, New York, North Carolina, Maryland-Virginia) met to draw up a constitution for a General Synod, a loose federation of synods in America with power to propose worship materials, to advise on points of doctrine and discipline, and to promote unity. The Ohio and Tennessee synods sent no representatives, fearing any central authority and being suspicious that the new organization might yield in its allegiance to the German language or to the Augsburg Confession. The New York Synod looked at the new General Synod constitution and waited sixteen years to join. The Pennsylvania Ministerium withdrew from General Synod in 1823 and stayed out for thirty years. Only heroic efforts by Samuel S. Schmucker preserved the existence of the General Synod as an agency through which new synods being formed, especially English-speaking ones, could cooperate to provide mutual support and train ministers. Schmucker was chief leader of the General Synod from 1820 to 1870. He was also head of its Gettysburg Seminary for some forty years during which time about five hundred men prepared there for the Lutheran ministry both inside and beyond the General Synod.[5]

Differences among American Lutherans were very complex. They brought with them the loyalties and aversions of an immense variety of continental backgrounds. There were advocates and opponents of rationalistic state churches, advocates and opponents of union churches with the German Reformed (Calvinists), advocates and opponents of intensely emotional personal piety. In America these differences were further compounded by interaction with all the neighboring American denominations.

On the liberal extreme of the spectrum were some who believed that in America the Lutherans should take their places as full members in a general Protestant consensus. They should learn and use English. They should join their Protestant compatriots to support the American benevolent societies for promotion of revivals, Sunday schools, Bible distribution, missionary expansion, and a host of good causes. They should cease non-essential teachings and practices which seemed to most Americans to be vestiges of Catholicism—the real presence of Christ's body and blood in the Lord's Supper, the practice of private confession and absolution, and the belief in baptismal regeneration. They should affirm that the Bible, the whole Bible, and nothing but the Bible is the rule for faith and practice and that in the Lutheran confessional standards the fundamental doctrines of the Bible were taught in a manner substantially correct. Thus the Augsburg Confession would be authoritative as far as it was observed to be in agreement with the Scriptures. This position could lead at once to full intercommunion with the German Reformed, as already practiced in some German provinces, and to ecumenical worship and work with a wide range of American Protestants. Such were the views for a time of Samuel S. Schmucker as head of Gettysburg Seminary, of Benjamin Kurtz as editor of the *Lutheran Observer*, of Samuel Sprecher as president of Wittenberg College, and of some continuing sections of the General Synod.[6]

On the conservative extreme of the spectrum were some who counted the continued use of the old language, generally German, as preferred or even essential for worship and for religious instruction. They had been gravely offended by the compulsory integration of Lutheran and Reformed churches by some governments in Germany and wanted no such compromise in America. They counted all the Lutheran confessional standards as authoritative statements of the apostolic faith restored in the Lutheran reformation, to be accepted by Lutheran members and clergy without question or further validation. This doctrinal priority was most often affirmed for the "unaltered" or first edition of the Augsburg Confession of 1529. They made stout profession of the real presence of Christ's body and blood in the Lord's Supper and so wished to prevent participation by any who might partake at a Lutheran altar unworthily. Religious fellowship with non-Lutherans was regarded as hazardous, tending to laxity and degeneration.[7]

Lutherans in America lived out their lives somewhere on this spectrum. Describing their positions became even more difficult because the whole spectrum kept moving to the right—in a conservative direction—during the nineteenth century. The extreme "American" position of Schmucker, Kurtz, and Sprecher lost favor. The older congregations and synods generally were not ready to desert their heritage for anything so radical. The newer Lutheran immigrants pouring in from Europe were already shocked enough with the ways of freewheeling American denominations. In their own churches they rejoiced for a while longer in the old language and the old loyalties and the old confessions. Incoming Germans were especially attracted to those Lutheran churches which provided schools to offer their children religious instruction in German. Preachers willing to leave Germany to serve in America were often motivated for mission service by a conservative personal piety to which they rallied the people in their new mission field.

So the liberal *Definite Synodical Platform* issued in 1855 and advocated by Schmucker and Sprecher was widely rejected. Members and institutions of the General Synod kept moving in a conservative direction. In 1864 the General Synod amended its constitution to include a more overtly positive affirmation of the Augsburg Confession as "a correct exhibition of the fundamental doctrine of the Divine Word." Indiana's two liberal synods promptly did the same. That was not enough to satisfy the increasingly conservative constituency. In 1860 the General Synod comprised two-thirds of Lutherans in America and ten years later only one-fourth.[8]

In addition to the General Synod, delegates of eleven other conservative synods met in Fort Wayne in 1867 to establish their own conservative umbrella organization called the General Council.[9] The most conservative synods, completely outside either the General Synod or the General Council, grew healthy and strong. Where Lutheran constituencies grew strong, joint churches with German Reformed kept fading from favor. Everywhere the sixteenth century Lutheran confessions and traditional Lutheran liturgy became the marks of America's Lutherans.

> Everywhere staunch advocates of "old Lutheranism" arose. Of course the movement towards historical Lutheranism encountered some stout resistance, and resulted in all kinds of internal discord, but whenever the issue was clearly joined, the result always favored the Lutheranism of the Augsburg Confession and the other symbolical writings. Conservative principles spread like contagion, and the rising generation of ministers soon caught it. Men spoke of the period as "the present transition state of the church," and such it was.[10]

Early Lutheran Missionaries in Indiana

The typical Lutheran in early Indiana was a German. Not all Germans were Lutherans by any means; Germans might be Catholic or Reformed or advocates of Lutheran-Reformed union or converts to American denominations or adherents of various small sects or completely unaffiliated or bitterly anti-church. However, many Germans were Lutherans and a few were in Indiana from the earliest settlement. They were widely scattered; early Lutheran missionary effort in Indiana was often described as an effort "to gather the scattered Germans."[11]

First came the horseback missionary explorers searching to see how many scattered Germans Indiana had and where they were. The variety of Lutheranism was represented among the missionary riders in Indiana from the beginning. George Forster crossed over from Ohio to visit Germans in Indiana's Harrison County in 1805. Mount Solomon Lutheran Church was organized there in 1810, and histories eventually recorded seventeen Lutheran churches existing at some time in the Corydon area. Samuel Mau had a Lutheran preacher's license issued by the Ministerium of Pennsylvania in 1789, just two years after the death of its founder Muhlenberg. Mau spent some time in the wilds of Indiana's Fayette and Union counties as early as 1807, ministering to a cluster of Germans who had settled there about 1804, and organized St. John Church. John Lewis Markert of North Carolina Synod toured Indiana in 1813 and continued some occasional ministry to Hoosiers during the years following. These were very small beginnings serving a very small German constituency. When General Synod was formed in 1820 there were only 153 Lutheran pastors to serve the whole nation. Markert was the only one regularly at work in Indiana. After 1819 he actually lived across the state line in Ohio supporting himself as a barrel and cask maker, but he kept on ministering occasionally to Lutherans in Indiana's Whitewater River area.[12]

The pace of missionary visitation quickened during the 1820s. Lutheran church bodies in the East were stimulated by their own curiosity about frontier opportunities and by letters from particular clusters of Lutheran settlers pleading that ministers be sent. The Pennsylvania Ministerium sent John Christian Frederick Heyer, Michael Wachter, Jacob Schnee, and Ludolf Myers. The Ohio Synod sent Andrew Henkel, Henry Heincke, and Jacob Gruber. The Tennessee Synod, a small group of conservatives which broke away from North Carolina Synod in 1820 to avoid connection with the liberals of General Synod, took a particular interest in Indiana. The whole Tennessee Synod had but six pastors when organized but soon augmented the work of its own John Markert in Indiana with missionary labors there by Jacob Zink, Abraham Miller, Christian Moretz, and various members of the Henkel family.

These Lutheran circuit riders of the 1820s included colorful characters. Gruber supported himself as a gravestone engraver. As he circulated with his preaching and catechizing, he would take orders for grave markers and promise delivery on the next trip. He organized churches in Clinton and Blackford counties. Heyer was a veteran Pennsylvania pastor commissioned for short term missionary service in Ohio, Kentucky, and Indiana and destined to become the first American Lutheran missionary to India in 1839.[13] Schnee was an accomplished printer and livestock farmer as well as a pastor and his desire to found a religious community involved him in real estate dealings with both the Rappites and Owenites. After his trip west in 1821 he reported that Posey County on the Wabash in Indiana would be a good place for a preacher to make his home. Seven years later he leased 806 acres at New Harmony and settled there himself.[14] Zink was a missionary well past his prime according to the report of Jacob Schnee.

> In the State of Indiana there is a great need for a travelling preacher in order to assist old Mr. Zink. He is very weak in his preaching, and the congregations fall apart under him. There are many Germans—but the delicate matter is which road to take—if one were to find a young pastor then they no longer want to listen to Zink, and if he is allowed to continue, the congregations will perish. I am letting the Synod decide. I take him to be a good man with pure doctrine, but so poor and insignificant as a preacher that I know no one like him.[15]

The Henkel family deserved to be called a Lutheran institution or a regime.

> Paul Henkel had five sons who entered the ministry of the Lutheran church. Three of them, Philip, David, and Andrew, and one grandson, Eusebius S. Henkel, helped plant confessional Lutheranism in Indiana. David is said to have been the real theologian and kept the presses rolling at New Market, Va. with his confessional writings. He served in Indiana from 1824 to his death in 1831. His older brother Philip is reported to have organized five congregations in 1831 alone: St. John's in Clear Creek Township, Monroe County; Zion, Bean Blossom Township, Brown County; Salem, White River Township, Morgan County; Philadelphia, in Parke County; and St. John's, Bluff Creek, Johnson County.[16]

Besides the labors of these legitimate Lutheran missionaries, Indiana received the ministry of a few charlatans who passed themselves off as Lutheran ministers in order to exploit congregation members. With a synodical scene so chaotic, there was no regular procedure for establishing credentials or for protecting the people from impostors. Heyer reported in 1836 that a teacher named Hohenholz (variously spelled Uhnholz or Hohnholz) had assumed the role of minister for a time at Saint Omer in Decatur County. Hohenholz was later expelled from a church in Quincy, Illinois, for immoral practices and still later charged as an impostor at Syracuse, New York. Heyer said that Lutheranism in Harrison County "has got somewhat into disrepute, on account of unsuitable men, who at different times have visited this section of country, and preached among the people as Lutheran ministers."[17] Missionary Friedrich Konrad Dietrich Wyneken also crossed the trail of a Lutheran impostor.

> In Benton where there are nearly 40 families of Germans, I could not get more of a congregation than 12 persons to whom I might preach . . . Some time since, a certain Schlabach, a cooper by trade . . . after he had been dishonourably chastised by certain people, on account of his shameful treatment of his wife, left the place, to the benefit of the congregation. I met with the traces of this uncalled preacher in several other congregations, not far from Lafayette, in Tippecanoe county, endeavored to find him but only obtained the information, that he had gone further West. This increases the evil, that men of this stamp disgrace our office and make the word of life despicable in the eyes of people.[18]

Such a German population as Indiana was building could not be ignored. Previously not an assigned part of any Lutheran synod, the state was claimed at the same time by two new synods formed in 1835. They had little to do with each other, being at opposite ends of the Lutheran spectrum.

An Early Conservative Synod

First there was the Synod of Indiana (later Union Synod, Indiana Synod, and Indiana-Chicago Synod) which was organized as a synod of the nation's most conservative sort. At its first meeting on 15–18 August 1835 at St. John Church in Johnson County there were representatives of some ten congregations. Deacons Abraham Miller, Conrad F. Picker, and Ephraim R. Conrad were present as candidates to be examined and were ordained to the pastoral office. Ministerial leaders were John L. Markert of Fayette County, Christian Moretz of Morgan County, and Eusebius S. Henkel of Monroe County—all "Henkelites" from the conservative Tennessee Synod. They stoutly supported the Augsburg Confession and Luther's Small Catechism as statements of the true faith unalterable by human vote. They scorned the more liberal and ecumenical views of the General Synod in northeastern United States and the whole range of interdenominational benevolent societies.[19] The synod grew slowly, numbering perhaps twenty-five hundred communicants at its greatest strength. Its life was stormy.

> The Synod of Indiana continued after 1835 in such a frail condition that it seemed about to collapse at any time. It suffered from both theological and practical shortcomings. Theologically, one of its more serious deficiencies was in the marginal education of its pastors. Virtually the only training received by candidates for ordination was from parish pastors who themselves were poorly trained. Thus the clergy were not equipped to deal adequately with departures from orthodoxy . . . On the practical side, the Synod of Indiana was also weak with respect to parish organization. Instead of providing definite boundaries within which pastors resided and built up strong congregations, the Synod was considered a unit wherein the clergy were traveling preachers. Since the . . . Synod had an inherited hostility to missionary societies as well as theological seminaries, the expansion of its membership and programs was hard to accomplish.[20]

Ephraim Rudisill was the clergyman who dominated the Synod of Indiana for years. He was a power in debate and author of popular treatises against the Baptists and Campbellites. However, in a context of Lutheran theology he was nothing less than eccentric. His flirtations with Universalism and with a non-Lutheran doctrine of immediate destruction of unsaved souls at death divided the synod into factions and destroyed its peace. Samuel Good, Rudisill's chief advocate in Tippecanoe County, was charged by his opponents with rejecting the denomination's teaching on resurrection, original sin, and the Holy Ghost; deprecating portions of the Bible; and ordering church councils to burn Luther's catechism.

The Synod of Indiana dissolved in 1859 and "buried the records." Its successor, Union Synod, was actually a reconstitution, a new beginning within twenty-four hours with seven ministers and fourteen congregations continuing after the collapse. They were still under the influence of a somewhat chastened Ephraim Rudisill. After twelve years the reconstituted synod built up again to perhaps fifteen hundred communicants. Its future growth was to be associated with membership in the General Council, with shared sponsorship of Chicago Lutheran Theological Seminary, and with such active mission work in the northern areas of Indiana and Illinois that its name changed to Chicago Synod in 1896.[21]

An Early Liberal Synod

On the other hand there was the Synod of the West (later Olive Branch Synod and its sister Synod of North-ern Indiana) which was organized as a synod of the nation's most liberal sort. Its original constitution mentioned only one Lutheran confession, acknowledging that the doctrinal articles of the Augsburg Confession were "substantially correct." It would share communion with Methodists and Presbyterians; it would join other Protestants in support of such benevolent enterprises as the American Bible Society, the American Tract Society, the American Sabbath School Union, and other interdenominational organizations promoting temperance, education, and missions. But there was always dissension among its members.

John Jacob Lehmanowsky was a retired professional soldier holding the rank of colonel in the armies of Bonaparte. He was also a teacher, physician, gentleman farmer, touring lecturer, and philanthropist. Maryland Synod had licensed this mature layman as a Lutheran minister for the western frontier in May of 1835. At the age of sixty-two he went from his home in Indiana to attend the first meeting of the Synod of the West at the Methodist Protestant Church in Louisville on 4–6 October 1835. Of his ordination the following year he said: "I was ordained to the holy gospel ministry by the laying on of the hands of the elders who were such in truth, men who had toiled and sacrificed for the work of the Master. The service was a very plain one; yet I felt that it meant promotion on the field of battle at the hands of fellow soldiers."[22] Lehmanowsky became a notable contributor to Lutheranism in several states but he often felt frustrated by the Synod of the West.

> Not only were the men and means lacking with which to occupy the fields standing ripe to the harvest, but there was a worse lack in the almost utter absence of oneness of spirit and purpose. At times, when united effort was needed for the carrying through of the work of the Church and hardly a trace of this unanimity could be found, I used to think almost with longing of the spirit that made the armies of Napoleon all but irresistible. This was a spirit of vain glory or of evil; yet it was an *esprit de corps*, and it drove the armies on to victory. In those little synodical bands there seemed at times to be almost more opinions than men, and the only spirit that all had in common was the spirit of individualism, leading each one to consider himself the centre of the universe, about which all should revolve.[23]

The brethren did not like for Lehmanowsky to exhort them to unity or to chide them for lack of it. Lehmanowsky later repented a terrible urge to commit mayhem on one irritating colleague. He responded at the last instant to a call "Hold! this is not Napoleon's army."[24]

Disunity remained the mark of this early Synod of the West. When it voted to subdivide along narrowed geographical lines in 1846, the Indiana portion—some fourteen ministers and over one thousand communicants—so disintegrated that its identity was largely lost.[25] Olive Branch Synod was organized afresh as a successor synod in 1848; no Indiana ministers from the old Synod of the West appeared at the organizing convention. Now the Olive Branch Synod and its counterpart Synod of Northern Indiana (from 1855) were clearly representative of the liberal Lutheranism of the eastern General Synod, even of the more extremely "American" position of Schmucker and Sprecher. In Indiana these liberal synods grew. They sponsored missions and Sunday schools; their congregations multiplied and churches were built. By 1870 they included thirty-eight ministers, eighty-five churches, and over four thousand communicants.[26]

There were strategists who felt from the beginning that polarization and division among the state's Lutherans would interfere with their work. The veteran John Christian Frederick Heyer was back in Indiana as a missionary early in 1836, this time under appointment of a new missionary society in Pennsylvania and reporting to its secretary Samuel S. Schmucker.

> Many of the Lutherans in Indiana State have emigrated from North Carolina and Tennessee, where they have imbibed prejudices against every thing connected with the General Synod. On various occasions I have conversed with these people, and pointed out to them wherein they misapprehended things. However, I think it is very important that an understanding should take place between the Indiana Synod and the Synod of the west; and I am pleased to learn that negotiations are now pending between some of the brethren to unite these two synods into one. The brethren Henkel and Miller are much in favor of such a measure, and I hope the object will be accomplished. Without this union some of the ruinous transactions which occurred in North Carolina might be witnessed again in Indiana. May the Great Head of the church bless our endeavors to promote peace and harmony within the borders of our beloved Zion.[27]

Ezra Keller was also a commissioned Lutheran missionary from Pennsylvania and was in Indiana later that same year.[28] His appraisal of Indiana's religion was candid. He said about two-thirds of the adult population trusted the truth of the Bible and respected the Christian religion but belonged to no church and so were "properly called Nothingarians." He divided the Baptists into "regular, Cambelite and Dunker" but chose to comment only on the first group. Regular Baptists in Kentucky and Indiana seemed to him to be different from the Regular Baptists he had known in the East. These western Baptists were "a people of whom it is hard to say good things." They wielded great popular influence, much of it directly opposed to the very causes Keller held dear. He said "Bible, Tract and Temperance Societies they hate with a perfect hatred . . . In their estimation a missionary is a perfect scoundrel, a base villan—a pest to human society. The Sabbath of the Lord they totally disregard and an educated ministry they will not have."

Keller saw in Indiana a great number of Methodist Churches and an even greater number of Methodist preachers. In fact, in some places it seemed to him that nearly all the adult Methodist men bore the title of preacher. He thought their pulpit efforts made them "an object of pity to some and a laughing stock to others." Presbyterians suited him better because "they have several colleges established, which are under the supervision of able professors and promise to be very useful." New Light Christians puzzled him. "What they believe I cannot distinctly tell," he said. "Some say they are people who wish to have a new creed but do not know how to make one which will abide the text of the Bible."[29] His own standard for a western minister was demanding.

> Let no one entertain the opinion that the weaker instruments should be sent to the West. This erroneous notion has been too prevalent in the ecclesiastical bodies of the East. If there be talent, learning and eloquence necessary in any part of the land, it is West of the Alleghany . . . In most places in this state a Lutheran minister should be able to preach in both languages, to endure privations, to suffer hardships and to labor with patience and hope amidst many discouragements.[30]

Keller was fresh out of Gettysburg Seminary. The Synod of the West made him welcome as an "advisory" member at its 1836 meeting and invited him to preach.[31] Gettysburg alumni George Yeager of Jeffersontown, Kentucky, and Peter Rizer of Corydon, Indiana, made their report to the synod on the state of Lutheranism in Indiana. They were very concerned about the "Henkelites" and about the conservative Synod of Indiana.

> In this state our church is tolerably extensive; yet it is still much scattered, and scattered as it is, more lamentable to record, it is much distracted by division; and more lamentable still, if possible, a large part of it is prejudiced against its own highest, dearest and best interests. Thus in Floyd, Harrison and Washington Counties. Though in these counties there are many members whose hearts are pure and faithful; yet there are numbers

of others who are of precisely the opposite character. Besides the most unreasonable prejudices, instilled and imbibed by the solemn teaching of some of their preachers, against all the liberal and evangelical efforts made by our brethren in other sections of the Church, the withering, blasting, and corrupting doctrine of absolute and unconditional Universalism has taken hold among them, and is worming itself like a deadly serpent into their hearts, and this, even if not approved of, is connived at by those their preachers to whom we have referred. But through all this, as the faithful heralds of salvation, it becomes us to look onward.[32]

Lutheran union for Indiana loomed large on the agenda of that 1836 meeting. Synod president Jacob Crigler urged union of effort and decisive action for the sake of Indiana. He appointed a committee to confer and negotiate with the Synod of Indiana to achieve union. Conferring and negotiating would not prove to be enough. The Synod of Indiana had come into existence in 1835 with a resolution "that the Hymn Book used by the Lutheran Tennessee Synod; the Augsburg Confession of Faith; Luther's Smaller Catechism, with the preliminary remarks; the treatise on the Person and Incarnation of Jesus Christ, by David Henkel, be recommended to Lutherans, as containing the Lutheran doctrine in its purity." Now it required as a basis of union that the Synod of the West separate from the General Synod, adopt a doctrinal stance compatible with this one of the Synod of Indiana (and Tennessee), and abandon "the falsely called benevolent societies of the present day—such as Tract, Temperance, Missionary, Bible and a host of such like 'fantastical' societies." The Synod of the West kept deploring the rigidities of the "Henkelites" of the Synod of Indiana. The Synod of Indiana kept charging the "Generalists" of General Synod, and so of the Synod of the West, with subverting and destroying Lutheran doctrine and discipline. Ezra Keller finished his missionary tour and went home. Within eight years he had become organizer and first president of Wittenberg College at Springfield, Ohio. He and his school became as much a center as Indiana's more liberal and English oriented Lutherans would know in the nineteenth century. But he was dead seventy-two years before the two pioneer synods of Indiana's Lutherans, much modified and matured, finally united. Union delayed until 1920. There came to be more pastors—a five-fold increase between 1836 and 1850—but not more unity.[33]

So nineteenth century Lutheranism in Indiana was a kind of theological smorgasbord. A later Lutheran commentator suggested as an appropriate collect: "O Lord, how often we have 'synoded' against Thee!" A pastor could take his congregational following into the liberal and ecumenical Synod of the West (later Olive Branch Synod and Synod of Northern Indiana) or into the conservative Synod of Indiana (later Union Synod or Indiana Synod). But only about half of Indiana's Lutherans belonged to either one of these Hoosier organizations by 1870. There was the option of belonging to the Joint Synod of Ohio and Other States which had more than twenty congregations in Indiana by the 1870s. It had become very conservative and rarely risked dilution of its orthodoxy by collaboration with other Christians, Lutheran or not.[34]

Missouri Synod

And after 1847 there was the greatest conservative attraction of all, the German Evangelical Lutheran Synod of Missouri, Ohio, and Other States.[35] The Missouri Synod story in the nation was epic, a growth from twelve small congregations to over five thousand congregations with more than 1.9 million baptized members during its first century.[36] Indiana's role in Missouri Synod's development was equally dramatic with leading characters like Wyneken, Sihler, and Husmann in residence and with much of the action taking place at Fort Wayne.

Fort Wayne was destined to have a substantial German population. The land was rich, the travel route known, and the promised canal exciting. The German Lutheran John Siebold came as a day laborer in 1822 and was soon an independent farmer. Skilled carpenter Martin Bargus came two years later by what became the regular route for Germans until the Wabash and Erie Canal approached Fort Wayne in 1835—from New York City to the Erie Canal, by lake to Detroit, by ox team from Detroit to the Maumee, and by pirogue down the Maumee. Some Germans were recruited along with the Irish to labor for ten dollars a month to construct the canal. Canal workers could buy land at favorable rates, even with the deflated scrip in which part of their wages were paid. The number of Irish immigrants to the Fort Wayne area leveled off after 1840 but the Germans kept pouring in. By the census of 1850 more than half of Indiana's foreign-born population of 54,426 was German. Among the northern counties over one-third of the entire alien population was concentrated in Allen County which includes Fort Wayne; 2,439 of Allen County's foreign born were Germans. These German immigrants, with their growing families, provided a matrix for the development of the Missouri Synod which occurred there.[37]

One particular factor in the story of the Germans and the Lutherans at Fort Wayne was Henry Rudisill. At the very end of the year 1829, Rudisill and his wife Elizabeth were rushed to Fort Wayne from Ohio to attend to a crisis in the business interests of his employer John Barr. Rudisill was only twenty-eight but he was already an expert merchant who could be trusted with the affairs of Barr, a Baltimore investor and a partner in purchasing the original plat for the founding of Fort Wayne. Rudisill managed Barr's local affairs with energy, keeping store, settling land accounts, and constructing both flour mills and sawmills in the vicinity of Fort Wayne. The village had only about 150 inhabitants when he arrived.[38] A reliable labor supply was essential and Rudisill filled his mail to Barr with requests for German immigrants.

> Hire some Germans from Germany and send them out to me German Emigrants are frequently arriving in Baltimore and would be glad of such an opportunity, you can hire them much lower than the Americans and I think they are more to be depended on[.] you can hire a good stout young man for 60 or 90 dolrs. a year[.] if you could get whole familys it would be better.[39]
>
> I feel very anxious to hear from you concerning the Germans[.] I would rather have 3 of them than 6 of our common hands.[40]
>
> I wish you by all means if you possibly can to send me the Germans[.] I would prefer the Wurtembergers as they are the most industrious and temperate[.] It is difficult to get good hands here or in Ohio.[41]

Immigrating Württembergers were likely to be Lutherans and the Rudisills, American-born Lutherans, favored German Lutheran immigrants. The enterprising Rudisill sent mail to church agencies as well. He wrote to the Emigrantenkommission and to the Missionsgesellschaft in Philadelphia and Baltimore asking them to send Lutheran immigrants to Fort Wayne.

Then Rudisill asked for a Lutheran pastor also. Pastor Jesse Hoover in Woodstock, Virginia, saw the appeal in a German-language church paper. He corresponded with Rudisill and, with the encouragement of Pennsylvania Ministerium, visited Fort Wayne in July of 1836 where he accepted the invitation to be pastor. Hoover was an 1833 graduate of Gettysburg Seminary, competent in both German and English, ready to support benevolent societies and to cooperate with German Reformed and American Presbyterians. The Presbyterian Church in Fort Wayne had no pastor when Hoover arrived with his family in fall of 1836. He preached English sermons regularly for the Presbyterians and operated an English school in the basement of the Presbyterian Church

which was then the only church building in town. Hoover was ministering to all the Germans in the area as well.[42] He organized a German Lutheran church at Fort Wayne.

> Having preached every alternate Lord's-day in the town of Ft. Wayne, I organized a church, the First Evangelical Lutheran Church in Ft. W. on the 14th of Oct. 1837. It consists of Seventy members, some of these live 8 miles from town. All these had certificates of church membership in Ger. except one who was rec. by a profession of faith etc. The greater number of them are hopefully pious and manifest their faith by their works. I have a pious, enlightened church council, who feel the importance of maintaining a proper standard of piety and discipline from the commencement. We have not however been without our difficulties. Some of our people are from Prussia and others from every part of Germany & the Netherlands with different prejudices and apprehensions of Christian propriety, lawful duty, etc, etc. It is easy to conceive that it requires a good deal of discretion to mould this heterogenous mass into one harmonious American church. But by the grace of God I have some prospect of success to a very considerable extent.[43]

The following spring he organized another in nearby Adams County.

> On the 11th of March Inst. I organized a church in the northern part of Adams Co., the Co. next south of Allen, of 23 members. This little church is in a flourishing condition. They have kept up a prayer meeting regularly since the latter part of last summer. Then I expect to have a flourishing S. School this summer. More of this anon. We have not yet commenced building churches. This we will have to do before long. There is a great number of Germans expected on this summer. At present the Ft. W. Ch. worships in a S. house. And the Friedens Kirche in Adams Co. worships in a cabin. I purpose if life and health are spared to visit other sections of this country this summer. I have thus far since July last confined my labors almost exclusively to the Germans as there is a supply of Eng. ministers and none who preaches Ger. except myself. And this no doubt will be the most proper course here after as there is an abundance of German labor for one man.[44]

The Fort Wayne community was especially appreciative of the ministry of Hoover among the expanding population of Germans. Because the German churches were yet in their infancy and Fort Wayne was "a dear place to live in, every article of subsistence being very high," the pastors of the Methodist, Baptist, and Presbyterian churches prepared an application letter and obtained an annual commission of three hundred dollars for Hoover from the American Home Missionary Society. These "citizens of Ft. Wayne" said in support of Hoover:

> The protestant german population is about three hundred and their number continualy increasing, two or three hundred more are expected in the spring, these people are generaly poor but industrious. Many of them have a small piece of land in the green woods and it is with much difficulty that they can maintain their families until they can make comfortable improvements . . . He has frequent calls to preach in other parts of this and the adjacent counties and he is the only minister in these parts from whom they can "hear in their own tongues wherein they were born the wonderful words of God." It is believed that these people will not long lean upon the benevolence of your society that the germans will soon be so numerous and in such circumstances as to be able to support their own minister.[45]

Jesse Hoover died of a heart ailment on 23 May 1838 at the age of twenty-eight.

When Jesse Hoover died at Fort Wayne, his unknowing replacement was already on his way to America. Friedrich Konrad Dietrich Wyneken was one of nine children of a village pastor in Hannover. His father died early but Wyneken was enabled to study theology at Göttingen and Halle. This formal training became warmed by personal piety under the guidance of a pastor von Hanfstengel in Hannover and by much devotional study of the Bible. Appeals in some missionary journals on behalf of the scattered Germans in America moved him to leave an academic post and cross the ocean to help them.

> With deep regret I must confess that as far as I know myself, neither love for the Lord nor for the orphaned brethren drove me to America nor a natural desire. Rather I went contrary to my will and after great conflicts, from a sense of duty, driven in, and by, my conscience. As much as it saddens me that I did not have and still do not have more love for the Lord and that He had to drive me like a slave, still in times of spiritual trials and temptations, doubts and tribulations, which came over my soul during my ministry, this was my comfort that I could say: I had to come to America. Thou, O Lord knowest how gladly I would have remained at home, but had I done this, I should not have been able to look up to Thee and pray to Thee; so I simply had to come.[46]

A devout sea captain gave him free passage. Pastor J. Haesbaert in Baltimore provided a brief American apprenticeship and connected him with the Pennsylvania Ministerium. That body sent him to gather the scattered Germans in Indiana. When he got to Adams County, Hoover's congregation there told him that Hoover had died. Wyneken wrote to Haesbaert.

> Eight days ago I arrived in Fort Wayne. Here as well as in two neighboring settlements I have already preached five times, baptized children, and read burial services. And now these people want me to stay—I advised the vestry of the church to write to the committee of their church body about this. Tomorrow I intend to continue my journey, and I expect to return in four weeks to receive the answer. I am ready to do the Lord's will, and I shall leave it to Him to direct the hearts of the members of the committee as He sees fit. I am satisfied with everything as long as I am certain that the Lord wants me to work here.[47]

Soon he had a reply releasing him from his missionary commission so he could take charge of the two congregations provided he would also minister to the scattered Germans all around.[48]

It was a momentous appointment. Wyneken quickly experienced the realities of ministry in northern Indiana. An attempted trip from Fort Wayne to visit the scattered Germans at Wolf Lake, Benton, Elkhart, South Bend, and Mottville in January of 1839 nearly ruined both Wyneken and his horse. Try as he might, there was no way for one part time missionary to serve northern Indiana's rising German tide. Wyneken was a strategist, never one to suffer in silence. He developed convictions about what should be done and kept telling the world about them. To the editor of *Die Lutherische Kirchenzeitung* in Pittsburgh he wrote:

> I believe that the only way to accomplish anything worth while in the vineyard of the Lord is to call missionaries for smaller sections of the country. The General Synod ought to make an appeal to the Lutheran congregations. It certainly is not right that 2,000 churches, and perhaps more, cannot support more missionaries. If we have [not] sufficient warriors in this country, then I am convinced that a strong appeal to the brethren in Germany, especially to the mission societies there, will bring us recruits enough to fill the ranks.[49]

That paper published many of his articles and letters. He kept up a constant correspondence with individuals and mission societies in Germany. The *Zeitschrift für Protestantismus und Kirche* in Erlangen published his writings.

Some help came—F. W. Husmann from Bremen to be a teacher at Fort Wayne in May of 1840; A. F. Knape sent from pastor Gossner of Berlin in May of 1841 to relieve Wyneken of his Adams County congregation; G. Jensen sent from Stade Mission Society in June of 1841 to help at Fort Wayne. Wyneken was convinced that brighter missionary fires must be set blazing back in Germany and that he was the man to kindle them. He knew where to place six ministers within the territory he himself had visited.[50]

> What I have in mind is the following: I desire with the help of God to have six or eight pastors come to America who are to parcel out a section of the country among themselves. A superintendent is to be at the head of all, who is to visit each circuit and who should be elected for a period of about four years. The preachers ought to visit their circuits first without attempting to organize the people into congregations. After some time, however, this ought to be done, but with such members only as have manifested their sincerity by Christian conduct. As a confessional basis the Augsburg Confession or, where the people are Reformed, a Reformed confession should serve. All congregations should be united together and, if possible, also become members of existing synods.[51]

The Mission Committee of the General Synod was convinced. They sent Wyneken and his new Adams County bride Marie Sophie Wilhelmine Buuck to Germany in October of 1841. They stayed until June of 1843. In Germany Wyneken was doing what he did best—describing the condition of America's scattered Germans and advancing plans to help them. He had already established good connections so he was welcomed to address congregations of missionary-minded pastors, missionary societies, and mission-oriented schools. At the university city of Erlangen he gained the support of professor Karl von Raumer. At Dresden and at Leipzig he helped organize mission societies.

Germans were fascinated by Wyneken's accounts of America and the religious conditions there. He became something of a sensation as a lecturer. Some of the material from his lectures was published in his pamphlet *Die Noth der deutschen Lutheraner in Nordamerika* which had wide circulation in Germany and later in America.[52]

> The area in which our German people settle is getting even larger, the number of those suffering spiritual need continues to grow; and it is getting harder and harder to watch over this tremendously large region and to help lessen the misery. Therefore my appeal to your hearts: Help in the name of Jesus! Help, because the need is ever more urgent. What will become of our brethren in ten or twenty years if there is no help? To the disgrace of the German name, the shame of the church, and to the eternal reproach before the Lord, a German populace which knows nothing of its God and Savior, will settle down in the West; and in the following centuries it will point fin-

gers at the people and the church, who, in spite of all the plenty in their homes, let their children languish.

> The sects which are working most zealously at tearing down the old neglected cathedral of the church in America, in order to build up their own chapels from the fragments, and with which I have had the most dealings, are the United Brethren in Christ, the so-called Albright people, and the Methodist-Episcopal sects. The latter is the most active of them all. Within the past several years, it has also established a mission among the Germans, which it heavily supports, and which, unless the Lord sends help very soon, will certainly even wipe out the name of the Lutheran Church in the west. That seems to be its intention, according to a statement by its strongest supporter, a man from Württemberg. At least, the latter mentioned to a Lutheran preacher that the Lutheran Church was so corrupt it would have to disappear even in name.[53]

After a long parody of a Methodist revival meeting with its "new measures" exhibited for the delight of the curious Germans he asserted: "There is hardly a Lutheran or Reformed congregation which does not have to suffer from these swarming pests. Many congregations have been completely scattered by them, others are constantly exposed to their attacks and banter, and complaints about these agitators come from all areas. For the faithful preacher they are a constant evil gnawing at the very marrow of his soul." American Methodists read the pamphlet too. They replied to Wyneken the next year with their own pamphlet entitled *Why Have You Become an Apostate?*[54]

Most crucial for Missouri Synod development and for the development of Wyneken himself was his association with pastor Johann Konrad Wilhelm Loehe of Neuendettelsau in Bavaria. Loehe was a village pastor but he was a one-man army. He had a congregation drawn from miles around to hear his earnest preaching in support of missions and evangelism. He had the cause of America's scattered Germans at heart, having been a reader of Wyneken's descriptions since 1840. He had made his church and village into a veritable missionary society, raising substantial funds for mission support.[55] In the second number of the *Sonntagsblatt* for 1841 he wrote

> Thousands of families, your brethren in the faith, possibly your brothers and sisters according to the flesh, are hungry for the nourishing meat of the Gospel. They cry out and implore you: Oh, help us! Give us preachers to strengthen us with the Bread of Life, to edify us through the Word of the Lord, to instruct our children in the doctrine of Jesus. Oh, help us, or we are undone! Why do you not help us? Is that your love for Jesus? Is that keeping His

Commandments? Consider the words: "What ye have done unto one of the least of these My brethren, ye have done unto Me." —It is literally true that many of our German brethren in western North America plead with us in such terms. Besides, in many places a new danger has arisen. In no other country are there so many Christian sects as in North America. Even now some have directed their attention and efforts to the settlements of our German brethren and fellow Lutherans. Strangers wish to reap while the Lord is calling His own. Shall our brethren no longer worship in the Church of their fathers, filled with the breath of the Lord, but instead recline in the miserable shacks of sectarianism? Shall German piety decay in the new world under the influence of human propaganda? I beg of you, for Jesus' sake, take hold, organize speedily, do not waste time in consultations. Haste, haste, immortal souls are at stake.[56]

Loehe was operating a program at his own parish to train some "emergency men" (Nothelfer) in a short course designed to get them into service quickly in the neediest missions as Lutheran teachers and possibly ministers. The course included "cursory reading of the Scriptures, the Book of Concord, church history, geography, English grammar, composition, penmanship, singing, piano, methods in reading and writing, Christian doctrine, pastoral theology, catechetics, liturgics, homiletics, participation in divine services and in congregational life."[57] Encouraged by Wyneken's visit in 1842, Loehe decided to send the first two graduates of his course to America. He would focus his missionary effort on building up the Lutheran Church in America, publish a monthly paper, and organize the Kingdom of Hannover into missionary districts in support of American missions. Loehe and Neuendettelsau became world renowned for missions. From 1846 to 1853 their missionary output was directed specifically to a school in Indiana.[58]

> At the time of the organization of the Missouri Synod, Loehe had prepared and sent to America 23 emergency men. By 1853, the year in which Loehe and the Missourians parted, 82 candidates of theology, emergency men, and students for the Fort Wayne seminary had come to America through his efforts. Most of them joined the Missouri Synod after its organization.[59]

Wyneken was an inspiration for Loehe's missionary zeal. Loehe was an influence on Wyneken's doctrinal stance, an advocate of the return to Lutheran confessionalism then widespread in Germany. Loehe was a leader in the liturgical renewal within German Lutheranism and championed the reappreciation of the sixteenth century formulations of Lutheran doctrine. Before Loehe's mis-

sionary workers sailed for America, they pledged their allegiance to the confessional writings of the Lutheran Church. Loehe told them which American synods were orthodox enough for them to join. This movement toward strict Lutheranism became evident in Wyneken during his stay in Germany.

Back in America Wyneken had been sent to the Indiana frontier by the Pennsylvania Ministerium. He was a member of the liberal Synod of the West, an affiliate of the General Synod which had arranged for his trip to Germany. At Fort Wayne his congregation was composed of Lutherans and Reformed. For two years he had continued to receive support from the American Home Missionary Society, chiefly funded by Presbyterians and Congregationalists, as Jesse Hoover had done. Now in Germany his *Notruf* deplored any union with the German Reformed.[60] For his German audiences he identified a large body of English-speaking Lutherans in America who were breaking away from the faith of their fathers and spreading false doctrine. He said Gettysburg Seminary was in the hands of this faction of "Methodistic" Lutherans "and instead of being a nursemaid of the Lutheran Church, if everything remains the same, it will turn into a snake, which it has raised in its bosom, and into a powerful tool to help destroy the Church."[61]

Wyneken's direction was firmly set. When he returned to Fort Wayne he drew the line between Lutheran and Reformed so sharply that his Reformed members withdrew to form a new congregation. No more German Reformed preachers were to be allowed in the Lutheran pulpit and no more non-Lutherans could share in the Lutheran communion. At the Synod of the West in October of 1844 and at the General Synod in May of 1845 he stated his position against their inclusiveness and then withdrew from both. Early in 1845 he left Indiana to become pastor of St. Paul Church in Baltimore. It turned out to be infested with Reformed also; soon eighty members there withdrew to organize another congregation. Loehe cheered: "Wyneken is herewith beginning a war which he may carry on with the deepest peace of soul, a war in which all true children of the Lutheran Church will have to join him."[62]

On his way from Fort Wayne to his new church in Baltimore, Wyneken stopped at Pomeroy, Ohio, to visit Lutheran pastor Wilhelm Sihler. At the age of forty-four, Sihler was just entering the Lutheran ministry. He was a Prussian army officer, a doctor of philosophy via the universities of Berlin and Jena, and a professor. He was more lately the subject of a dramatic conversion, a most zealous student of the Scriptures, and a champion of the

Lutheran confessions after he had studied them as a member of the Dresden Mission Society.

> Here he also met Dr. Rudelbach, a recognized leader of confessional Lutheranism, who created in Sihler the desire to study the Symbolical Books of the Lutheran Church. The study of the Book of Concord convinced Sihler that the Lutheran Church was the only true visible Church of God on earth, aroused in him an abiding opposition to the Roman Catholic Church, and filled him with contempt for the Reformed Church and abhorrence for any church unionism or religious compromise.[63]

While wrestling with inclinations to enter the ministry, he chanced to read a copy of Wyneken's *Notruf*. "Like a flash of lightning, it pierced my soul," he said, "as though God spoke with emphatic words to me, 'You must go!'"[64]

Sihler's north German friends and his colleagues in the Dresden Mission Society fortified him for American service with trunks of clothing plus ten ducats and five hundred rubles. Dr. Rudelbach gave him a Latin certificate of his maturity in divinity. Pastor Loehe at Neuendettelsau gave his approval and some hope of a professorship at Columbus, Ohio. At Bremen Sihler visited friends and relatives of Wyneken. Though not a member of Loehe's school, he traveled to America with Loehe's blessing and in the company of one of Loehe's graduates. The Lutherans he met on the east coast of the United States were not nearly Lutheran enough to please him. Neither were his colleagues in the Joint Synod of Ohio or the members of the two congregations he served at Pomeroy. He took stringent measures to purge Reformed elements from them all.[65]

By the time Wyneken visited Sihler in Ohio early in 1845, both men had been reading *Der Lutheraner* which Carl Ferdinand Wilhelm Walther first issued from St. Louis on 7 September 1844. In fact, they were the only two pastors to be sent copies of the first issue.[66] It was a publication so painstakingly and conservatively Lutheran that it pleased Wyneken, Sihler, and all the Loehe missionaries.

> The purpose of the periodical shall be: (1) to acquaint the reader with the teaching, the treasures, and the history of the Lutheran Church; (2) to offer proof that this church is not one of the many sects in Christendom, that it is not a new, but the old true church of Jesus Christ on earth, that it, therefore, has by no means died out, yea, cannot die out, according to Christ's promise "Lo, I am with you alway, even unto the end of the world"; (3) to show how a true Lutheran can have true faith, live a Christian life, suffer patiently, and die a blessed death; (4) to point out, refute, and warn against current false,

> seductive doctrines, and especially to unmask those who falsely call themselves Lutherans, who under this name spread misbelief, unbelief, and religious fanaticism and arouse hurtful prejudices against our church in the minds of non-Lutherans.[67]

Walther has often been regarded as the father of the Missouri Synod and his *Lutheraner* the unifying center for its early life. Walther's Saxons in Missouri were recognized as the group's primary theologians. But Sihler and his colleagues from the school of Loehe furnished much of the Missouri Synod's energy.

Sihler succeeded Wyneken as pastor at St. Paul Church in Fort Wayne in July of 1845. Loehe wanted an American theological seminary to which he could send his stream of German ministerial recruits. Sihler offered to found and operate such a seminary at Fort Wayne. The first eleven students arrived in October of 1846 along with three theological candidates, one of whom was to serve as their teacher. But Sihler was always its chief teacher and president. It was he who arranged for both the education and the care and feeding of the seminarians, housing and teaching many of them in his own home with his young wife and a family which eventually grew to nine children.[68]

It was Sihler who wrote Walther for more copies of *Der Lutheraner* to distribute and who corresponded with him about uniting the Saxons with the Loehe men to establish a new orthodox synod. That project moved with remarkable speed. Convened at Cleveland by Sihler and others in September of 1845, the Loehe men delegated Sihler and J. A. Ernst to go to Walther's home in St. Louis to meet and negotiate with Walther and the Saxons. At this first joint meeting the following spring the two parties proceeded at once to draft a constitution for the new synod. Sihler and Walther were among the draft's signers. Six weeks later Sihler hosted the second joint meeting at Fort Wayne beginning 2 July 1846. All sixteen pastors present signed the Fort Wayne draft and six other clergymen sent word of their approval of the plan.[69] Sihler said:

> The main purpose of this meeting was, in the presence of and with the participation of the Eastern brethren [Loehe men from Indiana and Ohio and places east of St. Louis] to go over anew the basic articles of the draft of a truly faithful Lutheran synodical constitution, drawn up by Pastor Walther at St. Louis and to reach a conclusion—which occurred then, at the expiration of about a week, to the satisfaction of all in general. Naturally here, as in St. Louis, the Saxon brethren had to push the thing along, for we Easterners were pretty much novices for this ticklish and difficult work.[70]

The Fort Wayne draft was printed in the issue of *Der Lutheraner* for 5 September 1846 and actual organization was scheduled for Chicago in April of 1847. Men sent to America by Loehe outnumbered the Missouri Saxons present. Indiana had more charter members than any other state, mostly from Allen and Adams counties. Two of the three officers selected to effect the Synod organization listed Fort Wayne addresses—F. W. Husmann as secretary and Wilhelm Sihler as treasurer. Sihler preached on Synod's opening day on Acts 2:42. In the election of regular officers for the new synod he was chosen vice president, examiner, and collocutor.[71] Requisites for membership of pastors and congregations included

Acceptance of the Scriptures of the Old and New Testaments as the written Word of God and the only rule and norm of faith and practice. Acceptance of all the symbolical books of the Ev. Lutheran Church as a true and correct statement and exposition of the Word of God, to wit, the three Ecumenical Creeds (the Apostles' Creed, the Nicene Creed, the Athanasian Creed), the Unaltered Augsburg Confession, the Apology of the Augsburg Confession, the Smalcald Articles, the Large Catechism of Luther, the Small Catechism of Luther, and the Formula of Concord. Renunciation of unionism and syncretism of every description, such as serving union congregations composed of members of churches with different confessions as such; taking part in the services and sacramental rites of heterodox congregations or of such of mixed confession; joining the heterodox in missionary efforts or in the publishing and distribution of literature; exclusive use of doctrinally pure agendas, hymnbooks, and catechism in church and school; providing the children with a Christian school education.[72]

Parochial schools were to be very important to the new synod. In the days before Indiana had effective public schools, any Lutheran church or pastor was very likely to operate a parish school for general education. After public schools were operative, and after most other Lutheran groups had settled for parish confirmation instruction rather than a full curriculum, Missouri Synod held fast to the ideal of a parochial school in every parish offering a complete elementary course. The first Lutheran teachers were at least the equal of Indiana's early public school teachers. The pastor was often obligated to be schoolmaster as well, but full time lay teachers were desired.[73]

The Lutheran lay teacher Friedrich Wilhelm Husmann was one of the firstfruits of Wyneken's cries for more help for Indiana from Germany.

In Fort Wayne Husmann became the first teacher of St. Paul's congregation, whose pastor at that time was Wyneken. Wyneken and Husmann became intimate and lifelong friends. Besides teaching in Fort Wayne, he also taught, as time and opportunity presented itself, in two other Lutheran settlements, one eight miles, the other eighteen miles from Fort Wayne. The entire distance, through dense forests, had to be made on foot.[74]

Husmann set a high standard in Fort Wayne's parochial schools from 1840 to 1845 before becoming a missionary pastor in the area himself.[75]

Wilhelm Sihler began at once to train teachers as well as preachers in the school he opened for Loehe at Fort Wayne in 1846. Fourteen of the first seventy-two men leaving Sihler's school went out as teachers. Fort Wayne had more Lutheran parochial schools than any other place in the state. The cumulative list for all of Indiana grew to 766 teachers who had served in seventy-two Missouri Synod parochial schools up to the end of 1941. Typically they were men who were "called" in the same sense that pastors were called and remained a long time in office.[76]

The center at Fort Wayne kept growing. It was always the site of a Missouri Synod theological seminary, or a college to prepare young men to go to theological seminary, or a college to train teachers for parochial schools. Sihler was there at the center of it all for forty years—pastor of the city's largest Lutheran church who heard the private confessions of many of his congregation members prior to each celebration of communion; primary actor and strategist in all synod affairs; author of well over a hundred articles in *Der Lutheraner* and *Lehre und Wehre* and of a popular pamphlet against the Methodists which sold twelve thousand copies and was translated into English, Norwegian, and Swedish; president of whatever Lutheran schools were in operation at Fort Wayne; professor of exegesis, dogmatics, isagogics, symbolics, and pastoral theology; continuing mentor for the host of pastors and teachers produced by that school system and president of the regional district so that he personally conducted an inspection of each parish and its school regularly. So in 1857 a theological seminary, a pre-seminary department, a teachers' seminary, and an academy all occupied one campus at Fort Wayne and Sihler was head of the entire institution. Most students paid no tuition and very little room and board. Congregations in Allen and Adams counties, especially Sihler's St. Paul Church, were large supporters of the schools and constantly poured in gifts of food and clothing for the students.[77]

Most of the students for church vocations during the formative years of Missouri Synod between 1846 and 1874 came directly from Germany. Of the eighty-nine students during the first nine years at the seminary at Fort Wayne, only one was American born. The earliest German settlers in the Midwest hardly thought of themselves as potential clergymen or as candidates for the academic discipline required for that learned profession. It was Loehe at Neuendettelsau who gathered, supported, inspired, and sent the rising ministers and teachers.[78]

After Loehe cut off his connection, because he felt the new Missouri Synod granted too much autonomy to local congregations, the synod contracted with Pastor Friedrich Brunn at Steeden and Pastor Theodor Harms at Hermannsburg. Between 1861 and 1865, Brunn sent a total of fifty men. The contingent from him was twenty-one in 1866, eighteen in 1868, and twenty-one in 1870. Eventually he sent more than two hundred professional workers to the Missouri Synod, always aiming to select the ablest and the most orthodox. Finally the situation reversed. Germany actually developed a shortage of teachers and preachers; America's Missouri Synod needed less ministerial manpower from Germany. In 1878 the synod resolved to close the school at Steeden and to pension Brunn.[79]

It was a most effective leverage. The tremendous need for Lutheran church workers among the mass of German immigrants in the American Midwest was balanced by a rich source of such workers in Germany, the whole action supported by fund raising on both sides of the ocean and energized by an excitement for both expansion and orthodoxy in America. Fort Wayne was a fulcrum for the operation; Sihler was the very pivot of it. He died full of honors in 1885.

> Sihler's funeral was magnificent, with 60 to 70 brethren in the cloth attending, hundreds of schoolchildren in the procession, thousands of people on foot, and with nearly 200 carriages following in the van. It was a great tribute to a remarkable man who was sincere even when mistaken; true, devout, and spiritual . . . He grew to manhood in the Prussian aristocracy and lived out his days in the American democracy. He was confirmed in the state church but lived to become one of the leaders of a free church. He reached maturity indifferent to the claims of religion and ended up dedicating his all to religion.[80]

This stiff-backed German, later called wrong-headed on nearly every social issue, slow to accept the use of English, opposed to full church fellowship with every kind of Christian but his own, met the full tide of German immigration in the midst of a band of colleagues united and prepared to do serious ministerial work.[81]

Missouri Synod and its base at Fort Wayne attracted constituents. If a Lutheran pastor or teacher was needed,

Fort Wayne might have an alumnus to send when nobody else did. Ministers of "Old Lutheran" sympathies arriving from Germany rallied to Missouri Synod. Established American pastors, attuned to *Der Lutheraner* and its fellowship of subscribers rising toward twenty thousand and seeking a compatible synod home, might lead their congregations into Missouri Synod.[82] A pastor or missionary sent from Missouri Synod might split an existing congregation to purge the German Reformed. His exclusive claims might offend some other ecclesiastical neighbors. But once established he was likely to be a link in a continuing chain of Missouri Synod ministers who were prepared to do pastoral work and to build. He and his congregation would have the support of a synod which actually provided supervision and developed high morale. Charges of exclusivism by outsiders only bound the Missouri Synod forces together and made them more consistent champions of their formulation of Lutheran doctrine. With such conviction and discipline, Missouri Synod accumulated a substantial fraction of existing Lutheran work outside Fort Wayne at such Indiana locations as Columbus, Darmstadt, Evansville, Farmer's Retreat, Indianapolis, Lafayette, Lanesville, and Seymour.[83]

To the incoming Germans, Missouri Synod offered the whole range of church life in the familiar German language, German schools immediately available for the children to preserve their appreciation of German culture, unabashed orthodoxy advanced by convinced teachers, and appeals for strenuous philanthropy in support of this denomination's obvious needs for schools, missions, and institutions of mercy. The same ethnicity which could be a divisive force was harnessed as an equally powerful force for growth and loyalty. When Sihler came to Fort Wayne there was one Lutheran Church in the town; when he died there were ten, an order of parish multiplication nearly equaled across the state by the end of the first twenty-five years. Indiana had five Missouri Synod pastors in 1847; in 1872 there were forty-eight.[84] In states with a higher concentration of German immigrants—Illinois, Missouri, Wisconsin, and Michigan—the Missouri Synod grew even faster so that the national count rose from twenty-two pastors in 1847 to 415 pastors in 1872. The whole enterprise was much indebted to Fort Wayne.

Friedrich Konrad Dietrich Wyneken came back home to Friedheim in Adams County in 1859. Along with his wife and many children he brought to Indiana with him the office of president of Missouri Synod, a superhuman responsibility which he had already borne for nine years.

It required participation in all the national conventions, participation in all the district conferences, and even preaching in all the individual congregations on a scheduled rotation which finally had to be expanded from three years to six years. His daughter said: "The journeys Father necessarily was called upon to make as President, took him to many and distant sections of the country and often were strenuous and hazardous trips. He made them by canal boat, riding on huckster wagons, or by any means of transportation which was available. These journeys aged Father before his time, so that in 1864 he resigned from the Presidency."[85]

Scandinavian Lutherans

Scandinavians were scarce among Indiana's pioneers. Scandinavian Hoosiers were mainly Swedes who entered the state from Chicago after 1850. Pastor Erland Carlsson, his assistant A. Andreen, and the student Eric Norelius came from Chicago to make occasional preaching visits in Indiana beginning in 1854. On 18 February 1855 Carlsson organized a congregation of Swedish Lutherans at West Point in Tippecanoe County which included settlers gathered from Lafayette, Yorktown, West Point, Milford, and Attica. This West Point church did not survive because so many of the Swedish settlers moved on to Minnesota and other states. However twenty-nine of its members had been from Attica; the Attica and Lafayette region did continue to exhibit Swedish Lutheran activity.[86]

Another such area was at Bailytown and LaPorte. A Swedish Lutheran conference in Illinois in September of 1858 expressed the "almost certain hope" that the Swedish congregations at Bailytown and Attica would each be sending in twenty-five dollars in support of a Scandinavian professor for the faculty of the Lutheran college in Springfield.[87] That same year the conference report of vacancies had a paragraph for Indiana.

> In this state there were enumerated: Bailytown, Porter Co., where good prospects of a congregation are found. Further in LaPorte, where a church is already built, and Attica, where an important field is open. The Lutheran church there is said to have about 200 persons. About $1,000 have been subscribed for a church building and work on it is to begin in the fall. It was agreed that there is work and bread enough for a pastor in Indiana.[88]

Pastoral supply was always hard to arrange. The December meeting of the same conference hoped the Attica area could "be supplied with a pastoral visit once a month, for the time being." As for the Bailytown and LaPorte area "it was resolved that the brethren in Chicago visit them as often as they can."[89]

These feeble beginnings of Scandinavian Lutheran activity in Indiana were not very important so far as numbers were concerned. Scandinavian Lutherans did not arrive in Indiana in substantial numbers until the factories and steel mills came years later, and even then Indiana's German Lutherans outnumbered them thirty to one.[90] Still Carlsson's organization of the church at West Point was a very significant event in the history of Swedish Lutherans. Carlsson and his colleagues belonged to the Synod of Northern Illinois which was founded in 1851. It was a mixture of American and Scandinavian congregations, an affiliate of General Synod which accepted the Augsburg Confession as "mainly correct." Everywhere the tension was high between "Old Lutheranism" and "New Lutheranism." Schmucker's liberal *Definite Synodical Platform* appeared to allege errors in the Augsburg Confession and so polarized the synod more completely when it was published in September of 1855.[91]

> Within the Synod of Northern Illinois the effect was disastrous: it widened the breach between the symbolical Scandinavians, and their conservative allies, and the so-called American Lutherans. The Scandinavians stigmatized their adversaries as "platformists" and "pseudo-Lutherans," whereas the liberals lamented that their brethren from Europe were bigoted and semi-Romanist and alien to the spirit of American institutions.[92]

It was Carlsson who marked out an acceptable resolution for the Scandinavians several months before Schmucker's treatise appeared. When he organized the West Point congregation in Indiana he named it "The Swedish Evangelical Lutheran Congregation of Indiana." Its confession said: "As Christian in General, and as Evangelical Lutheran in particular, this congregation acknowledges that the Holy Scriptures are the only sufficient and perfect norm for the faith and life of man; and accepts not only the oldest symbols (the Apostolic, the Nicene and the Athanasian creeds), but also the unaltered Augsburg as a short but true summary of the chief doctrines of Christianity." Individual members were reminded of their profession previously made in the Swedish Lutheran Church and all were asked: "We wish simply to know if also in this country you will hold fast to our old, unchangeable faith and doctrine. In the name of this congregation, therefore, I ask you, if you with honest hearts will remain faithful to that confession, which you have already made before the Lord's altar, and in accordance with the same will be faithful to the Augsburg Confession."[93]

It was this combination of respect for the old Swedish Church forms with a firm and personal confessional requirement, formulated and tested in Indiana, which "contained the root ideas of the constitution later worked out for the Augustana congregations." Scandinavian ethnicity was strong in support of it. By June of 1860 the Swedish and Norwegian congregations had withdrawn and organized their own Augustana Synod. Ten years later the Norwegians and Danes separated from Augustana to organize yet another.[94]

Growth and Consolidation

It was the great influx of German immigrants following 1850 which gave Indiana's Lutheran churches special opportunity to grow. "Germans constituted by far the largest element among European immigrants. Of the 54,426 persons of foreign birth resident in Indiana in 1850, according to the United States census, 29,324 or 53 percent were natives of the German states. By 1860 the number had more than doubled—to 66,705 or 56 percent of the whole. In 1870 the number was 78,060 or 55 percent. Ten years later the total had grown but slightly, to 80,756 and the percentage remained the same.[95] The total number of foreign born was never more than 10 percent of the state's population but they tended to cluster with their own kind. These German immigrant clusters with their familial descendants made a substantial population segment. *Der Lutheraner* was so impressed it printed the extreme estimate in January of 1860 that there were 895,360 Germans living in Indiana.[96]

Before that great influx of Germans the way of a Lutheran missionary in Indiana could be very hard. Darius Hoyt found that true at Lafayette as late as the 1840s. Ezra Keller had looked at Lafayette when he was touring Indiana for the Pennsylvania Ministerium in 1836. Keller reported that Lafayette was a flourishing town needing a missionary. Some Lutherans there were despairing of getting a minister and were joining other churches.[97] It was Darius Hoyt who finally came to be that first Lutheran pastor in residence at Lafayette, moving into town with his bride of one year at the end of October 1845 and beginning his preaching on the afternoon of 2 November. He was a Yale graduate sent by the Home Missionary Society of the Lutheran General Synod, an "American" type of Lutheran who cooperated with other Protestants. He rented a room at the school to hold services, enlisted excellent support in the community, and made an impressive impact on Lutherans and others

for miles around. Just before his death of typhoid at age twenty-eight, he sent off a letter to the Home Missionary Society telling them what missionary work was like for a Lutheran in Indiana.

Hoyt said eastern people seemed overcome by "a species of religious romance" about western mission work. He wished to correct this. "It would be well for such to remember that human nature is always and everywhere the same. The tokens of depravity are sufficiently visible in the East. In the West, the will is not one whit less perverse, nor is the heart less obdurate."[98] He said a Lutheran missionary had even more to contend with than most others. His church was unknown. Not one in ten Hoosiers had heard its name nor one in a hundred knew what it taught or did. Even former Lutherans had forgotten it! Those Hoosiers who did claim to know a little about Lutherans thought they were "a set of Dutch that have no religion but to christen their children and take the sacrament." Others would remember that there were several varieties of Lutherans who fought among themselves. The ground was already occupied by other denominations. Lutherans had already joined other churches; even if converted now under Lutheran preaching they were likely to join other churches where their friends and kin were members. Lutheran ministers were few and isolated from each other. To attend a conference required sixty or seventy miles horseback on impossible roads; to attend synod meant one to two hundred miles of the same. Other denominations already had attractive church buildings while the Lutheran missionary was in some out-of-the-way rented space. People were wary of joining when they knew they would soon be asked for money to build a church. Hoyt thought the Home Missionary Society should raise and send money west for Lutheran church buildings.[99]

As the immigrant flood occurred, Lutheran churches multiplied in the major towns. Indianapolis had only Pastor Abraham Reck to gather the Lutherans in 1836.

On the 23rd day of the same month [April 1836] we arrived safely in Indianapolis, and settled about $4\frac{1}{2}$ miles north east of town, where I secured a little home for my family, went to house-keeping of anew, after breaking up the old foundations—began to preach in three different settlements of Lutherans, and attempted also in a fourth place to set the sole of my foot, but could not as yet, for there were only about a half dozen of European Germans in Indianapolis, who belonged to the Protestant Church. I also began catechetical instructions in my home, and continued them three or more months when on the 6th of August last, we organized a little church or society in my barn, when eleven male members signed the constitution. In the mean time these few members exerted themselves in a praiseworthy manner, and put up a house of worship 30 x 35 feet, of logs; and on the 30th of October we had the first communion, the first confirmation of 15 persons, in the first Lutheran house of worship in this region of Indiana. There communed 49 Lutherans on this solemn occasion, and a few Presbyterians, and a few Methodists. But what made the season still more interesting was this, our young brother Ezra Keller just happened with us, as Missionary of the East Pennsylvania Synod, and preached and aided in the solemnities of the occasion, much to the satisfaction of the hearers, and I hope their edification also. About half the summer I and part of my family were laid up with the acclimating process, ague and fever, which with myself, twice turned into violent bilious besides as yet. We need, dear brother, many pious ministers and believing prayers, as well as money, to build up our wasted, our neglected Zion in the West.[100]

But the census of 1850 reported eleven Lutheran churches in Marion County. The conservative Synod of Indianapolis existed from 1846 to 1852; at its peak in 1850 it enrolled nineteen congregations and twelve pastors.[101]

At Richmond the Quakers were displaced as the dominant population group by the close of the Civil War. Germans had begun coming to Richmond about 1833 and proceeded to alter the town's ethnic and ecclesiastical complexion. About the turn of the century a historian commented:

I find that almost every German who came to Richmond was thoroughly religious, and with the exception of one man who had become disgusted with the alleged dissipations of several Catholic priests in Germany, I am unable to learn of a single one of the early Germans who did not, upon his arrival, join one or the other of the German churches.[102]

By 1900 Richmond had 3,354 persons with German names in the city directory listing 10,990 persons over age fifteen. Of the town's 8,569 church members, 3,043 were of German extraction. There were three Lutheran churches using English exclusively, one using English in the Sunday evening services and Sunday school, and one refraining from the use of English in the church as well as from fellowship with churches using English. Richmond had 144 students in Lutheran parochial school in 1900; they transferred to public school as they began the eighth grade.[103] Late nineteenth century historians of Vanderburgh County had some difficulty keeping Evansville's German Lutherans assorted and labeled. They agreed that

within about fifty years there had come to be three congregations of them. Trinity congregation of "about 1,000, including the children," worshipped in a grand Gothic structure 90 feet by 45 feet with a steeple 145 feet high.[104]

Indiana reported sixty-three Lutheran churches to the census in 1850.[105] By 1906 this number had grown to 305 Lutheran churches in the state with the Missouri Synod membership already larger than all the other Lutheran varieties combined. That religious census of 1906 indicated that the total Lutheran family in Indiana had grown to be about the same size as the Presbyterians and the United Brethren, not in the same statistical class with Baptists and Disciples and four times outnumbered by the Methodists against whom Wyneken and Sihler had reacted so stoutly.[106] They were recognizable everywhere by their confessional and liturgical tradition. They were well established and growing even beyond their own ethnic group, soon to become the largest of the "placed Protestant" churches. And here at the turn of the century they were entering what Lutheran historian Abdel Ross Wentz called "an age of larger units," engaged in the centripetal process of overcoming the divisions into which their history had flung them for so long.[107] It was not as if the Lutherans had come to Indiana as a unity and then divided. Rather they came as many separate entities and invested most of two centuries forming their new identity.

In 1990 the Lutherans were the fourth largest Protestant family in Indiana. Two hundred ten churches with 78,727 adherents belonged to the Evangelical Lutheran Church in America, a denomination resulting from a long process of union by members of at least nine earlier Lutheran fellowships. Two hundred nineteen churches with 109,895 adherents belonged to the continuing Lutheran Church—Missouri Synod which had written so much of its history among the Hoosiers. Five additional churches with "Lutheran" in their denominational name reported one congregation each in the state with adherents for the five totaling just over one thousand.

NOTES

1. Abdel Ross Wentz, *A Basic History of Lutheranism in America*, rev. ed. (Philadelphia: Fortress Press, 1964), 5–21.

2. Wentz, *Basic History*, v.

3. Wentz, *Basic History*, 42.

4. Wentz, *Basic History*, 50–51, 65.

5. Sydney E. Ahlstrom, *A Religious History of the American People* (New Haven, Conn.: Yale University Press, 1972), 520; Wentz, *Basic History*, 74–75, 77, 80.

6. Kendall F. Svengalis, "Theological Controversy among Indiana Lutherans, 1835–1870," *Concordia Historical Institute Quarterly* 46 (Summer 1973): 73–78.

7. Lewis W. Spitz, *Life in Two Worlds: Biography of William Sihler* (St. Louis, Mo.: Concordia Publishing House, 1968), 123–71; Svengalis, "Theological Controversy," 75–77.

8. Spitz, *Life*, 131.

9. Wentz, *Basic History*, 142–49.

10. Wentz, *Basic History*, 129.

11. The writings of Rudolph F. Rehmer describe the pioneer Lutheran preachers in Indiana. Concerning the earliest traveling missionaries, see his "Sheep without Shepherds," *Indiana Magazine of History* 71 (March 1975): 21–84.

12. Carson R. Defenderfer, *Lutheranism at the Crossroads of America*, Commissioned by the Indiana Synod of the United Lutheran Church in America (N.p., 1948?), 15, 17; Henry G. Waltmann, *History of the Indiana–Kentucky Synod of the Lutheran Church in America* (Indianapolis, Ind.: Central Publishing, 1971), 2, 8; Rudolph F. Rehmer, *Lutherans in Pioneer Indiana* (Lafayette, Ind.: Commercial Printing, 1972), 8.

13. Rudolph F. Rehmer, "Letters of Lutheran Traveling Missionaries Keller and Heyer 1835–1837," *Concordia Historical Institute Quarterly* 47 (Summer 1974): 86; Defenderfer, *Lutheranism*, 17; Wentz, *Basic History*, 65, 102.

14. Mary Lou Robson Fleming, "Jacob Schnee: Preacher, Publisher, Printer and Utopian Community Pioneer," *Pennsylvania Folklife* 32 (Spring 1983): 128–38; Mary Lou Robson Fleming, "Jacob Schnee: Pioneer Lutheran Minister" (Unpublished manuscript, 1985), 66–70, 92.

15. Fleming, "Jacob Schnee: Pioneer," 69.

16. Rehmer, *Lutherans*, 9; see also Defenderfer, *Lutheranism*, 16.

17. Rehmer, "Sheep," 31, 51–52.

18. "Report of the Executive Committee of the Missionary Society of the Synod of Pennsylvania, Containing Brother Wynecken's Report," *Concordia Historical Institute Quarterly* 20 (October 1947): 128.

19. The history of the Synod of Indiana is sympathetically told in Martin L. Wagner, *The Chicago Synod and Its Antecedents* (Waverly, Iowa: Wartburg Publishing House Press, 1907), 69–72, 75–174. See also Svengalis, "Theological Controversy," 78–82.

20. Waltmann, *History*, 9; see also Wagner, *Chicago Synod*, 68–69.

21. Henry G. Waltmann, "The Struggle to Establish Lutheranism in Tippecanoe County, Indiana, 1826–1850," *Indiana Magazine of History* 75 (March 1979): 44; Defenderfer, *Lutheranism*, 35–44; Svengalis, "Theological Controversy," 82–86; Wagner, *Chicago Synod*, 72–75, 83–88, 96–103; Waltmann, *History*, 12.

22. William A. Sadtler, *Under Two Captains* (Philadelphia: General Council Press, 1902), 209.

23. Sadtler, *Under Two Captains*, 211.

24. Sadtler, *Under Two Captains*, 205–12.

25. During the chaotic period of realignment begun in 1846, four conservative pastors withdrew from the Synod of the West and organized a Synod of Indianapolis. They were John F. Isensee, John George Kunz, F. W. Wier, and J. J. Meissner. By 1852 most of its membership had chosen to unite with other conservative Lutheran

bodies so the Synod of Indianapolis ceased to exist. See Willard D. Allbeck, *A Century of Lutherans in Ohio* (Yellow Springs, Ohio: Antioch Press, 1966), 130; Wagner, *Chicago Synod*, 104.

26. Svengalis, "Theological Controversy," 89–90.

27. Heyer to Schmucker, 28 May 1836; Rehmer, "Sheep," 49.

28. Michael Diehl, *Biography of Rev. Ezra Keller* (Springfield, Ohio: Ruralist Publishing, 1859), 68–74; Rudolph F. Rehmer, "Letters," 72, 84–85; Defenderfer, *Lutheranism*, 21.

29. Rehmer, "Sheep," 65–67.

30. Ezra Keller to Samuel S. Schmucker, 14 December 1836; Rehmer, "Sheep," 69.

31. Rehmer, "Letters," 72; Defenderfer, *Lutheranism*, 23.

32. Defenderfer, *Lutheranism*, 23.

33. Svengalis, "Theological Controversy," 79; Wagner, *Chicago Synod*, 74–77; Rehmer, "Letters," 72; Defenderfer, *Lutheranism*, 24; Waltmann, "Struggle," 31. For a chart of Lutheran synodical developments 1820–1970, see Waltmann, *History*, 3.

34. Wentz, *Basic History*, 99; Waltmann, *History*, 11.

35. Hereafter called Missouri Synod from the name Lutheran Church—Missouri Synod which it adopted in 1947.

36. Wentz, *Basic History*, 202.

37. Charles R. Poinsatte, *Fort Wayne during the Canal Era 1828–1855* (Indianapolis, Ind.: Indiana Historical Bureau, 1969), 57, 59–65; James H. Madison, *The Indiana Way* (Bloomington, Ind.: Indiana University Press, 1986), 173; Elfrieda Lang, "An Analysis of Northern Indiana's Population in 1850," *Indiana Magazine of History* 49 (March 1953): 17–60.

38. Rudolph F. Rehmer, "The Origins of Lutheranism in the Fort Wayne Area 1829–1847," *Old Fort News* 30 (Spring 1967): 6; Walter A. Baepler, *A Century of Grace: A History of the Missouri Synod 1847–1947* (St. Louis, Mo.: Concordia Publishing House, 1947), 56; George R. Mather, *Frontier Faith: The Story of the Pioneer Congregations of Fort Wayne, Indiana, 1820–1860* (Fort Wayne, Ind.: Allen County–Fort Wayne Historical Society, 1992), 99; Poinsatte, *Fort Wayne*, 55–56.

39. Rudisill to Barr, 8 January 1830; Poinsatte, *Fort Wayne*, 55.

40. Rudisill to Barr, 30 January 1830; Poinsatte, *Fort Wayne*, 56.

41. Rudisill to Barr, 16 January 1830; Poinsatte, *Fort Wayne*, 56.

42. George R. Mather, "Fort Wayne Celebrates the Arrival of the First Lutheran Pastor: Jesse Hoover," *Old Fort News*, 50 (1987): 11–12; Poinsatte, *Fort Wayne*, 162.

43. Jesse Hoover, Fort Wayne, to Milton Badger, American Home Missionary Society, New York, March [no date] 1838; Mather, "Fort Wayne," 12.

44. Jesse Hoover, Fort Wayne, to American Home Missionary Society, New York, 19 March 1838; Mather, "Fort Wayne," 12–13.

45. To Milton Badger, American Home Missionary Society, New York, December [no date] 1837; Mather, "Fort Wayne," 12.

46. Wyneken to A. Biewend, 29 November 1842; Baepler, *Century*, 54.

47. Wyneken to Haesbaert, 1 October 1838; Baepler, *Century*, 5–6.

48. Rehmer, "Origins," 10; Baepler, *Century*, 54–56.

49. Wyneken to Friedrich Schmidt, Pittsburgh, 25 January 1839; Baepler, *Century*, 57.

50. Baepler, *Century*, 55–58.

51. Wyneken to Friedrich Schmidt, Pittsburgh, [no date] 1841; Baepler, *Century*, 58.

52. Friedrich K. D. Wyneken, *Die Noth der Deutschen Lutheraner in Nordamerika* (Erlangen, Germany: Theodor Blaesing, 1843), 48.

53. Friedrich K. D. Wyneken, *The Distress of the German Lutherans in North America*, trans. S. Edgar Schmidt, ed. Rudolph F. Rehmer (Fort Wayne, Ind.: Concordia Theological Seminary Press, 1982), 29–30.

54. Baepler, *Century*, 59–60; Wyneken, *Distress*, 10, 32.

55. Baepler, *Century*, 65–66.

56. Baepler, *Century*, 66.

57. Baepler, *Century*, 67–68. The Book of Concord was published in 1580, the fiftieth anniversary of the Augsburg Confession, as a collection of confessional documents with authority for Lutherans. Besides the Apostles', Nicene, and Athanasian creeds, it contained the Augsburg Confession, Apology of the Augsburg Confession, Schmalcald Articles, Luther's Larger and Smaller Catechisms, and the Formula of Concord.

58. Baepler, *Century*, 68–69.

59. Baepler, *Century*, 69.

60. Gustav E. Hageman, *Friedrich Konrad Dietrich Wyneken* (St. Louis, Mo.: Concordia Publishing House, 1926), 40–42; Wyneken, *Distress*, 4, 6; Baepler, *Century*, 61, 69.

61. Wyneken, *Distress*, 47.

62. Baepler, *Century*, 61–62, 64.

63. Baepler, *Century*, 77–78.

64. Baepler, *Century*, 78.

65. Ernest G. Sihler, "Memories of Dr. William Sihler, 1801–1885," *Concordia Historical Institute Quarterly* 2 (July 1932): 54; Spitz, *Life*, 31, 33–41; Baepler, *Century*, 78–79.

66. Baepler, *Century*, 52.

67. "Walther's Editorial in the First Issue of *Der Lutheraner*," trans. Alex W. C. Guebert, *Concordia Theological Monthly* 32 (October 1961): 656–57.

68. James L. Schaaf, "Wilhelm Loehe and the Missouri Synod," *Concordia Historical Institute Quarterly* 45 (May 1972): 61; Spitz, *Life*, 45–50; Baepler, *Century*, 70, 82; Rehmer, *Lutherans*, 21.

69. Baepler, *Century*, 82, 87–93; Spitz, *Life*, 83–84; Schaaf, "Wilhelm Loehe," 59.

70. Baepler, *Century*, 94.

71. Spitz, *Life*, 84–85; Schaaf, "Wilhelm Loehe," 59; Baepler, *Century*, 104–5. The full original name of the new synod was The German Evangelical Synod of Missouri, Ohio, and Other States (Die Deutsche Evangelische Synode von Missouri, Ohio, und anderen Staaten).

72. Baepler, *Century*, 99–100; see also Spitz, *Life*, 84.

73. William J. Kirchhoff, "A Century of Lutheran Elementary Schools in Indiana" (Master's thesis, Butler University, 1942), 28.

74. E. S. H. Husmann, "Biographical Sketch of Pastor F. W. Husmann, 1807–1881," *Concordia Historical Institute Quarterly* 1 (April 1928): 8.

75. Friedrich Wilhelm Husmann, *Diary of Pastor Friedrich Wilhelm Husmann*, trans. Otto F. Stahlke (Fort Wayne, Ind.: Concordia Theological Seminary Press, 1985?, 138 p.).

76. Carl Stamm Meyer, "Secondary and Higher Education in the Lutheran Church—Missouri Synod, 1839–1874" (Ph.D. diss., University of Chicago, 1954), 228; Kirchhoff, "Century," 29–31, 36–37. For examples of curricula and schedules for Missouri Synod schools from 1854 to the 1880s, see Kirchhoff, "Century," 20–24.

77. Herbert G. Bredemeier, *Concordia College, Fort Wayne, Indiana, 1839–1957* (Fort Wayne, Ind.: Fort Wayne Public Library, 1978), 56; Spitz, *Life*, 44–45, 82–83, 103, 165–170; Baepler, *Century*, 80; Meyer, "Secondary," 239–247, 370.

78. Spitz, *Life*, 86; Meyer, "Secondary," 402.

79. Carl Mauelshagen, *American Lutheranism Surrenders to Forces of Conservatism* (Athens, Ga.: University of Georgia, 1936), 153; Spitz, *Life*, 157. For a full account see "Expanding Needs in America Met with Imported Workers" in Meyer, "Secondary," 395–444.

80. Spitz, *Life*, 176–77.

81. Spitz, *Life*, 100, 104–71.

82. Wentz, *Basic History*, 113–15.

83. Mauelshagen, *American Lutheranism*, 135; Rehmer, *Lutherans*, 11; Waltmann, "Struggle," 41–43.

84. Baepler, *Century*, 113.

85. Emma Wyneken, "Memories of the Wyneken Household," *Concordia Historical Institute Quarterly* 14 (July 1941): 40–41; Hageman, *Friedrich*, 52–53; Baepler, *Century*, 116.

86. *Selected Documents Dealing with the Organization of the First Congregations and the First Conferences of the Augustana Synod and Their Growth until 1860*, vol. 2, Augustana Historical Society Publications, vol. 11 (Rock Island, Ill.: The Society, 1946), 80–89.

87. *Selected Documents*, vol. 1, Augustana Historical Society Publications, vol. 10, 141–42, 152; Wentz, *Basic History*, 124.

88. *Selected Documents*, 1:142.

89. *Selected Documents*, 1:151–52.

90. Waltmann, *History*, 14.

91. *The American Origin of the Augustana Synod*, Augustana Historical Society Publications, vol. 9 (Rock Island, Ill.: The Society, 1942), 5–6.

92. *American Origin*, 6.

93. *Selected Documents*, 2:80–81.

94. *Selected Documents*, 2:80; Wentz, *Basic History*, 124–26, 189.

95. Emma Lou Thornbrough, *Indiana in the Civil War Era 1850–1880* (Indianapolis, Ind.: Indiana Historical Bureau and Indiana Historical Society, 1965), 547; see also Spitz, *Life*, 78–80.

96. Madison, *Indiana Way*, 173; Kirchhoff, "Century," 8.

97. Diehl, *Biography*, 73.

98. Waltmann, "Struggle," 49.

99. Waltmann, "Struggle," 47–52.

100. *Lutheran Observer*, 30 December 1836.

101. Rudolph F. Rehmer, *Early Lutheranism in Indianapolis* (Lafayette, Ind.: Commercial Printing, 1985), 1–3, 6.

102. Fred J. Bartel, *The Institutional Influence of the German Element of the Population in Richmond, Indiana*, Papers of the Wayne County Historical Society, vol. 1, no. 2 (Richmond, Ind.: Nicholson Printing, 1904), 17–18.

103. Bartel, *Institutional*, 12, 20–24.

104. *History of Vanderburgh County, Indiana* (Madison, Wis.: Brant and Fuller, 1889), 299–300; Joseph P. Elliott, *A History of Evansville and Vanderburgh County, Indiana* (Evansville, Ind.: Keller Printing, 1897), 244–45, 272–73.

105. Definitions of "church" and reports of the number of "churches" vary widely. Evidently the census of 1850 counted only congregations with church buildings and had reports of only sixty–three Lutheran structures in the state. Tippecanoe County

had seven small Lutheran congregations in 1850, three of them with church buildings; yet the 1850 census reported only one Lutheran church in Tippecanoe County. On the basis of an extensive review of church records and collateral sources, Henry Waltmann said "approximately 190 Lutheran or part-Lutheran congregations were formed in Indiana before the end of 1850." See his "Struggle," 31, 46. For an actual list of forty-three Lutheran congregations established in Indiana by 1850, see Rehmer, *Lutherans*, 5.

106. Edwin S. Gaustad, *Historical Atlas of Religion in America* (New York: Harper and Row, 1962), 48.

107. Wentz, *Basic History*, 241–356.

EPISCOPALIANS

At the very time that Englishmen were discovering and exploring America, the churches in England were working out their several identities. It became plain that no single national church could comprehend all English Christians.[1] Presbyterians and Congregationalists and Baptists and Quakers were among those who defined their own places within the English heritage.

One major continuing body of English Christians has been called Anglican, Church of England, or Episcopal. It was often officially established and supported by the English government. The early versions of its *Thirty-Nine Articles* and of its *Book of Common Prayer* were formulated during the Reformation of the sixteenth century when it took a position with Lutherans and Reformed over against the claims of Catholicism. Among its teachers were Thomas Cranmer (1489–1556) and Richard Hooker (1554?–1600). Alongside its reformation heritage this church has been equally urgent in affirming its direct continuity with the primitive Christian church both in the content of its teaching and in the succession of its bishops. The Lambeth Conference of 1888 offered four articles as a basis for Anglican participation in ecumenical dialogue:

(a) The Holy Scriptures of the Old and New Testaments, as "containing all things necessary to salvation," and as being the rule and ultimate standard of faith; (b) The Apostles' Creed, as the Baptismal Symbol; and the Nicene Creed, as the sufficient statement of the Christian faith; (c) the two Sacraments ordained by Christ himself— Baptism and the Supper of the Lord—ministered with unfailing use of Christ's Words of Institution, and of the elements ordained by Him; and (d) the Historic Episcopate, locally adapted in the methods of its administration to the varying needs of the nations and peoples called of God into the Unity of His Church.[2]

In the early years of the American colonies this church had recognition, prestige, and preferred status. Some proprietors and governors and colonial legislative bodies gave it official priority. In this Church of England only a bishop could ordain ministers, consecrate churches, and confirm communicants. No bishop ever set foot on the soil of the American colonies. So the functioning of the Anglican congregations was at the same time encouraged and handicapped. The bishop of London did designate a few American clergy as church administrative agents called "commissaries," Thomas Bray of Maryland and James Blair of Virginia being the most famous of them. Bray organized missionary supporters in England into the Society for the Propagation of the Gospel in Foreign Parts which sent 309 missionaries to America before the Revolution. His concurrent Society for Promoting Christian Knowledge founded about forty libraries in America at locations from Boston to Charleston.[3]

The revolt of the colonies crippled the Church of England in America. It is true that Anglican clergyman William White was chaplain of the Continental Congress. It is true that George Washington, Thomas Jefferson, Patrick Henry, John Jay, Robert Morris, John Marshall, Charles Lee, Henry Lee, John Randolph, and many more

American patriots were Episcopalians.[4] But it is also true that the King of England was titular head of the Anglican Church. Missionaries of the Society for the Propagation of the Gospel felt the force of their oath of allegiance to the king. When the war came most clergy fled to England or Canada.

> Two-thirds of Virginia's rectors left their parishes during the war. William White, the future bishop, was for a time the only Anglican priest in the whole state of Pennsylvania. Even Jacob Duché, who gave a moving invocation at the First Continental Congress, later joined the Tory exodus. At the war's end, there were but five priests in New Jersey, four in Massachusetts, one in New Hampshire, and none in Rhode Island or Maine. Nor was it only the clergy who remained loyal to the king. Among the Anglicans of New York, New Jersey, and Georgia, Loyalists were probably in the majority; and they were strong in Virginia, Massachusetts, and Maryland as well. Over seventy thousand of them left the country during the war or immediately after. A large part of those who were able to leave were merchants, wealthy landowners, or former royal officials, and since these classes were predominantly Anglican many very prominent parishes were depleted.[5]

After the Revolution the Anglicans in America still believed in bishops but had none. They had no organization of churches and no preferment or funding as an established church. Their support from the Society for the Propagation of the Gospel stopped abruptly in 1784. Their traditional association with England was now a burden.

It took until 1789 for the various remnants of the church to combine to form the Protestant Episcopal Church in the United States (called The Episcopal Church since 1969). That consolidation finally provided an independent American identity for Anglicans. They had three canonically consecrated bishops so they could consecrate more bishops to extend and serve the church according to need. They had an American revision of the *Book of Common Prayer* and a new constitution. There was a democratic structure with lay representation, elected bishops, and strong vestries at the local level. At the same time these American leaders affirmed their English heritage. "This church is far from intending to depart from the Church of England in any essential point of doctrine, discipline, or worship," they said.[6]

Early Episcopalian Missionaries in Indiana

By the time the Episcopalians got organized in 1789 the American population was already galloping off to the West, exercising that freedom of religion provided by the Northwest Ordinance of 1787. The Episcopalians were slow to follow.

> For twenty years after the convention of 1789 the Episcopal Church, its strength seemingly spent by the tremendous effort of reorganization, lapsed into lethargy and inaction. Spiritual vitality was at a low ebb in the Church; economic distress was acute. With the loss of the former S.P.G. revenues in the North and the disendowment of the colonial establishments in the South, the long and painful process of educating Episcopalians to support their Church by voluntary offerings was begun. Crippled by the loss of potential lay leaders among the emigrating Loyalists and hampered by a severe shortage of clergy, the Church was slow to recover from the disastrous effects in the recent war . . . The Church during these two decades received little or no inspired leadership from its first bishops. William White, a saintly scholar, was not an aggressive figure, while Samuel Seabury, vigorous enough, died in 1796. Bishop Provoost showed little enthusiasm for Church affairs in New York, resigning in 1801 to occupy himself with botanical studies. Claggett of Maryland discovered the diocese in so deplorable a condition, its churches neglected, its clergy unable to be supported, that he despaired of accomplishing anything at all. Bishop Madison of Virginia did not even try. After one visitation of his congregations, he devoted himself entirely to his presidential duties at William and Mary College.[7]

Philander Chase was one notable Episcopalian who did give some attention to the Northwest. He was a freelance missionary to Ohio, Indiana, Michigan, and Illinois. He was elected bishop for Ohio when that diocese was formed in 1818 and bishop for the Diocese of Illinois at its founding in 1835. So he knew about the situation in Indiana. It was his expressed opinion that Indiana was completely lost to the Episcopal Church because mission work had been so long delayed.[8]

Chase was wrong. Episcopalian missionaries for Indiana were coming even if they were slow.[9] From its beginning Episcopal work in Indiana needed to be conducted by missionaries and established in urban settings. Neither Episcopal missionaries nor urban settings were in good supply in Indiana's early years.

> In striking contrast to other denominations, Baptists and Disciples of Christ especially, the Episcopal Church in Indiana was urban from its very foundations in a state overwhelmingly rural.[10]

> By 1840 Indiana had only three cities of more than 2,500 people—Madison, New Albany, and Indianapolis. Rapid urban growth in the 1840s left eight cities of this

size by 1850, and thus sufficient to be labeled urban by the census bureau. Even the very largest cities in 1850—New Albany, Indianapolis, and Madison—had just over 8,000 people and were still small towns in most essential ways.[11]

In 1820 there was no minister of the Episcopal church in Indiana, Tennessee, Illinois, or Missouri and probably none in any of the organized territories. That year the Episcopal church founded the Domestic and Foreign Missionary Society but three years after its foundation not a single missionary had been sent. The society could never send more than an occasional rider to Indiana.[12] Henry Moore Shaw seems to have been a kind of Episcopal free lance at Vincennes, sharing in the temporary establishment of an Episcopal church there in 1823 and the next year head of the town's struggling state seminary. After service in Louisville (1825–30) and in Mobile (1831–32), he was back at Vincennes in 1834 and elected state senator from Knox County for the 1835–36 session of the legislature. He moved off into ecclesiastical oblivion in Texas. Henry H. Pfeiffer was an Episcopal missionary whose district was Hindostan in Martin County and parts adjacent. He visited Indianapolis and baptized a child there about 1823. After about two years he returned to Pennsylvania.[13]

The year 1835 began a new era for Episcopalians in Indiana. On 9 March the Missionary Society appointed Melancthon Hoyt specifically as missionary to Indianapolis with an annual missionary allowance of $250 plus $75 for "an outfit." He could learn of only four or five Episcopalians in the area but began regular services in the courthouse and sent back a report of the potential importance of Indianapolis. This preacher who wore no beard but did wear a gown was something of a novelty in town. By the end of the year Hoyt concluded that annual support for his ministry would be no more than twenty-five dollars from the Indianapolis congregation; he moved to Crawfordsville which he thought might contribute four times that amount. So the first Episcopal church cornerstone in Indiana came to be laid at Crawfordsville 8 June 1837.[14] Hoyt moved on from Indiana in 1838. The building at Crawfordsville was not finished and consecrated until many years later. Hoyt's tenure was short; yet his arrival was symbolic of a new seriousness among Episcopalians about missions. Systematic weekly or monthly collections across the denomination raised mission funds from $1,500 in 1829 and $16,443 in 1832 to $27,621 in 1835 and $55,249 in 1836.[15] Another notable day was 28 August 1835. That day the General Convention of the denomination declared that every Episcopalian was a missionary of the church and that there was one missionary society—the whole church itself. No longer would missions be the province of a separate and voluntary missionary society.[16]

Jackson Kemper, Missionary Bishop

A crucial agent of the new missionary era was to be the "missionary bishop." The canon as passed by the General Convention read: "The House of Clerical and Lay Deputies may, from time to time, on nomination of the House of Bishops, elect a suitable person or persons to be a Bishop or Bishops of this Church, to exercise Episcopal functions in States and Territories not organized as Dioceses."[17] They did not tarry. The missionary bishop authorized in August was consecrated in September at Saint Peter Church, Philadelphia. Bishop George Washington Doane preached the sermon. This office of missionary bishop was a completely new thing for Episcopalians, Doane said, and so this consecration was an event which had never occurred before.

> If there be, in Indiana or Missouri, in Louisiana, Florida or Arkansas, some scattered handfuls here and there of Churchmen—or if, obedient to the Saviour's mandate, to preach the Gospel unto every creature, we send our heralds of the Cross to China, Texas, Persia, Georgia, or Armenia—upon what principle can we neglect, or on what ground can we refuse,—since from their feebleness and poverty they cannot have a Bishop of their own, or in their ignorant blindness, they do not desire it,—to send to them, at our own cost and charge, and in the Saviour's name, a Missionary Bishop?[18]

The missionary bishop's name was Jackson Kemper. He was valedictorian of his class at Columbia in 1809 and trained in theology by the powerful John Henry Hobart, soon to be bishop of New York. He was for twenty years assistant to and a chief source of energy for enterprises of the aging William White who held the three United Parishes of Philadelphia besides his duties as head of the Board of the Episcopal Academy, bishop of Pennsylvania, and presiding bishop of the Episcopal Church in America. Visible across the church for his ability and activity, Kemper was particularly known as a champion of mission work. During four years at a parish in Norwalk, Connecticut, he founded several missions and approximately doubled the number of parish communicants. He had gone on missionary tours to the Pennsylvania frontiers, to Wisconsin, and to the South. He was a member of the Board of the denomination's Missionary Society and of General Theological Seminary.

Twice a widower, he could presently travel without moving a family. So his colleagues collected some three thousand dollars for the enterprise and sent him off to be missionary bishop of Indiana and Missouri.[19] At that moment Indiana had one missionary with no church and Missouri had one church with no missionary. Later they made some additions to his jurisdiction—Iowa, Wisconsin, Kansas, and Nebraska.[20]

It was on a Friday the thirteenth that Jackson Kemper first laid eyes on his new diocese. That was 13 November 1835. He said "Indiana looked woody, interesting, and inviting." For the next fourteen years he would be the head and symbol of Episcopalians in the state. His annual tours were to the larger towns. So his first visit was a river trip to the metropolises of Madison and New Albany with 2,500 inhabitants each, Vincennes with 1,600, Lawrenceburg with 1,000, Terre Haute with 900, Jeffersonville with 700, and Evansville with 300. He must scout out the rising western population centers and return east every year in search of men and money to meet the needs. Wherever a town had even a handful of Episcopalians he would encourage them to meet wherever they could for regular services. To the most promising clusters he would try to send a missionary to build up the congregation.[21]

Henry Caswall, rector at Madison, described the services of parishes with missionary clergymen as he knew them in 1839. On Sunday the people expected morning and evening prayer including two sermons. Some clergy went well beyond this to add a third service or lecture on a weeknight or superintend a Sunday school. Communion was generally administered once a month.

> The ordinary clerical costume is much the same as in England, consisting of a suit of black, and a white neckcloth. The usual dress of a bishop is in no respect different from that of any other clergyman. In regard to the vestments used in divine service, it may be remarked that they are not designed to indicate collegiate distinctions. A bishop wears the usual full dress, with lawn sleeves, when performing acts peculiarly episcopal. At other times he appears in the vestments of an ordinary presbyter. The latter consist of a surplice, with a black silk scarf, a pair of bands, a gown of black silk, and sometimes a cassock and a sash . . . In the performance of common prayer, the whole congregation join in the responses, and the psalms and hymns are given out by the clergyman. In the reading of the Creed a disagreeable confusion sometimes arises when a stranger officiates. In my own parish, on one occasion, a bishop performed the services in the morning, and two priests in the afternoon and evening. The bishop read the article on the descent into hell, as it

stands in the English Prayer Book; the first presbyter read the substitute permitted in America, "He went into the place of the departed spirits"; and the second omitted the article altogether. Very frequently the clergyman says one thing and the congregation another; and occasionally individuals, disapproving of their pastor's choice, repeat with marked emphasis the phrase which he rejects.[22]

Caswall said the pioneer Episcopal congregations were generally composed of highly intelligent and respectable people. They appreciated intellectual sermons, expecting them to be presented with some of the "oratorical genius" which was "necessary to clerical success in republican America." Commonplace, old, or borrowed discourses would never do.[23]

To those congregations which persisted, Kemper would return to confirm communicants and consecrate church buildings. Each parish was a unique and risky adventure. Its record of growth or failure was etched year by year upon the bishop's heart. Clergy and delegates at each annual convention, after nine parishes formed the Diocese of Indiana in 1838, would receive an account of Kemper's travels in the state and a town by town report of the infant churches.

Diocese of Indiana

Only a dedicated missionary could have avoided discouragement. When the Diocese of Indiana was organized in 1838 there were nine clergymen and nine congregations. Of the parishes, only the church at Lafayette was self-supporting. Its rector was wealthy and generous so he chose to serve without pay. In 1839 there were sixteen Episcopal parishes in Indiana. Evansville, Fort Wayne, Indianapolis, Jeffersonville, Lafayette, Madison, Michigan City, New Albany, and Richmond were served by clergy. The other seven—Bristol, Crawfordsville, Lawrenceburg, Logansport, Mishawaka, Terre Haute, and Vincennes—were vacant. Good clergy were hard to find. After serving briefly in an Indiana parish, a clergyman tended to move to try another church or to leave the state.[24] At the convention of the Diocese of Indiana in 1842 Kemper told the clergy assembled—all missionaries but one—"The days of severe trial and of great discouragements have, I trust, passed."[25] But the special convention called in 1844 to elect a bishop declined to act. About half the parish clergy had left the state again.

> The Diocese of Indiana is as yet too poor and feeble to support a separate Diocesan. The Churches are few, the congregations small, most of them embarrassed as yet with the first efforts to erect Churches or residences for

their pastor, or having them still to erect. The Communicants number less than five hundred, and most of them are poor in this world's wealth. In certain of the Dioceses, some one Parish takes the lead in population and property, and the Diocesan can be sustained by becoming its rector, and receiving its sufficient salary. But in the Diocese of Indiana no such case occurs. All the Parishes are feeble. No one pastor, it is believed, receives more than three hundred dollars apart from the allowance from the Board of Missions.[26]

Kemper said to the Diocese of Indiana in July of 1847, "The difficulties we have encountered in organizing, building up, and sustaining parishes have been peculiarly great, and could not be easily comprehended by our eastern brethren." Only six or seven of the twenty-one parishes were holding services every Sunday.

> Shall we look to the east for fellow labourers? Only two of our present number, besides myself, came directly from there. Years have elapsed since the Alleghanies were crossed by a clergyman whose face was directed towards these regions. Were the work the work of man—were we seeking for fame, honours or wealth, I would bid you despair, I would exhort you to abandon a field which is so peculiarly difficult, and where we have but little sympathy or assistance. But, brethren! we are winning souls to Christ, in his name, and with his commission.[27]

Episcopalians were educated people. They and the standards of their church required an educated ministry. Kemper wanted Episcopal schools, a full range of them from parochial schools to a theological seminary. At the first meeting of the Diocese of Indiana in 1838 a committee was appointed to consider the expediency of establishing a college in the state. There was a flicker of interest at Lafayette and at Indianapolis. But when Kemper's Missouri constituency and the Missouri legislature realized that he had actually secured $20,000 back east to open a western college, they moved at once to charter Kemper College on a campus about five miles from St. Louis. The school was a source of great joy to Kemper, and of heartbreak when it closed because of indebtedness in 1846. At the third meeting of the Diocese of Indiana in 1840 Kemper urged the organization of parochial schools. The committee appointed to respond reported warily "that general education should be pervaded with a religious spirit; that the Church should secure and direct that religious influence, in the best way, for the good of her children; that they recommended to each parish to keep the importance of parish schools in view, and, when good opportunities to form them presented themselves, to avail themselves of them." Episcopal educational institutions in Indiana were destined to be limited to a small and fluctuating number of academies at secondary level.[28]

Kemper's theological seminary also developed outside Indiana. Kemper was recruiting clergy for the West at General Theological Seminary in New York in 1841. Three young seminarians arranged to move west that year and to settle in Wisconsin under Kemper's jurisdiction as a semi-monastic missionary group. Their early commitment to celibacy was somewhat eroded when group member William Adams married Kemper's daughter. Adams teamed up with Azel Cole to make Nashotah House into a seminary which Kemper and his successors were glad to commend to those Hoosiers who believed in economical theological education on western ground.[29]

If Kemper's feeble parishes in Indiana were slow to commit themselves to support schools, they were prone to overcommit themselves in building their local churches. Abhorrence of debt drove the bishop to strong language. "The ruinous practice of erecting and adorning churches before funds have been secured" he called it. He wanted every church fully paid for before it was consecrated. He urged that "early and untiring efforts be made to free each parish from debt." Clergy were to exercise "the strictest economy." Madison congregation had to sell its church building.[30] New Albany got rebuked.

> This congregation has been much injured by a large debt, which I regretted to find was not yet cancelled. When shall we learn to be humble-minded, and to build according to our means? If our Eastern brethren will assist in sustaining our missionaries for a few years, we ought not to expect them to aid us in the erection of handsome churches. Our chief aim must be for a spiritual building—a flock gathered from the world and its fatal influences—a flock that will rejoice in praising God, through the great Mediator, in an upper room or a log building, if they cannot afford a better.[31]

It was a repeated theme. Two wishes were highlighted when the bishop addressed the diocesan convention in 1843: "You know my sentiments concerning the inexpediency, folly, and indeed great wickedness of debts; and you likewise know my desire, from the increase and pressure of duties, to be relieved from the charge of the Diocese."[32]

Finding a bishop for the pioneer Diocese of Indiana was about as difficult as getting rid of debts. Diocesan conventions worked at it sporadically for six years. The 1843 convention elected Thomas Atkinson of Maryland to be bishop at a salary of $500, but he declined. In 1844 an election was attempted but delayed. In 1846 Atkinson was elected again at a salary of $500, with permission to take charge of a parish as well. He pleaded ill health. In 1847 Samuel Bowman of Pennsylvania was nominated and confirmed and in 1848 Francis Vinton of New York; both declined. In 1849 George Upfold of Pennsylvania was elected and consecrated. Upfold had visited Indiana earlier in 1849 and had preached at Indianapolis. The convention members evidently felt assured that he would accept if elected.[33]

Along with his sorrows, Bishop Kemper knew many joys during his fourteen years in Indiana. There was real mutual affection between him and Indiana's Episcopalians. He was their first choice to be Indiana's bishop, elected unanimously by both clergy and laity in 1838 and in 1846. He declined. However, Kemper declared his intention to stay with his first missionary field so long as he was needed. Some pioneer clergy like Benjamin Halsted, B. B. Killikelly, James Runcie, and Ashbel Steele gave him solid support.[34]

St. John Church at Lafayette and its first clergyman Samuel Roosevelt Johnson were a source of much satisfaction to him. Johnson was an alumnus of Columbia College in New York who had left good ecclesiastical opportunities in the East in order to go with Kemper to his new missionary field. After some exploration, Johnson chose Lafayette as a good place to establish a new church. He refused to accept any salary. He himself gave the congregation three city lots on which the new church was built in 1838. In appreciation of his gifts and services, the congregation built Johnson a house, a "splendid edifice" which cost $3,000. Here was Indiana's only self-supporting congregation of Episcopalians until Michigan City reached that status in 1846. Here was a colleague ready to travel with Kemper and to volunteer for most any diocesan duty. Lafayette was at the top of all the early assessment lists for support of the bishop. Johnson and Lafayette kept handing out assistance to other congregations—to Delphi, to Crawfordsville, and to Evansville.[35] After eleven years in Indiana, Johnson was ordered back east to become professor of theology at General Theological Seminary. Kemper said:

> I cannot speak his praise, or express the love and gratitude which all of us will ever cherish towards one whose simplicity and godly sincerity, whose generous and self-sacrificing spirit were pre-eminently useful from the commencement of our struggles . . . He accompanied me when I first came to the west; selected for his residence the place where he might be most useful without any reference to health, sustained himself and family, and bore all his own expenses during many a long journey

which he made with me and at my request; and devoted all his energies—his fine scholarship, his sound judgment, his able preaching and his admirable pastoral abilities—to the welfare of our infant church.[36]

The congregation at Indianapolis grew slowly at first but Kemper never doubted the preeminence and potential of the state capital as a location for Episcopal work. He tried to get Melancthon Hoyt to stay at Indianapolis rather than move to Crawfordsville. He took personal pleasure in building an Episcopal constituency there.

> In the year of 1837, the real birth of Christ Church parish took place. Early in the year, Bishop Kemper spent two weeks at the newly built (1836–7) Browning's Hotel, Washington Hall, located on the south side of Washington Street between Pennsylvania and Meridian on the present location of the W. T. Grant Company store. Those persons with Episcopalian leanings hospitably invited him into their homes as a matter of course, and showed him warm courtesies . . . Bishop Kemper remained in Indianapolis until February 8. He was busy talking with potential contributors to the fund for building a church. He recorded: "Dr M[ears] says he St. C. will give 500 towards building a Ch." Mr. Briggs promised one hundred dollars. It was estimated that between twenty-five hundred and three thousand dollars could be raised. He preached at the Methodist Church on Sunday the 29th of January, as stated in the diaries of himself and Calvin Fletcher.[37]

He secured the services of missionary James B. Britton to begin work at Indianapolis in July of 1837 for an allowance of "$400, & an outfit." The founders of the congregation signed the association agreement that month, plans were advertised for a church building in the fall, and "the choir attempted a chant for the first time on Christmas Day."[38] Churches without clergy were a great concern to Kemper wherever they were, but a vacancy at Indianapolis was particularly painful.

Kemper often took time to supply ministry to this church himself. During the unpleasantness at the time of the Old School–New School division among the Presbyterians in 1837–38, several substantial Presbyterian members moved over to Christ Church and became Episcopalians.[39] In 1841–42 the pressure was in the other direction. The pulpit at Christ Church was vacant and Henry Ward Beecher was the popular preacher at Second Presbyterian Church. Kemper came to the aid of Christ Church again.

> During Passion W. & Easter—8 days, I celebrated our full services 14 times & pr. 6 written and 18 ext. sermons. I think I may truly say I will never do so again.

Last monday & tuesday I really suffered.—& perhaps am not yet fully rested. But what could I do?—to hear 3 bells—Baptist, & Old & New School—ringing every morning at 8—and every night at 7—during our solemn week when we had peculiar & prescribed services—and to know that the 2 Luth: with the Methodists were worshipping at the same time! Our people attended—but very few others: and now it will take the best clergyman a year to regain the footing we once had here. The course of Beecher is to my mind very unsatisfactory and alarming. All he requires of a person is to join the Church—repentance, doctrine, practice—are not urged—join & every thing will follow: it was his way—he was not converted until after he had joined the Ch! He professes the greatest liberality—constantly prays in public that our Ch may be supplied—and steadily calls upon every member who attends his meeting more than once. If told our Ch is preferred, the answer is, never mind, join up—& I'll hand you over to the Epis: Ch. Ought not the manner in which such men procure our baptised members be exposed, and denounced as insulting and intrusive?[40]

A particular boost to the morale of Kemper and of Indiana Episcopalians was the conversion of Andrew Wylie, a Presbyterian clergyman and president of Indiana University. Wylie was put off by the tediousness and divisiveness of his fellow Presbyterians. In 1840 he expressed his unhappiness by publishing a blast entitled *Sectarianism Is Heresy*.[41] That year he was confirmed by Kemper and sought ordination as an Episcopal clergyman. Kemper reported the application to the fourth convention of the Indiana Diocese in 1841; in 1842 he noted Wylie's admission to deacon's orders. Kemper's biographer described the ordination service:

On the second Sunday in Advent [1841] Andrew Wylie was ordained deacon, being upward of fifty years of age. It was felt to be a deeply interesting, indeed momentous event in the history of the infant Diocese of Indiana. The ordination took place at New Albany, and Samuel Roosevelt Johnson was the preacher. In his sermon he set forth in incisive terms the doctrine of a catholic deposit,—a trust, not subjective, but "a witness which God has given His Church, independent of us, transmitted to our care, which we must accept and faithfully declare and hand over to the generation which shall succeed, without addition, diminution, or reserve" . . . The ordinand cordially assented to these sentiments,—indeed, the preacher and he were the formative ecclesiastical influences of the diocese.[42]

Wylie himself reported to the convention of the Diocese of Indiana in 1845.

The undersigned respectfully reports, that during the past year he has been enabled, in the good providence of God, to preach in the chapel of the University once every Sabbath, offering prayers according to order and forms prescribed by the Church. He is encouraged to hope that these labors have not been in vain in the Lord. The nature of his duties in the University has been such that he has not been able to preach elsewhere, except on one occasion.[43]

His reputed plans to establish an Episcopal congregation in Bloomington were cut off by his sudden death in 1851.[44]

The growth in the number of Indiana congregations was enough to give Kemper cause to celebrate. When he began his service as missionary bishop in 1835, Indiana had no Episcopal parishes at all. As early as 1837 Kemper could say "we trust, through Divine grace, to prove, in the course of a few years, that if Indiana was ever lost to the Church, she is regained." When he surrendered the jurisdiction of Indiana to Bishop George Upfold in 1849, there were twenty-three parishes. These were in a diocesan organization which appeared to have enough identity and momentum to survive.[45]

To the eye of incoming bishop George Upfold, the Diocese of Indiana offered challenge aplenty. He was consecrated its bishop in December of 1849. As his work began in 1850, Indiana was reporting a population of 988,416 persons. All the Episcopal parishes combined reported 549 communicants. The Methodists reported 754 church buildings in Indiana in 1850, the Baptists 385, the Presbyterians 295, the Christians 161. For that year the Episcopalians were glad to count 24.[46] Kemper had been warning that missionary funds from the national church were being cut back.

I regret to state to you, brethren, that the missionary appropriation for the year commencing the 1st of October, has been very much reduced. I asked for $5,500, and have the promise of only $3,000. Under these painful circumstances many important questions arise. What places shall we sustain? Who of the clergy can make sacrifices, and to what amount? At every station it has now become the sacred duty of the laity to make renewed and increasing exertions. Aid cannot be expected much longer. We are grateful, I trust, truly grateful for the past: and we cherish the hope that at a future day the whole Church will rejoice at having had the privilege to build up the Diocese of Indiana. But this is our day of trial.[47]

The parishes must come to self support and Upfold must lead them to do it.

Kemper's own salary of $2,000 per year plus travel expenses had been paid by the Board of Missions. The only way Indiana could afford its own bishop was to make George Upfold rector of the larger of the two self-supporting churches in the Diocese. He moved into that good house built for Samuel Roosevelt Johnson at Lafayette. His beginning episcopal salary from Hoosier sources was $100 per year, in addition to his salary of $600 as rector of St. John Church of Lafayette, out of which he paid $300 for an assistant. This desperate beginning was soon remedied. However, developing an adequate base among all the churches to pay for salary and housing for the bishop was to be a work of many years. Most parish clergy were missionaries themselves. Henry Caswall estimated in 1839 that a typical Episcopal clergyman in Indiana received $250 per year from mission funds toward a total stipend of $600.[48]

Indiana's new bishop was the missionary he needed to be, on the road from the start. Some six months after his consecration, when the diocesan convention met at Christ Church in Indianapolis, he had already visited all of the parishes and missions but two, consecrated three churches, ordained three priests, baptized twenty-two persons, confirmed ninety-eight persons, and administered Communion nine times. Often he could travel by steamboat and increasingly by the new railroads.

> The location of these early parishes indicates much about the dispersion of the Episcopal Church in Indiana. Madison, Lawrenceburg, Jeffersonville, New Albany, Evansville, Vincennes, New Harmony, Lafayette, Terre Haute were all important river towns, while Fort Wayne, Logansport, and Delphi were situated on the Wabash and Erie Canal. Bristol, Mishawaka, LaPorte, and Michigan City were on or near routes of migration from New England and New York. Richmond was the eastern terminus of the National Road in Indiana. Indianapolis was significant as the state capital, and Crawfordsville was becoming an important market center for a rich agricultural hinterland. None had a population as large as ten thousand souls in 1850, but they were among the largest cities in the state throughout the entire period.[49]

He formed new parishes at Attica, Cannelton, Connersville, Elkhart, Goshen, Hillsboro, Lima, Warsaw, and Worthington.

Like Kemper, Upfold hated church debt, commending the kind of "plank church" developed by the congregation at Lima which cost about fifteen hundred dollars including furniture. Like Kemper, he wanted schools. But because of his situation his major theme had to be support from the membership for clergy and church institutions since the diocese must begin to stand on its own. Some of his missionary clergy were actually suffering poverty and

the bishop must be their champion. Renting of pews may be necessary for a time; "a clergyman cannot live on a mere abstract principle, and he must not be starved to sustain such a principle."[50] On his rounds of confirmations, ordinations, consecrations, and conventions he called on the people to sacrifice by giving.

> There is money enough expended annually, monthly, daily, on personal and purely selfish gratifications, on dress and ornaments, on the decoration of our houses, on furniture, articles of taste, social entertainments, amusements, such as Musical Concerts, Histrionic Exhibitions, Menageries . . . to enable us to meet all the calls, and they are many and frequent . . . and leave a large surplus besides, for other fields of missionary enterprise. Twenty-five cents, fifty cents, a dollar, nay, when children are indulged to go and see the show, even five dollars, and ten dollars, are deemed of no account, in patronizing the numberless vagabonds who perambulate the country to minister merely to our amusement. They are sure to open the purse wherever they go, and whatever their pretence. On these occasions no considerations of economy are entertained. But when the cause of missions, or the support of the ministrations of our holy faith, or any other object for the promotion of the glory of God, and the salvation of men, is presented, and an appeal made in their behalf, then all at once "a killing frost" comes over this liberality, the purse suddenly contracts and refuses to open, the pinching of poverty is felt, economy is studied, and a three cent piece, a five cent piece, at most a dime, is regarded as a very generous and creditable contribution.[51]

And he called the clergy to sacrifice by staying on the job.

> Do not your discouragements arise sometimes, nay, often, from an erroneous estimate of the position you occupy and its capabilities—or from morbid sensitiveness to apparent indifference or neglect on the part of some of those to whom you minister—or from an entire misconception of the estimate which your people have of you and of your ministrations, and a too ready listening to gossiping fault-finders, croaking complainers, and meddlesome busy bodies, who are to be found every where? Now instead of looking these apparent impediments in the face, and attempting to surmount them, there is often too ready an assent to what is erroneously apprehended, or too much consequence attached to the complaints and fault finding retailed, and preparation is made at once to run away from them. Whereas, were there a little more patience and perseverance exercised, quite another result would be soon perceived.[52]

In 1855 Upfold was finally free of parish duties at Lafayette because of $1,000 per year assured from the churches to cover his salary and travel. In 1857 he shifted his official residence and office from Lafayette to Indianapolis.[53] The episcopate for Indiana was stabilizing. Upfold was bishop until 1872 but he became so crippled by arthritis by 1860 that he could hardly conduct visitations. In August of 1865 Joseph Cruikshank Talbot was elected bishop coadjutor.

> By the time he presided at his first convention as coadjutor, there was no mistaking who was actually in charge. His strong role as *episkopos* clearly reverberated in his first address to the convention. In it he sounded themes that would recur again and again: (1) Parishes should have committed priests, prepared to give leadership and to stay long enough for the church to take root; (2) the diocese must be put on a sound financial footing; (3) the diocese should strongly support education efforts; (4) there should be conformity to the canons and the Book of Common Prayer; (5) everyone—lay and clergy alike—must become imbued with mission.[54]

In Talbot the Diocese of Indiana had a bishop of great energy and charisma. His background was in business and banking. As a rising young pastor he had led Christ Church in Indianapolis in building its "model church of the West" on the Circle in 1857. From 1859 to 1865 he was successor to Jackson Kemper as missionary bishop of the Northwest—Nebraska, the Dakotas, Wyoming, Utah, and Montana. Now he was back among friends in Indianapolis, full of large expectations which almost everyone really wanted to meet. Talbot was a missionary who knew at once that Indiana was a mission field. In 1868 he gave a statistical report showing thirty-two parishes, more clergy than ever before, and a three fold increase in confirmations. At the same time he pointed out that the state population surrounding those small parishes was 1,638,500. In fact, he said, sixty-seven Indiana counties without even one Episcopal parish had a total population of 1,229,500. A committee responding to the bishop's address solemnly called the roll of the names of sixty-four Indiana counties, from Adams to Whitley, completely without benefit of Episcopal clergy.[55]

Talbot did his part. During the sixteen years when his health persisted he confirmed 5,323 persons for the diocese. At the conventions he advocated free churches without rented pews. He demanded substantial gifts of money for houses for clergy; for proper support for clergy; for life insurance for clergy and their wives; for endowment for the episcopate; for proper residences for the bishops; for a theological seminary for Indiana; and especially for missions which he wanted to operate directly by his own cathedral staff. He wanted parochial schools. And none of this was to come from the proceeds of fairs or balls or gambling.[56]

He certainly did not get everything he wanted. Running aground on Hoosier realities, he sometimes had to beg for arrears in his own salary. The Standing Committee once commented unkindly that payment of assessments for the bishop's salary would probably improve if the bishop would visit more "even though it should . . . confine him to work in the Diocese as long every year as the parochial clergy generally continue at their posts."[57] Talbot died, sick and worn out, in January of 1883.

> No other era in the history of the diocese witnessed the kind of dynamic growth that characterized the Talbot years. He had more than doubled the communicants in the diocese. He had enabled 22 new churches to be built, and encouraged the building of rectories and church improvements in 15 parishes. Nine new parishes were organized during his episcopate, as were eleven missions. He provided an enduring foundation of apostolic orthodoxy for the church in Indiana.[58]

David Buel Knickerbacker became bishop in May. When he was just out of seminary, he had taken a mission church in Minneapolis when that place was a village of two hundred persons. In twenty-six years as its rector he had led the parish to national recognition for missionary performance. As soon as he was well acquainted with Indiana he announced his policy "to regard this whole state as a grand missionary field for the Church of the Living God, and unfurl its standard in every county."[59]

> In his first annual report to the convention in June 1884, Bishop Knickerbacker described the diocese as he found it. In a state with two million population, the Episcopal church had only 3884 communicants. In a state with ninety-two counties, the Church had a presence in only thirty-three. There were forty organized parishes, five organized missions, and two unorganized missions; of these nearly half, twenty, were without ministers or services. The clergy in the diocese numbered twenty-three, of whom two were disabled.[60]

Off he went like a missionary whirlwind across the state for his eleven years as Indiana's bishop. Communicant membership was about seven thousand when he died.[61] During his tenure twenty-five churches, fourteen rectories, and twelve parish houses were built. Clergy increased from twenty-three to forty. There was actually an endowment of $39,000 for the episcopate. Bishop and Mrs. Knickerbacker were themselves generous contributors. A full time missionary archdeacon was at work doing church extension.[62]

Knickerbacker wanted the Diocese of Indiana divided, a move advocated by his predecessor as early as 1876. "It will come in time," Knickerbacker said. It came four years after his death when 12,820 square miles of northern Indiana became the Diocese of Michigan City in April of 1899 (Diocese of Northern Indiana after 1919). The southern 23,225 square miles remained the Diocese of Indiana (Diocese of Indianapolis after 1902). An increasingly urbanized Indiana was just able to support them both.[63]

"High Church" Concerns

The years of Episcopal missionary effort in Indiana coincided with the years of greatest ecclesiastical excitement related to the "Oxford Movement" among Anglicans. Generally this movement reflected a concern for apostolic succession in Anglican clergy; for integrity of the *Book of Common Prayer*; for study of patristics to encourage a return to beliefs and customs of the early centuries of the church; for beautification of churches, ancient intonation of services, and the wearing of vestments; for traditional sacraments, especially frequent celebration of the Eucharist; for restoration of near-monastic communities. Much energy was expended everywhere in discussion of "high church" and "low church" and "broad church" stances, not always carefully defined.[64]

> The internal elasticity of American high church attitudes prevents any overly narrow theological definition of the movement. Even on such a question as whether episcopacy was absolutely essential for the existence of a true church (*esse*) or simply necessary for its well-being (*bene esse*), no unanimity of opinion can be found . . . Rather than by absolute agreement on all theological articles, the high church writers considered in this study were united by a common assumption and approach. All accepted the normative importance of the primitive church for all modern theological and ecclesiological issues. Second . . . they emphasized the identification of the present Episcopal Church with the primitive church and saw in this identification the key for defining the position of the Episcopal Church both to the other evangelical churches and to the society at large . . . On this key attitudinal difference all of the persons considered under the rubric "high church" would have concurred—the Episcopal Church was an alternative to evangelical theology and culture and not part of it.[65]

The issue took on a more emotional charge when such prominent persons in the movement as John Henry Newman in England (1845) and Bishop Levi Silliman Ives of North Carolina (1852) converted to Catholicism.[66]

Under Bishop Charles P. McIlvaine, Ohio had a strong evangelical or low church tradition. Indiana's Episcopalian leaders, on the other hand, were always high church. Some have alleged there was actually a tacit agreement about 1835 that the high churchmen would have direction of domestic missions while the low churchmen would have charge of the foreign field.[67]

Bishop Kemper's teacher and mentor was John Henry Hobart of New York, the most prominent high church pioneer in America. During his years in the East, Kemper was recognized as a consistent friend and member of the high church party. He was a trustee of General Theological Seminary, an institutional focus for high church activity. He was resident provider and champion for Nashotah House with its semi-monastic heritage and sacramental zeal. He addressed his Hoosiers in convention as "Catholics of the primitive stamp." His valued colleagues Samuel Roosevelt Johnson and Andrew Wylie were high church.[68]

But when rumors were spread about Romanizing tendencies in the bishop and among his clergy, that was too much for Kemper. At the annual convention of the Diocese of Indiana in 1845 he delivered a blast against Romanism. It was, he said, "the most formidable evil with which we have to contend." He urged his clergy to study the rise of Romanism and the necessary Reformation "which was established in our Mother Church by the blood of those glorious martyrs Ridley, Cranmer and Latimer."

> All hope of union with a Church which is usurping and idolatrous, which abounds in superstitious practices and claims infallibility and supremacy, is absurd if not impious. Her members are to be met, if met in argument at all, calmly and ably, with the sword of the Spirit, which is the word of God. And those among us, if there be such, who cherish what may be called Romanizing tendencies, which at times perhaps amount to nothing more than a romantic feeling, and undefined admiration for some of the solemn but vain ceremonies of the Church of Rome, are to be entreated with kindness and won, by scriptural arguments and well known facts, to the old paths in which we tread, as did the early Confessors, before Popery and its defilements were known.[69]

In 1846 a letter from a communicant in LaPorte had been published, intimating that domestic mission offerings were lagging because of Puseyism and semi-papal views among the western clergy.[70] Speaking to the 1847 convention in Indiana, Kemper defended again. "You and I, my brethren, have had some strange accusations circulated against us," he said.

I am sure I can say in the name of all of you, that we receive the Book of Common Prayer as the daughter of the Bible, and the best exposition of its hallowed and inspired truths; that we receive it in its plain and natural sense; that we are not only satisfied with it, but are grateful to God for it; and that our highest aim is to carry out in all their fulness, its rich and glorious designs; and that whereinsoever Pusey or Noel or any other divine has attempted to obscure its language or lessen the force thereof, we condemn him as wrong. Wishing only to be known as sound and consistent Churchmen, we repudiate all factions. Believing in the divine origin of the Church, her sacraments and her ministry, we have no fear with respect to her final success and triumph. And under all circumstances, and at every sacrifice, we will seek her peace and prosperity.[71]

Bishop Upfold was also "a staunch Churchman of the Hobart school." He was at pains to demonstrate his church's apostolic succession but equally careful to show how that lineage was separate from Rome. He considered the submission of Bishop Levi Silliman Ives to be "apostasy to the corrupt communion of the Church of Rome . . . treachery to the Church which had trusted, honored and cherished him."[72]

At the convention in 1869 Bishop Talbot used high church language to remind his Indiana clergy that they were special guardians of "the sacred deposit of truth which God has entrusted to our keeping." They were to "watch with jealous care" to "keep it safe and unimpaired" for their own times and "to be handed down by us to the latest generation." This reminder he followed immediately with a reading of the solemn warning against Romanism from the House of Bishops. They were to beware of the attempts some were making to disparage the Anglican Reformation or to substitute medieval beliefs and usages for those the reformation had recovered from earlier and purer ages.

Especially do we condemn any doctrine of the Holy Eucharist which implies that after consecration the proper nature of the elements of bread and wine does not remain; which localizes in them the bodily presence of our Lord; which allows any adoration, other than that of our Blessed Lord Himself . . . We would at the same time deprecate most earnestly those extravagancies in Ritualism recently introduced, which tend to assimilate our worship to that of a Church, not sectarian but hostile to our own.[73]

Bishop David Knickerbacker (1883–1894) liked the round of the holy days of the church. "Year by year the whole life of our Lord passes before us in the Prayer Book, keeping us constantly in mind of this wondrous familiar story on which rests our religion," he said. A trip to the Third Lambeth Conference in England in 1888 heightened his interest in Anglican tradition.[74]

The Diocese of Northern Indiana, established in 1899, was called "perhaps the nearest thing in the Episcopal Church to what is often termed a 'monochrome diocese,' i.e., a diocese in which one kind of churchmanship completely predominates." An unfriendly commentator said of a consecration service there in 1944:

The Bishop of Northern Indiana . . . was consecrated in St. James Church, South Bend, in late October. The service according to a picture in an Anglo-Catholic weekly, was very, very Catholic. Copes and mitres there were in profusion. Candles, too, and a pot of incense or so. And there were three monks . . . Oh, it was very, very Catholic and blessings were as thick as gooseberries in July.[75]

A diocesan historian simply accepted the high church commitment and the price he thought must be paid for it.

In many quarters Northern Indiana is viewed as a citadel of Anglo-Catholicism. It is true that from its early days the diocese has stood forthrightly and without equivocation for the full Catholic tradition of Anglicanism, including a strong sacramentalism. Regardless of the accoutrements of worship, the Holy Eucharist has been central in the life of most parishes for decades. For this a price had to be paid. That price has been exacted in the numbers of people to whom we have been unable to minister because they were repelled by—or warned away from—"high church" practices: the vestments, the genuflections, the sign of the cross, the bells and smells (sanctus bells and incense), the Holy Communion as the chief service of Sunday worship, Friday abstinence, the confessional. Obviously not all of these are of equal importance. Some may be characterized as *adiaphora* (matters of indifference to Christian faith). Unfortunately, both the clergy and the laity share a tendency to get emotionally involved and fail to make the necessary distinctions—fail to distinguish the wheat from the chaff. Thus over the years a steady attrition has resulted, particularly among those who have transferred into Northern Indiana from areas representing a different tradition. As the old controversies between the "high" and "low" fade away, however, this attrition should diminish likewise.[76]

Regional Growth and Stabilization

Episcopal strength in Indiana remained far below that in Ohio, Illinois, Michigan, Minnesota, Missouri, and Wisconsin, both in total number of adherents and in percentage of the population. Every new bishop of an

Indiana diocese was quick to tell the world that his jurisdiction was essentially a mission field. As late as the end of the nineteenth century, Bishop Hazen White said the percentage of Episcopalians in the state's general population was "so small that an ardent Churchman hesitates to mention it save in bated breath."[77] The Diocesan Board of Missions said in 1901: "Indiana is peculiarly a missionary jurisdiction. There are no thrilling, hair-breadth escapes by land or water or encounters with savages to record, but for downright hard work and the cultivation of unremitting patience in the midst of hard-headed opposition and warped religious partisanship few places can produce a parallel."[78]

Between 1838 and 1888 304 Episcopalian clergymen served in the Diocese of Indiana. Ten stayed more than fifteen years but the others left so regularly and so quickly that average tenure in the state was only 3.9 years for that first half century.[79] And in 1888, at the end of half a century of effort by the diocese, $4,900 of mission funds were still being granted as stipends to missionaries in Indiana. Rector William M. Pettis of Lafayette, writing for that fiftieth anniversary, slipped into present tense when he spoke of "the peculiar and difficult nature of the field."

> There was, and is, a dense ignorance of the Church among all classes of people in Indiana, and a great indifference to religious things. Moreover, in their free and easy style, they do not readily take to anything like the formality of rites and ceremonials, or fixedness of expression. The man with the gown, the set forms of a book, a manuscript sermon, and an Apostolic lineage, is not the one to whom the people of Indiana most readily turn.[80]

Work in Indiana is harder than opening an altogether new field, he said, because it is "the recovering of lost ground, the redeeming of lost opportunities."[81]

Persons given belated opportunity to hear the Episcopalian claims were not always grateful, especially if the effect was to lead away members from other churches. "Upward switching" of members from other denominations was a significant source of Episcopalian growth.[82] So the Presbyterian minister Asa Johnson was alarmed when an Episcopal priest was located in Peru in 1846, a very high churchman. "He is very bold and arrogant in his claims . . . He has been round among my members & given them tracts & told them they did not belong to the Church." In his next quarterly report Johnson said "The Episcopalians are making great efforts . . . They are a mischievous people." But the priest had gone back to New York by the end of the year and Johnson reported that Episcopal influence in Peru was declining.[83]

The efforts of a remarkable series of missionary-minded bishops were crucial in planting the Episcopal Church in Indiana. They sought out handfuls of constituents, cultivated the loyalty of these clusters of members until several became first missions and then parishes, and labored to consolidate every inch of gain. By the turn of the century the fruit of all this was about seven thousand Episcopalians in about forty parishes and twenty-five organized missions. Later church expansion came particularly at Indianapolis, at urban centers in the northern part of the state, and at major university centers. Bishop Richard A. Kirchhoffer (1939–59), Bishop John Pares Craine (1959–77) and leading layman Eli Lilly provided leadership for an especially exciting burst of ministry and growth in the decades immediately following the Second World War.[84]

In 1990, forty-three of Indiana's ninety-two counties still had no Episcopal congregation. Numerical strength in the state had approximately doubled in the twentieth century to total eighty-one churches with 21,102 adherents including 14,431 members. Nearly 22 percent of the adherents were in Marion County. Other counties reporting over six hundred Episcopal adherents were Allen, Elkhart, Hamilton, LaPorte, Madison, Monroe, St. Joseph, Tippecanoe, and Vigo.

NOTES

1. Sydney E. Ahlstrom, *A Religious History of the American People* (New Haven, Conn.: Yale University Press, 1972), 218.

2. *Oxford Dictionary of the Christian Church* (London: Oxford University Press, 1974), 795.

3. William W. Manross, *A History of the American Episcopal Church* (New York: Morehouse Publishing, 1935), 42, 45–47, 61; Ahlstrom, *Religious History*, 219–21.

4. Frank S. Mead, *Handbook of Denominations in the United States*, 7th ed. (Nashville, Tenn.: Abingdon Press, 1980), 122.

5. Ahlstrom, *Religious History*, 368.

6. Powel Mills Dawley, *The Episcopal Church and Its Work* (Greenwich, Conn.: Seabury Press, 1955), 23–24; 45–47; Ahlstrom, *Religious History*, 368–70.

7. Dawley, *Episcopal Church*, 48–49.

8. Robert J. Center, *Our Heritage: A History of the First Seventy-Five Years of the Diocese of Northern Indiana* (South Bend, Ind.: Petersen, 1973), xi; Edward Clowes Chorley, *Men and Movements in the American Episcopal Church* (New York: Charles Scribner's Sons, 1946), 41–42, 117–20; William S. Perry, *History of the American Episcopal Church 1587–1883*, 2 vols. (Boston: James R. Osgood, 1885), 2:251; *Historical Magazine of the Protestant Episcopal Church* (hereafter cited as HMPEC), 4:198; 17:4–5; *Journal of Proceedings . . . of the Protestant Episcopal Church in the Diocese of Indiana*, 1847:21; Manross, *History*, 248–52; Dawley, *Episcopal Church*, 55–56.

9. There is little truth but much insight in the popular comment that the Baptists came on foot; the Methodists on horseback; the Presbyterians with the roads; the Episcopalians by Pullman. The remark does show too little respect for the battered bones of the Episcopal missionary Bishop Jackson Kemper who is said to have traveled 100,000 miles on horseback. See Center, *Our Heritage*, xiii.

10. *A History of the Episcopal Diocese of Indianapolis 1838–1988* (hereafter cited as *HEDI*) (Dallas, Tex.: Taylor Publishing, 1988), 34; see also Charles Latham, "A Missionary Church" (Paper presented at the meeting of the Indiana Historical Society, Spring Mill Park, 14 May 1988, 18 p.).

11. James H. Madison, *The Indiana Way* (Bloomington, Ind.: Indiana University Press, 1986), 95.

12. Manross, *History*, 254; Center, *Our Heritage*, xi; *HMPEC*, 15:169–208; 17:3–43.

13. Eli Lilly, *History of the Little Church on the Circle: Christ Church Parish, Indianapolis, 1837–1955* (Indianapolis, Ind.: Christ Protestant Episcopal Church, 1957), 28–30.

14. Lilly, *History*, 33–35; *HEDI*, 8, 142.

15. Henry Caswall, *America and the American Church* (London: J. G. & F. Rivington, 1839), 256–65. Caswall wrote this work while rector of Christ Church, Episcopal, at Madison, Indiana.

16. Latham, "Missionary Church," 6.

17. *HMPEC*, 4:171; see also *HMPEC*, 15:202–8.

18. *HMPEC*, 4:192.

19. Greenough White, *An Apostle of the Western Church* (New York: Thomas Whittaker, 1900), 70; *HEDI*, 11, 13; *HMPEC*, 17:5.

20. Perry, *History*, 2:251; Latham, "Missionary Church," 6.

21. Lilly, *History*, 34; Latham, "Missionary Church," 7.

22. Caswall, *America*, 294–95.

23. Caswall, *America*, 296.

24. Richard W. Mote, "The History of the Episcopal Church in the State of Indiana, 1838 to 1954" (Master's thesis, Butler University, 1955), 12; *HMPEC*, 17:8; Lilly, *History*, 55; *HEDI*, 33, 67.

25. *Journal of Proceedings*, 1842:3, 16.

26. *Journal of Proceedings*, 1844:6.

27. *Journal of Proceedings*, 1847:11–12.

28. Perry, *History*, 2:253–54, 259; White, *Apostle*, 87, 128; *HMPEC*, 4:198, 17:7; Mote, "History," 30–33, 52–57, 73.

29. Manross, *History*, 259–60; *HMPEC*, 4:204–5, 208; 17:14.

30. Perry, *History*, 2:254, 57; *HEDI*, 25, 192.

31. *Journal of Proceedings*, 1845:16.

32. *Journal of Proceedings*, 1843:12.

33. Perry, *History*, 2:253–58; *HEDI*, 32.

34. *Journal of Proceedings*, 1871:34.

35. White, *Apostle*, 83; *HMPEC*, 17:5; *HEDI*, 186; *Journal of Proceedings*, 1846:20; 1847:26–27, 29; 1848:13, 16; 1853:15.

36. *Journal of Proceedings*, 1847:11.

37. Lilly, *History*, 36–37, 39.

38. Lilly, *History*, 41–46.

39. Lilly, *History*, 51; Latham, "Missionary Church," 8.

40. Lilly, *History*, 71, citing Bishop Kemper's Letters, vol. 26, no. 28, April 3, 1842. See also Lilly, *History*, 67 and *Journal of Proceedings*, 1842:14.

41. Anton T. Boisen, "Divided Protestantism in a Midwest County," *Journal of Religion* 20 (October 1940): 362; Andrew Wylie, *Sectarianism Is Heresy* (Bloomington, Ind.: n.p., 1840, 132 p.).

42. White, *Apostle*, 104.

43. *Journal of Proceedings*, 1835:30.

44. *HEDI*, 128–29.

45. *HMPEC*, 4:198; 17:9; *HEDI*, 15.

46. *HEDI*, 33, 38.

47. *Journal of Proceedings*, 1845:13. See also *Journal of Proceedings* 1847:20.

48. *HEDI*, 28, 31; *Journal of Proceedings*, 1847:35; *HMPEC*, 17:8; Caswall, *America*, 305–6.

49. *HEDI*, 33–34.

50. *Journal of Proceedings*, 1854:19, 28–29.

51. *Journal of Proceedings*, 1856:29.

52. *Journal of Proceedings*, 1855:33. See also *Journal of Proceedings*, 1856:17.

53. *Journal of Proceedings*, 1855:24; Lilly, *History*, 124.

54. *HEDI*, 43.

55. Lilly, *History*, 110–35; *HEDI*, 42; *Journal of Proceedings*, 1868:22, 52–53.

56. *Journal of Proceedings*, 1869:11, 22–23; 1870:24–36, 43–47; 1871:23, 53–54; 1872:23–24, 37–38.

57. *HEDI*, 45; *Journal of Proceedings*, 1871:18.

58. *HEDI*, 47.

59. *Journal of Proceedings*, 1886:27.

60. *HEDI*, 50. See also *Journal of Proceedings*, 1884:14–15.

61. *Journal of Proceedings* for June 1894, p. 109, shows 6,788. Knickerbacker died 31 December 1894.

62. *HEDI*, 53–55; *Journal of Proceedings*, 1894:10–14, 29–30.

63. Mote, "History," 69; *HEDI*, 57, 70.

64. These developments in America are described with care in Edward Clowes Chorley, *Men and Movements in the American Episcopal Church* (New York: Charles Scribner's Sons, 1946, 501 p.).

65. Robert Bruce Mullin, *Episcopal Vision/American Reality: High Church Theology and Social Thought in Evangelical America* (New Haven, Conn.: Yale University Press, 1986), xiv–xv.

66. Manross, *History*, 266–74, 284–85.

67. Manross, *History*, 275, 278. See also McIlvaine's *The Christian Minister's Great Work* (Cincinnati, Ohio: H. W. Derby, 1850, 44 p.), a sermon preached at Indianapolis at the consecration of Bishop George Upfold; *HMPEC*, 4:176, 207.

68. Samuel R. Johnson, *The Rainbow: A Sermon Preached in Christ Church, Indianapolis, July 11, 1846* (Indianapolis, Ind.: Morrison and Spann, 1846), 12; see also his *O Worship the Lord in the Beauty of Holiness: A Sermon at the Consecration of St. Mary's Church, Delphi, Indiana, on Thursday, August 21, 1845*, 24–30; Chorley, *Men and Movements*, 167, 252–55, 264–69; White, *Apostle*, 104, 113, 120; *Journal of Proceedings*, 1845:7; *HMPEC*, 4:207.

69. *Journal of Proceedings*, 1845:19–20.

70. White, *Apostle*, 120; *HMPEC*, 4:207. After John Henry Newman withdrew from the Oxford Movement in 1841, Edward Bouverie Pusey was England's principal champion of the high church movement. He searched for a basis for union of Catholics and Anglicans.

71. *Journal of Proceedings*, 1847:21–22.

72. George Upfold, *The Ministry of Reconciliation, Its Authority and Responsibility* (Indianapolis, Ind.: Austin H. Brown, 1854, 55 p.); *HEDI*, 38–39; *Journal of Proceedings*, 1855:20; 1888:168.

73. *Journal of Proceedings*, 1869:24–25.

74. Sarah S. Pratt, *Episcopal Bishops in Indiana* (Indianapolis, Ind.: Pratt Poster, 1934), 83; *HEDI*, 54.

75. Center, *Our Heritage*, 34.

76. Center, *Our Heritage*, 91–92.

77. Manross, *History*, 326–27; Edwin Scott Gaustad, *Historical Atlas of Religion in America* (New York: Harper and Row, 1962), 68; *Churches and Church Membership in the United States 1990* (Atlanta, Ga.: Glenmary Research Center, 1992), 12–36; *HEDI*, 67.

78. *Journal of Proceedings*, 1901:26.

79. *Journal of Proceedings*, 1888:58–61; the ten who stayed more than fifteen years were John H. Drummond (31 years), John B. Wakefield (31), George B. Engle (24), Robert M. Chapman (23), George Fisk (22), James Runcie (20), Joseph S. Large (18), Thomas R. Austin (17), Ashbel Steele (17), and Edward A. Bradley (16).

80. *Journal of Proceedings*, 1888:188.

81. *Journal of Proceedings*, 1888:16, 193.

82. Wade Clark Roof and William McKinney, *American Mainline Religion* (New Brunswick, N.J.: Rutgers University Press, 1987), 162–63; *HEDI*, 34–35.

83. Asa Johnson, Peru, to Milton Badger, American Home Missionary Society, New York, 10 February 1846, 4 May 1846, 8 December 1846, 16 February 1847.

84. *HEDI*, 67–68, 94–114.

GERMAN REFORMED CHURCH

The German Reformed Church in the United States was historically linked with all the other European branches of the Reformed family—Swiss, French, Dutch, and British (Presbyterian).

Pennsylvania became the preferred state for German Reformed people in America. Some had settled early in New York, Virginia, and Carolina but most of them landed at Philadelphia directly from the provinces of southwest Germany. There may have been as many as thirty thousand immigrants of German Reformed background in Pennsylvania in 1750. Generally they came from the valley of the Rhine River where electoral prince Frederick III had found Zwinglians and Calvinists and Lutherans in violent disagreement when he ascended the throne at Heidelberg in 1559.

> But neither ultra-Lutheranism nor radical Calvinism was to have a berth in the Palatinate. The Elector bade both parties cease the controversy. Indeed, he expelled both leaders and thus paved the way for the introduction of a mediating and irenic Melanchthonian Lutheranism . . . The Reformed type which arose in the Palatinate was congenial to the spirit of Bucer and Melanchthon. The Zwinglian and Calvinistic point of view was preferred to that of orthodox Lutheranism, and yet the new position was so little "Reformed" in the Genevan sense, that it is difficult at times to discern the Calvinistic earmarks. The development toward this modified form of Calvinism was indeed considered by some of the Lutheran provincial churches to be the logical completion of the

Lutheran Reformation. In this modification of Calvinism and approximation to Lutheranism lies the genius of the Reformed Church in the United States.[1]

Frederick enlisted two young theologians named Zacharias Ursinus and Caspar Olevianus to prepare a catechism expressing this Reformed understanding he advocated. The result was the Heidelberg Catechism published in 1563. The German Reformed Church regarded the Scriptures as its primary authority. A formulation of the faith it counted scriptural was in this beloved Heidelberg Catechism. Within twenty-five years it was translated into Dutch, French, Polish, English, Lithuanian, Bohemian, and Romanian. Church historian Max Goebel said "The Heidelberg Catechism may in the true sense of the term be considered the flower and the fruit of the whole German and French Reformation. It was Lutheran inwardness, Melanchthonian clearness, Zwinglian simplicity, and Calvinistic fire, harmoniously blended."[2]

Frederick himself defended this catechism before the assembly of German princes at Augsburg in 1566. German cities and principalities which followed the lead of his Palatine church and became this mediating type of Reformed included Nassau (1578), Bremen (1581), Hanau (1596), Anhalt (1597), Baden-Durlach (1599), Lippe (1600), and part of Hesse (1604). In this movement sixteenth century Lutherans and Reformed approached each other more closely than anywhere else in Europe. Later the impact of pietism, as advocated by Philip Jacob

Spener (1635–1705) and others, heightened the zeal of both Lutherans and Reformed for heartfelt religion, for clean morals, and for practical ministries to the needy.[3]

John Philip Boehm and Michael Schlatter

In the 1680s the tide of Reformed population began to flow from the German Rhineland territories and from Switzerland to America. People fled from terrible wars, poverty, and persecution; sometimes it seemed as if the Palatinate would be entirely depopulated. These continental congregations had a hard time adjusting to the frontier of America and to the welter of sects in Pennsylvania. There was no prince to offer stability or to gather taxes for church support. Impoverished churches back in the Palatinate could not send enough leadership to staff a new church organization in America. Schoolmaster John Philip Boehm conducted services as a lay reader for some of his neighbors in southeastern Pennsylvania. At their urging he administered the Lord's Supper to the congregation at Falkner's Swamp on 15 October 1725. He secured ordination in 1729, even though he had no formal theological education. One result was the gathering and preservation of many German Reformed congregations because of Boehm's horseback itineration of thousands of miles over the whole region between the Delaware and Susquehanna rivers. Another result was a controversy in the church over the procedure of his ordination.[4]

After settling the ordination issue on appeal, the more prosperous Synods of Holland or Dutch Reformed agreed to take charge of the German Reformed churches in America. The Classis[5] of Amsterdam was their agency for this mission and Michael Schlatter was the man sent to regularize the organization of America's German Reformed churches. Schlatter arrived from Holland in 1746 and was soon pastor for the German Reformed churches at Philadelphia and Germantown. Like his good friend Henry Melchior Muhlenberg who was working the same areas at the same time on behalf of the Lutherans, Schlatter kept traveling endlessly in Pennsylvania, Maryland, and Virginia to organize and strengthen congregations wherever he found German Reformed people. He asked them to pledge to pay a specific amount to support a pastor. Sixteen charges were quickly gathered, each consisting of several preaching points.[6]

At the end of 1747, Schlatter formed the German Reformed Synod (called a "coetus") at Philadelphia. Three ministers came from Europe to add strength in 1748. In 1751 the American Coetus sent Schlatter to Europe on behalf of the German Reformed churches of America. He

came back with six young ministers named Otterbein, Stoy, Waldschmid, Frankenfeld, Wissler, and Rubel; with seven hundred German Bibles for free distribution; and with twelve thousand pounds to be invested for income for the benefit of churches in Pennsylvania. The incoming Reformed preachers were well educated. They became men of influence in the eighteenth century at such Pennsylvania centers as Philadelphia, Lancaster, Easton, and York. Individual German Reformed churches were prominent in New York City and in the cities of Frederick and Baltimore in Maryland.[7]

The German Reformed church knew about the challenge of America's westward-moving frontier but had limited means for reaching out to it. Several of its prominent eastern congregations and preachers functioned as independents instead of adding their strength to the missionary efforts of the Reformed synods. Pastor John Peter Miller had damaged the denomination's morale in 1735 by leading the elders and several members of the Reformed Church at Tulpehocken, Pennsylvania, into the celibate communal experiment of the Seventh Day Baptists at Ephrata. Just when things seemed to look promising under the leadership of Michael Schlatter, he lost the confidence of his German-American constituents. He left his missionary position in the mid-1750s and became a military chaplain.[8]

The American synod (coetus) took an action in 1791 to declare its independence: "Resolved, that the Coetus has the right at all times to examine and ordain those who offer themselves as candidates for the ministry, without asking for or waiting for permission to do so from the fathers in Holland."[9] There was now a new name—Synod of the German Reformed Church in the United States of America. There were some 178 congregations but almost all of them were in eastern Pennsylvania and 55 of them were vacant. There was no college or theological seminary, no mission board, no church paper. Churches from Nova Scotia to South Carolina were calling on the new synod for pastors but there were none to send. John William Weber was the only German Reformed pastor at work beyond the Alleghenies. He was gathering churches in Westmoreland, Fayette, and Armstrong counties and organizing the first congregation of any denomination in Pittsburgh.[10]

The new *Synodalordnung* (Rules of Synod) described what candidates for its ministry should be and do. Remarkably, candidates began to appear, some from Germany but even more from among the sons of Reformed clergy in America. At first they studied in the homes and congregations of active pastors. Between 1793 and 1825 the number of ministers in the Synod grew from twenty-two to eighty-seven. After March of 1825 candidates for the ministry could study at the Theological Seminary of the Reformed Church which was first at Carlisle, then at York (1829), next at Mercersburg (1837), and finally at Lancaster (1871) in Pennsylvania.[11]

Western Synod

The increasing ministerial corps began to move out of eastern Pennsylvania to probe the frontier. By 1825 thirteen German Reformed ministers had settled west of the Alleghenies. The Classis of Ohio resolved itself into an independent Synod of Ohio in 1824 so it could ordain its own ministers more conveniently. "The business of the church can be as satisfactorily transacted in Ohio as in Pennsylvania," these westerners said. That Synod of Ohio was more popularly known as the Western Synod, since it soon had congregations beyond Ohio's boundaries.[12]

Reformed ministers and missionaries brought many familiar issues into the new western Synod of Ohio. Was use of the German language essential in the immigrant churches or could English be tolerated? Should they join in unions with German Lutherans or be strictly Reformed? If Reformed, should they take a high church view of the nature of the church, sacraments, and ministry like that of the "Mercersburg" party or a more low church view like the "Old Reformed"? Should they receive members by preparation in the traditional catechetical school or press for emotional conversions using American revival techniques? Where should they take their place between the advocates of total abstinence from beverage alcohol and the general German tolerance for drinking?[13]

This Western Synod became and remained a second center of strength for the German Reformed. It took pride in its American-style campus established in 1850 at Tiffin, Ohio, for its theological seminary and Heidelberg College.[14] At the same time it undertook a ministry to the new "foreign Germans," many of whom were pouring directly from Germany into the American Midwest. These new Germans were not primarily Reformed people from the Rhine Valley and Switzerland as the early immigrants to Pennsylvania had been. They were more likely to be Lutherans or Rationalists than Reformed. As new arrivals they were stoutly loyal to their German language and culture. The German Reformed Church, at home with English and long acclimated to America, had limited success among them.

The year 1863 was a year of celebration. It was the three-hundredth anniversary of the Heidelberg Cate-chism. That year the long-separated Eastern and Western synods united to form a General Synod of the German Reformed Church in the United States. Mission work was now more deliberate and directed toward the American Midwest. E. V. Gerhart laid Reformed Church foundations among the Germans in Cincinnati; H. J. Ruetenik established the first Reformed congregation and a German publishing house in Cleveland. For the Midwest the General Synod sought bilingual ministers familiar with recent changes of theological mood in Germany and prepared for the aggression of Rationalism. Three new "German District Synods" were developed within the General Synod to meet the needs of recent German immigrants. These new synods were outstanding among the Reformed for their energy and devotion. A favorite benevolent ministry among German Reformed was care for orphans, especially for children made homeless by the violence of the Civil War.[15]

Indiana Ministries

Indiana received the attention of German Reformed clergy belatedly. They were needed to minister to clusters of German speakers. Most of the younger generation of Reformed preachers in the East were not competent for this; of the thirty-nine German Reformed seminary students in America in 1835, it was reported that only seven or eight could preach in German.[16] Both the Eastern and Western synods and some classes had missionary intentions but effective missionary effort for Indiana came slowly. Jacob Larose probably explored Indiana briefly as a German Reformed missionary as early as 1805.[17] Gerhard Zumpe of Ohio's Classis of Miami served small congregations of Indiana's Germans in Union County and Clay County for more than two decades before 1853.[18] A "Classis of the West" for Indiana and Illinois was organized in 1837 but was not able to sustain itself and dissolved by 1840.[19] W. K. Zieber was appointed superintendent of Reformed Church missions for Indiana, Illinois, and Iowa in 1857 and traveled that wide area for two years.[20]

Some substantial Reformed ministry developed in Northern Indiana among that concentration of Germans in the area around Fort Wayne in the counties named Allen, Adams, Huntington, Miami, and Wells. Peter Herbruck visited from Ohio in summer of 1840. Huntington was a village of about eighteen houses at the time. Herbruck said he was the first German Reformed minister to visit some of the communities. As he traveled, the faithful kept him busy conducting funerals, administering the

Lord's Supper, and baptizing children. In 1854 Peter Vitz set out from Germany with his wife and two children. One child was buried at sea. His wife died in Wisconsin four months after their arrival in America. With the remaining five-year-old son, Vitz went to Tiffin, Ohio. At the school there he prepared for the Reformed ministry. In 1856 he was ordained and sent to the Germans living south of Fort Wayne in Indiana. He and his second wife organized flourishing churches at Magley, Decatur, and Saint Lucas in Adams County; they also served at Lafayette and Newville. Five sons of this Vitz family became pastors in the German Reformed church and three daughters became the wives of ministers, nearly all serving in areas where their father pioneered.[21]

In the major center at Fort Wayne, German Reformed people were united with German Lutherans at first. As one German-speaking congregation they organized First Evangelical Lutheran Church in 1837 and built a meetinghouse. But when Friedrich Konrad Dietrich Wyneken, the second pastor, returned in 1843 from an extended stay in Germany, he had become an extremely strict Lutheran. Those members who persisted in Reformed belief and practice were denied communion and were denied use of the building for separate services in their Reformed tradition. About seventy withdrew. They asked Mercersburg Seminary for assistance in securing a pastor. In summer of 1844 Andrew Carroll arrived and organized them as the German Evangelical Reformed Congregation of St. John. By January of 1845 they had a frame house of worship at Washington and Webster Streets and in 1847 they topped it with a spire.

In its early years the St. John congregation received substantial help from the Presbyterians. They used the facilities of First Presbyterian Church until they could build a meetinghouse of their own. Presbyterian missionary agencies, both New School and Old School, provided a series of grants to ensure a continuous German-speaking ministry for this sister church of the Reformed family. The alliance with Presbyterians involved the German Reformed of Fort Wayne in the ecclesiastical politics of the Old School and New School Presbyterians for a time. From 1847 to 1856 St. John Church and its pastors were full affiliates of the Old School Presbytery of Fort Wayne. One such pastor, Johann Jacob Bossard of Switzerland, was competent in language and scholarship to minister as well to a substantial minority of French Reformed families in and near Fort Wayne. In 1856 the St. John Church, led by its new pastor John L. Klein, was dismissed by letter from the Old School Presbytery of Fort Wayne to the St. Joseph Classis of the German Reformed Church of America. In 1858 St. John Church was of sufficient stature to host sixty ministers and elders meeting as the Synod of the German Reformed Church in Ohio and Adjacent States. Under Klein's leadership the congregation proceeded to build a school 24 feet by 36 feet for their seventy-five scholars.[22]

St. John Church at Fort Wayne was the site for the first meeting of the new Synod of the Northwest being formed in 1867. This was one of the three new "German District Synods" designed by the General Synod of the Reformed Church. It was formed to meet the needs of the "foreign Germans" who kept pouring in, Germans not likely to be reached without a ministry in their own language. This German Synod of the Northwest located its orphanage at Fort Wayne in 1883.[23] In its bilingual report for 1903–4, the Reformed Church orphanage at Fort Wayne reported 87 children, 1 hired man, 1 cook, 1 seamstress, 2 nurses, 9 horses, 10 cows, 15 calves, 30–75 pigs (31 had been butchered for meat during the winter), and 150 chickens. Indiana churches from the German Synod of the Northwest sending support for the orphans were in Fort Wayne (2), Vera Cruz, Magley, Huntington, Decatur, Auburn, Berne, and Marion. The English-oriented Indiana Classis included scattered churches all the way to Kentucky and Tennessee. Its Indiana congregations aiding the orphans at Fort Wayne were at Indianapolis (5), Poland, Linton, Terre Haute, Lafayette, Crothersville, and Jeffersonville.

The national religious census of 1906 showed clearly where German Reformed strength lay. That year there were 177,270 members in Pennsylvania and 50,732 members in Ohio; these were the states with the denomination's chief leadership and major institutions. Wisconsin was a distant third with a membership of 8,386 based on the nineteenth century mission work of H. A. Muehlmeier and his colleagues in the Classis of Sheboygan. Indiana showed surprising strength by ranking fourth among the states with 8,289 members in 58 congregations. The General Synod for the entire denomination held its meeting at Fort Wayne in 1875.[24] Although far removed from Pennsylvania, Indiana entered the twentieth century with more German Reformed than Episcopalians or Cumberland Presbyterians but somewhat fewer German Reformed than Dunkers. The 1934 merger of the Reformed Church in the United States with the Evangelical Synod of North America brought an enlarged but belated awareness of the name Reformed for most Hoosiers.

NOTES

1. Carl E. Schneider, "The Genius of the Reformed Church in the United States," *Journal of Religion* 15 (January 1935): 33–34.

2. Schneider, "Genius," 34. See also Joseph H. Dubbs, *History of the Reformed Church, German*, American Church History Series, vol. 8 (New York: Christian Literature Co., 1895), 226.

3. Dubbs, *History*, 226–27, 230–31; Schneider, "Genius," 40.

4. John B. Frantz, "John Philip Boehm: Pioneer Pennsylvania Pastor," *Pennsylvania Folklife* 31 (Spring 1982): 128–33; Dubbs, *History*, 247–50.

5. Among Reformed churches a "classis" (plural "classes") is a regional governing body consisting of ministers and representative elders from congregations in a designated area—comparable to a diocese, conference, or presbytery.

6. Dubbs, *History*, 249, 278–89.

7. Dubbs, *History*, 281–82, 284–85, 294.

8. Dubbs, *History*, 258–63, 285–87, 296–303.

9. Dubbs, *History*, 323.

10. Dubbs, *History*, 324–26, 330.

11. James I. Good, *History of the Reformed Church in the U.S. in the Nineteenth Century* (New York: Board of Publication of the Reformed Church in America, 1911), 12–20; Dubbs, *History*, 331–36, 352–59.

12. Dubbs, *History*, 335, 383.

13. Good, *History*, 195. The positions of the Reformed theological parties are treated at length by Good, *History*, and briefly by Sydney E. Ahlstrom in *A Religious History of the American People* (New Haven, Conn.: Yale University Press, 1972), 615–21. See also John B. Frantz, "Revivalism in the German Reformed Church in America to 1850" (Ph.D. diss., University of Pennsylvania, 1961, 314 p.).

14. Good, *History*, 122; Dubbs, *History*, 386.

15. Dubbs, *History*, 396–406.

16. George R. Mather, *Frontier Faith: The Story of the Pioneer Congregations of Fort Wayne, Indiana, 1820–1860* (Fort Wayne, Ind.: Allen County–Fort Wayne Historical Society, 1992), 195.

17. Good, *History*, 194.

18. Gerhard Zumpe, Evansville, Ind., letter to American Home Missionary Society, New York, 9 May 1851.

19. Carl E. Schneider, *The German Church on the American Frontier* (St. Louis, Mo.: Eden Publishing House, 1939), 81.

20. Good, *History*, 626.

21. David Dunn et al., *A History of the Evangelical and Reformed Church* (Philadelphia: Christian Education Press, 1961), 125.

22. Mather, *Frontier Faith*, 195–202.

23. Good, *History*, 644.

24. Good, *History*, 570, 630–31; Dubbs, *History*, 404–5.

About "Evangelical" Churches

In Indiana the word "Evangelical" on a church cornerstone is only an invitation to further inquiry. (1) Both Lutheran and Reformed churches freely used "Evangelical" in their names as a synonym for "Protestant." It spoke of their convictions that salvation is the gracious gift of God alone and that the Bible is the Christian's supreme authority. The hosts of Indiana churches marked "Evangelical Lutheran" can be assumed to be connected to some one of the regular German Lutheran synods. (2) Some Prussians in Europe grew tired of the complications of maintaining two Protestant state churches early in the nineteenth century. They pressed for a united church of Lutherans and Reformed which they named "Evangelical." King Frederick William III of Prussia championed the new union; it developed in several other German provinces. So this "Evangelical" union was viewed as the good old German church back home by many immigrants to America. They established it anew in St. Louis about 1840. These "Evangelicals" came to Indiana from the west and had established 91 congregations of their German Evangelical Synod of North America with 21,624 communicants in the state by 1906. The union of this group of German Evangelicals with the German Reformed in 1934 produced the Evangelical and Reformed Church with substantial strength in the state. (3) Jacob Albright (1759–1808) was a German immigrant in Pennsylvania who experienced a personal conversion and a call to preach under the ministry of local revivalists. The classes of his converts held an organizing conference in 1803. They ordained Albright and made him head of the fellowship which became the Evangelical Association. These "Evangelicals," essentially Methodist in structure and operation but strongly attached to the German language, came to Indiana from the east. By 1906 the number of these "Evangelicals" or "so-called Albrights" in Indiana ranked fourth among the states with 8,787 communicants in 112 congregations. (4) Twentieth century usage may name an independent church "Evangelical" to announce its position over against whatever is designated liberal or modern. On this usage, see the article "Evangelical Protestantism" by Joel A. Carpenter in Encyclopedia of Religion in the South, *ed. Samuel S. Hill (Macon, Ga.: Mercer University Press, 1984), 239–43.*

EVANGELICAL SYNOD OF NORTH AMERICA

Reversing the usual direction, the Evangelical Synod of North America came to Indiana from the west. Once, in the 1500s, the German Reformed had sought to unite Lutheran and Reformed statements of faith in the area of Heidelberg and the Palatinate. The confession they produced, the Heidelberg Catechism, came from Europe to America with a large German population moving to Pennsylvania. Now, in the 1800s, the Evangelicals effected an actual confessional union of the Lutherans and Reformed in the area of Prussia. The united church they produced came from Europe to America with a large German population moving to Missouri.

King Frederick William III (1797–1840) was moving toward unity in his Prussian state in the early 1800s but the Protestant state churches of his realm showed little unity. Lutherans and Reformed sometimes shared use of the same church building but kept right on feuding over doctrine, polity, and liturgy. Rationalists and Pietists within both branches opposed each other. Frederick took October of 1817, the three-hundredth anniversary of Luther's posting of his Ninety-Five Theses at Wittenberg, as the occasion to promulgate a new Protestant union.

> Doctrinal equations were to be avoided. Lutherans were not to become Reformed, nor were Reformed to become Lutherans, but, united in essentials, they should now become "Evangelicals." Together they should now merge into a new, revitalized, evangelical Christian Church, according to the spirit of their blessed Founder.[1]

What Frederick got was not unity but an explosion. Lutherans wrote ninety-five new theses in opposition to his plan and Frederick's union church became just one more element added to the former discord.

Frederick's patience wore thin. In 1830, the three-hundredth anniversary of the Augsburg Confession, he introduced a common book of worship to be used by all the churches. At the capital in Berlin, Lutherans who had always said the Lord's Prayer with "Vater Unser" were expected to say it with "Unser Vater" and to see the bread of communion broken in the Reformed style. This time Frederick did not hesitate to make martyrs. Lutherans and Reformed who resisted got fines and prison. A resistant Lutheranism came out of this but so did a union Evangelical church.

> The Union Church thus established was widely hailed by the populace and spread to other provinces, where the decision to accept or reject was frequently referred to the local congregation. Most success attended the movement in the West: in the region along the Rhein in Westphalia, Baden, Nassau, and in both Hesses. In 1818 it was introduced into the Bavarian Rheinpfalz, in 1820 into Bernburg, and in 1827 into Dessau.[2]

German immigration to America in the 1830s began sweeping directly from ports of entry into the great western river valleys. Illinois and Missouri were favorite German destinations. By the middle of the nineteenth century perhaps one-fourth of the population of Saint

Louis was German. The German mother church of many of these immigrants was the Evangelical union.[3]

Evangelical Society Organized at Saint Louis

Louis Eduard Nollau sent out an invitation to Evangelical ministers he knew on 28 September 1840.

> For some time a number of German Evangelical brethren who are in charge of United Evangelical congregations have felt in their solitude and isolation the need of fellowship and fraternal cooperation. This feeling has become stronger of late on account of opposition of the English Lutheran synods, and, for those living in the neighborhood of St. Louis, of the Ultra Lutherans. In order to establish and foster such fellowship, we purpose, if God wills, to hold a fraternal gathering on Wednesday, October 14, 1840 in Gravois Settlement. It is not intended at this time that this meeting shall be a gathering of a "synod," but for the time being it shall simply afford an opportunity to become mutually acquainted. Some important matters will be deliberated upon, and a covenant of fraternal fellowship will be made.[4]

Nollau of Gravois, Hermann Garlichs of Femme Osage, Philipp Heyer of St. Charles, and Georg Wall of St. Louis attended from Missouri. Karl Daubert of Quincy and Johann Riess of Centerville attended from Illinois. These six pastors got acquainted, passed twenty-four resolutions, and constituted themselves as the German Evangelical Society of the West (Der Deutsche Evangelische Kirchenverein des Westens). Johannes Gerber and Joseph Rieger signed on as charter members but were unable to attend the first meeting.

The new group wanted very much to keep a low profile. Priests (Pfaffen) and Synod Lords (Synodalherren) were negative labels the Rationalists who were a part of this generation of Germans would be quick to apply. These pastors wanted their organization to be a Kirchenverein, a simple pastoral conference or association or society with the right to examine and ordain applicants for admission. Nevertheless the rationalist press got word of their meeting and moved at once to expose them as an established church organization of Pfaffen and Synodalherren bent on destroying all liberty.[5] The conservative Lutherans also had no kind word for the Evangelical group.

> The Saxon Lutheran clergy, thoroughly acquainted with the European-German point of view, were well qualified to serve the German settlers in the West and thus share with the Evangelical pastors the burden of a common struggle against the rationalism and infidelity of the day. However, this was not to be. Instead, there was planted

in Missouri a new Lutheran denomination, which, by its energetic opposition to the labors of the Evangelical pastors, forced the latter in self-defense to effect an independent organization.[6]

For their part, the newly immigrant Evangelicals were not open to overtures from Congregationalists and Presbyterians and German Reformed who noted their doctrinal kinship or from Episcopalians who pointed to common liturgical interests. Even the General Synod Lutherans, particularly those of the Synod of the West whose stance appeared so completely compatible, were rebuffed. All these were too Americanized or too English or too eastern or too Puritan to be acceptable. Confessionally and liturgically they chose to follow "our Evangelical mother church in Germany."[7] A Bekenntnis-paragraph of 1848 explained a bit further.

> We recognize the Evangelical Church as that communion which acknowledges the Holy Scriptures of the Old and the New Testament as the Word of God and as the sole and infallible rule of faith and life, and accepts the interpretation of the Holy Scriptures as given in the symbolic books of the Lutheran and the Reformed Church, the most important being: the Augsburg Confession, Luther's and the Heidelberg Catechisms, in so far as they agree; but where they disagree, we adhere strictly to the passages of Holy Scriptures bearing on the subject, and avail ourselves of the liberty of conscience prevailing in the Evangelical Church.[8]

A book of worship (Agende) was published in 1857; editions of a new Evangelical catechism appeared in 1847 and in shortened form in 1862. An Evangelical denomination preserving their particular German heritage was the eventual result, the German Evangelical Synod of the West by 1866 and eventually the German Evangelical Synod of North America.[9]

For a while the Evangelical Society barely survived. Of the eight charter members, Nollau and Garlichs traveled to Germany and served the Society only intermittently thereafter. Gerber mysteriously dropped out of active participation. Heyer resigned at the Society's request. From 1840 to 1845 attendance at the annual meetings never exceeded five and in 1842 only three members were present.[10]

Ministers from German-speaking Europe

The driving force which gave the Evangelical Society power was its connection with the foreign mission societies of German-speaking Europe, notably those maintaining missionary schools at Basel, Barmen, and Bremen.

Germany had a surplus of theological candidates, many with respectable educational credentials but little hope of appointment as pastors. These were young men reared and trained in German pietism. They were strongly motivated for missionary service. The German-speaking population of America made an exciting foreign mission field in which these candidates could gather congregations without meeting a language barrier. The foreign mission societies and their schools kept routing these young candidates to the Evangelical Society for examination, ordination, and placement in the American West. Four of the founders of the Evangelical Society had been sent from Basel and Barmen. Eleven of the thirty-one preachers in the Society's first decade came from the missionary society and school at Basel. Of the 156 clergy who were members of the Evangelical Society in the period 1840–66, 50 were definitely known as sons of Basel and Barmen. Between 1833 and 1937 the Basel mission society sent 287 missionaries to America of whom 158 became Evangelical ministers. While some charter members of the Society were being lost during the first decade, their number was more than made up by new ministerial recruits from Germany.[11]

The drawing force which gave the Evangelical Society opportunity was the hunger of many western German immigrants for ministers to provide services and sacraments on their familiar pattern. Most could not understand enough English to comprehend the sermon of an American preacher or participate in the service. What they did see and understand of America's informal worship and self-educated clergy appeared to them to be chaos and confusion. Evangelical missionary Arend Lueken said:

> It is sometimes rejoicing beyond expression to see and hear how happy it makes old persons when they hear once again a sermon in their mother tongue . . . Easter a man came twenty seven miles to partake the sacrament of the Lord's Supper with us. A countryman, living about fifty miles from Terre Haute, sold his farm and bought one here again only that he might have opportunity to hear the services of God in his own language and denomination.[12]

Assistance of American Home Missionary Society

In the early years the connection of a German Evangelical missionary and his potential German congregation in America was often assisted by the American Home Missionary Society (hereafter abbreviated AHMS), a national agency supported and directed mainly by Presbyterians and Congregationalists. The AHMS had both money and a desire to provide ministry to Germans in the West. Assisting the Evangelical foreign missionaries arriving from Germany was seen as cooperation with Providence. Lyman Beecher said:

> Oh I have looked on upon the masses of Germans rushing like an avalanche upon this land till I trembled and my heart grew faint. I have been praying these many years, and Prof. Stowe and I have often considered the matter, and we have prayed over it, and have been on the point of sending circulars to the evangelical ministers of Germany, that they must do something for the Germans among us. And now our prayers are answered. God is converting the Germans in their own land, and here too, and driving them away by persecution, that they may come over here and work among their countrymen.[13]

Evangelical leaders Rieger and Wall were friends and clients of the American Tract Society and the AHMS even before they became founders of the Evangelical Society. At its first meeting the Evangelical Society decided to "whole-heartedly cooperate with such benevolent societies as are laboring for the advancement of the Kingdom of God."[14]

The year 1846 was a kind of turning point. The flow of ministers and candidates had increased so that six were ordained that spring. One of the six was Henry Toelke who was a native of the German principality of Lippe and had come to America as a missionary from the Langenberg Society in 1843. After an apprenticeship of about two years in New York and Pennsylvania, he applied to the Evangelical Society in Missouri for a license and was directed to Evansville. A colony of Evangelicals from Lippe had settled in Vanderburgh County in 1836 and had organized St. Paul Church and St. John Church in German Township. By the end of the 1840s Toelke was preaching occasionally at both of these places plus carrying on a much more ambitious work at Evansville. By 1849 Evansville had 7,000 inhabitants including some 2,500 Germans, many of whom were Evangelicals from Lippe.[15]

Toelke was busy bringing in more Germans. By his own estimate 120 German families plus many single persons were living in Southern Indiana in 1850 because of information he himself had sent; he said their relatives and friends in Germany would follow. Toelke also had an annual commission for $200 from the AHMS "to labor among the destitute Germans." This sent him horsebacking over adjacent counties, twice to Dubois County in 1848, probably to Jasper, Dubois, and Duff.[16]

Toelke's work at Evansville grew happily; he added a new congregation named Salem about eight miles from town "on high and hilly land near the Ohio" and preached there most Sunday afternoons. Equally exciting were the prospects at a new colony of German settlers from Lippe now located in Knox County. They were about seventy-six miles north of Evansville in an area known to Toelke and his friends as Bethlehem and later called Freelandville. The church Toelke organized there in 1847 was named Bethel. When his Zion Evangelical Church in Evansville had twenty-nine members, Bethel Church in Knox County had about forty. When Evansville added fifteen members, Bethlehem added twenty-eight. By the summer of 1850 Toelke had moved to Bethlehem and settled on a piece of Congress land which had only a well and a stable. Attendance at worship at Bethel Church was 100 to 120 adults.[17]

Toelke reflected the ecclesiastical tension in which an Evangelical Society missionary and his church often labored on the Indiana frontier. He was a pious German with a desire to promote heartfelt religion. He thought that orthodox but unconverted members, church officers, and preachers combined to make dead churches which were easy prey for vigorous sectarians and proselyting groups. The AHMS expected the ministry of its missionaries like Toelke to produce heartfelt religion made visible in conversions, revivals, Sunday schools, prayer meetings, contributing local auxiliaries to mission and benevolent causes including temperance, inspired ministerial candidates, and self-supporting churches.[18] Toelke seemed to be a model missionary in all these respects. His reports of conversions and of deathbed testimonies were frequent and fervent. In a year when his own meager salary was not fully paid, he led his Germans at Evansville to send $30 back to the missionary society in Prussia, $26 to the American Tract Society, and $12 to the AHMS. He exemplified the ecumenical stance of his Evangelical Society and of the AHMS by increasing his proficiency in English and by occasionally attending or even leading the meetings of Presbyterians.[19]

At the same time Toelke had the traditional role of pastor to many solid Germans in his congregations who resisted an emphasis on emotional religious experience and regarded most of the AHMS agenda as arrogant bigotry. They wanted German confirmation, quiet and regular and at the usual age. Confirmation should lead to full communicant membership in a congregation worshipping in the old German style and at peace with old German habits. Toelke shared their displeasure with such groups as the German Methodists and United Brethren.

These he called sects because he felt they were unsound in doctrine, uneducated for ministry, and inclined to pirate away religious immigrants with their stress on emotion and perfection. But he was an honest and earnest evangelical who wanted incoming members to show evidence of regeneration by the Holy Spirit. He finally eased his own tension over these things by joining the New School Presbyterians.[20]

Toelke was the key man for Southern Indiana in the early days of the Evangelical Society. However the Society and the AHMS teamed up to send and assist four more missionaries. Toelke's Zion Evangelical Church in Evansville continued to receive missionary support after his departure to Knox County. Zion Church was considered essential in Evansville because the large United German Evangelical Church in that city did not meet pietist standards: "How much of real Evangelism it has within it, may be estimated by a simple statement that its members may celebrate the Lord's Supper in the morning—be found in the bar room drinking and playing cards in the afternoon and then in the ball room in the evening and that on the Lord's day."[21] Gerhard H. Zumpe of the German Reformed Church in the United States succeeded Toelke briefly at Evansville beginning in 1851. Even with $150 in aid from the AHMS he could not support his family there and moved away the following year.[22]

Some members of Zion Church had been previously acquainted with Pastor Christian Schrenk in New Orleans and invited this Basel graduate to Evansville in 1852. After one year the church officers notified the AHMS that they now wished to support Schrenk as their pastor and to be regarded as a self-sustaining church. They had already paid for one parsonage and meetinghouse. They sent $5 as a token of their warm feelings for the AHMS. Schrenk was at Zion Church for two periods of pastoral service totaling fifteen years. Before the end of his tenure Zion congregation had a large brick church based on a foundation wall two feet thick at the base, sixteen inches thick up to the Gothic windows, twelve inches thick to the roof, and topped by a spectacular steeple.[23]

Similarly cheering was the ministry of John Wettle in Indiana. Wettle was a graduate of Basel, ordained by the Evangelical Society in the watershed year of 1846. He was a perennial missionary of the AHMS but received his first Indiana appointment in 1856 to a new congregation at Sandersville in Vanderburgh County. It was a model of AHMS success. Five men of the congregation had built a new church building just before Wettle arrived. He promptly introduced some English services and a bilingual Sunday school; when the communicant membership was 40, an average congregation was 150. By 1859 the original 5 families had increased to 100 families who were attending preaching and Wettle had organized a new preaching station nearby. The request for annual assistance had decreased to $75. Wettle's letter of 1 March 1861 thanked the AHMS for support during the church's infancy and declared that the congregation was now self-supporting.[24]

The case of missionary Louis Austmann was more painful. When he arrived from Lippe in Germany he lacked the customary educational preparation for ministry and was ordained by the Evangelical Society in summer of 1850 with reluctance. His ministry in Indiana had actually begun in 1849. It included service at Tersteegen and Salem in Posey County near Evansville, at Mount Vernon, at Newburgh, and at Boonville. It was at most points marked by catastrophe, controversy, and unhappiness. His church officers in Posey County finally wrote to the AHMS to charge him with nonfeasance and to inquire what they were to do if Austmann sued the church officers as he had threatened.[25]

Evangelical Institutions

Harbingers of the future of the Evangelical Society appeared in some reports of these young missionaries serving in Indiana. In June of 1849 Henry Toelke went by steamboat from Evansville to Saint Louis "to meet our Synod." He was impressed by the steamboat boiler explosion at Evansville which killed about twenty persons. He wrote of the cholera epidemic in Saint Louis on account of which he stayed an extra week to assist an overworked pastor. He also noted the two really big pieces of news from the Evangelical Society meeting of that year. First, there was the decision to build an Evangelical theological seminary on Femme Osage Creek in the backwoods of Warren County, Missouri. And at the same meeting the Society decided to begin publishing a monthly church paper called the *Messenger of Peace* (*Friedensbote*). There was a body of Evangelical Society leaders in Missouri and Illinois more able, more educated, and more sophisticated than the scattered handful of missionaries in Indiana. With only twenty-two ministers in the Evangelical Society and with a largely unorganized and undisciplined constituency, they dared to undertake these two costly ventures. They sought support everywhere; they simply would not let these new denominational enterprises fail.[26]

Toelke was certainly motivated. In February of the following year he reported that his combined membership of about a hundred Germans at Zion church in Evansville and Bethel church at Bethlehem had given $15 for home missions, $15 for foreign missions, $35 for the American Tract Society, and $70 for the new theological seminary! When the members of Zion congregation at Evansville were unable to sustain Gerhard H. Zumpe as their own pastor early in 1852 and were just finishing paying for their own new church and parsonage, they kept sending support for a poor theological student and making contributions to higher education. In 1853 Christian Schrenk again reported that Zion church in Evansville had made a contribution to the theological seminary of the German Evangelicals in Missouri.[27]

By 1852 that seminary at Marthasville in Warren County (later to be Eden Seminary at Saint Louis) had a printing press on which to issue denominational publications. The president of the seminary—Wilhelm Friedrich Binner and then his successor Andreas Irion—was also chief editor.[28] Every month, and semi-monthly after 1858 for the same fifty cents per year, the *Friedensbote* went out to western homes. This paper became a kind of soul of the young church. Its stated intention was to avoid theological controversy and specialize in nurture. It offered church families constant commentary on scriptural passages and the catechism. It printed hymns, sermons, poems, stories, and biographies of Christian men and women. It brought news of home and foreign missions, of district and general conferences, of ministerial candidates examined and ordained, of new churches established and dedicated, of all the phases of life of sister congregations. Affection and loyalty to these institutions, and to Elmhurst College located in Illinois in the next generation, brought unity, growth, and denominational identity to these Evangelicals. Where there had been 8 pastors in the Evangelical Society in 1840 and 25 pastors in 1850, there were 122 in 1866. Of the 122, 26 were in Indiana.[29]

For many years the society's complexion remained strongly German. The children must be acclimated to America, but not too fast. Instruction for confirmation was expected to be in the German language. Out of love for the mother tongue a few of the stronger churches operated full scale parochial schools. Seminary and college professors had to be completely competent in both German and English.[30]

> The Society continued to be served by a wholly foreign-born ministry. Of the 139 [of 156 clergymen of the Society to 1866] whose birthplaces could be ascertained, fourteen came from Switzerland, two from Alsace, and the remainder from Germany. Without exception, they were all committed to the German traditions. Of the

overwhelmingly German contingent . . . 38, or 30.8 percent, hailed from pietistic Wuerttemberg, the next highest numbers having emigrated from Lippe-Detmold (11), Hanover (11), and Prussia (10). It is equally clear that, measured by their socio-economic background, *Kirchenverein* pastors came mostly from the lower economic groups, with relatively few whose families belonged to the higher, professional classes.[31]

Many of the first students at the seminary at Marthasville came from Germany with little or no preparation.

> Some had not even attended the public or parochial schools and were a treasured burden to men like Binner and Birkner, who lovingly sought to introduce them into the intricate ways of Greek grammar. Under such conditions most elementary methods were used, the study of dogmatics being little more than an advanced exposition of the catechism . . . Of the nine new students in 1855, only three could write acceptably; the remainder could not write a line without a mistake.[32]

Carefully the faculty took such candidates wherever they were educationally and brought them up to traditional ordination standards.

In the first sixteen years of its history (1850–66), the seminary at Marthasville sent fifty-one men into the Evangelical ministry. Gradually the Evangelicals of the American Midwest began sending their native-born sons to their college and seminary and into service of their church. Families and congregations were enlisted year by year on behalf of missions. The support of the whole membership was needed if the seminary was to survive and thrive as a place for pastors and missionaries to be trained. Beginning in 1853, women in Evangelical congregations formed organizations (*Frauenvereine*) in order to respond to appeals for assistance from Marthasville. Missionaries were not only for foreign fields, as the continental German mission societies had been prone to understand, but also for home missions and church extension, especially among German-Americans. And there must be care for the poor, the sick, the orphaned, the disabled. Evangelical institutions of mercy tended to be in Missouri and Illinois rather than in Indiana. However Indianapolis became the site of an Evangelical orphans' home and Evangelical "deaconess hospitals" were opened at both Indianapolis and Evansville.[33]

Vitality in Southwestern Indiana

Indiana shared fully in the growth. The state had six churches being served by Evangelical pastors at the end of the Society's first decade in 1850. By 1866, when the Society was finally willing to be called a synod and took its intermediate name of German Evangelical Synod of the West, Indiana had added thirty-five for a total of forty-one congregations served at least for a time by Evangelical pastors.[34] Most of the churches were concentrated in the southwest corner of the state around Evansville. However the Evangelical expansion and amalgamation kept extending from west to east into Ohio and New York. Indiana was joined with the eastern territories in the Eastern District in 1856 to create the most vital area of Evangelical growth. This lively district kept motivating the mother Evangelical Society to write a constitution, to define its internal relationships, and to play a responsible role as the major denomination it had become. At the annual conference at Evansville in 1866 this national fellowship of Evangelicals officially adopted a new constitution by which they finally laid aside the name "society" and became a "synod." Professor Adolf H. Baltzer of the seminary accepted election as the first full-time president and located his new office at Saint Charles, Missouri, conveniently close to Marthasville.[35]

Religious census takers of 1906 found this family of Evangelicals to be a mature American denomination named the German Evangelical Synod of North America. By that year the states with largest membership were Illinois (59,973), Ohio (35,138), Missouri (32,715), and New York (26,183). Indiana was fifth with only ninety-one church organizations but with a membership totaling 21,624. Nearly a hundred years from the time of their earliest organization in America, these German Evangelicals merged with their kindred Germans of the Reformed Church in the United States to form the Evangelical and Reformed Church in 1934. When being German was no longer so important, they merged with the Congregational Christian Churches in 1957 to form the United Church of Christ. It was the combined strength of the German Evangelical Synod of North America and the German Reformed which gave the United Church of Christ a very substantial presence and many tall church spires in Indiana. In 1990 this merged fellowship reported 60,773 adherents in 173 congregations in the state, eleventh in size among the 89 reporting denominations.

NOTES

1. Carl E. Schneider, *The German Church on the American Frontier* (St. Louis, Mo.: Eden Publishing House, 1939), 11.

2. Schneider, *German Church*, 11.

3. Sydney E. Ahlstrom, *A Religious History of the American People* (New Haven, Conn.: (Yale University Press, 1972), 755; Schneider, *German Church*, 14–24.

4. Schneider, *German Church*, 106–7.

5. Schneider, *German Church*, 33–35, 107–9, 113–29.

6. Schneider, *German Church*, 105; see also Schneider, *German Church*, 103–5, 372–75.

7. Schneider, *German Church*, 68–69, 99–102, 110, 129–32.

8. Schneider, *German Church*, 409.

9. Schneider, *German Church*, 414–17, 448–55.

10. Schneider, *German Church*, 133–37.

11. David G. Gelzer, "Mission to America: A History of the Work of the Basel Foreign Missions Society in America" (Ph.D. diss., Yale University, 1952, 374 p.); Schneider, *German Church*, 155–57, 161, 328.

12. Arend H. Lueken, Terre Haute, to American Home Missionary Society (hereafter cited as AHMS), New York, 1 August 1849 and 1 May 1850.

13. Lyman Beecher in an address to the annual meeting of the American Tract Society at Cincinnati; Schneider, *German Church*, 387, citing *Report of the American Tract Society* (1847), 97.

14. Schneider, *German Church*, 89–91, 110.

15. Schneider, *German Church*, 147–48.

16. Schneider, *German Church*, 188; Henry Toelke, Evansville, to AHMS, New York, 10 January 1849 and 27 February 1850; the AHMS files include fourteen letters sent by Toelke from his mission field in Indiana between 1848 and 1851.

17. Henry Toelke to AHMS, New York, 2 March 1848, 13 August 1850, and 8 November 1850.

18. Henry Toelke to AHMS, New York, 19 November 1849 and 10 May 1850; "Missionary Aid to German Churches," *Home Missionary* (January 1851): reprinted in Schneider, *German Church*, 493–95.

19. Henry Toelke to AHMS, New York, 10 January 1849, 28 May 1849, 27 February 1850, and 8 November 1850.

20. William McCarer, Evansville, to Milton Badger, AHMS, New York, 10 November 1850; Henry Toelke to AHMS, New York, 18 November 1849 and 14 May 1851; Schneider, *German Church*, 148.

21. Wilhelm Hinspeter, Evansville, to AHMS, New York, 14 July 1852.

22. Schneider, *German Church*, 189; Gerhard Zumpe to AHMS, New York, 9 May 1851 and 12 February 1852; the AHMS files include ten letters by Zumpe from his mission field in Indiana between 1851 and 1853.

23. Schneider, *German Church*, 155, 226–29; Gerhard Zumpe to AHMS, New York, 4 March 1852; Wilhelm Hinspeter, Evansville, to AHMS, New York, 14 July 1852; William McCarer, Evansville, to AHMS, New York, 20 March 1854.

24. Schneider, *German Church*, 150, 209; J. P. Voelker, Sandersville, to AHMS, New York, 15 September 1856, 15 September 1857 and 15 September 1858; M. Hersch, Sandersville, to AHMS, New York, 15 April 1860; John Wettle, Sandersville, to AHMS, New York, 15 June 1858, 15 September 1858, 15 September 1860 and 1 March 1861; AHMS files include twenty-five letters by Wettle from his Indiana mission field between 1856 and 1861.

25. Elfrieda Lang, *History of Trinity Evangelical and Reformed Church, 1853–1953, Mount Vernon, Indiana* (St. Louis, Mo.: Eden Publishing House, 1953), 99–101; Ernest Krumme, Tersteegen, to AHMS, New York, 13 April 1854; the AHMS files include eleven letters by Austmann from his mission field in Indiana between 1851 and 1857 and several others about him.

26. Toelke to AHMS, 17 August 1849; Lang, *History*, 66–68; Schneider, *German Church*, 299–318.

27. Henry Toelke to AHMS, New York, 27 February 1850; Gerhard Zumpe to AHMS, New York, 4 March 1852; Christian Schrenk, Evansville, to AHMS, New York, 25 May 1853.

28. Schneider, *German Church*, 458–460 includes a list of publications.

29. Schneider, *German Church*, 287, 461–62.

30. *Brief History of the Indiana District of the Evangelical Synod of North America, 1886–1938* (St. Louis, Mo.: Eden Publishing House, 1938), 13–14; Schneider, *German Church*, 320.

31. Schneider, *German Church*, 441.

32. Schneider, *German Church*, 314.

33. Schneider, *German Church*, 248, 328–48, 442–43; *Brief History*, 12, 14.

34. The original six were St. Paul, St. John, and Zion in Vanderburgh County; Zion at Lippe and Salem at Black Hawk Mills in Posey County; and Bethel in Knox County. The thirty-five additional were at Holland, Cumberland, Huntingburg, Vincennes, Inglefield, Haubstadt, Evansville, Andrews, Bippus, Bremen, Newburgh, Cannelton, Kasson, Elberfeld, Indianapolis (2), Hickory Branch, New Albany (2), Stewartsville, Boonville, Urbana, Wabash, Sugar Creek in Hancock County, Santa Claus, Lawrenceburg, South Bend, Edwardsport, Bourbon, Central Point, Fulda, Madison, Farmer's Retreat, Buffaloville, and Warrenton. It was not uncommon for churches supplied wholly or in part by Evangelical ministers to function as independent or union German for years before officially joining the Evangelical Society. See Schneider, *German Church*, 511–14; *Brief History*, 8–9.

35. Schneider, *German Church*, 387–96, 446–48, 453–54.

CONGREGATIONALISTS

Congregationalists developed in the English reformation of the 1500s and 1600s. They were generally Reformed in theology; after 1648 a part of the doctrinal basis for a Congregational covenant was likely to be the Westminster Confession. They were a strand of Puritanism which became increasingly unwilling to participate in the episcopal government and church traditions of the official Anglican Church as they knew it.

A few of them wanted churches completely independent and separate from the state. But most of them wanted to convince all regenerate English people to make covenants to form themselves into individual regenerate congregations. These taken together would constitute a true Church of England which was Congregational, obedient to the Bible only, and the religious basis for a nation which could then be or become a holy commonwealth. Failing to implement this experiment in England, they emigrated to America to establish their biblical commonwealth. Not many modern Americans raise cheers for their Congregational state church which endured for two hundred years in parts of Massachusetts and Connecticut. Both internal and external forces kept eroding that arrangement. Much more weighty than their fading establishment were the contributions of Congregationalists to education, to missions, to benevolent enterprises, and to the ordering of both civic and cultural institutions in the new nation. Wherever they went and wherever they sent their agents, their impact was large all out of proportion to their numbers.

Congregational churches were usually organized by immigrants from the New England states. Early Indiana had few settlers from the New England states and got few Congregational churches. In 1850 only 2 percent (10,646) of Indiana's population was from New England. Even if one assumed that settlers coming to Indiana from New York were only New Englanders once removed, New Yorkers plus New Englanders would still have totaled only 3.5 percent of the population in 1850. Nor was the rate of immigration from New England increasing. Five times more Indiana residents in 1850 had come from foreign countries than had come from New England. The census of that year showed one hundred Congregational churches in Ohio, forty-six in Illinois, twenty-nine in Michigan, thirty-seven in Wisconsin, and fourteen in Iowa. Indiana had two—one each in LaPorte and Vigo counties.[1]

Heavy Investment in Indiana

That slim statistic disguised a heroic investment in Indiana's development by the Congregationalists. They were among the earliest and most persistent in raising money for missions and in sending missionaries to the new territory and state. Indiana's population from the South and from the Middle States was not very hospitable to the New England missionaries so their results were not phenomenal. And whatever progress they did make usually translated into gains for Presbyterians. These were the days of the Plan of Union in which Congregationalists and

Presbyterians agreed to unite their effort to offer a trained ministry to the rising West. Preparing to serve a population from the South and the Middle States, welcoming the support of an established Presbyterian denominational structure, and following a pattern already familiar in New York and Ohio, the Congregational missionaries almost routinely connected themselves with the western presbyteries and founded Presbyterian churches. Later there were complaints that Congregationalism seemed to be a stream which rose in the East and flowed westward into Presbyterianism. When the Congregationalists held their first general convention in two hundred years at Albany, New York, in 1852, one of the speakers said "They have milked our Congregational cows, but have made nothing but Presbyterian butter and cheese."[2]

Congregationalists John F. Schermerhorn and Samuel J. Mills explored the West in 1812–13 for the Connecticut and Massachusetts churches. Samuel J. Mills and Daniel Smith explored again in 1814–15. They reported that Indiana needed missionaries.[3] So the Connecticut Missionary Society commissioned four men for Indiana in 1816. Isaac Reed, graduate of Middlebury College in Vermont and licentiate of Fairfield Congregational Association, worked part time for the Connecticut Missionary Society in Indiana. He was busy founding Presbyterian churches. In 1827 "The Rev. Mr. Crow," missionary of the Connecticut Missionary Society in Indiana, wrote to the home office: "I may venture to affirm that nearly one–half the Presbyterian churches of Indiana have been planted by your missionaries. Twenty years ago the first church, located at Vincennes, Knox county, was formed and called after the Territory the 'Indiana Church.' Now we have about sixty churches and sixteen ministers."[4]

The pace of Congregational support for Indiana only quickened when the Connecticut Missionary Society, other New England societies, and the Domestic Missionary Society of New York united to become the American Home Missionary Society (hereafter written AHMS) in 1826. Money and men for western missions came from both the Presbyterians and the Congregationalists; the Society seemed to take little account of the origins of either. But any roll of Indiana's Presbyterian missionary pioneers must include Isaac Reed, Benjamin Cressy, Martin M. Post, Caleb Mills, Edmund O. Hovey, Henry Little—all sons of New England. And Congregational money was sharing in the support of Indiana Presbyterians all the way from the salary of pioneer preacher Nathan B. Derrow in 1816, to Henry Ward Beecher's $400 per year at Lawrenceburg in 1837, and to the com-

missions of an army of young missionaries among the increasing population of northern Indiana. A Congregational historian said: "We find in 1830 the National Society [AHMS] had eighteen missionaries in Indiana, appropriating to their support $3,367. The number continued to increase as time went on. For several years upwards of fifty missionaries were employed in the state. In 1851, the number rose to sixty-three."[5]

Limited Number of Congregational Churches

If Presbyterian churches were the regular issue of Congregational effort in Indiana, Congregational churches seemed for a long time like irregular issue and an odd lot. The first one known in the state was at Bath, in Franklin County, formed in 1833 as part of a revolt against the local Old School Presbyterian preacher who literally locked the New School Presbyterians and New England sympathizers out of the church. They took the name Congregationalist. A few such refugee congregations from the Old School–New School controversy among Presbyterians in that area organized the First Congregational Association of Indiana in 1837. It was almost entirely dependent on the leadership and labor of AHMS missionary Moses Wilder. It faded after Wilder left the state for Ohio in 1839.[6]

At Terre Haute a Methodist from Massachusetts, trained in theology by a Presbyterian in Baltimore, riding horseback to Saint Louis in search of a missionary field in the West, was invited to stop and establish a nonsectarian church for the improvement of the town's image. All seventeen of the charter members were Presbyterians.[7] The church remained independent of denominational connection from its founding in 1834 until it combined with four or five small preaching points in the area to form the Evangelical Congregational Association of the Wabash Valley in 1844.[8]

In Warrick County there was a "Congregational" church at Boonville and another in Ohio Township beginning in 1839. Calvin Butler of Connecticut was their minister, along with a mixture of other employments, for about twenty years. Butler viewed his efforts, much limited by sickness, as the basis of a small island of religious and cultural hope in the sea of destitution which was southwestern Indiana; there were no other AHMS appointees in seven contiguous counties. The Society kept supporting him there out of a kind of courtesy and a view that doing less would be culpable somehow. Butler's ministerial colleagues were Presbyterians and he participated as a full member within the Presbyterian organization. Combined membership in the two churches was fifty in 1841.[9]

The churches at Ontario and Orland, so far north in Indiana that they belonged to the Presbytery of St. Joseph in Michigan, became "Congregational" in 1843 and 1848 respectively. Ontario held to Congregationalism partly because of a condition in the deed of its property forbidding change. In 1846 the missionary there reported that he was also minister for a Presbyterian church nearby. Ontario had only five male members to provide support but "increased its membership by more than one third" within the year.[10] Missionary Jacob Patch reported from Orland in 1848 that his church there had lately changed to a Congregational form of government but remained under the care of St. Joseph Presbytery. Patch referred to himself as a Presbyterian. The Orland congregation had lately constructed a union church building which Congregationalists would share with the Baptists and Methodists. "By uniting the 3 denominations in the same congregation," Patch said, "the people at Orland have long kept up regular preaching, 2 sermons each Sabbath. They wish to keep the congregation together (and their choir of singers) & so are trying to build a church edifice that they can occupy as they have the school house."[11] Neither of these churches represented a great resurgence of Hoosier Congregationalism.

There was a cluster of "Congregationalism" in northeastern Indiana about 1853, characterized by abolitionist principles and the conviction that the Presbyterian churches were not strenuous enough in their actions against slavery. Churches named Pisgah, Ohio, Liber, Westchester, and Buena Vista went independent. Liber College in Jay County was an institution of this group, a pioneer like Union Literary Institute in Randolph County (Quaker) and Eleutherian Institute in Jefferson County (Baptist) in opening its doors to students regardless of race. Before 1858 these churches formed the Upper Wabash Valley Association.[12]

The characteristics of these early Congregational clusters in Indiana were (1) a few New England families; (2) served by a minister who had been a Congregationalist in New England; (3) organized to exert leverage on Presbyterians in the interest of adhering to a principle or of securing relief from a Plan of Union arrangement which had become burdensome. Almost all of the pastors, except M. A. Jewett at Terre Haute, were supported by the AHMS. That society became increasingly sensitive about being evenhanded with Congregationalists and Presbyte-

rians. None of the early clusters, except Terre Haute, had sufficient constituency to anchor a Congregationalist program and structure for the state. That role fell to some rising population centers in northern Indiana and to Indianapolis.

Congregationalists in Richmond organized in 1835 but merged with the New School Presbyterians in 1839. Elkhart Congregationalists separated from the Presbyterians; a small but loyal fellowship survived. Michigan City developed a Congregational church by separation from the Presbyterians after a bitter struggle in 1841. That congregation not only survived but enjoyed a series of revivals, built an impressive new church, and was host to the Western Congregational Convention in 1846. Nathaniel A. Hyde was first pastor for the new Plymouth Congregational Church of Indianapolis in 1857, a church destined to become one of six Congregational churches at the state capital before the century's end and a national pioneer in urban ministry. Plymouth Church became a natural ecclesiastical center. The General Association of Congregational Churches and Ministers of Indiana was organized there in 1858.[13] Hyde later summarized the situation of the Congregational fellowship:

> After forty-five years of its abundant and fruitful missionary labors, this is what it has to show in the State: Three churches in Terre Haute and vicinity; four in the Northern counties with one exception still trammelled with a mixed government, and even claimed by another denomination; four in the Eastern counties, and two or three preaching stations; one at the capital and two weak enterprises in Hamilton county (Westfield and Cicero); three or four small congregations in the south end of the State, undiscovered at the time of which we are speaking; a total of eighteen churches. In the first statistical tables of churches of our name in the State, published in 1858, thirty names appear, but it is now certain that some of these names had no right to a place in that list, they were merely preaching points and not organized churches. Not more than eighteen or twenty names held their places in subsequent reports, and three or four of these were only semi-Congregational churches, being enrolled as belonging to Presbytery. This small body of churches, we have seen also, has united in an organization for fellowship, and taken their place among the State Associations. This review, it must be confessed, is not flattering to our denominational pride; yet it is something to have discovered that Congregationalism, by its missionaries and money, had done a grand service in organizing Christian institutions in this State; it is something to have this striking

illustration of the unsectarian and catholic spirit of Congregationalism, exalting, as it did, the general interests of Christ's kingdom above the interests of its own church order.[14]

When the New School Presbyterians withdrew from the AHMS to found their own denominational mission board in 1861, that Society was left to the Congregationalists. A few more churches were founded in Indiana. Lyman Abbott was an able preacher who increased the parish visibility as pastor at Terre Haute from 1860 to 1864, but he was hardly a zealous Congregationalist.[15] He went so far as to say: "Although my position is entirely undenominational, and I hope to cooperate cordially with all Evangelical Christians, I cannot personally forget . . . those principles of ecclesiastical liberty, which I inherited from a Puritan ancestry."[16]

A new era began when Nathaniel A. Hyde won the Society's commitment to more serious work in Indiana and agreed to become the superintendent of missions for Indiana in 1867. Northern Indiana was "the most hopeful part of the field," he said. "The old plan of union churches were there, and they held on to some of the principles of our polity; there were individuals also in each one of them who longed for Congregational liberty."[17] Hyde got the Northern Association of Congregational Churches of Indiana established with only one church in it at the start. He was a veritable bishop for the Indiana Congregationalists until he returned to Indianapolis as pastor of the Mayflower Congregational Church in 1872. E. Frank Howe, Lyman Abbott's successor at Terre Haute, was Hyde's close friend and co-worker, helping him to organize the Central Association in 1867. Howe visited Illinois in 1867 and wrote to the AHMS: "Certainly we as Congregationalists cannot afford to lose this dark—very dark—peninsula of Indiana in the midst of the light we are spreading on both sides of it."[18] The pattern of aggressive missionary superintendency was established; in 1887 it was heightened by new promises from the AHMS and by the appointment of Edward D. Curtis as missionary superintendent. In 1861 there were 19 Congregational churches in Indiana with 754 members; in 1894 there were 55 churches with 3,463 members; the census of 1906 reported 58 churches with 5,405 members.[19]

Congregationalists took pride in the fact that the nationwide youth movement called Christian Endeavor originated in a Congregational church, that the first such society in Indianapolis was in Mayflower Congregational Church, and that by 1895 they had 32 societies of Christian Endeavor with 1,083 members in the state.[20] At the turn of the century the census indicated 54 Congregational Sunday schools in Indiana with 4,663 scholars and 550 officers and students. Yet the Congregational Church in Indiana was always a small enterprise. When it combined its English heritage with the German traditions of the Evangelical and Reformed Church to form the United Church of Christ in 1957, the merged denomination still looked very German in Indiana. The leaven of Congregationalism in that body in Indiana was a very modest testimony to the significance of its contribution to the state.

Oscar Carleton McCulloch at Indianapolis

The Congregationalist who became best known was Oscar Carleton McCulloch, minister of the Plymouth Congregational Church of Indianapolis from 1877 to 1891. Plymouth had been a rather traditional Congregational church under its first four pastors from 1858 to 1877. It was theologically orthodox but not stiff, socially active against slavery and strong drink and bad morals, and zealously patriotic. Its historian said, "On the business and financial side, Plymouth Church pursued a very steady and uniform course. It was always in debt." In fact, in 1877 it had surrendered its church property to W. H. English who held a mortgage on it.[21] Then Oscar C. McCulloch became pastor and out went orthodoxy. McCulloch's watchword was "open door," so church membership was based on conduct and aspiration alone.

> All persons are eligible for membership who will unite with us on the basis of these principles and pledge themselves to carry out the objects of this church, it being distinctly understood and agreed that the applicant is not committed to any philosophy of faith, and that Christian spirit and Christian character shall be the only requisites of membership.[22]

When David Starr Jordan, professor of natural history at Butler University, expressed his desire to become a member, the church committee raised no questions about his beliefs. Jordan had not been baptized and "did not like the form as it was only a form." McCulloch waived the baptism, commenting "It is one of the forms that will soon disappear resting as it does on a misconception of a text."[23]

Lack of orthodoxy might have made McCulloch controversial but not famous. What made him famous was the remarkable social ministry into which he led Plymouth Church and the community. A biographer said, "His genius for organization and his leadership were responsible for almost every philanthropic agency established in Indianapolis within the fourteen years of his residence in that city."[24] He organized the charities, systematized and united solicitation for their support, and regularized them to be efficient and to resist exploitation. Plymouth Church needed a new location and building. McCulloch said his plan for the building was to put brick and mortar around the idea "that they might have life more abundantly." At Meridian and York streets there took form an institution which was a church and a school and a lecture hall and a library and a social center and a gymnasium and an orchestra room and a relief center and an office building for Indianapolis social agencies. In the pulpit was McCulloch advocating the right of labor to organize and strike, control of unethical business practices, right to a fair wage and reasonable working hours, abolition of child labor, improved living conditions for the poor, and amelioration of every evil of industrialization then visible in Indianapolis. Not everybody was favorably impressed. Dwight L. Moody said that making social work the focus of the church's attention was as futile as cultivating crab apples. McCulloch was never deterred. He called his work "preparing the way for the Lord."[25] Besides his impact on the constituency of Plymouth Church and on the city of Indianapolis, McCulloch figured largely as an officer and a constant participator in the National Conference of Charities and Correction.[26] He was both host and president for the eighteenth annual session of that Conference held at Indianapolis in 1891. Near the end of that year he died at the age of forty-eight.

NOTES

1. Frederick Kuhns, "A Sketch of Congregationalism in Indiana to 1858," *Indiana Magazine of History* 42 (December 1946): 343–44.

2. *Proceedings of the General Convention of Congregational Ministers and Delegates in the United States, Held at Albany, N.Y. on the 5th, 6th, 7th, and 8th of Oct., 1852* (New York: n.p., 1852), 71; Colin B. Goodykoontz, *Home Missions on the American Frontier* (Caldwell, Idaho: Caxton Printers, 1939), 149–51; Williston Walker, *The Creeds and Platforms of Congregationalism* (Boston: Pilgrim Press, 1960), 524–41; Robert Hastings Nichols, "The Plan of Union in New York," *Church History* 5 (March 1936): 29–51.

3. John F. Schermerhorn and Samuel J. Mills, *A Correct View of That Part of the United States which Lies West of the Allegany Mountains, with Regard to Religion and Morals* (Hartford, Conn.: Peter B. Gleason, 1814), 30–31; Samuel J. Mills and Daniel Smith, *Report of a Missionary Tour through That Part of the United States which Lies West of the Allegany Mountains* (Andover, Mass.: Flagg and Gould, 1815), 10–11, 15–16.

4. Nathaniel A. Hyde, *Congregationalism in Indiana* (Indianapolis, Ind.: Carlon and Hollenbeck, 1895), 14; this correspondent was John Finley Crowe, Presbyterian minister at Hanover and founder of Hanover Academy.

5. Hyde, *Congregationalism*, 16. Almost all of these missionaries are heavily represented in the correspondence files of the American Home Missionary Society (hereafter cited as AHMS). See L. C. Rudolph, Ware William Wimberly, and Thomas W. Clayton, *Indiana Letters*, 3 vols. (Ann Arbor, Mich.: University Microfilms International, 1979).

6. Kuhns, "Sketch," 346–48.

7. On page 348 of his "Sketch," Kuhns showed the name of the nondenominational missionary as Mark A. Jewett and reported seventeen charter members. Lyman Abbott showed the name as Merrick A. Jewett and suggested eleven charter members. See Lyman Abbott, *Reminiscences* (Boston: Houghton Mifflin, 1915), 190–93. In his correspondence with the AHMS he was always M. A. Jewett.

8. Kuhns, "Sketch," 348–50; Hyde, *Congregationalism*, 27–30.

9. Kuhns, "Sketch," 351. The AHMS files include many letters sent by Calvin Butler from his mission field in Indiana between 1829 and 1849.

10. Kuhns, "Sketch," 350; Hyde, *Congregationalism*, 21–22; D. McGee Bardwell, Lima, Lagrange County, to Milton Badger, AHMS, New York, 21 June and 15 July 1846.

11. Jacob Patch, Orland, to Milton Badger, AHMS, New York, 28 February 1848.

12. Emma Lou Thornbrough, *The Negro in Indiana* (Indianapolis, Ind.: Indiana Historical Bureau, 1957), 173; Hyde, *Congregationalism*, 30–32; Kuhns, "Sketch," 352.

13. Hyde, *Congregationalism*, 21, 37–38; Kuhns, "Sketch," 349–50, 352.

14. Hyde, *Congregationalism*, 40–41.

15. Abbott, *Reminiscences*, 187–232.

16. Lyman Abbott, Terre Haute, to AHMS, New York, 24 March 1865.

17. Hyde, *Congregationalism*, 45.

18. E. Frank Howe, Terre Haute, to David B. Coe, AHMS, New York, 25 May 1867.

19. Hyde, *Congregationalism*, 59–60.

20. Hyde, *Congregationalism*, 60.

21. Junius B. Roberts, "Plymouth Church, Indianapolis," *Indiana Magazine of History* 7 (June 1911): 53–54.

22. Roberts, "Plymouth Church," 57.

23. Genevieve C. Weeks, "Oscar C. McCulloch Transforms Plymouth Church, Indianapolis, into an 'Institutional' Church," *Indiana Magazine of History* 64 (June 1968): 95.

24. Genevieve C. Weeks, "Religion and Social Work as Exemplified in the Life of Oscar C. McCulloch," *Social Service Review* 39 (March 1965): 38.

25. Genevieve C. Weeks, *Oscar Carleton McCulloch, 1843–1891: Preacher and Practitioner of Applied Christianity* (Indianapolis, Ind.: Indiana Historical Society, 1976), 101, 165–218; Weeks, "Religion and Social Work," 39, 41.

26. McCulloch's work in the genetics of paupers brought him national recognition, especially his report and publication *The Tribe of Ishmael* (Indianapolis, Ind.: Charity Organization Society, 1888, 7 p.); see Weeks, *Oscar Carleton McCulloch*, 171, 215–17. It later brought a reckless charge that he was a principal social engineer for and a principal contributor to the worst form of modern genocide. See Hugo P. Leaming, "The Ben Ishmael Tribe," in *The Ethnic Frontier*, ed. Melvin G. Holli and Peter d'A. Jones (Grand Rapids, Mich.: William B. Eerdmans, 1977), 97–141.

SOCIETY OF FRIENDS

Members of the Society of Friends were nicknamed Quakers because George Fox told a British judge he should tremble at the word of the Lord. Quakers arose in England out of the radical left wing of Puritanism. George Fox (1624–1691) found not comfort but despair in England's churches, established or sectarian. What he did find in the 1640s was his own experience of the indwelling presence of Jesus Christ so that "the whole earth had a new smell."

> Gradually the results of his study, his thinking, his inquiries and the travail of his spirit began to crystallize out in clear convictions, in "openings" of truth, such as that "all Christians are believers and are born of God"; that a university education does not make one a true minister of Christ; that God does not dwell exclusively in temples made with hands; that every man is enlightened by the divine light of Christ; that God ministers directly and inwardly to human needs apart from ecclesiastical agencies; that there is an ocean of infinite life and love that can overflow and swallow up the ocean of human sinfulness, misery and despair; that it is possible to be delivered from the power of sin in this life—to "come into the state that Adam was in before his fall."[1]

His beliefs and enthusiasm found ready converts. Soon there were groups of Quakers (also called Children of Light, Friends, or Friends in Truth) drawing their religious faith and life from the divine light of Christ within (also called the Light, the Light of Christ, the Light Within, the Spirit of Christ, the Spirit, the Seed, the Root, that of God within you, the Truth, the Inner Light, or the universal and saving Light). The term "Inner Light" might designate God as knowable to and within persons; the capacity in all persons to perceive, recognize, and respond to God; and God as inwardly known.[2]

Fox and his followers wanted meetings for worship to be occasions for silent listening unless or until a member had a "leading," a truth or experience or exhortation or message or prayer or song to share. Such leadings were tested against the Bible and consensus of worthy Friends past or present. In ethics and social matters, Fox was an activist.

> Among the reforms and social movements in which he pioneered were care for the poor and aged, prison reform, just treatment of the American Indians, provision for the insane, opposition to drunkenness, capital punishment, and slavery. He insisted on honesty and truthfulness in all affairs, renounced oaths, believed in the one-price system in trade and just wages for working people. He was opposed to all kinds of war and refused any participation in it. He taught that governments exist for the benefit of the people as a whole and are bound by the moral law. He believed in religious democracy in the church based on the equality of all, both men and women, before God; and championed the right of women to preach. He refused to conform to customs which gave one class honor, power or wealth at the expense of others. His insistence upon simple dress, upon the singular pronouns in addressing all classes, upon refusing to doff the hat to (so-called) social and political

superiors sprang from the same spirit of Christian democracy.[3]

Fox and many of his early followers were aggressively missionary. For a time the English authorities viewed them as disrespectful, provocative, and dangerous. American colonies with established churches were often hostile to Quakers as well; four were hanged in Massachusetts between 1659 and 1661. The religious toleration of Rhode Island made it a Quaker refuge. Treatment of Quakers in America changed from persecution to toleration and even to localized privilege in the late 1600s as English Friends became major proprietors of colonies in areas which were to become Pennsylvania, New Jersey, and Delaware. Quakers also settled in the South in the late 1600s. In the Carolinas they enlisted many of their members from among the general unchurched population.[4]

> By the year 1700 Friends meetings had been established in all the English colonies. Friends owned or had recently owned the Jerseys, Pennsylvania and Delaware; they had a controlling influence in Rhode Island and the Carolinas; they had considerable influence in New York, especially on Long Island, and in Maryland; and they had won the struggle for toleration in New England and Virginia. At that time Friends were the greatest single religious organization in the English colonies as a whole, both in their influence and in their promise . . . It is estimated that about 1750 there were fifty thousand in the colonies.[5]

Friends communities kept growing and seeking out fresh lands in the South. About 1730, Virginia granted 100,000 acres of land in the Shenandoah Valley to a company predominantly Quaker. Indian troubles in Virginia encouraged immigration southward and strengthened Friends settlements in Guilford and Orange counties of North Carolina after 1750. Soon after 1760 prosperous settlements of Friends were formed in Union and Newberry counties of South Carolina and in Columbia County in Georgia; some of these families came from the Northern colonies and some directly from England and Ireland.[6]

In the course of the 1700s the Quakers in America made decisions which cost them much of their evangelistic and political power. They advocated a principle of non-violence while the main body of colonists waged war with the Indians and the British. In the context of a citizenry whose wealth and culture were linked to slave labor and slave trade, they came to a growing conviction that slavery was entirely wrong. Surrounded by massive non-Quaker immigration, they wrote "disciplines" and established non-professional church officers (ministers,

elders, overseers) dedicated to safeguarding their principles and way of life. They became a "quiet" and "peculiar" people who chose to be in the world but not of the world. Non-Friends they called "the world's people" or "persons not in profession with us."

The population of Quakers on the southern frontier still expanded, though not as fast as that of the surrounding non-Quakers. They increased by nurturing their children as birthright members of the Society of Friends. Quakers on the southern frontier had many children. A primary duty was to safeguard these children from the world. Generally they wished to give the children an education up to their own rudimentary level, already somewhat eroded by life for a generation or more in the woods. Generally they chose to avoid the hazards of higher education for their children, their members, and their ministers alike.[7]

Quaker Indian Missions

Early Quaker visitors to Indiana came from the East; they wanted to help the Indians. When the Indians were defeated at the Battle of Fallen Timbers in 1794 and ceded vast tracts of western land to the United States in the Treaty of Greeneville in 1795, Quaker yearly meetings in both Philadelphia and Baltimore immediately acted on their concerns about the needs of the Indians of the Northwest Territory. The Pennsylvania Quakers had advice for the Indians of the whole region.

> We were made glad when we heard that the sober good People among you were disposed to promote Peace & brighten the old Chain of Friendship with the white People of the united States; and that many of you have a desire that you may be instructed in tilling the Ground, to live after the Manner of the white People, which we believe you will find to be more comfortable for you & your Families than to live only by hunting; and we think it will be also good for your young People to be learnt to read & write, and that sober, honest, good Men should be sent among you for Teachers.[8]

The actions of Baltimore Yearly Meeting had a more precise impact on Indiana. The Baltimore Quakers discussed "the difficulties and distresses to which the Indian natives of this land were subject." There followed "a deep consideration and enquiry whether . . . there was not something for us as a Society to do for them, towards promoting their religious instruction, and knowledge of agriculture, and useful mechanic arts." They asked the quarterly and monthly meetings to "open subscriptions among our members for their relief." They appointed a

"Committee for Promoting the Improvement and Civilization of the Indian Natives." They sent delegations to confer with Indians in Ohio in 1796, 1797, and 1799. Then in 1802 principal chiefs of the Miami and Potawatomis on their way to Washington, D.C., to visit President Jefferson—Little Turtle, Five Medals, and others—met with the committee in Baltimore.

Now the Quaker committee at Baltimore had a real focus for their effort in Indiana. They "concluded to address Congress" about the incompatibility between a government policy to civilize Indians and a parallel trade policy which kept supplying them whiskey; "a law passed, which in some measure provided a remedy for the evil." In 1803 they sent to Fort Wayne "a considerable number of implements of husbandry." They responded to a letter of thanks for these implements from chiefs Little Turtle, Five Medals, and others by sending a Quaker delegation to Fort Wayne in early spring of 1804, a delegation including Philip Dennis who brought along his team of two horses and volunteered to stay all summer. They said: "His desire is to cultivate for you, a field of corn; also to shew you how to raise some of the other productions of the earth. He knows how to use the plough, the hoe, the axe, and other implements of husbandry."[9]

Dennis set up his demonstration farm at a site the Indians provided on the Wabash about thirty-five miles southwest of Fort Wayne.

> He raised about 400 bushels of corn, besides a quantity of turnips, potatoes, cucumbers, water-melons, pumpkins, beans, parsnips, and other garden-vegetables; which he directed to be divided amongst the Indians on their return from their hunting camps; and left with the family of Indians, with whom he resided, upon the farm he had cultivated, 23 hogs and pigs, seven of which were in good order to kill, and he expected would weigh 1500 lb. These he engaged the agent to attend to the killing and salting of. They were small when brought to the farm in the spring, and had no other food than what they gathered in the woods. With some assistance, which he obtained from Fort-Wayne, he cleared and enclosed under a substantial fence twenty acres of ground, and built a house, thirty-two feet long and seventeen feet wide, a story and a half high, with floors and partition.[10]

Since this project had the express approval of Secretary of War Henry Dearborn, the fencing and farming operation continued after the departure of Dennis under the encouragement of John Johnston and William Wells, federal Indian agents at Fort Wayne, and of Chief Little Turtle. But by the time Quaker William Kirke came to Fort Wayne in 1806 to replace Philip Dennis as demon-

stration farmer, his good intentions and his substantial federal grant of $6,000 were largely wasted by being caught in an ongoing power struggle between Johnston and Wells.

The Quaker attempt to civilize Indiana's tribes through agriculture was thwarted. One more delegation from Baltimore in 1810 was treated with courtesy and "handsomely entertained" by the United States troops and agents at Fort Wayne but found at least as much whiskey and violence as agriculture among the tribes. Government agencies responsible for Indiana were soon more concerned to subdue the new confederation of Indian forces led by Tecumseh and The Prophet than to teach the Indians how to farm.[11]

Quaker Settlers from the South

Indiana's first Quaker settlers came from the South. They were of the quiet and separated sort. The migration was remarkable.

> One of the great folk movements in American history was the migration to Ohio and Indiana of southern Friends during the first forty years of the nineteenth century. By the time this movement ran its course, North Carolina, the center of the Society of Friends in the South, was largely denuded of its Quaker inhabitants, and a town on the Whitewater [Richmond, Indiana] had replaced Philadelphia as the center of Orthodox Friends in the United States.[12]

The country north of the Ohio River looked good to the southern Quakers. There was cheap and fertile land for their large families. There was a fundamental ordinance that slavery would be forever prohibited. Slavery had gotten to be a major consideration for Quakers in the South. After years of increasing sensitivity heightened by the traveling ministry of John Woolman and his colleagues, Quakers had divested themselves of slaves and had declared themselves opposed to slavery on principle. Yet the institution seemed to be fastening ever more tightly on the South; Tennessee entered the Union as a slave state in 1796 and Kentucky adopted a proslavery constitution again in 1799. Some of the black persons set free by Quakers were actually reenslaved by North Carolina law. Friends feared their children would be competing with slave labor and would become enmeshed in the slave system. Quaker traveling minister Zachariah Dicks was in South Carolina and Georgia in 1803 warning Friends to come out of slavery. So when they went west they went northwest, first to Ohio and then to Indiana.[13]

The Andrew Hoover family, including ten children, traveled five weeks from Randolph County, North Carolina, to Stillwater in Montgomery County, Ohio, in 1802 "to better our circumstances."[14] In 1806 his son David traced a section line west "rather accidentally" and reported to his father that he thought he had "found the country we had been in search of. Spring water, timber, and building-rock appeared to be abundant, and the face of the country looked delightful." The Hoovers were the first Quaker family in Indiana; David Hoover later laid out the town of Richmond in the Whitewater Valley and eventually became clerk and judge of the Wayne County Circuit Court. Others soon followed. David said: "Jeremiah Cox, John Smith, and my father, were then looked upon as rather leaders in the Society of Friends. Their location here had a tendency of drawing others, and soon caused a great rush to Whitewater; and land that I thought would never be settled was rapidly taken up and improved."[15]

Friends migrating to Wayne County in Indiana were not all poor settlers. Most came with wagons and with enough horses among them to double team the wagons through the most difficult mountain stretches. One family history recorded: "The road, when there was one was exceedingly poor and rough. The trails were bad and there were no bridges. They were forced to hitch logs of trees they cut by the way for brakes to the wagons when descending the steep rugged places."[16]

Andrew Hoover came to Indiana "worth rising of two thousand dollars"; Jeremiah Cox "came to the territory worth 35 hundred dollars"; John Smith, "tho not worth more than two thousand dollars when he arrived in the Territory he by selling lots etc became quite wealthy for the times, and was liberal to a fault in the support of the Church and contributions to aid poor travelling ministers in their outfit etc."[17] Educational level varied among the Quaker pioneers but was usually quite low. David Hoover said of his boyhood in North Carolina:

> As to education, my opportunities were exceedingly limited; and had it not been for my inclination and perseverance, I should, in all probability, at this day be numbered among those who can scarcely write their names, or perhaps should only be able to make a "X" in placing my signature to a written instrument. In order to show the state of society in my early youth, as an evidence of the intelligence of the circle in which I was raised, I can say of a truth, that I never had an opportunity of reading a newspaper, nor did I ever see a bank-note, until after I was a man grown.[18]

With a healthy rate of immigration and with good community stability, Quaker development at Richmond came quickly. In the fall of 1806, Friends held meetings in the cabin of Jeremiah Cox. In 1807 West Branch Monthly Meeting in Ohio, the nearest Friends meeting, granted a so-called "indulged" meeting for worship to these Friends at Cox's Settlement. In 1808 a log meetinghouse was built half a mile northeast of the settlement; Quakers preferred having these houses at a quiet spot in the woods. In 1809 there were at least two hundred members so the Whitewater Monthly Meeting was organized, the first Friends organization within the present bounds of Indiana. About eight hundred Friends, mainly from Cane Creek and Back Creek in North Carolina, from Cane Creek in South Carolina, and from Mount Pleasant in Virginia were received by Whitewater Monthly Meeting between 1809 and 1812. Quaker migration to Indiana slowed during the Indian unrest during the War of 1812 but then increased, the Whitewater Meeting now so well known that southern immigrants came directly to Indiana without stopping over in Ohio.[19]

There were smaller clusters of Quakers in other parts of the state. When William Hobbs moved his young family to Indiana in spring of 1812, he settled on the headwaters of Blue River in what later became Washington County. He had been born in Randolph County, North Carolina, one of eight children of illiterate parents who were once Episcopalians. When his parents united with the Friends at Back Creek in North Carolina, young William found his place. After several "tendering" experiences from about age eleven, he found his personal peace at the age of twenty-one.

> The Lord was pleased to speak peace to my tried mind. When about my daily labor, my mind being turned to Him in prayer, it was very intelligibly sounded in my inward ear, "If thou wilt be faithful in following that inward witness that has so long been pleading with thee, thy sins shall be forgiven and I will be with thee and be thy preserver" . . . I then thought the rest of my days, let them be few or many, with His divine aid, should be spent in serving so merciful a Savior Who had so long borne with me, a poor sinner, Who had so long striven with me, in His matchless mercy.[20]

His fellow members at Back Creek supported his development as a leader in family visitation.

The few Friends around his new home on Blue River in Indiana thrust Hobbs into leadership. They insisted that he "time the meeting." The group was so small at first that he thought of leaving it to move to a somewhat stronger meeting at Lick Creek in Orange County but finally decided against that. In fall of 1813 a monthly meeting was established for Lick Creek and Blue River together. Hobbs was appointed an elder. In July of 1815 the Blue River Monthly Meeting was established.

> Society at this time seemed to prosper. Three ministers moved to our meeting from North Carolina and some others began to appear in that way who seemed in the life, and we had lively meetings. The Masters presence was often felt to be in our midst, and Friends were much in harmony and unity one with another, and several were added to us by convincement, and became useful members.[21]

From this base in Washington County Hobbs became a person of stature in Quaker affairs—leading in the new Blue River Quarterly Meeting; attending Ohio Yearly Meeting in 1819; helping to form Indiana Yearly Meeting in 1820 and serving as a member of its "Meeting for Sufferings," an executive committee with substantial duties between annual sessions; assisting traveling preacher Priscilla Hunt on a journey of six months to visit meetings in North Carolina and Virginia; visiting by appointment among the constituent meetings of Indiana Yearly Meeting, especially during the painful period of the Hicksite division.[22]

At the age of fifty-one Hobbs felt a clear call to be a minister, an honored but entirely unpaid and non-professional office among Friends. He said: "It was very clearly communicated to my inward ear, that I was called to the ministry. Other service had heretofore been required of me but now I must shortly tell others what the Lord had, in mercy, done for me."[23] He began to speak in meeting, a normal first step in response to a call to ministry.

> While sitting in a meeting for worship at Driftwood, a few words were brought to my mind with so much weight, that I ventured to express them, for which I felt much peace of mind. After that, when I felt drawn thereto, I ventured to relieve my mind with as few words as I could, though I appeared but seldom, being desirous not to appear without being immediately called upon and qualified by the Great Head of the Church, Who alone is able to give strength and ability to do His work, but sometimes under so great discouragement that I was almost ready to conclude that surely the Master did not call for it at my hands, because I did not feel the impression as strong and clear as some others I had read about. Sometimes under these discouragements I would hold back, till it would feel like fire in my bones, and as I would give up to be faithful, I would feel the incomes of

the Father's love; but still much tried at times because the motion seemed so small.[24]

His fellow members in Blue River Monthly Meeting did not hasten to record Hobbs as a minister; they encouraged his continued work as an elder instead. Almost three years after the death of his first wife in 1836, Hobbs married Anna Unthank of Newport in Wayne County, "a well approved minister of our Society." Then the Blue River Friends acknowledged his ministry and approved proposals of the two sixty-year-olds to follow their concerns for visiting and peacemaking among Friends in Indiana and Ohio.[25]

Worthy enough of a place in the history of Indiana Friends in his own right, William Hobbs was even better known as the father of Barnabas C. Hobbs, born in Washington County in 1815. Barnabas was the beneficiary of his father's zeal for the Society of Friends and of his father's circle of friends. Judge Benjamin Parke at Salem invited Barnabas to work for him, to live in his house, and to use the resources of his library while attending the school then operated in Salem by John I. Morrison. This opportunity set Barnabas on a path to Cincinnati College, to leadership in several Quaker schools including Bloomingdale Academy and Earlham, and to the office of Superintendent of Public Instruction for the State of Indiana. Barnabas was recorded a Friends minister in 1853 and held the crucial office of clerk of Western Yearly Meeting from its inception in 1858.[26] Thus a part of a new elite in Quaker education came out of the Friends meetings in Washington and Orange counties.

Another Friends settlement developed on the Wabash a few miles south of Terre Haute. This became Honey Creek Monthly Meeting in 1820. Friends were quick to enter when central Indiana opened for settlement. They settled White Lick in Morgan County in 1820 and made it a monthly meeting in 1823. Driftwood Meeting was formed in Jackson County in 1820 near the later site of Seymour; it included a Quaker settlement at Sand Creek in Bartholomew County. Within a decade the Society established meetings in Randolph, Parke, Hendricks, Henry, Marion, and Boone counties. These represented substantial communities; monthly meetings were established only in places where there was evidence of considerable strength.[27]

Quaker Concentration in East-Central Indiana

The Whitewater area kept receiving the largest number of Indiana's Quakers. Settlements of Friends with established monthly meetings by 1820 included "New Garden, eight miles north of Richmond in Wayne County; Silver Creek, two miles west of Liberty in Union county; West Grove, near Centerville in Wayne County; Springfield, near Economy in Wayne County."[28] When Indiana Friends were authorized to establish Indiana Yearly Meeting in 1821, its headquarters was at Richmond. To house the huge annual gathering they built a brick meetinghouse 100 feet by 60 feet with side walls 25 feet high. It was constructed between 1822 and 1829 and was one of the wonders of the West.[29]

Some Friends destined to make great impact on the state of Indiana were members of the Coffin family. William and Priscilla, parents of ten children, moved from Nantucket to New Garden in Guilford County, North Carolina, in 1773. They were Quaker elders. Their children and hosts of grandchildren were a part of the Quaker migration from North Carolina to Indiana. Their grandson Levi Coffin settled at New Garden in Wayne County, Indiana (renamed Newport in 1834 and Fountain City in 1878), in 1826. As a merchant in that place and in Cincinnati he was reputed to have assisted over 3,000 runaway slaves in their escape and was dubbed "president of the underground Railroad."

Another grandson, Elijah Coffin, horsebacked from North Carolina to Indiana in 1818 to visit his sister Hannah near the later site of Milton in Wayne County. Quakers had poured in there so fast that Hannah and her husband had an "indulged meeting in our barn." From the time of that visit Elijah made plans to move north. When he returned in September of 1824 it was with a contingent of about forty of his family members and friends. They made the wagon trip to Milton by way of the Cumberland Gap and the Wilderness Road in about four weeks. They observed that most mountaineers they saw on that route "were living in rude log cabins on a low plane of civilization and morality, steeped in ignorance, shiftless and coarse. Drink was the prevailing curse. They raised small patches of barley and Indian corn, from which they manufactured liquors in domestic stills, erected on springs, brooks and creeks."[30]

Elijah Coffin and his wife Naomi had little property. Having sold their small farm in North Carolina at a low price, they arrived in Indiana with "a horse, a small amount of household property, and about two hundred and fifty dollars in money." Their daughter Miriam was three and one-half years of age and their son Charles was eighteen months. They bought forty acres of woods and built a log house. Charles later said of Wayne County's pioneer period that the streams in the forest were about

double their later size in the cleared land; that the vast amount of walnut timber was used lavishly because it was easily split into rails; and that all early commerce centered on Cincinnati, over sixty miles each way with four-horse wagons over impossible roads. Elijah had almost no formal education; by strenuous application and study on his own initiative he had parlayed a basic ability to read and cipher into a level of learning well above that of his neighbors. In his log house at Milton he "took up" a school.[31]

In North Carolina Elijah had enjoyed a reputation as an outstanding young Friend. In a Society normally dominated by elderly elders, he had actually been appointed clerk (presiding officer and crucial interpreter of meeting actions) of the North Carolina Yearly Meeting at the age of twenty-four. He had visited among Quaker meetings in other parts of America. Now in Indiana he was again invited to positions of leadership—monthly meeting clerk, quarterly meeting clerk, and when not quite twenty-nine clerk of Indiana Yearly Meeting. Some members protested his serving as clerk because his hat brim was not wide enough but the objection was not sustained.

As an elder who declined designation as minister, Elijah Coffin was the clerk of Indiana Yearly Meeting beginning in 1827 and continuing for twenty-nine years. Dozens of Quaker leaders who visited Richmond from other meetings in the United States and Great Britain stayed at his house.[32] His six-foot frame had instant recognition when he visited gatherings of Friends across the nation. His prominence in banking and in business at Richmond gave him availability, local stature, and means to support his concerns. His concerns encompassed a whole galaxy of Quaker interests. In spite of some Quaker opposition, his concerns also included ecumenical efforts with other Christians engaged in Bible distribution and Sabbath schools. He involved his son Charles in these causes as well.[33] During his years as clerk Elijah's hand was in most of the enterprises of the largest yearly meeting in the land and his leadership was responsible for many initiatives. During the troublesome divisions over doctrine and over abolition of slavery, he earned a reputation for stability and level-headed counsel. To think of Indiana Yearly Meeting was to think of Elijah Coffin.

Elijah Coffin ended his official career as clerk of Indiana Yearly Meeting in October of 1858 and officially withdrew from the banking business in Richmond in 1859. His son Charles, the one who had taken his first baby steps alongside the wagons crossing the Appalachians from North Carolina, succeeded him both as chief officer of the bank and as clerk of Indiana Yearly Meeting.

Charles was thirty-five; both appointments recognized his record of service in community and in meeting. Charles F. Coffin was clerk of Indiana Yearly Meeting for twenty-seven years. Elijah, retired from business, continued to invest himself in church work from his base in Richmond until his death in 1862. During his final illness Elijah was a regular reader of the *Missionary Herald* in order to keep well informed about the progress of world mission. Rhoda M. Coffin, wife of Charles, was a teammate for him, his match in effectiveness and zeal for church or social causes. These three members of the Coffin family, surrounded and supported by an army of kinfolk and dedicated Friends, furnished more than half a century of stimulating leadership during the very years in which Orthodox Quakerism in America underwent a major transformation. They were major agents in the process.[34]

The center of activity at Richmond attracted some Quaker leaders of great potential from outside the state. Timothy Nicholson was a talented young Friend in North Carolina, so favorably known and so obviously successful as an educator that he was invited to move north to Pennsylvania to open a preparatory department for Haverford College in 1854. After six years as faculty member and superintendent at Haverford, rising center of Quaker academia, Nicholson followed an earlier decision to move to Richmond, Indiana, and go into business there with his brother John. He arrived in 1861 and was immediately accorded a place among Quaker leaders. He was appointed an elder by 1865—just in time to undertake responsibility for advocating and counseling Indiana's young Quakers drafted for military service and to travel to Indianapolis with Barnabas C. Hobbs and others to negotiate with government agencies on their behalf; just in time to represent Indiana Yearly Meeting in the herculean task of administering a program of aid for liberated slave families in the South, working from his desk at Richmond; just in time to get deeply involved, alongside the Coffin family, in the effort of Indiana Yearly Meeting to reform terrible conditions in the prisons of Indiana.[35]

> Except in Indiana . . . it appears that no organization of Friends officially undertook prison reform. Elsewhere efforts in this direction were made individually or in cooperation with other associations. In 1867, the Meeting for Sufferings . . . of Indiana Yearly Meeting appointed a committee of six, of which Timothy Nicholson was a member, "to organize a system for the reformation of juvenile offenders and the improvement of prison discipline."[36]

Prison reform required a relentless campaign of forty-two years. The state legislature of 1889 finally named a nonpartisan, unpaid, and advisory Board of State Charities to have continuing rights of inspection and report for all the penal, reformatory, and benevolent institutions of the state including the county infirmaries, orphans' homes, and jails. That meant twelve state institutions and more than two hundred county institutions to visit annually or more often. By then Charles and Rhoda Coffin had moved off to Chicago. The Congregational reformer Oscar Carleton McCulloch died in 1891 just as the work of the new state agency was shaping. Nicholson spent about forty days each year visiting institutions; he was the most influential member of that board for nineteen years. Every step toward prison improvement had to be earned by a combination of pressure and diplomacy. Never recorded as a minister and never paid for his service, Nicholson seemed to be at the center of official administration and action for nearly every enterprise of Indiana Friends. Unofficially the office of his bookstore and publishing business was a radiation point for Indiana's Quaker activities for sixty-three years. "Things must be looked after," he said.[37]

Allen Jay grew up in Indiana Yearly Meeting, for a time in the state of Ohio but at Marion in Grant County, Indiana, after 1850. His family favored education. His Uncle Eli and Aunt Mahalah Jay actually went to Oberlin College for two years and to Antioch College for four years in the face of the expressed displeasure of many members of West Branch Quarterly Meeting. They became educational heavyweights among Indiana Friends at Farmers' Institute, at Spiceland, and for fourteen years at Earlham College where they "touched and aided . . . several thousands." Allen studied briefly at Friends Boarding School at Richmond (Earlham College after 1859), and at Farmers' Institute near Lafayette, and at Antioch College in Ohio alongside his Uncle Eli and Aunt Mahalah.

Following the evangelistic interests of his father and of a Quaker minister transferred from Blue River Meeting named Jeremiah Grinnell, Allen became an evangelistic Quaker elder before he was thirty and a recorded minister when thirty-three. With permission of the meetings involved, he sometimes visited twenty or more Quaker families per day with conversation and personal messages about their spiritual condition. It appeared that his ministry was to be in the East; he was for many years in educational administration and fund raising in North Carolina and Rhode Island. But in 1881, at the age of fifty, he came back to Indiana to do his educational administration and fund raising for Earlham College. There in Richmond he took his place among the benevolent elite of Indiana Yearly Meeting, involved at every level in defining the shape of the Quaker fellowship. Timothy Nicholson said Allen Jay was "first Friend in America in his personality and influence . . . we were intimately associated in Earlham and in church activities, and our love was similar to that of David and Jonathan."[38]

Old Quaker Ways

When William Hobbs came to Blue River in 1812 and Elijah Coffin to Whitewater in 1824, Quaker life and worship was of the quiet, peculiar, and separated sort. When Barnabas Hobbs, Charles and Rhoda Coffin, Timothy Nicholson, and Allen Jay were young people that pattern was still discernible. The closest associations of Friends were likely to be with other Friends. Quaker clothes were distinctive—plain buttons only as necessary; plain cut suits for men without collars, lapels, or cuffs; broad brimmed hats for men, black ones from John Suffrin's in Richmond or light yellow ones from Beard's Hatter Shop in North Carolina; stiff, plain bonnets for women. Quakers said "thee" or "thou" instead of "you." They called the days of the week and the months of the year by common numerals so that "Sunday, January 1" became "first-day, first-month." Quakers were not to participate in "public fasts, feasts, or what are termed holy days." That included Christmas.[39]

If feasible Quakers attended meeting on first-day and again at an agreed time in midweek. There were no sacraments. There was no singing. The meeting was unprogrammed. Conduct at meeting was participatory in the sense that all shared in disciplined and silent waiting. The meeting might be entirely silent for an hour or longer. More often, one or more men or women would be led to vocalize a prayer, a concern, an admonition, a sermon short or long, one or more quotations from the Bible. Silent or vocal, the meeting ended when the two persons at the head of the special seating section for officers exchanged a handshake. It was usually the same persons who spoke in meeting for worship, elders or ministers saying accustomed things in accustomed style, often in a special sing-song tone. Visiting traveling ministers with credentials from other meetings were somewhat more likely to speak. For a regular member to begin speaking in meeting was a serious matter very carefully noted. Allen Jay and his wife Martha attended meeting at Pine Creek on the upper Wabash.

> There was no minister or elder belonging to it. Neither had there been for some twelve or fifteen years. There were few who spoke in meeting except Enoch Moon. His communications were largely made up of Scripture quo-

tations. Occasionally some one else spoke. Vocal prayer was rarely, if ever, heard, unless some traveling minister came along, which was not very often . . . During the year 1859, in our silent meeting on First-day morning, I rose and spoke a few words in the way of ministry. It was a memorable day to me. It had an effect on the congregation. It made me a "speckled bird" from that time forward.[40]

Quaker men kept their hats on in meeting except during prayer to indicate that they regarded one place to be as sacred as another. Women and men were separately seated in the meetinghouse. During a meeting for worship the dividing shutters between the men and women were opened so that the one meeting was shared by all. To change to a meeting for business the shutters between the two sections were closed to permit simultaneous business meetings for men and women. The business meetings for women were not second class; separate minutes were kept for women and men. Messengers were sent between the two when they were acting on matters of mutual concern. In meetings for business the role of the clerk was crucial. There was no other presiding officer. No votes were taken. The sense of the meeting was judged by the clerk according to the quality and quantity of the indications of support and recorded as a minute of the official action for authentication by signatures of officers.[41]

Monthly meetings were significant scenes for the regular religious and social life of all members. Quarterly meetings united Friends gathered from a wider area to share oversight and fellowship and to mingle with weighty Friends who attended as accredited visitors.[42] Yearly meetings were massive week-long events which stretched the hospitality of Richmond. Joseph John Gurney described the Sunday scene in 1837.

> Never, to the best of my knowledge, have I witnessed so remarkable an assemblage of people, as that which was convened for public worship, at Richmond, on the commencement of the Yearly Meeting for Indiana—Friends and others, arriving on horseback, or in the grotesque carriages of the country, almost without end. The horses, hitched to nearly every tree of the wood which surrounded the vast red-brick meeting-house, formed in themselves a curious spectacle. It was supposed that about 3000 people were accommodated within the walls; and nearly as many, unable to obtain a place in the house, were promenading by the hour together on the premises. It is the constant custom of the people in the surrounding country to attend the "Quaker's Meeting" on this particular occasion . . . [for] the opportunity . . . of walking and talking with their neighbors. It was however, for those within, a time of great solemnity and refreshment.

On the following morning we proceeded to the business of the Church. All strangers had now withdrawn; the great shutters which divide the house in two, were let down; the one compartment was filled by the men—the other by the women.[43]

When the Quakers were zealous to be a separate people, they gave much attention to discipline. The *Discipline* of Indiana Yearly Meeting provided nine specific queries to be put to every Quaker meeting at least once each year. A report was made of the answers returned.[44]

First query. Are all meetings for worship and discipline attended? Do Friends avoid unbecoming behavior therein? And is the hour of meeting observed?

Second query. Do Friends maintain love towards each other, as becomes our christian profession? Are talebearing and detraction discouraged? And when differences arise, are endeavors used speedily to end them?

Third query. Do Friends endeavor, by example and precept, to educate their children, and those under their care, in plainness of speech, deportment and apparel? Do they guard them against reading pernicious books, and from the corrupt conversation of the world? Are they encouraged frequently to read the holy scriptures?

Fourth query. Are Friends clear of importing, vending, distilling, or the unnecessary use of spiritous liquors; of frequenting taverns, or attending places of diversion? And do they observe moderation and temperance on all occasions?

Fifth query. Are the necessities of the poor, and the circumstances of those who may appear likely to require aid, inspected and relieved? Are they advised, and assisted, in such employments as they are capable of; and is due care taken to promote the school-education of their children?

Sixth query. Do Friends maintain a faithful testimony against a hireling ministry, oaths, military services, clandestine trade, prize goods, and lotteries?

Seventh query. Are Friends careful to live within the bounds of their circumstances, and to avoid involving themselves in business beyond their ability to manage? Are they just in their dealing, and punctual in complying with their engagements? And where any give reasonable grounds for fear in these respects, is due care extended to them?

Eighth query. Are Friends careful to bear testimony against slavery? Do they provide, in a suitable manner, for those under their direction, who have had their freedom secured; and are they instructed in useful learning?

Ninth query. Is care taken to deal with offenders seasonably and impartially, and to endeavor to evince to those who will not be reclaimed, the spirit of meekness and love, before judgment is placed upon them?[45]

Requirements could be locally expanded, narrowly interpreted, and minutely prescribed. The size of headstones for Quaker graves was often specified. Prohibition of a hireling ministry could mean not only careful avoidance of the creation of any paid religious functionaries for Quakers and great reluctance to pay or reimburse any costs for approved ministerial visitors but also prohibition of attending any services of any denomination which supported its clergy, inviting any participation among Quakers by any members or ministers of any denomination which paid its clergy, or associating with any such denomination even in benevolent work.[46] The exclusiveness became very painful in the case of marriage. To "marry outside the meeting"—marry a partner who was not an Orthodox Friend or wed in a place or manner other than that prescribed by the *Discipline*—was almost certain to bring disownment.

There was some early uneasiness among Quakers about scheduled Bible study and about regular family devotions or Scripture reading in Quaker homes. If any structure in worship was to be so carefully avoided at the meetinghouse, was not regular or structured worship in the home equally dangerous? When Quaker traveling minister William Williams of Indiana had "told his thoughts" to his host family about some of their poor behavior, they concluded he was some sort of preacher and asked him to lead evening devotions for the family. He declined because "we, as a people, did not believe that we could perform such things at our own stated times." And how were Quakers to relate the content and authority of the Bible to the content and authority of enlightenment by the Inner Light? What place would there be in Quaker thought for orthodox Christian doctrines concerning the Holy Spirit, the person and work of Jesus Christ, the Fall, Original Sin, and the Atonement?[47]

Hicksite Quaker Minority

These perennial questions became immediate and poignant for Indiana's Quakers when Elias Hicks offered himself as Quaker champion of the priority of the Inner Light. He reduced or dismissed a whole range of orthodox Christian beliefs. "For a man to look for a Savior or salvation any where else, than in the very centre of his own soul, is a fatal mistake," he said, "and must consequently land him in disappointment and errour." Standing as a restorer of primitive Quakerism, Hicks taught that Jesus Christ was the son of God in the same way that all persons are except that Jesus Christ obtained divinity by perfect obedience to the Light. Hicks held that the

Bible was valuable but without special authority, being far inferior to revelation still being provided to living persons by the Inner Light.[48]

Elias Hicks seemed a long way from Indiana. He was a farmer-minister from Jericho, Long Island. His following to some extent represented a protest movement among lower middle class Quakers in the East against wealthy and well established Orthodox Quakers who had made peace with the teachings of America's evangelical denominations.[49] However the issues raised were explosive and the traditional free exchange of credentialed visitors among the meetings provided a potential entry point for the Hicksite debate on every Quaker agenda in the land.

> The break first came in Philadelphia in April 1827. Hicks's followers despaired of gaining control of the yearly meeting or of even obtaining justice within it and called a conference in which they set up what they claimed to be the true Philadelphia Yearly Meeting. The Hicksites in New York were bolder. They not only insisted on recognizing the Philadelphia Hicksites as the legitimate yearly meeting there, but in a roughshod fashion they also tried to force out all the officials who dared to oppose them. At Ohio Yearly Meeting there was a near riot in which the clerk suffered a broken rib. Even in Baltimore Yearly Meeting, where almost all Friends were Hicksites, and in Indiana, where the overwhelming majority were Orthodox, there were numerous incidents of bitterness.[50]

Indiana Yearly Meeting was only six years old when the separation came. Orthodox messengers hurried to Richmond in 1827 to warn of the Hicksite wave approaching, messengers including editor Elisha Bates of the anti-Hicksite *Miscellaneous Repository* along with evangelical leaders from England and Ohio and North Carolina. By meeting time in October the three visiting Hicksites from the East could not even get their credentials read at Richmond. Indiana Yearly Meeting approved instead a "Testimony and Epistle of Advice" which took a stand against Hicksite positions and condemned Elias Hicks by name. With long quotations from George Fox, Indiana Yearly Meeting demonstrated that primitive Quakers were really orthodox evangelicals and not Hicksites. Indiana Yearly Meeting would not acknowledge Hicksite meetings or extend religious fellowship to Hicksite members.

When Elias Hicks himself came to Richmond the following year, in September of 1828, the cause was so firmly in the hands of the Orthodox that Hicks did not even attend the sessions of Indiana Yearly Meeting. He held a meeting in an adjacent barn. The Hicksites who now controlled large sections of the Society of Friends in the East were not strong enough in Indiana Yearly Meeting to bid for control or to stage a serious contest with the orthodox evangelicals. They set up a small Indiana Yearly Meeting of their own, its annual sessions alternating between their larger congregations at Waynesville in Ohio and at Richmond in Indiana. They had twenty meetings in Indiana by the end of 1828. Their history in Indiana was generally a story of genteel decline.[51]

Thus the Orthodox were always by far the larger Quaker group in Indiana. Yet the memory of the Hicksite separation and the continuing presence of Hicksite meetings kept affecting Indiana's Friends. Henry Hoover said of his father Andrew, "The unfortunate separation in '27–8, sealed his enjoyment in Church matters, and was a steady theme of sorrow and pain and I think quite probably hastened his dissolution." Elijah Coffin, the clerk of Indiana Yearly Meeting, saw his father and brother go with the Hicksites while his step-mother remained an Orthodox minister. Coffin's father-in-law, Benajah Hiatt, refused to speak to his Hicksite brother Silas.

William Hobbs expressed the pain of separation at Blue River: "Nearly half of the members of our Monthly Meeting separated, and among them were some of my near kin." The two parties tried for a time to share the Blue River meetinghouse but in January of 1829 the Hicksites locked out the Orthodox who then spent over $500 to build anew. Between 1828 and 1831 Hobbs visited widely across Indiana Yearly Meeting helping subordinate meetings adjust to the division. The conclusion generally was that persistent Hicksite Quakers were to be discredited and disowned.[52]

Orthodox Gurneyite Majority

Over against what they saw as Hicksite heresies, Indiana's Orthodox Quakers took firm positions regarding the authority of the Bible as well as the divinity of Christ and his work of atonement. Except for the omission of sacraments, they became very close in doctrine to the main body of evangelical Protestants in the United States. In this movement a prominent leader and most winsome spokesman was Joseph John Gurney of England.

> Outwardly, Quakerism as Gurney interpreted it was not much different from quietism. He held to the spirituality of the sacraments, the importance of silence, and the traditional view of the ministry. He also accepted all of the outward regulations of the plain life. But Gurney revolutionized the Quaker conception of certain vital points of

doctrine: the role of the Bible, the place of early Friends, the guidance of the Inner Light, the nature of justification and sanctification, and the relationship of Friends to other denominations.[53]

Gurney elevated the authority of the Bible over direct revelations from the Inner Light. Like contemporary evangelical Protestants and revivalists he viewed justification—acceptability before God—as the result of a simple act of faith and belief in Christ. He believed that salvation produced good works and that Quakers could and should collaborate even with non-Quakers in promoting such causes as temperance, antislavery, Bible reading, and prison reform.

Gurney's teaching caused some dissension and division in eastern meetings of Friends but in the West its evangelical character was welcome. As part of a triumphal three-year visit in America he attended Indiana Yearly Meeting in 1837. At Richmond he was naturally a guest in the home of Elijah Coffin. Charles Coffin was then a boy of fourteen. He later reminisced:

> I have the most profound love and affection for him. He was one of the best specimens of manhood I have ever seen; six feet high, well proportioned, impressive manners. He was a great orator, a strong writer and sound in evangelical faith. He was a man that was raised amid wealth and refinement, but he devoted himself not to the making of money but to work for the good of his fellow men. I recollect some of his "opportunities" in my father's house and especially of his speaking to me. Some of his remarks made an impression upon my mind that has never been erased.[54]

As a mark of their agreement with Gurney and in clear distinction from any Hicksite tendencies, Orthodox Quakers in Indiana were also called "Gurneyites." Eighty-five years after the Hicksite separation of 1827, Orthodox revivalist Luke Woodard published from Plainfield one more compilation of Hicksite errors intended to prove that the unrepentant ones were heretics, Unitarians, and kin to a deadly modernism.[55]

Early Quakers had been reluctant to enter politics or to take disputes involving believers before civil courts in view of the injunction in Matthew 5:25–26. However Indiana's Quakers were from the South where their settlements had learned to wield some political clout against slavery and against required military service. Faced with Hicksite claims for possession of meetinghouses, cemeteries, schools, and church records, the Orthodox in Indiana were soon ready to go to civil courts to prove that they were the only true Society of Friends. Faced with what they considered to be Hicksite invasions and disorder, they were ready to call in officers of the law to defend the priority of orthodoxy. In fact they constituted such a unified body of citizens in their area of concentration (e.g., Whitewater Valley counties like Wayne, Randolph, Henry, and Union) that they often held the balance in election of local officers and state legislators. Thus their support was courted and they won political offices themselves.

> Between 1829 and 1842 at least 26 Quakers ran for the state legislature, most of them successfully. Only two sessions of the legislature in those years did not have at least one Friend, usually more, as a member. In 1840 the Whigs placed Wayne County State Senator Achilles Williams, a Friend with an impeccable Quaker pedigree, on the state ticket as a Harrison elector. Williams's faith was not incompatible with considerable political acumen. He followed Harrison's victory by using his connections to land for himself a considerable political plum, the Richmond postmastership.[56]

On the wider political scene they came to provide solid voting blocs first as Whigs and then as Republicans.

Abolitionist Friends

An instance of the tension between politics and Quaker principle arose in 1842. Henry Clay was seeking the Whig nomination for president. He had good connections in the Whig stronghold of Richmond and came there on Saturday during yearly meeting for a speech before an immense audience. Next day Friends leaders escorted Clay to the huge yearly meetinghouse and seated him on one of the raised seats at the head of the meeting. But Henry Clay was a slaveholder! A Hicksite abolitionist had confronted him on Saturday with a petition bearing about two thousand signatures asking him to free his own slaves and had gotten a brusque answer. It was too much for abolitionist Friends in Indiana. They had been sensitized and organized by Arnold Buffum, a disowned Quaker and an agent of the American Anti-Slavery Society living at Newport (now Fountain City). Buffum involved hundreds of Quakers in antislavery activities between 1839 and 1841; in 1841 they formed the Liberty Party. Also at Newport, Buffum and Benjamin Stanton had been publishing two abolitionist journals called the *Protectionist* and the *Free Labor Advocate*. Abolitionist Friends were willing to join their labors with strenuous and strident and unpopular abolitionists anywhere in a common cause of abolishing slavery.[57]

The Orthodox majority in Indiana Yearly Meeting was embarrassed by all this. In 1841 it had banned the use of

Quaker meetinghouses for antislavery meetings and advised Friends not to join antislavery societies that included non-Quakers "who do not profess to wait for Divine direction." Proposed antislavery writings were to be submitted for approval before publication. When abolitionist Friends did not comply, the Yearly Meeting took action to remove eight of them from the meeting's influential executive group called the Meeting for Sufferings. That happened on the very day that Clay arrived, so at the same time the abolitionists were put down and a slaveholder publicly honored. The abolitionist Friends moved off to their stronghold at Newport and formed the Indiana Yearly Meeting of Anti-Slavery Friends. They felt that slavery was so evil that every alliance against it was permissible and immediate action essential. Even the Yearly Meeting could be divided on behalf of principle. About two thousand of Indiana Yearly Meeting's twenty-five thousand members separated.

It was hard for the Orthodox majority to appreciate the issue. They deplored the separation and felt the pains of Hicksitism all over again. When the separatists called them "pro-slavery" they protested that none of them wanted slavery. However in 1842 the majority did want patience and order. They said the abolitionists brought "reproachful abuses to our Society and to other respectable Churches" and threatened "the place and influence which, as a Society, we have heretofore had with rulers of our land." Some looked askance at Levi Coffin's traffic in refugee slaves. They stayed with the Whigs and assured Henry Clay that the extremes of the abolitionists did not represent the real position of Quakers. Following 1848 they supported the Free Soil Party; "the three Quaker counties of Wayne, Randolph, and Henry provided almost a quarter of the Free Soil vote in the state." When the Republican Party was organized, almost all Quakers joined it and voted for Lincoln in 1860. They were stoutly for the Union with votes, relief work, and propaganda.[58]

Calls for military service did create a crisis for Quakers who were committed to nonviolence. Indiana Yearly Meeting reaffirmed its commitment to pacifism. Conscientious objectors to military service who refused to serve, and on the same principle refused to pay someone else to serve, and on the same principle refused to pay a fine which would employ a substitute, suffered some harassment and occasional prosecution under state law. After hearing such Quaker leaders as Charles F. Coffin, Timothy Nicholson, and Barnabas C. Hobbs, Governor Oliver P. Morton and top officials in Abraham Lincoln's staff quietly intervened to prevent wholesale confiscation of Quaker property or imprisonment of Indiana Quakers.

Union sympathy was so strong that at least 1,198 Indiana Friends, about a quarter of all the males of military age, simply volunteered for the Union army. In spite of soul searching by Quaker meetings about a proper response to this violation of discipline, most soldiers suffered no punitive action from their meetings.[59]

Charles Osborn was outstanding among Indiana's Anti-Slavery Friends. Osborn was a pioneer crusader for immediate and unconditional abolition, having led in the organization of the Tennessee Manumission Society in 1814 and having published his *Philanthropist* for that cause in Ohio in 1817–18.[60] In 1819 Osborn moved to Indiana and gave himself to a traveling ministry on the model of John Woolman. Any plan for gradual emancipation or colonization was not acceptable to him. As enthusiasm for immediate abolition built up in the 1830s under leadership of William Lloyd Garrison and others, Osborn was among its zealous promoters. He was willing to labor in the cause alongside Friends or non-Friends. For this activity Osborn was among the eight removed from executive leadership in Indiana Yearly Meeting in 1842, personally referred to as "gone, fallen, and out of the life." He exited with those who chose to form the new Indiana Yearly Meeting of Anti-Slavery Friends. Levi Coffin at Newport was a widely recognized and publicized member.[61]

Walter Edgerton at Spiceland was a most persistent supporter of the antislavery organization. He prepared his *History* to show the grievous errors of Indiana Yearly Meeting and to be a complete vindication of Anti-Slavery Friends.

> I have omitted no document issued by either of the Yearly Meetings, or their representatives, bearing upon the controversy, that I could reasonably obtain; indeed, none of any particular importance . . . No good can result to any Church by covering up its wrongs, or by suffering the impression to remain, that those who were really in the right were the transgressors, when a plain, unvarnished exhibition of historical facts can remove it, even if such exhibition should unfold grievous errors in the Church.[62]

Edgerton had some cause to be disgruntled. Indiana's Anti-Slavery Friends were a healthy correction during a period of political expediency. They performed a significant educational role for which they got little credit or respect. Their documents sent off as painstaking proofs of the necessity of the abolition of slavery on the basis of the Gospel and of Quaker writings were often ignored or opposed anonymously in the press by other Friends. No Orthodox Quaker meetings felt obligated to receive or reply to their communications. Friends in the London Yearly Meeting long ignored their pleas but in 1845 sent a committee prepared only to urge them to cease their separation.[63]

As the temper of the northern states and the voice of the larger Indiana Yearly Meeting became more overtly antislavery, most abolitionist Friends returned to the old Yearly Meeting. The Indiana Yearly Meeting of Anti-Slavery Friends simply dissolved in 1857. It ended without apologies, disownments, reinstatements, or formalities of reunion. Elijah and Charles F. Coffin, deplorers of the separation and frequent targets of its attacks, helped to negotiate its conclusion.[64]

Another factor may have been at work in the relations between Indiana Yearly Meeting and the separated Yearly Meeting of Anti-Slavery Friends. In 1843 the New England Yearly Meeting had disowned John Wilbur. Some five hundred of Wilbur's followers separated and reorganized. Every yearly meeting across the land had to decide whether to recognize these Wilburites, possibly dividing itself in the process. The issue was Joseph John Gurney. The followers of Wilbur pointed out that Gurney, and the large majority of Orthodox Quakers who concurred with him, had broken with old Quaker ways. Wilburites wanted the old quietism—the plain life, the strict discipline, the separation in worship and work from other religious groups. They feared that Gurneyites had elevated the Bible above the Holy Spirit within, had slighted or twisted the authoritative writings of the first three generations of Quaker writers, and had opened themselves to dangerous innovations like organized Bible schools and revivals. This Wilburite controversy hit Indiana Yearly Meeting right on the heels of the antislavery separation. Indiana Yearly Meeting wanted nothing to do with any more separations. Elijah Coffin wrote: "[We] have suffered so much . . . and undergone so much in the conflict . . . that we must keep 'hands off' from everything which gives them strength and support."[65]

Indiana Yearly Meeting wanted little to do with Wilburites, being contented and committed followers of Gurney. However the same Charles Osborn who was an abolitionist was also a critic of Gurney. And the same Walter Edgerton who was clerk of the Indiana Yearly Meeting of Anti-Slavery Friends was hotly opposed to Gurney. He would one day be disowned for publishing his *Modern Quakerism Examined and Contrasted with That of the Ancient Type*.[66] When Anti-Slavery Friends criticized the Indiana Yearly Meeting as corrupted by wealth and worldliness, those publications had a Wilburite ring. Such a combination of abolitionism and Wilburism was

not easy for the leaders of the Indiana Yearly Meeting to hear. Abolitionists they would become, but not until later. Wilburite sentiments would find limited and belated expression in Indiana in a very small body of Conservative Friends organized late in the century to protest Quaker participation in the holiness revivals.

Quaker Acculturation

Indiana's Quakers certainly were changing fast by 1860. When they first entered the state early in the 1800s they counted on maintaining their peculiar identity and unity and discipline by keeping separate from the world and its ways. They felt their traditional faith and life were right and best. But as the century advanced they found the world modifying their terrain in very attractive forms. The world came to successful Quakers with cookstoves to replace fireplaces, two-story houses with cellars to replace log cabins, carriages with spirited horses to replace farm wagons. Plain-cut clothes could display richness and quality; in fact plain dress almost completely disappeared among western Quakers between 1860 and 1870. Post offices multiplied and roads increased. Especially impressive was the railroad "bringing the markets to our doors." Non-Quakers, often Methodists by affiliation or inclination, surrounded and infiltrated all the communities.[67]

Bernhard Knollenberg has commented on the striking change in Richmond during the 1850–60 decade. In 1850 Richmond was a trading and local manufacturing center for the surrounding farm community, its population about 3,000. By 1860 it was the eighth largest town in the state, population 6,603. In 1850 it was an isolated backwoods settlement dominated by Quakers in dress, manners, and concepts. By 1860 it was relatively cosmopolitan and closely linked by rail to a thousand other similar communities. Its newcomers were mainly Germans, Irish, and other non-Quakers. "Though the presence of many men and women still wearing the Quaker garb long continued to give Richmond some of its old flavor, it was no longer either a bucolic or even a predominately Friends community."[68]

Education changed for Indiana's Quakers. At first they had been advocates of rudimentary reading and ciphering, about the level the better trained of them possessed when they immigrated from the South. Quaker meetings were expected to maintain such elementary schools and to arrange to pay tuition for the children of families too poor to pay their own. Teachers were employed and supervised by the meetings. Religion was thus integrated with literacy in safe schools. Even that minimal education made Quakers stand out conspicuously in Indiana where there was no effective public school system before 1850. Twenty-two counties in Indiana reported that 16 percent of their residents over twenty years of age were unable to read and write in 1840. That same census showed the Quaker stronghold of Wayne County with almost 100 percent literacy.[69] Between 1840 and 1850 Indiana's population increased 50 percent but the illiteracy rate increased 100 percent. Indiana Yearly Meeting reported for 1851

> that the Monthly Meetings had conducted 114 schools that year, with an enrollment of 3,551; with sessions lasting from six weeks to twelve months. In addition, Friends' teachers had taught in ninety-one public schools, showing how Quakers were transferring their influence to the district schools. By 1860, the decline of the Monthly Meeting schools was quite apparent: their enrollment for that year being only 1,546, while 3,699 Friends' children attended district schools. Friends were still careful, however, to maintain a guarded education for the children, for of the 3,699 students in district schools, 2,069 of them were still being taught by members of the Society. The main reason for this was that the practical-minded Friend could see no reason for supporting two schools; so he sent both his children and their teacher to the district school and obtained the same education for one-half the . . . cost.[70]

White's Manual Labor Institute in Wabash County was an elementary school based on an initial gift by Josiah White of Philadelphia; it continuously served under-privileged children with special needs, notably Indian children in its early days. In 1881 the Indiana Yearly Meeting said:

> A striking fact in these reports is that our children are almost entirely getting their education in the Public Schools. It is gratifying to know that these schools have greatly improved in the past few years, both in the character of the instruction, and in the time of their continuance . . . It is also an important consideration that many of these schools are virtually under the control of Friends, they being in many instances the teachers as well as the trustees or directors. This opportunity for elevating the character of the schools, and making their moral tone such as we should wish our children to attend, ought to be carefully improved. We certainly owe it to the communities in which we live, as well as to our children, to do what we can to surround the public schools . . . with a high moral and social influence. And much can be done in this direction without exciting any fear of undue sectarian influences.[71]

Any Hoosier who could read was likely to encounter Quaker literature. Quakers were busy putting their books into all libraries. Tract circulation by Indiana Yearly Meeting ran to 66,000 in 1852, 55,000 in 1854, and 122,608 in 1860 reaching a total for that year of over one million pages. In their literature Quakers were for justice to Indians and blacks. They were against war, intemperance, and dancing.[72]

The real change came as some small fraction of Indiana Friends pressed on for education in the "higher branches." The most progressive parents wanted better opportunities for their children. The most successful students glimpsed the range of knowledge and hungered for more. Where there was an educated teacher, he could simply expand the curriculum to teach the ablest students as much as he himself knew. An able teacher or succession of teachers combined with a responsive constituency might produce an "academy."

Well ahead of state public education again, the Quakers of Indiana produced about twenty academies, seminaries, and high schools. They were secondary schools; the best of them in their best periods offered a persistent student a level of training about equal to a modern undergraduate college. Academies named Bloomingdale, Farmers' Institute, and Spiceland were among the best known. Western Yearly Meeting said in 1884:

> As the primary schools have been absorbed by the public system, our obligations with respect to higher education have been increased, and in the effort to meet these obligations the present gratifying state of advancement has been reached. From one high school in the Yearly Meeting—Bloomingdale Academy—at the beginning of this organization (1858) there are now three excellent academies under the exclusive management of Quarterly Meetings, and three others of equal strength and efficiency, which, to all intents and purposes, are Friends' Schools. Not only is it expected that these institutions shall be under the management of teachers thoroughly educated for their profession, and of the most pronounced Christian character, but that a positive religious influence shall characterize all the training and associations of the pupils. The study of the Bible is a regular and prominent part of the curriculum and devotional exercises, in ways adapted to circumstances, are made a part of the daily programme.[73]

In fact these secondary schools blended into or were superseded by a tax supported system of public high schools in the early 1900s. The Quakers were very reluctant to see their secondary schools supplanted but found no alternative.[74]

There was one exception. It was only reasonable that a center so prominent as Richmond should have a Quaker school and that its school should become outstanding. Whitewater Monthly Meeting School at Richmond got its own brick building near the yearly meetinghouse in 1834. Charles Coffin attended there in the winter of 1834–35. When Barnabas Hobbs was its teacher, in 1845–46 and again in 1850–51, it was highly reputed. Concurrently a committee was attempting to raise money for a Quaker boarding school of good quality at Richmond, this as a project by and for the whole of Indiana Yearly Meeting. Allen Jay said: "In 1833 this committee reported that they had received $137. In 1834 they reported $11.50 received; in 1835 they reported nothing received; in 1836 they reported $7.00 received." Excitement rose when construction was actually projected but the panic of 1837 slowed the schedule. Friends Boarding School finally opened in one partially completed building in June of 1847. Among its supporters were the Coffin family at Richmond and William Hobbs of Blue River.[75]

Barnabas C. Hobbs became superintendent of this new Boarding School from 1848 to 1850. The opening circular read:

> The scholars shall use the plain scripture language, and be clothed in plain dress, becoming the appearance of Friends; having respect to decency and usefulness, and avoiding imitation of the changing fashions of the world . . . Such girls as have arrived at sufficient years will be expected to have plain stiff-plait bonnets, and other dress corresponding. The boys will be expected to bring hats, as caps will not be allowed; and their coats, vests, and jackets are to be made with plain collars, to stand up, and not with rolling or falling collars . . . The committee expect to be able to employ competent Teachers and other Officers; and to provide for instruction in the following and probably some other branches of learning, viz: Spelling, Reading, Writing, Arithmetic, Geography, Ancient and Modern History, Grammar, Rhetoric, Composition, Algebra, Geometry, Mensuration, Surveying, Astronomy, Natural Philosophy, Chemistry, Physiology, Botany, Mineralogy, Geology, Natural History, Mental and Moral Philosophy, Evidences of Christianity, and the Latin and Greek Languages.[76]

At the end of the second term were added political economy, political grammar, French, trigonometry, and Bible. Development was always slow and difficult, but by 1859 this boarding school became Earlham College at Rich-

mond, named for the British estate of Joseph John Gurney, and began to award bachelors' degrees to its graduates. Now there was a school where young Friends could have a guarded and religious education. Timothy Nicholson became a trustee of Earlham in 1862; he poured his energy into the school for more than sixty years.[77]

Quaker integration into the contemporary literary world was not just a matter of going off to school. The convenient post offices brought newspapers and magazines—the *Friends Review* from Philadelphia but also the *National Era* with the latest news off the telegraph. Leaders among the Friends were acquiring and discussing books beyond the standard Quaker works. Alert to their stake in political decisions, they studied the issues in the *Palladium* from Richmond or the *Free Territory Sentinel* from Centerville.[78]

Advocates of Revivalism and Holiness Practices

Young Quakers most in touch with the contemporary atmosphere of change found some of the old religious ways to be stifling. Elijah Coffin's daughter-in-law Rhoda said:

> The Society of Friends after many, many years of vitalizing active service, in which they bore a strong testimony for spiritual worship and against formalism, had, through this protesting against formalism in other churches, become very formal. While there were many able, conscientious Christians here and there, striving to serve the Lord in the way they thought right, the Church as a whole had lost much of its vitality. As is always the case, so was it now—strikingly so—while engaged in finding fault with what others were doing, criticising, judging and protesting, the life was sapped by a system of quenching and "thou shalt nots." The younger people had no means of showing their love to God by any active service. They were required to use certain modes of dress and language, abstain from all relaxations and amusements; music and singing were prohibited. Even singing a hymn at home was very doubtful, not to be encouraged, an evidence of "creaturely activity" of which there was great fear. It was a narrow path, a "guarded education," but the guards were so strong and high that the breathing of the pure air of contact with other Christians was almost shut off. The pure flow of Christ-like thought was obstructed by repression.[79]

His grandson Elijah spoke of the days of his father:

> The effect of the "Great Separation" (of 1828) still hung over everything. Quietism was at its highest point, and a

great horror of "creaturely activity" filled the minds of many of the good people who were at the head of the meeting. "Creaturely activity," in those days was the term applied to any movement out of the regular rut or routine. Elders were appointed for life, and people, who were under thirty-five years of age, were rarely appointed as members of committees. Speaking, or vocal prayer, by any not of the authorized ministry, was quietly discouraged, and if persisted in, was privately reproved by the elders . . . Conditions existed similar to those of that period when the Puritans of New England were in absolute power. Hicksites, Spiritualists and Infidels were regarded as lost beyond redemption. Presbyterians and Episcopalians stood a chance of salvation, if they would only repent. Methodists were the most highly respected, but no Religious intercourse at all was held with other churches, and only a moderate amount of social intercourse was permitted. Friends were sufficient unto themselves. Members who fell by the way, were practically ostracized.[80]

Luke Woodard said that for many "Quakerism was a mere form, in its avowed opposition to forms—a kind of system of negations."[81]

Young Quakers were more drawn to occasions which involved their emotions in intense religious commitment and then gave them opportunity for individual expression and profession of their faith. Religious emotion had been no stranger at the old-style quiet meetings. Tears came frequently. Hearts were "tendered" and new commitments made to live the consecrated life. Visitation with families in their home setting could be searching. Quaker parents looked hopefully for signs of personal religious commitment in their offspring who were Quakers by birthright. The experience of Allen Jay illustrated the movement toward a new kind of speaking in meeting which would set an expectation of conversion and provide a motivation toward that goal. Jay described the variety of Quaker preaching going on at Randolph, Ohio, during his teen years. He said his father changed the tenor of the gathering when he began to speak about 1846: "The ministry of my father was different. He was given to speak to conditions of meetings and individuals. Often his communications were so direct that meetings were impressed and individuals were led to surrender their lives to God."[82]

When Jay had established his own young family at Pine Creek preparative meeting near Farmers' Institute Academy in Tippecanoe County, Indiana, he took charge of a first-day class of about twenty young Friends. Several of them began offering vocal prayer in the class, in devotions in their homes, in devotions at the close of social gatherings of community young people, and in the nearby academy. In spring of 1859 Jay was favorably impressed by Quaker minister Jeremiah A. Grinnell who transferred from Blue River to Pine Creek.

He was a man twenty-five years ahead of his time. He understood the signs of the times . . . He produced a great change in our meeting without hurting the feelings of those who differed from him. In two years all were ready to go with him as he led the way. He knew how to bring out and develop the gifts of young people better than any person I ever knew in all of my wide acquaintance.[83]

When family visitation began "every member of the committee was heard in prayer and testimony." By August of 1860 Allen Jay and his wife were appointed elders, their interests decidedly oriented toward youth work and revival.[84] Jay said:

There was created a hungering for the Gospel. The membership was moved by the Spirit to seek something definite in the way of religious experience. As I have said, we felt it in our school at Farmers' Institute, where a number of children were converted, and in the neighborhood prayer meetings, which were held in the homes. When we met socially, we would often read a portion of Scripture and have a time of prayer before closing. This went on quietly from 1861 to 1865. Jeremiah A. Grinnell was the human instrumentality that God used to lead it forward so quietly and wisely that but little opposition was ever raised against it.[85]

In Richmond the same evangelical impetus among the youth found support among the influential Coffin family. It was not unusual for Friends to seek and receive permission to hold a special evening gathering while the Indiana Yearly Meeting was in session. Such permission was requested and granted for a youth meeting on Sunday, 7 October 1860. It was understood that regular ministers would not be in charge of this youth assembly. The sponsors hoped at least one hundred would attend. Elijah Coffin recorded in his journal that at 7 P.M. the lower floor of the meetinghouse was packed plus some in the gallery, an attendance "not less than two thousand." The young people were told that the meeting was in their hands. Some adults who had signed the request testified briefly, Charles and Rhoda Coffin for the first time. Then came the surprise. "There had been absolutely no urging to speak, no calls for converts to rise. Everything was orderly. But more than 150 people either prayed, or rose to tell of their intention to serve their Master, and their desire to become Christ's children. The meeting lasted from seven o'clock until midnight and was difficult to close even then."[86] One Quaker elder even tried to sing a hymn.

Quaker minister Sybyl Jones from Maine asked to meet at a later date with those who had spoken at the youth meeting. Those later meetings began the next Sunday evening at the home of Charles and Rhoda Coffin and continued as a prayer meeting there every Sunday evening for nearly seven years. In retrospect Charles Coffin called it "the most wonderful power for good in the life of the [Friends] Society in America."[87]

There was opposition to these deviations. However the prayer meeting in a private home was not easily subject to official censure. Elijah and Charles and Rhoda Coffin were persons of great conviction and stature among Quakers. Rhoda said:

> Many Friends came to see us to persuade us to give up the Prayer Meeting, but all who attended advised us to continue . . . During the Yearly Meeting in 1861, previous to our Father Coffin's death, although very feeble, he felt he had a message for that body. He was taken to the Meeting House and made a most earnest plea for the liberty of holding Prayer Meetings. All who heard him felt that it was his dying effort, and he stood before them so feeble and emaciated, and pleaded so earnestly, he won every heart. His address was incorporated in the "Minute on the State of Society," which as usual was sent to all of the subordinate Meetings.[88]

Indiana Friends would never be the same. In addition to the body of outspoken young converts, there was a substantial corps of Quaker leaders ready to encourage them.[89] Conversion was an urgent part of their message and the new birth for all was their goal. From 1860 the preaching at sessions of Indiana Yearly Meeting at Richmond generally urged "the necessity of individually making a definite covenant with God and experiencing individually the regenerating work of grace in the heart." From 1861 provisions for worship at this annual meeting included outdoor preaching by experienced evangelistic ministers to exhort the crowds to seek conversion. In the winter of 1866–67 twenty young men were converted in one term at Earlham College, and before the end of the year almost the whole student body was swept into the movement. Walnut Ridge meetinghouse in Rush County was the scene of a noisy revival in 1867, especially among young Friends recently influenced by Methodists. Raysville and Spiceland in Henry County held meetings with some revival manifestations. Some time after the events at Walnut Ridge, a few of the participants behaved irrationally and were charged with "ranterism" and "fanaticism."[90]

Indiana Yearly Meeting began experimenting in 1867 by approving some "general meetings" to be held outside the usual meeting structure and schedule. They were established to benefit members who said they were too far out of the orbit of Richmond to participate fully in the events of Indiana Yearly Meeting. So a team of weighty Friends, often including clerk Charles F. Coffin or committeeman Timothy Nicholson, would spend three or four days at some location away from Richmond to offer able preaching plus instruction and discussion. Subjects might include "conversion, sanctification, worship, silence, peace, the ministry, baptism and communion, marriage, and the plain life." Conversion was certainly the hottest of the topics. As these general meetings passed into the hands of revival preachers, they tended to become revival meetings.[91]

In the city of Richmond itself the evangelical energies focused especially on a new meeting set off in regular order in 1864 as "Richmond Preparative Meeting" and composed mostly of members residing south of Main Street and west of the city. It was closely linked to Charles and Rhoda Coffin and to the prayer meeting for young Friends long held in their house. Rhoda said:

> In these Meetings there was the greatest freedom and liberty of action, "to do what our hands found to do"— Sabbath Schools, Bible Classes, Reading Circles which met at different homes, Tracts and Tract Readings, Cottage Prayer Meetings, etc. The missionary spirit was soon apparent; our Friends desired that the Gospel should be carried to those who sat in darkness. Louis and Sarah Street, members of our Meeting, felt called upon to go to Madagascar where they labored most successfully for twelve years. This was like the leaven. The influence was felt and resulted in many others going out in different directions, in different places, and finally in the establishment of the Foreign Mission work in which American Friends are now engaged. Prayer was offered night and day for direction, for guidance in the spiritual upheaval which soon followed. The Prayer Meeting became the center of great activities. A great revival came upon us. For six months this Church was the recipient of great grace, hundreds were brought to a full acceptance of new life. Three hundred and seventy-five were added to the Church. The revival spread all over the city.[92]

Charles F. Coffin was recorded a minister in 1866. He conducted prayer meetings on Friday evenings and men's meetings on Sunday evenings.[93]

Richmond had grown enough by the war years to spawn most varieties of vice and to include many poor families broken and displaced by the Civil War. Quaker women at Richmond, led by Rhoda Coffin, established

The Home for the Friendless. They raised $8,000 for a building and $1,000 per year for operating costs. Measureless contributions in kind included "forty wagonloads of firewood and provisions" from surrounding neighborhoods for the first of what became annual "donation days."[94]

Charles and Rhoda led the prayer meeting troops in the founding of a Friends Mission School for Richmond's children. Charles was superintendent; Rhoda was chief teacher.[95]

> With two pupils I opened my infant class. We had a goodly number of teachers and devoted workers. We soon learned that singing was essential. The adoption of this exercise caused grief to some honest Friends and, strange to say, gave us much trouble . . . We built our new Meeting House on what is now Eighth street, the second story for a church, and the ground floor for our Christian work. The citizens contributed largely to the fitting up of the basement for our school. There was in time as many as eight hundred children enrolled at one time. Five hundred and twenty-three of these were in my class, aged from three to fifteen. I obtained a thorough knowledge of every scholar, and of their homes. I threw my whole strength and interest into it, and sought to bring them into a knowledge of Christ.[96]

Friends in Indiana still had much silent and unprogrammed worship; they had no pastors or sacraments. But their religious goals were increasingly articulated like those of their Protestant neighbors. They entered benevolent work with other churches in many good causes and soon excelled in their behalf. Quakers like the Coffins, Barnabas Hobbs, Allen Jay, and Timothy Nicholson welcomed the renewal among Friends and were not fearful of emotional intensity. They wanted less of the old Quaker legalisms and more testimonial participation by ordinary members in the meetings. Their voice was the *Friends Review*. These were moderate reformers with a mindset of many Quakers in the educated middle class.[97]

As the revival quickened following 1868 there developed a group of Quaker ministers who were full-time religious workers and professional revivalists. They claimed they were simply recovering the aggressive evangelism of the early Quakers like George Fox. Speaking in meeting was soon assumed in their case wherever they appeared; they could be depended upon to excite the membership and the community. Sympathetic meetings to which they belonged were willing to give them credentials for their work in very general terms so that they became travelers able to go wherever there was opportunity and support. Since Quakers generally retained some

bias against a "hireling ministry" and had no tradition of ministerial support, they were not quick to provide a living for such full-time evangelists. Quaker revivalists often conducted campaigns for Methodists. They learned how to begin by preaching to the prisoners at a town jail and then expand that opening into a campaign at the town's center.[98]

Esther Frame was converted as a youth among the Methodists in Boone County, though her mother was a Friend.

> One stormy night, while the elements were warring without, and the heavens seemed brass above me, I felt myself sinking, and I sank and sank until my feet touched the purple flood, and I was covered all over with glory, then I came up whiter than snow and my soul was filled with joy. I was so happy I could not tell it. As I went home that night, though it was dark and the storm was raging without, my soul was illuminated by divine grace and it seemed to me that I almost flew, and there seemed a light all about me. There was no greater punishment for me than to keep me away from meeting and school.[99]

She was full of conviction that she must preach, compelled by the voice of the Lord saying "Preach my Gospel." Overcoming some resistance she transferred from the Methodists to the Friends where men and women had equal opportunity to be ministers, carrying her husband with her into Friends meeting and into evangelistic service. The Quakers at Concord in Wayne County were accustomed to meet for quiet waiting on Sunday and Wednesday at 11 A.M. in a meetinghouse less than half filled. What came into that quiet waiting in 1867 was Esther and Nathan Frame. Esther said: "The spirit that they had waited for so long to move them, and for which they had many times silently asked, was about to waken a slumbering church and touch many lips with live coals from off God's holy altar and anoint them to preach the glad tidings of salvation." Esther was soon speaking all the time and Nathan on Sundays when his school was not in session. The meetinghouse was now filled. Not yet recorded as ministers, the Frames could not appoint meetings but they announced "tract reading meetings" in private homes. The tracts were evangelistic and the comments hortative. Revival broke out and fed back from the homes into the meetinghouse.[100]

From the summer of 1868 the Frames developed into a team of evangelistic travelers—reviving local meetings; visiting hundreds of families; moving from services at the Anderson jail to a street meeting there. Esther was always the curiosity and the spellbinding star. Nathan said of the Anderson meeting:

Esther preached to them with a power that held that company of men and women of all grades of society perfectly entranced. It was a new and strange thing for a Quaker woman to preach, and especially on the street. Her message to them was a most wonderful one, and before the sermon was ended there were as many as five hundred gathered at that street meeting, and they stood there quietly the full two hours that the meeting lasted, and all that time there was perfect order and quiet reigned.[101]

The Frames shared at many points in the revival of 1869 at Richmond. Rhoda Coffin called it "a great revival" with "hundreds . . . brought to full acceptance of new life" and "three hundred and seventy-five . . . added to the Church." The Cincinnati *Gazette* for 24 May 1869 said: "A Mrs. Frame, perhaps, is one of the most remarkable preachers in this revival,—tall, graceful, and commanding in appearance, and a voice full of music, she can enchain, and melt into tears an audience sooner, than any person it has ever been our pleasure to hear . . . Her success has been remarkable. Presbyterians, Methodists, and other churches, are now vieing with each other to have her preach to their congregations."[102]

The Frames were now engaged in nationwide interdenominational evangelism, doubly a crowd pleaser everywhere for the novelty of being Quaker evangelists with one team member an obviously more than equal woman preacher. An observer of a meeting at the Methodist Church at Union City in Indiana in June of 1871 reported: "The novelty as well as the sublimity of the services were greatly heightened when Esther Frame, as if moved by an irresistible impulse, threw her soul into the most devotional song we ever heard sung." They preached often on the equality of men and women and encouraged young Quaker women at Knightstown who professed a call to preach. Indiana was not neglected, being recipient of at least forty-two campaigns by the Frames. At the Bloomingdale meeting in November of 1888, Barnabas C. Hobbs attended most of the meetings and took part in the exhortation. At Columbus in spring of 1891 there were 506 conversions and 300 accessions to the host Methodist Church. The Cincinnati *Gazette* for 17 April 1891 said "No one who hears her preach will ever ask the question 'Can a woman preach?'"[103]

The Frames knew other Quaker revivalists from Indiana Yearly Meeting, some more famous than themselves. Luke Woodard, Dougan Clark, Jr., and John Henry Douglas were all involved in that impressive all-night meeting at Richmond in 1860. Woodard called it "one of the most marked instances I have ever witnessed of the out-pouring of the Spirit upon a whole congregation." Woodard was a Wayne County Friend who experienced conversion about 1858.

> As I was at work alone in my field, the scene of Calvary where my Savior bore my sins in His own body on the tree, was presented to my mind; the Holy Spirit impressed upon my heart with inexpressible vividness the thought that it was for me—that He loved me and gave himself for me. No sooner had I grasped this by appropriating faith, than my sense of condemnation was gone, and joy and peace took its place, and I sank upon the ground and wept tears of joy.[104]

Soon afterward he first spoke in public meeting and was recorded a minister by New Garden Meeting in 1862. On a tour to Iowa in 1865 he met Esther Frame at her father's house. "She was at that time young, gaily dressed, and apparently not very religious, and was not a member of our church. In an interview with her I told her I believed it was the will of God that she should join the Friends Church and preach the gospel. She promised she would."[105]

From the beginning of his ministry, Woodard was a champion of revivals. "General meetings" like those authorized by Indiana Yearly Meeting were finding favor nationwide and became essentially revivals. Woodard went as evangelist to a number of these in New York and Ohio. Frequently his colleagues in conducting these revivals were John Henry Douglas and David B. Updegraff. At Glen Falls, New York, in 1872 a Friend said "Luke Woodard lays the foundation and teaches the way; John Henry Douglas presses them in; and David B. Updegraff fixes them so they will stand."[106] In winter of 1873–74 this trio led a revival at Spiceland in Indiana. Spiceland may well have been the largest meeting of Friends in the world with about 800 members, besides the Academy with perhaps 200 more.[107] Douglas of Indiana Yearly Meeting and Updegraff of Ohio Yearly Meeting were the most powerful of the Quaker revivalists. By the early 1870s they were on an endless round of revival meetings, recognized as chief preachers everywhere.

David B. Updegraff was bringing Quaker evangelism a new teaching. In fall of 1869 John S. Inskip stayed at Updegraff's home at Mt. Pleasant, Ohio. Inskip was a Methodist. He was founding president of the National Camp Meeting Association. He was one of the nation's most able advocates of the doctrine of perfect holiness or entire sanctification understood as a distinct second act of grace following salvation, a second act of grace which brings complete deliverance and purification from all sin.

By the end of Inskip's visit, Updegraff was convinced. He had been converted and saved under Methodist preaching at Mt. Pleasant in 1860. "I was converted through and through, and I knew it. I was free as a bird. Justified by faith, I had peace with God." Now in 1869 came that second experience of sanctification which Inskip had urged him to claim.

> Every "vile affection" was nailed to the cross . . . It came to be easy to trust Him, and I had no sooner reckoned myself "dead unto sin and alive unto God" than the Holy Ghost fell upon me just as I supposed He did at the beginning. Instantly I felt the melting and refining fire of God permeate my whole being . . . I was deeply conscious of the presence of God within me, and of His sanctifying work.[108]

The next Sunday Updegraff rose in Quaker meeting to tell his experience and to witness for sanctification as he now understood it.

From that time Updegraff's message was always this doctrine of holiness. Every person, church member or not, should be sure to receive the new birth through an experience of conversion, but that was not yet the goal. Conversion was to be followed by a second experience of sanctification by which every trace of residual sin was removed. Every Quaker, young or old, birthright or not, should expect and insist on these two experiences. Since either or both could be lost by backsliding, either or both might always need to be regained or renewed. The experiences might come, by God's grace, at any time and in any way. However the proven means for seeking them included stirring holiness preaching, singing, testimony, heartfelt repentance, and continuing fervent prayer. So in the revival meetings at Farmington, New York, in August of 1871, Updegraff's theme was "the higher life within the reach of all prayerful and faithful ones." That autumn Luke Woodard was working with Updegraff in Michigan where there were "conversions and renewals and . . . the profession of the experience of entire sanctification of others."[109] Woodard had been reading holiness literature, became convinced, and received the blessing himself.

> The blessing came to me in the city of Adrian, Mich., where I had been attending, with other ministers, a series of meetings . . . It was the response of submissive, appropriating faith, and it was answered by an indescribable sense of the presence of the Holy Ghost, and a sweet peace that filled my mind and heart . . . Since that time I have taught both by voice and pen, the doctrine of sanctification, and that as an experience, it is realized subsequent to regeneration through the baptism with the Holy Ghost, on the condition of definite consecration,

and the prayer of faith, and I have ground to believe that my teaching has been blessed to many.[110]

John Henry Douglas of Indiana Yearly Meeting encountered holiness teaching about 1870. Rehearsal of his own spiritual pilgrimage convinced him that he was both converted and sanctified, but for reasons of good order he kept silent about the latter. While working with David B. Updegraff in a general meeting at Brooklyn, New York, in 1871, Douglas publicly announced his belief and experience and became a holiness crusader. "This began a new era in my work for God," he said.[111]

Dougan Clark, Jr. was trained as a physician but chose to accept a position as teacher of foreign languages at Earlham College. He was a shy professor-scholar who was quietly reading some holiness teachings in private. Updegraff convinced Clark that all he needed to do to become sinless was to claim the experience publicly in faith. Upon doing so, Clark said all his being became filled with wonderful peace, that he was "dead to self and sin, alive to Christ, and filled with the Holy Ghost." He changed at once into a zealous holiness preacher and writer. He said "In the three weeks that followed my sanctification I did more good than in three years before."[112]

When Earlham College established a Biblical Department in 1885, Clark was its head. He assumed constant revival as a proper context for Quakers. Sanctification as a second blessing was central in his understanding of a proper Quaker theology.

> Now observe that in this experience [conversion] it is sins that are washed away in the blood of Jesus— removed as far off as the east is from the west,—and never again brought into remembrance against us. But as for sin it still remains in the heart. It exists but it does not reign. Its power is broken, so that by the grace of God and constant watchfulness and prayer, it may be kept from all committed sin. It is a spurious conversion which does not preserve its possessor from actual sinning. But sin, the inward principle of evil is not and cannot be gotten rid of by a process or an act of forgiveness. It requires another and a subsequent work of grace to destroy the body of sin, and the individual who is the subject of this second experience, becomes thereby a sanctified or a holy man. His heart is cleansed from the remains of carnality, and he enters into the experience of holiness.[113]

During his nine years as department head he linked Earlham to the national holiness movement, not least to the influence of his particular friend J. Walter Malone who opened a holiness center in Cleveland called the Friends

Bible Institute and Training School. Elbert Russell remembered a revival led by Malone at Earlham College in fall of 1890. Student leaders were converted. Attendance at prayer meetings became general and practically all the students joined Christian associations.[114]

The Frames were also consistent advocates of holiness teaching. The testimony of Esther included a sanctification experience in 1868, preceding even that of Updegraff. "Then last of all I threw myself down upon the altar and said 'Lord take poor Esther, too,' and the altar sanctified the gift, and fire came down from heaven, and sweet incense has been arising ever since, and there has never been a cloud that has for a moment come between me and my father's face and I was wholly sanctified and filled with the spirit." Reports of revivals led by the Frames regularly included conversions, renewals, and believers who "obtained the blessing of perfect love" or "professed to be cleansed from all sin."[115]

It was these highly visible holiness revivalists who produced models for Indiana's Quaker meetings, Quaker youth, and Quaker ministers for a period following 1870. A new generation of ministers arose who were products of these revivals and dedicated to evangelism on this pattern. Quakers provided some preachers for other revivalist groups, e.g., Seth Rees to lead the emerging Pilgrim Holiness Church (later Wesleyan) and Ambrose Jessup Tomlinson to found the pentecostal Churches of God in Tennessee. They received an even greater influx of holiness revivalists from other denominations.[116] Thus many Quaker revivalists were short on Quaker background and long on linkage with other holiness groups.

A small body of conservative Friends felt that holiness was indeed always to be sought but that sanctification was a lifelong process furthered by continued quiet waiting, tenderings of heart, renewals of commitment, and the discipline called "bearing the cross." They opposed "Second Advent views, water baptism, instantaneous conversion and sanctification, and the entire apparatus of the revival."[117] Old-fashioned conservatives among the Quakers were no match for the revivalists. When Spiceland Meeting was revived in the winter of 1873–74

There were a number engaged in exhortation and vocal supplication, besides many others singing, while others were down at the mourners' benches, and most of the rest on their feet, who had arisen at the call of the preacher, all going on at the same time. Meanwhile children, and even young women, evidently terrified and wild with fright, were crying, women hastening through among the men, and men among the women. Over seven hundred people, virtually the entire membership

of the meeting, ministers and elders, young and old, were converted or sanctified by a team of revivalists led by Updegraff.[118]

Walter Edgerton of that Spiceland Meeting published a strenuous critique of such revivals and their departure from Quaker tradition. Neither Updegraff nor the revivals got restrained; Edgerton was the one who was disowned for "creating disunity."[119]

Some conservatives at Plainfield protested noisy prayer gatherings among Quakers at the annual session of Western Yearly Meeting. By 1877 the practice had increased until almost every other house in the village had a prayer meeting of fifteen or twenty people. These were often held until after midnight with singing, loud praying, public testimonies and shouting. The decision of Western Yearly Meeting favored the revivalists rather than the conservative protestors. When a small group of conservatives then declared their separation from Western Yearly Meeting, a revivalist sang a hymn to them as they departed and counted their going good riddance.[120]

Quaker revivalists moved their journal to Chicago and considerably strengthened it under editor Calvin Pritchard in 1883.

In the reorganized *Christian Worker* the revival party found a reliable mouthpiece. "First a Christian, second a Friend," was the *Christian Worker*'s motto. It advocated a thoroughgoing revival platform that included preaching, singing, vocal prayer, altar calls, and mourners' benches. It was an uncompromising defender of "scriptural holiness"—instantaneous, second-experience sanctification—and an enemy of Unitarianism, infidelity, sectarianism, and traditional Quakerism. Pritchard epitomized the attitudes of holiness Friends of the last quarter of the nineteenth century. Revivalism had become a permanent feature of Quakerism, they asserted, and should be part of the life of every Quaker. No meeting could do without revivals, because no other method worked so well in producing conversions and sanctifications.[121]

In the *Christian Worker* Updegraff called the conservative Quakers "fossil remains" and Dougan Clark said they wanted only the "kind of holiness . . . that somebody had two hundred years ago."[122]

What had occurred among Indiana's Orthodox (Gurneyite) Quakers was a holiness revival revolution. Barnabas C. Hobbs told the Friends at London Yearly Meeting in 1878 that they could not understand what had happened to the Orthodox Quaker meetings in Indiana. "No one can without seeing it. Our meetings were shaken as by a vast whirlwind."[123] Walter Robson of that British meeting certainly knew because he had visited the sessions of both Western Yearly Meeting at Plainfield and Indiana Yearly Meeting at Richmond just the year before. He was awed by the size. "In this [Western] & Indiana Y.M.'s (both in the state of Indiana) are over 25,000 Friends—truly a powerful army!" He saw the conservative separation at Plainfield at which "99 men were counted out of the house" and "a similar scene . . . the other side of the shutters in the Women's Y.M." For Sunday there were about 3,000 carriages present and so a crowd of perhaps 12,000. At Plainfield one revivalist preached for perhaps 2,500 in the meetinghouse while a second revivalist preached for another 5,000 outside on the grounds. They sang "There Is a Fountain" and "Shall We Gather at the River." Conservatives, Robson said, had no sympathy "with the hymn singing &c that has such constant place among Friends here." He thought the town of Plainfield looked like a country fair. "Stalls for refreshments (all tee-total) were well supplied and patronized."[124]

Everything was even bigger for the 1877 gathering at Richmond since "Indiana is still the largest Y. meeting in the world tho' there have already been three great off-shoots from it—Kansas, Iowa & Western." Robson stayed at the home of Charles and Rhoda Coffin. Both John Henry Douglas and David B. Updegraff were very prominently present. Robson described Sunday, the meeting's big day.

> A very thrilling devotional meeting at 8. Large & earnest confessions & professions from all parts of the house . . . The scene was very wonderful. Train after train arriving at the depot, crowded with passengers, the streets near & the meetinghouse ground, full of vehicles, the roads lined with refreshment stalls, all teetotal, the one great centre of attraction being the two meeting houses & the preaching stand in the grounds. I suppose 10 to 15 thousand would be present altogether.[125]

He worked as a member of an evangelistic team of at least a dozen, preaching long both inside the meeting-house and out. "We were all greatly favored & many wept," he said. "Hundreds of black faces among the white people. Of course we all roared as loud as we could so as to reach as many of the thousands as possible & I am glad to hear were very well heard."[126] Robson shared in the height of excitement at this very hub of Orthodox Quakerdom, the Sunday evening service inside the Friends meetinghouse at Richmond.

> A scene of indescribable solemnity was being acted, "an Altar of prayer." Friends old & young, smart & very plain, kneeling in rows, sometimes quite still, often ejaculating short earnest prayer for a baptism of the Holy

Ghost, some praising God with a loud voice that their prayers were answered. Dear David Updegraff & J.H.D. quietly moving about among the kneeling throng, sometimes in prayer themselves & at others quietly whispering words of comfort or of counsel. I never realized such agonising in prayer before. It was a scene never to be forgotten. Did not get home till past 11 o'clk, tired, but very thankful for a day of uncommon blessing.[127]

Robson found that total eradication of sin in the believer was a lively topic for discussion at both Plainfield and Richmond, that state enthusiastically claimed by several.[128] By the time Elbert Russell attended Western Yearly Meeting at Plainfield in 1889, there were still excursion trains from Indianapolis and the crowd of about 10,000. Every local youth with a horse and buggy felt honor bound to take his best girl to Plainfield on yearly meeting Sunday. Russell said: "Religious services were held in the meeting house morning, afternoon, and night, where some of the leading ministers of Quakerdom spoke. A large part of the crowd were not interested in the meetings and never went in the meeting house at all. In order to reach as many of the visitors as possible, five or six preaching stands with rude benches were provided in the afternoon here and there on the grounds and even in the streets down town."[129]

The continued evangelism multiplied converts. Many who professed conversion were already birthright Friends.[130] A large number of converts also came from outside Quakerism; between 1881 and 1889 Indiana Yearly Meeting, with a membership of about 18,000, had more than 9,000 applications for membership. These new members were generally ill prepared for quiet or unprogrammed services. They had been converted under charismatic preachers in an evangelistic setting. They looked for continuing preaching in continuing evangelistic services.

The yearly meetings named committees of elders, overseers, and the customary non-professional ministers to watch over the new Friends lest they drop away. A Committee on Ministry for Indiana Yearly Meeting was appointed in 1880 to care for new members, to direct evangelists, and to see that meetings were provided with ministers.[131] Such committees were necessarily limited. The professional revivalists and their converts were accustomed to an exciting personal narrative of religious experience by each of their preachers including a narrative of a personal "call" to the revivalist ministry. Several of the revivalists were also accustomed to receiving sufficient free will offerings to support them in their full-time work. Luke Woodard and Esther Frame and David Updegraff advocated a full-time Quaker clergy fully supported for their work. This was squarely opposed to the old Quaker tradition that ministers should support themselves in a secular trade and that meetings should abhor a hireling ministry.

Change came relentlessly. The number of paid Quaker pastors slowly increased.

> Several evangelists—Robert W. Douglas, Luke Woodard, and Nathan and Esther Frame—claimed to have been pastors before 1875, but their tenures were brief and unofficial. The first true pastorates were those of the Frames in Muncie, Indiana, and John Henry Douglas in Glen's Falls, New York, in 1878; Isom P. Wooton in Des Moines and Jacob Baker in Selma, Ohio, in 1880; and Dougan Clark, Jr., in Cleveland in 1882.[132]

The revision of the *Discipline* adopted by Indiana Yearly Meeting in 1878 eliminated the query against a hireling ministry.[133] Some notable Quaker moderates in Indiana opposed the trend toward a pastoral system: Timothy Nicholson, Charles Coffin, Barnabas Hobbs. They lost. When Indiana Yearly Meeting approved the pastoral system in 1897, it was simply recognizing what already existed. The system was no panacea. Quakers had no ready source of trained pastors and no tradition of supporting a clergy.

> As late as 1907, less than a third of the meetings in Indiana Yearly Meeting had full-time pastors. Old members of one small, rural meeting in Indiana remember how they felt compelled to have regular preaching but could pay almost nothing. Often they simply opened their pulpit to anyone willing to fill it, subjecting themselves to a procession of cranks. There were few criteria, educational or otherwise, for recording ministers besides a "call," and harried yearly meetings often recommended untested and unsuitable fledgling preachers for pastorates.[134]

Resistance to Holiness Revival Program

Eventually some weighty Quakers resisted the holiness revival program. Indiana Friends like Allen Jay, Charles F. Coffin, Timothy Nicholson, and Barnabas C. Hobbs were advocates of heartfelt religion. Yet they had reservations about the level of emotionalism which had developed in Quaker revivals and especially about the emphasis given to promoting instantaneous sanctification as a second and separate experience. They felt that holiness teaching and holiness preachers were impatient to have this doctrine crowd out everything else. Hobbs included quotations from Quaker scholars in his *Earlham Lectures* published

by Nicholson at Richmond in 1885. One quotation said that the expression "entire sanctification" was not scriptural. Another said that the Spirit of Christ leads believers into all truth "yet not all at once, but as we poor, low, weak mortals are made able to bear, from one degree of convincement, illumination, sanctification, understanding, experience, and knowledge, to another . . . in order to be fitted for a far greater glory, and full establishment in a more excellent world to come." Another stressed the kind of spiritual discipline by which the seeker gradually advances from one degree of grace to another. The moderate critics found support and reinforcement in the *Friends Review* published in Philadelphia.[135]

The sharpest confrontation came less about holiness revivals than about baptism and the Lord's Supper. Quakers traditionally called these "ordinances" rather than "sacraments" and did not observe them. Timothy Nicholson explained it to a Methodist:

> I then proceeded to show in a few words that water baptism was not a Christian but a Jewish ordinance: "John said, I indeed baptize with water but He shall baptize with the Holy Spirit. The first Christians were Jews and while Jerusalem remained they would continue the Jewish customs. Jesus did not baptize with water. Paul was one of the first to break away or give up Jewish ways, and he tells us he baptized only a few; that he was sent not to baptize but to preach the gospel. So with the Passover. It was Jewish and would be observed while Jerusalem remained, by Jewish Christians. What is called the Lord's Supper was merely the passover, so called by Christ himself. He knew they would continue at least for awhile to keep it; therefore He said, 'Do it in remembrance of me,' I am the real paschal lamb, not the lamb slain in Egypt. John, the most spiritual of the disciples, and who is supposed to have written after the destruction of Jerusalem, and who narrates in whole chapters what Jesus said and did at the last passover, says not a word about keeping this feast permanently. So Friends do not believe that Christ instituted any rite or ordinance to be continued by his followers, not even foot-washing; and that we have far more scripture to sustain our position than have those who contend for the keeping of the so-called ordinances."[136]

On the other hand, some of the leading Quaker revivalists claimed that these ordinances were symbols commanded by Christ. Therefore they said that Quaker preachers should be tolerated if they chose to advocate or practice them.

Luke Woodard, John Henry Douglas, Dougan Clark, and David B. Updegraff were among those who favored toleration. Clark and Updegraff were actually baptized, and Updegraff seemed ready to mount a campaign to bring the ordinances to the Quakers for their own good. Toleration of Quaker ministers advocating the ordinances was too much to ask. Luke Woodard lost his honorary position as head of New Garden Monthly Meeting. Updegraff was accustomed to making the rounds of Quaker yearly meetings with instant recognition and generous prerogatives. The yearly meeting at Richmond in 1879, with Charles F. Coffin and Timothy Nicholson in control, denied Updegraff's request to hold devotional meetings. In 1880 that meeting would not even receive his credentials. When he persisted he was rebuked and silenced.[137]

Timothy Nicholson and eleven other Friends began publishing the *Morning Star* at Indianapolis to combat Quaker adoption of the ordinances. Nicholson also published a pamphlet of seventy-two pages citing Quaker authorities against adoption of the ordinances. Indiana Yearly Meeting took a clear stand in opposition to the ordinances. One by one all the yearly meetings but Updegraff's Ohio took action against receiving any minister who had been baptized or who had partaken of the Lord's Supper.[138] Dougan Clark returned to the Earlham faculty after having been baptized in Ohio in the summer of 1894. President Mills and the college trustees did not wish to make a public issue of Clark's baptism. When no students applied for his courses, Clark simply resigned. Whitewater Quarterly Meeting advised other meetings not to receive him as a Quaker minister any longer.[139]

New head of Earlham's Biblical Department was Elbert Russell. He was selected as a safe but innocent Earlham graduate to succeed the controversial Dougan Clark. Soon he was a student of contemporary biblical theology, possessor of a University of Chicago doctorate, and full of ideas gained from modern biblical studies which he offered in periodicals and in sessions of Earlham Bible Institute each summer. At Chicago he committed himself "to the gospel of universal love as the essence of Christianity." He was for "overcoming and supplanting evil by the positive spiritual powers of truth, justice, good will, and brotherly cooperation and sharing for the common good." All this was not the theological vocabulary of the holiness revival stalwarts. Russell was not always conciliatory toward them. When Esther Frame preached her famous sermon on "Homecoming in Heaven" for Western Yearly Meeting he would not rise on invitation either with those who claimed to be sanctified or with those who wanted to go to heaven.[140]

There came what Russell saw as "the inevitable conflict between the older evangelical leaders and the newer liberalism." He counted John Henry Douglas, Luke Woodard, and the Frames among the "older evangelical leaders" and Woodard as the most dogmatic. Allen Jay was a leader of the revival movement but Russell said Jay was "tolerant in spirit" and that he "kept an open and progressive mind."[141] Holiness Friends continued to preach the necessity of a conversion experience, ideally followed by a subsequent experience of entire sanctification. They urged continuous revivals to promote these experiences and repudiated old Quaker notions of quietism and the Inner Light. Most of all they became defenders against liberalism, against the teaching of evolution, and especially against the claims of modern biblical studies. They developed their own schools such as Friends Bible Institute at Cleveland, Ohio, and Union Bible Institute at Westfield, Indiana. This Quaker constituency and their schools found natural fellowship with other Bible colleges, denominational and non-denominational, engaged in the same kind of defense of fundamentals.[142]

Leadership of Orthodox Quaker structure was eventually retained in the hands of a small but very influential body of the moderates who sought stability rather than holiness effervescence, a modicum of respect for older Quaker traditions, and a new level of cooperation among their kind who controlled most of the yearly meetings. The cooperation became impressive. Around the supper table at Timothy Nicholson's house in Richmond in 1886, leaders from six yearly meetings agreed that it was time to convene representatives from all the yearly meetings in a general conference. Barnabas C. Hobbs was present and enthusiastic in support. In 1887 representatives of all the Orthodox (Gurneyite) yearly meetings in America, augmented by delegations from London and Dublin, met at Richmond and were called to order by Nicholson.

One document the general conference produced and approved was called the Richmond Declaration of Faith. It was distinctly evangelical but did not please the holiness revivalists. Updegraff said it paid too little attention to practical soul-saving and was a dangerous creed. General conferences continued every five years thereafter. Eleven yearly meetings of Orthodox Quakers approved a Uniform Discipline and constitution. On this basis the general conference possessed delegated authority beginning in 1902 and was named the Five Years Meeting. It was an effective agency for cooperation, for example in the development of the American Friends' Service Committee during the First World War. What it could not restore or provide was unity, not to mention uniformity, in Quaker ranks.[143]

Quakers had entered Indiana in the early 1800s as a quiet, separated, and relatively uniform group in their faith and life. By the end of the 1800s they seemed bound to embody every variation of American Protestantism. There was a handful of conservatives (Wilburites) bent on preserving the old ways. There was a small liberal group (Hicksites) urging the priority of each person's experience of the Inner Light and heavily influenced by Unitarians or Universalists. Within the major Orthodox body there was a larger liberal constituency symbolized by Elbert Russell at Earlham and Rufus Jones at Haverford, open to modern biblical studies and social gospel motivations. Within the major Orthodox body there was also a portion of the membership linked to the years of Quaker revivals, prone to the vocabulary and concerns of revivalists. At a Friends meeting for worship one might find any Protestant practice except the observance of the sacraments. Concerns for peace and relief of suffering nearly always found expression. No theological wind could blow to which this fellowship would not be bared.[144]

According to the religious census of 1906, just over one-fourth of all American Quakers of any kind lived in Indiana. Indiana (with 29,255) had more than twice the number of Orthodox Quakers in Ohio (with 12,394) and more than three times the number in any other state. Hicksite Quaker membership in the state was small with 1,013 members in nine meetings and the conservative Wilburite membership was even smaller with 353 members in seven meetings. As the twentieth century progressed the number of Friends in Indiana declined. The national headquarters of the Friends United Meeting remained at Richmond. In 1990 this denomination reported 12,380 members (an estimated 15,489 adherents) in 112 congregations in Indiana. Thus they were somewhat larger in number than the Seventh-day Adventists but smaller than the Episcopalians. Earlham College continued to be a focus of the Quaker heritage and a location of valuable archives.

NOTES

1. Elbert Russell, *The History of Quakerism* (New York: Macmillan, 1942), 23.

2. Russell, *History*, 48–51.

3. Russell, *History*, 25–26. See also Hugh Barbour and J. William Frost, *The Quakers* (New York: Greenwood Press, 1988), 4, 40–46, 98–101.

4. Russell, *History*, 123.

5. Russell, *History*, 124–25.

6. Harlow Lindley, *The Quakers in the Old Northwest* (Cedar Rapids, Iowa: Torch Press, 1912?), 3–4.

7. Jack D. Marietta, *The Reformation of American Quakerism, 1748–1783* (Philadelphia: University of Pennsylvania Press, 1984), xi–xvi.

8. Luther M. Feeger, "Message of Pennsylvania and New Jersey to Indians of the Old Northwest," *Indiana Magazine of History* 59 (March 1963): 57.

9. *A Brief Account of the Proceedings of the Committee, Appointed by the Yearly Meeting of Friends, Held in Baltimore, for Promoting the Improvement and Civilization of the Indian Natives* (London: Phillips and Fardon, 1806), 31.

10. *Brief Account*, 38–39.

11. Joseph A. Parsons, "Civilizing the Indians of the Old Northwest," *Indiana Magazine of History* 56 (September 1960) 207–13; John S. Tyson, *Life of Elisha Tyson* (Baltimore, Md.: B. Lundy, 1925), 58–77; *Brief Account*, 9–43.

12. Bernhard Knollenberg, *Pioneer Sketches of the Upper Whitewater Valley: Quaker Stronghold of the West* (Indianapolis, Ind.: Indiana Historical Society, 1945), 18.

13. Russell, *History*, 246–49; Lindley, *Quakers*, 5–10.

14. Large families were common. Andrew Hoover's father "left eight sons and five daughters, all of whom had large families." His wife's father "left one son and seven daughters by his first wife and seven sons by a second wife." David Hoover, "Memoir of David Hoover," *Indiana Magazine of History* 2 (March 1906): 18; Knollenberg, *Pioneer Sketches*, 19.

15. Hoover, "Memoir," 19–20; Knollenberg, *Pioneer Sketches*, 20–21.

16. Mary Coffin Johnson, *Charles F. Coffin* (Richmond, Ind.: Nicholson Printing Company, 1923), 63.

17. Knollenberg, *Pioneer Sketches*, 19, 27, 29.

18. Hoover, "Memoir," 17–18.

19. Ethel Hittle McDaniel, *The Contribution of the Society of Friends to Education in Indiana* (Indianapolis, Ind.: Indiana Historical Society, 1939), 125; Knollenberg, *Pioneer Sketches*, 42–43, 53.

20. William Hobbs, *Autobiography of William Hobbs* (Indianapolis, Ind.: Indiana Quaker Records, 1962), 5.

21. Hobbs, *Autobiography*, 9.

22. Hobbs, *Autobiography*, 7–9, 11–16.

23. Hobbs, *Autobiography*, 18.

24. Hobbs, *Autobiography*, 18.

25. Hobbs, *Autobiography*, 22–23.

26. Elizabeth H. Emerson, "Barnabas C. Hobbs, Midwestern Quaker Minister and Educator," *Quaker History* 49 (Spring 1960): 21–35.

27. McDaniel, *Contributions*, 126–27. The general organizational hierarchy of Quaker meetings proceeded from monthly meeting to quarterly meeting to yearly meeting, each with special functions, higher authority, and larger jurisdiction. There was a system for appointing representatives, but any member present could take part in business meetings at any level. There was no authority in the Society higher than the yearly meeting. Indiana Yearly Meeting was by no means coterminous with the state boundaries. From 1821 to 1858 Indiana Yearly Meeting extended from the Scioto River in Ohio to the Pacific Ocean. In 1858 the Western Yearly Meeting was set off to include much of western Indiana along with the state of Illinois. Most of the leadership and

action of Indiana Yearly Meeting did center at Richmond in Indiana. Plainfield in Indiana became headquarters for Western Yearly Meeting. So references to either of these yearly meetings were likely to relate very significantly to Indiana.

28. McDaniel, *Contribution*, 126.

29. Opal Thornburg, *Whitewater: Indiana's First Monthly Meeting of Friends* (N.p., 1960?), 4; Knollenberg, *Pioneer Sketches*, 54.

30. Levi Coffin, *Reminiscences of Levi Coffin, the Reputed President of the Underground Railroad*, 3d ed. (Cincinnati, Ohio: Robert Clarke Company, 1898), 1, 5–6; Johnson, *Charles F. Coffin*, 51–52, 61, 63.

31. Elijah Coffin, *The Life of Elijah Coffin* (Cincinnati, Ohio?: E. Morgan and Sons, 1863), 286–87; Johnson, *Charles F. Coffin*, 61, 63–68.

32. Rhoda Mary Johnson Coffin, *Rhoda M. Coffin: Her Reminiscences, Addresses, Papers and Ancestry* (New York: Grafton Press, 1910), 62; Coffin, *Life*, 20–21, 299; Johnson, *Charles F. Coffin*, 71.

33. Coffin, *Life*, 107–8, 157–58, 160, 183–86, 189, 294–95; Johnson, *Charles F. Coffin*, 103, 129, 163, 175–76.

34. Thomas D. Hamm, *The Transformation of American Quakerism: Orthodox Friends, 1800–1907* (Bloomington, Ind.: Indiana University Press, 1988, 261 p.); Coffin, *Life*, 170, 301–2; Johnson, *Charles F. Coffin*, 62–63.

35. Walter C. Woodward, *Timothy Nicholson, Master Quaker* (Richmond, Ind.: Nicholson Press, 1927), 37–55, 64–69, 75, 77–78, 83–135; Johnson, *Charles F. Coffin*, 137–48; Coffin, *Rhoda M. Coffin*, 64–68, 91–99.

36. Woodward, *Timothy Nicholson*, 84.

37. Woodward, *Timothy Nicholson*, 68–69, 93–94, 101, 105, 200.

38. Allen Jay, *Autobiography of Allen Jay* (Philadelphia: John C. Winston, 1910), 46, 57–60, 67–74, 82–89, 92–93, 126–28, 321–402; Woodward, *Timothy Nicholson*, 227.

39. James Baldwin, *In My Youth* (Indianapolis, Ind.: Bobbs-Merrill, 1914), 91, 372; *Discipline of the Society of Friends of Indiana Yearly Meeting* (Cincinnati, Ohio: Mirror Press, 1835), 21; Johnson, *Charles F. Coffin*, 92.

40. Jay, *Autobiography*, 78–79, 82.

41. Jay, *Autobiography*, 38–40; Johnson, *Charles F. Coffin*, 107–9; Baldwin, *In My Youth*, 475–78.

42. *Semi-Centennial Anniversary, Western Yearly Meeting of Friends Church* (Plainfield, Ind.: Publishing Association of Friends, 1908), 106–7.

43. Joseph John Gurney, *A Journey to North America, Described in Familiar Letters to Amelia Opie* (Norwich, Eng.: J. Fletcher, 1841), 36–37.

44. John William Buys, "Quakers in Indiana in the Nineteenth Century" (Ph.D. diss., University of Florida, 1973), 17–31.

45. *Discipline of the Society of Friends of Indiana Yearly Meeting* (Cincinnati, Ohio: Mirror Press, 1835), 61–62.

46. Luke Woodard, *Sketches of a Life of 75* (Richmond, Ind.: Nicholson Printing, 1907), 216–17; Jay, *Autobiography*, 44, 126–27.

47. William Williams, *Journals* (Cincinnati, Ohio: Lodge, L'Hommedieu, and Hammond, 1828), 198; Coffin, *Life*, 289–90; Johnson, *Charles F. Coffin*, 93; Jay, *Autobiography*, 25; Hamm, *Transformation*, 49.

48. Knollenberg, *Pioneer Sketches*, 59; Hamm, *Transformaion*, 16.

49. Robert W. Doherty, *The Hicksite Separation: A Sociological Analysis of Religious Schism in Early Nineteenth Century America* (New Brunswick, N.J.: Rutgers University Press, 1967, 157 p.); Hamm, *Transformation*, 16.

50. Hamm, *Transformation*, 18.

51. H. Larry Ingle, *Quakers in Conflict: The Hicksite Reformation* (Knoxville, Tenn.: University of Tennessee Press, 1986), 229–31, 242; Seth E. Furnas, Sr., *A History of Indiana Yearly Meeting* [Hicksite] (N.p.: Indiana Yearly Meeting, Religious Society of Friends, General Conference, 1968), 34–98; Buys, "Quakers," 38.

52. Thomas D. Hamm, "Indiana Quakers and Politics, 1810–1865" (Paper presented at the meeting of the Indiana Association of Historians, 14 March 1987), 6; Ingle, *Quakers*, 242; Knollenberg, *Pioneer Sketches*, 30; Hamm, *Transformation*, 18–19, 51; Hobbs, *Autobiography*, 13–16.

53. Hamm, *Transformation*, 20–21.

54. Johnson, *Charles F. Coffin*, 101.

55. Luke Woodard, *A Historical Sketch of the Schism in the Friends Church in the Years 1827–1828 Known as the Hicksite Separation* (Plainfield, Ind.: Caller Publishing Company, 1912), 4, 14–19.

56. Hamm, "Indiana Quakers," 10.

57. Charles Osborn, "Henry Clay at Richmond," *Indiana Magazine of History* 4 (September 1908): 117–28; Hamm, "Indiana Quakers," 13–15; Buys, "Quakers," 115–16.

58. Walter Edgerton, *A History of the Separation in Indiana Yearly Meeting of Friends* (Cincinnati, Ohio: Achilles Pugh, 1856), 48–58, 61–62, 73–92; George W. Julian, *The Rank of Charles Osborn as an Anti-slavery Pioneer* (Indianapolis, Ind.: Bowen Merrill, 1891), 262, 264; Charles Osborn, *Journal* (Cincinnati, Ohio: Achilles Pugh, 1854), 419; Jay, *Autobiography*, 104–9; Russell, *History*, 366–68; Hamm, "Indiana Quakers," 14, 17–20.

59. Jacquelyn S. Nelson, *Indiana Quakers Confront the Civil War* (Indianapolis, Ind.: Indiana Historical Society, 1991, 303 p.); Jay, *Autobiography*, 95–97; Johnson, *Charles F. Coffin*, 119–23; Woodward, *Timothy Nicholson*, 73–77; Hamm, "Indiana Quakers," 20–21.

60. Julian, *Rank*, 234–36, 248. Julian makes much of the priority of Osborn among abolitionists in the nation since he "proclaimed the doctrine of immediate and unconditional emancipation when William Lloyd Garrison was only nine years old" and "edited and published one of the first anti-slavery newspapers in the United States."

61. Julian, *Rank*, 243–63; Edgerton, *History*, 33–39; Coffin, *Reminiscences*, 223–47; Buys, "Quakers," 131–33.

62. Edgerton, *History*, iv.

63. Edgerton, *History*, 129–49, 324–52.

64. Ruth Nuermberger, *The Free Produce Movement* (Durham, N.C.: Duke University Press, 1942), 33; Coffin, *Life*, 300; Johnson, *Charles F. Coffin*, 104–7.

65. Hamm, *Transformation*, 33.

66. Walter Edgerton, *Modern Quakerism Examined and Contrasted with That of the Ancient Type* (Indianapolis, Ind.: Printing and Publishing House, 1876, 31 p.).

67. The increasing appeal of the contemporary culture to Hoosier Friends is sensitively shown in Baldwin, *In My Youth*, 379–410. See also Coffin, *Rhoda M. Coffin*, 35, 49–50, and Hamm, *Transformation*, 52.

68. Knollenberg, *Pioneer Sketches*, 137–38.

69. McDaniel, *Contribution*, 221; Johnson, *Charles F. Coffin*, 94–95; Knollenberg, *Pioneer Sketches*, 126.

70. Buys, "Quakers," 52–53.

71. McDaniel, *Contribution*, 212.

72. Buys, "Quakers," 76–79, 92, 101–10, 157–58, 197–99.

73. McDaniel, *Contribution*, 176–77.

74. Quaker academies, seminaries, and high schools are listed and described in McDaniel, *Contribution*, 191–209. See also McDaniel, *Contribution*, 174–75, 212–20 and Coffin, *Rhoda M. Coffin*, 20, 39.

75. Opal Thornburg, *Earlham: The Story of the College 1847–1962* (Richmond, Ind.: Earlham College Press, 1963), 31; Johnson, *Charles F. Coffin*, 79–83, 94–95; Coffin, *Rhoda M. Coffin*, 43–45; Jay, *Autobiography*, 327–31; Coffin, *Life*, 292–93.

76. Thornburg, *Earlham*, 47–48.

77. Thornburg, *Earlham*, 28–79; Jay, *Autobiography*, 326–37; Woodward, *Timothy Nicholson*, 166–73.

78. Baldwin, *In My Youth*, 379–84; Johnson, *Charles F. Coffin*, 97; Hamm, *Transformation*, 39.

79. Coffin, *Rhoda M. Coffin*, 79–80.

80. Johnson, *Charles F. Coffin*, 89–90.

81. Woodard, *Sketches*, 16.

82. Jay, *Autobiography*, 46.

83. Jay, *Autobiography*, 83.

84. Jay, *Autobiography*, 79–81, 83, 86.

85. Jay, *Autobiography*, 110.

86. Johnson, *Charles F. Coffin*, 116.

87. Johnson, *Charles F. Coffin*, 115–17; Coffin, *Life*, 217; Coffin, *Rhoda M. Coffin*, 81; Hamm, *Transformation*, 61.

88. Coffin, *Rhoda M. Coffin*, 82–83.

89. The Coffins were important and symbolic persons in the renewal. They were by no means alone. For names of other renewal leaders see Hamm, *Transformation*, 42–48; Johnson, *Charles F. Coffin*, 116–17.

90. Jay, *Autobiography*, 110; Hamm, *Transformation*, 63–66, 75–76; Woodard, *Sketches*, 23–25.

91. Woodward, *Timothy Nicholson*, 183–84; Hamm, *Transformation*, 72.

92. Coffin, *Rhoda M. Coffin*, 85–87.

93. Johnson, *Charles F. Coffin*, 133–35.

94. Alice Almond Shrock and Randall Shrock, "Private Duty and Public Responsibility: Richmond's Home for Friendless Women, 1867–1972" (Paper presented at the meeting of the Indiana Association of Historians, 14 March 1987, 18 p.); Coffin, *Rhoda M. Coffin*, 144–45.

95. Coffin, *Rhoda M. Coffin*, 134–38; for names of other leaders in this school see p. 138.

96. Coffin, *Rhoda M. Coffin*, 134.

97. These are examples of Quakers in what Thomas D. Hamm has called "The Renewal Movement"; see pages 36–73 in his *Transformation of American Quakerism*, including his fuller list of renewal leaders on pages 43–45.

98. Nathan T. Frame, *Reminiscences of Nathan T. Frame and Esther G. Frame* (Cleveland, Ohio: Briton Printing, 1907), 14–15, 57–60, 64, 82–84.

99. Frame, *Reminiscences*, 28–29.

100. Frame, *Reminiscences*, 39–53.

101. Frame, *Reminiscences*, 68.

102. Coffin, *Rhoda M. Coffin*, 87; Frame, *Reminiscences*, 75–81.

103. Frame, *Reminiscences*, 134, 380–81, 411–12, 441, 445–47, 456, 485–86, 495–96, 524.

104. Woodard, *Sketches*, 6.

105. Woodard, *Sketches*, 12, 21; Johnson, *Charles F. Coffin*, 115–16.

106. Woodard, *Sketches*, 19–34, 64–76, 94; Hamm, *Transformation*, 88–90.

107. Walter Robson, *An English View of American Quakerism: The Journal of Walter Robson 1877* (Philadelphia: American Philosophical Society, 1970), 94; Woodard, *Sketches*, 72–73; Hamm, *Transformation*, 84.

108. J. Brent Bill, *David B. Updegraff: Quaker Holiness Preacher* (Richmond, Ind.: Friends United Press, 1983), 16–17.

109. Woodard, *Sketches*, 30, 65.

110. Woodard, *Sketches*, 9–11.

111. Hamm, *Transformation*, 83.

112. Hamm, *Transformation*, 82.

113. Dougan Clark, *Instructions to Christian Converts* (Chicago: Fleming H. Revell, 1889), 79–80.

114. Elbert Russell, *Elbert Russell: Quaker* (Jackson, Tenn.: Friendly Press, 1956), 56, 80; Russell, *History*, 505; Thornburg, *Earlham*, 196–97; Hamm, *Transformation*, 160–61.

115. Frame, *Reminiscences*, 44, 444, 467, 477.

116. Hamm, *Transformation*, 87, 101–3, 144–45, 161; *Encyclopedia of Religion in the South*, ed. Samuel S. Hill (Macon, Ga.: Mercer University Press, 1984), 782, 825.

117. Hamm, *Transformation*, 100.

118. Hamm, *Transformation*, 84.

119. Walter Edgerton, *Modern Quakerism Examined and Contrasted with That of the Ancient Type* (Indianapolis, Ind.: Printing and Publishing House, 1876, 31 p.); Walter Edgerton, *Walter Edgerton's Disownment by Spiceland Monthly Meeting* (N.p., 1877); Hamm, *Transformation*, 93–94.

120. Willard Heiss, *A Brief History of Western Yearly Meeting of Conservative Friends and the Separation of 1877* (Indianapolis, Ind.: John Woolman Press, 1963), 3–6; Robson, *English View*, 69; Hamm, *Transformation*, 90–91; Russell, *History*, 430.

121. Hamm, *Transformation*, 103–4.

122. Hamm, *Transformation*, 110.

123. Hamm, *Transformation*, 90.

124. Robson, *English View*, 68–75.

125. Robson, *English View*, 89.

126. Robson, *English View*, 81, 90; Gregory S. Rose, "Quakers, North Carolinians, and Blacks in Indiana's Settlement Pattern," *Journal of Cultural Geography* 7 (Fall/Winter 1986): 35–48.

127. Robson, *English View*, 90.

128. Robson, *English View*, 76, 78, 88.

129. Russell, *Elbert Russell*, 45.

130. Woodard, *Sketches*, 41, 123. Most biographical studies of nineteenth century Quakers in Indiana include an account of their conversion, e.g., Hobbs, *Autobiography*, 3–5; Coffin, *Life*, 15, 304; Jay, *Autobiography*, 23–24, 100–1; Johnson, *Charles F. Coffin*, 102; Coffin, *Rhoda M. Coffin*, 15.

131. Hamm, *Transformation*, 125; Buys, "Quakers," 281–83; Thornburg, *Whitewater*, 11.

132. Hamm, *Transformation*, 127.

133. Thornburg, *Whitewater*, 11; Russell, *History*, 484; Johnson, *Charles F. Coffin*, 176–77.

134. Hamm, *Transformation*, 129.

135. Barnabas C. Hobbs, *Earlham Lectures* (Richmond, Ind.: Nicholson and Bro., 1885), 90, 91, 105; Hamm, *Transformation*, 111–20.

136. Woodward, *Timothy Nicholson*, 180–81.

137. Hamm, *Transformation*, 131–32; Buys, "Quakers," 288.

138. Woodward, *Timothy Nicholson*, 187–88; Hamm, *Transformation*, 132.

139. Thornburg, *Earlham*, 197–98; Russell, *Elbert Russell*, 80.

140. Russell, *Elbert Russell*, 82, 85–114, 125; Russell, *History*, 508–9.

141. Russell, *Elbert Russell*, 101.

142. Hamm, *Transformation*, 161; Russell, *History*, 507, 540.

143. Woodward, *Timothy Nicholson*, 189–94, 197–98; Hamm, *Transformation*, 138; Russell, *History*, 517.

144. Hamm, *Transformation*, 172–73.

BRETHREN (DUNKERS)

Alexander Mack was a citizen of Schriesheim near Heidelberg, and so a member of the Reformed church there. His conviction was that saving faith must involve a much more thorough awakening and conversion than that state church required or provided. He and some scattered associates dropped out of regular state church activities among Lutherans and Reformed and moved to Schwarzenau in Wittgenstein, temporarily a more tolerant place.

> In the year 1708, eight persons consented together to enter a covenant of a good conscience with God, to take up all the commandments of Jesus Christ as an easy yoke, and thus to follow the Lord Jesus, their good and faithful shepherd, in joy and sorrow, as his true sheep, even unto a blessed end. These eight persons were as follows, namely, five brethren and three sisters. The five brethren were George Grebi, from Hesse-Cassel, the first; Lucas Vetter, likewise from Hessia, the second; the third was Alexander Mack, from the Palatinate of Schriesheim, between Mannheim and Heidelberg; the fourth was Andrew Bony, of Basle, in Switzerland; the fifth, John Kipping, from Bareit, in Würtemberg. The three sisters were, Joanna Noethiger, or Bony, the first; Anna Margaretha Mack, the second; and Joanna Kipping, the third. These eight persons covenanted and united together as brethren and sisters into the covenant of the cross of Jesus Christ to form a church of Christian believers. And when they had found, in authentic histories, that the primitive Christians, in the first and second centuries, uniformly, according to the command of Christ, were planted into the death of Jesus Christ by a threefold immersion into

> the water-bath of holy baptism, they examined diligently the New Testament, and finding all perfectly harmonizing therewith, they were anxiously desirous to use the means appointed and practiced by Christ himself, and thus according to his own salutary counsel, go forward to the fulfillment of all righteousness.[1]

In summer of 1708 these five men and three women participated in baptism in the Eder River, one unnamed brother baptizing Mack and Mack then baptizing his baptizer and the others. So began the Brethren movement, its members sometimes called Dunkers, Tunkers, or Dunkards because of their style of baptism by immersion. They were missionary from the start, gathering followers in Switzerland and the Palatinate and elsewhere.

To their European neighbors these Brethren resembled some other small groups of Reformed and Lutheran people later called "radical pietists" who were seeking a more mystical and heartfelt religion in their conventicles outside but alongside the state churches. Brethren also resembled the Mennonites, descendants of sixteenth century Anabaptists who separated entirely from state churches and formed free congregations by baptizing adult believers committed to their understanding of a New Testament model. Alexander Mack and his fellow believers had early contacts and close connections with both the radical pietists and the Mennonites. Neither was quite right to satisfy the yearning of the Brethren for a pattern which would follow Christ fully. Some radical pietists would not risk a sharp separation which might destroy the stability of the established churches; some Anabaptists did not require baptism by immersion. The Brethren insisted on both. Life was precarious for all dissenters. They were under persistent pressure to conform to the official church of their territory or to flee.[2]

The Brethren moved to America. Peter Becker led the first group of twenty families from Krefeld to Pennsylvania in 1719; they settled at Germantown. Alexander Mack led a second migration of thirty families to Pennsylvania, after a stay in the Low Countries, in 1729. A third migration was led by John Naas in 1733. By 1740 most of the baptized membership, perhaps a total of 250, had moved to America. No identifiable remnant of the fellowship persisted in Europe. The Germantown group began holding regular meetings in fall of 1722. When some attending asked to be baptized, Peter Becker was chosen their first minister in America. He was leader for the baptism and love feast held on 25 December 1723.[3]

Lively missionary activity followed. One new convert, J. Conrad Beissel, led off a large group of the membership to form a rival communal society of Seventh Day German Baptists called Ephrata. Nevertheless the Brethren multiplied and expanded into the new land. A census by Baptist historian Morgan Edwards in 1770 listed forty-two ministers and over 1,500 baptized Brethren; Edwards thought there must be five times that number of persons related to the Brethren. Their search for land had taken their congregations to Maryland, Virginia, and the Carolinas. They were also quick to move west with the frontier after the American Revolution. Dunker families were in Kentucky before 1790. Ohio received Brethren settlers before 1800 and soon had a concentration of Brethren congregations west and north of Dayton in Montgomery and adjoining counties.[4]

Brethren Life and Practice

It was the intention of the Brethren to be followers of Jesus, to conform their faith and lives to the admonitions and example of the New Testament while taking particular care not to drift carelessly with the ways of the world. Given the opportunity of freedom in a new land, they kept working out the implications of their intention, a process of identity and consolidation occupying a couple of centuries. To their American neighbors the early Brethren looked in some ways like Quakers: plain speech, plain dress, no oaths, no military service, no professional clergy, close knit fellowship with their own kind, exclusion or avoidance of violators of group discipline, direction by an annual meeting which gave official re-

sponse year by year to carefully formulated queries. However, the Quakers were generally dissenters from Great Britain, very resistant to use of sacraments which they called "ordinances." The Brethren, on the other hand, were generally dissenters from German-speaking Europe. Brethren had stout convictions about the biblical mandate for their ordinances and a particular affection for them besides.

Correct ordinances among the Brethren included baptism by immersion three times face forward (trine immersion) immediately followed by the laying on of hands in confirmation. The early baptisms were generally performed in an outdoor body of water; George L. Studebaker reported from Mississinewa in Indiana in 1885 that two were made willing to follow Jesus so "the ice was cut and they were baptized."[5] The "love feast" was the high point of Brethren liturgical and sacramental life, a time of deep emotional satisfaction to the believers. Celebration of a love feast included (1) general sharing of hospitality with a wide representation of members and visitors; (2) preparation to insure that all participants in the supper were in peace and unity; (3) footwashing after the example of Jesus recorded in John 13; (4) the Lord's supper eaten as a shared meal—usually meat, soup, and bread; (5) the holy communion or eucharist with bread and cup after the supper. Generally baptism, footwashing, and ordination of elders included exchange of the holy kiss, brother to brother and sister to sister. The sick might be anointed on request as indicated in James 5:14–16.[6]

The regular Annual Meeting of the Brethren dated back to a visit by the Moravian protector and leader Count Nikolaus Ludwig von Zinzendorf. He came to America in 1742 with a plan to unite all the German denominations. Zinzendorf's plan was not agreed to by the Brethren but they convened a meeting to discuss the proposition. This meeting formalized their previously less-structured practice of mutual consultation and visitation and proved so useful that they continued the sessions each year. The Annual Meeting was soon the final authority for the whole body of Brethren in matters of procedure and discipline. Given the zeal of the Brethren to follow Jesus and to conform to ancient church usage while resisting the incursions of the world, there was constant need for decisions by the Annual Meeting concerning particular instances or practices.

> Brethren church government was never strictly congregational. All important church actions required the presence and assistance of representatives of the larger brotherhood . . . Congregations were organized under the guidance of visiting elders, ministers were called to

office in their presence, and serious matters of church discipline were decided with their aid. When the counsel of these "adjoining elders" could not settle an issue, it was taken to the highest level, the Annual Meeting. Such questions, called queries after Quaker practice, were carefully noted and answered. These decisions were circulated in writing to all congregations for the guidance of members. After 1837 minutes were printed in German and English for greater ease in distribution.[7]

In 1856 districts were sanctioned "for the purpose of meeting jointly at least once a year, settling difficulties etc." thus lessening the load of business on the Annual Meeting. If a complaint involving a congregation could not be resolved locally or by counsel with elders from neighboring congregations, a visitation committee from the district or annual meeting might be necessary. Unrepentant violators could be "put in avoidance."[8]

Issues among Brethren were not often about doctrines of God, Christ, Holy Spirit, or the nature of the church. Nor were they often about such primary Brethren distinctives as trine immersion or the basic components of the love feast. On these matters there was considerable unity and a continuing fellowship even through division. The focus for dissent and decision was more often on the line to be drawn between Brethren practice and worldly practice. Could a member of the fellowship manufacture whiskey, keep slaves, accept interest on loans, go to war or pay for a substitute if drafted, take part in militia muster, take an oath, vote, go before a civil court, serve on a jury, hold public office, receive public poor relief, remarry if divorced, wear a mustache without a beard or trim the beard in a worldly fashion, join a lodge, use tobacco, invite an outsider to speak in a Brethren church, escape debt by declaring bankruptcy, buy insurance, own musical instruments, or wear jewelry? All these were forbidden by the Annual Meeting at some time. Practice was always evolving. Calls for official guidance were many and varied.

It is probably sufficient to point out some of the things that came up in Annual Meeting that were more or less seriously opposed. Gambling, music schools, carpet in houses, college education, preaching by women, attending a theatre, acting as auctioneer at a sale, taking out patent rights, attending revivals or camp meetings, using the benediction at the close of worship, having pictures taken, paying attention to phrenology and mesmerism, buying bank stock or other stock, use of lightning rods, holding prayer meetings, attending spiritual "rappings" (seances), working on public works, attending county fairs, self-defense with deadly weapon, erecting large tombstones, taking public collections, use of sleigh bells, use of pen names, receiving of wedding fees by a minister, establishment of colleges or academies, discounting notes, use of church bells, use of flowered wall paper, paying of ministers, use of fashionable "burial cases" and hearses, attending Centennial or World's Fair, a trained ministry, having birthday dinners or feasts, going to skating rinks, attending woodchopping or quilting parties with their evening play, joining labor unions, offering reward for stolen goods, use of term "Reverend," taking part in debating school or lyceums, having "exhibition" at close of school term, use of hymn books with notes for public worship, joining farmers' clubs, building baptistry in church, having musical instrument in church, attending soldiers' reunion, playing cards, checkers or other games, use of magic lanterns in churches or colleges, wearing of neckties, borrowing of money for use in trading. All of these were at some time since 1778 opposed to some extent by decisions of Annual Meeting. Many of them were absolutely banned.[9]

Patterns of Brethren Settlement in Indiana

Indiana received its initial stream of Brethren settlers from North Carolina and Kentucky. There was preaching at Olive Branch in Clark County as early as 1803; congregations with southern roots established Lost River congregation in Orange County in 1819 and White River church in Lawrence County about 1821. There was a Bethel church in Harrison County. Before 1825 there were Brethren settlements of southern background in Jackson, Washington, Monroe, and possibly Dubois counties. The communication of these southern Brethren with the Annual Meeting of the Brethren back east was not very good and what communication there was caused uneasiness. One Indiana group, following Kentucky ministers Adam Hostetler and Peter Hon, were evidently ignoring traditional Brethren practices while being influenced by frontier revivalism. Hostetler and Hon were expelled from the church sometime between 1816 and 1820 and formed an independent Brethren fellowship which included the southern Indiana congregations. But the new association was soon in controversy because Peter Hon and Abraham Kern of Lawrence County persuaded most of the churches to baptize by immersion once backward like Baptists rather than three times face forward like Brethren.

In 1827 John Wright of Washington County, leader of a small group of independent Baptist churches, suggested a merger between his group and the Dunkers. By then young Joseph Hostetler of Orange County was an influential preacher in the independent Brethren group and a reader of the *Christian Baptist* published by Alexander

Campbell. The Blue River Baptists of the Wrights and the independent Brethren association agreed to form one organization and called themselves Christians. The New Lights in the area, led by Beverly Vawter, were also brought into the negotiations. By a series of stages and negotiations nearly all of these Indiana congregations became part of the "Restoration" movement led by Alexander Campbell. As many as 2,400 Brethren in as many as fifteen Ohio Valley congregations thus changed their identity and were lost from the Brethren tradition.[10]

Southern Indiana was to remain largely devoid of Brethren. When the Southern Indiana District of the Brethren was established in 1868 it included nearly two-thirds of the state. However its churches were actually in central Indiana. The thirty-two most southern counties in Indiana remained a Dunker mission field. Not one county seat in those counties had a Brethren church as late as 1917 and there were only three small Brethren churches in the thirty-two counties. Central and northern Indiana received the larger Brethren immigration from the East, typically from Ohio and especially from the Miami Valley area of Ohio. The Brethren were farmers. Central and northern Indiana offered excellent land at low prices.[11]

Some of those arriving already had experience as leaders of Brethren congregations.

> Selection by lot ceased early in Brethren history. In earliest times, ministers were chosen by consensus. As membership grew, an election procedure evolved in which the congregation met in the presence of two visiting or adjoining elders who, after prayer, took the spoken votes. All members were permitted to vote for candidates of unusual promise for ministry; nominations were not permitted. The individual given the most votes was received as a minister with the hand clasp and the holy kiss. This procedure applied to choosing ministers and deacons; elevation to the eldership was by common consent of the membership.[12]

The office of elder was the third or highest degree of ministry among Brethren. When a congregation had two or more elders, one was usually called the presiding elder or elder-in-charge. Such elders attended to the whole range of ministerial needs of the congregation but also linked the congregation with the wider brotherhood. In the early days they received no pay or reimbursement of costs for their service at home or abroad. Yet they traveled frequently and widely. They provided the substance of the structures for both annual and district meetings and they felt an obligation to do missionary service.[13]

When Elder Jacob Miller of the Bear Creek congregation in Ohio heard that fourteen Brethren from Pennsylvania and Virginia had settled near Four Mile Creek in Union County, Indiana, he began visiting and preaching there. In 1809 he and Elder John Hart organized the Four Mile Church, first Brethren congregation in the state. From the congregation John Moyer and Daniel Miller were chosen for the ministry; Christopher Witter and Joseph Kingery were chosen to be deacons. The church grew rapidly both by immigration and conversions and by 1813 there were Lower Four Mile and Upper Four Mile congregations. Both kept selecting ministers from their membership. Some of these ministers moved with the bands of Brethren locating in Hamilton, Howard, Miami, St. Joseph, Wabash, and Wayne counties and built up congregations among them. That is the way Indiana's second congregation of Brethren was founded on Nettle Creek in Wayne County. Ministers from Four Mile congregation began preaching there and gathered a nucleus of members west of the later site of Hagerstown. The Nettle Creek Church was organized in 1820 with Elder David Miller from Ohio in charge. Public services related to Nettle Creek were soon being held up and down the creeks and rivers of the region where Cambridge City and Hagerstown would later stand.[14]

North-central Indiana was to become the chief concentration point for Indiana's Brethren. Elder Daniel Cripe was reputed to have been the first white settler to plow a furrow on Elkhart Prairie where Goshen would later stand, and to have contributed his only lamb for the first love feast in the region. Elkhart congregation was gathered about 1830. Brethren ministers David Miller and Aaron Miller settled in St. Joseph County just northwest of the future site of South Bend. They and their families were a basis for Portage Prairie Church. Other ministers were elected as the congregations grew and multiplied. Elders James Tracy and Jacob Berkey were northern Indiana experts at church extension. Between 11 December 1835 and 7 February 1839 thirty-five German Baptists arranged to purchase more than 10,000 acres of land in the area northwest of the future site of North Manchester. Their tracts ranged in size from 40 to 1,760 acres. These Brethren were the basis of Eel River congregation.[15] Otho Winger has named Indiana's "main mother churches" for the Brethren.

> Four Mile in Union and Wayne Counties, 1809; Nettle Creek, in Wayne and Henry Counties, 1820; Raccoon, now Ladoga, 1826, in Montgomery and Putnam; North Fork, now Pyrmont, 1829, in Carroll, Clinton and Tippecanoe; Bachelor Run, 1830, in Carroll, Howard, Cass and White; Elkhart, now West Goshen, 1830, in Elkhart; Portage, 1831, in St. Joseph; Mexico, 1838, in

Miami, Fulton and Wabash; Eel River and Manchester, 1838, in Wabash and Kosciusko; Turkey Creek, 1838, in Elkhart and Kosciusko; Mississinewa, 1841, in Delaware; Salimony, in 1845, in Huntington and Wells; South Bend, 1846, in St. Joseph and Elkhart; Yellow River, 1848, in Marshall and Kosciusko; Somerset, 1848, in Wabash, Miami and Grant; Rock Run, 1850, in Elkhart and Lagrange; Clear Creek and Sugar Creek, 1850, in Huntington and Whitley; Stony Creek, 1850, in Hamilton and Madison; Blue River, 1852, in Noble and Whitley; Cedar Creek, 1853, in Allen, Noble and Dekalb; Pine Creek, 1854, in St. Joseph and Marshall; White, 1858, in Montgomery, Clinton and Tippecanoe; Walnut Level, 1867, in Wells, Adams and Jay.[16]

The national religious census of 1850 did not display the true strength of the Brethren in Indiana. That census recorded the number of church buildings and seatings reported by each denomination. Brethren congregations had not hurried to produce church buildings. While Indiana's Methodists were reporting 778 buildings, the Baptists 428, the Presbyterians 282, and the Christians 187, the Brethren reported only 5. These Brethren were farmers and they simply held their services in their houses, barns, and groves. Four Mile and North Fork (Pyrmont) churches did that for more than thirty years, and Nettle Creek for more than twenty years, before building the first Brethren meetinghouses in Indiana.[17]

> People would come for miles to attend these services; either afoot, or on horseback or in a two horsed wagon. In the latter case the company usually consisted of the entire family and such neighbors, who had no conveyance of their own. Thus a missionary spirit was started which in recent years has grown to much greater proportions. Arrived at the place of meeting, the services would be opened by singing and prayer; then some brother would preach, and after preaching, other ministers, if present and sometimes deacons, who always sat on a bench, either immediately before or behind the preachers, would exhort. Services would then be closed with singing and prayer; after which dinner was served at the expense of the brother at whose house the meeting was held, and several hours were spent in social intercourse before returning home . . . In like manner were the lovefeasts held; the barn of some brother who lived near the center of the district, was usually chosen for this purpose. Some brother who could afford it, considering it a privilege to give a young beef for this purpose. The sisters furnished the bread; none but the best was thought fit for this service.[18]

When Elder "Uncle John" Metzger built his own home in Clinton County he made it 25 feet by 40 feet plus porches and designed it especially as a gathering place for the Brethren. Even when a central church building was finally constructed, half of the Sunday services might be held at outlying points for the convenience of families living at a distance.[19]

Raccoon congregation (later Ladoga) in Montgomery and Putnam counties was formed about 1826 among immigrants from Ohio who settled on Big Raccoon Creek. Elders William Smith from Ohio and Daniel Miller from Four Mile Church gave it early leadership. Twenty-two years after establishment the congregation built its first meetinghouse and called it Cool Spring. Raccoon was the congregational base for Robert Henry Miller, Indiana's best known nineteenth century leader of the Brethren.[20]

Robert Henry Miller

Robert Henry Miller was born in Kentucky in 1825. He moved to Montgomery County, Indiana, with his parents at about age seven. The family settled near the later site of Ladoga. Miller was studious, attending log schoolhouses as available and enrolling in Waveland Presbyterian Academy for a time. At home he read some law and earned amateur status locally as a debater and speechmaker. In religion he was influenced by his father who was "a strong Baptist." He became greatly interested in a Methodist camp meeting at Waveland at age nineteen but did not join the Methodists partly out of respect for his father. He also discussed religion with the Universalists. Then in 1846 he married Sarah C. Harshbarger, daughter of a deacon in the Brethren congregation. He became increasingly interested in Brethren doctrines. He and his wife were baptized in spring of 1858. In August of the same year he was elected to the ministry by unanimous vote of Raccoon Church. Soon he was elder-in-charge at Raccoon and in demand as a preacher far beyond the local congregation. Annual Meeting came to Nettle Creek in Indiana in 1863 and Miller became visible on the national scene.

Not one of the Brethren to be absorbed by Campbellites, Miller debated them in Putnam County (1861), in Howard County (1869), in Hamilton County (1872), in Wabash County (1875), and in Miami County (1876). He debated a Methodist in Virginia and two Campbellites in Missouri, the last of these debates published and widely circulated.[21] James Quinter had represented the Brethren in six debates between 1866 and 1869; his published debate on baptism with a Lutheran in Carroll County, Indiana, could be had for a dollar a copy in 1868.[22] Quinter was glad to acknowledge a new champion and allow Miller to be recognized as the brotherhood's greatest debater. In 1876 Miller consolidated the arguments from his debates in *The Doctrine of the Brethren Defended; or, the Faith and Practice of the Brethren Proven by the Gospel to Be True*.[23] Its introduction said: "We offer this volume to the public as a defense of the faith and practice of our church on the subjects we have here discussed. As we believe it is due to our church and to the reader that the reasons for our faith should be plainly given, we have attempted to do so, giving our views on a number of the main points of doctrine and practice in which we differ from some of the popular churches of our age."[24] It remained for decades the primary piece of Brethren apologetic. At the same time Miller was prominent in denominational affairs.

> He served on the Standing Committee twelve times . . . He was a member of most of the important committees appointed by Conference [Annual Meeting]. Few men were sent on more committees to churches than he. He was very resourceful in meeting a trying situation. He had the happy faculty of stating a proposition in such a way that it would give the least possible offense. He would frequently suggest compromises by which all contending parties could be satisfied. No difference how great the excitement or provocation, he always kept cool.[25]

It was not an easy time to give such heavy commitment to itinerant ministry among Brethren. The districts were authorized in 1868 to collect and disburse funds for missionary evangelists but the membership remained distrustful of money-raising efforts so that effective organization was very slow. Brethren generally did not pay salaries to ministers.[26] So Miller was often away from home on missions which provided no financial support whatever. He and his family were often sick. His son died in September of 1877; his daughter died in February of 1880; his wife died in March of 1880. About this time he failed financially and his assets had to be distributed. Shortly after his wife's death in 1880 Miller was offered the presidency of Ashland College at Ashland, Ohio.

> We have accepted a position in Ashland College as its president because we feel it our duty to do so under the circumstances . . . To oppose education in this age and this country is to die; though it may be slow it will be sure, because the rage of learning is all around us now; a free school for eight months in the year in reach of all, and higher schools all over the land . . . We want every science and art, and business and calling, all turned to help in the great work of saving men. We cannot do this by opposing them; we must take hold of them ourselves,

rid out the evil, turn all the good to service for God. To this end we can do more in the proper training of the young than in any other.[27]

It was not an easy time to be president of a Brethren college. A large percentage of the Brethren did not want to change the old separated ways of the fellowship and saw the college as a dangerous agent of innovation. Another segment of the Brethren membership wanted speedy modernization of the fellowship (revival meetings, salaried pastors, Sunday schools, lively literature) and saw the college as a tool for making these improvements quickly. Miller always represented the moderates, the conservatism of the Annual Meeting, the policy of cautious change advocated by James Quinter in the *Gospel Visitor* and by Miller himself in his periodical writings. Ashland College trustees sided with the progressives and Miller resigned his presidency effective 31 December 1881. He went back to Indiana as elder-in-charge of North Manchester (also called Manchester) church.[28]

It was not an easy time to be in charge of a Brethren congregation either. What had been a heated difference of opinion represented on the extremes by the "Old Orders" and the "Progressives" came to serious splits within the Brethren churches in the early 1880s. In the congregations church members were choosing sides. During a crucial decade Miller gave leadership to sustain the central moderate majority. Brethren communities in the area were large. The North Manchester *Journal* said in 31 May 1883: "The annual communion meeting of the German Baptists or Brethren at their church 2 miles west of town on Thursday last was well attended. As is the custom of this people, they gave a good dinner to all who would eat. They had made ample preparation . . . About 1200 ate dinner that day, and the supply of food was not visibly affected."[29] His West Manchester congregation had finished a new brick church building in August of 1892; in March of the following year Miller's funeral was the first and one of the largest ever held there. Educator Robert Henry Miller died unaware that North Manchester itself was destined to become a major educational center for Brethren in the state.[30]

Brethren Divisions

Divisions among Indiana Brethren were painful because they were a people who valued peace and unity so much. Yet divisions among the Brethren seemed inevitable. There was within the fellowship an unyielding determination to describe and restore the details of biblical practice and to signal their nonconformity to the world.

At the same time all who attempted separation from the contemporary world were continually battered by the demands and appeals of a rapidly changing culture. Brethren were influenced by the arguments and practices of other evangelical Protestants. Technological change, public schools, and rural prosperity modified the old ways.

The very size of the brotherhood and its gatherings came to demand accommodation to the world and its economy. Indiana first hosted the Annual Meeting of the entire denomination at Jonathan Wyland's new barn (80 feet by 40 feet) in Elkhart County in 1852; "possibly near five thousand" attended of whom about one thousand were members of the Brethren church.[31] By 1868 the Brethren and visitors attending the Annual Meeting at elder Jacob Berkey's barn five miles from Goshen were delivered by railroad "within sixty rods of the meeting." The *Gospel Visitor* gave advice:

> To the brethren and sisters going to Yearly Meeting next Pentecost in Elkhart county, Ind. This is to inform you that the B. & O. R.R. company will return free of charge all members who have attended the meeting and paid full fare going from Columbus, Ohio, to the point of starting. Thus those who take the road at Baltimore will be returned free of charge to that point, those from Washington City, D.C., to that point, &c, &c . . . And as this very liberal company has given to the brethren 600 miles of their road for half fare, I think we should patronize it. And as the Pittsburg, Fort Wayne & Chicago Railroad has never given the brethren east of the Ohio River any advantages, I think we should avoid it.[32]

Caring for that annual meeting crowd at Berkey's simply outran the capacity of old-fashioned and home-centered hospitality. Some local Brethren households were putting up as many as sixty or seventy visitors. All were fed free of charge but twenty-three congregations in the Northern Indiana District were asked to contribute hard cash totaling $2,622.73 to pay for such essential items as $173\frac{2}{3}$ bushels of wheat, 175 bushels of corn, 6,598 pounds of beef, 165 pounds of coffee, 260 pounds of sugar, 8 pounds of pepper, $836\frac{3}{4}$ pounds of butter, $68\frac{1}{2}$ gallons of apple butter, 1 barrel of salt, and 145 gallons of pickles.[33] The Annual Meeting and the district meetings were to make decisions permitting adjustments to the modern world at a tolerable rate while maintaining true faith, order, and peace. However, questions about the authority of the annual and district meetings themselves were always becoming grounds for more divisions.

So the Hostetler Brethren (also called "Honites" and "Kentucky Dunkards") relaxed Brethren distinctives, de-veloped an affection for revivals, organized as an independent association, and led a couple of thousand of their Indiana constituents into merger with the Campbellites. In 1848 a special council under auspices of the Annual Meeting met at Delphi, Indiana, to resolve differences of the fellowship at large with followers of Peter Eyman and George Patton. Unsatisfied with the decisions, the "Oimanites" organized an independent church (New Dunkard Church of God) which numbered a few hundred members in half a dozen counties of Indiana. They baptized with a single backward immersion, practiced footwashing in the single mode before the Lord's supper was placed on the table, and allowed some participation in civil government. The Leedy Brethren in central Ohio were single mode footwashers, out of connection with the Annual Meeting after 1858. Indiana had some "Leedyites" in Whitley County.[34] Divisive feelings ran high in the brotherhood in the late 1870s.

The divisions of 1881 and 1882 were of a whole new order of magnitude. There were the traditionalists who were nicknamed the "Old Orders." Their periodical was the *Vindicator*. When control of the Annual Meeting seemed to be passing out of their hands in 1881, about 5,000 of them withdrew and organized as the Old German Baptist Brethren. Essentially they wanted Brethren faith and practice as it had been before 1850, including footwashing in the double mode. Their Annual Meeting endorsed old Brethren practices, the most visible being their uniformity of dress which they still maintain:

> Men can be recognized by their black broadrim hats, plain "frock" coats with "stand-up" collars, and broadfall pants. Most of the men wear beards but shave their upper lips. Women can be recognized by their dark bonnets, white prayer coverings (caps), and long dresses with matching capes over the shoulders and matching aprons. Upon meeting one another (except on the street and in public places) the salutation is always the handshake and the holy kiss exchanged brother to brother and sister to sister.[35]

Their Annual Meeting then continued the perennial process of deciding which particular products and processes of modern technology could be accepted; electricity, telephones, and automobiles have gradually been accepted but radios and televisions have not. Very small groups named the Old Brethren and the Old Brethren German Baptists, around Camden and Wakarusa in Indiana, found so much innovation uncomfortable. They separated again in order to adapt to the world at a still slower pace, the latter still limited to horse-drawn buggies for transportation. Indiana generally ranked second among the states in the number of Old Order German Baptist Brethren—790 members in 13 organizations in 1906. Their counties were generally Elkhart, Kosciusko, Wabash, Cass, Carroll, Clinton, and Madison.[36]

There were also the liberals who were nicknamed the "Progressives." Their spokesman was Henry R. Holsinger of Pennsylvania with his publications the *Christian Family Companion* and then the *Progressive Christian*. He felt commissioned to bring the Brethren into the modern world with higher education, salaried clergy, free personal choice of dress, organized missions, Sunday schools, and protracted evangelistic meetings. Said he:

> The church was in great need of reformation. One unfortunate feature in the state of the church at this time was that the congregations were in the care of incompetent bishops [elders] . . . I can even now close my eyes and name a dozen churches with whose elders I was personally acquainted who could not read intelligently a chapter from the Bible or a hymn from the hymnbook, nor write an intelligent notice or announcement of a communion meeting for the paper. Some of them could deliver a pretty fair discourse in an extemporaneous way, more or less satisfactory to the people of the community in which they lived, but the more discreet of them could not attempt to preach at a strange place or in a town . . . Such men as those just described composed the examining board for the candidate to the eldership in ninety-nine cases out of one hundred . . . From this grade of elders the standing committees of the general conference were elected, for none except ordained elders were eligible to the standing committees. From their ranks, also, were selected the members of the various committees sent to the churches by annual meeting. These, with the council of adjoining elders, constituted the consistory, and held the fiat of the Tunker power, from which there was no appeal.[37]

Holsinger was particularly apt at infuriating the bulk of the Brethren leaders year after year after year. James Quinter was the contemporary giant among Brethren preachers, editors, and agents for slow and gradual change. As early as the Annual Meeting at Berkey's barn at Goshen in 1868, Quinter responded icily to an attack by Holsinger: "We kindly submit to br. Holsinger whether it would not be best before the Annual Meeting is so severely censured, or any of its officers charged with delinquency of duty, in our public papers, to consider the subject well, and inquire into it, and be sure the case will justify on Christian principles such a public exposure."[38] Robert H. Miller of the Standing Committee of the Annual Meeting cautioned Holsinger against spreading dissension and strife. Holsinger took no such counsel in

what he considered matters of principle. A large body of polemic literature accrued.

Finally, in 1881, a committee of the Annual Meeting was appointed to visit Holsinger at his church in Berlin, Pennsylvania, and deal with him "according to his transgressions." Holsinger made the visit a dramatic confrontation. When the next Annual Meeting for the whole brotherhood convened at John Arnold's farm near Milford, Indiana, in 1882, it appeared to be the largest assembly of Brethren members ever held. The Cincinnati, Wabash, and Michigan Railroad was bringing them nearly to the meeting gates. The Berlin Committee presented its recommendation that "Brother H. R. Holsinger cannot be held in fellowship in the Brotherhood, and all who depart with him shall be held responsible to the action of the next Annual Meeting." After a day of discussion the committee's report was overwhelmingly sustained. In a series of steps and stages about 5,000 Brethren withdrew with Holsinger to form the Brethren Church (often designated Progressive or Ashland).[39] "The Bible, the whole Bible, and nothing but the Bible" was their motto. They restated their allegiance to the distinctive doctrines of the Brethren:

> 1. That the ordinance of baptism is trine immersion only.
> 2. That feet-washing is a divine institution, and should be practiced in the public worship by all saints, in connection with the Lord's Supper. 3. That the Lord's Supper is a full evening meal, and is to be eaten in the night, as a divine institution, in the public worship of God, in connection with the communion of bread and wine.
> 4. That the eating of the communion bread and the drinking of the communion wine, in connection with the Lord's Supper, is a divine ordinance, to be thus kept and obeyed by the church, in her public worship.
> 5. That the "holy kiss" is a divine institution, to be practiced by all the saints in the public worship of God.
> 6. That the various separate and collective congregations, while absolutely and truly congregational in government, yet each and all have a divine relation to each other, and to the whole church as the body of Christ; and that, therefore, the faith, character, and practice of each and all are under the same divine law of government, under Christ and the Holy Spirit, to each other, as the Word of God teaches.[40]

They said they were conservators of original Brethren ideals but progressive in applying these ideals to modern life. In the division the Progressives came to control Ashland College in Ohio and made it a center for education and administration.[41] Control of the Annual Meeting over local congregations was carefully limited among Progressives.

Indiana was well represented among Brethren Church (Progressive) members and leaders, adding new congregations and eventually becoming the denomination's largest district. Jonathan H. Swihart at Bourbon, Indiana, had become a persistent protester against what he considered the despotism of the Annual Meeting. He had led his following into the Congregational Brethren about 1879 and used his *Gospel Messenger* on their behalf. In 1882–83 he promoted the merger of his Congregational Brethren with Holsinger and the Progressives. Swihart was an elder-in-charge of several congregations and a traveling evangelist said to have organized thirty-two churches and led about 3,500 persons to Christ. Stephen H. Bashor was an evangelistic minister with close ties to the Progressive congregation at Mexico, Indiana. He had already received 1,400 into the church in the first two years of his preaching and became the most notable Brethren revivalist. The pioneer Progressive leader Henry R. Holsinger himself was pastor at Berne, Indiana, in 1886–87. Progressives built retirement homes in Indiana at Flora and South Bend.[42]

Indiana was destined to become even more prominent in this Progressive Brethren family due to further division within the group. Progressive leaders Louis S. Bauman, Alva J. McClain, Homer A. Kent, and Robert Paul Miller were among those caught up in the issues of fundamentalism and dispensationalism stirring the churches in the early years of the twentieth century. They and their colleagues became concerned about evidences of liberalism and modernism among their fellow Brethren, especially at Ashland College. They established Grace Theological Seminary in 1937 and withdrew in 1940 from the Brethren Church (from this time often designated Ashland Group or Ashland Brethren as well as Brethren Church or Progressives) to form what became the Fellowship of Grace Brethren Churches (Grace Brethren). Winona Lake, near Warsaw, Indiana, had been a favorite place for Brethren gatherings since 1892. The president at Winona said other assemblies at that place were numbered by thousands but the Brethren were counted by acres. Following relocation of Grace Theological Seminary there in 1939, Winona Lake gradually became the institutional center for the new Grace Brethren—seminary, college, publishing house, retirement home, denominational offices, and missionary headquarters. Grace Brethren came to combine their progressive and fundamentalist heritage with a zeal for evangelism and missions using contemporary techniques. At the same time they maintained their loyalty to certain Brethren distinctives such as trine immersion and the threefold communion service with footwashing and Lord's supper followed by the bread and cup.[43]

In 1906 Indiana was second only to Pennsylvania (with 3,885) in the number of Brethren Church (Progressive) members. Indiana reported 3,800 Progressive members in 29 congregations with 2,564 Sunday school scholars. Following the division, both the Ashland Group and the Grace Brethren continued to grow. Their Indiana strength was in the same north-central counties, especially Elkhart, St. Joseph, Wabash, and Miami.

The departure of the "Old Orders" and the "Progressives" seemed to free the parent body for a new period of growth and expansion. That continuing parent body was called the German Baptist Brethren or the German Baptist Brethren (Conservative). By 1908 so few of the members used German that they abandoned that language designation and renamed their denomination the Church of the Brethren. Following the separations of 1881–83 they were still about ten times the size of either of the departing groups and by 1900 they had more than regained their level of national membership. Their *Gospel Visitor* evolved into the *Gospel Messenger* (1883) advocating cautious accommodation to the contemporary world and to mainstream Protestantism. Church of the Brethren districts became increasingly active in organizing to support missionary and benevolent causes. J. P. Miller led a group in Southern Indiana District to establish an orphans' and old folks' home at Sulphur Springs in Henry County.[44]

Levi Miller was a champion of benevolent causes in his Mexico congregation. At the meeting of the Middle Indiana District in 1889 he said:

I propose to make a donation of 15 acres of land and erect a building 36 x 50 feet, and make a deed to the middle district of Indiana for the same, for the benefit of the poor members and the orphan children of said district. It will be a home the poor can call their own. Let it be called the Old Folks' and Orphan Children's Home.[45]

In 1892 he was back saying:

I propose to, by consent of this meeting, erect another building on the same lot and near to the Old Folks' Home as a refuge or temporary home for homeless children. This building shall be 36 x 54 feet, two stories high and shall have a basement under the whole building. This building I propose to complete and then give it to the middle district of Indiana, for the above named purpose.[46]

That year the Superintendent's salary at the Home in Mexico was $287.50; he received $428.19 "for the support of the Home" and $388.13 "for general use."

Of the $338.13 paid to the Superintendent for general use he paid $14.00 for a cow, $53.06 for house supplies, $21.22 for clothing, $162.03 for eatables, $3.84 for tobacco, $32.25 for doctor bill, $38.50 for hired girl and $63.23 for sundries. Brother Welty, an inmate of the Home, who came last November, being a physician, treats the inmates free of charge, thereby saving a large doctor bill.[47]

Reports of the next seventy-five years showed the home at Mexico receiving more than 1,500 children, most of them promptly placed in families.[48]

Lacking the resistance of the most vocal of the Old Orders, the annual and district meetings allowed gradual liberalization of church practice until the Church of the Brethren seemed more progressive than the Progressives. Enforced plain dress was going out; they said nonconformity could be an internal spirit or attitude instead of a required garb. Sunday schools came to be considered essential; Joseph Amick told the Middle Indiana District that more than 500 of Indiana's Brethren children had passed through Methodist Sunday schools into Methodist churches in 1878 alone. Missions and evangelism with revivals were clearly in favor and were part of the reason for the church's growth.

> The first series of meetings [in northern Indiana] were held in the Portage Prairie church in February, 1865. The preaching was done by Elder Daniel B. Sturgis, assisted by the home ministers. The next church to hold a series of meetings was the Rock Run. In February, 1867, Jacob Cripe of Portage Prairie district conducted a two week's meeting, which resulted in the conversion of more than sixty souls. From this time on protracted meetings have been very common. Though at first some opposed it.[49]

Architecture and church furnishings were becoming like those of other Protestants. Annual Meeting of the Church of the Brethren in Muncie in 1893 warranted the frivolity of igniting a gas well to provide a Wednesday evening exhibition.[50]

Change still did not come without pain. When the 1911 Annual Meeting recommended plain dress for members of the Church of the Brethren but did not require it, discontent simmered among remaining conservatives. Discontent compounded as B. E. Kesler kept advocating the old standards in his *Bible Monitor* published from Missouri. Discontent boiled over into one more separation at a meeting at Plevna, Indiana, in June of 1926. Those departing took the name Dunkard Brethren and cited a list of evidences of lowered standards: neckties, stylish hats, fashionable hairstyles, remarriage of divorced persons, lodge memberships, union memberships, church

camps, salaried ministers, participation in politics, encouragement of higher education. They advocated nearly all the old practices of plain dress and separated living short of horse and buggy. Indiana's Dunkard Brethren congregations were in Elkhart, Miami, and Howard counties; their leader B. E. Kesler came to live at Goshen.[51]

Higher Education

Higher education was a hard cause to sustain even among the main body of Indiana Brethren. Alexander Mack and his colleagues in the days of the church's founding had been friends of learning but the urgency for simplicity, plainness, and separation from the ways of the world seemed to undercut a drive for excellence in education among Brethren on the American frontier. Education beyond basic literacy looked like luxury and might be sin. The Annual Meeting consistently opposed ventures in higher education by Brethren before 1858. The *Gospel Visitor* sent out from Ohio by elders James Quinter and Henry Kurtz was tolerated as a private journal circulating among Brethren beginning in 1851. These editors and their successors cautiously advocated higher education along with Sunday schools and evangelistic missions, later prodded toward these innovations by the Progressives.[52]

The *Visitor* had friends in Indiana. W. R. Deeter and George Studebaker of Mississinewa church in Delaware County sent in reports of missionary work and revivals for publication. In June of 1869 Deeter said "We have a flourishing Sabbath school in operation. The *Gospel Visitor* is fast growing in favor with the brethren here." Thirty were reported baptized following meetings conducted by James Quinter at Mississinewa in April of 1868; fifty-six were baptized at Bush Creek congregation in Randolph and Jay counties. Jesse Calvert and Jacob Cripe were holding meetings at Pierceton in fall and winter of 1868–69 and twenty-nine persons were received. John Hoover at Marshall wrote "I truly think that the *Visitor* is the best publication now in use except the Bible, and I feel like bidding God speed to the publication thereof."[53] Such pockets of support for the *Visitor* were no indication that the main body of Indiana Brethren were won over to that publication's cause of higher education. As late as the 1870s the Middle Indiana District advised against providing children education beyond the elementary level lest they become puffed up.

The 1858 Annual Meeting, held with Indiana's Bachelor Run congregation ten miles from Delphi in Carroll County, did make some new room for higher education.

Among the more than sixty queries on the meeting's agenda was one about an academy which editors Kurtz and Quinter wanted to open in Ohio.[54] "We desire to know whether the Lord has commanded us to have a school besides our common schools, such as the one contemplated in the *Gospel Visitor*? If we are, ought we not to have it soon? And if it is not commanded of the Lord, ought we to have one? And is it right to contend for or against such an institution publicly through the press, since our different views may become a stumbling block before the world? And if it is once decided ought we not to keep forever silent about it?" The answer was: "Concerning the school proposed in the *Gospel Visitor*, we think we have no right to interfere with an individual enterprise so long as there is no departure from gospel principles."[55] This was no ringing endorsement; the Annual Meeting did not commit the fellowship to build Brethren schools or to champion them. Anything tending toward a professional, formally educated, or salaried ministry was certain to be viewed with alarm.[56] Still the door was opened and there was a minority of Hoosier Brethren among those motivated to open schools.

Samuel Murray became an advocate of higher education. He was the itinerant elder most responsible for establishing and nurturing Brethren life in the Middle Indiana District. He built up congregations at Pipe Creek and Salamonie, was married five times, fathered sixteen children, and lacked one day of living one hundred years. Murray and Daniel Smith met with others at Antioch (later Andrews), Indiana, in 1870 to formulate a request that Middle Indiana District "approve the establishment of a school among the Brethren, where our children may receive a better and more thorough education than they can at our public schools" and "devise some means to meet the wants of the school relative to educational facilities." Their suggestion was really to establish a college at Antioch within Salamonie congregation. There was opposition and the Middle District took no action.[57]

In the same year of 1870 Northern Indiana District was more supportive. The citizens of Bourbon, Indiana, in Marshall County, offered to donate land and buildings for a college if the Brethren would establish and continue a first class institution of learning in their town. Encouraged by the District, a group of Brethren acting as trustees contracted to provide a college "after the order of Oberlin College, State of Ohio, except the theological department." It was the first Brethren "college" in America. The next year the Annual Meeting received a query: "Does the Annual Meeting of 1871 claim Salem College of Bourbon, Ind., to be under the auspices of our Broth-

erhood?" The official reply was: "It does not regard it as a church school, or conducted by the general Brotherhood, though it is under the auspices of members of the church and is supported by those who patronize it, and not by donations of the church."[58]

In fact the Salem College trustees were about to be sacrificed. There was rhetoric on behalf of the school. Progressive physician and elder Peter R. Wrightsman said:

There are now hundreds of our Brethren's children away from home, receiving their education in high schools of other denominations, some of the teachers of which are Universalists, infidels and deists, and to say the least may do their best to explain away the plain, simple commandments of Christ's church. Now shall we, who profess to be the true followers of Christ, lie still and suffer these sectarians thus to poison the minds of our dear children? God forbid! Brethren, forbid it. But some tell us, "It is just to make preachers and they will want a salary for preaching." This is a very slender objection. This is by no means the object of establishing a school. It is to keep the Brethren's children under the religious influence of our own church. The time has come when the youth will have an education. If parents do not send them where they will have the advantage of a high school or college, many of them will go to other denominational schools and there will be taught the peculiar views of those sects. How much better to have such a school among the brethren, and teach them the true Christian doctrine.[59]

The Honorable Barnabas C. Hobbs, State Superintendent of Public Instruction, presented a powerful dedicatory address. The school's advertising claimed it was "of equal rank with the best colleges of Europe and America." Besides offering a college course, it provided for an academy, a commercial school, a school of music, and a school of painting. The tuition per term at Salem varied from seven to fifteen dollars, depending on the department in which the student was enrolled.[60] Enrollment grew from eight students at the opening in December of 1870 to more than one hundred. But in 1874 Salem College was closed, casting a heavy personal debt on its trustees.

Indiana's Brethren still seemed to lack a sufficient base of educators and supporters to operate such a school. The failure slowed the educational efforts of Indiana Brethren at a time when Brethren were busy founding colleges or high schools in Pennsylvania, Ohio, Illinois, Virginia, Kansas, and California. Southern Indiana District thought it saw an educational opportunity in 1892. The citizens of Ladoga offered the building of their former normal school to the Brethren and promised additional backing. There was serious pledge taking all around but the amount promised was far short of the $40,000 agreed upon as a minimum to open the school. Schools begun as Pleasant Hill College at Warsaw (1871) and Burnett's Creek Normal School at Burnettsville (1872) were soon discontinued.[61]

The successful effort in higher education for Indiana's Brethren finally began at North Manchester in 1895. At that town the United Brethren in Christ had a college building of sixteen rooms, a campus of ten acres, and more financial problems than they could solve. Brethren trustees acquired the property from the United Brethren as a site for a Brethren "College and Bible School." By ceaseless fund raising, by enlisting the support of several districts in the major denomination of Brethren, and by developing a body of officers and friends who refused to be discouraged, Manchester College became a regional rallying point for Brethren training and mission. Hundreds of teachers, ministers, missionaries, and community leaders eventually issued from the school. With the addition of Bethany Bible School (later Bethany Theological Seminary) in Chicago in 1905, the Church of the Brethren was on its way toward replacing its free and plural ministry with a professional and salaried clergy.[62]

When the majority body of Brethren made their report to the 1906 religious census they were approaching the 200th anniversary of the Schwarzenau baptisms in the Eder River, soon to take their new name as Church of the Brethren. They numbered 76,547 members in America. Pennsylvania had 18,889 of the members. But Indiana was second with 9,949 members in 103 congregations and 7,992 Sunday school scholars. They were well along in the process of acculturation. Their distinctive plain dress was still observable but passing. In church the members of this main body of Brethren were recognizable among evangelical Protestants chiefly by their preference for trine immersion and by their observance of love feasts in three parts. Outside church they were likely to be known for their service and relief work. Their heritage of nonresistance was attenuated but far from lost.[63] Some Brethren youth served as soldiers in the World Wars; more accepted some form of noncombatant service. Brethren cooperated with Friends, Mennonites, and others to develop alternatives to military service such as civilian programs of service and relief. Several of these efforts earned international recognition and took on continuing institutional form. Brethren leadership, including Indiana leadership, was strong in such major programs as the Heifer Project and the Christian Rural Overseas Program (CROP).

All members of the Brethren shared the restoration vision of Alexander Mack and his friends, a vision of following Jesus and of nonconformity to the ways of the world. Every eventual organization of them in Indiana embodied its own range of convictions within it, the members regarding one another as conservatives or liberals. Every continuing organization of them in Indiana had to learn to live in the presence of other substantial branches of the same Brethren family who defined their separation from the world somewhat differently and drew the lines of nonconformity at quite different places. In 1990 the Church of the Brethren with 17,388 and the Brethren Church (Ashland, Ohio) with 5,307 represented a combined total of 22,695 adherents, an estimated numerical strength for these two in Indiana about equal to that of the Episcopalians, the Church of God (Anderson, Ind.), or the Latter-day Saints.

NOTES

1. Martin G. Brumbaugh, *A History of the German Baptist Brethren in Europe and America* (Mount Morris, Ill.: Brethren Publishing House, 1899), 37–38.

2. *The Brethren Encyclopedia*, 3 vols. continuously paged (Philadelphia: Brethren Encyclopedia, Inc., 1983), 815–16, 1079–80; *The Church of the Brethren, Past and Present* (Elgin, Ill.: Brethren Press, 1971), 10–14; Brumbaugh, *History*, 16–44.

3. John C. Wenger, *The Mennonites in Indiana and Michigan* (Scottdale, Pa.: Herald Press, 1961), 423; *Church of the Brethren*, 14.

4. David B. Eller, "Hoosier Brethren and the Origins of the Restoration Movement," *Indiana Magazine of History* 76 (March 1980): 3; Donald F. Durnbaugh, *The Brethren in Colonial America* (Elgin, Ill.: Brethren Press, 1967, 659 p.); *Brethren Encyclopedia*, 112–13, 177; *Church of the Brethren*, 16.

5. Ralph G. Rarick, *History of the Mississinewa Church of the Brethren, Delaware Co., Indiana* (Elgin, Ill.: Brethren Publishing House, 1917), 100.

6. *Church of the Brethren*, 57, 59; *Brethren Encyclopedia*, 762–65.

7. *Brethren Encyclopedia*, 176.

8. *Church of the Brethren*, 69.

9. Jesse H. Ziegler, *The Broken Cup: Three Generations of Dunkers* (Elgin, Ill.: Brethren Publishing House, 1942), 43–44.

10. Eller, "Hoosier Brethren," 3–15.

11. Otho Winger, *History of the Church of the Brethren in Indiana* (Elgin, Ill.: Brethren Publishing House, 1917), 169–77.

12. *Brethren Encyclopedia*, 434.

13. *Brethren Encyclopedia*, 432–33.

14. Winger, *History*, 59–62, 101; *Brethren Encyclopedia*, 505.

15. Owen Opperman, *A Brief Sketch of the Brethren, Generally Known as Dunkards, of Northern Indiana* (Goshen, Ind.: News Printing Co., 1897), 7–16; Lester H. Binnie, *Early Brethren Families in the Eel River Congregation in Kosciusko and Wabash Counties, Indiana* (Albion, Ind.: The Author, [1974]), 5.

16. Winger, *History*, 15–16.

17. Winger, *History*, 60, 101, 121–22.

18. Opperman, *Brief Sketch*, 16–18.

19. M. M. Eshelman, *A Model Life; or Uncle John Metzger on Earth* (Mount Morris, Ill.: Brethren Publishing House, 1898), 26–27; Winger, *History*, 102.

20. Otho Winger, *The Life of Elder R. H. Miller* (Elgin, Ill.: Brethren Publishing House, 1910, 269 p.); Winger, *History*, 72–75, 388–94.

21. Robert H. Miller, *The Miller and Sommer Debate* (Mount Morris, Ill.: Brethren Publishing House, 1898, 533 p.).

22. James Quinter, *Is Immersion the Mode of Christian Baptism Authorized and Proved by the Bible?* (Indianapolis, Ind.: Douglass and Conner, 1868, 304 p.); *Gospel Visitor* 18 (July 1868): 256.

23. Robert H. Miller, *The Doctrine of the Brethren Defended; or, The Faith and Practice of the Brethren Proven by the Gospel to Be True* (Indianapolis, Ind.: Printing and Publishing House Print, 1876, 404 p.).

24. Miller, *Doctrine*, iii.

25. Winger, *History*, 392.

26. Alvin E. Conner, *Sectarian Childrearing: The Dunkers, 1709–1900* (Gettysburg, Pa.: Brethren Heritage Press, 1987?), 130–35; *Minutes of the Annual Meeting, 1868*, 6–7; *Brethren Encyclopedia*, 1136–37.

27. Winger, *Life*, 87–88.

28. Winger, *Life*, 41–82.

29. Binnie, *Early Brethren*, 25.

30. Winger, *History*, 85, 394.

31. Opperman, *Brief Sketch*, 27.

32. *Gospel Visitor* 18 (April 1868): 126; 18 (May 1868): 157.

33. *Gospel Visitor* 19 (January 1869): 30; Winger, *History*, 212.

34. Eller, "Hoosier Brethren," 1–20; Winger, *History*, 458–59; *Brethren Encyclopedia*, 297–98, 631–32, 689, 734. Concerning footwashing, page 481 of the *Brethren Encyclopedia* commented: "In the early and mid-19th century, Annual Meeting prescribed the double mode, in which one person washed and another dried the feet of several persons. This pattern is continued by the Old German Baptist Brethren in the 20th century. The western or Far Western Brethren, Congregational Brethren, Progressive Brethren (Brethren Church), and eventually, the Church of the Brethren, favored the single mode, in which one participant washed and dried the feet of one other person."

35. *Brethren Encyclopedia*, 967.

36. *Brethren Encyclopedia*, 964–70.

37. Henry R. Holsinger, *Holsinger's History of the Tunkers and the Brethren Church* (Lathrop, Calif.: Pacific Press, 1901), 473–75.

38. *Gospel Visitor* 18 (July 1868): 255.

39. Winger, *History*, 216–20; *Brethren Encyclopedia*, 179, 181–85, 621–22.

40. Homer A. Kent, *Conquering Frontiers; A History of the Brethren (The National Fellowship of Brethren Churches)* (Winona Lake, Ind.: BMH Books, 1972), 122.

41. Kent, *Conquering Frontiers*, 96–107; *Brethren Encyclopedia*, 181–82.

42. *Brethren Encyclopedia*, 92–93, 182, 334–35, 622, 821, 1245.

43. Winger, *History*, 227; *Brethren Encyclopedia*, 484–85, 1351.

44. Winger, *History*, 179, 201; *Brethren Encyclopedia*, 298–305, 561, 818–19, 983.

45. *Minutes of District Meetings of Middle Indiana, 1877–1913* (Flora, Ind.: Hoosier Democrat Print, 1913?), 35.

46. *Minutes of District Meetings*, 49.

47. *Minutes of District Meetings*, 52.

48. *Brethren Encyclopedia*, 333–36, 965–66.

49. Opperman, *Brief Sketch*, 33–34. See also *Brethren Encyclopedia*, 930–31.

50. Winger, *History*, 200, 223; *Brethren Encyclopedia*, 298–305.

51. *Brethren Encyclopedia*, 407–10, 690, 1451.

52. *Manchester College: The First Seventy-five Years*, (Elgin, Ill.: Brethren Press, 1964), 14–17; Winger, *Life*, 83; *Brethren Encyclopedia*, 427, 561.

53. 19 (July 1869): 223; 18 (January 1868): 26; 19 (February 1869): 61; 18 (December 1868): 380–81; 19 (February 1869): 61; 19 (May 1869): 155.

54. Winger, *History*, 208–9.

55. Winger, *Life*, 84.

56. *Brethren Encyclopedia*, 427–28, 603–5.

57. Samuel Murray, *A Short Autobiography of Elder Samuel Murray* (N.p., 1896), 20; Winger, *History*, 253–54, 399–401; *Brethren Encyclopedia*, 897.

58. Winger, *Life*, 85.

59. Winger, *History*, 258–59.

60. Kent, *Conquering Frontiers*, 88.

61. *Manchester College*, 18; *Brethren Encyclopedia*, 231–32.

62. Winger, *History*, 255–304; *Brethren Encyclopedia*, 125–28, 785–86, 1138.

63. Rufus D. Bowman, *The Church of the Brethren and War, 1708–1941* (New York: Garland Publishing, 1971, 348 p.). *Brethren Encyclopedia*, 298–305.

EVANGELICAL ASSOCIATION (ALBRIGHTS)

Not all religious Germans chose to found churches modeled after any of the ones in their fatherland. Some of the pietists seeking intense personal experience of religion and disciplined daily life found more kinship with America's revivalists. On the frontier they functioned with the zeal and systematic efficiency of the Methodists and had similar results.

Such a one was Jacob Albright (1759–1808) who was born in Pennsylvania but who never learned English well. In a way he was Lutheran. His parents were Lutheran. He and his wife united with the Bergstrasse Lutheran Church in Lancaster County. A Lutheran catechism was one of his study resources as he began his ministry. In a way he was Reformed. His wife came from that church. After some of their children died in an epidemic in 1790 he sought the services and counsel of a Reformed minister under whose guidance he experienced a conversion in 1791. "All fear and anxiety of heart disappeared," he said. "Joy and blessed peace inbreathed my breast. God gave witness to my spirit that I had become a child of God." In a way he was a Methodist. His search for close Christian fellowship led him to join a Methodist class and to study that church's order enough to become a licensed Methodist exhorter in 1796.[1] He learned from all these connections but he let them all lapse and became a sharp critic of existing fellowships.

> You Lutherans, of course, think you have Luther, and that he was a converted man; that you have the catechism; but your sinful lives prove that you are not Lutherans, for you live contrary to God's word and Luther's teaching. And you, German Reformed—what does it mean to be Reformed? It means to be restored, to be converted from sin and the world, to God; but your lives prove that you have turned from God and towards the world. You Dunkards and Mennonites, with your peculiar dress and outward plainness, by which you comfort yourselves, you will be lost without the new birth, notwithstanding you have large farms and earthly possessions. Be not astonished that I said unto you, "You must be born again," for these are the words of our Savior and Judge.[2]

Organized like Methodists

His real drive, his divine call as he felt it, was to preach in German to the Germans like himself who understood English poorly if at all and whose needs he believed to be overlooked by all the churches. He simply began to do it. By 1800 he sought to conserve and strengthen his converts by gathering some of them into three classes in Methodist fashion.[3] One of his class members described the events.

> We therefore accept as a gift from the Lord, that which he wrought through his servant Jacob Albright, the Evangelical preacher; for we perceive that it has pleased the Lord to work, and spread abroad his knowledge through the counsel and direction of this godly man. Under the direction of this devout preacher, various persons united themselves, in the year of our Lord 1800, to

pray with and for each other, in order that they might be saved from sin and flee from the wrath to come. In order to begin and carry out this good and momentous work, they decided to spend each Sunday in social prayer, and to set apart every Wednesday evening for prayermeeting. Studiously and with diligence they sought to avoid everything evil and sinful and to do all manner of good as far as God gave them strength and ability. The number of those disposed to attend such meetings soon increased and the work grew from year to year, as the records will show. This was the origin of the united Evangelical Association, the operations of which at first extended throughout the Counties of Berks and Northampton in the State of Pennsylvania. Because of their peculiarly earnest manner in worship, and more especially because Jacob Albright, by the grace of God, was the instrumental cause of their solemn union, they were at first called "The Albrights," by other Christian denominations.[4]

By 1803 there were five classes and there were two young men assisting Albright as preachers.

During this year the Association resolved to introduce and establish an ecclesiastical organization, and accordingly elected Jacob Albright to the office of Elder among them. He was consecrated, that is ordained, by the other preachers in a suitable manner, by the laying on of hands, and thereby authorized to administer all the affairs belonging to a Christian Church, and to exercise the duties and offices belonging to an Evangelical preacher. With one accord they chose the Holy Scriptures as their rule of faith and conduct. A written license was granted to Albright by which the Association recognized him as a genuine Evangelical preacher, and authorized him to appoint other competent persons as co-laborers.[5]

This was no longer just a loose fellowship but a distinct organization. Regular annual meetings of the Albright brethren began in 1807. John Walter, George Miller, and John Dreisbach were providing a new generation of leadership. There were traveling preachers, class leaders, and exhorters structured like the Methodists. The first annual conference in November of 1807 elected Jacob Albright bishop and appointed him "to prepare and publish a brief compendium of church rules—a Discipline—for the instruction and edification of the societies." But six months later Albright died. The new *Discipline* was presented to the 1809 conference by George Miller.[6] A catechism written by John Dreisbach was also approved that year. Printed license forms for preachers issued in 1807 called the group "The Newly-formed Methodist Conference." The 1809 conference resolved that the name should be "The So-called Albrights." The 1816 General

Conference took as the official name "The Evangelical Association."[7]

Jacob Albright favored episcopal government and was the first bishop elected by and for his people. Yet after his death they continued their work for more than thirty years without a bishop. The annual and general conferences, not very carefully differentiated, simply met and conducted the church's business. They elected presiding officers and secretaries as needed. They named a committee each year to station the preachers. John Walter, George Miller, and John Dreisbach were ordained as elders, recognized as official visitors among the congregations, circuits, and big meetings. Other senior preachers, whether or not ordained as elders, functioned as supervisors and counselors as well.

Along with the primary duty of oversight of the circuits and preachers, the conferences acted to remind their membership of their identity as a plain people. In 1818 "It was unanimously resolved that none of our ministers be allowed to wear gloves during Summer, nor to use silver-plated bridle bits or stirrups, or loaded whips, and in no case to adorn their person with large watch keys; this resolution to be positively observed by all of our ministers whether they be connected with the Annual or with the Quarterly Conferences." The General Conference of 1839 disapproved lavishness of dress because "splendid apparel is always expensive, and we may become spendthrifts in clothing as well as in eating and drinking."[8]

When the members of the General Conference of 1839 finally elected a bishop to succeed Albright they chose a man known for his frugality and simplicity, an unpretentious bachelor who wore plain clothes and darned his own socks. John Seybert was a Pennsylvania native who began preaching soon after his conversion at age nineteen. He opposed adornments, frivolous amusements, secret societies, alcoholic beverages, and tobacco. He was a serious horseback scholar, an effective revivalist, and a respected presiding elder in the East. He also had understanding of and affection for the West based on his own experience. He had personally planted the church in the unreached area of Erie and Warren in Pennsylvania and made that field an Evangelical stronghold. His malaria was western, having been contracted in the swamps of the frontier circuits of Ohio.[9]

Western Missionaries

Missionary enthusiasm was in the air at the time of Seybert's election. The new bishop's "Call to the Ministry of the Evangelical Association" pled the cause of "the thousands of poor Germans in the states of Michigan, Ohio, Indiana, Illinois, etc., who wander amid perils in the moral desert in great throngs, like sheep without a shepherd." That 1839 General Conference also established "The Missionary Society of the Evangelical Association of North America." John G. Zinser and Absalom B. Schaefer were conference delegates voting in the bishop's election. Both were wholly committed to a ministry on the westernmost frontier of the Evangelical Association—Ohio, Indiana, and Illinois. Bishop Seybert was elected in March of 1839. In September he began a missionary tour which included 132 days in the territory of the newly authorized Ohio Conference. At the western limit of his first tour as bishop, on Miami Circuit, he barely crossed Indiana's eastern border.[10]

Much of that western work was available for the bishop's attention in 1839 and following years because of Absalom B. Schaefer (1797–1869), who was both a product and a producer of the surge of missionary effort for the Evangelical Association in Ohio. Born in a community of "European Germans" in Virginia, catechized and confirmed a Lutheran, employed as a supervisor of canal construction in Ohio, converted in 1829 under the ministry of Evangelical preacher George Schneider of Lancaster Circuit in Ohio, Schaefer began preaching about three months after his conversion. As a local preacher visiting from Lancaster Circuit, Schaefer had helped conduct the first Evangelical "big meeting" in Indiana—at Abington in Wayne County in October of 1835.[11] Absalom Schaefer and John Lutz, riding the frontier Miami Circuit in 1836–37, heard calls from Indiana but could not respond.[12]

> It is more or less the case at each preaching place, that folks are looking to us for council and instruction and are beginning to forsake the old empty wells which give them no water. Furthermore we have received word from the interior and western part of Indiana, and along the Wabash River, that many there are earnestly desiring the Bread of Life. We would have visited them at once and rendered service there had that been possible. But in the meanwhile our circuit has already grown so large, with so many preaching places, that we cannot leave it.[13]

Assigned to his home area of Ohio's Lancaster Circuit in 1839, Schaefer was highly visible as a founder of local missionary societies to raise money to support missionary work farther west. In the Ohio Conference, just authorized in 1839 and formed in 1840, Schaefer was conference secretary, senior rider in the wilds of the circuit farthest west, and such a promoter of missions that

this frontier conference was soon supporting mission work not only in western states but also in New York City and in Canada.[14]

It was hard for Schaefer to keep his mind on Indiana. His Miami Circuit included Dayton, Ohio. He and his associates were under orders to give that place special attention. The work at Dayton was exciting; an Evangelical Association class was formed there in 1841. Schaefer preached there once every three weeks, twice as often as at other circuit points. "We travel through fifteen counties, six in Ohio and nine in Indiana," he said. "Although we preach every day and sometimes twice a day, yet it requires from seven to eight weeks to make one round on the circuit. We trust that conference will appoint four men instead of two for this field." Schaefer was always adding preaching points so his circuits demanded to be divided and served by more workers. He reported that German preaching places could be added in almost every portion of Indiana. Invitations came almost every day and from many places. "But on account of the wide expanse of our circuit we had to refuse."[15]

Schaefer's supervisor was presiding elder John G. Zinser who had five circuits in his new Ohio District. It was also hard for Zinser to keep his mind on Indiana. The Chicago area kept dominating his agenda. When northern Illinois was still very thinly settled, some Evangelical Association members from Warren, Pennsylvania, moved there. They were friends of Bishop John Seybert since Seybert had been their circuit rider and evangelist back in Pennsylvania. In 1836 and 1837 these bands of believers formed classes at Des Plaines, Naperville, and Moline. They built the first church building of the Evangelical Association west of Ohio. Their work in the area was so successful that German-speaking people from Chicago came twenty miles to the meetings and Evangelical circuit riders were soon at work in that city.[16] Zinser visited in 1840.

> Last Sunday I preached in Chicago to an attentive assembly of European Germans. The Word seemed to have had a stirring effect upon the people. O, how it makes me sad when I see the lamentable religious condition of the German people in this city! I feel as though, if the circumstances would permit, that from this hour on I would give myself as a missionary to the Germans here. It appeared to me that unless a man give his full time and effort in this center, nothing much can be accomplished. O, how great is the harvest, and how few the laborers![17]

So Evangelical leaders always seemed to be crossing Indiana on their way from their strongholds in Ohio to their strongholds in Illinois. "On his way to Illinois" in 1841, Bishop Seybert went from a camp meeting in Fairfield County, Ohio, to visit both the Whitewater and Fort Wayne missions in Indiana.[18] His loop through northern Indiana gave him a memorable month, including his fiftieth birthday.

> To-day I am fifty years old. Oh I would dissolve in tears of gratitude and praise to God, and appear in deepest humility before His throne of grace for the love with which He has crowned my days. I have now lived through half a century, in which millions not so old as I, have passed into eternity. O God! O God! O God! what shall I render unto Thee, because Thou hast borne me with so much patience until this day? I will present unto Thee my soul and body as a sacrifice, and devote all my future days to Thy service.[19]

At Fort Wayne he preached a sermon at Brother Keim's in the evening. Next day on the road he witnessed a Hoosier celebration of the Fourth of July—"as usual with shooting, swearing, carousing, dancing and drinking." It was, he said, "the way our western nominal Christians give thanks to Almighty God for national independence and personal liberty of conscience."[20] On his way to Fort Wayne he had gotten terribly lost in the forest and had run for miles to catch his runaway horse. Small wonder that with the Indiana crossing complete "it was a great delight to the bishop to meet his old friends from Warren, Pennsylvania, in their new Illinois home."[21]

Then on his return from the Illinois camp meeting in August, back in Indiana at South Bend, his horse seemed determined to die then and there. Only a miraculous cure got the beast on the road again. Nevertheless Seybert remained an unshaken enthusiast for the West. After the 1841 adventures he set off for home "preaching through Indiana and Ohio as he went, and attending campmeetings." Later visits were happier. In June of 1848 the bishop dropped in from a tour in Michigan to preach at Mishawaka. "The demonstrations of the congregation were so great that the Bishop was obliged to cut his sermon short and sit down, unable to proceed." In October of 1848, somewhere in Indiana, "Seybert preached to them from Psalm 126, and the Lord blessed the friends so powerfully that some of them were, so to speak, 'spiritually drunken.' It has been noticed, that he often took that text on such occasions, when he intended to pour out the 'best of the wine.'" He was disappointed if preaching was ever "so superficial that the services were perfectly quiet."[22]

Indiana District and Indiana Conference

When it came time to erect a new conference west of Ohio in 1844, they named it Illinois Conference, tossing in Indiana's three circuits and 562 members as a part of it to be called Indiana District. Absalom Schaefer agreed to become presiding elder of Indiana District with the assured privilege of returning to Ohio after two years.[23] Actually he stayed five years, went back to serve Dayton from 1849 to 1856, and then returned to serve in Indiana nearly ten years more. The Indiana District as Schaefer first served it extended from Defiance, Ohio, to Mt. Carmel, Illinois, including the entire state of Indiana.[24]

By the time Indiana District became Indiana Conference in 1851, it had 13 preachers, 1,285 members, and 16 church buildings. It warranted a respectable place on Bishop Sybert's calendar. His service record for that year read: "In Pennsylvania, one hundred and six days; in New York, fifty days; in Ohio, sixty days; in Michigan, eleven days; in Indiana, thirty-four days; in Illinois, eighty-one days; in Canada, only three days; in Wisconsin, fourteen days; in Maryland, six days; total: three hundred and sixty-five days . . . My journey was five thousand one hundred and sixty-nine miles long."[25] The Evangelical Association built considerable strength in northeastern Indiana, especially on the upper Wabash and its tributaries, merging with the denomination's substantial population in Ohio. Solomon Altimos, working down from Michigan, had begun the work among the Germans in the Fort Wayne area in 1839; John Hall was appointed to create a circuit there in 1841.[26] Evangelical itineration in northern Indiana in 1851 included:

ST. MARY'S CIRCUIT: Consisted of the following classes: Fuhrman, 7 miles northwest, and Salem, 2 miles east of Decatur; Furthmiller, 9 miles east; Five Points, 9 miles south-west; Reserve, Bethlehem, 12 miles south of Ft. Wayne; Gottschalk (Salem) and Vera Cruz, in Wells County . . .

ELKHART CIRCUIT: Composed of Ott's or Salem, Ebenezer, Benton, Waterford, Middleport (Dunlaps), Schwartz's, Loose's, Smith's, Harrison Center, Canada, Union Township, Elkhart County . . . Mishawaka, Coalbush, in St. Joseph County, Barren (now Bremen), Hepton and Heim's in Marshall County, Oster's, near Milford, North Webster, near Larville, Strickler's, near Warsaw, in Kosciusko County.

DEKALB MISSION: Was made up of Stroh's and Husselman's, between Waterloo and Auburn; Diehl's, four miles south of Butler, Schutt's and Kramer's, south of Edgerton,

Brunnersburg, near Defiance, Dickman's and Kuhn's, north of Brunnersburg, Miller's, north-west of Avilla, Schlichtenmeyer's, near Kendallville, west, Dutch St. (Wolcottville), Eshelman's (Wright's Corner), Lima and Van Buren . . .

MIAMI MISSION (FULTON CIRCUIT): Embraced Barnheisel, New Ark, Condo's, Walter's, Sharpie's, around Bunker Hill; Silver Lake, in Kosciusko Co., Meyer's, Leininger's, Stetzel's, in Huntington Co.; Young's and Laketon, in Wabash Co.; Salem and Zwingeisen's, Leidersford, Lake Bruce, South Germany, in Fulton Co.; Zechiel's, Twin Lakes, Maxinkukee, Flora, in Marshall Co.; two appointments south-west of Logansport, and others.[27]

In the central part of the state there was a cluster of members on the upper Whitewater and White rivers. Absalom Schaefer lived for several years at East Germantown (renamed Pershing in 1918) where he had assisted at the state's second Evangelical Association big meeting in 1836. The first Evangelical Association church building in the state was erected there in 1844.[28] In 1851 the Evangelical itineration pattern in central Indiana included:

WHITEWATER CIRCUIT: Comprised of New Lisbon, Cambridge, Zion Church, East Germantown, Pennville, Jacksonburg, Winchester, and probably others.

HAMILTON MISSION: Embodied Indian Creek, Stony Creek, Clarksville, Dicks, Cicero, Pendleton and Whitewater appointments.[29]

About half of Indiana's counties, those in central and southeastern and northwestern sections of the state, had no congregations of the Evangelical Association. But in the southwestern tip of the state a very lively Evangelical area developed, first as an extension of Mt. Carmel Circuit in Illinois and then as Dubois Circuit. Its description in 1851 read:

DUBOIS CIRCUIT: Embraced Huntingburg, Maple Grove, Warrentown (Tabor), Elberfeld, Kohlmeier, near Sommerville, a class in a Methodist Episcopal Church, in Paris, Posey Co., Boonville, Evansville, Rockport, Zoar, Miller's, near Rockport, Ind.[30]

Huntingburg was a particular center of Evangelical vigor. A local preacher named Jacob Trometer led a Christmas morning revival there in 1843. "God's power was greatly manifested . . . Children from 10–12 years of age were mightily gripped by God's Word and converted."[31] When

Bishop Seybert visited the Huntingburg area in 1848 to attend a scheduled camp meeting, he was delighted with the development at Maple Grove.

I attended a camp-meeting at Maple Grove, near Huntingburg, where our friends bought 40 acres of good timber land from the Government for the sum of $50.00. They have built well-covered log-tents, and a preacher's stand and tent, right close to their church, so that the church can be used in case it rains. This property is consecrated to God by a people who, in their poverty, have made a place for the saving of souls. Where can the like be found among the rich converted Americans? No wonder that the windows of heaven were opened over us, and sinners were converted and believers greatly blessed.[32]

In 1851 a new German immigrant named Melchior Mayer was converted at a quarterly meeting at Huntingburg. "Here I fully learned to know myself, and felt that a change of heart must take place," he said. "I became a penitent, acknowledging my sins, and continued until I found peace, joy and conscious salvation on November 30, 1851." Mayer became a class leader in 1852, a preacher on probation in 1854, and a traveling preacher for Dubois Circuit in 1855. There were fifty accessions for the Evangelical Association on his circuit for the year 1855–56. Though he went on to serve at Evansville and at many other places in the state, Mayer often returned for "blessed camp-meetings" at Huntingburg. When the South Indiana Conference met at Huntingburg in March of 1887, Mayer "located" from the itineracy having traveled 75,330 miles and preached 4,407 times.[33]

The Evangelicals had impressive urban work in Dayton and Chicago and Milwaukee. However, urban work was not typical for the Evangelical Association in Indiana. Instead there were scattered rural "fields" served by itinerant or shared preachers. There were thirteen such traveling preachers in Indiana Conference at its formation in 1851.

This great field challenged the "Brave Thirteen" to noble battle. With faith and courage they went forth in the name of their Lord and Master to possess the field and make it subject to the Kingdom. Little attention was paid to English-speaking people, which was surely a mistake, but with holy abandon they went to seek the lost sheep of the "Fatherland," especially as they were found in the rural districts. The cities were considered impregnable, and the seat of all corruption and beyond cure, and generally "passed by on the other side."[34]

Preachers were normally permitted to stay no longer than two consecutive years on a circuit and a presiding elder no longer than four consecutive years on a district. So there was a constant round of emotional farewell occasions.

> When the preacher, at the close of his sermon, declared that he was determined by the grace of God, in spite of tribulations, hardships and adversities, to be faithful until he had finished his course and received the crown in the kingdom of glory and proposed to the audience, that each one who would meet him there should lift up his right hand, immediately the hands would go up, floods of tears burst forth, and deeply moved souls would give vent to their feelings, while they felt as if their heartstrings would be torn asunder. Sometimes the emotions would utter themselves also in shouts of praise at the prospect of a happy re-union in the better world.[35]

Training and Paying the Preachers

In the early years there were no established educational qualifications for the Association's preachers. Bishop John Seybert was a student of theology who wanted his preachers and members to be students as well. He was personally involved in transporting large quantities of printed materials in German to the Ohio Conference on the frontier. Indiana's Evangelical Association preachers were distributors and sellers of books; John Zinser and Absalom Schaefer were among Seybert's most zealous book customers. The Evangelical Association's printing establishment at New Berlin, Pennsylvania, and especially the paper *Der Christliche Botschafter* after 1836, provided grist for preachers who would study.[36]

Somewhat defensively, the General Conference of 1843 made a statement about education. There had been charges that Evangelicals considered formal education "as altogether superfluous, yea even as dangerous and injurious." Conference was quick to assert that an educated person "without a divine call and the unction of the Spirit" was indeed unqualified for ministry. Even a "comparatively illiterate" man with a call was better. Just as quickly the conference acknowledged that the man who was genuinely called of God and endowed with the Holy Ghost had a much greater advantage and wider usefulness if he had some education. It concluded: "This Conference recommends to all its candidates for the ministry, and to all its ministers generally, to take proper measures to store their minds with as large an amount of useful information, as they possibly can, or to endeavor to become learned and literary men, who have also the unction of the Holy Spirit."[37]

The aged John J. Kopp, an Evangelical circuit rider since 1832 and former presiding elder of the Indiana District, described the itinerants and their congregations as he liked to remember them.

> We preachers endeavored to become very useful to our hearers for their salvation, therefore we studied our texts and prayed much in secret for divine help. We also practiced fasting and abstinence. At first we fasted every Friday, later on every quarter, namely on the Friday before Quarterly Meeting, and fasting was also enjoined upon the members. When the friends gathered for worship, they came in a prayerful spirit and devotional frame of mind, and in the meeting they did not look about much; they collected their thoughts and gave attention to the Word of God. The preachers declared the whole counsel of God, sinners were called to repentance and Christians were urged to practice earnestness, honesty and faithfulness in the service of the Lord. The foolish fashions of a vain world, especially in the matter of dress, were not softly dealt with, but cleanliness and propriety were enjoined by precept and example . . . When in those years a preacher lacked unction in preaching, some one would pull at his coat as a token that he should give way to some other one. And in all things we were concerned that all the glory should be given to God. In making pastoral visits we questioned old and young as to the conditions of their souls, and especially professors as to how they were progressing spiritually; thereat the Lord frequently opened the hearts of the people, and when we then closed our interviews with prayer, great good was the result.[38]

In the annual reviews of ministers at the conferences there were many lapses to be dealt with among the part-time local preachers. In 1817 "two were deposed and expelled from the Association on account of unchristian conduct, and three were deposed from the ministry for neglect of duty, the Conference declaring it to be improper to grant a preacher's license to men who preach but a few times during a year or perhaps not at all, and who neglect those duties which are for their own edification and for that of the church."[39] The full-time itinerants came to be more carefully instructed and better disciplined. The first examinations for junior preachers in the Indiana Conference were held in 1853.

> In the early part of the history of the Conference, examiners would ask the examinees to sit in a row. Then he would question them on the studies they were to be examined in. The examiner would usually begin at the upper end of the row, like in a spelling class, and ask the first question. After the answer was given with a mien of some knowledge, and with apparent confidence that the

answer was correct, then the examiner would go down the row and ask each one, "Was the question answered correctly?" If they believed that the first one gave a correct answer, they would assent by "Ja"; if not, they were to give a better answer. The examinees soon observed the usual rule where questioning began, and the less informed would try to have the best informed among them head the row. If they thought he answered well, then they usually would bow their heads with a "Ja" (Yes), and look wise.[40]

Better examination procedures were adopted along with restraints on some conference members who were unreasonably zealous in their questioning.

The services of the early Evangelical Association were emotional.

> A lively worship was highly appreciated. The preaching was to be full of "power," the "praises of God" must be heard from the "children of God" besides the cries of penitents; and at campmeetings a "shout in the camp of King Emmanuel" was expected to take place. In short, no one was satisfied without "victory" in preaching and in the exercises . . . The Quarterly Conference, which was usually held on Saturday forenoon had for its object to ascertain whether all the officers and members of the congregation had conducted themselves as Christians, so that they might be admitted as worthy guests to the Lord's Supper. On Saturday afternoon and frequently also on Sunday morning the presiding elder would deliver a "sermon for Christians," in which Christian experience, life and duties were described clearly and keen applications made.[41]

Everywhere these enthusiastic Germans were subject to the displeasure of both secular opponents and the more traditional German churches. When communicants or constituents of those churches were "converted" to membership in the Evangelical Association, disapproval could become violent. Absalom Schaefer and John Lutz on their Miami Circuit were labeled "deceivers."[42] G. G. Platz reported a glorious camp meeting at Dill's farm in Wayne County in August of 1845.

> There was good behavior on the part of the outsiders until Tuesday night, when the hordes of Satan gathered about, armed with clubs and knives, presaging evil. During the preaching, a sham-battle was played, hoping to lure us out, and when they failed in this, they rushed in upon us, as we surrounded the altar and were praying with the many penitents. For an hour or more, we had a serious and rough time. God's people fell upon their knees and prayed earnestly, sinners cried mightily to God for pardon, while these hoodlums mocked and filled the air with their profanity. The ringleader called

himself a Lutheran, and orthodox, and put us down as deceivers.[43]

John Henry Ragatz was an Evangelical itinerant. He wanted his uncle in Switzerland to understand his ministry in the American Midwest so he wrote at length from East Germantown (later Pershing), Indiana, in July of 1849. Evangelicals did not consider the ministry an ordinary profession, he said. They believed the Bible indicated that God would supply and call ministers to serve the people as prophets, shepherds, and teachers. Such ministers, responding to the call, preached "what we know" and "what we have seen." Primarily "we know that we have come from death to life, and hence we also exhort all persons to repent and seek forgiveness for their sins from God through Christ, and to live righteously and in peace before God, the Father of our Lord." For his uncle, who would be thinking in terms of European territorial parishes, Ragatz described itineracy. "We travel from one vicinity to another to preach," he said," and are satisfied if we have food and clothing." Since the motto of the itinerants was "consecrated to the Lord," they had no fear and did not hesitate to face uncertainties.

Ragatz wanted his uncle to sense the size and structure of the Evangelical enterprise.

> Our Association extends from New york to Iowa and Wisconsin, and from Indiana north to Canada. It is divided first into a general conference, which meets once every four years; secondly into five annual conferences; thirdly the several conferences are divided into districts, each of which is served by one or two pastors . . . These districts are, in the fourth place, divided into classes of from fifteen to forty or still more members, as may be most convenient for the neighborhood. Each such group has a class leader and an exhorter, whose duty it is to call together their body twice each week for prayer meeting. No one can become an Association member until we first see and hear from him that he is whole-heartedly desirous of the salvation of his soul.[44]

He also explained about pay. "Since the relation among the members of the Association is so close, almost like a family, it does not cost us much to travel, for we are entertained everywhere by our brothers in Christ." To meet costs not covered by hospitality, each rider was to collect freewill offerings on his circuit every quarter and turn in the money to the annual conference along with his own travel expense account. This money would be applied proportionally toward salaries and travel expenses of the preachers as far as it would reach. "The salary of an unmarried pastor this year was sixty-two dollars and that of a married one twice as much," Ragatz said, "but out of this we are obliged to provide ourselves with our horses and conveyances, for one must ride horseback or in a little carriage, as there is often as much as forty miles to be covered in going from one preaching place to another, and the roads are on the whole very bad."[45]

In the early years all Evangelical preachers within each annual conference received equal salaries, well below the standard officially established by conference. East Pennsylvania Conference made history in 1841: "The preachers received their salary in full—that is to say: each single preacher received $60—each married preacher $105 and $15 for each child under fourteen years, together with 'reasonable traveling expenses'! This was the first time in the history of any Conference that this occurred; it was therefore something altogether new and cheering."[46] In 1861 Indiana Conference declared a new basis: "Salaries on circuits were, from now on, independent of each other, so that each circuit preacher could keep the amount paid, in excess of his fixed salary, instead of distributing it to those who fell short."[47]

Evangelical Association statistical units and categories did not neatly match those of the federal census takers. So the 1902 statistics for the fiftieth anniversary of the Indiana Conference of the Evangelical Association, a body not quite coterminous with the boundaries of the state, reported 69 "fields" (9 stations, 16 circuits, 44 missions) containing 162 "appointments" served by 70 itinerant preachers and 56 local preachers. The conference claimed 10,549 communicant members and 12,867 scholars in its 149 Sunday schools.[48] For the state of Indiana proper the federal religious census of 1906 reported 8,787 members of the Evangelical Association in 112 "organizations"—less than Ohio (14,932), Pennsylvania (13,294) and Wisconsin (13,280), but more than Illinois (8,660).

From German to English

Very slowly the Evangelical Association made room for the English language. Its founder, Jacob Albright, was not competent in English and understood his mission as ministering to Germans in the German language. Evangelical elder John Dreisbach conferred with Francis Asbury about union with the Methodists in 1810. Asbury thought the German language would not exist long in the United States. He advised the Albright people to learn English and become Methodists. However, Dreisbach was among those who believed that German would not only persist but increase, so he considered a continuing German ministry to be fundamental. In the face of this

difference of opinion, union with the Methodists was delayed 158 years.[49]

In 1830 a young preacher named John Hamilton urged the Evangelical Association to move quickly from German to English usage. He also advocated some radical views about abolishing all organizations and doctrinal statements. As an adverse reaction to this man and all his views, the General Conference of 1830 dismissed him from the Association and specified "that no more preachers shall be received into the traveling connection who are not somewhat proficient in the German language." John Seybert, elected bishop in 1839, had received elementary education in both German and English but never became fluent in the latter. He wanted Evangelical Association churches and Sunday schools to be German. He said that English-speaking people were already amply provided for by other churches. If the Evangelical Association did not help the Germans in the United States, nobody else would. He believed God had commissioned the ministry of the Evangelical Association specifically to bring the light and life of the gospel to the neglected German population.[50]

The adoption of English was delayed but could not be denied. In 1834 the General Conference acted to allow any annual conference to organize an English conference within its bounds if it had as many as ten English preachers. An edition of the English Discipline appeared the next year and an improved and enlarged English Hymnal in 1846. Indiana Conference permitted a journal of its proceedings to be taken in English after 1875 so long as there was a parallel official journal in German.[51] In Indiana Conference in the fiftieth anniversary year of 1902 there were 1,228 subscribers to the English church paper called the *Evangelical Messenger* established in 1847 compared to 794 subscribers to the German church paper called the *Christliche Botschafter* established in 1836. Among the Sunday school papers the *Christliche Kinderfreund* numbered 749 Indiana subscribers while the *Sunday School Messenger* had 2,391. The national trend toward English usage developed fast enough to alarm German speakers so they demanded and received three conferences to be designated German and remain German.[52] Local congregations were divided in their language preference; preachers were mixed in their language abilities. One Hoosier preacher joked rather painfully. "When the Presiding Elders wanted a congregation to change over, they sent me. After hearing me attempt to preach in German, the people readily changed to English."[53] Many members or prospective members simply grew weary of the language issue and joined the Methodists.

After surviving the anti-German bias of the First World War and a thirty-year schism in its own ranks over ethnicity, episcopacy, and sectionalism, the Evangelical Association chose to move toward a union seriously discussed 130 years before—union with their German kinsmen the United Brethren in Christ.[54] This national merger in 1946 resulted in a major church in Indiana where both groups were substantial, an Evangelical United Brethren denomination larger than the Presbyterians or the Lutherans and fifth largest in the state. Merger with the Methodists came in 1968.

NOTES

1. J. Bruce Behney and Paul H. Eller, *History of the Evangelical United Brethren Church* (Nashville, Tenn.: Abingdon, 1979), 68–72; James I. Good, *History of the Reformed Church in the U.S. in the Nineteenth Century* (New York: Board of Publication of the Reformed Church in America, 1911), 653.

2. Raymond W. Albright, *History of the Evangelical Church* (Harrisburg, Pa.: Evangelical Press, 1942), 52.

3. Behney and Eller, *History*, 71–73.

4. Sylvanus C. Breyfogel, *Landmarks of the Evangelical Association* (Reading, Pa.: Eagle Book Print, 1888), 11–12.

5. Breyfogel, *Landmarks*, 13.

6. *Disciplines* of the Albrights were always very similar to the Methodist *Disciplines*. Elder John Dreisbach carried the Methodist *Discipline* of 1805 as his standard until the Albrights produced their own. See Behney and Eller, *History*, 131, 143–48.

7. Behney and Eller, *History*, 73–82, 91, 94; Breyfogel, *Landmarks*, 17–18, 30.

8. Breyfogel, *Landmarks*, 34; Behney and Eller, *History*, 147.

9. Behney and Eller, *History*, 148–52.

10. Samuel P. Spreng, *The Life and Labors of John Seybert* (Cleveland, Ohio: Evangelical Publishing House, 1888), 194–95, 204; Roy B. Leedy, *The Evangelical Church in Ohio* (Harrisburg, Pa.: Evangelical Press, 1959), 72–75, 78; Samuel H. Baumgartner, *Historical Data and Life Sketches of the Deceased Ministers of the Indiana Conference of the Evangelical Association 1835 to 1915* (N.p.: The Conference, 1915), 11.

11. For early Evangelicals "big meetings" usually began on Saturday and ended Sunday evening. Later they became "quarterly meetings," often the occasions for celebrating the Lord's Supper. "Camp meetings" were larger. They were coordinated in the schedules of preachers and circuits over a wide area and were likely to last a week. Camp meetings were rallying points for the membership, instruments for evangelism and church extension, schools for new preachers, and validation points for ministerial candidates on the track toward ordination.

12. Baumgartner, *Historical Data*, 261–67.

13. Leedy, *Evangelical Church*, 75.

14. Leedy, *Evangelical Church*, 61, 76–77, 84–87, 104.

15. Leedy, *Evangelical Church*, 87; Baumgartner, *Historical Data*, 267.

16. Reuben Yeakel, *History of the Evangelical Association*, 2 vols. (Cleveland, Ohio: Thomas and Mattill, 1894), 1:258–62, 282–83; Behney and Eller, *History*, 134; Spreng, *Life*, 233; Leedy, *Evangelical Church*, 61–65, 82, 87–89.

17. Leedy, *Evangelical Church*, 87.

18. For the Evangelical Association a "mission" was a hopeful early stage of a circuit, served by a circuit rider developing an increasing series of preaching points.

19. Spreng, *Life*, 231.

20. Spreng, *Life*, 230–31.

21. Leedy, *Evangelical Church*, 88.

22. Spreng, *Life*, 231–32, 236, 282, 284.

23. Leedy, *Evangelical Church*, 111, 117; see Baumgartner, *Historical Data*, 270 which says the assured privilege was to return after four years.

24. Baumgartner, *Historical Data*, 261–71.

25. Spreng, *Life*, 300.

26. Leedy, *Evangelical Church*, 60, 88; Baumgartner, *Historical Data*, 11–12.

27. Baumgartner, *Historical Data*, 22–23.

28. Baumgartner, *Historical Data*, 14; Leedy, *Evangelical Church*, 61, 115.

29. Baumgartner, *Historical Data*, 22–23.

30. Baumgartner, *Historical Data*, 23.

31. Baumgartner, *Historical Data*, 14–17; Leedy, *Evangelical Church*, 105–14.

32. Baumgartner, *Historical Data*, 18. See also Spreng, *Life*, 284–85.

33. Baumgartner, *Historical Data*, 197–202.

34. Baumgartner, *Historical Data*, 21.

35. Yeakel, *History*, 1:451.

36. Spreng, *Life*, 228–29; Leedy, *Evangelical Church*, 91–101; Behney and Eller, *History*, 141–44.

37. Yeakel, *History*, 1:356–57.

38. Yeakel, *History*, 1:452.

39. Breyfogel, *Landmarks*, 31. See also Breyfogel, *Landmarks*, 46, 75, 79, 92; Albright, *History*, 164; Yeakel, *History*, 1:446.

40. Baumgartner, *Historical Data*, 359.

41. Yeakel, *History*, 1:449–50.

42. Baumgartner, *Historical Data*, 11.

43. Baumgartner, *Historical Data*, 15.

44. John Henry Ragatz, "A Circuit Rider in the Old Northwest: Letters of the Reverend John H. Ragatz," translation and notes by Lowell J. Ragatz, *Wisconsin Magazine of History* 7 (September 1923): 95.

45. Ragatz, "Circuit Rider," 95–96.

46. Yeakel, *History*, 1:326.

47. Baumgartner, *Historical Data*, 338.

48. Baumgartner, *Historical Data*, 25.

49. Yeakel, *History*, 1:108–10; Behney and Eller, *History*, 87.

50. Behney and Eller, *History*, 140, 143, 149; Albright, *History*, 238–39.

51. Harry O. Huffman, *History of the Indiana Conference North of the Evangelical United Brethren Church* (Nappanee, Ind.: Evangel Press, 1968), 12; Behney and Eller, *History*, 143; Leedy, *Evangelical Church*, 112.

52. Yeakel, *History*, 1:443; Behney and Eller, *History*, 144, 198; Baumgartner, *Historical Data*, 25.

53. Huffman, *History*, 13.

54. Breyfogel, *Landmarks*, 30.

UNITED BRETHREN IN CHRIST

A particularly effective blending of German piety with American revivalism occurred in the United Brethren in Christ. They had notable leaders. These highly visible leaders were representatives of an army of colleagues less well known.

Philip William Otterbein (1726–1813) was in some sense a founder of the United Brethren. Otterbein was a German Reformed clergyman. His grandfather, father, and all five of his brothers were German Reformed clergymen. He lived, worked, and died a German Reformed clergyman in good standing. Some of his religious intensity rooted in his home life and in Herborn Academy in the German province of Nassau where all the male members of his family studied theology. A biographer said: "Throughout his ministry Otterbein showed the influence of Calvinistic thought in its warm expression in the Heidelberg Confession, the doctrine of the covenants, and the depth of religious feeling and moral rectitude of Pietism. These influences came upon him from every member of his family and from the religious spirit of his theological teachers in the Herborn Academy, especially Professors John Henry Schramm, Valentine Rau, and John Eberhart."[1]

Otterbein's ideal of personal religious discipline found expression in his first pastorate at Ockersdorf in Nassau where he organized the more responsive members of the laity into small Bible study and prayer groups within the larger congregation. This pious interest showed in his response to a missionary calling. Michael Schlatter came

looking for Reformed ministers to return with him to serve the struggling Germans in America. Otterbein, not quite twenty-six, was ready to pass the examination of the Amsterdam Classis and set sail for Pennsylvania.

> When it became known that six young pastors had arrived, the congregations immediately issued calls. Otterbein accepted a call from the congregation in Lancaster and made the journey westward over seventy miles of rough wagon trail. He served the Lancaster church for six years from 1752 to 1758. Following that pastorate he served two churches in the area of Tulpehocken, Pennsylvania, from 1758 to 1760, the church in Frederick, Maryland, from 1760 to 1765, and the church in York, Pennsylvania, from 1765 to 1774. This constituted his early ministry. His last pastorate was in Baltimore from 1774 to 1813. While serving these early pastorates Otterbein also responded to the needs of people living in remote areas. To do so he traveled on horseback or, where there were passable roads, by carriage. Such places were Pequea, Reading, Oley, Conewago, Lebanon, Paradise, Bermudian, and Kreutz Creek in Pennsylvania and Antietam, Pipe Creek, and Middletown in Maryland . . . In each place he organized a prayer and study group, the *collegium pietatis*, which he had used in the church at Ockersdorf. This called for lively lay participation to which the more staid members of his churches objected.[2]

Otterbein reported a personal religious experience, a direct assurance of God's saving grace, while in his parish at Lancaster in 1754. Then he laid aside his silk robe and sermonic essays and spoke to the people more confidently and directly. No matter where he served as pastor, Otterbein served at the same time as an itinerant preacher seeking converts outside the normal orbit of "respectable" churches. Other German Reformed pastors and some lay preachers shared the itinerant work with him. As they gathered their hearers into classes under local leadership, they conferred with each other about ways to give their class members oversight. For example, when they met at Pipe Creek, Maryland, in 1774 they said: "The ground and object of these meetings is to be, that those thus united may encourage one another, pray and sing in unison, and watch over one another's conduct. At these meetings they are to be especially careful to see to it that family worship is regularly maintained. All those who are thus united are to take heed that no disturbances occur among them, and that the affairs of the congregations be conducted and managed in an orderly manner."[3]

While Otterbein was shaping his ministry to the Germans in America, Martin Boehm (1725–1812) was finding his way as well. The two men did not seem very similar. Otterbein was European; Boehm was a native Pennsylvanian. Otterbein was university educated; Boehm was somewhat self-taught. Otterbein was a mainstream Reformed churchman; Boehm was Mennonite with little concern for historical creed or structure. Otterbein baptized babies by sprinkling as children of the covenant; Boehm recognized only adult believers as candidates for baptism by pouring. Otterbein was a childless widower without real property; Boehm was a wealthy farmer with a large family. Their lives were cast together when Boehm was chosen by lot to be a minister for his local congregation in Lancaster County. Reduced to stammering and to lamenting his lack of fitness, he appealed for divine mercy. The words of Jesus came into his mind: "I am come to seek and save that which is lost." He reported "In a moment a stream of joy was poured over me."[4]

From that time on Boehm preached, not only by invitation in local Mennonite congregations but also on a broad itinerant circuit among Germans in Pennsylvania, Maryland, and Virginia. Preachers, both German and English, were raised up among his converts. Boehm and his preachers were among the denominations sharing in "great meetings" scheduled several days at a time at convenient farms or groves. Boehm called such a meeting for Whitsuntide of 1767 on the farm of Isaac Long in Lancaster County, Pennsylvania. At that place there was a timber and stone barn 108 feet in length. Otterbein, pastor at nearby York, attended the meeting and heard

Boehm's sermon preached on the threshing floor of the big barn. It was the same gospel of regeneration which he preached; Boehm's personal experience of the assurance of God's saving grace was like his own. After the sermon Otterbein went forward to embrace Boehm and exclaim "We are Brethren" (Wir sind Brüder).[5]

Otterbein and Boehm soon recognized their common evangelistic enterprise. At the same time they were colleagues with their obvious theological kin, the Methodists. Francis Asbury and Philip Otterbein overcame the barrier of Otterbein's broken English to become good friends. At Asbury's invitation Otterbein shared in the ordination of Asbury as a Methodist bishop at the "Christmas Conference" in Baltimore in 1784. Boehm was on the membership list of a Methodist class which met at Boehm's Chapel. He found great comfort in meeting with the Methodists. But the Methodists were mostly English speakers and the Methodist bishop did not hesitate to wield his authority. Otterbein and Boehm felt a bond of German ethnicity and an affection for ecclesiastical freedom which was even stronger than their bond with Methodists. They kept expanding their work among the Germans in their own way. They enlisted additional Reformed and Mennonite preachers for the movement. They commissioned lay participants to serve as preachers. In 1789 and 1791 they and their preachers met in conferences.

> No minutes of the meetings are extant, but two historians of the United Brethren Church, Henry Spayth, writing in 1819 and 1850, and John Lawrence, writing in 1860, both depending on prior sources, give a total list of twenty-two preachers who were in attendance at the meetings or who were regarded by those in attendance as members of the fellowship. The church background is known of all but four of these men. Ten—William Otterbein, George A. Geeting, Adam Lehman, John Ernst, John George Pfrimmer, Henry Weidner, Henry Baker, Frederick Schaffer, Christian Crum, and Benedict Schwope— were of the Reformed Church; six—Martin Boehm, Christian Newcomer, John Neidig, Martin Crider, John Hershey, and Simon Herre—were Mennonite; Abraham Troxel was Amish; Christopher Grosh was Moravian. The four whose religious affiliation is not known were Benedict Sanders, G. Fortenbach, Daniel Strickler, and J. Hautz. Of the ten Reformed preachers only Otterbein, Geeting, and Schwope had been formally ordained.[6]

United Brethren Organize

Their conference of 1800 has been generally accepted as the formal beginning of the United Brethren Church.[7] By then being United Brethren in Christ was probably the primary religious identity of those gathered. Boehm's broad associations with other religious fellowships had led to his excommunication by the Mennonite leadership by 1780. The chief ministry of George Adam Geeting (1741–1812) was in the evangelistic services and great meetings at his own meeting house plus itineration reaching five states; the German Reformed synod was processing charges against him on the grounds that he was "fanatical." Otterbein remained an active German Reformed pastor but the United Brethren competed for his best attention. Geeting was secretary for the annual conferences from 1800 to 1812 and prepared an official compilation of the minutes. The compilation indicated that Otterbein and Boehm were chosen as bishops in 1800, variously called "elders" and "superintendents" but clearly understood to be bishops. There was no ordination of ministers by United Brethren until 1813 but all conferences from 1800 authorized men to preach and assigned them to their circuits or districts.[8]

Otterbein was seventy-four years old when elected a bishop for the United Brethren and Boehm was nearly seventy-five. By 1813 Otterbein, Boehm, and Geeting were dead with the structure and direction of the United Brethren still undecided. The emerging leader was Christian Newcomer (1749–1830), a Mennonite turned traveling preacher about 1777 under the ministry of Otterbein and Boehm. He identified himself increasingly with the revival movement. On 5 May 1813 the conference named him bishop. Because he believed the United Brethren must develop a stabilizing structure, he had been gathering converts into formally organized classes at his preaching points even before his election, as early as 1809.[9] Three-quarters of a century after Newcomer's election, a United Brethren historian regarded his ministry as crucial in forming the denomination's identity:

> From 1813 to 1820 was an unsettled period in our denominational history. Its founder had been a member of the Reformed Church. Before his death, it had drawn largely from the Mennonites, through the labors of Boehm, Newcomer and others. As the Reformed element waned, the Mennonite increased in strength. Unaccustomed to much organization, and desiring the utmost simplicity, it is questionable whether the United Brethren Church might not have been sacrificed, had it not been for the strong hand and native tact of Newcomer. He was the re-founder of the Church, and, humanly speaking, had it not been for the tact and good sense, and the piety

of this man of God, we might not, as a denomination, be in existence to-day.[10]

It was Newcomer who had followed the German population westward and organized the Miami Annual Conference in 1810. It was his Miami Conference which had petitioned Otterbein "to ordain, by the laying on of hands, one or more preachers, who afterward may perform the same for others." Newcomer was one of the first three United Brethren ordinands, the ones ordained by the aged Otterbein and Methodist elder William Ryland in October of 1813. Newcomer was always in the saddle, supervising both the eastern constituency and the westward expansion.

> In 1795 he began to record his activities in the *Journal*. Using his farm home in Washington County, Maryland, as his base, he rode many times on horseback, usually with one or two companions, in four different areas or "circuits": (1) north into Pennsylvania west of the Susquehanna as far as Tyrone, Mount Union, and Lewisburg, then across the river to the eastern side, south through Lancaster County, and then to his home; (2) east in Maryland toward Baltimore and then back to his home; (3) south into the Virginia Valley and back to his home; and (4) beginning in 1799, westward into southwestern Pennsylvania. He made this journey five times, thus crossing the Allegheny Mountains ten times. In 1810, when he was sixty-one years old, he extended the western trips and usually rode through Wheeling, across southern Ohio, into Kentucky as far as Lexington, through Louisville into southeastern Indiana, to Dayton, Ohio, and through north central Ohio to Akron, through Pittsburgh and Bedford and back to his home. This journey he made nineteen times, once each year until 1829—except 1811, the year his wife died. Thus he crossed the Alleghenies on these extended trips thirty-eight times, making a total of forty-eight crossings. He usually left on these extended trips in early spring and returned home in midsummer in time to take his grain cradle and help harvest the grain crops on his farm.[11]

Though he rode these episcopal circuits until he was eighty, he did not live to see the union with the Methodists and with the Evangelical Association which he desired. His constituency resisted adopting a Discipline to be a basis for these unions until the best opportunities for union had passed. The First General Conference, in 1815, did adopt and publish a Discipline. It provided for bishops chiefly administrative, elected for four year terms, in charge of an itinerant system which no church authority was ever to be permitted to abolish.[12]

John George Pfrimmer in Southern Indiana

Growth of the United Brethren in Christ in Indiana was remarkably early and remarkably sustained. A veteran preacher named John George Pfrimmer moved to Corydon in 1808. This man was an immigrant Alsatian surgeon broadly educated in French and German, brought up in the Reformed Church, a convert among the early United Brethren in 1790 who began at once to preach, a participant in the formative conferences of 1791 and 1800 which confirmed the leadership of Otterbein and Boehm, and a highly successful itinerant in Pennsylvania. He was one of the inner circle of the brotherhood, known to all its early leaders.[13]

Pfrimmer had heavy responsibilities at Corydon. There was his medical practice and his farm of 160 acres of government land to be attended. Territorial governor William Henry Harrison appointed Pfrimmer a county judge and enlisted his assistance in the development of county and territorial government. Harrison also employed Pfrimmer in an unsuccessful attempt to operate some mills in the area. His family grew to include six children; the piano he brought to Corydon to assist in their instruction was one of the state's first. At the same time Pfrimmer developed such a following in religious work that he began to organize the people into societies of the United Brethren even before the United Brethren had ordained their first ministers or adopted a Discipline—Pfrimmer Chapel five miles northeast of Corydon in 1812, Stonecypher Church on the farm of Henry Stonecypher three and one half miles southeast of Corydon in 1813, a church among the Pennsylvania Germans near Charlestown in 1813.[14]

In 1814 Pfrimmer reported on the Indiana work to the Miami Conference of the United Brethren meeting in Ohio and began his active membership in that body. His leadership was promptly recognized. He was formally ordained an elder at the conference session in 1815. At the conference session in June of 1816 a collection of $2.72 was taken among the preachers and "given to Br. Pfrimmer in order to purchase a book and record all of the proceedings of this Conference." At the same 1816 session Pfrimmer functioned as assistant to Bishop Newcomer and was named presiding elder of a new district including southeastern Indiana and northern Kentucky.[15]

After that 1816 conference session at Andrew Zeller's in Ohio, Pfrimmer and Bishop Newcomer rode west together to look at parts of Pfrimmer's new district. Having passed through Madison and Lexington, they took a pilot to show them the way through the forest to Henry Steinseifer's. Newcomer wrote in his journal:

I am now in Clark county, State of Indiana, more than 100 miles west of the State of Ohio. We came today to an elevated spot of ground from whence we had a view all around to a considerable distance; here I humbled myself on my knees in gratitude to God, who in mercy has preserved me in this wilderness to the present time: ultimately we reached the house of a Mr. Swartz, where we took some refreshment and rode to John George Pfrimmer's, where we staid for the night . . . I reached Corydon, in Harrison county. A Convention of the people is at present assembled here to form a State Constitution. I visited Mr. Reis and returned to Pfrimmer's . . . I preached here to a numerous congregation, both in the German and English languages. The people appeared to be greatly affected, nearly all of them shed tears; I bid them farewell, rode to Mr. Zeller's, thence to John Bauman's and staid for the night.[16]

Pfrimmer was a pioneer for the United Brethren in Indiana. He organized at least fifteen churches between 1812 and 1821, mostly in Harrison, Floyd, and Dearborn counties, and supervised much of the work from the time he joined the Miami Conference in 1814 through 1823.[17] However it is important to see him in the full context of the United Brethren itinerant plan. Thirty-five United Brethren preachers worked in Indiana and Kentucky between the time Pfrimmer settled in Harrison County in 1808 and the time Indiana Conference was organized in 1830. Bishop Newcomer and the Miami Conference kept fulfilling their roles so that by 1819 Pfrimmer was in charge of the Indiana Knobs Circuit but the powerful and popular preachers Jacob Antrim and John C. McNamar had Indiana circuits as well. In 1820 Pfrimmer was the senior one of three preachers on the Indiana Knobs Circuit but there were three other riders staffing two additional circuits.[18]

By 1827 the significance of the United Brethren in Indiana was recognized again when Bishop Newcomer convened the Miami Conference at Corydon, Indiana. It was his first episcopal tour in a carriage; he was seventy-eight. John George Pfrimmer died in 1825 and Christian Newcomer in 1830 but the work of the United Brethren in Indiana hardly felt a change of pace. The year Newcomer died the new Indiana Conference held its first session at Stonecypher Meetinghouse in Harrison County. Bishop Henry Kumler Sr. presided, a leadership role he was to take repeatedly for United Brethren conferences in Indiana. Presiding elders were named for East and West districts. Preachers were assigned to circuits named White Water, Tanner's Creek, Flat Rock, Charlestown, Orange, Corydon, Coal Creek, and Wea. Indiana Conference accepted an invitation to hold its second meeting in 1831 at the home of Margaret Hoobler in faraway Fountain County on Indiana's western border.[19]

The Hoobler Family and the Wabash Conference

Volunteering to house and feed sixteen United Brethren preachers complete with horses for a seven-day conference held no terrors for Margaret Hoobler.[20] She was a Brown, member of a Pennsylvania family which had many friendly links with Bishop Christian Newcomer. Her brother Peter and four sons of Peter came to be United Brethren preachers, one a bishop. Her own sons John and William became preachers and her daughter Mary a substantial contributor to the church.[21] In her accounts of her own younger days Margaret Hoobler would tell how she "walked thirty miles to watch night meetings, sixty miles to two-days meetings and ninety miles to camp meeting, over the hills of Pennsylvania. They would take a wagon in which were bedding, children and provisions. The older ones walked, stopping with some christian family and have meeting there at night. Next morning the family with whom they had tarried would join and go along to another family, and so on, until the place of worship was reached and people from all directions assembled; they had a most glorious meeting."[22]

But Margaret's husband Jacob died in Pennsylvania, leaving her to be Widow Hoobler with seven children to provide for. She migrated with a mixture of Browns and Hooblers who relocated in southwestern Ohio in 1822. One computation indicated that a score of United Brethren preachers came out of their communities at Taylor's Creek a few miles west of Cincinnati. In 1826 the Hoobler and Brown families furnished the nucleus of a colony that migrated 200 miles northwest to Indiana's Wabash country. One group located at a bend of the Wabash, a few miles west of Lafayette. Margaret Hoobler built her large house, designed as a dwelling and a place of worship, at the forks of Coal Creek in Fountain County. There followed an outbreak of United Brethren societies in the region.[23]

John Hoobler was Margaret's eldest child, a resident convert at Taylor's Creek and protege of Bishop Henry Kumler. He came to the Wabash bearing his license to preach. As soon as he had built a cabin for his family he began his evangelistic work—one class three miles from home where he found Jacob, John, and David Bonebrake and families along with "Father and Mother Baker and their children"; another class gathered around a cluster of former United Brethren lately arrived from Butler County,

Ohio; another class at Lopp's Prairie where Simon Brown had located. He preached every two weeks for each of these classes. In September of 1827 he traveled to Ohio to report to Bishop Henry Kumler: "Three classes, forty or fifty members (I guess at the number) whose lives are commendable. Congregations large and getting larger. Prospects good."[24]

The bishop gave John Hoobler his approval and a sufficient examination to have him admitted to annual conference membership the following spring. For twenty-two years Hoobler was an itinerant for Indiana and Wabash conferences, for nine of them a presiding elder—this in addition to two terms as a representative in the Indiana legislature and twenty years of preaching in Illinois.[25] His nephew Adam Shambaugh has written that John Hoobler was a master at preacher recruitment.

> Every young man and some old ones that gave evidence at his conversion that he had the gift of relating the story of Jesus and his love, was at once put on the stand. His theory was that if any young or old man could move people to tears in talking of heaven and glory, such a one the Lord had need of . . . He excelled all other men I ever knew finding young preachers; having found them, to work they had to go. Setting by to cheer them on, "amen" followed "amen." "God bless the brother and help him to preach." "That is truth, oh, Lord send it home." Another "amen" and so on until a pretty good message was given to the people. Was it any wonder then that Hoobler had a train of preachers half as long as the Wabash River. All loved him, and he loved them all. I never heard him say one unfriendly word against any of his boy preachers, nor did I ever hear one boy say anything but tender words of love for him . . . Following are some of the young men who were authorized to minister in the house of the Lord: George Kite, Robert Baker, Samuel Potts, William Hoobler, Samuel C. Zuck, George Davis, Abraham Eckles, Jacob Dice, Walden Smith, Wm. H. Brown, John A. Nast, Jeremiah and Jacob Kenoyer, Andrew Winset, George Myers, James Timmons, William Harett, Bres. Freeman, Jackson Baily and others whom I can not name now.[26]

For expansion into northern Indiana the bishops and the conferences were by no means wholly dependent on Browns and Hooblers. Concurrent with the earliest white settlement, the upper Wabash was integrated into the regular United Brethren itinerant system with valued workers annually assigned. Frederick Kenoyer, son-in-law of John George Pfrimmer, rode horseback 180 miles from Harrison County to Warren County to the first stop on his pioneer assignment to the Pine Creek Circuit. At the invitation of Aaron Rawlings near Annapolis in Parke

County, Kenoyer established a new class. It became the basis for the Rawlings camp meetings begun in 1835 and conducted every year for a quarter of a century. These camp meetings plus the ones held annually at the farms of Jesse David and "Father Baker" near Lafayette kept energizing United Brethren in all that region. Presiding elders and circuit riders depended largely on camp meetings to reach the unchurched.[27]

Miami Conference sent John Denham to Wabash Circuit in 1829. He wore long hair as a reminder of his rescue from early backsliding and was "somewhat eccentric" but became a recognized expert in the perpetual frontier conflicts with Campbellites over baptism.[28] James Griffith entered Indiana Conference as a charter member in 1830. As a guest at Margaret Hoobler's for the conference session of 1831 he was assigned to Coal Creek Circuit in the upper Wabash and spent forty-five years of his life as preacher and presiding elder for northern Indiana.[29]

By the time Wabash Circuit had become Wabash Conference and was holding its 1836 session at the home of the Hooblers, John Hoobler was already surrounded by a whole company of itinerant colleagues. Conference minutes recorded that "Josiah Davis and John Hoobler were chosen presiding elders. The assignments were as follows: Upper District, Josiah Davis, P. E.; St. Joseph, James Griffith, William Robertson; Pine Creek, Frederick Kenoyer; Wea, William Davis. Lower District, John Hoobler, P. E.; Coal Creek, Elijah T. Cook, William Hoobler; Vermillion, James Davis, Ephraim Shuey."[30] Growth from this northern Indiana base was explosive. Six years later, in 1842, the Wabash Conference was extending its boundaries to include the state of Illinois plus some outposts in Iowa and Wisconsin. That year it reported fifty preachers, thirteen applicants for licensure, and about twenty circuits or missions. The gain in membership for this conference for 1843 alone was 2,144. The conference kept multiplying by forming new conferences named Lower Wabash (1858), Upper Wabash (1858), and St. Joseph (1845).[31]

Early Openness to English

One cause of the notable growth of Wabash Conference in the early 1840s was the ministry of a particular conference missionary. Wabash Conference received John Calvin McNamar by transfer in 1841 but his place in his denomination's history had been assured long before that. In 1812, when United Brethren preachers were assumed to be German, this Scottish school teacher was converted at a meeting in Andrew Zeller's barn near Germantown in Ohio. After his conversion he wanted to preach and was recognized in 1812 as an exhorter. There is no indication that he became competent to preach in German or that he was required to do so. Miami Conference received him into its fellowship of preachers in 1813, ordained him in 1816, and assigned him to the "Lawrenceburg to Corydon Mission" in Indiana in 1820. Indiana was to be his place. When Miami Conference met for the first time on Indiana soil at Charlestown in August of 1823, McNamar was present. His colleagues named him secretary for the conference session and assigned him to White Water Circuit—the counties of Fayette, Franklin, Union, and Wayne. They appointed him repeatedly to missionary duty in the state, evidently valuing the effect of his English preaching. In 1826, 1829, 1831, and 1834 they elected him presiding elder. When Indiana Conference was formed in 1830 he was a respected charter member. And when the bishop failed to attend Indiana Conference in 1831, 1834, and 1835 McNamar presided over the sessions. As a Wabash Conference missionary in the early 1840s, McNamar conducted "celebrated campaigns" in Clay and Owen counties.[32] Thus he added strength to the United Brethren all across the state, not least in the central area which became White River Conference in 1846. A historian of the Indiana Conference of United Brethren said McNamar "had marvelous success in evangelistic service. He was among the first English preachers in Indiana, and won many to the ministry, who became English preachers."[33]

This was an indication of the openness of the United Brethren to the use of English. They were not ashamed to be German but not resistant to English. For them the important thing was to get the people to hear. From the earliest days of the movement, its founders who could preach in English did so if there were hearers limited to English. It was common for them to hold joint meetings and evangelistic tours with Methodists so that a preacher from the United Brethren like Otterbein could preach to the mixed congregants in German and a Methodist like Francis Asbury could preach to them in English.[34] When the United Brethren bishop Christian Newcomer came to Indiana as the state was forming in 1816, he made it a matter of record that he preached in Indiana in German and in English.

English quickly took a place in United Brethren publications. When Indiana Conference was organized in 1830 there were two secretaries—Craven Linn for English and George Brown for German.

The General conference of 1817, after revising the *Discipline*, ordered that the original be printed in German and a translation into English also be published. One hundred English copies were made. In the 1820's General and Annual Conferences had two secretaries, one German and one English. By 1837 the English language had become predominant. The General Conference of that year was conducted in English. It ordered the *Discipline* to be printed primarily in English and then in German. Six thousand copies of the English *Discipline* were made and two thousand of the German translation.[35]

The denominational paper named the *Religious Telescope* published its first issue on the last day of 1834. It was printed only in English from its beginning. In the Wabash country James Davis was converted in 1830. He was the first convert of John Hoobler to become a preacher, a young man illiterate in any language. First he learned to read English, carrying his English spelling book on his first circuit. Next he added a German spelling book to begin mastery of the second language. Frederick Kenoyer, at work in the Wabash country in the early 1830s, was a good singer and preacher "using both English and German languages at pleasure." It was Indiana's McNamar who came to symbolize such openness to English; he received the reputation and the epitaph as "first English preacher" among the United Brethren.[36]

Some German members lamented the continuing shift to the use of English. They were treated with courtesy. A new German periodical entitled *Die Geschäftige Martha* was issued for them beginning in 1840. The early United Brethren generally avoided division over language or religious tradition. United Brethren with Mennonite and Baptist heritage might prefer baptism of adults only and that by pouring or immersion. Those with Methodist or Reformed associations might prefer to baptize by sprinkling and include children as members of the covenant. These differences did not disrupt the United Brethren. They followed the preference of the persons involved. Occasionally they practiced footwashing where footwashing was important to the members who were of Dunker background, this with a caution in the Discipline of 1825 against extreme emphasis on this rite. They were unyielding against the general German fondness for alcoholic beverages and for freewheeling recreation on Sunday. Some of the earliest preachers and members, including Otterbein, used alcoholic beverages but the practice passed and abstinence became a membership requirement.[37] There was no substantial division among United Brethren over these things. Not even the issue of slavery could divide the United Brethren. The General Conference of 1821 took action on the subject: "Resolved that in no sense of the word shall slavery in whatsoever form it

may exist, be tolerated in our church, and that no slaveholder, making application for membership, shall be received, and that if any member by found to possess slaves, he cannot remain a member, unless he manumit his slaves as soon as notified to do so by the annual conference."[38] Controversy was between anti-slavery people who wanted instant abolition and anti-slavery people who wanted to allow more time to work for a more amicable national settlement. The denomination was not torn.[39]

Division over Secret Societies

What did divide the United Brethren was a conflict over secret societies. Could a person be a member of the Masonic Order and at the same time a member of the United Brethren? There was a social dimension to this conflict.

> The United Brethren was almost entirely a rural church in the State of Indiana during its earlier history. Most of their church societies were compelled to worship in private homes in those early years. The log building was the one in common use for many years, for home, school and church. As late as 1880 nearly one-half of the Church societies in Indiana Conference worshiped in school houses. The preachers in those days could not devote all their time to church work, for the reason that their salaries were meager, and wages were low, and their families had to be provided for. Many of the preachers were farmers, and they could only give a part of their time to church work. These were the conditions that prevailed well up in the fifties.[40]

But members and ministers who wanted to belong to lodges were generally the more affluent, often the town and city dwellers. The issue was sharpened in anti-Masonic statements by conferences in 1826, 1827, 1829, and 1833. Joseph A. Ball admitted at the 1832 session of Indiana Conference that he had previously joined the Masons but he repented the act and was restored as a preacher. The new constitution for the denomination in 1841 said "There shall be no connection with secret combinations." That closed all lodges and some temperance societies to United Brethren. Such a constitutional provision also required a majority of two-thirds to modify. An increasing number of prominent church members wanted to be members of secret societies. They kept petitioning General Conference to drop or modify the antisecrecy rule. Successive General Conferences rejected the petitions but with declining majorities. The result was a polarization of the United Brethren membership and ministry. The "Radicals" stood fast for the antisecrecy rule. The "Liberals" wanted the rule dropped or modified.[41]

Indiana had some "Liberals" who were among the first to show organized resistance. After the 1869 General Conference had responded negatively to a petition for modification and had made the enforcement against secret societies even more rigid than before, members of White River Conference held a convention at Indianapolis to protest. They called the antisecrecy rule impractical and injurious. At the next meeting of White River Conference some of these protesting members were expelled and others withdrew from the United Brethren. First United Brethren Church of Indianapolis was devastated by the conflict.[42]

Indiana had even more "Radicals." Milton Wright, respected bishop and editor of the *Religious Telescope*, father of aviators Wilbur and Orville, was a native of Rush County and an alumnus of Indiana's Hartsville College. He was the most impressive representative of the "Radicals" in the nation. When his successor as editor of the *Religious Telescope* seemed to lean toward the "Liberals," Wright began publishing his own antisecrecy periodical from his home at Richmond. Then a new constitution was ratified at the General Conference of 1889 which made cautious provision for membership in secret societies, allowed easier procedure for modifying the constitution, provided for lay representation, and approved reconstruction of the "Confession of Faith." It was more than Milton Wright could tolerate. He was the bishop who withdrew with fifteen General Conference delegates that year claiming to be the true Church of the United Brethren in Christ. There were court battles at many levels including a test case concerning the property of Sugar Creek Church in Wayne County which was appealed to the Indiana Supreme Court. The legal name of the group led by Wright came to be the United Brethren in Christ (Old Constitution). The older preachers and local preachers were more solidly against secret societies and so sided with the "Radicals" in larger proportion.[43]

In the course of the controversy between 1883 and 1889, most Hoosier "Radicals" concluded that they valued their convictions against secret societies but they valued the unity of the church even more. Southern Indiana and the Wabash region actually lost only a few members when division finally came. Stronghold of the "Radicals" was Milton Wright's home conference, White River Conference in central Indiana. Even there only 2,896 members went with the "Radical" denomination while 5,569 remained. Nearly half of the ministers of that conference withdrew. Halleck Floyd of White River Conference had assisted in editing a "Radical" periodical for a time and was elected a bishop of the Old Constitution

branch alongside Wright and two other colleagues in 1889.[44]

Education

There were few educational opportunities for ministers or members among the United Brethren during the early decades of the movement. The educational ideal was preserved but it was somewhat overshadowed by the emphasis on revival. References were often made to the educational acumen of Otterbein as an example. Francis Asbury of the Methodists had described Otterbein as "towering majestic above his fellows in learning, wisdom, and grace, yet seeking to be known only of God and the people of God."[45] In his rules drawn up for his own church in 1785 and used as a guide by most of the early United Brethren, Otterbein said:

> The preacher shall make it one of his highest duties to watch the rising youth, diligently instructing them in the principles of religion, according to the Word of God. He should catechize them once a week and the more mature in years, who have obtained knowledge of the great truths of the gospel, should be impressed with the importance of striving, through divine grace, to become worthy recipients of the Holy Sacrament.[46]

Some preachers did gather the children of their communities for instruction and counsel. It is a matter of record that John George Pfrimmer did this kind of schooling in Pennsylvania and it is assumed that he did the same soon after his arrival in Harrison County in Indiana. Pfrimmer is traditionally credited with forming the first United Brethren Sunday school in the nation at Corydon in Indiana.[47]

Another pioneer educator for the United Brethren was Aaron Farmer of Indiana. After riding the Orange Circuit—in counties named Orange, Washington, Harrison, Floyd, and Clark—he came to the 1829 meeting of Miami Conference with a proposal to publish a church paper. It was to be a monthly named *Zion's Advocate* and to be issued from his home in Salem. The conference approved and gave advice: "I. That *Zion's Advocate* was to contain doctrine consonant with the church of the United Brethren in Christ. II. It is not to be devoted to unprofitable controversy. III. It is to be printed on good paper and neatly executed. IV. It is to be edited by Aaron Farmer." But the conference provided neither money nor sufficient patronage to keep the paper going. After two years it ceased.[48] Editor Farmer went on to become a most effective evangelist and presiding elder for the United Brethren in Indiana. His Indianapolis District in 1838 included about half the state. Farmer's publication in Indiana was the first periodical issued anywhere by the United Brethren. It was a groundbreaker for the *Religious Telescope* and the denominational publishing house to be established in Ohio in 1834.[49]

Examination procedures were established for United Brethren preachers by the General Conference of 1841.

First, the candidate had to be approved as a Quarterly Conference licentiate by a two-thirds vote of a class or congregation. He had to give "satisfactory evidence of his . . . call, experience, soundness of doctrine, and attachment to our church and government." Second, after holding that status for at least one year and passing a prescribed doctrinal examination, he was received as a member of the Annual Conference on probation. Third, after three years of probation, if judged worthy by a majority vote of the Annual Conference, he was approved for ordination as an elder. It was recommended that the candidate spend the three years of probation in studying selected books which included the Bible, general history, church history, philosophy and logic, grammar and elocution, and theology.[50]

Then the list of readings was expanded, made mandatory, and combined with required essays to be written by the candidate. Many conferences established "Committees on Reading Courses" and then "Conference Institutes" to supervise and counsel ministerial candidates without formal education as well as to conduct their examinations.[51]

What the United Brethren of Indiana wanted was a college. In 1847 the voters of Haw Creek Township in Bartholomew County acted to build their new schoolhouse in the center of the town square at Hartsville. It was 25 feet by 50 feet and two stories high. They agreed to turn the building over to the United Brethren if the church would operate a school there. Four conferences in Indiana were supporting the institution by 1852. It was "Hartsville Academy" and then "Hartsville University" and then "Hartsville College." After Hartsville College passed to "Radical" hands and burned, Indiana Central University at Indianapolis became the denomination's next project in higher education.

Mr. William L. Elder, of Indianapolis, Indiana, made an offer to some of the ministers of the United Brethren Church, that if the Church would sell a stipulated number of town lots in his new addition, at a fixed price per lot, he would deed eight acres of ground to the Church for a college campus, and that he would erect a forty-thousand dollar Administration Building thereon,

with no further cost to the Church . . . A charter was secured in 1902 . . . In 1904 the Administration building was erected. The school was opened in 1905.[52]

In the meantime General Conference had established a seminary at Dayton, Ohio, in 1871. In appreciation of a gift of $50,000 from John M. Bonebrake of Veedersburg, Indiana, a place on Coal Creek in Fountain County with Hoobler associations, it became Bonebrake Theological Seminary. The shape of ministerial education of the future was evident at the meeting of Indiana Conference at Dale in August of 1905. Conference voted to establish an official relation with Indiana Central University at Indianapolis and "Monroe Crecelius was voted ordination upon his graduation at the seminary at Dayton, Ohio." The seminary had to overcome some indifference and even some opposition but it had become an official agency of General Conference and a place where ministerial standards would be set.[53]

Official statistics came late among United Brethren. When it was proposed to the Conference of 1802 to provide oversight for converts by recording the names of all the members and by taking a count, the conference refused. Most preachers opposed "numbering Israel" because of the biblical accounts in II Samuel 24 and I Chronicles 21 of God's displeasure at census taking. No numerical records of church membership were kept in the first five decades; the first accurate numbering was made in 1857. United Brethren in Indiana knew their church had been growing. There were reports in the *Religious Telescope* like the one from Wiley Jones on Fall Creek Circuit:

The first display of the power of the Lord occurred at a protracted meeting held on Lick Creek at Brother Lambert's schoolhouse . . . about three miles southwest of Pendleton, commencing February 22 and ending March 1, 1840. The brethren seemed to have been engaged for weeks wrestling with the Lord for a blessing, and when assembled all seemed to have the same mind, and come up to battle with the Captain of our salvation at their head. On Sabbath morning, in the prayer-meeting the Lord manifested himself powerfully near. Sinners were pierced to the heart, mourners crowded to the altar, thirty-eight professed conversion and nineteen united with our church. Again at the quarterly meeting held on Fall Creek at Brother Barnes schoolhouse . . . nine miles distant from the former revival, commencing April 4, 1840, the Lord again wonderfully blessed us. I never witnessed a more wonderful display of divine power. God's children were happy, sinners cried for mercy, mourners were comforted and leaped for joy, and backsliders like the prodigal, returned to their "Father's house." It was a memorable time. Nearly thirty were converted from the love of sin and death to the pure love of God shed abroad in their souls. Sixteen joined our church. May the good Lord preserve them. Generally the times are good, and the prospects are flattering around the circuit.[54]

L. S. Chittenden received 700 persons into the church in 1842 on the Corydon Circuit alone.[55]

Receiving the full compilation of their growing membership every year after 1857 was exhilarating. For 1860–61, Indiana Conference in southern Indiana had 203 preaching places and 158 classes but only 48 meeting houses; its 5,958 members were served by 26 itinerant and 38 local preachers. White River Conference in central Indiana had 167 preaching places and 139 classes but only 50 meeting houses; its 4,197 members were served by 23 itinerant and 25 local preachers. Lower Wabash Conference had 221 preaching places and 146 classes but only 24 meeting houses; its 3,745 members were served by 26 itinerant and 18 local preachers. Upper Wabash Conference had 202 preaching places and 144 classes with only 32 meeting houses; its 3,694 members were served by 20 itinerant and 27 local preachers. St. Joseph Conference in extreme northern Indiana had 241 preaching places and 175 classes with only 38 meetinghouses; its 4,095 members were served by 30 itinerant and 31 local preachers. This report made plain that the United Brethren in Indiana were strong and that they were strong all over the state—in fourth place among Protestant churches in Indiana by the census of 1880.[56] This report also illustrated the continuing affection of the United Brethren for the itinerant system and their practice of multiplying small neighborhood preaching places. So at the Indiana Conference session of 1848 the charge for J. L. Stearns was listed as "Corydon" but that charge was understood to have preaching places at "Corydon, J. Hottel's, Burnes', Sister Applegate's, New Amsterdam, Cold Friday, Potato Run, Peter Hottel's, Haas' (now known as Mt. Lebanon), Jordon's, Allen's, and Macedonia, called Corydon."[57]

Some strategists at the turn of the century did complain that United Brethren preachers in Indiana Conference needed to shift from their rural and itinerant character and be more aggressive about establishing churches in towns and cities. One said: "In different parts of southern Indiana, the United Brethren Church holds the ground as the leading church. Yet it is established in less than half a dozen of the county seats within its territory. With men and money furnished, many of the towns and cities could be occupied quickly, thus conserving and strengthening the results reached in the rural sections."[58]

Penetration of towns and cities came late but was impressive, especially in White River Conference of central Indiana. Terre Haute founded eight United Brethren churches between 1865 and 1923; Indianapolis founded seven between 1844 and 1925; Marion founded four between 1887 and 1905; Muncie founded four between 1901 and 1914; and Wabash founded two, in 1887 and 1905.[59]

In the religious census of 1906 the "Old Constitution" branch of United Brethren reported a national membership of 21,401 with 4,641 of that number in Indiana. Their denominational headquarters, publishing establishment, and a college were located at Huntington, Indiana. At the same time communicants in the major United Brethren denomination totaled 274,649. Ohio ranked first with 65,191 and Pennsylvania second with 53,397, but Indiana was third with 48,059 and none of the remaining states had half so many. In 1906 Indiana reported 600 United Brethren Sunday schools with 43,211 scholars and 6,561 officers and teachers—a vigorous base for still more growth before the eventual union of the major branch with the Evangelical Church (Albrights) in 1946 and with the Methodists in 1968.

NOTES

1. J. Bruce Behney and Paul H. Eller, *History of the Evangelical United Brethren Church* (Nashville, Tenn.: Abingdon, 1979), 33. See also Joseph H. Dubbs, *History of the Reformed Church, German,* American Church History Series, vol. 8 (New York: Christian Literature Co., 1895), 304, 311.

2. Behney and Eller, *History,* 34–35.

3. Arthur C. Core, *Philip William Otterbein* (Dayton, Ohio: Board of Publication of the Evangelical United Brethren Church, 1968), 115; Behney and Eller, *History,* 35–36.

4. Behney and Eller, *History,* 41.

5. Behney and Eller, *History,* 42.

6. Behney and Eller, *History,* 56, 104.

7. In the early years the members of this group were wary of the word *church.* They used the terms *society, association, fellowship,* and *brotherhood.* The word *church* first appears in the minutes of the Miami Conference in 1814. Legal incorporation under the name Church of the United Brethren in Christ did not come until 1890. See Augustus C. Wilmore, *History of the White River Conference of the Church of the United Brethren in Christ* (Dayton, Ohio: United Brethren Publishing House, 1925), 72–73; Frederick A. Norwood, *The Story of American Methodism* (Nashville, Tenn.: Abingdon, 1974), 107; Behney and Eller, *History,* 99.

8. Behney and Eller, *History,* 43, 58, 97–98, 100, 105; Norwood, *Story,* 106.

9. Paul R. Koontz and Walter E. Roush, *The Bishops, Church of the United Brethren in Christ,* 2 vols. (Dayton, Ohio: Otterbein Press, 1950), 1:130; Henry A. Thompson, *Our Bishops,* (Chicago: Elder

Publishing Company, 1889), 148; Behney and Eller, *History*, 62–63.

10. Thompson, *Our Bishops*, 149–50.

11. Behney and Eller, *History*, 63, 102–3.

12. Behney and Eller, *History*, 106–8, 114–17; Thompson, *Our Bishops*, 151.

13. William M. Weekley and Henry H. Fout, *Our Heroes; or, United Brethren Home Missionaries* (Dayton, Ohio: United Brethren Home Missionary Society, 1908), 44–46.

14. Adam B. Condo, *History of the Indiana Conference of the Church of the United Brethren in Christ* (N.p.: Published by order of the Indiana Conference, 1926?), 15–16, 128.

15. Christian Newcomer, *Christian Newcomer: His Life, Journal and Achievements*, ed. Samuel S. Hough (Dayton, Ohio: Board of Administration, Church of the United Brethren in Christ, 1941), 185; Behney and Eller, *History*, 61.

16. Newcomer, *Christian Newcomer*, 185–86.

17. Condo, *History*, 27–29 lists their names and many of their charges.

18. Condo, *History*, 132, 327.

19. Newcomer, *Christian Newcomer*, 267; Condo, *History*, 35–36.

20. Wilmore, *History*, 38–40.

21. Adam Shambaugh, *Early Days on the Wabash River, Indiana* (Glen Elder, Kans.: n.p., 1890. Reproduced . . . by Rev. M. E. Reed, Winamac, Indiana, 1969), 9, 22–27, 30. Shambaugh's family moved from Pennsylvania to Fountain County, Indiana, in 1827. His mother was Margaret Hoobler's daughter. Shambaugh never had charge of a circuit or joined an annual conference but as a local preacher received some 3,000 persons into the United Brethren in Indiana and Wisconsin.

22. Shambaugh, *Early Days*, 22–23.

23. Augustus W. Drury, *History of the Church of the United Brethren in Christ* (Dayton, Ohio: Otterbein Press, 1924), 386–88; Wilmore, *History*, 38–40, 62; Shambaugh, *Early Days*, 23.

24. Shambaugh, *Early Days*, 7–8.

25. Wilmore, *History*, 64–65.

26. Shambaugh, *Early Days*, 20–21.

27. Shambaugh, *Early Days*, 9–10; Wilmore, *History*, 61, 63–64.

28. Wilmore, *History*, 67; Shambaugh, *Early Days*, 15–18.

29. Wilmore, *History*, 36, 38, 41, 87–88.

30. Wilmore, *History*, 62.

31. Daniel Berger, *History of the Church of the United Brethren in Christ* (Dayton, Ohio: United Brethren Publishing House, 1897), 279, 582, 587; Wilmore, *History*, 70.

32. Drury, *History*, 373, 385; Condo, *History*, 140–41; Wilmore, *History*, 30–32, 37, 67, 70, 79.

33. Condo, *History*, 141.

34. Behney and Eller, *History*, 55.

35. Behney and Eller, *History*, 120–21.

36. Condo, *History*, 35; Behney and Eller, *History*, 127; Wilmore, *History*, 63, 77; Shambaugh, *Early Days*, 10, 13; Drury, *History*, 373.

37. Behney and Eller, *History*, 120, 122–23, 127, 162–64.

38. Behney and Eller, *History*, 124.

39. Behney and Eller, *History*, 119, 165–67.

40. Condo, *History*, 107.

41. Condo, *History*, 37; Behney and Eller, *History*, 126, 183–84.

42. Paul R. Fetters, *Trials and Triumphs: A History of the Church of the United Brethren in Christ* (Huntington, Ind.: Church of the United Brethren in Christ, 1984), 245; Drury, *History*, 465, 487, 724; Wilmore, *History*, 118.

43. Drury, *History*, 474–76, 503–4; Fetters, *Trials and Triumphs*, 302–3; Wilmore, *History*, 196–97, 209; Behney and Eller, *History*, 184–87.

44. Wilmore, *History*, 204–5, 231; Condo, *History*, 66, 78, 80–81; Berger, *History*, 584; Fetters, *Trials and Triumphs*, 301, 304–5, 308.

45. Edwin H. Sponseller, *Crusade for Education: The Development of Educational Ideals in the Church of the United Brethren in Christ* (Frederick, Md.: The Author, 1950), 67–73; Behney and Eller, *History*, 106, 121.

46. Sponseller, *Crusade*, 70. See also Condo, *History*, 111.

47. Grover L. Hartman, *A School for God's People: A History of the Sunday School Movement in Indiana* (Indianapolis, Ind.: Central Publishing Company, 1980), 7–8; Sponseller, *Crusade*, 71, 73; Condo, *History*, 112; Drury, *History*, 309–10; Behney and Eller, *History*, 61.

48. Weekley and Fout, *Our Heroes*, 62. See also Condo, *History*, 134, which says the paper lasted about twelve months and Wilmore, *History*, 49, which says it lasted four years.

49. John Lawrence, *History of the Church of the United Brethren in Christ*, 2 vols. (Dayton, Ohio: United Brethren Printing, 1861), 2:260–67; Weekley and Fout, *Our Heroes*, 63–66, 68; Wilmore, *History*, 49–51; Behney and Eller, *History*, 127; Condo, *History*, 332.

50. Behney and Eller, *History*, 158.

51. Condo, *History*, 63, 91; Wilmore, *History*, 227.

52. Condo, *History*, 122.

53. Condo, *History*, 93; Wilmore, *History*, 180, 275; Behney and Eller, *History*, 179, 233–34, 243–44, 256–57, 268–69.

54. Wilmore, *History*, 52–53.

55. Behney and Eller, *History*, 117; Drury, *History*, 718.

56. Lawrence, *History*, 2:424; Wilmore, *History*, 195.

57. Condo, *History*, 56.

58. Drury, *History*, 721. See also Condo, *History*, 88, 89.

59. Wilmore, *History*, 293–308.

SHAKERS

Shakers once lived in Indiana. They usually called themselves believers—members of the United Society of Believers in Christ's Second Appearing. They believed that the same Christ spirit that dwelled in the person of Jesus of Nazareth had made a second appearance in the person of Ann Lee of Manchester, England, who was therefore the spiritual Mother of all the new creation of God. Ann Lee came to prominence in England as a member of a group of religious enthusiasts led by Jane and James Wardley whose members used frenzied dance in their worship service. They were nicknamed Shaking Quakers. The dancing followers of Mother Ann Lee were similarly nicknamed Shakers and came to use the name of themselves.[1]

Mother Ann Lee and seven followers came from England to New York just before the American Revolution. They took form as a celibate and communal group at the rural town of Niskeyuna (later called Watervliet). Their converts in America came from the same ferment of pious, evangelical, mystical, and millennial enthusiasm they had known in England. An especially important initial group of converts came out of a "New Light Baptist" revival at New Lebanon, New York, in 1779–80. When Ann Lee and her elders made their missionary journeys through Massachusetts and Connecticut in the years 1781 to 1783, New England Baptists excited by revivals were especially attracted. Mother Ann Lee died in 1784. Joseph Meacham, Lucy Wright, and David Darrow were successors who gave shape and direction to the Shaker movement.[2]

Since the same spirit existed in Christ Jesus (Father), in Ann Lee (Mother), and now in the Shaker society whose members were the true people of Christ, these believers understood themselves as a community already living in the millennium. As millennium dwellers they were to be set apart from the world and to be a living judgment upon all creatures of the world around them. Among themselves they were to enjoy peace and happiness but they were also to be empowered to suffer much for the sake of the gospel. The true church was made up of those who had suffered and had gained power over all sin. Ann Lee had proclaimed that the fundamental nature of sin was lust and that all activity associated with sexual impulses was evil. The weightiest part of "bearing the cross" for Shakers was separation from every sexually related thought or action, including marriage and the natural family. Living free of sin also meant renouncing private possessions in order to avoid selfish claims or gratifications. Shakers developed a theology involving a God both male and female, a liturgy involving dancing and enthusiastic praise, a spiritual literature including gifts of revelations and poetry offered by the members, a discipline which included exhaustive confession of sins to the elders, and an official ministry for governance including both men and women.[3]

Each society or separate "family" grouping within a Shaker society was normally governed by two elders and eldresses assisted by deacons and deaconesses. All were expected to do manual labor. All were expected to submit their wills to the will of the United Society of Believers as expressed by the official ministry. There was failure. But there was also the attraction of the security and comfort of the Shaker extended family, of the efficiency of Shaker technology and agriculture, of the opportunity for rising in the Shaker leadership structure, and of the religious excitement of living in a community which claimed to receive revelation and prophecy day by day because of the indwelling spirit of Christ.[4]

Shakers Move West

By 1800 eleven Shaker communities had been founded in the East with the one at New Lebanon in Columbia County, New York, as the location of the central ministry and seat of authority. Shakers were also alert to the reports of evangelical awakenings and revival exercises on the western frontier. Issachar Bates was one commissioned to be a western missionary.

> In the latter part of December 1804 I was sent for to go to Lebanon. Soon after I arrived, Elder Ebenezer invited me into his room we sat & talked awhile about common matters. At length he asked me how I felt, towards them precious souls, that God was at work with in the west. I told him, I wondered why they had not been visited before this time. He said the Church, could not feel a gift to send till now; but now the door was opened. Now said he, I want to know your faith, supposing the lot should fall on you, to go for one; are you man enough, to leave your family once for all, & all your friends in these parts: & hasard your life in that wild part of the world for Christs sake, & for the sake of them poor souls whom God is preparing for salvation? I answered thus— my faith is in the gift of God that is in the Church; & that faith I will obey, come life or come death. Well said he, that will do; for the Church have appointed,—Elder John Meacham, Benjamin S. Youngs and Issachar Bates; to start for that country, the first day of january 1805. You will receive further counsel: so you may prepare yourselves. Now, all my former hopes, of my fixed home at Watervliet; were all blown up to the moon.[5]

Meacham, Youngs, and Bates were off to sound out the centers of revival excitement in Kentucky, Ohio, and Indiana.

Through the efforts of these missionaries, and those of their successors and converts, five new Shaker communities were formed in the West within a decade. Bates described his missionary message:

> Which work we inured ourselves to, like Gods hunters; & went through this wild wooden world, by day & by night; hunting up every soul that God had been preparing for Eternal Life, or for death unto death; to give them the offer of that treasure which God had committed to us. Which is Eternal Life; in obedience to the gospel of Christ & Mother, in this day of his second appearing. Which life to obtain, they must honestly confess all their sins before a witness of God, thing by thing; & forsake them by taking a final cross against the world, flesh, & all evil in their knowledge: and by righting all their wrongs with their fellow creatures: and to subject themselves to the teaching of those, appointed from time to time to minister unto them. This was our gospel: & I am one witness among many, that there is not one soul who has received the gospel, in the love of it; & have obeyed it from the heart: but have now Eternal Life abiding in them: and are justified & accepted of God. And on the other hand, that there is not one soul, who has ever received it, & turned away from it by disobedience; but are now, or shortly be, gasping, and strugling under the power of second death; which never dies.[6]

Union Village in Warren County, Ohio, was their first foundation, basis of a strong community which provided regional oversight for all the western groups. Watervliet society in Ohio was gathered later in Montgomery County. Three Presbyterian ministers in Kentucky, leaders in the Cane Ridge revival, were among those who joined the Shakers. South Union in Logan County and Pleasant Hill in Mercer County near Harrodsburg were the new Kentucky communities.[7]

Busro Community in Indiana

Indiana's Shaker colony was the one farthest west.[8] In June of 1808 Shaker Elder Issachar Bates and three male associates "crossed the Ohio R. into Indianna & went to Busserun on the Wabash; & in that place & the borders of Illinois, we staid three weeks; in which time 70 persons confessed their sins." At a "great meeting" on Sunday, 12 June, Shaker converts John Dunlavy and Matthew Houston were among the preachers before "4 or 500 spectators." Kentucky Shakers had kinfolk in the area to open the way. Early Indiana converts transferred three land parcels totaling about 1,300 acres to the new fellowship.[9] Elder Bates visited Indiana Territory headquarters at Vincennes that first summer and asked Governor William Henry Harrison if there were laws to protect the believers. He said "The same law . . . that there is in any of the United States. You have the right to preach your faith and any one has a right to embrace it. So you need not be uneasy; I will protect you." But when Bates and three male associates returned in September they were accosted by "a mob of 12" who told the celibates they would trim their hats and trim their coats and trim other unnecessary parts sending them out dead or alive if they remained until Saturday night. Harrison did come to their defense promptly with a magistrate and constable so the troublemakers were stilled and the missionaries reassured.[10]

Methodist circuit rider Peter Cartwright confronted Busro's leaders William Brazleton and Robert Gill in fall of 1808, reclaiming eighty-seven of the Shaker converts and organizing them into a Methodist society.[11] Busro's need for order and support warranted a midwinter visit by Issachar Bates, Benjamin Youngs, and Richard McNemar in January of 1809. They set out from Union Village (Turtle Creek) in Ohio with provisions for only five days for what became a deadly exposure of sixteen days on foot through more than 200 miles of forest and icy floodwaters across the breadth of southern Indiana. Bates recorded that perilous journey in a ballad of sixteen stanzas soon added to the Shaker song repertory to the tune "Judgment."[12]

In August Elder David Darrow came from Union Village in Ohio to visit Indiana with a top-level delegation of Shaker men and women. From 1805 to 1825 Darrow was in effect the bishop over all the Shaker settlements in the West, fully recognized as such by the central ministry in New York. Richard McNemar (also known as Elder Eleazar) became his chief advisor. The Indiana settlement at Busro always depended heavily on Darrow's missionary energy and oversight. Of this first visit he said:

> The occation of my going was . . . such as to fix a Seat or Senter for the Society—& the place to build their meeting house, & other buildings when they get able etc—Considering their Circumstances—it was evident it was a gift of God in my going—for the brethren could not have done what was necessary to be done without me—our Visit & labors among them gave them great satisfaction & Strength—the whole number of believers we left there was: 229—Those above 15 years old— 116—the chief part of them are as strong in faith as any believers—the believers at busroe are settled on the north end & West Side of a large dry rich prairie—Containing upwards of: 3000—acres of land & So level that we Could see their Cabbins for five or six miles before we got to them . . . we expect it will not be more than one or two years before some will have to go & live there to take care of them.[13]

Visiting delegations now began passing freely between the organized Shaker communities at Busro and Union Village.[14]

Between 1809 and 1811 Busro added more than 100 members as part of the relocation of Shaker congregations from Eagle Creek and Straight Creek in Adams County, Ohio, and from Red Banks (Henderson) in Kentucky.[15] Shaker history in Indiana was marked by a series of painful migrations best described in "Memorandum of Remarkable Events" by Samuel Swan McClelland.[16] Members from the Ohio congregation at Eagle Creek moved to Busro in March and April of 1811. Some drove the cattle and sheep on foot the distance of 300 miles. Some took the horses overland to Jeffersonville where they met their riverboat parties and loaded three wagons off their boats for a cross-country haul of 120 miles to Busro. Two companies of boats were loaded at the mouth of Red Oak River to travel for a terrible month and a half down the Ohio and up the Wabash rivers generally in flood and once in a storm which raised the river eight feet.[17] One Shaker traveler wrote in a letter dated 24 June: "Now picture to yourselves for a moment one of the family boats loaded to the brim with goods, being piled on the roof and everywhere, and crowded with women and children as thick as one could stand beside the other."[18]

Busro Evacuated

Just as the shock of integrating all the new settlers from Eagle Creek was being absorbed by Indiana's young community of Shakers, there came the terrors of war. During 1810 and 1811 there were rumors of Indian attacks about to come. Then in July of 1811 there were at Busro a couple of hundred Indian warriors gathering to go to Vincennes with Tecumseh to negotiate with Harrison. "These hungry creatures were about us nearly three weeks singing and dancing to the Great Spirit." Then after the negotiations failed at Vincennes there were at Busro the soldiers of Governor Harrison sent close on the heels of the departing Indians "to keep them from pilfering from the inhabitants. But this was like setting the dog to watch the butter—for they did more mischief in one night, than the Indians had done all summer." Then in September there were at Busro the "wicked Pottawatomies" who stole the excellent four-horse mill team from the Shakers and mauled the pacifist search party of believers sent in pursuit, taking from them two horses more.[19]

On 17 September "the army began to come on"—one company of light horse and two companies of riflemen— to train at Busro for the upcoming Battle of Tippecanoe. Issachar Bates said:

> The contractor used our shop in the dooryard for a store house, and made a slaughter yard at the back of it. Here

it was, drums and fifes, blood and whisky! Alas! alas! here they staid, waiting for the troops to come on. They had their washing, baking, some lodging, and all their forage for their horses, from us, though they paid for it, and behaved with civility toward the Believers. Yet, alas! alas! about the 26th the whole army came, with the Governor, and encamped at the same place. In their army were 500 regular troops from New England, commanded by Col. Boyd, from Boston.[20]

Soldiers returning from the Battle of Tippecanoe brought sick and wounded for the believers at Busro to attend. Earthquakes cracked some of Busro's brick houses and toppled chimneys during the winter of 1811–12.[21]

After a brief but fearful period in which the Indians remained stirred up and the frontier largely undefended, soldiers came back to Busro in strength in summer of 1812. The nation had declared war against England. Troops were marshalling to go north to fight Tecumseh and the British. Samuel McClelland said:

> Malitia troops were now almost dayly collecting—they made their encampment in the commons close by our houses—In, and out, of which they come and went without molestation—and without regart to even common good behaviour—Our gardens and fields were rich and afforded plenty for them and their horses—Our cattle and hogs they butchered and destroyed in a most savage wasteful manner . . . The Press Gang come on and seized a number of our horses some saddles and some axes—as they were in haste to get up to Fort Harrison it being then besieged by the Indians—this circumstance caused us considerable trouble by breaking our teams &c. . . . The army was soon increased to about 1000—our houses was converted to Barracks. our nurcerys into horse lots, and our fields into race grounds— In short the whole place looked as tho' a host of Pharos plages had passed over it.[22]

All the while the Shakers were in tension about being drafted for military service or being fined because they would not fight. Some whites even blamed the Indian hostilities on the Shakers and declared that if the Indians did not kill the Believers they were ready to do it.[23]

It was too much. The Shakers chose neither to wait for peace on the Wabash frontier nor to accept Harrison's offer of temporary location in the safety of Vincennes. Issachar Bates wrote: "It was all tumult upon tumult—war! war! people all forting, & armies coming among us, till the greater part of our people were so filled with fear; that they could not rest day nor night: so we held a council, & concluded to move out of that place, & go among our brethren in other States; where there was not so much

danger."[24] They packed up as much as they could save and carry. They left a delegation of five or six at Busro "to take care of whatever they could among the tumultious multitude." They agreed to head south to camp at Red Banks (Henderson) on the Kentucky side of the Ohio and there await directions from the ministry at Union Village. The result was a strangely circuitous pilgrimage of 522 miles from Busro to Union Village. This painful Shaker exodus began on 15 September 1812, a year and season when as many as twenty of the believers had to be transported while prostrated with fevers.[25] McClelland described the scene: "The whole camp consisted of about 300 human souls—250 head of sheep—100 head of cattle—14 waggons—and one Keel boat—and Perianger—and one canoe. The waggons were so crowded with plunder that it was difficult for the sick to be taken along with any tolerable degree of comfort—tho' a number of sick went on board of the boat." The physician Calvin Morrel recorded his memory of "the tribulation and almost endless perplexities of moving a company of more than 300 Men, Women, and children through mud and mire and storms of rain, with old wagons, worn out gears and balky horses, upwards of 400 miles."[26]

First rendezvous of the boat and wagon groups was at Red Banks on 29 September. After another 112 miles, thirty believers and the sheep stopped at the South Union community in Logan County, Kentucky. After another 140 miles, a few more believers stopped at Pleasant Hill community in Mercer County, Kentucky. The remainder pressed on, a few miles a day, 150 miles further to arrive at Union Village in Warren County, Ohio, on 10 November. Indiana was an aching memory. "Our hearts were saddened when we realized how we had been cast out from our beautiful home at Busro, from our fruitful fields and well tilled gardens, to make a weary pilgrimage of hundreds of miles, which could only be through great anxiety of spirit and severe toil of body."[27]

Busro Restored

By the next summer they were thinking about moving back to Indiana! In 1813 there was favorable word from the War Department about prospects for peace on the western frontier so they began preparing for the return. Eighteen fourteen was another year devoted to moving. Traffic back to Busro was brisk that spring and summer. Those who had remained there were "imployed in the business of preparing the fields for the plow—halling rails, makeing and repareing fences &c." These resident agents ordered a new supply of white plates, pitchers, cups, teapots, and spoons. Some believers returned by water; the Shaker keel boat and flat boat were plying the rivers. Some came overland and brought the horses. William Davis arrived with the cattle on 29 May.[28]

So a new decade of Shaker life began in Indiana. This time they were developing their village on a new location at the south end of their property near Busseron Creek. They used the new name West Union, seeming to indicate a permanent settlement parallel to Union Village in Ohio and South Union in Kentucky. They built a new dam and a mill house which was 40 feet square and 72 feet to the ridge beam. The new frame barn was 65 feet by 28 feet. The four older houses were augmented in 1820 by a new brick house 50 feet by 44 feet. The old meetinghouse was moved to the new location. It was 48 feet by 50 feet with walnut planks for seats around the walls and the floor clear for dancing; the second floor, reached by two flights of stairs, provided nine rooms as a residence for the ministry. Archibald Meacham said: "When the members started to sing and 'labor,' the sounds produced were comparable to 'mighty thunderings.' They would sometimes stamp, roar, and speak in unknown tongues for about two hours, and when the ritual was completed the people were 'as wet with sweat, as tho they had plunged into a river.'" The new sawmill began sawing in May of 1819. Construction at West Union continued strongly until 1825.[29]

The Shakers acquired 1,280 acres across the Wabash in Illinois Territory and built mills there. They provided nearly every kind of pioneer craft for themselves and for their region—blacksmith shop, doctor shop, skin shop, weave shop, fulling mill. They manufactured furniture, cutlery, brooms, baskets, woven straw hats, and spinning wheels. Their farms were fruitful; Shakers excelled in production of seeds, nursery stock, and livestock. Nor was Shaker inventiveness dead at Busro. In 1821 "a mill for washing clothes was built and accidentally, its first motion broke two fingers on the left hand of one of the Sisters."[30]

In their earliest days they had been resented by their Hoosier neighbors as family breakers, non-patriots, and heretics who danced in church. Folk tales made much of their celibacy or charged them with failure to measure up to their profession. As they became better known and were less active in proselyting, they found more acceptance among their neighbors and even admiration from traveling visitors.[31] Philip Mason enjoyed the hospitality of the Shakers twice on his trip from Vincennes to Fort Harrison and return in 1816:

At Busseron Creek we found a society of Shakers, with a fine farm and snug buildings. We stopped with them over night and found comfortable lodgings and good table fare, the first that we had had since leaving home. These people had mills on the creek and were engaged in erecting a splendid flouring mill . . . They are what is called the Shakers or Shaking Quakers, and lived in a community as a family, and seemed in possession of many comforts and conveniences, and appeared happy.[32]

William Hebert of London was favorably impressed in 1823.

They have their capacious granaries, fine mills, and machinery of various kinds, but they adhere to their object of living in christian fellowship, in a state of plenty and independence of the world. They are not merchants or money-changers, and when visited by strangers, entertain them gratis. This you will allow to be really respectable.[33]

They were in happy interrelation with other Shaker communities. By 1822 Shaker brothers and sisters often traveled between Busro and Union Village in carriages or on horseback, a distance of 300 miles requiring eight to eighteen days. They had serious conversations with the Rappites at nearby New Harmony. George Rapp's daughter Rosina and granddaughter Gertrude studied English at the Shaker settlement in 1816; four Shakers also visited the Rappites at New Harmony that year to explore the possibility of merger.[34]

Busro Terminated

Yet the colony endured only briefly. One problem was sickness. The Wabash bottom land was fertile but frequently flooded and poorly drained. Scores of Shakers died; persons new to the area were terribly vulnerable. Of 1814, the very year of the return to Indiana, Samuel McClelland said: "Several of our people were taken with chills and fever and no medical applications seemed to relieve them. During the summer season several persons were called from this to another life much to our sorrow and a great loss to the community." He said of the middle of August in 1818 "the fevers began . . . and went on with violence so that before the scene was closed, there was but 7 of the whole Society that escaped without takeing a pritty smart brushing."[35] Issachar Bates said of the middle of August in 1819:

The fever came on us with fury. The first attack was on a number of our best members. Elder Archibald was also taken down. They were taken with such violence that in a few hours their breath would stop, and no medicine had any effect. Then we betook ourselves to pray, and obtained help from God, so that we made war with the Destroyer. When any were violently seized, we assembled in the meeting-house, and labored until they were released, which frequently took place, till finally we obtained a confident promise from God, that we should have our lives for a prey, although we should all be sick. After this, confidence was gained, and medicine operated well. Six or eight were taken in a day, till a hundred were down at once.[36]

Another problem was rebellion, especially among "the children." Practicing believers lived as celibates but many converts brought children into the community with them. These young people were gathered under caretakers and teachers. In 1812, for example, Busro had seventy-five boys and fifty-six girls in their new two-story school-house. There were about seventy children in 1817. In 1820 an order of "young believers" was established under direction of Henry Miller. These rising young adults on the fringe of the community did not respond happily to rules requiring eternal celibacy and submission to the authority of the Shaker ministry.[37]

Some of the children took on the ways of neighboring backwoods Hoosiers. Elder Issachar Bates complained in 1817 that in the Illinois unit of Busro there was not one man among them "but what can cut off a wood-peckers head with a rifle ball at the distance of six or eight rods—or course a bee through the woods to his hive in a few minutes—but not one among them all (two years ago) that knew how to hang a sithe, or use it when it was hung—or how to use since any other farming tool except an axe." Some heard exciting talk about democratic rights in the outside world, even the enthusiastic social theories of the Owenites after they arrived at New Harmony. It was painful to have such children leave the colony; it was even more painful to have them stay as challengers to community order.[38]

The problems became crucial by 1826. The year 1825 brought a cold winter followed by a drought. Shaker history recorded: "The death rate this year was large and the unhealthiness of the place began to be more and more a matter of discussion. The country was but sparsely settled, and the low lands could not be sufficiently drained, so that as warm weather approached the atmosphere was charged with malaria." In August of 1826 McClelland reported, "The fever now rages with violence in almost every quarter of the Village—three of the New comers are already dead and a number more appear to be dangerously ill." John Dunlavy was one of the Presbyterian

ministers who converted to Shakerism, "an able Minister of the Gospel, perhaps the ablest defender of Mothers pure Gospel of any man that has yet believed in the Western country." In September of 1826 Dunlavy visited Busro and died there.[39]

Apostasies increased, especially among the children. McClelland said: "From the 8th of May to the 7th of September [1825], there was 13 members left the Society and went to the world—eight men and five women—all young people." Membership was down to 152 by Christmas of 1825. There was less missionary effort to replenish the membership and there were fewer massive revivals to multiply Shaker converts.[40] Elder Archibald Meacham concluded something must be done about the West Union children whom he called stout youth, troublesome and unruly, too big to be subject to any order or rule whatever, with no more thought or consideration about the salvation of their souls than the beasts that perish. "A few days ago we felt that the time was come," he said, "that those who would not confess their sins honestly and take up their cross could have no further privilege here with us . . . In going through with the purging work there was a number that would not comply . . . they were well known to be very corrupt and deceitful; therefore they were purged out and dismissed from any further privilege among believers."[41]

Meacham was not very happy with the results of the purge and in July of 1826 set out for the Shaker headquarters at New Lebanon for more advice. At the same time the ministry of the western headquarters at Union Village was writing to New Lebanon:

> It has been a matter of considerable doubt in the minds of some of the people at West Union for years, whither that place would finally be an abiding residence for believers—In consequence of sertain difficulties & imbarisments which have attended that place hitherto, of course it might be expected that such could not feel the same interest in building it up as they othorwise would do . . . It appears that dissatisfactions, & discouragements are becoming more & more prevalant among the remaining few . . . if it should be finally thought most adviseable . . . for the believers to evacuate that place we shall acquiess in it.[42]

Elder David Darrow had died in summer of 1825; there died with him much of the Shaker missionary zeal on which Indiana's settlement at West Union depended.[43]

By 1826 Indiana was also acknowledged as one of the centers of overt rebellion against the old lines of Shaker authority. Daniel Rankin of Busro was an active collaborator with John Whitbey, Richardson Whitbey, and Robert

Barnett at Pleasant Hill in their attempt to break the control of the regular ministry over Shaker government and economy. Shaker elder Benjamin S. Youngs said they were "puffed up with new discoveries of light and knowledge & full of ministrations, commissions from the school of infidel philosophy and corruption . . ." John Whitbey was under the influence of Robert Owen at New Harmony, traveled to New Harmony in 1825, and with the aid of the Owenites published his attack on the Shakers entitled *Beauties of Priestcraft; or, A Short Account of Shakerism* (1826).[44]

Shaker hopes for exemption from militia fines also came to a test in 1826. The fines amounted to a substantial assessment with so many men involved. Shakers refused to do the military service or to pay the fines even if the money was designated for the state's education fund. They argued that all their property was held in common and so could not be attached for the failure of any individual member to pay his fine. This argument failed as they lost their case in court.[45]

The result of all this was the end of West Union. Richard McNemar brought the official word on 19 November 1826. Among the ministry of all the societies in the East and the West "it was universally thought and felt best for all the people to rise once more and move away from Busro, and so abandon the place forever!" There were only about one hundred members left to move, most of them women. They signed over all interest in the remaining property to Shaker trustees Nathan Sharp and Francis Voris, clearing the title for later sale of both the Indiana and Illinois tracts to a Virginian named Grider.[46] Issachar Bates came from Union Village by carriage to be with the stricken colonists and to bring them the gift of a ballad entitled "An Encouragement for the Busroe Believers to Remove."

> What seasons of sorrow and feelings of horror
> I've borne on the plains of Busroe;
> No mortal has known it but now I will own it
> That Busroe Believers may know.
> Thro' war and confusion apostate delusion
> With fevers our bodies were torn
> Grim death's horrid features green flies and musketoes
> O heavens what have I not borne.[47]

The members and the pieces of portable property were divided into three groups—one to go to Union Village, one to go to Pleasant Hill, and one to go to South Union. Twenty-four believers set out for South Union in four wagons on 10 March 1827. The remaining persons and much of the "plunder" were then freighted out to the Wabash, part of the way through "water and mud . . . up to the waggon beds." First leg of the river trip for them on this final Indiana pilgrimage was in the relative luxury of the steamboat Lawrence, but there was no mood of celebration. "Just 35 minutes after 5 o. clock [20 March 1827] we pushed off from McCartyes landing, and bid a final Adieu to all our hard earned and dear-bought Possessions on Busro Prairy—The pen, even of the learned, would fail should it undertake to discribe the feelings of this unfortunate people." The boat ran well and about 7 P.M. tied up for the night at Vincennes. McClelland said: "Many of the citizens being acquainted with us, and sorry for our departure gathered on the bank and strove to entertain us with music boath Instrumental and vocal—with many good wishes for our welfare . . . This sleepless night was mostly spent in solemn meditation."[48]

NOTES

1. Stephen J. Stein, *The Shaker Experience in America: A History of the United Society of Believers* (New Haven, Conn.: Yale University Press, 1992), 3–7.

2. Stephen Marini, *Radical Sects of Revolutionary New England* (Cambridge, Mass.: Harvard University Press, 1982, 213 p.); Arthur E. Bestor, *Backwoods Utopias* (Philadelphia: University of Pennsylvania Press, 1950), 31; Sydney E. Ahlstrom, *A Religious History of the American People* (New Haven, Conn.: Yale University Press, 1972), 493; Stein, *Shaker Experience*, 7, 10–12, 39–118.

3. Stephen J. Stein, *Letters from a Young Shaker: William Byrd at Pleasant Hill* (Lexington, Ky.: University Press of Kentucky, 1985), 34–38; Stein, *Shaker Experience*, 45, 91–94, 133–35.

4. James Guimond, "The Leadership of Three Experimental Communities," *Shaker Quarterly* 11 (Fall 1971): 109–13.

5. Issachar Bates, *A Sketch of the Life and Experience of Issachar Bates*, 152–53. Bates, *Sketch*, will be cited as reprinted in *Shaker Quarterly* 1 (Fall 1961): 98–118, 1 (Winter 1961): 145–63, and 2 (Spring 1962): 18–35.

6. Bates, *Sketch*, 159–60.

7. Stein, *Shaker Experience*, 57–66, 114; Bestor, *Backwoods Utopias*, 32.

8. The location sixteen miles north of Vincennes was sometimes designated by the name of the creek spelled Busseron or Buseron or Busserun. The name of the village might be written Busro or Busroe. Shakers generally called the community West Union. All these names refer to the same settlement. In 1991 Donald Janzen, Donald Pitzer, and John Martin Smith located the perimeter of the Center Family Dwelling at Busro as part of a research project for the Communal Studies Association and the Indiana Historical Society. See Stein, *Shaker Experience*, 63–64, 92–94, 126; *Communal Studies Association Newsletter* 16 (September 1991): 3.

9. Bates, *Sketch*, 19; Mary Lou Conlin, "The Lost Land of Busro," *Shaker Quarterly* 3 (Spring 1963): 44; John P. MacLean, *Shakers of Ohio: Fugitive Papers Concerning the Shakers of Ohio, with Unpublished Manuscripts* (Columbus, Ohio: F. J. Heer Printing,

1907), 277–78; Diana M. Sheffler, "A Historical Study of the Shakers at the Busseron Settlement in Indiana" (Master's thesis, Indiana State University, 1968), 23.

10. Conlin, "Lost Land," 44–45; Sheffler, "Historical Study," 25–26; MacLean, *Shakers*, 278; Marguerite Melcher, *The Shaker Adventure* (Princeton, N.J.: Princeton University Press, 1941), 71–72.

11. Peter Cartwright, *Autobiography of Peter Cartwright* (New York: Carlton and Porter, 1857), 52–55.

12. "A Ballad by Elder Issachar Bates," *Shaker Quarterly* 2 (Summer 1962): 60–66; MacLean, *Shakers*, 278; Melcher, *Shaker Adventure*, 72–73.

13. Conlin, "Lost Land," 46–47.

14. MacLean, *Shakers*, 280; Stein, *Shaker Experience*, 108–17.

15. MacLean, *Shakers*, 271–76, 281–82, 330; Sheffler, "Historical Study," 30.

16. Printed in *Manifesto* 15 (1885): 110–12, 139–41, 164–66, 183–85, 205–7; also printed in and cited here from MacLean, *Shakers*, 281–328.

17. MacLean, *Shakers*, 271–76, 281–83, 330; Sheffler, "Historical Study," 30, 47.

18. Conlin, "Lost Land," 48.

19. MacLean, *Shakers*, 280, 286–89, 330–32; Conlin, "Lost Land," 50.

20. MacLean, *Shakers*, 333.

21. MacLean, *Shakers*, 287–88, 333.

22. MacLean, *Shakers*, 290.

23. MacLean, *Shakers*, 330–33; Sheffler, "Historical Study," 37–40.

24. Bates, *Sketch*, 22.

25. MacLean, *Shakers*, 290, 334–37, 346; Bates, *Sketch*, 22–23; Sheffler, "Historical Study," 54.

26. MacLean, *Shakers*, 290, 335.

27. MacLean, *Shakers*, 290–305, 337.

28. MacLean, *Shakers*, 307–10; Conlin, "Lost Land," 55; Sheffler, "Historical Study," 60–61.

29. MacLean, *Shakers*, 277, 309, 315–18; Conlin, "Lost Land," 50, 55–58; Sheffler, "Historical Study," 65–68.

30. *Manifesto* 15 (August 1885): 185.

31. Melcher, *Shaker Adventure*, 76–78.

32. Philip Mason, *A Legacy to My Children Including Family History, Autobiography, and Original Essays* (Cincinnati, Ohio: Moore, Wilstach and Baldwin, 1868), 108–9.

33. Harlow Lindley, *Indiana as Seen by Early Travelers* (Indianapolis, Ind.: Indiana Historical Commission, 1916), 337. For additional reports by travelers see Bestor, *Backwoods Utopias*, 42–50.

34. *Manifesto* 15 (September 1885): 205; Donald E. Pitzer, "New Harmony's First Utopians, 1814–1824," *Indiana Magazine of History* 75 (September 1979): 247, 257.

35. *Manifesto* 15 (August 1885): 184; MacLean, *Shakers*, 315.

36. MacLean, *Shakers*, 339–40.

37. Conlin, "Lost Land," 52; Sheffler, "Historical Study," 67; MacLean, *Shakers*, 317.

38. Conlin, "Lost Land," 56; Stein, *Shaker Experience*, 125–28.

39. *Manifesto* 15 (September 1885): 205–6; MacLean, *Shakers*, 323; Stein, *Letters*, 144.

40. MacLean, *Shakers*, 321; Sheffler, "Historical Study," 92.

41. Conlin, "Lost Land," 58.

42. Conlin, "Lost Land," 59.

43. MacLean, *Shakers*, 68, 70–71.

44. Stein, *Letters*, 27, 120–24, 153.

45. Sheffler, "Historical Study," 85–86.

46. MacLean, *Shakers*, 324, 341, 344; Stein, *Letters*, 68.

47. Conlin, "Lost Land," 59.

48. MacLean, *Shakers*, 326.

RAPPITES

George Rapp (*1757-1847*) lived in Württemberg where Duke Karl Eugen ruled the state and was also head of the Evangelical Lutheran church within his realm. Duke Karl was a disgrace to his offices. George Rapp was a loyal subject in civil matters but a persistent rebel against every form of religious authority beyond the sincerity of his own convictions. In April of 1785 George Rapp and his wife Christina were before the church council in their home town of Iptingen explaining why they had absented themselves from the church services and the sacraments. George claimed a personal conversion by the inner light. He rejected all trained clergy. He had a volatile mind which he fed on volatile parts of the Bible and on some other books the church did not recommend. His wife was a faithful follower in 1785. So were Christian Hörnle, a farmer, and Michael Conzelmann, a shoemaker.[1]

There followed nearly twenty years of tension. From their meetings in private houses Rapp and his growing body of separatist followers drove the local clergy to distraction with their verbal attacks on church members, on pastors, on sacraments, and on the content of Lutheran preaching. They said that all of these as known in the state church would be destroyed along with all agencies of evil and that they, the separatists, would inherit the earth. They claimed direct inspiration and power because of the work of the Holy Spirit in them as individuals by means of an inner light. Rapp's library and repertory kept increasing. Along with their favorite *Berleburg Bible*, he and his followers read from the works of the pietist

Michael Hahn and the mystic theosophist Jakob Böhme. They were attracted to idealistic pictures of the primitive Christian church which could be painfully contrasted with the corrupt government of which the state church of Württemberg was a part. They studied a conversion narrative called *Precious Drops of Honey from the Rock of Christ* and a work of mysticism and millennial promise by Christoph Schutz entitled *The Golden Rose; or, Testimony of the Truth about the Golden Age of the Thousand-Year and Eternal Reign Now so Close at Hand and the Return of All Things Connected with It.* Higher authorities of church and state were very slow to support local officials by acting against these separatists. There was no civil disobedience involved and upper-level officials favored restraint in enforcing religious requirements to avoid creation of martyrs.[2]

Given opportunity by the tolerance, Rapp became immensely popular. People kept flocking to Iptingen to hear him. When officials in a council session bade him be silent because he was no prophet, he said "I am a prophet, and I am called to be one." When they ordered him to prison for two days, all the believers offered to go with him. He was issuing pastoral letters to his followers from 1793. They presented their articles of faith to the Württemberg government in 1798. They advocated heartfelt conversion from sin, daily communion with God, pursuit of Christian perfection, strict standards for taking communion, and preparation for the second appearance of Christ with its work of kingdom building. They opposed infant baptism, confirmation, oaths, and military service. They wished to set up their own separate congregations and schools on their own principles. In July of 1798 Rapp's nephew Friedrich Reichert (later adopted as his son Frederick Rapp) joined him to become treasurer and business manager for the new fellowship. When George Rapp preached at Knittlingen in February of 1803, the audience was so large that doors and windows were removed from the building so that people outside could hear him.[3]

Finally the government struck. The ruler of Württemberg by then was Friedrich II who was an elector and wanted to be king. He would not tolerate the disunity of this large and well-organized separatist church which would not recognize the jurisdiction of the ruler in matters of religion. The royal decree of 27 December 1803 left the separatist church little room to live. George Rapp had not waited for the decree. There were some 2,000 members in his organization. They sent their leader George Rapp and three other brethren to America in late summer of 1803 to inquire about the country. Frederick Rapp was holding the church treasury and the organization together in Württemberg as well as he could.[4]

Rappites in Pennsylvania

George Rapp found that exploring the United States was a big job. He was inclined to locate his colony in the Muskingum River valley in Ohio and met with President Thomas Jefferson in July of 1804 to ask for special credit arrangements to buy 40,000 acres there. Jefferson explained that such a request could be granted only by Congress. Meanwhile the flock from Württemberg was pouring in—300 in the ship *Aurora* on 4 July 1804 and 257 more with Frederick Rapp on the *Margaret* on 19 September. There had to be a location without delay. "George Rapp with Society" was the signature on the contract to buy a tract of about 9,000 acres on the Connoquenessing River in Butler County near Pittsburgh in December of 1804. The next February somewhere between 400 and 500 members signed the articles of association to be the Harmony Society. The estate and property of all members was signed over to "George Rapp and his Society." Members pledged obedience to the regulations and superintendents "in such a manner that not only we ourselves endeavor, by the work of our hands, to promote the good and interest of the congregation, but also to hold our children and families to do the same." George Rapp and his society were to provide "necessary instruction in church and school which is needful for

temporal and eternal felicity" and "all the necessaries of life, as lodging, meat, drink, and clothing, etc."[5]

Rapp and his followers came to America in a mood of intense religious expectancy. Rapp clearly identified his society with the biblical Sunwoman (Revelation 12:1–6), the true church now being led into the American wilderness to a safe place prepared for it. The Lord was coming soon in a judgment which would mean the destruction of evil Europe with its established churches. At the Lord's return this elect Rappite community would surely have a very special role to play. One of the songs the emigrants sang on their way was

> Up and away, in America
> the sheep's pasture is still to be
> there the Sunwoman is to flee
> that she be removed at the time of evil
> then judgment will break out to avenge.[6]

In the flush of this enthusiasm George and Frederick Rapp saw plenty of candidates to become members of the society. Frederick said there could be 20,000 emigrants from Württemberg alone if the American government would provide some support.[7]

On the Connoquenessing the Rappites did the work in which they always excelled—successful farming, building, manufacturing, and commerce. The Rapps and other society supervisors kept increasing their competence in English. Relations with the world beyond the society were increasingly in the competent hands of Frederick Rapp. At the same time community loyalty and religious intensity increased. In 1807 and 1808 the community experienced a religious revival which heightened their expectation of the Lord's return and their drive to perfection. Celibacy was adopted in 1811, not as a signed agreement but as a discipline and testimony following the apostolic advice in view of the imminent return of the Lord that even those who have wives would do well to live as if they had none (I Corinthians 7:29). George and Christina Rapp had agreed to cease sexual relations while still in Württemberg. George Rapp's charismatic control of the society strengthened as well, reinforced by his practice of hearing confessions of members.[8]

Rappites in Indiana

This was the Harmony Society which came to Indiana. In the ten years from 1804 to 1814 the Pennsylvania site had been marvelously improved; a simple list of buildings and improvements filled two pages. The society had become nationally and internationally famous especially because of very favorable descriptions in *Sketches of a Tour to the Western Country* by Fortescue Cuming and in *Travels in the United States of America* by John Melish.[9] But the dragon of the world was still harassing the true church, the Sunwoman, as indicated in Revelation 12:13. In Pennsylvania the harassment looked like encroachment of unsympathetic neighbors, taxes, military draft or assessments in place of military duty, and rising prices for land. The Rappite treasury was strong. George Rapp's original vision of a place for the Lord's prepared people in the western wilderness was also strong. His word from the Lord was Revelation 12:14, "And to the woman were given two wings of a great eagle, that she might fly into the wilderness, into her place, where she is nourished for a time, and times, and half a time, from the face of the serpent." The Rappites had tried in 1805–6 to buy an entire township in Indiana on very special credit terms as they sought to fix their first location in America. The bill embodying that proposal passed the Senate but failed by one vote in the House of Representatives on 18 February 1806. Now they would look west again.[10]

In April of 1814 George Rapp, John L. Baker, and Ludwick Shriver were scouting the Ohio River valley for a new site which could accommodate many new immigrants from Germany and provide a navigable river. They wanted water power, mild climate for the culture of grapes, and fertile soil. On 10 May Rapp wrote from Vincennes:

> The place is 25 miles from the Ohio mouth of the Wabash, and 12 miles from where the Ohio makes its curve first before the mouth. The town will be located about $\frac{1}{4}$ mile from the river above on the channel on a plane as level as the floor of a room, perhaps a good quarter mile from the hill which lies suitable for a vineyard. The hill is worth more than the land because it has many stones for building. For fifty miles around none is to be found otherwise. The river has plenty of fish and when the water falls many barrels full can be caught by people who know the places and who come from a distance of 40 and 50 miles. In short, the place has all the advantages which one could wish, if a steam engine meanwhile supplies what is lacking.[11]

This time the Sunwoman church in the wilderness wanted vast acreage. Its agents had time and money so they could move deliberately and from a position of strength. Following Father Rapp's instructions they purchased their land along the Wabash River in Indiana and Illinois, a holding large enough to protect Harmony from the incursions of outsiders and to give control of several miles of river frontage. Frederick Rapp kept the transfer

orderly. By spring of 1815 between 800 and 1,000 persons plus livestock, supplies, and equipment had been moved to Indiana.[12]

In many ways it seemed a change for the bigger and better. Harmony on the Connoquenessing had 9,000 acres with improvements remarkable enough to warrant a sale price of $100,000. Harmony on the Wabash (also called New Harmony or Neu Harmonie) soon became even more impressive.

> Within less than five years, according to an inventory of its holdings, its buildings and real estate were valued at over $140,000. Included were 150 log dwellings, a brick house for George Rapp, three other brick buildings, a frame church, a frame tavern and stable, mills, stills, a brewery, craft and trade shops, a steam mill and other mills, a dyehouse, granaries, barns and sheep huts, stables, and corncribs. There were 1,450 acres of cleared land . . . When the entire property was advertised for sale in 1824 it included twenty-one substantial brick houses, four of them 60 by 80 feet and three stories high, twenty-five weatherboarded houses, eighty-six log dwellings, two churches, a brick store- and warehouse, plus factories, mills, shops, granaries, barns, and other structures. The streets of the town were tree-lined and there was a five-acre garden with labyrinths, orchards, and vineyards. Out of town were 3,000 acres of fenced farm land and the total land holdings in Indiana and across the Wabash in Illinois ran to about twenty thousand acres. The asking price was $150,000.[13]

Whether log, frame, or brick, Rappite buildings were stout and were expertly made, seeming ready to endure for eternity or at least a millennium.

Frederick Rapp, always the colony's best representative to the world, was in his prime as business manager. Harmony's reply to a "manufacturers' census" in 1820 listed 2 grist mills (5 pairs of stones), 2 sawmills, 1 oil and 1 hemp mill, 6 carding machines, 520 spindles, 11 weaving looms, 4 stocking weaver looms, and one steam engine. In a year they processed 10,000 pounds of wool, 5,000 pounds of cotton, 5 tons of hemp, 1,000 hides, and 1,000 deerskins. Market value of the year's manufactures was reported as $50,000. Items listed included:

> Superfine, fine & course cloths; Cassimers, Cassinetts flanells; Blankets, Lincy swansdown; plaide, stripes Chambrey & white; Cottons blue & white yarn; upper, Sole, & sadler Leather; Various kinds of Blacksmith work; Tin ware, spinning wheels; Ropes, Cordage, Leather Gloves; Shoes & Boots, wool & furr hats; Sadles Bridles & Harness; Stokings, Socks, mittens & caps; Flax, Rope, hemp & pumgan seed oil, Earthen ware; strong Beer,

Peach Brandy Persico; Rye & corn whisky, wine; wagons Carts & Ploughs; flour, Beef, Pork, Butter.[14]

Harmony was selling manufactured goods and produce through its own agents in Louisville, Pittsburgh, Saint Louis, and New Orleans. Society-operated stores were opened in Indiana and Kentucky and Illinois. Harmony's religious symbol of the golden rose on its manufactured goods had become a recognized mark of quality across the United States and in some markets of Canada, England, Scotland, the Netherlands, France, Switzerland, and Germany. The stature of Frederick Rapp was recognized when he was named a delegate to the Indiana Constitutional Convention of 1816 and in 1820 served on a commission to choose a site for the permanent state capital. He answered the distress call of the state treasurer with a loan of $5,000 from the Harmony Society in 1823.[15]

Ferdinand Ernst of Germany visited in 1819. "On July 18 toward 8 in the evening I got into the vicinity of Harmonie. The clock in the tower struck 8—a joyful sign of culture for a traveller who has covered 800 miles without having heard the striking of a bell. When I arrived at the inn, it seemed as though I found myself in the midst of Germany." Ernst was awed by the colony's machinery and declared Harmony well on its way to being "the most beautiful city of western America." A "Mr. Courtney" from England visited in the same year and was most favorably impressed. William Hall from Illinois, lately an immigrant from England, said in 1821, "The Government, Arrangement, & results produced at this Place are truly astonishing." He saw 300 acres of wheat, Indian corn "upwards of 10 ft. high & as clean as a Garden," 1,400 Merino sheep, and a very large herd of cows. Scientific observer Henry R. Schoolcraft was impressed with the degree of specialization at Harmony, the "exact division of labour which pervades their whole system. Every individual is taught that he can perform but a single operation, whether it be in the various manipulations of the cotton or woollen manufactory, or in the simple business of the farmyard. By this means, no time is lost by changing from one species of work to another: the operator becomes perfect in his art, and if he possess any ingenuity, will contrive some improved process to abridge or facilitate his labour."[16]

Rappite Religious Doctrine and Practice

The leaders of Harmony knew that their marvels of commerce and technology were only incidental. Harmony's real significance was its unique role in the unfolding plan of God. The society's senior merchant John L. Baker ran their store in Shawneetown, Illinois, in 1823 and yearned to be at home with the other members in Harmony. He spent his free time at night and on Sunday reading and meditating on the cosmic importance of Harmony. Of his local neighbors in Illinois and Indiana he said: "It is hard to live with such an evil and perverse kind as most of these people here are, who serve sensuous pleasure to a point of wastefulness, and have neither courage, strength, nor will to acquire the means in some kind of proper manner, who help themselves with loafing, cheating, and gambling, and who steal their bread from the few who are industrious." Surely the Scriptures were being fulfilled in this degeneration and these were the last days. The God who preserved Noah, rescued Lot, and watched over his elect was shielding Harmony for his purpose. Baker wrote: "He surely is protecting the poor little group in the Harmonie, so deserted and hated by all the world, until the evil powers of hell are exhausted and Christ her saviour will reveal himself, then well unto you, you who are now sad, you who must deny yourself everything, except that which hard-fought-for virtue grants you 'the peace of God.'"[17]

Frederick Rapp was always quick to point out to all inquirers that the basis of Harmony was neither political nor economic. To a New York promoter of communes he said:

> It appears from your letter, that you look upon us more as a political than a religious society, which, however, is not the case, for our Society is based entirely upon religious principles, and everything is arranged according to the model of the first church after Acts of the Apostles in the 2d and 4th chapters. No one possesses the least as his own. Everyone who wants to join this Society must be here at least for 3 months before on trial, so that he becomes acquainted with our principles and rules, and when he decides to become a member, he must surrender forever all his property and possessions, and may never demand it back again, but if he should become dissatisfied and wished to leave the congregation, he gets travel money, according to his condition and the decision of the elders of the congregation . . . We do not encourage the state of matrimony, because physical propagation cannot take place in the following of Jesus, since those who belong to Christ crucify not only their flesh but also their lusts and desires. There can be only one religious opinion here, for without being of the same mind, no union of the spirit and, consequently, no communal life would be possible . . . Our number is about 900 persons. We own about one township of land, the title is in the name of all.[18]

His reply to a Swedenborgian in Boston expanded on the terrible state of the world, the approaching kingdom of

Jesus Christ, and the expected role of the Harmony Society in the coming age.[19]

> Our Community stands proof, firm and unmoveable upon its Rock of truth, the World and hell have but very few Means remaining untried to overthrow Harmonie, and yet she Stands, and will also well maintain her Ground, for the strength of faith which penetrates into the invisible Realm of Spirits will even reach him whom all Power is given in Heaven and upon earth, he will for certain be Sufficiently interrested to promote the preparations of his approaching Kingdom wherever he finds people for it; and with that belief Harmonie is prepossessed in a high degree. The signs of the times pointed out to us by the scripture let us apprehend sufficiently, that the coming of the Lord is not far off . . . Our Community remains pure without using constraint or rigor, but everything is governed and managed priestly after the order of Melchisedec, we also believe for Certain that the nigh approaching Kingdom of Jesus Christ will be governed and conducted in the same manner as well here upon earth as in the Realm of Spirits, and alltogether Humanly untill no adversary to truth and Jesus remains unsubdued, which the Scripture of the Old and New testament tells us Sufficiently, besides many other Witnesses of truth.[20]

Meanwhile "to keep up and inculcate with energie the doctrine of the Christian Religion, as well as the rules and ordonnances of the Community it requires a Man for Superintendant as mentioned above whom all others obey in Spiritual or temperal Regulations and submit to his Orders, depending all upon one Will."[21]

The one man with the one will for Harmony was George Rapp. His control was hardly questioned during the Indiana years. The new articles of agreement drawn up for all members to sign in 1821 made his governance even more secure. Frederick Rapp did manage large areas of the temporal affairs of the society but Frederick himself and all those temporal affairs still remained subject to the authority of George Rapp.[22] The detailed rules and regulations which society members were to obey were not written but were embodied in George Rapp. They were interpreted by George Rapp. Failures in practice, real or fancied, were confessed to George Rapp. He directed major operations of planting and harvest, marching 60 women out to reap and bind oats, or the whole community out to save a harvest from bad weather, or 160 people to plant 45 acres of Indian corn in a single afternoon.[23]

Members were entitled to the instruction needed for their temporal and spiritual well being. Rapp provided free education for Harmony's children which was half a century ahead of the state in general. Vocational training was excellent. Rappites lived in the midst of music both instrumental and vocal; music lessons were available to everyone. Bible study, catechism, and religious music were central in the school curriculum. Rapp had a printing press which issued religious books, including his own *Thoughts on the Destiny of Man* (1824), the first work of religious philosophy printed in Indiana. Always the chief teacher was George Rapp himself. He was the perennial preacher who kept the group identity clear. He gathered the community at least twice every Sunday. On a Sunday afternoon in October of 1819 the Harmony band led the whole membership three-quarters of a mile to the banks of the Wabash where Rapp "addressed them in German in a most animated & pathetic manner." Of the Harmonist church building Ferdinand Ernst said in 1819: "In the church I found neither an altar nor other decorations. On an elevation of about 3 feet there was a seat for Rapp, beside this a desk, on which lay a Bible. Each Sunday he speaks here to the people and is reported occasionally to call himself a prophet of God."[24]

In 1822 George Rapp led the community to begin building a grand new church. The old frame church was hot in summer. The Harmony craftsmen were capable of accepting a challenge to their skill and devotion. Most of all, Rapp saw the time as right in the prophetic calendar. He was always alert to events of world history and to cosmic events such as comet sightings. These, linked with the writings of mystics like Johannes Tauler, Jakob Böhme, Emanuel Swedenborg, or Johann Herder, and always related to millennial passages in the Bible, were the stuff of Rapp's thoughts and dreams. These combinations were the subjects of many of his evening religious discussions. Now the Sunwoman church had endured its times of hardship and was ready to stand forth prepared before the world. The church building was not quite complete when William Hebert visited Harmony.

> They are erecting a noble church, the roof of which is supported in the interior by a great number of stately columns, which have been turned from trees of their own forests. The kinds of wood made use of for this purpose are, I am informed, black walnut, cherry, and sassafras. Nothing I think can exceed the grandeur of the joinery, and the masonry and brick-work seem to be of the first order. The form of this church is that of a cross, the limbs being short and equal; and as the doors, of which there are four, are placed at the ends of the limbs, the interior of the building as seen from the entrances, has a most ample and spacious effect. A quadrangular story or compartment containing several rooms, is raised on the body of the church, the sides of which inclining

inwards towards the top, are terminated by a square gallery, in the centre of which is a small circular tower of about ten feet in height, which is surmounted with a silvered globe . . . I could scarcely imagine myself to be in the woods of Indiana, on the borders of the Wabash, while pacing the long resounding aisles, and surveying the stately colonades of this church.[25]

Outside, over the north door, they placed the symbols of their identity, a sunburst window and a golden rose with the year 1822. Karl J. R. Arndt's investigation of the meaning of that golden rose has based it on Luther's translation of Micah 4:8, "And thou, O tower Eder, a stronghold of the daughter of Zion, thy golden rose shall come, the first dominion, the kingdom of the daughter of Jerusalem." The end of the second flight of the Sunwoman which had brought the society to Indiana was drawing to a close. The time had come for the next step in building the divine economy and the city of God.[26]

Rappites Return to Pennsylvania

But not in Indiana. The home on the Wabash seemed spacious but the years there were marked by restrictions. The society did not grow by immigration as the Rapps had expected. There were some additions but the membership in the long term did not increase. Between 800 and 1,000 members had come from Pennsylvania to Indiana and that remained the maximum membership. The religious establishment liberalized back in Württemberg and not so many persons of Rapp's persuasion were leaving; a new prophet there said the flight of the Sunwoman would be to Russia rather than to the United States, so some believers went to Russia instead.[27] Germans who did write to inquire about Harmony on the Wabash were often indentured servants working off their passage cost or other debts in America's eastern cities. Some virtually demanded that the Rapps pay their debts and provide transportation to Harmony. George Rapp responded testily to some applicants:

Did we not do our duty and fulfill it? Did not brother Friedrich . . . free many godless people of the world who begged him for it, and many of them ran off on the way, and our money was lost? Did we not risk $7,000 cash money in this, to which our sweat and work clung, and few even thank us for it . . . We have learned a lesson with our countrymen, the fewer who come to us now the more we like it, for the narrow path to Life is too distant for them and too strange, and they mostly bring a heart full of offense, which they have collected by hearsay, covered slightly with a bit of natural love to their

dear friends and acquaintances, and when this has disappeared the first stays on in the heart and expresses itself in jealousy and lack of good will, and thus such people instead of heaven have hell.[28]

Fredrick Rapp told Harmony's agents in Pittsburgh to beware of advancing aid to any incoming Germans unless he specifically recommended them because "most of the people in Germany within a few years past, became depraved in such a degree, that neither Calamity, favor nor gospel are able to produce a change in their corrupted heart."[29]

Persons born in America were hardly accepted at all. Chester Chadwick of Kentucky wrote twice in late summer of 1822. He had a wife, six children, no property, and a great affection for "the Apostolick plan of a Society" in which he could withdraw "from the bustle & cares of the world." As part of his application he included a poem of sixteen lines. Frederick Rapp explained to him the rigors of being in a society "alltogether Religious" and of being "obidient to the ordained superintendants." Since Chadwick did not understand German and so could not benefit from Harmony's church or school, Rapp advised him to "content yourself for a while yet the best way you can" since the end of the age should come soon anyway.[30]

The Wabash was navigable but far from ideal, being often high, or low, or frozen, and always a long way by slow boats from the major markets. Business was difficult in the hard winter of 1822–23 when there was no mail delivery to Harmony from the east for a full month; some mail from Cincinnati actually took four or five months to arrive. Neither the vineyards nor the Germans proved very comfortable in the climate of the Posey County bottoms. In spite of good management and care, 219 Rappites died beside the Wabash.[31]

To their Hoosier neighbors the German-speaking Rappites often appeared clannish and arrogant. When George Rapp would not pay what they considered fair wages for their labor in clearing a site for the first Rappite arrivals in 1814, they threatened him. Rapp said "I am rather unsafe here . . . I do not go more than one or two miles from the house." It was a great convenience for the region to have the stores and the excellent mechanical services developed by the Rappite colony. These were widely admired and patronized. However these Germans were strictly business. They offered a hundredweight of flour for three bushels of merchantable wheat and four bushels of meal for five bushels of corn, which local customers said was a grinding toll above the going rate. For merchandise or services they required payment in hard money or United States notes. Money flowed to the Rapps who returned little of it to the region and answered to nobody. Since the society needed very little from its neighbors, there was very little real trade. Some local citizens concluded: "If an ordinary merchant could come among us, and set up a store, as he grew rich he would increase his expenditure, and the money would circulate and enrich those who supplied him with meat, bread, &c.; but these people spend nothing, and therefore we should be very glad to see their society destroyed."[32]

Inevitably there were exaggerated estimates of Rappite profits and resentment against this group which professed no attachment to worldly goods but showed such expertise in acquiring them. Rappite control of so much river frontage was resented. Charges of monopoly and price gouging were carried to the state legislature. The Rappite grist mills were essentially declared public utilities and regulated by a state law painfully interpreted by the circuit court of Posey County. Frederick Rapp grumbled: "We will never grind for customers . . . We are determined more and more to limit ourselves to ourselves . . . The world can no longer bear us, and we cannot bear it, until it is judged."[33]

In January of 1820 tensions with the neighbors turned violent. William Harris came to Harmony to assault two Rappites and was himself assaulted by nine community members including Frederick Rapp. Next day Harris returned to Harmony with armed reinforcements who rioted there for two hours. The matter inflamed local public opinion against the Rappites and dragged on in the Posey County court for months. Frederick Rapp was disgruntled when the local jury fined the Rappites more heavily than the rioters.[34]

Engaging in politics was an avocation dear to Hoosiers. Here again they were troubled by Rappites, particularly by the possibility of block voting by Rappites. Candidates felt compelled to seek or manipulate the Harmonist vote. Ratliff Boon wrote Frederick Rapp in 1821:

I am confident that the present Election [for state senator] will depend Entirely on your votes, you have the power to Elect who you please, many of the people in the Country say, it is not worth their while to vote, for Harmonie can Elect Just who they please . . . If you Should determine to vote for [Elisha] Harrison in this Election, you will loose many good friends in different parts of this district, and in fact it will raise opposition in the different parts of the State, I will only ask you to divide your votes Equal, or be silent as to the senator . . . You must know that you have already a number of Enimies in consequence of your decided power to regulate Elections.[35]

Suspicions about the society usually centered on the power of George Rapp and the practice of celibacy. Some unfriendly neighbor in Indiana sent a letter to the newspaper called the *Morgenröthe* in Harrisburg, Pennsylvania, saying that the Rappite society on the Wabash "manufactures almost all articles except children." Frederick Rapp sent a careful correction.

The writer says that the begetting of children or sexual intercourse of married people is forbidden in the Harmonie and that in the last 5 years no more than 1 or 2 children were born, which is false and a lie and an erroneous statement which has been spread among the public for the last 12 to 15 years, and which is kept in circulation still by people without religion and reason, although our school, which always contains 80 to 100 children from 6 to 12 years of age and still contains such, contradicts this statement sufficiently. Also every reasonable person and one who knows human nature would easily see that a society of about 800 people could not live under a law of that kind and live in peace and unity for so many years. The Harmonie Society consists only of people who live the religion of Jesus practically and who pursue sanctification. Among these there are some of both sexes who have so advanced in sanctification and who by means of the power of the gospel of Jesus Christ and His vicarious atonement have been so enobled in their virtue, that they of their own free will have given up carnal intercourse and devote themselves fully to prepare for Christ and His Kingdom, which kind of people have always existed and still exist, although their number has always been small.[36]

During the winter of 1823–24 Frederick Rapp began inquiring again about large tracts of land—one of about a million acres near Wheeling which might be available for twenty-five cents per acre; one "upwards of 300,000 acres" in western Virginia. On 5 May 1824 Frederick Rapp and two colleagues purchased the new site just eighteen miles down the Ohio River from Pittsburgh. Settlement began immediately; corn was planted on the new site by 13 May.[37]

This time they moved by steamboat. The Rappites in Community House No. 2 at Harmony on the Wabash wrote in German on the house step: "On the twenty-fourth of May, 1824, we have departed. Lord, with Thy great help and goodness, in body and soul protect us." This first load pushed off about 4 P.M. George Rapp went with them and Indiana saw him no more.[38]

The move was a religious event. George Rapp was sure that the Lord's providence had been keeping this new place for his society.

There was absolutely no doubt in George Rapp's mind about the necessity of the third move of God's elect. His calculations of the time of the sunwoman assured him that he was to lead his people from the comforts of the Wabash into a new land which the Lord, his and their God, had provided for them, for on this land they were to build the Divine Economy, and God would make of them a great people.[39]

That was the message in the pastoral letter he sent to those still in Indiana on 19 June. It summarized the preparation he had been giving them. The keynote passage was Genesis 12:1–2, one they knew well. "Get thee out of thy country, and from thy kindred, and from thy father's house, unto a land that I will show thee. And I will make of thee a great nation, and I will bless thee, and make thy name great; and thou shalt be a blessing." Whoever seriously wanted the heavenly kingdom should leave "the fat valley of Sodom" and hurry like the homesick to the new promised land. The person who wished to be useful to mankind should leave nature and selfishness behind, deny his own will, take as companion and fellow absolute obedience to the truth and the divine laws.

> And we also have now again been commanded: leave your present abode, leave your fatherland for I want to make of you an exemplary people of blessing and faith. Whoever of you now believes and recognizes this, how joyously, how confidently can he continue his pilgrimage. He will sleep as gently in nature under a hut of boards as in the most beautiful furnished and papered house. He will fear neither robbers nor vicious beasts, because faith in the word of God is the spirit's nourishment. That gives courage. One feels one's inner energies and turns oneself over and leaves oneself without conditions to the direction and leadership of the Lord.[40]

By 5 May 1825 they had purchased and launched their own new steamboat, arranged the sale of Harmony on the Wabash to Robert Owen for $150,000, produced a large stock of goods in the factories on the Wabash to supply their customers during the transition, and moved to Pennsylvania. George Rapp had just finished writing his *Thoughts on the Destiny of Man*. It was fired with the vision of a "divine economy"—an earthly city which would be at the same time a true harmony, a heaven on earth, a kingdom of God. The name of the new place to embody that ideal had become Economy.[41] Frederick Rapp had the vision too.

> It seems, few men are able to comprehend the great events which have taken place in our community. The present time may be compared with the time of Jesus Christ, when he appeared among his nation. Who paid any attention to Him? Although, in spite of all this, His aim came true! So, of course, our community will also attain its aim, regardless of whether more or less pay attention to us. Keep patience, soon the winter will be gone and the long expected spring of the golden kingdom will appear, for the enjoyment of all good men on earth as in Heaven.[42]

George Rapp lived to be nearly ninety years of age in the new location at Economy in Pennsylvania. He made a series of poor judgments because of his infatuation with a young community member named Hildegard. About 175 members of the community and a settlement of $105,000 were lost in a schism led by Bernhard Müller (also known as Count Leon) who claimed to be a more reliable prophet and alchemist than the aging Rapp. Frederick Rapp was saddened and disillusioned in the course of these events. Frederick Rapp died in 1834 at the age of sixty but George Rapp lived on for thirteen more years, even more comfortable in his self-assurance for lack of Frederick's restraint. While decreasing in numbers and respect, his society remained immensely rich and powerful. Between 1834 and 1847 he shored up his security by accumulating a "church fund" of some $500,000 in gold and silver held secretly at his own house.[43]

Historians have seen in George Rapp at least some degree of exploitation and abuse of authority. After years of Harmony studies, Karl J. R. Arndt has written: "The most disappointing, disillusioning and yet undeniable result of my long and thorough research into the history of Rapp's determination to build the City of God on earth is the inescapable fact that an element of doubt and uncertainty, if not premeditated 'pious' fraud, clings to most important documents of Rapp's Society as far as its honesty toward the members of the Society is concerned."[44]

Evidently Rapp stole no money. In his view the interests of George Rapp, and of the Harmony Society, and of the kingdom of God were simply one. He liked to cite in his own behalf the biblical example of the craftsmen employed by King Josiah to restore the temple in Jerusalem when "there was no reckoning made with them of the money that was delivered into their hand, because they dealt faithfully" (II Kings 22:7). He applied to himself the passage from Isaiah which said "the government shall be upon his shoulder" (Isaiah 9:6). His people were to trust and obey him; he was to tell them exactly as much as he felt it was good for them to know. He never lost the supreme confidence that he acted always as a veritable agent and prophet of God. For years he kept everything in readiness awaiting the divine signal to bring his society to the land of Israel. His final earthly day was 7 August

1847. He said "If I did not so fully believe that the Lord has designed me to place our society before his presence in the land of Canaan, I would consider this my last."[45]

NOTES

1. *George Rapp's Separatists, 1700–1803: A Documentary History*, comp. and ed. Karl J. R. Arndt (Worcester, Mass.: Harmony Society Press, 1980), 67.

2. *George Rapp's Separatists*, 84–102, 111, 175, 228; Karl J. R. Arndt, "Luther's Golden Rose at New Harmony, Indiana," *Concordia Historical Institute Quarterly* 49 (Fall 1976): 112–22.

3. *George Rapp's Separatists*, 152, 162, 184, 192, 230, 272–79, 329.

4. *George Rapp's Separatists*, 404–12.

5. Karl J. R. Arndt, *George Rapp's Harmony Society, 1785–1847* (Philadelphia: University of Pennsylvania Press, 1965), 65–68, 72, 74.

6. *George Rapp's Separatists*, 357.

7. *Harmony on the Connoquenessing, 1803–1815: A Documentary History*, comp. and ed. Karl J. R. Arndt (Worcester, Mass.: Harmony Society Press, 1980), xxii; *George Rapp's Separatists*, 441; Arndt, *George Rapp's Harmony Society*, 56.

8. Donald E. Pitzer and Josephine M. Elliott, "New Harmony's First Utopians, 1814–1824," *Indiana Magazine of History* 75 (September 1979): 248–52; *Harmony on the Connoquenessing*, xxvi, 459, 461; Arndt, *George Rapp's Harmony Society*, 97–104.

9. Fortescue Cuming, *Sketches of a Tour to the Western Country* (Pittsburgh, Pa.: Cramer, Spear and Eichbaum, 1810, 504 p.); John Melish, *Travels in the United States of America*, 2 vols. (Philadelphia: Printed for the Author, 1812).

10. *A Documentary History of the Indiana Decade of the Harmony Society, 1814–1824*, comp. and ed. Karl J. R. Arndt, 2 vols. (Indianapolis, Ind.: Indiana Historical Society, 1975, 1978), 1:xii; *Harmony on the Connoquenessing*, 137–69.

11. *Documentary History*, 1:8.

12. *Harmony on the Connoquenessing*, 970–74; *Documentary History*, 1:xii–xiii.

13. *Documentary History*, 1:xiii.

14. *Documentary History*, 2:130–33.

15. Pitzer and Elliott, "New Harmony's First Utopians," 235–36, 241–42; *Documentary History*, 1:xiii; 2:691, 701, 754.

16. *Documentary History*, 1:744–46, 799–801; 2:247–49, 256.

17. *Documentary History*, 2:717.

18. *Documentary History*, 2:338–39, 363–64.

19. *Documentary History*, 2:401–3, 511–15.

20. *Documentary History*, 2:512–14.

21. *Documentary History*, 2:514.

22. There is evidently no truth in the story that George Rapp faked angel footprints in stone to underscore the authority of his revelations. In the Indiana decade he needed no such amateur hoax to guarantee his place. See Arndt, *George Rapp's Harmony Society*, 335; *Documentary History*, 1:613–15; 2:259–60, 524–25.

23. *Documentary History*, 2:187–89, 257, 524, 569; Arndt, "Luther's Golden Rose," 117; *Harmony on the Connoquenessing*, xxvi, 459.

24. Donald E. Pitzer, "Education in Utopia: The New Harmony Experience," in *Indiana Historical Society Lectures 1976–1977* (Indianapolis, Ind.: Indiana Historical Society, 1978), 75–101; Pitzer and Elliott, "New Harmony's First Utopians," 242–48; *Documentary History*, 1:746, 784; 2:917–19.

25. Harlow Lindley, *Indiana as Seen by Early Travelers* (Indianapolis, Ind.: Indiana Historical Commission, 1916). 334–35.

26. Arndt, "Luther's Golden Rose," 113–18; Pitzer and Elliott, "New Harmony's First Utopians," 232, 252, 281–85.

27. Pitzer and Elliott, "New Harmony's First Utopians," 252.

28. *Documentary History*, 1:676.

29. *Documentary History*, 2:42–43.

30. Lindley, *Indiana as Seen by Early Travelers*, 333; *Documentary History*, 2:442–43, 465–66, 525–26, 783.

31. Lindley, *Indiana as Seen by Early Travelers*, 336–37; Arndt, *George Rapp's Harmony Society*, 300–301; *Documentary History*, 2:168–70, 510–11, 516–17.

32. *Documentary History*, 1:78, 440–41; 2:158, 248, 527.

33. Lindley, *Indiana as Seen by Early Travelers*, 331–37; *Documentary History*, 1:440–43; 2:118, 157–59, 179, 523–27.

34. *Documentary History*, 2:9–13, 19, 44, 75–79, 118–19.

35. *Documentary History*, 2:253.

36. *Documentary History*, 1:775; see also Arndt, *George Rapp's Harmony Society*, 209–10 and *Documentary History*, 2:389, 486–93.

37. *Harmony on the Wabash in Transition, 1824–1826*, comp. and ed. Karl J. R. Arndt (Worcester, Mass.: Harmony Society Press, 1982), 5–7, 653; *Documentary History*, 2:759, 769–70, 786, 793–94.

38. Arndt, *George Rapp's Harmony Society*, 306.

39. *Harmony on the Wabash in Transition*, xv.

40. *Harmony on the Wabash in Transition*, 44.

41. Arndt, *George Rapp's Harmony Society*, 308; *Documentary History*, 2:917–19.

42. Arndt, *George Rapp's Harmony Society*, 305; see also *Documentary History*, 2:880.

43. *George Rapp's Years of Glory*, comp. and ed. Karl J. R. Arndt (New York: Peter Lang Publishing, 1987), 4; Arndt, *George Rapp's Harmony Society*, 449–531, 552–53; Pitzer and Elliott, "New Harmony's First Utopians," 256.

44. *Harmony on the Wabash in Transition*, 597.

45. Arndt, *George Rapp's Harmony Society*, 577; see also *George Rapp's Years of Glory*, 1073.

OWENITES

On the evening of 25 February 1825, Robert Owen spoke in the Hall of Representatives at the United States Capitol in Washington, D.C. The subject of the speech was a series of world-shaping events about to occur on the banks of the Wabash River in Indiana. Incoming president John Quincy Adams was present for the speech as was his predecessor James Monroe. Also in the audience were several members of the Cabinet, of the Supreme Court, and of the Congress. Full text of the speech was immediately printed in the *National Intelligencer* and separately issued at Washington in pamphlet form. To Owen it seemed only right that his tremendous news should be heralded at the very heart of this young republic. "The subject which I shall endeavour to explain is, without exception, the most important that can be presented to the human mind," he said. "And, if I have been enabled to take a right view of it, then are changes at hand, greater than all the changes which have hitherto occurred in the affairs of mankind." He believed a new age had begun. "At this time, a match has been applied to a train, that, if I mistake not, will dispel past errors, until old things shall pass away, and all shall become new, and beautiful, and delightful, bringing unnumbered and unlimited blessings to everyone."[1]

Robert Owen and Religion

Owen was an evangelist. His good news was word of a social millennium about to dawn. What was being introduced at the Wabash was a gift and model to be eagerly embraced by "the world at large." In this first address in the Capitol he focused on the certainty of his own principles and on his previous success as a reformer. "Having discovered that individuals were always formed by the circumstances, whatever they might be, which were allowed to exist around them, my practice was to govern the circumstances; and thus, by means imperceptible and unknown to the individuals, I formed them, to the extent I could control the circumstances, into what I wished them to become." As an industrialist he was sure that "a few hours daily of healthy and desirable employment, chiefly applied to direct modern mechanical and other scientific improvements, will be amply sufficient to create a full supply, at all times, of the best of every thing for every one." He stepped gingerly around the subject of religion at first. He was negative toward sects, classes, or parties which divide man and "make him one of the most unjust and irrational of all beings." He was positive toward the goals of truth and benefit for fellow creatures which he was sure real religion and real martyrs have always wanted.[2]

On 7 March 1825 Owen spoke for three hours at the same Hall of Representatives in the Capitol at Washington with President Adams again among those in attendance. In the language of unrelieved social determinism which he espoused everywhere, he reiterated the first principle of his new "science of circumstances."

The first principle of the science is derived from the knowledge of facts, that external circumstances may be so formed as to have an overwhelming and irresistible influence over every infant that comes into existence, either for good or evil; to compel him to receive any particular sentiments or habits, to surround him, through life, with the most agreeable or disagreeable objects, and thus, at pleasure, make any portion, or the whole of the human race, poor, ignorant, vicious, and wretched; or affluent, intelligent, virtuous, and happy.[3]

And he asked to be more clearly understood about religion. On the infrequent occasions when he spoke of a pure religion, a genuine religion, a universal religion, or a rational religion he meant "the daily undeviating practice, in thought, word, and action, of charity, benevolence, and kindness, to every human being with whom we come into communication, or have any transactions, near or remote." It was a religion to be entirely derived from the evidence of human senses. None of his hearers could have ever seen or understood such religion before, he said, because it was "now for the first time declared amidst this enlightened assembly."[4] There were always some who urged him to apply his principles to the present state of society, not to disturb it but to promote union and harmony among the variety of social structures that exist. Not a chance! All religion as previously or currently known or organized anywhere in the world had to go.

> The fact is, and I am most anxious that all parties should fully understand me, the system which I propose now for the formation and government of society, is founded on principles, not only altogether different, but directly opposed to the system of society which has hitherto been taught and practised at all times, in all nations . . . The old system has been influenced, in all ages, by some imaginary notions or other, under the name of religion, but which notions have been, in all countries, uniformly opposed to facts, and, in consequence, all minds have been thereby rendered more or less irrational . . . The old system keeps its votaries in ignorance, makes them mere localized beings, and the perpetual slaves of a combination of the most inferior and worst circumstances, and, in consequence, society is a chaos of superstition, passion, prejudice, poverty in many, and ignorance of their real interest in all.[5]

This conviction of the necessity to clear the ground of all existing religions was one he had established long before coming to America from Great Britain. As a boy in his native town of Newtown in Wales he was energetic, intelligent, and independent. Admiring people of the town loaned him a great variety of books, many on religious subjects. Religious instruction offered by his

parents who were members of the Church of England and especially by three of his aunts who were Methodists he seems to have regarded as attempts to convert him and as invitations to a contest of will. Years later in his autobiography he said: "But certain it is that my reading religious works, combined with my other readings, compelled me to feel strongly at ten years of age that there must be something fundamentally wrong in all religions, as they had been taught up to that period."[6]

From age ten to age twenty he learned his way in the business world at Stamford and London and Manchester. Generally he had great appreciation for his employers who trained him. Often he shared in the religious life of the merchant family to whom he was apprenticed. Mr. McGuffog belonged to the Church of Scotland; Mrs. McGuffog belonged to the Church of England. They attended a service at each church every Sunday and Robert Owen always went with them to both. The McGuffogs got along happily under such an arrangement but to Robert Owen what he heard were "contending sermons."

> But the more I heard, read, and reflected, the more I became dissatisfied with Christian, Jew, Mahomedan, Hindoo, Chinese, and Pagan. I began seriously to study the foundation of all of them, and to ascertain on what principle they were based. Before my investigations were concluded, I was satisfied that one and all had emanated from the same source, and their varieties from the same false imaginations of our early ancestors . . . It was with the greatest reluctance, and after long contests in my mind, that I was compelled to abandon my first and deep rooted impressions in favour of Christianity,—but being obliged to give up my faith in this sect, I was at the same time compelled to reject all others, for I had discovered that all had been based on the same absurd imagination, "that each one formed his own qualities,—determined his own thoughts, will, and action,—and was responsible for them to God and to his fellowmen." My own reflections compelled me to come to very different conclusions. My reason taught me that I could not have made one of my own qualities,—that they were forced upon me by Nature;—that my language, religion, and habits, were forced upon me by Society; and that I was entirely the child of Nature and Society;—that Nature gave the qualities, and Society directed them. Thus was I forced, through seeing the error of their foundation, to abandon all belief in every religion which had been taught to man.[7]

Owen the Industrialist

Taking up a fortunate opportunity, he invested his small savings and his great energy in a rapidly expanding new enterprise at Manchester, "spinning cotton by new and curious machinery." Owen's speedy rise in the business world now became meteoric. Before he was twenty he was established as supervisor and rising partner in a cotton mill employing 500 men, women, and children at the machines. In his new prominence he was welcomed into the Literary and Philosophical Society of Manchester and into an evening discussion group at Manchester College where he was known as "the one who opposed the religious prejudices of all sects." On spinning mill business in Scotland he met and courted Caroline Dale, eldest daughter of David Dale whose wide holdings included New Lanark's cotton spinning mill. Before he could buy New Lanark and marry Caroline, the issue of religion had to be faced. David Dale was a wealthy industrialist but also a Presbyterian minister in Glasgow and superintendent for some forty congregations of his independent Presbyterian denomination. Owen did not yield.

> I took my ground with him on the error of all religions in placing any virtue in the faith or belief in their respective dogmas. I held that belief never was and never could be in the power of anyone . . . And as all religions were based on the presumed power of man to believe or disbelieve by the power of an independent will of his own creation, and as this supposition was opposed to all facts, all the religions of the world were emanations of disordered or misinstructed minds . . . I told him I could no more force my mind to believe that which he had been made conscientiously to believe, than he could force his own mind to believe as I had been compelled to believe; that that which had been forced into his mind as divine truth, was made to appear to me as ignorant human falsehood, and which, whenever brought under discussion with me, I was conscientiously compelled to endeavour to disprove.[8]

They agreed to disagree and lived for seventeen years in deep mutual affection.[9]

About the first of January in 1800, Robert Owen "entered upon the government of New Lanark." Owen was the resident director and for the next twenty-five years the major factor in shaping the town's life. He said "I had now, by a course of events not under my control, the groundwork on which to try an experiment long wished for, but little expected ever to be in my power to carry into execution." Under the non-resident ownership of David Dale, the mills at New Lanark had been better than most.[10] Under the resident direction of Robert Owen the situation was marvelously improved. The improvement had to be made in spite of partners who wanted no changes which might lower their profits. The improve-

ment had to be made in the face of resistance by the Scots at New Lanark to this invasion of outlander Englishmen who were always changing the machines, changing the work procedures, and changing the standards. Owen made it all work. The town got cleaned up. Stealing and drunkenness dropped. No children under ten were employed in the mills; no more children were imported from the parish workhouses. The company store in the village soon earned a reputation for excellent goods at a fair price. Under Owen's eagle eye, the mills actually increased production levels and profits concurrent with the social improvements.

Best of all, there was the school. It kept expanding and improving. When Owen was free to carry out his ideas fully in 1816, he built an excellent new building to house his Institution for the Formation of Character. It offered full time education for children of the villages of New Lanark and Old Lanark from the time they could walk until age ten plus part-time continuing education for all who were ten and older. Owen was very personally involved in the school's operation. He was testing his theory of the forming of character by control of circumstances, of developing pupils in an atmosphere of participative happiness.[11]

Owen's "New Views of Society"

Though he was spinning mill supervisor, adviser and assistant to his father-in-law, and director of schools, his chief mission from the summer of 1802 had become "to openly propagate my new views of society." For the next fifty-five years the most characteristic remark about him was "Mr. Owen explained his principles." Everywhere and with everybody he was always asserting that the character of man is formed for him and not by him. For Owen this was not endless repetition of one idea. It was the lifting up of a revolutionary insight with implications which must reconstitute the world. The implications were improved working conditions; a share of the prodigious output of the new industrial techniques for the workers; and especially a deliberate program of education which would transform the character of people everywhere by governing their circumstances. The world was full of people who were poor and miserable; he intended to make them prosperous and happy. For any who might say this was impracticable, one part of his explanation of his principles was always a recital of the success of his experiment at New Lanark. Thousands of people from Great Britain and many foreign lands came to New Lanark to see.[12]

At this time Britain's best leaders were troubled about deplorable social conditions developing in the new era of machines, factories, and urbanization. Robert Owen was very rich and articulate. He understood industry and could illustrate his presentations with hard data about industrial life. He was privileged to explain his principles in the drawing rooms of the great and in the halls of church and state. In 1813 and 1814 he put his principles into print in four essays. Five publishers distributed the printed essays. Owen had forty copies specially bound and sent them off to the rulers of Europe, Napoleon's copy by private courier. These essays were published together as *A New View of Society* in London in 1816.[13] In following years he published at least 130 tracts besides articles and speeches. Generally they were all the same.

His critics said he was too repetitious, too insistent, too strong in his presentations, and nearly obsessive. In later years his oldest son thought Owen's manner was "too vehement and absolutely irritating." His second son thought the enjoyment of this reformer was much more in contemplation than in reality. His biographers have spoken of his "autointoxication" and "self-delusion." He was, to say the least, single minded.[14]

His mission kept being complicated by his aversion to organized religion. His opposition to such religion was candid and widely known. Out of love and respect for his wife, he allowed her to involve their seven children in her branch of Presbyterianism, an orientation his strength was capable of reversing with little more than a word. His oldest son reported one brief boyhood conversation with his father which undid all the years of his mother's instruction. "My father, either with or without design, had laid the axe at the very root of my religion; and though I was myself unconscious, even for years afterward, of its effect, yet did the whole tree wither and die of that single blow at last."[15] Robert Owen's *New View of Society* was not primarily concerned with religion. However it did lay the blame for the bulk of the world's ills on inconsistencies based in the church and its doctrines "which have created, and still create, a great proportion of the miseries which exist in the world." Its doctrines had generated "superstition, bigotry, hypocrisy, hatred, revenge, wars, and all their evil consequences." The church had been teaching people erroneously that they were responsible for their own character. Church and clergy could not be counted on to be reformers since they taught this basic error of accountability; they were also disqualified as reformers because they would hardly act contrary to what they believed to be in their own financial interests.[16]

Owen's Campaign for His "New Views"

Robert Owen thought his "simple, plain, honest enunciation of truth, and of its beautiful application to all the real business of life" would quickly sweep the world. When victory seemed to lag, he used the years between 1815 and 1817 to lobby for social and educational reform among the manufacturers, the officers of government, and the agencies of Parliament. He still seemed to have the ear of persons of influence but must have realized that his power within the British establishment was fading. Some enemies enlisted a clergyman at Old Lanark to accuse him of making a treasonous speech at the opening of his new school in 1816. When he testified for child relief before the Factory Committee of the House of Commons, a powerful committee member took the occasion to question Owen himself about his religious beliefs. After he did a lot of work to prepare a report for the Association for the Relief of the Manufacturing and Laboring Poor, a report requested of him by the archbishop who was chairman, he and his report were passed off to a parliamentary committee which kept him waiting for two days in the committee anteroom and then informed him that his report would not be needed after all.

Owen immediately published his report in the newspapers. Relying on his reputation as a reformer and a friend of workers, he announced his intention to take his program directly to the British public. He called a public meeting for 14 August 1817 in the large room at the City of London Tavern "to consider a plan to relieve the country from its present distress, to re-moralise the lower orders, reduce the poor's rate, and gradually abolish pauperism with all its degrading consequences."[17]

In his published Report to the Association and in his address at London on 14 August, his reform proposal had taken the shape of founding cooperative villages, self-supporting communities of 500 to 1,500 persons in which the circumstances would be rightly controlled to produce good character, plenty, and happiness for all. He offered drawings and financial projections for such communities. He was sure that when this experiment was rightly started anywhere to serve as a model, not just the host of unemployed but the population of the whole world would soon organize itself into such happy villages. Using his own funds, he blanketed Britain with thousands of copies of the newspapers carrying full texts of these exciting plans. He was, he said, "beyond comparison the most generally popular character living."[18]

Then came Owen's second address at the City of London Tavern on 21 August 1817. The subject was religion. It expressed his abiding conviction that the ground for reform must be cleared of all existing religious organizations. What he said more sedately in his *New View of Society* he now sharpened.

> Knowing that what I should say at the meeting would be published the next day in every London morning and evening newspaper, that the public mind was highly excited upon the subject, and that what should be said by me would be widely circulated over the civilised world;—and knowing also that unless a deathblow could be given to all the existing false religions of the world, there could be no hope for man's liberation from the bondage of ignorance, disunion, and misery;—and feeling that in my then position I was the only individual living who had the slightest chance to accomplish such a task,—I resolved to dare the deed.[19]

He was willing to sacrifice his popularity and "to lay the axe to the root of all false religions." He was sure all religions but his own were false.

> Then my friends, I tell you, that hitherto you have been prevented from even knowing what happiness really is, solely in consequence of the errors—gross errors—that have been combined with the fundamental notions of every religion that has hitherto been taught to men. And, in consequence, they have made man the most inconsistent, and the most miserable being in existence. By the errors of these systems he has been make a weak, imbecile animal; a furious bigot and fanatic; or a miserable hypocrite; and should these qualities be carried, not only into the projected villages, but into Paradise itself, a Paradise would be no longer found![20]

The meeting ended in chaos instead of in the appointment of a committee as he had hoped. The *Times* of London printed the speech but this time printed a rebuttal as well. In every explanation of his principles from that day forward he could expect to be questioned about his religion. Generally there would be hints or accusations that he was an infidel. "I soon found I must prepare for the full extent of opposition which my so public uncompromising denunciations against all the religions of the world naturally excited," he said. "And this opposition continued without ceasing for upwards of thirty years, following my footsteps wherever I went, using all the unfair means of established power and prejudices to frustrate every attempt I made to practically benefit poor suffering ill-used humanity." With typical bravado he declared a victory and moved on. He said 21 August was "the most important day of my life for the public:—the day on which bigotry, superstition, and all false religions, received their death blow."[21]

New Harmony in Indiana as a Demonstration Cooperative

Though his role was now changed from lobbyist to private agent, Owen was no less a reformer. He was rich, highly visible, and fired with zeal for expression of his principles through the founding of limited cooperative communities. He still maintained an amazing network of acquaintances internationally who knew of his dedication to reform and of his experiment at New Lanark. He was not a revolutionary and hardly an advocate of democracy. It was not up to the masses to take economic or political power to themselves. Rather it was up to privileged rich men like himself to give humanity a demonstration of the one true path to social redemption.[22] He was alert to other experimenters and looking for opportunities. In August of 1820 he wrote to George Rapp at Harmony on the Wabash. He wanted "a correspondence . . . in the expectation of procuring a correct account of your establishment." He sent Rapp "copies of such works as I have already published."[23]

Owen was estimating the cost of land and equipment for an experimental community of 1,200 in Britain to be nearly $500,000 and his own fortune was only $250,000. Nobody else was coming up with cash. Then came the American opportunity. Richard Flower was agent to sell the Rappite land and equipment at Harmony on the Wabash for $150,000. Owen could afford to buy that himself. He talked with Flower in August of 1824, sailed to America to inspect the property in October of 1824, and signed papers on 3 January 1825 for purchase of the whole 20,000 acres and 180 buildings. His son said:

> The success of the Rappites, such as it was, wonderfully encouraged my father. He felt sure that he could be far more successful than they, without the aid either of bodily and mental despotism or of celibacy. Aside from rational education, which he deemed indispensable, he trusted implicitly, as cure for all social and industrial ills, to the principle of co-operation.[24]

During his stay in the United States from November of 1824 to June of 1825, Owen enjoyed a splendid honeymoon period among the Americans. The speeches in the Hall of Representatives at Washington, D.C., were symbolic of his reception among the nation's top leaders in business, academics, and politics. Most of the hours of every day he was explaining his principles and showing his sketches. His plan enlisted several educators and scientists as well as general members for his community. Eight or nine hundred prospective community members poured into New Harmony in spring of 1825. Owen spoke to those present on 27 April. "I am come to this country . . . to introduce an entire new state of society; to change it from an ignorant, selfish system to an enlightened social system which shall gradually unite all interests into one, and remove all causes for contest between individuals." In May he told them at New Harmony that the United States, and particularly the states west of the Alleghenies, seemed especially prepared and ripe for change to his principles. Soon blacks and Indians would also be organized.[25]

Constant Controversies about Religion

Owen was frank about his religious views during this first sweep of America early in 1825 but not especially confrontational. After his addresses in the Hall of Congress in Washington there was a flurry of twenty-four letters in the *National Intelligencer* debating his plan and its religious implications. Owen noted in the second of those addresses that his works were now published and distributed in America. So his views of religion were not hidden. Wherever he encountered clergy or Rappite leaders in his travels, religious differences were soon delineated. Frederick Rapp said Owen's principles "are in no way to be differentiated from those of the fallen angels who also said, we do not wish to be slavish worshippers of a Godhead, we are free."[26]

Evidently Owen felt that his insights about religion must be made still more plain. America must clear its ground of the old erroneous institutions to make way for his rising new system. While at sea between Liverpool and New York in October of 1825, he composed a letter to America. It was delivered to the New York newspapers on 7 November and widely published.[27]

> It is true you have derived many advantages from your European ancestors, but it is equally true that you have transplanted a very large portion of their errors and prejudices; you cannot therefore, enjoy to their full extent, the benefits to which I refer, until these errors of the old world have been removed . . . Belief and disbelief, love and hatred, are not under the control of the will. It is therefore irrational in the extreme to maintain, that man can be accountable for either, and most unjust and injurious to force any such absurdity into the infant mind. Yet all religions and laws have been hitherto founded on this error. Hence their want of success; hence the present irrational state of the human mind in every part of the world; and hence nearly all the evils, except those of climate, which afflict the inhabitants of the United States.[28]

On this second grand tour in late 1825 and early 1826, Owen visited New York and Philadelphia and left his model of a proper building for New Harmony with the president at the White House. But things were different now. The religious press was producing criticism in articles and pamphlets. After his speech at the Franklin Institute in Philadelphia he was cornered with a question about the Scriptures. For nearly an hour he argued that the Old and New Testaments were no more the word of God than any other writings. This position was widely denounced in print. Owen was becoming better known as a heretic in religion than as a heretic in economics. In spite of his assurances that residents of New Harmony would be guaranteed freedom of worship, Owen was often pressed to explain how persons could be convinced believers in his principles as well as convinced Christians.[29]

Perhaps the irritation of the religious opposition he felt in America influenced his address for the next Fourth of July at New Harmony. He offered alongside the American Declaration of Independence of 1776 his own Declaration of Mental Independence of 1826, an "event likely to prove, in its consequences, as important as any which has occurred in ancient or modern times."

> I now declare, to you and to the world, that Man, up to this hour, has been, in all parts of the earth, a slave to a Trinity of the most monstrous evils that could be combined to inflict mental and physical evil upon his whole race. I refer to private, or individual property—absurd and irrational systems of religion—and marriage, founded on individual property combined with some one of these irrational systems of religion . . . Religion, or Superstition,—for all religions have proved themselves to be Superstitions—by destroying the judgment, irrationalized all the mental faculties of man, and made him the most abject slave, through the fear of nonentities created solely by his own disordered imagination.[30]

In this hour, the fulness of time as he saw it, he declared that he had given the deathblow to tyranny and despotism over the human mind.[31] Beginning with the printing of the new declaration on 12 July 1826, each issue of the *New Harmony Gazette* carried three designations of date: (1) date in the year of the Christian Era; (2) date in the year of American Independence; and (3) date in the year of Mental Independence.

In early January of 1828, Owen was explaining his principles in a series of lectures in New Orleans. Resident clergy used the local papers to express their opposition. Such aggravation provoked Owen to lay the axe to the root of religion one more time. He inserted an ad in the

New Orleans papers offering to meet all or any of the clergy in public or private discussion.[32]

> I propose to prove, as I have already attempted to do in my lectures, that all the religions of the world have been founded on the ignorance of mankind; that they are directly opposed to the never-changing laws of our nature; that they have been, and are, the real source of vice, disunion, and misery of every description; that they are now the only real bar to the formation of a society of virtue, of intelligence, of charity in its most extended sense, and of sincerity and kindness among the whole human family; and that they can be no longer maintained except through the ignorance of the mass of the people, and the tyranny of the few over that mass.[33]

The clergy in New Orleans did not respond but Alexander Campbell of Virginia eventually did. Campbell was editor of the *Christian Baptist*, dedicated to subsuming all denominations into one expanding fellowship of biblical believers called Disciples or Christians.

Frances Trollope of England, a keen if somewhat acid observer of American life, was a member of the overflowing crowds attending the debate in Cincinnati 13–21 April 1829. It was, she said, "a spectacle unprecedented . . . All this I think could only have happened in America. I am not quite sure that it was very desirable it should have happened anywhere." She was amazed that neither of the participants really answered the other. The debate was to "commence each day at 9 o'clock, A.M. intermit at 12, recommence at 3 P.M. and continue until the parties agree to adjourn." Owen used his familiar anti-religion speech as an opener, stating what Trollope called "his mature conviction that the whole history of the Christian mission was a fraud, and its sacred origin a fable." Timothy Flint, Congregational-Presbyterian minister and one of the moderators, was impressed that the audience "received with invincible forbearance, the most frank and sarcastic remarks of Mr. Owen, in ridicule of the most sacred articles of Christian belief."[34]

For the remainder of the fifteen sessions Owen simply made the debate an occasion for advocating his own favorite idea. He kept reading and expanding his "Twelve Laws" affirming the complete dependence of character on environment. "Twelve truisms," Mrs. Trollope called them, which could hardly be twisted into a refutation of the Christian religion. "Mr. Owen is an extraordinary man, and certainly possessed of talent," she said, "but he appears to me so utterly benighted in the mists of his own theories, that he has quite lost the power of looking through them, so as to get a peep at the world as it really exists around him." The debate was a national event,
widely publicized and published because of its symbolic character. In the drama Robert Owen of New Lanark and New Harmony was a willing national symbol of unbelief.[35]

The Experiment's Legacy to Indiana

The Owenite community at New Harmony did not work. In a way it existed for about two years—from early 1825 to early 1827. In another way it never came into existence at all. At New Lanark in Scotland Robert Owen had given decades of hard work and close personal direction to establish the character of his community. At New Harmony on the Wabash he failed to provide realistic steps to move from grand assertions of principle and ideal sketches or models to an actual working community. Hundreds of prospective community members pressed in quickly without adequate preparation or selection. The population was always shifting. Owen himself was often absent; he left the colony at a particularly crucial stage of its infancy between June of 1825 and January of 1826. Even when he was present, his actions seemed erratic, changing the structure from a preliminary society to a constitutional society to a personal directorship by himself somehow nebulously linked with a constitution. All these structures were very feeble; he did not deed the bulk of his land at New Harmony to any of them.[36]

By spring of 1827 the experimental community was gone. William and Robert Dale Owen said it in the *New Harmony Gazette* for 28 March. "New Harmony, therefore, is not now a Community but, as was originally intended, a central village out of and around which communities have formed and may continue to form themselves." Robert Owen's investment of some $200,000 had produced no model village on the Wabash to illustrate his new system. He made at least two farewell addresses during the last week in May of 1827. In the speech on 27 May he called the remaining splinter groups at New Harmony "ten social colonies," thus declaring a kind of victory before departing for Scotland on 1 June. He returned to New Harmony for fleeting visits in spring of 1828 and spring of 1829 but exercised little influence. Some of the continuing residents would hardly give him a hearing and called him "Old Bob" behind his back.[37]

Nevertheless, the legacy of Robert Owen to Indiana and to America was very impressive. Because of their interest in the new world and because the remainder of their patrimony was invested in land on the Wabash, four sons (Robert Dale, William, David Dale, Richard) and one daughter (Jane) of Robert Owen made New Harmony their home base. These were energetic and educated persons. All four sons were trained in their youth at the highly regarded school of Philipp Emanuel von Fellenberg at Hofwyl in Switzerland; they were lifelong scholars, scientists, and community leaders.

Robert Owen collaborated with William Maclure to invite a notable cluster of educators and scientists to share the experiment at New Harmony. Maclure was a financial partner with Owen in New Harmony, a world citizen, a geologist, and a substantial patron of both education and science. So at a time when the study of science in Indiana was primitive at best, New Harmony had world class natural scientists Thomas Say and Charles Alexandre Lesueur in residence. Maclure was in constant contact with New Harmony and was always sending valuable books and materials. David Dale and Richard Owen were studying and popularizing science. The press at New Harmony kept issuing illustrated scientific works. European scholars of science came to visit. Donald Carmony and Josephine Elliott have stated in their study of New Harmony: "The scholarly research and publications by Maclure and other scientists associated with the model community doubtless exceeded that from all Indiana colleges and universities prior to the Civil War." At a time when schools in Indiana were poor and scarce, New Harmony offered instruction by educational pioneers such as Marie Duclos Fretageot, Joseph Neef, William Phiquepal D'Arusmont, and various members of the Owen family.[38]

Robert Owen's aversion to all existing religions was also part of his legacy. He did not appear to have much success in clearing the ground of all religion nationally. At the end of the eight days of the Owen-Campbell "debate" in Cincinnati in 1829, Alexander Campbell asked those to stand who prized the Christian religion. Nearly the whole audience of more than a thousand promptly rose. When he asked those who were "friendly to Mr. Owen's system" to rise, only three or four stood.[39] Nevertheless Owen's rationalism made its imprint.

During the days when Owen's experimental community was operating at New Harmony, freedom of religion was said to be guaranteed. Sunday was free from all but the most necessary kind of work. Representatives of any denomination could have a place for worship by arrangement. Mrs. Pears said in April of 1826 that Sunday at New Harmony was actually "only used as a day of recreation, visiting and amusement, military operations, and with some few of work." However residents who chose to use Sunday as a day for games, drills, or festivities were to show respect by keeping the town square quiet if there were meetings at the church. As William Pelham described them in letters to his son, these meetings at the New Harmony church were by no means typical Indiana services for Sunday. In fall of 1825 most of the Sunday meetings seem to have been conducted as lectures by Robert Jennings who "refused a good living and church from the Universalists" in order to support Robert Owen's principles at New Harmony and lead in liberal education for the rising generation. Pelham wrote in September of 1825: "On Sunday the Rev. Mr. Jennings commonly delivers a lecture in the forenoon (without any formal text) in which he explains the manner of receiving religious impressions. I have not yet heard one of his Sunday lectures, but from several conversations I have had with him, I can plainly see that he will never try to stupify the understanding of his hearers with unintelligible dogmas, and incomprehensible jargon." When Mr. Jennings was absent for two Sundays, William Owen and another community member addressed the congregation, reading and expounding some extracts from the works of Robert Owen.[40]

There were evangelical preachers from outside but they found little hospitality. Pelham said "A Baptist preacher came into the town and announced his intention of delivering a discourse in the evening in the Church. Accordingly a large congregation assembled, and listened to him with great attention. He is certainly one of their first rate preachers, and he managed his matters with much address. The next evening—(Friday) Mr. Jennings delivered a lecture in the same place, and ably demonstrated the sandy foundation of the ingenious gentleman's arguments, without any pointed allusion to him or his arguments." When the unnamed Baptist attempted a rejoinder to Jennings, most of the congregation chose not to listen. They went off to the Hall, formerly the big Rappite church, for music and dancing. "Last Sunday afternoon," said Pelham, "we were regaled with a truly christian harangue from a rambling shaking quaker who happened to be here."[41]

In 1826 William Maclure prepared a petition to the Indiana legislature for an act to incorporate his education projects separately as the New Harmony Education Society. It was "overwhelmingly rejected by a Senate distrustful of the heterodox views that prevailed at New Harmony." Maclure said it was difficult to attract outside pupils to his schools at New Harmony because of "immense prejudices, not to say a kind of horror, excited against Mr. Owen's natural marriages and other theories."[42]

When the community experiment ended in spring of 1827 and all residents were notified they must make their own way, that did not bring any quick resurgence of traditional religious practice. The *New Harmony Gazette* continued. The non-religious orientation of the resident members of the Owen family was plain. The Pestalozzian educators at New Harmony wanted to distance themselves from any traditional Christian views that human nature needed redemption. Whatever their practice in private, none of the scientists was a public advocate of pious life.[43]

There had been one early separation of a handful of community members with Methodist sympathies. They leased 1,200 acres from Robert Owen and founded Macluria where the atmosphere for Christianity could be more friendly. Its members were of small influence and its life was short.[44] Constance Fauntleroy Runcie later reported reminiscences of her aunt who was among "the few who assembled together on the Lord's day for divine service" at New Harmony.

> Large stones were hurled against the door, and overhead still larger ones were rolled up and down, making a noise like thunder; or a half-dozen men in heavy boots would wait until service had begun, then one after another, with great noise, would shuffle in, waiting only a few moments to shuffle out again, intent upon tormenting and disturbing the little congregation. And later on, when hoping to build for themselves a little church, the subscription paper was torn to atoms, and they were unable to collect even a small amount.[45]

Worst of all, said the aunt, "was to know and feel yourself misunderstood and despised; to be accounted deficient in common sense, and considered mentally inferior because you confessed Christ crucified."

Robert Dale Owen and Frances Wright

Crucial events for the preservation of Robert Owen's testimony against religion occurred at New Harmony in summer of 1826. Frances Wright visited for some weeks at the neighboring settlement of Richard and George Flower at Albion in Illinois. Actually she spent much of that time at New Harmony. Those were heady days at New Harmony. There were still impressive remnants of the Rappite construction and order. Robert Owen was in residence, having come from another triumphal tour of America early that year along with Maclure's remarkable collection of scientists and educators known as the "boatload of knowledge." He was shoring up his already tottering community with non-stop assertions and spirited discussions of his principles, the ones he would enunciate in July in his "Declaration of Mental Independence." Frances Wright was impressed.[46]

Frances Wright was impressive herself. She was a handsome woman with enthusiasm and an agile mind. She was a Scottish heiress in a small way and was committed to make the most of her life and her funds in social reform. She loved the American republic and democratic principles. She was author of *A Few Days in Athens* (London, 1822), *Views of Society and Manners in America* (London, 1821), and a play entitled *Altdorf* produced in New York and published in Philadelphia (1819). Her literary and republican interests had brought her the attention and affection of General Lafayette; she and her sister had stayed for extended periods at his estate named LaGrange forty miles from Paris. While traveling with Lafayette on his visit to America in 1824–25 she had seen the horrors of slavery and decided to make freeing the American slaves her primary cause.[47]

On the same trip Miss Wright had encountered Robert Owen explaining his principles in Washington, D.C. Her creative stroke was to join her campaign against slavery with Robert Owen's vision of the model community. She decided to purchase and operate a southern plantation on which slaves could experience the efficiencies and education of an Owen-style cooperative. There the slaves would easily produce enough for their own support and out of surplus production establish their freedom by reimbursing the plantation for their own purchase price. By the time she arrived at New Harmony in 1826 she already had a Tennessee plantation of at least 640 acres of former Chickasaw land near Memphis and more than a dozen slaves being prepared for freedom. Nashoba she had named it.[48]

Now in the stimulation of the discussions at New Harmony she added to her program of eliminating American slavery two of the priorities of Robert Owen—to lift from Americans the yoke of the Christian religion and of the institution of marriage as presently conducted. Both freedom from religion and advocacy of sexual equality across race lines became principles for Nashoba.[49]

On this visit to New Harmony she also enlisted Robert Dale Owen, the eldest son of Robert Owen. In later years Robert Dale called his years of collaboration with Frances Wright "an earnest sowing of wild oats" and speculated what his life might have been if he had been influenced by some "cool-headed dispassionate friend" instead of Frances Wright. "I required to be restrained, not urged," he said, "needed not the spur, but the guiding rein." He commented, "I found no such mentor, but met, instead, with a friend some ten years my senior, possessing various noble qualities, but with ideas on many subjects, social and religious, even more immature and extravagant than my own. This new acquaintance mainly shaped, for several years, the course and tenor of my life."[50]

At the age of twenty-four Robert Dale Owen found Frances Wright quite compelling. When she read some of his more radical opinions in the *New Harmony Gazette*, she told him that he was one of the few persons she had ever met with whom she could act in unison. By the following December, General Lafayette, William Maclure, Robert Owen, and Robert Dale Owen were among the ten trustees to whom Frances Wright conveyed Nashoba's now 1860 acres "in perpetual trust for the benefit of the negro race." The combined efforts of Robert Dale Owen and Frances Wright in both America and Europe could do little to stabilize or even to establish Nashoba. Its intended purpose of freeing slaves had been swallowed up by controversy and mismanagement. The experiment had totally collapsed by spring of 1828, object of the fear and fury of many religious critics. Frances Wright accepted the invitation of Robert Dale Owen and moved from Nashoba to New Harmony in June. By July they were joint editors of the *New Harmony Gazette*.[51]

Their primary target for reform now shifted from slavery to religion. Robert Dale Owen had focused the attention of the *Gazette* more sharply on religion when he returned to New Harmony in March of 1828. There was less editorial matter on cooperative communities and the industrial revolution and labor relations and political economy. In place of these topics appeared "virulent attacks on sectarianism and the clergy, more than half of Owen's editorials up to the middle of June dealing directly with such topics."[52] In April Owen wrote:

> I do not believe the Christian revelation; but if I did, I could not live as they do . . . I am a sceptic. I doubt the accuracy of all predictions regarding our fate beyond the grave . . . Believing as I do that the religions are in error, I deeply regret that error. It can produce only evil continually. Either it makes a man a hypocrite, or a weak inconsistent trifler; or else it abstracts his thoughts from the things of this world.[53]

For Frances Wright the new location at New Harmony and the new reform emphasis on religion was a happy change. Her strength was in articulation of a combination of zeal and reform ideas which could be packaged to grip the public mind. Opposition to organized religion had become a matter of great urgency for her. Revivalists were claiming victories all around. In the years since 1816 Christian activists in the East, and their sympathizers everywhere, had been developing a coalition of voluntary societies with interlocking directorates aiming to evangelize the nation, e.g., American Bible Society (1816), American Sabbath School Union (1824), American Tract Society (1825), American Home Missionary Society (1826). They were raising funds, developing a corps of missionary agents, and utilizing the new mass printing media with a goal of providing a Bible in every family, a Sunday school in every neighborhood, a pastor in every locality, and good reading material in abundance. There was an interest in enforcing observance of Sunday nationally as a Christian sabbath and in places there was even talk of a "Christian party in politics." Frances Wright was a natural defender against any such Christian collusion. One weapon was the *New Harmony Gazette* which had changed its name to *Free Inquirer* by fall of 1828.[54]

Even more important, Wright discovered her power as a lecturer. Being a woman lecturer was a novelty. Being a woman lecturer against organized religion, and a powerful lecturer at that, guaranteed her visibility. Frances Trollope spoke of "the splendour, the brilliance, the overwhelming eloquence" of Wright as orator.

> It is impossible to imagine any thing more striking than her appearance. Her tall and majestic figure, the deep and almost solemn expression of her eyes, the simple contour of her finely formed head, unadorned, excepting by its own natural ringlets; her garment of plain white muslin, which hung around her in folds that recalled the drapery of a Grecian statue, all contributed to produce an effect, unlike any thing I had ever seen before, or ever expect to see again.[55]

In July of 1828 Wright gave three lectures at the Cincinnati Court House; in August she repeated them in a theater there. The results were satisfying, she said. "A kindling of wrath among the clergy! A reaction in favor of common sense on the part of their followers! An explosion of public sentiment in favor of liberty, liberality, and reforms in education! And a complete exposure of the nothingness of the press."[56]

Wright's series grew to six lectures. As they were later published the lectures began and continued at length in praise of what she counted the only true knowledge. Such knowledge was fact limited altogether to sensation since "nothing can be known where there is nothing to operate on our senses." History could not be admitted as knowledge. Certainly religion had no basis at all. Dealing so largely with things unseen and unknown, it had no substance for instruction or discussion. One of the lectures included a catalog of abuses by religion and by the clergy "whose power lies in the weakness of those they rule, or in the ignorance of those they lead." The Jesuits in France, "resuscitated for a while by the imbecile Bourbons," persecuted all teachers but their favored religious ones, she said. In the same way superstitious Americans were now blocking the efforts of good Pestalozzian teachers. She said all her studies, reading, reflection, and observation had not discovered anything significant for humankind beyond this earth and she doubted that her hearers could find anything significant beyond this earth no matter how much time and treasure they spent. In fact, she was sure far too much treasure had already been misapplied in construction of big church buildings and far too much time misemployed by professional persons to staff them.[57] She held religion accountable for war and for abuse of women.

> The rivers of the earth run blood! Nation set against nation! Brother against brother! Man against the companion of his bosom; and that soft companion, maddened with the frenzy of insane remorse for imaginary crimes, fired with the rage of infatuated bigotry, or subdued to diseased helplessness and mental fatuity, renounces kindred, flies from social intercourse, and pines away a useless or mischievous existence in sighings and tremblings, spectral fears, uncharitable feelings, and bitter denunciations! Such are thy doings, oh religion.[58]

In September of 1828 Frances Wright was back at New Harmony, working hard to make the *Gazette* pay its way as the only publication in the West free of religious influence. Robert Dale Owen's biographer has characterized the place.

> In the summer and autumn of 1828 a backwoods town in Posey County was fast becoming the most important freethought center in the United States. Under its new editors the *Gazette* was unquestionably the ablest journal of its kind. Jennings had returned with plans to establish a boarding school employing Pestalozzian methods and inviting the patronage of liberals. Using New Harmony as a base, Frances Wright electrified the Ohio and Mississippi Valleys with her lectures on free enquiry and just knowledge. And to the banks of the Wabash must be traced the earliest recorded approval in America of the Neo-Malthusian movement. The first fruits of the Owen community were not socialism, education, or science but a militant, free discussion of religion, morals, and sexual relations.[59]

Soon the public campaign against religion moved from the Wabash to the East. Frances Wright could get even larger audiences there. "New Harmony is out of the ques-

tion," she said. Her first appearance at New York drew a crowd of "from 1500 to 2000 people." She said "the same spirit of enquiry and reformation seems to exist throughout the land, and to require only the match to burst into flames." By the end of 1828 she had established herself in New York. She needed a paper to give immediate answer to her critics in the New York press so she began issuing a New York edition of the *Free Enquirer* in January of 1829. In April Robert Dale Owen joined her there. Madame Fretageot was somewhat relieved to have them out of New Harmony. "Robert Dale is going there for helping an institution on the plan of Epicurus in Athens, as well as the continuation of his paper under the title of *The Free Enquirer*," she said. "Thus we lose them all, and if I am not mistaken it will prove beneficial to our establishment in removing the public opinion from our place."[60]

In New York Owen was primarily the editor and Wright the lecturer, but Owen took the rostrum more and more frequently. They based their campaign for the mind of the world in their Hall of Science, the converted building of the Ebenezer Baptist Church which Wright had bought at auction.[61] They offered the *Free Enquirer*, published weekly at $3 per year. They provided reprints from the *Free Enquirer* and other low cost literature for freethinkers. In 1830 the list of literature for sale included seventeen titles by Robert Dale Owen in a variety of formats, two collections of addresses and seven fables by Frances Wright, the Owen-Campbell debate—these products from the New Harmony circle augmented by works of Shelley, Paine, Voltaire, Condorcet, and Hume.[62]

Wright and Owen constantly conducted courses of lectures, especially on Sundays. They advocated women's rights and divorce for incompatibility and birth control and the labor movement and debtors' rights and free schools. None of the things they stood for seemed to them to be compatible with organized or orthodox religion. So opposition to religion was the most immediate cause of all. Owen published his unbelief.

> Enough, I am now a sceptic. I live for this world, because, I know nothing of any other. I doubt all revelations from heaven, because they appear to me improbable and inconsistent. I desire to see the thoughts and efforts of mankind directed solely to the improvement of their own and their fellow-creatures' condition on this earth . . . I have crossed in safety, and found the opposite shore fair and pleasant; a land of freedom and of virtue, whence terror is banished, and where tranquility reigns.[63]

But tranquility was hardly his style. The vigor of their movement depended on resistance by professional clergy. Owen taunted the New York clergy to pay them more attention, "to step openly forward and attempt to stem a heresy that grows and strengthens even at their very doors, and already numbers thousands among its converts."[64]

> We pitched our tent in this city, chiefly because here the clerical profession was the most numerous, its resources the most concentrated, its influence the most overruling . . . I perceive no remedy for these errors, so long as it is considered a trade to support the orthodox creed. But I do not perceive the necessity nor the advantage of such a trade. Some day or other the world will see it abolished . . . I have laboured—and while health and conviction remain with me—I will labor, by exhibiting its worse than inutility, to hasten its abolition. Let those who think with me, aid in this righteous endeavor.[65]

For many months they kept asserting that they were riding a tide of victory.

> Let them muster their forces, they will not find them too many. Let them strengthen their interest; they will require it all, ere long . . . Our numbers are few; but let the priest and his followers look to it! These are sceptical times . . . The institutions of the country are in our favor; the independence of its inhabitants is in our favor; the awakening spirit of enquiry is in our favor; and, though prejudice and intolerance be powerful, yet prejudice and intolerance are diminishing, in proportion as light spreads and intelligence increases. If our opponents are many and zealous, yet are their weapons blunted and their best resources gone.[66]

Victory was elusive. One Quaker physician in Wilmington prepared a particularly annoying compilation of the more extreme statements of Wright and Owen. He interlaced this with his own critical comments and circulated the work widely in at least three editions.

> But, after having denied, in the face of the world, the existence of a God—ridiculed the idea of Providence—scoffed at the doctrines of the immortality of the soul, and a future state—reviled the Author of Christianity, his immediate followers, and all Christians indiscriminately; and telling us that it is not abuses merely, that you declaim against—that the whole system of Christianity, in all its parts, is an abuse—that you have not misled in this matter—that you understand religion to mean "that spiritual knowledge which teaches how to live here, that we may attain happiness hereafter"—after such unequivocal testimony of your real purpose, that mind must be possessed of a perception strangely perverted, that would infer that you are governed by the praise-worthy motive of reforming religion, and not destroying it![67]

New Harmony as Owen Family Home

News of the end of the Owenite mission from the Wabash to New York came in the issue of the *Free Enquirer* for 13 October 1832. After nearly four years in New York there was no longer any claim of thousands of converts. Frances Wright pled fatigue and poor health. She married the *Free Enquirer* printer William Phiquepal D'Arusmont, earlier of New Harmony, and took up residence in Europe. Her letter sent from Paris for publication in the *Enquirer* said "I resign to others the task of prosecuting free enquiry." Robert Dale Owen said he also must leave New York and get back to Indiana to work with his brother William. "After four years of public service, I feel myself called upon to give my time, for a season to private business. It is, perhaps, almost as essential to public usefulness, as to private peace of mind, that one should be secure in a pecuniary independence, however small; and this is especially necessary in the case of a heretic." His property in Indiana could support him if he would attend to it himself. This he would do with no plan for any radical social experiment. "We dream of nothing more than of encouraging, by every means in our power, honest, industrious, intelligent men and women, to become our neighbors, by purchase or otherwise. We look to each one possessing his own house and lot, or his own little farm." He looked forward to "many friends of human improvement . . . tried and valued personal friends of our own . . . gradual association for many general objects . . . a rational school . . . public lectures, public assemblies, a reading room perhaps, and so on."[68]

All this change of scene represented no weakening of conviction. On his way from New York to New Harmony a year earlier, Robert Dale Owen had preached as an itinerant missionary of freethought at Hudson, Albany, Ithaca, and Buffalo in New York as well as in Cleveland, Ohio. On the morning of his wedding to Mary Robinson on 12 April 1832, he underscored his principles in a statement for his friends. "We have selected the simplest ceremony which the laws of this state recognize, and which . . . involves not the necessity of calling in the aid of a member of the clerical profession; a profession . . . we do not recognize, and the influence of which we are led to consider injurious to society." The statement appeared in the *Free Enquirer* for 2 June. When he was assisting Robert Owen in London during the winter of 1832–33, he wrote controversial and antireligious editorials for his father's weekly, *The Crisis*, and supervised production of English editions of his own freethought writings. He kept announcing that Frances Wright would be moving back to Indiana to help him establish a residential center for reformers at New Harmony like the one they had known at New York, but she did not return.[69]

If there was no change of conviction, there was at least a change of tempo. Robert Dale Owen's role in Indiana was less that of a freethought crusader and more that of an estate manager and family man. His biographer commented:

> For Owen, removal from New York brought to a close a definite period in his life. It may be too much to say that after 1833 he no longer deserved to be called a reformer, but it is a fact that after that date he was seldom an active participant in the multifarious humanitarian crusades that mark our middle period. Owen was ever the child of his surroundings, and in the next two decades his ties with the old associates in the East were to snap, one by one. In the years that were to come his thought and action were influenced by a new environment, one not so congenial to a radical reformer, that of the democratic, individualist, and self-assertive West.[70]

As his interests turned to public service and to politics, Owen was confronted with some of his earlier freethought statements. When he ran for Congress in 1839 he lost, partly because some Whigs circulated a handbill about his career as a radical reformer. A Whig paper cited a long exchange of letters in the *Free Enquirer* in 1829–30 (separately published in 1831, 1832, 1833, 1840, 1842, 1852, 1854) between Owen and a Presbyterian minister named Origen Bacheler, and charged Owen with denial of the "authenticity of the Christian religion" and of "the existence of a God." Women, whose rights Owen had always stoutly defended, were organizers against him on religious grounds in that campaign. His freethought writings may also have played some part in his defeat as a candidate for re-election to Congress in 1847.[71]

New Harmony still had the image of a place where religion was not highly regarded.[72] Constance Fauntleroy, daughter of Robert Owen's daughter Jane, grew up at New Harmony in the 1840s. She was secure in the affection of her extended family and very appreciative of her opportunities in music, science, and literature. Persons of world reputation were residents or frequent visitors; animated discussions ranged over wide areas of knowledge. She was aware of herself as a gifted and privileged child.

> To one subject only I cannot remember my attention being directed—the subject of religion—and with the Bible we were practically unacquainted . . . A tradition there was that all the Bibles of the town had been burned in the public square. This I never believed . . . Among all

this culture and mental vigor there was a little band of ignorant and poor people, who were called religious, and had a small meetinghouse somewhere, a place we never frequented, as we despised this class of people, setting them down as weak and ignorant, taking no notice of their proceedings, and pitying them as persons only worthy of our compassion and contempt.[73]

Given the extremes of the positions and the publicity of the past, perhaps the most remarkable thing was the efficient dissolution of the hostility of religious people toward New Harmony. Robert Dale Owen became an effective campaigner and was elected to Congress in 1843. On 28 May 1851 he was celebrated in an oratorical fest at the Hall of the Indiana House of Representatives in Indianapolis. The hall was specially decorated and so crowded that more than 500 persons had to be turned away. The silver pitcher presented to him was inscribed "Presented to the Hon. Robert Dale Owen, by the women of Indiana, in acknowledgement of his true and noble advocacy of their independent rights to property in the Constitutional Convention in the State of Indiana, convened at Indianapolis, 1850." In one part of his acknowledgment speech he seemed to be replying to those who still called him infidel. "There is much said about modern Infidelity. Shall I tell you who is the practical Infidel? The man, who has no abiding faith in the Good and the Beautiful. The scoffer—at human virtue. The sceptic—in human progress. The doubter of man's capacity for self-government. Above all, beyond all, the unbeliever in woman's goodness."[74] His service as a state agent in the purchase of arms and war supplies during the Civil War gave him visibility and public approval. David Dale Owen and Richard Owen, sons of Robert Owen based at New Harmony, distinguished themselves as geologists and as teachers of science.

Owens as Spiritualists

The year 1858 was a kind of gathering point for Owenite religious history. In 1858 Robert Owen died quietly in England. He was an unrelenting foe of all known religions to the end, stoutly so in his autobiography written in his mid-eighties.

> There is no sacrifice at any period, which I could make, that would not have been willingly and joyously made to terminate the existence of religion on earth.[75]

> Let it be told in the voice of thunder to all the devotees of all the religions of the world, that religion has ever been the bane of humanity, and the cause of all its

crimes, irrationalities, absurdities, and sufferings, and that until these deadening superstitions, based solely on the irrational notion that man can do good to God, shall be removed root and branch from humanity, man will remain an insane fanatic and bigot, madly destroying, unconsciously, his own happiness and the happiness of his fellows.[76]

He was buried beside his parents in the churchyard at Newtown, buried with conventional religious services to spare offense to the Christian villagers.[77]

Robert Owen himself had been a convert to Spiritualism since 1853 when some unsolicited rappings on a table at the home of a medium named Mrs. Hayden had been interpreted as a message from the spirit world for him. All of the community experiments based on his principles in Britain and America had failed. Nevertheless he remained supremely confident in his last years that his principles must and would transform the world, a conviction now reinforced because of "the daily aid which I receive from superior Spirits who promise effective assistance until success shall be assured." Through mediums he was receiving messages from Thomas Jefferson, Benjamin Franklin, the Duke of Kent, Grace Fletcher, and a great many others—even an entire "Address to the World" sent from superior Spirits by way of "an experienced medium in the United States" and published complete in the introduction to his autobiography. Some members of his family at New Harmony deplored this "strange infatuation" with spirits as "sad hallucination."[78]

In 1858 Robert Dale Owen of New Harmony completed his five years of service as United States chargé d'affaires to the Kingdom of the Two Sicilies. From the time he left Naples that autumn, he was always engaged to some extent in the investigation and then the promulgation of Spiritualism. An impressive experience with spirit writing at the home of the Russian plenipotentiary at Naples in 1856 had set him off on "a course of study that eventually changed the whole feelings and tenor of my life." In 1860 he published a large book of 528 pages entitled *Footfalls on the Boundary of Another World*. It was a collection of narratives of hauntings, clairvoyance, and somnambulism with cautious affirmation of existence after death. The book sold 20,000 copies and drew international notice.[79] His biographer has noted how the tenor of Owen's religious views had changed. "Owen in 1860 spoke of the Scriptures as if they were a superior authority, of God's omnipotence as if there were a God, and of the Creator's intentions as if these could be known. Nature no longer loomed as the ultimate criterion of right and wrong; its place was taken by a personal

deity, a fact which clearly distinguished the younger Owen as a spiritualist from the elder."[80]

In 1872 Robert Dale Owen published an even larger book of 542 pages entitled *The Debatable Land between This World and the Next*. This time the caution was gone. He was now a crusader for Spiritualism in his own style. He dedicated this second book to the Protestant clergy whom he pictured as besieged by skeptics and overwhelmed by Catholics. He offered them his support. What they needed was sensory and scientific evidence for their faith. This he could now provide—a union of creedless Christianity with the empirically provable manifestations of Spiritualism.[81]

> When the conditions are favorable, and the sensitive through whom the manifestations come is highly gifted, these may supply important materials for thought and valuable rules of conduct. But spiritual phenomena sometimes do much more than this. In their highest phases they furnish proof, strong as that which Christ's disciples enjoyed—proof addressed to reason and tangible to the senses—of the reality of another life, better and happier than this, and of which our earthly pilgrimage is but the novitiate. They bring immortality to light under a blaze of evidence which outshines, as the sun the stars, all traditional or historical testimonies. For surmise they give us conviction, and assured knowledge for wavering belief.[82]

Catholic editor Orestes Brownson was not much impressed with Owen's offer to come to the rescue of the Protestants. Brownson did the review of *Debatable Land* for the *Catholic World*.

> Mr. Owen, though he has since been a member of Congress, and an American minister at Naples, was formerly well known in this city as associated with Frances Wright in editing the *Free Enquirer*, as the author of an infamous work on moral physiology, and as an avowed atheist. He now claims to be a believer in the existence of God, and in the truth of the Christian religion; but his God has no freedom of action, being hedged in and bound hand and foot by the laws of nature, and his Christianity is a Christianity without Christ, and indistinguishable from unmitigated heathenism. How much he has gained by his conversion, through the intervention of the spirits, from atheism to demonism and gross superstition, it is not easy to say, though it is better to believe in the devil, if one does not mistake him for God, than it is to believe in nothing . . . Certainly, he holds that, as it is, Protestantism is losing ground . . . As things now go, the whole world will become Catholic, and the only way to prevent it, he thinks, is to accept the aid of the spirits. We are not so sure that this aid would suffice,

for Satan, their chief, has been the fast friend of Protestants ever since he persuaded Luther to give up private Masses, and has done his best for them, and it is difficult to see what more he can do for them than he has hitherto done.[83]

And in 1858 there began to circulate in Indiana a report that a granddaughter of Robert Owen was teaching a Sunday school at New Harmony itself. She was Constance Fauntleroy, who had gone abroad at age sixteen with her mother and sister to "complete her education." They sailed with Robert Dale Owen and his family on their way to Naples in 1852; they lived in Europe for five years, chiefly at Stuttgart in Germany. Along with the music, art, and literature of the Continent, Constance discovered active practice of the Christian religion.

> For the first time that I can recollect, my attention was intelligently fastened upon a prayer; and I must have been fully twenty-one years of age, I think. The language fascinated me. I loved German, and the lofty style of thought and composition took possession of me. I read it for the beauty of the language alone. The sonorous phrases pleased my ear, the noble construction of the prayers appealed to my love of exalted thought and feeling, and, finally, it made me wish to see the Bible, that I might understand what all this meant.[84]

For a time she kept her devotions secret, fearing ridicule and disapproval by her family. When she confessed her mother said "My dear Constance, you have been purposely kept free from all prejudice and superstition. Your soul has been a blank, a white page, kept free by me, that when the time came for you to think and choose for yourself, you might yourself write your religion there. Go and be baptized, but take heed to walk worthy of your belief. Show by your actions the inner belief of your soul." On the trip home she was baptized in Cincinnati by an Episcopal clergyman named Butler. He was amazed at her ignorance—no attendance at worship or preaching, no instruction, no creed, no catechism.[85]

While Constance Fauntleroy had been in Europe the precarious mission congregation of Episcopalians at New Harmony, founded in 1841 and named St. Stephen Church, had built a "very neat" church building.[86] When its services were irregular for lack of clergy, Constance faced the need. She attended worship with a neighboring Methodist congregation but concurrently she developed her own lay ministry at St. Stephen.

> During all this time I carried on a Sunday-school, with about one hundred and twenty-five members. I have no remembrance of a vestry in those days, but virtually took the key of the church in my own possession. Not knowing it to be contrary to the custom of the Church, I would write and deliver short sermons to the children from the pulpit. I also visited from house to house where the parents were quite indifferent toward religion, and the children often had to rise and dress themselves on Sunday morning, eating a cold crust of bread for breakfast, as the parents took no interest in their religious training, and would not rise in time to get them ready for Sunday-school. On one occasion nearly the whole school demanded baptism, to which I did not dare accede in the face of the opposition of the parents; and a more eager, interested set of children I have never since seen. Now and then a missionary, sent by Bishop Upfold, would officiate, and before my leaving New Harmony eighteen (I think) were baptized, and thirteen presented to the bishop for the apostolic rite of confirmation.[87]

Several members of the Owen family made decisions to practice Christianity. Constance Fauntleroy married James Runcie, the Episcopal missionary under whose occasional ministry the New Harmony church building had been erected. She was, she said, the only clergyman's wife she had ever known up to the time of her marriage and had to begin preparation for her role by learning the creed and the service. In her autobiographical account published in 1881 she reported "Fifteen of my immediate family have been baptized and confirmed, besides bringing to baptism some eighteen or twenty of their children. Among them were Robert Dale Owen's two daughters, the wife and two grown sons of Richard Owen and their wives (himself, being absent from New Harmony, was received into the Presbyterian denomination about the same time), my own sister, and the two daughters of my father's sister."[88]

When Robert Dale Owen died in 1877, his services conducted by the same Presbyterian minister who had performed the wedding ceremony for him and Lottie Kellogg the year before, the obituaries in the public press were extraordinarily full and the eulogies unequivocal. Focus was already shifting from the irreligion of New Harmony's first founders to the scientific, educational, cultural, political, and religious contributions of persons related to that community.[89]

Twentieth century developments added a new dimension to the religious heritage of New Harmony. Kenneth Owen, native of New Harmony and descendant of Robert Owen through his son Richard, married Jane Blaffer of Houston. Jane Blaffer Owen was especially sensitive to the unique religious history of New Harmony. She energized efforts to conserve some of the buildings remaining from the early communities. Mrs. Owen also commissioned construction of a nondenominational religious center, a "Roofless Church" with appropriate sculptures and gardens. It received first award of the American Institute of Architects in 1961. Herself a student and friend of internationally known theologian Paul Tillich at Union Theological Seminary in New York, she enlisted his approval and interest in planning a Paul Tillich Park adjacent to the religious center. Tillich presented the address on Pentecost Sunday of 1963 and said "I, Paul Tillich, give my name to this place, and dedicate the ground of the park and the Cave of the New Being to a new reality." When he died in 1965 his ashes were interred at the park and a lecture series in his memory was established at the Roofless Church.[90] Several agencies continued to develop New Harmony as a historical site. Visitors received their accounts of New Harmony's religion in the context of restored buildings, a program of cultural events, a restaurant and inn, a research library, and a modern museum.

NOTES

1. Arthur E. Bestor, *Backwoods Utopias* (Philadelphia: University of Pennsylvania Press, 1950), 111–12; Robert Owen, *Two Discourses on a New System of Society; as Delivered in the Hall of Representatives of the U. States, in the Presence of the President of the United States, the Ex-President, Heads of Department, Members of Congress, &c. on the 25th of February and 7th of March, 1825* (Philadelphia: Atkinson and Alexander, 1825), 3, 21.

2. Owen, *Two Discourses*, 10–11, 13, 15, 17; for a discussion of the relation of Owen to millennialism, see J. F. C. Harrison, *Quest for the New Moral World; Robert Owen and the Owenites in Britain and America* (New York: Charles Scribner's Sons, 1969), 92–139.

3. Owen, *Two Discourses*, 25.

4. Bestor, *Backwoods Utopias*, 112; Owen, *Two Discourses*, 25–26.

5. Owen, *Two Discourses*, 27–28.

6. Robert Owen, *The Life of Robert Owen. Written by Himself. With Selections from His Writings and Correspondence*, 2 vols. [1 and 1A] (London: Effingham Wilson, 1857–58), 1:4.

7. Owen, *Life*, 1:16.

8. Owen, *Life*, 1:71–72.

9. Owen, *Life*, 1:22–28, 36.

10. Frank Podmore, *Robert Owen: A Biography*, 2 vols. continuously paged (New York: D. Appleton and Company, 1907), 82–83; Robert Dale Owen, *Threading My Way* (New York: G. W. Carleton, 1874), 34–36; Owen, *Life*, 1:57.

11. Owen, *Life*, 1:56–64, 79–81, 134–42; Podmore, *Robert Owen*, 126–60; Owen, *Threading My Way*, 113–15.

12. Owen, *Life*, 1:xxvi–xxviii, 76, 143; Robert Owen, *A New View of Society and Report to the County of Lanark* (Baltimore, Md.: Penguin Books, 1970), 9.

13. Owen, *Life*, 1:107–12. For publication sequence of the four essays and their combination, see Bestor, *Backwoods Utopias*, 68.

14. Robert Dale Owen, *To Holland and New Harmony. Robert Dale Owen's Travel Journal, 1825–1826*, ed. Josephine M. Elliott (Indianapolis, Ind.: Indiana Historical Society, 1969), 233–34; William Owen, *Diary of William Owen from November 10, 1824, to April 20, 1825*, ed. Joel W. Hiatt (Indianapolis, Ind.: Indiana Historical Society, 1906), 129–30; William Maclure, *Education and Reform at New Harmony. Correspondence of William Maclure and Marie Duclos Fretageot 1820–1833*, ed. Arthur E. Bestor (Indianapolis, Ind.: Indiana Historical Society, 1948), 327; Owen, *New View*, 11, 25–27; Bestor, *Backwoods Utopias*, 217.

15. Robert Dale Owen, *Prossimo's Experience. On the Study of Theology. Safest to Believe; or, The Balance Struck* (London: J. Watson, n.d.), 8–9.

16. Podmore, *Robert Owen*, 175, 180; Owen, *Threading My Way*, 75–88; Owen, *New View*, 148–49, 182–85.

17. Bestor, *Backwoods Utopias*, 70; Owen, *Life*, 1:117–21, 126–33.

18. Podmore, *Robert Owen*, 217–41; Bestor, *Backwoods Utopias*, 70–81; Owen, *Life*, 1:154–58, 189.

19. Owen, *Life*, 1:159–60.

20. Owen, *Life*, 1A:115.

21. Owen, *Life*, 1:162, 190–91.

22. Owen, *New View*, 44–54; Owen, *Life*, 1:191–92.

23. *Documentary History of the Indiana Decade of the Harmony Society 1814–1824*, 2 vols., comp. and ed. Karl J. R. Arndt (Indianapolis, Ind.: Indiana Historical Society, 1978), 2:89–90.

24. Owen, *Threading My Way*, 244; Bestor, *Backwoods Utopias*, 102–3, 110.

25. Thomas Pears, *New Harmony: An Adventure in Happiness, Papers of Thomas and Sarah Pears*, ed. Clinton Pears, Jr. (Indianapolis, Ind.: Indiana Historical Society, 1933), 12–13; *Harmony on the Wabash in Transition, 1824–1826*, comp. and ed. Karl J. R. Arndt (Worcester, Mass.: Harmony Society Press, 1982), 537; Bestor, *Backwoods Utopias*, 104–14.

26. Donald Macdonald, *The Diaries of Donald Macdonald 1824–1826* (Indianapolis, Ind.: Indiana Historical Society, 1942), 159–74, 257–58; Owen, *Diary*, 87; Owen, *Two Discourses*, 24; *Harmony on the Wabash in Transition*, xxvii; Bestor, *Backwoods Utopias*, 125.

27. Macdonald, *Diaries*, 308; *Harmony on the Wabash in Transition*, 702–5.

28. *Harmony on the Wabash in Transition*, 702–3.

29. Bestor, *Backwoods Utopias*, 131–32; Macdonald, *Diaries*, 316; Pears, *New Harmony*, 48–49, 61.

30. *Harmony on the Wabash in Transition*, xx.

31. *Harmony on the Wabash in Transition*, xviii, xxii.

32. Robert Owen, *Debate on the Evidences of Christianity; Containing an Examination of the "Social System" and of All the Systems of Scepticism of Ancient and Modern Times. Held in the City of Cincinnati, Ohio, from the 13th to the 21st of April, 1829; Between Robert Owen, of New Lanark, Scotland, and Alexander Campbell, of Bethany, Virginia*, 2 vols. in 1 (Bethany, Va.: Printed and published by Alexander Campbell, 1829), 1:11–12.

33. Owen, *Debate*, 1:30.

34. Frances Trollope, *Domestic Manners of the Americans*, ed. Donald Smalley (New York: Alfred A. Knopf, 1949), 147–53; Earl

I. West, "Early Cincinnati's Unprecedented Spectacle," *Ohio History* 79 (Winter 1970): 5–17; Owen, *Debate*, 1:6.

35. Trollope, *Domestic Manners*, 151, 153. The debate as edited by Campbell was published in a book of some 550 pages from Bethany, Virginia, and from Cincinnati, and from London. Indiana historian Jacob Piatt Dunn called it "the most read book in the world for the next few years—certainly the most universally read in the [American] West." Jacob Piatt Dunn, *Indiana and Indianans*, 2 vols. (Chicago: American Historical Society, 1919), 2:1102.

36. Donald F. Carmony and Josephine M. Elliott, "New Harmony, Indiana: Robert Owen's Seedbed for Utopia," *Indiana Magazine of History* 76 (September 1980): 161–261; Pears, *New Harmony*, 7–96.

37. Podmore, *Robert Owen*, 320; Owen, *Threading My Way*, 289–93; Bestor, *Backwoods Utopias*, 180–81, 198; Carmony and Elliott, "New Harmony," 179; Maclure, *Education and Reform*, 396–97, 400, 405; Pears, *New Harmony*, 86–87.

38. Patricia T. Stroud, *Thomas Say: New World Naturalist* (Philadelphia: University of Pennsylvania Press, 1992, 340 p.); Walter B. Hendrickson, *David Dale Owen: Pioneer Geologist of the Middle West* (Indianapolis, Ind.: Indiana Historical Bureau, 1943, 180 p.); Reuben G. Thwaites, *Early Western Travels 1748–1846*, 32 vols. (Cleveland, Ohio: Arthur H. Clark, 1906), 22:163–65. On early education at New Harmony see Donald E. Pitzer, "Education in Utopia: The New Harmony Experience," in *Indiana Historical Society Lectures 1976–1977* (Indianapolis, Ind.: Indiana Historical Society, 1978), 91–98. Excellent primary materials on education at New Harmony are in the correspondence of William Maclure and Marie Duclos Fretageot published as *Education and Reform at New Harmony*. For a statement of the larger impact of the whole Owen experiment at New Harmony, see Carmony and Elliott, "New Harmony," 179–87.

39. West, "Early Cincinnati's," 17; Trollope, *Domestic Manners*, 153.

40. Harlow Lindley, *Indiana as Seen by Early Travelers* (Indianapolis, Ind.: Indiana Historical Commission, 1916), 370; Miner K. Kellog, "Recollections of New Harmony," *Indiana Magazine of History* 64 (March 1968): 56–59; Alice J. G. Perkins and Theresa Wolfson, *Frances Wright: Free Enquirer* (New York: Harper and Brothers, 1939), 154; Richard W. Leopold, *Robert Dale Owen: A Biography* (New York: Octagon Books, 1969), 35; Pears, *New Harmony*, 83; Macdonald, *Diaries*, 292.

41. Lindley, *Indiana as Seen by Early Travelers*, 370–71.

42. Maclure, *Education and Reform*, 375, 384.

43. Gerald L. Gutek, *Joseph Neef: The Americanization of Pestalozzianism* (University, Ala.: University of Alabama Press, 1978), 71–122; Maclure, *Education and Reform*, 301, 304, 312, 318, 322, 346–47, 404; Kellog, "Recollections," 59; Hendrickson, *David Dale Owen*, 64–65.

44. Carmony and Elliott, "New Harmony," 174; Leopold, *Robert Dale Owen*, 34.

45. Constance Owen Fauntleroy Runcie, *Divinely Led; or, Robert Owen's Granddaughter* (New York: James Pott, 1881), 12.

46. Celia Morris Eckhardt, *Fanny Wright: Rebel in America* (Cambridge, Mass.: Harvard University Press, 1984), 126–30; Perkins and Wolfson, *Frances Wright*, 146–47.

47. Perkins and Wolfson, *Frances Wright*, 37–42, 64–65, 123–24; Eckhardt, *Fanny Wright*, 21–107.

48. Perkins and Wolfson, *Frances Wright*, 124–27, 137–45; Eckhardt, *Fanny Wright*, 87, 108–26.

49. Perkins and Wolfson, *Frances Wright*, 153–54, 175; Eckhardt, *Fanny Wright*, 134–36.

50. Owen, *Threading My Way*, 296, 323.

51. Perkins and Wolfson, *Frances Wright*, 182–207; Eckhardt, *Fanny Wright*, 136–68; Owen, *Threading My Way*, 299–300.

52. Leopold, *Robert Dale Owen*, 56.

53. *New Harmony Gazette* 3 (30 April 1828): 214–15.

54. Leopold, *Robert Dale Owen*, 56–57; Perkins and Wolfson, *Frances Wright*, 209–11; Eckhardt, *Fanny Wright*, 170–71, 180.

55. Trollope, *Domestic Manners*, 73.

56. Perkins and Wolfson, *Frances Wright*, 213, 215; Eckhardt, *Fanny Wright*, 171–84.

57. Frances Wright, *Course of Popular Lectures . . . Delivered by Frances Wright, in New-York, Philadelphia, Boston, &c.* (London: James Watson, 1834), 56, 59, 63, 66–68.

58. Wright, *Course of Popular Lectures*, 64.

59. Leopold, *Robert Dale Owen*, 61–62.

60. Maclure, *Education and Reform*, 404–5; Perkins and Wolfson, *Frances Wright*, 229–30; Eckhardt, *Fanny Wright*, 190–91.

61. Leopold, *Robert Dale Owen*, 66–69.

62. *Popular Tracts* (New York: Published at the Office of the Free Enquirer, 1830), separately paged; this citation from catalogue, pp. 1–4 at end.

63. Robert Dale Owen, *Prossimo's Experience. On the Study of Theology. Safest to Believe; or, The Balance Struck* (London: J. Watson, n.d.), 11–12.

64. *Free Enquirer*, 3 (7 November 1829): 24.

65. Robert Dale Owen, *An Address on the Influence of the Clerical Profession*, 2d ed. (London: J. Watson, 1835), 15, 20.

66. *Free Enquirer* 1 (5 November 1828): 14.

67. William Gibbons, *An Exposition of Modern Scepticism, in a Letter Addressed to the Editors of the Free Enquirer*, 3d ed., rev. and enl. (Wilmington, Del.: R. Porter, n.d.), 28.

68. *Free Enquirer*, 4 (13 October 1832): 406–7.

69. Leopold, *Robert Dale Owen*, 71–72, 104, 110–11, 113–14, 116–17.

70. Leopold, *Robert Dale Owen*, 120.

71. Leopold, *Robert Dale Owen*, 106, 166, 238; Dunn, *Indiana and Indianans*, 2:1105.

72. Virginia Twigg, "St. Stephens, the First Church in New Harmony," *Indiana History Bulletin* 5, extra no. 1 (March 1928): 8.

73. Runcie, *Divinely Led*, 10–14.

74. *Proceedings at the Presentation to the Hon. Robert Dale Owen of a Silver Pitcher, on Behalf of the Women of Indiana, on the 28th Day of May, 1851* (New Albany, Ind.: Kent and Norman, 1851), 11, 16.

75. Owen, *Life*, 1:102.

76. Owen, *Life*, 1A:iv–v.

77. Leopold, *Robert Dale Owen*, 326–27; Bestor, *Backwoods Utopias*, 90.

78. Owen, *New View*, 7; Carmony and Elliott, "New Harmony," 179; Podmore, *Robert Owen*, 600–614; Owen, *Life*, 1:xxxii–xi; 1A:xxxiv–xxxviii; Runcie, *Divinely Led*, 11; Leopold, *Robert Dale Owen*, 322.

79. Leopold, *Robert Dale Owen*, 321–39, 379–416; Robert Dale Owen, *Footfalls on the Boundary of Another World* (Philadelphia: J. B. Lippincott, 1860), 3–6; Robert Dale Owen, *The Debatable Land*

between This World and the Next (New York: G. W. Carleton, 1872), 1, 281–87.

80. Leopold, *Robert Dale Owen*, 331.

81. Owen, *Debatable Land*, 9, 23–26, 32–170.

82. Owen, *Debatable Land*, 175.

83. *Catholic World* 14 (March 1872): 803–4.

84. Runcie, *Divinely Led*, 19.

85. Runcie, *Divinely Led*, 21, 24–25.

86. Twigg, "St. Stephens," 7–10; *Journal of the Proceedings of the Fifth Annual Convention of the Protestant Episcopal Church in the Diocese of Indiana . . . May 26 to . . . May 29 . . . 1842*, 8–9; Runcie, *Divinely Led*, 28.

87. Runcie, *Divinely Led*, 29–30.

88. Runcie, *Divinely Led*, 32–33, 35.

89. Leopold, *Robert Dale Owen*, 415.

90. Rudiger Reitz, *Paul Tillich und New Harmony* (Stuttgart: Evangelisches Verlagswerk, 1970, 128 p.); Richard Asher, "Paul Tillich and New Harmony, Indiana," *Studies in Indiana German-Americana* 1 (1988) 25–38.

AMISH AND MENNONITES

During and following the Reformation of the sixteenth century in Europe, churches were state churches with territorial arrangements. There were Catholic churches in Catholic territories, Lutheran churches in Lutheran territories, Reformed churches in Reformed territories. Terrible wars in the name of religion and precarious balances of power were commonplace. A fourth major religious group, the Anabaptists, was so diverse as to make generalization difficult. Generally, they had no territory and resisted the alliance of church and state in the territories in which they lived. They felt that Lutherans and Reformed had begun a reformation based on the Scriptures but had stopped short of full obedience. Genuine Christianity would mean (1) churches only as voluntary gatherings of adults professing faith and recognizing only the authority and leadership of the Holy Spirit in response to the preached Word—no state churches or infant baptism; (2) strenuous following of Christ in life by obedience to the New Testament which for many meant no sword bearing, no litigation, no oath taking; (3) obedience to officers of the state so long as there was no conflict with the Word but no responsibility for the operation of the state or discipline of its citizens since admonition and discipline of the body of believers was concern enough; (4) avoiding bondage to possessions and practicing strenuous philanthropy in a New Testament pattern. They were aggressively missionary and spread widely, especially where German and Dutch were spoken.

To established church and state authorities, hard pressed for stability and even for survival, these separating congregations looked extremist and irresponsible and subversive. The church already available had room and need for all the holiness and good works these people could muster. The authorities responded in fear and anger and, faced with stubborn conviction, with violence. As an uncomplimentary name, they labeled the rebels Anabaptists—those who deny, negate, or refuse to recognize a Christian baptism and who baptize their adherents again, a thing forbidden since the time of the Donatists in the fourth century.[1]

Anabaptists who persisted were prosecuted as heretics and as violators of law. Protestants and Catholics were divided on many issues but could agree that Anabaptists were intolerable. Under the intensity of persecution, when many stable leaders had been taken away, there were millennial and apocalyptic excesses which were associated with Anabaptists and used to discredit them further. Hundreds were put to death. Most attempted to move from areas of intense persecution to areas of less intense persecution—generally to the Low Countries or to the lands of independent princes in what is now Germany and eastern Europe. They were seldom permitted to own land themselves but a prudent prince might prize their industry and protect them as tenant farmers as long as he chose. The Anabaptists were turned hard inward upon themselves for survival, understanding themselves as islands of Christian martyrs in a hostile world. Reports of cheap land and religious freedom in the new world of America sounded to them like good news. Some were in that first boatload of Germans which arrived at Philadelphia from Krefeld in 1683. They kept coming and searching out the good cheap land—south into Virginia, northwest into Ontario, especially west into Pennsylvania and Ohio. Eventually some 64,000 made the trip.[2]

As northern Indiana was being settled and developed, families of these German-speaking Anabaptists arrived. After three hundred years of battering they had lost most of the missionary zeal which had gotten them into so much trouble in the 1500s. Now they wanted mostly to get plenty of good land and to be left alone. Most of them had lived in Pennsylvania or Ohio before coming to Indiana. As the price of land rose in those states, they sold out and purchased larger acreage for their growing families on the Indiana frontier. The name Anabaptist was generally left in Europe and was hardly heard in Indiana. Some Anabaptists (*Doopsgezinden*) remained in the Netherlands. Some with a heritage in Austria and in eastern Europe became known as Hutterian Brethren, eventually settling in strength in the western plains of the United States and in western Canada but not in Indiana. The ones who came to Indiana were almost entirely of Swiss and German descent and were called Mennonites. The name Mennonite came from a respected Dutch Anabaptist named Menno Simons; he actually had little to do with the Swiss and Germans whose descendants came to Indiana but they were known by his name. Some of the Mennonites arriving were also called Amish.[3]

The decades following the arrival of this body of Swiss and German pilgrims in Indiana proved to be times of strain and stress for them. The stress points were not so much major theological doctrines concerning God, Jesus Christ, the Holy Spirit, the Church, or the nature of the Christian life. The *Dordrecht Confession of Faith* of 1632 was widely agreed upon as a statement bringing together biblical truth on these subjects and a basis for instruction. Eighteenth century worship practices of the groups had been very similar, the old traditions preserved with special care by the Amish. A service held every second Sunday in the house or barn of a member was conducted in some mixture of forms of German. There were hymns from a German hymnal (the old Anabaptist *Ausbund*), readings from the German Bible according to an assigned annual sequence, at least two sermons with others present given opportunity to add testimony, and prayers either silent or read from the Prayerbook (*Die Ernsthafte Christenpflicht*). There was also general agreement that they were to be a plain and nonresistant people, living in the discipline (*Ordnung*) of a beloved community (*Gemeinde*) in humility (*Demuth*) and yieldedness (*Gelassenheit*). But how were these traditional congregations to relate to such nineteenth century staples of American religious life as frequent church services conducted in English in special meetinghouses, new hymns with rollicking tunes, Sunday schools, revivals, religious publishing enterprises, and missionary organizations led by professional executives? Each congregation or local district had ministers and usually its own bishop to provide guidance. How far could these leaders and their people allow adoption of popular kinds of clothing, haircuts, farm machinery, automobiles, electrical appliances, telephones, or public education? Could they allow such changes and still signal to their own members and to the world that this was a fellowship with a very special heritage of community discipline and humility? Both the Amish and the Mennonites took a variety of positions on these questions.[4]

Amish

The name Amish came from Jakob Ammann of Erlenbach in Switzerland. He stood fast for his conviction that purity of the fellowship required true believers to practice the *Meidung*, the systematic shunning or avoidance of unworthy and excommunicated persons. Shunning was sometimes based on such scriptural texts as Matthew 18:17, I Corinthians 5:11, II Corinthians 6:14–18, or II Thessalonians 3:14. Ammann saw no salvation outside a properly disciplined Mennonite fold; he could not have fellowship with any who did not practice shunning. He personally excommunicated his opponent Hans Reist and all Swiss elders and ministers who would not agree with him. Having solicited support for his interpretation in Switzerland, Alsace, and South Germany, he brought about a division of the churches in 1693–94. Twenty-seven of sixty-nine Mennonite preachers sided with him. Ammann contended for uniformity in dress—hats, garments, shoes, and stockings. He opposed trimming of the beard and attending any services in the state churches. He introduced footwashing, previously practiced in Holland, as a church ordinance among his Swiss followers. The name Amish did not persist in Europe but was to loom large in the American West.[5]

Four Amish men scouted settlement sites in the good lands of Iowa, Illinois, and Indiana in 1840. They liked Indiana's Elkhart County best.

> In the following year of 1841, four families made preparations to move to Indiana: Daniel S. and Barbara Miller and five children (Samuel, Polly, Jonathan, Rachel, and

Barbara), Preacher Joseph and Elizabeth Miller and four children (Lydia, Polly, Daniel, and Joseph), Deacon Joseph and Barbara Borntreger and five children (Lisi, Christian, Barbara, Hansi, and David) and Christian and Elizabeth Borntreger and two children (Lydia and Maria). These four families loaded their most necessary things on wagons, of which each family had one, and three one-horse spring wagons, for at that time there were no railroads. On June 3, 1841, these twenty-four persons left Somerset County, Pennsylvania, and set out westward.[6]

They settled east of Goshen; non-Amish Mennonites were already in the county's western side and besides the Amish felt that the "nice prairie-land" to the west was already too expensive. Five families came from Ohio that fall; the first Amish service was held in the fall of 1841 in the home of Daniel S. Miller in Lagrange County. At least twenty families arrived in 1842, some from Pennsylvania and some from Ohio.[7]

From the beginning there were differences within the ranks between the more conservative Amish immigrants from Somerset County, Pennsylvania, and the more progressive ones from Holmes County, Ohio. These pioneer Amish divided briefly in 1845 and split permanently in 1854. Conservative chronicler Hans (John) Borntreger of Pennsylvania lineage named four preachers as the ones responsible for the innovations, especially Jonas Troyer who had just come from Ohio in April of 1854 and was ordained a bishop by Isaac Schmucker that year. "Wherever the Lord builds a church," said Borntreger, "Satan builds one beside it." According to Borntreger these preachers and their followers "no longer wanted to conform to the former rules and regulations and had much to say in opposition." They "declared their freedom and started a new church" causing "a serious, deplorable, and complete split." They built meetinghouses. And Jonas Troyer introduced a new practice by performing some baptisms in a flowing stream. Borntreger wrote: "Looking back over the outcome of the above history, it is quite evident that carnalmindedness and lust of the eye were the main reasons for discord and division; for four things which Christ cannot tolerate in His church are especially noticeable: (1) Expensive clothing after worldly fashion; (2) Serving in public office; (3) Complete commercialism; (4) The wisdom of this world."[8]

This split of 1854 established the identity of the Old Order Amish for the first time in Indiana. In Elkhart and Lagrange counties they were that smaller conservative portion of the Amish who signaled their faithfulness in discipline and humility by adherence to old ways such as religious services on alternate Sundays in their own houses or barns; use of German language in services; use of slow German hymns from the *Ausbund* without part singing; distinctive seventeenth century garb; limitation of formal education to elementary level; resistance to worldly technology such as electricity, automobiles, photography, telephones, and modern farm machinery. They refused Sunday schools, revivals, and missions organized by professional bureaucracy. Within the Old Order Amish there came to be further shadings of affiliation announced by such differences as style of buggy, placement of pockets in clothing, or dimensions of hat crowns or brims. A modern student of Amish ways wrote: "Gohn Brothers clothing and yard goods store in Middlebury, the supplier of most 'store bought' clothing to the Old Order Amish communities in Northern Indiana, stocks more than a dozen different varieties of the black felt hat for the various groups . . . The Amish man buys the hat used by his group as a consciously-employed symbol of the *Gemeinde* and of its unique interpretation of the Amish way."[9]

Indiana's Old Order Amish have maintained an average of more than seven children per family. When Bishop Moses Borkholder of Marshall County died in 1933 at the age of ninety-five, he had 565 living descendants. Very few Amish children deserted their faith entirely. In some areas as many as one-third fed into somewhat more liberal bodies of Amish or Mennonites. Most remained Old Order Amish and eventually made that church the largest Mennonite denomination in the state. There were 22,300 adherents in 149 churches in 1990.[10]

Beginning with Elkhart and Lagrange counties they adopted a new practice of solidly filling in large blocks of land with Old Order Amish families for the convenience of their group life and discipline. Besides the forty-four congregations in Elkhart and Lagrange counties, substantial settlements were formed in Adams, Allen, Daviess, and Marshall. As the size of families and the price of land conspired to deny many couples their own acreage, more than half of the heads of households among the Old Order Amish in northern Indiana came to be employed off the farm in such work as carpentry, masonry, factory labor, and even tourism. Predictions that such vocational adaptation would destroy the traditional character of the Old Order Amish have been at least premature. They have generally gone to outside work in groups within which they have maintained their language and identity.[11]

Members of Indiana's Old Order Amish generated several entirely new groups. Henry Egly was a deacon in his church in Adams County, a relatively liberal Amishman with a heritage from Europe by way of Ohio rather than

Pennsylvania. During the course of recovery from a prolonged illness, he experienced a spiritual rededication. When he was ordained a preacher in 1854 and a bishop in 1858, the tenor of his message was the importance of a personal experience of heartfelt conversion and of the assurance of salvation. He said his fellow Amish lacked spiritual vitality and were too formal. He rebaptized some who had not experienced regeneration at the time of their first baptism. He extended membership to some persons whom their Amish congregations were shunning. About half of his congregation agreed with him. The other half asked him to resign. Congregations of "Egly Amish" formed at Berne, Woodburn, Grabill, Lafayette, and Fort Wayne in Indiana; the states of Ohio, Illinois, Kansas, Tennessee, and Michigan had congregations as well. Officially they took the name Defenseless Mennonite Church in 1908 and then Evangelical Mennonite Church in 1948. Their emphasis was always evangelism and in that interest they gradually adopted meetinghouses, multiple services, Sunday schools, English language, evangelistic preaching, and musical instruments. Beginning in 1911 their foreign missions included a major share in the successful Congo Inland Mission in Africa. Headquarters for their continuing program of missions and evangelism was established at Fort Wayne.[12]

A further development from this group with large impact on Indiana came near the end of the century. A group of Egly Amish under the leadership of Joseph E. Ramseyer became convinced that baptism should be by immersion; Amish and Mennonites generally baptized by pouring, either at their places of worship or at a stream site, but not by immersion. Ramseyer also concurred with holiness churches in teaching that a Christian should seek and expect a second work of grace as a crisis experience, an infilling or baptism of the Holy Spirit following conversion and regeneration. Based on his understanding of the Bible, he placed a primary emphasis on urgent expectancy of the second coming of Jesus Christ, to be accompanied by a resurrection of the righteous dead and a period of great tribulation, followed by a thousand years of peace under Christ's sovereignty.

After five years of deliberation the General Conference of the Egly Amish meeting near Berne, Indiana, excommunicated Ramseyer in 1896. Ramseyer had precipitated the decision by being rebaptized by immersion in August of that year. Two years later a new organization called the Missionary Church Association was established at Berne. Henry Egly's son Joseph was in it. Joseph Ramseyer was its primary leader and able evangelist for the next forty-six years. Known as the Missionary Church Association, and as the Missionary Church after its merger with a kindred Mennonite group in 1969, this fellowship grew steadily on foreign mission fields and at home. Indiana became the state with the largest share of Missionary Church membership—14,009 adherents in 69 churches in 1990. Its denominational headquarters were located at Fort Wayne; its institutions for higher education were established as Fort Wayne Bible College (later becoming Summit Christian College and in 1992 a branch of Taylor University) at Fort Wayne and Bethel College at Mishawaka.[13]

A few Indiana congregations were among those designated by the statistician at the turn of the century as Conservative Amish Mennonites—more conservative than the increasingly progressive main body of Amish Mennonites but less conservative than the Old Order Amish. Jonathan Troyer was preacher from 1886 and bishop from 1895 to 1930 at the Townline Conservative Amish Mennonite church in Lagrange County near Shipshewana. Griner and Pleasant Grove congregations were daughter churches of Townline. A Conservative Amish Mennonite Conference developed with ordained representatives from at least seven states. Mennonite historian John C. Wenger said: "It has sometimes been remarked facetiously that the coming of the automobile accounts for the growth of the Conservative Amish Mennonite congregations. That is, a number of Old Order Amish families transferred their membership to the Townline congregation where the automobile was permitted." By the 1940s Conservative Amish Mennonites still dressed much like Old Order Amish, although their use of more color did earn them the name "Pinky Amish" around Goshen. However they had grown apart from the Old Order in unmistakable ways. They had meetinghouses with services every Sunday, some services in English, Sunday schools, summer Bible schools, and revival meetings. At home they had automobiles, tractors, electricity, and modern appliances. In 1957 they dropped the word Amish from their name to become the Conservative Mennonite Conference.[14]

Old Order Amish felt the Conservatives were far too liberal. Back at the Casselman River congregation in Somerset County, Pennsylvania, the Amish bishop Moses D. Yoder led his congregation to place any and all members who would defect in that direction under strict ban. But there was a problem. His successor Moses M. Beachy did not believe that persons who simply left to join another church should be put under the ban when there was no other accusation against them. He would not enforce such a ban. Hard lines were drawn between parties in the congregation and the eyes of the Amish world watched with interest. Finally four respected ministers from outside were called to Casselman River in 1925 to help settle the controversy, one of them Bishop Eli J. Bontreger of Shipshewana, Indiana. The conflict was not resolved. After the split in 1927, one of the congregations was known as Beachy Amish. This group soon acted on some additional convictions—to allow automobiles if painted all black, electricity, and Sunday schools. They became counselors to other Old Order Amish with similar views. Moses M. Beachy traveled to Miami County, Indiana, in 1939 to assist in forming a congregation.

In 1940 Beachy Amish ministers from Pennsylvania met with Old Order Amish near Nappanee, Indiana, considering the dissatisfactions of Bishop David O. Burkholder. When the Old Order ministers withdrew from the conference table on 28 April 1940, they silenced Bishop Burkholder as an Old Order preacher. Moses M. Beachy promptly restored Burkholder as a minister in his fellowship. In Indiana the Beachy Amish were often called Burkholder Amish because David O. Burkholder assisted in the formation of congregations in the vicinity of Nappanee, Middlebury, and Odon. There were 946 adherents in 10 congregations by 1990. They offered Indiana an Amish fellowship more conservative than the Conservatives—old modes of dress, German language, unison hymn singing, men bearded after marriage, precaution generally against pride in apparel or home decoration. At the same time they intended to demonstrate that they could make free use of the world's automobiles, electricity, and farm machinery without so much as the appearance of being worldly.[15]

Mennonites

The most successful early settlement of Mennonites in Indiana was in Elkhart County, west of Goshen. At first the families came slowly—Jacob Brown in 1839; Jacob Coppes in 1844; old Martin Hoover with his son John and John Smith with his son Joseph in 1845. Then thirty families came in a single year in 1848. Frequently the older immigrants had been born in Pennsylvania and their children in Ohio. Not all of them remained in Indiana and there was a great deal of buying, selling, and moving as they accommodated their large families. In 1849 they built a meetinghouse a mile north of Southwest—a place southwest of the county seat at Goshen. That Elkhart County congregation was named Yellow Creek. It became a real religious center and mother church for the Mennonites of northern Indiana. A history printed in 1874 named six distinct congregations within it, maintaining services at eleven different places:

> Yellow Creek church, in Harrison township; Holdeman's church, in Olive township; Blosser's church, in Union township; Christophel's church, in Jackson township; Shaum's church in Baugo township; Elkhart church, in the town of Elkhart; Union meeting-house, in Locke township; Jones' school-house, in Harrison township; Stump's school-house, in Union township; and Clinton church, in Clinton township. The latter also holds regular services in the Union meeting-house, at Forest Grove, in Middlebury township.[16]

All district conferences were held at Yellow Creek; at the 1862 conference forty-six converts were baptized and the number taking communion was variously estimated between three hundred and six hundred.[17]

Jacob Wisler was a preacher from the beginning of services at Yellow Creek and was its bishop beginning in 1851. He had been ordained bishop by conservative Bishop Abraham Rohrer of Wadsworth, Ohio, and continued to take conservative counsel from Rohrer. Wisler loved what he considered the good old Mennonite ways. He wanted to keep Mennonite practices just as they were when he arrived in Indiana in 1848—quiet, restrained, and conducted in ancient patterns. When Preacher Joseph Rohrer and Deacon John Oyer favored more exuberance in the services, Wisler let them go join the Evangelicals (Albrights). Then two of the nation's most able Mennonite preachers moved to Elkhart County. They were too much for Wisler to control; they were destined to violate his conservative standards and to eclipse him in the history of the church.[18]

Daniel Brenneman

At about the age of twenty-two, Daniel Brenneman was converted, married, and ordained to the Mennonite ministry in less than one year's time. In Ohio he earned wide approval as a bilingual preacher of great energy and as an excellent bass singer. When he moved under Wisler's oversight in Elkhart County in 1864 he quickly learned that all parts of the services were always to be in German rather than English and that hymn singing was to be unison with no place for harmonic parts. This was hard news for Brenneman who said it "seemed very absurd and unreasonable." He "thought it not necessary to pay much attention to it." When Wisler was silenced for a time for improper discipline of a congregation member, it appeared that Brenneman and his more progressive ideas might be winning favor at Yellow Creek. That was not to be. Reports arrived in 1873 that a revival had broken out among the Mennonites in Ontario. Ministers Daniel Brenneman of Elkhart County, Indiana, and John Krupp of Branch County, Michigan, "concluded to go over and be convinced as to the right or wrong in the movement." Krupp visited the Canadian revival once; Brenneman went twice, baptizing thirty of the revival converts on his second visit.[19] Both were caught up in the revival. Mennonites John Krupp and Samuel Sherk began conducting "experience meetings" at Jones schoolhouse in the vicinity of Yellow Creek meetinghouse. John F. Funk described them.

> The protracted meeting at Jones continues and much excitement prevails throughout the county. On Wed. 10 were baptized, some in the water, some under the water forward, some under the water backward. Meetings were continued during the week. Several prayer meetings were held in which considerable disorder prevailed. And Daniel Brenneman also takes part with them and seems to justify their course . . . Much ado was made, loud crying and weeping, howling that could be heard a long distance—half a mile. Sitting or lying around on the floor, and making great confusion, shouting, jumping, and so on.[20]

At the district conference at Yellow Creek on 25 April 1874 twelve officers signed the document listing three reasons Brenneman was expelled until "he shall acknowledge his error" and "reconcile himself with this and other churches where he has been cause of offense." Brenneman did not see how he could disown the revival when he felt it was exactly what the Mennonites needed. He and his followers did not feel they could join any of the "popular churches" such as the Methodists, Baptists, or Christians. They felt that "minor churches" such as the Brethren (Dunkers) or the Quakers were not satisfactory. So they established the Reformed Mennonite Church beginning with about eighty-six members in 1874. Brenneman was an unceasing evangelist. He published a hymnbook called the *Balm of Gilead* and a church magazine entitled the *Gospel Banner*. The church evangelized; it merged with other small Mennonite bodies of similar interests, changing its name in the process; it gathered over 3,000 members in Indiana and established its publishing company at Elkhart. Finally it joined with the Missionary Church Association in 1969 to form the Missionary Church with headquarters in Fort Wayne and with two colleges in Indiana. Thus the legacy of Mennonite preacher Daniel Brenneman of Yellow Creek in Indiana was an energetic midwestern denomination close akin to America's holiness evangelicals in the Methodist family.[21]

John F. Funk

The second Mennonite preacher to come to Elkhart County and become more popular than Bishop Wisler was John F. Funk. His Mennonite home church in Bucks County, Pennsylvania, offered little activity for young people so Funk sampled the Sunday services, Sunday schools, prayer meetings, and revivals of neighboring Protestants. At the age of nine he memorized 648 Bible verses in a single year and was awarded a New Testament by Superintendent Leidy, recent convert of an Evangelical (Albright) revival. At Chicago, in the lumber business with his brother-in-law, he continued his lively religious interests. He was converted under Presbyterian ministry. Funk said:

> On one occasion the Rev. Mr. Brooks prayed earnestly. His prayer was offered for me. I knew it. It just suited my case. The Spirit of God followed me to the counting room [bookkeeping office of the lumber company] and pressed itself home to my heart all the day long. I could not escape it. There was no peace of mind, and I knew not what to do, but, upheld by his rich grace, I despaired not. I trusted in Christ and I prayed. God heard my prayer, and the next day I felt quite a different being, so happy,—so cheerful,—a joy unfelt before. It was that sweet, peaceful serenity of mind which none but the Christian can feel. And I began to experience what I had so long desired to, and which so often before had brought doubt to my mind, when I heard Christians tell of the unspeakable joy they felt, and made me wonder whether there was truth in it. But now I found it to my great joy, to be an indisputable fact.[22]

But Funk did not choose to become a Presbyterian. His evenings and Sundays in Chicago were packed with Bible study, teaching, superintending, and street ministry. In some of his activity he was a co-worker with Dwight L. Moody but he did not choose to imitate Moody. What he wanted to do was to be a Mennonite and to help the Mennonites in some specific ways he had in mind. "I felt that I also owed a duty to the church of my choice," he said, "and while my own church had few contributions to Gospel activities and active mission work, having no Sunday schools, no continued meetings, no missionary work of any kind, and was almost altogether inactive in all kinds of church work, I felt that I had there also a duty to perform." Mennonites had no church paper. Funk and his wife Salome began issuing the *Herald of Truth* from their home in Chicago in January of 1864, each issue produced concurrently in German as *Herold der Wahrheit*. He was to edit the *Herald* for the next forty-five years. On weekends he often commuted sixty miles to preach for a Mennonite congregation at Gardner, Illinois, and was ordained to the ministry there in May of 1865. The burden of ten hours a day at the lumber company plus all the editing and all the ministry drove Funk to decide among his priorities. He sold his share of the lumber company for $10,000 and focused his energy on ministry to his fellow Mennonites.[23]

This was the thirty-two-year-old dynamo who moved to Elkhart on 6 April 1867. Funk had attended conferences at Yellow Creek in Elkhart County in 1862 and 1864. He knew what a lively Mennonite center it was. Elkhart would be a better location for influencing Mennonite affairs than Chicago. John and Salome Funk came to Elkhart with $2,500 worth of newly purchased printing equipment. They set up their print shop in the rented basement of a drugstore and had the May issue of the *Herald* ready to mail on schedule.[24]

John Funk and his message were already known among Mennonites because his *Herald* was the primary Mennonite paper, with more than 2,000 subscribers. He and his fellow contributors to the *Herald* believed that the Mennonites were in crisis. Mennonites had a respected theological heritage and a literary history; both now appeared endangered on the American frontier. Elkhart's presses operated by John Funk and his colleagues published 118 books and reprinted 62 others for his people— doctrinal books, inspirational books, prayer books, catechisms, confessions, hymnbooks, study manuals, biography, church history, biblical literature. These included the thousand-page *Martyr's Mirror* and the seven-hundred-page *Complete Works of Menno Simons* in both German and English. Funk's *Herald* was always lifting up a moderately progressive revision of Mennonite ideals.[25]

Every Mennonite church was essentially a gathering of baptized believers but many Mennonite children were not being instructed or enlisted to confess their faith and to take their places as adults in the church. A sure way to kill off churches was to do nothing for the children and simply let the old members die. Other denominations with youth programs would keep their young people and attract the Mennonites as well. Funk wanted Mennonite Sunday schools to teach Bible and German and English and singing. "O! beloved brethren, consider the matter well, and see whether it would not be highly necessary for our churches everywhere to establish Sunday schools, so that the children may not grow up in ignorance and remain unacquainted with God and his commandments," he wrote. "It is truly astonishing how little our young people, generally, know about this matter; there-

fore, we should make every effort to instruct them and bring them to Jesus." The *Herald* was always lifting up the need for Sunday schools, telling how such schools could be conducted, describing the best schools as they went "evergreen" or year round, and reporting the excitement of Sunday school conventions. Since there was no suitable literature for Mennonite Sunday schools, Funk got the necessary instruction books and quarterlies written and published them. The first Mennonite general Sunday school conference in the nation was held at Clinton Frame church near Goshen on 5–8 October 1892.[26]

Funk knew that preaching was poor in many Mennonite congregations; the sermons in German could be long, repetitious, and not palatable to youth. Small and scattered congregations might have no preaching or communion services or baptisms at all for extended periods and no place to appeal for help. Funk did not want revival extremes. He was among those voting in 1874 to expel his friend and collaborator Daniel Brenneman after Daniel and the excommunicated John Krupp entered into "prayer and experience meetings." One charge was that women were being allowed to testify in them. However the *Herald* kept reporting good results of evangelistic meetings carefully conducted. Funk kept advocating both systematic evangelism among established congregations and missionary assistance for struggling ones.[27]

When John and Salome Funk came to Elkhart in 1867 there was no Mennonite Sunday school in the state. There were five Mennonite churches in the county's countryside but none at the growing town of Elkhart. The new Prairie Street Church which they helped to establish there about 1870 became their congregational focus and a kind of model for progressives. Here was a year-round Mennonite Sunday school with regular teacher training. Eventually it developed branch schools at three other Elkhart locations. Funk was the church's minister; sometimes he was Sunday school superintendent as well. The church's calendar changed from the traditional pattern of one worship service every two weeks to services twice on Sunday plus an added Sunday meeting for youth. More and more of the services were conducted in English. Bible classes and singing classes met on weeknights. Prairie Street Church at Elkhart pioneered with a series of evangelistic meetings and the Funks' daughter Phoebe was one of the first to be baptized. Indiana Conference finally authorized some systematic evangelism among the scattered members and small churches in 1881. In 1892 Funk was ordained a Mennonite bishop with oversight of Elkhart County west of Goshen.[28]

Funk kept enlisting and supporting additional Mennonite leaders. His brother Abraham Funk was a stalwart partner with him in the publishing business. John S. Coffman accepted Funk's offer of $500 per year to move from Virginia to Elkhart in 1879 to help with the *Herald*. Coffman seemed to help with everything— with the *Herald*, with Sunday schools, with singing schools, with missions to struggling congregations, with soliciting support for higher education at Elkhart Institute, and with evangelism. There were so many invitations to conduct meetings that Coffman found he could be "preaching all the time," and he eventually did just that. He became America's best known Mennonite evangelist.[29] John Horsch and Menno S. Steiner were younger editorial associates at the *Herald* on their way to national leadership among Mennonites. Prairie Street Church at Elkhart was point of origin for the Mennonite Evangelizing Committee which developed into a denominational mission program and for the Mennonite Aid Plan to provide disaster relief for Mennonites forbidden to purchase commercial insurance.[30]

Funk and Coffman wanted Mennonite higher education for Mennonite young people lest such youth be alienated from their heritage while attending secular or denominational institutions. Elkhart seemed a logical place for a Mennonite school. They attended discussion of the subject with Elkhart leaders in the reception room of Funk's Mennonite Publishing House. Funk did not think the Mennonites were ready for such a project and took no further leadership in it. John S. Coffman and Henry A. Mumaw, another younger colleague whom Funk had brought to Elkhart, were among those who did give leadership to the founding and operation of Elkhart Institute. It became a Mennonite school in 1895, not because of adoption by any official church action but in the sense that all nine members of the board of directors were Mennonites and the school's advertising was aimed at Mennonite young people whose vocations or personal interests pointed them toward higher education.

When expansion seemed essential, the citizens of the county seat at Goshen subscribed $10,000 and invited the Elkhart Institute to relocate there in 1903 as Goshen College. Maintaining an ongoing and sometimes heated dialogue with church members and authorities, Goshen College provided a continuing focus for educational and cultural influence. Religious and missionary zeal were often rekindled through the school. Goshen College Biblical Seminary was added in 1933 and a School of Nursing in 1951. Scholars at Goshen spoke to the Mennonite community and to the scholarly world about the nature of the Anabaptist-Mennonite heritage, clearing away centuries of misrepresentation. The Mennonite Historical Society, founded in 1924 at Goshen, with its *Mennonite Quarterly Review*, and the Mennonite Historical Library at Goshen became recognized among church historians everywhere as supporters of research. Mennonites were back in higher education to stay.[31]

Not all of Indiana's Mennonites wished to be reformed or improved in the ways which Funk and his colleagues advocated. Innovations looked to some like corruptions of the good old ways. Before John F. Funk ever moved to Elkhart County, Bishop Jacob Wisler pointed to the danger that Mennonites might all become like Methodists before they knew what was happening. A later historian said:

> The Civil War offered the most immediate and direct challenge to Mennonite identity, and many Mennonites failed to meet the challenge. But in the long run, Sunday schools and the *Herald* may have changed the church even more . . . At the Yellow Creek congregation of Elkhart County, the battle reached its highest pitch. Tension between progressives and conservatives arose and mounted in the early 1860s. In 1866 conflict erupted at the Indiana Conference meetings, and for the next six years various ministers and groups of ministers sought to heal the wounds. All Mennonite eyes followed the fighting, for the issues at hand were not merely local.[32]

Two years after Funk's arrival in 1867, Bishop Wisler and about a hundred of his people began to hold their own worship services separately. The schism was final in 1872. The Wisler Mennonites said they must have peace from their tormentors and just wanted to be left alone. Similar withdrawals in favor of the old ways followed among Mennonites in Ohio, Virginia, Pennsylvania, and Ontario between 1872 and 1900. Indiana's Wisler Mennonites wanted the old pattern of worship without Sunday schools but in the twentieth century they did come to allow use of automobiles and telephones. This was too much for Bishop John W. Martin of Elkhart County. He and his followers withdrew from the Wisler church in 1907 to become the Old Order Mennonites, some of whom have stayed with horse and buggy and shunned modern inventions.[33]

Cooperations and Mergers

More remarkable than the Mennonite separations were their cooperations and eventual mergers. John F. Funk was no Mennonite paragon; his impatience and anger were factors in the Wisler separation. He became a prosperous town dweller. The Wisler Mennonites said that Funk's carriage and furniture were too fancy and that he kept a dressy coat for special occasions in addition to his plain one. He gathered at Elkhart a cluster of reformers who wanted to get things done. They were less oriented to the profound Mennonite principle of humility and more engaged in what they considered the essential business of saving the churches through work—progressive work, direct work, active work, aggressive work. Abram B. Kolb, Funk's son-in-law and a fellow reformer at the *Herald*, warned in 1898 that modern Christianity seemed to have become "all work—one continued earnest, active, hurrying, rushing, hustling, pushing world of active work." Young people brought forward by participation and leadership in Sunday schools, youth meetings, and conventions could seem altogether too forward for some of the old-fashioned church members back home.[34]

All of the new energy was amply counterbalanced by inertia in the membership. Funk certainly knew that any proposed change might require years of suggestion in the *Herald* and persistent gentle advocacy among local leaders before finding any fruition in the local congregations. Quickening did come. A substantial body of Mennonite bishops, ministers, and leading families came to believe that something must be done, especially for their large families of children now constantly exposed to the English language and to modern American influences. They took lessons from Elkhart and from observation of their Protestant neighbors.[35]

And the Amish, the main body of Amish Mennonites which had not separated as Old Order Amish in 1854, were made welcome to join in. Both Amish and Mennonites read the *Herald*. Amish and Mennonites bought Funk's publications and established similar Sunday schools. Amish and Mennonites organized and led their Sunday school conventions together. Amish and Mennonites invited evangelists like John S. Coffman to conduct evangelistic meetings; they shared in the missionary efforts of the pioneer Mennonite Evangelizing Committee. Amish attended Elkhart Institute and Goshen College along with Mennonites.

Finally, in 1898, the Amish joined with Mennonites to form a new general conference. For many years the two groups had freely attended each other's district conferences. In 1916 those in Indiana and Michigan were the first to actually merge at the district conference level. With Indiana and Michigan districts in the lead, the merger spread across the continent and made the resultant Mennonite Church the largest of the Mennonite

bodies in North America. As a result the name Amish was left to the smaller body of Old Order Amish and became increasingly associated with the most conservative groups.[36]

John F. Funk did not finish his earthly work in a blaze of glory. His business was devastated by bankruptcy and fire. Then the church took over publishing as its own enterprise and located that enterprise not at Elkhart in Indiana but at Scottdale in Pennsylvania. Funk was forced to retire from the office of bishop at the age of sixty-seven in 1902. Yet historian Harold S. Bender has called him "more responsible than any other one man (teamed with J. S. Coffman) for the general character of the Mennonite Church in the 20th century in its middle-of-the-road position between tradition on the one hand and undirected progress on the other." For the crucial nineteenth century quickening of the Mennonites, John F. Funk was the key person and Elkhart, Indiana, was his place.[37]

Mennonites at Berne

The dialect of one cluster of Indiana's Mennonites was Swiss. A few families from the Jura Mountains in the canton of Bern located on the line between Wells and Adams counties in 1838 and organized the Baumgartner Mennonite congregation. Then in 1852 a group of eighty-two Swiss came directly to Indiana from the Jura Mountains, almost all Sprungers or their relatives by marriage. They formed their settlement in Adams County and called it Berne. In 1860 they built their first meetinghouse. Immigration and natural increase made theirs a strong church. When they needed to select a new preacher in August of 1868, seventeen men of the congregation were nominated. Three women of the congregation had nominated "Sammie" (Samuel F.) Sprunger whose only formal education had been five short terms in country school and who was not yet twenty. Of the seventeen nominees, the lot fell on Sammie. The slip in the hymnbook he chose said "Lord, Knower of all hearts, indicate which one Thou hast chosen."

Sammie was immediately ordained but took the advice of the pastor of the neighboring Baumgartner congregation that he get some education before beginning his work at Berne. He chose to enroll in the new Wadsworth Institute in Ohio. Wadsworth was a school of the General Conference Mennonites, a recent union of more liberal immigrant groups in the American West formed with the aim of stirring Mennonites from their lethargy.[38] The school was headed by a university-trained professor from

Germany and favorably inclined toward missions, evangelism, and youth work. Sammie attended three years. When he came home to Berne for a visit the people were shocked that he wore a different coat, that he stood up instead of humbly remaining seated when invited to speak in meeting, and that he dared to use high German in church instead of Swiss dialect. When he returned to his congregation after graduation in 1871, the majority refused even to hear him. He preached to his minority of followers on alternate Sundays when the meetinghouse was not in use and to the nearby Baumgartner congregation.

By 1886 the three Berne congregations had merged. Under Sprunger's preaching there came a revival that year in which over one hundred persons professed their faith. Before the end of Sprunger's ministry in 1913 he was the leading publisher for the General Conference Mennonites through the Mennonite Book Concern which he established at Berne. The church had a brick meetinghouse with a seating capacity of 2,000 and was the largest Mennonite congregation in North America. Its membership did not hold fast to Swiss garb or to German language. They installed a pipe organ and adopted open communion. Their distinction was an openness to world mission and service.[39]

World Service

All varieties of Mennonites were likely to be under particular stress in times of war. As citizens they were called to serve in the armed forces and to raise funds in support of the war effort. Some could not do either as a matter of conscience. During the Civil War Indiana's constitutional provision was followed which said "No person conscientiously opposed to bearing arms shall be compelled to do militia duty; but such persons shall pay an equivalent for exemption." Cost to individual Mennonites ranged from $200 to $600. The situation was more threatening during the First World War. In some localities Mennonites were treated as pro-German or disloyal. In some camps conscientious objectors were abused. A few were court-martialed, given dishonorable discharges, and sent to prison at Fort Leavenworth. Consideration of these excesses probably helped to motivate the provision in the Selective Training and Service Act of 1940 that persons "who by reason of religious training and belief" were conscientiously opposed to all forms of military service should "be assigned to work of national importance under civilian direction." A similar law was enacted in 1951. Mennonites, Brethren, and the Society of Friends

cooperated in efforts to organize and fund qualified civilian direction and administration for projects in refugee relief, care of the sick, and emergency construction. As a result the image of Mennonites as persons unusually committed to a mission of serving the needy was heightened both inside and outside the church.[40]

Mennonites did not make the option of exemption from military service any cause for withdrawal from international involvement. In fact, twentieth century Mennonites were notable for their programs of worldwide service. Between 1941 and 1969 the Mennonite Central Committee, joint relief agency for foreign assistance, sent tons of shoes, bedding, clothing, food, soap, and medical supplies valued at about $50 million. Of the 5,241 persons who undertook assignments in ninety foreign countries under auspices of the Mennonite Central Committee between 1920 and 1969, 412 were from Indiana. In the 1980s Mennonite Central Committee contributions totaled about $20 million in cash and $10 million in material aid each year. By 1990 about 85 percent of Goshen College undergraduates were spending one trimester abroad.[41]

Indiana's Mennonites did not get a slice in the Census Bureau's circle graph reporting the size of religious bodies in the state in 1906, being simply thrown into the category of "all other." Nor was any Mennonite group listed in the Census Bureau's 1916 chart reporting membership of fourteen major denominations in the state. Yet the Mennonite presence continued to be very strong in Indiana. The states of Pennsylvania with 30,550, Ohio with 35,200, and Indiana with 22,300 represented 72 percent of the Old Order Amish adherents reported for the U.S.A. in 1990. Adding that report of 22,300 Old Order Amish to the report for the Mennonite Church (17,976), the Mennonite General Conference (3,084), the Evangelical Mennonite Church (1,417), and the Beachy Amish (946) gave a Hoosier Mennonite total of 45,723 that year without counting 14,009 adherents in the daughter Missionary Church.

In the 1990s the nation's largest Mennonite relief sale, to support the work of the Mennonite Central Committee, was being held annually in northern Indiana. It had become a celebration of Mennonite-Amish peoplehood. Central office of the Mennonite Board of Missions and Charities had been located at Elkhart since its founding in 1906 and was joined there in 1988 by the national headquarters of the Mennonite Church. The two largest Mennonite denominations were cooperating to offer ministerial training at the campus of Mennonite Biblical Seminary at Elkhart. Both the Mennonite Historical Library and the national archives of the Mennonite church were at Goshen. So were the headquarters of Mennonite Mutual Aid, an Indiana nonprofit corporation serving Mennonite institutions and members by managing assets of some $175 million on their behalf. Its purpose was "to provide a means for members, congregations, and church communities in the United States to carry out the historic Anabaptist and New Testament practice of stewardship of material and financial resources, and to share in times of crisis and hardship." Its eight constituent corporations provided a wide range of options for insurance, investment, and church development.[42]

In 1990 Indiana's whole Mennonite family was about equal in size to the Churches of Christ or the Assemblies of God in the state and approximately twice as large as the Episcopal Church or the Society of Friends. Some of its members were in seventeenth century clothes, riding by horse and buggy to German service in a house church in Lagrange County; others, in their twentieth century Sunday best, sang in English around the organ in great meetinghouses at Berne or at Goshen College.

NOTES

1. Cornelius J. Dyck, *An Introduction to Mennonite History: A Popular History of the Anabaptists and the Mennonites* (Scottdale, Pa.: Herald Press, 1967), 103–11.

2. John C. Wenger, *The Mennonites in Indiana and Michigan* (Scottdale, Pa.: Herald Press, 1961), 6–8; Dyck, *Introduction*, 145–47.

3. Mennonite is the broader term which includes the Amish. Those siding with Jakob Ammann (b. 1644) who began immigrating to the American colonies before the Revolution were more accurately named Amish Mennonites. However the shortened form Amish was also used for them. As the Amish Mennonites took their place in American culture a majority of them merged their district conferences with the larger Mennonite (not Amish) conferences and became referred to as Mennonites—a uniting process begun with a conference merger in Indiana in 1916 and completed generally by the 1920s. This left the name Amish to refer primarily to the Old Order Amish, those who had declined merger with other Mennonites and held fast to the worship, organization, costume, and language used by Jakob Ammann and his associates about the year 1700. However, the designation Amish also includes kindred groups such as the Beachy Amish who maintain a distinctive garb, language, and community separation but have elected to use such evangelistic means as Sunday schools and such products of technology as automobiles, electricity, telephones, and modern farm machinery. The Conservative Mennonite Conference, with eleven congregations and over a thousand members in Indiana in 1985, was known officially as the Conservative Amish Mennonite Conference from 1910 to 1957. See *Mennonite Encyclopedia: A Comprehensive Reference Work on the Anabaptist-Mennonite Movement*, 5 vols. (Scottdale, Pa.: Mennonite Publishing House, 1955–90), 1:93–97, 254; 2:86, 854–65; 3:587; 4:43–47; 5:192, 431.

4. Theron F. Schlabach, *Peace, Faith, Nation: Mennonites and Amish in Nineteenth-Century America* (Scottdale, Pa.: Herald Press, 1988), 207–10; James C. Juhnke, *Vision, Doctrine, War: Mennonite Identity and Organization in America 1890–1930* (Scottdale, Pa.: Herald Press, 1989), 21–79; *Mennonite Encyclopedia*, 2:69–70; 3:612–13, 897–907. For service forms as preserved among the Old Order Amish see John A. Hostetler, *Amish Society* (Baltimore, Md.: Johns Hopkins Press, 1968), 52–57, 102–23, 171–89; John Umble, "Amish Service Manuals," *Mennonite Quarterly Review* 15 (January 1941): 26–32; Joe Wittmer, *The Gentle People: Personal Reflections on Amish Life* (Minneapolis, Minn.: Educational Media Corporation, 1990), 12–14, 45–53, 60–64, 91–95.

5. *Mennonite Encyclopedia*, 1:90–92; Hostetler, *Amish Society*, 28–35. For an alternate theory of the derivation of the name, see James E. Landing, "Amish Settlement in North America: A Geographic Brief," *Bulletin of the Illinois Geographical Society* 12 (December 1970): 65.

6. Hans E. Borntreger, *A History of the First Settlers of the Amish Mennonites and the Establishment of Their First Congregation in the State of Indiana, along with a Short Account of the Division which Took Place in This Church*, trans. Elizabeth Gingerich (Topeka, Ind.: Dan Hochstetler, 1988), 5–6.

7. Landing, "Amish Settlement," 67; *Amish and Mennonites in Eastern Elkhart and Lagrange Counties, Indiana, 1841–1991* (Goshen, Ind.: Amish Heritage Committee, 1992, 44 p.).

8. Borntreger, *History*, 3, 10, 12.

9. Stephen B. Harroff, "Living the Set-Apart Life: Sights and Sounds of the Amish Way," *Old Fort News*, vol. 44, no. 1 (1981): 4; Hostetler, *Amish Society*, 134–38, 249–54.

10. Gerald E. Markle and Sharon Pasco, "Family Limitation among the Old Order Amish," *Population Studies* 31 (July 1977): 270; Hostetler, *Amish Society*, 81–82.

11. Thomas J. Meyers, "The Old Order Amish of Northern Indiana from 1840 to 1984" (Paper presented at the meeting of the Indiana Historical Society, Indianapolis, 3 November 1984); Landing, "Amish Settlement," 65–69.

12. William C. Ringenberg, "Development and Division in the Mennonite Community in Allen County, Indiana," *Mennonite Quarterly Review* 50 (April 1976): 114–31; Wenger, *Mennonites*, 403–7; *Mennonite Encyclopedia*, 2:164, 264–66; Schlabach, *Peace*, 115–16.

13. *Mennonite Encyclopedia*, 2:266; 3:710–11; 4:250; Wenger, *Mennonites*, 416–18; Schlabach, *Peace*, 115–16.

14. Karl Baehr, "Secularization among the Mennonites of Elkhart County, Indiana," *Mennonite Quarterly Review* 16 (July 1942): 135–36; *Mennonite Encyclopedia*, 1:700–2; 4:739; 5:192; Wenger, *Mennonites*, 408–12.

15. Alvin J. Beachy, "The Rise and Development of the Beachy Amish Mennonite Churches," *Mennonite Quarterly Review* 29 (April 1955): 118–40; *Mennonite Encyclopedia*, 1:254; Wenger, *Mennonites*, 418–20.

16. *An Illustrated Historical Atlas of Elkhart Co., Indiana* (Chicago: Higgins, Belden & Co., 1874), 8.

17. Lynn Bender, "The Yellow Creek Mennonite Settlers: A Study of Land and Family," *Mennonite Quarterly Review* 46 (January 1972): 70–83; Wenger, *Mennonites*, 17–18, 61–62; Schlabach, *Peace*, 39.

18. John C. Wenger, "Jacob Wisler and the Old Order Mennonite Schism of 1872 in Elkhart County, Indiana." *Mennonite Quarterly Review* 33 (April 1959): 112–13.

19. John C. Wenger, "Documents on the Daniel Brenneman Division," ed. J. C. Wenger, *Mennonite Quarterly Review* 34 (January 1960): 48–50.

20. Wenger, "Documents," 52–53.

21. Wenger, "Documents," 55–56; *Mennonite Encyclopedia*, 1:417–18; 3:603; 4:774; Schlabach, *Peace*, 110, 113–14; Wenger, *Mennonites*, 379–84.

22. William W. Dean, "John F. Funk and the Mennonite Awakening" (Ph.D. diss., University of Iowa, 1965), 60.

23. Dean, "John F. Funk," 61–77.

24. Dean, "John F. Funk," 72–73, 77–78; Wenger, *Mennonites*, 62.

25. Dean, "John F. Funk," 78–83.

26. Dean, "John F. Funk," 86–112.

27. Dean, "John F. Funk," 140–77; 257–58.

28. Dean, "John F. Funk," 95, 113–39, 157.

29. Barbara F. Coffman, *His Name Was John* (Scottdale, Pa.: Herald Press, 1964), 122–25, 143, 279; *Mennonite Encyclopedia*, 1:633–34; Dean, "John F. Funk," 173–77.

30. Dean, "John F. Funk," 159–60, 236–37, 254.

31. John Umble, "The Elkhart Institute Moves to Goshen," *Mennonite Quarterly Review* 9 (January 1935): 37–59; John Umble, *Goshen College 1895–1954* (Goshen, Ind.: Goshen College, 1955, 284 p.); Wenger, *Mennonites*, viii, 35, 49; Dean, "John F. Funk," 270–74.

32. Joseph C. Liechty, "Humility: The Foundation of the Mennonite Religious Outlook in the 1860s," *Mennonite Quarterly Review* 54 (January 1980): 6.

33. Wenger, *Mennonites*, 366–71; Wenger, "Jacob Wisler," 108–31, 215–40; *Mennonite Encyclopedia*, 4:47–49, 965; Schlabach, *Peace*, 220–23.

34. Schlabach, *Peace*, 221, 320.

35. John Umble, "Seventy Years of Progress in Sunday School Work among the Mennonites of the Middle West," *Mennonite Quarterly Review* 8 (October 1934): 166–79.

36. *Mennonite Encyclopedia*, 3:29–30, 612; Dean, "John F. Funk," 274–75; Schlabach, *Peace*, 210–11.

37. *Mennonite Encyclopedia*, 2:422; Dean, "John F. Funk," 262–66.

38. *Mennonite Encyclopedia*, 2:465–71; 5:329–32; Schlabach, *Peace*, 127–39.

39. Naomi Lehman, *Pilgrimage of a Congregation: First Mennonite Church, Berne, Indiana* (Berne, Ind.: First Mennonite Church, 1983), 1–48; *Mennonite Encyclopedia*, 1:298–99; 4:605–6; Wenger, *Mennonites*, 356–59.

40. Harold S. Bender and C. Henry Smith, *Mennonites and Their Heritage* (Scottdale, Pa.: Herald Press, 1964), 142–44; Guy F. Hershberger, "Historical Background to the Formation of the Mennonite Central Committee," *Mennonite Quarterly Review* 44 (July 1970): 225–44; Robert Kreider, "The Impact of MCC Service on American Mennonites" *Mennonite Quarterly Review* 44 (July 1970): 245–61; Wenger, *Mennonites*, 21–23, 38–41, 45–51; Schlabach, *Peace*, 173–200.

41. John Hostetler, "Mennonite Central Committee Material Aid, 1941–1969," *Mennonite Quarterly Review* 44 (July 1970): 318–23; Paul Classen, "Statistics on Mennonite Central Committee Personnel," *Mennonite Quarterly Review* 44 (July 1970): 324–29; *Mennonite Encyclopedia*, 3:605–9; 5:560–62.

42. *Mennonite Encyclopedia*, 3:592–94, 615; 5:432, 564–67, 572–73.

Village Creek Primitive Baptist Church,
Fayette County

Below, Battlefield Chapel, Battle Ground

Powers Church, Steuben County

Mount Pleasant Beech African Methodist Episcopal Church, Rush County

Above, Little Cedar Grove Baptist
Church, Cedar Grove

Walnut Ridge Friends
Meetinghouse, Rush County

McCutchanville United Methodist Church,
McCutchanville

Hanover Presbyterian Church, Hanover

Christ Episcopal Church, Madison

Below, Old Brookville Church, Brookville

First Baptist Church, Huntington

St. John Episcopal Church, Crawfordsville

First United Methodist Church, Columbus

Indianapolis Hebrew Congregation,
Indianapolis

Above, St. John Catholic Church,
Indianapolis

Christ Temple, Indianapolis

St. Paul Lutheran Church,
Indianapolis

St. George Greek Orthodox Church,
Lake County

Tyson United Methodist Church, Versailles

Calvary Tabernacle, Indianapolis

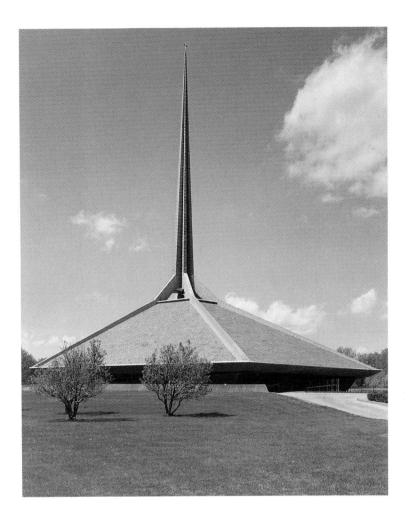

North Christian Church, Columbus

Church of God, Anderson University, Anderson

Sts. Peter and Paul Catholic Cathedral,
Indianapolis

Central Christian Church, Indianapolis

Sacred Heart Basilica, Notre Dame

Second Presbyterian Church,
Indianapolis

Islamic Center of North America, Plainfield

Worship Structure, Angel Mounds Site, Vanderburgh County

Roofless Church, New Harmony

St. Meinrad Archabbey and
Seminary, St. Meinrad

Convent Immaculate Conception, Ferdinand

Chapel of Immaculate Conception, Oldenburg

MORAVIANS

Moravia and Bohemia, later included in Czechoslovakia, were evangelized by Christian missionaries Cyril and Methodius from the Greek Catholic Church in the 800s. There followed a long history of resistance to the increasing predominance of Roman Catholic sovereigns and clergy over the region. John Huss and Jerome of Prague became resistance leaders; they were martyred in 1415 and 1416 respectively. In 1457 the continuing resistance movement formed a church fellowship using various forms of the name "Brethren," increasingly "The Unity of the Brethren (Unitas Fratrum)" or "The United Brethren (Fratres Unitatis)." They had perhaps 200 essentially Protestant societies with 10,000 adult male members in Bohemia and 100,000 in Moravia before the rise of the German and Swiss reformers in the 1500s. They related very cordially to such sixteenth century reformers as Luther and Calvin. When the terrible wars in the name of religion found a kind of territorial conclusion in the Peace of Westphalia in 1648, these Brethren were given no place in the settlement. Their church was destroyed. Their last bishop, John Amos Comenius, died in exile at Amsterdam in 1670. Their identity seemed lost.[1]

Then they were reconstituted. A carpenter-evangelist named Christian David became acquainted with some families in Moravia who remembered their Brethren heritage and wanted to find a safe place to practice their faith. David made connections with Count Nicholaus Ludwig von Zinzendorf in Saxony who agreed to give them asylum. Those who could began making their

escape to Saxony as early as 1722. They began their new building in an undeveloped place and called it Herrnhut. Zinzendorf was and continued to be a Lutheran. He was influenced by those pious Lutheran leaders Spener and Francke and was himself a graduate of what was then a most religious university at Halle. Since his family insisted that he be a lawyer and civil officer instead of a full time religious worker, he had resolved to make his own village of Bertholdsdorf into a model Christian community. By 1727 he had become so moved by the faith and practice of these immigrant "Moravians" in his territory that he served as their bishop for a time and invested his whole fortune in their mission. "I, as far as I can, will help to bring about this renewal," he said. "And though I have to sacrifice my earthly possessions, my honours, my life, as long as I live I will do my utmost to see to it that the little company of the Lord's disciples shall be preserved for Him until He comes."[2]

Zinzendorf was under constant investigation and periodic exile for his support of the Moravians. He and his followers took their displacement as a sign that they were to be a Diaspora, a scattered people like salt for the earth. Their small army simply undertook to win the world to discipleship of Jesus Christ. In every place where they were allowed to form one of their communal societies—Herrnhut, Herrnhaag, Marienborn, and a score of other places in Europe—they worked to support themselves, to serve their immediate locality with ministry and education, and to school themselves for new missionary endeavor. Besides their European districts for evangelism, they pioneered as Protestant missionaries in Greenland, Labrador, Alaska, North America, the West Indies, Demerara, the Mosquito Coast, Surinam, Cape Colony, Kaffraria, German East Africa, Victoria, Queensland, Kashmir, Tibet, and Jerusalem.[3]

It was their missionary drive which brought the Moravians to America. Augustus Gottlieb Spangenberg led a party of nine to Georgia in 1734 to evangelize the Creek Indians, the Cherokee Indians, and the black slaves. Twenty Moravians coming to Georgia as reinforcements in 1736 were shipmates of and contributors to the conversion of John Wesley. At least partly because of war and disease the settlement in Georgia dwindled and failed. Its remnants were led from Georgia to Pennsylvania by George Whitefield in 1740. There they established their semi-communal settlements named Bethlehem and Nazareth which became bases for thirty-one centers of itineracy, for schools, and for missions to the Indians. A similar colony established by 1763 at Salem, North Carolina, became their focus for southern responsibilities.[4]

It was their missionary drive which brought the Moravians to the border of Indiana. Their Indian converts among the Mohicans and Delawares kept being driven westward from New York to Pennsylvania to Ohio. Beginning in 1772 in the Tuscarawas Valley of Ohio, they formed three settlements of Christian Indians called Schonbrünn, Gnadenhütten, and Lichtenau. All were viewed with suspicion and destroyed. During the war between the Americans and the British, neither the missionaries nor their converts would bear arms for either side. Ninety Indian men, women, and children were massacred without resistance at Gnadenhütten by American settlers in 1782. One remaining group of Moravian Indians, led back from Canada by the missionary David Zeisberger in 1798, reestablished a small colony at Goshen on the Muskingum.[5]

Mission to Delawares in Indiana

There were Delaware Indians in Zeisberger's Ohio colony who were in touch with the Delawares now roaming Indiana Territory with nine villages on the upper waters of the West Fork of White River. In the exchanges among these Delawares, Zeisberger thought he heard a clear invitation for the Moravians to send Christian teachers to the Indiana Delawares. Officials of the Moravian Church in Pennsylvania acted on Zeisberger's report of the opportunity in Indiana. Abraham Luckenbach and John

Peter Kluge volunteered for the White River Mission. Zeisberger had suggested that at least one of the missionaries to Indiana be married. Luckenbach and Kluge were both single but Kluge was willing to marry; Anna Marie Ranke accepted her choice by lot to be his wife and to be a missionary to the Delawares.[6]

The account of the mission was recorded in heartrending detail in the diaries and correspondence of the missionaries. The "invitation" turned out to be anything but clear. What the more powerful of the Indian leaders really wanted were recruits for their Delaware confederation rather than missionaries. Without the welcome they expected, the missionaries dragged themselves the last hundred miles of their trip, the overland portion, in a month of sickness and privation. Earlier Moravian successes among the Indians could not be duplicated in the current hostile atmosphere of Indiana. They spent themselves in instruction and religious ministry for the Indians but their station near the present site of Anderson bore little fruit. A few Christian Indians gathered there from earlier settlements. Some sick persons cared for at the Moravian mission chose to be baptized and to remain at the settlement. Abraham Luckenbach reported, "During the five years of our work on the White River, only two persons, who were in health, were baptized, namely, a Pottewatemi and a Monsy woman."[7]

Whiskey traffic alone seemed enough to end the mission in despair. The Indians were being destroyed by the flood of whiskey shipped to Fort Hamilton or Fort Wayne by white traders and then retailed on the trails and in the villages by the Indians themselves.[8] Moravian witnesses wrote:

> They poured this horrid drink, by the pint, down their throats . . . Several times, indeed, we tried by kindness to restrain them from their dreadful drinking. But in vain, and when we did not cease making protestation to them in order to dissuade them from their drinking, they got angry and told us to leave them alone . . . They screamed all night in the woods and acted like madmen. No one who has not seen an Indian drunk can possibly have any conception of it. It is as if they had all been changed into evil spirits . . . If the hurtful beverage was not brought in by the traders, it was not too far for the Indians, when about to celebrate certain heathen festivals, to go four or five days' journey to the Ohio River and bring from five to six horse loads, after which the whole Indian village concerned would be plunged into the most pitiful and terrible state, since nearly all the inhabitants of both sexes, children and minors not excepted, gave themselves over to drink, and people from other Indian towns

came on horseback to assist in the wickedness, which seldom passed off without wounds and bumps, yes, and seldom without homicide and murder.[9]

The mission's literal death blow came from the heavy influence of the Shawnee Indian prophet Tenskwatawa, brother of Tecumseh, and finally from a personal visit of Tenskwatawa in March of 1806.[10]

> [Tenskwatawa] called himself a prophet and said that he knew everything that had happened and what was now happening and that he had been sent by the Great Spirit to hold a court of judgment, and drive away all bad men. Now a time of suffering began; no one was safe either day or night. It seemed as though the very air was full of evil spirits. Murder and arson were the order of the day. An old Delaware chief was burned alive before our eyes, and our interpreter, Brother Joshua, had also to end his life in the flames. Moreover, an old Indian sister fell a sacrifice to their superstition. We ourselves never knew at what hour we too would be murdered and for 6 long mos. had to hide ourselves almost every night in the woods.[11]

The Moravian missionaries actually waited for permission from church authorities before they would abandon the work among the Delawares. Their diary for September of 1806 included this entry.

> 15th. The pack horses were loaded and on the 16th, toward noon, we left the White River. Before doing so, however, we once more recalled the many proofs of the gracious assistance and protection of our dear Lord and Saviour which we enjoyed here during the 5 years and 4 months of our stay in this place. We had much to be grateful for in many respects, and with a feeling of shame and sadness in our hearts, we thanked Him for all His help and commended our seedtime of tears to Him. With this our mission here came to a close.[12]

They returned to Pennsylvania to further assignments in church service, the Luckes with three babies born among the Indians at the White River Mission.

Indiana Moravians at Hope

Moravians wrote a second significant chapter in Indiana's religious history, this time among the white Moravian settlers moving west. It was a crucial experiment in use of Moravian church funds for "home mission" to support the foundation of a new model of congregation. A Moravian historian said: "Had a deaf ear been turned at this time, it is likely that church extension would have perished stillborn, and the Moravian Church in America might have gradually shrivelled into a sect interesting chiefly if not exclusively to the antiquarian."[13]

The key missionary experimenter for Indiana was Martin Hauser. Beginning about 1825 some Moravian families had come from the South to Haw Creek and Flatrock townships in Bartholomew County in Indiana. They were from Moravian communities at Salem and at Hope in North Carolina. They were attracted to cheap and fertile land in an area free of slavery. Martin Hauser came from Salem to visit his family and friends in Bartholomew County in 1828 and found them eager to have a Moravian pastor. Hauser was no pastor but he was willing to fill the immediate need for a religious leader. He had ideas of his own about effective Moravian operations on the American frontier. He had been awakened to religion in the national Sunday school movement of the 1820s and was a champion of Sunday schools which could be led by laymen. He resisted what he considered the current Moravian notion that "only those brought up at the feet of Gamaliel or had D.D. affixed to their name, is properly called to officiate in public."[14]

Hauser felt that the self-sufficient and exclusive communities of Moravians, as they were then known in Europe and in the eastern United States, were poorly adapted to frontier conditions. The scattered settlement of private families in the American West required active evangelists gathering congregations of individual settlers in the American style. From the Provincial Elders' Conference of the Moravians at Salem, North Carolina, he got his credentials to be lay leader for the Moravian group in Indiana. From Ludwig David von Schweinitz, Moravian administrator of church property at Bethlehem, Pennsylvania, he got $200 in cash to purchase 160 acres of land in Bartholomew County. This land was to be a center for the new Moravian community of Goshen and to support a ministry for that new congregation.

Von Schweinitz of the Moravian headquarters in Pennsylvania took a lively interest in the project. In 1831 he traveled to Indiana himself to formally organize the congregation and to administer the sacraments in the new log church. His journal for the trip offered interesting commentary on both the religious life and the plant life of Indiana; he was an ordained clergyman and a trained botanist. Hauser had no formal theological education and little formal education of any kind but in 1833 he was invited east to Bethlehem, Pennsylvania, for ordination. He became Indiana's first settled Moravian pastor.[15]

The first mail arrived at Goshen's new post office on 10 March 1834; Hauser was the first postmaster. From postal authorities the Moravians learned that there was already a Goshen post office in the state so they changed their town's name to Hope. It was the oldest and has remained the largest Moravian congregation in Indiana, later augmented by three others in Marion County. The Moravians at Hope operated three schools in succession between 1841 and 1881. One of the schools was served as principal by John Henry Kluge whose birthplace was that early Moravian Indian Mission on White River.[16]

Martin Hauser lived to be seventy-six but he did not spend his mature years as regular pastor at Hope. He resigned in 1837 and was succeeded by William Eberman in November of 1838. Much of his remaining thirty-seven years he spent on "Diaspora trips" visiting frontier clusters of Moravians—Enon, Tough Creek, New Holland, Coleman's and Warren's schoolhouses in Indiana; West Salem, Woods Prairie, Wannboro, Albion, Olney in Illinois. Always he was raising the consciousness of Moravians about home mission needs. The patterns of congregational organization and of church extension which he advocated and pioneered in Indiana found only partial acceptance by Moravians generally. However, similar strategies were useful in later Moravian work, especially among the German settlers in Wisconsin.[17]

NOTES

1. Edward Langton, *History of the Moravian Church: The Story of the First International Protestant Church* (London: George Allen and Unwin, 1956), 11–54.

2. Langton, *History*, 59–68, 74–75.

3. David A. Schattschneider, "Yesterday's Lessons and Tomorrow's Mission," *Transactions of the Moravian Historical Society* 24 (1986): 47–58; John T. Hamilton, *A History of the Church Known as the Moravian Church* (Bethlehem, Pa.: Times Publishing Co., 1900,

631 p.); John T. Hamilton, *A History of the Unitas Fratrum, or Moravian Church, in the United States of America*, American Church History Series, vol. 8 (New York: Christian Literature Co., 1895), 429; Langton, *History* 93.

4. Hamilton, *History of the Church*, 80–82, 138–43, 241.

5. Lawrence H. Gipson, *The Moravian Indian Mission on White River: Diaries and Letters May 5, 1799, to November 12, 1806* (Indianapolis, Ind.: Indiana Historical Bureau, 1938), 5–11.

6. David Zeisberger, *Diary of David Zeisberger, a Moravian Missionary among the Indians of Ohio*, 2 vols. (Cincinnati, Ohio: Robert Clark and Co., 1885), 2:496, 500–2; Arthur W. Brady, "The Moravian Mission Settlement in Indiana," *Proceedings of the Mississippi Valley Historical Association* vol. 10, pt. 2 (1919–20): 287; Gipson, *Moravian Indian Mission*, 12–13.

7. Elma E. Gray, *Wilderness Christians: The Moravian Mission to the Delaware Indians* (Ithaca, N.Y.: Cornell University Press, 1956), 197–99; Brady, "Moravian Mission," 289; Gipson, *Moravian Indian Mission*, 86–101, 617. Gipson's work contains translation of substantial selections from the diaries and correspondence and from the autobiographies of Luckenbach and Kluge.

8. Gipson, *Moravian Indian Mission*, 18–19, 92–96; Brady, "Moravian Mission," 292.

9. Gipson, *Moravian Indian Mission*, 94, 96, 610.

10. Gipson, *Moravian Indian Mission*, 17–18, 392–93, 402–3, 407, 438, 556–64.

11. Gipson, *Moravian Indian Mission*, 589–90.

12. Gipson, *Moravian Indian Mission*, 454.

13. Hamilton, *History of the Church*, 358.

14. Earl R. Shay, "Martin Hauser: The Old Pioneer of the New Purchase," *Transactions of the Moravian Historical Society*, vol. 23, pts. 3–4 (1984): 81.

15. Ludwig David Von Schweinitz, *The Journey of Lewis David von Schweinitz to Goshen, Bartholomew County in 1831* (Indianapolis, Ind.: Indiana Historical Society, 1927), 205–85; Shay, "Martin Hauser," 81–86.

16. *History of Bartholomew County, Indiana—1888* (Columbus, Ind.: Avery Press, 1976), 118–21.

17. David A. Schattschneider, "Moravians in the Midwest—1850 to 1900: A New Appreciation," *Transactions of the Moravian Historical Society*, vol. 23, pts. 3–4 (1984): 47–69; Von Schweinitz, *Journey*, 226.

UNITARIAN UNIVERSALISTS

Indiana's early settlement was concurrent with the development of Unitarianism as an American denomination. Though the movements were contemporary they rarely came in touch with each other. The negative reaction to the revivalism of the Great Awakening as illustrated in Boston's Charles Chauncy; the continuous though unofficial drift of New England Congregationalism toward Unitarianism; the appointment of three liberal faculty members at Harvard between 1805 and 1810; William Ellery Channing's manifesto on "Unitarian Christianity" at the ordination of Jared Sparks in 1819; the actual division of congregations and their property from about 1820 to 1840, resulting in an approximate division of 135 Unitarian to 409 Congregational in Massachusetts; the actual organization of the American Unitarian Association in 1825—these were some of the processes and steps in the forming of the Unitarian Church in America.[1]

Hoosiers were certainly not oblivious to all this. Unitarians and their orthodox opponents were remarkably literate. The collective impact of New England journals edited by Unitarians and of authors and preachers and teachers who were Unitarians was very significant for all Americans. Indiana readers of theological journals knew some of the theological issues and some of the literature. A Unitarian paper of excellent quality called the *Western Messenger* issued alternately from Cincinnati and Louisville between 1835 and 1841. The intention of its clergy editors, notably James Freeman Clarke and William Henry Channing, was to inform and elevate the West. It

was a heavy burden. Much of the support for the precarious existence of the *Messenger* had to be collected from New England and from the members of the two western congregations served by the editors. Clarke left Louisville for New England in 1839 lamenting the lack of mental stimulus in the West: "all around me are flat, heavy, worldly, like Dutch marshes, and my feeble taper expires in this moral miasma." Channing's crisis of health and faith took him back to Cambridge, Massachusetts, in 1841 "for silence and rest, in which to seek for deeper truth and larger wisdom on all subjects."[2]

Unitarian Missionary Efforts in the West

Eastern Unitarians did care about the West. After they united to form the American Unitarian Association in Boston in 1825, they dispatched "a sturdy theological student" from Cambridge on a "mission of inquiry." This Moses G. Thomas did not assert his identity by preaching but he traveled all the way to St. Louis in 1826, half the distance through the twelve states on horseback. He reported much opportunity for Unitarians, including good possibilities at St. Louis and Cincinnati and Louisville and Indianapolis and elsewhere in the eastern part of Indiana if good ministers could be had.

> Because I have mentioned the foregoing places as favorable for missionary efforts I would have no person think that a preacher would immediately step into a fine meeting house or into ample means of support or even

into a church already organized; but rather into places where some have neglected religion because they have heard it presented in a manner repugnant to their reason and their conscience, others because they have seen it made a matter of "experiences," confessions and creeds, an austere, exclusive and gloomy system; into places where one must labor as becometh a minister of the gospel and reap the reward of his labors in seeing a church grow up around him. Preachers at first may promise themselves hearers in all these places but it will depend on their own powers whether they interest and retain them.[3]

Sixteen years after Thomas made his ride and report there were Unitarian churches established at St. Louis, Cincinnati, and Louisville but none at Indianapolis or elsewhere in Indiana.

Unitarians surveying the West were long intrigued by the New Light Christians, also known in Indiana as Christian Connection, "old" Christians, Christ-yans, New Lights, Marshallites, and Stoneites. These were a combination of (1) a New England group of "Christians" organized by Baptists Abner Jones and Elias Smith; (2) a southern group of "Christians" being the Republican Methodists of James O'Kelly renamed; and (3) a group of "Christians" emerging from Kentucky under the leadership of Presbyterian Barton W. Stone. There were thousands of these in Indiana. Unitarians rightly observed that many of them resisted the doctrine of the Trinity as they resisted any and all sophistication of formulation beyond the bare wording of the New Testament as they understood it. Critics of New Light Christians often accused them of being Unitarians. Unitarian James Clarke of Boston said in 1843: "Their cause is identical with ours [but] they are able to do more to advance it among certain classes of society. They are breaking the rough land and gradually preparing it for the higher cultivation we may give it." However, linkage with these sons of revival was not easy or natural for New England Unitarians. Even after the Unitarians cooperated with the New Light Christians to establish a theological school at Meadville just south of Lake Erie in Pennsylvania in 1844, few additional members or missionary preachers were gained from that fellowship for Unitarianism in Indiana. In Indiana the New Lights did not become readers of Unitarian publications and become Unitarians. They became readers of Alexander Campbell's publications and became Campbellites.[4]

George W. Julian, congressman from a heavily Quaker district in Indiana and leader of Hoosiers against slavery, expressed his personal indebtedness to the Unitarians. In 1843 there was no Unitarian congregation in the state but in that year Julian found a volume of the works of William Ellery Channing on the table of a law office in his home town of Centerville, Indiana. "It was a new revelation and at once breathed into me a new life," he said. He read other Unitarian books; he subscribed to three Unitarian periodicals; he sent to Boston and to Cincinnati for Unitarian tracts. He claimed that his hostility to slavery and his zeal against oppression and inequality were fired by such reading. But he proved to be no organizational pillar for the Unitarian denomination in Indiana. Julian was a seeker on a long migration from his Quaker youth and from his Methodist environment to eventual rejection of "every form and quality of supernaturalism." Having passed the age of seventy, in 1888, he acknowledged that "Unitarianism as a sect" had been an appreciated way station on his religious pilgrimage. "As a powerful and heroic protest against false dogmas, and a great stride towards the inevitable goal of Free Thought, I honor it," he said, "and thank it, more than words can express."[5]

Unitarian missionary work in the West did become more deliberate and better supported but continued to lag in Indiana. By 1869 there was a Unitarian congregation at Evansville and one at Indianapolis, thanks especially to the leadership of a western secretary of the American Unitarian Association named Carlton A. Staples. After a year of hesitation when Henry Blanchard left its ministry in 1877 and fifteen years of hesitation after George W. Cooke resigned in 1880, the Indianapolis church was reorganized in 1903, taking a place of community leadership. The federal religious census of 1906 reported 4 Unitarian organizations in Indiana with a total of 253 members—compared to Massachusetts with 189 organizations, Illinois with 22, Michigan with 13, and Iowa with 13. When the Universalist preacher Elmo Arnold Robinson arrived in Indianapolis in 1914 "a Rev. Mr. Wicks in Indianapolis was the sole Unitarian minister in the state." The census in the depression year of 1936 reported only one Unitarian organization in Indiana with 465 members. Thereafter church extension steadied—there were churches at Indianapolis, Evansville, Fort Wayne, South Bend, and there was a special effort to organize fellowships at university centers such as Bloomington and West Lafayette.[6]

Universalists

During Indiana's early years Universalism was much the stronger. When the Unitarians had two organizations in Indiana in 1870, the Universalists had about forty. Elmo

Robinson's survey of Universalism in Indiana in 1917 listed 255 "Universalist ministers who have lived in Indiana, together with the places where they have preached." At least 200 of them were nineteenth century preachers, typically part time and for a brief tenure.[7]

These Universalists were not generally the intellectual elite with the look of New England established clergy. They were more often recruits from the humbler eastern countryside and small towns, often disaffected Baptists or Christians or Methodists with very little formal education. They were Jeffersonian Anti-Federalists while the New England Unitarians were Federalists. They were in the denominational tradition of James Relly of London (1722–1778) and John Murray of New England (1741–1815) and Elhanan Winchester of Philadelphia (1751–1797) and Hosea Ballou of Boston (1771–1852), Universalists who affirmed a positive determinism that all would be saved no matter what their conduct or preference and denied the possibility of eternal punishment for any person. A Universalist profession of faith was approved at Winchester, New Hampshire, in 1803.

Article I. We believe that the Holy Scriptures of the Old and New Testament contain a revelation of the character of God, and of the duty, interest and final destination of mankind.

Article II. We believe that there is one God, whose nature is Love, revealed in one Lord Jesus Christ, by one Holy Spirit of Grace, who will finally restore the whole family of mankind to holiness and happiness.

Article III. We believe that holiness and true happiness are inseparably connected, and that believers ought to be careful to maintain order and practice good works; for these things are good and profitable unto men.[8]

Hosea Ballou said one of the excellencies of this formulation was its very ambiguity. It left room for variation about how much punishment there might be short of eternal, ranging from none at all in the doctrine of Hosea Ballou to fifty thousand years of purgation in that of Elhanan Winchester. That was not nearly long enough for most early Unitarians and orthodox Christians who believed that eternal punishment for those who elected sin and rejected the gospel was both scriptural and right. Further, the threat of eternal punishment after death was considered an important and probably essential motivation to morality and amendment of conduct in earthly life.[9]

There was also room in the Winchester Profession for variety in the extent to which Universalists accepted the inspiration and authority of the Bible. Universalists influenced by Deism, as Ballou was by the writings of Ethan Allen, were more inclined to make human reason the primary religious authority. That was a minority view in the early years.[10] Most nineteenth century Universalist ministers in Indiana accepted the Bible as authoritative and were expert at hurling proof texts. Universalist minister John H. Blackford described such ministry even in the latter half of the century.

Everywhere we were met by hostile, aggressive, often unfair opposition. Oral debates were common. Our preachers were compelled to qualify themselves to meet this opposition. The Bible was the arsenal from which they drew the weapons of their warfare. David was not more skillful with his sling than were they with Bible proofs in support of their contention. Goliath did not more certainly go down under the unerring aim of David than did the idea of a personal devil and an endless hell writhe in pain and die under the clear presentation and convincing logic of these early preachers. Those preachers knew the Bible. It was their textbook. They believed in it. When a proposition demanded a "thus saith the Lord" a "thus saith the Lord" was forthcoming.[11]

Universalist churches were congregational in polity with each church free to run its own affairs. In much of the West and certainly in Indiana there were few substantial Universalist congregations to serve as models, guides, and service points for all these independent groups in their denominational life. In 1834 the convention in New England became the General Convention of Universalists in the United States but for decades it had small resources for outreach to the West. Regional associations and conventions waxed and waned, gradually being superseded by the various state conventions. Until late in the nineteenth century Universalist ministers seemed to function as free agents, feeling little discipline or support from the loose ecclesiastical network.[12]

In Indiana other denominations were usually at work and to some degree established before the Universalist preachers arrived. To those frontier churches laboring to orient the lives of settlers in terms of orthodox beliefs energized by revivals, the Universalists seemed dangerous and subversive. Things were difficult enough without these invaders bringing confusion and division and loss of immortal souls. When Universalist preacher George Rogers knocked on many doors in Madison in 1837 trying to sell subscriptions to the *Sentinel and Star in the West* issued from Cincinnati, he found nobody was buying. Some citizens did ask where the paper was coming from and then said they were at least glad it was not being published any nearer.[13]

Two Lutheran pastors in Indiana came under the influence of the Universalist paper *Star in the West* published in Cincinnati, to the distress and disruption of the Lutheran Synod of Indiana. Eighty-six letters from Presbyterian missionaries in Indiana to their New York headquarters reported on the dangers of western Universalism. Charles Beecher said that Universalists, sharp set for debate, "trip up the clumsy circuit rider with his year's worth of spiritual provender." Some people were confused by such conflict, he said, but some looked on with glee at the theological cockfight. Baptists and Methodists and Christians developed and shared defensive techniques against Universalists. A body of polemical literature appeared.[14]

In some instances unrecognized Universalist preachers simply played the role of itinerant ministers without identifying themselves with the dreaded word "Universalist." But they came to assume hostility in almost every place and to demand hostility and to use the leverage of it to their own advantage. Finding any gathering of people, be it a congregation at church or a crowd celebrating the Fourth of July, they would rise to announce their intentions to offer one or a series of discourses. Early in the process they were likely to challenge another preacher or to be challenged by one. This guaranteed both a hearing and a crowd. There might be a single exchange or a series of exchanges or even a formal debate extended over several days with the possibility of publication. Elmo Robinson compiled a listing of thirty-two major formal debates involving Universalists in Indiana alone.[15]

In August of 1829 Universalist preachers Josiah Waldo and Jonathan Kidwell were "utterly unable to provoke the Methodists into debate at Louisville. In the process however of housing themselves and hassling the Methodists they gained a good audience and a good house." Things went better for Kidwell on a visit to Indianapolis in the winter of 1829. He preached several times in the State House, got challenged by a young Methodist named Edwin Ray, saw the state legislature adjourn so its members could attend the debate, and published his version of the substance of the speeches as *A Series of Strictures* which became a major propaganda piece for western Universalists.[16]

Jonathan Kidwell

Jonathan Kidwell was the first major contributor to Universalism in Indiana. He had been a Methodist preacher and then a Christian preacher but by 1815 he was on the circuit as a Universalist. Though he moved near Abington in Wayne County, Indiana, in 1826, he traveled seven

counties in eastern Indiana and nine in western Ohio as well as the environs of Louisville. As early as 1829 Kidwell claimed that the number of Universalists in his territory had increased from 200 to 2,000; he reported that in one season five Universalist church buildings were being erected. He was a leader in the Western Convention of Universalists which included Ohio and all the territory to the west. When the first Indiana State Convention was established in 1837, he was its president. Yet his place in the national Universalist fellowship was always marginal. He was an unceasing publicist, editor of papers called *Star in the West*, *Sentinel and Star in the West*, *Philomath Encyclopedia*, *Genius of Liberty*, and *Independent Universalist*. By 1831 his *Sentinel and Star in the West* had agents in twenty-two Indiana towns.[17]

To his delight, much of what Kidwell published in his papers was an affront to his denominational opponents. One of his favorite productions was his story of the good and simple girl named Amanda who was scared to a terrible death by the hellfire preaching of an Arminian and the predestinarian preaching of a Calvinist. Nor did he mind being an embarrassment to his fellow Universalists. He felt that the eastern Universalists seeking to strengthen their General Convention were constantly trying to dictate to Universalists in the West. He would tolerate none of that. Yankees were also inclined to abolitionism and for Kidwell abolitionism was a form of "political insanity."[18]

Kidwell was a defender of Robert Owen and of many of Owen's views about organized Christianity, agreeing that Jesus Christ was simply a man and that affirmation of his oneness with God was "a gross corruption of primitive christianity." He said the Pentateuch of the Old Testament was "a heterogeneous mass of vague traditions combined with Jewish history." He discarded the biblical account of creation, campaigned against the observation of Sunday as a special religious day, denied the divine inspiration of all the Scriptures, and rejected all supernatural revelation. For him the sacraments were "useless lumber." The Lord's Supper, even as a symbolic or memorial gesture, was intolerable, "nothing but a mock-supper; the mere relic of Papal ignorance and superstition . . . a piece of Catholic mummery."[19]

In 1832 Kidwell was commissioned by two western bodies to obtain subscriptions and to find a location for a Universalist school to be free from domination of all orthodox clergy and their theologies. He found and purchased the remains of a deserted town site called Bethlehem a few miles south of Richmond, Indiana. He changed its name to Philomath. His plan was to make Philomath the home of western Universalism, the location of the academy named Western Union Seminary, and the publication place of the *Sentinel and Star in the West*. The Western Universalist Convention held its 1833 meeting at Philomath. By 1836 the academy had two professors and a two-story brick building. In 1837 the town got a post office with Kidwell in charge. But the plan went awry. The *Star* returned to Cincinnati and came under new editorship hostile to Kidwell. The school attracted more criticism than support, leaving its sponsors and Kidwell deeply in debt at its failure.[20]

In the decade of the 1840s the leadership of Indiana's Universalists shifted from the native Kentuckian Kidwell and his pioneer supporters to a new echelon of preachers from the East. Cincinnati became their missionary center. George Rogers made Cincinnati his home base from 1836 to 1846. Though he seemed always itinerating, he functioned as an editor for the *Sentinel and Star in the West*, now critical of Kidwell. Rogers organized a Universalist society at Patriot, Indiana; he and his fellow editor Samuel Tizzard did a preaching tour in four counties of Indiana in 1837. John A. Gurley, minister for the First Universalist Society in Cincinnati, edited the *Star in the West* at Cincinnati from 1838 to 1854 and made it the leading Universalist paper of the area while the influence of Kidwell was fading.[21]

Enoch M. Pingree, a quiet young convert to Universalism from New Hampshire, learned the basics of frontier rhetoric in Ohio in the late 1830s and went on to become what his biographer called "considering his age . . . the most celebrated and successful controversialist in the world." Pingree said "I changed my manner of preaching from a quiet, dull, harmless reading of sermons, to a far more energetic, positive, and extemporaneous manner—so that I was called boisterous by some of my more quietly disposed friends." His manuscript book entitled "Controversial Theology" illustrated his method of overpowering opponents with outpourings of biblical texts. For about a decade he was an exciting Universalist presence on Indiana's southern fringe. The *Christian Teacher* for July of 1842 reported: "There has recently been a debate in Madison, Ia., between Br. Pingree, of Cincinnati, Ohio, and Rev. J. O'Kane, of Crawfordsville, Ia., which continued seven days and a half. The fruits of it—a Universalist society, consisting of 30 members, and nearly subscription enough to build a Universalist meeting house in Madison. Truth loses nothing by investigation." Pingree preached beside the Ohio River at Patriot and debated for five days with the Campbellite B. U. Watkins at Rising Sun. His published debates were part of the Universalist stock in trade of editor John A. Burley at the

Star in the West in Cincinnati. Pingree's pastorate at Louisville began in spring of 1843 but was limited by his poor health which led to his premature death in January of 1849.[22]

Erasmus Manford

It was Erasmus Manford who did most to displace Kidwell and to link the Universalists of Indiana to their national fellowship. After Manford came from New England and was itinerating from the hub of Universalist activity at Cincinnati in 1837, George Rogers encouraged him to take a tour of Indiana. His summary of his first tour of the state, from the middle of May through December of 1838, was "traveled twelve hundred miles—all on horseback—delivered one hundred and ten discourses, and received for compensation, one hundred and fifty dollars." For the next dozen years Indiana was to become his primary field and home base. "I have traveled through its length and its breadth," he said, "and preached in nearly every town within its borders."[23]

Jonathan Kidwell was established as a key leader of Universalists in eastern Indiana long before Manford arrived. Conflict between the two may have been inevitable. Kidwell was probably the least educated of the western Universalist ministers, admitting without apology that he was "an unpolished son of the forest . . . raised in the back-woods of Kentucky, under the hooting of the owl and the war-whoop of the red man, without even common education." Even his friend and admirer George W. Julian referred to the "occasional irruption into the neighborhood" of Kidwell, "soundly hated by all orthodox people . . . a man almost wholly without education but possessed of a broad and vigorous grasp of mind, a natural lover of controversy, and a perfect master of invective." On the other hand, Manford was probably the best educated of the western Universalist missionaries, having been apprenticed under three Massachusetts clergy.[24]

Kidwell was a zealous publisher, promoting his *Philomath Encyclopedia*, bruised by the recent loss of his *Star in the West* to Cincinnati, and at odds with the easterners Rogers, Gurley, and Pingree who had become leaders and publishers there. Manford also became Kidwell's publishing competitor. He said "I made Lafayette, Ind., the center of my operations, and commenced the publication of the *Christian Teacher*, a monthly publication of twenty-four pages, at one dollar per year. The first number was issued April, 1841."[25] Manford's paper came to be called in turn the *Christian Teacher*, *Western Olive Branch*, *Golden Era*,

Manford's Magazine, and *Manford's Monthly Magazine*. It was published successively at Lafayette (1841), Terre Haute (1843), Indianapolis (1846), Cincinnati (1848), Saint Louis (1850), and Chicago (1864). He was a particular friend of Rogers, Gurley, and Pingree at Cincinnati.

Kidwell concluded that such easterners as Manford and the Cincinnati group intended to put him out of the Universalist fellowship. He called them "silk-stocking gentry sent out West to enlighten the brethren." Manford he called a "conspirator," a "little bishop," and "this little excuse of a man." In return the easterners publicized Kidwell's extreme views on the sacraments, on the Scriptures, and on the person of Jesus Christ. They challenged not only his orthodoxy but also his claims to be an effective missionary.[26] Manford's paper said:

> What has been the result of his long residence here, and his preaching? How many churches has he been instrumental in gathering? How many meeting-houses have been built where he has labored much? We hesitate not to say, that not one flourishing church has been organized by him, and not one meeting-house has been erected where he has preached much. These are facts. There are about twenty-five churches in this state that are prospering, and most of them have been gathered within the past two years, by preachers who have moved here within that time.[27]

Kidwell had wielded great influence in the Indiana State Convention of Universalists formed in 1837 and in its component associations. In 1841 this pioneer Indiana convention responded with Kidwellian bias to a proposition for more unification under the General Convention: "Resolved, That the Universalists of Indiana are of age and consider themselves capable of self-government, and therefore can not submit to any dictation or control, either on the part of our brothers in the east or elsewhere, and that our delegates to the United States Convention be so instructed."[28] Kidwell was able to use the old state convention organizations to bring charges against Manford in 1846 and 1847 and to act to suspend him from the Universalist fellowship.

Manford responded to Kidwell's tactics by calling a meeting at his home in Indianapolis on 12 May 1848 where a new Universalist Convention of Indiana was formed, this one free of the influence of Kidwell and fully affiliated with the General Convention. Members of the new state convention asserted the necessity of accepting the authority of the Bible and expressed their support for Sunday schools. Kidwell died in 1849 and soon thereafter his printing press was destroyed by fire. The old

state convention, which had been Kidwell's base, dwindled and died while the new convention continued to meet annually to consider its agenda of denominational business.[29] Years later Manford wrote in summary:

> The strife between the Northern and Southern people, which ultimated in the late rebellion, disturbed the Universalist denomination in Indiana long before the war commenced. The contention though was not about slavery, but grew out of the antagonism between people from those two sections of country. Southern and Central Indiana was settled chiefly by emigrants from the South, and unfortunately they cherished prejudices against the Yankees. The Indiana State Convention would not join the United States Convention, because it was controlled by Northern people . . . After the new order of things was inaugurated, peace and harmony reigned in our councils, and the good cause was more prosperous.[30]

During his years in Indiana Erasmus Manford was an abrasive controversialist who seemed in perpetual motion. On his 300-mile circuit in western Indiana from his home in Lafayette; on his 900-mile trip to Terre Haute, Indianapolis, Richmond, Madison, and the Green River region in Kentucky; in his regimen of visiting nearly every Indiana county annually from his base in Indianapolis—he called horseback his favorite mode of locomotion and the saddle his home. From Lafayette in 1841 he published eighteen "Questions to Calvinists," all meant to be embarrassing. He compiled a list of thirteen respects in which "Calvinism and Popery" agreed. He wrote a very hostile description of a Methodist camp meeting which he attended about one mile from Ladoga, Indiana.[31]

Manford's *Twenty-five Years in the West* recorded in detail how he answered every objection and demolished all who dared to offer a rejoinder. He overcame a Christian at Connersville on page 64, a Quaker at Richmond on page 92, a Presbyterian at Frankfort on page 104, a Methodist Protestant at Lafayette on page 119, an Adventist at Franklin on page 182, and a Mormon near Terre Haute on page 211. He lashed back at Episcopalian opponents in Michigan City.

> In one of my lectures I gave a history of the "rise and progress" of the Episcopal Church. Stated that it was conceived in sin and brought forth in iniquity; that Henry VIII., universally admitted to have been the most beastly monarch that ever reigned in England, was the first Episcopalian, and the father of the sect; that church from Henry's day to this day has been a proud, arrogant, insolent, overbearing concern; in England it draws half of its support from unwilling pockets, from those who belong to other communions; that it cares not who

starves provided its priests, bishops, and lords live in indolence, race horses, chase foxes, and drink brandy; it never took but one short step from the Catholic Church, the mother of harlots, and it was creeping back into the arms of its old mamma.[32]

He reported in some detail on a missionary trip in 1843 to Spencer, Gosport, Bloomington, Martinsville, Morgantown, Franklin, Columbus, and Nashville. "In all these places the liberal faith had not before been preached," he said. "This was a laborious journey, for it was war, war, from the beginning to the end of it."[33] In the book Manford identified his antagonists by name and included a summary of their texts and arguments as well as his own.

In 1847 Manford published at Indianapolis a volume of 223 pages embodying his controversial letter exchange with Presbyterian Enoch Kingsbury and with a substitute for Kingsbury named H. Vincent. The next year his three-day debate with Campbellite Benjamin Franklin was published verbatim at Indianapolis in a volume of 368 pages.[34] Franklin began by expressing the widespread frontier concern about Universalism. He felt compelled to debate, he said, because "I most solemnly believe my positions to be true, and that the positions of my opponent are not only untrue, but detrimental to the morals of the country, the safety and happiness of man, in his relations to his family, the citizens of the community at large, and the civil government under which he lives, as well as his happiness in the world to come."[35]

Mrs. Erasmus (Hannah) Manford was an educated New York native, a convinced Universalist, a writer, a lecturer, and a teacher. Erasmus gave her full recognition as a publishing partner "writing editorial, helping mail the paper, and keeping the books." He said a woman should have equal rights to education, to ordination, to "sue and be sued, buy and sell, vote at the polls, and be president of these United States, if she can get votes enough."[36]

Evaluations of Universalism in Indiana

Universalist historians have pondered the reasons for the relative weakness of Universalism as an American denomination and its weakness in Indiana as a case in point. Given a history with a lively publication program, with leadership from urban centers at Cincinnati and Louisville, with a large investment in itineration, with a long list of preachers resident for a time in the state, with a state convention continuous from 1848 and administering some budget for missionary activity from 1891, with substantial efforts for the founding of Universalist schools at Philomath in the 1830s and at Logansport

about 1870, why did Elmo Robinson find Universalism at such a low ebb in Indiana when he came to be Universalist minister at Anderson and Pendleton in 1914? Only Indianapolis, Muncie, and Logansport had full time Universalist ministers that year. Many rural churches were merely maintaining a building for infrequent services.[37] The federal religious censuses recorded the decline in Indiana from 44 Universalist organizations with 2,506 members in 1906, to 24 organizations with 1,656 members in 1916, to 15 organizations with 1,286 members in 1926, to 8 organizations with 795 members in 1936. Total Universalist expenditures for the whole state of Indiana in 1936 were reported as $3,171, lowest in the list of states except for Georgia and Kentucky.

In fact the Universalist General Convention had been unable to provide effective direction anywhere until the 1860s and even then its efforts in Indiana were not sufficiently supported to produce systematic church extension. The Universalist church in Indianapolis lacked strength to assume its natural position of leadership. Jonathan Kidwell and Erasmus Manford and Abner H. Longley preached at Indianapolis but during many of the crucial early years there was no regular pastor. Benjamin F. Foster led Indianapolis Universalists between 1853 and 1869, "the most eminent clergyman of the denomination in Indiana." But Foster's position as state librarian was his full time obligation. As late as 1873 the Indianapolis church received financial assistance from the General Convention to assure its survival.[38]

State conventions and association meetings were prone to strenuous independence. It was Indiana Convention which exhorted the General Convention "to urge, by all suitable and proper means, the assumption of a general missionary work" in 1865. But when the inevitable request came from General Convention for funds to support a missionary program, Indiana took the request under advisement.[39] Individual preachers were accustomed to independence, early ones like Kidwell and Manford making freewheeling sweeps over great distances seeking subscribers to their papers.

The very power of the Universalists in controversy became cause for regret. The year before he died George Rogers of Cincinnati published his memoirs and allowed himself "the presumption of adventuring some advice" to his Universalist colleagues. He lamented "a majority of the polemical ebullitions" to which the people were compelled to listen by the hour.[40]

> To young preachers the inducement is strong to show off their smartness at the expense of opposing creeds: those creeds themselves, by their absurdities, often furnish a

large part of the temptation, and the gratification to the preacher's vanity, afforded by the approving smiles and nods, and after-meeting commendations of the auditors, fully makes up the residue. But ah, me! how little worth is this sort of incense! From whom comes it in general? From the wise? the good? the sincere? the lover of Christ's cause? Seldom from either. More generally, rather, from those who would applaud Paine's ribaldries, at the expense of all religion; from those who would grin approvingly at the insidious sneers of Hume and Gibbon; or indulge in full-mouthed laughter at the *Ecce Homo* of Chubb. The preacher is in bad keeping with his cause, methinks, who panders to the liking of such as these. That preaching doubtless is best, which most tends to lodge useful truths in the minds of the hearers, and which does this in a way most compatible with christian kindness to all.[41]

In their freedom many individual Universalist members or constituents were also little inclined to the kind of discipline in participation and support on which strong churches depended. Universalist historian Elmo Robinson of Anderson, Indiana, said:

Every truth may be abused; the acceptance of the negative elements of Universalism without a grasping of its affirmations produced "anti-hellians," who were often against every policy of denominational expansion and in favor of nothing . . . Church membership as an essential to future individual salvation was rejected; church membership as an opportunity to work for present social salvation was an ideal rarely visioned. Hence the most prominent Universalists were often not members of their own organization, and their children and grandchildren joined other churches.[42]

The Universalist campaign against the doctrine of eternal punishment of the damned also lost much of its urgency when the preaching or teaching of that doctrine simply went out of fashion. Protestants generally came to hold it gingerly, if at all, relegating it to historic formulations in bound books rarely opened. A policy of silence made universalists of all.[43]

Unitarian Universalist Union

Unitarians and Universalists, long diversified and divided among themselves, came increasingly to see common ground. Advocates of doctrines of the Trinity, or of biblical authority based on divine revelation, or of vicarious atonement linked to the death of Jesus Christ, or of the possibility of punishment for or purgation of sin after death—these had generally died out or withdrawn from both fellowships. Having given over ideas of special reve-

lation or infallible Scriptures, they adjusted easily to the claims of the expanding sciences and biblical criticism. Both sought a world of justice, peace, and plenty, focusing their support for that world reformation on human agencies since no divine presence or person was expected to intervene. They saw obvious advantages to cooperation with each other in their religious education and publishing activities.[44]

After years of discussion and negotiation the American Unitarian Association and the Universalist Church of America fully consolidated as the Unitarian Universalist Association in 1961. There were about 115,000 members of the newly merged denomination in the United States and Canada. A national survey of denomination opinion was reported in 1967.

Only 2.9 percent of the respondents believed God a 'supernatural being,' 23.1 percent chose to see God in Paul Tillich's terms as "the ground of all being." But 28.0 percent saw God as "an irrelevant concept" and 1.8 percent saw God as an actually "harmful" concept. The largest percentage (44.2 percent) took the middle ground of agreeing that "God may be appropriately used as a name for some natural processes within the universe, such as love or creative evolution" . . . Very few (10.5 percent) classed immortality as part of their belief; a majority (56.9 percent) would not define their religion as "Christian." Although 11.2 percent preferred the denomination to move closer toward either "liberal Protestantism" or "the ecumenical movement within Christianity," a large majority preferred a movement toward "an emerging universal religion" (36.7 percent) or "a distinctive humanistic religion" (52.0 percent).[45]

By the time of the merger most of the rural Universalist churches in Indiana had died; there were churches with ministers only at Muncie and Oaklandon. Some continuing Universalist families at Manchester, Terre Haute, West Lafayette, and Indianapolis entered the union. Essentially the merged denomination in Indiana was a youthful entity, largely a product of recent church extension by Unitarians. Twelve of the seventeen Unitarian Universalist societies in Indiana in 1970 had been formed since 1939.[46] In 1990 the nine Indiana counties reporting more than one hundred Unitarian Universalist adherents were Marion (1,151), Monroe (402), Delaware (304), Allen (271), Elkhart (178), Lake (170), Tippecanoe (164), St. Joseph (117), and Vanderburgh (103).

NOTES

1. Sydney E. Ahlstrom, *A Religious History of the American People* (New Haven, Conn.: Yale University Press, 1972), 356–57,

390–97; Earl Morse Wilbur, *A History of Unitarianism*, 2 vols. (Cambridge, Mass.: Harvard University Press, 1945–52), 2:379–441.

2. Robert D. Habich, *Transcendentalism and the "Western Messenger": A History of the Magazine and Its Contributors, 1835–1841* (Cranbury, N.J.: Associated University Presses, 1985), 102–3, 148–49; For comment on literary contributions by Unitarians, see *An American Reformation: A Documentary History of Unitarian Christianity*, ed. Sydney E. Ahlstrom and Jonathan S. Carey (Middletown, Conn.: Wesleyan University Press, 1985), xi–xii.

3. Charles H. Lyttle, *Freedom Moves West: A History of the Western Unitarian Conferences, 1852–1952* (Boston: Beacon Press, 1952), 24–25.

4. Henry K. Shaw, *Hoosier Disciples* (St. Louis, Mo.: Bethany Press, 1966), 27–36, 60–71; Lyttle, *Freedom Moves West*, 61.

5. George W. Julian, "A Search after Truth," *Indiana Magazine of History* 32 (September 1936): 250–58.

6. Elmo Arnold Robinson, "A New England Minister in Indiana, 1914–1917," *Indiana Magazine of History* 68 (June 1972): 137; Lyttle, *Freedom Moves West*, 95, 260.

7. Russell E. Miller, *The Larger Hope*, 2 vols. (Boston: Unitarian Universalist Association, 1979–85), 1:703; Elmo Arnold Robinson, "Universalism in Indiana," *Indiana Magazine of History* 13 (March 1917): 1–19, (June 1917): 178–86; Lyttle, *Freedom Moves West*, 95.

8. Miller, *Larger Hope*, 1:45–46.

9. David Robinson, *The Unitarians and the Universalists* (Westport, Conn.: Greenwood Press, 1985), 56–59; Ernest Cassara, *Universalism in America* (Boston: Beacon Press, 1971), 16, 24; Miller, *Larger Hope*, 1:45.

10. Cassara, *Universalism*, 18–21; Miller, *Larger Hope*, 1:127–33.

11. Thomas S. Guthrie, *Life and Works of Rev. Thomas S. Guthrie, D.D.* (Indianapolis, Ind.: Mail Press, 1912), xviii.

12. Cassara, *Universalism*, 28–30; for a list of Universalist associations in Indiana, see Robinson, "Universalism," 12–13.

13. George Rogers, *Memoranda of the Experiences, Labors, and Travels of a Universalist Preacher* (Cincinnati, Ohio: John A. Gurley, 1845), 185; Miller, *Larger Hope*, 1:208, 238, 695.

14. C. R. Defenderfer, *Lutheranism at the Crossroads of America* (N.p., 1948?), 35–41; L. C. Rudolph, Ware William Wimberly, and Thomas W. Clayton, *Indiana Letters*, 3 vols. (Ann Arbor, Mich.: University Microfilms International, 1979), 3:1239; Charles Beecher, Fort Wayne, to Milton Badger, American Home Missionary Society, New York, 28 March 1845; Robinson, "Universalism," 174–76.

15. Erasmus Manford, *Twenty–five Years in the West* (Chicago: E. Manford, 1867), 215–16; Cassara, *Universalism*, 10–11; Robinson, "Universalism," 177.

16. David A. Johnson, *To Preach and Fight* (Tucson, Ariz.: Philomath Press, 1973), 36; Jonathan Kidwell, *A Series of Strictures* (Cincinnati, Ohio: S. Tizzard, 1830), 13–20; Robinson, "Universalism," 5.

17. Robinson, "Universalism," 3–4; according to Robinson the towns were Milton, Richmond, Connersville, Indianapolis, Danville, Greencastle, Eugene, Attica, Lawrenceburg, Covington, Harrison, Patriot, Montezuma, Terre Haute, Leavenworth, Lafayette, Versailles, Bloomington, Rome, Brookville, Somerset, and Logansport.

18. Jonathan Kidwell, *An Original Essay on the Coming of the Son of Man* (Cincinnati, Ohio: n.p., 1830), 70–74; Miller, *Larger Hope*, 1:608, 619; Johnson, *To Preach and Fight*, 44.

19. Miller, *Larger Hope*, 1:207–10; Johnson, *To Preach and Fight*, 43–44.

20. Miller, *Larger Hope*, 1:210–12, 407–10; Robinson, "Universalism," 168; Johnson, *To Preach and Fight*, 40–42.

21. Miller, *Larger Hope*, 1:265, 695.

22. Henry Jewell, *Life and Writings of Rev. Enoch M. Pingree* (Cincinnati, Ohio: Longley and Brother, 1850), 57, 89, 128–49; Miller, *Larger Hope*, 1:695.

23. Manford, *Twenty-five Years*, 44, 60, 73.

24. Miller, *Larger Hope*, 1:209; Julian, "Search after Truth," 251; Manford, *Twenty-five Years*, 13–16.

25. Manford, *Twenty-five Years*, 103.

26. Manford, *Twenty-five Years*, 217; Miller, *Larger Hope*, 1:210; *Christian Teacher* 2 (February 1843): 107–10.

27. *Christian Teacher* 2 (May 1842): 108.

28. Robinson, "Universalism," 16.

29. Robinson, "Universalism," 18–19, 157; Manford, *Twenty-five Years*, 217–19.

30. Manford, *Twenty-five Years*, 217–19.

31. Manford, *Twenty-five Years*, 104, 153, 213; *Christian Teacher*, 1 (August 1841): 104–6; (September 1841): 141–42; (November 1841): 188–91.

32. Manford, *Twenty-five Years*, 131.

33. Manford, *Twenty-five Years*, 170–71.

34. Erasmus Manford, *Theological Discussion between Rev. E. Kingsbury, Presbyterian, and Rev. E. Manford, Universalist, on the Question of Endless Punishment* (Indianapolis, Ind.: E. Manford, 1847, 223 p.); Erasmus Manford, *An Oral Debate on the Coming of the Son of Man, Endless Punishment, and Universal Salvation. Held in Milton, Ind., Oct. 26, 27, and 28, 1847* (Indianapolis, Ind.: Indiana State Journal Steam-Press, 1848, 368 p.).

35. Manford, *Oral Debate*, 3.

36. Manford, *Twenty-five Years*, 213, 274; Miller, *Larger Hope*, 1:537, 558.

37. Cassara, *Universalism*, 28–31; Miller, *Larger Hope*, 1:56–59, 242–53, 480–83, 703, 2:9–29, 355–56, 624–25; Robinson, "New England Minister," 136–37; Robinson, "Universalism," 157–70, 186–87.

38. Miller, *Larger Hope*, 1:702.

39. Miller, *Larger Hope*, 1:258–59.

40. Rogers, *Memoranda*, 396; Miller, *Larger Hope*, 1:202–12, 242–58.

41. Rogers, *Memoranda*, 397.

42. Robinson, "Universalism," 186.

43. Miller, *Larger Hope*, 2:xi; Cassara, *Universalism*, 39–40.

44. Cassara, *Universalism*, 35–43; Miller, *Larger Hope*, 1:783–841, 2:xiii.

45. Robinson, *Unitarians*, 177.

46. The twelve were Fort Wayne (1939), Lafayette (1947), Bloomington (1949), South Bend (1949), Evansville (1951), Rushville (1952), Michigan City (1954), Terre Haute (1955), Elkhart (1961), Richmond (1964), Columbus (1967), and Indianapolis (1971). See Robinson, "New England Minister," 150.

RATIONALISTS

Robert M. Taylor has defined freethinkers as "persons who view institutional religion and its theology, doctrines, clergy, and scriptures as expressions of superstition and irrationality. Trusting in the superiority of natural law and scientific inquiry, freethinkers historically have organized, published, lectured, and debated in an attempt to persuade individuals to cast off the yoke of otherworldly concerns."[1]

Residents at New Harmony were the most famous rationalists in early Indiana. Frontier preachers called New Harmony "that seat of infidelity" and "Satan's seat." Mrs. Abby Soper who lived at New Harmony from 1831 to 1834 said it was the "center of infidelity at the West." Presbyterian Lewis Pennell reported that New Harmony had barely tolerated preaching before 1837 but early in that year he was politely received and heard by "a few leading infidels." The 1829 debate between Alexander Campbell and Robert Owen was for many a symbolic confrontation between Christianity and unbelief.[2]

Indiana Rationalists Reported

But the Owenites were not the only rationalists. Christian workers encountered them in many places. Presbyterian James Duncan saw fit to publish his sophisticated *Dialogue between an Atheist and a Theist* in Indianapolis when that city was in its earliest muddy infancy. Using the dialogue as a literary device, Duncan rehearsed classic proofs of the existence of God and asserted that "atheism

tends so directly to licentiousness, that it supersedes the very being of moral justice; and dissolves all the bonds of society."[3]

That Methodist champion Peter Cartwright reported his besting of "infidels" across the West. Biographies of Indiana's Methodist circuit riders frequently included accounts of such victories. At the risk of his personal safety, James Havens subdued an abusive unbeliever with prayer. Dudley Willetts, a Presbyterian layman gone Universalist gone Deist and then "settled down into bald atheism, having no God, and living in a world which had no God to govern it" for eleven years, had a particular aversion to Methodist mourners' benches and shouting. In a revival meeting led by Methodist revivalist John Kiger, Willetts announced his intention to renounce his atheism and then did so before a crowd of 1,500 witnesses. He finally confirmed his new being by both praying through to assurance of salvation at the mourners' bench and offering shouts of praise.[4]

Eastern missionaries were especially sensitive to evidences of Hoosier unbelief. They saw a western frontier swarming with children and in desperate need of morality, education, and ordered life. They were sure that the remedy lay in conversion to true piety, in Sabbath keeping, in organization of schools with libraries, in Bible distribution and study, in temperance or abstinence regarding alcohol, and in the establishment of churches. That any responsible citizen would refrain from supporting such essential enterprises frustrated them to the point of heartbreak. That any pioneer could face that need and actually work to oppose them was nearly inconceivable. They were almost certainly capable of writing essays on whatever technical distinctions there were among Rationalists, Freethinkers, Agnostics, Skeptics, Deists, Atheists, and Infidels but in practice they seemed to use the designations interchangeably, or to pile them up for effect, or to substitute Universalists as a term equivalent to any of the others. Universalists and Unitarians often answered charges that their churches were stations on the route to complete infidelity.[5]

At least 115 letters from Indiana's nineteenth century Presbyterian missionaries to their headquarters in New York commented on dangerous concentrations of opposing unbelievers. "There is more of religion, morality and orthodoxy at the East," said Nathan L. Lord from Plymouth. "We have more of skepticism, multiform error, and open wickedness." Plymouth was repeatedly reported as a center of "organized infidelity." The infidels there even wanted missionary John M. Bishop to publicize their rationalist lectures. "Infidelity is becoming consolidated in Vincennes," said James R. Alexander in 1830. The works of Thomas Paine were circulating and twenty Vincennes citizens subscribed to an anti-church paper from New York entitled *Priestcraft Unmasked.* Approached with a subscription paper for Alexander's support, one local infidel said he would give something really handsome if Alexander would leave the place. Benjamin C. Cressy wrote from Salem in 1832 that no county abounded in infidelity more than Washington County. "We have the low disciples of Paine and the unblushing Atheist of the Owen school." Cressy's lectures against these evils were "thronged with attentive hearers." Most young men and principal male citizens in Bedford were reported to be infidels in spring of 1834. Cressy preached there also and caused "the very foundations of infidelity to tremble." Vevay was rated a "very hard place" for ministry in 1833, once a stronghold of infidelity. Ulric Maynard said in 1830 that his mission field at Connersville was "flinty," being a "nest of Deists and Universalists," but he was elated that even a professed Deist in the county had given him 50¢ in support of the Sabbath school.[6]

There was a flowering of rationalist activity in the state about mid-century with correlations to increased Universalist activity, to the prominence of Spiritualism, and to an increase in immigrants of overtly irreligious kinds. In the extreme northeast corner of Indiana, in Steuben County, settlers from the lake region of western New York had formed a new kind of town in 1838. A twentieth century social scientist with no bias in favor of organized religion later described it.

> The founders of Aton [Angola] fully intended to exclude churches for all time. Under their influence spiritualism and free-love became dominant; and the village acquired a reputation far and near for irreligion and immorality. It was spoken of as "a hot-bed of infidelity and vice." As late as 1865, it is probable that nine-tenths of the population were spiritualists and given to free-love. During this decade the most noted mediums of the land made Aton their headquarters, among them Abbey Kelley Foster, Mrs. Griffin and Mrs. Seymour. The town newspaper of that time says: "They held many public services, conducted funerals, and did great miracles before the eyes of the public." In 1855 the publication of an "infidel" paper known as *The Truth Seeker* was begun. It was financed by the founder and leading man of Aton. Its motto was "For Free Thought and Free Discussion and Democracy. Against False Theology, Superstition, Bigotry, Ignorance, Aristocracies, Privilege Classes, Tyrannies, Oppression, and Everything that Degrades or Burdens Mankind Mentally or Physically." This paper is described as a "most vile and vicious sheet." It wielded a strong influence for some years and then removed from the town.[7]

Presbyterian missionary Almon Martin said in 1852 that Angola should really be called "Satan's Seat" since it was notable for Sabbath breaking and intemperance and its most influential men were either skeptics or infidels. After Abigail Kelley Foster and her husband Stephen Symonds Foster visited and further stiffened the people's resistance to church organization, Martin concluded that "only a change of inhabitants in Angola" could open it to ministry. He moved on to Ontario in neighboring Lagrange County in 1854. Missionaries Jacob Patch, Henry Warren, and Henry Little gave the same appraisal of the situation in Steuben County. Influential men of Angola were circulating the "infidel writings" of Andrew Jackson Davis; at their own expense they were systematically importing such eastern lecturers as Abigail Kelley Foster and Stephen Symonds Foster to attack the Bible, the churches, and the ministers. Following a tour of Steuben County in 1855, Jacob Patch and Henry Little reported that unless help was sent the county's four churches at Angola, Brockville, Salem, and York would fall victim to infidelity for which Steuben County was becoming a stronghold.[8]

John G. Brice found the situation at Winchester to be daunting in 1847. "Infidelity is rapidly on the increase," he wrote. "You can have no conception how much Universalism has increased during the past two years. I am acquainted with several who two years ago were prominent members in the Methodist Episcopal Chh, some of them class leaders, who are now open & avowed infidels. Sabbath breaking & profanity are fearfully increasing. What will be the result God alone can tell . . . Missionaries in the West must now double their efforts. Pray for me." He was adding a copy of "Nelson on Infidelity" to every Sunday school library. Brice's judgment of Winchester was confirmed in nearly every report of his successor Thomas Spencer. "This place is a strong hold for infidelity," Spencer said in April of 1848. In June he added that some zealous teachers and advocates of infidelity spent almost their whole time in the stores and shops reading and extolling "Davis' Revelations." The next year Thomas Spencer was trying to raise money to build a meetinghouse at Winchester. The village had more than one hundred families but more than forty men, heads of families, openly denied belief in the Holy Scriptures. Among these were the town's wealthiest and most influential men and the youth were under their influence.[9]

Winchester's elders J. B. Kepler and Samuel P. Ludy said at the end of 1849, "There is an open opposition to the gospel and a manifest disposition on the part of infidels and other nonprofessors to break down every thing like religion, or even morality." Andrew Loose began his work at Winchester in 1851 knowing that Randolph County was "one of the hotbeds of infidelity." He reported that some lecturers in the school districts, one named Henry C. Wright, were forming "so called Literary Societies, but really infidel clubs" which met on Sunday mornings to defame the Bible, the church, and the ministry. Loose debated "rationalists and infidels" in the area, some of them at Pleasant Ridge where "the relicts of a 'Phalanx' disappointed in their endeavors to remodel the world and, as facts prove, even themselves . . . hold their weekly meetings to discuss their theory, and kindred matters, in philosophy and religion, A. J. Davis and Spiritual Knockings, etc."[10]

Skepticism increased at Fort Wayne as the German immigrants multiplied in the mid–1840s. They told missionary John Bayer that the Bible was not all true and that the clergy preached only for money. D. S. Altman reported that a "strong current of infidelity" was prevailing in his field at Richmond, New Paris, Philomath, and Springersville. Philomath was known as "The Devil's Headquarters." Altman said it was not unusual to preach a "plain practical Gospel sermon" and hear some opponent saying after the service "That was a lie—it's all lies." Presbyterian pastor William H. McCarer kept saying that the faith of many Germans around Evansville was rationalism and bold infidelity even if they were attending church.[11]

Abraham Hurst in Wabash County said "Universalists and infidels are numerous and active." John Fairchild, a successor there nearly a decade later, said liquor was the major obstacle to his ministry because "it opens the floodgates of iniquity and every vice and crime naturally flows in its channel." But the second major obstacle was skepticism. Joseph Sadd and Jacob Conrad told of infidels at Monoquet and Warsaw in Kosciusko County, some of whom boasted they would give the debating society good reasons for not believing the Bible. Infidels were reported to be the prevailing influence at West Point in Tippecanoe County. William Brier reported in detail on the grip of overt infidelity there: "Twenty-five or thirty copies of the Boston blasphemy breathing Investigator are taken and a great number of infidel books and tracts are received and scattered through the country."[12]

Fourierists

Evangelists traveling Indiana also found Fourierists or Associationists. The French social prophet Charles Fourier officially sent word of his discoveries to the government of the United States in 1823 "pointing out the value of his plan for taming the ferocious Indians, attracting desirable immigrants from Europe and China, and even ameliorating the climate of the bleak new world." The United States consul at Paris wrote across the bottom of Fourier's letter "either a genuine curiosity or the emanation of a disturbed brain." Fourier died in 1837 without seeing or understanding America but his theory labeled Fourierism was to have its best experimental trial on the American frontier. It appeared in a pamphlet published in New York in 1838.[13] It was promoted especially by Albert Brisbane, a rich and energetic disciple of Fourier in New York State. Brisbane said "Association . . . will produce so much, and so fill the world with wealth, that the question will be how to consume it all!"[14] A late twentieth century researcher of Fourierism said:

> The Associationists, following Fourier, believed that humanity progressed in stages from "Savagery" through the competitive "Civilization" of the nineteenth century to "Harmony," which would arrive through the peaceful reorganization of society into cooperative phalanxes uniting approximately 1600 persons of all types and classes. The complex arrangements of Association would liberate the 12 stifled "passions" of human personality yet also ensure the order and equity lacking in individualistic, unplanned Civilization.[15]

Fourierism was similar in some ways to the utopian plan of Robert Owen, though the two developed independently. However Owen wanted industry and machinery to multiply production in his utopia. Fourier idealized rural life of an agrarian-handicraft kind, each modestly wealthy peasant tending his vine and trees and contributing his talents according to his best natural inclinations, all part of a symmetrical construction (phalanstery) which was in fact an elegant garden. Owen's ideal, never implemented, was abolition of private property and the distinctions which ownership entailed. Fourier's plan was a joint stock company, each member with shares which could be counted and all members getting rich together. Owen believed in an essential goodness of humankind which required only that he destroy the evil system of organized religion and provide at New Harmony and succeeding locations a proper setting and system for the formation of character. Fourier believed in such an essential goodness of humankind that the "elevation and refinement of the mass" would be accomplished simply by setting each individual free in a liberating environment. In that environment there would be "no tyranny or dictation—no control of the individual by the individual—no disciplining by monastic rules and regulations—no violation of individual will for the pretended good of the community—no subjection of man to arbitrary systems." Instead, phalanxes would be places where "independence, education, intellectual development, moral training, enjoyment of the arts and sciences, and extended social intercourse, are only necessary to elevate the whole Human Race to that noble standard which God intended they should attain."[16]

America found the Fourierists or Associationists very exciting in the 1840s. Albert Brisbane published his *Social Destiny of Man; or, Association and Reorganization of Industry* at Philadelphia in 1840. He sponsored or edited two periodicals called *The Phalanx* and *The Future*. In 1842 he contracted to contribute a regular signed column on this "perfect system of Democracy" for the front page of Horace Greeley's New York *Tribune*. These columns were widely noted and copied by other papers. He gathered the substance of them into a pamphlet entitled *Association; or, a Concise Exposition of the Practical Part of Fourier's Social Science* which went through ten editions of 1,000 copies each. The movement spread like a revival. At least twenty-nine phalanxes were formed in the United States, besides other communities influenced by Fourierist ideals.[17]

First and largest Fourierist community in Indiana was the Lagrange Phalanx on 1,045 acres about forty miles from Fort Wayne on the Wabash and Erie Canal near the village of Mongo. The *Lagrange Freeman* was recognized in July of 1843 as a newspaper favorable to Fourierism. In fall of that year a large building was under construction since "many of the most influential and worthy inhabitants of that section are deeply interested in the cause."[18] Phalanx Secretary W. S. Prentiss reported in February of 1844:

> We have now about thirty families, and I believe might have fifty, if we had room for them. We have in preparation and nearly completed, a building large enough to accommodate our present members. They will all be settled and ready to commence business in the spring. They leave their former homes and take possession of their rooms as fast as they are completed. The building, including a house erected before we began by the owner of a part of our estate, is one hundred and ninety-two feet long, two stories high, divided so as to give each family from twelve to sixteen feet front and twenty-six feet depth, making a front room and one or two bed-rooms. One hundred and twenty feet of this building is entirely new. We commenced it in September, and have had lumber, brick and lime to haul from five to twelve miles. All these materials can be hereafter furnished on our domain . . . We have about one hundred head of cattle, two hundred sheep, and horse and ox teams enough for all purposes: also farming tools in abundance; and in fact every thing necessary to carry on such branches of business as we intend to undertake at present, except money . . . We shall have about one hundred and fifty persons when all are assembled; probably about half of this number will be children. Our school will commence in a few days. We have a charter from the Legislature, one provision of which, inserted by ourselves, is, that we shall never, as a society, contract a debt.[19]

The Philadelphia Industrial Association was the second of Indiana's Fourierist communities. William McCartney, president, was to make available his farm in German Township of St. Joseph County. William C. Talcott, a Universalist minister turned non-Christian reformer, was to be the secretary who would actually form and manage the association. Of the money collected from the members, part was paid to McCartney toward the cost of the farm. The remainder was used to build a dining hall seventy-five feet long, a kitchen, a storeroom, and fifteen dwellings and to buy farming implements and horses. Talcott said: "There were, probably, more than a hundred persons, old and young, connected with us, from first to last; but I should not think more than about seventy living on the premises at once. During a part of the time they ate at a common table."[20]

The Fourier Phalanx one mile south of Moore's Hill in Dearborn County was the last of the Fourierist communities established before the Civil War. Alcander Longley, former resident in phalanxes in New Jersey and Ohio, chose a tract of 220 acres near the depot of the Ohio and Mississippi Railroad for his experiment. In 1857 and 1858 he promoted the venture through his paper called the *Philansterian Record* "published by persons who are endeavoring to establish the Fourier Phalanx, an Integral School of Science and Art." The first members arrived at the new location in February of 1858.[21]

Fourierists launched few overt campaigns against the Christian churches. They did not feel Robert Owen's compulsion to clear the ground of organized religion. Many of them expressed their ideals in vocabulary and symbols familiar to Christians—love, communion, unity, divine order, salvation of humanity. The Lagrange Phalanx was said to have "maintained schools and preaching in abundance." Most Fourierist associations in America had some form of Sunday service. However their religious kinship was more often expressed toward Transcendentalists, Swedenborgians, and Spiritualists than it was toward Methodists, Christians, Baptists, or Presbyterians. Even the great body of Protestants expecting the millennium were uneasy with Fourierist offers of their secularized paradise as fulfillment of the highest hope of humankind. Socialism as proposed and promoted by Robert Owen had been viewed by the churches as a subverter of Christianity. The less combative socialism of the Fourierists met less ecclesiastical opposition than Owen received but upon examination still seemed incompatible with the main body of Christian teaching. Fourier, like Owen, made social circumstances the primary locus of sin and evil. Participation in proper social organization offered the best hope to transform human relations and banish evil. On the other hand, the predominant evangelical churches regarded the unregenerate human heart as the locus of sin and evil. Transformation of that heart, and so of society, required personal regeneration of the sinner and continuing divine help for the believer living a life of self-sacrificing discipline. The two could agree that both individuals and society needed help; they differed sharply over which was the crucial motive force.[22]

Missionaries in Lagrange County eyed the Fourierists with suspicion. Rasselas L. Sears wrote of local Fourierists on 8 June 1843 "this class have become somewhat numerous in this region." Within a week the report of Christopher Cory gave more details with less sympathy. "In fact this social mania, which is but the leaven of French infidelity, has extensively prevailed in the eastern part of the County of Lagrange and in the western part of Steuben," he said. "During the winter and spring, two societies of this nature were in a forming state. Their design was to accommodate in one house 300 families more or less, to have but one dining room with three tables for three different grades, with prices accordingly." Two Presbyterian families in Kosciusko County embraced "this new scheme of association." Missionary Joseph M. Sadd regretted the Fourierists' campaign "against our views of depravity and some other things." He also regretted that their removal took away $40 in subscriptions, about one-fourth of the amount the people had promised to support his work.[23]

German Freethinkers

Freethought in Indiana often had a German accent, advanced by liberal German immigrants in reaction to the domination they had known at the hands of church and state in Europe. *Freie Presse von Indiana* was a freethought newspaper published in Indianapolis from 1853 to 1866. Some Indianapolis freethinkers took steps to protect their children from the impact of evangelical Christian culture. They organized a German-English Independent School in which the children could avoid Christian instruction but would be taught German language, literature, and music as part of the weekday curriculum. The school was in operation from 1859 to 1882. For the children there was also a religionless Sunday school supplied with books, two volunteer instructors, and one paid singing teacher. Organized freethinker groups developed among the concentrations of Germans at Evansville, Fort Wayne, and Indianapolis.[24]

The Indianapolis Freethinkers' Society (Freidenker-Verein) organized and approved its first constitution in spring of 1870. Carl Beyschlag gave the opening speech. Beyschlag was formerly a Protestant pastor in Württemberg, enthusiastic participant in the revolutions of 1848, prisoner at Asperg when the revolutions failed, and now immigrant to Indianapolis editing the *Freie Presse*. In the membership were a substantial body of educated merchants and professionals such as Clemens Vonnegut, Herman Lieber, William Kothe, Theodore Dingeldey, Charles Pingpank, and Philip Rappaport. The officers and board of trustees met as often as weekly and public meetings were regularly held on the first Sunday morning of every month, just as their neighbors were going to church. Their membership was twenty-eight in 1870 and eighty in 1882. When Hoosiers by thousands converged on Indianapolis for the centennial Fourth of July in 1876, the Freethinkers were among the marching units in the grand parade. Their interests were social, educational, scientific, and political but always overtly anti-religious. There were lectures on morality in the New Testament, religion and history, superstition, and the position of Jews in society. One lecture was entitled "What Has Free Thought to Offer in Place of Christianity?"[25]

That prince of infidels Robert G. Ingersoll did not usually deign to dispute with ordinary clergy, saying he would rather kill the dog of religion than deal with its fleas. However he did respond in print to questions submitted by four Indianapolis preachers. Clemens Vonnegut of the Indianapolis Freethinkers' Society translated the questions and Ingersoll's answers into German. Vonnegut also wrote and published his *Proposed Guide for Instruction in Morals from the Standpoint of a Freethinker* in German and in English. In it he briskly disposed of Christian belief in pages five through eight and then advocated a morality based on science and reason.[26]

Eccentric Rationalist "Scientists"

Science became the angel of Indiana's English-speaking rationalists too. Organized religion was their devil, especially the clergy of organized religion. There were a few regulars at the freethinkers' conventions who were basically eccentrics, like Bruce Calvert who lived on a rural acre in what is now Gary. Calvert lectured for pay at chatauquas, lyceums, and clubs. Alongside freethought his topics included nature, human kinship, vegetarian diet, cold showers, correct chewing of food, proper breathing, and nudism. His essays were on socialism, science and health, rational education, and shorthand. "Indiana's Prize Crank" the Indianapolis *Star* called him.[27]

Some of Indiana's freethought editors seemed rather cranky as well. Jasper Roland Monroe began publishing his paper in Jackson County in 1855, first as the *Rockford Herald* and then as the *Seymour Times*. He brought it to Indianapolis in 1882 as the *Age* and then as the *Ironclad Age*. It was, he said, "a Paper with Few Principles" and "the only straight atheistic paper now or ever published in the world or out of it." He claimed 3,000 subscribers in the late 1880s and his press turned out scores of freethought pamphlets and books intended to be an affront to religious society.

> The Ironclad Age is offensive to the eye of Sanctity. It is wicked because it is opposed to the trade of a minister, and because it has but few principles and scarce a politic. Most journals are over-loaded with principles, platforms, and politics; but by discarding most of these the Ironclad

Age is able to cruise around in the shallow waters of superstition in search of Goodness without a god, Happiness without a heaven, Salvation without a savior, And redemption without a redeemer. It is thus the only great paper in the Great West that is able to run without a god or devil or ghost . . . The irreverent proprietor of the Ironclad Age is paying five dollars ($5) a head for ghosts, little or big, old or young, male or female, holy or unholy, and he wants all he can get. He is also paying fifteen thousand dollars ($15,000) a head for virgin mothers, He has furthermore a standing offer of fifteen dollars . . . for one sane man who will swear he believes there once existed a tripple-headed god—a father who was his own son, Christ; a son Christ, who was his own father, god; and a ghost that was both father and son, yet distinct from either, and that these three were at once the "heavenly father," the "son of man," and the "holy ghost"—the three being one and the one three. Let one sane man swear he believes this stuff and get the reward.[28]

In 1891 Monroe was offering for sale nine works by or about Thomas Paine and the following six in addition:

> (1) *The Genealogy of Jesus*: his ancestors a bad lot . . . Just the thing to hand to your christian neighbor. 15c; (2) *The Bible, Is It Fallible or Infallible . . .* post-paid. 15 cents; (3) *Revelations of the Confessional*. Priestly outrages against women . . . By mail, 10 cents; (4) *Open Letter to the Clergy*. Plain truths in plain words . . . One of the most unanswerable essays out. Price. 10 cents; (5) *A Defence of Atheism . . .* This is an excellent little work and should be widely circulated. 10 cts; (6) *Science Versus Theology*. A practical treatise on the laws and properties of matter. Showing that ignorance of these laws gives rise to all theologies. . . 295 pages. Cloth, 65 cts, paper, 30 cts.[29]

A periodical called the *Iconoclast* was begun at Noblesville in 1881 by W. H. LaMaster who claimed it would "owe no allegiance whatever to gods or priests, angels or devils." It had moved to Indianapolis by 1882 but within a year was banned from the mails.

Even behind the strange titles and irreverent humor, almost all Hoosier rationalists of the late nineteenth and early twentieth centuries saw themselves as serious champions of science and depicted Christians as opponents of real progress. They spoke for freedom and reason and accused Christians of being oppressors led by evil "priests of Jehovah." Kersey Graves of Richmond was an excited amateur student of comparative religion, specifically of "Sir Godfrey Higgins' Anacalypsis" and "200 other unimpeachable historical records."[30] He set about destroying any Christian claim to priority or uniqueness.

Graves issued the *Biography of Satan* "Disclosing the Oriental Origin of the Belief in a Devil and Future Endless Punishment. Also the origin of the Scriptural terms: 'Bottomless Pit,' 'Lake of Fire and Brimstone,' 'Keys of Hell,' 'Chains of Darkness,' 'Casting Out Devils,' 'Everlasting Punishment,' 'The Worm that Never Dies,' &c.,&c." Encouraged by popular acceptance, Graves undertook

> the banishment of that wide-spread delusion comprehended in the belief in an incarnate, virgin-born God, called Jesus Christ, and the infallibility of his teachings, with the numerous evils growing legitimately out of this belief—among the most important of which is, its cramping effect upon the mind of the possessor, which interdicts its growth, and thus constitutes a serious obstacle to the progress both of the individual and of society. And such has been the blinding effect of this delusion upon all who have fallen victims to its influence, that the numerous errors and evils of our popular system of religious faith, which constitute its legitimate fruits, have passed from age to age, unnoticed by all except scientific and progressive minds, who are constantly bringing these errors and evils to light.[31]

The work to accomplish this was entitled *The World's Sixteen Crucified Saviors; or, Christianity before Christ. Containing New Startling, and Extraordinary Revelations in Religious History, which Disclose the Oriental Origin of All the Doctrines, Principles, Precepts, and Miracles of the Christian New Testament, and Furnishing a Key for Unlocking Many of Its Sacred Mysteries, Besides Comprising the History of Sixteen Heathen Crucified Gods.* He also did *The Bible of Bibles* to show "that the score of bibles which have been extant in the world teach essentially the same doctrines, principles, and precepts. There are to be found in the old pagan bibles the same grand and beautiful truths mixed up with the same mind-enslaving errors and deleterious superstitions as those contained in the Christian bible. And the same exalted claim is set up by the disciples of each for their respective holy books."[32]

These three works of Indiana's Kersey Graves went through a great many editions; they circulated nationwide in multiplied thousands of copies. His intention was to deny any supernatural basis for religion so that the errors and dogmas and superstitions of the Christian system "will vanish like fog before the rising sun, and be replaced by a religion which sensible, intelligent, and scientific men and women can accept, and will delight to honor and practice." A part of the science which Graves espoused and admired was contemporary Spiritualism. He pointed out that such "miracles" as healings, clairvoyant knowledge, walking on air or water, demonstrating marks of wounds on the body, and communication with invisible spirits were now routinely demonstrable by mediums. In the case of Jesus Christ "it was doubtless his frequent displays of several very remarkable phases of spiritual mediumship that contributed much to lead people into the error of supposing him to be God." Eventually a Cincinnati newspaperman named John T. Perry took notice of the prominence of Graves on the national scene by preparing critical reviews of *The Bible of Bibles* and *The World's Sixteen Crucified Saviors* for the Richmond *Telegram* and by publishing the reviews plus his interchange with Graves as *Sixteen Saviours or One? The Gospels Not Brahmanic.*[33]

Rationalist Organizations

Official organizations of English-speaking rationalists developed in Indiana early in the twentieth century. Their negative agenda was to put down Christian belief and practice past and present; their positive agenda was to elevate contemporary science. Sixty-seven persons met at Muncie on 3 January 1909 to form the Humanitarian Society. It was a social and educational body with a strong freethought bias. Attorneys George H. Koons and Minos Winfield Lee, both Universalists, were president and vice-president respectively. Physicians Herbert D. Fair and Thomas J. Bowles were secretary and treasurer. Fair was a Universalist who contributed articles to the *Truth Seeker*, including one entitled "Curious Capers of Christian Converts, with Critical Comments of a Contemporary Contemplator." Bowles, reared in the Christian church but gone agnostic, was the most zealous freethinker among the officers and a contributor to freethought papers.[34]

Hoosier freethinkers participated in regional assemblies of rationalists. When the Buckeye Secular Union met in Columbus, Ohio, in September of 1909, Thomas J. Bowles of Muncie and David W. Sanders of Covington and Indianapolis were among the Hoosiers in attendance. Bowles addressed the meeting on "The Decay of Orthodoxy." In November of the same year Bowles and Sanders shared in the creation of the American Rationalist Association at St. Louis. Sanders was elected to be secretary-treasurer and Bowles one of the vice-presidents.[35]

A letter by Sanders in the Indianapolis *News* for December 1909 announced something new. There would now be an Indiana Rationalist Association. Its formation and first meeting would take place at the Claypool Hotel in Indianapolis on 4 December. Speakers were to "expose the fallacy, follies, and vices of all so-called revealed religions and will urge that the real infidels and blasphemers are the priests and preachers of orthodoxy."[36] Language of the Association meetings was confrontational and triumphal. Former state treasurer John B. Glover welcomed the crowd of more than one hundred at the opening convention at the Claypool as leaders of a higher and better civilization, pioneers of human progress, and destroyers of the noxious weeds of superstition and fear. He added his own testimony:

> Theology has blasted the hopes and aspirations of humanity. It is the lash of the priest, who beats the poor and ignorant into subjection . . . There is nothing so certainly false as the Christian theology. It is false from foundation to turret. There is not one truthful dogma in the whole list from the "fall of man" to the deity of Jesus. Not one! . . . Prayer is the last resort of the foolish and worship is the folly of the feeble. Every man is the architect of his own god . . . the Bible is no more sacred than the Essays of Emerson or the sayings of Epictetus . . . That orthodoxy is passing must be apparent to every one who thinks.[37]

Elbert Hubbard addressed the second meeting in 1910; he predicted the "ultimate triumph of truth and reason and the annihilation of orthodoxy." President Bowles complimented his audience as persons enlightened and free. They were, he said, "men and women who believe that happiness is the only good and that science is our only saviour . . . men and women who believe that Gods and priests and devils are enemies of the human race and the chief obstacles to the progress and happiness of mankind—men and women who believe that holy days, holy books and divine revelations have been a curse to all the nations of the earth through all the dark and cheerless centuries." After a long catalog of the violations of humanity by the fiendish "priests of Jehovah," Bowles paid tribute to American freedom.

> With the heart of a fiend and the instincts of a wild beast the priests of Jehovah have hunted liberty around the globe, and have deluged the earth with tears and blood. We [Rationalists] are the only people in all the world that have completely rescued the goddess of Liberty from their blood-stained hands, and for this infinite blessing let the whole world rejoice and give thanks to that illustrious and immortal trinity of deities, Paine, Franklin and Jefferson, whose names and fame are as imperishable as the stars.[38]

And he expressed his faith in the unending blessings of science.

> Liberty and the sun of science are now filling the earth with light and love and in the not distant future our beautiful earth will become a peaceful and happy home for the whole human race, and men, women and children will sing songs of gladness far sweeter than Beethoven's symphonies, the earth will be studded with rock-built temples dedicated to science, to liberty and humanity; and in the midst of this most marvelous civilization, made possible by the death of the priests of Jehovah, will break out an universal anthem of joy that will reverberate around the whole circumference of the earth like the chimes of ten thousand mighty bells hung in the blue canopy above us.[39]

David W. Sanders was a persistent freethought evangelist, urging subscriptions to freethought papers and distributing hundreds of booklets. At its 1910 convention the Indiana Rationalist Association authorized Sanders to edit and publish a volume of portraits and writings of freethinkers with emphasis on Indiana. Sanders included some writings of his own in which he referred to Jesus as "the Jew." Said he "Verily Rationalism is better, much better, than Christianity which bids a man hate his wife and home, his parents and family, to follow a dead Hebrew." He wrote: "Those of us who believe there is any God, believe also that he is too wise and good to have inspired a book so rotten and vicious and hateful as the bible; or to have inspired such a mysterious, hopeless plan of our future salvation from sins not committed as is set forth in the so-called New Testament and preached by the Christian church."[40]

All of Indiana's organized centers of freethought were short-lived. The projected churchless town of Angola got a Methodist meetinghouse in 1855 and a Campbellite "protracted meeting" in 1867. By the religious census of 1906, Angola had 353 Methodists, 901 Christians, 130 Congregationalists, and 178 United Brethren—a percentage of church membership far above that of Indiana generally or that of the nation as a whole.[41] Sociologist Newell Sims said at the end of his three-year study in 1912:

> In contrast to former religious influences, Aton [Angola] is now one of the most thoroughly churched communities to be found anywhere. The beliefs of earlier years have disappeared. The families that championed them are now in the churches, together with the wealth, culture and talent of the town. The church is easily the most dominant social force in Aton, leading reforms, promoting improvements, and directing pleasure. More than three-fifths of the people are believed to be regular attendants. The ministry is the most influential class. Older residents take delight in pointing out the "wonderful change," and consider it the most significant phenomenon of the town's history.[42]

Experiments of the Fourierists quickly faded. The Lagrange Phalanx began building with great hope on its large acreage in 1843 but 14 June 1846 was the date of its last report published in Fourierist literature. A contemporary later reported "this Phalanx was wound up and settled in 1847 or 1848, and its members scattered." There was, he said, "too little care in taking in members" so that "many adventurers came in, some for want of a home, others to winter and leave in the spring." At the Fourierist community called Philadelphia Industrial Association formed in St. Joseph County in winter of 1844–45, president William McCartney was to provide the farm property at an appraised price of $20 per acre. When the time came to deed his farm, he decided to keep the best land for himself and transfer only the broken and marshy portion to the phalanx at the $20 rate. His associate William Talcott said the association continued about two years. The association failed, Talcott said, while McCartney succeeded in getting some of his land cleared up and improved for nothing. The phalanx at Moore's Hill in Dearborn County existed largely in the publicity of Alcander Longley. The first members arrived in February of 1858. By August Longley had abandoned Fourierism for other communal forms.[43]

The Indiana Freethinkers' Society began with solid support among German community leaders in 1870. By its third year president Clemens Vonnegut lamented that a lack of zeal on the part of members was jeopardizing the noble aims of the freethinkers. The society was reorganized in 1875, reached its greatest strength in 1882, and then went into decline. There were only four board meetings between 1884 and 1890. Clemens Vonnegut moved in September of 1885 that the society disband but his motion was not acted upon. In January of 1890 the remaining society assets were divided among four German groups with kindred interests.[44]

Even with a full slate of the town's professionals—two doctors and two lawyers—as officers, the Humanitarian Society of Muncie continued its schedule of weekly programs only from January through May of 1909. Its officers Herbert D. Fair and Thomas J. Bowles became notable in the ranks of the Indiana Rationalist Association organized at the end of 1909. The statewide Indiana Rationalist Association began with gusto at its conventions in 1909 and 1910 at the Claypool Hotel and mounted to an attendance of over 300 for its two-day session in 1911. Then it quickly ran down. By the 1912 meeting David W. Sanders had died of Bright's disease at the age of thirty-nine. At the age of seventy-six Bowles yielded the presidential chair. Libby Macdonald of New York City was the new president and Thusnelda Peemoller of Indianapolis the new vice president. There was an announced plan that the Indiana Rationalist Association would change its name to become the National Rationalist Association and encompass the whole country. In fact the Indiana Association itself was badly run down by 1912 with fewer than fifty members and a burden of debt. The administration of the new National Rationalist Association had little of Indiana in it. After a relocation to New York and then to California, it disappeared from view by 1915. So did most of organized freethought in Indiana.[45]

Between 1914 and 1924, Indiana's Thomas J. Bowles and John Wesley Whicker tried to shore up the American Secular Union with little success. There were other national freethought groups for Hoosiers to support—in 1949 there were the American Association for the Advancement of Atheism, the National Liberal League, the Freethinkers of America, and the United Secularists of America. In that year the *Truth Seeker*, primary freethought periodical published in New York since 1873, listed sixty-six subscribers from Indiana. Paul Kinney of Spencer, Indiana, served as first general secretary of the National Liberal League in 1946. The *Ripsaw*, a freethought paper, originated in South Bend in 1955. It merged with the *Free Humanist* in 1963 which became the *American Atheist* in 1964 under the editorship of Madalyn Murray O'Hair. Lloyd Thoren expressed his rationalist convictions by opening the American Atheist Museum near Petersburg, Indiana, in 1978. Eight years later he closed the museum and moved to California. The museum had about a thousand visitors each year, Thoren said. However, he feared that community life in Pike County as the child of an outspoken advocate of atheism might become agony for his daughter Jenny.[46]

Freethinkers could generally agree on goals of dechristianizing the nation and elevating scientific reason. However their ranks included a variety ranging from anarchists to Spiritualists, all stout for total liberty and averse to central direction. Organization and discipline were difficult to sustain. Within the spectrum of denominational groups, the Protestants and Catholics and Jews challenged any special privileges for each other with such vigor that the rationalist protests of evil alliance between church and state sounded like feeble echoes. It was also obvious quite early that pace setters in science were more visible in such church colleges as Notre Dame, DePauw, Hanover, Wabash, Earlham, Franklin, and Butler than in the membership of rationalist organizations. In fact, church scholars generally adopted the insights of science and biblical criticism with such alacrity that the churchmen themselves have been credited with paving the way to unbelief. One interpreter made such a charge in the late twentieth century in his book through a major university press. "In trying to adapt their religious beliefs to socioeconomic change, to new moral challenges, to novel problems of knowledge, to the tightening standards of science, the defenders of God slowly strangled Him. If anyone is to be arraigned for deicide, it is not Charles Darwin but his adversary Bishop Samuel Wilberforce, not the godless Robert Ingersoll but the godly Beecher family." Many of the favorite issues of the rationalists were taken up by their ecclesiastical opponents and the rationalists were outflanked.[47]

NOTES

1. Robert M. Taylor, "The Light of Reason: Hoosier Freethought and the Indiana Rationalist Association, 1909–1913," *Indiana Magazine of History* 79 (June 1983): 109.

2. Lewis McLeod, Dearborn County, to Absalom Peters, American Home Missionary Society (hereafter AHMS), New York, 15 March 1826; Calvin Butler, Evansville, to Absalom Peters, AHMS, New York, 14 February 1832; Abby Soper, New Harmony, to AHMS, New York, 11 March 1832; Lewis Pennell, Mount Vernon, to Absalom Peters, AHMS, New York, 6 March 1837.

3. Martin E. Marty, *The Infidel: Freethought and American Religion* (Cleveland, Ohio: World Publishing Company, 1961, 224 p.); James Duncan, *A Dialogue between an Atheist and a Theist, in which That Important Question Is Discussed, Whether the Universe of Nature Ever Was Created, or whether It Has Existed from Eternity without Being Created* (Indianapolis, Ind.: Douglass and Macguire, 1826, 40 p.).

4. Peter Cartwright, *Autobiography of Peter Cartwright* (New York: Abingdon Press, 1956), 162–63, 190–93, 329–33; William W. Hibben, *Rev. James Havens: One of the Heroes of Indiana Methodism* (Indianapolis, Ind.: Sentinel Co., 1872), 61–66; Theodore D. Welker, *Conflicts and Triumphs of an Itinerant: Rev. John Kiger* (Cincinnati, Ohio: Cranston and Stowe, 1891), 92–101; Marty, *Infidel*, 132–34.

5. Marty, *Infidel*, 88–104.

6. L. C. Rudolph, Ware William Wimberly, and Thomas W. Clayton, *Indiana Letters*, 3 vols. (Ann Arbor, Mich,: University Microfilms International, 1979), 3:1179, 1195, 1222, 1232; Nathan L. Lord, Plymouth, to AHMS, New York, 9 July 1852; John M. Bishop, Plymouth, to Milton Badger, AHMS, New York, 24 February 1846 and 9 April 1846; James R. Alexander, Vincennes, to Absalom Peters, AHMS, New York, 24 November 1829 and 12 January 1830; Benjamin C. Cressy, Salem, to Absalom Peters, AHMS, New York, 15 June 1832; Solomon Kittredge, Bedford, to Absalom Peters, AHMS, New York, 26 April 1834 and 29 July 1834; George McCulloch, Vevay, to Benjamin Rice, AHMS, New York, 16 April 1833; Ulric Maynard, Liberty, to Absalom Peters, AHMS, New York, 11 February 1830 and 1 May 1830.

7. Newell LeRoy Sims, *A Hoosier Village; A Sociological Study with Special Reference to Social Causation*, Studies in History, Economics and Public Law, vol. 46, no. 4 (New York: Columbia University, 1912), 63. There appears to have been no connection between the *Truth Seeker* which began publication in Angola in 1855 and the *Truth Seeker* which began publication in New York in 1873; see Sims, *Hoosier Village*, 63–64 and Taylor, "Light of Reason," 110.

8. Almon G. Martin, Angola, to AHMS, New York, 4 September 1852 and 2 December 1852; Jacob Patch, Orland, to Milton Badger, AHMS, New York, 6 August 1855; Henry Warren, Salem Center, to Milton Badger, AHMS, New York, 15 February 1856. The Fosters wanted radical action against slavery and for women's rights. Alienated from religion, they accused all churches of criminal lethargy in social matters. Stephen Symonds Foster had "unusual command of denunciatory language." His pamphlet *The Brotherhood of Thieves; or, A True Picture of the American Church and Clergy* (New London, Conn.: W. Bolles, 1843, 64 p.), went through more than twenty editions. Andrew Jackson Davis was a clairvoyant who progressed from Mesmerism to Spiritualism, delivering 157 lectures in Manhattan while in a state of trance and issuing twenty-six works which shaped the principles and vocabulary of Spiritualism. See *Dictionary of American Biography* 3:105, 542–43, 558–59.

9. John G. Brice, Winchester, to Charles Hall, AHMS, New York, 20 May 1847; Thomas Spencer, Winchester, to Milton Badger, AHMS, New York, 1 April 1848, 1 June 1848, and 2 July 1849.

10. J. B. Kepler and Samuel P. Ludy, Winchester, to AHMS, New York, 29 December 1849; Andrew Loose, Winchester, to Milton Badger, AHMS, New York, 10 April 1851, 4 November 1851, 2 August 1852. The "Phalanx" was probably Union Home Community formed in 1844 at Huntsville in Randolph County. See Arthur E. Bestor, *Backwoods Utopias* (Philadelphia: University of Pennsylvania Press, 1950), 240.

11. John A. Bayer, Fort Wayne, to Milton Badger, AHMS, New York, 18 December 1845; D. S. Altman, Richmond, to AHMS, New York, 23 June 1851, 28 July 1851, 1 October 1851, 31 December 1851, and 1 March 1852; William H. McCarer, Evansville, to AHMS, New York, 14 July 1952, 20 March 1854, 27 October 1856, 3 March 1857.

12. Abraham Hurst, Wabash County, to Milton Badger, AHMS, New York, 1 November 1850; John Fairchild, Wabash, to AHMS, New York, 29 August 1859; Joseph M. Sadd, Monoquet, to Milton Badger, AHMS, New York, 28 March 1846; Jacob E. Conrad, Warsaw, to Milton Badger, AHMS, New York, 17 June 1849; William W. Brier, Romney, to Milton Badger, AHMS, New York, 25 July 1848. The *Investigator* was Abner Kneeland's freethought periodical. Kneeland had completed his break with Christianity by 1829 and had come under negative judgment by such variant authorities as the Universalists and the State of Massachusetts. See Russell E. Miller, *The Larger Hope*, 2 vols. (Boston: Unitarian Universalist Association, 1979–85), 1:185–96.

13. Arthur E. Bestor, "American Phalanxes: A Study of Fourierist Socialism in the United States," 2 vols. (Ph.D. diss., Yale University, 1938), 1:1–2; *Two Essays on the Social System of Charles Fourier, Being an Introduction to the Constitution of the Fourienne Society of New-York* (New York: H. D. Robinson, Office of L'Estafette, 1838).

14. Albert Brisbane, *Association; or, A Concise Exposition of the Practical Part of Fourier's Social Science* (New York: Greeley and McElrath, 1843), 35; Arthur E. Bestor, "Albert Brisbane—Propagan-

dist for Socialism in the 1840s," *New York History* 28 (April 1947): 128–58; Redelia Brisbane, *Albert Brisbane: A Mental Biography with a Character Study* (Boston: Arena Publishing Company, 1893, 377 p.).

15. Carl J. Guarneri, "The Associationists: Forging a Christian Socialism in Antebellum America," *Church History* 52 (March 1983): 36.

16. Bestor, *Backwoods Utopias*, 77; Brisbane, *Association*, 28–29; Bestor, "American Phalanxes," 1:11–14.

17. Bestor, "American Phalanxes," vol. 1, table of contents, unpaged, and map on Plate 2 between pages 17 and 18. Other English-language socialist communities of the 1840s in Indiana were the Congregation of Saints in Lagrange County (1843), the Union Home Community in Randolph County (1844), and the Grand Prairie Community in Warren County (1845). See Bestor, *Backwoods Utopias*, 240.

18. John Humphrey Noyes, *American Socialisms* (Philadelphia: J. B. Lippincott, 1870), 397–403; Bestor, "American Phalanxes," 2:57.

19. Noyes, *American Socialisms*, 397–98.

20. Leonard Swidler, "The *Doktrin and Practis* of William C. Talbot," *Indiana Magazine of History* 57 (March 1961): 4; Timothy E. Howard, *A History of St. Joseph County*, 2 vols. (Chicago: Lewis Publishing Company, 1907), 1:306.

21. Bestor, "American Phalanxes," 2:54–55.

22. Noyes, *American Socialisms*, 403; Guarneri, "Associationists," 36–49; Bestor, "American Phalanxes," 1:267–68.

23. Rasselas Sears, Lima, Lagrange County, to AHMS, New York, 8 June 1843; Christopher Cory, Lima, Lagrange County, to Milton Badger, AHMS, New York, 13 June 1843; Joseph M. Sadd, Oswego and Monoquet, to Milton Badger, AHMS, New York, January [no date] 1844 and 1 April 1844.

24. Sabine Jessner, "On the First Sunday of Every Month: The Freethinkers and Liberal Thought in Indiana" (Paper delivered at the Indiana German Heritage session at the annual meeting of the Indiana Historical Society, Indianapolis, 7 November 1987), 3, 9; Emma Lou Thornbrough, *Indiana in the Civil War Era, 1850–1880* (Indianapolis, Ind.: Indiana Historical Bureau and Indiana Historical Society, 1965), 550; Taylor, "Light of Reason," 111.

25. Walter T. K. Nugent, "Seed Time of Modern Conflict: American Society at the Centennial," *Indiana Historical Society Lectures 1972–1973* (Indianapolis, Ind.: Indiana Historical Society, 1973), 32; Jessner, "On the First Sunday," 4–12.

26. Robert G. Ingersoll, *Works of Robert G. Ingersoll*, 12 vols. (New York: Dresden Publishing, 1915), 7:123–67; Robert G. Ingersoll, *Offener Brief an die Indianapoliser Geistlichkeit*, übersetzt Clemens Vonnegut, Sr. (Milwaukee, Wis.: Freidenker Publishing, n.d., 17 p.). The Ingersoll response was also published in Indianapolis by a rationalist paper called the *Iconoclast* and in separate booklet form as Robert G.Ingersoll, *An Open Letter to Indianapolis Clergymen* (Indianapolis, Ind.: Vincent Publishing, 1893, 64 p.); Clemens Vonnegut, *Proposed Guide for Instruction in Morals from the Standpoint of a Freethinker* (Milwaukee, Wis.: Freidenker Publishing, 1890, and Indianapolis, Ind.: Hollenbeck Press, 1900).

27. Robert M. Taylor, "Panaceas from Duneland: Bruce Calvert and *The Open Road*," *Traces* 1 (Winter 1989): 23–39.

28. Jasper R. Monroe, *Holy Bible Stories* (Indianapolis, Ind.: The Ironclad Age, 1891), pamphlet, unpaged.

29. George MacDonald, *Fifty Years of Freethought*, 2 vols. (New York: Truth Seeker Company, 1929), 1:302, 350, 2:114; Monroe, *Holy Bible Stories*, unpaged endpapers.

30. Godfrey Higgins, *Anacalypsis, an Attempt to Draw Aside the Veil of the Saitic Isis; or, An Inquiry into the Origin of Languages, Nations, and Religions*, 2 vols. (London: Longman, Rees, Orme, Brown, Green, and Longman, 1836).

31. Kersey Graves, *The World's Sixteen Crucified Saviors*, 4th ed., rev. and enl. (Boston: Colby and Rich, 1876), 10.

32. Kersey Graves, *Biography of Satan* (Chicago: Religio-Philosophical Publishing Association, 1865, 42 p.); Kersey Graves, *The Bible of Bibles* (Boston: Colby and Rich, 1879, 440 p.); Graves, *World's Sixteen*, 373 and unpaged endpaper advertisements.

33. Graves, *World's Sixteen*, 17, 357–58; John T. Perry, *Sixteen Saviours or One? The Gospels Not Brahmanic* (Cincinnati, Ohio: Peter G. Thomson, 1879, 146 p.).

34. Fair was the son of a Methodist preacher. His painful account of his liberation from the religion of his parents is in "The Religious History of a Hypocrite" in David W. Sanders *The Light of Reason*, published under the Auspices of the Indiana Rationalist Association, ed. David W. Sanders (Indianapolis, Ind.: Manual Publishing Co., 1912?), 103–6; Taylor, "Light of Reason," 113–16.

35. Taylor, "Light of Reason," 116–22.

36. Taylor, "Light of Reason," 122. This article offers the best available account of the Indiana Rationalist Association including descriptions and photographs of such leaders as Thomas J. Bowles of Muncie, David W. Sanders of Covington and Indianapolis, John Wesley Whicker (also spelled Whickar) of Attica, Schuyler LaTourette of Covington, Isaiah M. Miller of Upland, and William Y. Buck of Muncie.

37. Sanders, *Light of Reason*, 34.

38. Taylor, "Light of Reason," 125; Sanders, *Light of Reason*, 35.

39. Sanders, *Light of Reason*, 36.

40. Sanders, *Light of Reason*, 1, 142, 144.

41. Sims, *Hoosier Village*, 64–71.

42. Sims, *Hoosier Village*, 64.

43. *Counties of Lagrange and Noble, Indiana* (Chicago: F. A. Battey, 1882), 71; Howard, *History of St. Joseph County*, 306; Bestor, "American Phalanxes," 2:54–55, 57, 61; Swidler, "Doktrin and Practis," 4–5.

44. Jessner, "On the First Sunday," 12–14.

45. Taylor, "Light of Reason," 126–131. For a summary of the 1911 convention program of the Indiana Rationalist Association, see Taylor, "Light of Reason," 126.

46. Taylor, "Light of Reason," 131; *Dubois County Herald*, 30 December 1986, 3.

47. David N. Livingstone, *Darwin's Forgotten Defenders: The Encounter between Evangelical Theology and Evolutionary Thought* (Grand Rapids, Mich.: William B. Eerdmans, 1987, 210 p.); James Turner, *Without God, Without Creed: The Origins of Unbelief in America* (Baltimore, Md.: Johns Hopkins University Press, 1985), xiii; Marty, *Infidel*, 151–76.

About Swedenborgians and Spiritualists

Swedenborgians and Spiritualists were never the same; both have been at pains to make their differences plain. Yet their interests and constituencies have often linked and merged. Swedenborg said "I enjoy perfect inspiration . . . The inner sense of the Word of God has been dictated to me out of heaven." But he also communicated with other famous persons long dead. Spiritualist pioneer Andrew Jackson Davis claimed contact with notable spirits among the dead including Swedenborg. Sydney Ahlstrom wrote: "Mesmerism and spiritualism were so intimately related that for several generations they were deemed to be virtually inseparable. It is by no coincidence, therefore, that Swedenborg, too, became implicated. In fact, there is some ground for seeing Swedenborg as the greatest medium in modern times and the New Church as the first spiritualist church . . . The major outcropping of interest in intercourse with the other world, which came in 1848 with the Fox sisters' rappings, was not directly traceable either to Swedenborg or to the New Church; but it did conduce to so rapid a growth of spiritualism among Swedenborgian 'liberals' that the New Church was threatened by schism in the 1850s and after."[1]

NOTE

1. Sydney E. Ahlstrom, A Religious History of the American People (*New Haven, Conn.: Yale University Press, 1974*), 484, 487.

SWEDENBORGIANS

Emanuel Swedenborg (1688-1771) was the son of a Swedish Lutheran theologian and bishop. After his university studies he excelled as a civil servant in the Swedish Council of Mines. He published works on geology, anatomy, neurology, paleontology, physics, and astronomy. At the age of fifty-seven he made religion his primary concern. He said "heaven was opened" to him in 1745 and he received direction from God "to explain to men the spiritual sense of the Scripture." First step, between 1749 and 1756, was the preparation of the *Arcana Coelestia*, an enormous eight-volume commentary on Genesis and Exodus. By the time of his death in 1771, he had embodied his doctrines in "some forty odd volumes of theological writings."[1]

The works of Swedenborg were in Latin. They were not easy to comprehend in any language. He spoke in sophisticated detail of "correspondences" between the material world and a spiritual world, between the natural being and a spiritual being, between the literal letter of the Bible and its spiritual meaning. Scriptures were a mere record in words; their true spiritual meanings became known when their original correspondence as revealed to Swedenborg was supplied. Resurrection for believers was no radical event but simply a continuation of the spiritual being without the natural. The historic church and its old controversies were displaced. The time had come for a new church on earth, its nature manifested to Swedenborg by word and vision and effected by the second coming of the Lord Jesus Christ which oc-

curred in the spiritual world on 19 June 1770. The New Church declared its independence of much of tradition, both religious and social. It opened new vistas of an angelic order both present and eternal. The first Swedenborgian society was gathered near Manchester in England in 1778. English translations of Swedenborg's volumes kept appearing. In 1787 one group there took a stand as dissenters distinct from all older churches. It was customarily called the New Church or the Church of the New Jerusalem.[2]

Swedenborgians were soon in America. In June of 1784 James Glen advertised his first discourse "on the extraordinary science of Celestial and Terrestrial Connections and Correspondences, recently revived by the late honorable and learned Emanuel Swedenborg" in the *Pennsylvania Gazette* at Philadelphia. In June of 1816 the New Church congregation in Philadelphia laid the cornerstone for its new Temple, the entire cost of the building borne by William Schlatter.[3]

Johnny Appleseed

The New Church message came to the western frontier very early in the form of John Chapman, affectionately known to both history and legend as "Johnny Appleseed." The records of First Congregational Church of Leominster, Massachusetts, show that Johnny was born there on 26 September 1774. Nothing more is known of his early life. He emerged in Pennsylvania at the turn of the century as a person who could read and write well, who had attained some skill in the propagation and culture of fruit trees, who knew how to take care of himself in the wilderness of the frontier, and who had embraced the religious doctrines of Emanuel Swedenborg. This last is rather amazing since the total population of "receivers" of Swedenborgian teachings in all of the United States was something less than 400 as late as the organization of the first General Convention in 1817. Most of the leaders were personally acquainted. The body of receivers was well known to them.[4]

Johnny had a passion for his apple tree business. He could easily pick up apple seeds from the cider mills of established settlements. His aim was to produce young seedlings in great quantity in nurseries located just ahead of the arrival of large pioneer populations. They needed apple seedlings quickly; he would have the young trees growing and ready to sell. He first practiced this strategic planning and planting in Pennsylvania. In the early days he had to beg or rent or lease or establish squatter's rights on small patches of land to clear and fence and plant as his western nurseries. He got better at the business as the forests of central and western Ohio were transformed into farms and orchards. Now some of his tracts involved ninety-nine-year leases on as much as quarter sections of land. Tradition locates him at Fort Wayne with a boatload of apple seeds in 1830 and ready with cash to make strategic purchases at Indiana's new land office at Logansport when the Wabash and Erie canal project was assured— 42.11 acres on the north side of the Maumee about three miles downriver from Fort Wayne on 28 April 1834; 99.03 acres three miles further down the river almost at the Ohio boundary on 26 May 1836; 18.70 acres near his other holdings on the Maumee on 10 March 1836; 74.04 acres on the Wabash River in Jay County, just over the Ohio line, on 11 March 1836; 40 acres several miles northwest of Fort Wayne on 16 May 1838. Indiana became his home base from 1838 to 1845 but tending his nurseries scattered over Indiana and Ohio kept him padding barefoot year by year along the same pioneer trails. He became recognized and anticipated on these rounds; his reputation grew as a ragged, gentle eccentric. People accumulated and exchanged their stories about this strange character with an unusual business who chose an abnormally hard life. Somehow he was the personal symbol of his doctrine of the triumph of spirit over matter.[5]

Johnny had an equal passion for the doctrines of the New Church. He was never an ordained minister or a commissioned missionary. He was on the church's list of receivers of Swedenborgian teachings. His efforts were voluntary and unofficial. Wherever his message was welcome he explained how his hearers lived in another world at the same time they lived in this one, how they had a spiritual existence as well as a natural one. His death notice in the Fort Wayne *Sentinel* said "He always carried with him some works of the doctrine of Swedenbourgh, with which he was perfectly familiar, and would readily converse and argue on his tenets, evincing much shrewdness and penetration." Circulation of the works of Swedenborg was always New Church business. Johnny yearned for more copies to place in the new West. Swedenborg's volumes available in American editions during Johnny's lifetime included *Arcana Coelestia, The True Christian Religion, Divine Love and Wisdom, Divine Providence, Conjugial Love, Heaven and Hell,* and *The Four Doctrines.* England was also a major source of supply. William Schlatter was a most generous Philadelphia merchant who said in 1819 that he had given away about 6,000 "books and sermons on the sublime doctrines of the New Jerusalem." Johnny Appleseed got some of those; he had been corresponding with Schlatter since about 1815. But the bank chaos following 1818 crippled Schlatter's business and cut his funds available for church causes. About 1820 Johnny offered to exchange 160 acres of land for New Church literature. Schlatter did not know how to cope with such an offer since the peripatetic Johnny could hardly be located for negotiation and the book suppliers dealt only in cash.[6]

The zeal of this curious apple tree man and his offer of land in exchange for books brought him notice across the church. In England in 1817 a report of the Manchester Society for Printing, Publishing and Circulating the Writings of Emanuel Swedenborg quoted a letter about this "very extraordinary missionary of the New Jerusalam" in the western country who "can sleep anywhere, in house or out of house, and live upon the coarsest and most scanty fare" and "has actually thawed the ice with his bare feet." This rustic phenomenon, the report said, "procures what books he can of the New Church; travels into the remote settlements, and lends them wherever he can find readers, and sometimes divides a book into two or three parts for more extensive distribution and usefulness." As for the apple business, the report continued, "the profits of the whole are intended for the purpose of enabling him to print all the writings of Emanuel Swedenborg, and distribute them through the western settlements of the United States." The *Journal of the Proceedings of the Fifth General Convention of the Receivers of the Doctrines of the New Jerusalem* in Philadelphia, 3–5 June

1822, spoke of John Chapman, "from whom we are in the habit of hearing frequently." His strenuous example would "put the most zealous members to the blush." Johnny's apples were again said to be subservient to his mission. "His temporal employment consists in preceding the settlements, and sowing nurseries of fruit trees, which he avows to be pursued for the chief purpose of giving him an opportunity of spreading the doctrines throughout the western country." A western acquaintance put it more bluntly. "His main bump seemed to be to leave the books of Swedenborg whenever he could get anybody to read them, and leave them until he called again . . . His books were very old. He got them somehow from Philadelphia. He had great thirst for making converts."[7]

The results of Johnny's missionary efforts for the New Church were not obvious in Indiana. In Ohio he had been instrumental in gathering a Swedenborgian group near Mansfield and persuading church leaders in Philadelphia to approve a local converted Methodist minister named Richard Ensign first as its lay leader and then its ordained minister. He was generally credited with sowing New Church seeds which produced small societies between 1820 and 1840 in Ohio's Licking, Wayne, Muskingum, Richland, Cuyahoga, Medina, Huron, Portage, Erie, Sandusky, Shelby, and Lucas counties. By the time Indiana became the center of his operations, he was in his mid-sixties. His increasing raggedness and eccentricity harmonized well enough with his growing prominence as a character in folklore but did little to give him credibility in his role as missionary teacher. Johnny was never a blind or fanatical distributor of literature. He read his tracts and discussed them sensibly even if many never understood what he was talking about. However, those Hoosiers who encountered the old man only briefly could hardly get past the shock of his oddity to give his message a serious hearing. Those who were moved to wrestle with the doctrines of Swedenborg in print found them slow and heavy going.[8]

Early in 1845 somebody gave Johnny Appleseed word that cattle had broken into his nursery on the banks of the St. Joseph River near Fort Wayne. Now past seventy, he hiked fifteen miles in a single day to attend to the crisis. He died on March 18. If he indeed had hopes that his estate built up through the apple business would go to support New Church enterprise in the West, those hopes were disappointed. The family of his half sister had joined him in the hard work of developing the Indiana acreage and nurseries. They were entitled to payment for their labors. The land sold in separate blocks and the proceeds of those sales were soon consumed by legal ad-ministration costs. Most of those who later invested so much effort to determine the site of his grave were interested because of Johnny Appleseed's fame in literature and folklore. Few were receivers of the doctrines of his beloved New Church.[9]

George Field

For Swedenborgian missionary George Field the West was a sea of opportunity. In all those thousands of square miles of settlements were a host of people who thought there was some spiritual realm beyond the material world, some life beyond mere biological life. Few felt qualified to speak with certainty of spiritual details. Most had never so much as heard of Emanuel Swedenborg or the New Church. This was a void Field was prepared to fill. From the Scriptures elucidated by the revelations to Swedenborg he had volumes and volumes of spiritual details to offer.[10]

Field was a speaker of such power he could meet much of his own missionary expense by collections or admission charges at his public lectures. He was popular enough to be elected chaplain of the Michigan Senate. All he needed was minimal local contact or even healthy curiosity in a community to provide sufficient basis to advertise a lecture series, long or short. Subjects included: Heaven and Hell; Second Coming; Resurrection; Last Judgment; Miracles of Egypt; Meaning of the Son of Man; Sabbath; Divine Attributes; Language of Scripture; Baptism; Blood of the Lord; Interior Memory; Lot's Wife; Swedenborg; Divine Trinity; Spiritual World; Doctrines of the Church. One immensely popular series based on Genesis, in two lectures or seven or nine as the time available allowed, he sometimes referred to as "Creation, Deluge, &c." It begged for repetition. He presented it twice in Peoria, twice in Chicago, twice in St. Louis, and five times in Detroit.[11]

Field's hearers kept saying he should have these creation lectures published so he "wrote them out in full." Rejected by Lippincott, Harper, Appleton, and Scribner, he published the work himself in a book of about 500 pages and sold 1,000 copies. Local clergy were prone to correct, counteract, or oppose Field. Opponents often tried to embarrass him by citing Swedenborg's work entitled *Conjugial Love* which described a level of love even higher than conjugal love between husband and wife and offered some quite specific revelations about sexuality in both earthly and heavenly orders. Field relished confrontation. Newspapers looking to liven their columns with unusual subjects and with controversy found him good copy. Sometimes they reviewed his lectures in their entertainment pages.[12]

At the same time Field was a churchman, an organizer of New Church congregations. On his way from New York to his chosen mission field of Illinois, he was delayed for the winter of 1837–38 in the area of Detroit. His primary mission field changed to become Michigan and Indiana. In December of 1841 he lectured at Elkhart, Indiana, to a crowded schoolhouse. Everybody in town was talking about his subjects and a local storekeeper was sending for a stock of New Church books to sell. Early in 1842 he was back at Elkhart with his course of lectures on "Creation, Garden of Eden, Flood, &c.,&c." Mr. Babcock, "a preacher among the Christian Brethren," challenged him to a public discussion on the meaning of Christ's dying for the people. The hearers overflowed the house and gathered outside at the doors and windows. The debate moderators decided the weight of the argument favored Field. He left Elkhart with a list of twelve persons "very much and very favourably interested in our doctrines."[13]

This recognition at Elkhart brought him an immediate invitation to Goshen, borne by Thomas Harris who was a lawyer there. He was promptly challenged to debate Noah Cook, Presbyterian minister at Goshen. Cook offered to controvert Field's positions on the Creation, on the Deluge, on the person, character, and mission of Jesus Christ, and on the interpretation of church history. He would "endeavor to prove that Emanuel Swedenborg was a blasphemer, an insane person, or a knave." The debate lasted from 9 A.M. on Tuesday to 9 P.M. on Wednesday with 300 to 500 present. There was no vote but Field was sure he had won. "I then gave notice that I would, on [Sunday] evening, give a lecture on the claims and credibility of Swedenborg," he said. "The house was crowded, not less than 500 being present. My lecture was three hours long! Yet scarcely a person moved from his seat till I had concluded."[14]

Following this encounter, Field stayed on to present another lecture series in Goshen. Generous coverage given to Field in the *Goshen Democrat* and in the *Northern Indianian* further provoked Noah Cook so that the controversy was extended through newspaper correspondence for several weeks. Field's prospect list at Goshen included "Mr. and Mrs. Rollin, Mr. Carr, Mr. T. Harris, Mr. Brown, Mr. Chamberlin, A. M. Haskell and brother, and about a dozen others." Goshen became a particularly lively New Church center. Field was welcomed there each round of his missionary tour. Sometimes the members would hear Field's lectures at Goshen and then commute

to Elkhart to hear him there as well. Only a handful of western towns could raise enough money to establish a New Church library. Goshen may have founded the first such library in the region with its subscription of $30 in 1843; Ann Arbor, Michigan, followed several months later.[15]

Field extended his evangelism for the New Church at Mishawaka, South Bend, and Michigan City. At LaPorte he felt his work was miraculously aided by a premonition of his coming in the dream of a daughter in the family of a Baptist named Harvey Strong. In rural Elkhart County Mrs. Wealthy Evans became interested in New Church books. She wrote a letter to Mr. Price, her rector, explaining why she was withdrawing from the Episcopal Church to become a Swedenborgian. She and her neighbors the Smiths formed a pioneer New Church Sunday school with thirty scholars; Mr. Smith began reading a Swedenborgian sermon in public every Sunday. Field published Mrs. Evans's letter to her rector in the *Northern Indianian* thus fueling the continuing newspaper controversy.[16]

At this stage of his life Field was not looking for a place to locate. He sought the role of itinerant missionary. By the end of 1842 his work had gained enough attention and won enough friends to warrant regional organization. "The Association of Readers and Receivers of the Doctrines of the New Jerusalem Church in Michigan and Northern Indiana" was formed on 2 January 1843. It began with fifteen persons representing seven clusters of receivers and letters from six more, essentially a George Field support group. They subscribed $230 and told Field that as soon as he was ordained he could become their missionary. He was ordained by the General Convention in May as "a priest and teaching minister in the Lord's Church of the New Jerusalem, with power to conduct public worship, to celebrate the Sacrament of the Lord's Supper, marriages, baptisms, and funerals; and generally to perform all holy rites and Divine ordinances of the Church, except that of ordaining other priests and ministers."[17]

Field was advised to make his circuits or tours semi-annually, determining the length of each stay by the size of the place, the effect of his work, and the amount subscribed for his services. "Here was a range of country for me to visit, of nearly three hundred miles in length, from East to West," he said, "from Detroit to Chicago; and by cross country routes, often without any stages, from Goshen, Ind., to the heavy timbered lands of Livingston and adjoining Counties in Michigan. And whilst thus travelling, my three little children, now motherless, the oldest only eight years old, and the youngest only a year and a half, had to be put out to board. And what were the means provided for me to meet my expenses with?" The support for Field as a full time missionary never materialized. He soon had to return to supporting himself as teacher, as lecturer, and most of all as draftsman for the Surveyor General's office in Detroit. Still he kept making his missionary rounds. A small corps of additional New Church preachers and lecturers were developed to serve the Association, e.g., Abiel Silver, Jabez Fox, and Henry Weller, but Field was the most effective visitor.[18]

Field was an advocate of New Church uniqueness. Forms of the Christian Church which had gone before, such as the Catholic or Protestant, were "Old Church" and so of no value. The New Church sprang from a completely new understanding. "This is why those of the New Church have nothing in common with what they believe to be a Church that is Christian in name only." For his New Church he wanted ecclesiastical character and discipline. New Church preachers should be ordained in a regular way; he was uneasy with lay preachers and lecturers. He wanted the sacrament of the Lord's Supper to be kept and respected in the New Church. Admission to full society membership and to the Lord's Supper was to be limited to persons who not only received the "heavenly doctrines" but also were baptized by an ordained New Church minister. Previous baptisms had no validity. Thirteen persons at Goshen came to agree with him and he baptized them. During his days with the Michigan and Northern Indiana Association he baptized 170 adults and 147 children.[19]

Field was also wary of persons who claimed to have their own visions or revelations or spirit communications to add to those of Swedenborg. Early in 1852 he received a letter from Henry Weller who was his friend, convert, and fellow New Church preacher. Weller signed the letter as "The Lord's High Priest." He said he had been in personal communication with Swedenborg, dead since 1771, and was summoning a group of New Church leaders to gather to hear the new instructions and reconstitute the church aright. Field did not respond or attend. At its regular meeting in 1852 the Michigan and Northern Indiana Association dismissed Weller from its membership as in "a state of mind eminently unfitting him for the useful discharge of a pastor, or minister." Weller settled at LaPorte and gathered a society. His Swedenborgian-Spiritualist paper, *The Crisis*, said it was "edited by Henry Weller, President of the Society of the Lord's Church, LaPorte, Ind." Weller claimed the events of the past two years had broken up all the theologies of the day and threatened the destruction of all existing church organi-

zations. "We hold it an established fact that this world is now subject to continual, direct, open visitations from the Spiritual World," he said. "In the last month of the past year commenced upon ourselves a series of spiritual visions of a most extraordinary character."[20]

Swedenborgians in the American West found the convictions of George Field to be rather churchy and stiff. A majority of them were inclined to be a lot more loose, regarding such external observances as ordination, baptism, and the Lord's Supper as entirely optional. For ministers, some kind of testimony or evidence of a spiritual call to preach was sufficient. Ordination was counted by many as "mere ritual" and likely to be "an invention from the love of dominion." Field's western constituents admired him and valued his ministry. They invited him often and promised him more pay than they would ever deliver. They would tolerate his sacramental views so long as he did not insist they should be standards for the whole church. When he did insist, as he always did eventually on the basis of his understanding of both the Scriptures and Swedenborg, they would reluctantly vote him down and let him go. So he moved from Detroit and from St. Louis and from Adrian, Michigan. When the Michigan and Northern Indiana Association would not approve his ecclesiastical convictions expressed in sermon and as an enthusiastic minority report, he withdrew from the Association. Within a short time it collapsed.[21] "Thus, after twenty-five years of earnest and laborious effort to build up the Church in Michigan, did this Association, once so flourishing, and with such hopeful prospects, pass away into oblivion, with the things that were," Field said, "and because 'freedom' is so clearly recognized in the New Church, it was strained into the persuasion that every man is a law to himself, and that he is free to remove the Divine landmarks."[22]

Field's constituents in Indiana were always on his itinerant schedule and his pastoral agenda. Early in 1869 he moved to Richmond, Indiana. He had previously given eleven lectures in Richmond, including the series on Creation and Deluge. Local Swedenborgians made him welcome. Most of the regular patterns of his ministry were soon evident. He had brought the New Church library from Adrian with him; twenty-five persons at Richmond borrowed seventy-five volumes. Methodist minister Thomas Comstock accused Field of saying the Vicarious Atonement was a hoax. This provoked an exchange of fourteen articles in the Richmond *Telegram* between August of 1870 and January of 1871. But he was restless. "I remained about two years and a half in Richmond, where I preached and Lectured regularly every Sabbath; but, questioning my ability to successfully cultivate a mental soil composed mostly of Quakers, Spiritualists, Lutherans, Roman Catholics and the so-called Evangelists; all of whom seemed to be so well satisfied with their present convictions, as not to care to know about any other faith, I doubted the propriety of remaining there." In October of 1872 Field began work as a Swedenborgian pastor in Toronto, Canada, and Indiana lost its most impressive New Church champion.[23]

Few of the Swedenborgian societies in Indiana survived. For the religious census of 1906, the General Convention of the New Jerusalem in the United States of America reported 119 organizations in the nation. Massachusetts had 17 organizations; Illinois had 15; Pennsylvania had 9; Connecticut, New York, and Ohio each had 7. Indiana reported 3 New Church organizations with a total of 131 members. The next three religious censuses showed Indiana with only 2 New Church organizations and a total state membership of less than 80. For many years Indiana's most healthy New Church congregation was the one at LaPorte. Its record said: "A number of persons of LaPorte, Ind., having been readers and receivers of the doctrines of the New Jerusalem Church, as unfolded in the writings of Emanuel Swedenborg, met together on the 14th day of June 1859, and organized themselves, by due form of the law, into a society, called the 'New Jerusalem Association of LaPorte.'"

Henry Weller, now turned from his interest in direct visions and spirit communication, was elected pastor and served as such until his death on 7 June 1868. James and Sarah Andrew donated half a lot at the corner of Indiana Avenue and Maple Street in 1859; Sutton Van Pelt supervised the construction of a "neat temple." A corps of substantial citizens of the town invested themselves in New Church doctrine and practice, citizens with names like Andrew, Van Pelt, Weller, Teegarden, Forney, Weaver, Niles, and Scott. John Barron Niles, a Presbyterian become Swedenborgian, sent his sons William and Henry to the Swedenborgian college at Urbana, Ohio; William Niles and his sister Mary Relief Niles Scott were for a time the church's chief subscribers. In 1980 the General Convention of the New Jerusalem in the United States of America reported only one church in Indiana, the congregation at LaPorte with sixty members.[24]

NOTES

1. Marguerite Beck Block, *The New Church in the New World: A Study of Swedenborgianism in America* (New York: Octagon Books, 1968), 19–51; Sydney E. Ahlstrom, *A Religious History of the American People* (New Haven, Conn.: Yale University Press, 1974), 483–86.

2. Block, *New Church*, 38–39, 61–68.

3. Block, *New Church*, 74–78.

4. For the growth and persistence of Johnny Appleseed stories, see Robert Price, *Johnny Appleseed: Man and Myth* (Bloomington, Ind.: Indiana University Press, 1954, 320 p.); see also Steven Fortriede, "Johnny Appleseed: The Man behind the Myth," *Old Fort News*, vol. 41, no. 3 (1978): 3–19.

5. Price, *Johnny Appleseed*, 201–8.

6. Price, *Johnny Appleseed*, 114, 121, 125–31, 238–39.

7. Price, *Johnny Appleseed*, 119–33.

8. Price, *Johnny Appleseed*, 124–31, 135, 140, 209.

9. "The Burial Place of John Chapman," *Ohio State Archaeological and Historical Quarterly* 52 (April–June 1943): 181–87; Robert C. Harris, "Johnny Appleseed Source Book," *Old Fort News* 9 (March–June 1945): 1–31; Price, *Johnny Appleseed*, 236–37, 241–45; Fortriede, "Johnny Appleseed," 10–19.

10. George Field, *Memoirs, Incidents, and Reminiscences of the Early History of the New Church in Michigan, Indiana, Illinois, and adjacent States; and Canada* (New York: E. H. Swinney, 1879; New York: AMS Press, 1971), 332–42, 345.

11. Field, *Memoirs*, 32, 45, 133, 209–12, 239, 270.

12. George Field, *The Two Great Books of Nature and Revelation; or The Cosmos and the Logos, Being a History of the Origin and Progression of the Universe, from Cause to Effect, More Particularly of the Earth and the Solar System; the modus operandi of the Creation of Vegetables, Animals, and Man, and How They Are the Types and Symbols by which the Creator Wrote the Logos. Illus. by the First Chapters of Genesis* (New York: S. R. Wells, 1870, 501 p.); Field, *Memoirs*, 133–80, 248, 274–75; Block, *New Church*, 453.

13. Field, *Memoirs*, 17–19.

14. Field, *Memoirs*, 19–21.

15. Field, *Memoirs*, 24, 88, 105, 120.

16. Field, *Memoirs*, 28–30, 33–37.

17. Field, *Memoirs*, 63–74.

18. Field, *Memoirs*, 71, 133, 182, 189, 208, 214.

19. Field, *Memoirs*, iv, 110–12, 346, 351–68.

20. Field, *Memoirs*, 216–19; Block, *New Church*, 127–28.

21. Field, *Memoirs*, 195–270.

22. Field, *Memoirs*, 246.

23. Field, *Memoirs*, 275–76.

24. "Record of the First New Jerusalem Society of LaPorte, Indiana," bound volume in Papers of Emmet Hoyt Scott, 1842–1924, Lilly Library, Indiana University; Virginia L. Mauck, "The Niles Manuscripts, 1765–1925," *Indiana University Bookman* 13 (January 1979): 72–79; Saundra B. Taylor, "The Papers of Emmet Hoyt Scott, 1842–1924," *Indiana University Bookman* 13 (January 1979): 63–71; Elizabeth Munger, "LaPorte Society of the New Church Celebrates 125th Anniversary," *The Messenger: Official Publication of the General Convention of Swedenborgian Churches* (September 1984): 191–94.

SPIRITUALISTS

Reports of continuing communication with the spirits of the dead seem as old as humankind. Primitive peoples often tried to avoid such communication. Visits from restless spirits might be judgmental and painful. But spirits of the dead were also sought out at times for prophecy, guidance, healing, or protection. Shamans or witches or priests or drugs or physical excitation might aid the communication. The religions of Greece and Rome provided oracles for consultation. Some biblical passages reported messages directly from God, borne perhaps by prophets, angels, or ordinary persons. At the same time biblical passages displayed a distinct uneasiness toward any "consulter with familiar spirits or necromancer" of the types known among the neighboring pagan tribes (Deuteronomy 18:9–14). The desperate and rebellious King Saul who consulted with "a woman who is a medium" to call up Samuel from the dead was plainly in God's disfavor and not represented as a role model (I Samuel 28:7–25). Congregations of early Christians were bidden to "test the spirits" and to guard against false prophets; ecstatic speaking in tongues was to be evaluated and interpreted immediately by responsible persons in the midst of a responsible congregation (I John 4:1; I Corinthians 14:26–28). The Catholic church came to give cautious approval to invoking the aid of saints but rejected invocation of the uncanonized dead. Partly in reaction to what they understood as Catholic exploitation of claims to have influence or jurisdiction over the spirits of persons gone from the earth, Protestants generally abhorred every notion of direct communication with dead individuals. But everywhere, alongside the attempts at discipline by recognized religions, there was a persistent subculture involving ghosts, witches, demons, and spirits good or bad.

Things changed in the 1800s. "Modern Spiritualism" was born, for the first time a religious movement uniquely based on belief in and practice of regular communication with the dead. Spiritualism also entered a new era of secular promotion and high visibility. Persons in Europe experimenting with the "animal magnetism" theories of Franz Anton Mesmer and with the philosophical-theological ideas of Emanuel Swedenborg found that some of their subjects in trance claimed to be in direct communication with guardian angels and spirits of the dead. In New York state Andrew Jackson Davis reported having conversations with Swedenborg (1688–1771) and with the famous Greek physician Galen (130–200) during his mesmeric trances. Ever since 1837 America's Shakers at worship had been delivering particular messages of admonition or encouragement from their dead as "gifts" to their communities, but the general public hardly heard of them.[1]

In the 1840s Andrew Jackson Davis was such a dramatic and public clairvoyant and his friends were such efficient publicists that thousands of people soon heard of him. Davis gave a series of some 150 lectures in Manhattan while in a state of trance. These were transcribed by colleagues and a compendium of them published in

1847 as *The Principles of Nature*. The work included "an evolutionary account of the origin and growth of the universe, a system of mystical philosophy, an account of the relations between the spirit and the material world, and a plan for the reorganization of society on socialist lines." It went through thirty-four editions within thirty years and was supplemented by a periodical called the *Univercoelum* issued by Davis and his group.[2]

Then, with the insights and terminology of Mesmer, of Swedenborg, and especially of Davis already in the public mind, came the highly publicized "Hydesville Rappings" or "Rochester Knockings" in New York state. The Fox family, good Methodists, moved into a house in Hydesville, near Rochester, which was reputed to be haunted. The house seemed to live up to its reputation with unexplainable noises and manifestations. On 31 March 1848 Katherine and Margaret Fox, ages twelve and thirteen, demonstrated to their parents how their questions addressed to a persistent spirit visitor brought replies in the form of audible rappings. Regional religious authorities and secular newspapers took a lively interest; the investigations brought more publicity. Their elder sister Leah assumed some management of the girls' affairs. Before the process of demonstration and investigation ran its course their promoters included P. T. Barnum and their publicists included the nation's most noted newspaperman, Horace Greeley, who was himself a believer. Margaret became an international personality on tour. She captured the popular mind of America, at once a childlike clairvoyant and a flamboyant spiritualist medium.[3]

The power of the movement was not so much in the philosophy of Davis or the rappings of the Fox sisters. It was in the enlistment of thousands of mediums across the country eager to establish communication with the spirit world. It was in the tens of thousands and eventually millions of persons motivated to investigate and to experiment with spirit communication. Spiritualism seemed to have a special appeal for educated and professional people who were outside the congregational life of local churches but who were still teased by questions about life beyond physical death; for people who had recently lost a close friend or relative by death; for people who were disquieted by claims against religion made in the name of rationalism or science and who saw in the manifestations of Spiritualism acceptable scientific evidence for affirming a spiritual order; and for people who were imaginative reorganizers of society by communal experiment. Following the burst of publicity about Hydesville and Rochester, copied by papers everywhere, Spiritualism was soon thriving in both East and West. Boston had a Spiritualist paper called the *Banner of Light*; Chicago had its *Religio Philosophical Journal*. Spiritual circles and societies multiplied mightily in the East and Ohio was not long deprived.

> The first public demonstrations of Spiritualism in Cincinnati were given on 26th September 1850 by Mrs Bushnell who had developed mediumistic powers after having had experiences in the circles in New York State. In 1851 interest in Spiritualism in the city was greatly stimulated by the visit of the Fox sisters, and some three years later the Cincinnati *Daily Times* reported that at least fifty-nine seances were held regularly every night in the city, that hundreds were held occasionally, and that there were at least 310 practicing mediums. The circles were not restricted to any one class of society, nor to a particular religion. "Christians, Jews and Infidels are earnest in their inquiries. The number of investigators can be estimated only by tens of thousands."[4]

Prominent citizens of Columbus, Ohio, attended investigations of the phenomena at Rochester and returned home to establish Spiritualist circles. The Fox sisters visited Cleveland in 1851 and developed a number of mediums there.[5]

Indiana Mediums

In Athens County, Ohio, a farmer named Jonathan Koons discovered in the early 1850s that he and his eight children were all powerful mediums. Under spirit direction he built a separate log cabin exclusively for seances. The Poston family were among the many visitors who came to observe remarkable phenomena at Koons's Spirit Room. The Postons claimed the promise of the Ohio spirits that like results could be gotten anywhere if certain conditions were met. Poston developed a spirit room at his newly rented farm in LaPorte County, Indiana, and his daughter proved to be such a powerful medium that the demonstrations of the Postons of Indiana were fully the equal of their models in Ohio.[6]

Among the crowds attracted to the Poston circles was Charles Cathcart, an ex-congressman and something of a scientist. Cathcart came as a skeptic, invoking "Balaam's ass" and rigging a flash of light to burst out during a seance to spot any cheating. Soon the whole Cathcart family became convinced participants with their own spirit room open free to the public. "Old King" was the most regular resident spirit for demonstrations related to the Postons and the Cathcarts, serving as sage adviser, friend, counselor, and disciplinarian. Charles Cathcart had a flair for publicity. From LaPorte he sent out an open letter dated 22 February 1857 telling the nation's editors exactly how to set up a demonstration or seance. It was published in New York's *Spiritual Telegraph*. His repeated public offers of a large reward if any fraud could be detected had no takers.[7] The next year he reported to the *Spiritual Clarion* of Auburn, New York:

> Besides astonishing manifestations, speaking, spirit voices, lights, etc., we have now a series of beautiful pictures of the spirit land, painted by the late E. Rogers, of Columbus, Ohio, and exhibited through the magic lantern. There are forty-five scenes in all. I have spent a great deal in giving those manifestations to the world, and have never received and never will, any pecuniary return. I am grateful that I can afford to do so. The mediums will accept of a fair remuneration from those who can afford it, and if those who witness the exhibition of Rogers's paintings, see fit to give anything for the benefit of his widow and orphans, it will be faithfully handed to them and gratefully received.[8]

Angola, Indiana, founded in 1838 by settlers from western New York on an overtly anti-church basis, was for many years a kind of Spiritualist establishment. The works of Andrew Jackson Davis were circulated there; mediums of national reputation came "and did great miracles before the eyes of the public." Some at Angola were evidently of the kind lamented as "worthless and licentious individuals" and were denied the name Spiritualist by historian Emma Hardinge Britten. A modern academic historian of Angola reported that as late as 1865 "it is probable that nine-tenths of the population were spiritualists and given to free-love."[9]

World-class Spiritualists with Indiana connections were Robert Owen and his son Robert Dale Owen. After his communal experiment at New Harmony had failed, Robert Owen returned to Great Britain. Modern American Spiritualism crossed the ocean to seek him out there in 1853 in the person of a medium named Mrs. Hayden who brought him a message from the spirit world. Until his death, notably in his autobiography published in his old age, his testimony as a Spiritualist was unwavering. Even more impressive was the contribution of Robert Dale Owen. His two large books on Spiritualism sold thousands of copies; they were reviewed internationally. It was Robert Dale Owen who reportedly read a long paper on a Spiritualist theme to Abraham Lincoln which brought the comment "Well, for those who like that sort of thing, I should think it is just about the sort of thing they would like." The Owens gave the movement energy and a more respectable status in its early years.[10]

Spiritualist phenomena reported with some regularity by 1860 were: (1) "Rappings, Table-tippings and other sounds and movements of ponderable bodies"; (2) "Spirit Writings and Spirit Drawings," made without the conscious volition of the medium and sometimes called automatic; (3) "Trance and Trance Speaking," in which the medium in trance spoke messages from and sometimes reproduced the voices of the spirits; (4) "Clairvoyance and Clairaudience," in which the medium saw or heard spirits and could describe them or transmit their messages; (5) "Luminous Phenomena" occurring in seances in which radiant objects were seen to float in the darkness; (6) "Spiritual Impersonation," in which the medium reproduced the actions, manner, gait, deportment, or peculiarities of the communicating spirit; (7) "Spirit-Music," presented with or without physical instruments; (8) "Visible and Tactual Manifestations," such as the appearance and touch of spirit hands; (9) "Spirit intercourse by means of the Mirror, Crystal and Vessel of Water." Involuntary utterances of the medium might include speaking in tongues.[11]

An Indianapolis lawyer named John H. Bradley agreed with his friend Judge David McDonald to conduct a personal investigation of Spiritualism. Bradley claimed to have had little interest before being enlisted for the investigation by the judge. He had once attended "the performance of the celebrated Miss Fox" at Hartford and had encountered a dancing piano at a seance in the home of an acquaintance in Washington, D.C. Neither had powerfully impressed him. Bradley and McDonald agreed that if either died in the course of the investigation, the deceased partner would initiate communication with the survivor. The judge died. Bradley said the judge kept the communication pact. Bradley moved from skeptic to convert to advocate of Spiritualism. He became the challenger of every critic.[12]

Bradley of Indianapolis visited the trumpet medium Mrs. Shaffer at Dayton, Ohio, for whom many spirits took up the trumpet and spoke. He reported often and at length on the ministry of a Jeffersonville woman named Mrs. Keigwin, a medium for whom the spirits wrote messages on a slate. The answers were often long, done in excellent form, very rapidly, and always inverted so they were upside down to the medium who kept one hand above the table while the slate was held underneath. In fact, the spirit messages came on the slate even with Mrs. Keigwin bound and gagged. Not all of Mrs. Keigwin's sessions were limited to use of the slate. Bradley's deceased daughter was among the spirits who spoke to him audibly. He was awed by the receptive powers of Mrs.

Hollis at Jeffersonville who "now receives writings on the slate; the spirits talk to their friends through the trumpet, and without any trumpet, as loud and clear as mortals talk. You obtain, in plain and beautiful language, too, full and clear explanations of nature, of the next life and its circumstances, and of many things in this life that we do not otherwise understand."[13]

Because Bradley was such a convinced witness for Spiritualism, he was especially pained by its misuse. Deception was common. Charlatans fleeced the gullible. Mediums in need of a living from their vocation overextended their advertising and dramatics. The Fox sisters themselves eventually admitted misrepresentation. When an Indiana cheater was caught Bradley wrote "I am very glad that Judge Huff, Dr. Yeakel and others, who are well known, and most excellent and reliable men in Tippecanoe county, have exposed that abominable cheat and trickster, Church. They were deficient in duty only, in not ducking him in the Wabash river. Any society that tolerates his connection with them one moment after this exposure at Lafayette, will be unworthy of anybody's respect, and so far as they may pretend any connection with the investigation of the sublime and sacred theory of Spiritualism, should be at once and everywhere repudiated."[14]

At a Terre Haute seance the spirit hand shown by the medium had the same ink mark as the hand of the medium. The whistle blown by spirits had the same ink mark as the mouth of the medium. Bradley said "That exhibition, in any of its different phases, was not one of spiritualism at all, and ought not to have been written or spoken of as such. It had nothing to do with Spiritualism. It was plain, open jugglery, and the little girl ought to have been advertised under the patronage of Barnum, instead of that of the Society of Spiritualists . . . I am surprised that the honest and honorable men, who are really spiritualists, who reside there, and have gotten up their hall, who were present, did not take her by the ears and walk her out of the house. Dr. Pence did right, of course, to hand the people back their money." He reiterated that even spirit messages could not be received uncritically since there were agents of disturbance everywhere. "It is one of the important Providential designs of these manifestations to teach mankind that spirits in general maintain the characters that they formed to themselves during their early life—that, indeed, they are the identical persons they were while dwelling in the flesh—hence, that while there are just, truthful, wise, and Christian spirits, there are also spirits addicted to lying, profanity, obscenity, mischief, and violence, and spirits who deny God and religion, just as they did while in your world." Unhappy experiences at Spiritualist sessions were likely due to the mischief of some lower order of spirits.[15]

In spite of all the hazards, Bradley felt the extension of Spiritualism and the multiplication of mediums was essential for the good of humankind. A spirit told him there was someone born with the qualities and capacity to be a medium in nearly every family. He urged interested persons with a slate and a cover and a receptive attitude to experiment. These direct experiences of the spirits through capable mediums could have the objectivity and method of true science since "One simple, plain manifestation is worth a hundred theories or opinions. One true and perfect medium is worth a thousand lecturers."[16]

Bradley was certain that all earnest practitioners of Spiritualism would "soon find a rational and scientific ground on which to rest every real Christian doctrine—miracles, regeneration, resurrection, and all, with the great advantage of having the fact of immortality of the soul taken out of the sphere of mere faith, and made a plain, proven, fixed fact. And further, that hereafter they shall lead science, rather than be dragged in its trail, and that science shall be enrolled in the service of God's religion, and no longer, as it and its votaries have nearly always heretofore been, be on the side of materialism and infidelity." Out of his mediated communications with his daughter and Judge McDonald and many other spirits he accumulated an impressive body of Spiritualist testimony and doctrine. This he offered to the public in a series of articles in the *Indiana State Sentinel*. These newspaper articles he gathered and augmented with some further insights from his reading in Spiritualist literature and published the whole at Indianapolis in 1870 as *Some Examination of the Theory of Spiritualism*. It was popularly written, often in question and answer format, a veritable Hoosier catechism for Spiritualists or inquirers.[17]

Indiana kept on contributing Spiritualist leaders. The first known certificate recording the ordination of a Spiritualist "minister" was issued by an Indiana association in 1869.

Many . . . unorganized but zealous workers, remaining true to their convictions in the face of persecution, aided the movement. Among these were Julius A. Wayland, editor of the *Coming Nation*, of Greensburg, Indiana, and later of the *Appeal to Reason*, of Kansas; Dr. Henry Stockinger, one of the first graduates of Indiana University, later a student under Joseph Rodes Buchanan, professor of the Cincinnati Eclectic Medical College, father of psychometry, author and spiritualist; Dr. H. V. Sweringen, head of the Medical Association of Ft. Wayne, lecturer and writer; Hon. A. B. Richmond, of Switzerland county, M.D. and lecturer, later United States court attorney, author of books on legal questions; Mrs. Henrietta Elliott, propagandist, North Vernon; Mrs. L. L. Lawrence, noted as first to establish free dress cutting and making schools in Indianapolis and other cities. With voice and pen Mrs. Lawrence announced the discoveries made by her mother, "Grandma Davis" who became a remarkable medium at the age of eighty.[18]

Twenty delegates representing Indiana societies attended a national Spiritualist convention in Chicago in 1873.[19]

Camp Chesterfield

Effective state organization for Indiana Spiritualists came slowly. Mediums were individualistic and mobile; many were not anxious for oversight or regulation or the paying of dues. A crucial advocate of state structure was J. W. Westerfield of Anderson. Son of a Methodist circuit rider and never himself a practicing medium, Westerfield held gatherings of free-thinking elements of the population in a hall above his drugstore on the town square in the 1880s. Many of them adopted Spiritualism. In the concurrent effort to effect a state organization and provide a location for a Spiritualist camp, the Westerfield family of Anderson and the Bronnenberg family of nearby Chesterfield played prominent roles. The campsite location committee had thirteen members including five from Indianapolis. Crown Point asked consideration, offering location on a lake. The committee member from Anderson was J. W. Westerfield. Beginning in 1890 the new Indiana Association of Spiritualists, under Westerfield's presidency, met on the Carroll and Emily Bronnenberg property on the bank of White River at Chesterfield.

The Indiana Association of Spiritualists purchased thirty-four acres of Bronnenberg land in 1892, thanks largely to the generosity of Westerfields and Bronnenbergs. Camp Chesterfield then began its long evolution from tent town to shanty town to residential village with large provision for transients. Eventually the Bee Line Railroad offered excursion fares to Chesterfield; the Union Traction Company had a trolley spur which entered the camp gates, turned right, and reversed on a manual push-around within the grounds. In 1924 historian Anna Stockinger stated that Camp Chesterfield was the second largest Spiritualist camp in the nation, second only to Lily Dale in New York:

> The charming location and modern equipment make the Indiana camp an ideal retreat for thousands coming from every state in the union to investigate the phenomena of

Spiritualism in open light through certificated mediums, and to hear its philosophy explained by the highest talent in the ranks. Camp Chesterfield holds its six-weeks' session annually, beginning in July, with an average attendance of twenty thousand.

Stockinger noted the large number of Indiana's Spiritualist groups, by then generally designated as "churches," and all too optimistically estimated their "average general attendance" at half a million.[20]

The strength of Spiritualism had waned by the end of the 1920s, the extent and rate of its weakening hard to measure because of a lack of central reporting. There were exposures of fraud and deception. Accounts of a few experiments with free love and communal living tended to discredit the movement. In spite of repeated protestations of Christian orthodoxy by such Spiritualists as John H. Bradley at Indianapolis, most churches perceived Spiritualism as something other than Christian and sometimes clearly anti-Christian. Coverage of Spiritualism by both the church press and the secular press turned negative. Central leadership and discipline of ministry were often absent among Spiritualists; when attempted they were often unwelcome.

The National Spiritualist Association of Churches, formed in 1893, did play some stabilizing role. It offered and advocated standard definitions and principles for Spiritualists. Six "principles" were derived through spirit communication in 1899: (1) We believe in Infinite Intelligence; (2) We believe that the phenomena of nature both physical and spiritual are the expression of Infinite Intelligence; (3) We affirm that a correct understanding of such expression and living in accordance therewith constitute true religion; (4) We affirm that the existence and personal identity of the individual continue after the change called death; (5) We affirm that communication with the so-called dead is a fact, scientifically proven by the phenomena of Spiritualism; (6) We believe that the highest morality is contained in the golden rule, "Whatsoever ye would that others should do unto you, do ye also unto them." Two more principles were added in 1909: (7) We affirm the moral responsibility of the individual and that he makes his own happiness or unhappiness as he obeys or disobeys nature's physical and spiritual laws; (8) We affirm that the doorway to reformation is never closed against any human soul, here or hereafter. And the ninth principle came in 1950: We affirm that the precept of Prophecy contained in the Bible is a divine attribute proven through mediumship.[21]

According to definitions provided by the National Spiritualist Association,

Spiritualism is the Science Philosophy and Religion of continuous life based upon the demonstrated fact of communication by means of Mediumship with those who live in the Spirit World.

A Spiritualist is one who believes as a part of his or her religion, in the communication between this and the Spirit World by means of Mediumship, and who endeavors to mould his or her character and conduct in accordance with the highest teaching derived from such communion.

A Medium is one whose organism is sensitive to vibrations from the Spirit World and through whose instrumentality, intelligences in that world are able to convey messages and produce the phenomena of Spiritualism.[22]

Publications distributed by the National Spiritualist Association expanded the doctrines. Infinite Intelligence is an all pervading mind and power but not a personal God. Jesus of Nazareth was the greatest medium ever known, the greatest teacher ever known, the greatest spiritual healer ever known, but no person of a divine trinity or agent of vicarious atonement. Saul of Tarsus was a superb communicator with the world of spirit. The Bible is rich in Spiritualism from the mediums Abraham and Moses in Genesis and Exodus to the trumpet of Revelation 4:1.[23]

The last national religious census in 1936 listed twenty Spiritualist churches in Indiana in connection with the National Spiritualist Association of Churches, but most of Indiana's Spiritualists had discontinued any such national affiliation long before and so were not well represented in that census. Perhaps a score of churches continued into the 1980s, mostly in urban communities such as Anderson, Bloomington, Evansville, Fort Wayne, Hammond, Indianapolis, Muncie, Peru, and Terre Haute.

As scores of Spiritualist camp grounds in other states faltered and failed, Indiana's Camp Chesterfield persisted. A large part of this persistence was due to the leadership of physical medium and executive secretary Mable Riffle who served as its principal administrator from 1909 to 1961. Events at Camp Chesterfield attracted sufficient attendance to enlist a corps of very popular mediums who in turn perpetuated the good attendance. After World War II came new buildings of brick and stone—hotel, cathedral, cafeteria. The Hett Art Gallery and Museum was dedicated in 1955 to house a permanent exhibition of such items as trumpets, slates, spirit writings, and trance paintings along with mementos of famous mediums, not least a large display of items associated with the Fox family of Hydesville, New York. Mable Riffle and her colleagues wanted a Spiritualist college at Camp Chester-

field. The result of their labors was not a conventional college but an education center, a conference center, a book and literature distribution center, and a service point for a wide Spiritualist constituency.

In the 1990s, at the end of its first hundred years, Camp Chesterfield was home to twenty-seven mediums who lived on the grounds, a major portion of the center's resident faculty. Their specialties within the approved broad categories of physical mediums, mental mediums, and healing mediums were neatly placarded on signs before their houses. Many students working toward ministerial certification were among those who attended the three major week-long seminars—spring, summer, and fall—where a faculty of twenty offered a total of forty courses ranging from Aura to Yoga. In addition there were smaller weekend seminars, typically conducted by two teachers, about once a month. Visitors by auto and busload arrived from the Midwest but also from more distant places such as Florida, California, and Canada. They stayed for a weekend or a week or longer, almost any combination of study being available by prior arrangement with the resident mediums. Regular Sunday services and psychic fairs about once a month added more occasions for spiritual consultation and message work. There was really no off-season. Camp Chesterfield in Indiana had become what was probably the largest center for Spiritualist ministry and training in the world. Further ministry was offered by the Universal Spiritualist Association at its headquarters and Maplegrove Spiritualist Camp at nearby Anderson. The *National Spiritualist*, official paper of the National Spiritualist Association of Churches, was being edited in Indianapolis by Herbert Ray Worth, minister of the Psychic Science Spiritualist Church. Spiritualist study materials were being issued at Indianapolis from Summit Publications at 668 East 62nd Street.

The breadth of the constituency of Camp Chesterfield at the beginning of the camp's second century illustrated the divided state of Spiritualism. Camp Chesterfield was the headquarters of the Indiana Association of Spiritualists and scene of that association's annual convocation for business. The Indiana Association respected the standards and used approved educational materials of the National Spiritualist Association of Churches and its more prestigious Morris Pratt Institute in Wisconsin without being officially related to either. Students, resident mediums, and individual churches participating in Camp Chesterfield programs might be affiliated with any or all of a half dozen Spiritualist associations, or with none.

The whole varied Spiritualist enterprise was being stimulated and impacted by a new force, the popular mystical pantheism of a contemporary mass media medium named Shirley MacLaine. All the facets of the New Age Movement of MacLaine and the host of her constituents interfaced almost perfectly with units already well established in the curriculum at Camp Chesterfield. The "channeling" advocated by the New Age to contact and harvest the insights of the spirit world was precisely the familiar "message work" of the Spiritualists. Both were willing to share to some extent the vocabulary and symbolism of traditional Christians—God, Jesus Christ, Holy Spirit, salvation—but the understandings and definitions differed.

May Wright Sewall

The story of Hoosier Spiritualists might be told in part with an account of its churches. Regular church services often included prayer, music, singing, selections read from the *Spiritualist Manual*, a sermon or lecture, and spirit messages from the departed in any of several forms. The story of Hoosier Spiritualists might be told in part in the history of the diverse associations and of Camp Chesterfield. But Spiritualism always retained an esoteric quality which resisted regularization. Mediums were very mobile individual practitioners. Some clients chose to keep their experimentation private. Such a solitary case was that of May Wright Sewall. She was principal of the Classical School for Girls in Indianapolis for twenty-five years, a woman who played a leading role in many good causes both locally and nationally. Booth Tarkington said, "She was a very leading citizen, indeed, in those days of her greatest activity in Indianapolis," ranking in his judgment with Benjamin Harrison and James Whitcomb Riley as one of the three most prominent citizens of the city. In 1920, the year of her death, she published *Neither Dead nor Sleeping* about her experiences in Spiritualism.[24]

For May Wright Sewall this publication was one more public service, offering an assurance of a survival after death and of a continuity of relationship. As an educator she believed that psychic science would come to be taught in high schools and universities just as natural science was. She had gone to speak for women's suffrage at a Chautauqua meeting at Lily Dale in New York in 1897. In a sitting with a slate writer she had received written replies when neither slate nor written questions had passed from her own hands. After that time she had enjoyed almost daily communications from her dead husband, was given piano lessons by the recently deceased Anton Rubenstein, and recovered from Bright's disease after following direct instructions of a medieval priest. Mrs. Sewall showed the manuscript of her book to Booth Tarkington, who wrote: "It was to me dumfounding to find that for more than twenty years this academic-liberal of a thousand human activities, Mrs. Sewall, had been really living not with the living, so to put it. And as I read, it seemed to me that I had never known so strange a story." Indianapolis was dumfounded too, since hardly anybody would have suspected that this practical reformer was communicating with the spirit world. The very shock may have muted her testimony both as Spiritualist and as reformer.[25]

NOTES

1. Geoffrey K. Nelson, *Spiritualism and Society* (New York: Schocken Books, 1969), 3; Edward Deming Andrews, *The People Called Shakers: A Search for the Perfect Society* (New York: Oxford University Press, 1953), 152–76.

2. Andrew Jackson Davis, *The Principles of Nature, Her Divine Revelations, and a Voice to Mankind*, by and through Andrew Jackson Davis . . . (New York: S. S. Lyon and W. Fishbough, 1847, 782 p.); Nelson, *Spiritualism and Society*, 50–53.

3. Nelson, *Spiritualism and Society*, 3–7; Earl Wesley Fornell, *The Unhappy Medium: Spiritualism and the Life of Margaret Fox* (Austin, Texas: University of Texas Press, 1964), 3–23. Ages of the sisters are cited from Fornell; reports of their ages in other sources vary by as much as four years.

4. Nelson, *Spiritualism and Society*, 13.

5. Emma Hardinge Britten, *Nineteenth Century Miracles; or, Spirits and Their Work in Every Country of the Earth. A Complete Historical Compendium of the Great Movement Known as "Modern Spiritualism"* (New York: Lovell and Co., 1884), 431–34; Nelson, *Spiritualism and Society*, 13, 18–23, 130–52, 256–59.

6. Nelson, *Spiritualism and Society*, 14.

7. Emma Hardinge Britten, *Modern American Spiritualism: A Twenty Years' Record of the Communion between Earth and the World of Spirits* (New York: the Author, 1870), 307–41.

8. Britten, *Modern American Spiritualism*, 341.

9. Newell L. Sims, *A Hoosier Village*, (New York: Columbia University, 1912), 63; Britten, *Nineteenth Century Miracles*, 427–30; Fornell, *Unhappy Medium*, 33–39, 72.

10. Carl Sandburg, *Abraham Lincoln: The War Years*, 4 vols. (New York: Harcourt, Brace, 1939), 2:306.

11. Nelson, *Spiritualism and Society*, 29–30.

12. John H. Bradley, *Some Examination of the Theory of Spiritualism* (Indianapolis, Ind.: Indiana State Sentinel Print, 1870), 3–4.

13. Bradley, *Some Examination*, 28–34, 44–51, 197; Britten, *Nineteenth Century Miracles*, 434.

14. Reuben Briggs Davenport, *The Death-blow to Spiritualism: Being the True Story of the Fox Sisters, as Revealed by Authority of Margaret Fox Kane and Catherine Fox Jencken* (New York: G. W. Dillingham, 1888, 247 p.); Nelson, *Spiritualism and Society*, 7; Fornell, *Unhappy Medium*, 176–81; Bradley, *Some Examination*, 92.

15. Bradley, *Some Examination*, 106, 142, 144.

16. Bradley, *Some Examination*, 14, 40–41, 164.

17. Bradley, *Some Examination*, 109–10.

18. Anna Stockinger, "The History of Spiritualism in Indiana," *Indiana Magazine of History* 20 (September 1924): 281–82.

19. Nelson, *Spiritualism and Society*, 26; Stockinger, "History," 282.

20. *Chesterfield Lives* (Chesterfield, Ind.: Camp Chesterfield, 1986, 95 p.); Stockinger, "History," 282–84.

21. Peggy Barnes, *The Questionnaire for the Teacher and the Investigator* (Indianapolis, Ind.: Summit Publications, N.S.A.C., n.d., 58 p.); Peggy Barnes, *The Fundamentals of Spiritualism* (Indianapolis, Ind.: N.S.A.C. Publishing Center, n.d., 44 p.).

22. Barnes, *Questionnaire*, 3.

23. Barnes, *Questionnaire*, 4, 14, 22, 34, 42, 57; Barnes, *Fundamentals*, 7–8.

24. May Wright Sewall, *Neither Dead nor Sleeping*, with an Introduction by Booth Tarkington (Indianapolis, Ind.: Bobbs-Merrill, 1920, [44], 320 p.).

25. Jane Stephens, "May Wright Sewall: An Indiana Reformer," *Indiana Magazine of History* 78 (December 1982): 293–95; Sewall, *Neither Dead nor Sleeping*, [22–25].

JEWS

Jews are all those related by descent or conversion to an ancient Hebrew people of Palestine. Judaism is a religion associated with this Hebrew people which affirms belief in one God as revealed to Abraham, Moses, and the prophets. Lives of the believers are to be governed by the Hebrew Scriptures, notably the first five books or the Torah, interpreted by rabbinic traditions. Not all who count themselves Jews ethnically profess themselves to be believers in or practitioners of Judaism.[1]

Jews came early to America. There were reputedly at least two secret Jews aboard the ships of Columbus. A small group of refugees from Brazil came to Peter Stuyvesant's New Amsterdam in 1654. Theirs became the first Jewish congregation in North America. For the first 150 years the small clusters of American Jews were on the eastern seaboard. At the time of the Revolution there was not a single rabbi in the colonies. In 1800, as Indiana was opening to substantial white settlement, all of American Jewry probably did not exceed two or three thousand.[2] When larger immigrations of Jews did come, they showed a preference for location in cities. Early Indiana had some towns, few cities, and no such metropolis as New York, Philadelphia, or Chicago. The whole Jewish population of Indiana has often been about equal to the Jewish population of metropolitan Cincinnati.

Because there were so few of them, Jews in Indiana often lacked the support of a practicing Jewish community. Until 1824 not a single congregation existed within 500 miles of Cincinnati. Jewish tradesman John Jacob

Hays moved from New York to Cahokia on the Mississippi in 1793 and was thus within the bounds of Indiana Territory when it was formed in 1800. President Madison later appointed Hays to be Indian agent at Fort Wayne. He married Marie Louise Brouillet at Vincennes; their three daughters were almost certainly reared in the Christian faith. He lived out his years in Indiana and Illinois apart from Jewish society. Rutgers graduate Samuel Judah became a Vincennes lawyer in 1818, rising to notable service as state legislator and United States district attorney. He also married outside the faith and his children were not raised as Jews. The first native Jewish child west of the Alleghenies was Edward Isaac Israel, born to David and Eliza Israel (named "Johnson" by the Indians) at Connersville in 1819. David and his brother Phineas were traders with the Indians along the Whitewater River. The religious affiliation of Phineas is unknown. In 1820 David moved his family from Indiana to Cincinnati, thereby boosting the adult Jewish population of that city to six. He was prominent among the English Jews who formed a congregation there in 1824 and dedicated the city's first synagogue in 1836.[3]

German Jews in Indiana

By 1859 there were about 3,000 Jews living in Indiana, a number about equal to the Jewish population of the whole nation fifty years before. Basis of that remarkable increase was the massive immigration of Germans to the

United States. More than a million came to America between 1820 and 1855; 2 to 3 percent of them were Jewish. Almost all the German immigrants were pushed from Europe by bad conditions; they were pulled to America by hope for better opportunity. Jews felt these motivations especially. Laws on residence, property holding, and marriage were so restrictive for Jews that emigration seemed the only chance for many to own a home or establish a family. Those who came were often single men. They were mobile enough to move westward with the expanding frontiers and take their places naturally among all the other German speakers. An Indiana historian said:

> They settled in Hoosier towns with relative ease. As high as twenty per cent of them received assistance from Jewish charities in New York. Most began their western experience, as their predecessors had, by becoming petty retailers, representing urban merchants in the backwoods. They were more fortunate than their predecessors, however, because the tide of immigration which brought them to American shores quickened the westward movement and increased the size of western market towns. The Germans did not wander about as peddlers for long, but tended to go west with the idea of settling down immediately among their own kind. As early as 1825, there was a community of German Jews in Rising Sun, Indiana, twenty miles from Cincinnati. By the 1840s, river towns in all parts of the state—Madison, Evansville, Vincennes, Terre Haute, Indianapolis, Lafayette, Fort Wayne, LaPorte—had three or four Jewish families each, mostly of German stock, drawn there by prospects of good trading opportunities along the inland waterways.[4]

Economic life in Indiana went satisfactorily for this first wave of Jews from Germany. Nearly all of them established themselves well enough to live in comfort and to plan an even higher level of achievement for their children. Several provided models of excellence in business and in community service. But stable Jewish religious practice was always precarious in the small or medium-sized Hoosier towns. There were only a few families in each town. Some of the families were not religious; secular liberalism had its advocates among these Germans. There were Jewish fraternal groups, insurance plans, and burial societies enough to meet the social needs of those who craved no synagogue. Those more committed to traditional Jewish practice found it difficult to secure kosher meat where there was no local religious officer to certify it and no refrigeration to preserve it. Friday evening and Saturday were the proper times for weekly observance of Sabbath; these were also the times when rural Hoosiers swarmed to town and expected Jewish merchants to be attending to trade. Religious instruction for children, particularly the Hebrew language for Scripture study and prayer, was difficult to arrange. Members of religious families who enjoyed economic success were attracted from the towns to the larger cities where both business and religious communities provided more opportunity. Jewish young people who went away from a Hoosier town to college were more likely to gravitate to a major city than to return. Even where the desire was strong for regular worship, observance of holy days, provision of consecrated burial grounds, education of Jewish children, and support for Jewish needy, the cost of supporting a rabbi was a heavy burden for so few. As transportation improved it was tempting to rely on a nominal relation with a stronger Jewish community some distance away.

When Adam Gimbel arrived from Bavaria in 1835 he was impressed with the mountains of merchandise at New Orleans while the scattered western settlers had so many needs. He moved as a peddler along the Mississippi and its tributaries and on 24 May 1842 paid $5 at Vincennes for a "peddlar's license" at that place to "retail dry goods until the first Monday in June." Gimbel stopped at Vincennes. His brothers Solomon, Lehman, Karl, Moses, Isaac, Elias, Abraham, and Seleman joined him there as did his sister Gertreid. The family holdings at Vincennes came to include four stores, a wholesale liquor business, and major interest in the American Bank of Vincennes. Seven of Adam's ten sons lived to reach maturity, each of them receiving basic training for business in Vincennes. The family and its enterprises were admired and valued by the community. And all these Gimbels were by no means the only Jews in Vincennes. Yet Vincennes did not become a Jewish center. Adam Gimbel and his brother-in-law, Gertreid's husband, decided to sell out and move to Philadelphia in 1866. Family members and family interests gradually followed. Gimbel's opened stores in Philadelphia (1894), New York (1910), and Pittsburgh (1925). In 1928 Saks Fifth Avenue became a Gimbel subsidiary. Adam Gimbel's nephew Jake devoted most of his time and fortune to helping boys of talent to gain a higher education, some in Indiana but mostly in California. Jewish presence in Vincennes declined. The religion section in the history of Knox County compiled in 1911 gave Judaism three lines: "The B'nai B'rith is the name adopted by a congregation of Israelites who are at present without a rabbi, the functions of which office are performed by Daniel Oestreicher, who is secretary of the order."[5]

In 1854 the newspapers announced that the Lake Shore and Michigan Southern Railroad would pass through Ligonier. It was probably this news which attracted Frederick William Straus and Solomon Mier to this village of 300. Straus began with a small general store and brought his brothers Mathias and Jacob to Ligonier from Germany. The Straus brothers manufactured buggies. They traded some buggies for land and developed this interest into the largest farm brokerage firm in the United States. They founded the Citizens Bank. Solomon Mier and his sons also established a general store, bank, and land brokerage. Their carriage and buggy company even produced an automobile. Jewish cousins, nieces, aunts, and uncles came to live in Ligonier. There was Loeser in horses, Schloss in dry goods, Selig in cattle, Jacobs in general merchandise, and Wertheimer in grain, seed, and wool. There were Jewish families named Ackerman, Kahn, Kann, Levy, Mayor, Rose, Sachs, Schuster, and Solomon. They competed commercially until farmers brought their crops and livestock from thirty miles around to trade at Ligonier. They collaborated in the synagogue.

Congregation Ahavath Shalom was formed at Ligonier in 1865 and completed its building on Main Street in 1871. Many Jews in Ligonier were traditional at first—Bar Mitzvah for all boys at age thirteen; men wearing hats and prayer shawls during worship; observation of dietary laws including use of separate sets of dishes for milk and meat. However, family pews rather than separate seating were provided in the first synagogue and within five years the prayer book of liberal Reform Judaism was adopted. When the new temple was dedicated on Main Street in 1889, that champion of Reform Judaism Isaac Mayer Wise came from Cincinnati to preach the sermon. Ligonier's congregation was affiliated with the Union of American Hebrew Congregations. In the next decade English replaced German, and Hebrew school gave way to Sabbath school. Here was a Jewish community of some fifty-five families, more than 200 persons. They were well integrated into the economic, social, and political life and leadership of the town. For years following construction of their first synagogue building, they had resident rabbis. Yet the years following 1900 saw a steady decline. The older generation died off. The younger generation moved away. Jewish immigrants entering the United States were not attracted to a small Hoosier town. By 1904 a part-time rabbi from South Bend conducted services only on Friday nights and conducted school on Saturdays. By 1932 services were held only on High Holy Days, conducted by a lay person from Chicago, and the Sabbath school was closed.[6]

At Columbus, Indiana, it was David and Samuel Samuels who evolved from peddlers to prosperous merchants and woolen mill owners. They brought their parents over from Germany. Along with other Jewish families named Vogel, Schloss, Kantrowitz, and Elfmann, they took the name Congregation Chisak Emuna in 1861, advertised for a rabbi in 1862, and dedicated their new synagogue in 1871. The *American Israelite* of Isaac Mayer Wise in Cincinnati published a letter from Columbus dated 9 January 1877.

> Columbus contains only about 5,000 inhabitants, and is the only place between Louisville and Indianapolis on the J.M. and I.R.R., that numbers among its houses of worship a Jewish church, which numbers about fifteen or twenty members . . . We are to have a wedding in a few days, the contracting parties being Miss Rose Blustine, daughter of S. Blustine, Esq. of this place, and a Mr. Wolfensticker of Kentucky. Great preparations are being made to make the affair rank above any of a similar kind that has ever taken place in our vicinity.[7]

Another letter to the *Israelite* dated 1 August 1879 reported with pride and pleasure on an address by "our beloved minister Rev. Samuel M. Laski" to about 1,000 in attendance at an interdenominational Sunday school convention in Columbus. But a historian of Bartholomew County in 1888 said Rabbi Samuel M. Laski was more scholarly than popular and "under him dissensions arose which materially interfered with the prosperity of the church." Where once there had been thirty member families with some 180 persons, only five families remained. Meetings were being held in the synagogue only once or twice a year. Jewish families moving to Columbus either did not choose or were not able to revive the local synagogue.[8]

In 1921 there was no longer a Jewish congregation in Columbus. Those who wanted religious services traveled fifty miles north to Indianapolis or seventy miles south to Louisville. Jewish young people often found marriage partners among their gentile schoolmates. William E. Marsh offered what he considered proof that Columbus held no prejudice against Jews: "The only Jewish weddings I recall were all with Gentiles, and the marriages, I believe, were very happy. Rena Brunswick married a Christian boy; Pansy Beatty and Ivy Dunlap, daughters of leading Baptist families, married Ben Bloch and Morris Rosenbush—and made good Baptists out of them. Jessie

Spurgeon's first husband was a Jew. One of the Kaiser girls married Schuyler Harrington, one of the Times printers from North Vernon, a Gentile." In 1969 Columbus Hebrew Congregation needed to be formed anew, meeting monthly at the Unitarian Universalist Hall and served by a rabbinical student from Hebrew Union College.[9]

A historian of Muncie said, "The most striking quality of Muncie's Jewish population was its restlessness, as individuals moved in and out of town searching for greater economic opportunity." Those who remained in Muncie long enough, even though in majority from Orthodox homes, generally came to align themselves with Temple Beth-El which was a Reform synagogue linked with Hebrew Union College in Cincinnati. The congregation could hardly afford a full-time rabbi and was often served by students or very recent graduates of Hebrew Union College. In the heyday of the 1920s there were twenty-four Jewish businesses in Muncie supporting eighty or ninety Jewish families. Orthodox practice was difficult to maintain; liberal practice seemed more suited to the situation in Muncie. In the 1960s those interviewed understood themselves as part of a declining Jewish population.[10]

Morris Feuerlicht, class of 1901, was the first graduate of Hebrew Union College to become rabbi at Lafayette. Congregation Ahavas Achim had been gathered there in 1851 and had dedicated a new house of worship for its thirty-five families in 1868. Ten rabbis had come and gone by 1886. By 1904 Feuerlicht had also moved along to serve the state's largest Jewish congregation at Indianapolis. At about the same time Lafayette families named Spector, Wasserstein, Goldberg, Winski, Pearlman, Wolfe, Goodman, Salzman, and Elkin were busy with plans for improvement of the Orthodox synagogue. That congregation employed Rabbi Gershuny from Cleveland in 1908. Central to the plan was a move from their rented hall on the third floor of the Levy and Rice Shirt Factory to a new synagogue building.[11]

Such was the transient, divided, and often precarious nature of Jewish communities in many of Indiana's small and middle-sized towns. There were about 100 Jewish men, women, and children living in Whitley County in 1900. The Whitley county seat at Columbia City had a Jewish cemetery and a Ladies Hebrew Benevolent Society but no synagogue. Jews there who practiced their faith communally depended on the rabbis and services at Fort Wayne. Those in New Albany depended on Louisville. Those at Connersville and Richmond felt the attraction of Cincinnati, Dayton, or Indianapolis.[12]

Jews from Eastern Europe

There was an important new wave of Jewish immigration beginning about 1880. The number of recorded synagogues in America grew from 270 in 1880 to 553 in 1890 to 1,901 in 1916 to 3,100 in 1927. Indiana's Jewish population increased eightfold from 3,381 in 1877 to 25,000 in 1904, a level long retained. This new immigration wave furnished the strength to assure a continuing Jewish presence in Indiana. The half dozen families of Jews at Richmond had hardly viewed themselves as a Jewish community before World War I. It was the addition and integration of the later immigrants with names like Fivelowitz and Vigransky which provided a basis for a Jewish congregation and Sisterhood in 1919, a Jewish Council in 1948, a B'nai B'rith lodge in 1955, and the dedication of a synagogue in 1963.[13]

This infusion of the new immigrant energy did not occur painlessly or uniformly across Indiana's towns. The bulk of the later Jewish immigrants were not from Germany but from eastern Europe. Many were from closely knit Orthodox communities in a huge, backward, and desperately poor agricultural region extending from the Baltic Sea to the Black Sea. They set out for America from Russia, Poland, Lithuania, and the Baltic states. To the resident Jews of an earlier generation, these new arrivals were often an embarrassment. They had the handicaps of poverty. Intense community and Orthodox religious discipline had been a basis for their survival. Theirs was a proud ethnicity welded to Orthodoxy. Traditional garb was important. The family language was Yiddish, a fusion of middle high German and Russian and Romance elements usually written in Hebrew characters right to left. The language of prayer and Scripture study was Hebrew. Religious exercises could be loud and long, especially those related to death and burial. Ancient tradition governed many details of living.

Most of Indiana's earlier Jews had for some time been demonstrating that they were fully American rather than foreign ethnic. It was a gift of $10,000 from Henry Adler of Lawrenceburg which had especially encouraged Rabbi Isaac Mayer Wise to press on to organize the Union of American Hebrew Congregations in 1873, Hebrew Union College at Cincinnati in 1875, and the Central Conference of American Rabbis in 1889.[14] "American" was a central word in the vision of Wise for the future of Judaism. For him "America was Zion and Washington was Jerusalem . . . The destiny of freedom—and therefore of Judaism—was indissolubly linked with the glory and the future of America, whose Constitution was Mosaic in substance and whose movement was toward the Good Society."[15] He said in his paper, the *Israelite,*

Sell our magnificent synagogues? Dispose of our gorgeous temples? Yes, you had better sell them. In twenty years, if you go on as you do now, there will be no use for them. A synagogue without a preacher, without a good and eloquent preacher, is of very little use. In twenty years an American Jew will speak English only as a rule. We will have no English preachers. England educates none. America educates none. No preachers will be equivalent to no synagogues and no temples. In twenty years you will need none. You had better sell them at your first best chance. Therefore, sell out in time or go to work to educate eloquent ministers for the American Jewish pulpit.[16]

However varied the mixture of orthodoxy and liberalism in their beginnings, most of the synagogues of the nation had come into Wise's "Reform" fellowship by the early 1880s. That was certainly the bent of most of the congregations in Indiana where the proximity of Wise and of his college at Cincinnati made his influence all the stronger. Temple Israel of Lafayette was a charter member of Wise's Union of American Hebrew Congregations.[17] When Abraham Cronbach went from the 1906 graduating class of Hebrew Union College to be rabbi at Temple Beth-El in South Bend, he found the congregation leaders ultra-liberal. They wanted no Friday evening or Saturday services except on New Year and Day of Atonement. They wanted less preaching on Bible texts and more discussions of questions of the day. They wanted no Hebrew class.

One of the first pieces of information imparted to me upon my arrival in South Bend was that the purpose of the temple was to demonstrate to the Gentiles that all Jews are not as indecorous as the 'Pollaks'—Jews of East European origin. A few weeks before the congregation had been started, some of the older and wealthier Jewish residents had attended the funeral of an acquaintance who had retained some vestiges of Orthodox background. Those older residents, unfamiliar with Orthodox Jewish ways, were inexpressibly shocked at the bedlam of the Orthodox obsequies. There is nothing in Orthodox Judaism more repulsive to Reform Jews than the disorder of Orthodox funerals. That funeral so horrified the older Jewish residents of South Bend that, with a minimum of delay, they organized a Reform Temple for the purpose of convincing the Gentiles that there are Jews among whom funerals can be solemn and dignified.[18]

To the new immigrants from eastern Europe, this "American" Judaism looked like no Judaism at all. People who kept no kosher kitchen, sat with heads uncovered in mixed seating for services and prayers in English, tolerated organ music in their "temples" and employed singers who were sometimes Gentiles, drove their automobiles or rode the train to services on Sabbath or High Holy Days—such people, the East Europeans thought, could hardly claim to be Jews. Even after he graduated from Hebrew Union College in 1922 and began his service as Reform rabbi at Lafayette, Samuel H. Markowitz could not rid his mind of the question of his Orthodox father. "What is the difference between you and an ethically sensitive non-Jew? He doesn't pray daily; neither do you. He eats non-kosher food; so do you."[19]

Concentration in Urban Centers

The newer immigrants from eastern Europe kept arriving until they were a majority among Indiana's Jews. Some of them did go to the towns where they established or strengthened Jewish communities. Most of them settled in larger population centers where employment as well as ethnic and Orthodox support were more available. Thus 80 percent of Indiana's Jews came to live in five cities—Indianapolis, Gary, South Bend, Fort Wayne, and Evansville, in that order.[20]

Fort Wayne had formed the first Jewish congregation in the state in 1848. Among the founders of Achduth Vesholom were Frederick Nirdlinger, A. Oppenheimer, Sigismund Redelspeimer, and J. Lauferty. Nirdlinger opened his home for the first meetings. The twenty-six charter members named him congregation president. By 1854 they employed a rabbi and in 1859 converted an old German Methodist church into the state's most impressive synagogue. Isaac Leeser, editor of the Jewish monthly the *Occident* published in Philadelphia, came to Fort Wayne to give the dedicatory address. When Stephen Douglas visited Fort Wayne in the year of the synagogue dedication, Frederick Nirdlinger symbolized the full acceptance of the earlier echelon of Jews by riding in a carriage with the senator through the streets of the city. By the time Samuel H. Markowitz went to be rabbi at Fort Wayne in 1924 he found about 300 Jewish families living there. They were divided among his Reform congregation at Achduth Vesholom, the Orthodox B'nai Jacob congregation, and a group of fifteen or eighteen families who were too orthodox for the Reform but all unwilling to "associate with those Polacks" at B'nai Jacob.[21]

Besides the Reform Temple Beth-El served by Rabbi Abraham Cronbach at South Bend in 1906, there was an

Orthodox synagogue served by a rabbi who wore ear-locks, a long beard, a long coat, and a circular fur cap. Historians of Evansville in 1889 and 1897 reported Congregation B'nai Israel—organized in 1857, by 1864 at the corner of Sixth and Division in a temple costing $45,000 and seating 600, proprietors of a flourishing Sunday school, a society characterized as "wealthy and intelligent" which "contains some of the best citizens in the community." At the same time they took note of a later variety of Jews in Congregation B'nai Moses which had faltered for lack of a rabbi during its first decade but in 1880 had built a small frame synagogue on Ingle Street for $2,500 and opened a Hebrew day school.[22]

The city of Gary was founded in 1906. It had two synagogues from the start. Congregation Bethel was formed on 9 May 1910; October of the same year brought organization of Congregation B'nai Israel. When the family of Hyman Pass, native of Lithuania, moved to Gary in 1925, they considered the two synagogues to be "Reform" and "Orthodox-Conservative." Having "broken away" from religious observance and being preoccupied with subsistence merchandising seven days per week, the adults of the Pass family had little to do with either. Nevertheless daughter Jeanette counted Saturday school for the children "our recreation, our joy, our hobby, our happiness."[23]

It was Indianapolis which became the notable center of the state's Jewish population. As the new capital changed from a frontier village to a railroad, trade, and population center it also became the state's destination of choice for Jewish immigrants. Forty percent of Indiana's Jews eventually came to live in Indianapolis, a long-term average of about 1 percent of the city's population. Alexander Franco, Sarah Franco, and Moses Woolf became the city's first Jewish settlers in 1849. When Rabbi Isaac Mayer Wise of Cincinnati visited Indianapolis in July of 1855, he found Jews with German names like Dessar, Glaser, Dernham, Herrmann, and Altman. The next year the Indianapolis Hebrew Congregation was established. Forty-five men approved the constitution and by-laws, nineteen of them merchants in the clothing business.[24]

At the organizational meeting of Indianapolis Hebrew Congregation, $125 was pledged for purchase of cemetery land and in 1858 the congregation purchased three and one-half acres. The congregation used temporary quarters until the dedication of its new synagogue, a hall rented from John M. Judah, in 1858. Isaac Mayer Wise of Cincinnati was guest of honor at the dedication. A clus-

ter of secular and social organizations served the small Jewish constituency alongside the synagogue:

> Organizations established in the 1860s and early 1870s included the Indianapolis Hebrew Benevolent Society (founded January 1861); the Young Men's Literary and Social Union (founded December 1862); a B'nai B'rith lodge, Abraham Lodge No. 58 (founded 1864); a lodge of the Independent Order of B'rith Abraham (founded 1865); the Harmonia Club (founded 1867); the Young Men's Bachelor's Association; the Tree of Life Mutual Benefit Association (founded October 1870); and later in the 1870s, a chapter of the Order of Kesher Shel Barzel. The only women's group of the period, the Hebrew Ladies Benevolent Society, established in 1859, was both a charity society and a kind of women's auxiliary of the synagogue, and was organized at the suggestion of Judah Wechsler, then rabbi of the congregation. The first officers were all wives of congregational members.[25]

Five religious leaders were employed in turn during the early years as decisions were made which gradually produced a liberal Reform congregation. Then came a period of remarkable stability. In 1867 Mayer Messing became rabbi and remained with Indianapolis Hebrew Congregation for forty years, the leading rabbi in the state and a champion of civic and charitable causes. A new synagogue building was dedicated in 1868 with Isaac Mayer Wise on hand for the celebration. In 1904 Morris Feuerlicht joined Messing as his associate rabbi and eventual successor. Feuerlicht combined nearly half a century of congregational and civic leadership with thirty-one years on the Butler University faculty. In a way these prominent rabbis were symbols of the community status of the body of earlier Jewish settlers in Indianapolis—German speakers like many other Indiana citizens but also at home with English and fully Americanized; comfortable as full participants and leaders in business, politics, and civil affairs; accepted socially in any neighborhood of the city.[26]

Onto the city of Indianapolis, and especially onto the comfortable and acclimated earlier stratum of Jews, came the flood of later Jewish immigrants from eastern Europe. They began coming in strength in the 1890s. They equaled the earlier Jews in number by about 1900 and kept right on coming. The federal census of 1910 recorded 2,177 individuals in Indianapolis whose native language was Yiddish. The total immigrant Jewish population in that year—including native-born children—was probably between 4,000 and 5,000, or between 67 and 83 percent of the total Jewish population of the city.[27]

Gradual Integration

There was no real possibility of immediate integration of the newcomers into the existing Reform congregation. Each new group came with its own customs and traditions. Especially during the stress of relocation, cultural continuity was essential. Most of them settled in the area just south of the state capitol building on streets named Maple, Eddy, and South Illinois. There the major ethnic groups assorted themselves by neighborhood, establishing their own synagogues, charities, benevolent societies, and social organizations. The synagogue Sharah Tefilla began as a prayer group of Poles about 1870. The Hungarians formed Congregation Ohev Zedeck in 1884. The Russians founded Knesses Israel in 1889. Seven successful businessmen who were south side residents deplored the national rigidities of the immigrant synagogues but were not ready to affiliate with the liberals of Indianapolis Hebrew Congregation. They organized the United Hebrew Congregation in 1903, more decorous and liberal than most contemporary Orthodox and destined to become the south side's largest. Ironically, the founders of United Hebrew Congregation were all Galicians so their effort to transcend ethnicity was often tagged with the ethnic label Galician. Beginning in 1906, Indianapolis received a small community of Sephardic Jews from Monastir in Turkish Macedonia. Besides having oriental looks and ways, they spoke a Judeo-Spanish language called Ladino instead of Yiddish and held their cultural heritage with special tenacity. They organized Congregation Sephard of Monastir in 1913. Poorest of the south side synagogues was Ezras Achim, sometimes called the "peddlers congregation" because so many peddlers were in it.[28]

Jewish immigrants on the south side of Indianapolis helped one another. So far as their religion and pride would allow, they also received help from the city's more established native Jews. Individual north siders offered relief and employment. There was welfare assistance from the Hebrew Ladies Benevolent Society which by 1896 evolved into the Indianapolis section of the National Council of Jewish Women. The Jewish Welfare Federation of Indianapolis, formed in 1905, drew its first strength from influential Reform Jews on the north side like Abram L. Block, Louis Newberger, G. A. Efroymson, and Morris Feuerlicht. Its early aims, much oriented toward the needy south side, were "to establish a unified method of fund raising" and "to utilize the collected funds to support local and national Jewish organizations dedicated to the relief of the deserving poor, the prevention of want and distress, the discouragement of pauperism, and the provision of educational facilities for deserving Jews."[29]

Headquarters of the Federation until 1929 were in the Nathan Morris House and then in the Communal Building in the south side ghetto. Here a generation of south siders found emergency relief, free medical care, interest-free small loans, legal aid, a library, athletics, entertainment, meeting rooms for Jewish organizations, and a galaxy of classes aimed to speed up Americanization. New York City was so inundated with Jewish immigrants at the beginning of the 1900s that concerned philanthropists there established the Industrial Removal Office to locate some of the new arrivals further west. The Indianapolis Jewish Federation was that program's agent in Indianapolis.[30] Federation superintendent S. B. Kaufman explained in 1909: "It would be mentally and spiritually impossible for the poor and unfortunate Jewish immigrant to stretch out his hand for aid to an individual or an organization which is not his own. On the other hand, there is the powerful, charitable, sympathetic and brotherly tie which unites all Jews throughout the world, and it is their characteristic to help one another in the hour of distress." So in nine months of 1909 the Federation provided physician or hospital care for 21; transportation for 24 transients and board and lodging for 72; employment for 62 who had thus become self-supporting; legal assistance for 12; subsistence pensions for 8; rent money for 39; coal for 49; groceries for 20; interest-free small business loans for 8; foster care for 9 to 11 children; removal from New York and establishment in Indianapolis for 8 to 10 persons per month; kindergarten for over 100 children; all the classes, lectures, and entertainments at the Nathan Morris House; and $2,800 sent to six Jewish institutions outside the state.[31]

All the Jews of Indianapolis seemed always in motion, yet always in search of a mode of manageable and controlled change. They moved up the economic and social ladder and so from the south side of Indianapolis to the north, slowed but temporarily by the depression years of the 1930s.

In smaller cities such as Indianapolis Jews faced fewer barriers to success, partly because there were fewer Jews in competition. Without having experienced a great struggle, the immigrant garment worker or peddler was now often the proprietor of his own retail business—the pants presser had his clothing shop; the peddler his dry goods store; the shoemaker his shoe store—and his

American-born children often attended a university or perhaps even a professional school.[32]

When federal legislation severely restricted east European immigration in 1921 and the south side Jewish population thinned, Jewish institutions of Indianapolis also moved north and took on a more middle class character. Jewish patronage kept declining at the south side Communal Center; it kept increasing at the north side Kirshbaum Center after 1926 and at the Jewish Center after 1958. Everywhere Jews kept coming together. As ethnic identity and Yiddish language became less crucial, some stoutly independent congregations could begin to share the services of religious functionaries and of schools. Second generation Orthodoxy was less strenuous. The first marriages between German and eastern European Jews came in the 1920s. Even the Sephardics were intermarrying within the Jewish community by 1932. The Indianapolis brand of Conservatism, at least as exemplified after 1927 by the energetic new Congregation Beth-El Zedeck, was hospitable to liberal practice.[33]

At the same time there was movement within the more Americanized, native, liberal, and modern Reform Judaism toward a greater appreciation of historic Jewish custom and tradition. When Samuel H. Markowitz went from graduation at Hebrew Union College in 1922 to be rabbi for Temple Israel at Lafayette, he announced a lifelong crusade. "To train parents to create in the modern Jewish home an atmosphere indigenous to the twentieth century, yet saturated with traditional character and concept—that was my goal." He called it "re-Judaization of the modern Jewish home." He prepared and circulated materials for many family rituals. He wanted no more Jewish Christmas trees. By the 1960s this re-Judaization was taking place in the homes of many families of Indianapolis Hebrew Congregation as well. In the course of the 1970s the temple employed its first cantor, added a Jewish symbol to the rabbi's robe, restored the Bar and Bat Mitzvah ceremonies, and instituted a class to study the week's Torah portion before the Saturday morning service. The new cooperative Hebrew Academy offered complete day school education through grade seven for 186 Indianapolis children by 1981.[34]

Jews were also brought together by broad mutual interests. Regional newspapers named *Indiana Jewish Chronicle* (established 1921) and *Jewish Post* (established 1933) sought a larger constituency across cultural divisions. Since the Jewish community in Indiana was not large or highly visible, the Ku Klux Klan committed few actual acts of violence on its members. However the Klan's hostile rhetoric and its potential for evil necessarily drew Jews together in defense against it.[35] Every variety of Reform and Orthodox Jewry wanted an accurate representation of the worldwide Jewish community to counteract the poisonous propaganda of the Nazi years in Europe and the infection of anti-Semitism anywhere. Two hundred new refugees were living in Indianapolis by 1941. After the war massive help had to be sent to the survivors in Europe and Palestine. Indianapolis contributions to the United Jewish Appeal tripled from $196,000 in 1945 to $625,000 in 1946 and climbed to a record high of $1,004,600 in 1948. Zionism had often divided Indiana's Jews; Isaac Mayer Wise and his early colleagues in Reform Judaism wanted no Jewish state. But when Jewish survivors of the Second World War found no place of refuge and again when joint Arab forces were mobilized for the apparent purpose of destroying Israel in 1967, calls for support of Israel brought enthusiastic and united response. Federation projects city wide and world wide were always calling Indianapolis Jews to work together.[36]

The national upsurge in religious interest in the 1940s and 1950s was also a "Jewish revival" which crossed the lines of earlier divisions. To be religious was acceptable and an acceptable way to be religious was to be Jewish.[37] The Jews of Indianapolis gave their synagogues new priority. Membership in Conservative Congregation Beth-El Zedeck doubled between 1945 and 1958. Indianapolis Hebrew Congregation sold its old building at 10th and Delaware to the Reverend James Jones in 1957 and built anew at 65th and Meridian. United Orthodox Hebrew Congregation (combining Sharah Tefilla, Knesses Israel, and Ezras Achim) dedicated its new building on the north side in 1966. B'nai Torah, established by merger of Orthodox groups in 1957, moved in 1967 to its new synagogue at 65th and Hoover Road. Etz Chaim (Sephardic) bought the Pleasant View Lutheran building at 64th and Hoover Road. The Federation was busy securing funding and building a nursing home called Hooverwood and Park Regency Apartments for the elderly. Near the end of the twentieth century a Jewish historian could say: "Indianapolis Jewry today is a more unified and uniform community than it has been since the original German Jewish settlement of the mid-nineteenth century. The lines that divided groups—German versus eastern European, native versus immigrant, south side versus north side, peddler versus department store magnate—have blurred almost to the point of disappearing, as have the antagonistic positions of Zionist/anti-Zionist, atheist/Orthodox, etc. This has resulted in less conflict in communal affairs." Indianapolis Jews, except for a few recent war refugees, were American citizens of the second and third generations. They were graduating from universities at about twice the national rate and entering the professions which had once tried to exclude them.[38]

Concern about Vanishing

These highly educated middle class Americans did tend to have low birthrates. By the end of the 1960s the average number of children born to an American Jewish woman was 1.4; a rate of 2.1 was considered necessary to maintain a population. Some young persons reared in Jewish homes dropped out of Jewish institutions after marrying non-Jews. Their children were likely to be lost to the Jewish community. A study in the early 1960s showed that the number of Jewish marriages with non-Jewish partners in the counties containing Indianapolis, Gary-Hammond, South Bend–Mishawaka, Fort Wayne, and Evansville was a very substantial 38.6 percent. In the other eighty-seven counties this intermarriage rate for Jews was a striking 63.5 percent. There was no longer much expansion of Indiana's Jewish community by immigration. There was no strong tradition of seeking increase by conversion. The flow of upwardly mobile persons, such as educated Jewish youth, continued from states with low Jewish density such as Indiana to larger urban centers or to the Sunbelt or to the West Coast. The *American Jewish Year Book* for 1988 reported an estimated Jewish population of 19,900 for Indiana, less than one-half of one percent of the population of the state. Such demography has driven students to speak of "the disappearing small-town Jew" or even "the vanishing American Jew." Hoosier college towns such as Lafayette, Bloomington, Terre Haute, and Muncie have offered better than average opportunities for Jewish community but historian Lance J. Sussman ended his appreciative account of Congregation Beth Boruk and its antecedents at the college town of Richmond with the sobering thought that "the long term decline in Jewish population may prove insurmountable."[39]

In the face of that kind of realistic if somber assessment stood a very live Jewish community. The synagogues and their leaders, once combative, were well interrelated. Members affiliated with one of the smaller synagogues were often affiliated with a neighboring larger one as well. Some Jews were finding satisfaction in deepening their ethnic identity with an overtly religious identity. Jewish institutions were deliberately planning a range of religious, educational, and social activities to build loyalty and develop friendships naturally within the group. It was no longer universally assumed that marriage to a non-Jew meant loss of an active participant or of the children of such a marriage. Some non-Jewish spouses participated in the community life without conversion. Some non-Jewish persons joined synagogues to become "Jews by choice."[40]

NOTES

1. Judith E. Endelman, *The Jewish Community of Indianapolis: 1849 to the Present* (Bloomington, Ind.: Indiana University Press, 1984), 19–20. Statistical citations in this section will refer to ethnic Jews unless reported for particular synagogues. In some instances and periods only 25 to 40 percent of persons designating themselves as Jews were actively affiliated with a synagogue. Estimating the size of the community of faith is further complicated by the common practice of reporting synagogue membership only by number of families.

2. Sydney E. Ahlstrom, *A Religious History of the American People* (New Haven, Conn.: Yale University Press, 1972), 569, 572–73.

3. Joseph Levine, *John Jacob Hays: The First Known Jewish Resident at Fort Wayne* (Fort Wayne, Ind.: Indiana Jewish Historical Society, 1973, 13 p.); David Philipson, "The Jewish Pioneers of the Ohio Valley," *Publications of the American Jewish Historical Society*, vol. 8 (1900), 43–57; Endelman, *Jewish Community*, 10–11.

4. Ware William Wimberly, *The Jewish Experience in Indiana before the Civil War* (Fort Wayne, Ind.: Indiana Jewish Historical Society, 1976), 1, 7–8.

5. J. Solis-Cohen, "Jake Gimbel: Hoosier Philanthropist," *Publications of the American Jewish Historical Society* 48 (June 1959): 256–61; Richard Day, "A Report on the Gimbel Buildings," in *Memoirs and Reflections* (Fort Wayne, Ind.: Indiana Jewish Historical Society, 1983), 44–57; George E. Greene, *History of Old Vincennes and Knox County, Indiana*, 2 vols. (Chicago: S. J. Clarke Publishing Company, 1911), 1:431; Endelman, *Jewish Community*, 13.

6. Lois Fields Schwartz, *The Jews of Ligonier—an American Experience* (Fort Wayne, Ind.: Indiana Jewish Historical Society, 1978, 45 p.).

7. Gladys Kaminsky, *History of the Jewish Community of Columbus, Indiana* (Fort Wayne, Ind.: Indiana Jewish Historical Society, 1978), 5–7; "S. Blustine, Esq. of this place" was the grandfather of Rosebud Blustine who became known as screen star Joan Blondell.

8. Kaminsky, *History*, 13–15; *History of Bartholomew County, Indiana* (Chicago: Brant and Fuller, 1888), 516. Several Jewish families arriving after 1884 are named in William E. Marsh, *I Discover Columbus* (Oklahoma City, Okla.: Semco Color Press, 1956), 210–11.

9. Marsh, *I Discover Columbus*, 211; Kaminsky, *History*, 33–34.

10. Dwight W. Hoover, "To Be a Jew in Middletown: A Muncie Oral History Project," *Indiana Magazine of History* 81 (June 1985): 131–58; Whitney H. Gordon, "Jews and Gentiles in Middletown—1961," *American Jewish Archives* 18 (April 1966): 41–70; Whitney H. Gordon, *A Community in Stress* (New York: Living Books, 1964, 269 p.).

11. Richard P. DeHart, *Past and Present of Tippecanoe County, Indiana* (Indianapolis, Ind.: B. F. Bowen, 1909), 260–61; Morris M. Feuerlicht, "A Hoosier Rabbinate," in *Lives and Voices* (Philadelphia: Jewish Publication Society of America, 1972), 156, 162, 166; Israel Elkin, *Autobiography; as Related to Sarah Elkin Brown* (Fort Wayne, Ind.: Indiana Jewish Historical Society, 1980), 19–21.

12. A. K. Strouse, "History of the Jews of Columbia City and Whitley County," in *Jewish Life in Indiana* (Fort Wayne, Ind.: Indiana Jewish Historical Society, 1980), 1–18; Ruth Sapinsky, "Memories of a Hoosier Girl, 1893–1906," in *Articles by or about Indiana Jews* (Fort Wayne, Ind.: Indiana Jewish Historical Society, 1982), 23–31; Lance J. Sussman, *The Emergence of a Jewish Community in Richmond, Indiana* (Fort Wayne, Ind.: Indiana Jewish Historical Society, 1981), 7, 21.

13. Lance J. Sussman, "Reflections: The Writing of Indiana Jewish History," in *Memoirs and Reflections* (Fort Wayne, Ind.: Indiana Jewish Historical Society, 1983), 32; Ahlstrom, *Religious History*, 970; Sussman, *Emergence*, 1–89.

14. Israel Knox, *Rabbi in America: The Story of Isaac M. Wise* (Boston: Little, Brown and Company, 1957), 97–118.

15. Knox, *Rabbi in America*, 113–14.

16. Max B. May, *Isaac Mayer Wise: The Founder of American Judaism* (New York: G. P. Putnam's Sons, 1916), 276–77.

17. Ahlstrom, *Religious History*, 578-82; Endelman, *Jewish Community*, 58; Sussman, "Reflections," 34.

18. Abraham Cronbach, "Autobiography," *American Jewish Archives* 11 (April 1959): 27.

19. Samuel H. Markowitz, "Autobiography," *American Jewish Archives* 24 (November 1972): 145.

20. Sussman, "Reflections," 32.

21. Thomas B. Helm, *History of Allen County, Indiana* (Chicago: Kingman Brothers, 1880), 99; Wimberly, *Jewish Experience*, 19–20; Markowitz, "Autobiography," 147–48.

22. Cronbach, "Autobiography," 28–29; *History of Vanderburgh County, Indiana* (Madison, Wis.: Brant and Fuller, 1889), 304; Joseph P. Elliott, *History of Evansville and Vanderburgh County, Indiana* (Evansville, Ind.: Keller Printing Company, 1897), 274–75.

23. William F. Howat, *Standard History of Lake County, Indiana, and the Calumet Region*, 2 vols. (Chicago, Lewis Publishing Company, 1915), 1:411; Jeanette Pass Goldhar, "Growing up in Gary," in *Memoirs and Reflections* (Fort Wayne, Ind.: Indiana Jewish Historical Society, 1983), 1–2, 16–17.

24. Endelman, *Jewish Community*, 8–9, 14–16; Sussman, *Emergence*, 37; Sussman, "Reflections," 32.

25. Endelman, *Jewish Community*, 20.

26. Endelman, *Jewish Community*, 17–57.

27. Endelman, *Jewish Community*, 59–61.

28. Endelman, *Jewish Community*, 61–69, 116.

29. S. B. Kaufman, "The Jewish Federation of Indianapolis," *Indiana Bulletin of Charities and Correction* (December 1909): 420–23; Endelman, *Jewish Community*, 97.

30. Endelman, *Jewish Community*, 96–110, 131–32.

31. Kaufman, "Jewish Federation," 420–23.

32. Endelman, *Jewish Community*, 114.

33. Endelman, *Jewish Community*, 81, 117, 130–33, 142–52, 155, 170, 202–4, 239–40.

34. Markowitz, "Autobiography," 144–49; Endelman, *Jewish Community*, 227–29, 238–43.

35. Hoover, "To Be a Jew in Middletown," 151–55; Endelman, *Jewish Community*, 118–26, 154–55, 184–85.

36. Esther Kretzman Schwartz, "History of Zionist Organization and Hadassah in Fort Wayne, Indiana," in *Articles by or about Indiana Jews* (Fort Wayne, Ind.: Indiana Jewish Historical Society, 1982), 6–22; Knox, *Rabbi in America*, 111–14; Endelman, *Jewish Community*, 168–80, 188–94, 218–20.

37. Will Herberg, *Protestant, Catholic, Jew; an Essay in American Religious Sociology* (Garden City, N.Y.: Doubleday, 1956, 320 p.); Nathan Glazer, *American Judaism* (Chicago: University of Chicago Press, 1957), 106–26.

38. Endelman, *Jewish Community*, 196–99, 236–37, 241–43.

39. Sussman, *Emergence*, 35.

40. Erich Rosenthal, "Jewish Intermarriage in Indiana," *American Jewish Year Book* 68 (1967): 243–64; Endelman, *Jewish Community*, 252–54.

HOLINESS AND PENTECOSTAL DEVELOPMENT

The turn of the century appeared to be a time of religious health and vigor for Hoosier Protestants. By 1900 Indiana's population had grown large; the census of 1900 reported 2,516,462 persons. Indiana's churches had grown large too. In the religious census of 1906 there were reports of 210,000 Methodists; 205,000 Catholics; 108,000 Christians; 60,000 Baptists; 49,000 Presbyterians; 48,000 United Brethren; 34,000 Missouri Synod Lutherans. The state had grown rich in agriculture and industry and capital improvements. Change came rapidly, if unevenly, across the state. As early as 1854 four locomotives standing abreast made the Union Station at Indianapolis a sight worth seeing and an Indiana correspondent wrote the *Western Christian Advocate* of 4 January:

> Our wealth is now rapidly increasing and our railroads are waking up every Poor Old Rip Van Winkle in the land. The Methodists are rich people in Indiana, and their whole country is growing so rapidly that they will become immensely wealthy in a few short years more. The whole system of things is passing away, and for one, I say let it go; give us the new life of the new age; let us feel the impulse of a new power, the forerunners of the millennium. Away with the old fogies . . . To work is the way to live and to go to heaven. To make plenty money and keep it . . . is soul suicide; to make it and scatter it in blessings over our earth, is sober, Christian, God like action. This is an age of works. One reform produces another.[1]

By 1900 there were 6,471 miles of main track railroad in Indiana; in 1910 it was estimated that about 200 passenger trains arrived at Indianapolis every day. Ebenezer Methodist church near Brookville was satisfied to build an inexpensive frame church for $1,400 in the 1850s. But during the gas boom years of 1888 to 1893 Cadiz Methodists replaced a $4,600 structure with a $7,000 one; Alexandria added $4,500 to their $7,000 edifice; and Elwood built an $8,000 house of worship. By June of 1888, Lagrange held a mass march led by a cornet band to its new site on which a modern church with kitchen and dining hall was built for $17,200. Outside the gas belt, Grace Methodist Church of Richmond built a place of worship worth $40,000.[2]

The itinerant preachers who had worked so efficiently with local class leaders and local preachers on their circuits were generally displaced. The roles of these three now devolved upon the resident ministers. These professional ministers regularly sought education in college or in seminary or in their denominational course of study, a level of theological training generally higher than their congregational average. Except for a few sophisticated or traditionally liturgical congregations, most churches were still employing revivals or protracted meetings as a means of evangelizing, even as a regular means of admitting children from their own Sunday schools to full membership. Resident ministers conducted revivals or invited other resident ministers to conduct revivals for them. In 1905 there were 1,545 conversions reported in the Fort Wayne district of the Methodist church alone; in 1906 the North Indiana Conference added 8,433 such probationers.[3]

Almost all evangelical Protestants were influenced by the techniques of the host of highly visible public evangelists modeling on the international successes of Dwight L. Moody. A native Hoosier pastor named S. M. Vernon invited "boy evangelist" Thomas Harrison to conduct a revival at Roberts Park Methodist church in Indianapolis in 1881. The first 140 converts received were "largely from the Sabbath-school, and almost entirely made up of young people, ranging from fourteen to twenty years of age." That meeting continued for thirteen weeks and published the names of 1,218 converts.[4]

In 1894 the cities of Indiana became part of the evangelistic circuit for the flamboyant "baseball evangelist" Billy Sunday. Beginning in 1900 Billy Sunday spent part of every summer at the Winona Lake Bible Conference in Indiana. That year he hired his first song leader and firmed up his policy of requiring that a wooden tabernacle be erected instead of a tent wherever he held meetings. He bought a home at Winona Lake in 1910 and moved his family there from Chicago. In his career Sunday conducted over 300 separate revivals, spoke to more than 100 million people without the aid of radio or microphone, and brought 1 million people "down the sawdust trail." He preached his final sermon on 27 October 1935 at Mishawaka.[5]

Businessman E. Howard Cadle built a tabernacle seating 8,000 in Indianapolis in order to bring evangelist "Gipsy" Smith there for a revival about 1921. His intention was to make it one of a nationwide chain of tabernacles to be toured by headliners like Billy Sunday and Aimee Semple McPherson. Later he felt called to become a professional evangelist himself. He and his family focused their ministry on the tabernacle and became pioneers in religious broadcasting with a radio program called "The Nation's Family Prayer Period."[6]

Flourishing Church Organizations

By the turn of the century the major Protestant churches were sufficiently organized at national and regional levels to provide their congregations with channels of cooperation and service. Churches still jealous of their congregational autonomy sometimes resisted having one central denominational organization but produced a series of overlapping administrative structures on behalf of such individual causes as missions, Sunday schools,

youth work, and women's work. Church women had organized in the years leading up to 1900. They brought the churches to a whole new level of world awareness and participation. Women had always been primary persons in church operation and support, though excluded from church governance. Now in each denomination they got their own organizations, their own officers, their own budgets, their own causes. From the beginning they directed their new unions in support of missions. Appointment as a missionary was one of the earliest professional appointments open to a woman. Support of missionaries was a familiar cause which women saw to be desperately needy. Foreign missions generally came first, the interest soon broadening to include home missions or church extension as well.

About the time of the reunion of Old School and New School Presbyterians in 1869 "there was an awakening among the women of the Church, in foreign missions." Contributions from Presbyterian women in the region of the nation named "Northwest" climbed steadily from $14,666 in 1874–75 to $50,400 in 1882–83. The Woman's Presbyterian Board of the Northwest met at First Presbyterian Church of Indianapolis in 1876. The Woman's Missionary Society of First Church assumed support of missionary Loretta C. Van Hook that year; in 1883 they sent Grettie Y. Holliday from the membership of First Church to be a missionary in Tabriz, Persia. Indiana's Presbyterian women had been organized in support of frontier home missionaries and mission schools since the 1830s. After Sheldon Jackson became superintendent of Presbyterian Missions for the Rocky Mountain Territories in 1869, the boxes and dollars from women's missionary societies went especially to missions and schools for Hispanics and Native Americans in the West.[7]

In 1890 the Woman's Home Missionary Society of North Indiana Methodist Conference, a mere decade old, declared its purpose to be the "evangelization of not only the immigrants, but the Chinese, Mormons, Spanish, Indians, poor whites, blacks and depraved in the cities." When Indiana's gas boom went broke in 1893 and every factory in the gas belt shut down within a month, these Methodist women did not cease their mission giving. They had become permanent leaders in the denomination's mission and stewardship programs. In 1895 Presiding Elder Horace N. Herrick had become so convinced of the centrality of missions that he undertook to press that cause personally in every church in Muncie District, assisted by specially trained regional squads. The task was too much. By the time he got to

Eaton church "he seemed lost while making his address, finally stopping and inquiring where he was." The next year he tried again with a more decentralized plan and Muncie District reached a new high in mission support.[8]

Baptist women in Indiana increased their role in church leadership after the Civil War. In 1871 the Women's Baptist Mission Society of the West was formed. There was a local chapter in Indianapolis by 1873. The State Convention recognized organized women's work in 1874. In 1876 Eusebia Craven gave a ringing presidential address to the Women's Foreign Missionary Society meeting in Richmond:

> The Women's Baptist Missionary Society of the West was organized five years ago, with the approval and consent of the officers of the Missionary Union, to which society it is auxiliary. Its object is the Christianization and elevation of heathen women, and to accomplish this work two cents per week, or one dollar per year is asked of every Baptist woman. It is not expected that any contributions shall be taken from other objects. Its aim is to gather the fragments, that nothing be lost; by economy and self-sacrifice to devote yearly one dollar more than we otherwise give to the extension of Christ's kingdom . . . In our State are thirty Associations, composed of more than five hundred churches. Must one person be expected to do the work of interesting all these? Are there not thirty women whose hearts are interested, and who will each undertake an Association . . . Let us adopt the high aim of our society—every Baptist woman a contributing member of the society.[9]

In 1877 $700 more was received. Mrs. N. B. Leslie was chairman of a women's committee to promote Baptist home missions within Indiana. She simply began visiting the needy churches herself in 1901 and raising money to help them. In 1902 she told the State Convention they should "quit this playing at state missions and . . . put the money and the missionaries in this field." She stayed at visitation and fund raising herself until 1907 at which time a full time evangelistic staff of three was at work and a program under way leading to a dozen new churches, several dozen new church buildings, and a sharp increase in the number of pastors employed.[10]

Indianapolis women of the Christian Church had already organized themselves into a missionary society before the General Convention of 1874. They helped convince the Convention to approve the Christian Woman's Board of Missions for both home and foreign work, located the headquarters of the new national society at Indianapolis, and provided strong leadership to the organization for many years. From Indianapolis they issued the national publications *Missionary Tidings* for women and *Little Builders at Work* for children.[11]

Indiana's Sunday schools had become a potent force before the end of the 1800s. Sunday schools had begun in England for the discipline and education of concentrations of poor children employed as work gangs in factories. In America the Sunday school clientele was much broadened. Children of churchgoers and members of the middle class went to American Sunday schools as well as children of the poor and unchurched. Teachers were volunteers, often enthusiastic workers who had been converted in revivals. Along with the Ten Commandments and the Lord's Prayer and the Bible verses, the students absorbed the values and expectations of their teachers. They, in turn, became converts and took their places as adult evangelical Protestants.[12]

Indiana's early public school system was quite limited, especially so until the enactment of the Local School Tax Law in 1867. Early Sunday schools needed to teach many pupils to read and write. As Sunday school workers came to hand over the job of teaching reading and writing to the common schools, the common school workers assumed that the Sunday school teachers would still be there giving the same pupils instruction in basic religious doctrine. Without enunciated or official agreement they generally reinforced one another. For much of the nineteenth century this was a partnership on which thousands of Hoosier communities counted as primary bearers of their faith and culture.[13]

United Brethren preacher John George Pfrimmer probably had a Sunday school at Corydon by 1814; a group of "godly women" had a thriving Sunday school in Madison in 1816; Presbyterian preacher Isaac Reed gathered a Sunday school of sixty members at New Albany in 1819; physician Isaac Coe founded the first Sunday school in Indianapolis in 1823, asking scholars to bring "the testaments, spelling books or such other books as they have"; Presbyterian missionaries Ransom and Sarah Hawley founded a number of Sunday schools and grouped them in the Daviess County Sunday School Union in 1829; Baptist jurist Jesse L. Holman did the same in Dearborn County.[14]

Sunday school effort was wonderfully stimulated by the program of the American Sunday School Union (ASSU) launched in Philadelphia in 1824. This Sunday school union came to be linked with the American Education Society (1815), the American Home Missionary Society (1826), the American Bible Society (1816), and the American Tract Society (1825) in a mighty effort to elevate and evangelize the West. In 1830 the ASSU resolved that, in reliance upon divine aid, they would establish "a Sunday school in every destitute place where it is practicable, throughout the Valley of the Mississippi." For Indiana this meant that all the agents and missionaries of these five societies would be engaged in encouraging and founding Sunday schools in every center of population. It also meant that any interested person could ask the assistance of the ASSU in founding a Sunday school in any locality.

Sunday school libraries were one very exciting form of assistance. By the late 1830s a Sunday School and Family Library of "100 select volumes from 72 to 252 pages, substantially bound" could be had from the ASSU for $10. And if the Sunday school missionary could not raise even $10, half of that cost could be provided from funds raised in the East. Thirty thousand of the public libraries listed in the United States in 1859 were in Sunday schools, over half the total number. In many places these were the only sources of books available to those persons who could read. The excitement caused by the arrival of such a Sunday school library at a fictional spot in the Indiana wilderness was nicely portrayed in an ASSU publication entitled *The Daisydingle Sunday-School*.[15]

The ASSU took great pains to keep its agents and materials and schools undenominational, though there was always a bit of the odor of the East about them and some suspicion of Presbyterian influence. Every denomination had to overcome an initial resistance to the establishment of Sunday schools among its members. Except among a few persistent anti-missionary groups, the resistance soon faded. Typical practice of denominations was to adopt the Sunday schools, to take them over, and to make them tools for achieving denominational goals. Methodists on the national scene had formed their own Methodist Sunday-School Union in 1827. The fifth report of the ASSU, in 1829, showed that a majority of the 100 pioneer Sunday schools in Indiana were sponsored by Methodists. Methodist enrollment was generally highest and their libraries best.[16]

Christians formed their own State Sunday School Association in Indianapolis in 1867 "to enlist the entire brotherhood of this state in an effort to promote the interest in the Sunday school." Few things ever succeeded so well. A Disciples historian said: "The Sunday school movement created more interest, developed greater enthusiasm, and reached more people than any movement the Disciples had ever before embraced in Indiana." They had semi-annual state conventions, songs, picnics, special trains, and loads of Bible study. They divided the state into twenty-two Sunday school districts

with a vice president in each and employed a full-time Sunday school evangelist. By 1872 the Indiana Christian churches reported 550 Sunday schools with 6,000 teachers and 65,000 scholars. L. L. Carpenter claimed in 1875 that three-fifths of the additions to Christian church membership came through the Sunday school program.[17]

By the 1850s Sunday schools and prayer meetings had become generally accepted as legitimate Baptist enterprises, even "the hope of the church and a pledge of promise for the conversion of the world." There was an Indiana Baptist Sunday School Convention by 1867, a staff member on the payroll of the Publication Society assigned to the state for Sunday school promotion soon thereafter, and a report of 542 Baptist Sunday schools with 60,000 scholars by 1876. S. H. Huffman, a Hoosier layman with zeal for the schools, became Baptist Sunday school agent for Indiana in 1882. For nearly a quarter of a century he promoted the establishment of Sunday schools within the churches. He also made the Sunday school enterprise an effective engine for church extension, organizing scores of mission schools in unoccupied city areas. Strong churches developed from several of these.[18]

So the Sunday schools began undenominational and became denominational. In the era after the Civil War they were often impressively interdenominational as well. Expert promoters combined the denominational Sunday school units into regional organizations each featuring a full slate of officers and a full schedule of showcase events for boys and girls. At the fifth National Sunday School Convention in Indianapolis in 1872 a plan for uniform or international Sunday school lessons was approved. On any given Sunday at all the cooperating schools in the world—over 3 million English-speaking pupils and teachers by 1900—a member or visitor could expect to study the same Scripture passages and memorize the same verse as a "golden text." Teacher training materials multiplied in support of the uniform lessons. Indiana was in the interdenominational Sunday school movement early and enthusiastically.[19] State president William H. Levering reported in 1887: "The Indiana Sunday School Union was organized in 1865 and has held a state convention every year. It achieved full county organization in 1877. In 1886–87, at least one county convention was held in every county—a total of 165. There were also a number of district conventions. Many townships are organized. One county of 12 townships held 22 township institutes, another 28. Indiana has performed all this as a thank offering to God—never having paid a salary to any officer in its prosecution."[20]

The basic units in the interdenominational state structure were local Sunday schools, more Methodist than any other. State convention was at Fort Wayne in 1868.

On the second day, the agenda was interrupted to hear a concert by 2,000 singing Sunday school children. In gala dress, they hurried to meeting places in their churches and chapels at 2:30 from which they marched two abreast, led by the "splendid Jones Cornet Band," to the assembly point at Wayne Street Methodist Church, largest in the city . . . The children "fluttered along in white dresses and gay ribbons with beautiful flags and appropriate banners floating overall." Children of the host church sang "Glory be to God"; those from Second Presbyterian Church offered "The Volunteer Song"; from the English Lutheran Church "Land without a Storm"; and from Centenary Methodist "My House upon a Rock." The boys and girls from the German Reformed school, singing in German, "maintained the most excellent perfect time and won a merited applause." The other selections were "Sing Jesus' Name" by the combined chorus of the Third and Fourth Presbyterian Churches; "In a Manger Laid" by the Baptist Sunday school; "Won't You Volunteer?" by the Evans Mission and Bloomingdale schools; "O Christian Awake" by the Berry Street Methodist youth; and "Shall We Gather?" by the children of First Presbyterian Church. The program closed with all present singing the Long Meter Doxology.[21]

At the 1916 Indiana Sunday School Convention at Muncie, delegates heard a report of new record high statistics for the state—69,958 officers and teachers; 580,231 enrolled in 5,388 schools; 3,895 chartered adult classes.[22]

For the older youth there was Christian Endeavor which quickly found nationwide acceptance after its organization at Williston, Maine, by a young Congregational minister in 1881. It developed its own literature, its own non-denominational administration, and its own convention structure at county, state, and national levels. In it the young people felt a strong sense of their own proprietorship; it was designed to meet many social and spiritual needs. Unlike the Methodists and Baptists, the Christians did not hasten to rename Christian Endeavor or to displace it with their own denominational youth program. Instead they took pride in the extent of their participation. A Christian historian has written: "B. L. Allen was state superintendent of Christian Endeavor for the Disciples in 1897. He stated there were 500 Endeavor societies in the Christian churches of Indiana and that this was 100 more than any other communion in the state could claim . . . Christian Endeavor was in such flourishing condition that by 1899 the *Indiana Christian* began to carry a column on Christian Endeavor prayer meeting topics. This was in addition to another full column on the activities of the various societies."[23]

Most Baptists wanted the youth organization to be their own and to bear their own name. When a national Baptist Young People's Union (BYPU) was formed in Chicago in 1891, Indiana youth groups were quick to affiliate. A main emphasis was missionary work, particularly the designation of part of the dues for support of a state evangelist. The Baptist Publication Society helped with promotion. The BYPU spread rapidly over the state and in 1896 was joined by a junior union for children. Baptist associations began devoting one entire evening session of their regular meetings to youth work. For Indiana young people there were district rallies and summer assemblies and even international conventions of BYPU in which to develop and display their leadership. There were 10,345 BYPU members in Indiana in 1906.[24]

There were five sorts of societies for young people operative in the Methodist church by 1889. That year, at a convention in Cleveland, all agreed to merge into one—the Epworth League. Indiana districts soon formed Epworth League chapters at local churches and Epworth League divisions at district level. By 1892 the North Indiana Conference requested the national General Conference to include the president and vice president of each local Epworth League as members of the official quarterly conference of each local church. The action was taken.[25]

When the International Convention of the Epworth League met in Indianapolis on 20–23 July 1899, there was much talk about how great Indianapolis had become—largest inland city in the world, grandest monument in the world; prettiest cycle path in the world; electric street car system equaled by few cities and surpassed by none; site of more national conventions than any other six cities in America. There was also much talk about how great the Epworth League had become—19,500 chapters in the United States and Canada. In the host state of Indiana alone there were 800 Epworth League organizations in twenty districts. Nearly half of Indiana's 200,000 Methodists were "Leaguers." The conventioneers at Indianapolis studied Methodism, social righteousness, good citizenship, temperance, and missions. Everywhere there was singing and celebration.[26] For many Protestants the turn of the century provided an exciting environment with congregations growing and multiplying; Sunday schools and youth groups thriving; women taking new leadership of their own church organizations; mission and benevolence interest high at home and worldwide; a system of public schools, colleges, and seminaries sharing common values; and the whole enterprise supplied and energized by religious revivals.

Persistent Discontent

But there was also a persistent rumble of dissent within this Protestant prosperity particularly within the ranks of the Methodists, largest of the denominational families. Efficient bureaucracy, especially the line of direct authority from bishop and presiding elder (district superintendent after 1908) to circuit rider or resident minister, was viewed by many as the very essence of Methodism. Until 1870 only the ordained preachers were full participants in Methodist conferences.[27] Some critics withdrew because they opposed such structured church government and the unrestricted appointive power of bishops. Methodist Protestants separated in 1830 and remained separate until 1939, even after Methodists had modified their polity.[28] Methodist bishops, with heavy responsibility for preserving denominational peace and unity, were slow to side with abolitionists and to take a clear position against slavery. So some enthusiastic abolitionists among Methodists withdrew in 1843 as the Wesleyan Connection. After the Civil War era had brought general condemnation of slavery, about 100 Wesleyan ministers and many lay persons returned to the parent Methodist church but a more substantial portion of the Wesleyan body chose to remain separate. Free Methodists withdrew in 1860 in protest against what they saw as Methodist modernism, worldliness, and bureaucratic power.[29]

Nearly all these hot dissidents kept following the perennial precedent of breakaway revivalists by criticizing the lifestyle of the cooler membership of the parent body. How could people be called Christians if they conformed to the world by using tobacco or alcohol, wearing stylish clothes and jewelry, belonging to secret societies, frequenting public sports and entertainments, reading unworthy printed matter, or building fancy churches in which to be served by fancy preachers and choirs? True converts to the Christian life, they said, should rather be marked by virtuous speech and life evidenced by plainness and focused on faithfulness in worship, prayer, study of Scriptures, strenuous giving, and promotion of revivals.

There was a persistent yearning after older ways which were seen to be passing away—that revivalist circuit rider touching neighborhood hearers on a regular schedule, often narrating his personal and simple religious ex-

perience; the intimacy and excitement of the testimonies at class meetings limited to serious members only; camp meetings as concentrated occasions for evangelism served by preachers who could employ the sustained power of "rousements" and make the meetings into religious harvest times; emotional services everywhere with conversions strongly felt. Compared to these traditions the more recent evangelists, often poor imitations of Dwight L. Moody, seemed technical and impersonal. Their revival campaigns in tents or temporary tabernacles were sometimes reported in the newspapers under "entertainment." Events billed as revivals or camp meetings also dealt in recreation and became indistinguishable from chautauquas. Converts signed a card and shook hands with the preacher who was already packing to depart for another town, never to return. Critics doubted that these were converts at all. What could be expected of churches full of members such as these?[30]

Dissent about Sanctification

At the same time a difference was sharpening over definition of the Christian life and the language to be used to describe its stages. There was general agreement that profession of faith in Jesus Christ and a decision to be his follower was a saving appropriation of the promised grace of God. Such a professing candidate for baptism could be said to be justified in God's sight and to have entered into new life. Words like regeneration and conversion and justification and salvation were used and generally understood by all to apply to this new state. However, profession of faith was universally understood to be a beginning. The grace of God given in salvation or justification was to be followed by God's further work in the cooperating believer to put to death the power of sin and to strengthen the new life as the follower of Christ moved on to maturity. This further work was named sanctification. But people differed in their descriptions of the nature and process of sanctification. Those differences produced the greatest outbreak of new denominations in America's history and reinvigorated the whole evangelistic scene.[31]

A large body of the Christian world thought of sanctification as the very day-by-day pilgrimage of Christian life. Empowered by the continuing grace of God, the believer was to keep on dying to sin and coming alive to righteousness. In victory there was rejoicing; in defeat there was repentance; through endurance came new strength. Faithful living as a follower of Jesus Christ— normally including worship, Scripture study, prayer, sacraments, and church fellowship—might be expected to produce visible growth in grace and usefulness but no person regarded sanctification as completed in this life. Real sanctification came as a gift of God at life's end when the believer was perfected and passed to glory.

Many followers of John Wesley had a somewhat different understanding of sanctification. From the beginnings of his movement within the Church of England, Wesley had been an especially strenuous advocate of holy living. Based on the Scriptures, on the lives and writings of especially devoted Christians, and on the needs of the church and people as he saw them, he urged that conversion be followed by holy living with a special zeal. He believed he knew persons who had attained sanctification or Christian perfection in this life. Wesley was cautious. He did not make an unequivocal claim to that status for himself or focus attention on his own record of holiness. He did not equate Christian perfection with freedom from ignorance, error, or infirmity. It was not deliverance from temptation but could be freedom from compulsion to sin. It was, he said in his *Plain Account of Christian Perfection*, "the humble, gentle, patient love of God and our neighbor, ruling our tempers, words, and actions . . . As to the manner. I believe this perfection is always wrought in the soul by a simple act of faith; consequently in an instant. But I believe in a gradual work both preceding and following that instant. As to time. I believe this instant generally is the instant of death, the moment the soul leaves the body. But I believe it may be ten, twenty, or forty years before." All this was not a matter for mere theorizing. If this level of Christian life was indeed attainable, then he and his preachers should press the people to attain it. And people should not rest content short of this perfection. Wesley thought and wrote a lot about this subject. His *Plain Account* appeared in several editions. In 1789 it was bound in the *Discipline*, the official formulation of Methodist standards.[32]

Some historians have said that the Methodist understanding of Christian perfection or entire sanctification got pressed into the background in America. To cut down the size and weight of the *Discipline*, the doctrinal tracts including the *Plain Account* were long omitted from the American *Discipline*. Methodist circuit riders racing to evangelize the Mississippi Valley were primarily crusaders for conversions, not always ready to instruct in the intricacies of entire sanctification. That famous circuit rider Peter Cartwright was "strangely silent" on the subject.[33]

On the other hand, America's pioneer bishop Francis Asbury strongly urged his preachers to preach sanctification. Sensitive to the needs of thousands of new members converted in the heat of frontier revivals, he chose to preach to them less about the dangers of backsliding and more about pressing on to perfection. The reports from the camp meetings which he relayed in his newsletters tallied thousands "converted" and other thousands "sanctified." Asbury never clearly claimed the sanctified status for himself; his *Journal* alternated bursts of praise and assurance with admissions of failure and need. He was cautious about accepting some testimonies of others who claimed the blessing. "I hope it is so," he would sometimes say. In America where conversion often came with a wallop of emotion in a revival, sanctification often came with a second wallop of emotion in a revival.[34]

There were always some bishops and preachers keeping the Methodist understanding of the doctrine of sanctification lifted up before Americans in the manner of John Wesley's *Plain Account* and John Fletcher's *Checks to Antinomianism*. One of the most faithful was Matthew Simpson, president of Indiana Asbury University from 1839 to 1848 and reputedly the ablest preacher among the bishops of his generation. The article on "Christian Perfection" in his *Cyclopaedia of Methodism* read like a sermon often preached. American followers of Wesley were to be taught to identify their religious experiences as (1) justification or salvation or conversion first, and (2) sanctification or entire sanctification or second blessing or Christian perfection second. After the first event some old habit or appetite or meanness of spirit might be expected to recur and grapple for control of the believer's life. After the second event such residual evil was eradicated root and branch. Perfect love was then to reign. However, carelessness or disobedience could destroy it all.[35]

Holiness Organizations

An important group organized for action to preserve and advance what they counted to be crucial but endangered parts of the heritage of their Methodist church. They wanted Christians to oppose conformity to the world and every temptation to the prevalent laxity and halfheartedness. They wanted to lift up the goal and expectation of strenuous holy living. Most of all, they wanted to stimulate a universal hunger for the personal experience of Christian perfection. One early center for the movement was the home of Phoebe Palmer and her husband Walter C. Palmer in New York City. Mrs. Palmer's Tuesday Meeting for the Promotion of Holiness began in 1835 and was so popular it continued for thirty years beyond her death in 1874. Participants included Methodists and non-Methodists; there were homemakers, Methodist bishops, and hundreds of clergy. Visitors professing sanctification in the intensity of these meetings carried home their zeal for that experience. The enterprise grew large. Dr. Palmer ceased the practice of medicine to give full time to his holiness work. He gave Phoebe ownership of a holiness journal called *Guide to Perfection*. They built up its circulation to 30,000 monthly. Participants in mass meetings found the personal teaching and testimony of the Palmers powerful and convincing. The Palmers toured England for four years; they toured major American camp meetings and conducted revivals at Methodist colleges.[36]

With the number of enthusiastic clients so large and widely spread, a rallying convention for America seemed indicated. A camp meeting to be devoted entirely to holiness was scheduled at Vineland, New Jersey, in July of 1867. It was the first in a long series of national holiness camp meetings. That year they formed the National Campmeeting Association for the Promotion of Holiness with Methodist preacher John Inskip as president. Inskip was a holiness preacher of great influence and conviction. He was, for example, a primary agent in the sanctification of the Quaker David Updegraff who then led many holiness revivals among Indiana's large population of Orthodox Friends.[37]

Inskip and his colleagues promoted "national" holiness camp meetings across the country. In Indiana there was the one at Indianapolis in 1871, the one at Warsaw in 1881, the one at Acton in 1900, and the one at Greenwood in 1901. There were eleven national holiness camp meetings at New Albany in the period between 1894 and 1904 when New Albany's manufacturer and financier Washington C. DePauw was helping Inskip manage the holiness publishing business designed to supply the land with inexpensive holiness literature. DePauw had claimed the experience of sanctification on 21 September 1871 in one of Inskip's tabernacle meetings at Indianapolis.[38]

Inspired by the success of the national movement, local and regional holiness associations conducted camp meetings in many places. The Indiana State Holiness Association was formed in 1880 with Daniel S. Warner as its vice president. In addition to the multiplying associations, a large number of independent holiness evangelists circulated through the cities and towns or established themselves in local tabernacles. They condemned sin, lukewarm Christians, and worldly ways. They preached for conversion to be followed by a second experience of entire sanctification. Their converts did not always fit easily into the membership of established town and city congregations. The more successful independent evangelists and holiness associations tended to form societies or bands and eventually congregations or denominations. Often their enthusiasm for Christian charity and for evangelism found expression in missions supported only by faith, missions to the inner city around them or missions to foreign lands. They organized into new churches and denominations, they said, because their converts among the poor would never find a home with unsanctified preachers in middle class churches and they could not desert these new converts in the world like defenseless chicks before the hawks.[39]

The Methodist church became uneasy. Even bishops who were advocates of sanctification still felt they had to be responsible for preserving the peace and order of the church. Bishop Matthew Simpson conferred with Phoebe Palmer about his religious life, attended holiness camp meetings, and always preached Christian perfection but never felt he could testify that he had such an experience himself. Clergymen like Simpson, those who believed in the doctrine of Christian perfection or entire sanctification but could not confess the experience personally, came under great pressure as the holiness movement developed. The Methodist fathers Wesley and Asbury themselves never left a clear record of their sanctified state. However Phoebe Palmer and many of her colleagues in the holiness movement said that any truly sanctified person must publicly testify to the experience of entire sanctification or the devil would snatch that sanctification away. Few could be expected to attain perfect love unless a militant and joyous group kept bearing witness to it.[40]

Phoebe Palmer said that full, complete, and total surrender of the believer's whole being to Jesus Christ was the requirement for sanctification. Those honestly so surrendered should immediately claim sanctification and keep professing the blessing. Her successors suspected that persons who did not press on from conversion to the experience and testimony of entire sanctification were almost certain to backslide and be lost. For a long time there were also holiness preachers who believed or implied that genuine sanctification would be manifested in denial of the trappings of contemporary prosperity and fashion—ruffles, feathers, cosmetics, jewelry, corsets, tobacco, alcohol, frivolous amusements, lodges and secret societies, dancing, card playing, expensive churches with formal services. Dangerous intellectual formulas to be avoided were those employing the vocabulary of social gospel, evolutionary theory, biblical criticism, and socialism. Holiness spokesmen generally advocated a return to "old paths," rejecting selected segments of the contemporary church and world as modern, worldly, and un-Christian.[41]

Despite protestations of tolerance and good intent on all sides, mainline Methodists came into tension with the proliferating agencies so eager to revitalize Methodism by promoting the second crisis experience of sanctification. Very few Methodists gave up the doctrine of Christian perfection or opposed it; the encounter with holiness movements had only made the place of the doctrine in the Methodist heritage more clear. But many mainline Methodists were put off by what they considered the divisive methods of the holiness advocates.[42] The bishops' address of the general conference of the Methodist Episcopal Church, South, officially expressed the tension existing in 1894:

> There has sprung up among us a party with holiness as a watchword; they have holiness associations, holiness meetings, holiness preachers, holiness evangelists, and holiness property. Religious experience is represented as if it consists of only two steps, the first step out of condemnation into peace and the next step into Christian perfection . . . We do not question the sincerity and zeal of their brethren; we desire the church to profit by their earnest preaching and godly example; but we deplore their teaching and methods in so far as they claim a monopoly of the experience, practice, and advocacy of holiness, and separate themselves from the body of ministers and disciples.[43]

Those followers of the holiness evangelists who affirmed their scriptural basis for and their inner assurance of a personal conversion with a subsequent experience of entire sanctification, and who had organized themselves into classes, associations, bands, and congregations as special champions of entire sanctification in Methodist lineage, now channeled their strength into denominations bearing the names Wesleyan, Free Methodist, Pilgrim Holiness, Salvation Army, Church of God (Anderson, Ind.), and Church of the Nazarene. Indiana came to be "holiness heartland." These young churches grew rapidly to become a major component of the body of Hoosier faiths.

Indiana's Taylor University was founded by Methodists. It took the name of a Methodist who was a maverick bishop and free-wheeling independent missionary. By the time it was operating in its new location at Upland in 1893, it was especially attracted to the principles of the holiness movement. These principles were more basic to the school's identity than official Methodist control which ended in 1922. During the years before the Second World War, Taylor was recognized nationally as a safe school for holiness youth and an efficient training center for holiness preachers and missionaries.[44]

The National Campmeeting Association for the Promotion of Holiness evolved by 1970 into an international organization of holiness denominations and agencies named the Christian Holiness Association. Its headquarters was in Indianapolis from 1972 until it moved to Wilmore, Kentucky, in 1979; executive secretary Thomas H. Hermiz said he felt his office in Indianapolis was "right in the heart of the holiness movement in America."[45] From its world headquarters in Greenwood, OMS International (formerly Oriental Missionary Society) published its *OMS Outreach*. From its headquarters in Bedford, Evangelistic Faith Missions sent out its monthly *Missionary Herald*. From its headquarters in Marion, World Gospel Mission issued its *Call to Prayer*. From Westfield, site of its holiness school called Union Bible Seminary, the Central Yearly Meeting of Friends published its *Friends Evangel*. These missionary agencies had their roots in the faith missions of the turn of the century. From bases in Indiana they kept enlisting hundreds of missionary workers of many nationalities and developing substantial support in prayers and dollars among the constituency of holiness people.

Not all advocates of entire sanctification were related to Methodists. Congregational revivalists Charles Finney and Asa Mahan on the faculty of Oberlin College in Ohio concluded from their studies as early as 1836 that Christian perfection was a possibility and a duty to be preached. Finney's revival techniques for preaching were standard means for almost all holiness groups. Congregationalist Thomas Upham, professor at Bowdoin, was the first male admitted to Phoebe Palmer's Tuesday Meeting. Holiness ranks included the contemporary Baptist evangelist A. B. Earle and the Quakers David Updegraff and Dougan Clark.[46]

Most impressive of all was the ministry of the Presbyterian Robert Pearsall Smith and his Quaker wife Hannah Whitall Smith. The Smiths were among the American evangelists who advocated holiness and Christian perfection on an international scale. Between 1872 and 1875 they took holiness teaching to thousands in England, notably to a convention at Oxford in 1874 and at Brighton in 1875. Dwight L. Moody prayed for the success of the Brighton meeting, calling it "perhaps the most important meeting ever gathered together." Out of the work of the Smiths in the lake district of northern England there developed a perennial interdenominational conference center in the parish of Keswick. The Keswick Convention for the Promotion of Practical Holiness met annually beginning in 1875. In later years holiness teaching kept coming back from Keswick to the United States in the form of such persons as evangelist Dwight L. Moody; first president of Moody Bible Institute R. A. Torrey; father of Gordon College Adoniram J. Gordon; founder of the Christian and Missionary Alliance A. B. Simpson; and evangelist J. Wilbur Chapman who became mentor to Billy Sunday. Most of these persons were writers as well as preachers, covering the earth with holiness literature. Hannah Whitall Smith's book *The Christian's Secret of a Happy Life* sold over 2 million copies and was translated into most major languages.[47]

These non-Wesleyan preachers of holiness did not regularly adopt a Methodist paradigm for sanctification nor did they use a Methodist vocabulary to describe it. They were not likely to speak in Methodist fashion of the residual sin remaining after regeneration which needed a second crisis experience or a second blessing to effect its complete eradication in order for the believer to know entire sanctification and Christian perfection. They sought a baptism in the Holy Spirit as a gift of power for a higher Christian life. They sought the gift in a setting of emotional and spiritual intensity. Their baptism in the Holy Spirit might come at the time of their baptism or at another time. Whenever it came, instead of giving the gift the number two and associating it with an instant eradication of residual sin, they left it unnumbered and called it a special anointing or empowerment for service and victorious life. The goal was to grow in grace and usefulness in the strength of this gift, looking forward to the completion of sanctification at life's end. Large numbers of holiness people of this non-Wesleyan complexion remained in Reformed, Congregationalist, Presbyterian, Baptist, and Anglican communions.[48]

Pentecostals

Pentecostals received most of their early leaders and many of their early members from the holiness movements. Their affirmation of experience-centered religion linked to enthusiastic revivals, strict codes for behavior and dress, faith healing, expectation of the early return of Christ, and direct personal guidance by the Holy Spirit was shared with large segments of the holiness families. By the 1890s holiness people were often associating their experience of sanctification with the events of Pentecost described in the second chapter of the Book of Acts. Many holiness had been speaking of the sanctifying gift received as a baptism in the Holy Spirit and had been

using the imagery of holy fire.[49] All this came to a dramatic focus and visibility in a new series of events.

Charles Fox Parham was conducting the Bethel Bible School near Topeka, Kansas, for thirty-four students in 1900. He was of Congregational and Methodist background but had learned from a wide variety of holiness teachers. The school was interdenominational; ministers from several denominations were enrolled. Parham was a preacher of entire sanctification and claimed that experience. Yet he was looking for something even beyond holiness sanctification, convinced that "there still remained a great outpouring of power for the Christians who were to close this age." He was especially interested in a miraculous gift of foreign tongues as a tool to hasten world evangelism since he and his students expected the imminent return of the Lord. On the first day of 1901 his student Agnes N. Ozman requested Parham to lay hands on her head and pray for her to be baptized in the Holy Spirit with the evidence of speaking in tongues. Parham wrote: "I had scarcely repeated three dozen sentences when a glory fell upon her, a halo seemed to surround her head and face, and she began speaking in the Chinese language, and was unable to speak English for three days. When she tried to write in English to tell us of her experience she wrote in Chinese, copies of which we still have in newspapers printed at that time." Within the next few days Parham and about half of his student body received the miraculous experience of tongues. Parham became an evangelist in Kansas and in Texas for this faith with its new level of immediacy. By 1905 he had established several "Apostolic Faith" churches in the suburbs of Houston and opened a Bible school there to train missionary evangelists.[50]

William J. Seymour was for a short time a student in Parham's training course at Houston. Texas law required racial segregation but the black man Seymour was admitted to the fringe of the class. Seymour had been born the son of former slaves in Louisiana. He had migrated to Indianapolis in 1895 where he got a job as a waiter in a fashionable restaurant and joined a black Methodist church. An attack of smallpox took his left eye in Indianapolis but left him under conviction to be a preacher. His interests and opportunities were with holiness groups—with the God's Revivalist movement of Martin Wells Knapp in Cincinnati; with the Church of God Reformation movement of Daniel S. Warner in Indiana; with pastor Lucy Farrow in Houston who had experienced speaking in tongues under the influence of Charles F. Parham. Now, as an eager learner in Parham's school, he became convinced that his regeneration plus the second blessing of sanctification still lacked an essential baptism in the Holy Spirit which would be evidenced by speaking in tongues.

When Seymour went preaching this doctrine to a holiness congregation which had invited him to Los Angeles, they locked him out. He and some colleagues did soon receive the baptism powerfully and spoke in tongues. Beginning 14 April 1906, in a battered old building at 312 Azusa Street, they conducted a revival which grew to eclipse the ministry of Seymour's mentor Charles F. Parham. William J. Seymour was at the center of the work but he did not seem to make it depend on him. Men and women, black and white, might shout, weep, dance, fall into trance, speak and sing in tongues and interpret the messages. There were altar calls for salvation or for sanctification or for baptism in the Holy Spirit. Anyone moved by the Spirit might preach or sing. Some came to Azusa Street out of curiosity and others as religious seekers. Meetings were held three times a day, seven days a week, for three years. Hundreds of preachers traveled to Los Angeles. Most were convinced of the genuineness of what they saw. Many received baptism in the Holy Spirit and the gift of tongues and returned as missionaries to their congregations.

Newspaper accounts were circulated worldwide. The mailing list for Seymour's paper, *Apostolic Faith*, grew to 50,000. Many persons had spoken in tongues in the United States in the years preceding 1906. Many had described their sanctification in terms of a baptism in the Holy Spirit. But it was this meeting which lifted up an example before the eyes of much of the world of a baptism in the Holy Spirit regularly followed by the sign of tongues. For the pentecostal world that sign would now be an expectancy. Practically every pentecostal movement in the world would be able to trace its origin to the Azusa Street Mission.[51]

The American denominational scene, already difficult to describe during the multiplications and divisions of the holiness movement, now seemed to become wildly complex in the face of pentecostal claims and energies. One scholar compiled a list of one hundred pentecostal denominations in the nation. Eleven thousand pentecostal denominations developed worldwide. At least one-fourth of the congregations in the church directory of a typical American city or county came to be pentecostal in practice. A few guiding facts have been helpful in understanding the portion of the pentecostal story most directly relevant to Indiana. All of the older denomi-

nations maintained their traditional views of sanctification. Thousands of their members and friends left the older denominations to become Pentecostals. By one estimate, at least 80 percent of the members of black pentecostal congregations came from other churches. Nevertheless, the state's major holiness churches—Wesleyans, Free Methodists, Pilgrim Holiness, Salvation Army, Church of God (Anderson, Ind.), Church of the Nazarene—dissociated themselves completely from the pentecostal movement. In them speaking in tongues was not accepted as evidence of baptism in the Holy Spirit nor was it welcomed.[52]

The founder of the holiness denomination called Christian and Missionary Alliance declared speaking in tongues to be allowable but not encouraged, an ambiguity which eventually made that group essentially non-pentecostal. On the other hand, the Hoosier-born holiness leader A. J. Tomlinson underwent a baptism in the Holy Spirit on 12 January 1908 in the course of which he slipped out of his chair into a heap on the rostrum floor and uttered what he judged to be ten different languages. Denominations developed by him and expanded from Tennessee across the world—Church of God (Cleveland, Tenn.) and Church of God of Prophecy—have been thoroughly pentecostal.[53]

Pentecostal churches emerging from holiness groups with a rural southern tradition, such as the Churches of God based in Tennessee, were more likely to delineate a Christian life in three discernible stages. They expected an initial experience of regeneration or salvation, followed by an experience of entire sanctification as a second work of grace, followed finally by a baptism in the Holy Spirit evidenced by speaking in tongues. On the other hand, pentecostal churches influenced by non-Wesleyan traditions might omit or oppose any doctrine identifying a definite second blessing of entire sanctification or of Christian perfection. If they had learned from evangelists in the Keswick tradition, or from the holiness teachers of the Christian and Missionary Alliance, or from the Chicago and Los Angeles ministries of William Durham, they were likely to understand their experience of regeneration and baptism in the Holy Spirit as separate but possibly contemporaneous events giving entry to empowerment for a progressively sanctified life. For times of special need, additional "infillings" of the Holy Spirit might be sought and received. Such non-Wesleyan churches have been represented in Indiana by the largest of the white pentecostal churches, the Assemblies of God, and by the smaller group continuing the ministry organized by Aimee Semple McPherson as the International Church of the Foursquare Gospel.[54]

A new understanding of the nature of God was formulated by one branch of the non-Wesleyan Pentecostals. Its first focus was the Arroyo Seco World Wide Camp Meeting near Los Angeles in 1913, a month-long event with Maria Beulah Woodworth-Etter of Indianapolis as a headline preacher. At a baptismal service during the meeting, evangelist Robert E. McAlister of Canada pointed out that the church in the Book of Acts always baptized in the name of Jesus Christ and not with the use of the traditional formula "in the name of the Father and of the Son and of the Holy Spirit" from Matthew 28:19. Some ministers present were excited to further study by this observation. John G. Scheppe spent the night in prayer and toward morning ran through camp reporting that he had been given a personal vision of the power of the name of Jesus.

Frank J. Ewart pondered all this. Ewart was the influential pastor of the Pentecostal church at the corner of Seventh and Los Angeles streets which had been established by William Durham as a non-Wesleyan answer to the Azusa Mission revival. Ewart concluded that, correctly read, "the name" in the traditional formula of Matthew 28:19 was Jesus. So there was one true God whose one name was Jesus and who had revealed himself as Father and Son and Spirit which manifestations were never separate or eternal persons. It was only in Jesus, he concluded from Colossians 2:9, that the fullness of deity dwelled bodily. His further conclusion was that all new believers should be baptized in the name of Jesus and all earlier believers still alive should be rebaptized in that name only. Ewart and his assistant Glenn A. Cook set up a tank in a tent and rebaptized each other in the name of Jesus on 15 April 1914. Then they set out on their mission of teaching, baptizing, and rebaptizing according to the new insight. This Oneness, or Jesus Only, or Unitarian pentecostal doctrine found many followers and leaders in Indiana, embodied especially in the churches named United Pentecostal and Pentecostal Assemblies of the World.[55]

Among the gifts of the Spirit cataloged in First Corinthians 12:8–10 were healing, miracle working, and prophecy. Ministries featuring these gifts arose among or alongside the Pentecostals. Healing evangelists generally championed the Bible as the infallible word of God. However it was typical of them to testify as well to their own miraculous call from God, often in audible voice or in vision, to be authoritative interpreters, messengers, judges, prophets, and healers for their generation. They were often culturally deprived in their youth and lacked formal education but a few displayed such a concentration of purpose and evidence of charisma that they were recognized by their contemporaries as special channels of power. Extraordinary events did not surprise them or their followers. They were confident that God was restoring the apostolic faith among them for the end of the age; it was fitting that God's intervention be accompanied by signs and wonders. John Alexander Dowie, with his Christian Catholic church and his Zion City in the Chicago area at the turn of the century, was an eccentric healer and messenger of the imminent restoration of apostolic faith. He did not personally welcome the new pentecostal revival but after his own health declined many of his followers moved into the Assemblies of God or into Oneness Pentecostalism in the midwestern region.[56] Indiana produced two extraordinary pioneers among the healing evangelists.

Maria Beulah Woodworth-Etter

Maria Beulah Woodworth-Etter of Indianapolis was a forerunner of itinerant healing evangelists, a forerunner of women preachers of national reputation, and such a forerunner of the modern pentecostal movement that she really deserved recognition alongside Parham of Kansas and Seymour of Los Angeles.[57] She was born Maria Beulah Underwood in 1844 and reared in Ohio, daughter of an alcohol-addicted father who died of sunstroke in summer of 1856 leaving her mother with eight children for whom to provide. As one of the older children, Maria had to go to work for pay. There was no opportunity or support for formal education. She married Philo Harrison Woodworth, a Civil War veteran with a head injury whose health remained precarious. She was often sick too. They worked hard but "everything we undertook seemed to be a failure." Five of their six children died, a bereavement which left her husband marginally deranged.

Maria was very religious. At the age of thirteen she had responded to the invitation of an evangelist at a revival in Lisbon, Ohio, and joined the Christian church. "I asked the Lord to save me, fully, trusting myself in His hands," she said, "and while going into the water, a light came over me, and I was converted. The people saw the change, and said I had fainted." From that time on she participated in a full schedule of church activities and felt called to be a preaching evangelist, though that possibility seemed too remote to even bear discussion.[58]

When Maria was about thirty-five she renewed her personal profession of faith at a revival in Damascus,

Ohio, and began to preach in some places near her home. It was after the death of her fifth child, in 1880, that the persistent visions and voices bidding her to preach came to focus in an empowering experience. She said: "I came like a child asking for bread. I looked for it. God did not disappoint me. The power of the Holy Ghost came down as a bright cloud. It was brighter than the sun. I was covered and wrapped up in it. My body was light as air. It seemed that heaven came down. I was baptized with the Holy Ghost, and fire, and power which has never left me. Oh, Praise the Lord! There was liquid fire, and the angels were all around in the fire and glory."

The mark of her ministry was what she called "the power." At her meetings the power would come to provide her both biblical text and message. When she pleaded with sinners to get right with God and when she told believers of their potential for a more powerful and holy life, her congregations would be moved to weep and repent and seek victorious renewal at the mourners' bench. Both Maria and her hearers might enter trance.[59]

Philo Woodworth was not very religious. He had been converted in a Methodist church after their marriage but had become discouraged. Maria's local ministry was booming. Her biographer said: "In a period of about a year and a half she held nine revivals, organized two churches (one of these started with 70 members), organized a Sunday school of about 100 members, preached in 22 meeting houses and four school houses, and delivered 200 sermons. And all of this was on an ecumenical basis for eight separate denominations." Maria wanted to move on to more extended revival tours, to "go west" as she put it. Her husband resisted. If she insisted on preaching, he said, there were plenty of sinners available in Columbiana County.[60]

Finally she prevailed; they left the farm and set out as evangelists. Philo involved himself in business management of the campaigns and in operation of certain petty concessions on the revival grounds but was often an embarrassment. He was divorced for infidelity in February of 1891, married a teenager a month later, and died in 1892. After ten years as a widow, Maria married Samuel Etter of Hot Springs, Arkansas. Maria was associated with the United Brethren church from the beginning of her itineration until 1884 and then with the 39th Indiana Eldership of the Churches of God until 1904.[61] However denominational sponsorship was never a primary matter for her. She worked among the holiness of whatever denomination invited her and later among the Pentecostals wherever exciting openings occurred.

First it was "going west" in Ohio with revivals at Willshire, Fairview, St. Mary's Circuit, Lima, Dayton, and Zion. Then, in Indiana, it was Pleasant Mills, Fort Wayne, and Monroeville. It was in Indiana that she rose to national attention. In preparation for the Hartford City meeting in 1885, Maria's intercessors prayed that believers and sinners alike "might fall as dead men." They did. Highly visible persons such as two lawyers, a newspaper editor, and a loud local drunk were among the converts. Twenty reporters came to write their stories for such papers as the Cincinnati *Enquirer*, the Indianapolis *Journal,* the Fort Wayne *Gazette*, and the Fort Wayne *Sentinel*. There were reports in the *New York Times* for 24, 26, and 30 January.

Following meetings at Indiana towns named New Corner, Summitville, Fairmount, Columbia City, Elwood, Tipton, and Pendleton this now-famous woman came to spend three weeks in Kokomo in May of 1885. She had a new electrifying element of excitement. At the Columbia City meeting she had responded to divine instruction to pray for the sick and had discovered that she had the gift of healing. The Kokomo *Dispatch* criticized her campaign; the Kokomo *Gazette Tribune* encouraged it. The size of the crowds forced the meetings from the Friends church to the courthouse and finally to the skating rink. Not even the arrival of Barnum's circus could compete with her drawing power. Over 12,000 attended the closing baptismal service for eighty-two persons at Wildcat Creek. In a later account, Maria reported that at one peak of the Kokomo meeting 500 converts testified in a period of two hours and the power of God was felt for fifty miles around. She said twenty ministers were licensed out of the Kokomo converts.[62]

The meeting at Alexandria, Indiana, in September of 1885 was the biggest Woodworth-Etter would know in her forty-five years as an evangelist. The site was a grove five miles from town. The crowd was estimated to be at least 20,000. The Muncie *Daily News* for 21 September described the Alexandria scene.

Upon these chairs in the centre, stood Mrs. Woodworth, a handsome, somewhat stately lady, who looks to be on the sunny side of forty. She was dressed in black, sparingly trimmed with black lace, rather short sleeves, and a white neck-dress. Her hair was braided, dressed high on her head and confined with a conspicuous, old-fashioned tortoise shell black comb . . . By observing her listeners she seemed to read with an exquisite nicety what was passing in their minds, and know how to control the mind of the larger portion of the audience as one. After she had finished her talk, which at times was singularly eloquent, she commenced singing; the audience joined in with a noise that was deafening and appalling. The very tent seemed to swell and collapse as the thundering manifestation would grandly increase in volume, transfixing one with mute awe, astounded and dumbfounded . . . The demonstrations decreased as the distance increased from her as though her violent agitations produced vibrations, which lost intensity with distance. The most violent crowded on the stage, jumped up and down, wrestled, shook hands, hallooed and pushed off exhausted, and when worn out their places were filled with fresh converts . . . Dozens [were] lying around pale and unconscious, rigid and lifeless as though in death.[63]

At the end of the campaign at Anderson in 1886, thousands lined the banks of White River to see 194 converts march four abreast with arms locked to be baptized.[64]

Maria Beulah Woodworth-Etter can hardly be said to have located anywhere. Before the turn of the century she had been thrust onto the national scene. She conducted racially integrated revivals in the South to the astonishment of local whites. Her name and work came to be known in every major American city. She seemed always on the road, giving little thought to rest and sure that the returning Lord would soon seek her out to share in the rapture of the saints. Her written records taken together did not provide even an approximate record of her ministry or a tabulation of the results of her evangelism. Historian Vinson Synan said that she was the first woman preacher to gain fame in the United States and that she "recorded the most colorful and fantastic ministry in all pentecostal literature."[65]

But Indianapolis was special to her. Of the year 1886 she said: "Having long felt impressed that it was my duty to commence a work for the Master at the Capital of Indiana, we went from Muncie to that city and inaugurated what proved to be the hardest and worst contested battle ever fought for King Jesus." In 1904 she set up her tent in the southern part of the city where many healings and testimonies were reported. In the summer of 1905 she pitched her tent again on the same Indianapolis lot. Her next recorded entry of a campaign was at Indianapolis again in spring of 1912. By then Indianapolis had become her home base. From Indianapolis she circulated her books. There were at least eight of them plus two song books, all full of "marvels and miracles, signs and wonders, and acts of the Holy Ghost" drawn from her life and meetings. Such substantial parts of them were published in French, Italian, Danish, Swedish, Hindustani, and other dialects of India and South Africa that persons abroad were still sending letters addressed to her sixty years after her death.[66]

Most important of all, at Indianapolis she dedicated the 500-seat Woodworth-Etter Tabernacle in 1918. She said: "God showed me one night that I was to build a tabernacle here at West Indianapolis, Indiana, so that people from all parts of the country could come in and spend some time in a good spiritual mission, and get established in God. He showed me that the meetings should be of oldtime fashion and power, where people can get spiritual food to supply their needs for soul and body."[67] It was next door to her house at 2114 Miller Street, a kind of simple construction familiar among the glory barns of pentecostal churches for the next three decades. The Tabernacle was a place of security to which she could return for periods of ministry among close friends. It was a place for friends to visit her. Aimee Semple McPherson came to Indianapolis in her new seven-passenger Oldsmobile in 1918. "For years I have been longing to meet Sister Etter," McPherson wrote in her diary, "and have been talking about it more in recent months. I have longed to hear her preach and be at her meetings . . . Tomorrow Mrs. Etter's tabernacle will be open and I will have the desire of my heart. Glory!" Next day she wrote, "We rejoiced and praised the Lord together. The power of God fell . . . The Lord was there showering His blessings upon us." Aimee was on her way from New York to California where she was soon to found the Angelus Temple, to become the first woman to deliver a sermon on radio, and to develop the International Church of the Foursquare Gospel.[68]

At the Woodworth-Etter Tabernacle there was a constant lively agenda of worship, singing, preaching, shouting, glory marching, falling, healing, dancing, and speaking in tongues. The best meetings with the biggest crowds were those when pastor Maria was in town. But she was gone a lot. The rising pentecostal denominations rediscovered her and called her back to the sawdust trail. This was not surprising since Maria's language and manner had been essentially pentecostal throughout her ministry. Both the visitation of "the power" and speaking in tongues had been common in her meetings though she had not linked them precisely in twentieth century pentecostal fashion. People spoke in tongues at her meeting in St. Louis concurrent with the World's Fair of 1904. Of her meeting in Indianapolis in 1904 she said "One sister spake in unknown tongues all night. This was before the Holy Ghost fell at Los Angeles, California." Referring to her trance experiences, she reported that she herself had been carried away in the

Spirit many, many times, once seven hours under the power of God.[69]

It seemed to Woodworth-Etter that the earliest Pentecostals may have been too much excited about tongues. "I was left back," she said, "and could not do much with the movement at first." Speaking to ministers and workers at Montwait, Massachusetts, in a sermon entitled "Try the Spirits," she said that people should not do outrageous things and then count them to be of God. "Some people take every foolish thing for the Holy Ghost," she warned. "There are two extremes; one keeps the Holy Ghost from working except in a certain channel; and the other thinks everything is of the Holy Ghost . . . One is as bad as the other."[70]

Maria Beulah Woodworth-Etter did not join a pentecostal denomination but she bore positive witness to the events and interpretations of Azusa Street and regarded herself as one of the Pentecostals during her later ministry. The only difference was that her meetings became more noisy, she said. Her *Signs and Wonders*, published at Indianapolis in 1916, included "A Few Interpretations from Messages in Other Tongues," almost all being warnings of a judgment, or of the impending end, or of the present moment's being the occasion of a life or death decision for someone at the meeting, or of the necessity to proclaim the gospel message. She was a supportive friend to J. Roswell Flower and Alice Reynolds Flower as they were young people beginning their lifetime of ministry in what became the Assemblies of God.[71]

A young Pentecostal from Dallas attended her Indianapolis meeting of 1912. He was sure Maria was what Dallas needed. The result was her five-month Dallas campaign in which hundreds and perhaps thousands accepted the new pentecostal message and experience. So she was naturally invited to be a headliner for the famous Worldwide Camp Meeting at Arroyo Seco in Los Angeles in 1913. And she was on the road again to preach among the nation's Pentecostals holding meetings at such places as Alexandria, Minnesota; Atlanta, Georgia; Tampa, Florida; Philadelphia, Pennsylvania; Los Angeles, California; Chicago and Warren, Illinois; Sioux City and Des Moines, Iowa; Evansville, Indiana; Cincinnati, Ohio; Louisville, Kentucky; and the Winnebago Indian Reservation in Nebraska. Her eightieth birthday celebration, exhorting the crowd at the 1924 summer tent meeting in Indianapolis, was her last. She died on 16 September.

Sharing in her ministry of revivals and leading the continuing work at the Tabernacle at Indianapolis were her associates August Feick and Thomas Paino. The Paino family developed Maria's congregation from its small beginnings and through the ravages of arson into Lakeview Christian Center of the Assemblies of God—a church for 2,000 worshippers, an academy, a counseling center, a senior citizen housing complex, and a convalescent center.[72]

Maria Beulah Woodworth-Etter achieved successes; she also suffered many threats and much abuse. Her ministry seemed to inspire the ridicule of newspaper reporters. She was regarded by many as a woman out of her place. But Maria was not intimidated by opposition and she did not want other women to be intimidated. If the Apostle Paul told the Christian women of Corinth to be silent in church and ask instruction from their husbands at home (I Corinthians 14:34–35), that was a law not appropriate in this age of grace. What the Apostle was protesting was noisy contention—jangling in the house of God. If some women had to depend on their husbands for knowledge they would die in ignorance. "My dear sister in Christ, as you hear these words may the Spirit of God come upon you, and make you willing to do the work the Lord has assigned to you," she said. "It is high time for women to let their lights shine; to bring out their talents that have been hidden away rusting, and use them for the glory of God."[73]

William Marrion Branham

So Maria Beulah Woodworth-Etter was a pioneer Hoosier healing evangelist of national reputation. A later Hoosier named William Marrion Branham was even more visible. He circled the globe five times and became a Hoosier healing evangelist of international reputation. Branham was born into deep poverty in the eastern mountains of Kentucky on 6 April 1909; he was reared in deep poverty on a farm near Jeffersonville, Indiana. His own accounts of his religious life included a special sign of light at his birth; visions at age three and seven; providential oversight during the temptations of youth; plus a heavenly voice and three visions in connection with his conversion as a young adult in an old shed in the back of his house. He then received the baptism in the Holy Spirit and felt a calling of God to preach.[74]

In summer of 1933 he was an independent Baptist minister conducting a major tent revival in Jeffersonville. As many as 3,000 people attended the meetings in a single night. As he immersed 130 converts from the meetings in the Ohio River on 11 June, there was another experience of a heavenly light and voice. He later said "It liked to a-scared me to death." After that revival in 1933, he became minister of the Branham Tabernacle at

Jeffersonville. The ministry had to be part time and without compensation. Times were hard and the people were poor. In 1936 he declined invitations from some Oneness Pentecostals to conduct revivals for them, yielding to the prejudices of his mother-in-law against Pentecostals as "holy rollers" with a social status even lower than his own. His wife and daughter died in the Ohio River flood of 1937.[75]

The great crisis and the new era began in 1946. One interpreter said: "The times were ripe. Pentecostalism had become affluent enough to support mass evangelism. It had become tolerant enough to overlook doctrinal differences. Convictions were still deep enough that there was a longing for revival. As the older generation thrilled to memories of the miracle ministries of the 1920s, the young yearned for a new rain of miracles."[76] Branham took the lead. On Sunday morning of Memorial Day weekend of 1946 he told the congregation at Branham Tabernacle how an angel had visited and commissioned him as a healer on 7 May at a hideaway cabin in the woods near Charlestown. It was an account he would keep sharing throughout his ministry.

> Now, coming through the light, I saw the feet of a man coming toward me, as naturally as you would walk to me. He appeared to be a man who, in human weight, would weigh about two hundred pounds, clothed in a white robe. He had a smooth face, no beard, dark hair down to his shoulders, rather dark complexioned, with a very pleasant countenance, and coming closer, his eyes caught with mine. Seeing how fearful I was, he began to speak. "Fear not. I am sent from the presence of Almighty God to tell you that your peculiar life and your misunderstood ways have been to indicate that God has sent you to take a gift of divine healing to the people of the world. If you will be sincere, and can get the people to believe you, nothing can stand before your prayer, not even cancer."[77]

The angel promised Branham two signs. When he held the right hand of a seeker of healing with his left, there would come a "physical effect" in Branham's left hand if the seeker was being healed. If that feeling came and then went away, the disease was gone. Secondly, as the people came Branham would "know the very secret of their heart" even before they spoke. Both gifts were to be advertised characteristics of Branham's revivals.[78]

There followed a decade of evangelistic explosion. Branham went out in the role of prophet and agent of a final work of God before the second coming of Christ. There were great healing meetings in St. Louis and in Jonesboro, Arkansas, and in Vandalia, Illinois, and

through the western states. Branham now preached to and for Pentecostals and was actually able to bring both oneness and trinitarian Pentecostals into unity in his support. Pentecostal leaders Jack Moore and Gordon Lindsay became his expert agents and publicists. They issued reports of the signs and wonders in his meetings in a magazine called *The Voice of Healing*. Accounts of a tour in Canada said that 1,000 to 1,500 were often converted in a single service.

Branham said 35,000 persons received healing by the end of the first year of his healing campaign. In spring of 1950, Branham made the first tour of Europe by an American healing evangelist. In Finland and Norway opposition from the state church and secular press only increased interest so that as many as 7,000 persons attended. The campaign in South Africa in 1952 was the subject of a published book. Gordon Lindsay thought the altar call of 30,000 in Dunbar might be the largest of its kind in history. In 1954 Branham was preaching in Portugal, Rome, and India; the 1955 tour of Switzerland and Germany was successful. Witnesses said his simplicity and humility melted the hearts of his hearers everywhere. Branham thought in 1954 that converts at his meetings had numbered half a million.[79]

The heyday of healing evangelism conducted by itinerants, which had begun with such power in 1946, now ended. A historian of the movement wrote:

> The charismatic revival was born in the small pentecostal churches in the aftermath of World War II and nurtured by the generation of charismatic evangelists who established independent ministries in the late 1940s and early 1950s. The most successful of the revivalists quickly freed themselves from the domination of the small pentecostal churches and became autonomous powers in the pentecostal world. By the mid-1950s most of the pentecostal denominations, for a variety of reasons, had withdrawn their endorsements of the traveling evangelists. Some of the smaller evangelists were crushed by this development and forced to stop campaigning; the most successful had to reassess their plans and change their methods to build new bases of support.[80]

Beginning in 1955 Branham's great meetings failed financially.

Branham was poorly equipped to develop a radio and television clientele like that of the energetic evangelist Oral Roberts who came to dominate the healing revival. Branham also lacked the social and educational preparation for ministry to the more sophisticated charismatics in universities and mainline churches. Yet he remained widely recognized and honored. A biographer of Oral

Roberts said: "Roberts deeply respected Branham; he prized a 'rare photograph' taken during his 1948 visit to Branham's Kansas City campaign. Roberts was no follower; his mushrooming ministry was his own. But he was obviously flattered when Branham attended his Tampa crusade in 1949."[81]

The star of Oklahoma's Oral Roberts was rising while that of Indiana's William Branham was going down. For Branham the Lord did not come but the Internal Revenue Service did. Branham was evidently not a rascal but was certainly a poor accountant and the tax penalty exacted was $40,000, a debt he could never pay. As his popularity on the evangelistic circuit faded, he intensified his criticism of his fellow evangelists and of all denominations. Except to his most devoted followers, his doctrines seemed to grow eccentric. Among those devoted followers who commuted to his tabernacle in Jeffersonville he gave increasing emphasis to the role of a divinely commissioned eschatological messenger who was coming or had come to gather and prepare the true believers for the rapture. A body of those followers soon identified Branham as the prophetic messenger. When he died after an auto accident on 18 December 1965, shocked pentecostal leaders and healing evangelists mourned his departure. Followers delayed his burial until Easter of 1966 hoping for his return from the dead to usher in the rapture.[82]

Great expectation continued to exist concerning Branham's resurrection, or his role in the imminent second coming of Christ, or the vindication of his own divine identity, or the universal recognition of his teachings as authoritative word of God for the true believers. The staff at Branham Tabernacle in Jeffersonville has maintained about 1,100 of his sermons for circulation on tape and over 300 in print in 28 languages. Unofficial estimate of worldwide adherents to some form of the Branham "Message" in 1986 was 300,000—about 50,000 in the U.S.A.; strong churches and publication societies in Canada and Germany; significant following in India and Latin America, including 40,000 believers in Brazil; 25,000 in Zaire, reputed to comprise the fourth largest religious group in that African land.[83]

There were no longer many prominent pentecostal preachers of salvation and healing making the circuit in tents and local halls by the time William Branham died in 1965. However a few pentecostal evangelists kept entering the nation's households with even more direct efficiency by use of television. Hoosiers who turned on their sets might see and hear Oral Roberts who had moved from itinerant ministry to pioneer as a preacher-healer on radio and then television. Though he became a United Methodist in 1968, Roberts also remained faithful to much of his tradition from the Pentecostal Holiness church. He maintained that speaking in tongues was normative for every believer. At the helm of the Christian Broadcasting Network there was Pat Robertson, an ordained Southern Baptist who professed the experience of baptism in the Holy Spirit and had served as associate to a charismatic pastor in New York. Kenneth Copeland was a gospel crusader while a young man at Oral Roberts University and became a leading proponent of the "Word of Faith" message taught by Assemblies of God minister Kenneth E. Hagin at his Rhema Bible Training Center at Tulsa. And there was Lester F. Sumrall, ordained by the Assemblies of God at age nineteen. He moved to South Bend in 1963 where his church, school, and *World Harvest Magazine* became linked with an international chain of radio and television stations.[84]

Many hearers and supporters of such television ministries were members of non-pentecostal churches who were friends of high technology missions and of "old-time religion." Television viewers and donors cultivated by mail were motivated to support these ministries as agents of worldwide soul-saving, education, and relief of human misery. Peculiarly pentecostal notes might be muted by the preachers in deference to such a wide and varied body of contributors. But typical pentecostal expectancies were often expressed—for baptism in the Holy Spirit, for speaking in tongues, for direct revelations and visions, for healing, for urgent worldwide evangelism in view of the imminent return of the Lord.

Since television ministries generally made their way as independents, there was very little contribution, involvement, or control by the established pentecostal denominations. Established television evangelists might simply cut their denominational connection without disadvantage. When television evangelist Jim Bakker was charged with serious improprieties in 1987, the Assemblies of God followed its regular procedure and dismissed him for conduct unbecoming a minister. When television evangelist Jimmy Swaggart confessed to voyeuristic activities involving a prostitute, the Assemblies of God followed its regular procedure of requiring him to undergo a rehabilitation program. He refused and was defrocked by his denomination in April of 1988.[85]

Charismatics

Not all pentecostal manifestations were in churches acknowledged as pentecostal. There came to be people in unexpected places carrying Bibles, and lifting hands in praise of Jesus, and claiming continuing direct communication and guidance from God, and doing evangelism by personal witness, and describing life in terms of battling Satan with his powers of evil, and speaking in tongues, and prophesying, and healing. They were especially active among Catholics, Episcopalians, and Lutherans. They were also organized among the Baptists, Mennonites, Methodists, Presbyterians, United Church of Christ, and Wesleyans. In spite of efforts to resist by such churches as the Orthodox, Southern Baptist, and Missouri Synod Lutheran, every major denomination shared in the movement to some extent. These practitioners beyond the bounds of regular pentecostal fellowships came to be called Charismatics or Neo-Pentecostals. The phenomenon has been named the Charismatic Movement or the Charismatic Renewal.[86]

Some became Charismatics because they had been influenced by pentecostal evangelists ranging from the tabernacle of William Branham in the 1940s to the television PTL Club of Jim and Tammy Bakker in the 1980s. Some dated their baptism in the Holy Spirit from an invitation to a week at Camps Farthest Out. In 1951 a pentecostal dairyman named Demos Shakarian formed the Full Gospel Business Men's Fellowship International at Clinton's Cafeteria in Los Angeles. Oral Roberts was its first speaker. Chapters were organized in many places. A frequent format for this ministry was a weekend seminar in the restaurant or ballroom of a middle-class hotel featuring testimony of God's intervention in the daily living of one or more Spirit-baptized business men. A steady stream of laymen returned from these sessions to influence the intensity of life in their denominations.[87]

Most significant of all was the multiplication of traditional church pastors who claimed to have received baptism in the Holy Spirit and then shared that experience with their people. Rector Dennis Bennett of St. Marks Episcopal Church in Van Nuys, California, told attenders at the three services of his congregation on 3 April 1960 that he and some congregation members had received the gift of the Holy Spirit and had been speaking in tongues. Responding to official suggestions, he announced his resignation at the end of the third service that day and moved to a more hospitable setting in Seattle where he made his parish a center for development of Episcopalian Charismatics. It was a pattern to be repeated at some level in nearly every American denomination. There were impressive charismatic conventions across denominational lines. A high point was a conference in Kansas City in 1977 attended by more than 50,000. An array of independent and nondenominational charismatic fellowships developed as well, drawing much of their membership from mainline denominations.[88]

The Charismatic Movement was strongest among Catholics. A primary center within the Catholic Charismatic Renewal in America was at South Bend, Indiana, especially among the campus community of the University of Notre Dame. On 4 March 1967, Kevin and Dorothy Ranaghan were hosts to a prayer meeting in their home at South Bend. A visitor witnessed to recent charismatic events at Duquesne University and to his own pentecostal experience. His closing prayer was that all present might be filled with the Holy Spirit. The next night nine persons gathered at the apartment of Bert and Mary Lou Ghezzi; at their request the visitor from Duquesne laid hands on their heads and prayed. On 13 March nine from Notre Dame went to a prayer meeting at the home of Ray Bullard, president of the South Bend chapter of the Full Gospel Business Men's Fellowship and a deacon at Calvary Tabernacle of the Assemblies of God. About twenty Pentecostals, including several prominent ministers, were there. Seven or eight of the Notre Dame people prayed in tongues. News of the charismatic events was shared quietly from person to person at Notre Dame. Forty-five visitors came from Michigan State and the Lansing area on the weekend of 7–9 April for prayer and reflection with about forty persons at Notre Dame. Manifestations of the Spirit were intense and the "movement" now faced full publicity plus visitation by the curious. Two hundred people came to the regular prayer meeting on 14 April and the next two meetings were crowded. Then, as curiosity at the university died away, Protestants of many denominations began attending. Some Pentecostals prayed forcefully over one nun. The only prayer she could think of was "Sacred Heart of Jesus, get me out of here!" A charismatic prayer group developed among the Lutherans at Valparaiso University nearby and established friendly relations with colleagues at Notre Dame.[89]

The first cluster of seventy-five to one hundred persons involved in the movement—undergraduates plus several graduate students, three faculty members, three priests, three sisters, and several people from the South Bend–Mishawaka area—scattered in May of 1967 at the end of the school year. However charismatic prayer groups sprang up all over again among the summer session students. Conversions, tongue speaking with interpretation, and prophecy continued among the approximately fifty persons regularly involved. Steadying influences appeared so that acknowledged leaders were spoken of as elders and invitations to speak in other parts of the country were answered by teams of three or more visitors prepared to stay a full day or longer to provide instruction and stability. James Byrne and Peter Edwards offered to stay after graduation to anchor the work at Notre Dame. The house donated for them by Herbert True was named "True House" and became residence, meeting place, and administrative center.[90]

The "Michigan State weekend" in April of 1967 had been so powerful in the movement's beginning that a similar spring meeting for discussion and prayer was held for about 150 on 28–31 March 1968. About 500 attended the 1969 gathering including 25 or 30 priests and many Protestants including the pentecostal scholar David Du Plessis. In 1970 about 1,500 people came for what was officially titled "The Fourth National Conference on Charismatic Renewal in the Catholic Church." After this there was a Service Committee to coordinate the activities of Catholic Charismatics and a Communication Center in True House and a national newsletter. The international crowd of over 4,500 in 1971 had to be moved to Notre Dame's new Convocation Center. Two bishops and 147 priests shared in the closing liturgy. During the two-and-one-half-hour Mass the assembly moved from prayers into a spontaneous chorus of singing in tongues. Over 11,000 people came from sixteen countries in 1972.

For the estimated 22,000 at the conference in 1973 the general assemblies had to be held in the football stadium. Cardinal Leon-Josef Suenens of Belgium presented the homily and about 500 priests concelebrated the final Eucharist. Assemblies of God minister Russell P. Spittler said "I stood spellbound in June 1973, in Notre Dame's football stadium as more than 20,000 Catholics sang in the Spirit, each in his own divinely given tongue." That year the Communication Center, having outgrown True House and having employed eleven people, distributed approximately 350,000 books and 20,000 cassettes.[91]

After 1976, when attendance at the Notre Dame conference had reached 30,000, planning policy was modified to favor regional conferences and spiritual renewal centers of more manageable size. Thousands of local charismatic prayer groups were linked more closely to regular Catholic parish life. Some bishops appointed staff persons for liaison with the charismatic fellowships of their dioceses. Leadership also came to focus in special covenanted communities of Charismatics living under agreed disciplines providing at least for frequent sharing of meals and prayers. At South Bend the services earlier provided at True House were taken up by People of Praise, one of the oldest and largest of the covenanted

communities. People of Praise provided administrative leadership for major charismatic conferences at Notre Dame and elsewhere. Through a formal corporation at South Bend designated Charismatic Renewal Services, they became the major supplier of charismatic books, literature, and tapes for the nation.[92]

Pentecostal Development

To most Americans, the early Pentecostals looked odd. Those who came out of the holiness movement were full of social strictures. A pentecostal historian said: "There was hardly any institution, pleasure, business, vice, or social group that escaped the scorn and opposition of pentecostal preachers. Included in their catalog of 'social sins' were: tobacco in all its forms, secret societies, life insurance, doctors, medicine, liquor, dance halls, theaters, movies, Coca Cola, public swimming, professional sports, beauty parlors, jewelry, church bazaars, and makeup."[93] All the revivalistic body exercises of the holiness were there too, capped with the most electrifying sign of all, speaking in tongues. There was absolutely nothing like it to enliven a meeting, to excite the believers, and to disconcert the opponents. Meetings for worship or prayer were unstructured in a deliberate way, repetitive, noisy with the noise increasingly electronically amplified, and seemingly endless.

Pentecostal scorn for the world was answered in kind. There was "a constant hail of brick-bats on the tin roof" at the early pentecostal meetings in Indianapolis. Gangs harassed preachers and members. Persistent early Pentecostals visiting Allen Chapel A.M.E. church in Indianapolis were arrested and jailed for disturbing the services. Words were the most frequent weapons and Pentecostals, especially their healers, were labeled as crooked, weak, obsessed, satanic, sick, or insane. Even social psychologist Anton Boisen, whose scholarly analysis of religion in Bloomington and Monroe County was only mildly condescending, used the popular and all too communicative term "holy rollers." That was one appellation that several pentecostal denominations had specifically and officially repudiated.[94]

Pentecostals produced a substantial literature to reply to their despisers. Even more, they simply wore out the opposition with evidences of their own stability. No further major pentecostal groups were formed in the United States after 1932; there was shifting and consolidation and administrative organization but not much more splintering.[95] Members of Pentecostal denominations rose in the economic scale. Middle class persons joined the churches. Hoosier millionaires were sitting in congregations once labeled dispossessed. There were pentecostal believers in congregations which stressed strenuous plainness of dress and behavior; alongside them were underwriters of pentecostal causes dressed in expensive suits and accustomed to attending conventions of the Full Gospel Business Men's Fellowship in first class hotels. There were pentecostal fellowships charting detailed structures of dispensations and prophecies of cataclysmic events to take place at the imminent end of the age; alongside them were Charismatics seeking experiences to deepen spiritual life but interested in no prophetic structure whatever.

Pentecostals became more ecumenical. Eight trinitarian pentecostal denominations joined in a Pentecostal Fellowship of North America in 1948 and its membership expanded to include twenty-four groups. In 1970 Bishop Worthy G. Rowe of South Bend took the initiative to invite some 130 of the world's "Apostolic" organizations, mostly independent and oneness Pentecostals, to agree to work together. By 1987 the headquarters of this Apostolic World Christian Fellowship in South Bend reported seventy-nine cooperating organizations in fourteen nations and invited attendance at its sixteenth annual conference. Twelve pentecostal denominations joined with non-pentecostal Christians in the National Association of Evangelicals, making up a substantial majority of that body's membership.[96] In 1982 two films were widely shown which revealed a variety of pentecostal worship patterns in Indiana to thousands who would not have experienced them otherwise.[97]

As the church buildings grew more comfortable and the services more orderly and the music more complex and the ministry more academic, there were Pentecostals praying that all this affluence and order and learning might not become a "stone of stumbling." Some feared losing the very witness they wanted to bear to all classes in the world.[98]

NOTES

1. Roger H. Van Bolt, "Fusion out of Confusion, 1854," *Indiana Magazine of History* 49 (December 1953): 353.

2. Clifton J. Phillips, *Indiana in Transition: The Emergence of an Industrial Commonwealth, 1880–1920* (Indianapolis, Ind.: Indiana Historical Bureau and Indiana Historical Society, 1968), 229, 251; Herbert L. Heller, *Indiana Conference of the Methodist Church, 1832–1956* (Greencastle, Ind.: Historical Society of the Indiana Conference, 1957), 93–94; Horace N. Herrick and William Warren Sweet, *A History of the North Indiana Conference of the Methodist Episcopal Church* (Indianapolis, Ind.: W. K. Stewart Co., 1917),

146–47, 131–32, 214, 218.

3. Herrick and Sweet, *History*, 215.

4. J. C. Belman, *The Great Revival at Roberts Park M. E. Church and Other Churches* (Indianapolis, Ind.: Journal Company, 1881), 66, 244, 299–309.

5. William G. McLoughlin, *Billy Sunday Was His Real Name* (Chicago: University of Chicago Press, 1955), 16, 19, 157, 293; Lyle W. Dorsett, *Billy Sunday and the Redemption of Urban America* (Grand Rapids, Mich.: William B. Eerdmans, 1991), 50–61, 67–68, 86, 95–96, 103, 109, 115, 142–43.

6. E. Howard Cadle, *How I Came Back* (Indianapolis, Ind.: Cadle Tabernacle, 1932, 186 p.); Helen Cadle Dixon, *A Portrait of My Mother* (Indianapolis, Ind.: Cadle Chapel, 1968, 47 p.).

7. *Encyclopaedia of the Presbyterian Church in the United States of America*, ed. Alfred Nevin (Philadelphia: Presbyterian Encyclopaedia Publishing Co., 1884), 246–47, 1036–37; *Centennial Memorial, First Presbyterian Church, Indianapolis, Ind.* (Indianapolis, Ind.: First Presbyterian Church, 1925), 111–15.

8. Herrick and Sweet, *History*, 166–67.

9. Israel George Blake, *Finding a Way through the Wilderness. The Indiana Baptist Convention, 1833–1983* (Indianapolis, Ind.: Central Publishing Company, 1983), 77–78.

10. John F. Cady, *The Origin and Development of the Missionary Baptist Church in Indiana* (Franklin, Ind.: Franklin College, 1942), 269–71.

11. Henry K. Shaw, *Hoosier Disciples* (St. Louis, Mo.: Bethany Press, 1966), 193–94, 211–12, 253.

12. Anne M. Boylan, *Sunday School: The Formation of an American Institution 1790–1880* (New Haven, Conn.: Yale University Press, 1988, 225 p.).

13. Boylan, *Sunday School*, 33, 59, 160.

14. Grover L. Hartman, *A School for God's People: A History of the Sunday School Movement in Indiana* (Indianapolis, Ind.: Central Publishing Company, 1980), 5–11, 36; David M. McCord, "Sunday School and Public School: An Exploration of Their Relationship with Special Reference to Indiana, 1790–1860" (Ph.D. diss., Purdue University, 1976, 206 p.).

15. Robert W. Lynn and Elliott Wright, *The Big Little School*, 2d ed., rev. and enl. (Nashville, Tenn.: Abingdon Press, 1980), 41, 42, 57, 58; *The Daisydingle Sunday-School* (Philadelphia: American Sunday School Union, 1849, 64 p.).

16. Lynn and Wright, *Big Little School*, 45; Hartman, *School*, 14.

17. Shaw, *Hoosier Disciples*, 181, 203–8.

18. Cady, *Origin and Development*, 168, 173, 218–21.

19. "A Pinch of Harvard, a Heap of Tammany Hall," in Lynn and Wright, *Big Little School*, 90–116; "Harvest Time," in Hartman, *School*, 39–70.

20. Hartman, *School*, 39.

21. Hartman, *School*, 43–44.

22. Hartman, *School*, 66.

23. Shaw, *Hoosier Disciples*, 247–48, 284.

24. William T. Stott, *Indiana Baptist History, 1798–1908* (Franklin, Ind.:? n.p.], 1908), 326; Cady, *Origin and Development*, 233–34.

25. Herrick and Sweet, *History*, 158.

26. *Souvenir, Song Book and Official Programme, Fourth International Convention of the Epworth League, Held in Indianapolis, Ind., U.S.A., July 20, 21, 22 and 23, 1899* (Indianapolis, Ind.: Levey Brothers and Co., 1899, 158 p.).

27. *History of American Methodism*, 3 vols. (New York: Abing-

don Press, 1964), 2:273–75; Frederick A. Norwood, *Story of American Methodism* (Nashville, Tenn.: Abingdon Press, 1974), 258.

28. John C. Coons, *A Brief History of the Methodist Protestant Church in Indiana* (N.p., 1939, 73 p.).

29. Lee M. Haines and Paul William Thomas, *An Outline History of the Wesleyan Church* (Marion, Ind.: Wesley Press, 1981), 53–74; *History of American Methodism*, 2:39–47, 339–60.

30. Melvin E. Dieter, *The Holiness Revival of the Nineteenth Century* (Metuchen, N.J.: Scarecrow Press, 1980), 110.

31. Dieter, *Holiness*, 273–75.

32. John Wesley, *A Plain Account of Christian Perfection* (London: Epworth Press, 1952), 33, 35–37, 42, 62–69, 86–97, 112; John L. Peters, *Christian Perfection and American Methodism* (New York: Abingdon Press, 1956), 32, 201–15; Haines and Thomas, *Outline History*, 15–20. Some terms eventually used by holiness teachers to describe this status included sanctification, entire sanctification, Christian perfection, Christian holiness, second blessing, second definite work of grace, perfect love, heart purity, baptism in the Holy Spirit, fulness of the blessing, and full salvation. In this section they are used interchangeably.

33. W. T. Purkiser, *Called unto Holiness: The Second Twenty-five Years, 1933–58* (Kansas City, Mo.: Nazarene Publishing House, 1983), 21; Peters, *Christian Perfection*, 98; *History of American Methodism*, 2:340; Haines and Thomas, *Outline History*, 29–30.

34. L. C. Rudolph, *Francis Asbury* (Nashville, Tenn.: Abingdon Press, 1966; Bicentennial edition, 1983), 116–19, 157–64; Peters, *Christian Perfection*, 217–19.

35. Matthew Simpson, *Cyclopaedia of Methodism* (Philadelphia: Everts and Stewart, 1878), 704–7.

36. Charles E. Jones, *Perfectionist Persuasion: The Holiness Movement and American Methodism 1867–1936* (Metuchen, N.J.: Scarecrow Press, 1974), 2–3; Timothy L. Smith, *Revivalism and Social Reform* (New York: Abingdon Press, 1957), 124; Timothy L. Smith, *Called unto Holiness: The Story of the Nazarenes: The Formative Years* (Kansas City, Mo.: Nazarene Publishing House, 1962), 15, 23; Dieter, *Holiness*, 48, 131–33.

37. Jones, *Perfectionist*, 17–19, 21.

38. Jones, *Perfectionist*, 23, 184–86; Dieter, *Holiness*, 148.

39. Jones, *Perfectionist*, 47–49, 55–78, 90; Dieter, *Holiness*, 213, 232. Timothy Smith estimated there were 206 full-time holiness evangelists in America by 1888, most without regular assignment from ecclesiastical superiors; see his *Called unto Holiness*, 39.

40. Jones, *Perfectionist*, 90; Dieter, *Holiness*, 151–52; Smith, *Revivalism*, 115; Haines and Thomas, *Outline History*, 19–20.

41. Smith, *Revivalism*, 125–29; Jones, *Perfectionist*, 4–6, 83–87; Dieter, *Holiness*, 204–9.

42. Dieter, *Holiness*, 128, 221–25.

43. Jones, *Perfectionist*, 91–92.

44. William C. Ringenberg, *Taylor University: The First 125 Years* (Grand Rapids, Mich.: William B. Eerdmans, 1973, 184 p.).

45. Hermiz to L. C. Rudolph, 6 April 1990.

46. *The Higher Christian Life: A Bibliographical Overview* (New York: Garland Publishing, 1985), 19–23; Keith J. Hardman, *Charles Grandison Finney, 1792–1875, Revivalist and Reformer* (Syracuse, N.Y.: Syracuse University Press, 1987), 324–49; Smith, *Revivalism*, 103–13.

47. *Aspects of Pentecostal-Charismatic Origins*, ed. Vinson Synan (Plainfield, N.J.: Logos International, 1975), 83–97; *Dictionary of Pentecostal and Charismatic Movements* (Grand Rapids, Mich.: Zondervan, 1988), 407; *Higher Christian Life*, 22, 128–31; Smith, *Called*, 23, 25; Dieter, *Holiness*, 175, 186–88; Purkiser, *Called*, 19.

48. *Aspects of Pentecostal-Charismatic Origins*, 87–90.

49. Donald W. Dayton, *Theological Roots of Pentecostalism* (Grand Rapids, Mich.: Francis Asbury Press, 1987, 199 p.); *Aspects of Pentecostal-Charismatic Origins*, 41–53.

50. Sarah E. Parham, *The Life of Charles F. Parham, Founder of the Apostolic Faith Movement* (Joplin, Mo.: Hunter Printing Company, 1930), 48, 52–53; *Dictionary of Pentecostal and Charismatic Movements*, 660–61. For a detailed study advocating and defending the priority of Parham as a Pentecostal pioneer but revising Parham's account of events, see James R. Goff, *Fields White unto Harvest: Charles F. Parham and the Missionary Origins of Pentecostalism* (Fayetteville, Ark.: University of Arkansas Press, 1988, 263 p.).

51. Vinson Synan, *The Holiness-Pentecostal Movement in the United States* (Grand Rapids, Mich.: William B. Eerdmans, 1971), 103–15; *Dictionary of Pentecostal and Charismatic Movements*, 31–36, 778–81; Goff, *Fields*, 106–27.

52. *Dictionary of Pentecostal and Charismatic Movements*, 810–30; Synan, *Holiness-Pentecostal*, 177. Of 186 churches listed in the "Directory of Area Churches" in the *Herald-Times* of Bloomington, Indiana, for 24 June 1989, 60 were probably pentecostal in practice.

53. Synan, *Holiness-Pentecostal*, 133–35, 145–46; *Dictionary of Pentecostal and Charismatic Movements*, 197–202, 206–9, 846–48.

54. Synan, *Holiness-Pentecostal*, 147–53; *Aspects of Pentecostal-Charismatic Origins*, 81–97; *Dictionary of Pentecostal and Charismatic Movements*, 255–56, 518–19.

55. James L. Tyson, *The Early Pentecostal Revival* (Hazelwood, Mo.: Word Aflame Press, 1992), 169–201; Synan, *Holiness-Pentecostal*, 153–59; *Aspects of Pentecostal-Charismatic Origins*, 94–95; *Dictionary of Pentecostal and Charismatic Movements*, 290, 349–50, 644–51, 700–701, 860–65.

56. *Aspects of Pentecostal-Charismatic Origins*, 86–87; *Dictionary of Pentecostal and Charismatic Movements*, 248–49.

57. Wayne E. Warner, *The Woman Evangelist: The Life and Times of Charismatic Evangelist Maria B. Woodworth-Etter* (Metuchen, N.J.: Scarecrow Press, 1986), 145.

58. Warner, *Woman Evangelist*, 4–7; This biographer pronounces her name as Mah-rye-ah rather than Mah-ree-ah; see p. xii.

59. Warner, *Woman Evangelist*, 10–13. Evidently the "mourners' bench" could be any area designated to receive persons willing to ask or cry out for prayers, counsel, or receipt of the power. There might be an altar or chairs or benches for sitting or kneeling, or no furniture at all.

60. Warner, *Woman Evangelist*, 15–16.

61. This latter association was with the Church of God formed by John Winebrenner and not to be confused with the Church of God (Anderson, Ind.) formed by Daniel S. Warner. In fact both Maria Beulah Woodworth-Etter and Daniel S. Warner were Winebrennerians who had their credentials revoked for being such enthusiastic holiness preachers. See Warner, *Woman Evangelist*, 25, 31–32.

62. Maria B. Woodworth-Etter, *Signs and Wonders God Wrought in the Ministry for Forty Years* (Indianapolis, Ind.: Mrs. M. B. W. Etter, 1916), 74; Maria B. Woodworth-Etter, *Acts of the Holy Ghost; or, The Life, Work, and Experience of Mrs. M. B. Woodworth-Etter, Evangelist* (Dallas, Tex.: John F. Worley Printing, 1912), 128;

Warner, *Woman Evangelist*, 23, 37–44, 50.

63. Warner, *Woman Evangelist*, 53–55.

64. Warner, *Woman Evangelist*, 57–61.

65. David E. Harrell, *All Things Are Possible: The Healing and Charismatic Revivals in Modern America* (Bloomington, Ind.: Indiana University Press, 1975), 98; Synan, *Holiness-Pentecostal*, 120.

66. Woodworth-Etter, *Acts*, 141–45; Warner, *Woman Evangelist*, 163, 193.

67. Maria B. Woodworth-Etter, *Spirit-filled Sermons Preached by Mrs. M. B. Woodworth-Etter . . . With a Brief Account of Her Early Life and Particulars Regarding the New Tabernacle* (Indianapolis, Ind.: n.p., 1921), 202.

68. Warner, *Woman Evangelist*, 254–55, 285–87; *Dictionary of Pentecostal and Charismatic Movements*, 568–71.

69. Warner, *Woman Evangelist*, 255–61; Woodworth-Etter, *Acts*, 342.

70. Woodworth-Etter, *Signs and Wonders*, 493, 499–500.

71. Warner, *Woman Evangelist*, 12, 156, 206, 211, 266; Woodworth-Etter, *Signs and Wonders*, 567–69.

72. Warner, *Woman Evangelist*, 260–64, 283–84.

73. Woodworth-Etter, *Signs and Wonders*, 211, 215.

74. C. Douglas Weaver, *The Healer-Prophet William Marrion Branham: A Study of the Prophetic in American Pentecostalism* (Macon, Ga.: Mercer University Press, 1987), 22; Harrell, *All Things*, 28.

75. Weaver, *Healer-Prophet*, 22–27, 32–33.

76. Harrell, *All Things*, 20. In *All Things Are Possible* Harrell reports and analyzes the remarkable upsurge of healing revivals in America between 1947 and 1955. Branham was the pioneer and pacesetter. On the jacket of *All Things Are Possible* is a print of a picture valued among his followers as a photographic record of Branham preaching with a miraculous halo over his head.

77. Weaver, *Healer-Prophet*, 35–36.

78. Weaver, *Healer-Prophet*, 35–36.

79. Julius Stadsklev, *William Branham; A Prophet Visits South Africa* (Minneapolis, Minn.: Julius Stadsklev, 1952, 195 p.); Weaver, *Healer-Prophet*, 45–47, 50–52.

80. Harrell, *All Things*, 5.

81. Harrell, *All Things*, 36; see also David E. Harrell, *Oral Roberts: An American Life* (Bloomington, Ind.: Indiana University Press, 1985), 109, 148, 150–51.

82. Harrell, *All Things*, 39–40, 163; Weaver, *Healer-Prophet*, 107.

83. Weaver, *Healer-Prophet*, 152–59.

84. Edith L. Blumhofer, *The Assemblies of God*, 2 vols. (Springfield, Mo.: Gospel Publishing House, 1989), 2:78; *Dictionary of Pentecostal and Charismatic Movements*, 137, 226, 245, 759–62,

835; Harrell, *All Things*, 177–78.

85. Blumhofer, *Assemblies*, 2:186–90; *Dictionary of Pentecostal and Charismatic Movements*, 38–40, 142, 837–38.

86. *Dictionary of Pentecostal and Charismatic Movements*, 133–41, 160.

87. *Dictionary of Pentecostal and Charismatic Movements*, 131, 321–22, 781–82.

88. *Dictionary of Pentecostal and Charismatic Movements*, 53–54, 130–60.

89. Edward D. O'Connor, *The Pentecostal Movement in the Catholic Church* (Notre Dame, Ind.: Ave Maria Press, 1971), 38–107; Kevin Ranaghan and Dorothy Ranaghan, *Catholic Pentecostals* (Paramus, N.J.: Paulist Press, 1969, 266 p.); *Dictionary of Pentecostals and Charismatic Movements*, 111–17. For a description of a meeting of Catholic Charismatics at parish level and for a sociological analysis of the Catholic Charismatic movement, see Richard J. Boyd and Joseph E. Faulkner, *The Catholic Charismatics: The Anatomy of a Modern Religious Movement* (University Park, Pa.: Pennsylvania State University Press, 1983, 162 p.).

90. O'Connor, *Pentecostal Movement*, 75–91.

91. O'Connor, *Pentecostal Movement*, 95–99; *Aspects of Pentecostal-Charismatic Origins*, 242.

92. *The American Catholic Parish: A History from 1850 to the Present*, ed. Jay P. Dolan, 2 vols. (New York: Paulist Press, 1987), 2:366–67; Richard Quebedeaux, *The New Charismatics II* (San Francisco: Harper and Row, 1983), 233–39; *Dictionary of Pentecostal and Charismatic Movements*, 112, 122–24, 128, 160.

93. Synan, *Holiness-Pentecostal*, 190.

94. Morris E. Golder, *Life and Works of Bishop Garfield Thomas Haywood* (Indianapolis, Ind.: n.p., 1977), 3–4; Anton Theophilus Boisen, "Holy Rollers and Churches of Custom," in *Religion in Crisis and Custom: A Sociological and Psychological Study* (New York: Harper and Brothers, 1955), 8–20; Synan, *Holiness-Pentecostal*, 190–92.

95. Synan, *Holiness-Pentecostal*, 146–47, 222.

96. Synan, *Holiness-Pentecostal*, 207–8; *Dictionary of Pentecostal and Charismatic Movements*, 634–36, 703–4.

97. *Community of Praise*. Middletown film. 60 minutes. Shown on Public Broadcasting Service (PBS—WTIU) 7 April 1982; *Joy Unspeakable*. Video production of Indiana University Radio and Television Department. 3/8" u-matic videocassette and other video formats. Shown on Public Broadcasting Service (PBS—WTIU) 9 April 1982.

98. William W. Menzies, *Anointed to Serve: The Story of the Assemblies of God* (Springfield, Mo.: Gospel Publishing House, 1971), 372–83; Synan, *Holiness-Pentecostal*, 222–24.

WESLEYANS

When the Wesleyans organized separately from the Methodists in 1843, they met "to form a Wesleyan Methodist Church . . . free from Episcopacy and Slavery, and embracing a system of itineracy, under proper limitations and restrictions, with such disciplinary regulations as are necessary to preserve and promote experimental and practical godliness." Unyielding opposition to slavery and championship of abolition were primary planks in the platform. Even before the conference at Utica, New York, which brought the denomination into existence, Indiana was forming Wesleyan churches. First president of the new Wesleyan church was Orange Scott, a Yankee abolitionist. When he visited Indiana on his 1845 tour he found his Wesleyan antislavery kindred already thriving at Newport (later Fountain City).

> One sister stated that she had come over fifty miles to attend the Conference. She had once been a slave, I believe, though not very dark. Several spoke in the love feast who had been slaves. Hundreds of slaves every year pass through this state to Canada. At eleven o'clock I preached a long sermon for me (about one hour and a half) to, it was thought, about one thousand persons; many of whom could not get into the house, but who stood, both men and women, around the windows and doors during the whole of the exercises, though it rained smartly all the time . . . This [Miami] Conference is in a prosperous condition. It had only five stationed preachers two years ago. Since that time the Illinois and Wisconsin Conferences have been cut off from this, and

there still remains [sic] some thirty stationed preachers, and about seventeen hundred members. The preachers are devoted and in good spirits, and are prepared to go through mud and water to save souls.[1]

Wesleyan abolitionists were working alongside Indiana's Quakers to staff the "Underground Railroad." When Eliza of *Uncle Tom's Cabin* crossed the Ohio on floating ice, the man who helped her up the bank was William Lacy, later a Wesleyan circuit rider and president of Indiana Conference. Daniel Worth went as a Wesleyan minister from Indiana to North Carolina in 1857, hoping that his North Carolina nativity and family connections would get his abolitionism a favorable hearing. It was a false hope. He was jailed on Christmas Eve of 1859 for circulating antislavery books, sentenced to a year in prison, and released only upon posting of bond to guarantee his return to his family in Indiana. Other Wesleyan members and ministers also moved under pressure from North Carolina to Indiana. After the Civil War, in 1871, the Indiana Conference sent North Carolina natives Lindsay Fisher and Emsley Brookshire back to North Carolina as Wesleyan ministers to restore remnants of Wesleyan churches there. Tennessee received postwar ministers from Indiana as well and for a long time all the pastors with appointments in both Tennessee and North Carolina were carried on the Indiana rolls.[2]

Best known of Indiana's pioneer Wesleyan preachers was Aaron Worth who addressed the General Conference of the national denomination for the last time at Fairmount, Indiana, in 1919.

> At 10:30, Rev. Aaron Worth, the "Grand Old Man of Indiana," preached on the theme, "The Rejected Stone," using as a text Matt. 21:42. For 66 years he has been preaching an uncompromising gospel, a noble record of service. He is 84 years old and the only man now living (so far as is known) who attended the first General Conference, 76 years ago. It is impossible to do justice in reporting this sermon. The flow of his well-rounded and eloquent sentences, the richness of his tone, mellowed by life's winters, the joyfulness of his spirit, as, for half an hour this Father in Israel poured forth a rich and unctuous gospel, all united in making it a service very impressive. He spoke of Christ; poor, poorer than we will ever be, born in another man's barn, buried in another man's tomb. Christ the great corner stone offered Himself to His nation and church, but was rejected to their eternal loss. He was a precious stone, a tried stone, a living stone. His enemies tried to kill Him, and they did, but the third day He arose, tingling with immortal life and rode to the skies with death chained to His chariot wheels. He illustrated his truths by apt illustrations and from his own experiences as a champion of reform in anti-slavery, prohibition and woman's suffrage, all at first rejected but later successful.[3]

Worth was a candidate for governor of Indiana on the Prohibition Party ticket in 1892. He made a canvass of every county in the state, speaking twice a day for 110 days.

Thus for the early Wesleyans a reform lecture may have been even more characteristic than a traditional sermon. At the end of the Civil War, the early goal of abolition had been achieved. About a hundred of the nation's Wesleyan ministers and many lay persons returned to the Methodist Episcopal church. In Indiana the Wesleyans were not so ready to return. Only six Indiana ministers left their Wesleyan connection; Wesleyan membership in the state actually increased by 42 percent during the 1866–1867 conference year.[4]

Wesleyans supported reforms in addition to the abolition of slavery. They wished to escape what the founders were convinced was the tyranny of the presiding elders and bishops of the Methodist Episcopal church. They "advocated an end to war; called for the prohibition of the manufacture, sale, and use of alcoholic beverages; warned against the evils of tobacco; and opposed secret societies and lodges." They opposed profanation of the Sabbath, social or commercial events held in the churches, and immodest dress. Changes interpreted as lapses into worldliness or immodesty or sinful indulgence sparked protests at every stage of the denomination's life. There was much discussion of the length of hair and of the length of sleeves and of the wearing of jewelry, even wedding rings.[5]

Wesleyans Become Holiness Evangelists

Most important by far in the period following the Civil War was the heightened emphasis on personal evangelism. What had been primarily a crusade to reform society as a whole became primarily a crusade to reform individuals by religious conversion. There came to be less emphasis on racial justice; there came to be more emphasis on holiness doctrine and practice. The holiness revival in the nation and the rise of the holiness movement became the powerful new motivation for the Wesleyans. Holiness evangelist Mary E. Depew made a mighty impact on the Indiana Conference in 1876. There were General Conference statements showing increased urgency for entire sanctification in 1883 and 1885. The Indiana Annual Conference of 1887 made it official. "Resolved:—That no preacher of the Indiana Annual Conference shall be allowed to preach who is not in accord with the doctrine of holiness as taught by John Wesley, and set forth by our General Conference and Book of Discipline as being a work of grace in the heart subsequent to conversion." That same conference established three full time officers with considerable authority at the state conference administrative center: a president to be "the conference in the absence of the conference," a conference evangelist, and a conference missionary. The next year Indiana Conference authorized Olinda Davis, Lucy Simons, and Mossilene Crilley to organize the Woman's Missionary Society. The model for the new church was established. Church extension was now the primary program. That came to mean persistent holiness revival.[6]

One scholar said ordinary Wesleyan services might be austere enough with gospel songs, prayer, offering, special music, sermon, and lengthy invitation.

> But such a service could become electrifying with the addition of the right ingredients—if "the Spirit really moved." The singing was extremely spirited. During all parts of the service there could be exclamations of "Hallelujah," "Praise the Lord," "Well, glory." Each person felt free to express his own feelings of joy over what Christ had done and was doing for him. Some might leap to their feet suddenly and begin to jump up and down, waving their hands in the air and screaming at the top of their voices—sometimes with words, sometimes with

unbroken sound. Some would run, leap over pews, perform feats normally beyond their strength. Some would walk back and forth weeping for joy. Some would give vent to the "holy laugh." Some would simply sit with their faces shining, enjoying the rejoicing of others as well as their own inner peace and joy. Some would testify, describing how they were saved and/or entirely sanctified, or how God had healed them or answered some other specific request, Interestingly enough, glossalalia were not tolerated. Praying was almost always done while kneeling—not on padded prayer benches but on the floor, turning around and facing the pew on which the worshipper had been sitting. In many instances it was "concert prayer," with everyone praying at once and the person who had been asked to "lead" in prayer going unheard in the uproar. Sometimes the preacher would not get to preach because so many would "obey the Spirit" and "take their liberty." Those who wanted spiritual help came forward to kneel at a bench set out at the front, or to a prayer rail built along the edge of the speaker's platform. It was referred to as "the mourner's bench" or "the altar." Here the seeker after conversion, or sanctification, or healing, or reclamation from backsliding, or help for some problem, or the person interceding for another was expected to remain until he "prayed through." He was usually surrounded by "mothers and fathers in Israel" who hugged him, pounded him on the back, shouted encouragement in his ear, and prayed earnestly with him that he might "get the victory." Some might stay with him all night if such proved necessary.[7]

For them decorum was not really very important in the face of what they considered ultimate issues of heaven and hell. They felt that personal embarrassment was secondary if slaves of alcohol and tobacco were liberated, diseased bodies were healed, the dregs of society were turned into respectable citizens, and cruel wife-beaters and tyrants at home became loving husbands and fathers.

Indiana was open to the message and the method. Indiana's annual conference was a strong one among the Wesleyans from its formation in 1848. As it came to embody the vigor of the holiness revival, it supplied leadership for the whole denomination. Eber Teter of Boxley was chairman of the committee to propose a plan to organize the work of Indiana Conference under leadership of a full-time conference president. The conference membership liked his plan so well they adopted it and elected him to the enhanced office of president. Under his energetic leadership between 1887 and 1901, Indiana pastorates increased from seventeen to thirty-six, congregations increased from sixty-seven to ninety-five, membership grew by one-third, Sunday school enroll-

ment grew by two-thirds, and total contributions tripled. The Wesleyan campground established at Fairmount in Grant County during his presidency was a model, so well developed that both the Indiana Conference and the denomination's General Conference regularly met there. Teter moved on from Indiana to the staff and presidency of the General Conference where he put his distinctive evangelistic, theological, and administrative stamp on the whole denomination before returning home to die in Hamilton County in 1928. Most of Teter's early successors at the head of Indiana Conference were also called into service in the denomination at large. W. H. Kennedy of Indiana Conference became the first general missionary superintendent in 1891; Indiana men led the denominational department of home missions—evangelism and church extension—for its first forty-eight years. When the denomination formed a pension plan for ministers, they adapted an Indiana Conference plan.[8]

Indiana also became a Wesleyan educational center. The pioneering Indiana Annual Conference of 1887 authorized the committee on itineracy and elders' orders to conduct theological institutes for the training of ministers. The aim was to have the ministers at least a bit better educated than the general level of the constituency. Fairmount Bible School was opened at the denomination's permanent camp meeting grounds and graduated its first class in 1909. By 1920 it became the theological department of a new college located at Marion. Indiana Wesleyans were spared none of the pains and terrors of college funding and accreditation. Not all members were sure they wanted this educational thing. Wesleyan conferences outside Indiana provided very limited support. However, one-fifth of all Wesleyans were members of Indiana Conference by 1920; that year there were twenty-five Wesleyan churches within a radius of thirty miles of Marion. They managed to keep Marion College viable until it became in fact a senior college for the whole denomination rather than merely a local enterprise. Indiana Conference offered in 1955 to donate a site at Marion for a new denominational headquarters. Fire at the denominational publishing house at Syracuse, New York, hastened the decision to locate both the Wesleyan International Headquarters and the publishing house in Indiana.[9]

Merger with the Missionary Bands of the World

Wesleyan strength kept growing in Indiana because of persistent evangelism in holiness style. It also kept growing through merger, the uniting of components of that galaxy of independent missionary bands set off early in the modern holiness movement. One such faith mission group, inspired primarily by the ministry of a midwestern native named Vivian A. Dake, had sent out clusters of youth dependent entirely on divine provision to pray and preach in local groceries or schoolhouses. The more durable of these evangelists went on the same unsalaried basis to establish quite substantial missions in India and Jamaica. During the time they were in peripheral connection with the Free Methodist church they called themselves Pentecost Bands. When they could not accept the level of supervision prescribed by the Free Methodists, they incorporated independently in 1898 as Pentecostal Bands of the World. The religious census of 1906 reported seventy-five domestic missionaries and seventeen foreign missionaries on their rolls. In 1925 they changed their name to Missionary Bands of the World and in 1958 they merged with the Wesleyan Methodist Church. They brought with them to the Wesleyans their headquarters campground in Indianapolis, eight congregations in Indiana, and their very considerable missionary commitment.[10]

Merger with the Pilgrim Holiness

The 1958 merger of Wesleyans with the Missionary Bands of the World was small indeed compared to the 1968 merger of the Wesleyans with the Pilgrim Holiness. In Indiana the Pilgrim Holiness fellowship was about equal in size with the Wesleyans. It was even more aggressive and faster growing. And the Pilgrim Holiness body was an even richer blend of the enthusiastic evangelistic bands so characteristic of holiness movement beginnings, each bringing to the union its own force of unsalaried workers at missionary stations at home and abroad.

The Pilgrim side of Pilgrim Holiness bore the imprint of a Hoosier named Seth Cook Rees. When a youth of nineteen, Rees was converted in a Quaker meeting of holiness style in his home town of Westfield.

> I had not long been seated when the Spirit fell upon the congregation, and the meeting proved to be one of testimony and confession. When the meeting was well under way, a strange power came over me and I arose and confessed that I was an awful sinner. I was not on my feet thirty seconds, but I sat down a saint! Up to that time I had not attempted to pray. I had not shed a tear. Now my eyes were fountains; I wept like rain. The complexion of everything was changed. Every blade of grass, every drop of water and every bird of forest and field, seemed to dance with delight.[11]

Five months later he began his preaching career atop a dirt pile on the grounds of the Quaker Quarterly Meeting at Westfield. From the beginning he resisted restraint. "I conferred not with flesh and blood," he said. He claimed he conducted his ministry "under the immediate and perceptible guidance of the Spirit." Under the preaching of Quaker evangelists David B. Updegraff and Dougan Clark, he anguished his way to sanctification.

> At last there began to creep into my soul a tranquil feeling, a holy hush, a death-like stillness, a sweet, placid "second rest." I had let go, and He had embraced me in His arms. Eight hours later the conscious filling came, and from that hour I had convictions of certainty. "The old man" was "put off," "the body of sin" was "destroyed," "the old leaven" was "purged out," "the flesh" was "cut away," "the son of the bondwoman" was "excommunicated," "the carnal mind" was "crucified," and I was dead indeed unto sin. He did it. No credit belongs to me.[12]

Rees's Quaker connection came into question in 1886 when he and his wife accepted baptism with water, contrary to Quaker tradition. However holiness evangelism across denominational lines was becoming his real vocation. He developed into a holiness evangelist of commanding presence, mercurial but powerful and widely sought nationwide to conduct revivals. Sometimes his sponsors billed this marginal Friend as "The Earthquaker." In 1897 he united with Martin Wells Knapp at Cincinnati to form a proto-denominational holiness organization known as the International Holiness Union and Prayer League. C. W. Ruth, a holiness evangelist in Indianapolis, was its treasurer. Candidates for membership needed to possess heart purity or have an ardent desire for the experience. And they needed to sign a pledge: "I believe that Christ's baptism with the Holy Ghost is subsequent to regeneration, that it is for all believers, that it is an instantaneous experience, received by faith, cleansing the heart of the receiver from all sin, and enduing him with power for the successful accomplishment of all to which he is called."

The League's program was large—servicing a network of revivals over a wide area; forming missions, churches, rescue homes, and camp meetings; issuing a monthly periodical called *The Revivalist*; operating a school for evangelists called God's Bible School and Missionary Training Home which sent out independent faith missionaries to many foreign lands. It kept looking more and more like a denomination.[13]

Rees severed his connection with this bustling Cincinnati center after Knapp's death in 1901. He occupied himself in similar enterprises across the American West and by 1909 located his center of operations in Pasadena. There he joined his holiness colleagues in the newly formed Nazarene denomination and in 1912 was appointed pastor of the University Church at its rising Pasadena College. The idea was to place a powerful revivalist in the Nazarene college church to guarantee that the college would remain a center of spiritual fire. In the revival Rees helped to spark there "the Holy Ghost fell upon the whole fifty acres." His involvement in the controversy which followed that revival tested the very ability of the youthful Nazarene union to survive.

In the midst of the furor in 1917, Rees took his most immediate followers out of the Nazarenes and into a completely new covenant. They came to be called the Pilgrim Church. They soon set up Pilgrim Bible College in Pasadena and a missionary work stretching from Mexico to China. They gathered a few affiliate congregations in Texas and Kansas and began publishing *The Pilgrim*. It was this small body of constituents—475 members and 325 of them in Rees's congregation at Pasadena—which he brought to be the Pilgrim side of the Pilgrim Holiness union in 1922. But he brought more. In 1926 the General Assembly of the Pilgrim Holiness Church meeting at Frankfort, Indiana, called on him to be its general superintendent, an office he was to hold and shape as the denomination developed its administrative center at Indianapolis. He was seventy-two when elected. For the next six years his powerful personality, his national visibility, and his evangelistic drive gave the new merger strength to survive the lean years of its beginnings.[14]

The Holiness side of the Pilgrim Holiness merger was also a blending of independent holiness unions impelled to become church denominations in the interest of more effective organization. There was that continuing International Holiness Union and Prayer League set in motion by Martin Wells Knapp and Seth Cook Rees at the turn of the century and centered in Cincinnati. Faced with unordained candidates for missionary service, three ministerial members of the Union ordained Charles Cowman and his wife Lettie to go to Japan in 1901. By the end of 1905 the organization manual showed 248 ordained ministers or missionaries and 28 ordained deaconesses. Its name had changed to International Apostolic Holiness Union in 1900 and changed again to International Apostolic Holiness Church in 1913.[15]

Even more significant for Indiana was the Holiness Christian Church. It grew out of revivals following 1882 in the Philadelphia area, being first named the Heavenly Recruit Association. A historian described the develop-ment: "While the formation of a church was originally not their motive, the necessity of a distinct organization soon became evident. Seeing that so many churches had a form of godliness but denying the power thereof, that young converts had little opportunity to become established in holiness, it became urgent that classes should be formed for the spreading of scriptural holiness and the free exercise of vital godliness."[16] Next came the commissioning of itinerant ministers to serve the new class groups, and at the annual conference of 1894 C. W. Ruth of Indianapolis was elected presiding elder to station the preachers. Indiana Conference of the Holiness Christian Church was organized at Tipton, Indiana, in October of 1896.

At New London, Indiana, a Holiness Christian school was begun with a unique plan to move the institution periodically from congregation to congregation, students to be housed and fed by the church members. Holiness Christian minister Charles Calvin Brown got the school settled at Carlinville, Illinois, in 1905. He also opened an orphanage there and issued *A Voice from Canaan* as an official Holiness Christian paper. Brown was a native of Crawford County, Indiana, who ministered widely in Indiana and became the denomination's general superintendent in 1917. He lent his leadership when 2,167 members of this Holiness Christian Church merged with 8,000 members of the International Apostolic Holiness Church of Knapp and Rees origins to become the International Holiness Church in 1919. Over half the Holiness Christians in that merger were in Indiana—1,485 of the 2,167. Three years later Brown presided over the general assembly in which the 457 members of the Pilgrim Church centered in California merged with the International Holiness Church to form the Pilgrim Holiness Church. Growth by evangelism kept paralleling the merger activity. Indiana shared fully in this growth. Indiana District was the largest in the new Pilgrim Holiness Church.[17]

All the vested interests involved in the mergers plus all the traditional independence and suspicion of church authority had left the emerging Pilgrim Holiness denomination with a badly fragmented administrative structure. The general assembly chaired by Seth Cook Rees at Frankfort, Indiana, in 1930 dared to propose that all the administrative remainders be replaced by a unity of one general board, one general superintendent, and one general church headquarters. Kingswood in Kentucky and Frankfort in Indiana invited location of the headquarters but Indianapolis was selected.

During the move to Indianapolis the Pilgrim Holiness treasury was empty. Headquarters for a time was a residence at 839 North Capitol rented for $35 per month. Local volunteers did clerical work and bookkeeping and building remodeling and lodging of headquarters visitors. Evangelist E. V. Halt was also a qualified bookkeeper. He was invited to move from Terre Haute to Indianapolis to serve as general treasurer and manage the headquarters building and operate the publishing business and run the book sales room and insure regular publication of the denominational paper. Every Pilgrim Holiness church had a Sunday school. All needed Sunday school literature and supplies and Bibles and books. By 1945 the publishing business itself had grown strong enough to contribute $60,000 in cash toward the purchase of "an attractive and commodious office building," a proper headquarters and publishing house six stories tall at 230 East Ohio.[18]

Among the denomination's six Bible schools and colleges was Frankfort Pilgrim College at Frankfort, Indiana, founded in 1927 and in theory supported as well by Kentucky and Illinois as "patronizing territory." In 1950 merger continued in a small way as most congregations of the Trinity Gospel Tabernacle Association united with the Pilgrim Holiness. This independent association was an affiliation of several local congregations in southwestern Indiana with the larger congregation and radio ministry of A. L. Luttrull at Evansville. When membership of the Indiana District of the Pilgrim Holiness was large enough to divide in 1951, both the resulting Northern District and Southern District made lively growth, establishing camp meeting centers among the largest in the denomination.[19]

So the union of the Wesleyan Methodists with the Pilgrim Holiness in 1968 was a major gathering point for holiness people. There were about 6,000 members of each in Indiana with perhaps three times that number of constituents. Together they made Indiana the largest conference of the merged body named the Wesleyan Church. In 1990 Indiana's reports showed 238 Wesleyan churches with 34,025 adherents in the state. Marion College had been renamed Indiana Wesleyan University and Indianapolis was the site of the new Wesleyan world headquarters serving an international constituency of about 250,000 including congregations in some forty missionary districts.

NOTES

1. Ira Ford McLeister and Roy Stephen Nicholson, *Conscience and Commitment: The History of the Wesleyan Methodist Church of America*, 4th rev. ed., ed. Lee M. Haines and Melvin E. Dieter (Marion, Ind.: Wesley Press, 1976), 28, 45.

2. McLeister and Nicholson, *Conscience*, 586–89, 616–18.

3. McLeister and Nicholson, *Conscience*, 153–54.

4. Lee M. Haines, "A History of the Indiana Conference of the Wesleyan Methodist Church, 1867–1971" (Th.M. thesis, Christian Theological Seminary, Indianapolis, Ind., 1973), 1, 9.

5. Haines, "History," 1, 193–94.

6. Haines, "History," 9–18, 74, 82, 133; McLeister and Nicholson, *Conscience*, 96, 99.

7. Haines, "History," 120–21.

8. Lee M. Haines and Paul William Thomas, *An Outline History of the Wesleyan Church* (Marion, Ind.: Wesley Press, 1981), 80–81, 105; McLeister and Nicholson, *Conscience*, 217, 586–88.

9. Haines, "History," 72, 174–82; McLeister and Nicholson, *Conscience*, 515–28.

10. Charles E. Jones, *Perfectionist Persuasion: The Holiness Movement and American Methodism 1867–1936* (Metuchen, N.J.: Scarecrow Press, 1974), 66–69, 161–62; Haines and Thomas, *Outline History*, 103–4; Ida Dake Parsons, *Kindling Watch-fires: Being a Brief Sketch of the Life of Rev. Vivian A. Dake* (Chicago: Free Methodist Publishing House, 1915), 17–52. For a Hoosier woman's account of her life of service in Indiana as an unsalaried member of the Pentecost Bands and Missionary Bands of the World, see Maude H. Kahl, *His Guiding Hand* (Overland Park, Kans.: Herald and Banner Press, 1970, 280 p.).

11. Paul S. Rees, *Seth Cook Rees, The Warrior Saint* (Indianapolis, Ind.: Pilgrim Book Room, 1934), 9.

12. Rees, *Seth Cook Rees*, 17.

13. Paul Westphal Thomas and Paul William Thomas, *The Days of Our Pilgrimage: The History of the Pilgrim Holiness Church*, eds. Melvin E. Dieter and Lee M. Haines (Marion, Ind.: Wesley Press, 1976), 16; Jones, *Perfectionist*, 99–104; Rees, *Seth Cook Rees*, 11, 22, 46, 54–63.

14. Timothy L. Smith, *Called unto Holiness* (Kansas City, Mo.: Nazarene Publishing House, 1962), 140, 274–81; Thomas and Thomas, *Days*, 94–95; Rees, *Seth Cook Rees*, 86–97.

15. Haines and Thomas, *Outline History*, 126; Thomas and Thomas, *Days*, 51–52.

16. Thomas and Thomas, *Days*, 87.

17. Thomas and Thomas, *Days*, 63, 86–90, 94–95, 105.

18. Thomas and Thomas, *Days*, 124–38, 156–57.

19. Thomas and Thomas, *Days*, 161, 168, 239, 249, 270, 314; Haines and Thomas, *Outline History*, 154–55.

FREE METHODISTS

The story of the early years of the Free Methodists blended with the life story of Benjamin T. Roberts. He was born in July of 1823 in Cattaraugus County of western New York. Having become a precocious and well disciplined youth, he was combining school teaching with apprenticeship in the study of law. The year he was twenty-one he was converted. "The instrumentality was very humble," Roberts said. "A pious, but illiterate cooper, a very bad stammerer, gave in his testimony at the regular Sabbath afternoon prayer-meeting. I was there by the invitation of friends, and his testimony found way to my heart . . . Many who had power with God prayed for me; but I had to yield. Christ demanded an unconditional surrender; I made it The joys of pardon and peace flowed into my soul. My cup was full, my happiness was unspeakable."[1]

His conversion reoriented his vocation. After two preparatory terms at Lima Seminary he joined the class of 1848 at Wesleyan University in Middletown, Connecticut, to prepare for the Methodist ministry. While in college he kept teaching in district schools to help meet his expenses. Always he was attending and leading church meetings. His letters from college were full of holy intention and fervor for his chosen work. This commitment was intensified in winter of 1846 when a physician-evangelist named John Wesley Redfield conducted a series of revival meetings at the First Methodist Church in Middletown.[2]

"Dr. Redfield," as he was universally known, had earlier ended his own anguished search for entire sanc-

tification in the tent of Phoebe and Walter Palmer at a camp meeting near New York City. Phoebe Palmer "stated the preliminary steps to be taken," the first of which was a thorough consecration to God. Then she "made this entire consecration to appear as a reasonable demand." And she "showed the reasonableness of believing that God meant what he said, and that he would do what he said he would do, and that our faith must rest mainly on his promise." Dr. Redfield testified to his own receipt of the great blessing on these terms. Then he became a flaming advocate of old-fashioned Methodism and of entire sanctification. This sanctification was less to be sought as a grand new surge of feeling; it was more to be sought as an unreserved consecration to God of the person's whole being and potential.[3]

At Middletown Dr. Redfield left lukewarm church members little room for comfort. "The faculty, the official members, and the Church received and endorsed the truth. Such a work of God as followed we never witnessed. Professors in the college, men of outwardly blameless lives, saw they were not right with God, frankly confessed it, and laying aside their official dignity, went forward for prayers. The city and adjoining country were moved as by the breath of the Lord. For some eight or ten weeks, the altar was crowded with penitents, from fifty to a hundred coming forward at a time. The conversions were generally very clear and powerful." The preaching was sensational. "Glory to God," William C. Kendall once said of Redfield, "he rules the whirlwind and directs the storm." Nearly all the young men at Wesleyan College were among the 400 converts that winter. Twenty-six of the college students became ministers. William Kendall of the class of 1848 "received at this time the blessing of holiness under Dr. Redfield's labors." The success at Middletown gave Redfield hope that the cause of holiness and the quest for sanctification might be renewed in the Methodist church. Benjamin T. Roberts said "Such scenes of spiritual power I never had witnessed. The convictions I there received never left me."[4]

"Nazarites" and "Regency" in New York State

Roberts graduated with honors and enrolled in Genesee Conference, a young man on a fast track who moved up quickly to become pastor of the prestigious Niagara Street church in Buffalo at age thirty. His popularity among the Methodists did not last. In 1851 Roberts had attended Collins camp meeting. Evangelists Phoebe and Walter Palmer of New York City were there. "Mrs. Palmer . . . labored for the promotion of holiness with great zeal and success," he said. All the convictions earlier stirred in him by the preaching of Dr. Redfield were renewed and increased. "I deliberately gave myself anew to the Lord, to declare the whole truth as it is in Jesus, and to take the narrow way. The blessing came. The spirit fell upon me in an overwhelming degree. I received a power to labor such as I had never possessed before. This consecration has never been taken back."[5]

Now his revivals were holiness in theme and style. Roberts began writing articles in the *Northern Independent* about worldliness and other evils creeping into the Methodist church. He preferred to share revival ministries with a group of likeminded preachers including Asa Abell, William Kendall, Joseph McCreery, Fay Purdy, John Wesley Redfield, Loren Stiles, and Seth Woodruff. Roberts brought the stormy Dr. Redfield to preach at Niagara Street church. That revival of "several weeks" ended with at least as many protests as converts and no remuneration even for the evangelist's expenses. Redfield never contracted for or asked pay for his services or travel. Following the example of the apostle Paul indicated in Acts 20:34, he intended that his own hands should "minister to his necessities."[6]

Roberts himself was not reappointed to the stylish congregation in Buffalo; he was sent to rural Brockport and from there to Albion. Such displacement was all too common for the holiness preachers. Roberts wrote his father "It has been the case under the odd-fellow reign that if a minister was true to his vows and endeavored to carry out the discipline he was crushed. We are determined that this shall be done no longer." Joseph McCreery said there ought to be a "Nazarite Union" of holiness reformers to protect themselves from such abuse. No such union was actually formed; seventeen holiness reformers of Genesee Conference issued a joint statement that no such association ever existed. Loren Stiles said there seemed to be a "Regency" of powerful progressives in the Conference working to destroy the revivalistic reformers.[7]

So Genesee Conference, already noisily divided since Eleazar Thomas distributed a pamphlet opposing lodge membership in 1848, now became polarized between the holiness "Nazarites" and the progressive "Regency" although each refused to accept any such name. Said a member of the Regency:

Spurious reformers are as plenty as blackberries, and as contemptible as plenty. Incapable of comprehending the moral condition and wants of society around them, and also of understanding the modes or processes by which reformation is to be effected, they believe, or affect to believe, that they are the chosen instruments of some greatly needed social regeneration . . . We of Genesee Conference have such a batch of false prophets—such pseudo reformers among us. And such a group of regenerators as the Nazarites compose, we can not believe was ever before brought together by the force of a common belief in a divine call to a great work. Whence, or why the idea ever struck them that they were the chosen ministers of a new reformation, will probably never be rescued from the dimness and uncertainty of speculation. They probably felt a motion of something within them—it may have been a wind in the stomach—and mistook it for the intimations of a heaven-derived commission, summoning them to the rescue of expiring Methodism, and the inauguration of a new era of spiritual life in the history of the Wesleyan movement.[8]

In a manner already characteristic of him, Roberts attempted to define the issues clearly and then to describe them in an incisive essay. From Albion he sent his article "New School Methodism" for publication in the hotly anti-slavery *Northern Independent* in August of 1857. He wrote:

Already there is springing up among us a class of preachers whose teaching is very different from that of the fathers of Methodism. They may be found here and there throughout our Zion; but in Genesee Conference they act as an associate body. They number about thirty. During the last session of this Conference, they held several secret meetings, in which they concerted a plan to carry their measures and spread their doctrines. They have openly made the issue in the Conference. It is divided. Two distinct parties exist. With one or the other every preacher is in sympathy. This difference is fundamental. It does not relate to things indifferent, but to those of the most vital importance. It involves nothing less than the nature itself of Christianity.[9]

The New School Methodists hold that justification and entire sanctification, or holiness, are the same—that when a sinner is pardoned, he is at the same time made holy—that all the spiritual change he may henceforth expect, is simply a growth in grace.—When they speak of "holiness," they mean by it the same as do evangelical ministers of those denominations which do not receive the doctrines taught by Wesley and Fletcher on this subject. According to the Old School Methodists, merely justified persons, while they do not outwardly commit sin, are conscious of sin still remaining in the heart, such as pride, self-will, and unbelief. They continually feel a heart bent to back-sliding; a natural tendency to evil; a proneness to depart from God, and cleave to the things of earth. Those that are sanctified wholly, are saved from inward sin—from evil thoughts, and evil tempers. No wrong temper, none contrary to love, remains in the soul. All the thoughts, words and actions are governed by pure love.[10]

Differing thus in their views of religion, the Old and New School Methodists necessarily differ in their measures for its promotion. The latter build stock churches, and furnish them with pews to accommodate a select congregation; and with organs, melodeons, violins, and professional singers, to execute difficult pieces of music for a fashionable audience. The former favor free churches, congregational singing, and spirituality, simplicity and fervency in worship. They endeavor to promote revivals, deep and thorough; such as were common under the labors of the Fathers; such as have made Methodism the leading denomination of the land.[11]

Preachers of the old stamp urge upon all who would gain heaven, the necessity of self-denial—non-conformity to the world; purity of heart and holiness of life; while the others ridicule singularity, encourage by their silence, and in some cases by their own example, and that of their wives and daughters, "the putting on of gold and costly apparel," and treat with distrust all professions of deep Christian experience. When these desire to raise money for the benefit of the Church, they have recourse to the selling of pews to the highest bidder; to parties of pleasure, oyster suppers, fairs, grab-bags, festivals and lotteries; the others for this purpose, appeal to the love the people bear to Christ. In short, the Old School Methodists rely for the spread of the gospel upon the agency of the Holy Ghost, and the purity of the Church. The New School Methodists

appear to depend upon the patronage of the worldly, the favor of the proud and aspiring; and the various artifices of worldly policy.[12]

The article was a boon to his enemies. Only a few days later Roberts was before the Genesee Conference charged with nine counts of "unchristian and immoral conduct" toward his fellow conference members, all based on citations from his "New School Methodism." The Regency had a small but disciplined majority. Under the shadow of a formal reproof laid on him by the Conference, Roberts was sent off to be pastor to the farmers at Pekin. He called Dr. Redfield to Pekin to spend "some weeks" reviving the congregation. He was now receiving many invitations to conduct revivals himself. His friend George Estes of Brockport tried to help by preparing and distributing a pamphlet which included a reprint of the text of "New School Methodism" by Roberts along with an account of the 1857 trial quite uncomplimentary to the Regency. As a result Roberts was back before the Conference in 1858, fully blamed for the pamphlet gotten out by Estes and charged with contumacy. Both he and a Nazarite colleague named Joseph McCreery were expelled.[13]

Neither Roberts nor McCreery gave up their efforts for reform. Roberts moved his family to Buffalo from which base he carried on his work as a private publisher and evangelist. Beginning in 1858 holiness Methodists who supported "old paths" in general and Benjamin T. Roberts in particular held a series of "laymen's conventions." They prepared strenuous statements rehearsing the abuses suffered by the Nazarites and pointing out the errors of the Regency. They resolved to raise money to support Roberts ($1,000) and McCreery ($600) "to travel at large, and labor as opportunity presents." They named an "executive committee" to superintend the constituency arising from such travel and labor, soon a large and lively body of both members and preachers. They looked with favor on the gathering of these constituents into bands and independent churches while awaiting decision on the appeal of Roberts to the Methodist General Conference scheduled to meet in May of 1860. They declared their unwillingness to pay any support whatever to progressive pastors appointed over them. Attempts of the Conference to discipline the participants in these conventions only hardened their resolve. Roberts hoped to be exonerated by the General Conference of 1860 and so to strengthen reform among Methodists in Genesee Conference, but in the meantime he became in fact an itinerant superintendent for a separated holiness constituency.[14]

Western Laymen's Convention in Illinois

A second exciting center of support had developed in the area of St. Charles in northern Illinois. David Sherman had invited Dr. Redfield there in 1856 to conduct a holiness revival. Besides the converts, "some forty" had claimed entire sanctification. Dr. Redfield was later invited to conduct meetings in neighboring towns of Elgin, Marengo, and Woodstock. When Methodist authorities resisted the efforts of Redfield and his colleagues, an independent Western Laymen's Convention arose with a profile and program similar to the laymen's conventions developing in New York. Redfield was the central figure for the West but as early as 1859 Roberts went west to help. In June of 1860, Roberts went with a delegation from New York to the camp meeting and laymen's convention at St. Charles. He said: "As we came upon the ground we plainly perceived that God was among the people. At once we felt at home. Strangers are brought nigh by the blood of Christ. Dr. Redfield, whose labors for the promotion of holiness have been greatly blessed in Northern Illinois, had charge of the meeting. He was assisted by as promising a body of young ministers as we ever saw together—men of grace, gifts and physical vigor, who will yet leave their mark for good upon the world." For the business meeting in connection with this 1860 camp meeting at St. Charles, Benjamin T. Roberts was called to preside and John Wesley Redfield was among those enrolled. After that camp meeting they held local evangelistic meetings at St. Charles, Clintonville, Kishwaukee, Franklinville, Marengo, Bonus, Woodstock, and Queen Ann.[15]

Formation of Free Methodist Denomination

The Methodist General Conference of 1860 decided against the appeal from Roberts. Redfield and Roberts then worked expeditiously as a team at their centers in New York and Illinois to consolidate a new Free Methodist denomination. There was little argument about the denominational name. The independent bands and societies and conventions were already using the name Free Methodist. The organizing conference was called "for the purpose of adopting a Discipline for the Free Methodist Church." The name was understood to represent freedom from rented pews in the churches, freedom from slavery, freedom from lodge memberships, freedom from domination by unsympathetic Methodist officials, freedom from sin by way of personal sanctification, freedom of the Spirit in revival meetings and worship.

Dr. Redfield especially represented the West but his influence was great in both centers. Redfield had believed for years that separation was necessary and said the West was ready to form the new denomination without delay. Roberts, long hopeful that he could remain to reform the main Methodist body, agreed to proceed with the separation since East and West should move together. Loren Stiles wanted the Discipline of the new denomination to allow room for those who saw sanctification as a gradual work. Redfield said that "gradualism" had caused much of the previous mischief and insisted on a stand for instantaneous sanctification.[16]

They formed the new church organization at Pekin, New York, in August of 1860. Methodist articles concerning Roman Catholicism and concerning civil rulers were omitted from the Articles of Religion as no longer necessary. A new article on "Future Rewards and Punishment" was added as a defense against Universalists. The crucial new article entitled "Entire Sanctification" read:

> Justified persons, while they do not outwardly commit sin, are nevertheless conscious of sin still remaining in the heart. They feel a natural tendency to evil, a proneness to depart from God, and cleave to the things of earth. Those who are sanctified wholly are saved from all inward sin—from evil thoughts and evil tempers. No wrong temper, none contrary to love, remains in the soul. All their thoughts, words, and actions are governed by pure love. Entire sanctification takes place subsequently to justification, and is the work of God wrought instantaneously upon the consecrated, believing soul. After a soul is cleansed from sin, it is then fully prepared to grow in grace.[17]

The new Discipline for Free Methodists provided for election of local class leaders by the members; election of district chairmen by regional annual conferences with equal lay and ministerial representation; and election of general superintendents by national general conferences also of equal lay and ministerial representation. Benjamin T. Roberts was named first general superintendent, confirming his position as primary overseer for the fellowship. He was also its chief voice. The first issue of his monthly Earnest Christian had been dated 1 January 1860, eight months before the new denomination actually organized. He issued this paper for three decades and when the General Conference of 1886 mandated publication of a weekly to be called the Free Methodist he was made its editor as well. But leadership was no solo matter among Free Methodists. Conferences at all levels practiced their democracy by electing multiple supervisors. All supervisors worked in the midst of a yeasty fellowship of evangelistic preachers who responded freely to invitations to foster revivals anywhere without meticulous attention to parish, district, or conference boundaries.[18]

Growth was rapid for the first three decades. Ministers and members came over to the Free Methodists in western New York; Genesee Methodist Conference did not regain its old strength until 1878. Thirty-three annual conferences of Free Methodists were formed in the first thirty-three years, up to the death of Benjamin T. Roberts in 1893. The national holiness movement was rising. There was no other avowedly holiness denomination to welcome its adherents until the Wesleyans began urging the holiness stance about 1880.[19]

Free Methodism came to Indiana from Illinois by way of Michigan. Roberts had always found that vital center of Free Methodism in Illinois to be inspiring. When he and Redfield had the new *Discipline* established at Pekin in the East in August of 1860, it went within a month to Illinois to be enthusiastically adopted by the independents functioning there as the Western Laymen's Convention. Roberts was at St. Charles camp meeting in June of 1861 to preside over the first meeting of what had now become the Illinois Conference of the Free Methodist Church. Already there were twenty preachers and appointments to be made to fourteen circuits, each with at least six preaching points. Roberts said: "All the preachers profess and we believe enjoy the blessing of entire sanctification. They are devotedly pious, laborious young men, capable of doing a great deal of service in the cause of Christ upon a very small salary. One of them during the year walked 1,600 miles, visited and prayed with 1,000 families, and received thirty dollars. Such men are not easily to be put down when engaged in spreading holiness, with the Holy Ghost sent down from heaven."[20] Redfield died in 1863. Roberts paid him tribute:

> As a revival preacher he had no equal in this country. The great fundamental truths of the Gospel he presented with convincing clearness and overwhelming power. Vast audiences were wrought to the highest pitch of religious excitement under his awful appeals, and wherever he held meetings the country was moved for miles around, and hundreds of converts were added to the church of God. He was an uncompromising advocate of Christianity in its apostolic simplicity and purity, insisting that professing Christians should come out from the world and be separate, and be essentially different in their spirit and in their life, from those who made no pretensions to piety.[21]

Then it was Roberts who steered the work in both East and West.

New Circuits Include Indiana

Thomas Scott LaDue was a Congregational pastor at St. Charles, Illinois, trained at Beloit College and Chicago Theological Seminary. He had been converted by reading the works of Charles G. Finney and later reported an experience of entire sanctification. His congregation said, with some displeasure, that his preaching was like the local Free Methodist they knew named John Wesley Redfield. LaDue went "as naturally as a bird flies to its nest" to the Free Methodists, joining them at the camp meeting at St. Charles in 1861. Superintendent Roberts sent LaDue on many missions, including a scouting expedition into southwestern Michigan which made him the first Free Methodist preacher in that state in 1862. He also became Indiana's first Free Methodist preacher, extending his circuit across the state line from Michigan to serve for a time at Elkhart and Mishawaka.[22]

Edward Payson Hart was a young Methodist preacher in northern Illinois. He married a daughter of the Bishop family, lately expelled by the Methodists for being zealous independent revivalists and for attending the preaching of Dr. Redfield at Marengo. Hart soon joined the Illinois Conference of the Free Methodists. Early in 1863 Superintendent Roberts sent him from Illinois to investigate Free Methodist opportunities in Michigan. The Harts stayed in Michigan eleven years to develop the work, recognized as "Michigan and Indiana District" by 1865 and then as "Michigan Conference" begun with twelve preachers in June of 1866.[23]

One of the pioneer preachers who moved from service in Illinois to the new Michigan Conference was C. S. Gitchell, earlier a student at Garrett Biblical Institute at Evanston. Gitchell had a particular gift for forming new circuits and building new churches. In 1866 Gitchell "struck over into Indiana." Until 1879 Indiana's preaching appointments were listed as a part of Michigan Conference. Indiana congregations on the Michigan rolls included Dublin, Boston, Lawrenceburg, Fort Branch, Tippecanoe, Westville, and Indian Point. Of particular importance as anchors of the work in Indiana were the stable congregations organized by C. S. Gitchell at Attica and by Septer Roberts at Evansville.[24]

It was Free Methodism's early style to establish many preaching points and gather many congregations even if some were very small. Not all survived. In Wabash Conference churches disappeared at Indiana locations named Cannelton, Millstone, West Baden, Woods Chapel, Bloomfield, Boonville, Fort Branch, Frankfort, Marshfield, Antioch, Black Rock, Crawfordsville, Ashboro, and

Cardonia. Growth of the Wabash Conference had been fast when Free Methodism was bellwether among the holiness people; its growth rate leveled off and stayed low when a whole family of aggressive holiness denominations developed.[25]

In the twentieth century the state's larger towns and cities received more systematic attention. For January of 1985 six of the eight Free Methodist churches in Indianapolis averaged more than 100 persons at morning worship. So did the congregations at Attica, Bedford, Bloomington, Columbus, Evansville, Fort Wayne, Kokomo, New Castle, Vincennes, Warsaw, and Washington. By 1990 Indiana's Free Methodists reported 44 churches with 5,450 adherents and a Sunday attendance regularly exceeding the number of members. Missions were so basic that well over half of the world's quartermillion Free Methodist members lived outside the United States and Canada.[26]

Women of Wabash Conference, which included Indiana, shared enthusiastically in this Free Methodist missionary work after Daisy Fritchy got them organized in 1896. That first year they contributed $44.83 to missions. By 1985 their annual contribution was about $100,000. Sunday school attendance in the churches came to parallel attendance at worship; young people organized as Christian Youth Crusaders and Free Methodist Youth. Wabash Park Campground near Clay City became the setting for a continuing series of youth camps and for an annual Wabash Family Camp ranked as one of the nation's largest. For higher education there was a choice among Free Methodist colleges. Free Methodist ministers could receive counsel and support in their seminary training from the denomination's John Wesley Seminary Foundation. Free Methodists affiliated with the Christian Holiness Association, the National Association of Evangelicals, and the World Methodist Council. Their plans for union with the Wesleyans were disappointed three times.[27]

Hoosier Headquarters

A 1934 decision gave Free Methodists a particular prominence in Indiana. In that year the General Board considered four other sites but voted to move the Free Methodist Publishing House from Chicago to Winona Lake, Indiana. At Winona Lake they developed a printing operation producing some 70 million pages annually—books, pamphlets, Sunday school literature, the weekly *Free Methodist*, the monthly *Youth in Action*, the monthly *Sunday School Journal*, the monthly *Missionary Tidings*, and the monthly *Transmitter*. At Winona Lake they located the office of the general superintendent, renamed "bishop" since 1907, and nearly all the national denominational offices. Here was a meeting place for administrative gatherings; here was a location for ministerial seminars; here were the studios for the "Light and Life" radio broadcasts.[28] When decision time came in 1989, the Free Methodists chose Indiana again. In 1990 they established their new national headquarters and publishing center in Indianapolis, already a city with a substantial Free Methodist presence.

NOTES

1. Benson H. Roberts, *Benjamin Titus Roberts* (North Chili, N.Y.: The Earnest Christian Office, 1900), 4–5.

2. Roberts, *Benjamin Titus Roberts*, 9–18.

3. Joseph G. Terrill, *The Life of Rev. John Wesley Redfield, M.D.* (Chicago: Free Methodist Publishing House, 1904), 95–101, 139–43.

4. Terrill, *Life*, 4, 162–65; Roberts, *Benjamin Titus Roberts*, 9–21, 50, 109.

5. Leslie R. Marston, *From Age to Age a Living Witness: A Historical Interpretation of Free Methodism's First Century* (Winona Lake, Ind.: Light and Life Press, 1960), 174–78; Roberts, *Benjamin Titus Roberts*, 50–51.

6. Roberts, *Benjamin Titus Roberts*, 68–73; Terrill, *Life*, 3, 82, 279–81.

7. Wilson T. Hogue, *History of the Free Methodist Church of North America*, 2 vols. (Winona Lake, Ind.: Free Methodist Publishing House, 1938), 1:50–56; Marston, *From Age to Age*, 577; Roberts, *Benjamin Titus Roberts*, 103–4, 111, 138–39.

8. Benjamin T. Roberts, *Why Another Sect: Containing a Review of Articles by Bishop Simpson and Others on the Free Methodist Church* (Rochester, N.Y.: The Earnest Christian Publishing House, 1879), 114–15.

9. Roberts, *Why Another Sect*, 86.

10. Roberts, *Why Another Sect*, 90.

11. Roberts, *Why Another Sect*, 92.

12. Roberts, *Why Another Sect*, 92–93.

13. Roberts, *Benjamin Titus Roberts*, 127–28, 144–46, 149–66; Marston, *From Age to Age*, 191–94; Roberts, *Why Another Sect*, 160–85.

14. *History of American Methodism*, 3 vols. (New York: Abingdon Press, 1964), 2:350; Hogue, *History*, 1:193–207, 287–93; Roberts, *Why Another Sect*, 200, 202; Roberts, *Benjamin Titus Roberts*, 187–90.

15. Hogue, *History*, 1:265–86; Marston, *From Age to Age*, 227–28; Terrill, *Life*, 302–3; Roberts, *Benjamin Titus Roberts*, 222–23, 226–29.

16. Marston, *From Age to Age*, 240–45, 249–51, 253, 258–59; Hogue, *History*, 1:321–22; Roberts, *Benjamin Titus Roberts*, 232–33.

17. Marston, *From Age to Age*, 258.

18. *Wabash Centennial: The History of Wabash Conference, Free Methodist Church* (Camby, Ind.: Wabash Conference, 1985), 24–25, 40; Hogue, *History*, 1:319–34, 2:110; Marston, *From Age to Age*, 256–57, 266, 471–77.

19. *History of American Methodism*, 2:357; Marston, *From Age to Age*, 214, 268–71, 430, 438–39.

20. Marston, *From Age to Age*, 267–68; Hogue, *History*, 1:276–77, 352–55.

21. Roberts, *Benjamin Titus Roberts*, 331.

22. John LaDue, *The Life of Rev. Thomas Scott LaDue* (Chicago: Free Methodist Publishing House, 1898), 33–44, 50–51; Hogue, *History*, 2:15–19; *Wabash Centennial*, 7.

23. Marston, *From Age to Age*, 229–30; Hogue, *History*, 2:19–38.

24. Hogue, *History*, 2:27–28, 36, 107–10, 115–18; *Wabash Centennial*, 8–9.

25. Carl L. Howland, *The Story of Our Church* (Winona Lake, Ind.: Free Methodist Publishing House, n.d.), 114–17; *Wabash Centennial*, 15, 19, 46.

26. *Christian Courier* 49 (March 1985): 23; Marston, *From Age to Age*, 451–70; Frank S. Mead, *Handbook of Denominations in the United States*, 9th ed. (Nashville, Tenn.: Abingdon Press, 1990), 162.

27. *Wabash Centennial*, 43–57; Marston, *From Age to Age*, 553–56, 562–64.

28. Marston, *From Age to Age*, 481–89; Howland, *Story*, 105–10.

CHURCH OF GOD (ANDERSON, INDIANA)

The goal of Daniel Sidney Warner was a fellowship of Christian saints marked by holiness and unity. In his view holiness and unity were what the Christians of America needed. Holiness and unity were essential to restore the church on a New Testament model. Holiness and unity were essential to each other.

It was no new idea to call true believers to come to unity by declaring their independence from all existing creeds, books of order, clergy, church governments, sects, and denominational divisions in order to walk together in new freedom. Congregations sharing such a concept of reformation, especially as enunciated by Alexander Campbell and his colleagues, were common in Ohio. Warner was converted at a schoolhouse revival near Montpelier in 1865. This revival was conducted by an evangelist from the Churches of God in North America, a revivalist development from the German Reformed whose founding leader was a Pennsylvanian named John Winebrenner. Warner was a sincere and competent young convert who would have been welcome in any of several fellowships. He had attended Oberlin College for about two years and was a public school teacher. He chose to enlist with the Winebrennarian church under whose ministry he was converted. Warner felt this one at least had the right name for the one true church. And Winebrenner's position on unity became a matter of record. "There is but one true church; namely, the Church of God . . . It is the bounden duty of all God's people to belong to her, and none else . . . It

is contrary to scripture to divide the church of God into different sects and denominations."[1]

Warner entered the ministry of the Winebrennarian church in 1867. He did see some imperfections among its ministers such as selfishness and wire-pulling for the best salaries, but he served that communion with much affection and efficiency. During his first six years of ministry in Ohio and Indiana he preached 1,241 times and won 508 converts. As a home missionary in Nebraska he serviced fourteen preaching stations and organized six new congregations.[2]

In these early pastoral years Warner encountered the programs of the National Holiness Association. The Winebrennarian church was presbyterial in government and historical background, not much attuned to the yearning of many holiness leaders for the good old ways of Methodism. It was not very hospitable to extremely emotional camp meetings and not hospitable at all to pressures on its members to achieve a second crisis experience of entire sanctification. Warner also opposed the holiness teaching at first. However his father-in-law was active in the holiness movement, his wife professed the experience of sanctification, and many of his evangelistic colleagues were associated with the holiness cause. He agreed to investigate. Matters came to focus in 1877. Warner became convinced that second blessing holiness was biblical and right. After intense sessions of seeking at his own revival altar, he testified to the experience of sanctification on 7 July.

Holiness became the burden of his evangelistic preaching. His differences with the Winebrennarians sharpened. At the conference of the North Ohio Eldership in 1877 he was accused of inviting a "sect of fanatics calling themselves the Holy Alliance Band to hold meetings in the local Churches of God" and of bringing schism among those churches. At that conference the next year he was expelled, a case of mutual rejection. Warner said: "On the 31st of last January the Lord showed me that holiness could never prosper upon sectarian soil, encumbered by human creeds, and party names, and he gave me a new commission to join holiness and all truth together and build up the apostolical church of the living God. Praise his name, I will obey him!"[3]

Early Members in the Midwest

Warner still retained his affection for his Winebrennarian communion. He knew that the Northern Indiana Eldership was more hospitable to holiness doctrine and conduct. They had withdrawn from the larger fellowship of Winebrennarians after denouncing membership in lodges and secret societies. Warner's abilities and credentials were welcome with this Indiana group. He was appointed joint editor of their paper to contribute a page on holiness for each issue. After some merger and trading, he was proprietor of that paper. Renamed the *Gospel Trumpet*, it was issued first at Rome City, Indiana, and then at Indianapolis.[4]

Warner now understood his calling to be that of a holiness evangelist. He was a popular writer and leader in the national holiness movement and vice president of the Indiana State Holiness Association. His book of 493 pages on sanctification was issued in 1880 by the publishing house of the Evangelical United Mennonites at Goshen, Indiana. His holiness stance was clear.

> Having, therefore, a clear conviction that upon the preaching and testimony of entire sanctification as a distinct experience subsequent to justification, more than upon all else besides, depends the salvation of immortal souls, the safety of converts, the purity and consequent power, peace, and prosperity of the church, and the glory of God; and perceiving that this "second grace" is the ultimate end of Christ's death, and the great burden of the apostolic ministry, I was constrained to dedicate forever unto the Lord all the energies of my being for the promotion of this great salvation.[5]

He counted the idea of gradual growth into sanctification a "fatal delusion." And his "come-outer" position was already firmly stated. "Widespread holiness destroys denominations . . . If you are a true, intelligent Bible Christian, a holy, God-fearing man, you must cast off every human yoke, withdraw fellowship from, and renounce every schismatic and humanly constituted party in the professed body of Christ. Instead of belonging to 'some branch,' you will simply belong to Christ, and be a branch yourself in him, the 'true vine.'"[6]

Then in 1881 came two further insights. During a day of prayer in a church at Hardinsburg, Indiana, on 22 April he received as a revelation from the Spirit of God that he could hardly repudiate sects and still belong to the Indiana State Holiness Association which was an interdenominational fellowship anxious to avoid charges of being divisive. Members of that association had to actually state their denominational affiliation. Warner, "being dearly attached to the holiness work," nevertheless went directly to the 1881 association meeting at Terre Haute with an amendment "to have the sect-endorsing clause removed from the constitution." Driven to the choice, the association preferred to keep the clause and lose Warner. His editorial in June said "We . . . forever withdraw from all organisms that uphold and endorse sects and denominations in the body of Christ."[7]

In October of that same year he attended the meeting of his Northern Indiana Eldership at Beaver Dam in Kosciusko County. There he proposed some changes to make their form of government more biblical. When the eldership rejected his proposal he withdrew along with five local persons who supported his principles—"David Leininger, William Ballenger and wife, and F. Krause and wife." In another small and separated branch of the Winebrennarians, the Northern Michigan Eldership of the Church of God, about twenty persons withdrew and established a congregation at Carson City. Their statement of principles embodied convictions they had developed under Warner's preaching.[8]

> Whereas we recognize ourselves in the perilous times of the last days, the time in which Michael is standing up for the deliverance of God's true saints (Dan. 12:1), the troublesome times in which the true house of God is being built again, therefore,
>
> Resolved, That we will endeavor by all the grace of God to live holy, righteous, and godly in Christ Jesus, "looking for, and hastening unto the coming of the Lord Jesus Christ," who we believe is nigh, even at the door.
>
> Resolved, That we adhere to no body or organization but the church of God, bought by the blood of Christ, organized by the Holy Spirit, and governed by the Bible. And if the Lord will, we will hold an annual assembly of all saints who in the providence of God shall be permitted to come together for the worship of God, the

instruction and edification of one another, and the transaction of such business as the Holy Spirit may lead us to see and direct in its performance.

Resolved, That we ignore and abandon the practice of preacher's license as without precept or example in the Word of God, and that we wish to be "known by our fruits" instead of by papers.

Resolved, That we do not recognize or fellowship any who come unto us assuming the character of a minister whose life is not godly in Christ Jesus and whose doctrine is not the Word of God.

Resolved also, That we recognize and fellowship, as members with us in the one body of Christ all truly regenerated and sincere saints who worship God in all the light they possess, and that we urge all the dear children of God to forsake the snares and yokes of human parties and stand alone in the "one fold" of Christ upon the Bible, and in the unity of the Spirit.[9]

Annual camp meetings were established by these congregations at Beaver Dam in Indiana and at Carson City in Michigan.

In 1881 Daniel Warner had little to offer beyond a very contagious enthusiasm for holiness and unity, principles not uniquely his own and principles which so far had consistently gotten him excluded. His passion for these causes became the basis for the very substantial Church of God Reformation Movement. Because of its strenuous non-sectarian principles, this group resisted being designated as a church among other churches and especially resisted being designated as a denomination among other denominations. Its preachers called unbelievers to be saved and called believers to be sanctified. Church members were the most likely candidates to attend their revival meetings and church members were the movement's special targets. They were called to denounce all denominations including their own. They were urged to come out of sectism, not to join a new sect but to stand free with the now liberated saints who were by biblical definition the true Church of God. Persons who "came out" knew the excitement and terror of standing alone against all existing churches in the face of family and community disapproval. They also knew the intense security provided by the mutual support of their fellow saints in the movement.[10]

The Church of God reformers encountered Adventist opponents, especially around such Adventist strongholds as Battle Creek in Michigan. In the course of the confrontation the Church of God movement developed its own books and charts and batteries of Scripture texts showing how this movement which began in 1880 was the fulfillment of many biblical prophecies including

some favorite Adventist ones in the books of Daniel and Revelation. Herbert M. Riggle of the Gospel Trumpet Company debated B. E. Kesler at North Webster, Indiana, in 1915. Riggle had the claim of the scriptural and historical priority of the Church of God well schematized. "I gave a prophetic history of the Church as portrayed in prophecy and Revelation and confirmed by the testimony of history," he said. "I thus traced it from its morning glory down through the twelve hundred and sixty years of popery, through the three hundred and fifty years of Protestant Sectism to its final restoration in the same unity, organization, faith, purity and power of primitive times; a blessed state now enjoyed by hundreds of thousands who are being gathered in the blessed evening light. Thus, I established the identity of the church I have the honor to represent with that of the New Testament Church."[11]

The movement was never technically "millennial," claiming instead that Jesus Christ was already and always ruler of his spiritual kingdom and rejecting any notion of his establishing any physical earthly kingdom whatever. However the movement's preachers were gathering the saints in expectation of the Lord's imminent return to judge the world so there was no time to delay. Many of the converts became evangelists known as "flying messengers." It was not their primary goal to establish or oversee new congregations of the liberated saints. Their emphasis was more on their role as heralds being sure the call to the saints to come out of sectism was carried everywhere quickly because of the urgency of this new manifestation of God's will and plan.[12]

Daniel Warner was the prototype of such flying messengers. For four years beginning in 1884 his traveling "family" included "Mother" Sarah Smith, Nannie Kiger, Frances Miller, and Barney Warren. They were saints selected in part because they could sing such excellent and memorable four-part harmony that they could guarantee a crowd anywhere. At age sixty-one Mother Smith told her family "I am done cooking for farming" and set out to sing tenor in the evangelistic team. The Church of God leaders put their message into many songs. Their first songbook, *Songs of Victory* (1885), had ninety-four new songs written by Daniel Warner and Joseph C. Fisher. Team members could also preach, testify, visit, counsel, distribute literature, entertain children, and whatever additional work was required. They could enliven a camp meeting. They could enter a town, ride singing through the streets on a spring wagon, and challenge all churches in the area as sects of Babylon. "We never in all our travels took up a collection," Mother Smith said. "Through our labors God established his church in many localities in Ohio, Indiana, Michigan, Illinois, Iowa, Kansas, Nebraska, Colorado, and Canada. Bro. Warner was marvelously helped by the power of God in preaching the gospel. He was very frail in body, but being filled with the power of God the Lord always stood by him in delivering the Word. He would often preach from two to three hours at a time while the people listened with great interest. He preached from two to four times during the day and night, working at the altar with those who were seeking help, and also gave much instruction outside of meetings, prayed for the sick, wrote for publication etc."[13]

There came to be hundreds of such unpaid evangelists and volunteer family members working for the Church of God reformation. There were many eager candidates. No formal education was either required or available. Daniel Warner said in the *Trumpet* that the only credentials required for ministry were "to be filled with the Holy Spirit and have a reasonable knowledge of the English language." The *Gospel Trumpet* for 1895, the year of Warner's death, printed 384 "field" reports from evangelists and companies most containing accounts of several series of meetings, each lasting from one to eight weeks. The largest number of reports were from the Midwest. Twenty-six published reports that year were from workers in Indiana. That year 196 calls were printed in the *Trumpet* inviting an evangelist or company to come to their communities with the message of the movement. These invitations were from thirty-two states, two from Canada, and one from England.[14]

The *Gospel Trumpet*

When he broke with the Northern Indiana Eldership of the Winebrennarians in 1881, Daniel Warner also had the *Gospel Trumpet*. It did not look like much of a possession—a five-column, four-page folio about 13 x 20 inches issued semimonthly at a subscription price of 75¢ per year. It printed articles on holiness and the nature of the church, notices and reports of meetings, testimonies, letters, and some material reprinted from other papers. The paper had no real resources except a hand press capable of printing a single sheet at a time plus the persistence of Daniel Warner and his current partner Joseph C. Fisher. In winter of 1881 the only way Warner could keep the ink warm enough to flow was to print the paper in the kitchen of his home in Indianapolis. Fully committed to the printed word as a tool of reformation, Warner would not give up the *Trumpet* even though it became part of a contention in which his wife deserted him.

The *Trumpet* moved six times in its first seven years. It went wherever the reformation movement was becoming concentrated enough to provide financial support and some volunteer workers—Cardington, Ohio (1882); Bucyrus, Ohio (1883); Williamston, Michigan (1884). The *Trumpet* became the guiding voice of Warner to the movement. It became the news center for those exciting reports and calls from the field. It became enunciator and teacher of reformation doctrine essential for the movement's self-understanding. It became producer, printer, and purveyor of supporting materials for the work of the saints at every level. It became an instrument of discipline; false teachers or unruly preachers could be refused publication or even disclaimed by name. The movement would tolerate no denominational identity or structure of church government. The movement was to have no "man rule" but to be directed by the Holy Spirit. The *Trumpet* became the agency by which persons who were recognized as Spirit-directed could communicate with the fellowship. The *Trumpet* became "the office."[15]

In 1887 the future of the *Trumpet* looked particularly dark. Its location by then was Grand Junction, Michigan, close to a Church of God camp meeting site at Bangor but very little else. Publisher and business manager Joseph C. Fisher was divorcing his wife with intention to remarry. Daniel Warner said this was "not straight" and he would not publish even one more issue of the *Trumpet* with Fisher. Actually Warner was now traveling almost constantly as an evangelist, sending in *Trumpet* copy written on the wing. Fisher had $1,000 invested in the *Trumpet*. Even if he should be willing to sell, the new prospect for publisher and manager would need to come with $1,000 to buy Fisher out and be prepared to work without pay as all Trumpet family members did. Help came from Indiana in the form of Enoch Edwin Byrum.

Enoch E. Byrum and Noah H. Byrum

Enoch E. Byrum was born in Randolph County, seventh of thirteen children in a prosperous farm family. His parents were United Brethren and his conversion was in that context.

> It was . . . when I was fifteen years of age that I yielded to the wooings of the Spirit and began to seek the Lord earnestly for peace in my soul. For nearly a week I went forward every night for prayer. One night I became so much in earnest that I almost forget my surroundings and called mightily upon God to forgive my sins and save me. Suddenly I was filled with heavenly peace. I knew that my sins were forgiven and that the Lord

accepted me as his child, and I arose and faced the audience and testified that I was saved and was not afraid of the whole world.[16]

He felt called to preach but also felt obligated to stay at home to operate the family farms after his father died. He said: "After many prayers and earnest pleadings I yielded by telling the Lord that if he would only open the way for me to go to school, whenever he called me I would go and would preach, go to Africa, or whatever he called me to do I would do it." In rapid sequence his brother Fletcher offered to take over the farms, he enrolled in a series of schools culminating in Otterbein University in Ohio, and he seemed on the way to service as a United Brethren preacher.[17]

Byrum was at Otterbein when Daniel Warner and his company of singers held meetings at Byrum's home church in Jay County called Prospect Chapel. Warner's team convinced Byrum's mother, his brother Fletcher, his preacher cousin Henry C. Wickersham, and most of the Prospect Chapel membership to come out of sectism into the freedom of the Church of God. Several "sought and obtained a real experience of salvation." A number "obtained the experience of sanctification and were filled with the Holy Spirit."

Byrum sent warnings from college to his family to beware of these deceivers. His warnings were of no avail. Back home on vacation he was so impressed with the positive changes in his family, with the preaching at the local Church of God revival, and with a vivid dream he had about the futility of efforts to restore Prospect Chapel that he determined to come out of sectism and stand with the Church of God himself.[18] And he experienced sanctification.

I had been desirous of having an experience when sanctified that would cause me to leap and shout for joy. But now I had reached a place where I was consecrated to accept the experience regardless of what the manifestations might be. When the church question was settled I knew that the last point was yielded to the will of God unreservedly. Upon the authority of the Word of God it was my privilege to claim and receive the experience for which I had so long sought. So positive was I that my consecration was completely in accordance with the will of God that without any feeling in the matter I said, "I am sanctified." The question then came, "How do you know you are sanctified?" I said "Because the Word of God says so." Then came the witness of the Holy Spirit and altho I did not feel like leaping and shouting, there was as definite and positive a work wrought in my soul as there was when I was converted several years previously.[19]

At the end of the college term at Otterbein in June of 1887, Byrum, his schoolmate John C. Mayne, and his cousin Henry C. Wickersham headed for the Church of God camp meeting at Bangor, Michigan. Daniel Warner, one of the principal preachers for the meeting, was wrestling with the problem of saving the *Trumpet*. Wickersham suggested Byrum as a prospective publisher and business manager. He was a saint lately freed from sectarianism. His education was unintegrated but well above average. He had just enough money from the recent sale of his farm to buy out Fisher's publishing interest if Fisher would sell. And his consecration to ministry was such that he might work for no pay beyond food and raiment if convinced it was a call. Three or four days into the meeting Warner asked Byrum to accept the position. Byrum said his prayers and agreed. Fisher sold out and departed. Warner stayed only ten days, leaving Grand Junction with his evangelistic company on 1 July 1887 not to return until the following April.

Without experience in theological writing, editing, printing, publishing, or business administration, the 25-year-old Byrum became publisher, business manager, bookkeeper, managing editor, and overseer of every department of the *Trumpet* office and home. There were only a few marginal pieces of equipment worth a few hundred dollars, three women volunteers and one man who was leaving in two or three weeks, a building mortgaged to its full value, and a substantial body of unpaid bills. There were two publishing and mailing deadlines to be met each month. Writing copy was hard work; decisions about whose copy to accept and how much to modify it could be even harder. Within the first month Byrum welcomed his fifteen-year-old brother Noah who had just been converted by the Warner team at meetings near the Byrum home and consecrated to the publishing work. Noah became office and business manager for the *Trumpet*. He worked for the *Trumpet* for sixty years, the first thirty without a paycheck.[20]

The Byrums learned quickly from everybody; they recorded the events of the next three decades as an endless series of miracles. They served the army of flying messengers in the field and developed that army's loyalty. Daniel Warner grew tired by 1892, withdrew more and more from public ministry, and died in 1895. The Trumpet Company, assisted by many but directed by the Byrums, held the movement together and preserved its momentum. In 1892 the *Trumpet* doubled in frequency to become a weekly; in 1898 it doubled in size to eight pages. The administrative structure developed from a partnership to a stock company to a reconstituted corporation, long providing no pay for workers at any level and always providing no profit for any personal owners or stockholders. Everything was for the reformation movement.[21]

Besides the thousands of copies of the *Trumpet* for subscribers, there were multiplied thousands of copies to be given away or distributed at cut rate. When the ten-weeks-for-10¢ specials were run, devoted members across the Church of God would sacrifice grocery money if necessary to provide a ten-week subscription for every neighbor, minister, school teacher, or physician in their community. One such campaign piled up 220,000 temporary subscriptions.[22]

As the publishing establishment was upgraded, prayers were requested and reported concerning the individual facilities and pieces of equipment needed. There were many examples of donations providentially timed. In fact, the office of the Gospel Trumpet Company made a very responsible channel for benevolent giving. Noah Byrum reported to *Trumpet* readers: "The *Gospel Trumpet* publishing work has been only partially self-supporting . . . Individuals who are desirous of placing their money where it will work for God frequently do so by placing it where it will contribute to the support and advance of the publishing work. To a considerable extent the work receives its support from such sources. Thus while God demands the exercise of faith and trust for its prosperity, he also moves upon those who have means at their disposal to consecrate their substance unto the Lord." Gifts for missionary work also came to be sent to the *Trumpet* office where they were properly recorded and forwarded.[23]

Many chose to make a particularly personal gift by becoming volunteer laborers at the Trumpet Company. The varied spectrum of the movement's membership was represented in this volunteer "Trumpet Family." Many were young people. Many were school teachers. Some stayed for months. Some stayed for years. Besides their contributions to the heavy work of publishing, shipping, and maintenance, some Trumpet Family members used the communal life at the home as a training experience to prepare themselves to be evangelists or missionaries. Besides the *Trumpet*, the company produced an increasing volume of pamphlets, books, songbooks, picture cards, mottoes, and Sunday school materials.[24]

The Move to Anderson

The whole Gospel Trumpet enterprise eventually came to Indiana. Daniel Warner had moved it to Grand Junction, Michigan, in 1886 in a single railroad car. The Byrums had moved it to Moundsville, West Virginia, in 1898 in a train of nine freight cars, two passenger cars, and one baggage car. Sixty-nine Trumpet Family members were on board the train to Moundsville; another thirty-two traveled separately. The sides of the freight cars were placarded with 100 large scriptural mottoes. The family distributed about 100,000 leaflets "leaving a line of truth all the way along." In 1906 it came to Anderson, Indiana, with twenty-six railroad car loads of machinery and inventory plus two railroad passenger cars and a baggage car.[25]

A contingent of fourteen had gone ahead to Anderson to begin construction of a three-story concrete building with facilities to house a Trumpet Family of more than 200—rooms for residents, kitchen, dining room, bakery, parlor, library, sewing room, music room, laundry, and chapel. A large auditorium and an old people's home were begun in 1907. Finally, in 1909, construction began on a separate building for the Trumpet Company, 50,000 square feet actually designed and engineered for publication work. Even at Moundsville the big rotary press had been turning out two and one-half tons of printed material every week, over 2 million sheets per day. Now at Anderson there was room for expansion. During December of 1909 they mailed 360,000 copies of the *Trumpet*.[26]

After a decade at Anderson, Enoch Byrum retired. By then there were many articulate and responsible leaders at the Trumpet office and in the movement but as editor in chief of the *Trumpet* Byrum had remained the central person. Though he was never such a flaming evangelist as Daniel Warner, Byrum traveled tens of thousands of miles among the congregations and camp meetings at home and abroad to preach, to teach the movement's doctrine, and to resolve disputes. He supplied much copy for the *Trumpet* and wrote twelve books. He could wield the disciplinary power of the *Trumpet* over individuals and groups if necessary. When rural-oriented constituents organized a stout party to deny fellowship to more modern members who wore neckties as part of their contemporary business dress, Byrum donned a tie at camp meeting and stalled the attempt with minimal damage. Of the time in 1899 and 1900 when a sizable body of the Church of God preachers were teaching that sanctification was received at the time of conversion rather than later as a separate cleansing experience, Noah Byrum said "It became the duty of the *Gospel Trumpet* to renounce all who after repeated admonitions still held and taught the erroneous doctrine." As many as half of the Church of God preachers defected over this "anti-cleansing" issue but many of them returned to the movement later.[27]

The College and the General Assembly

Enoch Byrum was no mere echo of his predecessor. Daniel Warner had said that Christians might elect to consult a doctor of medicine under some conditions. Enoch Byrum was a more stringent advocate and practitioner of healing by faith and prayer, both local and long distance. Noah Byrum wrote in 1902: "Many requests for prayer are received from parties at a distance desiring healing. There has accumulated a pile of over 400 telegrams from thirty-three different states, Canada and Mexico; and there are also cablegrams from Europe. Over 600 anointed handkerchiefs were sent in 1901 to those requesting them. See Acts 9:12." Just before his death Daniel Warner had spoken of his intention to open a formal school for gospel workers. Enoch Byrum and his successor Fred G. Smith did not want such a school and certainly did not want a full-fledged liberal arts college such as a denomination might found.[28]

However the movement as a whole entered a period of substantial change after the return of the *Trumpet* to Indiana and after Byrum retired in 1916. There had been some restiveness under his authoritarian administration. The movement was always expected to function under the immediate direction and teaching of the Holy Spirit. The editor of the *Trumpet* was indeed a valued voice and agent of the Holy Spirit. But the whole body of preachers increasingly expected opportunity to express their own convictions about the direction in which the Spirit was leading.

That body of preachers had grown large. Since the railroads wanted to know exactly who was entitled to reduced fares for clergy, Enoch Byrum asked all Church of God ministers to send in their names and addresses. There were just over 300 names on the first list in 1896. The list in 1916 included 985 persons. That year 467 designated themselves as "pastor" or "assistant pastor." In 1919 the *Yearbook* indicated that 450 of the 1,097 congregations owned their own place of worship and that 925 of these congregations had resident pastors. Plainly the evangelists once known as "flying messengers" were settling down to local pastoral responsibilities. Congregations of persons who had condemned "steeple churches" and sectism were now erecting buildings in which they and their children could worship and study.[29]

In 1917 the ministers at the annual camp meeting at Anderson organized as the General Ministerial Assembly. From that date the ownership and control of the agencies of the Church of God, including the *Gospel Trumpet*, passed to the Assembly. From that date the Assembly elected all members of the Gospel Trumpet Company and must ratify the election of the editor in chief. The Assembly was not to be a representative body with any authority to take actions to govern local churches. It was to be a continuing voluntary association made up of those Church of God ministers who chose to attend and participate. As an association it had flexibility to organize, to take responsibilities for specific work, to delegate responsibilities, and to engage in contracts as its voluntary members directed. They believed it was not allowable to organize a government for God's church as the sects had attempted. But they counted it only good stewardship for a Spirit-guided assembly to organize the work undertaken for God's church in order to make it efficient.[30]

Fred G. Smith succeeded Enoch Byrum as the *Trumpet*'s editor in chief. His books *Revelation Explained* (1908) and *What the Bible Teaches* (1914) had gone through repeated editions and were circulated by thousands. They had become standard doctrinal works consolidating the view by which many Church of God constituents understood their movement to be the fulfillment of apocalyptic prophecy and the harbinger of the imminent end of the age. After publication of his *Last Reformation* (1917), Smith sought for a time to limit standard doctrinal literature for the movement to works published before 1924. This effort was not successful and Smith's support kept eroding. When his editorial term expired in June of 1930, he was not reelected. Under the following editorial leadership of Charles E. Brown, the *Trumpet* was open to a greater variety of viewpoints and unwilling to play the traditional role of judge. Even the question of which preachers should be allowed to report in the *Trumpet* and which preachers should be listed in the new *Yearbook* was referred to decision committees at state level.[31]

Church Agencies

The "office" of the *Trumpet*, well known as the movement's address, the administrative center, the supplier of approved materials, the preparer of lists of ministers, the manager of the central camp meeting site and the old people's home, and the clearing house for benevolent contributions, was now increasingly responsive to the General Ministerial Assembly. It served also as a launching base for several agencies formed to conduct the work of that voluntary association of ministers. The Missionary Board was formed in 1909 after significant work was already begun in a score of countries. The Board of Church Extension and Home Missions was formed in 1921 and the Board of Christian Education in 1923. National youth conventions began at Anderson in June of 1924. In 1932 an Executive Council was incorporated to become the legal arm of the General Ministerial Assembly and the agency for conducting the general business of the Church of God.[32]

Also at Anderson on 18 June 1932 a "great throng" of women marched from the tabernacle to the auditorium singing "Onward Christian Soldiers." This was the newly approved Woman's Home and Foreign Missionary Society. Money contributed through the Woman's Society was understood to be over and above the tithe. The Society grew to 30,000 members; annual contributions to the programs of church agencies from these women reached $1 million.[33]

The General Ministerial Assembly exercised no authority over local congregations but Russell Byrum's book *Problems of the Local Church* (1926) offered guidelines for management of such concerns as church officers, membership, budgeting, bylaws, business meetings, planning, erecting church buildings, pledging, offering envelopes, and conduct of a church trial. The collective bureaucracy for which these agencies were a foundation, along with the *Gospel Trumpet*, was often referred to by the Church of God constituency as "Anderson." But "Anderson" was also the site of the annual gathering of the General Ministerial Assembly and the concurrent camp meeting at which some 20,000 Church of God constituents might be in attendance.[34]

Another part of the center at Anderson was also begun in 1917. The system of care and allowances for the army of volunteer workers had become complex and unmanageable. The Gospel Trumpet Company chose to simply employ workers and pay them wages. Some workers, now on private pay, moved from the commune and so left space in the Trumpet home. The home at Anderson had been an early model for the national network of training places for gospel workers in the Church of God movement. Now the convenient space at the home plus energetic local leadership created an opportunity to form a genuine school at Anderson. Leaders at the *Gospel Trumpet* took on the organizing and the teaching as extra duty. Daytime workers at the *Trumpet* became nighttime students. The school set off on a long pilgrimage which was to lead to a fully accredited college with a three-year graduate school of theology at Anderson. John A. Morrison joined the faculty in 1919 and became the school's first president in 1925. Morrison, his dean Russell Olt, and his successor Robert H. Reardon led a growing body of colleagues in rallying support both in the constituency of the Church of God movement and in the city of Anderson to develop a campus and faculty.[35]

Some in the movement remained uneasy. They were uneasy with the General Ministerial Assembly meeting annually at Anderson which claimed to be a voluntary association but had something of the look of the "man rule" which the flying messengers had abhorred. They were uneasy with the growing body of agencies at Anderson which listed so many employees in the *Yearbook*. They were uneasy that the Church of God had made higher education its concern and embodied that concern in the college at Anderson. They were uneasy with a rising generation of college teachers who believed it was an essential service to the movement to present alternatives to some of those earlier interpretations of Scripture which identified the Church of God as a particular fulfillment of apocalyptic biblical prophecies. They were uneasy that the schools and agencies at Anderson were not sustaining the attack on all the "Babylon" of existing church denominations and were inclined to include ecumenical cooperation among the approaches to the goals of holiness and unity. Church of God agencies and individuals eventually came to be recognized as participants, somewhere short of full members, not only in the activities of the Christian Holiness Association and the National Association of Evangelicals but also of the World Council of Churches, the National Council of Churches, and the Consultation on Church Union.[36]

Such uneasiness, based in Ohio and rallied in support of the doctrines of Fred G. Smith, produced conflict and an assembly vote barely sufficient to continue the college in 1929–30. Again in 1934 the presidency of John A. Morrison and the future existence of the college were sustained in the General Ministerial Assembly by the slim margin of twelve votes.[37] Such uneasiness organized again around the publications, preaching, and radio ministry of L. Earl Slacum of Muncie during the period 1944–1951. Slacum took the role of watchman against what he considered "man-made organizations" and doctrinal heresies at Anderson. He published a paper named *Watchman* and led a sizable separation. This time Fred G. Smith supported the main body of the Church of God, asking his conservative friends to stay with Anderson rather than go with what was popularly called the Slacum or Watchman movement. Slacum became so displeased with the ecclesiastical structure he saw rising within his own separatist group that he repented of his separation and returned to fellowship with Anderson. Most members of the Watchman movement also returned. Some differences persisted; two groups maintained journals as their voices for continuing discussion.[38]

The Church of God was chastened and to some degree shaped by such tensions but its general direction and the location of its center had become clear. The *Gospel Trumpet* became *Vital Christianity* in 1962. The publishing arm of the Gospel Trumpet Company became Warner Press the same year. The General Ministerial Assembly became the General Assembly in 1965, reflecting the inclusion of some unordained members. Anderson College became Anderson University, largest school of the Church of God. In 1976 the Assembly recognized seminary training as "the normal, the ideal level of initial preparation for the future young minister."[39]

Through it all Indiana remained the movement's central place. Only Ohio had more congregations. The World Conference of the Church of God met for the first time in the United States in June of 1980. The meeting was at Anderson, Indiana. There the report was that Daniel Warner's vision of Christian holiness and unity was embodied in a movement with 4,438 ministers. There were 2,308 congregations with 177,736 members in the United States and Canada. There were 1,574 congregations with 141,738 members in other countries. Sunday morning attendance substantially exceeded the reported membership.[40] The reports for the Church of God in 1990 showed 22,569 adherents in 159 congregations in Indiana, a constituency comparable to the Mormons, the Episcopalians, or the Old Order Amish. The Indiana connection of the fellowship was often made visible in one additional way. In order to distinguish among groups choosing the name "Church of God," this one was commonly designated "Church of God (Anderson, Indiana)."

NOTES

1. John W. Smith, *The Quest for Holiness and Unity: A Centennial History of the Church of God (Anderson, Indiana)* (Anderson, Ind.: Warner Press, 1980), 37–49; *The First Century*, 2 vols. continuously paged, ed. Barry L. Callen (Anderson, Ind.: Warner Press, 1977–79), 1:25, 27–29, 130.

2. Robert H. Reardon, *The Early Morning Light: A Friendly Reflection on Some of the Main Events in the Life of the Church of God Reformation Movement during the First Fifty Years* (Anderson, Ind.: Warner Press, 1979), 17; Smith, *Quest*, 49–50; *First Century*, 1:130.

3. Smith, *Quest*, 37, 51–53; *First Century*, 1:43–47; Reardon, *Early Morning Light*, 19.

4. Smith, *Quest*, 54–55.

5. *First Century*, 1:251.

6. Daniel S. Warner, *Bible Proofs of the Second Work of Grace; or, Entire Sanctification as a Distinct Experience, Subsequent to Justification, Established by the United Testimony of Several Hundred Texts. Including a Description of the Great Holiness Crisis of the Present Age by the Prophets* (Goshen, Ind.: E. U. Mennonite Pub. Society, 1880, 493 p.); Charles E. Brown, *When the Trumpet Sounded: A History of the Church of God Reformation Movement* (Anderson, Ind.: Warner Press, 1951), 101–2; Smith, *Quest*, 388–39, 56–57; *First Century*, 1:258.

7. *First Century*, 1:49; Smith, *Quest*, 57.

8. *First Century*, 1:50–51.

9. Smith, *Quest*, 46–47.

10. Val. Clear, *Where the Saints Have Trod: A Social History of the Church of God Reformation Movement* (Chesterfield, Ind.: Midwest Publications, 1977), 73–76; *First Century*, 1:52–53, 58–60.

11. John A. Morrison, *As the River Flows: The Autobiography of John A. Morrison, First President of Anderson College* (Anderson, Ind.: Anderson College Press, 1962), 165–67; Reardon, *Early Morning Light*, 40–44; Clear, *Where the Saints Have Trod*, 44–45; Smith, *Quest*, 97–100; *First Century*, 1:71–73, 281, 287–93.

12. *First Century*, 1:71–73, 332, 375–83, 2:620; Smith, *Quest*, 59–80.

13. Noah H. Byrum, *Familiar Names and Faces* (Moundsville, W. Va.: Gospel Trumpet Company, 1902), 216–22; Smith, *Quest*, 66, 72–73.

14. Reardon, *Early Morning Light*, 39; Smith, *Quest*, 69–73, 79–80.

15. Harold L. Phillips, *Miracle of Survival* (Anderson, Ind.: Warner Press, 1979), 22–33; Smith, *Quest*, 45–46, 62–67; Byrum, *Familiar Names*, 50.

16. Enoch E. Byrum, *Life Experiences* (Anderson, Ind.: Gospel Trumpet Company, 1928), 46–47.

17. Byrum, *Life Experiences*, 56.

18. Byrum, *Life Experiences*, 63–73.

19. Byrum, *Life Experiences*, 73–74.

20. Byrum, *Life Experiences*, 75–89; Brown, *When the Trumpet Sounded*, 131, 133–36; Phillips, *Miracle of Survival*, 34–38.

21. Byrum, *Life Experiences*, 158–67; Byrum, *Familiar Names*, 104; Reardon, *Early Morning Light*, 28–32; Phillips, *Miracle of Survival*, 42–47, 62–64, 143–47; Smith, *Quest*, 147–48; Brown, *When the Trumpet Sounded*, 367–69.

22. Brown, *When the Trumpet Sounded*, 365; Clear, *Where the Saints Have Trod*, 61.

23. Smith, *Quest*, 132, 137; Byrum, *Familiar Names*, 180.

24. For periodic production statistics see Phillips, *Miracle of Survival*.

25. Byrum, *Familiar Names*, 154–56; Smith, *Quest*, 67, 141; *First Century*, 1:81–83.

26. Smith, *Quest*, 133, 144–45; Phillips, *Miracle of Survival*, 109–10; Byrum, *Life Experiences*, 164–67; Clear, *Where the Saints Have Trod*, 61.

27. *First Century*, 1:480–81; Brown, *When the Trumpet Sounded*, 131–33, 363–66; Reardon, *Early Morning Light*, 31–32; Byrum, *Life Experiences*, 146–58; Byrum, *Familiar Names*, 164. For a historical register of leaders in the publishing work of the Church of God, see Phillips, *Miracle of Survival*, 337–45.

28. Reardon, *Early Morning Light*, 34–37, 47; Clear, *Where the Saints Have Trod*, 68–69; Byrum, *Familiar Names*, 176.

29. Smith, *Quest*, 124–28, 131, 146, 148; *First Century*, 2:471.

30. Brown, *When the Trumpet Sounded*, 365, 369–70; *First Century*, 2:492–99, 677, 680–84.

31. Morrison, *As the River Flows*, 170; Reardon, *Early Morning Light*, 53; Brown, *When the Trumpet Sounded*, 366–67; *First Century*, 2:482–83.

32. Brown, *When the Trumpet Sounded*, 375–87; Smith, *Quest*, 114–22, 268, 338; *First Century*, 2:503–5.

33. Hazel G. Neal and Axchie A. Bolitho, *Madam President: The Story of Nora Siens Hunter, Founder and First President of the National Woman's Missionary Society of the Church of God* (Anderson, Ind.: Gospel Trumpet Company, 1951), 52–57; *First Century*, 2:503–5.

34. Dale Oldham, *Giants Along My Path: My Fifty Years in the Ministry* (Anderson, Ind.: Warner Press, 1973), 89–91; Smith, *Quest*, 224–25.

35. Linfield Myers, *As I Recall* (Anderson, Ind.: Anderson College Press, 1973), 19–25, 77–98; Phillips, *Miracle of Survival*, 147–53; Smith, *Quest*, 230–44; Morrison, *As the River Flows*, 122–27; Reardon, *Early Morning Light*, 45–75.

36. Smith, *Quest*, 426, 442; *First Century*, 1:302–3; 2:640–42, 646–49, 694–96, 705–8, 740–44.

37. Morrison, *As the River Flows*, 165–82; Reardon, *Early Morning Light*, 47–75; Smith, *Quest*, 246–51.

38. Smith, *Quest*, 325–35; *First Century*, 2:643–46, 556.

39. *First Century*, 1:395; Smith, *Quest*, 364–65, 395.

40. Smith, *Quest*, 431–32.

SALVATION ARMY AND VOLUNTEERS OF AMERICA

Both Catherine Mumford and William Booth were born in England in 1829. Eventually they became husband and wife, parents of a remarkable family of eight children, and founders of a robust holiness church called the Salvation Army.[1]

The Mumford family were Methodists. John Mumford was a coach builder of moderate means and a lay preacher of moderate zeal. Catherine and her mother were "deeply attached to Methodism," enthusiastic supporters of its causes and missions. Catherine was sent to school at age twelve but withdrawn at age fourteen because of "a severe spinal attack." Her mother distrusted schools but provided a solid program of studies for her only daughter at home. The basic curriculum was augmented with Bible, church history, and theology—Bunyan, Wesley, Fletcher, Mosheim, and Neander. By the age of twelve Catherine had mastered the arguments of many temperance publications of the day and was writing to magazines arguing for abstinence from alcohol.[2]

The Mumfords moved to London in 1844. The next year Catherine concluded a strenuous search for evidence of her own conversion.

> One morning as I opened my hymn-book, my eyes fell upon the words:
>
> "My God, I am Thine!
> What a comfort Divine,—
> What a blessing to know that my Jesus is mine!"

Scores of times I had read and sung these words, but now they came home to my inmost soul with a force and illumination they had never before possessed. It was as impossible for me to doubt, as it had before been for me to exercise faith. Previously not all the promises in the Bible could induce me to believe, now not all the devils in hell could persuade me to doubt. I no longer hoped that I was saved, I was certain of it. The assurances of my salvation seemed to flood and fill my soul.[3]

She joined the Methodist church with her family.

However Methodist life in the Brixton congregation of London did not measure up to the standards of Catherine Mumford and her mother. It seemed to them to lack the vitality of early Methodism. Members were cold, formal, and insulated against pointed queries about the state of their souls. Only a few people were being saved. Catherine thought *Lectures on Revivals* by the American revivalist Charles G. Finney was "the most beautiful and common-sense work on the subject I ever read." She was in sympathy with the American holiness evangelist James Caughey who was in turn much influenced by Asa Mahan and Charles Finney and a close associate of Phoebe Palmer.[4]

Caughey had been lighting American-style revival fires in England since 1841. Thousands flocked to his meetings; hundreds crowded the communion rails asking prayer. A newspaper reporter said: "When the solicitude of the souls of the departed after the eternal welfare of their friends below was dwelt upon, a universal sob burst from the assembly, and even the faces of the rugged and weather-beaten men were illuminated by the reflection of the lamps in the water upon their cheeks. At times this emotion assumed a more frantic character, shouts, groans, and all manner of pious ejaculations rising from all parts of the house, until the preacher's voice became inaudible, and the whole place resounded with wailings and cries." Caughey was too much for the local Methodist conference; at the height of his success they banished him from their churches. Also under suspicion was a party called "Reformers" who plagued their fellow Methodists with criticisms. Catherine openly admired Caughey and defended the Reformers; she soon lost her membership ticket as a Methodist. She began meeting with the Reformers and teaching a class of teenage girls in their Sunday school.[5]

William Booth

William Booth was of Anglican parentage and he was baptized by the vicar of St. Mary's in Nottingham two days after his birth. The family had been wealthy but lost their money. William was taken from school at age thirteen and sent into business as an apprentice to a pawnbroker. His father died less than a year later. In religion, William gravitated to the Methodists. He was a frequent attender at Wesley Chapel and member of Henry Carey's class.[6] His conversion came in 1844 when he acknowledged and confessed a sin committed by deceiving some friends.

> I remember, as if it were but yesterday, the spot in the corner of the room under the chapel, the hour, the resolution to end the matter, the rising up and rushing forth, the finding of the young fellow I had chiefly wronged, the acknowledgment of my sin, the return of the pencil-case—the instant rolling away from my heart of the guilty burden, the peace that came in its place, and the going forth to serve my God and my generation from that hour . . . I felt . . . that I could willingly and joyfully travel to the ends of the earth for Jesus Christ, and suffer anything imaginable to help the souls of other men.[7]

When he was seventeen Booth began to preach. The American James Caughey had brought holiness fire to Wesley Chapel in Nottingham in 1846. A reporter said: "The preaching of Mr. Caughey creates a very great sensation in the town; the chapel is crowded even in the aisles during every service, and at its conclusion numbers of penitents make their way to the communion-rails, near the pulpit, to seek, under the terrors of guilty consciences, benefit there. It was announced on Wednesday

evening, that 200 persons had given in their names as having received conversion under Mr. Caughey's ministry since he came to Nottingham, and we believe his visit will not soon be forgotten."

William knew at once that this was what preaching should be. His friends Will Sansom and David Greenbury convinced him that he could do such preaching himself. Before long he was leader of a youthful evangelistic group. The method was Caughey's but the location was in the streets among many poor who never attended church. And the message was always the divine miracle of conversion: a surrender to God, a change of heart, a total revolution of soul and life. He had experienced this. He had been the human means of producing it. Nothing in the world seemed to him to be so real or important. The Methodists at Nottingham made him a local preacher. He worked as a pawnbroker six long days every week, worked in the slums at night, and worked for Wesley Chapel on Sundays. When his apprenticeship at Nottingham ended in 1849, he took his Bible and headed for London.[8]

The Methodists at London were uneasy with the new pawnbroker-evangelist. He added his name to the roster of Methodist local preachers but there were twenty preachers on the circuit and hardly any preaching invitations for him. The more he saw of London the more he felt he had to preach. He asked to have his name taken off the Methodist preacher list so he could be free to schedule any hours he had free from his business to do open air evangelism on the streets and greens in his own way. The Methodists thought he was acting like one of the troublesome Reformers and withheld his ticket of membership as well. When the Reformers heard he had been expelled, they asked him to join them and he did. Edward Harris Rabbits was a prosperous business man among the Reformers. He had heard William's preaching in American revival style and offered to provide a salary of £50 per year if William would become a preacher for the Reformers. So on his twenty-third birthday William quit pawnbroking to become preacher for the Reformers' chapel on Binfield Road. Among his congregation members were Mrs. Mumford and her daughter Catherine. After three years of courtship and theologically loaded letters, William Booth and Catherine Mumford were married on 16 June 1855.[9]

It was not easy to find a compatible church context for their ministry. The Reformers were gifted in criticism but seemed headed for ecclesiastical chaos. They provided scant institutional stability to support a rising clergy couple. Catherine suggested the Congregationalists as a group that allowed their clergy maximum freedom, but after considerable negotiation William balked at the prospect of going to college and of making mental peace with a Congregational doctrine of election. The Methodist New Connexion seemed to fulfill their requirements. William was appointed assistant on their London circuit, his salary subsidized again by Mr. Rabbits and his duties basically evangelism. They allowed him to marry Catherine at the end of one year of probationary service instead of waiting the regular four.[10]

William had become successful in his chosen work. A biographer said of the four months preceding his marriage to Catherine:

> No less than 1,739 persons had sought salvation at nine separate centres, besides a considerable number at four or five other places . . . This gave an average of 214 for each circuit visited, or 161 for each week, and 23 for each day during the time that meetings were being held. At Longton, during the first visit there were 260 in nine days, and during the second visit 97 in four days. At Hanley, there were 460 in a fortnight; at Burslem, 262 in one week; at Mossley, 50 in five days; at Newcastle-under-Lyme, 290 in one week; at Bradford, 160 in a fortnight, and at Gateshead, a similar number in the same time. Not included in the above was Guernsey, where, during Mr. Booth's first visit, 200 souls sought salvation in the space of a fortnight. It was an ordinary occurrence for 40, 50, or 60 persons to come forward to the communion rail each night.[11]

Opposition to his methods arose among the members of the New Connexion conference. They voted to change his field of labor. Instead of the itinerant evangelism he loved, he got regular circuit duty at Brighouse. Both William and Catherine were unhappy with the change. She wrote: "He cannot help making comparisons between this and his former sphere of usefulness, and though this is unquestionably much easier, it is far less congenial. I don't think he will ever feel right in it, neither do I believe the Lord intends that he should. He generally adapts His instruments to the work He marks out for them, and He has undoubtedly adapted my dear husband for something very different to this. But we will wait awhile."[12]

At Brighouse Catherine tried her hand as a temperance lecturer. At Gateshead, their circuit with the New Connexion from 1858 to 1861, she did some street preaching. In 1859 she published a pamphlet which was a spirited defense of the right of women to preach, specifically of the preaching rights of Phoebe Palmer who was drawing big crowds at the time at Newcastle just across the Tyne. Of a

minister's speech attacking Palmer for preaching, Catherine said "It was delivered in the form of an address to his congregation and repeated a second time by request to a crowded chapel, and then published! Would you believe that a congregation half composed of ladies could sit and hear such self-depreciatory rubbish? They really don't deserve to be taken up cudgels for!" Then on a spring Sunday of 1860, when William was concluding his preaching to a congregation of about a thousand, Catherine surprised him by coming forward to speak from the pulpit for the first time. It was quickly announced that she would preach that night. From that time the Booths were evangelists of equal power and popularity.[13]

Booths and Sanctification

Early in 1861, at Gateshead, both Catherine and William wrestled with sanctification. She wrote: "My soul has been much called out of late on the doctrine of holiness. I feel that hitherto we have not put it in a sufficiently definite and tangible manner before the people—I mean as a specific and attainable experience. Oh, that I had entered into the fulness of the enjoyment of it myself. I intend to struggle after it. In the mean time we have commenced already to bring it specially before our dear people."[14] When they began preaching holiness, their people responded by finding the blessing. Of William she said on 4 February:

> I have much to be thankful for in my dearest husband. The Lord has been dealing very graciously with him for some time past. His soul has been growing in grace, and its outward developments have been proportionate. He is now on full stretch for holiness. You would be amazed at the change in him. It would take me all night to detail all the circumstances and convergings of Providence and Grace which have led up to this experience, but I assure you it is a glorious reality, and I know you will rejoice in it.[15]

A week later she wrote of the conclusion of her own exhausting search for the experience.

> When we got up from our knees I lay on the sofa, exhausted with the excitement and effort of the day. William said, "Don't you lay all on the altar?" I replied, "I am sure I do!" Then he said, "And isn't the altar holy?" I replied in the language of the Holy Ghost, "The altar is most holy, and whatsoever toucheth it is holy." Then said he, "Are you not holy?" I replied with my heart full of emotion and with some faith, "Oh, I think I am." Immediately the word was given me to confirm my faith, "Now are ye clean through the word which I have

spoken unto you." And I took hold—true, with a trembling hand, and not unmolested by the tempter, but I held fast the beginning of my confidence, and it grew stronger, and from that moment I have dared to reckon myself dead indeed unto sin, and alive unto God through Jesus Christ, my Lord. I did not feel much rapturous joy, but perfect peace, the sweet rest which Jesus promised to the heavy-laden. I have understood the Apostle's meaning when he says "We who believe do enter into rest." This is just descriptive of my state at present. Not that I am not tempted, but I am allowed to know the devil when he approaches me, and I look to my Deliverer Jesus, and He still gives me rest. Two or three very trying things occurred on Saturday, which at another time would have excited impatience, but I was kept by the power of God through faith unto full salvation.[16]

Nothing could keep them located on one circuit any longer. When the New Connexion conference of 1861 would offer only part-time assignment to mass evangelism, they simply resigned from the New Connexion. Chapels of the Anglicans and of all varieties of Methodists were generally closing to them now, as they were to Caughey and the Palmers. Their home would be London and their location wherever opportunity opened on the evangelistic platforms of the world.[17]

London Ministry and the "Army"

Location was further determined in 1865 when William accepted an invitation to lead an evangelistic tent ministry in the slums of east London. William was appalled by the need. Surely no people on earth matched the degradation there or needed salvation so much. For thirteen years he conducted the Whitechapel mission in tent, dance hall, warehouse, and finally a Christian Mission building. Getting attention was primary. Noisy marches attracted crowds. Much preaching was done in the "cathedral" of the open streets. A service was no place for readings, even of Scriptures. Preaching had to grip the crowd's attention fast and hold it powerfully. Interruptions by hecklers and physical abuse by street mobs were regular fare. William Booth said "Darkest England may be described as consisting broadly of three circles, one within the other. The outer and widest circle is inhabited by the starving and the homeless, but honest, poor. The second by those who live by vice; and the third and innermost region at the center is peopled by those who exist by crime. The whole of the three circles is sodden with drink."[18]

William learned that a most effective sermon was the testimony of a reclaimed drunk. Catherine reported:

"My husband says the people do not come so much to hear the preacher as to look at the Bills and Dicks, the prizefighters and bird and dog fanciers who have been converted, and that they come still more to hear them speak." A philanthropist named Samuel Morley contributed to the support of the Booth household. Catherine was a popular evangelist in the region's more fashionable halls and drawing rooms. Her earnings helped to keep the large family solvent.[19]

When William tried to send his converts to traditional churches, most of them would not go. Those who went to mainline churches were often unwelcome. Also he needed the converts with him as workers in the streets, in the processions, at the meeting places, and in the soup kitchens. Inch by inch he consolidated his people and resources into an institution called the Christian Mission with a building, a membership, a *Christian Mission Magazine*, a printed report for contributors, and a conciliar body of some authority called the Conference or Conference Committee. His oldest son Bramwell was prominent in the mission leadership. So was George Scott Railton who offered himself to be the mission's secretary in 1873, bringing to it an unflagging zeal and a positive flair for publicity.[20]

By 1877 William concluded that the Conference Committee was too cumbersome. A work with such unstable support serving such an unstable constituency required the flexibility of prompt decision and direction like an army. The army imagery appealed to William and Bramwell and George Railton. An army structure and vocabulary became the organization's mark. William became "the General." A local congregation was a "corps." Members became "soldiers." The teams of ministers, many of them teenagers and a majority of them women, became "officers" with designation of military rank. Life and conduct were governed by "regulations." The mission's paper became the *War Cry*. Prayer became "knee drill" and the hallelujahs or amens shouted during services were "volleys" fired. Those who died in service were "promoted to glory." There came to be bands and uniforms.[21]

The doctrine of holiness remained central throughout the evolving Army plan. William said in 1877 "Holiness to the Lord is to us a fundamental truth; it stands to the forefront of our doctrines. We write it on our banners. It is in no shape or form an open debatable question as to whether God can sanctify wholly, whether Jesus does save His people from their sins. In the estimation of the Christian Mission that is settled for ever, and any evangelist who did not hold and proclaim the ability of Jesus Christ to save his people to the uttermost from sin and sinning I should consider out of place amongst us." In the Army's constituting documents of 1878, article ten of the "religious doctrines" said "We believe that it is the privilege of all believers to be 'wholly sanctified.'" Catherine and Bramwell Booth were enthusiastic preachers of holiness. Catherine's addresses on the subject were widely circulated in England and America in three books entitled *Aggressive Christianity, Godliness,* and *Holiness.*[22] William wrote a book entitled *Holy Living; or, What the Salvation Army Teaches about Sanctification.* In question and answer form, it was a very lucid and practical exposition of the doctrine of "entire sanctification" understood as a second blessing subsequent to justification. Salvation Army meetings were often marked by emotional testimonies of cleansing from all sin. Salvationist theologian Samuel L. Brengle was critically injured in Boston when a drunk tried to kill him with a paving stone. His ministry during a long convalescence was largely limited to writing. A doctrine he especially liked to write about was holiness.[23]

The Army in America

The Salvation Army kept multiplying its forces and "opening fire" on new territories. Sometimes a cluster of converts from one of Catherine's meetings would become the nucleus of a new corps. Stations in the urban centers of the British Isles were soon linked in a network of divisions under district-generals. The United States was the first country the Army invaded outside the British Isles. The Shirley family was moving from Coventry in England to Philadelphia in 1879. Their daughter Eliza wanted to be transferred to a Salvation Army post at her new home in America. William did not see how he could spare any officers for an invasion at the time or how he could commission this seventeen-year-old lieutenant to open an American mission. He said that if the Shirleys could begin a work in America the Army might annex the operation later.

The slums of Philadelphia were very much like the slums of London. Wealth may have come to many churches but the poor who needed most attention got the least. The Army team of the teenager Eliza Shirley and her mother fought for a hearing and a space in Philadelphia in spite of heavy mob abuse. One of their early posters read "Two Halleluja Females from England will speak and sing on behalf of God and Precious Souls, Commencing Sunday, October 5th, 1879, in the Salvation Factory, Formerly used as a Furniture Factory . . ." Conversion of the notorious alcoholic "Reddie" provided

a testimony. The Philadelphia newspapers were scornful but increasingly thoughtful.[24]

The work of the Shirleys kept reminding William Booth of his promise. The force finally gathered in England for the official invasion of America was made up of the enthusiast George Railton and seven Salvation Army lassies. One farewell prayer by an English officer was "Lord, these ladies are going to America to preach the Gospel. If they are fully given up to Thee, be with them and bless them, and grant them success. But if they are not faithful, drown 'em, Lord! Drown 'em!"[25]

The invasion force arrived in New York 10 March 1880. Railton's audacity promptly captured media attention. Posters announced "The Salvation Army Will Attack the Kingdom of the Devil at Harry Hill's Variety Theatre on Sunday, March 14, 1880, commencing at 6:00 P.M. sharp." The theater owner had given them a booking expecting to use them for public entertainment; they took the opportunity in order to evangelize but soon proved they were dead serious. They were making their way in New York against great obstacles and mob abuse, aided by the testimony of their first converted alcoholic, "Ashbarrel Jimmy," but came into conflict with the New York police who would not allow Railton to preach in the streets. Railton promptly moved the Army "headquarters" to Philadelphia, leaving Captain Emma Westbrook to occupy New York.[26]

Railton was summoned back to England after less than a year. Most of the original seven women officers returned to England. But the Salvation Army was planted in America to stay. English officers kept coming over but by 1882 there were as many American-born officers as English ones in the United States. In the summer of 1880 there were eight corps in the United States, six of them in Philadelphia. By the summer of 1890 there were 410 corps in thirty-five states. The Louisville *Courier-Journal* said the Salvationists who "opened fire" there in April of 1883 were "indefatigable and wonderfully zealous." Captain William Evans, his wife, and a lieutenant began operations with a drum and concertina on a Chicago street corner in February of 1885. In spite of "storms of violence," Chicago became the greatest Salvationist center in the country.[27]

In 1890 William Booth published his book *In Darkest England and the Way Out.* The first edition of 10,000 copies sold out the day of its appearance. Within a year the fifth edition—200,000 copies—was advertised. The book was William's attempt at description of the indescribable plight of the urban poor. It was his proposed program for a remedy. It embodied his heightened concern for social services. Conversion of the urban masses was the goal, but many candidates for conversion were going to need a lot of preliminary help. William said that when a London cab-horse fell he was helped up. A horse would be given food, shelter, and work while he lived. How much more should poor slum victims be helped up with immediate food, shelter, rest, and work on their way to rehabilitation.[28]

Booth's social program caused great excitement in America. If this goal was to be reached anywhere in the world, surely it would be in the United States. So American Salvationists soon offered not only Army corps as community churches for evangelism and the promotion of holiness but also shelters and service centers designed to help the fallen get back on their feet. These were frequently places of last resort. "No man need steal, starve, or commit suicide; come to the Salvation Army." The typical center patron was a man addicted to alcohol. The typical program provided food, shelter, cleaning up, drying out, and an opportunity to work for a limited time in an environment supportive of his resolution to lead a new life.[29]

General William Booth sent capable Army leaders to America. However it did seem that after breathing the air of the new world for a time these leaders caused him trouble. They respected him but felt he never quite understood America. According to the Army's founding documents recorded in England, all Army property was held personally by William Booth and all Army authority resided in him alone including the unquestioned right to name his successor. The American commander succeeding Railton, Major Thomas E. Moore, could not make that fit comfortably with the laws of American states governing property. When he tried to convince William to establish a separate American corporation to hold Army property, he was ordered to turn over the American property and command to Major Frank Smith and move off to a new command in South Africa. He denied any intention to disobey the General but instead of going to South Africa he turned over all property and rights which he controlled in America to a corporation in New York, took a strong stance as "American general," and stayed to lead a schismatic body incorporated as "The Salvation Army of America." Moore's principle of American incorporation of Army property eventually triumphed. However his breakaway branch of the Army dwindled. Most officers returned to the parent organization in 1889; a few remained independent of the Booths, eventually taking the name American Rescue Workers.[30]

The Ballington Booths and the Volunteers of America

William sent his son Ballington to be commander in the United States in 1887. Ballington and his wife Maud were very attractive young leaders. Both were powerful and charismatic speakers. Both were prolific writers. They became American citizens. They reconciled a substantial body of officers from the Moore schism to the main body of the Army. They helped change the popular abuse of the Army to public acceptance and affection, making General Booth's visit to the United States in 1894–95 into a triumphal tour. They planned and supervised construction of a splendid new headquarters building for the Army on West Fourteenth Street in New York, a memorial to Catherine Booth. They enlisted thousands of "auxiliaries" for the Army—persons contributing $5 per year, receiving the *War Cry*, and committing themselves to pray for the Army and support its work. The lists of the auxiliaries and the constituents of Maud Booth's drawing-room meetings included many of America's most prominent citizens.[31]

It was customary for Salvation Army officers to be transferred frequently and for territorial commanders to change every five years. But when Maud and Ballington were "ordered to farewell" from the United States in January of 1896 a great public outcry arose. The Salvation Army had already achieved a large place in American favor and for many these young Booths personified it. Maud and Ballington announced their intention to obey orders and relinquish their command. But instead of taking a new assignment they said they would "quietly retire" and remain in the United States. In spite of the great show of support for them both inside and outside the Army, they made no effort to lead out a large body in secession or to seize all the Army property to which Ballington held title personally. In March of 1896 Maud and Ballington formed a completely new organization called the Volunteers of America. It was military in style for its first eighty-eight years, but always more democratic than the Salvation Army. The Salvation Army had never ordained its officers and had refrained from introducing sacraments since they were considered unnecessary, divisive, and a possible temptation to alcoholics. The Volunteers of America offered ordination for its ministers and sacraments for its members. The principles and programs of the Volunteers were similar to those of the Salvation Army, notable for a continuing emphasis on ministry to prisoners which Maud had made a high priority.[32] Numerical loss from the Salvation Army to the Volunteers was substantial but soon recouped. The General's second daughter Emma and her husband Frederick—known as the Booth-Tuckers—were able to gather the Army's property from Ballington and secure it under a New York corporation designated "For the spiritual, moral and physical reformation of the working classes; for the reclamation of the vicious, criminal, dissolute and degraded; for visitation among the poor and low and the sick; for preaching of the Gospel and the dissemination of Christian truth by means of open-air and indoor meetings." The Army's growth continued and the American tour of General William Booth in 1898 was again conducted in grand style.[33]

Evangeline Booth

A family tragedy brought the farewell of Frederick Booth-Tucker in 1904. Then the General sent America his most dramatic daughter Eva to be commander. It was not that Evangeline Booth could have been an actress. She was an actress. Her professionally staged lectures packed halls across the nation on behalf of the poor. She played the media like she played her harp, to the delight of all concerned. She became an American citizen and personified the Salvation Army for an American public now won from abuse of the Army to affection for it. Presidents Theodore Roosevelt, Taft, Wilson, Harding, Coolidge, Hoover, and Franklin Roosevelt each received her and endorsed the Army's work.[34]

When the United States entered the First World War, Eva offered the ministry of a substantial unit of her Army. This unit set up service huts and visiting teams alongside military installations in the United States. More remarkably, it secured permission and sent about 250 Salvationists among the American troops in combat in France, augmented by about twice that many persons employed overseas. Salvationists accustomed to wearing themselves out meeting basic needs for the homeless wore themselves out in ministry to the troops far from home. On instructions from Evangeline, they identified with the enlisted men and never went near an officers' mess. They appeared surprisingly close to the front lines. They held religious services and offered counseling. They moved messages and money to and from families back home. They did emergency sewing. They offered coffee and doughnuts and pie. If the soldier at the Salvation Army canteen had no money, they sold to him on credit. They mothered the sick and lonely. Evangeline had borrowed

$125,000 to send her first officers overseas early in 1917 but at the end of that year a public plea for $1 million for the Salvation Army war work was endorsed by President Wilson and quickly answered. American veterans' groups, service clubs, and fraternal organizations were the Salvation Army's fast friends from that time forward.[35]

In September of 1922 the New York *World* ran a front-page story saying Commander Evangeline Booth was about to be transferred from the United States. She said publicly that she was an American citizen and did not wish to leave. Her "orders to farewell" soon came from General Bramwell Booth. Such a great public furor resulted that Bramwell delayed her transfer until 1929. That year a High Council of the Salvation Army in London deposed Bramwell Booth and ended the Army's original autocratic form of government. Evangeline was a leader in the deposition of Bramwell and in the reform. She remained commander for the United States into the terrible early years of the Great Depression when the Army's relief expense increased by 700 percent. She was elected general of the entire Salvation Army in 1934. Her spectacular public sendoff to London included the congratulations of Franklin D. Roosevelt. It was a fitting conclusion to her American command of thirty years and the culmination of a dynasty of Booths.[36]

Money for the Army

Flexibility was always the genius of Salvation Army efforts in the United States. If the poor were burning in the summer and the Salvation Army had dollars, it bought them ice. If they were freezing in the winter and the Salvation Army had dollars, it bought them fuel. If they were starving, it bought food. If they were ragged, it offered clothing. If they were homeless it offered rest and shelter. If they were children it offered care and recreation; a psychology major from Indiana University directed the first Salvation Army boy's club at Rome, New York. If disaster struck, it could mobilize quickly to send aid. For those addicted to drugs, especially to alcohol, it was always seeking the right combination of immediate rescue and long-term rehabilitation. The list of needs seemed endless. Salvationists kept experimenting.[37]

There were never enough dollars. Flexibility in ministry had to be matched by flexibility in funding. Ideally each corps and service center would be self-supporting. However the memberships were always small. Attendance at the holiness meeting of the corps on Sunday morning might be minuscule and those present were not usually persons of means. Seventy to eighty percent of the client load at a service center might be alcoholics, most with difficult personality problems and a firm conviction that they really had no drinking problem. Perhaps 20 percent of these could be substantially helped and only a handful of the ones rehabilitated would become active Salvation Army members willing to accept the disciplines of the *Soldier's Manual*.[38]

So a corps might seek out an advisory board of substantial local citizens willing to help underwrite the local work. It might develop a league of auxiliaries, each member willing to make an annual contribution. It might solicit gifts through Salvation Army kettles or "mercy boxes." It might share in the apportionment of funds from the Community Chest or United Way campaigns. Federal, state, or local governments might contract certain social services through the Salvation Army.[39]

Service centers early arranged to collect community salvage material to be sold. Alcoholic center residents regaining stability to reenter the regular work force might be operating horse carts or light trucks on routes collecting paper, rags, and household or commercial discards. Friendly donors also contributed items worthy of immediate resale. As the market in paper and rags and scrap became more competitive and less reliable, the Army shifted its focus to the operation of thrift stores stocked with donated saleable materials. These, in turn, came to face rising competition from the popular flea markets and garage sales.[40]

Both Church and Charity

Salvationists have lived in a certain tension. Their Salvation Army has always been a holiness church. It has always been engaged in an evangelical crusade, a pursuit of salvation and sanctification. It has always insisted that personal salvation is the only ultimate remedy for human misery. It has resisted any division of its social and religious work, saying that all of its work is in response to the commands of Jesus Christ and so is 100 percent religious. Its federal legal status and tax exemption have never been claimed as a charitable organization but as a church. It has defined itself over and over as a branch of or an order within the church universal and has been a participant in the World Council of Churches at some level since that council's inception in 1954. It has played a very substantial role in the affairs of the Christian Holiness Association. Crowds attending the celebration of its American centennial in 1980 heard not only appropriate historical speeches but also sermons and "interminable altar calls."[41]

At the same time the Salvation Army has administered a highly valued complex of social programs for the world at large. These have required a constant influx of funds and donations from sources beyond its own small membership. At times the Army has been the nation's largest provider of rehabilitation for alcoholics. Its officers have been required to function not only as preachers and pastors but also as counselors, social workers, and administrators as well as very precise accountants to be sure that church and public funds were properly separated. Since 1960 candidates for this complex role have completed the two-year course of the Salvation Army School for Officers' Training plus a summer of field work. Many have added further study at college, one favorite training place being Asbury College at Wilmore, Kentucky. Continuing education throughout a career of Army service has been assumed.[42]

Indiana Operations

Indiana, less urbanized than many states, was not a pioneer producer of city slums. However the state did have some areas of heavy industry and concentrations of urban poor by the time the Salvation Army came to America in 1880. Hoosiers were certainly hospitable to its holiness emphasis. National Commander Thomas Moore made a six-day tour of 2,000 miles through Kentucky and Indiana in 1883, keeping nine speaking engagements. On that trip he presented Salvation Army colors to new corps at Louisville in Kentucky and at New Albany in Indiana. Some Salvationists from Indiana were present for the fourth anniversary celebration in Brooklyn in 1884.[43]

Indianapolis became the center of operations for the state's Salvation Army, offering the most prominent example of its service and flexibility. Work was first established in Indianapolis in 1889 when Ballington Booth was national commander. Location in the city shifted at least five times in the earliest years. Then Ensign McKenzee and Mr. W. Kruse opened a "Men's Shelter" at 38 South Capitol in 1901. Soon four or five men were collecting waste paper and rags to be baled and shipped to the mills. Adjutant Emma Westbrook, one of the original seven women who came to America with George Railton in 1880, visited Indianapolis several times.[44]

The religious census of 1906 reported fourteen Salvation Army corps in Indiana. At Indianapolis the state and city offices for the Army located in the newly purchased and remodeled building at 26 South Capitol in 1911. In the same building were the Industrial Home (formerly Men's Shelter) for 40 men, the Men's Hotel for 60 men, the Anti-Suicide Department, the Free Labor Bureau, a public bath house, a public laundry, and an auditorium to seat 250. The Central Salvation Army Corps was around the corner at 54 Kentucky Avenue. Financial statements reflected fund raising by collection of salvage; there were expenditures for horse feed, harness, horseshoeing, and repairs to wagons. But there was also a Salvation Army store in that new location at 26 South Capitol. In his history published in 1910, Jacob Piatt Dunn reported about 160 Indianapolis subscribers to the support of the Army's work. He said the Army's "really great work" was "the steady never-ending relief of the sick, and helpless, and destitute."[45]

During this era of National Commander Evangeline Booth, Brigadier and Mrs. George F. Casler sent out their Indiana report for 1920 from 26 South Capitol. As new state commander, Brigadier Casler had already visited the twenty-seven Indiana cities where there were Salvation Army operations. For the period 1 October 1919 to 26 September 1920 he reported in Indiana: "Indoor meetings held 8,950; attendance at indoor meetings 366,436; number of conversions 1,846; open [air] meetings held 6,117; attendance at open air meetings 992,424; hours spent by commanding officers in visitation 29,646; active workers or soldiers 1,068; copies of War Crys sold 102,658; Sunday school attendance 33,821; Young People's Legion and other junior attendance 64,969." Relief work in the state included "Coal supplied to poor, pounds, 341,800; meals furnished 5,147; temporary relief given 130; situations found for men 4,971; situations found for women 178; Christmas dinners 20,614; Thanksgiving dinners 1,874; children given toys 10,159."[46]

At Indianapolis alone, Brigadier Casler was expecting 3,000 for the 1920 "Christmas dinner" on 24 December and 3,000 for the "Christmas Tree Celebration" featuring treats and gifts for children on 28 December. Mayor Charles W. Jewett was to address "these unfortunates" on both occasions. Casler's report on the Army's prison work in Indiana in 1920 showed "Meetings held for prisoners 528; total attendance 10,423; prisoners interviewed 1,701; professing conversion 3,128; War Crys distributed 14,009; hours spent in visiting prisoners 955; discharged prisoners helped 112." In 1920 one special Salvation Army corps was formed among prisoners in the Indiana

State Reformatory at Jeffersonville, the largest and most remarkable such prison corps in the nation.[47]

The total number of Salvation Army corps in Indiana leveled out at about forty by 1926 and made no further increase. However upgrading of facilities and experimentation with programs continued. Indianapolis service center was doing salvage collecting with light trucks instead of horses by 1933. In that depression year the salvage force averaged thirty-three men at 127 West Georgia, including three former heads of businesses, a plumber, an electrician, and a tailor. Such men in rehabilitation received room, board, and $2 or $3 per week to process salvage and refurbish items for sale in the thrift store. A bed for a transient cost 25¢. Persons with no money at all for the store or hotel were sent to the relief department at 24 South Capitol.[48]

After the Second World War the Army in Indianapolis developed its property at 113-127 West Georgia and acquired the old Indianapolis street car barn for its warehouse. The Indianapolis service center was operating twelve stores by 1970; by 1980 the Indianapolis stores instituted evening hours and began accepting Visa and Mastercard. There were many cooperative projects—with the Girl Scouts to bring in bagsful of useful articles; with the National Trucking Company to deliver materials to victims of a tornado at Monticello; with Lilly Endowment and the Indianapolis Foundation to provide emergency fuel; with the United Methodist Women to develop the Lucille Raines Residence with housing for 100 persons. And there were term contracts—with the federal Public Inebriate Program to conduct a thirty-bed detoxification program; with the local court to operate a Public Drinking Driver Program; with the State Division of Alcoholism to operate an accredited halfway house; with the federal Public Inebriate Program to operate a "walk-in" to which any person could come, at any time of the day or night, to sit and rest and have coffee and rolls; with the Salvation Army to train rehabilitation center administrators. Other social service centers at such places as Gary, Fort Wayne, and Evansville were compiling their own records of usefulness.[49]

Counting Salvation Army membership was always complicated. Persons aided or enrolled or in residence at the Army's social service centers—in later years generally called adult rehabilitation centers—were not counted as Army members at all unless they chose to seek out an Army corps and enlist. Each corps—in later years often called a Salvation Army community center—was like a church congregation with an especially heavy social ministry. A corps generally included only a small number of senior soldiers, full adult members who had signed the "Articles of War" and committed themselves to live by the Army's *Orders and Regulations for Soldiers*. A much larger number of persons expected services from the staff, were involved in its youth programs, and were users of corps facilities.[50]

The Salvation Army's 1990 report for the United States showed only 127,577 adherents in 1,167 corps as the church at the heart of the Army's huge social programs. For Indiana that year the Salvation Army report was 4,500 adherents in 41 corps, a numerical strength a bit smaller than the Free Methodists and somewhat larger than the Unitarian Universalists. Counties with a number of Army adherents exceeding 200 were Allen with 252, Elkhart with 211, Howard with 251, Lake with 355, La-Porte with 259, Marion with 315, St. Joseph with 227, and Vanderburgh with 298.

Volunteers of America

The Volunteers of America remained under the military-style direction of the Booth family—Ballington, Maud, and their son Charles—from its founding in 1896 until 1958. Its operations were much like those of the Salvation Army, exhibiting the same flexibility in program and ingenuity in funding on behalf of the needy. Volunteers were in Indiana during the first year of their existence.

> Captain and Mrs. Murphy arrived in South Bend, Indiana, in September, 1896, with very little money and the assignment to start a post. In fourteen weeks they reported their accomplishments. They had conducted 147 indoor meetings, 95 open air meetings and 26 saloon meetings resulting in 126 "absolute conversions." They had visited 785 homes and spent 800 hours in visitation, providing lodging for 75 men and 68 meals for hungry men. They had sold 3,600 copies of the *Gazette* and 300 copies of the *Advance* and had managed to raise their running expense of about $15 a week.[51]

Fort Wayne post was established in 1916. It developed a shelter for homeless men, a sheltered workshop for men preparing to reenter the work force, a halfway house for offenders, and a counseling service for alcoholics. Terre Haute post, formed the same year, developed two group homes serving the handicapped, the developmentally disabled, and the elderly.

Volunteers of America were at work in Indianapolis as early as 1902, with Lieutenant Major F. J. Preston in residence and some ninety "sustaining members" enrolled. That Indianapolis post of the Volunteers, officially founded in 1922, developed a remarkable breadth of programs for the homeless, the chronically mentally ill, substance abusers, pregnant teens, adoptive parents, and poor people in need of free apparel and household goods. Services for offenders included legal counseling, electronic surveillance, work release, and transitional care. Six major programs in 1990 were operating with a combined annual budget of $2.4 million. More federally funded housing was in prospect for the Volunteers programs at Indianapolis and Terre Haute.[52]

Big changes occurred among the Volunteers in the 1980s. The Fort Wayne post was closed by flood damage in 1982. It was scheduled for reopening in 1990 offering programs for infants from needy families and electronic monitoring of offenders. The whole military model of organization was replaced with a corporate structure in 1984. Gone were the uniforms and much of the military vocabulary. Posts became branches. But the Volunteers of America were still avowedly "a Christian church with a special ministry." The "president/CEO" was to be a Volunteers minister elected to this "supreme command" by a Grand Field Council whose voting members were the Volunteers ministers with more than four years of service.

Ministers of the Volunteers of America could be ordained by the Grand Field Council after a four-year course of study and examination. Ordained ministers could administer sacraments, perform marriages, and conduct funerals. They could be assigned by the president to "manage a local church" wherever that served the purposes of the organization. However both ministers and "constituent members" of the Volunteers were free to maintain an active membership in other churches if there was no conflict in doctrine. Volunteers doctrine was spelled out in ten cardinal points, essentially evangelical Christian. The article on holiness did not include language defining sanctification as a second blessing or an experience subsequent to justification. It simply said, "We believe that the Scriptures teach and urge all Christians to be cleansed in heart from inbred sin, so that they may walk uprightly and serve Him without fear in holiness and righteousness all the days of their lives."[53]

NOTES

1. For a list of the Booth children and their achievements, see Herbert E. Wisbey, *History of the Volunteers of America* (N.p., 1954), 4.

2. Frederick Booth-Tucker, *The Life of Catherine Booth, the Mother of the Salvation Army*, 2 vols. (New York: Fleming H. Revell, 1892), 1:22, 30–33, 39.

3. Booth-Tucker, *Life*, 1:46.

4. Norman H. Murdoch, "Wesleyan Influence on William and Catherine Booth," *Wesleyan Theological Journal* 20 (Fall 1985): 98; Harold Begbie, *The Life of General William Booth, the Founder of the Salvation Army*, 2 vols. (New York: Macmillan, 1920), 1:163; *The Higher Christian Life* (New York: Garland Publishing, 1985), 124–26; Booth-Tucker, *Life*, 1:47–52.

5. Begbie, *Life*, 1:12; Booth-Tucker, *Life*, 1:63–71.

6. Begbie, *Life*, 1:15, 23, 40–44.

7. Begbie, *Life*, 1:54.

8. Begbie, *Life*, 1:10, 62–75, 87–90.

9. Robert Sandall, *The History of the Salvation Army*, 4 vols. (London: Thomas Nelson and Sons, 1947–1964), 1:4–7; Booth-Tucker, *Life*, 1:79–197.

10. Booth-Tucker, *Life*, 1:98–106, 162; Sandall, *History*, 1:6–7; Begbie, *Life*, 1:208.

11. Booth-Tucker, *Life*, 1:198–99.

12. Booth-Tucker, *Life*, 1:288–316.

13. Booth-Tucker, *Life*, 1:305, 334, 343–49, 357–68; Sandall, *History*, 1:8.

14. Booth-Tucker, *Life*, 1:382; Sandall, *History*, 1:9.

15. Booth-Tucker, *Life*, 1:383.

16. Booth-Tucker, *Life*, 1:385–86.

17. Begbie, *Life*, 1:294; Booth-Tucker, *Life*, 1:390–431, 488–89; Sandall, *History*, 1:15–17.

18. Edward H. McKinley, *Somebody's Brother: A History of the Salvation Army Men's Social Service Department, 1891–1985* (Lewiston, N.Y.: Edwin Mellen Press, 1986), 9.

19. Sandall, *History*, 1:43, 97–98, 2:3–4; Booth-Tucker, *Life*, 1:373–74.

20. Herbert A. Wisbey, *Soldiers without Swords: A History of the Salvation Army in the United States* (New York: Macmillan, 1956), 21–22; Sandall, *History*, 1:65–185, 373–76.

21. Sallie Chesham, *Born to Battle: The Salvation Army in America* (New York: Rand McNally, 1965), 50–53; Edward H. McKinley, *Marching to Glory: The History of the Salvation Army in the United States of America, 1880–1980* (New York: Harper and Row, 1980), 4, 39–44; Sandall, *History*, 1:31–124, 206–38.

22. Timothy L. Smith, *Called unto Holiness* (Kansas City, Mo.: Nazarene Publishing House, 1962), 25; Begbie, *Life*, 1:376–84; Sandall, *History*, 1:167, 209, 289; 2:29–30, 112–13, 127–28.

23. William Booth, *Holy Living; or, What the Salvation Army Teaches about Sanctification*, 3d ed. (London: Salvation Army Publishing Department, 1890, 31 p.); Begbie, *Life*, 1:379–84; Sandall, *History*, 2:138; McKinley, *Marching*, 34, 83; Chesham, *Born*, 76–77, 238.

24. Sandall, *History*, 2:49–52; McKinley, *Marching*, 4–9, 78a; Wisbey, *Soldiers*, 13–16, 38.

25. Chesham, *Born*, 57.

26. Wisbey, *Soldiers*, 4; McKinley, *Marching*, 10–17.

27. Wisbey, *Soldiers*, 35; McKinley, *Marching*, 20, 36–37.

28. William Booth, *In Darkest England, and the Way Out* (London: International Headquarters of the Salvation Army, 1890, 285 p.); Sandall, *History*, 3:79.

29. McKinley, *Somebody's Brother*, 8–12, 213; McKinley, *Marching*, 56–59; Wisbey, *Soldiers*, 99–105, 188.

30. Wisbey, *Soldiers*, 45–55; McKinley, *Marching*, 24–31; J. Gordon Melton, *The Encyclopedia of American Religions*, 3d ed. (Detroit, Mich.: Gale Research, 1989), 323.

31. Wisbey, *Soldiers*, 67, 79–80, 86–87, 91–95, 107; Wisbey, *History*, 15–20.

32. Wisbey, *Soldiers*, 106–17, 179; Wisbey, *History*, 20–43, 75–92; McKinley, *Marching*, 35, 72–79; Sandall, *History*, 2:130–34.

33. McKinley, *Marching*, 83; Wisbey, *Soldiers*, 122–24.

34. McKinley, *Marching*, 94–95, 107, 110; Wisbey, *Soldiers*, 142.

35. Margaret Troutt, *The General Was a Lady: The Story of Evangeline Booth* (Nashville, Tenn.: A.J. Holman, 1980), 152–64; McKinley, *Marching*, 120–28, 135, 256–58; Wisbey, *Soldiers*, 160–66; Chesham, *Born*, 152–69.

36. McKinley, *Somebody's Brother*, 93–99; McKinley, *Marching*, 161–68, 171–72; Chesham, *Born*, 197–203; Wisbey, *Soldiers*, 179–91.

37. Chesham, *Born*, 176–77; McKinley, *Marching*, 56–58.

38. McKinley, *Marching*, 188; McKinley, *Somebody's Brother*, 171–79, 212–13.

39. McKinley, *Somebody's Brother*, 33–34; McKinley, *Marching*, 60–61, 211–15.

40. McKinley, *Marching*, 57; McKinley, *Somebody's Brother*, 58–80, 87–90, 105–7, 158–60, 179–83, 212.

41. *The Salvation Army and the Churches: An Anthology of Selected Articles by Salvationist Authors, Past and Present, on the Relationship of the Salvation Army to the Established Christian Churches*, comp. Commissioner John D. Waldron (New York: Salvation Army Literary Department, 1986), 1–8, 87–136; Jean Caffey Lyles, "New Battle Plan for Booth's Army," *Christian Century* 97 (27 August–3 September 1980): 811–12; McKinley, *Marching*, xi, 33–34, 59, 218; Chesham, *Born*, 264.

42. McKinley, *Marching*, 109, 203–9; McKinley, *Somebody's Brother*, 172.

43. Wisbey, *Soldiers*, 44, 46, 70.

44. Unpublished data provided with letter of Mary Stanberry, Indiana Divisional Headquarters of the Salvation Army at Indianapolis, to L. C. Rudolph, 3 August 1990; Jacob Piatt Dunn, *Greater Indianapolis*, 2 vols. (Chicago: Lewis Publishing Company, 1910), 1:623.

45. Stanberry to Rudolph, 3 August 1990; Dunn, *Greater Indianapolis*, 1:623.

46. *The Salvation Army in Indiana. 1920 Annual Report. Financial and Statistical Statements of the Work Done in Indianapolis for the Year Ending September 26th, 1920* (Indianapolis: Salvation Army Divisional Headquarters, 1920), 5–6.

47. *Salvation Army in Indiana*, 3, 5, 6; McKinley, *Somebody's Brother*, 82; McKinley, *Marching*, 141.

48. "Industrial Home Leader Is Salvage Corps by Himself in Aiding Needy," *Indianapolis Star*, 15 January 1933, 7.

49. Stanberry to Rudolph, 3 August 1990; McKinley, *Somebody's Brother*, 66, 86, 207.

50. McKinley, *Marching*, 215–18.

51. Wisbey, *History*, 64.

52. Dunn, *Greater Indianapolis*, 1:623; data provided with letter of Sheila Ewing BeMiller, Volunteers of America, Indianapolis Branch, to L. C. Rudolph, Indiana University, Bloomington, 25 July 1990.

53. BeMiller to Rudolph, 25 July 1990.

CHRISTIAN AND MISSIONARY ALLIANCE

This fellowship began with Albert Benjamin Simpson. Fourth child of strict Covenanter Presbyterians at Chatham in Ontario, he decided as a teenager to study for the ministry. He was a gifted youth of great emotional intensity. He and the modern holiness movement were coming to maturity concurrently. He was fifteen in the great revival year of 1858 when evangelist H. Grattan Guiness of London preached at Chatham. Following a series of terrifying personal crises that year, he sought and received a conversion so decisive that he later compared it to the biblical account of the experience of Saul of Tarsus in chapter nine of the Book of Acts. In his ministerial preparation he was such a star that he was called directly from theological studies at Knox College in Toronto to be pastor of the large and prosperous Knox Church in Hamilton.[1]

During booming Presbyterian pastorates of just over eight years at Hamilton, just under six years at Louisville, Kentucky, and just under two years at New York City, he increasingly adopted the form of preaching, music, and revival familiar in holiness evangelism. At Louisville in 1874 he read *The Higher Christian Life* by William E. Boardman, a Presbyterian holiness pioneer associated with Keswick. Then he sought and received "the new light of the indwelling Christ and the baptism of the Holy Spirit." So he became a preacher of sanctification which was to be experienced as an immediate crisis but gradually fulfilled. "Sanctification," he said, "is divine holiness, not human self improvement, nor perfection" but "the inflow into man's being of the life and purity of His [God's] own perfection and the working out of His own will." It is gradual in that it is "complete but not completed; perfect but not perfected." God the Holy Spirit is no mere lodger in the personal temple of the sanctified believer; the Spirit has been given the whole house.[2]

On vacation at Orchard Park, Maine, in 1881, Simpson attended the healing services of Charles Cullis. Then he sought and received healing from his perennial despondency and exhaustion. And he became a preacher and practitioner of divine healing. He was an enthusiast for world missions, issuing his own missionary periodical from 1880 variously called *The Gospel in All Lands*; *The Word, the Work and the World*; *The Christian Alliance and Missionary Weekly*; and *The Christian and Missionary Alliance Weekly*. He was always preparing for Christ's return and focused his missionary drive on the text of Matthew 24:14: "This gospel of the kingdom shall be preached in all the world for a witness unto all nations; and then shall the end come." World evangelism might be costly and the task enormous but it was the means appointed and a priority above all others. In the same year as his healing, he accepted baptism by immersion by a Baptist pastor and resigned his connection with the Presbyterians.[3]

In one way of speaking, Simpson became an independent. For his fellowship he would simply follow the "divine pattern" of the New Testament as he perceived it. He built up a large independent constituency in New York which incorporated in 1883 under the name Gospel

Tabernacle. There were services each evening and three times on Sunday. Besides the tabernacle there was a healing home, a missionary training school, a mission to ruined women, and an orphanage. His vision was a ministry free of prejudices based on economic and social gradations and designed to appeal to lower middle class persons not being served by the mainline churches. Besides the tabernacle services at New York and at two locations in Canada, there was an endless series of city and summer resort conventions. These gatherings lasting two to ten days "succeeded in producing in one place and at once a Bible conference, a camp meeting, an evangelistic campaign and a missionary promotional meeting." The message was always the Fourfold Gospel which Simpson saw in the New Testament and claimed to confirm in his own experience: Christ as Savior, Sanctifier, Healer, and Coming Lord. Raising money to send missionaries was a major part of the excitement at the conventions. By 1893, 180 missionaries in association with Simpson worked on forty stations in twelve fields. They were unsalaried; 23 paid for this missionary expansion with their lives.[4]

In another way of speaking, Simpson never became an independent. In his final sermon at Thirteenth Street Presbyterian Church in New York he "concluded with an appeal that members of the church not follow him or bring upon him the stigma of having split the church." To the day of his death he insisted that his movement was not to be or become a denomination. He formed two "alliances." The Christian Alliance, organized in 1887, was to be a fellowship of earnest Christians without regard to denominational lines. These were to be spiritual athletes always lifting up the Fourfold Gospel and so offering saving benefits to every person who would hear. Everywhere it existed the Christian Alliance was to raise funds for missions. The Missionary Alliance, formed later the same year, was to use every dollar and ounce of energy available to enlist, train, send, and oversee a constantly increasing force of faith missionaries. These were to go to remote fields where competition with other mission agencies was unlikely. After ten years the two alliances realized how interdependent they were; they merged their work and their names to become The Christian and Missionary Alliance.[5]

Simpson's alliance was visible in the handful of independent tabernacles like his own Gospel Tabernacle in New York. It could be seen in action in the host of city and summer conventions conducted by Simpson and by the colleagues he enlisted. His biographer said: "The conventions gradually spread from Old Orchard and the New York Gospel Tabernacle to other areas: Vermillion,

Ohio (1887); Western Springs, near Chicago (1889); Round Lake, near Albany, New York (1890); and Atlanta, Georgia (1899). Eventually the conventions would move upward into Canada (1889) and westward to California (1908), until they spanned the nation."[6]

But if the power of America's "Fourfold Gospel people" was to be rallied in support of world evangelism, there had to be some further device for focusing their efforts. To meet this need they began forming and multiplying "branches." Members of a branch subscribed to a sixty-four word creed. Their meetings—at least monthly and more likely every week—were scheduled not to conflict with regular church activities in their community since so many participants were church members. Simpson always wanted his alliance and its local branches to be catalysts in the midst of the membership of existing denominations, champions in support of holy living and world missions. Much of the missionary support raised for the Alliance came from members of regular denominations, an arrangement fully in line with Simpson's published principles and one that Alliance officers were not quick to disturb.[7]

Development of an Alliance branch was nicely illustrated at Indianapolis. In gratitude for what she counted a marvelous healing in March of 1882, the mother of Alice Reynolds joined others in a "prayer circle" which soon came into connection with the rising holiness and healing ministry of A. B. Simpson in New York. A prominent Methodist pastor at Anderson, Indiana, incurred the wrath of his North Indiana Conference for espousing divine healing and holiness principles. This George N. Eldridge, with a wife and six children, "stepped out on faith alone" and moved to Indianapolis to form the "prayer circle" into an Alliance branch. "God provided a home for them in Irvington," said Alice Reynolds. "Friends were raised up to help financially, sick were healed and souls saved and sanctified." The Alliance branch members at Indianapolis developed their own "Gospel Tabernacle" on East Street just north of Massachusetts Avenue. "The chief meeting was on Sunday afternoon when happy hearts from various denominational churches all over the city came for spiritual food and refreshing." Hymns of A. B. Simpson were a part of the order.[8]

Simpson wanted such an Alliance branch in every population center and a district superintendent of the branches in every state. That was not accomplished. The best extension effort of the Alliance kept going overseas. In 1912 there were 259 missionaries in sixteen foreign fields. In North America that year there were only 239 branches and affiliated churches. Over half the groups in the United States were in Pennsylvania (55), New York (30), Ohio (22), Washington (17), and California (12).[9]

One limitation for Simpson and his Alliance was what a biographer has called the "trial by tongues." While the Christian and Missionary Alliance was young, the pentecostal revival occurred in Kansas and California. Emissaries from the Azusa Street meetings in Los Angeles brought an expectancy that persons really baptized in the Holy Spirit would speak in tongues. How was this to be related to Simpson's Fourfold Gospel exalting Jesus Christ as Savior, Sanctifier, Healer, and Coming Lord? So many Alliance people in the Ohio Valley branches were reported to be fired by the new pentecostal experiences that Simpson sent an investigator in 1907. On the basis of that investigator's report and of his own observations, he warned against the danger of counterfeit excitements but concluded that many had indeed been recipients of a new work of the Holy Spirit.

Simpson did not wish to advocate for others what he had not personally proved. For a long time he gave himself to strenuous disciplines to be sure he was not somehow resisting or blocking the new gift. He found many times of excitement and of comfort during his disciplines but after five years of searching he said "No extraordinary manifestation of the Spirit in tongues or similar gifts has come." He stated a goal of mutual respect. "We give and claim charity and liberty, that those who have not this experience shall recognize in the Lord those who have it and use it to edification. And that those who have it, shall equally recognize those who have not this special form of divine anointing, but have the Holy Ghost in such other gifts as He is pleased to bestow upon one and another 'severally as He will.' On this scriptural ground of truth, liberty and love, surely we can all meet, and no other is practicable without error, division or fanaticism."[10]

Faced with this "seek not, forbid not" policy, the branches varied widely in their responses to the rising Pentecostals. Testimony to the amazing events at Azusa Street in California came to the Alliance branch in Indianapolis in the form of a visitor on a Sunday afternoon in January of 1907. By Tuesday Grace Harrison had received the Spirit baptism and had spoken in tongues. Others were holding "tarrying meetings" with the visitor and were expecting the blessing. The Alliance branch superintendent, George N. Eldridge, was out of town when the visitor came. When he heard what was going on at Indianapolis, he telegraphed instructions to a deacon there to close the building against such activities. So it happened that the "cream of the Alliance" moved out to become the nucleus of a new pentecostal congregation which was destined to furnish leadership for Pentecostals worldwide.[11]

A. B. Simpson and his Christian and Missionary Alliance were influential in the development of both holiness and pentecostal churches. However the shape of the Alliance fellowship in the United States was not clear for a long time. People advocating a new baptism in the Holy Spirit and expecting the sign of tongue speaking to follow soon preferred the overtly pentecostal fellowships to the Alliance branches. Membership of the pentecostal Assemblies of God nearly tripled in Indiana in the decade between 1926 and 1936. Holiness people denying tongue speaking as any testimony to baptism in the Holy Spirit generally preferred one of the more aggressive non-pentecostal denominations. The Church of the Nazarene in Indiana more than doubled in the decade between 1926 and 1936, reaching a membership of 12,277. All the while Indiana's Christian and Missionary Alliance branches lagged—only 130 members in 1916; 228 members in 1926; 373 members in 1936.

The membership and the world at large were receiving mixed signals whether the Christian and Missionary Alliance really intended to act like a denomination or whether it intended to be an association sponsoring conventions and raising mission funds interdenominationally. Gradually it took denominational shape, deciding to win members and gather them into its own churches at home as it had always done in its missions. The overt reorganization came in 1974. Page eight of *Eternity* magazine for August of that year said, "After 87 years as a paradenominational organization dedicated to missionary activity, the Christian and Missionary Alliance has officially recognized what many people have known for years: the Alliance is a denomination."[12]

In 1990 the Christian and Missionary Alliance reported 271,865 adherents in the United States, a home constituency about equal to the Wesleyans or the Church of God (Anderson). Nearly ten times that number were overseas, speaking a couple of hundred languages in half a hundred nations which had received Alliance missions. Twenty-one of Indiana's ninety-two counties had Alliance congregations totaling 3,085 adherents. Allen with 336, Dearborn with 218, Marion with 472, and Wabash with 208 were the Indiana counties with more than 200.

NOTES

1. Robert L. Niklaus, John S. Sawin, and Samuel J. Stoesz, *All for Jesus: God at Work in the Christian and Missionary Alliance over One*

Hundred Years (Camp Hill, Pa.: Christian Publications, 1986), 18–27.

2. Niklaus, Sawin, and Stoesz, *All for Jesus*, 7–9.

3. Niklaus, Sawin, and Stoesz, *All for Jesus*, 38, 40–43, 82, 90, 100.

4. Niklaus, Sawin, and Stoesz, *All for Jesus*, 53–61, 82, 94.

5. Niklaus, Sawin, and Stoesz, *All for Jesus*, 44, 68–79, 99.

6. Niklaus, Sawin, and Stoesz, *All for Jesus*, 82.

7. Niklaus, Sawin, and Stoesz, *All for Jesus*, 82–83, 187.

8. Alice Reynolds Flower, "How Pentecost Came to Indianapolis" (Assemblies of God Archives, Springfield, Mo., n.d., typescript), 1–2.

9. Niklaus, Sawin, and Stoesz, *All for Jesus*, 102, 124–25.

10. Niklaus, Sawin, and Stoesz, *All for Jesus*, 112–15.

11. Edith L. Blumhofer, *The Assemblies of God: A Chapter in the Story of American Pentecostalism*, 2 vols. (Springfield, Mo.: Gospel Publishing House, 1989), 1:121–23; William W. Menzies, *Anointed to Serve: The Story of the Assemblies of God* (Springfield, Mo.: Gospel Publishing House, 1971), 70–72; *Dictionary of Pentecostal and Charismatic Movements* (Grand Rapids, Mich.: Zondervan, 1988), 163–66; Flower, "How Pentecost Came," 2–3, 7; Niklaus, Sawin, and Stoesz, *All for Jesus*, 111.

12. Niklaus, Sawin, and Stoesz, *All for Jesus*, 171–73, 179–80, 210–11, 226–28, 230.

CHURCH OF THE NAZARENE

In a way the story of the Nazarenes begins with Phineas F. Bresee in California. The group's first service was announced for 6 October 1895 at Red Men's Hall in Los Angeles. The Church of the Nazarene was formed two weeks later with eighty-two charter members. The following spring the congregation moved to Board Tabernacle—also later called "Old Tabernacle" or "Glory Barn"—on Los Angeles Street between Fifth and Sixth.[1]

It was in California that Bresee focused his charismatic ministry and to California that he invited the nation's best-known holiness evangelists to assist him. Persons fired by visits with Bresee in California were early advocates of a new national holiness denomination on the pattern he and his colleagues had developed there. The National Holiness Association was fading as an interdenominational focus for holiness constituents. It had always refused to function as an actual holiness church. The Methodist church had expressed its disapproval of holiness enthusiasts. The hunger of holiness converts for a church of their own plus what he viewed as the failures of Methodism convinced Bresee of the need to develop the Church of the Nazarene into a national denomination.[2]

Bresee was hardly a holiness pioneer. He was born in western New York in 1838 and educated to the extent of a couple of years in the academy at Oneonta. He was converted at a Methodist meeting in 1856 and soon thereafter licensed as an exhorter. The family then moved to Iowa where he moved quickly up the Methodist ministerial ranks to circuit assistant in 1857, preacher in full connection in 1859, and elder in 1861. Iowa conference knew him as a very successful pastor in a series of charges and as presiding elder of the Winterset district. Everywhere his record was success and revival. Then commitment to a venture in Mexican gold mining left him financially ruined and personally embarrassed. In August of 1883 he and his family left Iowa for California.[3]

From the beginning of his ministry Bresee had been a powerful revivalist. In retrospect he said he had experienced sanctification in the winter of 1866–67 but did not at first understand the experience or feature the doctrine in his preaching. In California he accepted an invitation to preach at First Methodist Church of Los Angeles and was promptly named its pastor. This church had in it an influential cluster of laypersons who professed and promoted holiness. With their encouragement Bresee had a confirming experience of his second blessing and developed into a champion of holiness. For a time the combination of his abilities and local excitement over the holiness message brought him support and success—spectacular increases in membership and salary at Los Angeles and Pasadena; presiding eldership of Los Angeles district; doctor of divinity degree; leadership in the Methodist-controlled University of Southern California; reputation in the National Holiness Association; status in the Methodist General Conference.[4]

But in fall of 1892 Southern California conference was presided over by Bishop John H. Vincent, who had no patience with "holiness cranks." Bresee's plan to make Los Angeles district a lively home base for holiness constituents was demolished when he was removed from the office of superintendent. His secondary plan was to ask for inactive "supernumerary relation" with the conference and devote himself to urban ministry in the large Peniel Mission at Los Angeles. There he hoped to make the mission a place of membership for holiness converts not likely to find a comfortable home in mainline denominations. In the end he and his plans were rejected by both the Methodist conference and the Peniel Mission. He was left without credentials and without a place to preach. So there was that new beginning in 1895 at Red Men's Hall and in 1896 at the new Board Tabernacle.[5]

Bresee had become a preacher of uncommon power. Freed from concerns about denominational disapproval, he made the Church of the Nazarene at Los Angeles what he liked to call a "center of fire." Congregations sensing the power of God shouted, sang, clapped, and "got the glory down." There was a church program of such extent and excitement that it overflowed into marching, singing, and preaching in the streets. There was visitation before and after the services including ministry to the poor. Other clusters of holiness people in the area formed congregations and asked Bresee to extend his leadership to them. Pastors and evangelists allied themselves with Bresee and with the Church of the Nazarene. He began issuing the *Nazarene Messenger* as a monthly newsletter in July of 1896. It grew to twelve pages by 1898, became a weekly in 1899, and by July of 1901 was plainly serving as a national paper for Nazarene news.[6]

By 1906 there were twenty-six Nazarene congregations—thirteen in California, five in Washington and Idaho, three in the plains states, and five in Illinois. The key congregations were in large cities. Bresee came to believe that centers of fire in the nation's large cities would soon shed light all over the land. And the Pacific Bible School, later Pasadena College, which Bresee and his friends founded, was also to be a center of fire. Bresee's preaching seemed always to delight his holiness constituents and he maintained a heavy schedule. However he did not choose to dominate his pulpits. Especially for revivals he liked to bring in prominent evangelists and singers from the East and Midwest. They gave his program life and variety. Incidentally, several of them became Nazarenes or at least carriers of good reports about Nazarenes wherever they went.[7]

C. W. Ruth

One of the most significant invitees was C. W. Ruth of Indianapolis. Ruth grew up in a pious family among the Evangelical Association (Albrights) in Pennsylvania. Apprenticed to a printer in Quakertown, he was led to conversion by a fellow worker in 1882 and sanctified soon after. His biographer said: "He became a diligent seeker for the experience of entire sanctification. One Sunday evening while walking down the sidewalk, toward church, conscious that his consecration was complete, Ruth looked heavenward with a prayer, when suddenly and clearly the Holy Spirit came into his being in purifying power. As the youth rushed into church to testify, billows of glory swept over his soul until his joy seemed to be utterly inexpressible and uncontainable."[8]

Ruth got a position as a printer in Indianapolis but really felt called to preach. He soon stopped printing and set out on a fifty-six-year career as an evangelist. Ruth was fascinated with the Bible text. As a young convert he liked to carry both the English and the German testaments in his pockets. He wore a score of Bibles to tatters turning their pages while preaching. As an evangelist his usual method was to reveal some crucial gospel theme in a sequence of passages turned to in the book, each in turn "discovered" with great surprise and delight. The theme he disclosed most often in Scriptures was holiness. His books on that subject included *Entire Sanctification a Second Blessing*; *Bible Readings on the Second Blessing*; *The Pentecostal Experience*; and *Temptations of the Sanctified*.

Ruth's fascination was contagious. His delight became the crowd's delight. He was very popular on the national holiness scene, claiming as early as 1903 to have seen more than 30,000 kneel at the altar. He was a member of the Holiness Christian church which had some strength in Pennsylvania and Indiana but he seemed to be a seeker after larger holiness unity. When leaders convened at Cincinnati in 1897 to form the Holiness Union and Prayer League, Ruth of Indianapolis was there. When the General Holiness Assembly met at First Methodist Church in Chicago in 1901, Ruth of Indianapolis was there.[9]

Bresee, then both pastor at Los Angeles and general superintendent for the Church of the Nazarene, invited Ruth to come to Los Angeles for a revival which he called a "home camp meeting." Ruth described the outcome.

> In the fall of 1901, Dr. Bresee called me as an evangelist to conduct an evangelistic campaign in what was then the "Old Tabernacle." God gave a most sweeping revival, during which time more than three hundred souls bowed at the altar. It was at this time I first met dear

Dr. Bresee; our acquaintance at once ripened into a most sacred and intimate friendship. Before the revival closed, Dr. Bresee, with his official board, waited on me and insisted that I remain indefinitely as associate pastor. After much prayer arrangements were completed, and I at once removed my family from Indianapolis to Los Angeles, and took the relationship of associate pastor with Dr. Bresee, and for one year and a half we walked in daily companionship and fellowship together . . . He appointed me as assistant general superintendent; I was made associate editor of the paper; during this time we built the new church; together we started what is now Pacific Bible College, myself acting as vice-president, as well as teacher of systematic theology and Bible holiness. We planned, and prayed, and wept, and rejoiced together. During that memorable eighteen months, we made perhaps fifteen hundred pastoral calls, conducted more than a hundred funerals, and never had a week without seeing souls saved and sanctified at our altars—more than one thousand having knelt at our altars for pardon and purity during the last twelve months, and the membership increased from six hundred to twelve hundred. I mention these things to indicate in some measure the blessing of the Lord that rested upon the Church of the Nazarene in its early beginnings.[10]

A part of the plan had been that Ruth would take a larger part of the local pastoral work at Los Angeles so Bresee could travel more in the interest of the wider Church of the Nazarene. In fact the roles were rather reversed. Bresee had the exciting California model for a new holiness denomination but Ruth had wider recognition than Bresee among holiness people outside the Far West. After only eighteen months at Los Angeles, Ruth returned to Indianapolis and to the evangelistic work he loved.

Wherever he was after 1901 this Hoosier was a crucial groundbreaker for the Church of the Nazarene. He had uncanny success at translating respect and affection for himself into respect and affection for his vision of the Nazarenes as the rising national holiness church. In 1902 Ruth was invited to conduct a revival at the mission hall of the Washington State Holiness Association in Spokane. At the end of a week they formed a Church of the Nazarene there, pioneer congregation for the Northwest. In 1903 a scouting trip by Ruth produced impressive results: a Nazarene church in Salt Lake City; a revival at North Harvey, Illinois, providing an early Nazarene foothold in Chicago; contacts at the annual camp meeting of the Eastern Illinois Holiness Association at Danville with leading persons who would eventually found Olivet Nazarene College; cultivation of his old friends in the Holiness Christian church of Pennsylvania; establishment

of new friends among the vital Association of Pentecostal Churches with a history dating back to 1887 and substantial strength on the east coast.[11]

Nor was the 1903 trip an isolated effort. Ruth was invited to conduct a revival in Brooklyn in June of 1906 for E. E. Angell of the Association of Pentecostal Churches. On the trip together from Brooklyn to the Association camp meeting at Haverhill, Massachusetts, Ruth so inspired Angell with the possibilities of uniting the holiness people of East and West that the two of them convinced the Association to send a delegation to the next Nazarene General Assembly in Los Angeles. Out of that action came the steps producing the merged Pentecostal Church of the Nazarene in Chicago in 1907.

Even as that substantial union linking East and West was being consummated, plans were afoot to merge next with the Holiness Church of Christ which had very considerable membership in the South. Ruth was already involved in union negotiations with this southern body and had fraternal delegates present from them in 1907 at Chicago. Part of the campaign for the continuing union was a 1908 midwinter revival to be led by Ruth at Texas Holiness University. He gave them what one called "the cleanest, closest, most thorough Bible preaching that many of us ever heard." When Bresee followed as a preacher a few months later, the college president and the whole faculty came forward to be among the 103 charter members of that pioneer Church of the Nazarene in Texas. Holiness bands that supported the college were enlisted as well.[12]

Merger with the southerners of the Holiness Church of Christ in 1908 gave the Nazarenes immediate national visibility—228 churches; 10,414 members; 7,780 enrolled in Sunday schools; five institutions of higher learning; three periodicals; and mission work in five foreign lands. More mergers and more growth by evangelism followed. Within three years of the union they doubled their national membership and nearly tripled their Sunday school enrollment.[13]

Slow Beginnings in Indiana

At first Nazarene activity in the West, East, and South seemed to bracket Indiana with little effect. None of the new denomination's schools, periodicals, or headquarters located in the state. There was some influence from the center of fire in Chicago. When Chicago Central district was formed in 1905, independent holiness congregations in the Midwest had more convenient access to the new denomination. A physician named M. F. Gerrish was among the leaders of such a congregation at Seymour beginning about 1900. They were a Holiness Christian church from 1902 to 1906 but withdrew from that communion to become Nazarenes in 1907. Blacksmith A. T. Harris went from Chicago in 1906 to form a Nazarene mission at Hammond. Chicago Central district superintendent T. H. Agnew organized a congregation at Terre Haute.[14]

Indianapolis was viewed as an essential place. In 1906 Bresee spoke of the state capital as a likely new center of fire. The moderator of Indianapolis Presbytery changed from Presbyterian to Nazarene but moved away at once to a pastorate in Pasadena. Superintendent Agnew told the district assembly: "Indianapolis has had much work on the line of holiness—much good work—and much undenominational and interdenominational and some no 'national' at all, until it is high time there was something doing in the line of good, solid, substantial, organized organic holiness work. Amen." Opportunity came in the form of an Indianapolis organization called the Young Men's Holiness League which was seeking to do something more to support and care for converts won in their evangelistic campaigns. Evangelist L. Milton Williams convinced them they should organize themselves into a church. Nazarene superintendent Agnew did the organizing. C. W. Ruth agreed to serve temporarily as their minister and was able to show Bresee this new Nazarene work at Indianapolis when Bresee visited in 1908. But when J. W. Short began his ministry at First Church of the Nazarene in Seymour in 1910, the only other Nazarene churches in Indiana were those at Terre Haute, Indianapolis, and Hammond. For the religious census of 1916 only 141 Nazarenes were reported for the whole state.[15]

Impact of Nazarene Evangelists

Nevertheless Indiana was in position to share fully in the explosive Nazarene growth just ahead. Indiana was in the midwestern belt of heaviest Methodist population. Many Hoosier Methodists had been sympathetic for a long time to holiness issues and methods; the National Holiness Association had shifted the center of its attention to the Midwest by the turn of the century. County holiness associations and independent holiness missions were candidates for organization as new Nazarene congregations. Methodists and others were restive during the years of the fundamentalist controversies in the major denominations, many of them ready to rally to the theological conservatism of the Nazarenes. Rural Hoosiers migrating to the cities were likely to be more attracted to the folksy warmth and enthusiasm of the Nazarenes than

to the formalism of mainline urban churches. Nazarene leaders multiplied.[16]

John W. Wines was a considerable gift of Indiana to the Church of the Nazarene. Reared in a lively family in east central Indiana in the 1860s and 1870s, he felt a variety of religious influences. There was a primitive Sunday school at Windfall, Indiana.

> Anyone might suggest a chapter and it was read and considered. There were not many who could interpret much of it. They didn't care to try. All believed every word of it. There was no higher criticism on those days, no monkey business, i.e. evolution. The Word was honored, believed, respected and treated decently. There were faint spurts of antinomianism and arminianism but no controversy. The Word of God was believed and honored. While it was a primitive way of doing things, I am sure God was not displeased with this awkward way of serving Him, for I am sure He knew that they were doing their best.[17]

He recorded his unfavorable impression of a Hicksite meeting and his favorable impression of an Orthodox Friends Sunday school at Richmond. At Tipton he attended the Presbyterian Sunday school and heard the once-a-month preaching of Isaac Monfort who came out from Cincinnati. A special meeting was held at the Presbyterian church.

> I was so wrought upon that I joined the church, and was more determined than ever to be good. I had no change of heart, and simply knew nothing of heartfelt experience. I should have been taken through and landed on the glory side then. I did go and ask John Van Sickle to forgive me for giving him that awful licking the other day. That didn't do any good, for John just doubled up his fists and declared I couldn't do it again. Isaac Monfort baptized me by sprinkling, and when I get to heaven and see him, I shall have to say that baptism satisfied me all the days of my life.[18]

When Wines finished common school, a neighbor named George Carlisle took the initiative to offer him an unsecured loan to attend Central Normal College at Danville, Indiana, to become a teacher. While teaching in Shelby County he met and married Martha A. Addison whom he called "the sweetest, prettiest, smartest little Quaker maiden that ever did exist" and "one of the gamest, most indefatigable, pugnacious warriors for the cause and against the Devil that man ever had to work with."[19]

She seemed always a few steps ahead. They taught school together for nine years. Mattie got converted. So did he.

I couldn't stand it. The burden got heavier and heavier. I went to the mourners' bench. I confessed and cried for mercy, but didn't get through. I made the murderer [a revival preacher who murdered the English language] go home with me. As soon as we got in the house I called for prayers. I lay on my face, side and back, prayed and cried. The Devil had me by the hair of the head and was dragging me into hell; he had me right on the edge of the pit. I smelled the sulphur; I felt the flames. He set his teeth and was fixing his muscles so that with one mighty effort he could fling me into the awful abyss. Just at that moment a nail-pierced hand took him by the throat and threw him out of my sight. I can hear his disappointed shrieks and chattering teeth yet as he went back to his place. Jesus then came and walked around on the outside and inside of me for awhile. He blew with His own breath where the kindling wood had been laid. It sprang up into a flame, it grew in volume and strength until it burned up my sins and carnality. And praise God, today the fire still burns.[20]

She got sanctified. So did he.

When wife and I were teaching school at Sulphur Hill, Indiana, sometimes called Geneva, while watering my horse at the town spring, God for Jesus' sake sanctified me wholly, and unloaded millions of tons of grace upon me and gave me the blessing, and a blessing that I shall never get away from . . . When I was sanctified, I made the consecration by bringing all the good that I had and said, "Take it, it is all yours. Friends, time and earthly store, all I know and all I don't know." He did and sanctified me for Jesus' sake. When I was converted my committed sins were forgiven and blotted out. When I was sanctified, the inbred sin, Psalm 51:5, was taken out. The "old man" was crucified and "killed dead."[21]

John Wines told Mattie he was compelled to preach the gospel. She said "So am I." They were on the United Brethren membership rolls following his conversion but when they moved to Geneva, Indiana, they joined the Methodist church. In the Methodist ranks he moved up quickly from exhorter to local preacher to conference member on trial to deacon to elder. They preached together on Methodist circuits for sixteen years. Evidently the Methodists recognized Mattie's usefulness as a preacher but gave her little status. "Mrs. Wines preached almost as much as I did on the circuit during the year. She received four dollars and fifty cents in cold cash for her ministry." John Wines gave clear testimony of Mattie's popular acceptance in commenting on a later pastorate. "Mrs. Wines served them Sunday about, I one Sunday and she the next. Her offerings were more than mine."[22]

John and Mattie Wines were effective Methodists, especially in revivals on the rural circuits. Their rapport with the people was good and their list of converts long. "I always did, and do yet, believe the Bible from lid to lid," said John, "from the standing still of the sun and the stomach disturbance of Jonah in the whale, to bobbed haired Samson, the Immaculate Conception, the Virgin Birth of Jesus, the Feeding of the Five Thousand, the Raising of Lazarus, the conversion of Saul of Tarsus, the sanctification of the one hundred and twenty on the day of Pentecost." Their holiness enthusiasm was tolerated. "We had no trouble in the M. E. Church and always preached holiness. I was expostulated with by one of my presiding elders and urged not to preach it. I told him the M. E. Church made me promise to preach it before they would admit me in the church, and now you urge me not to preach it. I added, the only difference I can see between us is this. I meant what I said, and you didn't mean what you required me to say."[23]

But they were becoming uncomfortable. John said: "Some three hundred and fifty souls were at the altar the last year we served Whiteland. About all of them were sanctified. I was called back three years afterward for a funeral. Only a few claimed full salvation. We felt that we must try to find a church home where our hard earned victories would be conserved." When the Methodist conference met at Washington, Indiana, in September of 1909, John M. Wines turned in his credentials to be canceled. Bishop McDowell marked them "honorably dismissed at his own request" and returned them. By then Wines was already supply pastor for First Church of the Nazarene in Indianapolis.[24]

John was personally received as an elder in the Nazarenes by Phineas Bresee in 1909; Mattie was ordained an elder by Chicago Central district in 1911. The original constitution of the Church of the Nazarene had specifically recognized the right of women to preach. John and Mattie Wines were called to a series of significant pulpits in Indiana, Illinois, and Ohio. For two years he was superintendent of the Chicago Central district when it included half of Illinois, all of Indiana, and all of Michigan. Not even the Ladies Aid could stand against them. John said: "We always opposed church suppers, festivals and all the commercialism in the churches . . . I never announced a Ladies' Aid Society meeting in my life, nor took a cent of money from them, nor have I ever received anything for my ministerial work except that which has been given me as a free will offering." This position led to confrontations with the devil in the form of organized church women. Said Wines, "They wanted to exist."[25]

When J. W. Short was a student at Asbury College at Wilmore, Kentucky, he asked a prominent visitor to campus in which church a young clergyman should invest his life's work. The answer was "Join the Church of the Nazarene and grow up with it, for it is the coming holiness church of the world." So Short went to Chicago to hear Bresee and concluded at once that the Nazarenes were to be his people. He was ordained to the ministerial rank of elder by Bresee in October of 1910. His wife Frances was the only child of John and Mattie Wines, also recent recruits to Nazarene ministry.

Frances became a Nazarene elder also; the Shorts were a ministerial team. "Let's get the glory down" was James Short's call to praise and prayer. He was an emotional preacher, given to telling his listeners about heaven with tears rolling down his cheeks. But he was also a powerfully practical administrator. When he became its superintendent in 1920, Indiana district had 52 churches and 2,512 members. When he left the district in 1926 it had nearly doubled to 102 churches and 5,008 members. By the time he returned as superintendent of Indianapolis district in 1948 there were about 250 Nazarene churches in the state with about 25,000 members. Indianapolis, with 17 churches, had become an important Nazarene center.[26]

E. O. Chalfant was a model of aggressive Nazarene expansion. He was born on a farm nine miles southwest of Muncie on 22 March 1882. Both his parents were sanctified on the same day in the year he was four so his home was "a scene of glory." He said his family was "radical" United Brethren. He was converted during his first year at Huntington College. Back at his home church three years later he vowed he would go to the church building and stay there until God sanctified his soul. "I kept right on pressing my claim. On the third day about six o'clock in the evening, God opened all the windows of heaven and sent down glory and peace and joy and love; something hit me on the top of the head and went to the soles of my feet like an electric thrill. I knew that the old man of sin was crucified, for I had the witness that I was sanctified wholly. I was completely dead to this world and was fully alive to God. That was September 15, 1902."[27]

The call to preach followed. "God not only called me to preach," Chalfant said, "but he called me to preach old-fashioned, second-blessing, radical, dying-out heart holiness." From 1903 to 1908 he was doing evangelistic campaigns, mostly in Indiana towns—Nashville, Mount Zion, Wilkinson, Moreland, New Castle, Greenfield, Jamestown, Andersonville, Morristown, Straughn. These meetings were loud and provocative.[28]

One of Chalfant's associates was the "Hoosier Evangelist" John T. Hatfield, former schoolmate of the "Hoosier Poet" James Whitcomb Riley. Hatfield's specialty was the use of noise to break up local lethargy and excess decorum. A colleague said "John Hatfield can preach longer and louder, and keep at it longer, and shout more, and jump higher, and get more people to the altar, and pray longer and harder, than any man that walks on the ground . . . He seems never to tire or wear out, but is always full of juice and freshness and fire and glory . . . He is one of the greatest puzzles to the devil that is now living; the devil never knows what he is going to do next; he is about as liable to preach in one end of the church as the other—no strings on that man!"[29]

Another associate was the Quaker evangelist Joe Williamson. At Andersonville the team "hit about every sin in that community." Chalfant said: "The next morning we found our new tent flat on the ground. We counted forty holes cut in the top, and forty holes in the sides. The vandals had also cut the canvas seats and the ropes from the stakes and brail poles, and broken the gasoline torches. To make the situation worse, there had been a torrential rain during the night." Chalfant's father had the tent fixed and they were soon going again.[30]

All the while Chalfant seemed to be seeking to place his independent holiness ministry in a more stable context. When he attended a Bible conference at Winona Lake to hear Billy Sunday, J. Wilbur Chapman, and Homer Rodeheaver, he saw that his own group "did not have a corner on God." When he went to a large holiness camp meeting with preachers of national reputation, he "saw a sane and sensible crowd that had great power." Most important of all "I chanced to read a front-page article in a prohibition paper about Doctor Bresee and the work he was doing in Los Angeles. I remember the article told of the great glory in this center. For the first time in my life I realized that there was a better way of organized holiness, and I longed to know more about Dr. Bresee's crowd."[31]

Moved by these broadening experiences, he told his parents he needed more education. On 20 October 1908 the family was able to contract to sell $1,000 worth of gravel to builders of a new turnpike. On 26 October Chalfant arrived at Kingswood College in Kentucky where he stayed until he "had earned two degrees." The atmosphere at this holiness college was very hospitable to Nazarene influence. Said President J. W. Hughes, "Many people are talking about the Nazarene church's being the coming church. It is not the 'coming church.' It is already here." Chalfant went to Chicago in October of 1913 to attend the annual meeting of the National Holiness Association and to talk with Bresee. He said "I could not get away from the conviction that the Lord wanted me to identify myself with Dr. Bresee's crowd. Thus it was in 1916 that I joined the Church of the Nazarene in Muncie, Indiana, and was ordained to preach by Dr. R. T. Williams, September 1, 1916, at Anderson, Indiana."[32]

Muncie was Chalfant's first pastorate. There he illustrated what was to be the vigorous style of his own ministry and of the rising Nazarene denomination in the Midwest. He and his people simply called on everybody in city-wide canvasses in 1916, 1917, and 1918. Before one fall revival they canvassed 12,000 homes. They budgeted substantial sums for advertising in both local newspapers. They conducted "prolonged tent campaigns" in those three years resulting in two new Nazarene churches in Muncie. In addition they organized a new church at Gaston and assisted in evangelistic campaigns at New Castle, Anderson, and Parker City. They brought in missionary speakers and led the district in giving for foreign missions. They raised $2,500 for Olivet Nazarene College. All the activity tripled the membership at Muncie First Church.[33]

In 1919 Chalfant was called to Indianapolis to the West Side Church of the Nazarene and so was loosed upon the state capital. West Side congregation had only a basement church; with concentrated effort they dedicated the completed structure in April of 1920. Then Pastor E. O. Chalfant and District Superintendent J. W. Short collaborated in a plan "to give the gospel to the entire city of Indianapolis." Besides the advertising and visiting, this involved buying a tent and equipment for $1,000 and then continuing to buy additional tents and multiplying tent meetings as far as money was available. "The churches proceeded to give hilariously. Out of those tent meetings came a number of Nazarene churches throughout Indianapolis and the vicinity. We had a total of twenty-one meetings at a total cost of ten thousand dollars, but we had literally thousands of souls at the altar."[34]

In 1922 the Hoosier E. O. Chalfant left Indiana to become superintendent of the Chicago Central district, then an area including Illinois and Wisconsin. His immediate goal for that district was 100 new Nazarene churches. Before his retirement he had organized 260. He praised the dedication of his ecclesiastical troops. "I have been superintendent on this district long enough to know that our preachers and their families will literally die for our cause. I see more than one spend his last nickel of insurance and then wear secondhand clothes to plant our church, and this has not been done only by the small places but by many in the larger places. I have seen some of our leaders die penniless. We should do everything we can to take care of these men and women who are dying for our cause."[35]

Chalfant intended to be no less dedicated. "If the Lord would let me choose my lot," he said, "I would choose to die on the firing line and not behind it. A number of years ago I asked Dr. R. T. Williams how he could stand the burdens of his position. He replied, 'I am not standing it; I am dying by inches.' And that is just what he did. I must do no less than that."[36] In his autobiography entitled *Forty Years on the Firing Line* Chalfant included an evangelistic exhortation.

> Have revivals—Evangelize every way, through Sunday schools, youth services, our colleges, visitation, tracts, radio, personal work, good advertising, holiness conventions, long-siege revivals, home mission campaigns, old-fashioned altar services. Here are the revival essentials: 1. Humbling ourselves before God. 2. Making adjustments with one another. 3. Complete separation from worldliness. 4. Soul travail in prayer. 5. Home visitation and personal work. 6. Attractive advertising. 7. Inspiring, uplifting songs. 8. Earnest, rugged holiness preaching. 9. Old-fashioned altar services. 10. Spiritual life and freedom.[37]

Chalfant's raucous Hoosier colleague John T. Hatfield was invited by Bresee to be a guest evangelist in California. He too became a Nazarene. Chalfant's Hoosier contemporary Charles A. Gibson moved from the Holiness Christian church to the Nazarene ministry in 1913. Beginning in 1920 Gibson invested more than thirty-five years of his life as superintendent for districts, a specialist at establishing Nazarene churches in vacant storefront buildings.[38]

Clarence and Bertha Talbert were a more humble husband-wife team of Nazarenes in Indiana. Clarence was a hired man and Bertha had been a hired girl; they had managed to acquire a few farm animals and to rent a small acreage to support themselves and their two daughters. Clarence became concerned about the irreligious condition of his life. His wife said Clarence prayed and "told the Lord to send something on him that would bring him back into the fold again . . . In three weeks time he had a nervous breakdown." Following his illness and his conversion he kept feeling a personal calling to preach but his United Brethren counselors thought he would need a dozen years of training, a thing manifestly impossible.[39]

Bertha said she did not know that she could be saved until she "heard holiness preached by some Spirit-filled preachers" when she was twenty-seven.

I really settled the question in my kitchen at home but that night February 9th, 1916 I went to the altar and prayed until I knew every sin was covered by the blood. They were having day meetings which the people in those days had time to attend. I was a candidate for holiness and as the preacher preached I felt again the message was for me. I went to the altar and put everything on the altar but failed to accept, but for two months I kept telling the Lord I wouldn't give up until I received the blessing. Two months later in the Stringtown Church of the Nazarene, the witness came and for three days I was walking in the clouds. The Dear Lord knew what I was going to need throughout my future life.[40]

Precarious plans were made that Clarence would go away to Union Bible Seminary at Westfield, Indiana, leaving her with the two daughters and the livestock on the rented five acres where they were established. Bertha said: "On Monday morning at 4:30 the Lord awakened me and told me he wanted me to go to Westfield also. I didn't question his wisdom but quickly said I would go." And after arriving at Westfield she felt further guidance. "As usual the superintendent of the school gave an opening address and then had slips passed to each one there on which they were supposed to write full senior, full junior or miscellaneous course. Just like a clap of thunder out of a blue sky the Lord told me to write full junior course which I did, starting to school the next morning, leaving my house to be put in order between class sessions."[41]

They spent four semesters in Union Bible Seminary. It was operated by a small band of holiness Quakers which had no churches to offer the Talberts. Wesleyans offered them churches but they "didn't feel clear to accept." Bertha said: "In April of 1923 some of the members of the Fortville Church of the Nazarene came to our home and intreated us to accept a church. We were not members of a Nazarene church at that time but after we accepted a church Rev. Charles Carmony who was a dear friend of ours and pastor of the Nazarene church in Morristown insisted we join his church so he could give us local license. I don't know if this was the proper way or not but anyway we were heartily accepted into our Assembly which convened in Old Indianapolis First Church in the fall." And she admitted: "When we took our first pastorate we weren't told anything about what we were supposed to do so we just started preaching and teaching, and when one good member of the Fortville Church mentioned budget, we didn't even know what she meant."[42]

Both Clarence and Bertha Talbert were considered qualified for a ministry which emphasized the conduct of revival meetings. They served a series of small Indiana churches well designed to illustrate the leaner dimensions of pastoral life. Recognizing the leanness, they took care to interpret each pastorate in terms of occasional victories and small progress. In her old age Bertha said: "I did not retire when my husband did. I felt for my own future needs I should work for Social Security which I did after my seventieth birthday. I have found that the small amount I have earned has been just the amount needed to keep me out of financial stress. I believe the Lord knew I had gone through enough of that."[43]

Nazarenes were not despisers of church government. Having learned the church procedures, Clarence and Bertha Talbert became lovers of good order. Bertha said: "Our business was carried on according to the Manual and was open to scrutiny."[44] The *Manual* embodied much of Methodist doctrine and organization but with somewhat more local autonomy and with special emphasis on evangelism and personal morality. The book included regular orders for reception of members, baptism, the Lord's Supper, matrimony, and burial of the dead. The Lord's Supper and the love feast were held monthly, alternating at biweekly intervals.[45]

Music of Haldor Lillenas

Nazarenes were singers and a Hoosier pastor gave great impetus to the church's musical ministry. Haldor Lillenas was a child when his family emigrated from Norway to the American West. As a young man he joined the lately formed Church of the Nazarene and prepared himself for the ministry at its newly founded Deets Pacific Bible College (later Pasadena College). In 1933 First Nazarene Church of Indianapolis called him from California to be its pastor. Lillenas called Indianapolis "our most successful pastorate." During his three years of leadership the congregation built a new church, bought a new parsonage, and increased its membership from 150 to 260.[46]

But what Lillenas really liked to do was write songs and compile songbooks. He had already published four paperback songbooks before coming to Indiana—*Special Sacred Songs, New Sacred Songs, Strains of Love, Special Sacred Songs No. 2.* These contained few standard hymns but many songs for solo or small ensemble use. More than half were by Lillenas himself; for the others he had secured permission or purchased copyright. He had time to write only a few songs in the Indianapolis pastorate. "It was with most earnest prayer that I sought guidance from my Heavenly Father with regard to my future work," he said. "I greatly loved the pastoral work and I became enamored also with gospel song writing."[47]

In 1925 he made the break. He resigned the pastorate. He and five others organized the Lillenas Publishing Company. From this Indianapolis company came a flurry of songbooks increasingly adapted for congregational singing—*Songs of Full Salvation, New Songs of the Old Faith, New Songs of the Old Faith No. 2, Great Gospel Songs.* These were successful because they circulated about 700,000 copies. They were also successful because they kept increasing the number of copyrights Lillenas held. In 1930 Lillenas Publishing Company was purchased to be operated as a wholly owned subsidiary of the Nazarene Publishing House at Kansas City, Missouri. Included in the purchase were 1,535 song copyrights and a contract for the services of Haldor Lillenas at Kansas City as manager of a newly organized Music Department. In the next forty years Lillenas Publishing Company issued 443 books. The parent Nazarene Publishing House assembled a collection of music copyrights unequalled by any other evangelical music publisher. The musical publications sold widely in the Church of the Nazarene but had phenomenal circulation as well through independent dealers to other churches.[48]

Rapid Growth and Maturity

The Church of the Nazarene, which had more than 10,000 members in 1910 and almost 100,000 members in 1930, reported 888,123 adherents (563,728 communicant members) in the United States alone in 1990. Beyond the American homeland was a worldwide Nazarene constituency at least half that large. There were ten Nazarene colleges and seminaries in the United States and thirty-six abroad.[49]

Denominational self-consciousness developed early among Nazarenes and increased. Central offices serving denominational work at home and abroad were in Kansas City, Missouri. So was a very large publishing plant. Nazarene women and youth formed effective organizations. Fundamental legislative and doctrinal authority was lodged in a quadrennial general assembly of elected ministerial and lay delegates. General Assembly also named a varying number of general superintendents and a general board to which much continuing central administration was committed. But there were scores of district assemblies led by district superintendents elected by delegates from local churches. Each local church called its own pastor, subject to the approval of its district superintendent.[50]

There came to be considerable variety among the congregations in such traditional holiness concerns as plainness of dress, wearing of jewelry, use of cosmetics, and level of participation in "worldly" amusements. In spite of frequent agitation, the national church did not choose to make, enforce, or change rules about such things detail by detail. It preferred to lift up positive models for faith and work. It offered more general guides for life style—godly walk and vital piety, avoidance of evil, Christian simplicity and modesty.[51]

Some observers of this profile of rapid growth, organization, and acculturation spoke of the swift transition of the Nazarenes from sect to church. According to this paradigm the poor, pietistic, protesting, perfectionist, unstructured sect of cultural outsiders became in a generation a middle class, socially respectable, highly bureaucratized church of cultural insiders. "The rise and fall of the Church of the Nazarene" John Matthews called it in a bitter pamphlet in 1920.[52]

In his widely circulated *Small Sects in America*, Elmer T. Clark made heavy use of a simplified sect-to-church typology, saying: "All denominations began as sects, and the evolution of a sect into a church has followed a routine." Then he followed the example of Merrill Gaddis in applying the pattern of sect-to-church transition with particular force to the Nazarenes. In 1937 he said the Nazarenes had already begun to ape the worst institutional traits of the Methodists. They were losing "the freedom, spontaneity, and democracy so essential to the perfectionist spirit." They were "in danger of drifting away from vital and into merely formal, verbal, or dogmatic perfectionism." Sydney E. Ahlstrom gave the Church of the Nazarene a scant two pages in his *Religious History of the American People* published in 1972. Yet he retained an imagery of the Nazarenes as "a remarkable instance of a nearly full sectarian cycle."[53]

Nazarene historians took some pains to correct such a cyclical understanding. Instead of seeing the Nazarenes as an instance of rapidly changing identity, they saw the Nazarenes as an instance of remarkable consistency. They said this body was never a sect as the term was commonly understood. This unabashed denomination began as a union, a veritable ecumenical union, among particular advocates of holiness of heart and life. That goal remained unchanged. Holiness was linked to both evangelism and entire sanctification through the whole of Nazarene history. Revivals remained a regular part of local church life. A personal testimony to entire sanctification was expected of ministers, faculty members, and church officers. It was urged for everyone.[54] One Nazarene historian said:

The pattern for experiencing entire sanctification was simple, although it might be stated in various ways. Christians were urged to acknowledge their need of a deeper work of grace and to respond to its offer by coming to the altar at the front of the sanctuary for prayer. They were taught to consecrate their persons, talents, possessions, and relationships to God with "no strings attached." They were instructed to ask specifically for the sanctifying fullness of the Holy Spirit. A final step was appropriating faith, which might be presented either as a determined grasp of God's promise based on one's conviction of the completeness of his consecration, or as a spontaneous reaction at the end of a process of "dying out." Whatever the conception of faith, it was to be sealed by a "witness of the Spirit," an inner assurance or rest that God had responded to the prayers offered by the impartation of His Spirit's fullness.[55]

Only California with 92,273 and Ohio with 90,659 had more Nazarene adherents than Indiana in 1990. With 68,131 adherents the Church of the Nazarene was by far the largest of the state's holiness churches.

NOTES

1. Timothy L. Smith, *Called unto Holiness. The Story of the Nazarenes: the Formative Years* (Kansas City, Mo.: Nazarene Publishing House, 1962), 110–12; C. T. Corbett, *Our Pioneer Nazarenes* (Kansas City, Mo.: Nazarene Publishing House, 1958), 17–19; E. A. Girvin, *Phineas F. Bresee: A Prince of Israel* (Kansas City, Mo.: Pentecostal Nazarene Publishing House, 1916), 101–10.

2. Smith, *Called*, 123–26.

3. Smith, *Called*, 91–95.

4. Smith, *Called*, 96–103.

5. Corbett, *Our Pioneer Nazarenes*, 15–16; Smith, *Called*, 103–9.

6. Smith, *Called*, 118–22.

7. Charles E. Jones, *Perfectionist Persuasion: The Holiness Movement and American Methodism 1867–1936* (Metuchen, N.J.: Scarecrow Press, 1974), 111–12; Smith, *Called*, 120, 130–31, 136–40, 212.

8. Corbett, *Our Pioneer Nazarenes*, 28.

9. Christian Wismer Ruth, *Entire Sanctification a Second Blessing, Together with Life Sketch, Bible Readings and Sermon Outlines* (Chicago: Christian Witness Co., 1903), 9, 13; Corbett, *Our Pioneer Nazarenes*, 28–31; Jones, *Perfectionist*, 91–104; Smith, *Called*, 129.

10. Corbett, *Our Pioneer Nazarenes*, 26–27.

11. Smith, *Called*, 129–30, 141–42. "Pentecostal" was a name commonly applied to themselves by holiness groups during the nineteenth century and the earliest years of the twentieth century. But when the term came to be especially associated with tongue-speaking fellowships, it was systematically eliminated from the names of the holiness churches and their institutions.

12. Smith, *Called*, 77, 206–18; Corbett, *Our Pioneer Nazarenes*, 31.

13. W. T. Purkizer, *Called unto Holiness: The Second Twenty-five Years, 1933–58* (Kansas City, Mo.: Nazarene Publishing House, 1983), 29.

14. *Fifty Years—and Beyond. A History of the Chicago Central District, Church of the Nazarene*, comp. Mark R. Moore (Kankakee, Ill.: Chicago Central District, Church of the Nazarene, 1954), 14.

15. Interview with James Wiley Short, Indianapolis *Star*, 15 November 1948, p. 16; Smith, *Called*, 150, 219, 224, 236; *Fifty Years—and Beyond*, 90.

16. Smith, *Called*, 35, 235, 237–38, 298–316; Jones, *Perfectionist*, 79–82.

17. John M. Wines, *Hoosier Happenings* (Kansas City, Mo.: Nazarene Publishing House, 1926), 34–35.

18. Wines, *Hoosier Happenings*, 52–53.

19. Wines, *Hoosier Happenings*, 53–54, 69.

20. Wines, *Hoosier Happenings*, 82–83.

21. Wines, *Hoosier Happenings*, 54–55.

22. Wines, *Hoosier Happenings*, 58–61, 65, 71.

23. Wines, *Hoosier Happenings*, 40, 71–72.

24. Wines, *Hoosier Happenings*, 69–71.

25. *Fifty Years—and Beyond*, 91, 147; Wines, *Hoosier Happenings*, 66–73, 76.

26. Wines, *Hoosier Happenings*, 54; Corbett, *Our Pioneer Nazarenes*, 67–72; Interview with James Wiley Short, Indianapolis *Star*, 15 November 1948, p. 16.

27. Everette Otis Chalfant, *Forty Years on the Firing Line* (Kansas City, Mo.: Beacon Hill Press, 1951), 7–15, 21; Purkiser, *Called*, 51–52.

28. Chalfant, *Forty Years*, 22.

29. John Thomas Hatfield, *Thirty-three Years a Live Wire: Life of John T. Hatfield, the "Hoosier Evangelist"* (Cincinnati, Ohio: God's Revivalist Office, 1913), iv, 19–20; Chalfant, *Forty Years*, 25–30.

30. Chalfant, *Forty Years*, 29.

31. Chalfant, *Forty Years*, 30–32.

32. Chalfant, *Forty Years*, 3, 32.

33. Chalfant, *Forty Years*, 35–37.

34. Chalfant, *Forty Years*, 37–39.

35. Chalfant, *Forty Years*, 42, 66; Purkiser, *Called*, 51–52.

36. Chalfant, *Forty Years*, 78–79.

37. Chalfant, *Forty Years*, 67.

38. Smith, *Called*, 132; Jones, *Perfectionist*, 113; Purkiser, *Called*, 52–53; Corbett, *Our Pioneer Nazarenes*, 91–96.

39. Bertha Belle Talbert, *Our Labors of Love* (N.p., 1966?), 9.

40. Talbert, *Our Labors*, 10.

41. Talbert, *Our Labors*, 12–13.

42. Talbert, *Our Labors*, 15, 22.

43. Talbert, *Our Labors*, 36–37.

44. Talbert, *Our Labors*, 36.

45. Frank S. Mead, *Handbook of Denominations in the United States*, 9th ed. (Nashville, Tenn.: Abingdon Press, 1990), 90–91; Smith, *Called*, 134, 216–17.

46. Haldor Lillenas, *Down Melody Lane: An Autobiography* (Kansas City, Mo.: Beacon Hill Press, 1953), 40–41; Smith, *Called*, 139–40.

47. Lillenas, *Down Melody Lane*, 41.

48. Eleanor Whitsett, *A History of the Lillenas Publishing Company and Its Relationship to the Music of the Church of the Nazarene* (Kansas City, Mo.: Lillenas Publishing Company, 1972), 5–9; Lillenas, *Down Melody Lane*, 41–43; Purkiser, *Called*, 244.

49. Purkiser, *Called*, 313; Mead, *Handbook* (1990), 90–91.

50. Edwin Charles Jones, *A Guide to the Study of the Holiness Movement* (Metuchen, N.J.: Scarecrow Press, 1974), 135; Smith, *Called*, 270–71.

51. Jones, *Perfectionist*, 177; Smith, *Called*, 293–97; Purkiser, *Called*, 61–66.

52. Smith, *Called*, 290–91.

53. Elmer T. Clark, *The Small Sects in America*, rev. ed. (Nashville, Tenn.: Abingdon Press, 1965), 16, 75–76. The content of this work was substantially the same in other editions issued in 1937 and 1949. Merrill E. Gaddis, "Christian Perfectionism in America" (Ph.D. diss., University of Chicago, 1929, 589 p.); Sydney E. Ahlstrom, *A Religious History of the American People* (New Haven, Conn.: Yale University Press, 1972), 818–19.

54. Smith, *Called*, 266–71, 321; Purkiser, *Called*, 9–11, 57–69; Mead, *Handbook* (1990), 90–91.

55. Purkiser, *Called*, 66–67.

ASSEMBLIES OF GOD

The pentecostal fellowships finding their organizational beginnings in America after 1900 quickly grew to become the largest Protestant church family in the world. According to David Barrett's *World Christian Encyclopedia* issued in 1982, world population included about 30 million Methodists, 40 million Presbyterians, 43 million Lutherans, 48 million Baptists, 50 million Anglicans, and 51 million Pentecostals. That did not count as Pentecostals some 10 million Charismatics, most of whom shared the pentecostal search for baptism of the Holy Spirit and the confirming evidence of speaking in tongues. The ecumenical scholar Walter J. Hollenweger predicted in 1984 that the world population of Pentecostals of all types combined, members of classical denominations plus Charismatics plus the burgeoning indigenous non-whites, would grow to 250 million by the year 2000. Thus Christianity as a whole would no longer be "a predominantly white man's religion."[1]

Largest of the "classical" pentecostal fellowships by the 1980s was the Assemblies of God with a constituency of about 18 million worldwide. Its organizational beginnings had seemed precarious. Most early Pentecostals abhorred denominations. They were busy casting off what they considered to be the dead forms of the organized churches in order to restore the Spirit-filled church of the New Testament. They viewed the current renewal of tongue speaking, healing, and spiritual gifts within their own religious movement as clear evidence that the Lord was about to return to judge and rule the world.[2]

A leading student of Assemblies of God history said of the movement's pioneers:

> They firmly believed that their experience was a divine encounter. Pentecostalism made religion alive and meaningful to a popular constituency both uninterested in the theological issues that racked most contemporary denominations and uninspired by respectable, complacent, middle-class Protestantism. It infused the present with cosmic significance, offered tangible solutions for every pressing problem, provided a community of likeminded believers, and introduced meaning, certainty, and mission into even the most humble existence. It offered assurance that true believers could circumvent the taint of historical process and rediscover the pure primeval fountain of perfect Christian experience, a message of restoration, and an apocalyptic vision.[3]

Since they did not expect to be in this world very long, early Pentecostals were reluctant to take part in traditional earthly organizations. Assured by their experiences that their lives were now pleasing God, they were intolerant of variant opinions and of any account of divine intention which differed from their own. So they were divisive and suspicious of any form of human organizational control.[4]

Yet they were drawn together. Their personal pentecostal experiences were so similar that they naturally joined in singing, praising, and speaking in tongues. They attended many of the same revivals led by the same evangelists. They supported the same magazines and read the same books. They had the same missionary zeal to evangelize the world before the Lord's return. Some leaders in the Church of God in Christ advocated a pentecostal convention to "preserve the work." This group had over 360 ministers of whom at least 84 were women. Their members were distributed over twenty states and five foreign countries but were typically white Pentecostals concentrated in Texas and the Southwest.[5] The call to a convention appeared several times in their periodical named *Word and Witness*.

First—We come together that we may get a better understanding of what God would have us teach, that we may do away with so many divisions, both in doctrines and in the various names under which our Pentecostal people are working and incorporating. Let us all come together as in Acts 15, to study the Word, and pray with and for each other—unity our chief aim.

Second—Again we come together that we [may] know how to conserve the work, that we may all build up and not tear down, both in home and foreign lands.

Third—We come together for another reason, that we may get a better understanding of the needs of each foreign field and may know how to place our money in such a way that one mission or missionary shall not suffer, while another not any more worthy, lives in luxuries. Also that we may discourage wasting money on those who are running here and there accomplishing nothing, and may concentrate our support on those who mean business for our King.

Fourth—Many of the saints have felt the need of chartering the churches of God in Christ, putting them on a legal basis, and thus obeying the laws of the land, as God says. See Rom. 13. We confess we have been "slothful in business" on this point, and because of this many assemblies have already chartered under different names as a local work, in both home and foreign lands. Why not charter under one Bible name, 1 Thess. 2:14. Thus eliminating another phase of division in Pentecostal work? For this purpose also let us come together.

Fifth—We may also have a proposition to lay before the body for a general Bible Training School with a literary department for our people.[6]

Assemblies of God Organized

The meeting place was familiar to Pentecostals. The Grand Opera House in Hot Springs, Arkansas, was a second-floor auditorium over a ground-floor saloon. Indiana evangelist Maria Beulah Woodworth-Etter had just conducted several weeks of meetings there in fall of 1913, reporting that "God was with us in power." Pentecostal preacher Daniel Charles Owen Opperman of Indiana followed her meetings with one of his short-term

Bible schools in the same hall. The meeting format was also familiar. Thursday through Sunday, 2–5 April 1914, were entirely given over to rousing pentecostal services and a spontaneous parade down the main street of Hot Springs.[7]

On 6 April they began a very cautious organization for business. What kind of statement of purpose or structure could be acceptable? The convention call had been "for saints who believe in the baptism with the Holy Ghost with the signs following." The 300 or so in attendance were primarily from the Midwest but represented seventeen states plus Egypt and South Africa. A committee consisting of one delegate from each state presented resolutions which had been combined into a "Preamble and Resolution of Constitution" which read in part:

Whereas, He [God] commanded that there should be no schism (Division, sectarianism) in His body, the General Assembly (Church) of the firstborn, which are written in heaven (Heb. 12:23); and

Whereas, We recognize ourselves as members of said General Assembly of God (which is God's organism), and do not believe in identifying ourselves as, or establishing ourselves into, a sect, that is a human organization that legislates or forms laws and articles of faith and has unscriptural jurisdiction over its members and creates unscriptural lines of fellowship and disfellowship and which separates itself from other members of the General Assembly (Church) of the first born, which is contrary to Christ's prayer in St. John 17, and Paul's teaching in Eph. 4:1–16, which we heartily endorse:

Therefore, Be It Resolved, First, That we recognize ourselves as a General Council of Pentecostal (Spirit Baptized) saints from local Churches of God in Christ, Assemblies of God and various Apostolic Faith Missions and Churches, and Full Gospel Pentecostal Missions, and Assemblies of like faith in the United States of America, Canada, and Foreign Lands, whose purpose is neither to legislate laws of government, nor usurp authority over said various Assemblies of God, nor deprive them of their Scriptural and local rights and privileges, but to recognize Scriptural methods and order for worship, unity, fellowship, work and business for God, and to disapprove of all unscriptural methods, doctrine and conduct, and approve all Scriptural truth and conduct . . . and to consider the five purposes announced in the Convention Call in the February, 1914, issue of "Word and Witness":

Resolved, Second, That we recognize all the above said Assemblies of various names, and when speaking of them refer to them by the general Scriptural name "Assemblies of God"; and recommend that they all recognize themselves by the same name, that is, "Assembly of God" and adopt it as soon as practicable for the purpose of being more Scriptural and also legal in transacting business, owning property, and executing missionary work in home and foreign lands, and for general convenience, unity and fellowship.[8]

This formulation pleased those present so largely that they sang the Doxology and broke out into a praise meeting all over again. They adopted the Preamble and Resolution as "the Constitution of the General Council of the Assemblies of God." They limited voting rights in the council to males. They authorized the ordination of women as evangelists and missionaries, preferably "under the proper oversight of some good brother whom God has placed in charge of the work." They issued a statement on marriage and divorce. They recommended two of the existing Bible schools as acceptable training places for the ministry. Of particular importance for later developments, they elected a body known as the "executive presbytery" to provide certain administrative services and to call the next meeting of the full council. Eudorus N. Bell and J. Roswell Flower were to serve as continuing officers. Bell's monthly *Word and Witness* and Flower's weekly *Christian Evangel* were adopted as the official papers.

Thus the Assemblies of God had an administrative center and a journalistic voice "to give advice wherever needed; to aid whenever asked in helping assemblies to keep in New Testament order; to forward mission funds, help the missionaries, give free counsel for Bible order and promote in love the interests of the kingdom of God." Ministers and missionaries were receiving their credentials from the Assemblies of God during the following spring and summer. By fall of 1914 there were 512 approved workers of whom 142 were women.[9]

Beginnings in Indiana

Indiana did not have many congregations of the Assemblies of God in the fellowship's first years. Plans to form a district council embracing Indiana, Ohio, and Michigan were announced for January of 1915 but evidently had small results. The religious census of 1916 showed 118 Assemblies churches in the nation. There was Texas with 25, Oklahoma with 13, Arkansas with 13, and Missouri with 11. Indiana reported none.

However that statistical report was misleading. Indiana was a source and training ground for Assemblies leadership from the start. Maria Beulah Woodworth-Etter, famous pioneer woman evangelist from Indianapolis, shared in pentecostal evangelism with Fred Francis Bosworth and Daniel Charles Owen Opperman, both founding members of the Assemblies in 1914 and named

among its executive presbyters. The congregation she established in her tabernacle in Indianapolis in 1918 eventually became the state's largest Assemblies church, known as Lakeview Christian Center. She befriended and encouraged the newlyweds Joseph James Roswell Flower and Alice Reynolds Flower as they began their pentecostal ministry so central to Assemblies history.[10]

Alice Reynolds Flower and J. Roswell Flower

Alice Reynolds and J. Roswell Flower came into Pentecostalism from the Christian and Missionary Alliance congregation in Indianapolis. Glenn A. Cook returned from California to his home town of Indianapolis in January of 1907 and attended the congregation's Sunday afternoon meeting for testimony, praise, and prayer.[11] Alice Reynolds later reported:

> He stood up to testify, his face radiant with the glory of God. He told us that God was pouring out His Spirit in Los Angeles, and he had just come from the Azusa Street meeting where God was baptizing believers with the Holy Ghost and fire, and they were speaking in tongues as on the day of Pentecost. He added the information that he had received this blessing himself and returned to the old home town to bear witness of God's working in his life. He spoke humbly, declaring there were some wrongs he desired to make right. This had an electrifying effect upon all who heard him as they listened to his words and saw the glory on his face. To a young woman, sitting beside me, I said, "I want whatever blessing that man has."[12]

Cook and those members who "tarried" with him to seek the pentecostal outpouring for themselves were quickly excluded from the Gospel Tabernacle of the Missionary Alliance. They formed a new congregation. Cook soon returned to Los Angeles but other leaders came. Thomas Hezmalhalch, a Methodist minister from England, had recently received his pentecostal baptism at Azusa Street Mission. He was in charge of the Indianapolis meeting on Easter Sunday of 1907. Alice Reynolds was praying to receive the baptism in the Holy Spirit.

> I did not know that many fell under the power of God, nor that each individual spoke in tongues. All I seemed to sense was a deep craving for the overflowing of His love in my heart. At that moment it seemed I wanted Jesus more than anything in all the world, and if this baptism of the Holy Spirit was to open the door to a fuller revelation of Him, then nothing was to hinder me from having it. Spontaneously I rose to my feet, lifting my hands with a glad note of praise, "Thank God for the baptism of the

Holy Spirit; praise, O praise the Lord" . . . As this praise came from my lips, for the first time in my life I felt the physical manifestation of God's power all through my being, and I sank to the floor. God's day of Pentecost had come to a hungry teenager. My mother, kneeling at a distance, became concerned, fearing I might not be ready for such a great blessing, but "Brother Tom" assured her that God knew His business. I needed no help, and no one could have hindered me, for wave after wave of glory swept over me until there seemed to be a shining path reaching from my opened heart right into the presence of God. In a few moments my jaws began to tremble, and the praise that was literally flooding my soul came forth in languages I had never known.[13]

She further described an event a week later in which "the Spirit of God touched six of us, scattered over the congregation, and we arose to our feet to sing in wonderful harmony of the heavenly choir. Even now the thrill of that experience lingers. There was no effort. From deep within me the melody rolled forth in exhilarating joy and worship. Thank God, this has been repeated many times since."[14]

Alice said her baptism in the Holy Spirit was indeed an act but even more an introduction to a state, to a Spirit-filled life. She spoke of "the constant glorious reality of Jesus." While attending high school and college she maintained a full agenda of church work in addition to the normal three services on Sunday. There were meetings in the church every night except Saturday. On Saturday night the young people held open-air services on the city's courthouse steps. "There were cottage prayer meetings in various parts of town," Alice said, "until the Pentecostal message was well spread abroad over Indianapolis. In unexpected places, God confirmed His Word with signs following. Although continuing my school activities, I was able to take part in most of these nightly services. Whenever possible I had the joy of leaving the city for special meetings in different localities, sometimes alone and at other times in company with others."[15]

Many out-of-town visitors rode the network of twenty-six interurban lines serving Indianapolis to attend services at the pentecostal mission. The Indianapolis *Star* kept reporting the meetings with emphasis on the unusual manifestations. Some citizens were troubled that so many young people and children were involved in the excitement. They appealed to Mayor Bookwalter to stop the services. The mayor himself attended and reported through the newspaper that he was very favorably impressed.[16]

J. Roswell Flower was a nominal or backslidden member of that Christian and Missionary Alliance congregation at Indianapolis. His parents were among those attending services of the excluded pentecostal faction. He was working in the office of attorney Coley Kinney to prepare for a career in law, and at a couple of other jobs besides. He was present at the evening service on 7 April 1907 at which the newly Spirit-filled Alice Reynolds and five others felt divinely moved to demonstrate the heavenly choir.[17]

As that revival continued, Flower was reclaimed. He said:

Some way, the Lord never gave me anything without I first believed Him for it. My conversion was very quiet, yet I knew that my sins were forgiven; my sanctification was taken by cold faith in the finished work of Christ, and it was not till some minutes afterwards, when I was on my feet testifying to the experience, that any feeling came. Then I sought for the baptism, and expected to speak in tongues, and really, without hardly knowing it myself, I was seeking tongues. I sought for about two years and at last had to come to the point where I realized I would seek several years more if I did not step out by faith and claim the promise. I stepped. Nothing happened. Several days later the Lord, to encourage me, gave me a big blessing, but no tongues, and I still had to believe and testify that I had received. Hallelujah! After I went to Kansas City, while alone in prayer, the Lord gave me a few words in tongues and I spoke them. Instantly the power of God struck me and coursed all through my being. I was filled with joy unspeakable and full of glory. Then for a whole month I had to stand right there believing God. He gave much joy and peace but no tongues. It was hard to learn the lesson. About this time the tempter came my way. Doubts and fears began to assail me on all sides, and I am sorry to say I listened to him. Immediately I began to lose out and before long had an awful battle on my hands. I seemed to be deserted by both God and man. I did not understand His plan for me and so grew fretful and morose. This continued for three long dreary months, and then the Lord sweetly spoke to me.[18]

There was another peak experience for him a few months later. "While I asked the blessing at the supper table," he said, "the power of God fell on me, and I was compelled to go off alone with God where he dealt with me in a very precious way for some hours. Then the following week He filled me and refilled me and laid me under His mighty power half a dozen times. Thus He was honoring faith and blessing me exceedingly abundantly above all that I had asked or thought. Oh, hallelujah! Faith is the victory!"[19]

Soon after his conversion on 14 April 1907, and even before receiving the confirming sign of speaking in tongues, Flower turned from a career in law to a career in ministry. He attended the pentecostal camp meeting at Alliance, Ohio, in June. In 1908 he began issuing a monthly magazine called the *Pentecost* (1908–1910). As a traveling preacher he became widely acquainted among early pentecostal leaders and a collaborator with many youthful contemporaries in an evangelistic ministry ranging as far as Nebraska.[20]

Alice Reynolds and J. Roswell Flower were married in 1911. They traveled and preached in northern Indiana and in Ohio. Their particular friends and mentors were David Wesley Myland and his wife Nellie Ormsby Myland. David Myland was trained as a Methodist minister but later identified with the Christian and Missionary Alliance which was more hospitable to his emphases on sanctification, healing, and the Second Coming. When he heard of the outpouring of the Spirit at Azusa Street in Los Angeles, he began preaching the pentecostal message. After an outstanding career of more than twenty years with the Christian and Missionary Alliance in the Midwest, he was among the Pentecostals who withdrew from that association in 1912 because of his conviction that tongue speaking was the only sure sign of Spirit baptism. His composition "The Latter Rain," reported by him as a divine gift received during his own baptism in the Holy Spirit on 3 November 1906, was known as the first distinctively pentecostal hymn. His book *The Latter Rain Covenant* (1910) was the first book of pentecostal theology widely circulated.[21]

Myland's work offered extensive exegetical support for those who came to understand references to "early rain" and "latter rain" in such places as Deuteronomy 11, Joel 2, and Zechariah 10 to refer to particular historical times of outpouring of God's Spirit. He wrote: "If it is remembered that the climate of Palestine consisted of two seasons, the wet and the dry, and that the wet season was made up of the early and latter rain, it will help you to understand this [Latter Rain] covenant and the present workings of God's Spirit. For just as literal early and latter rain was poured out upon Palestine, so upon the church of the first century was poured out the spiritual early rain, and upon us today is being poured out the spiritual latter rain." Many early Pentecostals came to define themselves as people of the latter rain, participants in a powerful end-time revival and in the fulfillment of scriptural promise.[22]

Myland came to Indiana. At the age of fifty-four he had elected to invest himself in pentecostal education. An Indianapolis woman donated the use of "a commodious stone house with ample acreage" at Plainfield. The *Latter Rain Evangel* for July of 1912 announced: "Brother Myland writes from Plainfield, Indiana, they are in preparation for their summer Bible School and Home, and will open for at least a three months' term for all those who desire sound scriptural teaching, healing, and help in the Christian faith and life." The new school was named Gibeah. Those who were able paid $4 per week for room and board. Those without funds earned their way by working in the home and on its grounds.[23]

The first class at Gibeah included several young pentecostal leaders already experienced in evangelistic work. Fred and Margaret Vogler, colleagues of J. Roswell Flower in evangelism in Indiana, were among those ordained by Myland at the end of the first term in September. Vogler was destined to establish the work of the Assemblies of God at Martinsville, to construct the Assemblies church building at the headquarters city of Springfield in Missouri, to evangelize much of Kansas for the Assemblies, and to become first director of the denomination's Home Missions and Education Department. Myland also ordained Flem Van Meter from Jasonville, Indiana, at the end of that first term. Van Meter was to become chairman of the Central District (Ohio, Indiana, and Michigan) for the Assemblies of God, a kind of pioneer example for the denomination's full-time superintendents all over the country.[24]

J. Roswell and Alice Reynolds Flower were cofounders and colleagues with the Mylands in that school at Plainfield. They were ordained by Myland at the end of the first term in September of 1912 and took a pastorate in Indianapolis the following year. But they were also among those who stayed on with the Mylands for the two additional terms the school was open. Myland encouraged Flower to begin publishing a pentecostal weekly called the *Christian Evangel* (later *Weekly Evangel* and after 1919 *Pentecostal Evangel*) and contributed regularly to it. In 1913 Myland and Flower organized the Association of Christian Assemblies for interested pentecostal churches in Indiana and surrounding states. This was a significant constituency for Flower to represent at the founding of the Assemblies of God at the convention in Arkansas the following year.[25]

At that pentecostal convention at Hot Springs in 1914, J. Roswell Flower, at age twenty-six, was already widely recognized and trusted. Eudorus N. Bell of Texas and Arkansas was named general chairman of the convention.

Bell was a theologically trained minister and editor of the *Word and Witness* through which the convention had been called. But young J. Roswell Flower of Indiana was also highly visible as secretary-treasurer. The crucial Preamble and Resolution of Constitution, prepared in committee, was presented to the full body of participants by committee members Thomas K. Leonard of Ohio and J. Roswell Flower of Indiana. Flower was named as one of the twelve members of the new executive presbytery. His *Christian Evangel* was named the weekly paper of the new Assemblies of God so his was the editorial voice most frequently heard.

Bell and Flower collaborated as editors and very cautious "executives." When Springfield, Missouri, was chosen in 1917 to be the location of the new denominational headquarters, J. Roswell Flower was commissioned to oversee the move. He supervised installation of the linotype cylinder press, and paper cutter for the publishing house. Flower had never been a missionary but as the missionary enterprise grew he was elected on the first ballot in 1919 to move to the new headquarters to become the fellowship's first missionary secretary-treasurer. Two years later he had the audacity to project an actual mission budget—$40 per month for each missionary, $20 per month for each child, $25 per month for maintenance of mission property, $500 travel expense for each missionary going to or returning from the field. That budget was meant to be something of a stimulant since the amount of proposed expenditures was twice as much as the current income.

Flower was a great friend of order and what he called "sanity." Too much stress on speaking in tongues, he said, might encourage Pentecostals to regard all tongue speaking as divine. In fact some was "purely human" and some was "certainly satanic." He was delighted that twelve "safe, sane and trained brethren" had been selected for the first executive presbytery. It was a high compliment for his colleague E. N. Bell when Flower said that Bell was the "sweetest, safest and sanest" man he had met in the pentecostal movement. But when Bell became convinced by the anti-trinitarian Pentecostals in summer of 1915 and was among the large number being rebaptized in the name of Jesus only, Flower stood fast against what he considered that ancient heresy. He prepared the way for the general councils of 1915 and 1916 which pledged the Assemblies to trinitarian orthodoxy and reinstated Bell who repented of his temporary defection.

By 1925 Flower felt that the good order of the Assemblies required adoption of a constitution. The general meeting of that year disagreed with his urgency, voting him out of office and delaying the adoption of a constitution until the next meeting in 1927. His subsequent work as pastor and superintendent in the Eastern District (New York, New Jersey, Pennsylvania, and Delaware) soon projected him into national leadership again and he spent the last twenty-five years of his ministry back at the Springfield headquarters.[26]

Flower was one of a rising group of Assemblies leaders who were wary of the instability caused by endless pursuit of new visions and revelations among Pentecostals. They also resisted the Wesleyan definition of sanctification as a second, instantaneous, cleansing experience. Showing their heritage from the Christian and Missionary Alliance and from the teaching of William Durham of Chicago, they taught that sinners received full pardon and full cleansing at conversion. They affirmed sanctification but understood it as an empowering by Spirit baptism to lead a progressively holy and "overcoming" life. They attempted to protect unstable missionaries from themselves, to protect stable missionaries from the unstable ones, to increase mission support, and to invest each mission dollar both equitably and efficiently. Flower said that when any gift was received "for the neediest missionary," two-thirds of the missionaries seemed to qualify.[27]

Flower was also among the Assemblies leaders who called attention to the kinship among evangelicals and advocated cooperation. He was among the 147 religious leaders who signed the call to St. Louis to form the National Association of Evangelicals in 1942. The Assemblies affiliated with this national association in fall of 1943 and Flower served on its executive committee. Some American Pentecostals—mostly white trinitarian ones—decided to try for more cooperation among themselves. J. Roswell Flower was secretary of their first meeting in 1948, chairman of the committee to frame a constitution, and first secretary for the resulting Pentecostal Fellowship of North America. When Pentecostals—mostly white trinitarian ones again—began holding ecumenical conferences on a worldwide basis in 1947, the Assemblies of God participated from the beginning. Assemblies officers J. Roswell Flower and a younger Hoosier named Thomas Zimmerman had great influence in the continuing World Pentecostal Conference.[28]

Flower helped develop educational policy for the Assemblies in the face of wide differences of opinion about education within the membership. He was in the 1947 delegation to an interdenominational conference at Winona Lake in Indiana which formed an accrediting agency to set standards for the nation's host of Bible institutes and Bible colleges. The Assemblies became a founding member of this accrediting association and its Bible colleges agreed to conform. Flower had reported in 1945 that there was growing demand for a liberal arts college for the Assemblies of God. After the Second World War the Assemblies made a token payment of one dollar to acquire government hospital property of some sixty-eight buildings on fifty-nine acres at Springfield, Missouri. Evangel College opened there in 1955 and was fully accredited a decade later. The theological seminary opened at Springfield in 1973.

The Flowers reared six children, five of them ordained for ministries in the Assemblies of God and the sixth a pastor's wife. Alice Reynolds Flower was an effective speaker and writer. She helped edit the church papers and wrote for them. Most of all she wrote devotional books; at least eighteen of these were published.[29]

Thomas Fletcher Zimmerman

In the year that J. Roswell Flower retired, the Assemblies of God named another son of Indianapolis to its leadership. Thomas Fletcher Zimmerman was converted at seven, baptized in the Holy Spirit at eleven, and felt a call to gospel ministry while in high school. After one year at Indiana University his money was all gone but he became a very effective pastor at Kokomo, Harrodsburg, and South Bend in Indiana and at several places beyond the state. In 1945 the Assemblies of God established a radio department and Zimmerman was chosen to direct it. He did a weekly radio program called "Sermons in Song." The general council of 1959 at San Antonio named him general superintendent, the denomination's highest office.

Zimmerman continued the interests of Flower and of his immediate predecessor Ralph M. Riggs in ecumenicity and in education. While in radio work he was a founding member and later the president of the National Religious Broadcasters. He presided over the National Association of Evangelicals, the Pentecostal Fellowship of North America, and the International Advisory Committee of the Pentecostal World Conference. Under his leadership the administrative structure of the Assemblies was reorganized. At the end of his twenty-six years as superintendent the Assemblies had eleven accredited colleges and a theological seminary. More than 1,200 day schools sponsored by Assemblies of God churches enrolled about 110,000 children.[30]

The direction of Assemblies development did bring some tensions, defections, and losses. Ten of its executive presbyters withdrew or were dismissed within its first four years. A few members and ministers were excluded because of the denomination's consistent policy with moral offenders, the most painfully obvious examples being television evangelists Jim Bakker and Jimmy Swaggart. Some withdrew in protest because the Assemblies kept developing denominational organization, institutions for education, and ecumenical connections.[31] Some said the Assemblies did not pay enough attention to holiness, especially to holiness defined in terms of such things as hair style, dress code, and personal adornment. Some found the Assemblies inhospitable to their newer religious insights and revelations, most notably the antitrinitarian (Jesus' name, Jesus only, oneness) Pentecostals and a new generation of workers of healing miracles claiming to represent a later latter rain. Some could not agree with the position of the Assemblies that persons receiving true baptism in the Holy Spirit would give unfailing initial evidence of that baptism by speaking in tongues. Relations remained tenuous with members of the Full Gospel Business Men's Fellowship International and with other Charismatics who might seek baptism in the Holy Spirit and give evidence of that baptism by speaking in tongues but then remain in denominations involved in creed, liturgy, infant baptism, or nonpentecostal life style.[32]

However the most striking characteristic of the Assemblies of God was not division or loss. It was growth. The membership, which had burgeoned from the handful of participants at Hot Springs in 1914 to a half million in the United States and nearly a million overseas during the career of J. Roswell Flower, doubled again during the superintendency of Thomas Zimmerman. Assemblies of God often preferred to speak of "adherents," persons of all ages who identified with an Assemblies church. That number near the end of Zimmerman's superintendency in 1984 was about two million in the United States and nearly thirteen million abroad.[33] Concentrations of Assemblies churches in the United States in 1990 were in Texas (1274), California (1123), Florida (576), Missouri (501), Oklahoma (490), and Arkansas (434).

Indiana District

Indiana shared steadily in the Assemblies growth. The 1916 religious census reported no Indiana churches but eleven were in the report for 1926, a number doubled to twenty-five by the census of 1936. A decade later the number had doubled again to fifty-two churches with about sixty ministers. That year Indiana became a separate district.

At the celebration of Indiana District's fortieth anniversary in 1986 the report was "430 ministers and 199 churches with over 30,400 people attending Sunday morning worship services." Indiana District alone was sending more than $2 million per year to foreign missions. Organized young people were sending "Speed-the-Light" contributions of transportation and communication equipment to foreign missionaries—over $1 million sent by Indiana youth in the district's forty years. Organized church women had aided in making down payments on parsonages at Brownsburg, Tell City, Seymour, Madison, Danville, Logansport, Shelbyville, Bicknell, Frankfort, and West Lafayette. There was an Assemblies lakeside conference center at Hartford City, a district office building in Indianapolis, and a "teen challenge center" in Indianapolis with housing and staff to serve as many as forty girls addicted to drugs or alcohol. Many of the Assemblies congregations were small but at Elkhart Calvary, Fort Wayne First, Marion Westside, Carmel Northview, and Evansville Calvary the Sunday morning worship attendance averaged over 500. South Bend Calvary and Lafayette First averaged 1,200 on Sunday morning and Lakeview Temple at Indianapolis 2,165.[34]

In 1990 the Assemblies of God reported 51,907 adherents in Indiana. That was larger than the number reported for the Churches of Christ and about equal to the reported adherents for the United Church of Christ.

NOTES

1. *World Christian Encyclopedia. A Comparative Study of Churches and Religions in the Modern World, AD 1900–2000,* ed. David B. Barrett (New York: Oxford University Press, 1982), 14, 64; Walter J. Hollenweger, "After Twenty Years' Research on Pentecostalism," *Theology* (London: SPCK) 87 (November 1984): 403–12.

2. Edith L. Blumhofer, *The Assemblies of God: A Chapter in the Story of American Pentecostalism,* 2 vols. (Springfield, Mo.: Gospel Publishing House, 1989), 1:7.

3. Edith L. Blumhofer, *Pentecost in My Soul: Explorations in the Meaning of Pentecostal Experience in the Assemblies of God* (Springfield, Mo.: Gospel Publishing House, 1989), 16.

4. Blumhofer, *Assemblies,* 1:18–22, 174, 199–200; Blumhofer, *Pentecost,* 13–15.

5. Blumhofer, *Assemblies,* 1:130–34.

6. Blumhofer, *Assemblies,* 1:201–2.

7. *Dictionary of Pentecostal and Charismatic Movements* (Grand Rapids, Mich.: Zondervan, 1988), 653; Blumhofer, *Assemblies,* 1:171–72, 198–201.

8. William W. Menzies, *Anointed to Serve: The Story of the Assemblies of God* (Springfield, Mo.: Gospel Publishing House, 1971), 101–2.

9. Blumhofer, *Assemblies,* 1:203–10; Menzies, *Anointed to Serve,* 97–105.

10. Wayne E. Warner, *The Woman Evangelist: The Life and Times of Charismatic Evangelist Maria B. Woodworth-Etter* (Metuchen, N.J.: Scarecrow Press, 1986), 156–89, 266; *Dictionary of Pentecostal and Charismatic Movements,* 94, 653.

11. Alice Reynolds Flower, "How Pentecost Came to Indianapolis" (Assemblies of God Archives, Springfield, Mo., n.d., typescript), 2–3, 7; Blumhofer, *Assemblies,* 1:122–23; Blumhofer, *Pentecost,* 41–60; Menzies, *Anointed to Serve,* 66–67.

12. Blumhofer, *Pentecost,* 49–50.

13. Blumhofer, *Pentecost,* 52–53.

14. Blumhofer, *Pentecost,* 54.

15. Blumhofer, *Pentecost,* 55.

16. Blumhofer, *Pentecost,* 57–58; Flower, "How Pentecost Came," 4.

17. Flower, "How Pentecost Came," 4–5; *Dictionary of Pentecostal and Charismatic Movements,* 311–13.

18. Blumhofer, *Pentecost,* 46–47.

19. Blumhofer, *Pentecost,* 48.

20. Blumhofer, *Assemblies,* 1:163; Menzies, *Anointed to Serve,* 67.

21. J. Kevin Butcher, "The Holiness and Pentecostal Labors of David Wesley Myland, 1890–1918" (Th.M. thesis, Dallas Theological Seminary, 1983), 70–71, 106; David Wesley Myland, *The Latter Rain Covenant and Pentecostal Power, with Testimony of Healings and Baptism* (Chicago: Evangel Publishing House, 1910, 215 p.).

22. David Wesley Myland, "The Latter Rain Covenant," *The Latter Rain Evangel* (June 1909): 15; Butcher, "Holiness and Pentecostal," 90–98; *Dictionary of Pentecostal and Charismatic Movements,* 494–96, 632–33; Blumhofer, *Assemblies,* 1:150–53; Blumhofer, *Pentecost,* 27–28, 107. For a discussion of a Latter Rain Movement associated with pentecostal manifestations and miraculous gifts a generation later, see Blumhofer, *Assemblies,* 2:53–79 and *Dictionary of Pentecostal and Charismatic Movements,* 532–34.

23. Butcher, "Holiness and Pentecostal," 108.

24. Butcher, "Holiness and Pentecostal," 109–11; Blumhofer, *Assemblies,* 1:170, 254, 327–28; Blumhofer, *Pentecost,* 101–16.

25. Blumhofer, *Assemblies,* 1:170; *Dictionary of Pentecostal and Charismatic Movements,* 311, 633.

26. *Dictionary of Pentecostal and Charismatic Movements,* 53, 311–12; Blumhofer, *Assemblies,* 1:144, 204, 222–39, 234, 292–94; Menzies, *Anointed to Serve,* 98–105, 114–21.

27. *Aspects of Pentecostal-Charismatic Origins,* ed. Vinson Synan (Plainfield, N.J.: Logos International, 1975), 84–95; Blumhofer, *Assemblies,* 1:123, 128–30, 185–89, 217–21, 292; 2:184; *Dictionary of Pentecostal and Charismatic Movements,* 25, 169–80.

28. Blumhofer, *Pentecost,* 37; Blumhofer, *Assemblies,* 2:13, 15, 24–25, 31–32, 47–49.

29. Blumhofer, *Assemblies,* 2:113–18, 122–26, 128; *Dictionary of Pentecostal and Charismatic Movements,* 312.

30. Edith L. Blumhofer, "Thomas F. Zimmerman: The Making of a Minister: A Look at the Indiana Roots," *Assemblies of God Heritage* 10 (Winter 1990–91): 3–5, 21–22; *Dictionary of Pentecostal and Charismatic Movements,* 910–11; Menzies, *Anointed to Serve,* 306–9; Blumhofer, *Assemblies,* 1:322; 2:130, 169.

31. Blumhofer, *Assemblies*, 1:422; 2:185–90. For an account of the remarkable ecumenical activities of Assemblies minister David du Plessis, see Blumhofer, *Assemblies*, 2:90–102 and *Dictionary of Pentecostal and Charismatic Movements*, 250–54.

32. Blumhofer, *Assemblies*, 1:220–43, 332–33; 2:53–79, 88–89, 183–84.

33. *The Indiana District of the Assemblies of God: Forty Years of Ministry* (Indianapolis, Ind.: Indiana District of the Assemblies of God, 1986), 32; *Dictionary of Pentecostal and Charismatic Movements*, 910.

34. *Indiana District*, 9–12, 21–22, 29–31.

ONENESS PENTECOSTALS

The modern history of oneness Pentecostalism began in April of 1913 at the Worldwide Camp Meeting at Arroyo Seco outside Los Angeles. Maria Beulah Woodworth-Etter of Indiana was a featured evangelist. In the tradition of the pentecostal revival set off at Azusa Street a few years before, people were saved and baptized in the Holy Spirit at the Arroyo Seco meeting—500 by one count. Hundreds of preachers were present. Ministers and workers on the platform testified to a vision that God would soon move "for the restoration of the Apostolic Faith on the earth." Speakers prophesied that God was about to do a "new thing." Robert E. McAlister of Canada preached the sermon before a baptismal service to be conducted at the stream nearby. He commented that baptisms recorded in the New Testament were done in the name of the Lord Jesus Christ as in Acts 2:38 rather than in the name of the Father, Son, and Holy Spirit as in Matthew 28:19.

Contrary to the wishes of McAlister and those of most of the preachers present, this issue of baptism in the name of Jesus became the "new thing" out of Arroyo Seco. There was "fiery discussion." John G. Scheppe spent the night in prayer and meditation; next morning he ran through the camp shouting that the Lord had revealed to him the truth on baptism in the powerful name of the Lord Jesus Christ. Participating in the events of this 1913 camp meeting were three who were destined to be pioneers for oneness Pentecostalism and to focus its impact on Indiana: Frank J. Ewart, Garfield T. Haywood, and Andrew David Urshan.[1]

The Oneness Issue

The revolution came only in part over the issue of baptizing exclusively in the name of the Lord Jesus Christ. Some holiness preachers had used this form without much special notice as early as 1901 and Andrew Urshan said he had used it regularly for converts at his meetings beginning in 1910. The revolution came with greater force because asserting that only the mighty name and power of Jesus should be invoked at baptism quickly brought a reconsideration of the very nature and name of God.[2]

In the Scriptures there were all those affirmations of God's absolute and radical unity. At the same time there were all the actions and interactions of Father, Son, and Spirit as described in the Bible and as reported in Christian experience. There was also the unwavering assertion of the full humanity and of the full divine lordship of Jesus Christ. More than a millennium before Arroyo Seco, Christians had developed forms of words as guides for speaking of these reported characteristics of God and of Jesus Christ. There were forms of words to express doctrines which ought to be retained without fail. There were forms of words posted as warnings about unfruitful directions which ought to be avoided.

The historical process of arriving at those forms was long, painful, and subject to non-theological motives. Ecumenical councils came to concur, sometimes uneasily and in the face of dissent, that in Scriptures and Christian experience Father, Son, and Spirit are clearly three and in identity nothing less than persons. Each is not the other. Yet the Father is God, the Son is God, and the Spirit is God—the same in essential being and equal in power and glory. Baptism was performed for centuries in the name of the Father and of the Son and of the Holy Spirit following Matthew 28:19. The traditional formulation also affirmed that Jesus Christ is nothing less than fully human and fully divine, both these natures complete in him "inconfusedly, immutably, indivisibly, inseparably."

Within a year of that camp meeting at Arroyo Seco the whole body of traditional doctrine concerning Father, Son, and Spirit was undergoing fresh pentecostal examination. The search for a renewed "apostolic" understanding brought an explosion of research and writing.[3]

For oneness Pentecostals the mighty God known by and embodied in his name which is Yahweh (tetragrammaton YHWH) in the Old Testament was fully identified and equated with the same one mighty God known by and embodied in his name which is Jesus in the New Testament. So the centrality and unity of the mighty God and the mighty name were reaffirmed. In the Matthew 28:19 passage which spoke of baptizing in "the name" of the Father, Son, and Holy Spirit, that singular "name" was affirmed to be Jesus. This was supported with the statement in Colossians 2:9 that in Jesus Christ "dwells all the fulness of the Godhead bodily."

For fear of tritheism there was great reluctance among oneness Pentecostals to grant the traditional ontological understanding of "hypostasis" or to use the barely equivalent English term "person" for Father, Son, or Holy Spirit. These three were recognized instead as expressions of a rich variety of roles, offices, modes, aspects, manifestations, and relationships of the one God in his disclosure to human persons. Separation of the divine and human natures of Jesus Christ was common. In fact scriptural accounts were to be analyzed to determine whether he spoke or acted in each particular instance in his role as God or in his role as man. It was permissible to say that in some biblical prayers the human nature of Jesus prayed to the divine Spirit of Jesus that dwelt in the same man.[4]

Many oneness Pentecostals did not protest being identified with groups in the ancient conciliar period who were named Modalistic Monarchians or Nestorians and their doctrines declined. They simply said these perennial and popular positions were right after all. Oneness Pentecostals did not use the traditional baptismal formula of Matthew 28:19. Most urged an expanded initiatory experience based on Acts 2:38—repentant and obedient faith; baptism by immersion in water in the name of Jesus for the remission of sins; reception of the baptism in the Holy Spirit accompanied by speaking in tongues.[5]

Frank J. Ewart and Glenn A. Cook

Frank J. Ewart was the real oneness pioneer. He was a Canadian Baptist minister who received the baptism in the Holy Spirit in 1908. At the time of the Worldwide Camp Meeting at Arroyo Seco, he was pastor of the neighboring pentecostal congregation formed by William H. Durham. The discussions of baptism at Arroyo Seco stimulated his mind. "The revelation of the absolute Deity of our Lord Jesus Christ burst upon me," he said. "I saw that as all the fullness of the Godhead dwelt in Jesus, bodily; therefore baptism, as the Apostles administered it, in the Name of the Lord Jesus Christ, was the one and only fulfillment of Matth. 28:19. Instantly I conferred not with flesh and blood, but not wishing to trespass on the rights of those with whom I was associated in the ministry, I formed a band of helpers, rented and pitched a tent on the east side of the city of Los Angeles, and began to proclaim my new revelation."[6]

The tent was in the town of Belvedere and his first sermon on Acts 2:38 was on 15 April 1914. His associate was pentecostal evangelist Glenn A. Cook of Indianapolis. They set up a tank in the tent and rebaptized each other in the name of Jesus. It was Ewart who developed the oneness theology which was to accompany and validate the revised baptismal practice. He preached it widely and published it through his periodical *Meat in Due Season*. "From the very inception of its proclamation," he said, "God witnessed to it with a mighty revival, and 'signs and wonders and gifts of the Holy Ghost' heralded its importance, because of its identity with the apostolic principles and practices. People came from all over America and were baptized into the Name of the Lord Jesus, receiving 'power, as the Holy Ghost came upon them' and went away to be Christ's accredited witnesses."[7]

Glenn Cook, always the traveler, carried the new message across much of the nation. When Cook rebaptized six Pentecostals in the river at St. Louis in spring of 1915, the youthful pentecostal leader J. Roswell Flower protested. Cook eventually threatened Flower with disaster if he resisted this truth. Flower sent word east that Cook was coming with an erroneous doctrine. The warning availed little. At Indianapolis veteran evangelists L. V. Roberts and Garfield T. Haywood, along with their congregations, were rebaptized in the oneness name of Jesus and entered the oneness movement.[8]

The early oneness revivals coincided exactly with the organization and infancy of the Assemblies of God. Some thought the whole Assemblies fellowship might become Oneness. By the time of the third general meeting of the Assemblies at St. Louis in October of 1915, many pentecostal ministers including Assemblies leaders had been rebaptized in Jesus' name. Glenn Cook had rebaptized L. V. Roberts in Indianapolis on 6 March; that summer Roberts rebaptized E. N. Bell at a camp meeting in Tennessee. Bell was the Assemblies' most respected theologian and editor. But at the fourth general meeting of the Assemblies at St. Louis in October of 1916 the Oneness were clearly out of favor. E. N. Bell stood firm for the trinitarian formulation and against further contention over baptism. The council adopted a "Statement of Fundamental Truths" which affirmed the traditional understanding of the Trinity. It passed a resolution recommending that its ministers use the words of Matthew 28:19 when baptizing.[9]

So about 150 ministers of oneness convictions were excluded. They shared with the Assemblies a non-Wesleyan view of sanctification, a rootage in nineteenth century revivalism with special debt to A. B. Simpson of the Christian and Missionary Alliance, and a conviction that Pentecostals baptized in the Holy Spirit needed to find some order and organization. They had no obvious place to go. Early in 1917 they organized temporarily as the General Assembly of the Apostolic Assemblies but that organization was so new and unrecognized that it could not provide its ministers exemption from military service or clergy rates on the railroads.

Garfield T. Haywood

Garfield T. Haywood of Indianapolis came to the rescue. He had held credentials since 1911 in a small but officially recognized West Coast fellowship called the Pentecostal Assemblies of the World. By a merger with the General Assembly of the Apostolic Assemblies in 1918, the Pentecostal Assemblies of the World became for a time the major oneness body in the nation. In the merged denomination Garfield T. Haywood of Indianapolis was first a "field superintendent" and then a "general elder." On the call to the denomination to meet in convention at Indianapolis in 1919, Haywood was designated "general secretary." The denomination's headquarters was located in Indianapolis that year.[10]

Garfield T. Haywood was black. His parents, Benjamin and Penny Haywood, migrated from North Carolina following the Civil War. They came north to Greencastle, Indiana, and Garfield was born there in 1880, third in what was to be a family of nine children. Three years later the family moved to the Haughville community in Indianapolis. There Benjamin Haywood invested his life for his family, rising each morning at 4 A.M., walking miles to the foundry, working long hours, and then walking home. Young Garfield got to enroll in Indianapolis Public School No. 52; he later entered Shortridge High School and completed two years there. Schooling developed his gifts in language and art. He found employment as a cartoonist for two black weeklies, the *Freedman* and the *Recorder*.

Even as a youth Garfield Haywood exercised leadership and warranted respect, serving as Sunday school superintendent in both the Methodist and Baptist churches and secretary for the local chapter of the Knights of Pythias. Henry Prentiss, a black colleague who had come from California with Glenn Cook in 1907, was continuing the pentecostal meetings in an old building on West Michigan Street. Haywood finally yielded to the entreaties of his friends to attend. At a service on a February night of 1908, he and his wife Ida and his sister Gertrude were struck to the muddy floor, claiming their baptism in the Spirit and speaking in tongues.[11]

Ida Haywood had no enthusiasm for being married to any "jack-leg preacher" but Garfield Haywood was the natural leader in the tiny congregation. By the end of 1908 Henry Prentiss had moved on and Haywood was pastor for its thirteen members. The growing congregation became Oneness. When the rebaptized Glenn A. Cook came from Frank J. Ewart in California in 1915 with the new message on baptism and its supporting theology, Haywood was convinced. Ewart and Cook were his personal friends; he had shared with them in a successful revival in California a few months earlier. He answered J. Roswell Flower of the Assemblies of God: "Your warning came too late. I have accepted the message and have been rebaptized." Many of his constituents followed him, 465 being rebaptized in the name of Jesus in 1915 in Indianapolis alone. Haywood's monthly *Voice in the Wilderness* became a very effective force in advancing oneness doctrine. By 1924 his congregation members had become too crowded in their building at Eleventh and Senate which seated about 1,000. That year they built Christ Temple at Fall Creek Boulevard and Paris Avenue.[12]

Haywood's Indianapolis congregation was genuinely interracial, for a long time about 60 percent black and 40 percent white. That large oneness merger he helped to effect for the nation in 1918, the Pentecostal Assemblies of the World, was also genuinely integrated at first. However the racial mix was too much for the social structures of the time to bear. The very excellence and prominence of a black man such as Haywood could be difficult for persons accustomed to having the races kept separate and unequal. He was sought after as a preacher; prominent in pentecostal councils; impressive as a writer and artist; admired as a poet and composer of hymns; and firmly established as an officer in the denomination. It was embarrassing to some to have their ministerial credentials regularly validated by the approval and signature of this black man. There were complaints that the mixed denomination must always hold its meetings in the North where racially integrated sessions and facilities could be tolerated. White ministers moved to separate in 1924, cutting the membership of the Pentecostal Assemblies of the World in half immediately.[13] Within a year three white oneness denominations were formed, the beginning of a bewildering period of oneness fragmentation, name changes, and mergers.[14]

The Pentecostal Assemblies of the World, now much more black in its constituency, maintained its headquarters in Indianapolis. Garfield T. Haywood was called upon to play an even larger role. When the denomination reorganized to be governed by bishops in 1925, he was named a bishop. In fact he was presiding bishop continuously from 1925 until his death in 1931. So he combined duties as pastor of Christ Temple, duties as chief administrator of the denominational headquarters, duties as editor of the denominational paper from 1925 to 1930, and episcopal duties as "roving ambassador" to the entire volatile constituency. It was a mark of his impact that a large percentage of black Pentecostals in the Midwest became Oneness; that most black oneness groups had their origin directly or indirectly in the Pentecostal Assemblies of the World; and that the Pentecostal Assemblies of the World headquartered in Indianapolis grew to report a membership of 500,000 in 1,400 U.S. and 1,400 foreign churches in 1987. Indiana was one of the top five states in number of constituents of the Pentecostal Assemblies of the World. A contemporary directory listed fifteen congregations in Indianapolis as well as Aenon Bible College at the international headquarters on Meadows Drive.

Sunday worship attendance at Christ Temple alone regularly exceeded 1,000.[15]

United Pentecostal Church

By 1945 some leaders of two substantial bodies of predominantly white oneness Pentecostals refused to be separated any longer. They declined to make an issue of some differences in the way they delineated the steps to the new birth. They proceeded to unite. Thus the Pentecostal Assemblies of Jesus Christ and the Pentecostal Church, Incorporated, merged to become the United Pentecostal Church.[16]

From the time of its formation, the United Pentecostal Church was the largest organization of oneness Pentecostals—1,838 ministers and about 900 churches at the time of union in 1945. It was destined to grow to 3,496 churches; 7,064 ministers; and 350,000 members in the U.S. and Canada in 1987. Another 680,000 foreign members were reported that year. It formed a church government strong at the center to encourage denominational loyalty, maintained an aggressive evangelistic program, operated its own publishing enterprise, and came to endorse nine Bible schools in the U.S. and Canada. This fellowship not only defined itself in terms of the oneness distinctives on baptism in the name of Jesus and a supporting non-trinitarian theology but also emphasized holiness concerns about such things as length of hair, modest dress, and degree of involvement in worldly amusements. Indiana District of the United Pentecostal Church was formed in 1946.[17]

Nathaniel Urshan

As the United Pentecostal denomination was developing, it built a special relationship with an Indianapolis congregation. Oneness pioneer preacher and missionary Andrew David Urshan of New York deliberately arranged to introduce his son Nathaniel to singing evangelist Jean Habig of the Calvary Tabernacle in Indianapolis. Nathaniel and Jean were married in 1941. Hoosiers followed their evangelistic ministry with special interest. In July of 1949 Calvary Tabernacle called Nathaniel Urshan as pastor. He was twenty-nine years of age.

The congregation at the Tabernacle at Indianapolis grew to become a valuable symbol and training center for the United Pentecostal Church in the region. Nathaniel and Jean Urshan kept traveling widely on preaching tours. Early in their Indianapolis ministry they broadcast a fifteen-minute radio program over WIBC five nights a week using the theme song "Whisper a Prayer in the Morning." More local broadcasts were added. The United Pentecostal denomination began its "Harvestime" international radio ministry over 33 stations in 1961. By 1969 it had expanded to 318 stations. Those weekly programs were recorded at Calvary Tabernacle in Indianapolis using the church's facilities and musicians.

Nathaniel Urshan was the Harvestime preacher for seventeen and one-half years without missing a broadcast. Urshan was invited to lecture at Harvard University on baptism in the Holy Spirit and speaking in tongues. He was a leader in a great many local community organizations and fund drives. When the United Pentecostal Church International met for its 1977 conference at Indianapolis, Senator Richard Lugar and Mayor William Hudnut addressed the convention. At that meeting Nathaniel Urshan was elected to move to Hazelwood, Missouri, as general superintendent, the denomination's highest office.[18]

Under succeeding pastors Calvary Tabernacle continued its leadership. The new sanctuary seated 2,800. A list compiled in 1985 named seventy-six ministers and twenty-four spouses of ministers enlisted from its membership. Indiana Bible College, an endorsed educational institution of the United Pentecostal Church, moved from Seymour to 3350 Carson Avenue in Indianapolis in 1988. Calvary Tabernacle's pastor Paul D. Mooney became president of the school and the congregation became "holder of the deed" to the college property. Calvary Tabernacle loomed large but by no means stood alone. Southern Indiana reflected the early work of oneness evangelist Ralph G. Cook. In 1987 there were seven United Pentecostal churches in Indianapolis, eight in the Bloomington area, and a total of 138 in the state.[19]

Perhaps half of Indiana's oneness Pentecostals in the 1980s were outside the two larger oneness denominations in the state. They were not counted among the Pentecostal Assemblies of the World or the United Pentecostal Church International. Often the statistics of their membership and ministry were not compiled or reported to any central agency. If they were listed in local church directories they often appeared simply as "independent" or "non-denominational" or "pentecostal" or "other churches." Oneness Pentecostals often preferred the name "apostolic" as a fitting expression of their rediscovery of the genuine apostolic Christianity which predated the apostasy of mainstream Christianity and its fall into a form of tritheism. However that name was not distinctive since it was used by many pentecostal groups and by non-pentecostals as well. More often the unaffili-ated congregation simply took a name describing their location (Brummett's Creek, Pine Grove, Stinesville) or expressing their religious mission (God's Way, Souls Harbor, Upper Room). There was mutual recognition, friendship, and even denominational organization on a limited scale among some of these kindred oneness congregations. At the same time there was a tendency toward extreme individualism and endless division.[20]

Apostolic World Christian Fellowship

Worthy G. Rowe, bishop and pastor of the widely respected Apostolic Temple in South Bend, was concerned for unity among oneness Pentecostals. In 1970 seventeen key ministers responded to his invitation to study the divided situation—the Pentecostal Assemblies of the World, plus the United Pentecostal Church International, plus the scores of oneness organizations with a dozen to a few hundred churches each, plus the hundreds of independent congregations. These leaders agreed to do something to provide opportunity for all oneness Pentecostals to worship together, to do joint planning, and to make a united effort at least on behalf of international missions. The result was the Apostolic World Christian Fellowship. Its early emphasis was on enlisting wide participation by securing from oneness organizations a "letter of intent" to affiliate with the new Fellowship. "Organization" was eventually defined as a body with at least twelve "authentic churches." The Pentecostal Assemblies of the World signed a letter of intent, entering the Fellowship with its hundreds of churches. The United Pentecostal Church declined to affiliate but its 7,000 ministers were included in the Fellowship's mailing list of 18,000 oneness clergy worldwide. There was also a special provision for independent oneness preachers to affiliate individually.

The Apostolic World Christian Fellowship was always lifting up scriptural calls to Christian unity and mutual support. The Fellowship was careful to disavow any intention to win oneness adherents or preachers from their current church connections. The letter of intent provided "that each church or group remain sovereign and each minister be answerable to his own organization for his conduct and teaching." So the Apostolic Temple at South Bend, Indiana, became a clearinghouse for worldwide communication and collaboration among oneness Pentecostals. The issue of the *Clarion* inviting registration for the 19th annual congress at South Bend in May of 1990 reflected an Apostolic World Christian Fellowship with over 100 persons in leadership roles to some degree, with

109 affiliated organizations in 14 nations, and with influence well beyond its affiliated membership.[21]

NOTES

1. Arthur L. Clanton, *United We Stand: A History of Oneness Organizations* (Hazelwood, Mo.: Pentecostal Publishing House, 1970), 15; Frank J. Ewart, *The Name and the Book* (Hazelwood, Mo.: Word Aflame Press, 1986), 39–40; *Seven "Jesus Only" Tracts* (New York: Garland Publishing, 1985), viii; *Dictionary of Pentecostal and Charismatic Movements* (Grand Rapids, Mich.: Zondervan, 1988), 644, 901; Vinson Synan, *The Holiness-Pentecostal Movement in the United States* (Grand Rapids, Mich.: Eerdmans, 1971), 153–59; Edith L. Blumhofer, *The Assemblies of God: A Chapter in the Story of American Pentecostalism*, 2 vols. (Springfield, Mo.: Gospel Publishing House, 1989), 1:222–39; *Aspects of Pentecostal-Charismatic Origins*, ed. Vinson Synan (Plainfield, N.J.: Logos International, 1975), 143–47; James L. Tyson, *The Early Pentecostal Revival* (Hazelwood, Mo.: Word Aflame Press, 1992), 169–201.

2. Clanton, *United We Stand*, 14; *Dictionary of Pentecostal and Charismatic Movements*, 646.

3. For some exposition of Oneness doctrine see David K. Bernard, *The Oneness of God*, (Hazelwood, Mo.: Word Aflame Press, 1990, 343 p.); Ewart, *The Name and the Book*; *Dictionary of Pentecostal and Charismatic Movements*, 644–51; *Aspects of Pentecostal-Charismatic Origins*, 143–68; *Seven "Jesus Only" Tracts*.

4. *Dictionary of Pentecostal and Charismatic Movements*, 648–50; Bernard, *Oneness of God*, 87, 171, 178.

5. Bernard, *Oneness of God*, 90–91, 125, 239–52, 318–20; *Dictionary of Pentecostal and Charismatic Movements*, 650.

6. Ewart, *The Name and the Book*, 40–41.

7. Ewart, *The Name and the Book*, 41; *Dictionary of Pentecostal and Charismatic Movements*, 290, 644.

8. *Dictionary of Pentecostal and Charismatic Movements*, 644; Blumhofer, *Assemblies*, 1:194.

9. Clanton, *United We Stand*, 18–21; *Dictionary of Pentecostal and Charismatic Movements*, 645; Blumhofer, *Assemblies*, 1:236.

10. Morris E. Golder, *History of the Pentecostal Assemblies of the World* (Indianapolis, Ind.: The Author, 1973), 48–49, 53, 61, 64; *Aspects of Pentecostal-Charismatic Origins*, 94–95; *Dictionary of Pentecostal and Charismatic Movements*, 644, 700–1; Clanton, *United We Stand*, 22–26.

11. Morris E. Golder, *The Life and Works of Bishop Garfield Thomas Haywood, 1880–1931* (Indianapolis, Ind.: The Author, 1977), 1–4; James L. Tyson, *Before I Sleep: A Narrative and Photographic Biography of Bishop Garfield Thomas Haywood* (Indianapolis, Ind.: Pentecostal Publications, 1976), 8–9.

12. Fred J. Foster, *Their Story: 20th Century Pentecostals* (Hazelwood, Mo.: Pentecostal Publishing House, 1981), 90–94; William W. Menzies, *Anointed to Serve: The Story of the Assemblies of God* (Springfield, Mo.: Gospel Publishing House, 1971), 113; Blumhofer, *Assemblies*, 1:224; Golder, *History*, 44; Clanton, *United We Stand*, 16–17, 189. *Seven "Jesus Only" Tracts* includes four tracts by Garfield T. Haywood, separately paged, the material largely reprinted from his periodical *Voice in the Wilderness*.

13. Golder, *Life*, 11; Golder, *History*, 79–80, 82–83; Clanton, *United We Stand*, 27–34; *Dictionary of Pentecostal and Charismatic Movements*, 646, 863.

14. This complex story can be traced in Clanton, *United We Stand* and in appropriate entries in the *Dictionary of Pentecostal and Charismatic Movements*. As one example, note on p. 647 of the *Dictionary* that as late as 1941 L. R. Ooton of Indiana led nearly 1,000 oneness ministers from the tri-state region of Indiana, Ohio, and West Virginia out of the Pentecostal Assemblies of Jesus Christ to form the Apostolic Ministerial Alliance.

15. Golder, *History*, 87; Golder, *Life*, 55; *Dictionary of Pentecostal and Charismatic Movements*, 349–50, 647, 701.

16. Foster, *Their Story*, 140–52; Clanton, *United We Stand*, 116–27; *Dictionary of Pentecostal and Charismatic Movements*, 647.

17. *Meet the United Pentecostal Church International* (Hazelwood, Mo.: Pentecostal Publishing House, 1989), 115–25; Clanton, *United We Stand*, 128–82; *Dictionary of Pentecostal and Charismatic Movements*, 647, 860–65.

18. Georgia Smelser, *Nathaniel A. Urshan: Champion of Our Faith and Legend in Our Time* (St. Louis, Mo.: Harvestime, 1985?), 36, 70–71, 78–80, 89–92; Clanton, *United We Stand*, 175–76, 193–95.

19. *United Pentecostal Church Directory, 1987* (Hazelwood, Mo.: United Pentecostal Church International, 1987), 225–29, Smelser, *Nathaniel A. Urshan*, 40–41; Clanton, *United We Stand*, 193–95.

20. *Seven "Jesus Only" Tracts*, vii; Clanton, *United We Stand*, 122–23; *Dictionary of Pentecostal and Charismatic Movements*, 19–20. For a discussion of black oneness bodies developing from the Pentecostal Assemblies of the World, see James C. Richardson, *With Water and Spirit* (Washington, D.C.: Spirit Press, 1980), 16, 36–99.

21. *Apostolic World Christian Fellowship Clarion*, 14 (February 1990).

CHURCH OF GOD (CLEVELAND, TENN.)

When *Ambrose Jessup Tomlinson* was born in 1865 he was so small and fragile that his head was the size of a teacup and he had to be carried about on a pillow. His father said "I hope we can keep him, don't thee?" His older brothers had died; five older sisters survived. His mother said she prayed "If this child is never going to amount to anything let him die. He is such a care. If Thou hast something special for him to do, heal him up and let him live."[1]

Tomlinson said he was "reared in a moral rural district among Quakers" but that his parents seldom attended religious services so he did not go. Holiness influence was strong in the Quaker community of Westfield, Indiana. Tomlinson heard his sisters singing "Oh, How I Love Jesus" and other revival hymns. During his secondary school years a revival "broke out" in a church near the school. Tomlinson said "My conscience and spiritual nature was thoroughly aroused," but he did not "profess religion." He said his conscience kept lashing him for years but he had other interests.

The premature baby had grown to be an intensely competitive and persistent young man. A later associate said "I learned that oppositions served to stir his zeal and determination to overcome and win the victory, which he did again and again." Tomlinson once said of the intensity of his own commitment "There is a kind of divine fury in me that refuses to be quiet or show any signs of retreat." Because he was fascinated with writing, his father allowed him to attend some extracurricular ses-

sions of writing school; he wanted to keep on writing and writing. At Westfield Academy he concentrated on athletics and drama. Most of all he enjoyed the excitements of Indiana politics. During one campaign he swore that if his party lost he would quit the United States and go to Australia. His party won. He stayed in Indiana and married Mary Jane Taylor in April of 1889.[2]

Tomlinson as Holiness Evangelist

His interests came to a focus on religion when lightning struck the house. He told his young wife "It's time for us to pray." They were awkward but persistent in Bible reading and devotions. Tomlinson said "I never let up until I got a real experience of salvation. My [playing] cards were soon cremated, and I was attending Sunday school." Under his superintendence the Sunday school doubled from thirty to sixty. Revival came to the congregation through the prayer meeting. Tomlinson felt compelled to preach for the little congregation and to study the Bible in preparation for preaching.[3]

Through that small Quaker congregation he found access to the wider holiness movement. His visiting mentor J. B. Mitchell of Ohio had attended Oberlin College and was a convert under the ministry of Charles G. Finney. Mitchell taught him Oberlin views of sanctification, missions, and the urgency of distributing clothes and Bibles to the poor. At God's Bible School in Cincinnati Tomlinson became acquainted with the literature and leadership of holiness. His nickname at the school was "The Prevailer." He became an avid reader, especially of holiness periodicals.[4]

When Tomlinson had learned of sanctification understood as a second blessing, a victory over the old carnal nature and residual sin, he did not rest until he could claim that experience. He spoke and wrote of his months of wrestling as a kind of cosmic conflict with the "old man."

> I was making a corn crop, and I suppose I prayed in nearly every row, and nearly all over the field. Though I worked hard every day, I frequently ate but one meal a day. I remember it as if it were but yesterday. I would leave the house at night at times, and stay out and pray for hours. I searched my Bible and prayed many nights till midnight and two o'clock, and then out at work again next morning by sun up. It was a hard fight, but I was determined for that "old man" to die. He had already given me much trouble, and I knew he would continue to do so if he was not slain. I saw it, and I knew he must be destroyed or I would be ruined, and my soul dragged down to hell by his subtle influence and cruel grasp. At last the final struggle came. It was a hand to hand fight, and the demons of hell seemed to be mustering their forces, and their ghastly forms and furious yells would no doubt have been too much for me had not the Lord of heaven sent a host of angels to assist me in that terrible hour of peril. But it was the last great conflict, and I managed, by some peculiar dexterity, to put the sword into him up to the hilt. It was about twelve o'clock in the day. I cried out in the bitterness of my soul: "Now! Now! You've got to give it up now! Now!" I felt him begin to weaken and quiver. I kept the "Sword" right in him and never let go. That sharp two-edged "Sword" was doing its deadly work. I did not pity him. I showed him no quarters. There we were in that attitude when all of a sudden came from above, like a thunderbolt from the skies, a sensational power that ended the conflict, and there lay the "old man" dead at my feet, and I was free from his grasp. Thank God! I could get a good free breath once more. It was an awful struggle, but the victory was won. That was about twenty years ago, but it is fresh in my memory yet. I was indeed sanctified wholly.[5]

His interest in politics faded completely. He said "I will only vote for Jesus."

Influenced by the example of J. B. Mitchell, he committed himself to a ministry to mountain people near the point of junction of the states of North Carolina, Tennessee, and Georgia. He and his family located at Culbertson, North Carolina, in October of 1899. He labored in that region as a colporteur for the American Tract and American Bible societies, as an evangelist penetrating remote places with enthusiastic prayer and preaching, and as a distributor of the necessities of life to the poor. He and his wife made their home into an orphanage and school. To report on the work and to solicit the support they so desperately needed, they published an eight-page monthly paper called *Samson's Foxes*. Some local people violently opposed Tomlinson's aggressive ministry and especially his published descriptions of the conditions of southern poor whites.[6]

He kept seeking for an acceptable church base for his life and ministry. He had an aversion to every type of church organization or creed. He had a zeal for restoration of a pure church based on the Bible alone. In fall of 1901 he traveled to Maine to visit Frank W. Sanford's Holy Ghost and Us Bible School and his religious community named Shiloh. Though he had been baptized before, he was baptized by Sanford in the Andrascogin River and joined Sanford's "Church of the Living God for the Evangelization of the World, Gathering of Israel, New Order of Things at the Close of the Gentile Age." He was back at Culbertson by the end of 1901, then for a time in Elwood, Indiana, working in a glass factory, then back at Culbertson at the end of May of 1903. Within a few days of his return this restless Hoosier found the church affiliation which would occupy the rest of his life.[7]

The fellowship he joined in 1903 was made up of friends he had known for several years. On one of his trips with his horse-drawn bookwagon as a colporteur in the mountains he sold five-cent New Testaments to two boys. They thought this religious man should meet their father who was "powerful religious." Thus Tomlinson met William F. Bryant and came to know the local holiness band led by Bryant and Richard G. Spurling. Baptist preacher Spurling of Cokercreek in Tennessee had enlisted some friends as early as 1884 in an effort to call all the churches in the area from their creeds and divisions into one restored biblical church.[8]

When their call seemed to go unheeded, this group met in the Barney Creek Meetinghouse on 19 August 1886 and heard an invitation to organize that restored biblical church themselves under the name of Christian Union: "As many Christians as are here present that are desirous to be free from all man-made creeds and traditions, and are willing to take the New Testament, or law of Christ, for your only rule of faith and practice; giving each other equal rights and privilege to read and interpret for yourselves as your conscience may dictate, and are willing to sit together as the Church of God to transact business as the same, come forward." Eight responded.

These were followed at a second invitation by Richard G. Spurling Jr., who was soon ordained by his father and became the group's pastor in his father's place. Five of the charter members were women; during the early years the ratio of female to male members was about two to one.[9]

The group center shifted a few miles across the state border into North Carolina because a revival occurred there. Three laymen from Cokercreek vicinity experienced sanctification which they understood and preached in Wesleyan terms—a second definite experience to eradicate residual sin and produce natural holiness. Their preachings at Camp Creek in Cherokee County resulted in the gathering of huge crowds at Shearer Schoolhouse. Spurling and the Christian Union moved their services there. When the three lay evangelists moved on, the merged congregations continued as Camp Creek church. Pastor Spurling was often traveling. In his absence William F. Bryant was the group's leader.

It was at some of the meetings of this Camp Creek congregation at Shearer Schoolhouse in Cherokee County, North Carolina, that "the Holy Spirit fell" in summer of 1896, ten years before the outpouring at Azusa Street in California. Persons in fervent prayer were caught up in ecstasy and spoke in unknown tongues. It was reported that more than 100 persons received the experience and several afflicted persons were healed. The revival boomed as people "prayed, and shouted, and exhorted until hundreds of hard sinners were converted."[10]

However the congregation was nearly destroyed. Some erratic participants elected to chasten themselves with extreme regimens of fasting and personal deprivation. Some fanatic teachers wanted to press on from this baptism of "holy fire" to further baptisms of "holy dynamite," "holy lyddite," and "holy oxidite." Some opponents in the region undertook to wipe out the whole enterprise with violence. At their meeting on 15 May 1902 Spurling and Bryant led the congregation to formulate guidelines and regulations to ensure order. The church now had a simple government. It adopted a new name—The Holiness Church at Camp Creek. After the disorders had come and gone a mere handful of members were left.[11]

Tomlinson at Camp Creek (N.C.) and Cleveland (Tenn.)

It was to a meeting of this small Holiness Church at Camp Creek set for 13 June 1903 that A. J. Tomlinson of Indiana was invited. The invitation was natural enough. They knew each other well. Tomlinson was regarded as more highly educated than Bryant or Spurling and had been a welcome guest preacher for the church. However this June meeting was a time of special expectancy. Tomlinson said he came there with the understanding that they were going to search the Bible to see if they could find the Church of God. He was gifted and dynamic but still religiously at loose ends. "It was my desire to learn, if I could, the Bible plan for the work I knew must be done in the last days," he said. "I had already searched and investigated many movements until my faith in them had been completely exhausted. I seemed to be like a ship at sea with no rudder by which it should be controlled."[12]

Tomlinson stayed at Bryant's house the night of 12 June. Early next morning he climbed Burger Mountain where he "prevailed in prayer" and received a vision of "the Church of God of the last days." This was to be a Church of God restored to the purity in which Jesus began it. It was to be rediscovered by stripping off the overlay of all the apostate denominations which had become so dormant and backslidden.[13]

During the meeting of the church members which followed, Tomlinson examined the fellowship thoroughly. He was especially uneasy that they had chosen to become a church organization regulated by a church government.

> I learned more about the organization at this time, and when I understood fully that they meant to stand for the whole Bible rightly divided and to take the New Testament as their only rule of faith and practice, it appealed to me, and I became very much interested at once. I poured in the questions, and Bible answers were given which perfectly satisfied all of my inquiries. I then said, this means that it is the Church of God. To this they assented. Then, I ventured to ask if they would be willing to receive me into the church with the understanding that it is the Church of God of the Bible. They were willing and soon proceeded in order. I took the obligation with deep sincerity and extreme sacredness never to be forgotten.[14]

Tomlinson and four others joined the Holiness Church at Camp Creek that day to bring the total membership to twenty. Spurling handed Tomlinson a Bible and said, "Will you take this as the Word of God, believe it and practice it, obey its precepts and walk in the light as God is in the light?" Tomlinson was received, ordained, and chosen as pastor of the Camp Creek church.[15]

Then the church grew. The growth came in part because Tomlinson's assignment to the Camp Creek congregation freed Spurling and Bryant for evangelism in the region. Camp Creek church itself added fourteen members during Tomlinson's first year including the new minister M. S. Lemons to add to the evangelistic force. The growth came even more because Tomlinson had found his place in a church which was ready for the investment of all his energies. Once he had screamed in prayer, "O Lord, give me responsibility." Now he received responsibility; turning opportunity into achievement was always his pure joy.[16]

To preach, to teach, to write, to study, to organize, to prevail in conflict—these were the stuff of Tomlinson's eighteen-hour work days. In 1904 he was chosen pastor for three churches. To these he added preaching assignments all around at places such as Jones and Baldknob in Georgia and Ducktown and Drygo in Tennessee. That year he took up residence in Cleveland, Tennessee, county seat for some 15,000 citizens of Bradley County and, approaching 5,000, the largest town in the area. Cleveland was a regular stop on the Norfolk and Western Railroad and Tomlinson had a railroad clergy permit. He began editing and printing a new paper entitled *The Way*.

In 1905 he recorded a revival at his Union Grove church near Cleveland: "July 8, went to Union Grove where we held meetings for three weeks. Quite a number of renewals, conversions and several professed sanctification. I baptized 19 and 23 received into the Church. The most wonderful meeting I was ever in. People fell on the floor and some writhed like serpents, some cried out until they were released from the devil, some fell in the road, one seemed to be off in a trance for four or five hours. The church seemed to be greatly edified and blessed." His tent meetings in Cleveland itself that year attracted hundreds and a congregation was established in the town.[17]

The churches wanted a general meeting in January of 1906; twenty-one representatives from the four congregations held an assembly in the home of J. C. Murphy at Camp Creek. They had tasted success. Their identity as a fellowship had become strong. They made a series of decisions to further guide and govern their organizational life. They expressed their intention to hold such an assembly each year. Yet their wariness of church structure appeared in a note in the minutes of that first meeting: "We hope and trust that no person or body of people will ever use these minutes, or any part of them, as articles of faith upon which to establish a sect or denomination. The subjects were discussed merely to obtain light and understanding. Our articles of faith are inspired and given us by the Holy Apostles and written in the New Testament which is our only rule of faith and practice."[18]

A Pentecostal "Church of God"

At the assembly of 1907 they decided that the name of their fellowship would be The Church of God. Its expansion continued in the three states and beyond. Tomlinson recorded the "explanation and obligation" developed for incoming members.

> As Jesus Christ is the sole founder and originator of His Church, and still retains the position as head and only lawgiver, all who connect themselves with His Church will be expected to obey His laws and government . . . The applicants for membership are expected to accept the teaching of repentance, water baptism (by immersion), sanctification subsequent to conversion, the baptism with the Holy Ghost on the sanctified life evidenced by the speaking in tongues as the Spirit gives utterance, the Lord's Supper, feet washing, eternal punishment for the wicked and eternal life for the righteous, divine healing, tithing and offerings, and the second pre-millenial [sic] coming of the Lord. Applicants must sever their connections with churches and lodges, if not already free from them. Men having two or more wives, divorced or undivorced, and women having two or more husbands, divorced or undivorced, should not publicly present themselves for membership, but if they wish to join the church they should apply to the pastor or church privately, and be examined as to the reasons for being so situated. Those using tobacco in any form should not present themselves for membership. The obligation is simple, and just what every true child of God desires to practice. "Will you sincerely promise before God and these witnesses that you will take the Bible as your guide, the New Testament as your rule of faith and practice, government and discipline, and walk in the light to the best of your knowledge and ability?" Having accepted the above explanation and obligation the applicants are usually asked to kneel in holy reverence before God, while the minister engages in prayer and asks God's guidance and blessings upon the new members, and to make them useful, and keep them true and faithful until Jesus comes or calls. When the prayer is ended a song is usually sung by the congregation, and all the members give them a glad welcome by extending to them the right hands of fellowship.[19]

Reports of the pentecostal outpourings in California following 1906 reinforced the local experiences. Tomlinson was the only Church of God minister who had not received the experience and he sought it earnestly. At the 1907 assembly his sermon topic was "The Baptism of the Holy Ghost and Fire." He was himself a "seeker at the altar" all that year. Gaston Barnabas Cashwell was a renowned holiness evangelist of North Carolina who received the baptism in the Holy Spirit at the Azusa Street mission in California in 1906. He was leading multitudes of holiness members into Pentecostalism. Tomlinson invited Cashwell to visit the Church of God assembly in January of 1908. After the conference Cashwell preached in the Church of God at Cleveland.[20] Tomlinson wrote:

> On Sunday morning, January 12, while he was preaching, a peculiar sensation took hold of me, and almost unconsciously I slipped off my chair in a heap on the rostrum at Brother Cashwell's feet. I did not know what such an experience meant. My mind was clear, but a peculiar power so enveloped and thrilled my whole being that I concluded to yield myself up to God and await results. I was soon lost to my surroundings as I lay there on the floor, occupied only with God and eternal things. Soon one of my feet began to shake and clatter against the wall. I could not hold it still. When it got quiet the other one acted the same way. Then my arms and head were operated. My jaws seemed to be set, my lips were moved and twisted about as if a physician was making a special examination. My tongue and eyes were operated on in like manner. Several examinations seemed to be taken, and every limb and my whole body examined. My body was rolled and tossed about beyond my control, and finally while lying on my back, my feet were raised up several times, and my tongue would stick out of my mouth in spite of my efforts to keep it inside my mouth. At one time, while lying flat on my back, I seemed to see a great sheet let down, and as it came to me I felt it as it enveloped me in its folds, and I really felt myself literally lifted up and off the floor several inches, and carried in that sheet several feet in the direction my feet pointed, and then let down on the floor again. As I lay there great joy flooded my soul. The happiest moments I had ever known up to that time. I never knew what real joy was before. My hands clasped together with no effort on my part. Oh, such floods and billows of glory ran through my whole being for several minutes! There were times that I suffered the most excruciating pain and agony, but my spirit always said "yes" to God.[21]

As part of that experience in trance he seemed taken on tour of many of the world's peoples and spoke to several in their own languages. "Judging from the countries I visited in the vision I spoke ten different languages." This experience was to be at the heart of Tomlinson's evangelistic testimony. He said: "I have traveled thousands of miles and told the simple story, and related my experience to thousands of people, and have seen hundreds baptized with the Holy Ghost, and every one who received Him spake in tongues as the Spirit gave them utterance."[22]

Tomlinson as Principal Leader

A. J. Tomlinson was by no means the only leader in the rising Church of God. Richard G. Spurling, William F. Bryant, and M. S. Lemons were respected pioneers. The expanding fellowship attracted a whole new generation of ministerial leadership. But A. J. Tomlinson did become the primary leader of the church, its most articulate, active, and visible member. The annual assemblies became the center of church authority and identity. At these assemblies Tomlinson presided and in many years served as clerk as well to compose the official record of decisions made. He was named chairman in 1906, moderator in 1907, general moderator in 1909, general overseer in 1910, general overseer by acclamation in 1912, and general overseer for life in 1914.[23]

Tomlinson wrote in 1914: "The Holy Ghost set me in as General Overseer again. This time it was made plain that I should continue in the position until Jesus comes or calls. Tears form in my eyes as I write. I am unable to express my gratitude to God for His strength and care bestowed upon me. I go deeper into humility as I launch out into victory. God is faithful and I want to be. Oh God, make of me whatever pleases Thee at any cost." With his correspondence and with his addresses he set the agenda for most assemblies. The responsibility made him tremble, he said. "I am in a narrow path, because of a fear that I might recommend something that is unscriptural, and would prove a great detriment to the cause we love so well, if it were accepted and put into action. On the other hand, if I should fail to recommend something, that, if neglected, would cause the great Church of God to deteriorate instead of progress as it has been doing, it would be a source of sorrow and sadness to me the longest day that I live."[24]

Because he operated the central office and did things well and gloried in the achievement, most assembly actions were his to implement. It was he who awarded or removed ministerial credentials. When this duty came to be shared with state overseers, the state overseers in turn were named by him and reported directly to him. The assembly established a church paper in 1910; Tomlinson was editor from the day the *Evangel* began publication. His addresses and articles made up an important segment of its content. In 1914 the *Evangel* changed from a biweekly to a weekly paper. Circulation climbed from 5,000 in 1917 to 15,000 two years later.[25]

When the church called for its own Sunday school literature in 1914, Tomlinson wrote the material just ahead of the press deadlines. The assembly favored the purchase of its own printing plant in 1916; Tomlinson handled the transaction in 1917 and was named publisher. He told the assembly of 1917 about the pressing need for a Bible training school for church workers. The assembly said such a school should be started soon with the Bible as the principal textbook. Tomlinson established it at Cleveland in 1918 and was its supervisor; nearly all of the students made their home with the Tomlinsons. He spoke to the assembly in 1919 about the need for an orphanage. It was located at Cleveland in 1920 and he was its superintendent.[26]

Tomlinson was repeatedly elected pastor of the church at Cleveland and often served as its Sunday school superintendent. The entire Cleveland area called on him for pastoral work, especially ministry to the sick and funerals for the dead. He said:

> Well, I could not possibly keep up and do the work I am doing if the Lord did not hold me up. But it is wonderful how my strength holds up, and the work I do. I can hardly tell all I do. I have my regular office work, editing, publishing the paper, Sunday School literature, one hundred and fifty to one hundred and eighty letters every week to answer or attend to, pastoral work, making peace sometimes among members, praying for the sick, preaching three or four times a week. Funeral of Sister Luda Clark today. Preached twice yesterday. I can't take time to give a detailed account of my work in my journal as I used to do. I work from sixteen to eighteen hours every day and have to hurry in everything I do. God gives wisdom, grace and strength. My heart magnifies the Lord for His wonderful help to me. How I love Him![27]

He was the church's most efficient fund raiser. As state conventions developed, he made rounds to oversee their annual meetings, solving problems and igniting revivals.

Church of God Doctrine and Practice

All the while Tomlinson was the church's foremost teacher. He had written as an axiom in the minutes of the first meeting that the assembly of the Church of God was not to be a legislative body. There was no need to write law. The only acceptable law and government was from God and was provided in the Bible. The duty of the Church of God, under guidance of the Holy Spirit, was to search out this law and obey it. The church's compilation of "teachings" issued in 1911 was simply an abbreviated list of twenty-five subjects, each with one or more Scripture citations. "The Church of God is theocratic," Tomlinson liked to say.[28]

Sometimes Tomlinson simply moderated a church meeting and gave his official scriptural answers to questions immediately as they were raised. He saw a parallel between himself and James the brother of Jesus who evidently presided and responded with authority at the assembly at Jerusalem described in Acts 15:13–21. More often he taught major points of doctrine by repetition in his articles in the weekly *Evangel*; in his addresses to the assemblies and the state conventions; in his special messages for Thanksgiving, Christmas, and New Year's Day; and in his calls to celebrate the anniversaries of Church of God events.[29]

Tomlinson came under increasing conviction that the Church of God was the very true church being prepared for the last days, the precise body Jesus would search out upon his return. It was the Church of God which had authority to baptize. In 1918 he himself sought and received baptism in water again, this time by a Church of God preacher. However the normal sequence in the plan of salvation was expected to involve three stages.[30] He wrote:

> How can people be saved from their sins if the preacher does not preach it that way? And how can we expect people to get sanctified if the preachers do not preach it and make it clear and plain as a definite experience following conversion? And the same is true of the baptism of the Holy Ghost. These experiences are obtained by faith, but people cannot have faith to enter into an experience that is not taught clearly and conclusively. And when the teaching is rather mixed and uncertain the experiences are more likely to be sought in an indefinite and mixed up manner . . . The first experience is the one that makes one a child of God, the second is the crucifixion or destruction of the "old man" or the "carnal nature," and the third is the baptism of the Holy Ghost and fire. These are the three definite experiences that our people cling to so tenaciously. And the Church of God stands for a recognition of these experiences without compromise. They are known as "born again," "sanctification" and "baptized with the Holy Ghost and fire" with the "other tongues as the Spirit gives the utterance" as the evidence.[31]

The Church of God was always trinitarian. Baptism by immersion was to be in the name of the Father, the Son, and the Holy Spirit as indicated in Matthew 28.[32] Sanctification and baptism in the Holy Spirit were then to be urgently sought. "Our preachers are instructed to preach sanctification strong and powerful," Tomlinson said. "Show that it is a definite experience and not obtained by a gradual growth. These gradual growth sanctificationists never do get sanctified. They are always getting sanctified, but never able to state truthfully that they are sanctified. But we know we are sanctified just as well as we know we are converted because we get it as a second definite work of grace. The 'old man' is crucified, and no longer lives in the heart to try to dominate over the new nature put in there at conversion." He warned those who seemed to be slow. "Jesus declares that the world cannot receive the Holy Ghost, so if you cannot receive the Holy Ghost and talk in other tongues like the rest of us, you must be of the world, because the world cannot receive Him. (John 14:17) I would be afraid to risk your chance after you have had the light as some of you have had for years. Look out, brother."[33]

The Lord's Supper for the Church of God was to be celebrated with bread and grape juice. Footwashing was also a sacred rite.[34] Tomlinson wrote:

> Sometimes the power has been so great during these feet washing services that it almost seemed the water was charged. When the feet or hands came in contact with the water the bodies of both persons thus engaged were jerked and moved about sometimes for minutes. Usually there is a fresh baptism of love that comes upon the participants. This is one means of drawing the humble worshippers closer together in a spiritual sense. The men and women separate and occupy different places in the house or tabernacle. They sing and shout and dance, play music, talk in tongues. This makes it a time of rejoicing and happiness. Take it all in all, this is a sacred and glorious service.[35]

Tomlinson was sure that a careful search of the Scriptures disclosed God's "money system" for the church. He spelled out his conclusions at length in his first book in 1913. Every member should pay tithes of all earnings and then make additional offerings "as he purposes in his own heart." Members should give their tithes and offerings directly to the church instead of "throwing them out here and there as they felt led to do." One tenth of all receipts were to be sent from the congregation to the state treasurer who was to send one tenth of his receipts to the general treasurer. This system, with later modifications to adjust the share for state and general treasurers, gave great impetus to church programs for evangelism, missions, publishing, and general expansion.[36]

Tomlinson was sympathetic toward the codes of behavior and dress typical of holiness bands. Saints should be visibly separated from the ways of the world. Such restriction and self-definition was of lively interest among the people; there eventually came to be a long list of "practical commitments," each with a biblical citation. Members were to abstain from alcohol, tobacco, drugs such as opium or morphine, personal adornment and cosmetics, short hair for women or long hair for men, movies, dances, carnivals, church bazaars, swimming with the opposite sex, chewing gum, secret societies, labor unions, swearing, and many current styles of dress.[37]

Tomlinson thought the use of medicine was a sign of weak faith and regretted that sick members called physicians instead of calling the elders of the church.[38] "I do not know the reason that God reserved the right to heal the human race when they get sick," he said, "but just so He did . . . When I learned this fact from the study of the Bible, I discarded all medicines and have never used any remedies from that time till this. And I have lived forty-two years since that time. Lived without the use of medicine. Instead of using my money for medicine and doctor bills, except in the case of childbirth, I have invested it in the work of the Lord. Since He is my physician, I have paid it to Him."[39]

Mark 16:17–18 in Tomlinson's Bible said that believers would speak with new tongues, heal the sick, and cast out devils. Further "they shall take up serpents; and if they drink any deadly thing it shall not hurt them." He resisted scholars who claimed that the best and oldest manuscripts ended with Mark 16:8 and that the verses later appended were certainly not intended as a guide for church practice. "Some people try to claim that that part of the Gospel of Mark does not belong to the Bible," he said, "but it is there and we know that all of these signs have followed our people for years at intervals. Many serpents have been taken up with perfect victory. The Church stands for the whole Bible rightly divided, and it is wrongly dividing to cut out tongues and serpents."[40] Tomlinson lived to see the 1928 assembly of the Church of God, Cleveland, Tenn., formally denounce serpent handling.

Though he had been wary of church order and government at first, Tomlinson later developed a great affection for them. "I admit that we have those in our ranks who oppose government and any kind of organization," he said, "but such are false teachers. They refuse to submit to government, and are holding themselves aloof and independent, every one for himself, even contending against any form of organization, and say they are members of Christ's church. It matters not how spiritual they may seem to be, or how honest they may be, they are dangerous characters, and enemies to Christ and His truth."[41] Evangelism demanded efficiency: "We are now on the march, march, march! The Jericho walls of opposition to our advancement must fall, fall, fall! And they will fall down flat before us in proportion to our faith, and our faith will materialize in proportion to our obedience and unity of action. Perfect organization and concerted action will save souls, and house them in the great Church of God by the thousands. No unity, no organization, no system, no obedience, no concerted action, will damn souls in the abyss of everlasting punishment by the millions."[42]

The people must be taught submission to the Church of God which is God's government, Tomlinson said. They must be trained to bow to authority. They must learn obedience here in order that they may rule during the millennium. A "Declaration" in 1920 stated: "The General Assembly of the Church of God is that organized body with full power and authority to designate the teaching, government, principles and practices of all the local churches composing said Assembly . . . We . . . do not recognize the right of any local church to withdraw from the General Assembly as a whole, but those who prove disloyal to the Government and teachings as promulgated from time to time by the General Assembly or otherwise disorderly are to be dealt with in individual manner and excluded as a member of said church."[43]

The most frequent message from Tomlinson was an exhortation to work. The time was short. Idle or ineffective preachers meant souls slipping away into hell every day. He set the pace and expected others to follow his example. The church had twenty members when Tomlinson joined in 1903. At the end of the next decade there were 3,056 members in ten states and the Bahamas.[44]

Tomlinson reported to the assembly in 1922, approaching the end of his first twenty years, that there were 21,076 members in 666 churches served by 923 ministers. "I delivered my annual address that brought a flood of applause and tokens of approval far in excess of any that had ever been delivered," he said. "For two hours, I suppose, amidst shouts, music by the brass band, and songs, cheers and weeping, about twenty-five hundred people marched by and shook my hand and many of the men fell on my neck and kissed me and wept for joy. One precious old mother kissed me, too. My hand was sore for two months from the tight grips of love. Nobody suggested such a move, and nobody ordered it. It was voluntary and spontaneous."[45]

And, as he went from that 1922 assembly on his rounds of the conventions, he rejoiced: "Multitudes are wonderfully blest. There seems to be no way to describe the manifestations of the Spirit as He operates on the people all through the services, through the preaching and all. The people cry, laugh, shout, dance, run, jump, talk in tongues, give interpretations, whole congregations fall on their knees and faces at times when the presence of the Lord seems so great. If every meeting could be described it would take books to tell it all."[46]

Rebellion and Impeachment

However great trouble lay just ahead for Tomlinson. There was always some opposition; his aggressive style and the volatile nature of his constituency guaranteed that.[47] But in 1922 there came a whole new level of rebellion. He failed to carry his agenda with the assembly— abolition of a constitution which he claimed had gone legislative and denial of a requirement that he share his authority equally in a three-man executive committee. Worse still, an investigatory committee of three was at work to see if all the affairs of the Church of God were in order. Tomlinson's accounts were hardly ready for inspection.

As the active agent in most Church of God enterprises, he had borne the heavy responsibility of arranging financing and had often handled this as a personal matter. His diary for 12 August 1919 said: "I am having quite a test of faith for the money to complete the building. No one knows my heaviness and apparent perplexities. I tell it to God only and He is blessedly giving me grace. The elders in council advised me to put up the building when they met in April. So I am doing my best. I have borrowed money largely on my own responsibility. I am trusting God to make me able to meet it." And for 16 June of the following year the entry read: "The Lord has given me favor with the bankers and businessmen until I can get anything I ask for. I have borrowed thousands of dollars at the bank with no security, and have used hundreds with no notes given, just my word. This is God's work. It is wonderful."[48]

Always inclined to expect resolution of financial problems by divine intervention, he had transferred funds among personal and church accounts in crisis while awaiting a miracle. Special trouble came during a brief experimental period when all the tithes were being sent through his hands at general headquarters for redistribution to church work at all levels.[49]

> In order to save the Church and publishing house from bankruptcy I felt compelled to use some of the tithes. I decided that I would rather suffer the shame and reproach of whatever would be heaped upon me and risk incurring the ill-will of all the ministers than for the shame and reproach of bankruptcy to be heaped upon

the Church . . . A little later a number of the notes on the orphanage property and the auditorium property came due besides a lot of bills and dues on both that had to be taken care of, besides the insurance and running expenses of the publishing house and the payments on the machinery. All of this required thousands of dollars, but I only used the tithes little at a time, each time with a hope that I would get enough back in a few days to replace them and save the ministers as well as the publishing house and Church.[50]

The investigating committee and its auditor said that about $31,000 had been wrongly distributed and that there was a shortage of $14,141.38. Neither side displayed the combination of patience and grace which would have been required to get the accounts unscrambled or to continue the dialogue. Ten of the twelve elders on the council hearing the case brought charges against Tomlinson ranging from disloyalty and conspiracy against the Church of God to usurpation of authority and misappropriation of funds. In the long run very little financial culpability was sustained against Tomlinson. He said of his accusers: "The decision put about $45,000 debt for them to settle, and our cost is not quite $2,000. They have to pay the $17,000 that they undertook to make me pay and accused me of stealing. They also failed to prove me guilty of stealing the $14,000 they charged against me. So we have won quite a victory after all." But in the short run Tomlinson, along with elders George Brouayer and S. O. Gillaspie who had remained loyal to him through the trial, were impeached on 21 July 1923.[51]

A New "Tomlinson Church of God"—
Church of God of Prophecy

Tomlinson's next steps were entirely in character. Having just invested the twenty years from 1903 to 1923 in developing one Church of God, he was ready to invest the twenty years from 1923 to 1943 in developing another. It was true that he had been discredited and impeached at age fifty-eight. But it was also true that he now knew very well what he wanted a true church to be and to teach, that he had practical experience in nearly every phase of the operation of such a church, and that a nucleus of at least 2,000 members chose to be loyal to him. There was hardly a change in his pace. The second twenty years, in the midst of a smaller but more intensely loyal fellowship, were in many respects more satisfying to him than his first twenty.

Claiming the role of rightful and continuing general overseer, he called a meeting of the council of elders for 24 July, just three days after the impeachment. Only loyal elders Gillaspie and Brouayer joined him in attendance. The three adopted a carefully worded "Declaration of Independence" showing how the main body had gone astray with its "man-made constitution" and declaring their stand for "the Church of God as originally organized and as set out in the New Testament." They notified the ten absent and opposing members of the council of elders that they had vacated their eldership and all their church offices. They provided for the filling of all vacancies. They challenged each church member to "determine whether he or she will continue with the Church of God adhering to God's law and God's Word instead of the man-made creed adopted at the Assembly."[52]

Tomlinson made his own house his continuing base at Cleveland. Having lost the publishing enterprise and the *Evangel* in the steps leading to his impeachment in July of 1923, he began a new publishing program by issuing the *White Wing Messenger* from his home beginning in September of that year. Having lost the use of the spacious auditorium of the Church of God in Cleveland, he was able to prepare a tiny new tabernacle with shavings for a floor as a meeting place for what he numbered the rightful eighteenth annual assembly in November of 1923. Early in 1924 he said "We now have one hundred and seventy ministers on our list lined up to help us in this great revolution." At the end of 1927 he reported more than 300 ministers.[53]

Tomlinson spent a lot of his time alongside his state overseers stirring up the churches. In 1925 he said

Manifestations and demonstrations are signs of life, but the absence of manifestations and demonstrations are signs of death to me. I do not mean to say that a person is dead spiritually if he has no manifestations of the Spirit, neither do I mean to say that everyone should shout or dance or demonstrate in some manner in every service, neither do I mean to say that when there are no manifestations in a service that all have backslidden, but I am only trying to encourage our people to get close to God and be so full of the Spirit until the demonstrations like at Pentecost can be repeated more frequently, and to teach our people to have their faith in the power of God more than in something that merely feeds the intellect.[54]

He told a state overseer: "You should become so enthused as you make up your plans that you will have your convention all the way through in your mind many times over, both day and night, before the time arrives. By your being enthused about it you will have a tendency to cause others to be enthused. I want you to also try to have the largest attendance and greatest display of local churches with their bands and banners. You can do great things if you will just think you can and work at it, which I am sure you will do. I sure have great faith and confidence in you."[55]

The annual assemblies at Cleveland were greatest of all. The one in 1933, a mere ten years after his expulsion, was "a continuous feast of eight days." Tomlinson reported "about five thousand registered attendance, with at least five thousand others that tried to attend but could not get inside, and many could not get near."[56] These general assemblies at Cleveland grew and grew. Registered attendance rose to 20,000 and estimates of total participation ran as high as 50,000. Clerks described an opening night in the enlarged and remodeled tabernacle in 1943, the last one moderated by A. J. Tomlinson.

> The whole tabernacle is alive with the children of God praising Him—some shouting, some dancing, some singing, some laughing, some waving flags, some running, some leaping. Oh how happy this company of two armies with banners is! Now they are marching in almost every direction in the huge Tabernacle. The brass bands break in with their music and the shouting continues. The Tabernacle is full of the presence and power of God. A new shower has fallen on this mighty host and surely we are praising Him . . . All over the vast audience one can almost see the streaks of fire as the folks shout, dance, leap and talk in tongues. This is a direct result of the very presence of God. The General Overseer climbs atop the Bible stand in honor to God.[57]

Once more there was an orphanage with Tomlinson as president. He got a short-term school going again in 1941. He organized church women as the Women's Missionary Band and church youth as the Victory Leaders Band. In the new fellowship Tomlinson remained a champion of church order, government, and authority. His missionary vision was that Church of God literature would eventually be published "in all the languages of the world" through a group of translators located at Cleveland. "In order to keep the doctrine and teaching clean, and to avoid falling into error and heresy, all the fundamental teaching will have to go out from headquarters. This then, means that a group of translators will be required to put our teaching into all the languages . . . We must have our teaching printed in every language so we can teach them and cause them to learn. It will not do to depend upon the Bible going alone." He expected to remain at the center of it all. "God's people need government," he said, "but laws and rules are almost if not wholly worthless without somebody in authority to see they are obeyed."[58]

A pleasure of his old age was acquiring and marking Church of God historical sites—the Bryant cabin, Burger Mountain, Shearer Schoolhouse. These acquisitions formed the base of "Fields of the Wood" (Psalm 132:6), a multimillion-dollar biblical theme park built on a beautiful mountainous site of 216 acres. It was developed and supported as Tomlinson planned by continuing gifts of the church people to a Church of Prophecy Marker Association. Tomlinson saw Fields of the Wood as a very practical tourist attraction for thousands of visitors each year and as a conference ground. It was a place to hold a service each year prior to the general assembly, perhaps to baptize or rebaptize some persons in the outdoor pool. Columbus Day was celebrated there with commentary on the discovery of America as an instrumental step to the founding of the Church of God. There were pageants for Thanksgiving and Easter. There were revivals and youth rallies.

But Fields of the Wood was also to be a memorial to the penniless Hoosier tract salesman who invested his life in the formation of two pentecostal Churches of God. He saw himself as a crucial part of God's plan to reveal his true church. There were predecessors such as Spurling and Bryant but they "only saw the light as through a glass darkly." Tomlinson said: "The zeal of the Lord has pressed me along up the line so much and with such force that I am inclined to the belief that God is using me in this last days work because He put me on the program somewhere back in eternity, and I just have to operate according to His will in order to carry on His work."[59]

He was excited by what he understood to be a providential connection between his joining the Camp Creek church in 1903 and the successful flights by the Wright brothers in the same state in the same year. It seemed significant that both he and Wilbur Wright were Indiana natives. It was all linked up in Isaiah 60, Tomlinson said. The Church of God was there in verse one which reads "Arise, shine; for thy light has come." The Wrights were there in verse eight which reads "Who are these that fly as a cloud?"[60]

A. J. Tomlinson wanted to remain on the earthly scene of action until the church was ready to be presented to Jesus Christ. He wanted to be taken up with the church when Jesus returned, to "scale the heights of the sky without any handholds" as he liked to say. But on 2 October 1943 he died in Cleveland, Tennessee, and was buried there. There was a funeral service on Sunday night, another on Monday night, and another on Tuesday afternoon. The final one on Tuesday night continued until about 3 A.M. on Wednesday. Thousands filed by the honor guards in the tabernacle where his body lay in state. Cleveland business and traffic stopped as his funeral procession made its way to the Fort Hill Cemetery.[61]

Because the designation "Church of God" was so central to their self-understanding, both denominations insisted on having that name. Actually the name had been previously used and neither could eventually claim it exclusively in secular affairs. The larger branch which impeached Tomlinson and continued its line of general overseers with Flavius J. Lee in 1923 was finally recognized by the Tennessee courts as the original and continuing body and so entitled to the church assets. It went on to become the second largest of the predominantly white American pentecostal denominations. It finally accepted a legal name with the location of its headquarters appended—"Church of God (Cleveland, Tenn.)."[62]

The smaller branch under continued leadership of Tomlinson was variously "Tomlinson Church of God" and "Church of God Over Which A. J. Tomlinson Is Overseer." When A. J. Tomlinson died in 1943 the office of general overseer passed to his younger son Milton A. Tomlinson.[63] That selection was made by the assembled state and national overseers who were influenced by a message received in tongues and interpreted in favor of Milton. A decade later the legal name of the smaller branch became "Church of God of Prophecy." In their congregational life both branches generally referred to themselves simply as "Church of God."[64]

Two Maturing Denominations

These young pentecostal Churches of God soon took their places on both the American and the foreign mission scenes as substantial religious fellowships. While A. J. Tomlinson presided over the assembly of the undivided body in 1915, a resolution was passed demanding more respect:

> Whereas, the Church of God is suffering undue reproach by the slanderous title "Holy Rollers" that is in common use before the public in referring to its members and work, be it known to all men everywhere and unto all nations that we, the Church of God . . . do hereby and hereafter disclaim and repudiate the title "Holy Rollers" in reference to the Church of God. In consequence of this decision, we herewith give general notice to the public that all reference to the Church of God by the use of . . . "Holy Rollers" by the public press or otherwise will be considered and treated as a slanderous and malignant offense.[65]

A. J. Tomlinson prepared a letter to be left in every home in Bradley County in 1940.

> Cleveland is the capital of the world for the Church of God of which A. J. Tomlinson is General Overseer . . . On account of our high standing as a world-wide religious institution, we court the favor and friendship of all of our home people, both in the city of Cleveland and Bradley County, who will doubtless have the joy and pleasure of assisting us in entertaining the millions of strangers and foreigners who will come to be with us in our great Assemblies year after year. We want these millions to feel a holy and sacred atmosphere, not only in Cleveland, but also all about over the county.[66]

Church of God mission work, once carried out by individuals or bands going out "by faith" under no discipline but their private word from God, came to be regularized under denominational officers. The increased guidance and regular support for missionaries was so effective that Church of God membership overseas came to exceed membership in the United States. Executives were appointed as needed to handle the work of other church departments—publishing, evangelism, education, women's work, youth work, clergy aid, and many more. A goal was to have a state overseer in every state and at least one contact person or group for the Church of God in every county.[67]

At its 100th anniversary in 1986 the Church of God (Cleveland, Tenn.) had become a billion-dollar institution. It had congregations and missions in 107 countries. World membership was 1,652,000 including 547,000 in the U.S. and Canada. The Church of God of Prophecy reported in 1987 a membership of 74,588 (2,085 churches) in the United States plus a membership of 172,153 (3,048 churches) in 89 countries outside the United States.[68]

As the Churches of God grew older and larger and increasingly middle class, their emphases changed. The aim of each was to control the change, to keep the essentials of faith without complete rigidity. Scholars noted the unity of the two fellowships on all major doctrines but commented on some variations in emphasis and in the rate of change. Services, revivals, and altar exercises of the Church of God of Prophecy appeared to be longer and more frequent. The Church of God of Prophecy gave much attention to that particular personal vision of the true church revealed to A. J. Tomlinson on Burger Mountain on 13 June 1903 and so to the Fields of the Wood shrine in which that occasion and revelation was symbolized. In the Church of God of Prophecy official holiness restrictions seemed more carefully maintained, along with some unofficial ones such as the prohibition of wedding rings.[69]

The Church of God (Cleveland, Tenn.) was more hospitable to formal education, developing an accredited college and a theological seminary at Cleveland, four other Bible colleges in the United States plus ten abroad, and institute-level schools in fifty-two countries. And the Church of God (Cleveland, Tenn.) was more open to ecumenical relationships with other churches, being among the founders of the National Association of Evangelicals (1942), the Pentecostal World Conference (1947), and the Pentecostal Fellowship of North America (1948). So these Churches of God became more open to mainstream America. And mainstream America became more open to these Pentecostals, often seeing in them a rock of conservatism stabilizing old-time values and morals.[70]

Indiana Constituency

The Churches of God came to Indiana slowly and from the South. A. J. Tomlinson visited his old home in Indiana in 1909. He was already a very successful revivalist, having established the Church of God in the town of Cleveland and having received his pentecostal baptism. He preached during this Indiana visit but established no congregation. Preacher Sam C. Perry brought the Church of God northward when he moved to London, Kentucky, in 1910 and made that state the sixth to be reached. In 1913 Tomlinson added Indiana and Illinois to his tour as general overseer.[71]

This was the period of prominence of an Evansville Methodist named D. P. Barnett. The Methodists put Barnett out of their ministry in 1912 when he and some members of his congregation were baptized in the Holy Spirit and spoke in tongues. He became the central figure in a sweeping pentecostal revival at Evansville but found Illinois even more inviting and moved there. In 1916 Barnett and his followers joined the Church of God. For several years Eldorado, Illinois, was the largest congregation in the Church of God.[72]

In the course of her work in Egypt and Palestine, faith missionary Lucy M. Leatherman of Greencastle, Indiana, reported that "the Church of God was revealed to her." She joined that fellowship in Georgia in 1916. In her subsequent work in Chile and Argentina she was a pioneer representative of the Church of God abroad. But she did not pioneer in Indiana. The United States religious census of 1916 found only one congregation of the Church of God in Indiana. It had fifty-seven members.[73]

Effective entry into Indiana came with the second decade when Tomlinson was attempting to place an overseer in every state. Indiana had an unbroken line of state overseers for the Church of God (later Church of God, Cleveland, Tenn.) beginning with S. O. Gillaspie in 1919.[74] C. H. Standifer was holding meetings at Shelburn in Sullivan County as early as 1920. Churches of God were organized at Shelburn and at Coalmont in Clay County in 1927.[75] There were four churches with 299 members in Indiana in 1926, eight churches with 586 members in 1936, and thirty churches in 1950. In August of 1952, during the tenure of state overseer C. R. Spain, the general assembly for the entire Church of God (Cleveland, Tenn.) met at Indianapolis, the second meeting in its history to be convened outside the South.[76]

After his impeachment in 1923 and the redirection of his energies to the smaller branch of the Church of God (Church of God of Prophecy after 1953), Tomlinson added Indiana to his tours of state conventions again. Each state convention was expected to be a rousing regional replica of the annual excitement at Cleveland. He attended Indiana conventions in 1931, in 1932, and in 1933. His diary for 7 June 1933 said: "I visited the old home near Westfield. The place is terribly desolate and made my heart ache as I looked around. My sisters are all dead, got to see two of my cousins and Aunt Esther. Charlie and Lulu are taking care of her. She is too old to walk but seems cheerful." The 1936 religious census showed the "Tomlinson Church of God" in Indiana with 7 churches, 281 members, and cash expenditures of $2,517 for all seven combined.[77] Indiana's Churches of God shared in the general growth of holiness and pentecostal bodies through the depression years. They benefited from the population flow from South to North. In spite of southern origins, both bodies came to resist social pressures for racial segregation. In the 1980s the Church of God of Prophecy was probably the most racially integrated pentecostal church in the world.[78]

The Church of God (Cleveland, Tenn.) reported 695,074 adherents in the United States in 1990. Southern states reported the largest number of congregations—Florida with 479, Georgia with 466, North Carolina with 417, Alabama with 382, and Tennessee with 346. Indiana recorded 10,212 adherents in 85 churches.

The Church of God of Prophecy, roughly one-sixth the size of its historical sister within the United States, had concentrations of its 2,101 congregations in North Carolina (190), Georgia (153), South Carolina (150), Tennessee (146), and Florida (125). However, a register of activities of the Church of God of Prophecy in Indiana for the year ending in July of 1989 included 427 converted, 233 sanctified, 193 baptized in water, 174 baptized in the Holy Spirit, 4,934 sermons preached, and 20,265 homes visited.[79] There were 42 of its congregations in the state reporting 1,764 adherents.

Thus the number of Indiana adherents in the two Churches of God related to the missionary effort of A. J. Tomlinson of Westfield totaled 11,976—about as many as the Seventh-day Adventists or half as many as the Mormons. Lake County and Marion County had over 1,000 adherents each. Eighteen additional counties reported more than 200.

NOTES

1. Lillie Duggar, *A. J. Tomlinson: Former Overseer of the Church of God* (Cleveland, Tenn.: White Wing Publishing House, 1964), 18, 349, 688, 763.

2. A. J. Tomlinson, *The Last Great Conflict* (Cleveland, Tenn.: Press of Walter E. Rodgers, 1913), 199–201; *Dictionary of Pentecostal and Charismatic Movements* (Grand Rapids, Mich.: Zondervan, 1988), 846; Duggar, *Tomlinson*, 18, 20, 288, 763, 802.

3. Tomlinson, *Last Great Conflict*, 201–3.

4. James Stone, *The Church of God of Prophecy: History and Polity* (Cleveland, Tenn.: White Wing Publishing House, 1977), 19; *Dictionary of Pentecostal and Charismatic Movements*, 846–47.

5. Tomlinson, *Last Great Conflict*, 203–4.

6. Charles W. Conn, *Like a Mighty Army: A History of the Church of God 1886–1976* (Cleveland, Tenn.: Pathway Press, 1977), 50; Duggar, *Tomlinson*, 22–29; Stone, *Church of God of Prophecy*, 21.

7. Shirley Nelson, *Fair, Clear, and Terrible: The Story of Shiloh, Maine* (Latham, N.Y.: British American Publishing, 1989, 447 p.); Edith L. Blumhofer, *The Assemblies of God: A Chapter in the Story of American Pentecostalism*, 2 vols. (Springfield, Mo.: Gospel Publishing House, 1989), 1:77–81; Duggar, *Tomlinson*, 29–31; *Dictionary of Pentecostal and Charismatic Movements*, 847.

8. Conn, *Like a Mighty Army*, 50.

9. Mickey Crews, *The Church of God: A Social History* (Knoxville, Tenn.: University of Tennessee Press, 1990), 17; Conn, *Like a Mighty Army*, 8–13; *Dictionary of Pentecostal and Charismatic Movements*, 847.

10. Charles W. Conn, *Where the Saints Have Trod: A History of Church of God Missions* (Cleveland, Tenn.: Pathway Press, 1959), 11–12; Conn, *Like a Mighty Army*, 18–27; Crews, *Church of God*, 10; *Dictionary of Pentecostal and Charismatic Movements*, 198.

11. Vinson Synan, *The Holiness-Pentecostal Movement in the United States* (Grand Rapids, Mich.: Eerdmans, 1971), 82; Conn, *Like a Mighty Army*, 26, 29–37, 42–45; Tomlinson, *Last Great Conflict*, 184–92; Crews, *Church of God*, 191; *Dictionary of Pentecostal and Charismatic Movements*, 309.

12. Conn, *Like a Mighty Army*, 50–51.

13. Synan, *Holiness-Pentecostal*, 84–86; Duggar, *Tomlinson*, 34.

14. Conn, *Like a Mighty Army*, 52.

15. Duggar, *Tomlinson*, 35; *Dictionary of Pentecostal and Charismatic Movements*, 207.

16. Conn, *Like a Mighty Army*, 52; Duggar, *Tomlinson*, 741.

17. Duggar, *Tomlinson*, 35–37; Conn, *Like a Mighty Army*, 71; Crews, *Church of God*, 5.

18. *Minutes of Annual Assembly of the Churches of East Tennessee, North Georgia and Western North-Carolina, Held January 26 & 27 1906, at Camp Creek, N.C.* (N.p., n.d.), 1.

19. Tomlinson, *Last Great Conflict*, 194–96.

20. Duggar, *Tomlinson*, 52–53; Conn, *Like a Mighty Army*, 76–77, 84–85.

21. Tomlinson, *Last Great Conflict*, 211–12.

22. Tomlinson, *Last Great Conflict*, 214–15.

23. Duggar, *Tomlinson*, 39–41, 68, 86, 136, 143, 156–57.

24. Duggar, *Tomlinson*, 156, 163–64.

25. *The Evangel Reader: Selections from the Church of God Evangel, 1910–1958*, comp. and ed. with introduction and notes by Charles W. Conn (Cleveland, Tenn.: Pathway Press, 1958), 9; Duggar, *Tomlinson*, 87, 110, 135–36, 152–53; Conn, *Like a Mighty Army*, 116–17, 146–47.

26. Duggar, *Tomlinson*, 158–59, 165–66, 179–80, 326; Conn, *Like a Mighty Army*, 152–53, 169; *Evangel Reader*, 9–10.

27. Duggar, *Tomlinson*, 166–67.

28. Tomlinson, *Last Great Conflict*, 59–61; Conn, *Like a Mighty Army*, 118–19; Duggar, *Tomlinson*, 170.

29. Tomlinson, *Last Great Conflict*, 59; Conn, *Like a Mighty Army*, 135–36.

30. Tomlinson, *Last Great Conflict*, 134–52; Duggar, *Tomlinson*, 149–51; Crews, *Church of God*, 8; Conn, *Like a Mighty Army*, 400.

31. Duggar, *Tomlinson*, 102.

32. Duggar, *Tomlinson*, 97–100.

33. Duggar, *Tomlinson*, 106, 687.

34. Tomlinson, *Last Great Conflict*, 92–99; Duggar, *Tomlinson*, 94–97.

35. Duggar, *Tomlinson*, 97.

36. Tomlinson, *Last Great Conflict*, 163–83; Conn, *Like a Mighty Army*, 141–42; *Dictionary of Pentecostal and Charismatic Movements*, 199.

37. Crews, *Church of God*, 38–68; Conn, *Like a Mighty Army*, 118–20, 401–2.

38. Crews, *Church of God*, 69–83; Duggar, *Tomlinson*, 40–48; Tomlinson, *Last Great Conflict*, 81–89.

39. Duggar, *Tomlinson*, 41.

40. Crews, *Church of God*, 83–91; Duggar, *Tomlinson*, 53; Conn, *Like a Mighty Army*, 189.

41. Tomlinson, *Last Great Conflict*, 55–56.

42. Duggar, *Tomlinson*, 165.

43. Duggar, *Tomlinson*, 170, 183–84; Conn, *Like a Mighty Army*, 171.

44. Duggar, *Tomlinson*, 100–2, 740.

45. Duggar, *Tomlinson*, 196, 227; Tomlinson, *Last Great Conflict*, 194.

46. Duggar, *Tomlinson*, 208.

47. Conn, *Like a Mighty Army*, 178; Duggar, *Tomlinson*, 82–85, 176.

48. Duggar, *Tomlinson*, 176, 182; Conn, *Like a Mighty Army*, 170–74.

49. Conn, *Like a Mighty Army*, 159–62, 175.

50. Duggar, *Tomlinson*, 200–1.

51. Conn, *Like a Mighty Army*, 175–78; Duggar, *Tomlinson*, 209–11, 314; *Dictionary of Pentecostal and Charismatic Movements*, 206.

52. Stone, *Church of God of Prophecy*, 50–51; Duggar, *Tomlinson*, 212–17.

53. Stone, *Church of God of Prophecy*, 51; Duggar, *Tomlinson*, 220–22, 233, 323, 648.

54. Duggar, *Tomlinson*, 261–62.

55. Duggar, *Tomlinson*, 790.

56. Duggar, *Tomlinson*, 431.

57. Duggar, *Tomlinson*, 743–44.

58. Duggar, *Tomlinson*, 330–31, 524, 618, 649, 654; *Dictionary of Pentecostal and Charismatic Movements*, 209.

59. Duggar, *Tomlinson*, 647; Tomlinson, *Last Great Conflict*, 187.

60. *Fields of the Wood* (Murphy, N.C.: Fields of the Wood, n.d.), 19; Duggar, *Tomlinson*, 597, 599, 644–46, 661–62, 665–79, 731.

61. Duggar, *Tomlinson*, 760–62, 801.

62. Crews, *Church of God*, xii; Synan, *Holiness-Pentecostal*, 88; Conn, *Like a Mighty Army*, 186–88; Stone, *Church of God of Prophecy*, 62–67.

63. Older son Homer A. Tomlinson, born in Westfield, Indiana, in 1892, was passed over for the position of general overseer. He then conducted an eccentric ministry known as the Church of God, World Headquarters and as the Church of God (Queens, N.Y.). Under his successor this became the Church of God (Huntsville, Ala.). In 1952, 1960, 1964, and 1968 Homer ran as a Theocratic Party candidate for president of the U.S. *Dictionary of Pentecostal and Charismatic Movements*, 202–3, 848–49.

64. Conn, *Like a Mighty Army*, 188; Duggar, *Tomlinson*, 345, 348; Stone, *Church of God of Prophecy*, 62–67; *Dictionary of Pentecostal and Charismatic Movements*, 206.

65. Conn, *Like a Mighty Army*, 130–31.

66. Duggar, *Tomlinson*, 657–58.

67. Conn, *Where the Saints Have Trod*, 14–15, 23, 25–38; *Dictionary of Pentecostal and Charismatic Movements*, 201.

68. Crews, *Church of God*, 19–37, 159; Conn, *Where the Saints Have Trod*, 11–48; *Dictionary of Pentecostal and Charismatic Movements*, 197, 201, 209.

69. Charles E. Jones, *A Guide to the Study of the Pentecostal Movement*, 2 vols. (Metuchen, N.J.: Scarecrow Press, 1983), 1:321; Stone, *Church of God of Prophecy*, 84–88; *Dictionary of Pentecostal and Charismatic Movements*, 207–9.

70. Crews, *Church of God*, 176–78; Conn, *Like a Mighty Army*, 254–57, 273–75; *Dictionary of Pentecostal and Charismatic Movements*, 200–2.

71. Duggar, *Tomlinson*, 70–71, 153; Conn, *Like a Mighty Army*, 114.

72. Conn, *Like a Mighty Army*, 124–27.

73. Conn, *Where the Saints Have Trod*, 17, 19.

74. Indiana overseers serving more than one year included S. O. Gillaspie 1919–21, J. L. Goins 1926–29, C. H. Standifer 1929–36 and 1937–38, Roy J. Staats 1938–40, C. M. Jenkerson 1942–44, A. C. Rains 1946–50, C. R. Spain 1950–54, James A. Stephens 1955–58, David L. Lemons 1960–64, Cecil B. Knight 1964–68, P. H. McSwain 1968–72, and Bennie S. Triplett 1972–76. Conn, *Like a Mighty Army*, 436–55.

75. "History of the Church of God in Indiana," Undated clipping typesigned Logan Silver, from the *Church of God Evangel* about 1950, supplied by the Indiana State Office of the Church of God, Cleveland, Tenn.

76. Conn, *Like a Mighty Army*, 429–30.

77. Duggar, *Tomlinson*, 397, 410, 430–31.

78. *Dictionary of Pentecostal and Charismatic Movements*, 200–1, 208; Crews, *Church of God*, 163–72.

79. Letter of the Rev. William L. Gaddis to L. C. Rudolph, 30 November 1990.

CHURCH OF GOD IN CHRIST

Charles Harrison Mason was born 8 September 1866 on a plantation called Prior Farm near Memphis. His parents Jerry and Eliza were first slaves and then tenant farmers. They were devout Missionary Baptists. In 1878 they fled from a yellow fever epidemic in Tennessee to be tenant farmers on swampy land on John Watson's plantation near Plumersville, Arkansas. Jerry died the next year. Young Charles was so wracked with chills and fever in 1880 that his mother despaired of his life. But he was miraculously cured. At Mount Olive Baptist Church he was baptized with praise and thanksgiving. From then on he served as a lay preacher, giving his testimony and working with penitents at the mourners' bench.[1]

Mason was licensed to preach and ordained in 1891. In 1893 he entered Arkansas Baptist College intent on improving his education for ministry. There he was introduced to biblical criticism which seemed to him entirely different from the religion which had sustained his parents and to which he was committed. He stayed at college less than three months. "The Lord showed me that there was no salvation in schools and colleges," he said, "for the way they were conducted grieved my very soul. I packed my books, arose and bade them a final farewell, to follow Jesus, with the Bible as my sacred guide."[2]

Mason was much more inspired by a new book he read—*An Autobiography; the Story of the Lord's Dealings with Mrs. Amanda Smith, the Colored Evangelist; Containing an Account of Her Life Work of Faith, and Her Travels in America, England, Ireland, Scotland, India and Africa, as an Independent Missionary.* Amanda Smith was a holiness evangelist with a Wesleyan understanding. She was a disciple of the Methodist holiness champion John Inskip. Her colleague on a missionary tour in Liberia was the freewheeling Methodist bishop William Taylor who "was one of Phoebe Palmer's trophies of grace." Having read the life story of that black woman, Mason wanted the second blessing of entire sanctification. He claimed the experience and preached his first holiness sermon at Preston, Arkansas, in 1893.[3]

Church of God in Christ as a Holiness Fellowship

Here was a zealous evangelist now on collision course with his Baptist forebears. His best friend and fellow worker was another black Baptist preacher of almost exactly the same age and also of slave parentage. Charles Price Jones claimed the experience of sanctification in 1894 and was a Baptist pastor in Jackson, Mississippi, when the two men met in 1895. Jones and Mason became participants and leaders in an independent movement to promote holiness. Their holiness publications, conventions, and revivals flourished in the region around Jackson. Baptists and Methodists became uneasy as their congregations divided. Jones and Mason were expelled by the Baptists. Following a powerful revival in an abandoned cotton gin shed at Lexington, Mississippi, sixty miles north of Jackson, Jones and Mason took steps to organize their independent congregations into a new holiness fellowship.[4]

Mason contributed the name Church of God in Christ based on I Thessalonians 2:14 and on a revelation he had received while walking the street in Little Rock. The group was incorporated at Memphis late in 1897, the first holiness body to be legally chartered in the South. Independent holiness preachers acquiring its ordination and credentials could administer sacraments, officiate at funerals, perform marriages, and qualify for clergy rates on the railroads. Expansion was rapid, especially in Mississippi, Arkansas, and Tennessee.[5]

Three Leaders Become Pentecostals

Mason was still a seeker after deeper consecration. His colleague Charles Price Jones pointed out that they still lacked the signs of healing the sick and casting out demons. So when reports came of the exciting pentecostal revival at Los Angeles, Mason went with John A. Jeter and D. J. Young for a five-week visit with his old friend William J. Seymour at the Azusa Street mission. All three received baptism in the Holy Spirit evidenced by speaking in tongues. Mason reported:

> The Spirit came upon the saints and upon me! After which I soon sat down and soon my hands went up and I resolved in my heart not to take them down until the Lord baptized me . . . The sound of a mighty wind was in me and my soul cried, "Jesus, only, none like you." My soul cried and soon I began to die. It seemed that I heard the groaning of Christ on the Cross dying for me. All of the work was in me until I died out of the old man. The sound stopped for a little while. My soul cried, "Oh, God, finish your work in me." Then the sound broke out in me again. Then I felt something raising me out of my seat without any effort of my own. I said, "It may be imagination." Then looked down to see if it was really so. I saw that I was rising. Then I gave up for the Lord to have His way within me. So there came a wave of glory into me, and all of my being was filled with the glory of the Lord. So when He had gotten me straight on my feet there came a light which enveloped my entire being above the brightness of the sun. When I opened my mouth to say glory, a flame touched my tongue which ran down in me. My language changed and no word could I speak in my own tongue. Oh, I was filled with the glory of the Lord. My soul was then satisfied. I rejoiced in Jesus my Savior, whom I love so dearly. And from that day until now there has been an overflowing joy of the glory of the Lord in my heart.[6]

Back at Memphis early in 1907, Mason and Young were eager to share their experience. But general overseer and presiding elder Charles Price Jones did not accept this pentecostal teaching. Jones and a substantial part of the church disfellowshipped Mason at the 1907 convocation in Mississippi and withdrew. By 1911 the Jones group had reorganized as the Church of Christ (Holiness) U.S.A. The fourteen congregations in Tennessee, Mississippi, Arkansas, and Oklahoma which sided with Mason and Pentecostalism kept their identity as the Church of God in Christ. Most were able to keep their church property as well. They promptly reorganized in 1907 under Charles Mason as general overseer and chief apostle or bishop. Their annual convocations were at Memphis and their periodical was *The Whole Truth*.[7]

Mason wrote to a pentecostal magazine: "I was put out, because I believed that God did baptize me with the Holy Ghost among you all. Well, He did it and it just suits me." He said of his expulsion: "My being debarred from Lexington, Miss., was to the glory of God. The Lord moved me out into new fields where souls were perishing for the living word. The Lord through me saved, sanctified and baptized thousands of souls."[8]

New Dynamic Denomination

The Church of God in Christ now combined the powerful leadership of Mason with the energy of the pentecostal revival and the attraction of an incorporated body offering legal status to its clergy. Mason seemed to be free of racial bias. For him "gathering together all races and peoples in unity" was a part of the same pentecostal plan as conversion, sanctification, baptism in the Holy Spirit, speaking in tongues, dancing before the Lord, and healing. Between 1909 and 1914 hundreds of pentecostal preachers, about as many white as black, came to carry the valued credentials of Mason and the Church of God in Christ. The growing body of white preachers eventually treated him shabbily, accepting the benefits of his certification and often of his ordination but denying his leadership. Actually a substantial number of the white preachers were in transit from his Wesleyan understanding of holiness as a second blessing of entire sanctification to a non-Wesleyan "finished work of Calvary" position.[9]

When the white preachers issued a call to meet at Hot Springs in 1914 to form the Assemblies of God, Mason and the black Pentecostals were generally omitted or excluded from the plan. Mason went to the Hot Springs meeting uninvited and gave his blessing in a sermon to that whole body of white clergy. As the Assemblies of

God denomination was going on to become the largest predominantly white pentecostal body in the United States, the Church of God in Christ was going on to become the largest predominantly black pentecostal body in the United States. In spite of the withdrawal of the white preachers and members, the Church of God in Christ claimed 345 churches with more than 25,000 members in 21 states and the District of Columbia by 1934. Already the transition to a northern and urban church was becoming plain; there were bishops in Detroit, Dallas, Chicago, Philadelphia, and Cleveland.[10]

By 1962, a year after Mason's death, the church membership had increased more than tenfold to 382,679. At least ten additional church bodies owed their origins to the work of Mason. Twenty years later, in 1982, the membership of the Church of God in Christ had extended to some forty countries and had multiplied ten times again to 3,709,661. Dynamic leadership was being provided by Mason's successor, his son-in-law James Oglethorpe Patterson who had become the first elected presiding bishop in 1968 and been returned for a series of four-year terms.[11]

Relationship to Race

Charles Mason evidently did not define his religion racially. In his early pentecostal years his movement was clearly interracial. Mason conducted major evangelistic meetings at Nashville and Little Rock at the invitation of white groups. He responded graciously to slights and to exclusion of blacks by the white Pentecostals who formed the Assemblies of God in 1914 and the Pentecostal Fellowship of North America in 1948. He himself continued to maintain excellent relations with white pentecostal leaders and was a welcome elder statesman at the Pentecostal World Conference at London in 1952. The Church of God in Christ was unique among black denominations in its openness to members of the charismatic movement, a group typically interracial.[12]

Yet interpreters of the Church of God in Christ have often been moved to express its essential character and account for its growth in racial terms. "It is the first church to have arisen from the authentic experience of black people rather than from an existing white organization," said Douglas Nelson. The director of public relations for the denomination told a reporter at the annual convocation at Memphis in 1957 "Bishop Mason happened to have the original rhythm of colored peoples." F. D. Washington, pastor of a 3,500-member temple in Brooklyn said at that same convocation: "This church is

the true spirit of the Negro. Here outlet is given for the emotions of the people who have been pent up for years. We had no traditions handed down to us, and it makes a church grow when its people can express themselves freely."[13]

Leonard Lovett, widely recognized historian of the Church of God in Christ, acknowledged some contrary scholarly opinion but generally supported those who argued for a uniquely black element in pentecostal origins.[14]

> When whites could not "Europeanize" pentecostalism . . . and purge it of its "Africanisms," they separated and formed their own denominations. Thus white pentecostals conceded to the pressures of a racist society. Black pentecostalism is what it is, for the most part, because of its own unique experience in America. Attempts to objectively evaluate black pentecostalism have been hampered by preconceived notions about such things as illiteracy, religious fanaticism, unrestrained emotionalism, and exhibitionism. Historically, some of these notions are justifiable, but they should not prevent a fair hearing. Black pentecostals would contend that their encounter with the Spirit defies theological interpretation at points because of its suprarational and supernatural character. Objective evaluations of black pentecostalism collapse before a dimension of spiritual effusion that cannot be prestructured, preplanned, preprogrammed or regulated.[15]

Social and Educational Impact

Certainly the story of the Church of God in Christ became a focus for a justifiable black pride. Fifth in a sequence of improving church buildings in Memphis was the Mason Temple completed in 1944, the largest black-owned meeting place in the United States. Church facilities in Memphis continued to develop. The annual convocations in that city grew to an attendance of 40,000. Bishop Patterson told the 68th annual convocation in 1975: "God has brought us to a position of prominence. We rightfully take our places . . . God has blessed us to ride in the best automobiles, live in the best homes, wear the finest minks and exclusive clothing, and to have large bank accounts. Our churches are no longer confined to storefronts, but we are building cathedrals."[16]

Mason's early aversion to formal education gave way in 1918 to his sponsorship of Saints Home School which became Saints Industrial School which became Saints Industrial and Literary School at Lexington, Mississippi. It became Saints College, a monument to black women educators Pinkie Duncan and Arenia Mallory. Mason's successor J. O. Patterson sent Leonard Lovett to establish the Charles Harrison Mason Theological Seminary in Atlanta in 1970. It was the first fully accredited pentecostal graduate school in North America. Scores of "Bible colleges" were opened as extension schools in American cities.[17]

This denomination played a deliberate role in social history even at the risk of violence and reprisal. When the controversial Malcolm X was assassinated in New York in February of 1965, it was the Church of God in Christ which stepped forward to arrange his funeral even in the face of threats. When Martin Luther King came to Memphis in 1968 to campaign on behalf of the garbage and sewer workers, the Church of God in Christ was his host. On the night before his death on 4 April, King made his memorable "I Have Been to the Mountaintop" speech from the pulpit of Mason Temple.[18]

Development in Indiana

The Church of God in Christ was predominantly black and increasingly urban. Heavy migration of blacks from the rural south eventually located its largest memberships in California, Texas, New York, and the states of the industrial Midwest. In spite of a large increase in the percentage of black population in the 1920s, Indiana was generally the least black, the least urban, and the least industrialized among her midwestern neighbors. But there were significant concentrations of urban blacks in Lake, Marion, St. Joseph, Vanderburgh, and Allen counties. To them the Church of God in Christ began offering its ministry in the 1920s, advanced by missionaries in the vigor of their youth. Benjamin Watkins was a Kentucky Baptist converted to pentecostal holiness in 1910. He moved to Evansville in 1919 where he established the denomination's first mission in the state. Until 1928 the pioneer congregations at Evansville and Newburgh were administered as units of the church in Kentucky.[19]

Possibilities in northern Indiana were the most exciting. William Roberts came to Chicago in 1916. Typical of the ministers "working out" or "preaching out" a church, he held a full-time secular job and devoted his off-duty hours to pastoral labors. Beginning as leader of a little mission of twelve members, he increased in responsibility until Bishop Mason appointed him overseer of the Church of God in Christ for Illinois and Indiana. Northern Indiana kept beckoning. During the 1920s United States Steel increased the output of its Gary works from 2.3 million tons to 4.4 million tons; Inland Steel Company doubled capacity at its Indiana Harbor plant to 2.2 million tons and the nearby plant of Youngstown

Sheet and Tube Company approached a one million ton capacity. Worker immigration pushed the black population to 18 percent in Gary and to 10 percent in East Chicago.[20]

Clarence E. Bennett, born in Tennessee as the ninth child in a family of ten boys and five girls, came to Gary in June of 1920. He had attended college at Carbondale and Chicago in Illinois. He taught rural schools in southern Illinois where he was sanctified and baptized in the Holy Spirit under the preaching of M. C. Clay. He was licensed to preach in 1918 by Bishop D. Bostick of St. Louis. In Gary he began assisting the members of a very marginal mission of the Church of God in Christ. His pay from United States Steel was enough to rent a storefront meeting place. Overseer William Roberts of Chicago named Bennett pastor of that Gary mission in December of 1920.

The strengthening congregation began a building fund in 1924 and constructed the first building for the Church of God in Christ in Indiana in 1926–27. By then there were eleven ministers of the denomination laboring among the industrial centers of the state: C. E. Bennett and T. H. Coffee of Gary; L. J. Hall and Robert Miller of East Chicago; E. A. McNeely of Michigan City; E. A. Loveless and R. A. Nelson of South Bend; E. Renicks of Elkhart; J. H. Boone of Fort Wayne; G. H. Boyce of Indianapolis; and L. W. Burnice of Terre Haute. Six of these ministers petitioned the national leadership for a separate jurisdiction for Indiana and advocated C. E. Bennett for state overseer.

The denomination's senior bishop Charles Mason and "mother" Lizzie Robertson as general supervisor of women came to Gary for Indiana's first state convocation from 27 July to 5 August of 1927. Overseer William Roberts of Chicago and "Mother" Nancy Gamble as regional supervisor of women were present as appointees of Bishop Mason and convocation leaders. The meeting place was Bennett's new Saints Home Church at 509 East Twentieth Street. At the national convocation at Memphis the following December, Bennett was officially named state overseer for Indiana with the churches at Evansville and Newburgh now a part of his jurisdiction. He was destined to preside over Indiana as overseer and then as bishop for the next forty-five years, "five years longer than Moses led the children of Israel" one biographer observed.

The national religious census of 1936 reported 18 Churches of God in Christ in Indiana with 599 members. By the time Bishop Bennett died in a train-auto collision in 1972, Indiana had at least 90 churches and missions in his First Jurisdiction in northern Indiana, besides the descendants of some 16 churches in southern Indiana which had been set off as the Second Jurisdiction in 1948. Under Bennett's successor, Bishop William O. Blakely of East Chicago, the First Jurisdiction grew again to more than 120 churches.[21]

The Hall Family

The people of the Church of God in Christ in Indiana often spoke of a symbiosis of that denomination with railroads. Several of the early preachers were employed as railroad crewmen or porters. They conducted services and encouraged missions along the lines wherever they climbed down from their trains. At least as impressive was the continuing involvement of Church of God in Christ pioneers with industrial labor as illustrated by the ministry of Lewis J. Hall. As C. E. Bennett had invested his paychecks from United States Steel in the pioneer congregation and earliest building at Gary in the 1920s, so pastor L. J. Hall supported his family and founded a bellwether church while on the payroll of Continental Steel at Kokomo in the 1940s.

In 1942 Continental was just gearing up to supply the armed forces with air strip mats, wire ammunition baskets, steel lockers, metal buildings, aerial bombs, and fuel containers; after the war it would expand even more in roofing, fencing, posts, nails, and many forms of wire. That summer of 1942 "Church Mother" Nancy Gamble, who was Hall's sister, came to Kokomo and rented a former fish market building at 1001 Kennedy Street for $10 per month. After a thorough scrubbing, that building of 720 square feet became temporary meeting place for a new Church of God in Christ as well as residence for fifteen persons in the larger family of Halls.

Pastor Hall was a native of Arkansas, saved at Tyler, Texas, in 1912, and called to the ministry in 1915. In 1925 he had opened the denomination's work in East Chicago with a street ministry in a vacant lot at the corner of Pennsylvania and McKinley streets. His paychecks from Inland Steel were essential in forming the East Chicago congregation in 1926 and erection of its church building in 1928. During his six decades of ministry he was to share in the building up of congregations in ten cities. Under such experienced leadership Grace Memorial Church of God in Christ in Kokomo grew steadily from that 720 square feet of rented space in 1942 to a building of 7,740 square feet owned by the saints. All of the ten Hall children surviving to adulthood became members of the Church of God in Christ, the four sons ministers. When son Milton L. Hall, having worked his years at Continental Steel and having succeeded his father as pastor, was elevated to bishop in 1988, Grace Memorial became headquarters church for the largest of the state's three jurisdictions.[22]

A church founded by heroic self-investment of a ministerial family could come to be regarded as family property, a perception always being balanced in the Church of God in Christ by a stout episcopal government. Modern tax laws came to restrict simple commingling of ministerial family finances with church finances and to require strict accounting to show separation between the two. Still the denomination's most effective pattern of church extension was a missionary pastor and wife supporting themselves, their family, and a substantial part of the cost of a developing church from the proceeds of their own regular employment. About 50 percent of the Church of God pastors in Indiana continued to hold secular jobs.

Every church record for Indiana demonstrated the prominence of women in the Church of God in Christ. Nancy Gamble was worthy of a biography in her own right. Mrs. C. E. (Anna Mae) Bennett was herself a lifelong evangelistic church worker throughout the state, conducting successful revivals at Gary, East Chicago, Michigan City, South Bend, Fort Wayne, and Indianapolis. A series of "state mothers," later called "state supervisors of women," itinerated the congregations promoting the work of women's organizations—Nancy Gamble, Emma Chambers, Urie Alford, Beulah Hatchett. Many a congregation was formed or sustained for years by a female evangelist. Every congregational photograph album was filled with the pictures of women as church mothers, missionaries, Bible bands, willing workers, Christian councils, pastor's aids, ushers, teachers, nurses, committee members, choir members, and sunshine girls. When the New Bethany church at Marion was burned in a race riot in 1970, seven women made up the central core of the tiny congregation pledged to assist the pastor in rebuilding.[23] None of the denomination's women members were ordained. Technically they could not administer sacraments or perform weddings or conduct funerals.

The Church of God in Christ in Indiana grew to include 33 churches in Indiana's Third Jurisdiction, 29 churches in the Second Jurisdiction, and 80 churches in the larger First Jurisdiction which had long been one of the nation's most vigorous.[24] The jurisdictions were not strictly geographical; membership statistics were not separately reported for the jurisdictions or for the state as a whole. Church leadership was clearly concentrated in urban areas, especially in the urban areas of northern Indiana. A list of the denomination's ministers in Indiana in 1983 included 135 pastors, 178 ordained elders, 128 licensed ministers, and 194 women evangelists. Of these 635 only 60 had addresses at places south of Indianapolis and 42 of them lived in Evansville or Terre Haute. One hundred forty persons in these four categories of ministry were in Indianapolis alone.[25]

NOTES

1. James O. Patterson, *History and Formative Years of the Church of God in Christ, with Excerpts from the Life and Works of Its Founder, Bishop C. H. Mason*, Reproduced by Bishop J. O. Patterson, Rev. German Ross, Mrs. Julia Mason Atkins (Memphis, Tenn.: Church of God in Christ Publishing House, 1969), 14–15; *Dictionary of Pentecostal and Charismatic Movements* (Grand Rapids, Mich.: Zondervan, 1988), 585–86.

2. *Dictionary of Pentecostal and Charismatic Movements*, 586; Patterson, *History*, 16, 21. Patterson gives the date of licensure as 1893. There was evidently a two-year delay in his full-time ministry because of the opposition of his wife.

3. Amanda Smith, *An Autobiography* (Chicago: Meyer and Brother, 1893, 506 p.); Timothy L. Smith, *Called unto Holiness* (Kansas City, Mo.: Nazarene Publishing House, 1962), 15–18, 40–41; Patterson, *History*, 15–16; *Dictionary of Pentecostal and Charismatic Movements*, 80, 585–87.

4. *Dictionary of Pentecostal and Charismatic Movements*, 79–80, 586; Patterson, *History*, 16.

5. *Encyclopedia of Religion in the South*, ed. Samuel S. Hill (Macon, Ga.: Mercer University Press, 1984), 161, 463; Patterson, *History*, 33, 63; *Dictionary of Pentecostal and Charismatic Movements*, 586–87.

6. Patterson, *History*, 19.

7. Lucille J. Cornelius, *The Pioneer History of the Church of God in Christ* (N.p.: The Author, 1975), 13; *Dictionary of Pentecostal and Charismatic Movements*, 80, 204–5, 587; Patterson, *History*, 17–20, 63; *Encyclopedia of Religion in the South*, 161. Cornelius names thirteen ministers at the 1907 meeting besides Mason; *Encyclopedia of Religion in the South* reports "some 12 other leaders and seven congregations."

8. *Dictionary of Pentecostal and Charismatic Movements*, 80; Patterson, *History*, 24.

9. Charles A. Jones, *Black Holiness: A Guide to the Study of Black Participation in Wesleyan Perfectionist and Glossolalic Pentecostal Movements* (Metuchen, N.J.: Scarecrow Press, 1987), 98; *Encyclopedia of Religion in the South*, 161; Patterson, *History*, 22–23, 36–39.

10. Vinson Synan, "The Quiet Rise of Black Pentecostals," *Charisma* 11 (June 1986): 50; Vinson Synan, *The Holiness-Pentecostal Movement in the United States* (Grand Rapids, Mich.: Eerdmans, 1971), 168–70; *Dictionary of Pentecostal and Charismatic Movements*, 61, 587.

11. James S. Tinney, "Black Pentecostals: Setting up the Kingdom," *Christianity Today* 20 (5 December 1975): 42–43; Patterson, *History*, 33, 63–64; *Dictionary of Pentecostal and Charismatic Movements*, 83, 205, 587, 663–64; Cornelius, *Pioneer History*, 89–90; *Encyclopedia of Religion in the South* 161; Synan, *Holiness-Pentecostal*, 179.

12. Patterson, *History*, 23; Tinney, "Black Pentecostals," 42; Synan, *Holiness-Pentecostal*, 169–70; *Dictionary of Pentecostal and Charismatic Movements*, 205, 587, 703–4.

13. *Encyclopedia of Religion in the South*, 161; "Church Celebrates 50th Anniversary," *Ebony* 13 (March 1958): 58.

14. *Aspects of Pentecostal-Charismatic Origins*, ed. Vinson Synan (Plainfield, N.J.: Logos International, 1975), 123–41; *Dictionary of Pentecostal and Charismatic Movements*, 76–86.

15. *Aspects of Pentecostal-Charismatic Origins*, 139.

16. Patterson, *History*, 71–75, 110–13; *Encyclopedia of Religion in the South*, 161–62; Tinney, "Black Pentecostals," 42.

17. Cornelius, *Pioneer History*, 45; Tinney, "Black Pentecostals," 42; *Dictionary of Pentecostal and Charismatic Movements* 83.

18. Gerold Frank, *An American Death* (Garden City, N.Y.: Doubleday, 1972), 10–21, 48–55; *Encyclopedia of Religion in the South*, 162; *Dictionary of Pentecostal and Charismatic Movements*, 587.

19. James H. Madison, *Indiana through Tradition and Change: A History of the Hoosier State and Its People 1920–1945* (Indianapolis, Ind.: Indiana Historical Society, 1982), 7–8, 206, 229–30, 384–89; *1976 Convocation Journal* (N.p.: First Jurisdiction of Indiana, Church of God in Christ, 1976), 24, 49; *Brief History—Church of God in Christ in Indiana* (N.p., n.d., 2 p.).

20. *1976 Convocation Journal*, 19; Madison, *Indiana through Tradition and Change*, 8, 208.

21. *Bishop C. E. Bennett and Anna Mae Bennett* (N.p., n.d., 1 p.); *History of Saints Home Church of God in Christ* (N.p., n.d., 1 p.); *1975 Convocation Journal* (N.p.: First Jurisdiction of Indiana, Church of God in Christ, 1975), 9; *Brief History*, 1–2; *1976 Convocation Journal*, 8, 11, 22, 24.

22. *The History of Faith Temple Church of God in Christ* (N.p., n.d., 2 p.); *1976 Convocation Journal* 23, 30–31.

23. *1976 Convocation Journal*, 36.

24. Letter of Milton L. Hall, Bishop of First Ecclesiastical Jurisdiction, Kokomo, to L. C. Rudolph, 13 February 1991.

25. *Church of God in Christ, Inc., International Directory 1983–1984* (Memphis, Tenn.: Church of God in Christ, [1984], 204–18.

INTERNATIONAL CHURCH
OF THE FOURSQUARE GOSPEL

Many have regarded Aimee Semple McPherson as an actress. Certainly she was nothing less. In a survey of Pentecostals, Walter J. Hollenweger counted her the most outstanding example of the woman preachers "who play the same role in the Pentecostal movement as great actresses in the rest of society." When she was just a child named Aimee Kennedy at her home near Ingersoll in Canada, she would line up chairs and lead an imaginary congregation in testimony, prayer, and song. Her role model then was her mother, a junior sergeant major in the local Salvation Army corps and superintendent of its Sunday school. Her father, an organist and choir director for the Methodists, taught Aimee piano and organ. The elementary schoolmates who tried to tease her about her Salvationist connections were soon marching the playground as members of her Army band and singing salvation songs. She displayed in the wider community what she modestly called "some little talent for elocution." Soon she was a popular leader in dramatic programs and the juvenile author of at least one play. "As I recited, the audience would laugh and clap and laugh again until the tears came to their eyes, and I was very popular indeed with the churches in those days," she said.[1]

When her high school textbook in physical geography introduced theories of earth formation and evolution of life forms which seemed to differ from the creation accounts she had learned at home and at Sunday school, she played out that personal crisis in belief before the eyes of thousands. Her long letter to the editor signed "a perplexed school girl" was printed in the *Family Herald and Weekly Star*, then Canada's major newspaper. It drew a flood of letters, a glittering international response which did little to encourage her quiescence. Her parents and the local citizenry were hardly a match for the dramatic vigor of her attack on the more placid denominational churches and their members in her home town. She cried out in prayer to the Almighty to show himself if he did exist.[2]

The answer to that prayer seemed to her to come in the form of a storefront pentecostal mission which had just opened in Ingersoll. She became a Pentecostal at age seventeen. A few months later, on 12 August 1908, she married the pentecostal evangelist Robert Semple under whose preaching she had been converted. Then she focused the whole of her dramatic power on that shared ministry. Even as "a slip of a girl" of eighteen she found she could hold a vast audience in a London hall for a sermon of an hour and a quarter during which time nobody seemed to stir. As a young widow of twenty-one with an infant daughter, she remarried in October of 1911. She said she told Harold McPherson before the wedding that she would have to respond if the Lord called her back to evangelistic service. Now with two babies, she was soon back on the platform full time.[3]

For a decade she crisscrossed America without a home base, overcoming formidable obstacles in an itinerant ministry which seemed dependent hour by hour on her personal dramatic powers. For tens of thousands she became the unforgettable "Sister Aimee." In her hands everything was graphic. She called her sermon on the parable of the Ten Virgins (Matthew 25:1–13) presented at Washburn in extreme northern Maine in 1917 "one of the many wonderful messages and dramas worked out in their midst which were beyond description."[4]

By the time she located in California and centered her program at the Angelus Temple in 1923, the marquee could advertise sermons "vividly illustrated." Even her Los Angeles speeding ticket turned into a dramatic inspiration for Aimee. Next weekend she was on the temple platform, wearing a police uniform and standing beside a motorcycle, crying out to her hearers to "Stop" speeding down the road to hell. The temple's 5,300 seats were almost always filled.

> Because I have always believed that the eye-gate was as important to the preaching of the gospel as the ear-gate, I began depicting Bible truths by means of "illustrated sermons," almost from the very day the doors of Angelus Temple were flung open. While I was criticized for this to a certain extent by those who did not understand, yet I was enabled by this simple method to preach to capacity crowds, while a number of minister friends of my acquaintance were forced to cancel many of their services for lack of attendance and interest. Through this means, thousands of souls which otherwise might never have entered a church door, were won to the Lord Jesus Christ. These illustrated messages were enlarged upon to a great extent by putting a number of them to music. The Temple band, organ, and choirs began presenting entire operatic scores composed by myself as God would give them to me in the stillness of the night, or while riding in a train en route to a speaking engagement in another city or state. These are usually featured during special seasons of the year, such as "The Bells of Bethlehem," and "Regem Adorate" (my first) at Christmas; "The Crimson Road" and "The Rich Man and Lazarus" at Easter, and so on.[5]

At the very hour of its dedication on New Year's Day of 1923, her Angelus Temple entered a float in the Pasadena Tournament of Roses parade and won second prize in its division. The Temple's 1925 float won the parade's highest prize, the sweepstakes trophy.[6]

When Sister Aimee disappeared for thirty-six days in spring of 1926, the event and its aftermath averaged three front-page stories per week in the Los Angeles papers for a period of five years. Newspapers and periodicals across America and some in Europe followed the developments. The basic division was between Aimee and her supporters who said she had been held for ransom by evil kidnappers and the skeptical press which suspected she had been holidaying in a new blue Chrysler coupe with the Temple's radio engineer. A district attorney's charges of perjury and obstruction of justice were dropped for lack of evidence and that district attorney himself later came under legal investigation. No other actress could equal such media attention.[7] There followed a series of monographic studies prone to analyze McPherson as actress.[8]

Life magazine covered her funeral in October of 1944 with five pages of photographs. There were the thousands of mourners standing in line hour after hour waiting to view Sister Aimee as she lay in state. There were the fantastic floral pieces in the shape of a harp, of Aimee's chair, of a globe, of foursquare symbols. Even at that era's low prices, it was estimated such a funeral and flowers would cost $40,000. And interment was in a $40,000 marble sarcophagus containing eleven crypts. The reporter called the ceremonies a fitting climax for her two decades of dramatic evangelism in California. The article recalled "the skill with which she applied theatrical techniques to the art of homiletics"—her robes of blue and white, her stance with her Bible in one hand and a bouquet of red roses in the other, her vibrant voice crying "Ushers. Jump to it. Clear the one-way street to Jesus!" Twenty-five hundred invitations were issued for the commital service at the mausoleum. Another 6,000 people brought flowers and crashed the gate. In her career she had the marks of an actress and the look of stardom all the way.[9]

The Religious Mission of "Sister Aimee"

However Aimee Semple McPherson did not understand or describe herself as an actress. She was primarily a religious woman on a religious mission. As Hollenweger pointed out, her dramatic roles were undertaken as her uniquely personal contribution in service of the Kingdom of God. Even her critics conceded that she made drama an effective agent in turning criminals into church members and addicts into healthy human beings. The real power was in the message, she said.

> Many people ask me to what we ascribe the success of the meetings in Angelus Temple and "on the field," the throngs, the interest of the people as they sit on the edge of their seats, hearts thrilled with the truth and simplicity of the old, old story, as they drink in the message. The secret of the power lies, not in oneself or one's surroundings, but in the message which is borne; not in personality, but in the Christ which shines above the personality . . . The gospel of Jesus Christ the same, yes-

terday, and today, and forever, meets these needs—a Christ Who still delivers from sin, heals the sick, strikes off the shackles of dope, breaks down the gates of brass, saws asunder the bars of iron Satan has made, and leads His people to freedom and victory![10]

She said "Any success which has followed my ministry is attributed to the motivating power of the Holy Spirit in my own life." If that ministry became an organization which circled the earth, that was "naught but the impelling force of the Blessed Holy Spirit Baptism." She was, in short, what she aspired to be—a pentecostal evangelist and eventually a teacher of pentecostal evangelists. And her ministry was an integral part of the whole familiar complex of the twentieth century rise and expansion of Pentecostalism.[11]

Her first religious teacher was her mother, a Salvationist "caught in the devil's net" doing farm work when she yearned to fulfill a calling as a holiness evangelist. Her mother prayed to have that evangelistic yearning fulfilled in this child. The next influential religious teacher was Robert Semple by whose preaching she came under conviction and then to conversion.[12]

> At the end of the third day, while driving home from school, I could stand it no longer. The lowering skies above, the trees, the fields, the very road beneath me seemed to look down upon me with displeasure, and I could see written everywhere—"Poor, lost, miserable, hell-deserving sinner!" Utterly at the end of myself—not stopping to think what preachers or entertainment committees or anyone else would think—I threw up my hands, and all alone in that country road, I screamed aloud toward the heavens: "Oh, Lord God, be merciful to me, a sinner!" Immediately the most wonderful change took place in my soul. Darkness passed away and light entered. The sky was filled with brightness, the trees, the fields, and the little snow birds flitting to and fro were praising the Lord and smiling upon me. So conscious was I of the pardoning blood of Jesus that I seemed to feel it flowing over me. I discovered that my face was bathed in tears, which dropped on my hands as I held the reins.[13]

And it was within the pentecostal plan as preached by Semple that she was baptized in the Holy Spirit.[14]

> Each time that I said "Glory to Jesus!" it seemed to come from a deeper place in my being than the last, and in a deeper voice, until great waves of "Glory to Jesus" were rolling from my toes up; such adoration and praise I had never known possible. All at once my hands and arms began to shake, gently at first, then violently, until my whole body was shaking under the power of the Holy

Spirit . . . How happy I was, Oh how happy! happy just to feel His wonderful power taking control of my being. Oh Glory! That sacred hour is so sweet to me, the remembrance of its sacredness thrills me as I write. Almost without notice my body slipped gently to the floor, and I was lying stretched out under the power of God, but felt as though caught up and floating upon the billowy clouds of glory. Do not understand by this that I was unconscious of my surroundings, for I was not, but Jesus was more real and near than the things of earth round about me. The desire to praise and worship and adore Him flamed up within my soul. He was so wonderful so glorious, and this poor tongue of mine so utterly incapable of finding words with which to praise Him. My lungs began to fill and heave under the power as the Comforter came in. The cords of my throat began to twitch—my chin began to quiver, and then to shake violently, but Oh, so sweetly! My tongue began to move up and down and sideways in my mouth. Unintelligible sounds as of stammering lips and another tongue, spoken of in Isaiah 28:11, began to issue from my lips. This stammering of different syllables, then words, then connected sentences was continued for some time as the Spirit was teaching me to yield to Him. Then suddenly, out of my innermost being flowed rivers of praise in other tongues as the Spirit gave utterance (Acts 2:4), and Oh I knew that He was praising Jesus with glorious language, clothing Him with honor and glory which I felt but never could have put into words.[15]

Immediately thereafter, at age seventeen, she felt personally called and ordained by God for ministry. "An intense, heaven-sent longing to be a soul winner for Jesus was born of the Spirit within my soul," she said. As Robert Semple's wife she was an especially efficient understudy as they pioneered for the Pentecostals at Stratford and at London in Ontario. They felt the Lord "impressed it upon their hearts" to go to Chicago to share in the ministry of William H. Durham at his North Avenue Mission. Aimee was already a full partner; both Semples were ordained there on 2 January 1909.[16]

Durham was a veteran of the earliest pentecostal developments in Los Angeles and one of the chief teachers of Pentecostalism in America. He was not a Wesleyan teacher of sanctification as a second definite perfecting experience. For him salvation was a finished work at Calvary. Those who were converted and baptized in the Holy Spirit as evidenced by tongues were to be continually moving on to perfection in the Spirit's strength. This was also the gospel of the Semples which they proclaimed as colleagues of Durham for more than a year and members of his evangelistic teams. Aimee said "Oh, the teaching and the deepening, and the experiences that were ours in the little North Avenue assembly . . . have meant so much in the years which have followed!" She was a valued team member who could testify to her experience, preach, play the piano, pray with penitents, and interpret messages given in tongues. Durham's aversion to church government and organization probably reinforced the independence and "faith mission" orientation of the Semples also. The congregation of pentecostal saints in Chicago sent the Semples off to evangelize China in 1910. Aimee said "We have never known what it was to have any earthly board behind us or any one person to whom we could look for support, yet God has marvelously supplied our every need."[17]

Robert Semple died of malaria in China in August of 1910. After an abortive attempt at life as a homemaker, Aimee Semple McPherson reentered the circuit life of itinerant pentecostal evangelists at the bottom in 1915.[18] The work was always hard and the settings often hostile. Over and over she had to find a hall in which to preach or cope personally with the eccentricities of tents. Pianos and pulpits and altars must be secured. There were years of overland travel, much of the time spent camping on roadsides because there was no money for hotels or restaurants. Aimee wrote:

> As Brother McPherson is away again, I am alone, playing, leading, singing, preaching, and praying at the altar, besides having the Bridal Call to prepare, it is only the power of God that can sustain me. It is still a marvel in my eyes, the wonderful way the Lord helped me while left alone at Key West, to drive stakes, tie heavy guy ropes, and battle to keep the tent up, amidst wind and rain, sometimes preaching all day and sitting up the greater portion of the night to watch the tents and keep driving the stakes in with the big sledge-hammer, as fast as the wind pulled them out, through the night watches, while a three day nor'wester was on.[19]

Sister Aimee's rise was rapid. She was among the nation's most effective pentecostal itinerants. Few harassed her as she preached. Those who came to hear her returned to hear her again. Her altars were thronged with those praying to be saved or to be baptized in the Holy Spirit. After some impressive healings, she was actually terrified by the throngs of diseased and crippled who appeared. "Is the whole world sick," she cried. But she was sure the age of miracles was not past. The first title in her book of *Divine Healing Sermons* was "Is Jesus Christ the Great 'I Am' or Is He the Great 'I Was'?"[20]

> Day and night I have but to close these eyes of mine to see again, through misty tears, the drawn, white, pain-blanched faces of the afflicted of my people. One moment I am all a-weeping for the multitudes shut outside the crowded doors and for the thousands we could never reach, though we toiled day and night. And the next, my face is smiling, mine eyes are made to shine a-through the tears, in remembrance of the thousands who went away skipping, with singing in their hearts; straightened of limb, clear of eye, and strong of faith; to take up again the broken, ravelled threads of life, and weave upon the loom some brighter, fairer picture of a happy, prayer-filled home, wherein the Saviour spreads His hands in gentle benediction and reigns supreme upon the altar there.[21]

Aimee's itinerary included small towns and obscure camps; it also included large cities and great halls—Mount Forest in Ontario; Providence in Rhode Island; Cape Cod in Massachusetts; Corono on Long Island; Jacksonville, Tampa, Durant, and St. Petersburg in Florida; Savannah in Georgia; Long Branch in New Jersey; Boston in Massachusetts; Huntington on Long Island; Montwait in Massachusetts; Washburn in Maine; Jacksonville, Pleasant Grove, Tampa, Miami, and Key West in Florida; Pulaski and Roanoke in Virginia; Philadelphia in Pennsylvania; Long Hill and Hartford in Connecticut; Montwait and Wooster in Massachusetts; New York City and New Rochelle in New York.[22]

Wherever she preached she left groups of followers, sometimes organized as new pentecostal congregations. These friends she encouraged and bonded as a body of subscribers to her magazine entitled the *Bridal Call* (after 1964 the *Foursquare Advance*). Beginning in June of 1917 it was issued monthly from Savannah, Georgia, and then from Framingham, Massachusetts, and eventually from Los Angeles. Every issue was to have "one article making plain the way of salvation, one on the baptism of the Holy Ghost, and one on the coming of the Lord and the preparation to meet Him." She was also an editor for a New England pentecostal monthly titled *Word and Work*.[23]

Sister Aimee said "California rang in my ears, and the Lord had been speaking to us for some time about making a trans-continental, tract distributing-Gospel auto tour." So in fall of 1918 instead of returning to Florida she set out for California with her mother and her two children in their new seven-passenger Oldsmobile "gospel car." On one side it said in gold letters six inches high "Jesus is coming soon, get ready." On the other side it said "Where will you spend eternity?" They conducted impromptu services wherever they found opportunity. They sowed down their trail with gospels and tracts as they went. They paused at Tulsa in Oklahoma in

November to conduct previously scheduled meetings which ended in an awesome revival.[24]

By the time she did her first preaching in California in 1919, Aimee Semple McPherson was already something of a national institution. California seemed an especially needy place. She said "divers doctrinal differences had gotten the eyes of many off the Lord" since the pentecostal outpouring at Azusa Street Mission a decade before. Certainly California was hospitable to her. Her meetings at Los Angeles began in Victoria Hall which seated about a thousand. From there they moved to and eventually over-crowded Philharmonic Auditorium, the largest in the city. At the end of this first series of meetings which she conducted in the state, volunteers built and furnished a home at Los Angeles for her and the family.[25]

Pentecostal Position

Sister Aimee's sermons did not suffer from lack of content. There was no confusion about what she wanted to preach. She was an orthodox Pentecostal of the non-Wesleyan, baptistic, reformed, or keswickian sort and was trinitarian. In 1919, before she was thirty, she was of such stature as a pentecostal teacher that she issued a popular autobiography. The book was entitled *This Is That*, the title based on a favorite pentecostal citation of the apostle Peter in Acts 2:16 "This is that which was spoken by the prophet Joel." It was issued by her own publishing outlet newly located in California. The book was a practical and doctrinal manual for Pentecostals done in Aimee's own inspirational style.[26]

This Is That included her personal testimony and testimonies of others about the ministry of the Holy Spirit through her. It included sermons for sinners, sermons for the born-again who had not yet received the baptism in the Holy Spirit, and sermons for Spirit-baptized believers who were to be pressing on to perfection. It attacked those who opposed Pentecostals. It explained to rigidly non-demonstrative persons that dancing, shouting, shaking, falling prostrate under the power of the Holy Spirit, speaking in tongues, and interpretation of messages spoken in tongues were normal manifestations which were no surprise to God and from which God's dignity needed no protection. It told seekers after baptism in the Holy Spirit how they should seek. It provided a compact compilation of "Twenty-four Questions a Young Worker Is Apt to Meet, and Answers." Her written works would eventually include half a dozen books and 180 songs plus scores of poems. She did words and music for seven sacred operas each two hours in length.[27]

McPherson's place in the pentecostal mainstream was symbolized by her ordination as an evangelist by the Assemblies of God in 1919. She preached to the annual meeting of the Assemblies in 1920 and held Assemblies credentials until she returned them to chairman E. N. Bell on 5 January 1922. There was no public conflict between them over the proper shape of pentecostal teaching; the parting was without prejudice. Reasons for the separation were probably matters of personal preference and a desire to avoid any embarrassment for either side. There was her divorce from Harold McPherson in 1921. The guarded status for women ministers within the ranks of the Assemblies fitted poorly with Aimee's central role in the life of the massive Angelus Temple then under construction. Aimee was increasingly a model for women who became pastors of large independent pentecostal churches.

Faced by protestors against preaching by women, she noted that women had been colleagues of Peter and Paul in their work. The same apostle Paul who seemed to counsel silence of women in Timothy 2:11–12 gave instructions in I Corinthians 11:5 on proper conduct of women doing public praying or prophesying. And for her there was something even more weighty. "The best reason in favor of a woman's right to preach the Gospel is that God's favor has attended it and blessed results follow. Called into the work at seventeen, I have been in active service practically ever since. I have seen thousands come to the altar laden with iniquity, then rising to their feet changed men and women." The fact was that she always considered herself directly ordained of God at age seventeen and her ministry not subject to validation by any later ordination. There was always an interdenominational flavor to her meetings. The exchange of ministerial leaders between her congregations and those of the Assemblies of God was especially notable.[28]

It would certainly not have been correct to think of the work of Aimee Semple McPherson as confined to Los Angeles or even to California after Los Angelinos built her a home in 1919. During the next five years she crossed the United States eight times to conduct some forty revival crusades in tents, theaters, and municipal auditoriums. She included such large cities as Philadelphia, Washington, St. Louis, and Denver. At the Denver meetings 12,000 crammed the auditorium every night for a month. Revivals in Canada, New Zealand, Australia, and Great Britain gave her international stature. After the dismissal of charges related to her disappearance in 1926, she reassured her friends with another national preaching tour—Denver, Kansas City, Topeka, Shenandoah, Des

Moines, Indianapolis, Chicago, Dayton, Syracuse, Omaha, Rochester, Baltimore, Washington, New York, Jacksonville, Dallas. A 1933 trip was "a 150-day nation-wide tour . . . during which I preached the gospel in forty-four cities, planted the Foursquare banner in twenty-one states, broadcast over forty-three radio stations, and delivered 332 sermons."[29]

However it certainly would have been correct to think of that house in Los Angeles as the new base for all her work and for all her tours after 1919. After searching for a suitable place to preach when she was at home, she decided in 1921 to build her own. Her elected site for Angelus Temple was at the corner of Park Avenue and Glendale Boulevard across the street from Echo Park. The temple was a massive dome of concrete and steel valued at $1.5 million. The money to build it came from many places but primarily, Aimee said, the building came "by the loyal help of saints in Denver, Colorado, in other cities where meetings were conducted, and by the rallying 'round of our old friends in Canada and across the sea."[30]

The Foursquare Gospel

When the temple was under construction in July of 1922, Sister McPherson was in a crusade at Oakland. She was preaching in a great tent to a crowd of more than 8,000 on the vision of the prophet in the first chapter of the book of Ezekiel. She was suddenly caught up with the imagery of fours, notably the imagery of the four cherubim with faces of man, lion, ox, and eagle. She saw the vision as the prophet's revelation of God but more particularly, in verse ten, as a type of the fourfold ministry of Jesus Christ. The face of a man symbolized Jesus Christ the Savior. The face of a lion symbolized Jesus Christ the Baptizer with the Holy Ghost. The face of the ox symbolized Jesus Christ the Great Physician. The face of the eagle symbolized Jesus Christ the Coming King. Represented here were four cardinal points of pentecostal doctrine: (1) experience of salvation by reception of Jesus Christ as Savior; (2) experience of baptism in the Holy Spirit as the gift of Christ; (3) miracles of healing for believers because Christ had already borne their infirmities; (4) expectation of the imminent return of Jesus Christ in glory. At this Oakland campaign she began the process of signing up thousands nationwide, including clergy and laity of many denominations, who would agree to affirm and support this foursquare message. They made up the body of the Echo Park Evangelistic Association, the organization which built and maintained the Angelus Temple.[31]

The foursquare symbolism then seemed to Sister Aimee to become evident everywhere in Scriptures. She said: "I have stated that the Foursquare message existed from eternity in type and shadow but for the last few years of time God has seemingly saved this special definition of His Word. The Foursquare Gospel is entirely based upon the Word of God and proclaims to a needy world the message of Jesus; the Saviour, Baptizer, Healer and Coming King."[32]

Foursquare symbolism was embodied in a Foursquare Flag with stripes of four colors and a corner insignia with a "4" in a square superimposed on a cross lying on an open Bible. It became the structure for "Foursquare . . . Not Round," Sister Aimee's "Famous Sermon Preached All Over the World." She said some people cut off a corner of the gospel by requiring no experience of being born again for incoming members; they say just come join the church as you are. Some cut off another gospel corner by failing to exalt baptism in the Holy Spirit; they say just take it by faith that you have this baptism which may not even be appropriate for today anyway. Some cut off a third gospel corner by denial of divine healing; they say the Lord has lost his power or his inclination to do this kind of thing any more. Some cut off the fourth corner when they lose the urgency of their cry that Jesus is coming soon. After each has taken off an essential corner, said Aimee, what is left is not the gospel but a poor round something which nobody wants. The world wants a Foursquare Gospel! Foursquare entered the new church's name. The denominational body headquartered at Angelus Temple and officially incorporated in 1928 was named the Church of the Foursquare Gospel.[33]

An International Church

Angelus Temple became a giant institutional center. Membership grew to about 10,000, perhaps the nation's largest single congregation. When Sister Aimee was at home she was likely to preach every weeknight and three times on Sunday, up to twenty-one times per week in special seasons of the church year. A prayer tower was added in 1923. Sister Aimee had been the first woman ever to preach a sermon over the airwaves. That was in San Francisco in spring of 1922. In 1924 she became the first woman to receive an FCC license to operate a radio station. That was her KFSG (Kall Four Square Gospel) at Angelus Temple, third station in Los Angeles. Radio seemed an ideal vehicle for her sermons, her healing services, and her evangelistic meetings occasionally conducted by radio hookups in as many as eight cities at the same time.

With McPherson spending much of her time in Los Angeles, pentecostal fellowships across the country kept inquiring about additional foursquare preachers to serve them. The L.I.F.E. (Lighthouse of International Foursquare Evangelism) Bible college was founded in March of 1923 to train pastors, evangelists, and missionaries. By 1926 there was a five-story building by the temple to house the college. Students who graduated from L.I.F.E. formed and served branch churches referred to as Foursquare Gospel Lighthouses. These branches "sprang up like mushrooms in nearly every locality," said Aimee. The Angelus Temple Commissary opened in September of 1927. This commissary assisted those who asked for help without embarrassing inquiry about church membership or immigration status. It nearly bankrupted the Foursquare corporation by aiding some 1.5 million persons during the depression years.[34]

McPherson's business decisions were not always happy ones but her primary goals remained clear. She wanted to secure the ministry of Angelus Temple, of the L.I.F.E. Bible college, and of a continuing fellowship of pentecostal soul winners. To that end she personally led the temple and the college in a period of revival and expansion through the 1930s. She sought and followed the stringent counsel of her business manager Giles M. Knight even at the cost of alienating her mother and daughter. She was able to pay off the debts of the depression years and to deliver the Foursquare institutions solvent to the leadership of her son Rolf. He was elected president for life as she had been.[35]

When Aimee Semple McPherson died in 1944 the International Church of the Foursquare Gospel had over 400 churches in North America plus 200 mission stations. Indicative of its evangelistic emphasis, 3,000 of its 22,000 members had graduated from L.I.F.E. Bible college and received ministerial credentials. Rolf McPherson announced his retirement from the presidency in 1987 and John R. Holland was elected to become his successor. By that year there were 1,250 Foursquare churches in the United States as part of 15,051 churches in 59 countries. Growth was especially strong in Brazil, the Philippines, Colombia, and Nigeria. Membership in the United States was 188,757 while worldwide membership totaled 1,100,000. United Foursquare Women shared substantially in disaster relief programs worldwide; more than 40 percent of Foursquare ministers were women. Annual giving for missions exceeded $4 million. The denomination was supporting about sixty Bible schools.

Rolf McPherson and his executive associate Howard P. Courtney had led the International Church of the Foursquare Gospel into full participation in several ecumenical fellowships—Pentecostal Fellowship of North America; Pentecostal World Conference; National Association of Evangelicals; National Religious Broadcasters.[36]

Development in Indiana

The International Church of the Foursquare Gospel came to Indiana in the 1930s and 1940s. Most of its standard bearers were graduates of Sister Aimee's L.I.F.E. Bible college alongside Angelus Temple. Howard P. Courtney graduated from the college in 1932, an alumnus of such caliber he was marked to be recalled to Los Angeles by the McPhersons to play a leading role in bringing the Foursquare Church to international prominence. Just out of the college, in his twenties, he took part for a few years in the Foursquare program of planting churches east of the Mississippi. It was he who established Indiana's first Foursquare church at Terre Haute in 1934. It was he who responded to inquiries of persons at Muncie to begin services there. It was he who maintained a lively interest in Indiana's fledgling congregations from Urbana, Illinois, where he was pastor in 1939 and supervisor of the Great Lakes District from 1940 to 1944.[37]

Harold and Frances Wood began their Foursquare ministry at Muncie on Mother's Day of 1939. The church was about three years old; attendance averaged about ten. Frances began adding recruits for a music program training choirs for all ages and a widely acclaimed male chorus. There were a lot of revival meetings both in the church and in the open air. Converts included community leaders. Harold became Foursquare state superintendent for Indiana. In 1941 the church initiated the "Preach the Word" radio broadcast over WLBC (Muncie) which could be heard from Terre Haute to Fort Wayne and easily at nearby Anderson and New Castle. Harold was the radio minister seven days a week for seven years until he moved from Muncie. The congregation made room for growth in 1942 by moving services into a tent while wrapping a new enlargement around all four sides of their old building.[38]

Lindsay Flowers worked at the Ball Brothers plant in Muncie and later at the bedsprings factory. He began attending the Foursquare church where he became volunteer janitor. He was also Sunday school superintendent for seven years without missing a Sunday. His wife Lovie Mae was teacher of the class for young married people. They were effective evangelists for their church, apt to fill their new 1940 Plymouth with children they recruited for Sunday school. Supervisor Howard P. Courtney had heard the appeal of a pentecostal family of Kentucky lineage living at New Castle to begin a church there in 1943. L.I.F.E. Bible college graduate Harold L. Meyers agreed to be organizing preacher. Muncie Foursquare members were to provide the band and give testimonies as the effort began. Lindsay Flowers played the trombone and Lovie Mae the trumpet in the march from the Henry County courthouse to the revival tent at 25th Street and Broad.

The Flowers family felt a particular attachment to New Castle. They had lived there briefly as newlyweds in 1931. Now from eighteen miles away at Muncie they had helped plant the tiny congregation. As Kentuckians they felt a cultural kinship with many New Castle residents who had come from Kentucky to work in the Chrysler factory. With increasing conviction they felt themselves called to prepare for full-time ministry and serve at New Castle. In 1946 they sold their property and set out with their two daughters for L.I.F.E. Bible college in Los Angeles. There they held jobs by day and attended school at night. Pastor Meyers moved from New Castle in 1948. Other graduates of L.I.F.E. Bible college served there only briefly. In 1949 the Flowers team was on duty at New Castle with their theology degrees, having declined appointment to any other place. His home church at Muncie gave Lindsay Flowers a new briefcase as a graduation present. At the presentation ceremony he lifted up the gift and said "I am going to be using this in New Castle for the next twenty years." The New Castle congregation officially enrolled as a Foursquare church in 1950. They promised the Flowers family $30 per week but actually averaged $10 per week the first year.

By the time Lindsay and Lovie Mae Flowers retired in 1975 average Sunday attendance at the new Foursquare church at 3200 South 14th Street in New Castle exceeded 400. It was the largest Foursquare congregation in the state and one of the largest in the Great Lakes District. Under succeeding pastors Joseph Babcock and Charles McDonald the new Flowers House Fellowship Center, completed in 1977 and named in honor of Lindsay and Lovie Mae, became the site of a state-licensed day care program for more than 100 children and of an elementary school program for nursery through sixth grades for another 100. This was the only parochial or private school for children in Henry County.[39]

One of the boys transported to Sunday school in the 1940 Plymouth of Lindsay and Lovie Mae Flowers at Muncie was Robert Barber. While the Flowers family was away at L.I.F.E. Bible college, the Barber family became interested in Muncie's Foursquare church and were "saved" under the ministry of Harold T. Wood. Young Robert Barber felt called to preach. After preparation for the ministry at L.I.F.E. Bible college in Los Angeles he became pastor of the Foursquare church at Kokomo in 1960. The Kokomo church had been founded by Dale Johnson about 1941. Average attendance in 1960 was 93 for Sunday school, the largest service. At the end of Barber's ministry of twenty years the average attendance for morning worship was 365. Barber then moved to take leadership of a second Kokomo congregation.[40]

The centers of strength in Vigo, Delaware, Howard, and Henry counties represented about 70 percent of Foursquare constituency in Indiana in 1990. The twenty Foursquare churches in the state reported a total of 3,890 adherents, a number roughly comparable to the Unitarians or the continuing United Brethren in Christ.

NOTES

1. Walter J. Hollenweger, *The Pentecostals* (Minneapolis, Minn.: Augsburg Publishing House, 1977), 487–88; Aimee Semple McPherson, *This Is That: Personal Experiences, Sermons, and Writings* (Los Angeles: Bridal Call Publishing House, 1919), 25–28; *Dictionary of Pentecostal and Charismatic Movements* (Grand Rapids, Mich.: Zondervan, 1988), 568; Edith L. Blumhofer, *Aimee Semple McPherson: Everybody's Sister* (Grand Rapids, Mich.: William B. Eerdmans, 1993), 23–59; Daniel Mark Epstein, *Sister Aimee: The Life of Aimee Semple McPherson* (New York: Harcourt Brace Jovanovich, 1993), 5–26; Robert Bahr, *Least of All Saints: The Story of Aimee Semple McPherson* (Englewood Cliffs, N.J.: Prentice-Hall, 1979), 286. Bahr and Blumhofer suggest the likely influence of Salvationist commander Evangeline Booth on Aimee.

2. Aimee Semple McPherson, *The Story of My Life* (Hollywood, Calif.: International Correspondents, 1951), 24–28; McPherson, *This Is That*, 30–35; Bahr, *Least of All Saints*, 285.

3. McPherson, *This Is That*, 36, 93–106, 380–82; McPherson, *Story*, 28–29, 82–87; Blumhofer, *Aimee Semple McPherson*, 60–134; *Dictionary of Pentecostal and Charismatic Movements*, 569.

4. McPherson, *Story*, 88–177; McPherson, *This Is That*, 153; Blumhofer, *Aimee Semple McPherson*, 95–180.

5. McPherson, *Story*, 234.

6. McPherson, *Story*, 196–97; Blumhofer, *Aimee Semple McPherson*, 232–80.

7. Aimee Semple McPherson, *In the Service of the King* (New York: Boni and Liveright, 1927), 260–313; Blumhofer, *Aimee Semple McPherson*, 281–300; Bahr, *Least of All Saints*, 267–68; McPherson, *Story*, 208–29; *Dictionary of Pentecostal and Charismatic Movements*, 570.

8. John J. Kershner, *The Disappearance of Aimee Semple McPherson; With a Scientific Analysis of Her Teachings, Activities and Emotions* (Los Angeles: The Author, 1926, 61 p.); Nancy Barr Mavity, *Sister Aimee* (Garden City, N.Y.: Doubleday, Doran, 1931, 360 p.); Robert Steele, *The Vanishing Evangelist*, by Lately Thomas [pseud.] (New York: Viking Press, 1959, 334 p.).

9. "Aimee Semple McPherson: Thousands Mourn at Famed Evangelist's Funeral," *Life* 17 (30 October 1944): 85–89; Bahr, *Least of All Saints*, opposite 138, 278.

10. McPherson, *Story*, 234–35.

11. Aimee Semple McPherson, *The Holy Spirit* (Los Angeles: Challpin Publishing Company, 1931), 11; Edith L. Blumhofer, *The Assemblies of God: A Chapter in the Story of American Pentecostalism*, 2 vols. (Springfield, Mo.: Gospel Publishing House, 1989), 1:251; Hollenweger, *Pentecostals*, 487–88.

12. McPherson, *This Is That*, 12–21, 36–43.

13. McPherson, *This Is That*, 42.

14. McPherson, *This Is That*, 43–57.

15. McPherson, *This Is That*, 49–50.

16. McPherson, *This Is That*, 59; McPherson, *Story*, 42–45.

17. McPherson, *This Is That*, 8, 67–78; McPherson, *Story*, 50; Blumhofer, *Assemblies*, 1:128–30, 173–74; *Dictionary of Pentecostal and Charismatic Movements*, 255–56, 569.

18. McPherson, *This Is That*, 107–14; Blumhofer, *Assemblies*, 1:249–53; *Dictionary of Pentecostal and Charismatic Movements*, 569.

19. McPherson, *This Is That*, 164–65.

20. Aimee Semple McPherson, *Divine Healing Sermons* (N.p., n.d., 146 p.); McPherson, *In the Service*, 221–30; McPherson, *Story*, 88–99, 164.

21. McPherson, *Divine Healing Sermons*, 9.

22. McPherson, *This Is That*, 113–207.

23. McPherson, *This Is That*, 141–42; *Dictionary of Pentecostal and Charismatic Movements*, 461–62.

24. McPherson, *This Is That*, 199–229.

25. McPherson, *This Is That*, 231–41; McPherson, *In the Service*, 207–11, 215–17; McPherson, *Story*, 151–54.

26. Aimee Semple McPherson, *This Is That* (Los Angeles: Bridal Call Publishing House, 1919, 685 p.); Blumhofer, *Aimee Semple McPherson*, 190–231; *Dictionary of Pentecostal and Charismatic Movements*, 462.

27. McPherson, *This Is That*, 7, 431–43, 465–77, 485–98; McPherson, *Story*, 241.

28. Bahr, *Least of All Saints*, 292; McPherson, *This Is That*, 11; *Dictionary of Pentecostal and Charismatic Movements*, 569–70; Blumhofer, *Assemblies*, 1:249–52.

29. McPherson, *Story*, 172–76, 228–40; McPherson, *In the Service*, 239–44; Blumhofer, *Assemblies*, 1:250–51.

30. McPherson, *Story*, 188–93; McPherson, *In the Service*, 239, 245–50.

31. Aimee Semple McPherson, *The Foursquare Gospel* (Los Angeles: Echo Park Evangelistic Association, 1946, 199 p.); McPherson, *Story*, 178–80.

32. McPherson, *Foursquare Gospel*, 21.

33. McPherson, *Foursquare Gospel*, 63, 189–99.

34. McPherson, *Story*, 197–98, 230–31; Bahr, *Least of All Saints*, 293–94; *Dictionary of Pentecostal and Charismatic Movements*, 462, 570.

35. *Dictionary of Pentecostal and Charismatic Movements*, 462, 570–72; Bahr, *Least of All Saints*, 280–82, 298–99.

36. *Dictionary of Pentecostal and Charismatic Movements*, 462–63.

37. *Dictionary of Pentecostal and Charismatic Movements*, 227–28; Letter of Howard P. Courtney, Glendale, Calif., to L. C. Rudolph, 29 January 1991.

38. Letter of Harold T. Wood, Lake Arrowhead, Calif., to L. C. Rudolph, 22 March 1991.

39. Betty Hagerman, *How a Pair of Shoes Built a Church* (New Castle, Ind.: Foursquare Gospel Church, 1983, 178 p.); Letter of Charles M. McDonald, New Castle, Ind., to L. C. Rudolph, 23 January 1991.

40. Hagerman, *How a Pair of Shoes Built a Church*, 65; Telephone interview of Robert Barber, Kokomo, Ind., with L. C. Rudolph, 6 December 1990.

CHURCH OF JESUS CHRIST OF LATTER-DAY SAINTS (MORMONS)

Joseph Smith, one of nine children of Joseph and Lucy Mack Smith, received his first revelation in a wooded area near his home. That was in Palmyra Township in western New York in spring of 1820. He was fourteen. In the midst of the claims of several Christian churches in his community, he prayed hard about which was the right one to join. The answer came in the form of a personal visit by God and Jesus Christ.

> I saw two personages, whose brightness and glory defy all description, standing above me in the air. One of them spake unto me, calling me by name, and said, pointing to the other—This is my beloved Son, hear Him . . . I asked the personages who stood above me in the light, which of all the sects was right—and which I should join. I was answered that I must join none of them, for they were all wrong, and the personage who addressed me said that all their creeds were an abomination in His sight: that those professors were all corrupt; that "they draw near to me with their lips, but their hearts are far from me; they teach for doctrines the commandments of men: having a form of godliness, but they deny the power thereof."[1]

Local persons to whom he revealed this incident were not supportive. He himself remained expectant and the next visitant came as he was praying in bed on the evening of 21 September 1823. This angel was a descendant of an ancient people named Nephites who were in turn descendants of immigrants arriving in America from the Holy Land in the days before the Babylonian Captivity of about 600 B.C.

I discovered a light appearing in my room, which continued to increase until the room was lighter than at noonday, when immediately a personage appeared at my bedside, standing in the air, for his feet did not touch the ground. He had on a loose robe of most exquisite whiteness. It was a whiteness beyond anything earthly I had ever seen; nor do I believe that any earthly thing could be made to appear so exceedingly white and brilliant . . . Not only was his robe exceedingly white, but his whole person was glorious beyond description, and his countenance truly like lightning . . . He called me by name, and said unto me that he was a messenger sent from the presence of God to me, and that his name was Moroni; that God had a work for me to do; and that my name should be had for good and evil among all nations, kindreds, and tongues, or that it should be both good and evil spoken of among all people. He said there was a book deposited, written upon gold plates, giving an account of the former inhabitants of this continent, and the source from whence they sprang. He also said that the fullness of the everlasting Gospel was contained in it, as delivered by the Savior to the ancient inhabitants.[2]

The visitation included repeated communications by the angel plus a vision of the place nearby where the gold plates were secreted. Joseph easily recognized the designated hill and found the plates. After meeting Moroni at the hiding place every year for a prescribed period of four years, Joseph was entrusted with the plates and began translating with the help of two "seer" stones which accompanied them. Persons aware of the process were generally hostile or bent on stealing the plates. There was limited and amateur assistance for the young prophet from his wife Emma and their parents. There was especially helpful support from incipient believers Martin Harris, Oliver Cowdery, and David Whitmer. In March of 1830 the translation of the plates was published in 5,000 copies by the printer Egbert Grandin of Palmyra as the *Book of Mormon*. The plates, after privileged viewings by selected witnesses, remained in the care of the angel Moroni.[3]

While translators Joseph Smith and Oliver Cowdery were praying in May of 1829 about the teaching concerning baptism for the remission of sins which they were finding in the plates, a heavenly messenger appeared. This was John the Baptist who laid hands on them ordaining them priests after the order of Aaron: "Upon you my fellow servants, in the name of the Messiah, I confer the Priesthood of Aaron, which holds the keys of the ministering of angels, and of the Gospel of repentance, and of baptism by immersion for the remission of sins; and this shall never be taken again from the earth, until the sons of Levi do offer again an offering unto the Lord in righteousness."[4]

Following the messenger's instruction the two baptized one another and ordained one another by the laying on of hands, that act accompanied by many manifestations of the Holy Spirit. At some unspecified time soon afterward, a visit by the apostles Peter, James, and John conferred on Smith and Cowdery the higher priesthood after the order of Melchizedek; with this ordination they were empowered to lay on hands for the bestowal of the Holy Spirit and to establish a church. So the authoritative line of the priesthood of former days, lost since the days of the apostles of Jesus, was fully restored.[5]

The task of this renewed priesthood of the latter days was to gather the whole remnant of God's saints to Zion in preparation for the Lord's return. They set to work at once. On 6 April 1830 a group of at least thirty believers were gathered at David Whitmer's log house at Fayette, New York. Six young men in that meeting took the official action to organize the church—Joseph Smith, Hyrum Smith, Samuel Smith, Oliver Cowdery, Peter Whitmer, David Whitmer. They acknowledged Joseph Smith and Oliver Cowdery as the church's founding elders. The elders served the sacrament and confirmed the membership of those present. Mormonism now had its corporate form around the living prophet at its center.

A basic organizational structure and much continuing direction was received by revelation. As the prophet later worded the belief in continuing revelation: "We believe all that God has revealed, all that He does now reveal, and we believe that He will yet reveal many great and important things pertaining to the kingdom of God." The members were very excited at being engaged afresh "in the very same order of things as observed by the holy apostles of old." Their missionary effort was heroic. A revelation years later, on 23 April 1838, would establish the name of the fellowship as "The Church of Jesus Christ of Latter-day Saints," but from the beginning those who met the missionaries used the shorter form "Mormons" until that name became widely accepted also.[6]

Mormons in Ohio and Missouri

Early followers were enlisted primarily in the East and gathered at such places as Colesville, Fayette, and Palmyra in New York. But the Mormons kept moving west as well. Revelations about the great gathering of the Saints at Zion were less concerned about setting a final date for the gathering and more concerned with Zion's location. It was certain to be in America. A disclosure through Joseph Smith in 1830 said the place would be "on the borders by the Lamanites." In Mormon history the Lamanites were a degenerate remainder of one branch of the ancient immigrants from the Holy Land and were identified as the American Indians. An obvious contemporary border with the Indians was Missouri and revelations to the prophet during his visit there in summer of 1831 fixed the location of Zion in Jackson County near the site of Independence.[7] On the basis of the prophecies some Mormons began to move west and take up land to be near this Jackson County location for Zion. Meanwhile there were impressive additions in Ohio, notably the enlistment of Campbellite preacher Sidney Rigdon along with about 150 members of his congregation. Joseph and Emma Smith moved to Kirtland near Cleveland in December of 1830. Missionaries and converts kept gathering there. By spring of 1831 membership at Kirtland was more than 1,000 and growing. It would be the chief Mormon administrative and evangelistic center for the next six years.[8]

Converts kept flowing in but the gathering places in both Missouri and Ohio fared poorly. The intention of the prophet and his followers was to restore the full order of God's kingdom which would naturally have a priority in the whole of the people's economic, political, social, and religious lives. To their neighbors these burgeoning communities with such ambitious projections of priority seemed clannish and probably dangerous. The result was suspicion, fear, and violence. The Mormons in Missouri were driven from Jackson County, most of them across the river to Clay County in 1834 and from Clay County to Daviess and Caldwell counties in 1836. Joseph Smith and those Mormons at Kirtland who continued to support him were forced to begin their departures from Ohio to Missouri in the winter of 1837–38. Then the Mormons were driven out of Missouri entirely in 1838–39 —"exterminated," the state's governor called it.[9]

Mormons at Nauvoo in Illinois

The Mormon exiles purchased land in several places, most notably a large swampy tract beside the Mississippi River in Hancock County, Illinois. This turned out to be the most dangerous place of all. There was no lack of church members. Missions at home and abroad sent thousands of Mormon immigrants streaming to Illinois. Their central city of Nauvoo grew to about 10,000 by 1844, contesting Chicago to be the largest of Illinois cities. It had generous powers of self-rule with Mormon officers in charge of all branches of its government and Joseph Smith as lieutenant general of a city militia called the Nauvoo Legion. When Mormons voted as a block they could decide some Illinois elections; fear of such political influence alienated both the Whigs and the Democrats.[10]

The Nauvoo years were an especially active period for Joseph Smith as prophet, seer, and revelator. In 1842 he began publishing a paper called *Times and Seasons*. Thousands attended his teaching sessions. He disclosed and refined doctrines concerning an eternal progression of persons from preexistent spirits through an earthly pilgrimage to possible exaltation to become gods. The route to exaltation involved a body of temple ordinances. Construction of a limestone temple 128 feet by 60 feet was undertaken at Nauvoo. Having earlier seen a vision of heaven including his brother Alvin who had died before the Mormon restoration of the kingdom, the prophet disclosed the missionary procedures operative among the dead. Those who could not hear the true gospel in life might believe and be saved in the spirit world. Since these could not accomplish their own physical baptism for the remission of sins or physically complete certain blessings and sealings in a temple, these crucial acts should be done on their behalf by the living. There were baptisms for the dead in the Mississippi River and then in the partially completed temple at Nauvoo.

Celestial marriage was a step toward exaltation. Conventional marriages "until death do us part" were regarded to be as temporal as these words indicated; family ties of worthy Mormons sealed in a temple by the restored authoritative priesthood were eternal. The highest exaltation was for worthy Mormons who entered "the new and everlasting covenant of marriage." That new and everlasting covenant provided for plural marriage.

> And again, as pertaining to the law of the priesthood—if any man espouse a virgin, and desire to espouse another, and the first give her consent, and if he espouse the second, and they are virgins, and have vowed to no other man, then is he justified; he cannot commit adultery for they are given unto him; for he cannot commit adultery with that that belongeth unto him and to no one else. And if he have ten virgins given unto him by this law, he cannot commit adultery, for they belong to him, and they are given unto him; therefore is he justified.[11]

The prophet recorded this revelation at Nauvoo in 1843 as an answer to his inquiries of the Lord about the biblical accounts of the marriages of Abraham, Isaac, Jacob, Moses, David, and Solomon. Its reception and practice were to be kept confidential but evidently became common report. Official announcement and approval of plural marriage was delayed until 1852.[12]

The Mormons kept needing more room but expansion as a self-governing kingdom of Saints always met opposition. Mormon agents were eyeing opportunities for expansion in the far West. Early in 1844 Joseph Smith and his counselors decided on another option for safe expansion—to run the prophet for president of the United States. It was a common millennial understanding that the governments of men would ultimately fail and be replaced by the just rule of God's kingdom. Perhaps this was the time for a crucial step toward the reign of righteousness which would at the same time provide freedom from persecution for Mormons and demonstrate the very best of government for all. Sidney Rigdon was vice-presidential candidate for the National Reform party. There was a political platform. Mormon missionaries became campaigners in many places, including northern Indiana. In June it all came crashing down. Mormon officers authorized destruction of a particularly scurrilous anti-Mormon newspaper at Nauvoo. Public resentment focused on this act of destruction and on a party of Saints imprisoned for the offense at the county seat town of Carthage. There guards connived with members of a mob who broke in to murder Joseph and Hyrum Smith, culmination of a long series of violent acts against Mormons.[13]

Chaos followed the death of Joseph Smith. The line and procedure for succession was not clear. Some believers accepted the leadership of such claimants as Sidney Rigdon, Lyman Wight, James Strang, and William Smith.

However it was the Council of the Twelve Apostles which assumed effective management of community life at Nauvoo. Brigham Young was a rising leader on his way to being designated as president of the council in 1847 and as the church's official prophet, seer, and revelator in 1852. He consolidated his supporters at Nauvoo for a time. They concentrated on construction of the temple and most of the worthy members completed their temple endowments there.[14]

Relocation in the Far West

But there was no real hope of establishing a separate Mormon kingdom east of the Mississippi. Nauvoo's favorable charter was revoked by the Illinois legislature. Harassment of Mormons was rising again. Mormon leaders were still putting out feelers for a safe location in the far West. In winter of 1845 several members of the Council of the Twelve Apostles were reading the available reports and maps about western explorations, especially John C. Fremont's description of his expedition in 1843–44. The following spring the advance company moved out seeking "some good valley in the neighborhood of the Rocky Mountains." The planners had in view some unclaimed valleys along the western slopes of the Wasatch Mountains. Because the anti-Mormon mobs were active again in Illinois, Mormons began crossing the Mississippi from Nauvoo in the bitter weather of February. Brigham Young finally said "this is the right place" over the Great Salt Lake valley in July of 1847 but the huge operation of relocating some 12,000 Saints to the area continued into succeeding years.[15]

The United States took title to that western region in 1848 following the Mexican War. At about the same time the Mormon leaders mapped a "State of Deseret" covering what later became all of Nevada and Utah plus parts of California, Oregon, Arizona, New Mexico, Colorado, and Wyoming. They placed its government in the hands of a body of churchmen called the Council of Fifty and sought to secure its admission as a state in the Union. Here would be room for all remnants from Illinois and all those thousands of Saints being recruited from many nations. Here Brigham Young and his followers could institute the whole restoration format—economic, social, political, religious—including the revelations of the Nauvoo years. By 1856 about 40,000 Latter-day Saints had arrived in the Great Salt Lake valley. Some later dared to hope that when the states of the North and of the South had exhausted each other in the Civil War the government of the Council of Fifty might be ready for

recognition as the most obviously righteous and rightful government for the nation until the Lord's return.

But it was not to be. The stream of Mormons came west but so did a stream of miners, railroad builders, speculators, and non-Mormon settlers bent on establishing their own farms and ranches. There could be no separated place of peace for a restored kingdom in control of all aspects of Mormon life. What eventually came was federal territorial government of the type regularly provided for national western lands. That government ignored the existence of any State of Deseret and increasingly challenged the right of Mormon leaders who held the high church offices to also exercise the executive, legislative, and judicial powers over the lives of their fellow citizens in the territory.[16]

Practice of Polygamy

The easiest target for opponents was the Mormon practice of polygamy.[17] Less than a tenth of Mormon men practiced polygamy and most who did had only two wives. Nobody seemed to want to be polygamists very much. But after the revelation and practice were openly acknowledged at a general church conference of Utah Mormons in 1852 and advocated there by Brigham Young and Orson Pratt, defense of the doctrine became a matter of Mormon allegiance. A Mormon historian said:

> In emphasizing how small was the percentage of Mormons who were directly involved in polygamy it is important to recall that all the central church leaders were polygamists. From the president down through the apostles and the Presiding Bishopric during the period, no general authority was a monogamist; the same was true of most bishops and stake presidents, as well as, for all practical purposes, their counselors. The privilege of polygamy was granted to the pure in heart and hence was a clear sign of worthiness for promotion in the Mormon hierarchy. Although no one ever explicitly said so in the nineteenth century, it appears to have been an effective device for gauging and assuring loyalty. As those who entered polygamy learned at the very beginning, it brought such a difficult clash with general moral assumptions that accepting it was a declaration of irrevocable commitment to the Prophet and his movement. It did the same with a man's first wife, with the plural wife, with the parents of the plural wife, and with their children. Self-image and self-respect were inextricably part of these plural relationships. The system was surely not contrived with anything quite this simple in mind, but in practice it served as a powerful reinforcement to existing loyalty.[18]

Mormonism's defense of the right of its members to practice plural marriage according to the revelation brought the united force of a national crusade against them—evangelical preachers and members, organized reformers both male and female, newspaper reporters and editors, writers of travel accounts, humorists and cartoonists, and finally national legislators with their statutes including stringent provisions for enforcement.[19]

By the turn of the century Mormonism was turning from its self-understanding as a restored physical kingdom of God with political, economic, and social powers. On 24 September 1890 President Wilford Woodruff issued a manifesto which said in part: "Inasmuch as laws have been enacted by Congress forbidding plural marriages, which laws have been pronounced constitutional by the court of last resort, I hereby declare my intention to submit to those laws, and to use my influence with the members of the Church over which I preside to have them do likewise." A general conference at Salt Lake City said unanimously on 6 October: "We accept his declaration concerning plural marriages as authoritative and binding." At that conference presidential counselor George Q. Cannon referred to the supporting authority of a passage from Joseph Smith which said the Saints need not cling to a revelation which threatened their very existence. President Woodruff later said his manifesto was a revelation from the Lord in its own right. "The Lord showed me by vision and revelation exactly what would take place if we did not stop this practice . . . He has told me exactly what to do . . . And when the hour came that I was commanded to do that, it was all clear to me."[20]

This new stand required some years of adjustment within the church and even more years for acceptance among an emotional national public which had very nearly equated Mormonism with polygamy. Continuing revelation was always a basic belief among Mormons. Here was a crucial example of doctrinal correction by new revelation, precedent for realignment and redefinition of belief and practice by new revelations given in response to prayerful inquiry by church leaders. It was a route followed almost a century later when new revelation announced in 1978 removed historic Mormon discrimination against blacks.[21]

Mormons beyond Utah

Mormon converts in Europe liked to migrate to Utah where they could enjoy life among their fellow Saints and have opportunity to marry in the faith. But even the resources of expanded and multiplied Mormon settlements in the American West could not support endless immigrations. National immigration laws slowed the flow. So did church policy. President Joseph F. Smith was telling European Saints in 1910:

> We do not desire, my brethren and sisters, that you trouble yourselves too much about emigration. At present we do not advise you to emigrate. We would rather that you remain until you have been well established in the faith in the Gospel and until each one of you has been the instrument, through the help of the Lord, in bringing one, or more, of your fellow men into the Church. Be not troubled about the Temple ordinances, but live in faith and confidence in the truths, and wait patiently, and if death should call you before the ordinances are attended to, your children will see to it that the work will be done, and even if you have no opportunity in this life to receive those ordinances, the Lord will open the way so that it will be done in the future.[22]

At the end of another decade the official word to missionaries by revelation was to stop preaching emigration. That was certainly the message during and following the depression years of the 1930s.[23]

Equally revolutionary was the emigration of Saints out of the "Mormon culture region" of Utah, southern Idaho, western Wyoming, eastern Nevada, northern Arizona, and eastern New Mexico in the 1940s. From this agricultural area of limited industry young Mormons moved to Los Angeles, San Francisco, New York, Chicago, Portland, Seattle, and Washington, D.C. In fact they went wherever duty or opportunity called them. This gave new substance to the twentieth century teaching of their church that the stakes of Zion were by no means limited to Utah. The great tent of the kingdom was worldwide and worthy Mormons should erect its supports wherever they were. A group of Mormon churches in a designated area similar to a diocese was called a "stake." Stakes were to be established only where there was sufficient leadership and membership to assure operation of the full program of the church without constant outside supervision. Local congregations within the stake might first be called "branches" and then advance to be called "wards." More than one branch or ward might use the same chapel building. In 1936 every stake was bidden to develop a mission. The intermountain West of America continued to hold a tremendous attraction as a center for the Mormons of the world but the "scattering of the gathered" had come. The increasing army of missionaries came to be at least as eager to develop organizations in new localities as to send their converts to the Rocky Mountain West.[24]

Mormon leaders wanted statehood for Utah. With that status the Mormon majority could elect their own governmental leaders at all levels and have their representatives in place in the national congress. They would no longer be subject to unsympathetic territorial and military officers. Statehood finally came in 1896 after polygamy was renounced and separation of church and state was ensured. Brigham H. Roberts was elected to the national House of Representatives. He was still living with his plural wives and in response to public outcry was denied his seat in the House. When Reed Smoot of the Council of the Twelve Apostles was elected senator in 1902 the issue was not polygamy but church domination of the process of political selection. Arguing on Smoot's behalf, the church denied any control of elections. President Joseph F. Smith declared as a witness before the Senate that Mormon members were allowed wide latitude of belief, even contrary to a message from the prophet, so long as their lives were moral.[25]

Integration of Latter-day Saints into the American mainstream seemed well on its way. Utah Mormons divided themselves among the national political parties without serious imbalance. Mormons began taking places in the nation's business life including offices in major corporations. Attitudes of the Saints on morality and family standards found great respect among Americans, especially among conservative Protestants. Genealogists became appreciative patrons of the massive archives compiled by Mormons to aid in the work of binding and sealing the whole human family in the faith. Visitors found unfailing hospitality at the church's sacred sites. The Mormon Tabernacle Choir won national affection for its unabashedly religious and patriotic music. Mormons were stoutly patriotic; their congregations were outstanding among the sponsors of Boy Scouts of America.[26]

Thus the Mormon missionary might say that all other churches were wrong and that only his group had the good news of a restored apostolic line of prophecy and priesthood. He might carry an unusual canon of Scriptures—Old Testament, New Testament, Book of Mormon, Doctrine and Covenants, Pearl of Great Price. He might deny the Trinity and describe a God of bones and flesh involved in the same eternal progression with all faithful Mormons so that "we are as God was and shall be as he is." He might describe a religious pilgrimage reaching from preexistent spirits yearning for the opportunity to be born all the way through to ineffable glory for those most worthy Saints become creative gods in the midst of their families sealed together through temple covenants for eternity. He might have little to say about salvation by grace through faith and more to say about continuing worthiness demonstrated by immersion for the remission of sins; reception of the Holy Spirit through the laying on of hands; progression in the steps of the priesthood of Aaron and Melchizedek; participation in the regular life and duties of the body of Saints and its auxiliaries; tithing 10 percent of gross wages or net income to the central church plus about 5 percent for local and regional purposes plus offerings for special causes; accepting a mission call or calls; and observing the "Word of Wisdom" by abstaining from coffee, tea, alcohol, and tobacco.[27] But he was no longer an outsider.

By the end of the 1980s this Mormon fellowship was maintaining about 30,000 missionaries in the field. There were over 4 million adherents in the United States and over 2 million more in ninety-five other countries and twenty territories. In scores of temples thousands of members were at work on behalf of the living and dead. The ideal of a separated Mormon kingdom had been indefinitely delayed. Across America all the movement's unusual characteristics became familiar and were accepted as the profile and behavioral marks of one more unit of the nation's Christian pluralism.[28]

Reorganized Church of Jesus Christ of Latter Day Saints

Not all religious descendants of Joseph Smith migrated to the Great Salt Lake valley after his death. Some were not convinced that the presidency of Brigham Young and the move he led to the far West represented the will of the Lord. Some who left Nauvoo as part of that trek stopped off along the way or chose to return to the Midwest. There was a continuing process of sifting and validation of claimants to the office of prophet, seer, and revelator. Second in size only to the contingent of Brigham Young was the group which finally coalesced in support of Joseph Smith III, the martyr prophet's eldest son. Sometimes they were called "Josephites." Some were from branches of the Saints in Wisconsin led by Jason Briggs and Zenas Gurley. Some were impressed with William Marks, a senior associate of the martyred prophet whose revelation at a conference in Illinois said: "Thus saith the Lord; oh thou man of God! In times past thou hast sat with my servant Joseph, the Seer; and in times near to come thou shalt sit in council with his son. When I called my servant Joseph he was as a lone tree; but when I shall call his son he shall be as one of a forest."[29]

In spite of testimonies that his father had named him to be successor, Joseph III himself was reluctant. He had been only a lad of eleven when his father was killed in 1844. Revelations and organization on his behalf were persistent from 1851 to 1860. On 6 April of the latter year he accepted an invitation to a church conference at Amboy, Illinois, and reported a revelation he himself had received. "I wish to say I have not come here to be dictated by any man or set of men. I have come in obedience to a power not my own, and shall be dictated by the power that sent me. God works by means best known to himself, and I feel that for some time past he has been pointing out the work for me to do." Now sensing a concurrence of divine direction, the conference unanimously "resolved that Brother Joseph Smith be chosen Prophet, Seer, and Revelator of the Church of Jesus Christ, and the successor of his father." Marks, Gurley, and two others then ordained him to the presidency of the high priesthood of the church. Thus the formation of the Reorganized Church of Jesus Christ of Latter Day Saints was completed.[30]

Joseph III guided the Reorganized Church for fifty-four years as they developed their structure and defined their identity. They affirmed the early history of the movement—the rejection of existing churches and restoration of an apostolic order of prophecy and priesthood; the earlier recorded revelations of Joseph Smith the martyr; the early missionary efforts and the heroic survival of remnants from Kirtland and Missouri. Essentially they denied as invalid some of the last revelations attributed to Joseph Smith the martyr and much of the resulting experimentation at Nauvoo. And they painstakingly refuted the right of succession of Brigham Young who was a persistent advocate of those later revelations and experiments. They said that plural marriage was first disclosed as a "so-called" revelation by Orson Pratt and Brigham Young in Utah in August of 1852. They said that Joseph Smith neither taught nor practiced polygamy nor would they tolerate it. They took the abstentions from wine, strong drink, tobacco, and hot drinks enjoined as the "Word of Wisdom" in Doctrine and Covenants 89 as healthful advice, and not requirements for participation in the full benefits of membership. They rejected the doctrines of the eternal progression of God and man, of levels of glory providing for the exaltation of the faithful to godhood, of eternal sealing ordinances for marriages and families, and eventually even of ministries or vicarious services on behalf of the dead.[31]

The Reorganized Church had successive headquarters at Plano in Illinois until 1881, at Lamoni in Iowa from 1881 to 1920, and since 1920 at Independence in Missouri. Independence became a center for the church's administrative and educational programs; it provided offices and an auditorium but no closed temple with secret ordinances. Thus even after the Utah Mormons rejected polygamy and any claim to the creation of a separate kingdom, these two larger groups of Saints remained very different. A civil court in Ohio in 1880 recognized the valid succession of the Reorganized Church by awarding it possession of the Kirtland Temple property. A similar case involving legitimate continuation came before a federal court in 1892 in Missouri. Possession of property in Independence was awarded to the Reorganized Church but then denied on appeal because the church had waited too long to press its claim. The Reorganized Church grew from about 300 members at the time of its formation to some 244,000 in thirty-seven countries and on tropical islands by 1990. It became recognized as the body of Saints most inclined to share with the wider family of Protestant Christians in joint education and in social action. In 1985 the church began ordaining some of its women members to the previously all-male priesthood offices. All of its president-prophets have been descendants of the martyred prophet Joseph Smith.[32]

Early Mormons in Indiana

Indiana was on the route each time the Mormons traveled between their early centers at Kirtland in Ohio and Independence in Missouri. Joseph Smith himself made the trip five times. In summer of 1831 he and Sidney Rigdon went from Kirtland to visit a substantial Mormon group about twelve miles west of Independence; this group of about sixty led by Newel K. Whitney had moved from Colesville, New York, by way of Kirtland, to the "land of promise." Smith and Rigdon also conferred in Missouri with members of the "Lamanite Mission" which Parley Pratt and Oliver Cowdery had been conducting among the Delawares of west Missouri. On this trip the prophet prayed earnestly about the location of Zion and was given a revelation.[33]

Hearken, O ye elders of my church, saith the Lord your God, who have assembled yourselves together, according to my commandments, in this land, which is the land of Missouri, which is the land which I have appointed and consecrated for the gathering of the saints. Wherefore, this is the land of promise, and the place for the city of Zion . . . Behold, the place which is now called Independence is the center place; and a spot for the temple is lying westward, upon a lot which is not far from the courthouse. Wherefore, it is wisdom that the land should be purchased by the saints, and also every tract lying westward, even unto the line running directly between Jew and Gentile; and also every tract bordering by the prairies, inasmuch as my disciples are enabled to buy lands.[34]

In 1832 Smith, Rigdon, and Whitney were leaders of a party sent from Kirtland to Independence to ease some of the rivalries and jealousies common between the two centers. They passed along Indiana on the Ohio River steamboat from Steubenville to St. Louis on the way out in April. On the return trip in June Smith, Rigdon, and Whitney elected to travel to Kirtland on the stagecoach by way of St. Louis and Vincennes. Near Greenville in Indiana the stage team ran away. Smith and Rigdon jumped out of the coach unhurt but Whitney's coat pulled him into the wheel so that his leg and foot were broken. Smith stayed with the recuperating Whitney at Mr. Porter's Public House at Greenville for four weeks. He got food poisoning; he dislocated his jaw; his hair fell out.[35] He wrote to his wife Emma:

I have visited a grove which is just back of the town almost every day where I can be secluded from the eyes of any mortal and there give vent to all the feeling of my heart in meaditation and prayr. I have called to mind all the past moments of my life and am left to morn and shed tears of sorrow for my folly in sufering the adversary of my soul to have so much power over me as he has had in times past but God is merciful and has forgiven my sins and I rjoice that he sendeth forth the Comferter unto as many as believe and humbleeth themselves before him . . . It would have been very consoling to me to have received a few lines from you but as you did not take the trouble I will try to be contented with my lot knowing that God is my friend. In him I shall find comfort. I have given my life into his hands. I am prepared to go at his call. I desire to be with Christ. I count not my life dear to me only to do his will.[36]

In May of 1834 Joseph Smith crossed Indiana leading the greatest show of Mormon strength seen in the state in the century. The Saints in Missouri had been dispossessed of their land without due process; they had been driven from Independence in Jackson County across the river to Clay and neighboring counties. The prophet in Kirtland received a revelation on 24 February 1834 calling various leaders there to organize what came to be called "Zion's Camp" to march nearly 900 miles to relieve the faithful. The intention was to look something like an army to show strength in Missouri so there were knives, axes, pitchforks, and some small arms. Joseph Smith traveled as "Squire Cook" with a big bulldog, a pair of fancy pistols, a sword, and a rifle.

At the same time the intention was to look enough like farmers to avoid suspicion and opposition along the way. The army left Kirtland with about 100 men and grew along the way to 205 including 11 women and 7 children. Their route through Indiana generally followed the National Road through Wayne, Henry, Hancock, Marion, Hendricks, Putnam, and Parke counties. Parley Pratt, a trusted colleague of Joseph Smith and a missionary well acquainted with Indiana, was recruiting officer for Zion's Camp. He visited clusters of Mormons in Ohio, Indiana, Illinois, and Missouri as the camp passed through to obtain additional men, arms, stores, and money.[37]

The Richmond *Palladium* for 24 May reported "a caravan of about two hundred Mormonites with a long train of wagons." There were rumors that the band would be challenged and dispersed by the governor at Indianapolis. But the Mormon narrator of the march said: "When near the place many got into the wagons, and, separating some little distance, passed through the city, while others walked down different streets, leaving the inhabitants wondering 'when that big company would come along.'" Three weeks after Zion's Camp had crossed the Wabash into Illinois, the Brookville *Indiana American* was still grumbling: "It is said the Mormon War in Missouri is about to be renewed. A fanatical leader, styled General Joe Smith, has sent in the form of a circular, his pretended revelations from on high, requiring the aid of the faithful to 'expel the infidels' from the Holy Land. About 500 are on the move, and they are armed with dirks, swords, pistols, guns, and other hostile weapons." Missouri authorities denied any legal relief or protection to the Mormons. Zion's Camp "was by the word of the Lord disbanded; some remained as settlers in that country, and others returned to their homes and families in Ohio." Joseph Smith stabilized the Saints in Clay County with their own organization as a "stake of Zion" and returned to Kirtland.[38]

Joseph Smith and Sidney Rigdon were at Terre Haute again on 12 October 1837 on their way to Far West in Missouri. They were to decide whether to approve the Far West area as a Mormon center so "the poor might have a place to gather to." Having declared it a place of "sufficient room," they set out for Kirtland early in November. They were to test the hospitality of Missouri again sooner than they knew. At the turn of the year "apostate mobocracy" took control at Kirtland. Brigham Young fled west on 22 December 1837. Joseph Smith and Sidney Rigdon departed by night on horseback on 12 January. Their families in covered wagons joined them at an arranged meeting place sixty miles west. The party was forced to travel in great secrecy because their enemies from Kirtland stayed hot on their trail for days.[39]

The prophet took a nine-day stopover at Dublin, Indiana, in mid-January, cutting wood for hire to "relieve his necessities" and without funds enough to continue his trip. He said to Brigham Young "You are one of the Twelve who have charge of the kingdom in all the world; I believe I shall throw myself upon you, and look to you for counsel in this case." Brigham's counsel was "rest yourself and be assured you shall have money in plenty to pursue your journey." A Mormon brother named Tomlinson from Dublin was able to sell his farm following the counsel of Brigham Young. At Young's suggestion, Tomlinson gave Joseph Smith $300 so he could proceed to Missouri. Brigham Young arrived at Far West 14 March 1838 and Sidney Rigdon arrived on 4 April.[40]

One more mass movement of Mormons across Indiana occurred in summer of 1838—the loyal 105 families with 256 males and 273 females migrating from Kirtland to join their leaders at Far West. They worked to earn their way, alternately stopping and traveling. They were on the National Road in Indiana from 31 August until 7 September when they completed the first 436 miles at Terre Haute and turned right on North Arm Prairie road toward Paris. Local citizens who saw the display of their night fires in camp at Knightstown declared the company "exceeded any they had ever before seen in all their lives." At Far West on 2 October 1838 they "encamped on the public square round the foundation of the Temple."[41]

The revelations of the Lord through which Joseph Smith commissioned his young colleagues to "take their journey" between Ohio and Missouri often bade them also to "preach by the way." They were to go two by two to "preach by the way in every congregation, baptizing by water, and the laying on of the hands by the water's side." The revelation of 7 June 1831 said "Let my servants Parley P. Pratt and Orson Pratt take their journey and preach by the way." At the same time Reynolds Cahoon and the prophet's younger brother Samuel H. Smith were commissioned to "take their journey" as were Levi W. Hancock and Zebedee Coltrin.[42]

Preaching by the way often meant preaching in Indiana. Cahoon and Smith responded to their calling in summer of 1831 and so became the first two Mormon missionaries to preach by assignment in the state. Levi Hancock and Zebedee Coltrin were almost too successful at Winchester in Randolph County in 1831. They baptized over 100 people and were warned to leave town or face tar and feathers. Hancock made a public defense of his rights based in part on his patriotic American heritage as the son of a Revolution veteran and a cousin of the first man who signed the Declaration of Independence. Then Coltrin preached and they baptized seventeen more.[43]

Parley Pratt and Orson Pratt were quick to learn the ways of contemporary Hoosier evangelism. They went across Indiana on foot from east to west in summer of 1831. For the return trip early in 1832 Parley Pratt was paired with John Murdock. At Vincennes Pratt and Murdock met fellow missionary Saints Dustin and Beebe who were full of complaints about high expenses. Pratt offered them some instruction about ecclesiastical travel on the early Indiana frontier. Itinerant preachers were expected to pray with and preach to the people wherever they stayed; the inhabitants were accustomed to provide traveling preachers food and lodging and ferriage without charging cash. Mormon missionaries needed to make their role as preachers very plain in order to receive such courtesy. Pratt's presence was such that he rarely spent a penny in cash while traveling. At Vincennes and Washington and Madison he was entertained free at the hotel. Near Madison he and Murdock stayed for "a week or two" with a Christian church minister and "preached to crowded congregations in all the region; he frequently going with us to introduce us and open the way."[44]

Orson Pratt took Brookville by storm early in 1835. He was invited for public preaching at the court house. This was followed by a three-hour debate with a Universalist which the audience decided overwhelmingly in favor of the Latter-day Saint. The Brookville *Inquirer* for 25 February said of Pratt:

> Though in some things he characterized the fanatic; yet, in the main, his doctrines were sound and his positions tenable. We would do injustice to the gentleman were we to omit stating, that in all the discourses, of the like character, that we have ever heard it has never fallen to our lot to hear so much harmony in the arrangement of quotations from the sacred book. No passage could be referred to that would in the least produce discord in his arguments. The whole of his discourses were delivered in a very clear and concise manner, rendering it obvious that he was thoroughly acquainted with the course he believed he was called upon to pursue, in obedience to his Master's will.

The *Inquirer* invited Pratt for a return engagement: "Send us a letter and we will give public notice when you will attend; and we have no hesitation in saying, that you will be heard by the largest congregation ever assembled in this county. Your expenses during your stay will be defrayed." G. M. Hinkle was evidently doing missionary work alone in Indiana in 1835 and 1836. He reported to Kirtland on 15 July of the latter year that he had baptized forty-four at Columbus in Bartholomew County and was meeting with success at Fairplay in Greene County. Elders Curtis and Bracken reported that autumn from Clark and Scott counties that "many are believing in these regions."[45]

In the hands of a team of earnest young missionaries who could preach in the frontier free style, early Mormonism had its attractions for Hoosiers. There was the great sense of freedom in concluding that all known denominations were wrong and were now displaced by a restored original faith of unquestionable authority. There was the very natural conclusion that the restoration of primitive purity, the fulfillment of prophecy, and the return of the Lord to his Zion should occur in this new world of America. Affirmations by the Mormons of a substantial place for the person and work of Jesus Christ and for the familiar Scriptures of the Old and New Testaments gave initial common ground with evangelicals. At a time when casting off Calvinism was in fashion, Mormon theology was the most extreme form of that repudiation. Rejection of infant baptism in favor of immersion of adults for the remission of their sins suited a large constituency. Reformers of frontier excesses could welcome the prophet's 1833 revelation of a "Word of Wisdom" disapproving use of alcohol and tobacco. The added canon of Mormon Scriptures, still modest in the early 1830s, gave primary place to events in America and offered dramatic explanation of the origin and place of the American Indians. The concept of communal life under inspired leaders in the midst of a body of committed saints was a recurrent frontier excitement. Before the major body of Latter-day Saints left the Midwest for the Rockies in 1846, there were Mormon organizations in at least twenty-four Indiana counties.[46]

In this era when the aim of the Saints was to gather at Zion, Indiana's outpost Mormon branches were not really intended to develop or grow strong. They were stopping stations for Mormon travelers. Said Caroline Barnes Crosby of Pleasant Garden Branch in Putnam County: "There was scarcely a week passed after the organization of the branch but that we had one or more of the elders or brethren of some description with us, and sometimes a half dozen at a time. Our house was called the Mormon tavern all the time we lived in Indiana, which was three and one half years." They were recruiting points to enlist Saints to send to the centers in Missouri or Illinois or Utah. Only an unusually strong Mormon branch in this

period would leave much cultural evidence. At Winchester some Mormon-style homes remained as did some tombstones displaying both the Bible and the Book of Mormon.[47]

Mormon missionaries who honed their skills in Indiana often went on to high offices in the church. Parley and Orson Pratt were ordained members of the Council of the Twelve Apostles before they were thirty. They became missionary figures of international stature, sending home shiploads of British converts. They were powers in the Great Salt Lake valley as well, and it would be difficult to envision the larger course of Mormon history without them. In 1835, the year the Pratts were named apostles, the Randolph County missionary veterans Levi Hancock and Zebedee Coltrin were numbered among the First Seven Presidents of Seventies. They survived the tribulations of Mormons in Missouri and in Illinois and pioneered with Brigham Young in Utah.[48]

Charles C. Rich moved to Indiana with his family soon after his birth in 1808 and lived near Vevay in Switzerland County until 1829. His conversion to Mormonism took place in Illinois in 1832; he set out from there in the company of two Mormon missionaries to visit Joseph Smith at Kirtland. In the course of the trip across Indiana he was ordained an elder while in Fountain County and preached his first sermons as the party moved on to visit the new Mormon branch at Winchester. On the return trip he stayed at Rising Sun for about two months. Rich became a Mormon colony leader in Iowa and California and Idaho. He was a general in charge of Mormon military affairs, husband of six wives, father of fifty-one children, and for nearly forty years a member of the church's Council of the Twelve Apostles.[49]

Hoosier converts took places of prominence as well. David W. Patten was baptized by his brother John in Greene County in June of 1832. He became a missionary preacher of pentecostal style and power and was named to the Council of the Twelve Apostles in 1835. He was a source of great encouragement to other Indiana converts arriving in Missouri. Had he continued in the office he held as president of the Twelve, he would have been a logical choice for second president of the church rather than Brigham Young. Instead a shot to the belly on 25 October 1838 made him one of the earliest Mormon martyrs.[50]

When Orson Pratt led his company into the Great Salt Lake valley two days ahead of Brigham Young, Joseph Egbert of Sullivan County was one of his advance party. Egbert soon brought his family to Utah where he lived out his life as an officer of the church. Horace S.

Eldredge of Indianapolis lost his property once as a refugee from Far West and a second time as a refugee from Nauvoo. In 1848 he headed for the Great Salt Lake valley where he became a merchant, banker, and civic leader. Alexander McRae and his wife became Mormons in Ripley County in June of 1837. McRae's position as captain of the 23rd Regiment of Missouri militia put him into prison at Far West but he escaped. His position as captain of the Nauvoo Legion put him on the losing side again in 1846. At Salt Lake City he became bishop of the Eleventh Ward and held that office for thirty-four years.[51]

Less illustrious among the Mormons from Indiana was John C. Bennett of New Albany. He issued degrees of doctor of medicine at a lively rate from his diploma mill incorporated as Christian College by act of the Indiana legislature in 1833. As early as 1839 he began offering his sympathy and expertise to Joseph Smith and the Saints. He brought useful skills in management, public health, military affairs, and legislative lobbying. He received the Lord's approval, somewhat qualified, as part of the prophet's revelation of 19 January 1841. Soon his abilities were rewarded with the offices of mayor of Nauvoo, chancellor of the University of Nauvoo, and president of the Nauvoo Agricultural and Manufacturing Association. As assistant president of the church he was second in command only to Joseph Smith in the Nauvoo Legion which he organized, outfitted, and trained. But he fell as quickly as he rose. After only eighteen months of Mormon membership he was accused of sexual infractions and excommunicated. His subsequent publications did the church great injury.[52]

The larger body of Mormons focused their efforts on gathering the Saints to the Great Salt Lake valley after 1847. Free lance missionary efforts declined. Appointed missionaries received some calls to eastern states, more calls to foreign fields, and almost no calls to the Ohio valley. As the more zealous members went west, the small Indiana branches faded. A historian of the larger Mormon body wrote: "The Mormon Church, once welcome among Hoosier pioneers, diminished to almost nothing in the fifteen years before the Civil War, and by the time missionary work began anew in the 1870s, it had disappeared from the state without a trace."[53]

Hoosier Resistance to Mormons

Reintroduction of Mormonism into Indiana after the Civil War was no easy matter. Reintroduction became the goal of a never-ceasing stream of missionaries from the Great Salt Lake valley, first in the familiar pattern of gathering converts and preparing them to move west. The first recorded missionary of the renewal was prestigious enough. He was John Morgan, born in Decatur County of Indiana and nephew of the famed Confederate general. Morgan was an honored veteran of the Union army committed to reconstruction of the South by preaching the Mormon gospel there. Even before he was named president of the Southern States Mission in 1878, Morgan and his fellow missionary Joseph Standing began preaching in Morgan's native state. In northern Indiana they were able to establish two missionary resting places in the neighboring communities of Covington in Fountain County and Johnsonville in Warren County. In 1883 missionary W. W. Pratt wrote to the *Bear Lake Democrat* in Utah from Fountain County in Indiana.

> I have been in this state one year, traveling in various parts of it in all directions and have had but very little success so far as converts are concerned. It is about six years I think since this field was opened by Elder John Morgan and others. During that time there have been 30 baptized and 12 children blessed. Nine adults and six children emigrated to Utah. There are 21 members now in this branch and a family of three in the south part of the state, that came from Scotland and failed to get to Utah, making a total membership now in this state of 24 members. There are also a few dry-land Mormons that intend to get baptized, but don't get ready.[54]

The family members in the southern end of the state were probably part of the handful of Mormons who had received permission to meet in a church about three miles from New Providence in Clark County. Joseph Standing was murdered by a mob in Georgia in 1879. Morgan led the extremely dangerous Southern States Mission until 1888 and added to this a very distinguished church career in Utah.[55]

The work in Indiana came under jurisdiction of the Northern States Mission in 1882. By the 1890s there were about twenty missionary elders working in Indiana, a number which remained nearly constant for the next thirty years. Typically these were men from the far West who had accepted a calling to be away from their people for a lonely and grueling missionary term. They generally worked in teams of two. During this early reintroduction period in Indiana they did not remain long in one place. On their rounds they distributed tracts, sold books, searched out prospects, and visited each Mormon family perhaps twice a year for two or three days. In this era they were not anxious to preach and were generally reluctant to debate.

Every year a harvest of a dozen converts or so would go from Indiana to Utah. Then more and more began staying in Indiana as part of a thin and patchy Mormon fabric in which members and missionaries depended desperately on each other for mutual support. The people made hero figures of the missionary elders. They affirmed their own faith strenuously and treasured accounts of miraculous victories and healings. Theirs was a holding operation through a time when the Mormon image was poor among their Hoosier neighbors. So long as Mormon leaders defended plural marriage, Indiana's public opinion would be outraged. So long as there were claims of a separate Mormon kingdom, frontier-minded Hoosiers would resist this as a violation of their national unity and a misuse of their western lands. Even though Mormons were rapidly moving away from these two positions toward American pluralism and even after the offending doctrines were officially renounced, the passing of most of a generation was required to allay local prejudice.[56]

Hoosiers were both consumers and producers of anti-Mormon polemic. Two early non-Mormon governors of Utah Territory, appointed by a tolerant Lincoln but personally committed to oppose Mormon authority claims, were from Indiana. So was John H. Beadle, editor of the *Salt Lake Reporter* and tormentor of Mormons in general, who was a native of Rockville. His most ambitious book was *Life in Utah; or, The Mysteries and Crimes of Mormonism. Being an Exposé of the Secret Rites and Ceremonies of the Latter-day Saints, with a Full and Authentic History of Polygamy and the Mormon Sect from Its Origin to the Present Time.* It went through at least three English editions plus three more under alternate titles plus translations into German and Russian.[57]

Schuyler Colfax, congressman from Indiana and speaker of the national House of Representatives, took a trip overland all the way to the Pacific in summer of 1865. During the preceding decade there had been hostility between the Mormons and the national government, even serious preparation for armed conflict. The counsel Colfax gave Brigham Young seemed moderate—seek a new revelation to end polygamy and thus remove objection to admission of Utah as a state. But the popular account of the trip published by his companion Samuel Bowles was decidedly hostile to Mormons. That account went through five editions. Colfax of Indiana, now as the nation's vice president, was back in Salt Lake City in 1869 urging compliance with a federal law of 1862 forbidding polygamy. Mormon elder John Taylor protested such an invasion of religious liberty. The two rounds of this spirited exchange were printed in the New York *Independent* and separately published in booklet form.[58]

Indiana's evangelical preachers rehearsed reasons they believed Mormonism to be an alien faith. Hoosier newspapers reported on Mormon issues currently before the nation. They sometimes printed warnings to local Mormon missionaries and reported instances of "white-cappings" by secret vigilante groups within the state. Two Mormon women were severely beaten by White Caps in Crawford County in summer of 1888.

There were also Indiana voices for moderation. When Brigham Young was on trial before federal judge James B. McKean in 1871–72, editor Fishback of the Indianapolis *Journal* was widely reported nationally and appreciated by the Mormons for writing: "It is unfortunate for the nation that it is in the power of such men as Judge McKean and the deputy district attorneys, Maxwell and Baskin, to precipitate a collision between the federal authorities and the Mormons, in a contest in which the government occupies a false and untenable position . . . We are convinced that the pending prosecutions are conceived in folly, conducted in violation of law, and with an utter recklessness as to the grave results that must necessarily ensue." In 1906 Indiana's senator Albert J. Beveridge risked popular disapproval by advocating the seating of Reed Smoot as senator from Utah. He deplored what he called unfounded charges and disgusting publicity. He made a plea before the full Senate for religious tolerance.[59]

The Mormon Mission Policy Change

Change for Indiana's Mormons came not only because of increasing tolerance among their neighbors. It came also because of the shift in organizational policy by the larger church. No longer was the primary missionary emphasis to be on calling out converts to migrate to the Mormon centers in the intermountain West. There was that new policy of establishing the stakes of Zion in every area, of raising chapels for branches or wards in every population center. In Indiana where resistance still lingered and membership was small, the change came slowly.

Mormon missionary elders rode the Monon Railroad to Robinson Station to cultivate a rural Greene County neighborhood with families named Lewis, Burch, Royal, Neal, Jackson, Wright, Strauser, Harper, Ashcraft, and O'Bannon. Amos (Ike) Lewis was a leader of the small Mormon fellowship. The simple meetinghouse the group erected in Center Township in 1898 was locally known as "Mormon Temple." Services were discontinued by the early 1920s and only the marked site of the building remained.[60]

Mormons at Indianapolis dedicated their first chapel in 1927. No other chapels were built in Indiana until after the Second World War. However missionaries did begin staying longer in one location, taking a room or apartment and aiming to form a continuing group. Some groups rented meeting places. Expectations became higher for individual members. They were not only to survive and to make their homes service stations for visiting missionaries. They were to become the teachers and officers needed by their local group, participate in regional activities, attend to their blessings and sealings in a temple if possible, and even be open to a call to mission.[61]

Ellen Cox Clayton and James Clayton

Ellen Cox Clayton reflected such a transition within one lifetime in her *Memories of Yesterday in Indiana*. At the turn of the century her father died, leaving her mother to rear four children in lean circumstances at Linton. They were "about the only Mormons in the city." The earlier Greene County church was defunct. What supported her was the fervency of her faith. "We as members of the Church then were so alone, but our very souls were aflame with longing and in the quest for further knowledge of this great truth," she said. "We truly had a testimony of its divinity."[62]

> I read the Book of Mormon from cover to cover. I could assimilate it page by page, and I was thrilled to the depths of my very soul. I found it so interesting I could hardly lay it down, and each chapter was a new revelation to me. Then I came to where Jesus made his visit to the Nephites after his death in Jerusalem, and my soul literally took fire. I found myself shaking like a leaf, and the tears flowing down my cheeks. Such a joy in my heart! Such happiness in my very being! I had never experienced anything like that before . . . I obtained my testimony of that precious book. When I had finished it I knew first hand that it was the word of God and I was willing to stake my very life on that fact. Truly it is the stick (book) of Joseph spoken of by Ezekiel, and goes hand in hand with the Bible. This I know.[63]

The Mormon missionary elders were the Saints' lifeline.

> They had a standard form of dress which was: black suits, black ties, and black stiff hats. Their suit cases were in the form of a folding top valice. When doing country tracting away from their headquarters, they usually carried a change of garments, some tracts and naturally a few Books of Mormon. Some carried an umbrella tied onto their valice . . . They missed many meals . . . The Elders would make a tour of the families whose names

appeared on the record, so every month or two we would all be visited by these missionaries. It is my opinion that these visits and the consequent cottage meetings and home teaching held the saints in the church and to their membership.[64]

Ellen Clayton was trained in business school and gifted in dramatics. Her husband James became a convert to Mormonism. He shared operation of a funeral home and cut flower business with his family members who were unsympathetic with his conversion. Two men and six women organized as Linton's branch of Latter-day Saints in 1927. She and her husband became father and mother to it, Ellen said. They had their marriage sealed at the Salt Lake temple in June of 1927. They were instrumental in organizing a school bus load of Hoosiers to travel from Linton to Logan Temple in Utah for ordinances and blessings in summer of 1933.[65]

By this time there were a few other branches with whom to share. Missionaries Corey and Cordon from Salt Lake City had baptized Charles Arm and Anna Faulting along with her two children in Indianapolis in 1891. By 1910 John Thomas and his family had moved to Indianapolis; meetings were held at the Faulting and Thomas homes.[66] Ellen Clayton said:

> In the early days of the church in Indiana members were few and we were all more or less persecuted, so we kept closely together where possible at all. If a conference was announced for Terre Haute they would contact the Linton Branch so that we could cooperate with them. If Linton was scheduled for a conference we would notify Terre Haute and other surrounding branches, and we would rejoice together in these meetings and a spiritual feast was assured. Indianapolis always notified Linton of conferences each three months and we usually attended. These meetings went a long way toward holding us together.[67]

Many miracle stories circulated among the members, "faith promoters" Ellen called them.

The Claytons moved to Indianapolis in 1942 and extended their ministry even further. When Ellen was sixty-five and James was sixty-nine they set out on two years of missionary service. "We attended the mission school in Salt Lake and what a wonderful week of learning it was," said Ellen. "Most of the General Authorities spoke to us, one following another, and such enlightening, inspirational talks. We had a full week of that, with a party on Saturday night, and, of course, Sunday was the climax."[68] Their assignment was to Anderson, South Carolina, two Hoosiers in the deep, deep South. The first thing they did was refurbish the church. James was branch president.

We tried to keep up our responsibilities as missionaries as well as the branch duties so we were very, very busy people. A struggling branch needs a lot of help and we gave it to them, assisting the Elders all the time, attending all missionary and zone meetings, serving when needed on the Stake Board, teaching, and visiting the weak members. We tracted. We had to entertain all stake visitors in our apartment, and often visiting Elders from the mission, and we had to chaperone the Elders in most of their discussions. We had to head the M.I.A., the Primary and serve in any capacity that needed us, and I taught the adult Sunday School class. The branch grew and flourished. We had 250 members when we left Anderson . . . When our time was up the saints in Anderson took it hard and our farewell party was more like a funeral.[69]

By the time Ellen Clayton recorded her *Memories* in 1978 she could include first-hand and personal knowledge of Mormon organizations in twenty-one Indiana towns.

Rapid Mormon Increase in Indiana

Some of this growth was provided by the Hoosier converts who found Mormon doctrine compelling and the Mormon structures a very effective place to invest their lives. Some of the growth came by Mormon migration from west to east. The years surrounding the Second World War called Mormon youths into military, industrial, and educational service across the nation. They settled wherever they found good opportunity. Some married non-Mormon spouses. Indiana became part of the newly formed Great Lakes Mission in 1949; the Mormon diaspora among the Hoosiers was one natural field for the evangelism of this missionary agency. Indiana organized its first stake in May of 1959—the Indianapolis Stake of Zion. Its wards were Bloomington, Columbus, Indianapolis, Indianapolis 2, Purdue, and Richmond. Its branches were Anderson, Connersville, and Kokomo. Still under oversight of the Great Lakes Mission were wards and branches at Evansville, Linton, Peru, Fort Wayne, South Bend, Terre Haute, and Vincennes.[70]

Aggressive missionary effort and supervision in the state coincided with a national postwar era in which being a church member seemed a natural part of being an American. By then Mormons were understood to be exemplary Americans and an admirable church people. Young parents were invited to the disciplines of the church's family-centered organizational life. Men once on the fringes of the church committed themselves anew in the work of chapel building.[71]

In 1919 Indiana had perhaps 250 Mormons in five branches, a branch being the smallest kind of Mormon congregation. Seventy years later there were eight stakes, a stake being the Mormon equivalent to a diocese. The stakes were Indianapolis, Indianapolis North, Bloomington, Lafayette, Evansville, Fort Wayne, New Albany, and South Bend. Stake boundaries did not coincide precisely with state boundaries but 1990 reports indicated 20,901 Indiana adherents in seventy congregations. To this the Reorganized Church of Jesus Christ of Latter Day Saints added some 1,700 in fifteen branches for a population of Saints in Indiana of approximately 22,600. This was a constituency similar in size to the Episcopalians, Old Order Amish, Church of God (Anderson, Ind.), or African Methodist Episcopal Zion.[72]

NOTES

1. *History of the Church of Jesus Christ of Latter-day Saints*, 7 vols. An Introduction and Notes by B. H. Roberts (Salt Lake City, Utah: Deseret News, 1902–32), 1:5–6.

2. *History of the Church*, 1:11–12.

3. Brigham Henry Roberts, *A Comprehensive History of the Church of Jesus Christ of Latter-day Saints, Century I.*, 6 vols. (Salt Lake City, Utah: Deseret News, 1930), 1:95–166; James B. Allen and Glen M. Leonard, *The Story of the Latter-day Saints* (Salt Lake City, Utah: Deseret Book Company, 1976), 40–46; Klaus J. Hansen, *Mormonism and the American Experience* (Chicago: University of Chicago Press, 1981), 4–10; Jan Shipps, *Mormonism: The Story of a New Religious Tradition* (Urbana, Ill.: University of Illinois Press, 1985), 25–39; *History of the Church*, 1:13–39, 48–51, 71–76.

4. *The Doctrine and Covenants of the Church of Jesus Christ of Latter-day Saints, Containing Revelations Given to Joseph Smith, the Prophet, with Some Additions by His Successors in the Presidency of the Church* (Salt Lake City, Utah: Church of Jesus Christ of Latter-day Saints, 1954), Section 13; *History of the Church*, 1:39.

5. *History of the Church*, 1:39–42; *Doctrine and Covenants*, 27:8–13, 128:20; Roberts, *Comprehensive History*, 1:177–86; Allen and Leonard, *Story*, 44–45. All worthy adult males among Latter-day Saints have been regarded as priests—typically priests after the order of Aaron from about age twelve and priests after the order of Melchizedek when more advanced standards of ministry are met and ordinances performed. They established no professional clergy.

6. Leonard J. Arrington and Davis Bitton, *The Mormon Experience: A History of the Latter-day Saints* (New York: Alfred A. Knopf, 1979), 16; *History of the Church*, 1:74–80, 85–86; 4:541; *Doctrine and Covenants*, 20:1–84; Hansen, *Mormonism*, 38; Allen and Leonard, *Story*, 47.

7. The Garden of Eden was later located near Independence as well. After Adam and Eve were cast out of the garden they dwelt in the land of Adam-ondi-Ahman in present-day Daviess County. During the great flood described in chapters six through eight of Genesis, persons drifted in the ark from this American Eden to

become the biblical peoples of the Near East. *Doctrine and Covenants*, 28:9, 52:2–5; 57:1–16; 116; Hansen, *Mormonism*, 67–70.

8. Samuel G. Ellsworth, "A History of Mormon Missions in the United States and Canada, 1830–1860" (Ph.D. diss., University of California, Berkeley, 1951), 188–89; *History of the Church*, 1:120–43; Roberts, *Comprehensive History*, 1:236–50; Allen and Leonard, *Story*, 47–56; Hansen, *Mormonism*, 39.

9. *History of the Church*, 1:426–40; 3:1–3, 149–340, 368–74, 403–559; Roberts, *Comprehensive History*, 1:314–68, 396–412; Allen and Leonard, *Story*, 89–93, 104–16, 120–34; Hansen, *Mormonism*, 113–46.

10. *History of the Church*, 4:267–73; Allen and Leonard, *Story*, 139–65, 173–83; Arrington and Bitton, *Mormon Experience*, 68–72; Hansen, *Mormonism*, 140.

11. *Doctrine and Covenants*, 132:61–62.

12. *Doctrine and Covenants*, 124:29–37; 127:5–10; 128; 131:1–4; 132:1, 15–26, 61–62; Roberts, *Comprehensive History*, 2:65–75, 90–110, 128–39; Allen and Leonard, *Story*, 164–71; Arrington and Bitton, *Mormon Experience*, 197, 199; Hansen, *Mormonism*, 81–82, 138, 163–72.

13. Roberts, *Comprehensive History*, 2:247–87; Allen and Leonard, *Story*, 185–98; Ellsworth, "History," 268, 285.

14. F. Mark McKiernan, *The Restoration Movement: Essays in Mormon History*, eds. F. Mark McKiernan, Alma R. Blair, and Paul M. Edwards (Lawrence, Kans.: Coronado Press, 1973), 207–15.

15. Allen and Leonard, *Story*, 198–215; Hansen, *Mormonism*, 107–8.

16. Allen and Leonard, *Story*, 252–53, 287; Hansen, *Mormonism*, 142, 210.

17. Mormon practice was polygyny of a carefully delineated kind but the broader term polygamy was almost universally applied.

18. Arrington and Bitton, *Mormon Experience*, 204.

19. Martha Taysom, "'Glory Is A Comin' Soon': A History of Mormonism in Indiana," 3 sections (Undergraduate Honors thesis, Indiana University, Bloomington, 1989), 2:2–5, 34–35; Aleah G. Koury, *The Truth and the Evidence: A Comparison between Doctrines of the Reorganized Church of Jesus Christ of Latter Day Saints and the Church of Jesus Christ of Latter-day Saints* (Independence, Mo.: Herald Publishing House, 1965), 35–36; Arrington and Bitton, *Mormon Experience*, 199; Allen and Leonard, *Story*, 343–47, 353–58, 390–400; Hansen, *Mormonism*, 141–46, 155–62.

20. Allen and Leonard, *Story*, 416. Woodruff's manifesto and its endorsement by a general conference were published at the end of *Doctrine and Covenants* as "Official Declaration."

21. Allen and Leonard, *Story*, x, 401–16; Hansen, *Mormonism*, 179–204.

22. Douglas D. Alder, "The German-Speaking Immigration to Utah 1850–1950" (Master's thesis, University of Utah, Salt Lake City, 1959), 69.

23. Jan Shipps, "The Scattering of the Gathered and the Gathering of the Scattered: The Mormon Diaspora in the Twentieth Century" (Juanita Brooks Lecture, St. George Tabernacle, St. George, Utah, on the occasion of the inauguration of Douglas D. Alder as president of Dixie College, 11 March 1987), 5–6, 19; Alder, "German-Speaking Immigration," 66–73, 114–18; Allen and Leonard, *Story*, 496–98.

24. Shipps, "Scattering of the Gathered," 6–8; Allen and Leonard, *Story*, 532, 537–38.

25. Allen and Leonard, *Story*, 438–45; Hansen, *Mormonism*, 173.

26. Allen and Leonard, *Story*, 424–25, 446–48, 474–75, 557, 575; Hansen, *Mormonism*, 103.

27. Booklets copyrighted and published by the Church of Jesus Christ of Latter-day Saints, Salt Lake City, Utah, entitled *Which Church Is Right* (1982, 19 p.); *Plan of Salvation* (1983, 26 p.); *What the Mormons Think of Christ* (1982, 28 p.); *After Baptism, What* (1982, 14 unnumbered pages).

28. George W. Cornell, "Growing Mormon Membership Begins to Rival Older Churches," *Herald-Times*, Bloomington, Ind., 28 March 1987.

29. Koury, *Truth and the Evidence*, 99.

30. Koury, *Truth and the Evidence*, 91–102; McKiernan, *Restoration Movement*, 210–18. The Reorganized Church generally wrote the name "Latter Day Saints" rather than "Latter-day Saints" and preferred to leave the name "Mormons" to members of the larger church whom they often called the "Utah Church."

31. McKiernan, *Restoration Movement*, 218–26; Koury, *Truth and the Evidence*, 6–10, 17–50, 61–90.

32. Frank S. Mead, *Handbook of Denominations in the United States*, 9th ed. (Nashville, Tenn.: Abingdon Press, 1990), 136; J. Gordon Melton, *The Encyclopedia of American Religions*, 3d ed. (Detroit, Mich.: Gale Research, 1989), 585–86; McKiernan, *Restoration Movement*, 343; Koury, *Truth and the Evidence*, 104–10; Letters of Richard P. Howard, Independence, Mo., to L. C. Rudolph, 12 February and 21 March 1991.

33. Roberts, *Comprehensive History*, 1:250–63.

34. *Doctrine and Covenants*, 57:1–5.

35. *History of the Church*, 1:271–72; Roberts, *Comprehensive History*, 1:282–90; *Doctrine and Covenants*, 78:8–10.

36. LaMar C. Berrett, "An Impressive Letter from the Pen of Joseph Smith," *Brigham Young University Studies* 11 (Summer 1971): 518–20.

37. Parley P. Pratt, *The Autobiography of Parley Parker Pratt* (New York: Russell Brothers, 1874), 122; Taysom, "Glory," 1:34–36, 45; *History of the Church*, 2:68–70, 272; *Doctrine and Covenants*, 103.

38. *History of the Church*, 2:70; Brookville *Indiana American*, 13 June 1834; Pratt, *Autobiography*, 125.

39. *History of the Church*, 2:514, 519, 521, 525, 529.

40. *History of the Church*, 3:1–3, 11, 13.

41. *History of the Church*, 3:133–36, 147.

42. *Doctrine and Covenants*, 32, 34, 52:10, 26, 29, 30.

43. Winchester *News-Gazette*, 22 September 1984; Taysom, "Glory," 1:6, 12.

44. Pratt, *Autobiography*, 72–84; Taysom, "Glory," 1:10.

45. Ellsworth, "History," 188; Taysom, "Glory," 1:11–12.

46. Richard T. Hughes and C. Leonard Allen, *Illusions of Innocence: Protestant Primitivism in America, 1630–1875* (Chicago: University of Chicago Press, 1988, 296 p.); *The American Quest for the Primitive Church*, ed. Richard T. Hughes (Urbana, Ill.: University of Illinois Press, 1988, 257 p.); Hansen, *Mormonism*, 63, 73–83. The list of twenty-four counties reported to have early Mormon organizations is from Taysom, "Glory," 1:29–31. The counties are Bartholomew (1836), Boone (1843), Clinton (1843),

Daviess (undated), Fayette (1842), Fountain (1831), Greene (1831 and 1835), Lake (1843), Marion (undated), Marshall (1841), Montgomery (undated), LaPorte (1841), Porter (1843), Putnam (1842), Randolph (1831–1840), Rush (undated), Shelby (1843), Sullivan (1835), Tippecanoe (1831), Vanderburgh (1836), Vermillion (1831 or 1832), Warren (1831), Warrick (1841), Wayne (undated).

47. Taysom, "Glory," 1:29, 32.

48. Andrew Jenson, *Latter-day Saint Biographical Encyclopedia*, 4 vols. (Salt Lake City, Utah: Andrew Jenson History Company, 1901–1936; reprint, Salt Lake City: Western Epics, 1971), 1:83–85, 87–91, 188–90.

49. Leonard J. Arrington, *Charles C. Rich: Mormon General and Western Frontiersman* (Provo, Utah: Brigham Young University Press, 1974), 3–4, 17–21.

50. Jenson, *Latter-day*, 1:76–79; Taysom, "Glory," 1:25–26.

51. Jenson, *Latter-day*, 1:196–97, 620; 3:70–71.

52. Andrew F. Smith, "The Diploma Peddler: Dr. John Cook Bennett and the Christian College, New Albany, Indiana," *Indiana Magazine of History* 90 (March 1994): 26–47; *History of the Church*, 5:xvii–xxi, 4, 12–13, 35–83; Roberts, *Comprehensive History*, 2:47–50, 140–47; *Doctrine and Covenants*, 124:16–17; Arrington and Bitton, *Mormon Experience*, 72–73; Koury, *Truth and the Evidence*, 12, 46–47.

53. Ellsworth, "History," 295, 307–16, and unpaged "Summary of dissertation"; Taysom, "Glory," 1:38.

54. Taysom, "Glory," 2:7.

55. William W. Hatch, *There Is No Law: A History of Mormon Civil Relations in the Southern States, 1865–1905* (New York: Vantage Press, 1968, 133 p.); Jenson, *Latter-day*, 1:204–5; 3:719–21; Taysom, "Glory," 2:7–8, 12, 36–37.

56. Taysom, "Glory," 2:9–18.

57. John H. Beadle, *Life in Utah* (Philadelphia: National Publishing Company, 1870, 540 p.).

58. Samuel Bowles, *Across the Continent: A Summer's Journey to the Rocky Mountains, the Mormons, and the Pacific States with Speaker Colfax* (Springfield, Mass.: Samuel Bowles and Company, 1866), 82–130.

59. Roberts, *Comprehensive History*, 5:400; Taysom, "Glory," 2:24–33.

60. Mary Burch, "Mormon Temple," Unpublished MS, 2 p.; "Mormon Elders Writing History of Old Temple in Greene County," Indianapolis *Times*, 28 December 1948, 4.

61. Taysom, "Glory," 3:9–16.

62. Ellen Cox Clayton, *Memories of Yesterday in Indiana: A Brief History of the Early Days of the Church of Jesus Christ of Latter-day Saints in Indiana* (N.p., 1978), iv.

63. Clayton, *Memories*, 144–45.

64. Clayton, *Memories*, 185.

65. Clayton, *Memories*, 34–38, 44–54, 65, 99; Taysom, "Glory," 3:14–16.

66. Clayton, *Memories*, 27.

67. Clayton, *Memories*, 157.

68. Clayton, *Memories*, 221.

69. Clayton, *Memories*, 224–25.

70. Taysom, "Glory," 3:3–6, 20.

71. Shipps, "Scattering of the Gathered," 13–17.

72. According to data provided by church historian Richard P. Howard and staff assistant Barbara Bernauer at Independence, Mo., the Indiana branches of the Reorganized Church of Jesus Christ of Latter Day Saints at the end of 1990 were at Byrneville, Centerton, Derby, Evansville, Fort Wayne, Fremont, Highland, Indianapolis, LaPorte, Leavenworth, New Albany, South Bend, Speedway, Wabash, and Washington.

ADVENTISTS

William Miller was born 15 February 1782, the first of sixteen children. He was reared on a frontier farm at Low Hampton, New York. The family was pious. His grandfather Elnathan Phelps was among the preachers who visited the house; two of his uncles were Baptist preachers. Only the most rudimentary schooling was available to him but he borrowed books and built a reputation as both a great reader and a competent writer. At twenty-one he married Lucy Smith and moved six miles to her home town of Poultney, Vermont. Poultney had the first public library in the state. Some of the village intellectuals were skeptics; some of the library books were by Voltaire, Volney, Hume, Paine, and Ethan Allen. Miller became a member of the town's literary society and a deist. He also became successively deputy sheriff, captain of the local unit of the Vermont militia, and a commissioned officer in the United States Army for service in the War of 1812. Though miracles were no longer in his repertory, he felt the victory of 5,500 Americans over 15,000 British at Plattsburgh must have been somehow providential. Patriotism and deism had been among his major affections but they attracted him less with the brutalities of the war fresh in his mind.

Settled again as a substantial farmer at Low Hampton, he was disgusted with himself because he kept seeing the grip of the habit of profanity he had brought home from the service. Perhaps it was to please his widowed mother that he attended services at the nearby church on Sun-days when the minister was present. He said he did not attend on the other Sundays because the lay reader read the sermons so poorly. So the church deacons selected the sermons and asked him to do the reading. This hearing of preaching, and especially the reading of a sermon on Isaiah 53, brought him to conviction and conversion in 1816.

> Suddenly the character of a Saviour was vividly impressed upon my mind. It seemed that there might be a Being so good and compassionate as to himself atone for our transgressions, and thereby save us from suffering the penalty of sin. I immediately felt how lovely such a Being must be; and imagined that I could cast myself into the arms of, and trust the mercy of, such a One. But the question arose, How can it be proved that such a Being does exist? Aside from the Bible, I found that I could get no evidence of the existence of such a Saviour, or even of a future state. I felt to believe in such a Saviour without evidence would be visionary in the extreme. I saw that the Bible did bring to view just such a Saviour as I needed; and I was perplexed to find how an uninspired book should develop principles so perfectly adapted to the wants of a fallen world. I was constrained to admit that the Scriptures must be a revelation from God. They became my delight; and in Jesus I found a friend. The Saviour became to me the chiefest among ten thousand; and the Scriptures, which before were dark and contradictory, now became the lamp to my feet and light to my path. My mind became settled and satisfied.[1]

He joined the Baptist Church at Low Hampton and began conducting regular prayers with his family. His home was a popular gathering place for young people and visiting ministers. He was a perceptive hearer of the preaching available to him. Using his Cruden's *Concordance* as a guide to parallel passages, he studied the Scriptures for whole days and nights over a period of two years. He wanted to satisfy himself and his deistic questioners that the Bible as a revelation of God was consistent and intelligible. Miller was a systematic student working with a list of fourteen rules of interpretation.

A Prophetic Chronology for the End

No stranger to the millenarianism common in his region, he found millennial messages disclosed in the Bible's apocalyptic and prophetic passages and found them to be more and more compelling. In general the New Testament writers expected an imminent, dramatic, visible return of Christ to usher in a new age. The work begun in his ministry, death, and resurrection was to culminate in his triumphant return. The Old Testament also had much to say about God's coming for judgment and salvation, coming to make all things new. For Miller these expressions of a salvation moving toward realization came to form one coherent and concrete plan, indeed an irresistible chronology. He believed that prophecies revealing this chronology were often embodied in figurative language but they always had been and would always be fulfilled in actual calendar time.[2]

By 1818 Miller was convinced that Jesus would return personally with all the holy angels to establish the kingdom of God. The righteous dead would be resurrected and gathered up with the living saints at that advent. The earth would perish in fire, a new earth to spring from its ashes. Historical and prophetic interpretation of the Book of Daniel was crucial for calculation of the time of the cataclysm. Daniel 8:14 read "Unto two thousand and three hundred days; then shall the sanctuary be cleansed." It was understood among many students of prophecy that a "day" in this text was figurative language for a year. "Cleansing the sanctuary" came to be equated with the fiery purifying of the earth at the Lord's coming. Miller added the 2,300 years to 457 B.C., the accepted date for the decree of Artaxerxes to rebuild the temple at Jerusalem. The conclusion was that the end would come "on or before 1843."[3]

Miller said "I was thus brought, in 1818, at the close of my two years' study of the Scriptures, to the solemn conclusion that in about twenty-five years from that time all the affairs of our present state would be wound up." In September of 1822 he composed a list of twenty articles of his faith. Eighteen were fitting enough for a regular Calvinistic Baptist. But then there were articles fifteen and sixteen. "I believe that the second coming of Jesus Christ is near, even at the door, even within twenty-one years,—on or before 1843. I believe that before Christ comes in his glory, all sectarian principles will be shaken, and the votaries of the several sects scattered to the four winds; and that none will be able to stand but those who are built on the word of God."[4]

Miller and Himes as Messengers

Others had previously used a similar computation pattern to predict the end somewhere between 1843 and 1847. But it was Miller who felt his conclusion was so plain and so undeniable that the world really must be warned to prepare. Warning the world was a work he undertook with great reluctance. First he waited nine more years because he was no preacher and could hardly be expected to be the one to take this issue to the public. Friends whom he badgered privately with his convictions reacted with extreme caution. "Occasionally, one would see the force of the evidence," he said, "but the great majority passed it by as an idle tale."[5]

In 1831 he was nearly fifty; a prominent citizen-farmer; a justice of the peace; a Sunday school teacher and superintendent; a lay reader, exhorter, and clerk of his home church at Low Hampton. There was no minister to conduct service for the neighboring Dresden Baptist Church on Sunday, 14 August. Miller was invited to talk to the group that day about the second advent—his first sermon. It was like the loosing of an avalanche. Instead of ending on that Sunday, the service at Dresden went on for a week during which all but two members of thirteen families were converted. When Miller returned home there was a letter from a Baptist pastor inviting him to present similar lectures and conduct a revival at Poultney.

In one way of speaking he became a great success. He was in constant demand. Inquirers sought him out for Bible teaching. By 1833 eight ministers and 100 "brethren" were convinced. He was licensed as a Baptist preacher that year. Wherever he preached—mostly for Methodist, Baptist, and Congregational churches in the towns of New York, New England, and eastern Canada in the early years—attendance increased, converts multiplied, and religious concern deepened. He won the crowds with plain-spoken sincerity; he had a great urgency to teach. Listeners sat spellbound for two hours at a time. His teachings were published in a series of articles in the *Vermont Telegraph* and in Boston's *Daily Times*. A sixty-four-page pamphlet of his teachings was printed in 1833 and reprinted in 1835. In 1836 came his book of 223 pages entitled *Evidence from Scripture and History of the Second Coming of Christ, about the Year 1843: Exhibited in a Course of Lectures*. "Miller's Lectures" was the book's popular name. There was a revised edition in 1838.

Yet Miller was frustrated. The ministers wanted him as a proven evangelist. Curious crowds and Miller's earnest preaching made a very productive combination. Miller wanted revivals too and rejoiced that there was renewed evangelical vitality wherever he went. But he wanted most of all to have his hearers urgently involved in preparation for the coming of the Lord about 1843 and to have all the preachers joined with him in raising the advent cry. A few hundred convinced believers and a mere handful of crusading ministers would not be enough, given the shortness of time.

A new era began in 1840. Miller was traveling in Massachusetts and New Hampshire in fall of 1839. Pastor Joshua V. Himes invited him to preach at Chardon Street Chapel in Boston. Much impressed with the preaching, Himes asked Miller what he was doing to get such a crucial message out to the world. Miller said "What can an old farmer do? I was never used to public speaking; I stand quite alone; and, though I have labored much, and seen many converted to God and the truth, yet no one, as yet, seems to enter into the object and spirit of my mission, so as to render me much aid. They like to have me preach, and build up their churches; and there it ends with most of the ministers, as yet. I have been looking for help—I want help."[6]

Himes was an experienced champion of religious and reform causes and now a true believer. Adventism took on a whole new dimension. Miller remained the chief prophet and teacher while Himes directed the campaigns. Invitations now multiplied for Miller in the cities as well as in the towns. Four years later he could say "I have preached about 4,500 lectures in about twelve years, to at least 500,000 people." The new edition of *Miller's Lectures* was in 5,000 copies. A paper called *Signs of the Times* began publication in Boston in 1840, had 1,500 subscribers by the end of that year, became a weekly in 1842, and developed a large national constituency.[7]

When Miller came to lecture in New York City in fall of 1842, he and Himes distributed a new paper there, 10,000 copies per day for four weeks. This *Midnight Cry* then became a weekly.[8] Adventist papers began and continued similarly at Rochester, Cincinnati, Philadelphia, and Montreal. Persons convinced of Miller's views could order the expanding "Second Advent Library" of pamphlets and books to use in evangelism among their friends. Himes sold thousands of adventist tracts for 2¢ or 3¢ each; he also sent bundles of them to editors and postmasters and ship captains for free distribution. In May of 1844 he said that more than 5 million copies of adventist newspapers and tracts had been distributed and the great concentration of effort for summer and fall of 1844 still lay ahead.

Adventist Campaigns and Conferences

Some 200 ministers and lay leaders of adventist persuasion attended the first general conference in Boston in October of 1840. The conference, and publication of its speeches, was so successful that at least fifteen more general conferences for adventist leaders were held from Maine to Pennsylvania during the next three years. In addition there were about 120 local and regional conventions of adventist believers between 1842 and 1844. There were adventist camp meetings using groves and tents in frontier style—31 in 1842, 40 in 1843, 54 in 1844—with a total attendance at these estimated to be at least half a million. Himes was inspired to commission construction of the largest tent in America. It was 55 feet high and 120 feet in diameter with room for 4,000 in seats and another 2,000 in the aisles. This "Great Tent" itself was enough to draw crowds at Rochester, Buffalo, and Cincinnati. In spite of the sense that the end was near and time was short, Adventists in many major centers erected "tabernacles" in order to have places to meet. The one dedicated in Boston in May of 1843 was described as "a model of neatness, simplicity, comfort and frugality." It cost about $4,000 above the value of the land and would seat 3,000. William Miller lectured to about 4,000 people in Cincinnati in summer of 1844. In the very face of the predicted end of the age the believers there had constructed their own building 80 feet square; according to the building code, its walls were of brick.[9]

The *Western Midnight Cry* and the *Day Star* of Enoch Jacobs at Cincinnati

Cincinnati was out of the main orbit of pioneer Adventism. David L. Rowe has concluded, "The first consistent quality of Millerism was its Yankeeness." It was most at home in New England, in upstate New York, in the upper portions of Ohio, Indiana, and Illinois, and in

Michigan. But Joshua Himes cared deeply about all the West. He wrote, "We mean that the West shall have the light, if we spend the last farthing we possess." By early adventist reckoning the year 1843 was expected to be the last year of time. During the precious last days of that summer and fall, Himes himself extended a western mission with George Storrs and the "Great Tent" all the way to the Ohio River frontier. He lectured at Louisville and in southern Indiana; Storrs traveled even more widely in the area.[10] During that visit Himes and Storrs invigorated the adventist community at Cincinnati and its weekly paper called the *Western Midnight Cry*.[11]

Joshua Himes had to hurry back to Boston by way of Philadelphia and New York. The masthead of the *Western Midnight Cry* continued to carry the designation "J. V. Himes, Publisher" through the issue for 7 February 1845 but the involvements of Himes with Cincinnati were occasional at best. Storrs also had to hurry back east in November "in consequence of ill health of himself and family." Drafted for the editor's post in Cincinnati was Enoch Jacobs, a Methodist Protestant minister from New York City now fully engaged in adventist activities. At Cincinnati in December of 1843 he was lonely for his wife and children. "We have left our family in New York, for a visit to this place, where we only intend to remain for a few weeks," he said, "and in accordance with the suggestions of the brethren, have consented to take charge of the paper while here." In January he was back from a high-speed round trip to New York "comfortably situated with our family in a 'hired house' where we shall probably tarry till the Lord comes, or as long as we can be useful to others." Joshua Himes sent word from Boston that the Cincinnati membership would now be expected to sustain the paper themselves so that "the truth will be quickly spread over the entire West."[12]

Jacobs became the chief voice of Adventism in the Midwest. He and his *Western Midnight Cry*—named *Day-Star* beginning with vol. 5, no. 1—were the primary adventist influences on Indiana in the Millerite era. Other adventist periodicals did reach the state. Louisville had a small adventist fellowship and listed its address among the sources of supply for adventist publications. But the real action centered in Enoch Jacobs and Cincinnati. Every week he got out 800 to 1,000 copies of his paper—gathered and arranged the articles, composed the editorials, bundled the papers, addressed the wrappers. Eventually he even set some of the type. Beginning in the summer of 1845 those copies delivered within thirty miles of Cincinnati he could send postage free. Recipients who were able to pay were to pay 50¢ a year. Those persons who would say plainly that they wanted the paper but could not afford it would receive it free.[13]

Enoch Jacobs intended to avoid debt. Each issue of his paper provided an ongoing record of receipts from subscribers and donors and he would not print a new issue until he had paid for the last one. Some reliable donors always met the deficit so the whole weekly sequence of issues was nearly unbroken. The *Cry* reproduced letters and articles by easterners William Miller, Joshua Himes, George Storrs, Charles Fitch, Josiah Litch, and many more. Multiple copies of eastern adventist papers received by Jacobs as exchange were also circulated in the West and subscriptions for them ordered on request. The text of *Miller's Lectures* appeared in installments in the *Cry*. Jacobs printed his own essays and was very generous in publishing long articles or letters submitted by readers.[14]

Lest some lose sight of the key issues among these oceans of print, he began providing a prominent ruled block of italic type in each issue headed "Fundamental Principles on which the Second Advent Cause Is Based."

> I.—The Word of God teaches that this earth is to be regenerated, in the restitution of all things, and restored to its Eden state, as it came from the hand of its Maker before the fall, and is to be the eternal abode of the righteous in their resurrection state. II.—The only Millennium found in the word of God, is the thousand years which are to intervene between the first and second resurrections, as brought to view in the 20th of Revelation. And the various portions of Scripture which are adduced as evidence of such a period in time, are to have their fulfilment only in the New Earth, wherein dwelleth righteousness. III.—The only restoration of Israel yet future, is the restoration of the Saints to the New Earth, when "the Lord my God shall come, and all his saints with him." IV.—The signs which were to precede the Coming of our Saviour, have all been given; and the prophecies have all been fulfilled but those which relate to the coming of Christ, the end of this world, and the restitution of all things. V.—There are none of the prophetic periods, as we understand them, extending beyond the [Jewish] year 1843. The above we shall ever maintain as the immutable truths of the word of God, and therefore, till our Lord come, we shall ever look for his return as the next event in historical prophecy.[15]

Cincinnati had an adventist Sunday school, adventist lectures every evening except Saturday plus three times on Sunday, and a great many additions to the fellowship by conversion. In mid-December of 1843 Jacobs predicted "one of the greatest revivals with which this city has ever been visited." Most issues of the *Cry* offered more than forty adventist publications for sale besides "Bibles,

Charts, Tracts &c.&c." W. H. Maull was among the Methodist local preachers who converted to Adventism. Maull exposed "the corruption and wickedness of the M.E. Church . . . in an address of three hours in length to a crowded congregation." Jacobs added Maull's attack on the Methodists to the printed works for sale and added Maull's name to the list of traveling adventist lecturers whose reports on work in Ohio and Indiana he regularly printed—S. A. Chaplin, H. B. Chittenden, J. B. Cook, N. Field, William J. Greenleaf, Lewis Hicklin, J. Jones, J. Kempton, John H. Kent, Isaac Kimball, J. D. Pickands, A. A. Stevens, J. White, Caleb Worley, William Young.[16]

Jacobs and a local committee convened a "Second Advent Conference" at Cincinnati to begin 7 March 1844 to "continue for one week or more." Miller, Himes, and Storrs were especially invited from the East. Fourteen other adventist preachers were invited by name along with "all other Second Advent Lecturers West of the Mountains." Lecturers Miller, Himes, and Storrs did not come but ten others did, including two from Indiana. Their presentations were "thronged with thousands who apparently listened as for eternity." Jacobs later scheduled more conferences, always "providence permitting."[17]

Jacobs rallied the supplies, labor, and money to build Cincinnati's adventist tabernacle. He provided a description and explanation for his readers. It was, he said "A perfectly plain building—eighty feet square, walls of brick, one foot in thickness, and twelve feet in height; with a square, or hip roof . . . If the brethren could have rented a place such as would accommodate our congregations at any price, even beyond the bounds of reason, we think they would have done it in preference to building; but it could not be done, and the Tabernacle is consequently going up, but we sincerely hope and pray that the Lord will come before it is done." He set up his own printing press to produce the *Cry* and other adventist literature. He even arranged to pay Himes $250 for five-sixths ownership of the "Great Tent" and used it for campaigns at Cincinnati, Louisville, and Madison.[18]

The Great Tent (providence permitting) will be pitched at Madison, Indiana, at the junction of Main Cross and Vernon Streets, in the west part of the city, sometime during next week, and the meeting commenced on July 7th, to continue eight or nine days, should the weather be favorable . . . Lectures may be expected from J. Litch, of Philadelphia, S. S. Brewer, of New York, and E. Jacobs, of Cincinnati, embracing all the great Scripture truths, relative to the Second Advent of our Lord and Saviour Jesus Christ, now especially "nigh, even at the doors." All are invited to come and hear, and then judge for themselves; remembering that if "we be beside ourselves, it is to God: or whether we be sober, it is for your cause." I have taken the entire responsibility of this appointment upon myself, trusting in God; without any assurance from a single individual, of receiving a dollar towards defraying the expenses, which will probably amount to more than $200.[19]

Response from Indiana

Jacobs printed a steady stream of letters and news from Adventists in Indiana. He cited a report from Jonathan H. Hardy of Lexington in Scott County with the comment "There is a good deal of excitement in that place upon the subject of the Second Advent. If the theory as taught by Mr. Miller, is correct, there are large numbers in that vicinity who wish to know it. It is a soul cheering doctrine, to think, that in about four months at most, the Saviour will come in his kingdom." Hardy said "I have tried to sound the Midnight Cry in the best manner I can." He had hardly ever spoken in public before but "got over the fear of man in great measure." Hardy became a regular writer for the paper.[20]

Traveling lecturer A. A. Stevens sent a report to the *Cry* after his first fifteen lectures at Indianapolis. "Last evening the house was more crowded than ever," Stevens said. "At the speaking meeting after lecture, some eight brethren testified to the power of the truth in making them better and happier. Among these were brothers Young, Dr. Muncel, one of the most learned men in these parts, Dr. Saunders, &c. Br. Jemerson, the Disciples' minister, attends continually and agrees with us almost entirely . . . The publications which I brought were literally scrambled for and devoured." John H. Kent was visiting adventist lecturer at Indianapolis early in 1844. His hearers filled the large meeting room of the courthouse on the evenings of 5 and 6 February. John Hobart wrote from Indianapolis the following spring wishing that Stevens and Kent could visit again. He and his family had been "constrained to a withdrawal" from their denomination, "the church being unwilling to open her doors longer to the advocates of Christ's speedy coming." Most other Indianapolis Adventists had been expelled also. They declared the denominations "disorderly and not walking according to the traditions and commandments of the apostles in this respect." In fall of 1845 John Hobart sent Jacobs an unprecedented gift of $50, enough for a substantial payment on the adventist printing press.[21]

George Ruebush reported from Johnson County, just south of Indianapolis, in October of 1845. He was disturbed by the advent's delay.

I am one that has long been upon the watch-tower, and have seen many clear and literal fulfillments of the words of the Lord:—But, O my soul! what trials, temptations, sorrow, and disappointments! My Lord has not yet been revealed. O with what anxiety, and desire did I look forward to the feast of Tabernacles, or ingathering at the year's end, Ex. 22:16, believing it to be in this month; but I have been again disappointed. I have been made to mourn, and to think much of the past mysterious ways of God. I have been led to ask myself, Can this be a "strong delusion"! Am I now believing a lie that I may be damned? If this is delusion, how am I to find the truth?[22]

S. A. Chaplin at Oswego in Kosciusko County wanted an experienced adventist lecturer to visit and an adventist chart for himself. Lacking these, he said, "I intend to try and do a little in giving the alarm." Chaplin was half-time pastor for the Baptists at Oswego but withdrew to be free for adventist lecturing. Besides the doctrinal essays sent from Oswego by Chaplin, the paper often printed correspondence from his parishioner R. Willard.

I think it altogether likely that those who are grounded in the truths of the second coming, will go by themselves, as they cannot be longer fed by the old mode of preaching half of the truth, and overlooking the better half . . . When the numerous evidences were brought forward from Holy writ, testifying that probationary time was near to its end, and the everlasting Kingdom was to be set up at the second Advent of Messiah, and that the destiny of all men would then be irrevocably fixed, it seemed high time to examine whether I had oil for my lamp. For sometime I felt it somewhat of a cross to leave my dear brethren with whom I had been so long associated; but when I reflected that "whosoever loveth father or mother, more than me is not worthy of me," I could no longer hesitate in my decision.[23]

Elizabeth S. Willard wrote frequently from the same Oswego address. In December of 1845 she said "the Lord has filled this 'weaker' earthen vessel so full that I fear harm will result if I do not let it run over . . . How can this highly esteemed brother [Pickands] give up the 'glorious appearing' of our Blessed Master in his 'glorious body' like to which our vile bodies are to be changed and fashioned . . . Just at the time when those who draw back are rejoicing that they are no longer with this divided, despised company, I am rejoicing, yea leaping for joy that I am counted worthy to suffer shame with the people of God." In spring of 1845 the Oswego Adventists were holding meetings five times each week. Oswego became a significant center for Adventism.[24]

Lewis Hicklin from neighboring Noble County also became a traveling adventist lecturer of sufficient stature to lecture in the tabernacle at Cincinnati and to "comfort the brethren" all across Ohio and Indiana. William J. Greenleaf led a generous congregation at Springfield on the Eel River near Oswego. He said he had a dollar to send to Jacobs "as all my wants are supplied by the good brethren here.[25]

At Aurora there were "many dear brethren and sisters . . . trimming their lamps and waiting for the coming of the Bridegroom." In fact, about twenty Adventists and a majority of the trustees asked to be removed from the membership of the Aurora Methodist Church. Some Adventists thought that the transfer of loyalty of the trustees gave them control of the Methodist property. Such perceptions soon faded. There was some local street talk about giving the Adventists rotten eggs instead. But an adventist band persisted. Jacobs visited them and kept printing long adventist discourses by D. Bartholomew of Aurora. A physician named B. Eastman at Paris in Jennings County sent letters heavy with prophecies of doom and of impending judgment. He hoped that "the great day will show that I have been the humble means of awakening a large portion of country, and bringing into the field several very able advocates." He himself was prominently mentioned among the lecturers at the adventist conference in Cincinnati in March of 1844.[26]

John Creek of Liberty in Union County wrote that the good work begun there by adventist lecturers Storrs and Stevens needed to be sustained. Jacobs replied that lecturer Kent would probably visit Liberty "if time lasts so long." Henry B. Bear was still writing from Liberty on 24 October 1845 "I did expect and hoped that the Lord would have come yesterday, but it seemed good in the sight of the Lord to try his children a little longer." In fact Liberty continued such an adventist center that Jacobs led a contingent of forty-three believers on an excursion from Cincinnati one snowy February weekend in 1846 to join in a conference at Liberty. That was "forty-four miles of bad traveling" each way.[27]

Milton J. Nelson of Mount Auburn in Shelby County did not want to be called a "Millerite" but asked on behalf of *Cry* readers in his neighborhood for explanation of the beast in Revelation 13:11. Jacobs obliged with a long explanation. Jacobs himself went thirty-six miles down the river in February of 1844 to lecture for three evenings at Rising Sun in Ohio County. There had been about thirty in the town "that professed strong faith in the Lord's soon coming," including J. Hamilton and the

Disciples preacher named Kempton who was "a firm believer in the Second Advent doctrine." Only the Universalists at Rising Sun were willing to make their building available to Jacobs.[28]

Lecturer Isaac Kimball toured for three weeks in Indiana early in 1844. He lectured at Laurel and at Burlington. He addressed full houses in the Methodist church and in the courthouse in Rushville. When he visited Mr. Lynville's meetinghouse in Fayette County, six local preachers "embraced the Second Advent doctrine" and a healthy adventist unit was formed.[29]

H. B. Woodcock of Connersville prepared a long and complex treatise relating the imminent advent to the 144,000 spoken of in Revelation 7:4. Jacobs printed it but without approval. Thomas Haines lived eight miles from Connersville in Fayette County. He was convinced by the preaching of adventist missionary J. B. Cook there in January of 1845. He was the only adventist believer in his home town of Brownsville. He claimed his neighbors were interfering with his mail and giving him no work. He said, "How I do wish oftentimes that I was in Cincinnati, on Sabbath days and week evenings, that I might mingle with the people my soul loves."[30]

Sarah Bishop was a regular correspondent from Madison.

> Ever since I embraced the doctrine of Christ's soon coming, I have felt like a pilgrim and stranger on the earth. I still attend the Methodist meetings, but our preachers preach Jesus so far away, and us so low down in the grave, and make things look so cold, dark, and dreary, that it affords no comfort to the soul that loves the appearing of the Lord. Such preaching is cold comfort indeed—such as I never again expect to enjoy . . . I have had a home in the Methodist church for thirty-eight years—it is a church that I have loved much, and within whose pales I have enjoyed much of the comforts of religion; but now, it seems no more like home to me. Strange as this may seem, every true advent believer that I know in this place says the same.[31]

She sent Jacobs 50¢ and said of the adventist periodicals "I am never so sleepy but what I can sit up till I read them all through—and find them to be meat in due season." She and her husband were leaders for Madison's adventist fellowship. They yearned for more visits by adventist preachers and continued to conduct their own meetings once or twice a week even after the expected dates for the Lord's return had passed. Jacobs visited Madison in 1845. "There are probably not more than twelve or fifteen decided believers in the Advent near in this place," he reported. "Yet they are enough to keep the whole city in commotion the most of the time. The principal charges, however, seem to be heaped upon Bro. Bishop."[32]

Missionary lecturers J. B. Cook and William J. Greenleaf experienced a flurry of activity among the Adventists at Kingsbury in LaPorte County in early spring of 1845. M. M. Catlin and Joseph Catlin were ordained and seventeen persons were baptized. Kingsbury congregation was reported that fall as "a very faithful band . . . highly favored." J. B. Cook went to Winchester on a groundbreaking mission for Adventism in summer of 1845. "The false rumors . . . had reached them, but the truth had not," he said. "Thus I gave it to them, as the Lord enabled me. The last day I was probably six hours on my feet, talking to them during afternoon and evening."[33]

Disappointments

The Lord did not physically come to earth in glory during 1843. Nor did he appear before the close of the Jewish year the following March or April as many were expecting. Himes had gotten out the millions of publications and had directed campaigns in America's major cities to give the final warning. Jacobs at Cincinnati had given away thousands of copies of his special issue of the *Cry* for 9 March and of other publications. But William Miller's message to his followers on 12 May 1844 said, "I confess my error and acknowledge my disappointment; yet I still believe that the day of the Lord is near, even at the door." Adventists made Habakkuk 2:3 their text: "If the vision tarry, wait for it." Himes sent a message "To the Friends and Supporters of the Advent Cause" dated 29 May 1844. He said:

> The time we have published to the world, in which we expected the prophetic periods to terminate, is now past. We were mistaken as to the definite time, but not in reference to the truth of the general theory . . . The Advent meetings, lectures, and papers should be sustained. The publications should be scattered: and not only keep what ground we have gained, but we should make advances into the ranks of those that are sleeping upon their arms. There should be no giving up—no going back.[34]

Himes and Miller returned to the national circuit leading a movement which had borne two disappointments but in which morale was still high.[35]

In summer of 1844 the advent expectancy came to focus on the "tenth day of the seventh month"—the Day of Atonement or 22 October. Such a fall date had been suggested by William Miller as early as May of 1843. It had been advocated during 1843 and 1844 by advent-ist lecturer Samuel S. Snow. It received a dramatic endorsement when presented by Snow at an August camp meeting at Exeter, New Hampshire, in an atmosphere suggestive of direct revelation. Immediately after the camp meeting Snow published his conclusions in four pages entitled *The True Midnight Cry*. The message quickly spread. Adventists everywhere were energized and the public was stirred. An editor of the *Advent Herald* later said "There seemed to be an irresistible power attending its proclamation, which prostrated all before it. It swept over the land with the velocity of a tornado, and it reached hearts in different and distant places almost simultaneously, and in a manner which can be accounted for only on the supposition that God was in it."[36]

Miller and Himes, now wary of setting times, were swept along by the force of the popular response which they did not control and could not explain. They fixed their own hopes once again on this new date. Himes put an announcement at the top of column one of his *Advent Herald* in Boston:

> As the date of the present number of the Herald is our last day of publication before the tenth day of the seventh month, we shall make no provision for issuing a paper for the week following. And as we are shut up to this faith,—by the sounding of this cry at midnight, during the tarrying of the vision, when we had all slumbered and slept, and at the very point when all the periods, according to our chronology and date of their commencement, terminate—we feel called upon to suspend our labors and await the result. Behold, the Bridegroom cometh; go ye out to meet him! is the cry that is being sounded in our ears; and may we all, with our lamps trimmed and burning, be prepared for His glorious appearing.[37]

Out in Cincinnati Enoch Jacobs issued a most impressive warning edition of the *Western Midnight Cry* on 12 October; 10,000 copies were printed to be distributed free. At the end of the last column for 19 October he said: "Reader! this is the last warning we expect to give you, and now at this eleventh hour we ask you, are you awake . . . Stay not for tomorrow's sun. Go to your heavenly Father and with a heart all broken and contrite on account of sin, yet pleading the merits of such an all-sufficient Saviour and you shall find peace; and on that day, for which all other days were made, when Jesus is revealed in flaming majesty to judge the quick and the dead, you shall with all the ransomed throng, have an inheritance in that blest world where sin and sorrow can never enter! Farewell!!" Adventists got their affairs in

final order once more and shared a fellowship of special intensity.[38]

A reporter for the Cincinnati *Chronicle* attended services at the adventist tabernacle on the night of 22 October. He said about 1,500 were present.

> Considering the crowd, the meeting was very orderly. Two or three attempts were made by a set of rowdies outdoor to raise a breeze by noise and clamor, but the assertion of the preacher, that a strong police was present, calmed the multitude, and he was enabled to proceed with what he at the close said was, in his opinion, his last warning to a sinful world . . . Before nine o'clock the benediction was pronounced, and the people advised to go quietly home and await the awful coming, which not unlikely might transpire at the hour of midnight.[39]

The passing of 22 October 1844 without the Lord's appearing was the "Great Disappointment." Expectations of Adventists had been very, very high for that day; the very nature of reality hinged on it. After its passing there remained an awful sadness.[40]

Opposition and Abuse

During the course of the announcements and disappointments, a painful polarization had occurred. Adventists were alienated from their neighbors, even from their evangelical Christian neighbors who also looked for the Lord's return. Pioneer Adventists said that prophecy was plain and the end was very near. Every other subject for study, sermon, or prayer must surely be secondary to this imminent cosmic event. They had little patience with people who said they would just confess the Christian faith, seek to live the obedient life, and rejoice in the advent whenever it came. On that basis, said Enoch Jacobs in sarcasm, all 40,000 Cincinnatians would be Adventists. From an adventist point of view, all practicing Christians were to be faithful watchmen. J. H. Spear of Manchester, Indiana, said no real believer would remain inactive and unconcerned in the face of such a soul-cheering event. "Surely if they loved his appearing they would not remain stupid in the cause of Christ." Enoch Jacobs asked what kind of answer such persons could possibly have when Jesus asked them how they could have known so clearly of his coming without crying out to the world to be ready.[41]

Regular church pastors and administrators found adventist lecturers and their local bands of supporters to be divisive. Church people developed defenses and they launched attacks. Denominational publications provided anti-adventist ammunition. An adventist movement which intended to focus attention on biblical expectations of the Lord's return actually brought the subject under suspicion on denominational agendas for at least a generation. William Miller preached in a great variety of churches; to the end of his life he wanted no separate adventist body. He wanted a great united effort in which all denominations would join to sound the news of the Lord's coming to the world. But by the time of the Great Disappointment the practice of mutual abuse was so well established that separation seemed the only option. Both sides went about the separation with gusto.[42]

Cruelest of all was the abuse of Adventists by the secular media. The very prominence of their campaigning made them an inviting target. Adventists sometimes took steps to balance and close their earthly accounts before an expected day of the Lord's appearing. Some stayed home from work for a time in order to participate in final church services. In one odd instance perhaps 5 percent of the Adventists in Philadelphia followed the instruction of a visionary named C. R. Gorgas and went to tents just outside the city to await the Lord's arrival. No "ascension robe" was ever documented anywhere. However newspapers copied each other with fictional stories of Adventists in special robes climbing to high places to be ready to set out for heaven. The imagery was perfect for exploitation by cartoonists and the linkage of Adventism with erraticism was firmly established in the public mind. At Cincinnati Enoch Jacobs said "Not one out of 500 of the reports in the public prints relative to Second Advent Believers, contain a single word of truth." Specifically of Cincinnati he said "The principal mouth-piece of the vile slanderers of God's truth, and those who love and practice it, is Greely Curtis, editor of the Daily Commercial. The falsehoods published in that paper have gone abroad, and have been copied in scores of papers throughout the land."[43]

The host of authors who incorporated adventist instability into their fictional works was to range from Nathaniel Hawthorne and Henry Wadsworth Longfellow to Richard Wright. But the most important disseminator of that negative image was the native Hoosier Edward Eggleston. His *The End of the World: A Love Story* was serialized in the New York magazine *Hearth and Home* in 1872. The book form sold 10,000 copies even in advance of publication which occurred both in New York and London that same year. At least eight more editions followed between 1872 and 1912. Eggleston said this novel was about the vices of "literalism and fanaticism" and not "a work of religious controversy leveled at Adventists." But the Indiana Adventists in Eggleston's story

were portrayed as fanatics, their ignorance and poor ethics unredeemed by their ascension robes or by their climbing to a bluff overlooking the Ohio to await the end.[44]

Adventist Alignments

Even after the Great Disappointment the adventist movement was far from dead. However, it was badly scattered and its own segments frequently opposed one another. Jacobs said:

> Every intelligent individual knows what the Advent movement has been for it lies within the compass of our recollection. This cause has witnessed a continued wide spreading prosperity, without a parallel in the history of the church, up to the autumn of 1844. At, and a season prior to, that time, a band of more loving hearts never made the hills and valleys ring with joyful notes of praise to God. Since that time, they have been rent into a thousand fragments. Numberless prayers, (that all who joined their voices in echoing the cry "Behold he cometh," might "be one,") have been unavailing. Tears have run down like water, but all in vain. The unaffected sorrow, upon seeing our dear friends "look back"—face towards "Sodom and Egypt," has led us to exclaim, O, that they had died! If some body had shot them, or knocked their brains out, or burned them alive, then we would have rejoiced in glorious hope of seeing them in the Resurrection to eternal life.[45]

Among Adventists in the East were many, including Miller and Himes and Storrs, who believed the end was near but were no longer inclined to give so much special significance to 22 October 1844 or to set another definite date. Jacobs at Cincinnati abhorred such a "safe position." If Miller was now willing to admit error and to play down specific dating, maybe Miller's work was indeed done as his *Apology and Defence* (1845) said. That whole publication, Jacobs said, "savored more of Egypt, the wilderness, and Kadesh, than it did of Canaan."[46]

Jacobs was still for ascertaining a precise corrected date from divine prophecy and proclaiming it as the "definite time." He opened the pages of his weekly to a whole series of new and reworked calculations of specific dates including several such calculations from Indiana. Their bases included renewed study of Jewish chronology and projected stages of the filling up of the sealed 144,000 referred to in the seventh and fourteenth chapters of Revelation. George Ruebush of Johnson County in Indiana sent in a prediction "clear as daylight" based on careful interpretations of the schedule of watches kept by the virgins awaiting the bridegroom in Matthew 25. Jacobs said he knew few if any "indefinite time" believers in the Cincinnati area.[47]

Jacobs also wanted to be a western bulwark against any who saw the Lord's coming as anything other than physical.

> It is known to our readers that a class of individuals have recently sprung up at the East, who take the ground that Christ has come spiritually, or that there is to be no other coming of Christ than what has already taken place in the past movements—while the manifestation for which we are to wait, is a change from the mortal to the immortal state. One reason why we have said so little on this subject, is, there is not a single instance yet come to my knowledge, of such faith being embraced by any second Advent believer west of the mountains—though the views of the brethren above referred to, have been laid before our brethren here for investigation. So far as we at the west, are concerned, nothing need be said upon the subject. We are too well satisfied with the plain declarations of the Lord on this subject, to abandon, for one moment, the idea of seeing "the Son of Man coming in the clouds of heaven with power and great glory."[48]

Adventist leaders in the East called a conference at Albany, New York, in April of 1845. It was held in the interest of harmony and hinted that adventist unity might require some church organization. Jacobs crusaded against any kind of ecclesiastical organization. To organize the true church of God would be treason against its Great Head. "I have been, and still am of the opinion that God has organised those that are waiting for the Lord from heaven, much better than it could be done by a score of conferences," he said. "We know of no authorised bond of union but love; and where this is broken no other bond can unite. I know not how our organization in this place could be improved. God has furnished us a discipline—his word; and He himself keeps our church register." John Hobart of Indianapolis agreed and wished the end had come before that "assemblage at Albany."[49]

Pioneer Adventists often used the imagery of the parable of the ten virgins in Matthew 25. In that gospel sequence the midnight cry was raised, the bridegroom came, those who were ready went in to the marriage feast, and the door was shut. According to a popular parallel, those who refused the adventist gospel would later face a closed door and be forever lost. But in life, as the vision tarried, adventist preachers with evangelistic interests began to question the shut door. Sincerely penitent and earnest new converts must surely be accepted

into the ranks of the saints. Jacobs saw no such opportunity. "Some are claiming that some few are being converted here and there, since the Midnight Cry was made," he said, "thereby acknowledging that the door is almost closed. Others again, acknowledge that the work has ceased, but charge it to the preaching of the delusive doctrine, of the door being shut . . . To my mind, no truths in the Bible are made more clear, than that Christ has received the Kingdom, and the door mentioned in Matt. 25:10, is shut." When W. H. Maull wrote to say he was returning to adventist evangelism, Jacobs called him a frail mortal deceived by Satan.[50]

Jacobs thought the example of Jesus in John 13 made footwashing a required ordinance for the church. His fellow western lecturer J. B. Cook concurred. His colleague J. D. Pickands made his support of footwashing part of his attack on "eastern brethren" with their "boasted propriety of behaviour." In fact, he said, they were backslidden and in the dark, given to lofty scorn and contemptuous pity, and guilty of pious phariseeism. Jacobs described and defended footwashing as practiced 7 July 1845 by about sixty men and thirty-eight women meeting in separate apartments of Sister Moore's house in Cincinnati. Not all Hoosier Adventists joined him in this conviction. When Jacobs lectured at Rising Sun in September of 1845, most members excused themselves from the footwashing service. D. Kimpton of Rising Sun and Joseph Fassett of Columbus consistently opposed footwashing as a church ordinance.[51]

Until January of 1846 Enoch Jacobs was highly respected among the Adventists. He and his paper made Cincinnati a major adventist center. His strenuous positions—definite time, anti-spiritualizing, anti-organization, shut door, footwashing—cost him few readers in the West. His spirited editorial style was appreciated and his regional readers were loyal. John Hobart of Indianapolis said he occasionally saw the "Advent Herald and Watch" from Boston but found little of interest in it except the foreign news. What he liked were the editorials and letters in the paper which Jacobs published. R. Willard of Oswego said "As your little 'Star' seems to be the only Western light we have, and all the Eastern luminaries gone out or to us eclipsed, we are naturally obliged to look to you for what light we have." Jacobs also kept building "a large and increasing list of subscribers at the East" where his conservative stance made him appear to many to be a champion of Adventism old style. As a person of influence he was sought after to attend national adventist conferences. O. R. L. Crosier urged Jacobs, Pickands, Cook, and Peavy to attend the one at Rochester, New

York, in November of 1845 but Jacobs noted in the paper that his expectations of going there were "thwarted." He announced his intention to attend the one at Cleveland beginning 1 January 1846 and asked special prayers for all who would attend.[52]

Jacobs printed in his paper several harbingers of a new unity and identity emerging for Adventism. Some of his correspondents were convinced that all people everywhere should pay strict attention to the fourth commandment, observing the seventh day of the week as the Sabbath rather than the first day of the week as the Lord's Day. Jacobs opposed them in painstaking editorials in which he related Sabbath keeping to the Lord's coming.[53] As for himself, he said:

> I have not the least unkind feeling toward those that are impressed with the duty of observing the seventh day as the Sabbath. If they regard the day to the Lord, it cannot be sin. The way I have observed it hitherto, is by sending off about 800 copies of the "Day Star" to the Sheep and Lambs of the flock, in every State in the Union, (except Delaware and Maryland,) and in the Canada's . . . On the first day I meet the brethren at the Tabernacle where little children are taught the words of Jesus in the morning, and lectures given three times throughout the day. Taking the authority of Jesus, I cannot tell which of these two literal days are the most Holy.[54]

James White and Ellen Harmon White

There were letters from James White to Jacobs. White was a member of the Christian Connection recruited for adventist itinerancy in Maine about 1842 under the preaching of Miller and Himes. White said: "I had neither horse, saddle, bridle, nor money, yet I felt that I must go. I had used my past winter's earnings in necessary clothing, in attending Second Advent meetings, and in purchase of books and the chart. But my father offered me the use of a horse for the winter, and Elder Polley gave me a saddle with both pads torn off, and several pieces of an old bridle." By 1845 he was being recognized not only as a powerful preacher and singer but also as a rising leader with executive potential.[55]

In his letter of 6 September 1845 White was respectful of Jacobs and of his conservative western constituency. "The 'Day Star' shines gloriously," he said. "We, 'down East,' are happy to catch a single ray from its brilliant light. Shine, ye little messenger, till the Glorious King of Zion bursts forth on the sons of the morning . . . We are pleased with the course you are taking in the 'Star,' as it speaks out plain on the present truth, and commandments of my Master. Go on, but look out for the Devil's

counterfeit—Look out for false tests!" After warning against some false leaders among Adventists who were "designing individuals professing great spiritual discernment," White commented: "It is true we may expect glorious manifestations of God's Spirit; and I think the Bible warrants us in looking for visions, and those who may be discerners of spirits, even in the last days of time. But in such case we can judge alone by their fruits. There is one Sister in Maine who has had a clear vision of the Advent people traveling to the City of God." He summarized the content of her vision briefly.[56]

That sister was Ellen Harmon (to be Ellen White after 30 August 1846) who was just achieving regional recognition by 1845 as a preacher and visionary prophet of Adventism. Ellen's family was Methodist until that church excluded them for espousing the teachings of William Miller. She was converted at the age of twelve at a Methodist camp meeting in summer of 1840 and baptized by immersion in the Atlantic Ocean. Of her experience kneeling with those seekers she said "In that short period, when bowed among the praying ones, I learned more of the divine character of Christ than ever before." She had suffered a serious injury to her head and face at the age of nine. In the course of her struggle with invalidism and her search for mature faith following conversion, she reported a vivid dream in which Jesus smiled on her and bade her "fear not." She was also reassured by the counsel of L. F. Stockman, a Methodist elder turned Adventist, that she was surely being prepared for some special work.[57]

Thus encouraged she developed into a valued evangelistic worker whose prayer, testimony, and exhortation were regularly sought by the adventist ministers of the Portland area. The vision spoken of by James White was the one Ellen experienced in December of 1844. This was shortly after the Great Disappointment of 22 October. The vision clearly identified the Adventists in their afflictions as the true people of God on their pilgrimage to the heavenly city. Enoch Jacobs in Cincinnati obtained the text of this vision from Ellen Harmon and was the first to put it into print "published at the request of many friends that have heard it read." Ellen said it "was not written for publication, but for the encouragement of all who may see it."[58]

The Prophecy Fulfilled in the Cleansing of the Heavenly Sanctuary

In April of 1845 Jacobs began receiving a new adventist paper called the *Day Dawn*. He said it was "published by Franklin B. Hahn and edited by O. R. L. Crosier."

Both were friends of Jacobs. Hahn sent Jacobs $2 for a subscription in September of 1845 and said of the Cincinnati paper "It is giving us the truth." Crosier wrote the same month urging Jacobs to attend the upcoming adventist conference at Rochester and briefly voicing his own understanding of the second advent: "I believe the Bridegroom has come: Matt. 25:10; and is yet to come; for Christ was Bridegroom both before and after marriage. But to say Christ entered the Holy of Holies, the tenth of the seventh month, is saying He is in the secret chamber. Well, in this, we have good company; for Paul said he had entered within the Vail, which is the Holy of Holies, Heb. 6: 19, 20." This was compatible with the insight which Hiram Edson reported receiving by revelation on that terrible morning of 23 October after the Great Disappointment: "While passing through a large field I was stopped about midway of the field," Edson said. "Heaven seemed open to my view, and I saw distinctly and clearly that instead of our High Priest coming out of the Most Holy of the heavenly sanctuary to come to this earth on the tenth day of the seventh month, at the end of the 2300 days, He for the first time entered on that day the second apartment of that sanctuary; and that He had a work to perform in the most holy before coming to this earth."[59]

Edson, Hahn, and Crosier enriched this understanding by demonstrating in detail the fulfillment of the role of the high priest in the law of Moses by the role of the true high priest Jesus Christ. They now understood that Jesus entered the second and last phase of his work of atonement by moving from the Holy Place to the Most Holy Place (Holy of Holies) in heaven on 22 October 1844. The "cleansing of the sanctuary," then, was not the coming of the Lord to cleanse the church or the earth as Adventists had mistakenly supposed, but his entry into the Most Holy Place to cleanse the heavenly temple and blot out sin. His coming to earth with the holy angels lay ahead.

When they wished to offer this insight beyond the range of their personal contacts and beyond the limited circulation of their own *Day Dawn*, they contracted with Jacobs for its publication in an extra double number of his paper dated 7 February 1846. Crosier supplied the copy in fifty foolscap pages. Hiram Edson and Franklin B. Hahn appended a letter. "We have prayerfully examined the subject presented by Brother Crosier in the light of God's word, and are fully satisfied it is meat in due season, and if properly examined and understood will settle many difficulties in the minds of many brethren at this time. In order to get it before the brethren, it becomes necessary to loan the money necessary for its publication, with the expectation that all who feel interested and have means will aid in the expense. The expense as near as we can now ascertain will be about $30. Brethren here, as in most other places, are poor, (but rich in faith) but we can bear one-half of the expense, and will more if necessary."[60]

Defection of Jacobs

Although Enoch Jacobs was an adventist theologian of considerable acumen, he made very little of these insights published in his own paper which were destined to shape the future of Adventism. In fact he was preoccupied with a whole new religious affection. At the adventist conference he attended at Cleveland beginning 2 January 1846, he had played his accustomed role of western conservative putting down the foolish easterners who were saying "Christ has come." Then on the last day of the conference he was totally reversed by a sudden conversion. "I began to tremble in every limb," he said. "O, if ever an Almighty arm arrested Saul on his way to Damascus, that arm arrested me . . . I sunk down in the dust before God."[61]

The result of this new conversion brought little joy to his colleagues at the Adventist conference. O. R. L. Crosier was so poorly pleased that he advised Jacobs to "examine yourself with a lancet." Jacobs himself was now shouting "Christ has come" but was using that statement to refer to his own intensely personal and near pentecostal experience. He spoke of a special spiritual manifestation, of a refreshing, of holy unction. He spoke of being born again with wholly new eyes to see the kingdom which was now fully present. He spoke of singleness of eye, and of spiritual eye scales removed, and of spiritual anointment with eye salve to reveal the glorious kingdom. Over and over and over he said the kingdom must be received "as a little child." To be sure that his readers understood that his new position was a radical departure from his previous Adventism, Jacobs printed a lengthy display of the differences in parallel columns. His new testimony rocked the Cincinnati adventist community as "almost every one of the brethren testify that the spirit of God bore it to their hearts, and caused them to tremble in every limb." His wife and daughter "received the testimony" and went "rejoicing in the kingdom." Correspondents from Indiana cheered his new experience. The adventist congregation in Cincinnati split. The large and vigorous party siding with Jacobs, about 100 strong, lost a battle for possession of the adventist tabernacle but met daily in private homes in a revival of great emotional intensity.[62] Jacobs wrote:

The work that God is performing among his people here, is truly astonishing. The majesty and glory of his truth is beyond every thing we had ever conceived . . . Our meetings are crowded at the private houses, and some souls are born of the spirit every evening. Never so clearly has it been manifest, that God has undertaken the work of delivering his people. I would have sooner gone to the stake, three weeks since, than believed what I now do. O how rich and unbounded his goodness! He has opened our eyes to see, and our ears to hear.[63]

This was the band of crusaders who went out forty strong to join the Adventists of Liberty, Indiana, for a conference at John Creek's house and the nearby schoolhouse on that snowy weekend of 14–15 February 1846. The content of the doctrine of the visiting group was somewhat amorphous and effervescent. Jacobs said the genuine adventist remnant heard his new message—that the kingdom had come and was to be received in a burst of emotional insight—"with inexpressible joy" while some "gnashed their teeth in rage" and "the countenances of others told of inward woe."[64]

Henry B. Bear was present, a Pennsylvania Millerite and survivor of the Great Disappointment who moved west as a seeker and settled near Liberty in June of 1845. Soon after arriving in Indiana he was sending verbal and monetary support to Jacobs. His letters for publication in the paper seemed to reflect the influence of Jacobs. Said he, "Those brethren that laid a foundation at the Albany conference, I do hope will soon see that their works will be burned up." Bear was a zealous student of all parts of the Bible. His particular contribution to the continuing adventist movement was his unwavering focus on the parables of Matthew 13:44–46 in which the kingdom of heaven was compared to a treasure hid in a field and to a pearl of great price. In each case the discoverer of the great treasure "sold all that he had." And Luke 12:33–34 plainly advised seekers of the kingdom: "Sell that ye have, and give alms; provide yourselves bags which wax not old, a treasure in the heavens that faileth not, where no thief approacheth, neither moth corrupteth. For where your treasure is, there will your heart be also."[65]

Henry Bear and his wife Julia Ann were fully prepared to sell all. What they wanted was guidance to the place where the true citizens of the kingdom gathered. So they were enthusiastic participants when Jacobs and the Cincinnati Adventists began conversations and then negotiations with the Shakers at nearby Whitewater Village. Henry Bear meditated on his bed. "My mind was called to the Shakers," he said, "to compare their love with that of the adventists. The principle of a united consecration convinced me of their superior love, for while the Shakers lived in common in their houses, the adventists were living, some in fine houses, and others in poor rented hovels. Some could, and would, ride in fine carriages, while others had to walk. In view of these facts I had concluded that the manifest love of the Shakers condemned that of the adventists." He was impressed that Adventists were still wearing jewelry and ornaments while Shakers were not. He said, "I was, before day, almost persuaded that the Shakers were in possession of the kingdom we were looking for and which had cost us so much tribulation."[66]

Bear visited Whitewater Village himself, confessed his sins in Shaker style, and told his wife this surely was the kingdom. He reported, "She received the news with gladness and said, 'This is too good news, I expected we would have much more trouble and tribulation before we would find a resting place.' She had no hesitancy in making the decision to enter into the inheritance."[67]

Jacobs led a delegation of about 100 Adventists to a convention with Shaker representatives at Whitewater Village. As many as 200 regional constituents of Jacobs may have responded to his call to Shakerism. He was ecstatic about finding a new haven from the uncertainties of Adventism. "O what an ocean of contradictory theories is that upon which the multitudes have been floating for the last 18 months. Do you not long for rest from these conflicting elements? Do you want to find a place where Advent work takes the place of Advent talk,—where 'I' is no longer the prominent idea in any theory—where the purity of wives and husbands is the purity of heaven, and where your little children are protected from the poisonous influence of the world?"[68]

Henry and Julia Ann Bear were examples of the number of Adventists who found a home among the Shakers. Henry Bear said: "In twenty-seven years' experience of Shaker life, I have not had any thing like as hard, difficult and dangerous trials as I had in my former experience. I have often said, 'not for all the world would I have missed going through my advent experience; nor for all the world would I want to go through it again' . . . In my former experience I had to act upon belief only, but now upon knowledge and in obedience to direct counsel from a visible lead. Here no evil spirits can come, believers to deceive; therefore it is much less difficult to obey, because certain."[69]

Enoch and Electa Jacobs were examples of the even larger number of Adventists for whom bearing the cross of Shaker celibacy eventually seemed impracticable. The Jacobs family of husband, wife, and the survivors among nine children had many tender bonds. Even during the strange interlude in Cincinnati when Enoch and Electa considered themselves under divine direction to live as brother and sister, Enoch said his wife was dearer to him than a hundred sisters in the Lord. In their later years they dropped from prominence among either Adventists or Shakers.[70]

Union of Sabbatarian and "Sanctuary Cleansing" Adventists

The rising star of Adventism by 1846 was a tiny association of sabbatarian Adventists in the East. Their derivation from the movement led by Miller and Himes was clear. However the remains of that movement—once estimated by Miller in terms of 200 ministers, 500 public lecturers, and 50,000 believers in 1,000 congregations—had become scattered and chaotic.[71]

The sabbatarian Adventists themselves were so small a part of the movement that they were not even represented at the conference seeking stability for Adventism at Albany in April of 1845. Among them was Joseph Bates, a converted sea captain from New Bedford, Massachusetts, full of religious energy. He had come through the pains of the Great Disappointment with a missionary passion for observance of the seventh day as Sabbath. There was Hiram Edson near Canandaigua, New York, representative of that understanding of sanctuary cleansing written out in full for him and Franklin B. Hahn in the long article by O. R. L. Crosier. By 1846 Bates had met with the Canandaigua group. They united in support of the sabbatarian and sanctuary doctrines.[72]

An even more important merger occurred in Maine. That vision of encouragement received by Ellen Harmon in December of 1844 was followed about a week later by another which bade her "go and relate to others what he had revealed to me." It seemed a heavy commission for a young woman known only in a small section of Maine and at a time when the extremes of some Adventists had brought all private visions under suspicion. However her messages in trance were so encouraging and compelling to observers and hearers that invitations began coming to her from neighboring states. James White gave solid support to her expanding ministry and became her husband in August of 1846.

Soon after Enoch Jacobs printed Crosier's long article and its letter of endorsement in his Cincinnati paper in 1846, Ellen White disclosed a vision message that this view of the cleansing of the sanctuary was true light. Later the Whites met Hiram Edson personally while engaged in a series of conferences to consolidate the sabbatarian Adventists. This occurred at a volatile meeting in David Arnold's barn in Volney, New York, in August of 1848. The thirty-five adventist leaders present represented about thirty-five different forms of adventist opinion. Ellen White in vision pointed out errors, rebuked the contenders, and again supported Edson's sanctuary doctrine.[73]

Beginning with her early writings, Ellen White undergirded the "old landmark" adventist view of conditional immortality which had been disseminated by George Storrs in Indiana and nationally. Only God was to be considered innately immortal. Since no separate immortal soul existed in humans, there was no place for its punishment at death. All the dead slept until the first resurrection at which point the saints, living and dead, were gathered and the evil left to later judgment and extinction. This teaching denied the very existence of spirits of the dead so essential in the resurgence of Spiritualism following the experiments of the Fox family in 1848.[74]

The Whites became well acquainted with Joseph Bates and studied his pamphlet *The Seventh Day Sabbath: A Perpetual Sign* (1846). They began keeping the seventh-day Sabbath themselves and on 7 April 1847 Ellen received a vision confirming that practice. In 1847 she said "I saw that the holy Sabbath is, and will be the separating wall between the true Israel of God and unbelievers; and that the Sabbath is the great question to unite the hearts of God's dear waiting saints." Later she said that God had not paid any particular attention to the desecration of the Sabbath before 22 October 1844. But since that date when Jesus opened the door in the Most Holy Place containing the Ark, the commandments shone out anew so that all Christians were bound to keep the seventh-day Sabbath.[75]

All were now to be tested on the Sabbath question. The old "shut door" doctrine, which would have the destinies of all persons forever fixed by their acceptance or rejection of the prophecy for 22 October 1844, was gradually abandoned. Ellen White's vision of 24 March 1849 described the opening and shutting of doors as heavenly events serving primarily to focus light on the duty of Sabbath keeping. By 1852 sabbatarian Adventists were urging their hearers generally to become followers of Christ and accept the authority of the Bible. This would certainly include accepting the doctrine of the Lord's imminent return, the teaching concerning events in the heavenly sanctuary, the belief in conditional immortality, and the observance of the seventh-day Sabbath. In 1850 Ellen White discouraged further precise date setting for

Christ's return saying that time had not been a test since 1844 and would never again be a test.[76]

The work of disseminating this body of doctrines fell heavily on James White. Ellen's highly personal ministry could often overcome resistance, correct errors, and determine direction at adventist meetings. When she was present it was customary to ask her for any testimony given to her for the church; arrangements might be made to have the text printed. Of her own role she later said "Again and again these brethren came together to study the Bible . . . When they came to the point in their study where they said: 'We can do nothing more', the Spirit of the Lord would come upon me, I would be taken off in vision, and a clear explanation of the passage we had been studying would be given me, with instruction as to how we were to labor and teach effectively." Joseph Bates was on the road as a tireless itinerant, enlisting advocates for the new truths of sabbatarian Adventism.[77] It was up to James White to consolidate every inch of gain the others made and to add his own contributions of stability and strategy. He inherited none of the great media machinery of Miller and Himes. Out of pure poverty and with a recognized constituency of sabbatarian Adventists probably no greater than one hundred, he began issuing a little paper in 1849. It was *Present Truth* which became *Advent Review* which became *Second Advent Review and Sabbath Herald* which became *Review and Herald*. As the constituency grew he became its chief supplier of papers, tracts, hymnals, and instructional materials.[78]

The Whites were constantly "in the field," engaged in evangelism and in a perpetual round of meetings wherever their fellow sabbatarian Adventists would convene. They saw the need for more organization. They dared to advocate this in a constituency particularly hostile to organization as a thing historically opposed to Adventism and associated with sects and creeds. Everybody seemed to remember the warning of George Storrs that "no church can be organized by man's invention but what it becomes Babylon the moment it is organized." By 1854 Ellen White's visions called for the church to "become established upon gospel order which has been overlooked and neglected." James White was doing a series of articles in the *Review and Herald* on the same theme. A whole new generation of evangelists and a growing publishing business required system and support.[79]

Seventh-day Adventists at Battle Creek

The whole enterprise shifted west. The original axis of the fellowship was among the Yankees in New England and

New York. Now the meetings, the charts, and the literature became more popular among the transplanted Yankees in the Midwest. In 1858 the *Review and Herald* gained one subscriber in New England and lost nine in New York. It gained 125 subscribers in Michigan and Ohio that year and another 120 from farther west. With the same effort, said James White, twenty converts could be won in the West to one in the Northeast. Joseph Bates had visited Michigan in summer of 1849 to teach the new truths to adventist remnants at Jackson. He intended to move on to take the message to adventist families in Indiana at Kingsbury in LaPorte County and at Salem Center in Steuben County. But instead he felt guided in prayer to stay in Michigan at Battle Creek. There he found a welcome at the home of a Presbyterian named Hewitt, formed a small congregation, and received the Whites for an evangelistic meeting at Hewitt's house the following spring.

The work at Michigan in general and at Battle Creek in particular was a source of joy for sabbatarian Adventists. Battle Creek was the scene of their first tent meeting in 1854 and of a new meetinghouse in 1855. When James White sought a better publishing center, local leaders including John P. Kellogg provided $1,200 to move the press and the whole operation to Battle Creek. Two years later they had a steam engine and power press. In 1857 the Battle Creek congregation built a meetinghouse to seat 300 so they could fulfill their role as conference center for the whole brotherhood. In Battle Creek the Whites built the first house they ever owned and leading adventist families concentrated there. In 1859 Battle Creek congregation developed a plan for systematic giving which was offered in the *Review* as a model for others.

In 1860 Ellen White endorsed the decision of a conference at Battle Creek to adopt the name Seventh-day Adventists.

> I was shown in regard to the remnant people of God taking a name. Two classes were represented before me. One class embraced the great bodies of professed Christians. They were trampling upon God's law and bowing to a papal institution . . . The other class, who were but few in number, were bowing to the great law giver. They were keeping the fourth commandment. The peculiar and prominent features of their faith were the observance of the seventh day, and the waiting of the appearing of our Lord from heaven . . . The name Seventh-day Adventist is a standing rebuke to the Protestant world. Here is the line of distinction between the worshippers of God and those who worship the beast and receive his mark.[80]

The Seventh-day Adventist Publishing Association was incorporated in 1861; James White served as its president and general manager for the next twenty years. The Michigan Conference of Seventh-day Adventists organized itself to service its ministry and manage church affairs, a model which many other conferences were to follow. At Battle Creek in 1863 the six existing conferences formed a general conference authorized to supervise all thirty ministers and to guide the work for 3,500 members in 125 churches.[81]

Role of Ellen White

James White died in 1881; his was the largest funeral Battle Creek had ever seen. Ellen White lived thirty-four years beyond the death of James. When she died at Battle Creek in 1915, twenty-four of her books were in circulation totaling more than 100,000 pages. Her so-called "conflict series" featured apocalyptic interpretation of the high drama of holy history from the creation to the final restoration. Its five volumes were *Patriarchs and Prophets*, *Prophets and Kings*, *The Desire of Ages* (a life of Jesus), *The Acts of the Apostles*, and *The Great Controversy*. Millions of copies of *The Great Controversy* circulated in at least seventy languages. Her manual entitled *Steps to Christ* was issued in at least 15 million copies. She had received several hundred visions. She contributed over 4,500 articles to adventist periodicals. Nine volumes of didactic materials called *Testimonies for the Church* were selected from her manuscripts. These works were constantly regrouped and reissued. Throughout her lifetime she added to her written works the impact of her direct personal counsel to the growing army of pastors and administrators.

Seventh-day Adventists were a "Bible only" people. However the gifts and presence of Ellen White were so useful in consolidating the identity and structure of the church that she came to receive great veneration. She was recognized as a prophetess and her writings functioned as a kind of canon of church teaching. She never claimed elevated status for herself, holding always that doctrine must be grounded in the Scriptures rather than based on her revelations. But on many occasions she did make the prestige accorded her a basis for leadership to set the church's course. To much of the membership she was the "spirit of prophecy" named in Revelation 19:10.[82]

Ellen White energized the church's support for its missionary ministry. "If there is one work more important than another," she said, "it is that of getting our publications before the public, thus leading them to search the Scriptures." Seventh-day Adventists became known for their colporteurs constantly traveling to sell books and tracts. Colporteurs were served by the presses of the Seventh-day Adventist Publishing Association and by the General Conference Tract and Missionary Society at Battle Creek. Eventually they were linked to a network of state tract and book societies. They were part of the same missionary army as the visitors constantly going out from local churches to distribute books, periodicals, and tracts. Nearly 1,750,000 tracts and periodicals were given away in 1884 alone; by 1960 sales of books and periodicals totaled $23,543,132.

Seventh-day Adventists sent missionaries overseas in the 1890s and dramatically multiplied these missions after the reorganization of 1901. Ellen White herself spent two years in Europe beginning in summer of 1885— England, France, Switzerland, Germany, Italy, and Scandinavia. During the years 1891 to 1900 she worked with her son William in Australia, New Zealand, and Tasmania, sending constant reminders to American Adventists of their global responsibilities. By 1926 the number of Seventh-day Adventists outside North America exceeded the number in the homeland; by 1985 over 80 percent of the 4.5 million members were "foreign."[83]

Advocates of Health

At a time when the health reforms of Charles G. Finney, Sylvester Graham, William Alcott, Horace Mann, and Lewis B. Coles were familiar in the land, Ellen White became an advocate of hygiene, fresh air, moderate diet featuring vegetables instead of meat, and abstinence from tobacco, tea, coffee, and alcohol. At a time when doctors Joel Shew, R. T. Trall, and James C. Jackson were pioneering water cure treatments, she became interested in sanitariums where therapy centered less on drugs and more on baths, exercise, and rest. There was a vision in 1848 revealing the harmful effects of coffee, tea, and the "filthy weed" tobacco. Soon after an experience using hydrotherapy on two of her own sons and a neighbor child, Ellen was given a vision of some forty-five minutes on 5 June 1863 with a broad health regimen for Adventists. Following two visits to the sanitarium of James C. Jackson at Dansville, New York, the second because a serious stroke had disabled her husband James, she experienced another important vision on Christmas night of 1865. Adventists were being too slow in implementing the health practices, she said. Church members should be caring for their bodies and the church should have its own health institution. General Conference of 1866 took action to begin publication of a journal called the *Health Reformer* and to establish the Western Health Reform Institute at Battle Creek. Both survived marginally until they came into the hands of John Harvey Kellogg, son of that Battle Creek pillar John P. Kellogg.[84]

With the encouragement and financial backing of the Whites, John Harvey Kellogg had attended R. T. Trall's Hygieo-Therapeutic College and followed that with a year each at the medical schools of the University of Michigan and of Bellevue Hospital in New York. Kellogg changed the name of the adventist journal to *Good Health* and soon had 20,000 subscribers. He changed the name of the institution to Battle Creek Sanitarium and proceeded to confer on it his own rising world renown. As a teacher of health professionals he had few peers. As a surgeon he performed some 22,000 major abdominal operations. As a humanitarian he housed up to forty orphans in his own home and supported two other orphanages in the town.

John Harvey Kellogg and Ellen White sold the public multiplied thousands of copies of their books on health. Hers were basically concerned with health practices as compliance with natural law, with proper treatment of the body as the temple of the Holy Spirit, with the place of healthful living in preparing a people fit for translation at the Lord's coming, and with governance of the sex drive. His increasingly extolled "biologic living." Both were for sunshine, fresh air, exercise, baths, and a diet of vegetables, fruits, grains, and nuts. Both were against meat eating (especially pork), stimulating drinks, tobacco, spices, sugar, medical drugs, unhealthy dress, and frequent sex. The sanitarium at Battle Creek grew to be the world's largest with two acres of floor space and room for 700 patients. Clientele included the rich and famous—William H. Taft, Henry Ford, John D. Rockefeller, Jr., Harvey Firestone. Along with his oversight Kellogg gave his patients lectures and new health foods—peanut butter (before George Washington Carver), granola, corn flakes, shredded wheat, milk from soybeans, grain substitutes for meat and coffee.[85]

Eventually there were problems. Kellogg had become the world's most famous Seventh-day Adventist but at the same time his interests had become more broadly social and less overtly adventist. He spoke much of the "undenominational and unsectarian" nature of his medical work and yearned for extension of his humanitarian programs in Chicago. His ridicule of adventist clergy and resistance to General Conference oversight of "his" medical enterprises polarized the church. He was repeatedly reproved by Ellen White and then expelled from church membership on 10 March 1907. The medical institution did turn out to be his; when he left the church he took it with him. His brother Will also left the church and took with him the ownership of the health food enterprises.[86]

But the adventist emphasis on health did not leave the church with the Kelloggs. Health and fitness had become an ineradicable part of Seventh-day Adventist doctrine. Ministers and conference officers were trained to conduct practical health programs. Nor did the church lose its regard for health institutions and for professional medical training. Some of the institutions were sanitariums of the more modest order advocated by Ellen White. More visible to the eyes of the world was the church's College of Medical Evangelists which survived the Kellogg defection, was fully accredited by the American Medical Association in 1922, and became Loma Linda University Medical School. It was but one unit of what would become Adventist Health Systems/United States, seventh-largest health system in North America which admitted 300,000 patients and serviced nearly 2 million outpatient visits in a single year.

Travelers commented on the excellence of adventist hospitals in many lands. Top students in adventist colleges were likely to be headed for medical studies. Adventists in military service were often in medical assignments. Within the church some tension remained between the doctors and the denominational body. Trained medical personnel were paid more than most church employees, were in constant interaction with secular colleagues, and were providing round-the-clock services difficult to integrate with strict observance of the seventh-day Sabbath. At the same time the medical establishment was credited with advocating a holism in which physical health and spiritual growth were fully united, perhaps the most important emphasis contributed by Adventism to modern theology.[87]

Adventist Education

James and Ellen White were concerned about education too. The end of the world did not come but children did and they needed schools. Ministers and administrators required training. Public schools were suspect. Ellen White received a vision on education in January of 1872 and wrote thirty pages on the substance of the principle given. Battle Creek was the natural place to begin. General Conference approved a school there in 1873. Ellen White had in mind an agricultural-vocational school combining study, work, and healthful living. Others had a vision closer to a traditional four-year college with a classical curriculum. The college image was more evident when Battle Creek College was established in 1874. Within a decade came the institutional forerunners of Pacific Union College in California and Atlantic Union

College in Massachusetts. There were also early colleges at Lincoln, Nebraska, and at Walla Walla, Washington, and at Cooranbong, Australia. Many adventist educators in America eventually wanted to be full participants in the national academic community. They wanted to prepare their young people for admission to accredited professional schools, not least their own accredited medial school.

Adventists thrived on education, becoming college graduates at a rate about three times the national average. Some tensions have arisen when the church's own academically trained critics have focused their criticism on adventist biblical interpretation, or on the role and authority of Ellen White, or on the vast corpus of her teaching materials. Adventists also developed great affection for their own system of elementary and secondary schools. Ellen White urged members to develop "wherever there are a few Sabbath-keepers . . . a day-school where their children and youth can be instructed. They should employ a Christian teacher, who, as a consecrated missionary, shall educate the children in such a way as to lead them to become missionaries."[88]

Adventists and Contemporary Society

In some ways Adventists appeared to be separate. They observed Sabbath from sunset on Friday to sunset on Saturday; persistent Sunday observers were long regarded by them as in danger of bearing the "mark of the beast." Unlike the Mormons who made America and American history a part of their holy history, the Adventists generally distanced themselves from American national goals and reforms. Publication and distribution of their printed materials were carefully kept in their own hands. The corps of clergy and their financial support were closely and centrally controlled.

Adventists replicated many secular service agencies. Their 1985 worldwide report showed 4,306 primary schools, 901 secondary schools, 94 colleges and universities, 152 hospitals and sanitariums, 78 nursing homes and retirement centers, 51 publishing houses, 322 periodicals, dozens of radio stations, and 28 food companies. Members often chose to live near their major church institutions. Adventists in such places might move from adventist home to adventist school to adventist college to adventist vocation to adventist hospital to adventist retirement center to adventist resting place awaiting the resurrection without leaving the very bosom of the church. In the history and literature of the movement there was always some odor of their rejection of the churches and the world which had once rejected them.[89]

In most other ways Adventists seemed very much a part of the American evangelical consensus. Their statements of belief began with testimony to the priority they accorded to the Scriptures of the Old and New Testaments. Their worship ways were those of familiar non-liturgical Protestants. They baptized by immersion and opened participation in their communion services to all Christians. Ellen White was instrumental in preserving traditional statements concerning Trinity and concerning justification by faith as adventist articles of faith. There was a long dialogue in the 1950s involving editor Donald Gray Barnhouse of *Eternity* magazine, several evangelical theologians, and the adventist contributors to a work entitled *Questions on Doctrine* (1957). They claimed to discover an essential unity of belief. Seventh-day Adventists did not join the World Council of Churches or the National Council of Churches but they often cooperated as observers and consultants. And pastors often joined local ministerial associations as Ellen White herself had suggested.[90]

Seventh-day Adventist Extension in Indiana

When Seventh-day Adventists came to Indiana not much was left of the original adventist enthusiasm and structure. John N. Andrews of Maine visited in fall of 1851 and said he found little trace of the work of William Miller and Enoch Jacobs in Cincinnati. The tabernacle was sold and the congregation fragmented. Joseph Bates was in the state occasionally beginning about 1850. It was his way to stay in a place no more than three or four days, to teach and to gather subscriptions for the *Review and Herald*, and then to move on. The paper would be the continuing preacher.

There were some remaining Millerites in the northernmost Indiana counties. Adventists Samuel W. Rhodes from Oswego, New York, and John C. Bowles of Jackson, Michigan, came to Indiana in 1851. They found Joseph and Jemima Catlin at Kingsbury in LaPorte County. Joseph was an ordained Millerite who had been a correspondent with Enoch Jacobs; he and his wife accepted the new truths and became Sabbath keepers. There was a tiny continuing congregation which met at the home of Mrs. Foxe at Salem Center in Steuben County, on occasion harassed by stoning and by blocking the chimney to "smoke 'em out." Evangelist John N. Loughborough of Rochester, New York, was able to give them encouragement. Loughborough also rallied a new group at North Liberty in St. Joseph County in the 1850s.

James and Addie Harvey became outstanding members of the North Liberty congregation. James was a delegate at the formation of the Michigan Conference in 1861, first conference to be organized in the new Seventh-day Adventist church. He was also a delegate at the formation of the nationwide General Conference in 1863. Of one of his expeditions as an adventist colporteur among Hoosiers, James Harvey wrote that he was kindly received, that he and his horse were generally entertained free of charge, and that the people received his papers with thanks. "I have now spent twenty days in going from house to house, offering our publications to the people, and explaining these things, and praying with some of the families," he said. "I have visited 220 families, and sold 52,986 pages, for which I have realized $40.59. I furnished the Young Men's Christian Association of Logansport, Ind., with four of our bound books, and gave away some tracts." Printed material remained a big part of adventist evangelism. A Hoosier wrote to the *Review and Herald* "I have never yet seen a Seventh-day Adventist preacher. I was converted by reading your works and comparing them with the Scriptures. The *Review* and the books are the only preachers I have seen of this faith. I highly prize the weekly visits of the paper. I am trying to lecture on the Sabbath, as best I can."[91]

The early Seventh-day Adventists in Indiana's northern counties were oriented toward Michigan. Influence from Michigan was even stronger after the adventist headquarters came to Battle Creek in 1855. Appeals to Battle Creek from scattered Indiana converts brought tours by groundbreaking preachers—Joseph Bates, Moses Hull, Joseph H. Waggoner, John N. Loughborough, John Brington, W. S. Ingraham, Dudley M. Canright, R. J. Lawrence. Salem Center organized the first Seventh-day Adventist church in the state in October of 1861. North Liberty congregation built the first meetinghouse in 1868. Two young brothers from the vicinity of Battle Creek came to Indiana in 1869. They were Elbert B. Lane and Sands H. Lane. From the time of their arrival Adventism in Indiana took on more of the look of a statewide campaign. By 1870 there were bands of Seventh-day Adventists at Sullivan, Russiaville, Cicero, Tipton, Spencer, Patricksburg, Fairfield, Erwin, Lancaster, Bowling Green, and Sulphur Springs.[92]

Michigan sent its tent for adventist camp meetings in Indiana at Tipton and Fairfield in 1870 and 1871. In June of 1872 Joseph Waggoner and Elbert B. Lane were conducting a camp meeting at Gosport. A storm destroyed the Michigan tent. Adventist leaders from across Indiana met to face the crisis. The leaders convened again in September at Kokomo in the new tent they had bought for Indiana. James Harvey made the motion that they form their own Indiana Conference. Harvey was named secretary; William Covert was president; Isaac Zirkle was treasurer. The charter churches were at Alto, Erwin, North Liberty, Patricksburg, and Salem Center. Statewide evangelism became the immediate conference goal. By the turn of the century adventist preaching had been offered in more than 300 places. Evangelists at work included Arthur W. Bartlett, William Covert, John Covert, J. P. Henderson, William Hill, N. W. Kauble, Sands H. Lane, David H. Oberholtzer, Joseph M. Rees, F. M. Roberts, J. S. Shrock, Victor Thompson, Luzerne Thompson, and W. A. Young. Continuing churches founded before 1901 included

> Marion, 1876; Lafayette, 1877; Alexandria, Noblesville, Bloomington (as Smithville to 1871, then as Unionville to 1916), and Wolf Lake, 1878; Hartford City, Kokomo, and Northfield, 1883; Middletown, 1884; Plymouth, 1885; Sullivan (as Dugger to 1892, then as Salem to 1937), 1886; Boggstown, Rockford (as Barber's Mill to 1932), Rochester, and Wabash, 1887; Indianapolis, 1888; Angola, 1889; Terre Haute, 1892; Knox, 1893; Elnora, 1895; Monon (as Honey Creek to 1929), 1896; Fort Wayne, Tell City (as Mt. Zion to 1917), 1897; Anderson, 1898; Connersville, Muncie, and South Bend, 1900.[93]

Adventists had learned to draw crowds. Well publicized lectures in tents in summer and in schoolhouses or halls in winter attracted inquirers. Unusual charts and literature helped. John Covert at Rigdon held special meetings for children. P. G. Stanley at Priam gave cooking demonstrations. Arthur Bartlett engaged in five debates at Wabash. Sands Lane debated a Campbellite pastor at Farmersburg for four days in summer of 1883, an event which brought a thousand hearers and gathered believers.

The believers were always a curiosity because they would not work on Saturday. Sands Lane said of his campaign at Sevastopol in 1879 "It made quite a change in the village—a merchant left his store, the shoemaker, harness maker, and the undertaker closed shop. Men came from the country with work, but were told they could not get it done till the next day." No state accepted Seventh-day Adventism like Michigan. Membership there was 3,809 by 1885. But Indiana's 920 members that year was comparable to Wisconsin with 1,525, Ohio with 944, and Illinois with 729. Indiana's adventist membership kept doubling every ten years to reach 2,226 in 69 churches in 1900.[94]

Indiana was spotlighted by the denomination in a painful way just as the new century began. Many Adventists in the 1890s had been expecting a great outpouring of the Holy Spirit fulfilling the scriptural reference to the "latter rain" in Joel 2:23. Adventist evangelist S. S. Davis was especially impressed by some "spirit-filled" Christians he came to know in his work with the Helping Hand welfare mission in Evansville.

When Davis was named revivalist for Indiana Conference, he went on the road with a new "cleansing message." His team used stimulating music—organ, violins, tambourines, flutes, horns, and a bass drum. Audience members raised their hands to heaven, shouted, and clapped. Some fell in trance and were escorted through the "garden experience" of Christ in Gethsemane by the circle of singing, praying, and shouting members. Those with the experience were counted born of God, cleansed from all degrees of sin, released from the power of death, and ready for direct translation at Christ's appearing. Theirs was "holy flesh." The movement swept through the Indiana leadership and polarized the conference generally. Some exhausted seekers wanted the experience but could not quite feel certain they had achieved it. The excitement was reaching into other conferences.

At a public session of the 1901 General Conference, Ellen White reasserted the basic rationalistic character of Adventism. She ended the "holy flesh" movement conclusively. She said the overconfidence of people convinced they were beyond the reach of sin would play right into the devil's hands. Excitement of the kind evident in Indiana was "not favorable to growth in grace, to true purity and sanctification of the spirit." She said "The Holy Spirit never reveals itself in . . . a bedlam of noise." The leaders involved accepted her reproof and correction. The entire executive body of Indiana Conference resigned. Indiana's membership remained static at about 2,000 from 1900 to 1930.[95]

The flow of adventist energy from Battle Creek to Indiana lessened. Battle Creek College moved to Berrien Springs, Michigan, in 1901 where it eventually became Andrews University. The national adventist headquarters and the plant for publishing the *Review and Herald* moved from Battle Creek to Washington, D.C. (Takoma Park) in 1903. However the national church structure was effective everywhere under the strong executive leadership of Arthur G. Daniells.[96] Workers in Indiana Conference were able to double the membership to exceed 4,000 by 1950 and 5,000 by 1960, even though six black congregations had elected to transfer out in 1945 to join the new segregated Lake Region Conference. For 1990 the state reported 11,459 Seventh-day Adventist adherents, about half as many as Old Order Amish or Church of God (Anderson) and twice as many as Free Methodists.

A church of rural people in its beginnings, Seventh-day Adventism in Indiana deliberately moved to take its place in the cities. Arthur W. Bartlett formed a Sabbath school in Indianapolis in spring of 1876. Indiana Conference began serious outreach to the capital city in 1883. There was a city mission and lecture room on Cherry Street in 1885 and a congregation with a building on Central Avenue in 1888. Denominational leaders Ellen White and A. T. Jones came to Indianapolis to preach. There were adventist camp meetings on the north side of the city in 1888, 1892, 1893, and 1894. Tent meetings were out of fashion by 1920 but Adventists built permanent camp meeting facilities on the premises of their Indiana Academy at Cicero just north of Indianapolis. In the city they offered a penny-a-dish cafeteria during the depression. They conducted preaching crusades, Bible study classes, vacation Bible schools, and radio programs. The general conference of the whole Seventh-day Adventist denomination convened at the Hoosier Dome in Indianapolis in 1990.

By 1990 at least half of Indiana's adventist membership was in the state's larger cities with more than one-fourth in Marion and Hamilton counties alone. The Indiana Conference headquarters located in the Indianapolis suburb of Carmel. The Adventist Book Center at Cicero supplied literature needs. Timber Ridge Camp offered year-round facilities on 196 acres of woodland and lake near Spencer. Bethel Sanitarium at Evansville symbolized adventist health concerns. Besides the boarding academy for grades nine through twelve at Cicero, there were fourteen Seventh-day Adventist elementary schools in the state in 1991. They were at Anderson, Bedford, Bloomington, Cicero, Columbus, Elkhart, Evansville, Fort Wayne (Roanoke), Greenwood, Indianapolis, Kokomo, Lafayette, Richmond, and South Bend.

NOTES

1. James White, *Sketches of the Christian Life and Public Labors of William Miller, Gathered from His Memoir by the Late Sylvester Bliss, and from Other Sources* (Battle Creek, Mich.: Steam Press of the Seventh-day Adventist Publishing Association, 1875), 43–44.

2. For an indication of the centrality of these biblical themes and the large body of passages involved, see articles "Eschatology" and "Parousia" in *Interpreter's Dictionary of the Bible*, 4 vols. (New York: Abingdon Press, 1962). Miller's fourteen rules of interpretation are in William Miller, *Memoirs of William Miller*, ed. Sylvester Bliss (Boston: Joshua Y. Hines, 1853), 70–72.

3. Richard W. Schwarz, *Light Bearers to the Remnant* (Boise, Idaho: Pacific Press, 1979), 42. Miller originally believed that the "cleansing" was for the Christian church but by 1842 broadened its application to the whole earth. Miller's predictive work had a base much wider than the text of Daniel 8:14. Having established the date of 1843, he found the whole Bible clarified and illumined. For one list of his supplementary proofs, see Francis D. Nichol, *The Midnight Cry: A Defense of the Character and Conduct of William Miller and the Millerites, Who Mistakenly Believed that the Second Coming of Christ Would Take Place in the Year 1844* (Washington, D.C.: Review and Herald, 1944), 507–10. Miller and his colleagues greatly expanded the supporting network of interpretation. For an illustrated prophetic chart issued by the Adventists in 1842, see the foldout pocketed in *The Disappointed: Millerism and Millenarianism in the Nineteenth Century*, ed. Ronald L. Numbers and Jonathan Butler (Bloomington, Ind.: Indiana University Press, 1987, 235 p.).

4. White, *Sketches*, 57, 62–63.

5. White, *Sketches*, 68.

6. White, *Sketches*, 129.

7. *Adventism in America: A History*, ed. Gary Land (Grand Rapids, Mich.: Eerdmans, 1986), 8; Nichol, *Midnight Cry*, 206–7, 282, 433–34. Those convinced by the conclusions and predictions of William Miller were early referred to as "Millerites." Since Miller regretted such a personalized usage and since the movement included many persons who differed with Miller in some particulars, the *Advent Herald* for 20 March 1844 suggested the name "Adventists."

8. The phrase "midnight cry" was a favorite with Adventists. It was adapted from the parable of the wise and foolish virgins in Matthew 25:1–13. The virgins awaited the coming of the bridegroom so they could go in with him to the marriage feast. During the long wait they slept. "And at midnight there was a cry made, Behold the bridegroom cometh; go ye out to meet him" (Matthew 25:6). Adventists felt they were the watchers warning the sleeping world.

9. M. Ellsworth Olsen, *History of the Origin and Progress of Seventh-day Adventists* (Washington, D.C.: Review and Herald, 1925), 107–41; Leroy E. Froom, *The Prophetic Faith of Our Fathers*, 4 vols. (Washington, D.C.: Review and Herald, 1946–1954), 4:455–527; Schwarz, *Light Bearers*, 31–45; *Disappointed*, 18–58; Nichol, *Midnight Cry*, 29–30, 38, 41–125, 137–38.

10. *Disappointed*, 13–14, 48–49; Nichol, *Midnight Cry*, 144; Froom, *Prophetic Faith*, 4:526, 807.

11. The *Western Midnight Cry* is reported to date from 1841 but extant files begin with vol. 2, no. 1, which is the issue for 9 December 1843. The name of the paper changed to *Day-Star* with vol. 5, no. 1 for 18 February 1845 but the volume and number sequence continued unbroken. See *Disappointed*, 185.

12. *Western Midnight Cry*, 2:4, 33.

13. *Western Midnight Cry*, 2:32; *Day-Star*, 6:26; 8:14.

14. *Day-Star*, 6:47; 7:1; 7:23.

15. *Western Midnight Cry*, 3:57. Beginning with the issue for 4 May 1844 a lengthy quotation from the *Advent Herald* was appended to this block of "Fundamentals" noting that the published time was indeed past but advising in the words of Habakkuk 2:3 "it will surely come, it will not tarry."

16. *Western Midnight Cry*, 2:4, 13, 16, 32, 41, 82.

17. *Western Midnight Cry*, 2:81; 3:9.

18. *Western Midnight Cry*, 3:65, 73, 81–82; 4:9; *Day-Star*, 7:28, 32.

19. *Western Midnight Cry*, 3:97.

20. *Western Midnight Cry*, 2:4, 66; *Day-Star*, 6:16; 7:36.

21. *Western Midnight Cry*, 2:5, 75; *Day-Star*, 6:12; 9:44.

22. *Day-Star*, 8:24.

23. *Day-Star*, 5:30. Some Oswego letters are typesigned A. Willard but are probably by the same correspondent.

24. *Western Midnight Cry*, 2:15; *Day-Star*, 6:14; 9:20.

25. *Western Midnight Cry*, 4:34; *Day-Star*, 7:18, 38.

26. *Western Midnight Cry*, 2:33, 50–51, 59, 66–67; 3:9, 36, 41; *Day-Star*, 5:29–30; 9:5.

27. *Western Midnight Cry*, 2:59; *Day-Star*, 8:14; 9:44, 55.

28. *Western Midnight Cry*, 2:67, 74; *Day-Star*, 7:5, 19.

29. *Western Midnight Cry*, 3:73, 75, 82–83; *Day-Star*, 7:1.

30. *Western Midnight Cry*, 4:31–32, 34–35; *Day-Star*, 6:5.

31. *Western Midnight Cry*, 4:28.

32. *Day-Star*, 5:11; 6:47.

33. *Day-Star*, 6:49; 7:29.

34. *Western Midnight Cry*, 3:94.

35. *Western Midnight Cry*, 3:9; White, *Sketches*, 282; Nichol, *Midnight Cry*, 158–73, 208–9; *Disappointed*, 48–51.

36. Froom, *Prophetic Faith*, 4:795; Nichol, *Midnight Cry*, 216.

37. *Disappointed*, 53.

38. *Western Midnight Cry*, 4:9, 16.

39. Nichol, *Midnight Cry*, 245. Nichol said this instance in Cincinnati was the only one his research disclosed in which a reporter actually attended a Millerite meeting on 22 October 1844 and wrote a firsthand account.

40. Froom, *Prophetic Faith*, 4:810–26; *Adventism in America*, 26–31; Nichol, *Midnight Cry*, 213–35; *Disappointed*, 50–52.

41. *Western Midnight Cry*, 3:22, 69–71, 91; *Day-Star*, 5:50.

42. Nichol, *Midnight Cry*, 147–49, 163–68, 211–12; *Disappointed*, 30–33, 122–29; *Western Midnight Cry*, 3:26–27; 3:57.

43. Malcolm Bull and Keith Lockhart, *Seeking a Sanctuary: Seventh-day Adventism and the American Dream* (New York: Harper and Row, 1989), 3–4, 8; Nichol, *Midnight Cry*, 237–51, 303–426; *Disappointed*, 128–29; *Adventism in America*, 20–25; Schwarz, *Light Bearers*, 51; *Western Midnight Cry*, 3:8; *Day-Star*, 9:55.

44. Edward Eggleston, *The End of the World: A Love Story* (New York: Orange Judd and Company, 1872), 7 (preface), 256–57.

45. *Day-Star*, 8:47.

46. *Day-Star*, 5:18–19, 36; 7:16.

47. *Day-Star*, 5:17, 36, 42.

48. *Day-Star*, 6:48.

49. Nichol, *Midnight Cry*, 280–83; *Adventism in America*, 33; *Day-Star*, 6:10–12, 14–16, 18–20, 22–23.

50. *Day-Star*, 6:3–4, 28.

51. *Day-Star*, 6:40; 7:2, 7–8, 14, 18–20, 33, 35, 40.

52. *Day-Star*, 6:16, 20, 26, 48; 8:41, 43, 45–46, 51; 9:3.

53. *Day-Star*, 7:3–7.

54. *Day-Star*, 7:12.

55. Froom, *Prophetic Faith*, 4:1057–58.

56. *Day-Star*, 7:17–18; other letters from White appeared at 7:26, 47; 8:35; 9:25.

57. Arthur W. Spalding, *Origin and History of Seventh-day Adventists*, 4 vols. (Washington, D.C.: Review and Herald, 1961–1962), 1:65.

58. Ingemar Linden, *The Last Trump: An Historico-Genetical Study of Some Important Chapters in the Making and Development of the Seventh-day Adventist Church* (Frankfurt am Main: Peter Lang, 1978), 92–93, 170–80; Spalding, *Origin and History*, 1:67–69; *Day-Star*, 9:31–32.

59. *Day-Star*, 7:28; Nichol, *Midnight Cry*, 458.

60. *Day-Star*, 9:36–44. For a brief indication of the article's salient points see Schwarz, *Light Bearers*, 62–63 and Linden, *Last Trump*, 131.

61. *Day-Star*, 9:24.

62. *Day-Star*, 9:23–24, 28–29, 32, 36, 44, 47, 55.

63. *Day-Star*, 9:29.

64. *Day-Star*, 9:44, 55.

65. *Day-Star*, 8:14; 9:52.

66. *Disappointed*, 224.

67. *Disappointed*, 226.

68. *Disappointed*, 173–85; *Day-Star*, 10:51.

69. *Disappointed*, 226.

70. *Day-Star*, 9:61; Schwarz, *Light Bearers*, 56; *Disappointed*, 183. There is a report that Enoch left the Shakers declaring he would "rather go to hell with Electa his wife than live among the Shakers separated from her." The nearly total absence of glib comments in his previous writing makes this story suspect.

71. Jonathan Butler, "From Millerism to Seventh-day Adventism: 'Boundlessness to Consolidation'," *Church History* 55 (March 1986): 50–64; *Disappointed*, 189–208.

72. *Adventism in America*, 38; Nichol, *Midnight Cry*, 280–83; Froom, *Prophetic Faith*, 4:545–49, 953–61; Olsen, *History*, 184–91; Schwarz, *Light Bearers*, 59–60, 63; Spalding, *Origin and History*, 1:111–13.

73. Froom, *Prophetic Faith*, 4:1021–48; Spalding, *Origin and History*, 1:193–94; Schwarz, *Light Bearers*, 67; *Adventism in America*, 40.

74. *Adventism in America*, 32, 250; Froom, *Prophetic Faith*, 4:1031, 1033, 1160, 1169; Spalding, *Origin and History*, 1:147; Schwarz, *Light Bearers*, 176; *Disappointed*, 203; Bull and Lockhart, *Seeking*, 74–75.

75. Schwarz, *Light Bearers*, 67; Linden, *Last Trump*, 180–82.

76. Linden, *Last Trump*, 127; Schwarz, *Light Bearers*, 69–70; *Adventism in America*, 40–41.

77. Olsen, *History*, 230; Linden, *Last Trump*, 133, 189–90.

78. Schwarz, *Light Bearers*, 72–78.

79. Schwarz, *Light Bearers*, 86; *Adventism in America*, 46–52; *Disappointed*, 149.

80. Linden, *Last Trump*, 115.

81. Schwarz, *Light Bearers*, 89, 91, 95–97, 113; Olsen, *History*, 223–25, 230; *Adventism in America*, 49–50, 54, 58–60, 62–63.

82. Olsen, *History*, 419–23; Linden, *Last Trump*, 128, 132, 142–43, 157, 189, 199–211, 280–92; Bull and Lockhart, *Seeking*, 19–32.

83. Schwarz, *Light Bearers*, 152–57, 214; *Adventism in America*, 140–41, 147, 196–97; Bull and Lockhart, *Seeking*, 111–14.

84. Linden, *Last Trump*, 311–66; Schwarz, *Light Bearers*, 106, 111–12; Bull and Lockhart, *Seeking*, 128.

85. John Harvey Kellogg's brother Will Kellogg set up a company to market corn flakes. A Battle Creek patient named C. W. Post modeled his famous "Postum" on John Harvey Kellogg's cereal coffee. See Bull and Lockhart, *Seeking*, 131.

86. Schwarz, *Light Bearers*, 206–10, 282–97; Bull and Lockhart, *Seeking*, 75–76, 130–33, 159–60, 168–70, 219–21; *Adventism in America*, 69–70, 107–9, 133–38; Linden, *Last Trump*, 340–45.

87. Bull and Lockhart, *Seeking*, 95, 144, 219–29, 244–55, 260–65; *Adventism in America*, 173–74, 203.

88. Schwarz, *Light Bearers*, 123–32, 200–3, 205, 628; Bull and Lockhart, *Seeking*, 19–32, 229–43; *Adventism in America*, 198, 211–30.

89. Bull and Lockhart, *Seeking*, 35–43, 95–108, 171–75, 207–18, 268; *Adventism in America*, 41–42, 46; Schwarz, *Light Bearers*, 312.

90. Schwarz, *Light Bearers*, 167–68, 183–93, 539–45; Bull and Lockhart, *Seeking*, 152–58; *Adventism in America*, 229.

91. *Seventh-day Adventist Encyclopedia* (Washington, D.C.: Review and Herald, 1966), 573; Spalding, *Origin and History*, 1:260–61; Olsen, *History*, 251–52, 416, 439.

92. *Seventh-day Adventist Encyclopedia*, 573.

93. *Seventh-day Adventist Encyclopedia*, 573–74.

94. *Seventh-day Adventist Encyclopedia*, 574; *Adventism in America*, 73–74.

95. Schwarz, *Light Bearers*, 446–48; Bull and Lockhart, *Seeking*, 64–65; *Adventism in America*, 104; *Seventh-day Adventist Encyclopedia*, 574–75.

96. Schwarz, *Light Bearers*, 280, 299–312.

CHRISTIAN SCIENTISTS

Mary Baker was born 16 July 1821 in Bow, New Hampshire, the daughter of Mark and Abigail Baker and the youngest of their six children. Mark was a respected citizen, an officer of the church and town, and an earnest Calvinist. Mary joined her parents in the Congregational Church at Sanbornton (later Tilton) in 1838 after some wrestling with the subjects of election and regeneration. From that time she always defined and defended herself as a Christian. The best narration of religious experience she could muster at the moment was the 23rd verse of Psalm 139: "Search me, O God, and know my heart: Try me, and know my thought: And see if there be any wicked way in me, And lead me in the way everlasting." This was so earnestly said, she related, "that even the oldest church members wept. After the meeting was over they came and kissed me. To the astonishment of many, the good clergyman's heart also melted, and he received me into their communion, and my protest along with me." As a child she was often sick and often absent from school. A favorite teacher at home was her brother Albert, eleven years her senior, local schoolmaster, and then graduate of Dartmouth in the class of 1834. Through Albert and his books Mary's education was greatly expanded.[1]

The stabilities of Mary's home and family kept collapsing. The death of her grandmother broke the tie to the Bow homestead and the family relocated. Her brother George, who was the son expected to maintain the family home and farm, moved off to Connecticut. Albert capped a rapidly advancing legal and political career by being nominated for the U.S. Congress but died at age thirty-one before the election. Mary married George Washington Glover in December of 1843 and moved south with him. Just over six months later Glover died of yellow fever and Mary returned pregnant to the family farm. When her mother died in 1849 and her father remarried in 1850, Mary went to live with her sister Abigail; her son George was entrusted to the care of Russell and Mahala Cheney. Mary married a dentist named Daniel Patterson in 1853. Patterson had difficulty providing for his nervous and sickly wife. He had no intention of taking on the additional role of stepfather for George, who went away to Minnesota with the Cheneys as his guardians. The Patterson marriage ended in separation in 1866 and in divorce on grounds of desertion in 1873. George came back east to visit his mother in 1879 after a separation of nearly twenty-five years.[2]

Search for Health and Healing

Mary continually sought good health. Beginning about 1853 she found some help in homeopathy, a system of medicine fast rising in popularity. Homeopathic therapy was based on determining the essential nature of an ailment and administering only minute quantities of drugs closely similar to the disease in their essence. Mary treasured her *New Manual of Homeopathic Practice* by Gottlieb Heinrich Georg Jahr, both for her own use and as a guide

in the treatment of others. She and Daniel Patterson observed that in many cases the amount of the drug could
be reduced to a trace or omitted altogether without affecting the rate of cure. The power of mind and the faith
of the patient were obvious factors in healing. When both
her interest in homeopathy and her health declined, she
tried hydropathy. In June of 1862 she went to William T.
Vail's Hydropathic Institute at Hill, New Hampshire. Vail
advocated baths, rest, simple diet, and fresh air. He also
observed that a number of his patients could be cured
simply by talking to them to get rid of their fears.[3]

Mary heard reports of cures by Phineas P. Quimby at
Portland, Maine. She and Daniel Patterson had written
Quimby earlier about treatment for her. In October of
1862 she left Vail's institute and became Quimby's patient
in Portland. Quimby was a powerful practitioner, having
progressed from mesmerism to a technique of healing
by the constructive power of thought. He understood
disease as a disturbance of the essential vapor or fluid
which constituted the identity of a person. He used no
medicines. Cure came by ascertaining the source of the
disturbance and bringing the patient to a dynamic understanding of both the symptoms felt and the energy
available for recuperation. As a focus for the power of
his person in this essential dialogue, Quimby might use
some physical rubbings or manipulations or applications.
He treated Mary. At times she was much better. She wrote
a letter in appreciation of Quimby to the Portland *Courier*
in November. She stayed at Portland until the end of
1862 and returned there for considerable periods during
the next two years. Though she later concluded "Quim-
byism was too short" to compare or equate with Christian
Science, she knew Quimby well as a mentor and colleague in healing endeavors until his death in January
of 1866.[4]

At their home in Lynn, Massachusetts, Mary and
Daniel Patterson became members of the Linwood Lodge
of Good Templars, a temperance society and social organization. Mary was soon elected "Exalted Mistress" of
the women's auxiliary. On 1 February 1866 she was on
her way with friends to the Thursday evening meeting of
the Good Templars when she fell on the ice at the corner
of Market and Oxford. Her injury was serious, thought
by many to be crippling and life threatening. In the midst
of general gloom about her condition she asked to read
her Bible in privacy. She read an account of one of the
healings of Jesus. She heard the words of Jesus flood into
her thought: "I am the way, the truth, and the life: no
man cometh unto the Father, but by me" (John 14:6).
She arose, dressed, walked to the next room unaided,

and reported she was healed. The nature and extent of
her injuries were to become matters of controversy. But
there was no denying that the moment of healing was for
her a time of life-changing insight. "Discovery" she called
it. "My immediate recovery from the effects of an injury
caused by an accident, an injury that neither medicine
nor surgery could reach, was the falling apple that led
me to the discovery how to be well myself, and how to
make others so."[5]

The New Discovery

In one way her new discovery and mission was in a con-
tinuum with her early thirst for spiritual truth, with her
exposure to secular social analyses through her brother
Albert, with the insights gleaned from homeopathy and
hydropathy, with the mentorship of Phineas P. Quimby,
and with her own increasing skill as a mental healer. She
said:

> The physical side of this research was aided by hints
> from homeopathy, sustaining my final conclusion that
> mortal belief, instead of the drug, governed the action of
> material medicine. I wandered through the dim mazes of
> *materia medica*, till I was weary of "scientific guessing,"
> as it has been well called. I sought knowledge from the
> different schools,—allopathy, homeopathy, hydropathy,
> electricity, and from various humbugs,—but without re-
> ceiving satisfaction. I found, in the two hundred and
> sixty-two remedies enumerated by Jahr, one pervading
> secret; namely, that the less material medicine we have,
> and the more Mind, the better the work is done; a fact
> which seems to prove the Principle of Mind-healing.[6]

In a more crucial way she saw her discovery as a new
thing, a revealed insight so important and so radical that
the world must be made to understand and benefit.
Proper perception of the very nature of reality was at
stake. With right orientation would come healing. "The
mental virtues of the material methods of medicine,
when understood, were insufficient to satisfy my doubts
as to the honesty or utility of using a material curative,"
she said. "I must know more of the unmixed, unerring
source, in order to gain the Science of Mind, the All-in-
All of Spirit, in which matter is obsolete."[7] God—often
named by her seven deific synonyms Divine Principle,
Life, Truth, Love, Soul, Spirit, Mind—is the sole causation. God causes only good. Therefore sin, evil, disease,
death, and matter have no true or ultimate causation
and no real existence. They exist only as errors in perception. In the face of Truth their claim to being dissolves
as a mathematical error goes out of existence when the

correct answer is discovered or as darkness disappears when the light floods in.

However sin, evil, disease, death, and matter have a terrible reality for all who are their captives. So it is necessary to refer to these things as part of the confrontation of error. Because of the awful grip of error it is appropriate to speak of deliverance as salvation, regeneration, conversion, or redemption. The infection of error is so deeply rooted that it is also a proper formulation to say that the death and resurrection of Jesus were indispensable for the salvation of mankind.

Jesus is victor over sin and death, the necessary mediator or way-shower demonstrating both the supremacy of good over evil and the superiority of Spirit over matter. Thus the new discovery, claiming recovery of the original meaning and intent of the Bible and avowedly Christian, expresses many of its insights in Christian terminology understood in non-traditional ways. Christian perfection, for example, is not a condition gained through a second blessing of sanctification or through a perfecting of the believer at death. It is rather the God-created condition of everyone, a condition only recognized when sin is progressively put off. God's creation is spiritual and perfect now, though this perfection is obscured from human view by a false material understanding of existence.[8]

Development of Christian Science

Healing was always very important to Christian Science. Healing was a concern of the discoverer. Students of Christian Science were to be healed and to heal. Most initial converts to Christian Science came because of healing. Beginning with the 226th edition in 1902, the last section of 100 pages in *Science and Health* was entitled "Fruitage," a compilation of testimonies of healing resulting from reading and study of this Christian Science textbook. At least 50,000 testimonies of healing have been published in Christian Science literature and many thousands more given in the churches and societies on Wednesday evenings.

But the discoverer and her followers made clear that healing is not the most important part of Christian Science. "Healing physical sickness is the smallest part of Christian Science," said Mary Baker Eddy. "It is only the bugle-call to thought and action, in the higher range of infinite goodness. The emphatic purpose of Christian Science is the healing of sin; and this task, sometimes, may be harder than the cure of disease; because, while mortals love to sin, they do not love to be sick."[9] Christian Science healing involves prayer, concentration, and sys-

tematic affirmation of truth along with denial of error. However Christian Science is not primarily a technique for healing but a way of life. Redemption is not only from sickness but also from error, sin, death, and domination by material standards. Demonstration of such a way of life is never easy. It requires a discipline that is fitly called "taking up the cross."[10]

After her healing and discovery in 1866, Mary studied.

> For three years after my discovery, I sought the solution of this problem of Mind-healing, searched the Scriptures and read little else, kept aloof from society, and devoted time and energies to discovering a positive rule. The search was sweet, calm, and buoyant with hope, not selfish nor depressing. I knew the Principle of all harmonious Mind-action to be God, and that cures were produced in primitive Christian healing by holy, uplifting faith; but I must know the Science of this healing, and I won my way to absolute conclusions through divine revelation, reason, and demonstration. The revelation of Truth in the understanding came to me gradually and apparently through divine power.[11]

"The Bible was my textbook," she said. Now she found her revealed Science in the Bible everywhere. She seemed to resolve early that she would not only employ the new truth as a preacher and healer herself but also expand her ministry by becoming a teacher of preachers and healers. Progress was necessarily slow. Her husband had left her and made little payment toward her support. Her place of residence shifted according to necessity, sometimes among hospitable Spiritualists. "Through four successive years," she said, "I healed, preached, and taught in a general way, refusing to take any pay for my services and living on a small annuity." Her reputation as a healer grew substantial. She had been a competent lecturer since her days with Phineas Quimby and now took a place both in public halls and in churches.[12]

She kept enlisting students until the small initial clusters developed into the Massachusetts Metaphysical College in Boston in 1881. Six of her students joined her in forming a Christian Scientist Association in 1876. In 1879 the association organized the Church of Christ, Scientist, "a church designed to commemorate the word and works of our Master, which should reinstate primitive Christianity and its lost element of healing." Called to be its pastor was Mary Baker Eddy, since 1 January 1877 married to Asa Gilbert Eddy, charter member of the Christian Science Association and the first of her students to establish himself in public practice as "Christian Scientist." Boston became the center of operation after her location there in 1882.[13]

Science and Health with Key to the Scriptures

All the while she had been writing. She wrote commentary on Genesis. She did several versions of "The Science of Man," a work partly in question and answer form used as a textbook in her classes and as a means to develop her own thought. "From 1866 to 1875, I myself was learning Christian Science step by step," she said, "gradually developing the wonderful germ I had discovered as an honest investigator. It was practical evolution. I was reaching by experience and demonstration the scientific proof, and scientific statement, of what I had already discovered. My later teachings and writings show the steady growth of my spiritual ideal during those pregnant years." On 30 October 1875 came the first edition of *Science and Health with Key to the Scriptures*, the work which embodied the fullest expression of her insights to that date and the one she called her "best witness."[14]

Within a decade of the publication of *Science and Health*, Christian Science had become highly visible in Boston. In 1885 Mrs. Eddy was invited to speak for ten minutes in defense of Christian Science before a select audience of about 3,000 at the Monday Noon Lecture at Tremont Temple. By the end of the century she needed to rent that same large hall for the annual meeting of The Mother Church in Boston, by then grown in membership to 17,000. Nor were Boston and New England the limits. Students from Mrs. Eddy's Massachusetts Metaphysical College (chartered 1881) and issues of her *Journal of Christian Science* (established 1883) were impacting the land. She taught a class in Chicago in 1884. By 1885 Christian Science was reaching to Colorado and to California. There were about 100 congregations by the end of the decade; there were over 4,000 professional practitioners by 1910. The national census reported 7 Christian Science church buildings in 1890, 253 in 1906, and 1,206 in 1926. Membership in 1936 had reached 268,915, 95 percent urban and 31 percent male. Mrs. Eddy could hardly be called a feminist but she spoke out for equality of the sexes everywhere and became a notable feminine role model.[15]

New Consolidation Centered in the Mother Church in Boston

In 1889 Mrs. Eddy had moved from Boston to Concord, New Hampshire. In June of 1892, at age seventy, she settled there at her estate called Pleasant View. Following a defection of students and followers in 1888 she had disbanded the Christian Science Association, closed her flourishing Massachusetts Metaphysical College, disorganized the original Church of Christ, Scientist, and temporarily inactivated the National Christian Science Association of class-taught practitioners. This was by no means a withdrawal from her role as discoverer, founder, and leader of Christian Science. It was a consolidation and a fresh start. She completed an extensive reworking of *Science and Health* in 1890, the fifth of seven major revisions. In the course of the 1890s she reestablished the whole church enterprise on a new organizational basis.

In every way central was The First Church of Christ, Scientist, in Boston. It was organized in 1892, known as The Mother Church, and soon housed in a very impressive structure. *The Manual of the Mother Church*, its governing law published in 1895 and honed through eighty-nine editions before her death in 1910, was at the same time the constitution for all Christian Science branch churches and members. In 1898 Mrs. Eddy established the major administrative agencies of The Mother Church which were to perpetuate a pure form of her church and teaching with the seal of her authority. Publications now added to the monthly *Christian Science Journal* were the weekly *Christian Science Sentinel* in 1898 and the *Christian Science Quarterly* with the assigned Lesson-Sermons for all Sunday services in 1899. On 8 August 1908, recently relocated in Boston and now age eighty-seven, Mrs. Eddy instructed the Board of Trustees of The Mother Church to produce a daily newspaper constructively reporting and sharing the social concerns of the world and to have it on the newsstands by Thanksgiving. First issue of the *Christian Science Monitor* appeared on November 25.[16]

Criticisms and Responses

Spectacular success brought critics. Magazines played to the popular fascination with Mrs. Eddy and the success of this belief so different from common sense perception. H. L. Mencken made comments in the *Bulletin of the Freethinkers of America*. There were hostile articles in the *New York World* and in *McClure's Magazine* in 1906. Mark Twain, always uneasy with his own religious identity, gave Christian Science his full and biting attention. He had done an article on the subject in *Cosmopolitan* in October of 1899 and a series of four articles in *North American Review* beginning in December of 1902. This material was included in his book *Christian Science*, published at the height of muckraking attacks on Christian Science in 1907 and issued in at least six editions.[17]

Mrs. Eddy was a fitting foil for the mercurial Twain: a woman quite at ease and secure in her religious discovery; a woman who had built and now directed a large and stable enterprise; a woman who demonstrated precious little of the craft of writing but rivaled the craftsman and bookman Twain by selling her books by multiplied thousands at what he reckoned extravagantly to be a profit of 700 percent. Sometimes he seemed almost respectful, calling her "in several ways . . . the most interesting woman that ever lived, and the most extraordinary." He wrote:

> It is apparent, then, that in Christian Science it is not one man's mind acting upon another man's mind that heals; that it is solely the Spirit of God that heals; that the healer's mind performs no office but to convey that force to the patient; that it is merely the wire which carries the electric fluid, so to speak, and delivers the message. Therefore, if these things be true, mental-healing and Science-healing are separate and distinct processes, and no kinship exists between them . . . But there is a mightier benefaction than the healing of the body, and that is the healing of the spirit—which is Christian Science's other claim. So far as I know, so far as I can find out, it makes it good. Personally I have not known a Scientist who did not seem serene, contented, unharassed. I have not found an outsider whose observation of Scientists furnished him with a view that differed from my own.[18]

"With her own untaught and untrained mind, and without outside help," Twain said, "she has erected upon a firm and lasting foundation the most minutely perfect, and wonderful, and smoothly and exactly working, and best safe-guarded system of government that has yet been devised in the world, as I believe."[19]

Off the record Twain spoke of "that shameless old swindler, Mother Eddy."[20] When she was eighty-nine and soon to enter the last year of her life, he replied to a Scottish correspondent:

> My view of the matter has not changed. To-wit, that Christian Science is valuable; that it has just the same value now that it had when Mrs. Eddy stole it from Quimby; that its healing principle (its most valuable asset) possesses the same force now that it possessed a million years before Quimby was born; that Mrs. Eddy the fraud, the humbug, organized that force and is entitled to high credit for that. Then with a splendid sagacity she hitched it to the shirt-tail of a religion—the surest of all ways to secure friends for it, and support. In a fine and lofty way—figuratively speaking—it was a tramp stealing a ride on the lightning express. Ah, how did that ignorant village-born peasant woman know the human ass so well? She has no more intellect than a tadpole—until it comes to business—then she is a marvel![21]

Jews said Christian Science was incompatible with Judaism because it was Christian. But Christian clergymen everywhere took up the inevitable play on words to insist that Christian Science was neither Christian nor scientific.[22] That is also the way John Harvey Kellogg of Battle Creek Sanitarium put it in his book on neurasthenia. Contemporary idealists Bronson Alcott, Ralph Waldo Emerson, and Borden Parker Bowne took care to distance themselves from Christian Science. H. Richard Niebuhr gave his own sharply negative opinion in his *Social Sources of Denominationalism*. Massachusetts and some other states introduced bills requiring that Christian Science practitioners pass the same examinations as doctors of medicine. Such bills generally failed because they infringed upon free practice of religion.[23]

Mrs. Eddy was not easily put down by critics. She replied to a few, a response to *McClure's*, for example, and one to Mark Twain to make plain that she was not personally an object of worship or adulation. She provided some answers to critics in her messages to the church on special occasions and in her *No and Yes* published in various editions after 1887. In the structure of The Mother Church she provided the office and branches of a Committee on Publication to disseminate truth about Christian Science and to challenge errors or misrepresentations wherever they appeared. Ultimately her followers and defenders took their stand on a sentence in her reply to Mark Twain: "What I am remains to be proved by the good I do."[24]

Equally disquieting were critics and dissenters within the movement. The fortuitous move of Mrs. Eddy to Boston in 1882 was occasioned at least in part by defection of eight of her students at Lynn in 1881. Her students were interested in becoming healing practitioners. Many were less interested in Christian Science as a radical recovery of the true nature of reality and as a whole redeeming way of life. When they could claim to heal and could develop a following, many chose to become her competitors. They took with them whatever of the technique and name and clientele of Christian Science they found useful.[25]

When Mrs. Eddy spoke before the 3,000 at Tremont Temple in 1885, she used about a third of her precious ten minutes to distinguish between Christian Science and the host of Boston's mental healers. When people confused her teaching with Spiritualism, New Thought, Unity, eastern mysticism, occultism, or any proponents of mind cure, she was at pains to correct them. And advocates of these beliefs within her organization could expect discipline even at the cost of schism. In the course of her career she had to distinguish her position from that of Phineas P. Quimby, Edward Arens, Emma Curtis Hopkins, Amanda Rice, Luther Marston, Ursula Gestefeld, Augusta Stetson, Julius Dresser, and Warren Felt Evans. Her kind of healing was not to be by thought control or by faith alone but by a combination of faith with an exciting new understanding. Demonstration of the power of human mind over matter was not her concern. Her discovery was such a preeminence of Divine Mind that both human mind and matter were as nothing.[26]

Christian Science Practice

The *Manual of the Mother Church* defines the marks of Christian Scientists. This constitution is brief but incisive in its detail, centering great authority in the Christian Science Board of Directors at The Mother Church. However, on a federal model, each local "branch church" is to be free to operate its own democratic government under and within the constitutional limits of the *Manual*. A society cannot be admitted as a branch with less than sixteen members, at least four of whom are also members of The Mother Church, and one approved practitioner whose listing appears in the *Christian Science Journal*. Practitioners who advertise must give ample time to that ministry and may be expected to charge fees sufficient to provide the practitioner a living. No church building is to be dedicated until it is paid for. Most Christian Scientists are members both of The Mother Church and of a local branch or society. There are no pastors in the traditional sense. The *Manual* states: "I, Mary Baker Eddy, ordain the Bible, and Science and Health with Key to the Scriptures, Pastor over The Mother Church,—The First Church of Christ, Scientist, in Boston, Mass.,—and they will continue to preach for this Church and the world."[27]

In the established order for a Sunday service at any branch, readers present designated selections from the Bible and from *Science and Health* as the prescribed Lesson-Sermon.[28] Readers do not preach. Hymn singing and prayer are parts of every service. There are no sacraments in the traditional sense. The order for the semiannual "communion service" adds to the regular service a reading of the "Tenets of The Mother Church," a brief period of kneeling in silent communion concluded by audible repetition of the Lord's Prayer, and the singing

of a version of the Doxology. The Wednesday night service order is also prescribed but becomes more personal and informal by inclusion of "experiences, testimonies, and remarks on Christian Science," typically thanksgiving for victories and healings. Reading rooms, usually outside the churches, are hospitable places of information and study for both members and non-members. Approved teachers and lecturers may be invited and sponsored as the *Manual* provides.[29]

Christian Science Pioneers in Indiana

Christian Science came to Indiana quite early. Some Hoosiers were won to the faith in the very decade in which Mrs. Eddy moved from Lynn to Boston. In most cases the initial conversions came as a result of healing. Anna B. Dorland and several other residents of Indianapolis were healed under the ministrations of Silas Sawyer of Milwaukee, a student of Mrs. Eddy. At their invitation Sawyer came to Indianapolis in 1885 to conduct classes. Sawyer's students formed the nucleus of First Church of Christ, Scientist, chartered in 1889. Mrs. Dorland herself went to study with Mrs. Eddy, becoming a teacher and practitioner of Christian Science in Indianapolis. Second Church was formed in 1903, using a series of meeting places to accommodate rapid growth. Jacob Piatt Dunn said of Second Church in his *Greater Indianapolis* (1910): "The membership of this church is about 400, but the average attendance is twice that number."[30]

George Prescott of Terre Haute was healed of a stomach condition in 1895 through Mrs. Dorland's help. The Prescotts began holding services at their home which led to organization of a society in 1898 and a church in 1902. Miss M. Elizabeth Wright of Terre Haute was healed in 1896. She resigned her position in the local public schools in order to devote full time to the study of Christian Science and the work of healing. She wrote "I was so filled with awe at this manifestation of God's power that I consecrated my life to God's work at that time and gave up everything I knew how to give up."[31]

A New Englander named Josephine Tyter moved to Richmond in 1887, studied with Mrs. Eddy the next year, and set up an office as a Christian Science practitioner and teacher. Anna Gartline, blind and confined to bed for eight years, was reported healed there and Richmond church was organized in 1896. The daughter of Clarence A. Buskirk was healed at Princeton. Buskirk was a lawyer, judge, state legislator, and state attorney-general.[32] He became a Christian Science practitioner and lecturer.

When my attention was first called to Christian Science, about eight years ago, I was prejudiced against it. But the restoration to health at that time of a member of my own household through its ministration, induced me to try to learn whether its teachings were true or false. Three able allopathic physicians had signally failed in the case, and Christian Science had succeeded. But this did not convince me. For myself and for my family I wished to feel very sure that I was not leaning upon a rotten staff. So far as I have been able to do so, I have studied the subject from the viewpoint of its religious claims, its philosophy or metaphysics, its influences over human conduct and character, and its merits as a curative agency in the various ailments which are manifested in the body. I cannot ask space, of course, even to outline my studies and observations along those lines, but I wish to render my testimony in behalf of the cause of truth. I wish to testify that I recognize in Christian Science the religion taught by Jesus of Nazareth, freed from the barnacles which have been fastening upon it during its voyage through nineteen centuries in the form of man-made creeds, dogmas, and theological subtleties and blasphemies.[33]

In Evansville the earliest services were organized in 1901 by a local public school teacher who had witnessed the healing of her brother in another city.

A resident of South Bend was healed of typhoid fever through the help of a practitioner from Chicago in 1887. A copy of *Science and Health* in the library of the South Bend Woman's Literary Club sparked a study class which developed into a Christian Science service early in 1898. Under the energetic leadership of Mr. and Mrs. Bradford Dickson, "class-taught and experienced practitioners" just arrived from Kansas City, the group incorporated in August of that year. Judge Clarence A. Buskirk became a leading member at South Bend; members of the Studebaker family contributed toward church construction.[34]

A report from Logansport in 1895 said there were nineteen students of *Science and Health* in that city. Ora B. Shaver moved to Fort Wayne in May of 1890, a "class-taught" Christian Scientist and the city's first subscriber to the *Christian Science Journal*. Another Christian Science family arrived at Fort Wayne in 1892 from Springfield, Illinois. This was the nucleus for the regular gatherings at Miss Shaver's house for the Christian Science readings, at that time using subjects coordinated with the International Sunday School Lessons. "Class-taught" Isaac and Louise Woods moved to Fort Wayne from Chicago in 1896, accommodated the meetings in their home, and became the first Christian Science practitioners from Fort Wayne to have an official listing in the *Christian Science Journal*. The growing group incorporated in 1898 but re-

ported the typical pattern of more persons interested in healing than in the disciplines of full membership. During the period 1890–1898, the *Christian Science Journal* listed Indiana teachers and practitioners at Indianapolis, Rolling Prairie, LaPorte, Lafayette, Richmond, Pendleton, Terre Haute, Elkhart, Greenfield, North Manchester, Marion, and Economy.[35]

Indiana Critics

There were Hoosier voices among the opposition. Clarence A. Buskirk cited abuses of Christian Science in the state's newspapers:

Why are Christian Scientists thus traduced, their doctrine misrepresented and ridiculed, and popular prejudice sought to be inflamed against them? Why are our Indiana newspapers plied with fake specials against them? Thoughtful persons may well ask whether some business interest or frightened profession is behind this nefarious work. And when the Christian Scientists are threatened with the courts of Indiana, and the legislature is asked to enact laws which overturn the most sacred principles of religious and personal liberty which are guaranteed to the humblest citizen of Indiana by our Constitution, no matter what his religion may be, the inquiry as to the motive behind it all becomes strenuous.[36]

When Mrs. Eddy died in 1910, Rationalist David W. Sanders of Covington was hardly respectful.

Thousands of Christian Scientists in America and Europe aver that they have been cured of all sorts of backaches, earaches, toothaches, broken legs, asthma, gluttonous appetites and various defects of body and character—and all by faith. The claim is made that Christian Science has cured Christians and others of the habit of gossip about one's neighbors, of the habit of being irritable and peevish, of the habit of smoking, spitting, coughing or sniffling in public; cured men of coming into the house with muddy boots. It is even claimed that it has cured many of the wicked habit of being sick, and of grieving over the death of friends.[37]

Sanders noted that Mrs. Eddy's final days, unlike those of many religious founders, were not marked by violence or poverty. In fact, he said, the new church built in Boston with her disciples' money cost a little more than the Indiana State Capitol. He expected Christian Science to quickly undermine the institutions of both Protestantism and Roman Catholicism and so "help humanity far along on its way to the 'Reign of Reason.'" Judge George Louttit published his novel *The Eddyite* through the Colonial Press in his home town of Fort Wayne. In Louttit's story, association with Christian Science plunged the protagonist David Korsan into a fearful degradation comparable to that of Simon Slade in the famous temperance novel *Ten Nights in a Bar-Room, and What I Saw There*.[38]

Not many people read Sanders or Louttit. Edward Eggleston was more dangerous. This native Hoosier, since the success of his *Hoosier Schoolmaster* in 1871 a New York editor and fiction writer of international reputation, issued *The Faith Doctor* in 1891. It was published serially in *Century Magazine* and then in book form in both New York and London that year. In his preface Eggleston apologized a bit for his hard treatment of Christian Science but claimed to be "treating the subject with fidelity and artistic truthfulness." In fact he seemed to be competing to create the most thoroughly unsavory character in literature. The practitioner Eleanor Arabella Bowyer was an insufferable opportunist and a charlatan. Neither she nor the jumbled teaching Eggleston put into her mouth could have found any welcome among the troops of Mrs. Eddy. Yet in the story Bowyer claimed that she was a Christian Scientist. And Eggleston the storyteller was content to ridicule his own ridiculous caricature. The first American edition of *The Faith Doctor* was exhausted on the day of publication. There were at least five more editions. The body of the novel was an attractive love story which assured wide circulation through lending libraries. Thousands who never saw a Christian Scientist got their negative impression in this dramatic form.[39]

In Indiana, as in the nation, Christian Science grew most impressively in its early years. In 1900 there were fifteen churches in the state. In 1926 there were eighty. The *Manual* states "Christian Scientists shall not report for publication the number of members of The Mother Church, nor that of the branch churches. According to the Scripture they shall turn away from personality and numbering the people." In view of this instruction, no count of Indiana members has been published since the census report of 6,737 for 1936. Forty-eight churches were reported in the state in 1990. Any traveler consulting the *Christian Science Journal* for a place of Christian Science worship in summer of 1991 would have noted that continuing Hoosier congregations were mostly in urban places: Anderson, Auburn, Bloomington, Boonville, Brazil, Carmel, Chesterton, Columbus, Connersville, Crown Point, Elkhart, Evansville, Fort Wayne, Goshen, Hammond, Huntington, Indianapolis (6 churches), Kendallville, Kokomo, LaPorte, Lebanon, Logansport, Madison, Marion, Michigan City, Mishawaka, Muncie, Nashville, New Albany, Peru, Plymouth, Princeton, Richmond, Rockville, Shelbyville, South Bend, Terre Haute, Valparaiso, Vincennes, Warsaw, West Lafayette. All but five of these offered Wednesday services as well. Twenty-nine practitioners and teachers listed Indiana addresses.[40]

NOTES

1. Mary Baker Eddy, *Retrospection and Introspection* (Boston: Allison V. Stewart, 1915), 6–7, 10, 13–15; Robert Peel, *Mary Baker Eddy: The Years of Discovery* (New York: Holt, Rinehart and Winston, 1966), 8–9, 27–28, 44–47, 50–51; Thomas C. Johnsen, "Christian Science and the Puritan Tradition" (Ph.D. diss., Johns Hopkins University, 1983, 366 p.).

2. Eddy, *Retrospection*, 6–7, 19–21; Peel, *Discovery*, 30–31, 116–19, 294.

3. Mary Baker Eddy, *Science and Health with Key to the Scriptures* (Boston: The First Church of Christ, Scientist, 1934), 151–56; Eddy, *Retrospection*, 33–34; Peel, *Discovery*, 135–39.

4. Stephen Gottschalk, *The Emergence of Christian Science in American Religious Life* (Berkeley, Calif.: University of California Press, 1978), 104–9; Peel, *Discovery*, 136, 146–92, 294.

5. Peel, *Discovery*, 188, 195–98; Gottschalk, *Emergence*, 31–34; Eddy, *Retrospection*, 24.

6. Eddy, *Retrospection*, 33.

7. Eddy, *Retrospection*, 33–34.

8. *Ecumenical Papers: Contributions to Interfaith Dialogue* (Boston: Christian Science Publishing Company, 1969, 44 p.); Eddy, *Science and Health*, 332–34; Eddy, *Retrospection*, 26; Gottschalk, *Emergence*, xxi–xxiii, 46–97, 219–21, 283–84, 287.

9. Mary Baker Eddy, *Rudimental Divine Science* (Boston: Allison V. Stewart, 1915), 2–3.

10. Mary Baker Eddy, *Manual of the Mother Church, The First Church of Christ, Scientist, in Boston, Massachusetts*, 87th ed. (Boston: Allison V. Stewart, 1910), 92; Robert Peel, *Mary Baker Eddy: The Years of Authority* (New York: Holt, Rinehart and Winston, 1977), 190, 440; Gottschalk, *Emergence*, 222–40, 250, 292.

11. Eddy, *Science and Health*, 109.

12. *Christian Science: A Century Later* (Boston: Christian Science Publishing Society, 1982), 18; Eddy, *Retrospection*, 15, 24–29, 40; Peel, *Discovery*, 202, 211–12.

13. Robert Peel, *Mary Baker Eddy: The Years of Trial* (New York: Holt, Rinehart and Winston, 1971), 6–11, 63; Eddy, *Retrospection*, 42–44; Eddy, *Manual*, 17–18; Gottschalk, *Emergence*, xvi.

14. Peel, *Discovery*, 230–36, 291.

15. Penny Hansen, *Woman's Hour: Feminist Implications of Mary Baker Eddy's Christian Science Movement, 1885–1910* (Ann Arbor, Mich.: University Microfilms International, 1989, 465 p.); Gottschalk, *Emergence*, xvi–xvii, 244.

16. Eddy, *Retrospection*, 43–45; Eddy, *Manual*, 17–19; Peel, *Authority*, 3, 9, 37, 307–14; Gottschalk, *Emergence*, 175, 184, 192, 259, 272–74.

17. Raymond J. Cunningham, "The Impact of Christian Science on the American Churches, 1880–1910," *American Historical Review* 72 (April 1967): 885–905; *Christian Science Controversial and Polemical Pamphlets*, edited with an introduction by Gary L. Ward (New York: Garland Publishing, 1990), iii–ix; Mark Twain, *Christian Science: With Notes Containing Corrections to Date* (New

York: Harper and Brothers, 1907, 362 p.); Peel, *Authority*, 202, 260–81; Gottschalk, *Emergence*, 66, 197–215, 245–46.

18. Twain, *Christian Science*, 267–68.

19. Twain, *Christian Science*, 102, 255–58.

20. Peel, *Authority*, 198, 446.

21. Mark Twain, *The Portable Mark Twain*, ed. Bernard DeVoto (New York: Viking Press, 1946), 789.

22. This was neatly balanced in Mrs. Eddy's comment on Science and the senses: "Natural science, as it is commonly called, is not really natural nor scientific, because it is deduced from the evidence of the material senses." She called her own discovery scientific because she saw it to be so consistently demonstrated and proved in practice. Eddy, *Science and Health*, 274.

23. John Harvey Kellogg, *Neurasthenia or Nervous Exhaustion, with Chapters on Christian Science and Hypnotism, 'Habits' and 'the Blues'* (Battle Creek, Mich.: Good Health Publishing Company, 1915), 151; Helmut Richard Niebuhr, *The Social Sources of Denominationalism* (New York: H. Holt and Company, 1929), 104–5; Gottschalk, *Emergence*, 79–80, 247–48.

24. Mary Baker Eddy, *The First Church of Christ, Scientist, and Miscellany* (Boston: Trustees under the Will of Mary Baker G. Eddy, 1913), 299–316; Mary Baker Eddy, *No and Yes* (Boston: Allison V. Stewart, 1915, 46 p.); Gottschalk, *Emergence*, xiii, 190; Twain, *Christian Science*, 333.

25. J. Gordon Melton, *The Encyclopedia of American Religions* (Detroit, Mich.: Gale Research, 1989), 105–12, 616; *Christian Science Controversial and Polemic Pamphlets*, iii–ix; Gottschalk, *Emergence*, 98–157; Peel, *Trial*, 95–101.

26. Gottschalk, *Emergence*, xxiii, 18, 71–72, 99, 103–5, 111–24, 126–57; Eddy, *Science and Health*, 468.

27. Eddy, *Manual*, 58, 73–74, 82.

28. Each of twenty-six subjects is developed afresh twice a year. The subjects are God; Sacrament; Life; Truth; Love; Spirit; Soul; Mind; Christ Jesus; Man; Substance; Matter; Reality; Unreality; Are Sin, Disease and Death Real; Doctrine of Atonement; Probation after Death; Everlasting Punishment; Adam and Fallen Man; Mortals and Immortals; Soul and Body; Ancient and Modern Necromancy, *alias* Mesmerism and Hypnotism Denounced; God the Only Cause and Creator; God the Preserver of Man; Is the Universe, Including Man, Evolved by Atomic Force, Christian Science.

29. Eddy, *Manual*, 83–96, 122, 125–26; Gottschalk, *Emergence*, 191, 193.

30. Unless otherwise documented, information on particular Indiana churches is from the office of the Manager of the Committees on Publication, The First Church of Christ, Scientist, in Boston, Massachusetts, received with a letter of Nathan A. Talbot dated 4 June 1984. See also Jacob Piatt Dunn, *Greater Indianapolis*, 2 vols. (Chicago: Lewis Publishing Company, 1910), 1:623, 625. Dunn provides dates of 1889 for class beginning and 1897 for incorporation at Indianapolis.

31. "Dedication," First Church of Christ, Scientist, Terre Haute, 11 September 1983, no page cited.

32. *A Biographical History of Eminent and Self-Made Men of the State of Indiana* (Cincinnati, Ohio: Western Biographical Company, 1880), District 7, 13.

33. Extracted undated from Evansville *Journal* in *Christian Science Sentinel* 5 (4 April 1903): 487.

34. "Seventy-Fifth Anniversary: South Bend's Church of Christ, Scientist," by Tom Kelsch, *Tribune* Staff Writer, [1973]. The level of training of these early "class-taught" leaders is not clear. Mrs. Eddy said that only those holding certificates from the Normal Course of the Massachusetts Metaphysical College could be considered legitimate Christian Science teachers. This was a level hard to maintain, especially after that college was closed in October of 1889. Independent teachers and their institutes were at work. Teaching was defined and regularized after the Board of Education was created in 1898. See Gottschalk, *Emergence*, 188.

35. *A Brief History of First Church of Christ, Scientist, Fort Wayne, Indiana*, prepared for the Religious Heritage Committee of the Fort Wayne Bicentennial Commission, 1976, 4; Hansen, *Woman's Hour*, 320.

36. Extracted undated from Indianapolis *Journal* in *Christian Science Sentinel* 4 (3 October 1901): 67.

37. David W. Sanders, *The Light of Reason*, published under the auspices of the Indiana Rationalist Association, ed. David W. Sanders (Indianapolis, Ind.: Manual Publishing Co., 1912?), 124.

38. George W. Louttit, *The Eddyite: A Christian Science Tale* (Fort Wayne, Ind.: Colonial Press, 1908, 223 p.); Timothy S. Arthur, *Ten Nights in a Bar-Room and What I Saw There* (Boston: L. P. Crown, 1854, 240 p.). Louttit may well have known this *Ten Nights* novel since it sold at least 400,000 copies.

39. Edward Eggleston, *The Faith Doctor: A Story of New York* (New York: D. Appleton, 1891, 427 p.).

40. Eddy, *Manual*, 48; *Christian Science Journal* 109 (June 1991): 17, 52.

JEHOVAH'S WITNESSES

Charles Taze Russell was born 16 February 1852 in Allegheny County, Pennsylvania, the second son of Joseph and Ann Eliza Russell. The family was Presbyterian. His mother told the boy "It is my hope and prayer that in God's providence you may become a minister of the Gospel." His brief formal education was in common schools supplemented by private tutors. Natural aptitude and personal initiative were the real energizers of his education. He was precocious. In his early teens he became a partner in his father's clothing business, sharing fully in its prosperity as it developed into a chain of stores.[1]

Russell's religious goals were more elusive. His mother had died when he was nine. With the support of his father he invested his enthusiasm for the faith in the Congregational church and in the YMCA. He was a teacher and a superintendent in Sunday school. He considered a career in foreign missions. He was particularly concerned to save as many as possible from the eternal torment of hell. By his later teens he came uneasily to question how a God of justice and love could permit such a torment to be. Unable to enunciate and defend his beliefs against an "infidel," he simply gave up the Bible along with all creeds. He said "I fell easy prey to the logic of infidelity." Both he and his father abandoned their traditional faith and church. Charles studied some oriental religions and rejected each in turn. Of a crucial night in 1869 he later said: "Seemingly by accident, one evening I dropped into a dusty, dingy hall in Allegheny, Pa., where I had heard that religious services were held, to see

if the handful who met there had anything more sensible to offer than the creeds of the great churches. There, for the first time, I heard something of the views of Second Adventism, by Jonas Wendell."[2]

Russell now became an excited student of the Bible all over again, seeing the Scriptures as an inspired book very rich in both doctrinal truth and symbolic prophecy. Following adventist guidance he saw in the Bible no evidence that a human being had an immortal soul. With immense relief he concurred with the adventist conclusion that none of the biblical words translated "hell" in English versions conveyed a meaning of eternal torment. Thus God was doubly freed from any charge of condemning souls to a hell of torment either for Adam's sin or their own. God was indeed the fully just and loving One who provided the whole unworthy human race with ransom from death. Russell abhorred the idea of a hell of torment; he loved the teaching of ransom for all. That ransom provided by God in Jesus Christ guaranteed an occasion for all, when resurrected from death as all would be in the coming millennium, to choose life under God's laws or death as total annihilation.

These doctrines were lifted up in the new Bible class which Charles Russell formed with his father and a few friends in Pittsburgh in 1870. They also rejected the doctrine of the Trinity; Jesus Christ could be regarded as a primary creature by whom all else was made and the most highly placed divine agent but in no essential way one with God. They distinguished sharply between spiritual beings and human beings. Christ, God, and the angels were the spiritual beings. Their spiritual bodies were normally invisible unless they chose some temporary form of materialization. Human beings, on the other hand, were always and altogether of the earth and fleshly. Thus Russell concluded that the return of Jesus to the earth need not and indeed would not be visible to humans. Having these convictions and money from his business to advance them, he published 50,000 copies of a pamphlet entitled *The Object and Manner of Our Lord's Return*. Christ would return invisibly to resurrect the dead. This marked Russell's departure from most contemporary Adventists who expected Christ to return very visibly indeed.[3]

A Prophetic Chronology for the End

Many Adventists had grown wary of date setting since the Millerite crises of 1844. Russell himself resisted the building of chronologies at first. However, prophetic speculation, chronological computation, and eschatology generally became more and more compelling. Never so plainly at the heart of his early system as his doctrine of God or his theory of ransom, it was the chronological insight which came to motivate his ministry as he discerned a divine plan. In 1876 he read *Herald of the Morning*, a periodical published by adventist preacher Nelson H. Barbour of Rochester, New York. Barbour's group agreed with Russell's that the coming of Christ would be invisible. Based on extensive biblically based parallels and computations, Barbour and his associates concluded that an invisible "presence" of Christ had already come to earth in 1874 and so that the Lord's "harvest" had begun. Russell went over the prophecies with Barbour and agreed. Russell funded publication of Barbour's *Herald* for a time and supported Barbour's production of the book *Three Worlds and the Harvest of This World*.[4]

This book *Three Worlds* contained an interpretation based on Nebuchadnezzar's dream of a great tree in Daniel 4. The "seven times" in this vision were viewed as seven years of 360 prophetic days thus producing the number 2,520. That number of years added to 606 B.C., Barbour's dating of the destruction of Jerusalem by Nebuchadnezzar, would mark 1914 as a very significant year.[5] So in 1914 one might expect that Christ's kingdom would come to hold full sway over the earth, that the Jews would be restored to God's favor, and that the Gentile nations of the world would go down to destruction. The dates 1874 and 1914 were crucial for Russell for the rest of his days. The "harvest" period between 1874 and

1914 he took to be the theater of his life work. His confidence in this divine plan put to rest all his previous questioning.[6]

Russell as Apocalyptic Teacher, Writer, and Corporate Director

Russell called a meeting of all the ministers in Allegheny and Pittsburgh in 1877. He explained the Scriptures indicating the arrival of the Lord's presence in 1874 and the divine plan for the years just ahead. He invited them to repent of their errors and join him in preparing the people for the end of Gentile times in 1914. They did not respond. Russell then took his message directly to the members of the churches.

> Since 1878 (and never before that) we have felt at liberty to call God's children out of the nominal churches to a position of freedom and liberty, where they would be free to serve Him fully, as well as to study his word and be taught of Him: saying "Babylon . . . is fallen and become a habitation of devils and a hold of every foul spirit and a cage of every unclean and hateful bird." (This falling of the nominal church and receiving into her bosom the corruptions of earth has been in progress for some time.) Now comes the message: "And I heard another voice saying, Come out of her my people that ye be not partakers of her sins and receive not of her plagues" (Rev. xviii.2–4).[7]

Russell went about this evangelism with such energy and imagination that the results were striking. By 1900 he was providing specially printed "withdrawal letters" for his people to send to the traditional churches they were leaving. He multiplied classes of "Bible Students."[8] Government of the classes was entirely local and completely democratic but they were influenced by receiving identical study materials from Russell. Most of them elected him to be their pastor every year. Baptism by immersion was a valued symbol but Russell did not insist on baptism as a requirement for membership.[9]

Russell's chief agency for teaching and administration was his periodical which eventually became the *Watchtower*.[10] It was first issued in 6,000 copies in July of 1879 with the comment: "This is the first number of the first volume of 'Zion's Watch Tower,' and it may not be amiss to state the object of its publication. That we are living 'in the last days'—'the day of the Lord'—'the end' of the Gospel age, and consequently in the dawn of the 'new' age, are facts not only discernible by the close student of the Word, led by the spirit, but the outward signs recognizable by the world bear the same testimony, and we are desirous that the 'household of faith' be fully awake to the fact." During Russell's lifetime regular circulation rose to 55,000. As fuller insights kept providing answers to his theological questions, Russell wrote a series of six substantial volumes entitled *Studies in the Scriptures*.[11] These became primary material for study among Bible Student classes, considered an essential guide and key to the Scriptures. The first volume alone, *Divine Plan of the Ages* with its explanation of God's dealing with man from his creation six thousand years ago to a thousand years in the future, had been printed in 4,817,000 copies before Russell's death.[12]

When there were only thirty classes across Pennsylvania, New Jersey, New York, Massachusetts, Delaware, Ohio, and Michigan in 1880, Russell visited them himself, doing six hours of study in a day with each. But by 1884 there were far more invitations than he could answer personally. He developed a traveling corps of assistants called "pilgrims" who could visit classes, give public lectures, speak at conventions, and teach with whatever charts and aids they could marshal. The number of these varied from fourteen to eighty during Russell's life. Russell was so loved and respected that the body of classes led and personified by him was counted by its members as that "faithful and wise servant whom his lord hath made ruler over his household, to give them meat in due season" typified in Matthew 24:45.[13] Here was the God-given messenger gathering and leading those redeemed people who were preparing for the Lord's coming.[14]

Russell's visibility was by no means limited to his own flock. He poured tens of thousands of dollars of his money into publications. *Food for Thinking Christians* appeared in the *Tower* for September of 1881. It was also separately distributed in 1,200,000 copies at mass meetings, to subscription lists of big city newspapers, or as handouts at Protestant church doors. In London 500 boys helped distribute the 300,000 copies sent to Great Britain. Such special separate issues of the *Tower* came out almost every year. He established a regular distribution network. By the end of 1882 he was receiving between 500 and 600 letters per week.[15]

Activity intensified as 1914 approached. The Watch Tower Bible and Tract Society had formed a Pennsylvania corporation in 1884; it added a subservient corporation in New York in 1909 in order to hold property for a headquarters and staff home in Brooklyn. Some 600 colporteurs were out selling literature and preaching between 1911 and 1913; about 600,000 printed volumes and over 35 million tracts were being placed each year.

In the augmented effort Russell himself took on giant stature. He traveled by special railroad car, or even special train, to speak to thousands at series of conventions in major American cities. He liked to put down the traditional notion of eternal torment of the damned with his sermon entitled "To Hell and Back." He denounced all those unresponsive secular and ecclesiastical institutions, proclaiming that their days were now numbered. He announced God's plan and calendar as he discerned it. He went abroad ten times between 1891 and 1913; he circled the globe in 1912.[16]

Much of Russell's travel was arranged and supported by his international newspaper syndicate which built up the bearded "Pastor Russell" as a global celebrity. It distributed his sermons which he dispatched to them every week by telegraph. At one time over 2,000 newspapers published these sermons for a combined circulation of some 15 million readers. Russell believed the urgency of the message warranted even more. He captured the popular mind with a technical marvel far ahead of its time. The "Photo-Drama of Creation" was a complex combination of sound recordings, color slides, and moving pictures to tell the history of the world from creation to the coming millennial reign of Christ—an eight-hour production to be shown in four two-hour segments. It was expensive in time, being planned from 1910 and not ready for screening until 1914. The free showings were expensive in money; fourteen of the twenty sets had to be taken off the road at the end of the first year. Yet the public at home and abroad responded so well that some 12 million attended the showings. Local classes paid $262.50 for a simplified version with still pictures.[17]

The Bible Students were not taken home to heaven in fall of 1914 as many had expected. Russell simply announced to those gathered at the Brooklyn home for breakfast on Friday, 2 October, "The Gentile times have ended; their kings have had their day." He had earlier pointed out to the *Tower* readers that their consecration to service was not to be until some particular date which might have been miscalculated but "unto death." The ongoing destruction of nations in the First World War did seem an impressive prelude. Surely the end would be coming soon. Meanwhile Russell cautioned against indolence. "Never have so many people been ready to hear the good Message," he said. "In all the forty years of Harvest there have not been such opportunities to proclaim the Truth as now present themselves. The great war and the ominous signs of the times are waking people up, and many are now inquiring. So the Lord's people should be very diligent, doing with their might what their hands find to do." He led the way himself. Having operated the Watch Tower corporation for 32 years, traveled a million miles as a speaker, preached 30,000 sermons, written 50,000 pages, dictated 1,000 letters per month, and directed an evangelistic enterprise with as many as 700 speakers, he died aboard a train while on the lecture tour on 31 October 1916.[18]

Joseph F. Rutherford as President of "Jehovah's Witnesses"

The Bible Student fellowship became very unstable following the death of Charles Taze Russell. As many as 1,200 congregations had elected him year by year to be their pastor. So far as this represented an organization at all, it was a loose banding of independent units based on the personal influence of Russell and on loyalty to him. They were yoked with him especially in a mission to the world which was focused on 1914. Now both Russell and the crucial year were gone. There had been an actual decline in activity in 1915 and 1916. Preachers exhorted the hearers at Russell's funeral to press on with the great work but only the expectancy of an imminent end of the age would seem to provide motivation for that. Russell had arranged for an executive committee to continue the publications. The annual meeting of the Watch Tower Society stockholders on 6 January 1917 elected Joseph F. Rutherford to be the new corporation president. However the corporation at this time was in no sense a church. It was merely the fellowship's agency for conducting business. If there was to be a continuing organized church in any kind of succession to the gathered people around Russell, any "faithful and wise servant" to be God's agent to give his prepared people "meat in due season," that entity remained to be identified and described. For the next twenty-five years Joseph F. Rutherford was to shape a major segment of the Bible Student movement, to clarify and define its doctrines, and to be in the fullest sense its president.[19]

Joseph F. Rutherford was born 8 November 1869 in Morgan County, Missouri. His father espoused Baptist doctrine but Joseph resisted. His father also wanted him working on the farm but Joseph intended to be a lawyer. He had to raise money both to pay for his own education and to hire a replacement to do his labor on the farm. He mastered stenography, became a court reporter at age twenty, and was admitted to the bar at age twenty-two. During his fifteen years of service in Missouri he was a trial lawyer, a public prosecutor, and occasionally a special judge. Out of sympathy for people earning their way

by selling books as he had done, he bought three volumes of Charles Taze Russell's *Millennial Dawn* (after 1904 *Studies in the Scriptures*) from colporteur Elizabeth Hettenbaugh in 1894. He found the volumes convincing.

There was no organization of Bible Students at Boonville in Missouri but Rutherford pressed on to become a preacher of Russell's doctrines in 1905, a baptized member in 1906, and legal counselor at the Watch Tower headquarters in Pittsburgh in 1907. He was a primary negotiator in the move of the Society headquarters to Brooklyn, having been admitted to the New York bar that year and admitted to practice before the United States Supreme Court. He was quickly recognized as an extraordinarily able pilgrim for the Bible Students, lecturing and debating throughout America, Europe, and the Middle East. No obstacle seemed to daunt him. His selection as president of the legal business corporation must have seemed obvious. Step by step he disclosed how the Watch Tower corporation was one with the church and how its governing body, responding to the president's direction, was indeed the "faithful and wise servant" channeling the very instruction of God to his people.[20]

First he had to revitalize everything. He removed dissenters and organized the Brooklyn headquarters for efficiency. He got more pilgrims on the road for supervisory visits to the congregations; more colporteurs and pioneers doing professional evangelism with a new monthly *Bulletin* to instruct and inspire them; more congregation members distributing pamphlets on the streets in front of churches on Sundays and house to house; more systematic repeat calls on persons showing some interest in the teaching to involve them in classes and chart talks. He offered a questionnaire to all male members of the congregations. Its twenty-two questions searched each individual's personal religious maturity and his knowledge of the basic six volumes of Bible Student doctrine. All who submitted answers received "some kindly suggestions and hints" in reply. Those with an 85 percent rating on the questions were considered teachers qualified to give public talks and chart talks. The aim was to motivate study.[21]

Charles Taze Russell had long attacked the traditional churches and almost all secular institutions as instruments of Satan soon to receive the destruction they deserved. Joseph F. Rutherford, his conviction coupled with immense personal force and a blunt manner, now raised this polemical rhetoric even higher. "Religion is a snare and a racket" was a favorite cry. He made affront his specialty.[22]

Timing became troublesome. The United States entered the First World War on 6 April 1917 and was seeking cooperation of the traditional churches in a united patriotic effort. Congress passed the Selective Draft Act on 15 June. But on 17 July Rutherford began distribution of *The Finished Mystery*, volume seven of *Studies in the Scriptures*. Among its controversial passages was a paragraph which read: "Nowhere in the New Testament is Patriotism (a narrow-minded hatred of other peoples) encouraged. Everywhere and always murder in its every form is forbidden; and yet, under the guise of Patriotism the civil governments of earth demand of peace-loving men the sacrifice of themselves and their loved ones and the butchery of their fellows, and hail it as a duty demanded by the laws of heaven."[23]

In December of 1917 Rutherford's people were distributing 10 million copies of a fiery issue of the *Bible Students Monthly* entitled "The Fall of Babylon—Why Christendom Must Now Suffer—The Final Outcome." Graphic illustration showed the structures of Protestantism, Catholicism, finance, and government being thrown down as parts of Babylon's imminent fall. In spring of 1918 Rutherford was issuing *Kingdom News* insisting on religious tolerance for many of his Bible Students who were now plainly at odds with the national mood. At the same time he was keeping the millennial heat on his usual targets of financiers, governments, and traditional churches with his new lecture later to be entitled "Millions Now Living Will Never Die."[24]

The axe fell. Canada banned *The Finished Mystery*, the *Bible Students Monthly*, and the Watch Tower Society. On 8 May 1918 Rutherford and seven headquarters associates were served warrants by the United States District Court charged with

> the offense of unlawfully, feloniously and wilfully causing insubordination, disloyalty and refusal of duty in the military and naval forces of the United States of America when the United States was at war . . . by personal solicitations, letters, public speeches, distributing and publicly circulating throughout the United States of America a certain book called "Volume VII. Bible Studies. The Finished Mystery," and distributing and publicly circulating throughout the United States certain articles printed in pamphlets called "Bible Student's Monthly," "Watch Tower," "Kingdom News" and other pamphlets not named.[25]

With his effort at unifying and revitalizing the Bible Students still in its infancy, Rutherford was put on a train for Atlanta on the Fourth of July under sentence of eighty years in the penitentiary. Local prosecutions and mob ac-

tions broke out against Bible Students across the country. Brooklyn headquarters closed in summer of 1918. An executive committee of five did manage to continue publication of the *Watch Tower*.[26]

Then came the end of the war on 11 November 1918. A groundswell of public and judicial opinion favored release of Rutherford and his seven colleagues. Legal appeal by the Watch Tower Society on their behalf was allowed, bail was granted, and on 14 April 1919 their convictions were reversed. A year later all charges were dropped. Rutherford had been reelected to presidency of the corporation in January of 1918 while in prison. Now he was ready to rally the fellowship to whole new levels of energy and unity. His prison experience had hardly mellowed his resentment of the traditional wielders of the world's power. Against these he positioned himself as spokesman for God's power, God's plan, and God's oppressed people. Everywhere he saw the prophecies and types of Armageddon; his writing brimmed over with the violence of the coming conflict. He and the world which he condemned kept inciting each other in a contest of bitter language.[27]

In 1919 the restored Watch Tower headquarters at Brooklyn installed a giant rotary press which came to be known as the "Old Battleship." Almost every year there was a new book. At each major convention Rutherford would sound a blast in violent language against all political, commercial, and ecclesiastical entities with special attention to the League of Nations, Federal Council of Churches, Communism, Fascism, and Catholicism. These agencies of Satan were about to be done away. Then the thousands attending the convention would shout approval of a prepared resolution embodying the speech theme. The resolution with supporting matter would roll off the press for distribution in multiplied millions of copies. "Behold, the King reigns," he told the convention at Cedar Point, Ohio, in September of 1922. "You are his publicity agents. Therefore advertise, advertise, advertise, the King and his kingdom." Distribution of 45 million copies of the 1922 resolution began the following month.[28]

Rutherford did part of his advertising by radio. In the days of crystal sets with earphones, he broadcast his first radio address from Metropolitan Opera House in Philadelphia on 16 April 1922. It was one form of the speech he had been making since 1918 entitled "Millions Now Living Will Never Die."[29] Soon he was exposing apostate religion and announcing the millennium over the Society's own stations WBBR on Staten Island and WORD at Batavia, Illinois. Fifty-three stations were linked together in the "greatest hook-up of broadcasting on earth" for a live broadcast from the Sunday session of the convention of Bible Students in the Coliseum at Toronto in July of 1927.

On the air the 1927 resolution "To the Peoples of Christendom" was thunderously approved. Rutherford delivered the speech "Freedom for the Peoples" in support of the resolution, roundly condemning clergy, Christendom, kings, rulers, statesmen, financiers, and big business. The resolution concluded:

> It must now be apparent to all thoughtful peoples that relief, comfort and blessings so much desired by them can never come from the unrighteous system of "Christendom" or "organized Christianity," and that there is no reason to give further support to that hypocritical and oppressive system. In this hour of perplexity Jehovah God bids the peoples to abandon and for ever forsake "Christendom" or "organized Christianity" and turn completely away from it, because it is the Devil's organization, and to give it no support whatsoever . . . For four thousand years the cherished desire of Jews has been God's Messianic kingdom. For nineteen centuries that kingdom has been the hope of real Christians. It is now at hand. True to his promise God by and through the reign of Christ will lift up the burdens of the peoples, free them from war, fraud and oppression, from sickness, suffering and death, and give to them a righteous government and the blessings of everlasting peace, prosperity, life, and happiness.[30]

Later the use of fifteen-minute recorded transcriptions for radio allowed him more flexibility than live broadcasting. By 1933, the peak year, 408 radio stations broadcast 23,783 of Rutherford's talks to six continents on this "wax chain."[31]

Rutherford counted growth by evangelism to be the Society's chief work and he was a man known for getting that work done. Doctrines disclosed and clarified during the period of his leadership always had the effect of putting many more congregation members into the door-to-door visitation work called "preaching" or "publishing." He began a new magazine called *The Golden Age* in 1919. One special issue in 1920 was printed in 4 million copies. Besides his magazines, Rutherford published an average of one book per year, eventually totaling some 36 million copies. These publications were intended for distribution by class workers house to house. Definite field work territories were assigned to congregations in 1920. The full-time evangelists called colporteurs or pioneers had earlier been the ones to submit a weekly report of their service activity. Now, beginning in 1920, every congregation member engaged in witnessing was required to turn in such a weekly report of work done. Any congregation wishing to be a full participant in this lively new enterprise was expected to request the Brooklyn headquarters to appoint a congregational "director" who would be representative of headquarters on the local scene and in charge of local activities.[32]

The rising church structure got its new name in 1931. Rutherford presented the resolution at Columbus, Ohio: "That we have great love for Brother Charles T. Russell, for his work's sake, and that we gladly acknowledge that the Lord used him and greatly blessed his work, yet we cannot consistently with the Word of God consent to be called by the name 'Russellites.'" Nor were any of the former corporation or "Bible Student" names appropriate. The focus was on the text "Therefore ye are my witnesses, saith the Lord, that I am God" (Isaiah 43:12). The conclusion was: "We joyfully embrace and take the name which the mouth of the Lord has named, and we desire to be known as and be called by the name, to wit, Jehovah's witnesses." This resolution was acclaimed by all present and at fifty extension conventions within a few weeks. Coupled with another resolution titled "Warning from Jehovah" presented over 163 radio stations at the same 1931 convention, the new name resolution circulated in 5 million copies including 132,066 delivered personally by Witness visitors to clergy, politicians, and business leaders in the United States and Canada.[33]

In 1935 Rutherford clarified the chief target of the church's intensified activity. Evangelism was no longer so much a search for the 144,000 anointed ones of Revelation 14:1–3, the joint heirs of the heavenly life with Christ. The gathering of that number had been in progress since 1874 and the ranks of such a small body manifestly filled except for an occasional replacement if a saint should fail in the continuing judgment. But references had long been made among Witnesses to two other classes for salvation. There was the "great multitude which no man could number" of Revelation 7:9–15. And there were the "sheep" of Matthew 25:31–46 and John 10:16. These "sheep" were sometimes called "Jonadabs" because they were considered prefigured in the reception and recognition of Jonadab as a person of good will and moral character in II Kings 10:15 and in Jeremiah 35:8–19.

Rutherford demonstrated scripturally to the assembly of Jehovah's Witnesses in Washington, D.C., in June of 1935 that the "great multitude" was synonymous with the "other sheep" or "Jonadabs." Theirs was no expectation of heaven. Theirs was a good hope that by declaring allegiance to Jehovah, by persisting in seeking the divine will, and by faithfully performing whatever was given them to do they would survive the destruction of the final cosmic battle of Armageddon or be resurrected following that great day. They would live forever on the earth which would be restored to its primitive peace and productivity. This vast body of living persons must now be sought out, enlisted as Jehovah's people, and baptized.[34]

Enlistment of such a vast concourse of "other sheep" called for the ultimate missionary effort. More of the simple but attractive "Kingdom Halls" began appearing as centers for Witness worship, study, and evangelistic training. Central direction, already generally accepted, was brought to official completion. In 1938 three issues of the *Watchtower* pointed to New Testament evidence of the central direction exercised by the twelve apostles and other mature brothers at Jerusalem. In the same way the right government for Jehovah's Witnesses as God's organization was government by the voice of God from the top down. Said the *Watchtower,* "Jehovah's organization is in no wise democratic. Jehovah is supreme, and his government or organization is strictly theocratic."[35] All congregations were requested to act on a resolution similar to the resolutions already adopted and submitted by major congregations in London, New York, Chicago, and Los Angeles:

> We, the company of God's people taken out for his name, and now at ———, recognize that God's government is a pure theocracy and that Christ Jesus is at the temple and in full charge and control of the visible organization of Jehovah, as well as the invisible, and that "THE SOCIETY" is the visible representative of the Lord on earth, and we therefore request "The Society" to organize this company for service and to appoint the various servants thereof, so that all of us may work together in peace, righteousness, harmony and complete unity. We attach hereto a list of names of persons in this company that to us appear more fully mature and who therefore appear to be best suited to fill the respective positions designated for service.[36]

Jehovah's Witnesses generally agreed. Now they lived and worked in complete confidence. They were within God's own visible organization. They were receiving constant communication and direction from the publications of the Society, "the visible representative of the Lord on earth." The structure was plain. Each congregation or company had its company servant; each zone of twenty or so companies had its zone servant; zones were gathered into regions under regional servants; organizations at national level might be named branches. The govern-

ing body of the Society appointed and directed the leadership at all levels. Any member expecting approval of Jehovah or his society must be active in the preaching.[37] Powering it all was the immediacy of Armageddon. Rutherford put a whole new level of emphasis on Armageddon as the righteous outbreak of God against the whole blasphemous world, the ultimate vindication of his holy name. He said, "God provided that the death of Christ Jesus, his beloved son, should furnish the ransom or redemptive price for man; but that goodness and loving-kindness toward mankind is secondary to the vindication of Jehovah's name." All living persons must be called to choose. They must enlist with Jehovah, Christ, and the Theocracy or be destroyed with Satan and his system at the coming battle on God's great day.[38]

Opposition to Jehovah's Witnesses

The Witnesses met resistance. As Rutherford weeded out dissenters and brought the movement under discipline, the Society had thousands of motivated members to be put to work. They were selling magazine subscriptions door to door after 1938; in 1940 they began selling *Watchtower* and *Consolation* on the streets. After protests caused commercial radio stations to cancel their broadcasts of the transcription records of Rutherford's talks, the Witnesses found they could broadcast by using the same records in players with loud speakers mounted in public places or on sound trucks. Beginning in 1934 they equipped thousands of their preaching publishers with portable phonographs taken house to house to play four-and-one-half minutes of President Rutherford on such topics as "Satan's Organization," "Purgatory," "Exposed," "Religion and Christianity," or "The End."

These activists were not always welcome. Some Witnesses were arrested for disturbing the peace, or trespassing, or promoting religious hatred, or peddling without a license, or selling merchandise on Sunday. The Witnesses adjusted quite well to these simpler charges, using the courts ably on their own behalf. Some local congregations of Witnesses taught their members how to conduct themselves if arrested or threatened with arrest. They consistently maintained that what they were doing house to house was "preaching," an activity protected by constitutional rights. A telephone call from a Witness team under coercion or arrest might bring a subsequent visit by a substantial force of colleagues. The enlarged troop would sometimes canvass the whole resistant community in a door-to-door blitz of an hour or two, thus overloading the local apparatus of the law with a host of committed persons quite willing to suffer incarceration and trial. Witness attorneys were also on call. The Watch Tower Society headquarters might intervene to provide legal defense or to challenge laws which seemed to violate constitutional rights.[39]

Once more it was international conflict which brought real crisis. By 1934 the Society had branches in forty-nine countries. Rutherford had been sensitized by confrontations with Hitler's demands for extreme expressions of national loyalty. Wherever Witnesses in Germany would not comply, their meetings and literature were banned and they faced imprisonment. During a question and answer period at the convention at Washington, D.C., in June of 1935, somebody asked Rutherford about the flag salute used by children of many lands in their schools. He responded that it was unfaithfulness to God to salute an earthly emblem as if ascribing salvation to it and that he himself would not do it. On 20 September Carleton B. Nichols, son of a Witness family, declined to salute the American flag at school. During the ensuing publicity the Associated Press asked Rutherford for an official statement of Jehovah's Witness policy. He gave it in his own way—a radio address "Saluting a Flag" broadcast coast to coast on October 6 and embodied in a booklet entitled *Loyalty* distributed in millions of copies. He said Jehovah's Witnesses respected the flag but the teaching of the Bible and their relationship to Jehovah forbade their saluting any such image. And he said believing parents were obligated to teach their children this truth.[40]

Many local school boards, local officers of the law, and local mobs expressed the public rage in a decade of terrible persecution. There were hundreds of violent incidents across the nation. From 1933 to 1951 there were 18,866 arrests of American Witnesses and about 1,500 cases of mob violence against them. Witness parents in Pennsylvania brought suit to prevent expulsion of their children from public schools. The case was decided in their favor in two federal courts but lost by a margin of eight to one before the Supreme Court of the United States in June of 1940. There were instances of expulsion of Witness school children in forty-three of the forty-eight states. Some Witnesses felt compelled to organize private "Kingdom Schools" to provide education for their children.[41] The *1941 Yearbook* of Jehovah's Witnesses said:

> Jehovah's Witnesses have been assaulted, beaten, kidnaped, driven out of towns, counties and states, tarred and feathered, forced to drink castor oil, tied together and chased like dumb beasts through the streets, castrated and maimed, taunted and insulted by demonized crowds, jailed by the hundreds without charge and held

incommunicado and denied the privilege of conferring with relatives, friends or lawyers. Many other hundreds have been jailed and held in so-called "protective custody"; some have been shot in the nighttime; some threatened with hanging and beaten into unconsciousness. Numerous varieties of mob violence have occurred. Many have had their clothes torn from them, their Bibles and other literature seized and publicly burned; their automobiles, trailers, homes and assembly places wrecked and fired, resulting in damages totaling very many thousands of dollars. This demonized violence has completely possessed the people and officials in hundreds of communities of America, so that they have falsely charged Jehovah's Witnesses with sedition and like crimes of being "against the government." This character of persecution flared highest in Kentucky, Missouri and Indiana.[42]

All this was further aggravated as the United States approached the Second World War. Patriotism was expected. The Selective Training and Service Act went into effect in 1940. Jehovah's Witnesses generally would not seek classification in Class 4-E along with other conscientious objectors to military service. They said they were already enlisted in the service of Jehovah. All of them requested exemption in Class 4-D as ministers. Local draft boards trying to establish comparable status for all churches and church members had difficulty considering the unpaid officers of a small company of Witnesses as ministers and even more difficulty counting the door-to-door "publishing" of the congregation members as preaching.

Witness patterns of response to draft law were not established. When their exemption as ministers was denied, should they refuse to report when summoned for service? Should they report to the designated place but not step forward in line for the induction ceremony? Should they step forward but not take the oath? Should they fully enter the service but decline to obey military commands? Government attorneys and lower federal courts long contended that Witnesses must enter the armed forces before they had a basis for defending themselves in the courts. All routes could lead to prison, usually federal prison. About two-thirds of American conscientious objectors imprisoned during the Second World War were Jehovah's Witnesses.[43]

Those who responded with violence to the abrasive behavior of Jehovah's Witnesses were doomed to failure. The Witnesses thrived on abusive responses. They recorded their persecutions at length in their books and circulated them for mutual encouragement. They kept the legal channels full of their cases. They had help from some Protestant, Catholic, and Jewish defenders of

Witness rights. Appeals from lower courts eventually resulted in victory for the Witnesses in forty-three cases before the Supreme Court of the United States, some crucial ones being actual reversals of earlier decisions by that body. It became customary for writers in many disciplines to acknowledge Jehovah's Witnesses as special champions of civil and religious rights. Edward Waite stated in the *Minnesota Law Review* as early as 1944 that Jehovah's Witnesses had done more to guarantee basic freedoms than any other religious group in America. Charles S. Braden gave them credit for the same role: "They fight by every legal means for their civil rights, the right of public assembly—sometimes denied them—the right to distribute their literature, the right of conscience to put God above every other loyalty. They have performed a signal service to democracy by their fight to preserve their civil rights, for in their struggle they have done much to secure those rights for every minority group in America."[44]

Presidency of Nathan H. Knorr

On 8 January 1942, in the midst of the excitement of a great war, the old war-horse Joseph F. Rutherford died. His presidency of twenty-five years had consolidated the fellowship. No substantial body of dissenters remained within the Witnesses. No major body of doctrine needed to be defined. The place of the Watch Tower Society as Jehovah's faithful and wise servant was firmly established. As a later Witness historian said, "The theocratic organization proceeded without a halt or stumble." Five days after the death of Rutherford a joint meeting of board members of the Pennsylvania and New York corporations elected Vice-president Nathan Homer Knorr to the presidency. He became president of the International Bible Students Association as well and so, before his thirty-seventh birthday, the voice of the theocracy for the whole worldwide church.[45]

Knorr was the ultimate insider. At age sixteen he became associated with a congregation of Bible Students in his home town of Allentown, Pennsylvania. At age seventeen he attended Rutherford's convention at Cedar Point, Ohio, and decided to resign from membership in the Dutch Reformed Church. He worked as a colporteur for the Watch Tower Society. At age eighteen he was among those baptized by immersion in the Little Lehigh River by Frederick W. Franz from the headquarters at Brooklyn Bethel. About two months after his baptism he took up residence at Brooklyn Bethel where he stayed. There he became so valued for his work in production, publication, and administration that he was elected as a

director and then as vice-president of both corporations. Knorr was a disciple of Rutherford and a zealous supporter of his policies. He still continued the blasts against Christendom as false religion and against the clergy as "the most reprehensible class on earth today." He issued a booklet against the doctrine of the Trinity and sent a copy to all Protestant and Catholic clergy. He hammered the League of Nations and the United Nations and all governments associated with such instruments of Satan.[46] Knorr's conventions dwarfed any ever seen before. Some were mobile assemblies with hundreds of delegates traveling by land, sea, and air to convention sessions around the world. Some were concentrated international gatherings, culminating in the Divine Will International Assembly of 1958. The Sunday session of that one overflowed Yankee Stadium and the neighboring Polo Grounds with more than 250,000 in attendance from more than 120 countries; 2,937 men and 4,199 women were baptized at Orchard Beach. Simple logistics and police requirements compelled division of the conventions into more manageable sections after that year. Knorr continued using resolutions given mass approval at Witness conventions and then turned into tracts—194,418 "roared out a unanimous Aye" to the resolution on Friday of the 1958 convention and 70 million copies of the tract were distributed in fifty languages. Thirteen large, high-speed rotary presses were rolling in the new thirteen-story printing plant in Brooklyn by the end of that year.[47]

But Knorr was never so extreme in his attacks as Rutherford had been. Under his leadership the Witnesses remained unworldly but became less anti-worldly. He had some changes in mind. He took a wife, thus ending the Society's official coolness toward marriage. Witnesses became interested in and at times preoccupied with weddings, families, sex, and children. The Witness organization was to be less personality centered at the top. There was less place for such a visibly overpowering individual leader as Rutherford had been. Society publications would be written anonymously. Such publications approved for the Society's imprint bore the authority of the whole governing body, the trustworthy voice of the faithful and wise servant. The organization's evangelistic face to the world, on the other hand, was to become more personal and appealing. The printed testimony cards and the portable phonographs with recorded speeches from Rutherford went out of use. Each congregation member must become not only a kingdom publisher technically but also a winsome witness relating personally to the personal concerns of every householder. There was to be less freeing of the conscience of the Witness by dumping a warning of what the world had coming in the imminent cosmic battle. There was to be more gentle invitation to study a body of divine truth and more demonstration by example of the benefits of theocratic living.[48]

Witnesses as Educators

Such goals committed Knorr and his associates to an infinite program of education. Just over a month into his presidency, Knorr set up a pioneer school at Brooklyn Bethel to offer an "Advanced Course in Theocratic Ministry." Before this development ran its course, nearly every congregation had its own Theocratic Ministry School meeting weekly to teach both content and method of public presentation. Beginning in May of 1942, every paragraph in major *Watchtower* articles bore a number matching a question at the foot of the page. The teacher in the weekly meeting for *Watchtower* study would invite answers to the footnoted question and have the paragraph with its supporting Scriptures read until it was mastered. Visiting overseers, such as circuit and district servants, were to accompany local Witnesses house to house as instructors. Then they were to appoint the more experienced visitors in the congregation to assist the new and inexperienced. And of course there was special training for overseers.[49]

The years of Knorr's administration produced a marvelous flow of printed helps. Between 1942 and 1974 *Watchtower* was published in 2,836,041,443 copies. In the same period *Awake!* (*Consolation* until 22 August 1946) printed 2,600,751,501 copies. Witness printing presses issued 352,513,470 bound books in those years: Bibles, including the Witnesses' own New World Translation; aids to Bible study; organization manuals; curriculum materials for use in the schools for Witness trainees and in the schools scheduled in the homes of prospects willing to join their neighbors in a study group. A series of basic doctrinal primers were especially popular. The Society issued *The Truth That Leads to Eternal Life* in 1968. Its first edition was a run of 15 million; by 1982, when its successor appeared, the total number of copies printed had reached 115 million.[50]

Knorr's most notable education enterprise was the school founded on the Kingdom Farm near South Lansing, New York, while the Second World War was still raging. At its opening in February of 1943, Knorr named it Gilead. It offered an intensive course in Bible, doctrine, and foreign language for a limited number of outstanding students who were selected and individually invited by the president's office. They were to become mission-

aries in new and hard places, ready to go wherever they were sent. The first class learned Spanish because the only fields open in wartime were in Cuba, Mexico, Costa Rica, and Puerto Rico. In 1960 the school moved to the headquarters at Brooklyn. It kept producing an elite corps of evangelists and administrators serving the organization around the world. For Rutherford the commission to go into all the world had pointed mainly to Canada, Great Britain, and Europe. Knorr's vision encompassed the earth. Witness history for the thirty-five years of his presidency following 1942 has been described as global expansion. By 1975 there were over 2 million Witness publishers, almost three-fourths of them outside the United States. Many thousands of the world's illiterate persons were taught to read using the simple and highly illustrated Watch Tower publications. The new orientation of their life and morals was expressed in Jehovah's Witness vocabulary.[51]

When Knorr died at age seventy-two in 1977, he was succeeded in the presidency by a man almost twelve years his senior. Frederick William Franz had set out from his home in Covington, Kentucky, to prepare for the Presbyterian ministry. While studying at the University of Cincinnati he became convinced by Watch Tower teachings and in 1914 became a Bible Student colporteur. In 1920 he was invited to Brooklyn Bethel. Working alongside Rutherford and Knorr, he became the Society's foremost biblical exegete and scholar, sometimes called "our oracle." His understanding of the nature and mission of Jehovah's Witnesses aligned fully with that of his immediate predecessors and the character of his presidency was similar to theirs.[52]

Growth in Spite of Defections and Criticisms

Large numbers of Witnesses have chosen to drop out of the Society, perhaps as many as 50 percent of the children of Witness homes. Other thousands have been disfellowshipped for dissenting in doctrine or for violations of discipline. Yet the persistent evangelism and ministry of teaching has kept renewing and increasing the total fellowship. There were 2,501,722 publishers preaching the good news at least part time in 1983, about 600,000 of them in the United States. Total attendance at the spring celebration of the Lord's Supper that year was 6,767,707.[53] By January of 1984 the *Watchtower* had reached a circulation of 10.2 million for each issue. Young people lost from Witness families were always being replaced with converts from the world. When 12 percent of the population of the United States was black, 18 percent of Jehovah's Witnesses were black. Conservative Catholics and Protestants were attracted to the Witnesses because of their firm authority structure, their strict moralism, and their aversion to liberal ecumenism.[54]

More important for evangelism than any body of prophetic texts or any selected date for Armageddon was the attraction of a committed body of believers. Here was a local cluster of people whose lives were completely intertwined with one another in five church meetings a week plus several hours of door-to-door ministry. The specifics of Witness doctrine were continually being shaped and reshaped by official revelation, by reiteration, or by omission. Projected dates related to the coming cataclysm were continually being adjusted. Such formulations and calculations could always be acknowledged to be inexact and be corrected. What was constant was the assurance of being very members of the people of Jehovah, regularly receiving his word through the Watch Tower communications. For Witnesses that faithful and wise servant of Jehovah remained completely trustworthy.[55]

Hundreds of outside writers, including many who were motivated but poorly informed, took up their pens to denounce this group which they labeled a "cult." Witnesses inside the fellowship were not to read such literature. Some well-informed writers attempted to become inside critics. Raymond Franz, nephew of president Frederick Franz, was forced to resign from the Society's governing body for questioning the accuracy of some Witness interpretations of the Bible. He was disfellowshipped in 1981. That same year professor M. James Penton of Lethbridge, Alberta, Canada, was disfellowshipped. Such exclusion brought a terrible sense of isolation for persons whose commitment to the Witness community was at the heart of their personal identity. Franz and Penton reflected in their books the sorrow and sense of injustice they experienced. Their cases and those of several contemporaries received considerable attention and comment in non-Witness publications. Regular members of Witness congregations were generally insulated from such critical evaluations.[56]

Development of Witnesses in Indiana

The Bible Students had early connections in Indiana. Outsiders called them Millennial Dawnists or Russellites. They often called themselves "friends." The *Advent Christian Times* for 18 July 1877 warned that N. H. Barbour, J. H. Paton, and C. T. Russell had been circulating with "age-to-come trash" among Adventists in Ohio and Indiana. "We were credibly informed that one of them boasted in Union Mills, Ind., [LaPorte County] a few days since, that they would break up every Advent church in the land. We guess not." Morgan Gambill followed the teachings of Russell as early as 1879. By 1914 his wife Ora and his brother Hezzie had joined in the work. The family was especially active in Sullivan and Greene counties with impact on much of southern Indiana.[57]

Samuel J. Fleming of Wabash, Indiana, was one of two *Watch Tower* readers who contributed about thirty bushels of "miracle wheat" to the Watch Tower Society in 1911. Russell hoped this extremely productive strain was a sign that the earth was soon to be restored to its original purity and productivity. He sold the seed at a dollar a pound to benefit the Society as the donors had suggested. The improved wheat was only a mutant strain or sport which soon lost its quality and embarrassed Russell before his critics.[58] In the early 1900s there were classes of Bible Students in Indiana at Brazil, Bloomington, and Columbus. The "cottage meetings" at Acton about 1913 were held at the home of a switchboard operator in the same room with the telephone exchange. After a few years that Acton class rented a lodge hall and were proud to paint "I.B.S.A." on a window to identify the regular meeting place of the International Bible Students Association. In 1923 the state's Bible Students held a convention at West Baden.[59]

Indianapolis, easily accessible by rail from much of the state, was a natural center for Bible Student activity. The city's Bible Students held their meetings in the early years at the Metropolitan School of Music in Odeon Hall at Fort Wayne and North Streets. Friends from Indianapolis went out to share in the prayer meetings and singing at Acton. Bible students could come to the capital by interurban for a full Sunday of fellowship and instruction. They also came for some major events. In 1916 that technical marvel called the "Photo-Drama of Creation" came to Indianapolis for showing at various locations including Tomlinson Hall over the city market, Hartman Theatre, and the Shelby Branch Library. Later that year Charles Taze Russell himself came to speak at the Murat Temple. And new president Joseph F. Rutherford gave a public lecture in Tomlinson Hall in 1919.[60]

One banner year was 1925 when the assembly of the International Bible Students Association came to Indianapolis for the full week of 24–31 August. Automobile loads of delegates and visitors kept rolling up to Cadle Tabernacle. By Monday afternoon 4,000 had arrived with a total of at least 12,000 expected. In addition to the downtown hotels, many private homes were thrown open for the visitors. Leaders of the Watch Tower Society from Brooklyn were present and prepared to make the major addresses morning, afternoon, and night. Seventy-five delegates took turns at the microphone during Tuesday's prayer and testimony meeting. Mayor Lew Shank found the auditorium all decorated with flags, bunting, and Bible texts. He told the convention, "The city is yours until you get ready to go back home." C. J. Woodworth of the Association responded to the mayor by describing Bible Students as models of efficient and moral citizenry. He was sure that a city which was national headquarters for the American Legion would be interested to know how to become good soldiers of Jesus Christ before the coming great battle of Armageddon. All states but three responded to Tuesday night's roll call as did a large delegation from Canada. Convention programs were broadcast over radio stations WFBM and WPRM. More than 50,000 Indianapolis homes were visited by Bible Students. Friday was a special Service Day. Some 6,000 workers gathered at the Tabernacle early in the morning for a "word of cheer from Judge J. F. Rutherford." Then they piled into about 1,000 automobiles intending to call on every family in the rural districts and towns within a thirty-mile radius of Indianapolis. Literature distributed would be at cost, or free to needy readers.[61]

President Rutherford was the crucial convention speaker. He had a special task in 1925. The year had become one of the "significant dates" for Bible Students. In *Millions Now Living Will Never Die* by Rutherford and in *The Way to Paradise* by William E. Van Amburgh, Bible Students had been encouraged to expect "full restoration" in 1925—the resurrection of Abraham, Isaac, and Jacob and the beginning of the millennium. Many excited Students were expecting to be changed to heavenly glory that year. A few had closed businesses, given up jobs, and sold their homes.[62] Now Rutherford and Van Amburgh were at Indianapolis and the year was more than half gone. Rutherford adjusted the expectation. In Wednesday's speech he said the world was certainly not to be burned in 1925. "Much was said last winter about the end of the world and the destruction of the earth by fire. The Bible plainly shows that the earth will never be destroyed."[63] And on Saturday he said:

> Do what the Lord wants you to do and quit guessing about the end of the world. Just as 1776 marked the birth of the United States, so 1914 marked the beginning of the kingdom of Christ, but we do not know when the final establishment of the kingdom will take place. It is our place to work for the Lord, and stop worrying about

getting off this earth to an easier place. God took Jesus away from the earth, the place of nativity of his enemies, and seated him in the position of favor in heaven. The enemy Satan continued his nefarious operations without interference, but this was to be permitted only until a fixed time in the Father's plan. Jesus must patiently wait on the Father until due time to act. He possesses all power in heaven and earth, but he can not use it against the devil until the order for action comes from God. The time must come when God must subdue the enemy.[64]

The Indianapolis *Star* and the Indianapolis *News* gave generous coverage to the 1925 convention. They were especially impressed with Rutherford's final address on Sunday afternoon. The *Star* said the auditorium seating 12,000 was filled so early that scores could not get in; the *News* said hundreds were turned away. Rutherford reiterated that God would never destroy Indiana or any other part of the earth but that God would bind Satan and set up a kingdom of righteous peace on earth.[65] He introduced a resolution called "Message of Hope" and spoke to the resolution with an address entitled "A Call to Action." Together they were a long and furious attack on the existing powers of business, government, and religion as the very tools and forces of Satan. Both called the people from the bondage of Satan to the service of Jehovah.

> World powers, science and philosophy, commerce and religion, have each in turn offered their respective remedies for man's relief. In the name and under the guise of democracy, these combine in offering their joint and several powers to meet the requirements of man. Together they claim to be the sunlight of the world, holding forth all the light that shines to enlighten and guide the human race. Intrigue, duplicity and trickery are freely resorted to by the political and commercial powers; science and philosophy are marked by vanity and self-sufficiency; while the religionists, both Catholic and Protestant, are conspicuous by their arrogance, self-conceit, impiety and ungodliness . . . Therefore in the name and in the spirit of the Lord, the Standard of God's Truth and Righteousness is here lifted up against the enemy and for the benefit of the peoples . . . We confidently appeal to the peoples to rally to the Divine Standard of Truth thus lifted up and thereby learn the way that leads to life and happiness. We call upon all the peoples of good will of every nation, kindred and tongue, to discard the errors invented by the enemy Satan and for many years taught by man, and to receive and believe the Divine Plan of salvation as set forth in the Scriptures.[66]

As Rutherford departed, the hearers crowded around to shake his hand. He said the Indianapolis gathering had been the "best convention of consecrated people ever held in America." The *Star* printed the text of the resolution and the address, about eight full columns. The pamphlet form of the resolution was distributed in about 50 million copies. Bible Students had been recommissioned at Indianapolis as agents of evangelism. The "sifting" related to disappointment over the prophecies for 1925 brought only a negligible drop in attendance for the annual Lord's Supper in May of 1926. On 26 July 1931 a convention at Columbus, Ohio, approved Rutherford's resolution to take the name "Jehovah's Witnesses." The next week, from 31 July to 2 August, Indianapolis was the site of one of the subsequent "extension conventions" which embraced the new name and mission.[67]

Prosecutions and Persecutions in Indiana

Indiana Witnesses met resistance during wartime. Reported among the sufferers during the First World War was Curtis Plummer of Brownstown who "was threatened and coerced by a mob composed of the county sheriff and business men" on 30 April 1918. Witness William Darby of Indianapolis was reported fired, though he was a veteran of thirty-two years of honorable service as a mail carrier. Things were worse for Hoosier Witnesses faced with patriotic demands during the 1940s. In Shelbyville police used their sound cars to warn citizens that Witnesses were in town and then drove the Witnesses to the edge of town where they seized their literature for burning. They stopped short of burning Bibles. At nearby Lewis Creek a church mob drove Witnesses down the street and out of town. There were hostile incidents at Clinton and Terre Haute.[68]

Connersville came to have the highest profile among Indiana towns resisting the Witnesses. "No Kingdom of God for Connersville" read an editorial headline in the liberal weekly *Christian Century* for 30 April 1941. The editorial deplored "the Indiana criminal syndication law." Witnesses Grace Trent and Lucy McKee of Connersville had been convicted under that law in the Fayette Circuit Court the previous September and sentenced to two years in the Indiana Woman's Prison. The charge was "riotous conspiracy" and "resistance to organized government." What they had actually done, said the *Century*, "was to distribute the literature of the sect—a right specifically upheld by the United States Supreme Court—and to refuse to salute the flag." For the *Century* this trouble at Connersville made an occasion to speak out stoutly for civil rights: "Liberty of belief under the Constitution is not only for the wise, the tolerant and the respectable. If it has any meaning at all—and it has—it implies liberty for

fools, bigots and crackpots, providing they confine their activities to preaching and do not step over the line into overt disturbance of the peace."[69]

To many citizens at Connersville the situation seemed much more dangerous. Witness literature and phonographs carried the extreme language of President Rutherford against all earthly powers. Rutherford's unyielding stand against saluting the flag had been publicized for five years. The media of the time were full of the news of war and of the impending draft of Hoosier sons. Those two Witness housewives looked strangely stubborn and suspicious even in their home town. Professional Witnesses brought to Connersville from the outside, like zone servant Rainbow and Cincinnati lawyer Victor Schmidt, received even less sympathy. The trial went on for five days. The arguments of the prosecutor heightened crowd resentment. When the verdict of "guilty" was finally pronounced about 9 P.M., a mob of 200 to 300 moved against the defenders and pursued them through most of the night.[70] Victor Schmidt's wife said:

> Almost immediately, a barrage of all kinds of fruit, vegetables and eggs began bombarding us. We were told later that the mobsters had unloaded a whole truckload of these items on us. We tried to run to our car, but were headed off and pushed to the highway leading out of the city. Then the mob rushed at us, striking the brothers and hitting me in the back, causing a whiplash effect. By now, a storm had broken in all its fury. The rain was coming in torrents and the wind was lashing furiously. However, the fury of the elements was insignificant in comparison with the fury of this demon-crazed mob. Because of the storm, many took to their cars and drove alongside of us, yelling and cursing us and always including Jehovah's name in their cursings. Oh how that pierced our hearts![71]

That was not the end of the Connersville conflict. The *Century* editorial of 30 April referred particularly to a second series of events beginning on 6 April. Witness leaders had decided to respond to the mob abuse at Connersville with a witnessing blitzkrieg of the type currently recommended by the Watch Tower Society's legal counsel. They recruited a group of seventy-five Witnesses from Ohio, Kentucky, and West Virginia. With a truckload of Watch Tower literature, phonographs, and records they descended on Connersville on Palm Sunday. Police chief William Traylor and deputies of sheriff Joseph W. Oser refused to be overwhelmed. They confiscated the materials and arrested all seventy-five. Prosecutor John R. Chrisman swore out one affidavit to cover them all, charging conspiracy to commit a felony by advocating overthrow of the government by force. The Fayette county jail was full. The group was held briefly in City Hall. Then they were farmed out to the county infirmary and to jails in Brookville, Liberty, and Rushville.

Bail for the Witnesses was $2,000 per person at first, arranged at lower levels during a week of negotiation so that all could be at liberty awaiting trial. Two lawyers from Cincinnati and two from Indianapolis appeared as early counselors for the Witnesses; Ira Holmes of Indianapolis continued as their attorney. When the case reached a superior court in Indianapolis, Frederick Franz came from Watch Tower headquarters in Brooklyn as an expert witness on the Society's behalf.[72] An editorial in the Indianapolis *Star* viewed the whole Connersville matter somewhat differently than the *Christian Century*.

> It is unfortunate that the solemn observance of Holy Week in Indiana has been complicated by demonstrations of the religious sect known as Jehovah's Witnesses . . . Some citizens have had difficulty trying to decide whether Jehovah's Witnesses are a subversive group or a too zealous religious organization. The public is tolerant of supposedly religious activities . . . The average sect which demonstrates religious faith receives due consideration from the authorities and the public. There is little opportunity for any to profess martyrdom's role if they do not overstep the bounds of religion for subversive tinkering with government and the American way of life. The state will not tolerate distribution of subversive literature under the cloak of religious zeal.[73]

Witnesses and American Society

Things were changing by the time Judge Rutherford died in 1942. The Witnesses won such solid backing in the upper judiciary by the early 1940s that few local charges against them as a group had any chance of support in the courts. Focus shifted to the cases of individual Witnesses refusing the draft. After the emotional pressures of the Second World War had subsided, and after groundbreaking decisions in the United States Supreme Court between 1953 and 1955, Hoosier officials came to concur that for purposes of draft classification all Witnesses were ministers. The world and the Witnesses continued to growl at each other and publish polemic literature. There was only limited progression of the group from sect to denomination. But the mood was never quite the same after Rutherford.

Presidents Knorr and Franz advocated teaching. The image of the Witness visitor became less that of a deliverer of prophetic warnings of doom related to Armageddon and more that of a neighbor offering "Bible literature" and invitations to home Bible studies. Witnesses kept taking great pains to prove themselves separated from the world. Yet the surge of growth following the Second World War brought ever more massive investments in printing machinery and in media equipment and in educational programs at both local and headquarters levels. Jehovah's Witnesses took their place as one of America's more solidly vested institutions. Far from being unconcerned about contemporary society, they sought to become models of community morality. Pending the cosmic struggle of Armageddon, still expected momentarily, they championed such immediate reforms as reduction of crime, stabilization of family life, and elimination of racial prejudice.[74]

Modern, well-lighted, and comfortably furnished Kingdom Halls became a familiar part of the landscape in Hoosier towns. William J. Whalen visited one in 1961 and published a description in 1962.

> For years the congregation of Jehovah's Witnesses in Lafayette, Indiana (population 35,000), had met in a converted store between a sheet metal shop and a fundamentalist gospel mission. Last year they built a handsome Kingdom Hall in an outlying residential area. The brothers of the congregation pitched in to dig the foundation, finish the electrical work, install the plumbing, paint the walls. They worked two or three hours a night, four or five on Saturdays, and still kept up their doorstep preaching and Bible meetings. The only labor which was not donated was that needed for laying concrete blocks. Cost of land, labor and materials: $12,000. One of the brothers, an architect, drew up the functional design which includes on one floor a 120-seat auditorium, literature counter, library, office, rest rooms and furnace room. The Lafayette congregation now meets in quarters which are the envy of the other 19 congregations in their circuit.[75]

The Lord's Evening Meal or Memorial on Nisan 14 was the biggest meeting of the year at Lafayette. The elements were passed but none of the congregation of more than 150 partook. All counted themselves as "other sheep" rather than members of the 144,000. Whalen described the five typical weekly gatherings of that congregation: public lecture at the Hall on Sunday afternoon; *Watchtower* study using the footnoted questions at the Hall on Sunday evening; theocratic ministry school followed by the service meeting at the Hall on Thursday evening; congregation book study at the Hall or in member homes on Sunday morning. Besides attending these meetings, the active Witness was expected to study the Bible and Watchtower literature at home and spend some ten hours per month in systematic coverage of the area with door-to-door evangelizing.[76]

In the 1960s the Witnesses took a step to identify themselves more clearly as models of conservative American citizenship. Study materials on "Subjection to Superior Authorities" opted gingerly for support of the regular agencies of civil law and order. So long as there were no demands contrary to God's law, Witnesses were to give obedience and cooperation to those political authorities which Jehovah permitted to exist until the rule of Christ's kingdom removed them. Just in time, said one Witness commentator: "How could we possibly have known that 1964 would see the civil-rights issue ferment and boil over into riots in the streets and civil disobedience, violent and passive . . . We might have found ourselves stuck with the same reasoning that the clergy have who involved themselves in marches, protests and social issues of the day. Just right on time, in 1962, at the summer assemblies, we were fed 'food at the proper time.'"[77]

Witnesses Oppose Blood Transfusions

But it was also in the 1960s that Witnesses clarified a doctrine which sharpened their separation from the main body of society. They took a firm position against blood transfusions. There had been decades of Witness comment about taking blood into one's body in view of the prohibitions in Genesis 9:36, Leviticus 17:10–14, and Acts 15:20, 28, 29. Transfusion entered the discussion more pointedly after a blood bank was established in Chicago in 1937. The *Watchtower* took a stand against transfusions in 1945 and many Witnesses complied after that date, though compliance remained a matter of individual conscience. Then in 1961 came the official booklet *Blood, Medicine and the Law of God*. From that time Witnesses accepting transfusions were generally disfellowshipped, a procedure made compulsory in 1971. The principle was further developed to forbid transfusions with one's own stored blood, transfusions for domestic animals, and the use of any products derived from blood such as certain food additives, cosmetics, and fertilizers.[78]

The transfusion policy faced opposition by the medical establishment and a series of court cases. Witness leaders in Indianapolis were among those who deliberately sought better rapport with doctors and hospitals. By 1988 a Hospital Liaison Committee of four elders was arranging meetings with a wide range of healthcare professionals to explain Witness principles on the use of blood and blood products. They compiled and circulated a list of over 200 doctors in the area who were willing to serve Witness patients and to respect their wish not to accept transfusions. Witness elders were prepared to provide counseling for members in Indianapolis hospitals.[79]

Doctrine and Practice

Jehovah's Witnesses in Indiana were visible among the Hoosier faiths because of their beliefs. God's name is Jehovah. Christ is the first of the creatures, God's son but in no essential way one with him. Christ died on a stake, not on a cross. Life did not evolve but was created, part of a quite sophisticated process involving aeons of time before the first Genesis "day," thousands of years within the span of the Genesis account, and gradual development of the universe. The earth will never be destroyed or depopulated. Satan is the present invisible ruler of the world. God's invisible forces will destroy the present system at the battle of Armageddon. Humankind is now in the "time of the end" which began in 1914 and extends until Armageddon comes. The wicked will be annihilated. Only a little flock of 144,000 go to heaven and rule with Christ. The "other sheep," people whom God approves, will live eternally on earth under the rule of Christ.[80]

Witnesses do not emphasize emotional conversion nor do they seek overwhelming religious experience; nearly every one of some eighty questions asked of applicants for immersion have to do with doctrine, authority, and discipline. Members are to keep biblical laws of morality, keep separate from the world, have no part in interfaith movements, and avoid taking blood into the body through mouth or veins. Birthdays, holidays, and civic occasions are generally passed without celebration. Witnesses do not join political parties, vote, or hold public office. They rarely participate in extracurricular sports, social organizations, or secular amusements. The use of tobacco is forbidden.[81]

Jehovah's Witnesses in Indiana were also visible because there kept being more of them. Indianapolis illustrated the growth. Witnesses built the city's first Kingdom Hall at College Avenue and 27th Street in 1929. About 1939 they developed a second in a building at 1226 East Southern Avenue, formerly a Baptist church. This "South Unit" had living quarters for a team of evangelists called pioneers who served in the city but also visited other towns to teach Bible classes and offer literature.

When the area was organized into circuits—groupings of about twenty congregations totaling 1,000 to 1,500 members—Indianapolis needed a place for circuit assemblies. Meeting in such places as schools, skating rinks, and armories was uncomfortable and inconvenient. The Witnesses acquired a large building at 1202 North Delaware Street which would seat 1,200. It had a baptismal pool plus room for kitchen, dining room, and apartments. This was renovated by volunteers and dedicated 15 October 1978 as the Indianapolis, Indiana, Assembly Hall of Jehovah's Witnesses.

Witness circuits were grouped in districts. There were district conventions at Terre Haute, Evansville, and South Bend but especially at Indianapolis—1952 and 1964 at the State Fairgrounds; 1968 at Victory Field (later Bush Stadium); 1981 and 1982 at Market Square. In 1991 there were twenty-eight congregations of Jehovah's Witnesses in the Indianapolis and Marion County area attended by some 6,000 persons.[82]

NOTES

1. Timothy White, *A People for His Name: A History of Jehovah's Witnesses and an Evaluation* (New York: Vantage Press, 1967), 14; *Jehovah's Witnesses in the Divine Purpose* (Brooklyn, N.Y.: Watchtower Bible and Tract Society, 1959), 17; *1975 Yearbook of Jehovah's Witnesses* (Brooklyn, N.Y.: Watchtower Bible and Tract Society, 1975), 35; M. James Penton, *Apocalypse Delayed: The Story of Jehovah's Witnesses* (Toronto: University of Toronto Press, 1985), 14, 308–9.

2. *Jehovah's Witnesses*, 14, 17; White, *A People*, 14–16; Penton, *Apocalypse*, 13–15.

3. Charles Taze Russell, *The Object and Manner of Our Lord's Return* (Rochester, N.Y.: Office of the Herald of the Morning, 1877, 64 p.); White, *A People*, 16–21.

4. Nelson H. Barbour, *Three Worlds, and the Harvest of This World: A Brief Review of the Bible Plan of Redemption, which Spans Three Worlds: "The World That Was," "The World That Now Is," and "The World to come"; with the Evidence That We Are Now in the "Time of Harvest"* (Rochester, N.Y.: Published by N. H. Barbour [and] C. T. Russell, 1877, 194 p.).

5. A prophetic "day" was often equated with a historical year. Thus 1,914 plus 606 equals the 2,520 arrived at from Daniel 4. However no position of Russell or his colleagues ever rested on one such simple calculation. Their chronologies were constantly discerned and corroborated from additional sources by the dozen and the score. See Penton, *Apocalypse*, 21–22 and Raymond Franz, *Crisis of Conscience* (Atlanta, Ga.: Commentary Press, 1983), 25–26.

6. Anthony A. Hoekema, *The Four Major Cults* (Grand Rapids, Mich.: William B. Eerdmans, 1963), 252–54; *Jehovah's Witnesses*, 18–19; *1975 Yearbook*, 36–37; White, *A People*, 22–23, 66–79, 104–8, 135; Franz, *Crisis of Conscience*, 25–27.

7. *Jehovah's Witnesses*, 37.

8. For agendas of Bible class meetings see *1975 Yearbook*, 42–45. The groups were called ecclesias, Bible Students, or International Bible Students. Some outsiders called them Russellites or Millennial Dawn People. The name Jehovah's Witnesses was even-

tually offered to the largest wing of the movement by president Joseph F. Rutherford in 1931 and quickly accepted. The initial letter "w" in witnesses was preferably written in lower case until 1976. See *Jehovah's Witnesses*, 125–26, and Heather Botting and Gary Botting, *The Orwellian World of Jehovah's Witnesses* (Toronto: University of Toronto Press, 1984), 848–85.

9. *Jehovah's Witnesses*, 18–19, 24–25, 40; White, *A People*, 100–101, 113–20; Penton, *Apocalypse*, 29–33.

10. Its name was *Zion's Watch Tower and Herald of Christ's Presence* (1879); *The Watch Tower and Herald of Christ's Presence* (1909); *The Watchtower and Herald of Christ's Presence* (1931); *The Watchtower and Herald of Christ's Kingdom* (January 1939); *The Watchtower Announcing Jehovah's Kingdom* (March 1939). It was published monthly from July of 1879 through December of 1891 and semimonthly thereafter. See *Jehovah's Witnesses*, 21.

11. This series was called *Millennial Dawn* from 1886 to 1904. The six volumes were *The Divine Plan of the Ages* (1886); *The Time Is at Hand* (1889); *Thy Kingdom Come* (1891); *The Battle of Armageddon* (1897); *The At-one-ment between God and Man* (1899); and *The New Creation* (1904). See *Jehovah's Witnesses*, 21–22, 30–32.

12. *Jehovah's Witnesses*, 21–22, 30–32, 50; White, *A People*, 29–30, 66.

13. *Jehovah's Witnesses*, 23–24, 34, 68–69; *1975 Yearbook*, 50; White, *A People*, 42–45, 122–37; Penton, *Apocalypse*, 34–35, 315.

14. The people being called out during Russell's days were understood to be members of the 144,000 referred to in Revelation 14:1–3. In this tradition they have been referred to as the Anointed, Body of Christ, Bride of Christ, Chosen Ones, Elect, Faithful and Discreet Slave, Holy Nation, Israel of God, Joint Heirs of Christ, Kingdom, Kingdom Class, Little Flock, New Creation, New Nation, Royal House, Royal Priesthood, Sanctuary Class, Sons of Levi, Spirit-Begotten, Spiritual Israel, Spiritual Sons, and Watchman. See Botting and Botting, *Orwellian World*, xxxii, 187 and Hoekema, *Four Major Cults*, 287.

15. *Jehovah's Witnesses*, 25–26; White, *A People*, 26–28.

16. *Jehovah's Witnesses*, 26–27; *1975 Yearbook*, 51–53, 61–64; White, *A People*, 42–43.

17. *Jehovah's Witnesses*, 42–43, 51–52, 54, 58–58; *1975 Yearbook*, 47, 53–60; White, *A People*, 46–57, 66–90.

18. *Jehovah's Witnesses*, 61–62; *1975 Yearbook*, 73–74, 76, 78–79; White, *A People*, 64–65; Penton, *Apocalypse*, 346.

19. *Jehovah's Witnesses*, 58, 64–66; *1975 Yearbook*, 79–80, 85; White, *A People*, 118–21, 154–59.

20. *Jehovah's Witnesses*, 34, 56–57, 65–66; *1975 Yearbook*, 871–83; White, *A People*, 180–84.

21. *Jehovah's Witnesses*, 66–73; *1975 Yearbook*, 85–90.

22. In the usage of this group a "Christian" equals a Jehovah's Witness. "True Christianity" is also a term referring to Jehovah's Witnesses. But "religion" (later sometimes expanded to "false religion"), "Church," and "Christendom" are generally negative names for what are regarded as collective evil forces outside and against Jehovah's Witnesses.

23. *1975 Yearbook*, 104.

24. *Jehovah's Witnesses*, 76–79.

25. *Jehovah's Witnesses*, 79.

26. *Jehovah's Witnesses*, 75–76, 81–83; *1975 Yearbook*, 98–101, 104–11.

27. *Jehovah's Witnesses*, 85–87; *1975 Yearbook*, 115–19; Penton, *Apocalypse*, 56; White, *A People*, 170, 225–36.

28. For accounts of a series of such conventions, resolutions, and tract distributions for 1922–28, see *Jehovah's Witnesses*, 101–19 and *1975 Yearbook*, 131, 135–39.

29. For one text of this address, see Joseph F. Rutherford, *Millions Now Living Will Never Die* (Brooklyn, N.Y.: International Bible Students Association, 1920, 128 p.), in *Jehovah's Witnesses I: The Early Writings of J. F. Rutherford* (New York: Garland, 1990).

30. Joseph F. Rutherford, *Freedom for the Peoples* (Brooklyn, N.Y.: International Bible Students Association, 1927), 20, in *Jehovah's Witnesses I* (New York: Garland, 1990).

31. *Jehovah's Witnesses*, 117, 120–22; *1975 Yearbook*, 139–44; White, *A People*, 192–95.

32. *Jehovah's Witnesses*, 95–96; *1975 Yearbook*, 122–26; White, *A People*, 175–76; Penton, *Apocalypse*, 58.

33. *1975 Yearbook*, 149–52, 156; *Jehovah's Witnesses*, 125–26; White, *A People*, 259–61.

34. *Jehovah's Witnesses*, 139–40; *1975 Yearbook*, 156–57; White, *A People*, 215–20, 284–96; Penton, *Apocalypse*, 72, 108–9; Hoekema, *Four Major Cults*, 279–90. Witness translations of Revelation 16:6 and Witness writings often prefer the spelling "Har-Magedon" rather than the familiar Armageddon widely used by others.

35. *1975 Yearbook*, 247.

36. *Jehovah's Witnesses*, 148–49.

37. Raymond Franz, *In Search of Christian Freedom* (Atlanta, Ga.: Commentary Press, 1991, 732 p.); James A. Beverley, *Crisis of Allegiance: A Study of Dissent among Jehovah's Witnesses* (Burlington, Ontario, Canada: Welch Publishing Company, 1986), 100–102; *Jehovah's Witnesses*, 148, 186–92; *1975 Yearbook*, 166–67, 246–47; White, *A People*, 361–62, 365–68, 374–81; Penton, *Apocalypse*, 68–69, 159–64, 211–52, 259.

38. White, *A People*, 270–83; Penton, *Apocalypse*, 69–70.

39. *Jehovah's Witnesses*, 123–24, 131–39, 175–79; *1975 Yearbook*, 153–54, 157–60, 162; White, *A People*, 315–17; Penton, *Apocalypse*, 68–69.

40. *Jehovah's Witnesses*, 128–30, 141–43; *1975 Yearbook*, 174–75; White, *A People*, 307–14; Penton, *Apocalypse*, 143.

41. *Jehovah's Witnesses*, 143–44, 179–82; *1975 Yearbook*, 168–90; White, *A People*, 321–34; Penton, *Apocalypse*, 88, 143, 146–51.

42. *Jehovah's Witnesses*, 181.

43. Charles B. Hirsch, "Conscientious Objectors in Indiana During World War II," *Indiana Magazine of History* 46 (March 1950): 63; *Jehovah's Witnesses*, 222–26; *1975 Yearbook*, 205–8; White, *A People*, 341–43.

44. Edward Waite, "The Debt of Constitutional Laws to Jehovah's Witnesses," *Minnesota Law Review* 28 (March 1944): 209–46; Charles S. Braden, *These Also Believe: A Study of Modern American Cults and Minority Religious Movements* (New York: Macmillan, 1960, copyright 1949), 382; *1975 Yearbook*, 172, 177–80, 208; White, *A People*, 340–48; Penton, *Apocalypse*, 88, 136–38, 155.

45. *1975 Yearbook*, 194–96; White, *A People*, 337–57.

46. *Jehovah's Witnesses*, 196–97; *1975 Yearbook*, 194–96, 228–29, 234–37; White, *A People*, 337–57.

47. James A. Beckford, *The Trumpet of Prophecy: A Sociological Study of Jehovah's Witnesses* (Oxford, Eng.: Basil Blackwell, 1975), 50–51; *Jehovah's Witnesses*, 283–92; White, *A People*, 356–57. For reports of the massive international conventions from 1946 to 1958 under Knorr's administration, see *1975 Yearbook*, 210–18 and Penton, *Apocalypse*, 86–88.

48. Beckford, *Trumpet of Prophecy*, 47–48, 52–55; *1975 Yearbook*, 197–98; Penton, *Apocalypse*, 78, 110–12, 252, 261–70; White, *A People*, 278–81; Botting and Botting, *Orwellian World*, 41–43.

49. *Jehovah's Witnesses*, 201–2, 213–16; *1975 Yearbook*, 199, 227; White, *A People*, 354–56; Penton, *Apocalypse*, 83–84; Botting and Botting, *Orwellian World*, 86–87.

50. *1975 Yearbook*, 241; Botting and Botting, *Orwellian World*, 79–80.

51. J. Gordon Melton, *The Encyclopedia of American Religions* (Detroit, Mich.: Gale Research, 1989), 531; *Jehovah's Witnesses*, 202–5, 220–21; *1975 Yearbook*, 200–202, 226–27; Penton, *Apocalypse*, 271–73, 293; White, *A People*, 353–54; Beckford, *Trumpet of Prophecy*, 49–50.

52. Penton, *Apocalypse*, 79–80.

53. Most congregations have no partakers of the bread and cup at the Lord's Supper. Those elements are only for members of the 144,000, their ranks now much depleted on the earth. It is the host of "other sheep" who share in the occasion but without partaking.

54. Penton, *Apocalypse*, 253–61, 270, 292–97, 355–56, 358; Botting and Botting, *Orwellian World*, 52–59, 148–50; White, *A People*, 368–74; Beckford, *Trumpet of Prophecy*, 93; Indianapolis *Star*, 23 April 1983, 12.

55. Joseph F. Zygmunt, "Prophetic Failure and Chiliastic Identity: The Case of Jehovah's Witnesses," *American Journal of Sociology* 75 (May 1970): 926–48; *Jehovah's Witnesses II: Controversial and Polemical Pamphlets*, edited with an introduction by Jerry Bergman (New York: Garland, 1990), vi; *Jehovah's Witnesses*, 100; *1975 Yearbook*, 145–47; Penton, *Apocalypse*, 65–171, 197–201; Beverley, *Crisis of Allegiance*, 86–94, 97–100; Botting and Botting, *Orwellian World*, 60–75, 94–95, 153–57, 186; Beckford, *Trumpet of Prophecy*, 219–223.

56. Raymond Franz, *In Search of Christian Freedom* (Atlanta, Ga.: Commentary Press, 1991, 732 p.); Franz, *Crisis of Conscience*, passim; Beverley, *Crisis of Allegiance*, passim; Penton, *Apocalypse*, xiii–xv, 89–90, 117–23, 295–302; Botting and Botting, *Orwellian World*, 90–92. For a substantial bibliography including much controversial material, see Jerry Bergman, *Jehovah's Witnesses and Kindred Groups: A Historical Compendium and Bibliography* (New York: Garland, 1984, 370 p.).

57. Bergman, *Jehovah's Witnesses and Kindred Groups*, xvii.

58. *1975 Yearbook*, 70–71; Penton, *Apocalypse*, 43.

59. Arnold G. Kleine, "Information Regarding the Early Beginnings of Jehovah's Witnesses in Indiana." Prepared by Indianapolis City Overseer Arnold G. Kleine to accompany letter to L. C. Rudolph, 4 October 1991, p. 1.

60. Kleine, "Information," 1.

61. *Jehovah's Witnesses*, 109–10; *1975 Yearbook*, 137; Indianapolis *Star*, 24 August (p. 9), 25 (p. 1, 8), 26 (p. 9), 27 (p. 1, 3), 28 (p. 1, 3), 29 (p. 1, 8), 30 (p. 1, 7), 31 (p. 1, 3, 8); Indianapolis *News*, 24 August (p. 10), 25 (p. 1, 24), 26 (p. 15), 27 (p. 1, 19), 28 (p. 19), 29 (p. 1, 2), 31 (p. 13).

62. William E. Van Amburgh, *The Way to Paradise: A Brief History of the 7,000 Years of Sin . . . Brief Scriptural Biographies of Michael Who Became the Christ, and of Lucifer Who Became the Devil* (Brooklyn, N.Y.: International Bible Students Association, 1924, 254 p.).

63. Indianapolis *News*, 26 August 1925, 15.

64. Indianapolis *News*, 29 August 1925, 1–2.

65. Indianapolis *Star*, 31 August 1925, 1.

66. Joseph F. Rutherford, *The Standard for the People* (Brooklyn, N.Y.: International Bible Students Association, 1926), 55–57.

67. Indianapolis *Star*, 31 August 1925, 1, 3, 8; *Jehovah's Witnesses*, 110, 125–26; *1975 Yearbook*, 149–50; White, *A People*, 259–61; Penton, *Apocalypse*, 62; Kleine, "Information," 2.

68. *Jehovah's Witnesses*, 82–83; Kleine, "Information," 3.

69. *Christian Century* 58 (30 April 1941): 581.

70. *1975 Yearbook*, 186–88; Franz, *Crisis of Conscience*, 11–12.

71. *1975 Yearbook*, 186–87.

72. Franz, *Crisis of Conscience*, 11–12; Indianapolis *Star*, 8 April 1941 (p. 10, 19), 10 April 1941 (p. 16); Indianapolis *News*, 7 April 1941 (part 2, p. 8), 8 April 1941 (p. 12).

73. Indianapolis *Star*, 8 April 1941, 10.

74. *Jehovah's Witnesses in the Twentieth Century* (Brooklyn, N.Y.: Watchtower Bible and Tract Society, 1979, 32 p.); White, *A People*, 327; *Jehovah's Witnesses*, 228–31; Beckford, *Trumpet of Prophecy*, 221; Penton, *Apocalypse*, 3–7, 139–40, 284–87.

75. William J. Whalen, *Armageddon Around the Corner; A Report on Jehovah's Witnesses* (New York: John Day, 1962), 101–2.

76. Whalen, *Armageddon*, 101–13. Congregational schedules are also described in Penton, *Apocalypse*, 241–42 and in Bergman, *Jehovah's Witnesses and Kindred Groups*, xxxii–xxxv.

77. *1975 Yearbook*, 237–38; Penton, *Apocalypse*, 139–40, 283.

78. *Blood, Medicine and the Law of God* (Brooklyn, N.Y.: Watchtower Bible and Tract Society, 1961, 62 p.).

79. Jerry Bergman, "Blood Transfusions: A History and Evaluation of the Religious Objections and a Consideration of the Biblical and Medical Arguments," in *Jehovah's Witnesses II*, 552–54, 589–91, 600; *1975 Yearbook*, 222–25; White, *A People*, 394–96; Penton, *Apocalypse*, 153–54, 202–6; Kleine, "Information," 4; Franz, *Search*, 286–311.

80. *Life—How Did It Get Here? By Evolution or by Creation?* (Brooklyn, N.Y.: Watchtower Bible and Tract Society, 1985, 255 p.); Penton, *Apocalypse*, 185–87, 196–97; Hoekema, *Four Major Cults*, 270–79, 327–44; *1975 Yearbook*, 148–49; Botting and Botting, *Orwellian World*, 30–33, 88–89, 117–18.

81. *1975 Yearbook*, 147; Botting and Botting, *Orwellian World*, 31–32, 76–78; Penton, *Apocalypse*, 274–84.

82. Kleine, "Information," 2–4.

SOME MAJOR MINORITIES

As the twentieth century began, the imaginary center of United States population was near Columbus, Indiana. Many people thought that Indiana was then and continued to be typical America. Historian Frederick L. Paxson said it to the Ohio Valley Historical Association in 1916:

> Indiana approximates an average of America and closely resembles the composite that the various corners of our country might represent could they be brought together and intermingled. It is an average that makes a State with fewer of the very rich, with fewer of the very poor, with fewer of the foreign born, with a larger proportion of the home born than most of our other States; that makes a community born within itself, enlarging its own traditions and carrying on its own ideals; and because of the trend of its history it is singularly American in its point of view.[1]

Outsiders and Hoosiers themselves were likely to describe Indiana as average America with an emphasis on the rural. In 1920 about 70 percent of the state's residents lived in rural homes or in small towns with population between 2,500 and 25,000. Ninety-five percent were American-born. Ninety-seven percent were white. About 75 percent of church members were Protestants.[2]

That kind of averaging could be misleading. Hoosiers whose image of their state was rural and whose image of their fellow citizens was white, Protestant, and native-born always had to make some regional corrections. The neighboring states of Illinois and Ohio did become urban earlier than Indiana, but in the years just after 1880 manufacturing actually grew in Indiana much more rapidly than in the country as a whole.

There were still the old cities on the rivers—Madison, New Albany, Jeffersonville, Evansville, Vincennes, Terre Haute—dealing in water transported merchandise of every kind but especially processors of wood and flour and pork and metals and boats and glass and alcoholic beverages. When Indianapolis, in Marion County, got its railroads built, it quickly eclipsed the older cities, producing three times more manufactured products than any other city in the state by 1880 and ranking as the fifth largest meat packing city in the nation by 1919. Yet by 1919 the concentration of industry in Gary, Hammond, and East Chicago had put Lake County output ahead of Marion County; Marion and Lake counties together reported 48.8 percent of the manufactured products of the state that year. Canned foods, farm implements, automobiles, and steel were items added to the list of the state's products, along with a hundred more. Northern Indiana cities of South Bend, Fort Wayne, Anderson, Kokomo, Michigan City, Muncie, Mishawaka, Elkhart, Marion, Richmond, and LaPorte became important industrial centers before 1920. That year manufacturing overtook agriculture in the production of wealth in Indiana.[3]

Indiana Ethnics

Nor did the state's people neatly fit a white Anglo-Saxon, Protestant stereotype. Germans had come down the river from Cincinnati, up the rivers from New Orleans, and from the northeast by way of the Great Lakes. Hosts of the state's "native-born" were actually children born in Indiana to the large families of recent immigrants from Germany. In the religious census of 1916, Catholics numbered 272,283 to pass the Methodists and become the largest single religious body in the state. German immigrants to Indiana often arrived with some experience as farmers or craftsmen, skills familiar and welcome in the young state. They were soon "Americanized," a process speeded by the patriotic pressures of the First World War.[4]

Besides invigorating Indiana's Catholic church, the Germans added their strength to Protestant denominations which they brought with them from the homeland or elected to form or to join on the American scene—Lutherans, Reformed, Mennonites, plus Evangelicals and Brethren of several kinds. There were German Methodists too. William Nast, a college professor converted in Pennsylvania at a Methodist camp meeting, made Cincinnati his base for missionary work among the Germans of the region. He established a German version of the *Christian Advocate* entitled *Der Christliche Apologete* in 1839 and helped to multiply German preachers in the Methodist frontier style. The result was formation of twenty-eight German Methodist churches in Indiana with particular strength in the area around Evansville, Boonville, Dale, and Santa Claus.[5]

Even less in line with the Hoosier stereotype than the Germans was Indiana's dividend from the massive immigration from southern and southeastern Europe between about 1870 and 1920. Indiana's share seemed small. While the nation was receiving millions of Italians, Poles, Croats, Slovenes, Serbs, Czechs, Slovaks, Hungarians, Greeks, Russians, and Romanians, Indiana's total of all foreign-born plus their first generation children remained about 500,000 and a steadily declining percentage of the total population. That included almost 10,000 Mexicans by 1930. The impact of these later immigrants was heightened because they were concentrated in a few places. They gravitated to the industrial cities—to the railroads, factories, and mines. Sometimes they had been recruited in their homeland by agents of such Indiana manufacturers as James Oliver, the Studebaker brothers, or United States Steel.[6]

Indianapolis had Indiana's largest foreign-born population in 1920 with 16,968 persons from twenty-nine lands of origin. Besides those from the familiar western European lands, the state capital had hundreds from Greece, Hungary, Italy, Poland, Romania, Russia, and Yugoslavia. Not far behind Indianapolis were Gary, East Chicago, and South Bend. These four cities plus Hammond and Fort Wayne accounted for half of Indiana's 150,868 foreign-born. In Clinton, Michigan City, Mishawaka, and Whiting at least 15 percent of the residents were foreign-born.[7]

Some of the later immigrants followed an early intention to accrue a bit of money and hurry back to buy land or start a business in their native country. The larger percentage who stayed had to make a place for themselves at the bottom of the social and economic ladder. Adult males fortunate enough to find regular employment in such favored industries as Studebaker or Oliver or Singer Sewing Machine might earn $1.50 to $2.00 per day. To secure rent money, families added boarders to their already cramped conditions. Contribution of wages from both parents and children seemed essential for the family's survival. The surrounding culture kept reminding the immigrants that they were smelly, poor, ignorant, and of small value. Employers exploited them with little regard for health or safety. Organized labor wished them gone. The South Bend *Tribune* for 24 October 1905 printed a resolution of a local labor union.

> Whereas, this tide of immigration brings with it the germs of anarchy, crime, disease and degeneracy . . . Resolved, that we demand the enactment of such laws as will shield us from the depressing effects of unrestricted immigration, to the end that the American laborer may not only be protected against the product of the foreign pauper labor, but that we may be protected against direct competition in our own country by the incoming of the competitive alien.[8]

African Americans resented the foreigners' willingness to displace them at the lowest end of the wage scale. The Lutheran Sallie Wyatt Stewart of Evansville became the state's most prominent leader of organized black women. In her presidential address to the annual convention of the Indiana State Federation of Colored Women's Clubs in 1924 she put the rhetorical question "What has the immigration of the foreign population meant to the Negro in years past?" She answered it had meant the "crowding of the Negro out of the factories and a limitation on the kinds of employment open to him." She said "It has meant a lessening of the Negro's bargaining ability as there were hundreds of unlettered foreigners whose daily habits permit them to work for lower wages than the Negro can well live on."[9]

Immigrant laborers, many of them temporary bachelors, were likely to drink alcohol to warm their recreational singing, dancing, and occasional brawling. Now they lived in a state so zealous for temperance that former governor James F. Hanly himself had joined the Christian reformers stumping the state on behalf of total prohibition.[10] Most of the later immigrants were Catholics but they hardly felt at home in Indiana's Catholic church. It lacked their home language in church and school. It seemed rich in institutions ruled by Irish or Germans who expected the newcomers to get past their limitations as immigrants and get on with being good American Catholics loyal to the national and Roman hierarchy.

The members of each ethnic group naturally drew together to affirm their national pride and to preserve their cultural heritage. They organized, and seemed sometimes to overorganize, for mutual support. Out of their poverty they formed clubs for fellowship, associations to rescue one another in crisis, churches for worship, schools for children—all to be conducted in the traditional language and in their national manner. For families the church and school were especially crucial links to bridge the painful gap between members of the first generation still attached to the ways of the old country and their children fast taking their places in the culture of the new land.

It was typical for an association of ethnic laymen in a Hoosier industrial town to take initiative to begin religious services, to plan for a church in their own tradition, and then to campaign to secure a priest qualified in their language and tradition. Such a priest had a large role to play. Besides leading in worship and sacrament, and besides providing cradle to grave pastoral ministry to all members of all the families, he was almost certain to be teacher and possibly the chief or sole administrator in the parish school. He was a representative figure and spokesman for his people before the larger community and interpreter of the community's requirements to his people. For his constituents needing help with English paperwork, needing advocacy for employment, or needing assistance before the law, he was a primary resource. Yet his leadership was always under review of the association of ethnic laypersons which had secured his services.

So at Indianapolis there came to be Holy Rosary Catholic Church for the Italians and Holy Trinity Catholic Church for the Slovenes. Holy Trinity also had Hungarian and Polish members. But also at the capital were Holy Trinity Greek Orthodox Church, St. Stephen Bulgarian Orthodox Church, St. George Syrian Orthodox Church, St. Nicholas Serbian Orthodox Church, and SS. Constantine and Helen Romanian Orthodox Church. Adolfs Grosbergs established a ministry for Latvians after 1950. Hispanic Catholics, arriving in increasing numbers after 1960, often worshipped at St. Mary Church which normally had one Spanish-speaking priest on its staff.

Koreans had formed three Protestant churches (Presbyterian, Methodist, Baptist) in Indianapolis by 1980 and organized a Korean Catholic mission in 1991.[11]

The Calumet region had the richest ethnic variety. There was Holy Trinity Catholic Church at Gary and St. John the Baptist Catholic Church at Whiting for the Slovaks. There was St. Adalbert Catholic Church at Whiting for the Poles. The Calumet area developed a fine flowering of churches preserving Eastern church liturgies. Holy Ghost, St. Basil, and St. George Churches at East Chicago used Byzantine rites. Gary offered SS. Constantine and Helen Greek Orthodox plus parishes for Romanian Orthodox, Serbian Orthodox, Syrian Antiochian Orthodox, and Russian Orthodox. At Michigan City there was St. George Syrian Orthodox; Hammond had St. Michael Ukrainian Orthodox.[12]

By 1910 the Poles at South Bend had multiplied in their Catholic parishes of St. Hedwig (1877), St. Casimir (1898), St. Stanislaus (1900) and St. Adalbert (1909) until they accounted for a third of the city's population and land area. For a time the enrollment at St. Hedwig School exceeded that of any other parochial or public school in the city. St. Andrew Greek Orthodox and SS. Peter and Paul Serbian Orthodox churches were also in South Bend. Fort Wayne had parishes for Romanian Orthodox and Syrian Orthodox. There were St. Michael Greek Orthodox Church and St. Bavo Belgian Catholic Church in Mishawaka. A few of the later immigrants were Protestants, the Hungarian Reformed for example, but their numbers in Indiana were small. Gary had its Romanian Baptist and Hungarian Baptist churches.[13]

The flow of new immigrants from southern and southeastern Europe slowed during the First World War. It nearly stopped after 1924 because of national legislation imposing strictly selective immigration quotas. Loyalty to European ethnic institutions generally waned as the children of new generations lost competence in the old languages and were led by intermarriage or economic advancement to move from the old neighborhoods. Churches and ethnic societies, with their recurrent celebrations and reunions, were among the more persistent preservers of ethnic tradition.[14]

Ministries to Ethnics

Indiana's existing Protestant and Catholic churches, established a generation or more and now at home on the American scene, paid some attention to the influx of immigrants and blacks. Scores of individual members and church organizations responded to them as persons in need. They provided distribution points for food and clothing, family health clinics, classes in English and citizenship, recreational activities, and Sunday schools.

Among the many providers were Presbyterians with programs at Neighborhood House in Gary and Hill Crest Community Center in Clinton. Episcopalians founded St. Antonio Episcopal Mission for Italians and Hispanics in Gary. Methodists established a mission for Italians in Indianapolis; in Gary they shared in a massive ministry through Stewart House and Friendship House.[15]

Two graduates of Butler University formed Christamore in Indianapolis. The Christian Church also played a key role in support of both Flanner House and the American Settlement in Indianapolis. Baptists established the East Side Christian Center (later Edna Martin Christian Center) in Indianapolis and Brooks House of Christian Service in Hammond. Oscar Carleton McCulloch made Plymouth Congregational Church of Indianapolis into a center for a whole range of social ministries.[16] Churches were linked with the founding and support of the black YMCAs and YWCAs in Evansville, Muncie, and Indianapolis. The YWCA, in turn, was founding sponsor of the International Institute of Gary which was oriented more toward preservation than toward elimination of ethnicity.[17]

Catholic bishop Herman J. Alerding approved an East Chicago mission for Italians to be established by the Carmelite Sisters of the Divine Heart of Jesus in 1913. Alerding and his priest appointee John B. de Ville also labored for Americanization of immigrants through the Gary-Alerding Settlement House, the city's largest and most elaborate after 1923. The Our Lady of Victory Missionary Sisters, an Indiana Catholic order lately founded by John Francis Noll, made a special mission of Spanish language assistance to thousands of Mexicans attracted to Indiana steel mills but subject to abuse and sometimes to abrupt deportation.[18] Every kind of church agency and mission organization among the recent immigrants carried an immense burden of relief work during the terrors of the Great Depression. For example, in the month of March of 1931 alone the "soupline" of the famous Katherine House of Christian Fellowship in East Chicago served 10,443 free meals—typically vegetables, small portion of meat, bread, and coffee—at a cost of a little more than seven cents per meal.[19]

African Americans in Indiana

Indiana's total black population also seemed small. It was only about 1 percent of the state's total population from its earliest years through 1860 and had only grown to 2.8 percent by 1920. However the impact of this minority in Indiana was also heightened by its concentration in a few urban centers.[20]

Slavery was early declared illegal in Indiana. Both the Northwest Ordinance of 1787 and Indiana's state constitution in 1816 said "There shall be neither slavery nor involuntary servitude . . . otherwise than for the punishment of crimes, whereof the party shall have been duly convicted." The constitution's Bill of Rights added "nor shall any indenture of any negro or mulatto hereafter made or executed out of the bounds of this state be of any validity within the state." This legal stance was not intended as any welcome whatever to black immigration. The majority of Hoosiers did not want black slaves in the state but they did not want black free persons either. They said they feared inundation with a flood of poor black refugees from the South.[21]

Under pressure from the general public and the governor, the legislature passed a "black law" in 1831 requiring any black entering the state to post a bond of $500 as a pledge of solvency and good behavior. That law was not widely enforced. If Indiana was inhospitable and often hostile to blacks, other places were even worse. So immigration to Indiana continued—free blacks from other free states; manumitted slaves required to leave certain parts of the South because free blacks were not tolerated there; fugitives escaping from slavery. The census of 1850 reported 11,262 blacks widely distributed in Indiana. Counties with the largest concentrations were Marion (650), Randolph (662), Vigo (748), and Wayne (1,036). Quaker communities were especially likely to befriend and support blacks.[22]

The continuing increase in black population and controversy over enforcement of the 1831 black law provoked the strenuous Article XIII in the new state constitution of 1851. It stated flatly "No negro or mulatto shall come into, or settle in the State, after the adoption of this Constitution." Article XIII was submitted to the voters separately and was ratified by an especially large margin.[23]

The Civil War and three federal amendments in the years 1865 to 1870 made drastic changes. They made blacks free persons, citizens, and voters. Blacks could legally move north to a better hope, however feeble. In Indiana blacks had not been allowed to vote, to testify in court against whites, to serve on juries, or to attend public schools. Some of the limitations, such as the infamous Article XIII, were nullified by the courts and legislatures within a decade. However restriction of blacks was continued for a century by local laws, by social enforcement of traditional legalisms never officially enacted, and by denial of educational or economic opportunity.[24]

Meanwhile the flow of blacks to Indiana, though not uniform, was continuous. The state's black illiteracy rate got worse, from 15.5 percent in 1860 to 26.4 percent in 1880. New arrivals from the South went to Indianapolis and the northern Indiana cities. Blacks from the older towns along the Ohio River also moved to Indianapolis and the northern Indiana cities. Second generation members from the score of black farm settlements in Indiana went to the cities for better opportunities so these rural communities disappeared and black farmers became rare.[25]

So in 1910 Indianapolis had the highest percentage of black population of any Northern city in America with over 100,000 residents; the black percentage for Boston was 2 percent, for Chicago 2 percent, and for New York 1.9 percent but for Indianapolis 9.3 percent. When Indiana had 80,810 blacks in 1920, 43 percent of them (34,678) lived in Indianapolis. From 1930 to 1949 Indianapolis was remarkable as a Northern city with two separate public school systems as racially segregated as the dual systems of the South. During that period all Indianapolis blacks electing to attend public high school were required to go to Crispus Attucks.[26] By 1960 one in every five persons in Indianapolis was black and in 1990 blacks there numbered 165,570.[27]

Gary became the second great attraction for black Hoosiers. It was founded as a completely new industrial city on Lake Michigan in 1906. European immigrants moved in to make steel. In 1910 there were only 383 blacks there but by 1920 there were 5,299. European immigration slowed. However, as some powerful industrial unions eased racial discrimination, blacks kept flowing from Mississippi, Alabama, Arkansas, Georgia, and Tennessee to search for opportunities in Gary. The 1970 census indicated that 25 percent of the white population had moved from the city in the previous decade while 23,500 blacks had arrived. That year Gary was 55 percent black. There were also substantial black minorities at East Chicago, South Bend, and Fort Wayne as well as smaller black communities in such industrial towns as Anderson, Kokomo, and Muncie. Evansville was the only southern Indiana city with a large black population.[28]

Black Churches

Progress in racial integration in Indiana was resisted by whites out of prejudice and fear. Then it was resisted by blacks out of racial pride. In the face of repression and deprivation, blacks set up a whole institutional structure of their own—clubs, lodges, teams, newspapers, organizations for mutual support in sickness or crisis. The most impressive, powerful, useful, effective, and highly valued among these institutions were the black churches.[29]

There were a few black Methodist members in the predominantly white churches at first—13 in Lawrenceburg and Whitewater in 1812, 11 in Madison in 1823, 442 in the entire Indiana Methodist Conference in 1839. But only a very small minority of blacks and whites ever managed to continue in church membership together. Wounds of repression and segregation, past and current, kept interfering with fellowship. Policies of racial restriction in housing separated black and white neighborhoods and so divided their churches. A survey of Marion County Protestant churches as late as 1951 reported that fifty-four churches responding would accept members of another race but twenty-three would not.[30] Some commentators explained separation by invoking a primitive African mystique which made black religion qualitatively different.[31]

For whatever complex of reasons or causes, blacks generally gathered in churches of their own. There were some black congregations within the predominantly white mainline denominations such as Second Christian, Witherspoon Presbyterian, and St. Philip Episcopal in Indianapolis in 1920. A separate Lexington Conference for black Methodists within the larger Methodist denomination had 4,004 members in Indiana in 1956. Evansville's Grace Lutheran Church, Missouri Synod, was a black congregation with a white pastor. St. John parish in Evansville was for black Catholics.[32]

But the most impressive action was among black churches within separate black denominations, typically Methodist and Baptist.[33] In these receptive settings many black people, long denied formal education and social opportunity, hastened to develop themselves into articulate leaders. From deprived illiterates they moved within a generation to find places in their own churches as bishops and superintendents and musicians and youth leaders and committee members. Black women took positions of responsibility in the churches and received recognition for their leadership. In an inhospitable world members of these congregations took care of one another.

In Bloomington, the church comprised much of the social life of the early Black settlers. They frequently went to church three times a day or went and stayed all day. The church offered companionship and recreational opportunities: the choir, the Missionary Society, dinners, neighborhood clubs, sewing circles, various jobs at the church, plays, and picnics. At church socials, many young Black men and women became acquainted and later married.[34]

Yale psychiatrist James P. Comer described the black Baptist Church in East Chicago, Indiana, in which his father was a deacon and in which he grew up in the 1940s. He said the church "was the place to discharge frustration and hostility so that one could face injustice and hardship the rest of the week." He added:

> The black church had another important function: it was a place for participation and belonging. The deacons, trustees and ushers were ten feet tall on Sunday. This was not Inland Steel, Miss Ann's Kitchen nor the bank. This—the church—was theirs. In retrospect, the trustees were like the city board of finance and the deacons were like the city council. There was a little bit of respect for everybody.[35]

Black ministers became highly visible community leaders. From the strength of these church centers pastors and people could act to bring about some social change. The church became the matrix of black culture and of many valued black institutions.[36]

So when the Works Progress Administration (WPA) researchers for the Indiana Records Survey came counting churches in Indianapolis at the end of the 1930s they found black churches named Allen Chapel, Bethel Church, Coppin Chapel, St. John Church, and St. Paul Church of the African Methodist Episcopal denomination. For the African Methodist Episcopal Zion church they found Alleyne Chapel, Caldwell's Chapel, Jones' Chapel, Kyle's Mission, Messiah's Temple, Penick's Chapel, and St. Mark Church. The Colored Methodist Episcopal denomination had Phillips Memorial and Trinity Church. Of black Baptist churches the city had seen explosive expansion. One association (General Missionary Baptist State Convention of Indiana, Inc.) reported thirty-nine black churches in Indianapolis named Antioch, Bethlehem, Beulah, Galilee, Gethsemane, Good Hope, Good Will, Greater Ebenezer, Greater St. John, Greater St. Luke, Macedonia, Mount Helm, Mount Horeb, Mount Lebanon, Mount Sinai, Mount Vernon, Mount Zion, New Baptist, New Era, New Light, New Mission, North Side, Pilgrim, Good Samaritan, Second Baptist, Seventeenth Street, St. James, Tabernacle, Trinity, and Twenty-Fifth Street. And a second association (Indiana Baptist Association) added twenty-six more in the city named Bethesda, Corinthian, Eastern Star, Emmanuel, Fall Creek, First Baptist of Irvington, First Baptist of West Indianapolis, Friendship, Garfield, Metropolitan, Mount Calvary, Mount Carmel, Mount Nebo, Mount Olive, Mount Paran, Mount Pilgrim, New Bethel, New Liberty, North Indianapolis, Olivet, St. Paul, St. Mark, Shiloh, South Calvary, Tried Stone, and Union.

The Calumet area along Lake Michigan was no match for Indianapolis but listed thirteen African Methodist Episcopal churches and seventeen black churches affiliated with Baptist conventions plus ten "Independent Negro Baptist Churches" in Gary alone named Gospel Mission, First Free Baptist, Grant Street, Lillie, Morning Star, Mount Olive, Progressive, Providence, Purity, and Zion.[37] These were some of the churches in 1940 when blacks made up only 3.6 percent of the population of the state and 18 percent of the population of Gary. The percentage of blacks in the state would more than double to 8.8 percent by 1990, still lower than any neighboring state except Kentucky and well below the 12.1 percent of black population for the nation as a whole. By then Gary, with 93,982 blacks in a total population of 116,646, had known a black majority for more than twenty years. In East Chicago ethnic minorities made up 81 percent of the population, about half of them Hispanic and about one-third black.[38]

Ku Klux Klan

What Indiana needed for the years of immigration and urban concentration was a generous measure of grace and restraint. What Indiana got was professional promotion of hatred and polarization culminating in the resurgence of the Ku Klux Klan. There was a continuing undercurrent of anti-Catholicism in the state. When Alessandro Gavazzi came to America in 1853, he was welcomed to speak on 29–30 October at Indianapolis on the evils of the Church of Rome, on the dangers of Catholic schools, and on the horrors of the Inquisition. During the next year secret lodges of the anti-Catholic "Know Nothing" party organized at such Indiana towns as Lawrenceburg, Versailles, Madison, New Albany, and Rushville. The party's claim of 87,000 members in its Indiana "wigwams" was probably exaggerated. The Know Nothings were soon eclipsed nationally by debate over the larger slavery issue and went into decline everywhere by 1858.[39]

But as the number of incoming Catholics increased, fears of degradation and conspiracy persisted. What if their drinking and violence undercut the nation's moral character? What if they chose to control elections wherever they lived simply by block voting? What if they subverted the traditional Protestant character of the public schools? What if they consolidated and wielded their economic power through organized labor? What if the conspiring world hierarchy of Catholic clergy shaped them into an agency to give control of America to the Pope? In 1876 Richard Wigginton Thompson of Indiana published his book entitled *The Papacy and Civil Power*. He said there was an irreconcilable conflict between papal theory and popular government. President Rutherford B. Hayes named Thompson to be Secretary of the Navy that year, symbolic of contemporary Republican championship of traditional public schools and openness to anti-Catholicism.[40]

A new organizer of anti-Catholic sentiment was the American Protective Association (A.P.A.), formed in the law office of Henry Francis Bowers at Clinton, Iowa, on the afternoon of Sunday, 13 March 1887. By the elections of 1894 it was claiming a membership of almost 2.5 million organized coast to coast with immense political power. Perhaps 100,000 of these members were actually in the A.P.A. as a lodge, a secret fraternal order with rituals, robes, officers, titles, and exciting conventions. The remainder were more loosely linked to the A.P.A. as a federation of existing groups now united in the cause of anti-Catholicism. The A.P.A. never grew great in Indiana. The state A.P.A. council would not tolerate the use of sensational "former priests" as lecturers. Membership lists were leaked so the secret members feared exposure or boycott. One Indianapolis A.P.A. officer was charged with corruption and forced to resign his office as city street commissioner. Before the 1894 elections governor Claude Matthews of Indiana attacked the A.P.A. in his speech to the state's Democratic convention after which the delegates put a condemnation plank into the party platform. The A.P.A. reported that Indiana's organization ranked seventeenth among the states. Its claim of a Hoosier constituency of 75,850 was inexact and almost certainly exaggerated.[41]

The campaign of the Ku Klux Klan following 1921 had a whole new level of intensity. There was still the host of white Hoosier Protestants devoted to their religion and culture, sure that these best served the goals of God and country. They felt that persons of their principles and persuasion should be in charge, training and leading a virtuous national populace. The continuing increase of other religions and cultures was disquieting. In the hands of the postwar generation and its leaders, national virtue seemed to be eroding. Rich men and giant corporations served their own ends and seemed beyond the influence of honest ordinary citizens. Prohibition had closed the taverns and gotten numbers of poorer drunkards off the streets. However anybody with eyes could see

there was a new and more affluent coalition of illegal booze, crime, and political corruption. Surely there was a need for action to set things right. There was a popular yearning to join, especially to join a group with secrets, with impressive garb and rituals, with galaxies of offices and titles, with wealth and power, with stout affirmations of mutual loyalty, with a constant agenda of fun, and with a repertory of written and oral stories designed to demonstrate insider group superiority. This was fertile ground for the agents of a resurgent Klan. Indiana was soon in the hands of the nation's ablest Klan sellers. They offered a range of hates and were ready to sell whichever ones the hearers of the moment would buy. They simply fleeced the Hoosiers without mercy.[42]

In late summer of 1920 Evansville organized the first klavern of the Klan north of the Mason-Dixon. The state's Klan structure was to become the nation's largest and most politically powerful. Klan officers did not intend to provide complete membership information. There are estimates that about one-fourth of Indiana's white native-born Protestant males became Klan members. Perhaps one-fourth of white native-born Protestant females became Women of the Klan. There were Klan programs for all ages. For a brief period Indiana was permeated and sometimes dominated by a Klan presence which claimed to be secret but was at the same time highly visible and inescapable. Targeted as enemies were Catholics, blacks, Jews, immigrants, Mormons, labor radicals, bootleggers, moonshiners, theater owners, dance hall operators, radical feminists, and abusers of women. This explosion of nativism and bigotry artfully directed to the goals of power and greed would mark the image of Indiana forever.[43]

Everybody paid David Curtis Stephenson. He was a rascal demagogue from Oklahoma, not much handicapped by either principle or religion. Operating at Evansville after brief military service in the First World War, he was given opportunity to expand his talent for sales and organization in the service of coal interests. Whatever he touched grew large and was described by him even more largely. When he gravitated to membership in that first northern klavern of the Klan in Evansville, nobody saw its potential so clearly as he.

The Klan had been founded in the South in 1865 to dominate the former slaves. There was much talk of protecting pure white womanhood and much violence against any blacks trying to exercise their new citizenship. Enforcement of the law crippled that first Klan. A resurgent "Second Klan" came into being in 1915 in the South following the persistent crusading of a Methodist minister named William J. Simmons and the popularity of a movie entitled *Birth of a Nation*. Patriotism, purity of the white race, and opposition to Catholic conspiracy were the new themes. When that formula proved very popular, two Georgia promoters named Edward Young Clarke and Elizabeth Tyler took the enterprise from the inefficient preacher and made themselves rich. Hiram Evans of Texas, in turn, took control of the Klan from them. There was real money to be made. The recruiter who signed up a new Klan member got one-fourth of the $10 initiation fee.[44]

No Klan salesman equaled D. C. Stephenson. In 1922 the Klan powers at Atlanta sent Stephenson from Evansville to the Klan office at the state capital. He set up his coal office near the state house as a nerve center for all his enterprises. He helped establish the Klan paper called the *Fiery Cross* and build its circulation to 50,000 copies within a year. Every time a new Klan member paid the initiation fee of $10 in Indiana Stephenson got his fourth of it. There were 117,969 new members in Indiana alone between 25 June 1922 and 21 July 1923.

Stephenson was no stranger to violence. He directed a semi-legal vigilante group called the Horse Thief Detective Association which was capable of any necessary terror. However his main interest was not the kind of violent enforcement which had marked the original Klan in the South or was being practiced by the resurgent Second Klan in Texas. Young people petting in a parked car or a persistently unfaithful spouse might receive a warning Klan visitation. A damaging rumor broadcast by the "poison squads" of Indiana Klan women was a more frequent chastisement than the whips of the troops of the Klan's grand dragon. Indiana had much Klan show and serious intimidation but few actual beatings or lynchings.[45]

Stephenson wanted a huge and disciplined Klan membership because of the money it yielded. At the grand Klan rally at Kokomo on the Fourth of July in 1923, to be remembered as the largest meeting in the history of the Klan, Stephenson was inaugurated grand dragon of the realm of Indiana and given charge of Klan organizing in seven other Northern states. He received commissions from the thousands of new members plus a share of profit from sales of robes, handbooks, and paraphernalia. So he had plenty of money for cars and bodyguards and a big house in the stylish Irvington section of Indianapolis and even a yacht for parties on Lake Michigan. He shared in a grand plan of some Hoosier klansmen to purchase Valparaiso University and make it a Klan school.[46]

Most of all Stephenson wanted a huge and disciplined Klan membership for the political power to be achieved through its block voting. Candidates who wanted to assure their election by nailing down a large block of support were made to pay in many ways for Klan endorsement. The military efficiency of the Klan made it a force in some Indiana elections in 1922 and dominant in elections at state level in 1924. Stephenson dreamed of building a power base which could control election of the president of the United States.[47]

Instead of supporting his grand hopes, the Indiana Klan divided into warring factions only partly under his control. Stephenson ravished and raped Madge Oberholtzer of Indianapolis in 1925. Oberholtzer died. Stephenson was indicted for murder and went to penitentiary for thirty years. He who had done so much to energize the rise of the national Klan became the chief agent of its decline. Most people hastened to deny association with such an unsavory organization. In 1928 the *Indianapolis Times* was awarded a Pulitzer Prize for its anti-Klan campaign.[48]

In its days of power the Ku Klux Klan took on many churchly forms. It deliberately blended with Protestant membership and found among many Protestants at least a silent assent. It marched to "Onward Christian Soldiers" and the Klan hymn was "The Old Rugged Cross." There was much talk of "allegiance to the Master" and every klansman's stated model was said to be "the living Christ." At their meetings Klan members read the Bible, sang hymns, and recited the Lord's Prayer. Able Protestant preachers were recruited as speakers. The Klan provided ceremonial orders for baptism of babies and for induction of youth, women, or adult males into their appropriate Klan divisions. Rituals often focused on the Ten Commandments. There were well publicized Klan donations to needy persons and to worthy causes.

Leaders spoke of the Klan as the church "in action," a uniting of church people of all denominations who wanted to get something done. The Klan wanted especially to be seen as a champion of public morality. A historian has cited one handout of Indiana's Klan:

> Remember, every criminal, every gambler, every thug, every libertine, every girl ruiner, every home wrecker, every wife beater, every dope peddler, every moonshiner, every crooked politician, every pagan Papist priest, every shyster lawyer, every K. of C. [Knight of Columbus], every white slaver, every brothel madam, every Rome controlled newspaper, every black spider—is fighting the Klan. Think it over. Which side are you on?[49]

To accomplish its mission the Klan fed on churches and church people. Organizers opening a new territory often made their approach through Protestant congregations. A minister convinced of the worthiness of Klan goals could be offered a free membership, an opportunity to become a recruiter and so receive a portion of each initiation fee, or a place on the roster of Klan speakers. Some pastors arranged that most dramatic event for a church in which a fully garbed Klan deputation would interrupt the worship service on signal and stride up the aisle in silence to present a cash contribution.[50]

Quaker minister Daisy Douglas Barr was a powerful speaker widely known across the state because of her crusades for evangelical religion, patriotism, temperance, women's rights, and Republican politics. She personally recruited 75,000 Indiana and Ohio women into the Women of the Ku Klux Klan. Preachers who would not cooperate with the Klan might be put under immense pressure by influential congregation members.[51]

The Klan marshalled its horse troops, marching bands, singing groups, and orators for scores of initiation ceremonies, fireworks displays, picnics, patriotic parades, carnivals, cross burnings, and mass rallies. In 1923 alone there were estimated crowds of 16,000 "somewhere in Howard County" in February; 50,000 at Valparaiso in May; 10,000 at Franklin in June; 50,000 in the woods near Mooresville in July; somewhere between 10,000 and 200,000 at Kokomo in July; and 30,000 in Richmond in October. For such events the church organizations were mobilized along with the whole community to care for the crowds. Where the local newspaper was friendly to the Klan, a common enough arrangement, news and announcements for the churches and the Klan could be happily commingled.[52]

The Indiana Klan also used the church to define itself negatively. Its enemy was Catholicism. Zealous Klan members saw themselves as essential defenders against Catholic invasion and conspiracy. Catholics were so dangerous that any charge against them could be believed and disseminated. Catholic teaching against heresies was translated into a sinister Catholic plan to exterminate Protestants. The Catholic hierarchy and its host of obedient members surely intended to destroy the public schools, overthrow the civil government, and bring the papal seat to America. Catholic churches and institutions were reported to be storing guns to accomplish all this.

Monasteries and convents were labeled places of entrapment and immorality. "Former priests" and "escaped nuns" were frequent speakers on the Klan circuit. The *Fiery Cross*, published weekly from Indianapolis and sold

on street corners, advertised the lectures of Helen Jackson who claimed to have escaped from a convent in Michigan. There were also ads there for Jackson's autobiography entitled *Convent Cruelties*. Before the 1924 election D. C. Stephenson sowed northern Indiana with 100,000 copies of the bogus "Knights of Columbus Oath," an invention too violent and bizarre for civilized citation. Indiana Klan members did revile blacks and Jews and foreigners generally but the language of these assaults was mild compared to wild rhetoric against Catholics.[53]

There were persistent voices against the Klan. Election victories of its candidates were convincing for a time but far from total. Mayor Lewis Shank of Indianapolis opposed the Klan though he lost his job for doing it. George R. Durgan of Lafayette, William E. Wilson of Evansville, Arthur Greenwood of Washington, Joseph P. Turk of Indianapolis, and James W. Hill of Franklin were among those who dared to be anti-Klan political candidates. The Democratic state convention of 1924 put an anti-Klan plank in its platform. Wendell Willkie went from Rushville to the national Democratic Convention that year determined to oppose the Klan there. At South Bend a Klan rally planned to include speeches, parades, bands, and cross burning was broken up by local residents including some Notre Dame students. The Klan managed to rush out thousands of copies of a pamphlet entitled *The Truth about the Notre Dame Riot on Saturday, May 17th, 1924* and turn the incident into a Klan recruiting bonanza.[54]

Victims of the Klan responded with courage, the *Indianapolis Freeman* and the *Indianapolis Recorder* for blacks and the *Indiana Jewish Chronicle* for Jews. The *Indiana Catholic and Record* and its editor Joseph Patrick O'Mahoney were persistent voices against the Klan from the time it appeared in Indianapolis in 1921. *Tolerance* was a journal published by the American Unity League in Chicago and well circulated in Indiana. It was quick to expose the Klan's extreme positions and actions. It especially liked to obtain secret Klan membership lists and publish the names as it did for 12,208 Indianapolis Klansmen in spring of 1923. The Klan list reported in *Tolerance* for May 13 reported names and addresses for the ministers of twenty-eight Klan churches in Indianapolis—twelve Methodist, six Baptist, three Presbyterian, one Quaker, one Free Methodist, two Christian, two Nazarene, one United Brethren. It included twenty-one other Klan ministers in the city whose churches were unknown. A few local newspapers dared to oppose the Klan in print, for example, the Muncie *Post-Democrat*, the Winchester *Democrat*, and the Richmond *Palladium*.[55]

Among the churches, the Indianapolis Diocese of the Protestant Episcopal Church denounced the Klan. So did one regional Methodist newspaper and the Church of the Nazarene. Rabbi Morris Feuerlicht leaped into a Klan parade and ripped the hoods off some marchers. At least three Indianapolis ministers were among those forced from their pulpits for resisting the Klan. At Seventh Christian some church members were so displeased they burned a cross in front of the house of Clay Trusty, their anti-Klan pastor. The Klan's *Fiery Cross* reported the story. James M. Eakins left Memorial Presbyterian under pressure after preaching an anti-Klan sermon.[56]

At Englewood Christian, Frank Elon Davison called his personal attempts to prevent invasion by the Klan his "baptism by fire." Davison was a native of Brownsburg, alumnus of Butler University and Yale Divinity School, and pastor at Spencer and Sheridan before coming to Indianapolis. In February of 1923 the Englewood members surprised him with a party for his thirty-sixth birthday, expressing their affection with gifts and speeches urging him to spend the rest of his life in that pastorate. That spring more than 200 members were added during a revival which Davison conducted.

> At the close of that meeting a committee of three elders waited on me in my office. These good friends of mine said they wanted to make me the greatest preacher in the state. They further stated that they had two hundred men and their families ready to join the church if I would line up with a certain 100 per cent American organization. They hinted that I would be invited to make many speeches for that organization for which I would receive handsome remunerations. I did not quarrel with my brethren but when they demanded an answer, I opened the New Testament and read to them the story of the temptations.[57]

The official board at Englewood went ahead with plans and public announcements in preparation for a state-wide meeting of the Klan in the community hall of the church. Davison announced to the congregation on Sunday morning that the proposed Klan meeting was being held at the church without the consent of the pastor and over his protest. There was front page publicity for a few days; Davison came under immense pressure from fellow ministers serving the Klan and from local Klan supporters.

> The elders of the church called me into a meeting one night with the evident purpose of asking for my resignation. Dr. George Brown, professor at the College of Missions, was apparently the only elder unsympathetic to

the Klan. However, most of the elders could remember some service I had rendered them, their families, or the church. No one in the group could be found to move for my resignation. When Dr. Brown called the elders to their knees and he started the prayers, my emotions gave way. I left the room and went to my office. The office overlooked the community hall. A preliminary meeting to the state gathering was being held in the hall. I could hear the shouts and cheers of the men in that group. It did not take much effort to imagine that they were shouting for my blood—at least for my scalp. With my head upon my desk I wept. When prayers were over, Dr. Brown slipped into my office and, without saying a word, he held my hand while I sobbed out my heartache.[58]

Then Davison's resignation was accepted. He exchanged the pastoral ministry for work in a local bank until he could receive a call to a pastorate in another state.

John Francis Noll

Indiana was burdened with the nation's largest Klan generating nastiness against Catholics. At the same time the state produced and supported one of the nation's most effective and prolific Catholic defenders. John Francis Noll developed a Hoosier institution to speak up for Catholics. He invested his entire ministry in Indiana and became a kind of Hoosier Catholic institution himself, thriving well before the resurgence of the Klan and continuing long after its demise.[59]

Noll grew up in Fort Wayne knowing no language but English. Command of plain English was to become his best working tool. His stepmother, a recent convert, gave him Catholic instruction at home and then sent him to Cathedral School which was taught by Holy Cross Brothers. After his early interest in the priesthood was verified he was sent to Saint Lawrence College, operated by Capuchins in Wisconsin. There he had to learn German because textbooks were written in it and midwestern parishes would demand German competence. At seminary at Mount Saint Mary's in Cincinnati he was good in theology and especially good in apologetics, the answering of attacks on the faith. At age twenty-three, in 1898, he was ordained a priest and the next year became pastor at Kendallville, Indiana. Missionary duties were added until he was also priest for Ligonier, Millersburg, Rome City, and Albion.

As an earnest Catholic Noll found it irritating that the communities he served knew very little about Catholicism and that most of the things they did know about Catholicism were lies. He felt personally responsible for informing the whole of any town in which he labored, for teaching the heretics, infidels, and schismatics as well as the faithful. He was a born promoter and he loved to "argue religion," standing forcefully for his faith. So much malicious misinformation was being circulated about Catholics that he could generally gain support by simply exposing the lies and then appealing to his hearers' sense of fair play. Hoosiers still enjoyed a denominational fight. He was always prepared for a confrontation, the more publicity the better. First there were public lectures on the Catholic faith at Millersburg with some converts gained. Then there were public lectures at Kendallville and an interchange with the local Church of Christ preacher after which the latter left town.

Particular game for Noll were the anti-Catholic lecturers, often billed as "ex-priests," who toured the state lifting offerings from crowds in return for heavy doses of what Catholics came to call "Puritan pornography," lurid illustrated tales of evil doings in convents and confessionals. When Noll challenged them in Rome City and Lagrange and Hartford City he found they were showmen who had never been priests at all and did not know even the rudiments of Catholic faith.

Some Catholic laymen went with him to rout a lecturer at Farmland; one of them was moved to put up $10,000 to pay the "ex-priest" if he could disprove any of the charges which Noll made. It was a tactic Noll used consistently from then on. An early published form of the challenge offered $10,000 reward to any anti-Catholic lecturer who could offer proof that

(1) The Catholic Church forbids her people to read the Bible (in South America or any country); (2) Indulgences are sold; (3) A fee is charged for Confessions; (4) Catholics worship images or pictures; (5) Catholics owe political allegiance to Rome; (6) The Catholic hierarchy is seeking to control American politics; (7) Immoralities are common in convents or monasteries; (8) The Catholic Church is seeking to destroy the Public School system; (9) Girls are detained in convents against their will.[60]

The reward was also offered "for proof of the genuineness of the K. of C. Oath, or of the Jesuits' oath; for proof that the Jesuits ever taught that 'the end justifies the means,' etc., etc." By October 28 of 1928, on the eve of the election involving presidential candidate Alfred E. Smith, this reward list had been extended to proof that

(12) The Catholic Church refuses to acknowledge as valid the marriages of Protestants; (13) Catholics are given undue government patronage; (14) Our country would be benefited by closing the parochial schools; (15) The Assassins of Lincoln, Garfield, McKinley were Catholic; (16) Lincoln's "Dark Cloud" utterance is genuine; (17) Catholics believe that the Pope should rule in a temporal way over the world.[61]

In spite of such combativeness against critics of Catholicism, Noll developed a reputation as an internal healer and peacemaker for troubled Catholic parishes. In this role he was appointed priest at Besancon and then at Hartford City. In these places he discovered new personal gifts and new means to use in his drive to get Catholicism fairly understood. The real need was for an instructed Catholic laity. One problem was a shortage of instructional material which laypersons would actually read. At Besancon the congregation was in a bitter dispute about building a parochial school. Noll issued a healing pamphlet on Catholic devotion and character for the membership to try to get them beyond all the controversy over the school question. He called it *Kind Words from the Priest to His People*. It was so much appreciated that he mailed out sample copies to other priests and soon had orders for thousands of copies. The demand never seemed to let up.

At Hartford City Noll experimented with a congregational newspaper called *The Parish Monthly*, a publication he secured from Thomas Price in North Carolina and augmented with four pages of his own local items and ads as a wrapper. He soon found that he did not need to order the North Carolina filler since he really preferred to write the full thirty-two pages per month himself. This "patented core" he sent as sample copy to other parishes and soon had 200 parishes subscribing. It was destined to become *Family Digest* and to increase in circulation to 160,000 copies per month.

Bishop Herman J. Alerding recognized the ability and impact of this young apologist and appointed him pastor at Huntington where he had an assistant and better facilities. Noll made Huntington, Indiana, the most prolific center for Catholic instruction in the nation. By a remarkable turn of events he bought a large printing establishment on time payments. Now he could transfer all his printing business from Muncie and Hartford City and still have extra printing capacity. On 5 May 1912 he issued volume one, number one, of *Our Sunday Visitor*, destined to become and long remain the most widely circulated Catholic weekly newspaper in the United States. Like all his other publications, it arose from Noll's concern about anti-Catholicism and from his zeal for an instructed Catholic laity.

Noll was taking on the big time Catholic haters now, especially *The Menace*, established in 1911 and published in Aurora, Missouri. *The Menace* specialized in stories of Catholic conspiracies and of young damsels abused behind convent walls. Its circulation rose to a million, expanded by initial free deliveries to America's front porches by night. Its success brought a rash of imitators with such names as *The Peril, The American Defender, The American Sentinel, The Beacon Light, The Crescent, The Converted Catholic Evangelist, The Crusader, The Emancipator, The Guardian, The Good Citizen, The Jeffersonian, The Liberator, The Masses, The Patriot, The Silverton Journal, The Sentinel of Liberty, The Torch, Watson's Magazine,* and *The Yellow Jacket*. Most of these papers built circulation by sending promoters on tour, often advertised as former priests or nuns, to give lurid lectures, take up offerings, and solicit subscriptions. Their speeches were often memorized from script supplied by editors of *The Menace*.[62]

Noll duplicated two pages of *The Menace* and on their reverse side printed a Catholic answer in newspaper format. This he mailed to practically every Catholic pastor in the United States asking if the pastor would patronize such a Catholic paper named *Our Sunday Visitor* to be delivered weekly in bundles in time for distribution at the church door on Sunday for one cent a copy or fifty cents per year in advance. First press run was 35,000. By the end of the first year circulation was 200,000; by the end of the second year circulation was 400,000; eventually circulation exceeded 800,000.[63]

After 1913 he promoted his own writing through *Our Sunday Visitor* and secured wide readership. He issued *For Our Non-Catholic Friends*, in later editions entitled *The Fairest Argument*, mostly a collection of non-Catholic quotes which embarrassed Protestants or favored Catholicism. In *Our Sunday Visitor* he ran a long series of articles in dialogue form, a catechumen named "Jackson" acting as straight man for "Father Smith" whose responses covered the whole field of Catholic belief and practice. This series was run twice in its entirety in *Our Sunday Visitor*; was issued in book form as *Father Smith Instructs Jackson*; went through sixty large English editions by 1952; was adopted as the text for the correspondence course provided nationally for Catholic enquirers; was translated into Spanish, German, Hungarian, Chinese, and Japanese and issued in Braille. Over 1,500,000 persons had owned the book by 1952.

Alongside *Our Sunday Visitor* for laity, he shared in development of a periodical for priests, first called *The Acolyte* and later *The Priest*. Writing for this added further to the load of periodical copy he regularly produced. When he saw a need for life-related religious instruction books for Catholic high schools, he produced a four-volume set called *Religion and Life* in six weeks, keeping two secretaries busy with its dictation. His articles and books and pamphlets took on a more international tone after his first world tour. All the while he was pastor, developer of church property, charter member of Rotary, and a leading citizen of Huntington. By bringing together at Huntington a small religious order from Chicago and an initial gift from a California donor, he became co-founder and chief patron of Victory Noll, an order of sisters for home mission work, especially for work among Hispanics in the West.

At age forty-nine Noll succeeded Herman J. Alerding as bishop of Fort Wayne Diocese, conducting his editorial and publishing work alongside his labors as bishop just as he had combined them with pastoral labors earlier. Catholic education had been a lively interest with him earlier. Now it became a consuming episcopal concern. He wanted Catholic young people to be in Catholic elementary and high schools. *Our National Enemy Number One: Education without Religion* was his book on the subject. He felt the state should be paying the parochial school the same amount of money per child that the state would be forced to pay if that Catholic child went to public school.[64]

John Francis Noll of Indiana died in 1956. An era in the life of the Catholic church was dying with him. He was comfortable with the non-scholarly conservative views of many Catholics of his time: (1) Jesus left the Twelve Apostles a detailed blueprint for a church including seven sacraments with precise matter and form, the papacy vested with supreme and universal jurisdiction, the monarchical episcopate, and a particular body of doctrines, liturgies, and laws; (2) that church is primarily the visible Catholic hierarchy whose members are to teach, rule, and sanctify with specifically defined gifts of authority and infallibility; (3) laypersons are in a more secondary and dependent status, to be taught, ruled, and sanctified; (4) the Catholic church alone is the one, true Church of Christ from which other churches have lately broken away in error and so are without any valid claim to rights.[65]

Noll was at home in the pattern of pious practices associated with Mary, the saints, the consecrated wafer of the Eucharist, and the rosary which had flowered among Catholics of the nineteenth and twentieth centuries.[66] He personified much of Catholic heroism in the era before the Second Vatican Council. If people told lies about

Catholics, he exposed them as liars. If people wanted a Catholic to debate, he was ready. If the danger was modernism or socialism or communism, he was the champion of conservative Catholicism. If American Catholics needed to find their identity as both Christians and Americans second to none, he wrote out the rationale for that every week and delivered it to the church door, a penny a copy with quantity discounts. At a time when there seemed to be always more Catholics needing more Catholic churches, more Catholic schools, more Catholic priests and members of orders, and more Catholic institutions, he set a marvelous pace of work and achievement in service of the church.

Catholicism Renewed

But times changed.[67] The great rush of Catholic immigration ended. The relative size of the Protestant and Catholic communities stabilized. Between 1916 and 1955 the national membership of 128 Protestant bodies increased by 94.2 percent while the Catholic church increased by 92.4 percent. Catholicism was no longer viewed as an "immigrant faith" in search of American identity. The year before Noll died Will Herberg published the first edition of his book entitled *Protestant, Catholic, Jew*. "For being a Protestant, a Catholic, or a Jew is understood as the specific way, and increasingly perhaps the only way, of being an American and locating oneself in American society," said this popular book. "Not to be a Catholic, a Protestant, or a Jew today is, for increasing numbers of American people, not to be anything, not to have a name."[68] In Indiana towns most Catholics had become American insiders in their own eyes and in the eyes of others.

Other changes had been happening. Some rudimentary elements of the Catholic heritage were being recovered and enunciated. Within the Catholic church the liturgical movement was bridging the gap between altar and people; the biblical movement was training a corps of scriptural scholars; the social action movement was applying the social teachings of the church; the lay apostolate was involving more laity in the work of the church; the ecumenical movement was studying divided Christendom, the missionary movement was proceeding increasingly under native leadership. Most important of all, as part of a theological renewal, a basic understanding of the church as the people of God found encouragement.

Catholic seminarians at Saint Meinrad or West Baden or Oldenburg or Fort Wayne in Indiana still learned the theology of the old Latin textbooks and manuals. Their churches knew the older style of John Noll and *Our Sunday Visitor*. But Catholic seminarians, and college students, and members of religious orders, and parish members of scholarly inclination were very likely to know some writings of such authors as Karl Rahner, Yves Congar, Henri de Lubac, Edward Schillebeeckx, Hans Küng, and John Courtney Murray who were among those laying the foundations for the documents of Vatican II.[69]

John L. McKenzie was a native son of Brazil, Indiana, internationally respected professor in the Jesuit theological college at West Baden (1942–60) and at Notre Dame (1966–70). He was president of the Catholic Biblical Association from 1953 to 1964. His book *The Two-Edged Sword*, published in 1956, provided an introduction to contemporary Old Testament studies for thousands. His goal during fifty years of teaching and publication was to bring Catholics to excellence as Bible students, willing and able to use the best tools of biblical scholarship.[70]

John A. O'Brien was professor of theology at Notre Dame for forty years (1940–80), author of forty-five books and a specialist at winning converts. His *Faith of Millions* went through twenty-seven editions in ten languages. Yet his stance was not belligerent. O'Brien advocated and cultivated interfaith connections, in one specific instance a rapprochement between the Masons and the Knights of Columbus. His irenic writing and conduct earned him a place as an ecumenical leader. McKenzie and O'Brien of Indiana became national figures in Catholic Renewal well before Vatican II.[71]

When Pope John XXIII officially opened the Second Vatican Council in Rome on 11 October 1962, he said "The council now beginning rises in the Church like daybreak, a forerunner of most splendid light. It is now only dawn." The sixteen council documents issued between 1963 and 1965 constituted a fresh statement of the nature of the Catholic church. Indiana's Joseph Ritter, native of New Albany and graduate of St. Meinrad Seminary, was a cardinal and member of that council. He did not elect to be a silent participant. He assumed leadership among the progressives and intervened repeatedly on behalf of religious liberty, ecumenism, and the collegial nature of the church.[72]

Whether or not they had yet internalized the new documents describing the theological basis and nature of the church, both Catholics and Protestants were impressed with prompt changes in Catholic practice. The Mass went entirely into English with the priest facing the people. Congregation members reared to believe that only the priest should talk in church were now expected to read the Bible aloud from the lectern and to take their parts in the liturgy and to sing. One lamented:

Latin's gone, peace is too; singin' and shoutin' from every pew. Altar's turned around, priest is too; Commentators yellin': "Page 22." Communion rail's gone, stand up straight! Kneelin' suddenly went out of date . . . rosary's out, psalms are in; hardly ever hear a word against sin. Listen to the lector, hear how he reads; Please stop rattlin' them rosary beads . . . I hope all changes are just about done; That they don't drop Bingo, before I've won.[73]

Every person in authority from the parish priest to the Pope was to function in the midst of a council and to take its advice seriously. Instead of simply praying occasionally for the conversion of Protestants, the Catholics were to meet with and pray with Protestants as separated brethren. Most of the stereotypes of Catholic behavior, precious to Catholics and Protestants alike, were either removed or declared to be of less than central importance.

The Shape of Renewal

After the initial excitement, Vatican II was followed by a period of crisis in the American Catholic church. Richard McBrien of Notre Dame wrote in 1980:

The symptoms of this present crisis do seem clear enough: the sharp decline in Mass attendance and in vocations to the priesthood and the religious life; the higher incidence of divorce and remarriage; the widening of theological dissent; diversity and pluralism to the point of confusion and doubt in theology, catechetics, and religious education generally; the rejection of papal authority in the matter of birth control, and resistance to that authority on other issues such as the ordination of women and priestly celibacy; the ecumenical movement's challenge to Catholic identity and distinctiveness; the alienation of young people from the Church; the abiding social and cultural dominance of science and technology, with its correlative impact upon traditional spiritual values and motivation; the continuing and inevitable involvement of the Church on both sides of the historic struggle between rich and poor, oppressor and oppressed; the raised consciousness of women in the Church.[74]

In the face of the crisis Catholics all the way from Rome to the local parish were tempted to draw back. Almost all priests voiced support for the conciliar decrees but a few pastors had pretty well exhausted their capacity for change when they began offering Mass in English facing the people. In some parishes the membership divided. At the extreme conservative end of the spectrum were a few who tried to take the church back to Mass in Latin only and to all the old ways. Authorities disciplined them but then allowed some of the familiar practices for pastoral reasons.[75]

Mary Jo Weaver in Indiana was a voice from another group at the extreme liberal end of the spectrum.

Against a traditional interpretation that confines nuns to convents and women to the home, Catholic women have bonded with those who believe that the gospel is to be found in the lives of oppressed peoples. Surprisingly, they have discovered that, as women, they themselves are among the oppressed and so can look to their own marginalized situation as a locus of divine revelation. Through their participation in Catholic feminist organizations and their support of the Womanchurch movement, they have radicalized yesterday's questions and imagined a future in which patriarchal institutions cease to exist. Those meeting in Chicago in 1983, for example, were not overconcerned with the question of women's ordination: for them it was a given that women could and would celebrate the Eucharist, and their actions (there, and later in small groups all over the country) questioned, not so much whether women could be priests, but whether priests, as presently constituted in Roman Catholicism, were necessary. The Second Vatican Council's slogan for the laity—"We are the church"—has been taken seriously by women as they leave the patriarchal institution but refuse to leave the community of Jesus.[76]

Surrounded by such diversity the main body of Indiana's Catholics, committed to continuous reform, worked out the shape of ongoing parish life. The number of Hoosier Catholics kept growing; the state's 1960 membership of 611,415 became 717,799 by 1980.[77] At the same time the number of priests, monks, and nuns kept declining. Polls in the 1980s and 1990s indicated that a majority of American Catholics would welcome married clergy and those favoring ordination of women were approaching a majority. There was no indication that church authorities were about to approve either practice.[78]

The Archdiocese of Indianapolis, largest of five Catholic dioceses in Indiana, reported a decline from about 220 priests in 1970 to 130 priests in 1992 and several of the remaining ones were nearing retirement. Of the 111 theological students at St. Meinrad Seminary that year only 17 were affiliated with Indianapolis Archdiocese so the number of priests to be ordained from there could be expected to remain low. The Archdiocese made headlines in Southern Indiana newspapers in spring of 1992 with a preliminary proposal to close seven churches and to "cluster" sixty-three others in yoked pastoral arrangements to share the services of priests.

Compensating for the loss of clergy was a striking increase of lay leadership. Some Catholic laymen completed their qualification as deacons. As deacons they could administer parish organizations. They could be authorized to preside at baptisms and weddings as well as distribute Communion and preach. By 1982 there were 4,725 American deacons.[79]

In the 1992 proposal of the Indianapolis Archdiocese to close seven churches and cluster sixty-three were a dozen other churches suggested for assignment to the leadership of "parish life coordinators." Many of these coordinators were women, often nuns now taking a leadership role in a parish instead of doing their traditional duties in a school. They could perform a very wide range of parish ministries, arranging visits by a priest for essential clerical acts. The *Newsletter* of the Sisters of St. Benedict at Ferdinand, Indiana, for April of 1987 listed nineteen sisters of that order alone engaged in some form of parish ministry in southern Indiana.[80]

At every level short of sacrament in all types and sizes of Catholic churches the renewal enlisted an army of men and women to serve as decision makers in parish councils and committees, to plan worship, to read Scriptures, to lead prayers, to lead singing, to distribute communion, to provide religious education, to lead youth programs, to visit the sick or elderly, and to represent their church in a variety of community services. The Catholic church, once prone to leave everything to the clergy, had become distinguished for its lay participation.

NOTES

1. *The Indiana Centennial, 1916* (Indianapolis, Ind.: Indiana Historical Commission, 1919), 330–33.

2. James H. Madison, *Indiana Through Tradition and Change: A History of the Hoosier State and Its People 1920–1945* (Indianapolis, Ind.: Indiana Historical Society, 1982), 3.

3. Emma Lou Thornbrough, *Indiana in the Civil War Era, 1850–1880* (Indianapolis, Ind.: Indiana Historical Bureau and Indiana Historical Society, 1965), 404–24; Clifton J. Phillips, *Indiana in Transition: The Emergence of an Industrial Commonwealth, 1880–1920* (Indianapolis, Ind.: Indiana Historical Bureau and Indiana Historical Society, 1968), 271–322.

4. Thomas T. McAvoy, "The Formation of the Catholic Minority in the United States 1820–1860," *Review of Politics* 10 (January 1948): 13–34; Thomas T. McAvoy, "Catholic Education in Indiana," *Indiana History Bulletin* 23 (January 1946): 55–61; Phillips, *Indiana in Transition*, 463.

5. Carl Wittke, *William Nast: Patriarch of German Methodism* (Detroit, Mich.: Wayne State University, 1959, 248 p.); Orrin Manifold, "American United Methodism Bicentennial and Indiana

United Methodism's Beginnings" (Address at Spring History Workshop of Indiana Historical Society, Turkey Run State Park, 11 May 1984), unpaged.

6. Frank A. Renkiewicz, "The Polish Settlement of St. Joseph County, Indiana, 1855–1935" (Ph.D. diss., University of Notre Dame, 1967), 33–34.

7. James J. Divita, *Ethnic Settlement Patterns in Indianapolis* (Indianapolis, Ind.: Marian College, 1988) [119 p., 58 maps] 16–18, 49; Phillips, *Indiana in Transition*, 361–70; Madison, *Indiana Through Tradition and Change*, 13–15.

8. Leo Vincent Krzywkowski, "The Origin of the Polish National Catholic Church of St. Joseph County, Indiana" (Ph.D. diss., Ball State University, 1972), 118–19.

9. Darlene Clark Hine, *When Truth Is Told: A History of Black Women's Culture and Community in Indiana, 1875–1950* (Indianapolis, Ind.: National Council of Negro Women, 1981), 60.

10. Jan Shipps, "J. Frank Hanly: Enigmatic Reformer," in *Gentlemen from Indiana: National Party Candidates, 1836–1940*, ed. Ralph D. Gray (Indianapolis, Ind.: Indiana Historical Bureau, 1977), 237–68; Robert C. Kriebel, *Where the Saints Have Trod; The Life of Helen Gougar* (West Lafayette, Ind.: Purdue University Press, 1985, 238 p.); Phillips, *Indiana in Transition*, 97–101, 128, 494–98.

11. *A Directory of Churches and Religious Organizations in Indiana*, 3 vols. in 4 (Indianapolis, Ind.: Historical Records Survey, 1941, unpaged); Divita, *Ethnic Settlement Patterns in Indianapolis*, 39, 42, 43, 76, 85, 100.

12. *Directory of Churches*.

13. Dean R. Esslinger, *Immigrants and the City: Ethnicity and Mobility in a Nineteenth-Century Midwestern Community* [South Bend] (Port Washington, N.Y.: Kennikat Press, 1975, 156 p.); Donald J. Stabrowski, *Holy Cross and South Bend Polonia* (Notre Dame, Ind.: Indiana Province Archives Center, 1991, 89 p.); Renkiewicz, "Polish Settlement," 45.

14. Divita, *Ethnic Settlement Patterns in Indianapolis*, 54–55, 66, 110–12.

15. James J. Divita, "The Indiana Churches and the Italian Immigrant," *U.S. Catholic Historian* 6 (Fall 1987): 330–33; Ruth Hutchinson Crocker, *Sympathy and Science: The Settlement Movement in Gary and Indianapolis to 1930* (Ann Arbor, Mich.: University Microfilms International, Ph.D. diss., Purdue University, 1982), 260–376, 424–80; James J. Divita, "Hill Crest Mission," *Trailmarker* 13 (February 1985): 3; James B. Lane, *City of the Century: A History of Gary, Indiana* (Bloomington, Ind.: Indiana University Press, 1978), 56–58, 174–77; *Steel Shavings* 12 (issues unnumbered 1986): 15–16; James W. Lewis, *The Protestant Experience in Gary, Indiana, 1906–1975: At Home in the City* (Knoxville, Tenn.: University of Tennessee Press, 1992), 53–58.

16. Israel George Blake, *Finding a Way Through the Wilderness: The Indiana Baptist Convention, 1833–1983* (Indianapolis, Ind.: Central Publishing Company, 1983), 236–38; Genevieve C. Weeks, "Religion and Social Work as Exemplified in the life of Oscar C. McCulloch," *Social Science Review* 39 (March 1965), 38–52; Crocker, "Sympathy and Science," 100–259.

17. Darrel E. Bigham, *We Ask Only a Fair Trial: A History of the Black Community of Evansville, Indiana* (Bloomington, Ind.: Indiana University Press, 1987), 149–50, 186–88, 212; Hurley Goodall and J. Paul Mitchell, *A History of Negroes in Muncie* (Muncie, Ind.:

Ball State University, 1976), 20–21; Madge Dishman, "Paving the Way," *Black History News and Notes* 22 (August 1985): 5–7; George L. Knox, *Slave and Freeman; The Autobiography of George L. Knox* (Lexington, Ky.: University Press of Kentucky, 1979), 23; *Steel Shavings* 17 (issues unnumbered 1988): 29–32.

18. Divita, "Indiana Churches," 335–36; Crocker, "Sympathy and Science," 377–423; Lane, *City of the Century*, 71–76; *Steel Shavings* 13 (issues unnumbered 1987): 52.

19. *Steel Shavings* 17 (issues unnumbered 1988): 34–35, 37–41.

20. Divita, *Ethnic Settlement Patterns in Indianapolis*, 2; Phillips, *Indiana in Transition*, 370–78.

21. Emma Lou Thornbrough, *The Negro in Indiana; A Study of a Minority* (Indianapolis, Ind.: Indiana Historical Bureau, 1957), 5, 23.

22. Henry Ellis Cheaney, "Attitudes of the Indiana Pulpit and Press toward the Negro, 1860–1880" (Ph.D. diss., University of Chicago, 1961, 501 p.); Gregory S. Rose, "The Distribution of Indiana's Ethnic and Racial Minorities in 1850," *Indiana Magazine of History* 87 (September 1991): 246–57; Coy D. Robbins, *1850: Free Colored Persons in Indiana, Based on 7th U.S. Population Census Data* (Bloomington, Ind.: Indiana African American Historical and Genealogical Society, 1990, 2 p.); Thornbrough, *Negro in Indiana*, 31–63. Research of the Indiana Historical Society reported in its *Black History News and Notes* and of the Indiana African American Historical and Genealogical Society reported in its *Ebony Lines* has heightened interest in the history and contributions of this substantial free black element in Indiana's early population.

23. Thornbrough, *Negro in Indiana*, 68.

24. Coy D. Robbins, "The Sundown Laws in Indiana," *Ebony Lines* 3 (Fall 1991): 19–21; Herbert L. Heller, "Negro Education in Indiana from 1816 to 1869" (Ed.D. diss., Indiana University, 1951, 310 p.); Thornbrough, *Negro in Indiana*, 231–54.

25. Xenia Cord, "Black Rural Settlements in Indiana before 1860," *Black History News and Notes* 27 (February 1987): 4–8; Carl Lyles, "The Story of Lyles Station, Indiana," *Black History News and Notes* 11 (November 1982): 4–6; *This Far by Faith: Black Hoosier Heritage* (Indianapolis, Ind.: Indiana Committee for the Humanities, 1982), 1–2; John W. Lyda, *The Negro in the History of Indiana* (Terre Haute, Ind.?: n.p., 1953), 19–28; Emma Lou Thornbrough, *Since Emancipation: A Short History of Indiana Negroes, 1863–1963* (Indianapolis, Ind.?: Indiana Division American Negro Emancipation Centennial Authority, 1963?), 13, 18; Cheaney, "Attitudes of the Indiana Pulpit and Press," 201, 249.

26. Judy Jolley Mohraz, *The Separate Problem: Case Studies of Black Education in the North, 1900–1930* (Westport, Conn.: Greenwood Press, 1979), 123–30; Stanley Warren, "The Evolution of Secondary Schooling for Blacks in Indianapolis: 1869–1930," *Black History News and Notes* 29 (August 1987): 4–7 and 30 (November 1987): 4–7; Rosie Cheatham Mickey, "Russell Lane and Secondary Education in Indianapolis: 1927–1949," *Black History News and Notes* 19 (November 1984): 5–8; *Ebony Lines* 2 (Summer 1990): 6. Other counties with segregated black high schools were Harrison (Corydon Colored), Vanderburgh (Lincoln), Lake (Froebel and Roosevelt), Clark (Taylor), Jefferson (Madison Colored), Posey (Booker T. Washington), Floyd (Scribner), Gibson (Lincoln), Spencer (Rockport).

27. Divita, *Ethnic Settlement Patterns in Indianapolis*, 2, 39, 74, 89, 108.

28. Powell A. Moore, *The Calumet Region: Indiana's Last Frontier* (Indianapolis, Ind.: Indiana Historical Bureau, 1959; reprinted with an afterword by Lance Trusty, 1977), 676–77; Thornbrough, *Since Emancipation*, 16–19.

29. Robert A. Lowe, "Racial Segregation in Indiana, 1920–1950" (Ph.D. diss., Ball State University, 1965, 204 p.). For a description of black institutions in the city of Bloomington, see Frances V. Halsell Gilliam, *A Time to Speak: A Brief History of the Afro-Americans of Bloomington, Indiana, 1865–1965* (Bloomington, Ind.: Pinus Strobus Press, 1985), 26–36; For the black institutional range in the city of Indianapolis, see Divita, *Ethnic Settlement Patterns in Indianapolis*.

30. *Official Report of the 1951 Study on Racial Attitudes of the Protestant Churches of Indianapolis and Marion County*, Sponsors: National Council of Churches of Christ in the United States and the Race Relations Committee of the Church Federation of Indianapolis (Indianapolis, Ind.: n.p., 1952, 9 p.); Bruce E. Miller, "A Report of a Study of Racial Integration in Seven Churches" (D.Min. study, Christian Theological Seminary, 1973, 21 p.); Cheaney, "Attitudes of the Indiana Pulpit and Press," 342.

31. This is a distinction hard to maintain in view of multiracial experience among American Pentecostals. See sections on Pentecostals in this volume. See also Winthrop Hudson, "The American Context as an Area for Research in Black Church Studies," *Church History* 52 (June 1983): 157–71 and C. Eric Lincoln and Lawrence H. Mamiya, *The Black Church in the African American Experience* (Durham, N.C.: Duke University Press, 1990), 1–7. For a professional analysis based specifically on Muncie, Indiana, which concluded "the structure of black religious beliefs appears to be quite similar to whites and appears to be quite American," see "Black-White Differences in Religiosity: Item Analysis and a Formal Structural Test," by Cardell K. Jacobson, Tim B. Heaton, and Rutledge M. Dennis in *Sociological Analysis, a Journal in the Sociology of Religion* 51 (Fall 1990): 257–70. For evaluation of several current understandings of the nature of America's black church, see Leon McBeth, "Images of the Black Church in America," *Baptist History and Heritage* 16 (July 1981): 19–28.

32. Gayraud Wilmore, *Black and Presbyterian: The Heritage and the Hope* (Philadelphia: Geneva Press, 1983, 142 p.); Orrin Manifold, "American United Methodism Bicentennial and Indiana United Methodism's Beginnings," unpaged; Lincoln and Mamiya, *Black Church*, xii; Divita, *Ethnic Settlement Patterns in Indianapolis*, 46; Bigham, *We Ask Only a Fair Trial*, 221.

33. In this book black pentecostal groups have been treated earlier in the Holiness and Pentecostal sections.

34. Gilliam, *A Time to Speak*, 26.

35. James P. Comer, *Beyond Black and White* (New York: Quadrangle Books, 1972), 16–17.

36. Earline Rae Ferguson, "The Woman's Improvement Club of Indianapolis: Black Woman Pioneers in Tuberculosis Work, 1903–1938," *Indiana Magazine of History* 84 (September 1988): 238–39, 251; Emma Lou Thornbrough, "The History of Black Women in Indiana," *Black History News and Notes* 13 (May 1983): 1, 4–6; Lincoln and Mamiya, *Black Church*, 6–10, 16–19; Gilliam, *Time to Speak*, 77–83.

37. *Directory of Churches*.

38. Moore, *Calumet Region*, 676–77.

39. Carl F. Brand, "The History of the Know Nothing Party in Indiana," *Indiana Magazine of History* 18 (March 1922): 47–81; (June 1922): 177–206; (September 1922): 266–306.

40. Richard Wigginton Thompson, *The Papacy and Civil Power* (New York: Harper and Brothers, 1876, 750 p.).

41. Donald L. Kinzer, *An Episode in Anti-Catholicism: The American Protective Association* (Seattle, Wash.: University of Washington Press, 1964), 10, 95, 118, 124, 148, 177–79.

42. Leonard J. Moore has described the dynamic of the Klan in Indiana in terms of a popular swell of progressive reform. Kathleen Blee voiced a more common and more convincing explanation when she wrote "It was financial opportunism that shaped the Klan's rebirth and a sophisticated marketing system that fueled its phenomenal growth." Leonard J. Moore, *Citizen Klansmen: The Ku Klux Klan in Indiana, 1921–1928* (Chapel Hill, N.C.: University of North Carolina Press, 1991, 259 p.); Kathleen Blee, *Women of the Klan: Racism and Gender in the 1920s* (Berkeley, Calif.: University of California Press, 1991), 18.

43. Madison, *Indiana through Transition and Change*, 45–75; Moore, *Citizen Klansmen*, xii, 2, 44–75; Blee, *Women of the Klan*, 7, 70–72, 125, 172–73.

44. M. William Lutholtz, *Grand Dragon: D. C. Stephenson and the Ku Klux Klan in Indiana* (West Lafayette, Ind.: Purdue University Press, 1991), 16–21; Blee, *Women of the Klan*, 12–23. Division of fees and profits varied, a constant source of negotiation and conflict.

45. Moore, *Citizen Klansmen*, 10, 14–17, 24, 92, 212; Lutholtz, *Grand Dragon*, 29–32, 55–60; Blee, *Women of the Klan*, 3, 123–53.

46. Vance Trusty, "All Talk and no 'Kash': Valparaiso University and the Ku Klux Klan," *Indiana Magazine of History* 82 (March 1986): 1–36; Moore, *Citizen Klansmen*, 19; Lutholtz, *Grand Dragon*, 84, 95–103, 276–77.

47. Moore, *Citizen Klansmen*, 151–83; Lutholtz, *Grand Dragon*, 151.

48. Lutholtz, *Grand Dragon*, 178–314; Blee, *Women of the Klan*, 94–98; Moore, *Citizen Klansmen*, 181–83.

49. Martin E. Marty, *Modern American Religion*, vol. 2: *The Noise of Conflict 1919–1941* (Chicago: University of Chicago Press, 1991), 95.

50. Norman F. Weaver, "The Knights of the Ku Klux Klan in Wisconsin, Indiana, Ohio, and Michigan" (Ph.D. diss., University of Wisconsin, 1954), 11–16, 159–61.

51. Dwight W. Hoover, "Daisy Douglas Barr: From Quaker to Klan Kluckeress," *Indiana Magazine of History* 87 (June 1991): 171–195; Blee, *Women of the Klan*, 103–11. For descriptions of other church women prominent in the Klan, see Blee, *Women of the Klan*, 111–22.

52. Blee, *Women of the Klan*, 128–29, 135–39, 167–70; Moore, *Citizen Klansmen*, 76–105, 121–22; Lutholtz, *Grand Dragon*, 61, 63, 74–76, 83–93.

53. Weaver, "Knights of the Ku Klux Klan," 18–22, 159–61; Blee, *Women of the Klan*, 86–91; Lutholtz, *Grand Dragon*, 57–64.

54. *The Truth about the Notre Dame Riot on Saturday, May 17, 1924* (Indianapolis, Ind.: Fiery Cross Publishing Co., 1924, 21 p.); Lutholtz, *Grand Dragon*, 44–45, 140–44; Moore, *Citizen Klansmen*, 25–26, 158–59.

55. Deborah B. Markisohn, "Ministers of the Klan: Indianapolis Clergy Involvement with the 1920s Ku Klux Klan" (Master's thesis, Indiana University, 1992, 80 p.); Joseph M. White, "The Ku Klux Klan in Indiana in the 1920s as Viewed by the *Indiana Catholic and Record*" (Master's thesis, Butler University, 1974, 107 p.); Moore, *Citizen Klansmen*, 24, 187; Lutholtz, *Grand Dragon*, 65–72, 78–80; Blee, *Women of the Klan*, 66–68.

56. Lutholtz, *Grand Dragon*, 61.

57. Frank Elon Davison, *Thru the Rear-View Mirror* (St. Louis, Mo.: Bethany Press, 1955), 75–76.

58. Davison, *Thru the Rear-View Mirror*, 76–77.

59. Richard Ginder, *With Ink and Crozier: A Biography of John Francis Noll, Fifth Bishop of Fort Wayne and Founder of Our Sunday Visitor* (Huntington, Ind.: Our Sunday Visitor, 1952, 285 p.).

60. *Seventy Years of Our Sunday Visitor, 1912–1982*, ed. Robert P. Lockwood (Huntington, Ind.: Our Sunday Visitor, 1982), 13.

61. *Seventy Years*, 62.

62. *Seventy Years*, 9; Ginder, *With Ink and Crozier*, 108–9.

63. *Seventy Years*, xii; Ginder, *With Ink and Crozier*, 112, 135.

64. John Francis Noll, *Our National Enemy Number One: Education without Religion* (Huntington, Ind.: Our Sunday Visitor Press, 1942, 312 p.).

65. Richard P. McBrien, *Catholicism*, 2 vols. (Minneapolis, Minn.: Winston Press, 1980), 2:571–72, 603; Richard P. McBrien, *The Remaking of the Church; An Agenda for Reform* (New York: Harper and Row, 1973), 23–35.

66. Ann Taves, "Context and Meaning: Roman Catholic Devotion to the Blessed Sacrament in Mid-Nineteenth-Century America," *Church History* 54 (December 1985): 482–95; Jay P. Dolan, *The American Catholic Experience: A History from Colonial Times to the Present* (Garden City, N.Y.: Doubleday, 1985), 92–93, 122–23, 209–11, 384–87.

67. Indiana scholars associated with the University of Notre Dame have been especially active interpreters of Catholic renewal. Richard P. McBrien offered a clarification of the old and the new in his *Remaking of the Church: An Agenda for Reform* (New York: Harper and Row, 1973, 175 p.). He followed that with two large volumes entitled *Catholicism*, offered "as a bridge between the Church of yesterday and the Church of today, and between conservative, traditionally-minded Catholics, on the one hand, and progressive renewal-minded Catholics on the other" (Minneapolis, Minn.: Winston Press, 1980), 1:xvi. Jay P. Dolan put the changes in context in *The American Catholic Experience: A History from Colonial Times to the Present* (Garden City, N.Y.: Doubleday, 1985, 504 p.). Dolan and three colleagues detailed the transformation more sharply in *Transforming Parish Ministry: The Changing Roles of Catholic Clergy, Laity, and Women Religious* (New York: Crossroad, 1989, 366 p.). Joseph M. White described the effect of Catholic seminaries on the reform and the effect of the reform on the seminaries in *The Diocesan Seminary in the United States: A History from the 1780s to the Present* (Notre Dame, Ind.: University of Notre Dame Press, 1989, 489 p.). Mary Jo Weaver, with a doctorate from Notre Dame and a faculty position at Indiana University, voiced feminist impatience with the slow pace of reform in her *New Catholic Women: A Contemporary Challenge to Traditional Religious Authority* (New York: Harper and Row, 1985, 270 p.) and in "Feminist Perspectives and American Catholic History," *U.S. Catholic Historian* 5 (Summer-Fall 1986): 401–10. The Notre Dame Study of Catholic Parish Life, an unparalleled scientific research at parish level conducted with Lilly Endowment funding between

1981 and 1988, produced a galaxy of reports, articles, and monographs. See Jim Castelli and Joseph Gremillion, *The Emerging Parish: The Notre Dame Study of Catholic Life Since Vatican II* (San Francisco: Harper and Row, 1987, 222 p.); *Report, Notre Dame Study of Catholic Parish Life* ed. David C. Leege and Joseph Gremillion (Notre Dame, Ind.: University of Notre Dame, 1984–1989), nos. 1–15. Establishment of the Cushwa Center for the Study of American Catholicism at Notre Dame in 1975 formed an institutional base to support an ongoing series of projects, conferences, and publications often related to modern Catholicism. See *Cushwa Center: Report of Activities 1975–1991* (Notre Dame, Ind.: Cushwa Center, 1992, 39 p.).

68. Will Herberg, *Protestant, Catholic, Jew: An Essay in American Religious Sociology*, rev. ed. (Garden City, N.Y.: Doubleday and Company, 1960), 39, 40.

69. "Transitions in Catholic Culture: The Fifties," *U.S. Catholic Historian* vol. 7, no. 1 (1988), i–iv, 1–138.

70. John L. McKenzie, *The Two-Edged Sword: An Interpretation of the Old Testament* (Milwaukee, Wis.: Bruce, 1956, 317 p.); Gerald P. Fogarty, *American Catholic Biblical Scholarship: A History from the Early Republic to Vatican II* (San Francisco: Harper and Row, 1989), 258–59, 326–33; Emmanuel Charles McCarthy, "In Appreciation of a Catholic Scholar," *America* 164 (18 May 1991): 534–35.

71. O'Brien, John Anthony, *The Faith of Millions: The Credentials of the Catholic Religion* (Huntington, Ind.: Our Sunday Visitor, 1938, 538 p.); "A Living Landmark Passes: Rev. John A. O'Brien (1893–1980)," *Notre Dame Magazine* 9 (May 1980): 8; "John Anthony O'Brien," in *Contemporary Authors: First Revision*, vols. 1–4 (bound together and paged consecutively): 719–20.

72. James Johnson, *Joseph Cardinal Ritter* (Notre Dame, Ind.: University of Notre Dame Press, 1964, 48 p.); McBrien, *Catholicism*, 2:646–67; McBrien, *Remaking of the Church*, 35–57.

73. *The American Catholic Parish: A History from 1850 to the Present*, 2 vols., ed. Jay P. Dolan (New York: Paulist Press, 1987), 2:363.

74. McBrien, *Catholicism*, 1:12.

75. *American Catholic Parish*, 2:363–69.

76. Weaver, *New Catholic Women*, 134–35. In a later work Weaver expressed a feminist position more poignantly: "Many Catholic women find themselves in a double bind: living with misogyny and oppressive institutional structure is torture, but rejecting a church suffused with rich spiritual symbolism and a sacramental reality is starvation. What can such women do?" See her *Springs of Water in a Dry Land: Spiritual Survival for Catholic Women Today* (Boston: Beacon Press, 1993), xii.

77. *American Catholic Parish*, 2:384–86. Growth by diocese: Indianapolis from 184,281 to 202,087; Evansville 70,910 to 91,701; Fort Wayne-South Bend 139,015 to 147,438; Gary 154,349 to 190,033; and Lafayette 62,860 to 86,540.

78. George Gallup, Jr. and Jim Castelli, *The American Catholic People: Their Beliefs, Practices, and Values* (Garden City, N.Y.: Doubleday and Company, 1987), 54–57, 180; George Gallup, Jr. and Sarah Jones, *100 Questions and Answers: Religion in America* (Princeton, N.J.: Princeton Religion Research Center, 1989), 90–91; *Report. Notre Dame Study of Catholic Parish Life* 7 (March 1986): 3–9.

79. Dolan, *American Catholic Experience*, 437–40. See also *Transforming Parish Ministry: The Changing Roles of Catholic Clergy, Laity, and Women Religious* by Jay P. Dolan, R. Scott Appleby, Patricia Byrne, and Debra Campbell (New York: Crossroad, 1989, 366 p.).

80. *Newsletter* 13 (April 1987); Indianapolis *Star*, 24 February 1992, A-1, A-6; Bloomington *Herald-Times*, 24 February 1992, A-7; *Indiana Daily Student*, 2 March 1992, 4.

About Black Methodists

Blacks responded to the gospel presented by early Methodist preachers in America. They were char-ter members in some of the earliest Methodist churches. In 1786 black Methodists numbered 1,890 or about 10 percent of the American membership. Black and white Methodists worshipped together in early America. During the years of tension leading to the achievement of full black freedom, black and white congregations separated.

Four major groups of black Methodists eventually developed strength in Indiana. First, congre-gations continuing as integral parts of the Methodist Episcopal Church in the North achieved separation by having their own black Lexington Conference within that larger denomination. Second, those tracing their roots to an early separate church called "Bethel" in Philadelphia and organized in 1816 with Richard Allen as their first bishop became the African Methodist Episcopal Church. Third, those with linkage to an early separate church called "Zion" in New York and organized in 1820 with James Varick as their first bishop eventually took the name African Methodist Episcopal Zion Church. Fourth, loyal black congregations of the Methodist Episcopal Church in the South were set off with their property to form a new sister denomination called the Colored Methodist Episco-pal Church after the Civil War; it later changed that name to Christian Methodist Episcopal Church and moved into the urban North as a part of the massive migration of its members.

Besides conducting worship and the full range of life care ministries, these black Methodist churches had the special concern of providing education for their congregations of slaves or former slaves and their children. All of them eventually came to be full participants in the National Coun-cil of Churches and the World Council of Churches.

AFRICAN METHODIST
EPISCOPAL CHURCH

Richard Allen was born a slave child in Philadelphia in 1760. Benjamin Chew sold the whole family—Allen's parents and the four children—to a farmer named Stokeley near Dover in Delaware. In this new neighborhood Allen heard Methodist preaching. At the age of seventeen he was converted.

> I was awakened and brought to see myself, poor, wretched and undone, and without the mercy of God, must be lost. Shortly after, I obtained mercy through the blood of Christ, and was constrained to exhort my old companions to seek the Lord. I went rejoicing for several days and was happy in the Lord, in conversing with many old, experienced Christians. I was brought under doubts, and was tempted to believe I was deceived, and was constrained to seek the Lord afresh. I went with my head bowed down for many days. My sins were a heavy burden. I was tempted to believe there was no mercy for me. I cried to the Lord both night and day. One night I thought hell would be my portion. I cried unto Him who delighteth to hear the prayers of a poor sinner, and all of a sudden my dungeon shook, my chains flew off, and, glory to God, I cried. My soul was filled. I cried, enough for me—the Saviour died. Now my confidence was strengthened that the Lord, for Christ's sake, had heard my prayers and pardoned all my sins.[1]

Allen felt called to preach. "I was constrained to go from house to house, exhorting my old companions and telling to all around what a dear Saviour I had found," he said. "I joined the Methodist Society and met in class at Benjamin Wells's, in the forest, Delaware state. John Gray was the class leader. I met in his class for several years." It was a considerable concession for a farmer of the time to allow slaves to attend religious meetings at all. However the lives of Richard Allen and his brother so impressed their owner that Stokeley allowed them to attend meetings, gave permission for interracial meetings on his own property, and then became a convert himself. This led to a joint plan with Stokeley by which the Allen brothers could work to earn $2,000 and purchase their freedom.[2]

So Richard Allen, a free black handicapped by illiteracy and poverty, began his itinerancy. He preached. As a teamster hauling salt from Rehoboth in Delaware to supply George Washington's army, he established regular preaching stops all along the route. After the war he followed preaching opportunities among both blacks and whites in Delaware, New Jersey, and Pennsylvania. He generally worked for and among Methodists. He said: "I received nothing from the Methodist connection. My usual method was, when I would get bare of clothes, to stop travelling and go to work, so that no man could say I was chargeable to the connection. My hands administered to my necessities."[3]

His reputation grew. He and Harry Hosier were the only black preachers present when the Methodist Episcopal Church in America was organized in Baltimore in 1784. Methodist bishop Francis Asbury asked Allen to travel America with him as an unpaid preaching colleague, but Allen declined the offer, saying: "I thought people ought to lay up something while they were able, to support themselves in time of sickness or old age."[4]

Richard Allen in Philadelphia

Philadelphia became Allen's special place. The Methodist superintendent there had often invited him to visit. He was officially licensed to preach at St. George Methodist Church in 1784. He could preach at the less popular times and places in Philadelphia or go out to such towns as Atglen, Attleborough, Columbia, Ben-Salem, or Radnor. He said "It was not uncommon for me to preach from four to five times a day." He earned a respected place in the Philadelphia business community and a network of influential friends. He brought more black attenders to St. George Church than the members of that church could easily accommodate either in space or in spirit. "We felt ourselves much cramped," Allen said of the members of his black society formed in 1786. "They were considered as a nuisance." In 1787 a number of blacks were embarrassed and abused during worship service even while kneeling in prayer. Allen led the group which walked out of St. George never to return.[5]

To Allen's chagrin, one portion of his exiled followers elected to leave Methodism altogether and unite with the Church of England. Allen himself was a thoroughgoing Methodist.

> I was confident that there was no religious sect or denomination would suit the capacity of the colored people as well as the Methodist; for the plain and simple gospel suits best for any people; for the unlearned can understand, and the learned are sure to understand; and the reason that the Methodist is so successful in the awakening and conversion of the colored people, the plain doctrine and having a good discipline.[6]

Finally he did get a separate black Methodist congregation for Philadelphia. It met on a lot he purchased himself and in an old blacksmith building he bought and hauled to the lot with his own teams. Bishop Francis Asbury preached on the occasion of its formal opening in July of 1794. The highly respected Methodist leader John Dickins prayed that the new church "might be a bethel to the gathering in of thousands of souls" so it took "Bethel" as its name. Allen became the first black ordained Methodist when Asbury ordained him a deacon in 1799.[7]

But there was no stopping place. These black Methodists intended now to have their church be one place in which they would think for themselves, talk for themselves, act for themselves, and determine their own ministry because it would be supported from their own scarce means. The larger Methodist Church asserted its claim to jurisdiction over this church property and its right to appoint the ministers. There followed a series of tests in ecclesiastical and in civil courts which made the separation of the black church complete in 1816. The same process was going on between black and white Methodists in other cities. At Baltimore Daniel Coker was the ex-slave and preacher who took leadership of those separating from the Strawberry Alley and Lovely Lane Methodist churches. They organized an independent black church in 1816, actually a few weeks before Bethel in Philadelphia became fully independent.[8]

A.M.E. Church Organized

When Richard Allen sent an invitation to assemble as a convention of independent black Methodist churches in 1816, sixteen delegates responded: five from Philadelphia; six from Baltimore; one from Wilmington, Delaware; three from Attleborough, Pennsylvania; and one from Salem, New Jersey. They organized the African Methodist Episcopal Church (hereafter A.M.E.), thoroughly Methodist in doctrine and discipline. Coker and Allen were elected bishops but Coker withdrew in favor of Allen who was then consecrated by five regularly ordained ministers on 11 April 1816. Growth of the new denomination was impressive. By the end of the first decade in 1826 the annual conferences of Philadelphia, Baltimore, and New York were united in a general conference. All were meeting regularly and keeping proper records. Membership was 7,594. In many places there were clusters of black Methodists ready to move to establish a church of their own.

Growth could not come in the South until 1863. A huge black congregation in Charleston had been totally wiped out in 1822 because of the regional fear of slave insurrection. The best places to expand were among the free blacks in the Middle Colonies and in the West. By the time Richard Allen had been eulogized in Baltimore and Philadelphia and buried in Bethel Cemetery in March of 1831, his church had leaped across the Alleghenies. Philadelphia Conference reported five churches in western Pennsylvania and six in Ohio in 1824. Allen's successor Morris Brown organized Western Annual Conference (sometimes called Ohio Conference) in August of 1830 for the 15 ministers and 1,194 members west of the mountains.[9]

William Paul Quinn for the West

William Paul Quinn was at the June meeting of the New York Annual Conference in 1833. Quinn was born in Calcutta, India, converted in Pennsylvania in 1808, and licensed to preach in 1812. He had lost his A.M.E. ministerial status while serving an independent Methodist church. His application "to reunite with the Connection" had bounced from conference to conference for five years. Now, in 1833, New York Conference readmitted him as a full member but promptly sent him off to hard duty on the western frontier. He was one of seven itinerant ministers at the Western Conference meeting at Pittsburgh that year, destined to become a leader in the westward expansion.[10]

When the barber Augustus Turner gathered Indianapolis blacks in his log cabin to form Bethel A.M.E. Church in 1836, Quinn was one of their circuit preachers. When the black Indiana Conference was established at a settlement of black farmers called Blue River in Rush County in 1840 to encompass all the territory west of Ohio, the circuit riders included George W. Johnson for the Richmond Circuit, Robert Jones for the Indianapolis Circuit, and Shadrack Stewart for the Terre Haute Circuit. Quinn, in addition to riding his own circuit in Illinois, was to oversee all the others. He functioned, in fact, as special appointee of general conference in charge of missionary work in the West.[11]

The A.M.E. churches multiplied among Indiana's free blacks. Reporting more than fifty members to the Indiana Conference at some time between 1840 and 1845 were Jeffersonville (52), New Albany (55), Vincennes (105), Indianapolis (175), Paoli (65), Cabin Creek in Randolph County (88), Blue River in Rush County (102), Terre Haute (74), Salem (58), and Richmond (119). About forty additional Indiana locations were on the conference rolls.[12]

Quinn's missionary report to the General Conference of 1844 was electrifying. He described the black population of Indiana and Illinois, probably 18,000, as a body of rising farmers and craftsmen who had "every constituent principle among them, when suitably composed, to make them a great and good people." Among these blacks west of Ohio the A.M.E. church already had 72 congregations with 2,000 members, 1,080 of them communicants in 47 established churches. Serving them were 7 traveling elders, 20 traveling preachers, and 27 local preachers. There were 50 Sunday schools with 200 teachers (100 of them black), and 2,000 scholars. Forty temperance societies had been organized and 17 camp meetings conducted. Quinn's report said:

> This grand region of missionary enterprise is truly an interesting spot to excite the benevolent sympathies of the spirit of missions, being broad in its extent, inviting in its agricultural qualities, and grand in its commercial position. There is an immense mine of mind, talent and social qualities, all lying measurably in embryo, but by a proper direction of the missionary hammer and chisel, they can all be shaped to fit in the great spiritual building of God.[13]

The general conference had been considering election of another bishop, since bishops Morris Brown and Edward Waters were about seventy. After making this report on the West, Quinn was promptly elected and consecrated a bishop. An A.M.E. historian has called Quinn "hero of the epoch 1840–1860" and "trailblazer west of the Allegheny Mountains." His duties as administrator and presiding officer took him all across the church but he maintained a special presence in Indiana. The denomination was to provide him a house "somewhere in the West" but when no church house materialized he chose to live among friends in Richmond, Indiana, and to build his own home there. From that center he conducted his decades of episcopal labor until he died and was buried there in 1873.[14]

Daniel A. Payne for Education

The same general conference at Pittsburgh which elected Quinn a bishop in 1844 took a crucial stand for education. The A.M.E. founder Richard Allen and most of his ministerial associates had come out of the deprivation of slavery and were illiterate. So were a very significant number of the itinerant ministers up to 1844. The A.M.E. preacher Daniel A. Payne became the denomination's unrelenting crusader for educational improvement. Payne had been a free black school teacher at Charleston, South Carolina, until forced by law to close his school in 1835. He moved north and studied for two years at Gettysburg Theological Seminary in Pennsylvania on a scholarship provided by a society of the Lutheran seminary students.[15]

At Gettysburg Payne's Christian convictions deepened and his decision for the ministry became firm. He said: "I was lying upon my bed, lamenting and pondering over the future, when I felt a pressure from on high that constrained me to say with the Apostle Paul: 'Woe is me if I preach not the Gospel!'"[16]

Payne issued a series of five "epistles on the education of the ministry" leading up to the 1844 general conference and was the one who made the motion to establish a course of studies for the education of ministers. The conference exploded in protest; only after heated discussion, reconsideration, and a second vote was the study program adopted:

> I. For exhorters—First year—the Bible, Smith's English Grammar, Mitchell's Geography, our own Discipline, Wesley's Notes. Second year—Original Church of Christ, History of the Methodist Episcopal Church, Watson's Life of Wesley.
>
> II. For preachers—First year—Smith's English Grammar, Mitchell's Geography, Paley's Evidences of Divine Revelation, History of the Bible, Homes' Introduction (abridged). Second year—Schmucker's Popular Theology, Schmucker's Mental Philosophy, Natural Theology, or Watson's Institutes. Third year—Ecclesiastical History, Goodrich's Church History, Porter's Homiletics and D'Aubigne's History of the Reformation. Fourth year—Geography and Chronology of the Bible, with a review of the above studies. After the adoption of this system of studies, Conference decreed that they should be placed as an appendix to the Discipline.[17]

The adoption of such words was a mere beginning but the A.M.E. leadership never let go of the educational ideal. At the 1848 general conference Bishop Quinn presented the first written Episcopal Address. In 1852 the education agitator Daniel A. Payne was elected an A.M.E. bishop, bringing to that office his passion for improvement and order. His written Episcopal Addresses became a point of conference pride.[18] In 1856 one part of his address read:

> Respecting the ministry we feel, as heretofore, that we all ought to cultivate our minds by the study of every science—physical, mental, and moral—so that we may be better qualified to study the Bible. No man should be more enlightened than the Ambassador of the Cross, because no position is so commanding and no office freighted with such important results as his. Of all the ministers of Christ there are none who have more need of being thoroughly educated than those in the African Methodist Episcopal Church.[19]

The regional conferences took up the education theme. Indiana Conference, still including Illinois and Missouri churches, reported organizing a historical and literary society in 1856. That year Indiana's committee on education was thankful that a few colleges of "our white friends" were "placed within the reach of our people . . . Avery, Xenia, and Illinois Institutes." It reported 1,484 pupils in the day and Sunday schools of Indiana Confer-

ence. Ministerial candidates Hall, Strother, Trevan, Cain, Rush, and Nelson were examined in eight subject areas at Indiana Conference in 1858. None passed the examinations. Except for Strother they were "deficient in all areas" and bidden to keep studying. There was once a dream of establishing an A.M.E. institution of higher education in Indiana Conference but sponsors of that effort reported failure in 1851 because of the discriminatory "black laws."[20]

That A.M.E. college finally became a reality in Greene County, Ohio. The larger Methodist Episcopal denomination provided a campus there and opened Wilberforce University in 1856. North Indiana Conference (predominantly white) was meeting in Muncie in September of 1856. Enthusiasm for the report of the new Wilberforce campus for blacks was so high that conference attenders themselves made up a cash contribution of $202.50 on the spot.[21]

In 1863 the A.M.E. church purchased the Wilberforce property and became sole owner of what claimed to be the first institution of higher education founded by blacks in the United States. The effective agent in the whole enterprise was Bishop Daniel A. Payne, who moved to the campus and simply made the school succeed. When it needed staff he was professor and president. When it burned he enlisted the friends to rebuild it. Wilberforce University, and its theological department which became Payne Theological Seminary, was a symbol of the A.M.E. conviction that its blacks must excel in teaching and learning.[22]

When Payne came to Indianapolis to preside over the Eighteenth General Conference of the whole denomination in 1888, the Indianapolis News of May 7 called the meeting "one of the most significant religious events that ever occurred among the colored people of Indiana." Next day the Indianapolis Sentinel noted that the delegates were "the most educated and refined portion of the colored race." The delegates represented the 2,540 ministers and 405,000 members of what was then the largest black denomination in the United States. Actually the excitement of electing four bishops made that 1888 conference riotous enough to have been the death of the 77-year-old bishop, but even through this commotion his presiding and especially his preaching kept lifting up his ideal of a church of order and educational excellence.[23]

Educated A.M.E. Pioneers in Indiana

This continuing emphasis on education meant that many pioneer A.M.E. preachers in Indiana were educated persons. On his way to becoming the first black Senator in the history of the United States and head of Alcorn University, Hiram R. Revels was in Indiana studying at "a Quaker Seminary in Union County" about 1844 and serving as an ordained A.M.E. preacher before 1856.[24]

Bethel Church in Indianapolis was served by a series of articulate ministers who became community leaders: Aeneas McIntosh, James Curtis, T. W. Henderson, Morris Lewis, John W. Townsend, R. R. Downs, D. A. Graham, T. A. Smythe, Charles Sumner Williams, R. L. Pope, Roscoe Henderson, John A. Alexander, and Jonathan A. Dames. Bethel Church pastor Elisha Weaver, with assistance of six other A.M.E. preachers as editors, was publishing the *Repository* at Indianapolis from 1858 to 1861 to serve the A.M.E. literary societies of the Baltimore, Indiana, and Missouri conferences.[25]

Physician and preacher Willis R. Revels, brother of Hiram R. Revels, was pastor at Bethel Church in Indianapolis during the Civil War and twice pastor at Allen Chapel in that city. He was a colleague of Payne in drafting the first ministerial course of study in 1844. With his "superior intellectual training" he was "in advance of any of his compeers" and "one of the outstanding characters of Indiana Conference." For many years Willis Revels seemed to be at the center of every general conference assignment which required careful formulation in writing.[26]

James M. Townsend of Ohio came from Civil War service and studies at Oberlin College to invest his life among Indiana's A.M.E. churches. He was pastor at Terre Haute and at Indianapolis but became best known in his long career at Richmond where his constituents elected him to the state legislature in 1884. Samuel Smothers, colleague of Quakers as principal and model teacher of the Union Literary Institute in Randolph County until he entered the Union Army, returned from that service to be A.M.E. minister in several Indiana cities.[27]

John H. Clay came north from Georgia to Indianapolis as a servant and friend of an Indiana captain mustered out of the Union Army after the war. He was able to attend school and became an A.M.E. preacher in 1875. Clay was key organizer for a plan which brought hundreds of freed blacks from North Carolina to Indiana. He was pastor in turn at Greencastle, at Bloomington, at Terre Haute, and at the state's largest black Methodist congregation in Indianapolis.[28]

African Methodist Episcopal churches operated schools for blacks before public schools were open to them. A historian of early blacks in Indianapolis said:

Bethel AME organized the earliest school for Indianapolis blacks. In 1858, Reverend Elisha Weaver served as its principal and Lucy Jefferson assisted him. Geography, grammar, history, and physiology were offered in addition to the three Rs. In order to raise money for the school Weaver and Jefferson staged exhibitions of their pupils' work. In 1859, Bethel AME organized an educational society to raise funds for the school. The black community was the school's main source of support, through monthly dues and donations, as well as tuition payments.[29]

When public schools became available in 1869 they directed their young people to them, counting education as the route to the fullness of freedom. From 1886 the A.M.E. church published Christian education materials which were used by many black Sunday schools.[30]

Growth and Maturity

Out of A.M.E. congregations ranging from such farm communities as Lyles Station and Old Beech to Allen Chapel in the capital city came pioneering black youth prepared to take positions of responsibility and leadership. Indiana's state federation of black women supported Mary Evans of Allen Chapel in her studies at Wilberforce University and Payne Theological Seminary. She graduated in 1911. She later returned to Indianapolis to serve as pastor of Wayman Chapel (1915–16) and of St. John A.M.E. Church (1923–28). Mary Evans was an evangelist of national reputation, credited with some 30,000 conversions.[31]

Moses Broyles had noted the black Methodist preeminence in education when he came to the black Baptist congregation in Indianapolis in 1857. "The Baptist Church had very little influence in the community," he said. "All religious influence was in the A.M.E." But it was especially the black Baptists who poured into Indiana from the South during and following the Civil War. At the same time much A.M.E. denominational energy was diverted into its great "invasion" of the South after the way was opened there by federal troops in 1863. Eclipsed by this influx of Baptists and competing with three other varieties of black Methodists, the A.M.E. church in Indiana came to occupy a kind of eminent plateau.[32]

For years some A.M.E. operations in Kentucky, Missouri, Illinois, and a variety of Southern states were part of Indiana Conference. The size of the mother conference would shrink temporarily as these mission areas came of age and were set off. Within the state of Indiana itself the

A.M.E. church kept growing modestly. On his way back east from the California Annual Conference in 1874, Bishop A. W. Wayman visited A.M.E. churches at Crawfordsville, Rockville, Terre Haute, Indianapolis, Peru, Marion, and Richmond. He seemed to have a fondness for dedicating Indiana church buildings—Mitchell and Noblesville in 1873; Crawfordsville, Peru, Richmond, and Terre Haute in 1874; Kokomo and Seymour in 1875.[33] At the time of the last federal religious census in 1936, when the A.M.E. denomination had multiplied nationally to nearly half a million members and had mission work in nine foreign fields, Indiana reported 7,396 members in 51 churches. All but 186 members lived in cities.

Indiana Conference had become and remained a stable structure which gathered annually under guidance of the bishop for its primary business of preaching, praying, singing, developing support for missions and education, and electing delegates or officers. The presiding elders (superintendents) of the Southern District and the Northern District commented on the condition of each congregation and gave encouragement to the ministers appointed. There were progress reports on ministerial candidates and detailed published reports of the ministry of the licensed female evangelists. Conference minutes during the Great Depression still contained long lists of individual donors who gave amounts ranging from 25¢ to $6 each as "Dollar Money" for denominational and benevolent purposes far beyond their own debt-ridden parishes.

Generally there was an address at the annual meeting of Indiana Conference on "The State of the Church" and another on "The State of the World." The "World" address for 1935 said:

We are naturally better acquainted with depression and oppression than any other race in America . . . In normal circumstances we have been lynched, ostracized, jim-crowed, scattered, torn and peeled more than any other people. Everything everywhere has been employed to make us feel our inferiority. And oh! how we have longed again and again for a new birth of freedom—(1) An economic freedom; (2) a political freedom; (3) a social freedom. Freedom to work anywhere; to vote any ticket; to associate and affiliate with whom we please. This emancipation will never come until we strike the first blow. We must not wait for chance . . . Some say, leave the race question alone, it will settle itself. It will settle itself, but not to our advantage. We must make jobs for our own race by encouraging race business enterprises. Patronize our own group as much as we can. Trade with those where we may be employed. We men must take the

lead in this endeavor. The grand old A.M.E. Church is an example of what may be done through self-help.[34]

By 1990 the A.M.E. was the largest of the black Methodist denominations with about 2.2 million members. In Indiana there were 8,983 A.M.E. members in 53 congregations in 1990, a state membership comparable in number to the Church of God (Cleveland, Tenn.) or the Seventh-day Adventists.[35]

NOTES

1. Richard Allen, *The Life Experience and Gospel Labors of the Rt. Rev. Richard Allen*, Bicentennial edition (Nashville, Tenn.: Abingdon Press, 1983), 15–16.

2. Allen, *Life Experience*, 16.

3. Allen, *Life Experience*, 23.

4. *History of American Methodism*, 3 vols., ed. Emory Stevens Bucke (New York: Abingdon Press, 1964), 1:602; Allen, *Life Experience*, 19, 23.

5. Allen, *Life Experience*, 24–29.

6. Allen, *Life Experience*, 29.

7. *History of American Methodism*, 1:603; Allen, *Life Experience*, 81.

8. Daniel A. Payne, *History of the African Methodist Episcopal Church* (Nashville, Tenn.: Publishing House of the A.M.E. Sunday-School Union, 1891), 3–12; *History of American Methodism*, 1:603–6, 2:526–27; Allen, *Life Experience*, 81.

9. Charles Spencer Smith, *History of the African Methodist Episcopal Church* (Philadelphia: Book Concern of the A.M.E. Church, 1922; Johnson Reprint, 1968), 15; *History of American Methodism*, 1:606–9.

10. R. R. Wright, *The Bishops of the African Methodist Episcopal Church* (Nashville, Tenn.: A.M.E. Sunday School Union, 1963.) 283–86; Lori B. Jacobi, "More Than a Church: The Educational Role of the African Methodist Episcopal Church in Indiana, 1844–1861," *Black History News and Notes* (February 1988): 4; Payne, *History*, 96–97.

11. Frances Stout, "Brief History of Bethel AME Church," in *Directory, Bethel A.M.E. Church, Indianapolis, Indiana, September, 1953*, unpaged; Payne, *History*, 131, 137; Smith, *History*, 16; Jacobi, "More Than a Church," 4; *History of American Methodism*, 2:532.

12. Coy D. Robbins, *African Methodist Episcopal Churches Located in Indiana Black Communities, 1840–1845, Based upon Statistics Given in the Minutes of the Indiana Conference of the A.M.E. Church* (Bloomington, Ind.: Indiana African American Historical and Genealogical Society, 1990, 2 p.).

13. Payne, *History*, 171.

14. Payne, *History*, 170–72; Smith, *History*, 97–98, 101, 106.

15. Payne, *History*, v, vii, 393–94. Payne named the twenty-two students who sponsored him and dedicated a book to them in 1866; see Daniel A. Payne, *The Semi-Centenary and the Retrospection of the African Methodist Episcopal Church in the United States of America* (Baltimore, Md.: Sherwood and Company, 1866), 3. The journal of the crucial A.M.E. General Conference of 1844 is reprinted in Smith, *History*, 413–29.

16. Charles D. Killian, "Bishop Daniel A. Payne: Black Spokesman for Reform" (Ph.D. diss., Indiana University, Bloomington, 1971), 21.

17. Payne, *History*, 169–70.

18. Paul R. Griffin, "A Brief Account of the Development and Work of African Methodism in Ohio and Indiana," *Black History News and Notes* 23 (November 1985): 4–8; Wright, *The Bishops*, 285.

19. Smith, *History*, 38.

20. Payne, *History*, 260, 402, 405; Jacobi, "More Than a Church," 4–7.

21. Horace N. Herrick, *History of North Indiana Conference of the Methodist Episcopal Church* (Indianapolis, Ind.: W. K. Stewart Company, 1917), 56–57.

22. C. Eric Lincoln and Lawrence H. Mamiya, *The Black Church in the African American Experience* (Durham, N.C.: Duke University Press, 1990), 52–54; Payne, *History*, 400, 423–38; Killian, "Bishop Daniel A. Payne," 107–29.

23. Charles D. Killian, "Daniel A. Payne and the A.M.E. General Conference of 1888: A Display of Contrasts," *Negro History Bulletin* 32 (November 1969): 11–14; Killian, "Bishop Daniel A. Payne," 155–77.

24. Joseph H. Borome, "The Autobiography of Hiram Rhoades Revels together with Some Letters by and about Him," *Midwest Journal* 5 (Winter 1952–53): 79–92; Clarence E. Walker, *A Rock in a Weary Land: The African Methodist Episcopal Church during the Civil War and Reconstruction* (Baton Rouge, La.: Louisiana State University Press, 1982), 117–18.

25. Frances Stout, "Brief History of Bethel AME Church, Indianapolis, Indiana," in *Directory, Bethel A.M.E. Church, Indianapolis,* *Indiana, January, 1956,* unpaged; Jacobi, "More Than a Church," 4–7.

26. Smith, *History*, 56–57, 62, 98, 102, 111, 121, 373, 415, 417–19, 433–63, 465–545, 550–57.

27. Emma Lou Thornbrough, *The Negro in Indiana: A Study of a Minority* (Indianapolis, Ind.: Indiana Historical Bureau, 1957), 176–77, 301, 374–75.

28. Arnold Cooper, "Rev. John H. Clay and the 1879 Black Exodus to Greencastle, Indiana: A Case Study of AME Church Leadership," *Black History News and Notes* 42 (November 1990): 4–7.

29. Earline Rae Ferguson, "In Pursuit of the Full Enjoyment of Liberty and Happiness: Blacks in Antebellum Indianapolis, 1820–1860," *Black History News and Notes* 32 (May 1988): 6.

30. Payne, *History*, 493–98; Smith, *History*, 200–201, 345–47.

31. Luther Hicks, *Great Black Hoosier Americans* (N.p., 1977), 28–29; Judge Kelly, *First History of Allen Chapel A.M.E. Church, Indianapolis, Ind.* (N.p., 1916), 43; Hine, *When Truth Is Told*, 15, 57; *Ebony Lines* 2 (Fall-Winter 1990): 10–11.

32. Moses Broyles, *The History of the Second Baptist Church of Indianapolis* (Indianapolis, Ind.: Printing and Publishing House, 1876), 28; Payne, *History*, 465–74.

33. Smith, *History*, 107–8, 112.

34. *Proceedings of the Ninety-Seventh Annual Session of the Indiana Conference of the African Methodist Episcopal Church. Held in Bethel A.M.E. Church, Rev. R. C. Henderson, D.D., Pastor, Indianapolis, Indiana, September 25–29, 1935*, 56.

35. Lincoln and Mamiya, *Black Church*, 407; Letter of Leonard N. Williams, Sr., to L. C. Rudolph, 8 February 1994.

AFRICAN METHODIST EPISCOPAL ZION CHURCH

When Richard Allen of Philadelphia issued his call for a meeting of representatives of independent black Methodist churches in 1816, nobody came from New York. That was not due to any shortage of blacks in New York. Blacks there numbered thousands since keeping slaves was fashionable and legal until 1827. Nor was there any lack of contact between black and white Methodists. There were blacks in the pioneer John Street Church from the start, 70 black and 290 white members in 1789. Nor was there any lack of racial conflict in John Street Church. Humiliation of blacks was routine. Black leaders and preachers had little opportunity. Local preacher James Varick led a group of about thirty black Methodists to withdraw from John Street Church in 1796 and form the first black congregation in New York. Methodist bishop Francis Asbury approved the separation so long as the black society remained in the regular Methodist structure.[1]

A.M.E. Zion Church Organized

But when the New York blacks had finished and dedicated their own "Zion" church building in 1800, they wanted control of that property legally in the hands of their own black board of trustees. They also wanted full ecclesiastical standing and prerogatives for their black preachers. After many frustrations they withdrew completely from the larger Methodist body on 26 September 1820. The *Discipline* they adopted showed them to be thoroughly Methodist in belief and practice. They wanted to get some of their preachers ordained in the full ministerial rank of elder. However the white Methodist bishops would not do such ordination for a separate denomination. Neither would Bishop Richard Allen of the African Methodist Episcopal Church founded in Philadelphia ordain elders for this New York group unless they came under his jurisdiction. In fact, Allen was supporting a competitive branch of his own church in New York. Finally three ordained Methodist Episcopal elders now functioning as independents consented to come to Zion Church to establish its clergy by ordaining three elders on 17 June 1822. Next day six more elders were ordained. Elder James Varick was consecrated bishop on 30 July 1822.

By this time certain black congregations moving toward independence in New Haven and on Long Island and in Philadelphia had begun to look to New York for counsel and for ordained preachers. Varick, mixed blood child of a manumitted slave mother, motivated by the excitement of his freedom and a Methodist conversion, was now a bishop with a constituency. The African Methodist Episcopal Zion (hereafter A.M.E. Zion) denomination was on its way.[2]

The A.M.E. Zion church did its early growing in the North and East. By 1831 there were 1,689 members in conferences named Philadelphia and New York. By 1860, just ahead of black emancipation, 197 preachers had been on its rolls as itinerants, 92 of them still active in 6 annual conferences. As the issue of abolition had sharpened in the 1830s, black preachers were outlawed in most Southern states. So the A.M.E. Zion clergy were excluded from the great Southern mass of the nation's black population. Based in the North but speaking to the conscience of the nation, this church became an especially visible champion of emancipation and the abolition of slavery. Its first *Discipline* in 1820 had said without equivocation "We will not receive any person into our societies who is a slaveholder."[3]

Frederick Douglass was probably the nation's most famous black abolitionist, an orator eventually welcomed to international platforms and to the company of presidents Grant and Benjamin Harrison. He was a poor, green fugitive slave in the late 1830s when he began developing his gifts as sexton, Sunday school superintendent, steward, class leader, clerk, exhorter, and then a preacher at the A.M.E. Zion Church of New Bedford, New York. Later at Rochester, New York, he rose to prominence as editor of the anti-slavery newspaper *The North Star* and operator of a major northern terminus of the Underground Railroad.[4]

Douglass was always linked with such freedom fighters of the A.M.E. Zion church as Sojourner Truth, Harriet Tubman, Jermain W. Loguen, and William Howard Day. The former slave Isabella Baumfree became Sojourner Truth from her base in the membership of the A.M.E. Zion church in New York. Harriet Tubman was a fugitive slave, such a famous personal conductor of slaves up the Underground Railroad in the 1850s that slaveholders offered a reward of $40,000 for her capture. She located as a devout A.M.E. Zion member among her antislavery colleagues in Auburn, New York, and gave the church twenty-five acres of land there as a site for an old people's home.[5]

Strength in the South

With such abolitionist energy and reputation, the A.M.E. Zion church was well positioned to enter the South during the later stages of the Civil War. There were black Methodist congregations there ready to change affiliation. There were emancipated blacks now free to choose a church for the first time and in need of every kind of ministry. There were federal forces ready to open the way for an institution so obviously Northern. The A.M.E. Zion church named Joseph Jackson Clinton to be bishop for the South. Among the notable A.M.E. Zion missionaries in 1863–64 were James W. Hood in North Carolina,

Wilbur G. Strong in the deep South, and William F. Butler in Kentucky.

The A.M.E. Zion church which had been a vociferous but small denomination based in the North now became large, national, and especially strong in the South. The General Conference meeting at Montgomery, Alabama, in 1880 recognized that fifteen regional conferences of A.M.E. Zion churches had been organized in the South. The school established in North Carolina that year became the denomination's Livingstone College. The census of 1906 showed 673 A.M.E. Zion churches in North Carolina, 385 in Alabama, 193 in South Carolina, and 144 in Mississippi. New York had the largest number of A.M.E. Zion churches of any northern state, a mere 75.[6]

Indiana listed only eight A.M.E. Zion congregations in that religious census of 1906. The denomination had been slow to spread west in its early days. Missouri Conference, including Indiana and the whole Midwest, was not organized until 1890. At the state's largest concentration of black population in Indianapolis there was a very small church named Jones Chapel after Bishop Singleton T. Jones of Kentucky. When Jeremiah M. Washington, one of A.M.E. Zion's most able preachers was appointed to it from 1883 to 1885, Jones Chapel added 362 adult members and 450 Sunday school scholars. Evansville also had an early congregation as did South Bend.

Real growth in Indiana came as a return surge of A.M.E. Zion strength from the South. Part of it was the mighty twentieth century black migration from the South to the northern industrial cities. This included thousands of A.M.E. Zion members and additional prospects for evangelism. The Quadrennial Address of the Bishops to the 1920 General Conference said this influx "tested the ability and resources of some of our bishops and pastors to house them." The bishops named Indianapolis as one of the places where the A.M.E. Zion church "profited largely" from this migration.[7]

George Lincoln Blackwell

Another gift from the South was the North Carolinian assigned to be bishop of Missouri Conference in 1908. George Lincoln Blackwell was an honor graduate of Livingstone College and of Boston University School of Theology, the first university graduate to become a bishop in the A.M.E. Zion church. At the age of forty-six he had already served with distinction as minister in three states, as professor and dean at Livingstone College, as manager of the denomination's publication house, and as the denomination's general secretary.

As missionary bishop for the Midwest Blackwell moved quickly to divide the huge territory into three more manageable conferences named Missouri, Indiana, and Michigan. It was his principle to multiply leadership. "A new presiding elder district, like a new Annual Conference, gives opportunity to a new set of men to fill new important positions," he said. "Then too, to acquire new territory or even build or buy a new church, gives new hope and kindles new inspirations. So the making of these new districts has engendered a pleasant rivalry and a holy contest among the brethren."[8]

Blackwell organized an Indianapolis District and put W. H. Chambers in charge of it. Early workers in that Indianapolis District included J. H. Manley, H. Mickey, H. J. Callis, W. Rowan, T. A. Fenderson, A. J. Shockley, W. J. Winfield, P. H. Wright, and C. Holmes. The bishop's mind was a register of places where A.M.E. Zion expansion should be supported. J. J. Kennedy worked at Terre Haute; G. W. Henly at Gary; A. M. Taylor and S. W. Weller at South Bend. Indiana pastors John Wesley Wood, Benjamin G. Shaw, and Stephen G. Spottswood went on to consecration as bishops.

The bishop, his wife Annie W. Blackwell, W. H. Chambers of Indianapolis, and John Wesley Wood of Indianapolis became key persons in developing the A.M.E. Zion foreign mission enterprise which would later include scores of schools and churches with thousands of members in Africa. Mary Elizabeth Washington of New Albany was the most prominent woman in Zion Methodism in Indiana from 1900 to 1920, vice-president of the denomination's Woman's Home and Foreign Missionary Society for sixteen years. An A.M.E. Zion historian said "this gifted evangelist gave great impetus and spiritual ozone to the missionary cause in the Midwest and throughout the denomination." The denomination's Foreign Missions Board was first incorporated on 5 May 1920 in Indianapolis.[9]

A.M.E. Zion at Indianapolis with the Klan in 1924

So foreign missions were high on the agenda when the A.M.E. Zion church came to Indiana for its quadrennial general conference in May of 1924. It was an exciting time in Indianapolis, now a city of 358,760. The Ku Klux Klan, at the height of its power, flexed its muscle in the primary elections on May 6 to make Ed Jackson the Republican nominee for governor and to dominate selections at many other levels. However Indiana's resident grand dragon D. C. Stephenson had been notified of his suspension from "all rights and privileges" as a Klan member with charges cited. This suspension was sent out from Atlanta addressed to "all Genii, Grand Dragons and Hydras, Great Titans and Furies, Giants, King Kleagles and Kleagles, Exalted Cyclops and Terrors, and to all Citizens of the Invisible Empire." Klan no. 1 at Evansville was ordered to try Stephenson as a tribunal. The communication was signed: "Done in the Executive Chambers of His Lordship, the Imperial Wizard, in the Imperial Palace, in the Imperial City of Atlanta, Commonwealth of Georgia, on this the Seventh Day of the Fourth Month of the Year of our Lord, Nineteen Hundred Twenty-four, and on the Deadly Day of the Weeping Week of the Appalling Month of the Year of the Klan LVII. By His Lordship, H. W. Evans, Imperial Wizard."[10]

On May 12 Stephenson called Hoosier Klansmen to an assembly at Cadle Tabernacle. His purpose was to defy the Atlanta headquarters by adopting a new constitution declaring the complete independence of the Hoosier Klan. Now Grand Dragon again by his own seizure of power, Stephenson rallied his Hoosier followers with inflammatory speeches. Indiana citizens were 92 percent native-born with the best blood and traditions in America, he said. "God help the man who issues a proclamation of war against the Klan in Indiana now," he cried. "We are going to Klux Indiana as she has never been Kluxed before . . . I'll appeal to the ministers of Indiana to do the praying for the Ku Klux Klan and I'll do the scrapping for it . . . And the fiery cross is going to burn at every crossroads in Indiana, as long as there is a white man left in the state."[11]

Indianapolis newspapers were running headlines about Klan victories in the elections and about Stephenson's defiance. At the same time they were reporting the national A.M.E. Zion church gathering in the city. The denomination had grown large, now exceeding 2,500 congregations. Its general conference brought some 3,000 black delegates and visitors from all parts of the country, from Africa, and from South America into Klan-sensitized Indianapolis. They had their own agenda. They stayed in session twenty-three days. S. D. Davis of Jones Tabernacle was host pastor. Mrs. S. D. Davis and Mrs. Mary Jackson of Indianapolis were prominent among the officers as the Fifth Quadrennial Convention of the Woman's Home and Foreign Missionary Society opened its convention. On the very election eve when Klan operatives were canvassing the city's voters the black women were raising $50,000 for a new training school for Africa.

Besides the full measure of devotional and inspirational services, delegates at the daily general conference sessions at Tomlinson Hall over the city market heard reports from thirty committees and faced major decisions. Would laypersons now be given equal representation in general conference? Four bishops had died since the last general conference in 1920. Would this conference simply elect four new bishops as replacements from among the forty or so competent candidates or select five and send one off as missionary bishop to supervise the work in Africa as an African delegation was urging? There was redistricting to do. There were twenty-five general officers to elect. Were they willing to negotiate toward organic union with two other black Methodist denominations? They elected five bishops and approved a record denominational budget of $220,000 before going home.[12]

A.M.E. Zion at Indianapolis with George Wallace in 1964

Forty years passed before the A.M.E. Zion church returned to Indianapolis for its general conference. In 1964 the delegates found the city in the grip of racism once again. There had been a resurgence of the Ku Klux Klan in the South to resist civil rights for blacks. The most visible opponent to national civil rights legislation was George C. Wallace of Alabama. He always called his racism "states' rights." It was primary election time and Wallace was seeking the nomination as Democratic candidate for president. Indiana looked promising to him. He made his headquarters in a suite at the Claypool Hotel and stumped the state in the days before the election on May 5—Indianapolis on Thursday, Fort Wayne and Muncie on Friday, Crawfordsville on Sunday, and back to the Claypool to await primary election returns on Tuesday. Media giants like Walter Cronkite came to Indiana to repeat Klan stories from the state's racist past and to report on the Wallace campaign.

About 5,000 A.M.E. Zion delegates and visitors from the United States, Africa, South America, and the Virgin Islands opened their fifteen-day Indianapolis conference on primary election day. I. Benjamin Pierce of Jones Tabernacle was host pastor. During the daily sessions at the State Fairgrounds the 490 official delegates conducted the business of a denomination now grown to a membership of about one million. They heard the combined report of the twelve bishops. They considered again whether to enter a union of the three black Meth-

odist churches. Bishop C. Ewbank Tucker was assigned supervision of a district including Indiana, Tennessee, Arkansas, and Mississippi. There was a new financial system and a denominational budget for the coming fiscal year of $1,250,000.[13]

In spite of the revival of old tensions and the candidacy of George Wallace, the racial situation in Indiana was very different for this visit of the A.M.E. Zion conference in 1964. Under leadership of Governor Matthew E. Welsh, Indiana had taken a very progressive civil rights position among midwestern states in 1963. The state's Civil Rights Commission was empowered to issue legal cease and desist orders against discriminators. In Indianapolis mayor Albert H. Losche had also supported action to stop racial abuses and to secure civil rights.[14]

With reports coming in about civil rights marches in the South, the Indianapolis N.A.A.C.P. had sponsored a massive civil rights march and rally in July of 1963. A historian said of the event:

Never before had Indianapolis experienced such an awakening among the churches. The executive secretary of the Church Federation of Greater Indianapolis, Dr. Laurence T. Hosie, gave strategic counsel to Protestant church leaders. In turn he received the cooperation of top flight church executives and bishops. Prelates like Richard C. Raines of the Methodist Church and John Craine of the Episcopal Church made personal as well as official efforts to motivate cooperation from their churches. Church executives like John Fox of the Presbyterians, Barton Hunter of the Disciples of Christ, and Richard Muterspaugh of the American Baptists aided in promoting attendance and walked in the march. The Interdenominational Ministers Alliance under the leadership of its president, E. J. Odom, provided finances and leadership. The march and rally shared the public limelight with the national convention of the Knights of St. Peter Claver, a Negro Catholic men's organization. Following the NAACP march and rally the Catholic lay group moved to the climax of its convention with a processional around St. Rita's Catholic Church and His Eminence, Laurian Cardinal Rugambwa of Africa appearing in a solemn pontifical field mass on the church lawn. Rugambwa, the first Negro cardinal in the Catholic Church, addressed an estimated 10,000 assembled for the pontifical mass.[15]

All Indianapolis papers supported the demonstration and the cause. A delegation of some 300 Hoosiers, mostly church people under church sponsorship, went east in that same month of July for the civil rights "march on Washington." Wallace lost the Indiana primary in 1964.

He tried to claim that his 30 percent of the vote constituted a victory but it was Matthew E. Welsh, standing in for President Lyndon B. Johnson and standing squarely for civil rights legislation, who swept the election. The Indianapolis newspapers, so cautious in the face of the power of the Klan in the 1920s, were now embarrassed that Wallace had even minority support. They hastened to explain it away as voter opposition to Welsh's tax policy rather than to civil rights.[16]

Governor Welsh called Wallace "a pseudo-candidate chanting old slogans to a crowd of true believers who have long sought a spokesman who could show them the way to vote against democracy and brotherhood without suffering the pangs of conscience." He said "No American in good conscience can join this man Wallace for he is on the road to ruin, and he must walk alone." All Christian Church (Disciples) preachers in Indiana were requested to preach on ethical issues the Sunday before the primary, warning against half-truths and appeals to racial prejudice. Archdeacon Frederic P. Williams of the Episcopal Diocese of Indianapolis addressed civil rights marchers at Richmond on May 17. That same Sunday Theodore M. Hesburgh, president of the University of Notre Dame, said to 2,000 freedom marchers at South Bend: "After 10 years of frustration, culminating in the tragic comedy now taking place in the U.S. Senate, we are facing as a nation, the moment of truth."[17]

Bishop W. M. Smith got front-page coverage in the Indianapolis *News* when he made the Mother's Day address to the 1964 A.M.E. Zion General Conference at the State Fairgrounds. He was hardly a feminist visionary when he lamented what he saw as a loss of respect for the modern woman. "It remained for the 20th century to pull her down and make her like a man," he said. "The 20th century tolerance has won for women the right to become intoxicated, the right to smoke in public, and the right to be half-dressed. We call it progress. No people ever became great by lowering standards." But he was the traditional voice of his denomination now in tune with a majority of Hoosiers when he called George Wallace and Mississippi senator James Eastland "roadblocks in the path of democracy-loving people" who would not be able to halt the progress of freedom. He said the black "is on the march to the city called Freedom" and will not turn back until he has made it his home.[18]

The A.M.E. Zion church reported 22,661 adherents in Indiana in 1990, a number comparable to the Episcopalians or to the Church of God (Anderson, Indiana). The adherents concentrated in the state's most urban counties: six congregations in Marion with 10,328; five congregations in Lake with 10,187; two congregations in St. Joseph with 972; one congregation in Madison with 438; and one congregation in Vanderburgh with 389.

NOTES

1. William J. Walls, *The African Methodist Episcopal Zion Church* (Charlotte, N.C.: A.M.E. Zion Publishing House, 1974), 35–50, 86.

2. *History of American Methodism*, 3 vols., ed. Emory Stevens Bucke (New York: Abingdon Press, 1964), 1:613; C. Eric Lincoln and Lawrence H. Mamiya, *The Black Church in the African American Experience* (Durham, N.C.: Duke University Press, 1990), 56–60; Walls, *African Methodist*, 56, 65–83, 94.

3. Walls, *African Methodist*, 131, 144, 169; *History of American Methodism*, 1:614.

4. Walls, *African Methodist*, 149–62. Douglass came to Muncie in September of 1880. He recalled that the last time he spoke in Indiana, before the Civil War, he had been egged and mobbed at Pendleton. Now he was sponsored by Delaware County's black Republicans and greeted by a cheering crowd of 5,000, his visit one of the city's most spectacular events. See Hurley Goodall and J. Paul Mitchell, *History of the Negroes in Muncie* (Muncie, Ind.: Ball State University, 1976), 4–5.

5. Walls, *African Methodist*, 149–62.

6. Walls, *African Methodist*, 185–99; *History of American Methodism* 2:570–72.

7. Walls, *African Methodist*, 221, 251.

8. Walls, *African Methodist*, 222–23, 251–53, 263, 340–42.

9. Walls, *African Methodist*, 222–23, 384, 407, 596–98, 608–9.

10. Indianapolis *News*, 14 May 1924, 2.

11. M. William Lutholtz, *Grand Dragon: D. C. Stephenson and the Ku Klux Klan in Indiana* (West Lafayette, Ind.: Purdue University Press, 1991), 137. According to the Indianapolis *Times*, 13 May 1924, this meeting at Cadle Tabernacle which elected Stephenson as grand dragon for the realm of Indiana also elected a slate of realm officers: (1) grand klaliff (vice president)—Earl Sigmon of Indianapolis; (2) klokard (lecturer)—the Rev. H. B. Farrell of Frankfort; (3) kludd (chaplain)—the Rev. G. S. West of Brazil; (4) kligrapp (secretary)—Harry Pfeifer of Con nersville; (5) klabee (treasurer)—Dr. Harry Clauson of Columbus; (6) klarogo (inner guard)—George Wilcox of New Castle; (7) klexter (outer guard)—Dr. H. H. Alexander of Princeton; (8) kladd (custodian of paraphernalia)—C. O. Lighthouse of Fort Wayne; (9) klan nighthawk (courier and investigator)—Dr. M. L. White of Indianapolis; Indianapolis *Star*, 13 May 1924, 1, 3.

12. Indianapolis *News*, 3 May 1924, 39; 6 May 1924, 23; 7 May 1924, 6, 40; 9 May 1924, 43; 12 May 1924, 1, 10, 34; 13 May 1924, 2, 3; 14 May 1924, 2; 15 May 1924, 26; Indianapolis *Star*, 13 May 1924, 1, 3; Indianapolis *Times*, 13 May 1924, 2.

13. Walls, *African Methodist*, 281–82, 625; Indianapolis *News*, 1 May 1964, 2; 2 May 1964, 7, 14; 4 May 1964, 1; 5 May 1964, 1; 6 May 1964, 33, 35; 7 May 1964, 4; 9 May 1964, 5; 11 May 1964, 1; 13 May 1964, 8; Indianapolis *Star*, 7 May 1964, 22, 30.

14. Emma Lou Thornbrough, "Breaking Racial Barriers to Public Accommodations in Indiana, 1935 to 1963," *Indiana Magazine of History* 83 (December 1987): 301–43; James H. Madison, *The Indiana Way: A State History* (Bloomington, Ind.: Indiana University Press, 1986), 241–47.

15. William Kappen Artis Fox, "The Involvement of Negro Protestants in Cooperative Christianity in a Metropolitan Area" (Master's thesis, Butler University, 1964), 109–10.

16. Indianapolis *Star*, 7 May 1964, 30; Indianapolis *News*, 4 May 1964, 1.

17. Indianapolis *News*, 1 May 1964, 2; 18 May 1964, 19, 27.

18. Indianapolis *News*, 11 May 1964, 1.

CHRISTIAN METHODIST EPISCOPAL CHURCH

The nation's Methodist Episcopal Church divided north and south over the issue of slavery in 1844. There were many black members in the Methodist Episcopal Church, South, an actual black majority in South Carolina. As they were emancipated these freed black Methodists were invited and exhorted by both black and white missionaries from the North to change their affiliation to one of the Northern-based Methodist denominations. Those who elected to be Methodists could dissociate themselves from former Southern slaveholders by joining the African Methodist Episcopal Church or the African Methodist Episcopal Zion Church or the Methodist Episcopal Church (Northern). Most of them did so. But several thousand chose to stay with their familiar Methodist Episcopal Church, South.[1]

C.M.E Church Organized

Beginning in 1866 those who remained were accorded their own congregations and annual conferences within the old denomination. In 1870 eight of these black annual conferences—Tennessee, Kentucky, Georgia, Mississippi, South Carolina, Alabama, Arkansas, and Texas—convened at Jackson, Tennessee, as a general conference to form a new denomination. Until 1954 it was called the Colored Methodist Episcopal Church in America (hereafter C.M.E.).

Relationships of this new church with the main body of white Southern Methodists continued close and sup-

portive. The *Discipline* they adopted was essentially that of the Methodist Episcopal Church, South. They received legal title to many of the Southern Methodist properties. The former masters supplied leaders and money to get the new denominational structure well started. The C.M.E. church made much of being "set up" in good order by its mother church as a distinct branch of the great Methodist family rather than "set off" as some kind of move to be rid of an unwanted orphan people. In the interest of peace and in the tradition of contemporary Southern Protestantism, the new denomination expressly forbade political activity on church property in its early years. This meant no use of church buildings for meetings or speeches or actions designed to keep the South under military rule or political domination from the North.[2]

Such a policy of cooperation rather than confrontation often earned them the scorn of their black competitors. Such stinging designations as "bootlicks" or "Rebel church" or "old slavery church" or "white folks' niggers" left scars which would complicate later attempts at black Methodist union. In fact the C.M.E. church was strikingly similar to its sister denominations of black Methodists. It was different in that it was somewhat later and somewhat smaller. It was more wholly Southern in its origins; only four of the church's first forty-five bishops were born outside the South. But like the others it soon provided the church and the nation an impressive black leadership, seven black bishops by 1894 and all of them former slaves. Bishops Lucius Holsey of Georgia and Isaac Lane of Tennessee were outstanding.[3]

The C.M.E. church sought education for its members and ministers. Institutes named Paine and Lane grew to be colleges; smaller institutes and academies like Holsey Industrial School served the needs of blacks getting started. The General Conference of 1910 raised requirements in the course of study for ministers. Formation of a Women's Missionary Council in 1918 energized mission enterprises in Ghana, Nigeria, and Haiti. Later in the century women were included in the ordained ministry.

From an early nonpolitical posture and social quietism, the C.M.E. church gradually moved to support ethical positions familiar to Methodist bodies and to the National Council of Churches. The C.M.E. general conferences issued their own statements to the world conscience on housing, employment, education, capital punishment, and especially civil rights.[4]

The C.M.E. church came to Indiana in the twentieth century and from the South. In July of 1899 the Fourth International Epworth League Convention was welcomed to Indianapolis by Governor James A. Mount. It was a mass meeting for thousands of Methodist young people and their counselors from the United States and Canada. The C.M.E. church had adopted the Epworth League as its society for young people and received an invitation to send representatives to the Indianapolis convention. With the invitation came some remarkable information: "Delegates of the two races will not be separated. Every person attending the Convention, White or Colored, will have the privilege of sitting where he pleases. There will be no color line."[5]

Charles Henry Phillips

Charles Henry Phillips of Tennessee and Randall A. Carter of Georgia were members of the C.M.E. delegation of twelve who took prominent parts in the Epworth celebration at Indianapolis. Phillips was invited to preach "on the Sabbath at 10:30 A.M. in one of the leading churches." Carter addressed the convention session in the English Opera House at 10:30 A.M. on Friday.

> Rev. R. A. Carter, D.D., introduced as of the Colored Methodist Church, compared God to the ocean and man's spiritual nature to the shallow bays and harbors that must be deepened. The ever-flowing waters of unnumbered centuries completed in the rock-ribbed strata of the earth what primeval upheavals began. By their ceaseless activity mighty gorges yawn and deep-rolling streams move on in

majestic sweep where tiny rills rolled and weakly streams purled and played when creation was young. His entire address was like gorgeous rhetoric.[6]

It was Phillips who was destined for special prominence in the C.M.E. church as "the Prince of Colored Methodism." Tenth in a family of twelve children, he had professed his faith as a Christian at the age of sixteen. Of his conversion on 26 December 1874 he said "I felt a change of heart; I knew that I had found redemption and forgiveness of my sins in the blood of Christ." At age twenty he was licensed to preach. Church agencies helped him attain college degrees in both liberal arts and medicine. From his vocation as a youthful school principal he accepted the challenge of Bishop W. H. Miles to full-time ministry in the C.M.E. church. For more than sixty years he was a role model for clergy and a symbol of the dignity and quality to which the denomination aspired.[7]

When Charles Henry Phillips and his wife were part of the delegation to the Epworth convention in Indianapolis in 1899, he had already served as pastor in Memphis, in Washington, D.C., and in Louisville. He was editor of the denomination's periodical *The Christian Index*. On 15 May 1902, at the age of 44, he was elected bishop by an overwhelming majority. Phillips was one of the leaders who understood the dynamic of black migration. In an Episcopal Address he said: "What will happen to the CME Church when more than one half of its membership removes from its present dwelling place, its younger and most aspiring membership, to the North, the East, and the Northwest, if it is not there 'to meet and fold its own'? We must follow our membership wherever it goes or in a few years be emasculated."[8]

The work of Phillips as bishop in the Midwest and the Far West was to be the foundation for much of the later C.M.E. growth. That growth was increasingly in the North and West. In the South the C.M.E. circuits were often groupings of small rural congregations. The pattern in the West and North, on the other hand, was formation of large urban congregations, many of them named "Phillips." The Southwest Missouri and Illinois Annual Conference was for a time the largest in the entire denomination.[9]

Bishop C. H. Phillips did not forget Indianapolis. He encouraged an Indianapolis local preacher named J. F. Taylor to organize a C.M.E. mission there. Taylor came to visit the Tennessee Conference where Phillips was presiding in 1906. Tennessee Conference took the Indianapolis work as its own mission and assigned Taylor there as its first pastor. Presiding Elder H. J. Johnson of Nashville took Indianapolis into his district and held the first C.M.E. quarterly conference there the following December.

Bishop Phillips had a special affection for Indianapolis. He visited the mission himself in February of 1907. In 1908 he was back to purchase a lot on Drake Street, to get a Mr. Lambert to build a church building 30 by 50 feet, to finance the project, and to pay it out of debt. This was Phillips Chapel, the first C.M.E. church in the state of Indiana. Later Phillips sent Indianapolis a pastor named G. I. Jackson, an especially able congregation builder. The product of that pastorate was "one of the largest and most representative Church edifices in the Connection." Phillips Chapel in Indianapolis had become Phillips Temple.[10]

In Gary J. Claude Allen helped the Israel Church build a beautiful building during the years of the Great Depression. Allen was elected a C.M.E. bishop in 1954. However, it was Indianapolis which remained the center of the state's C.M.E. strength. In 1985 Phillips Temple listed a staff of seven ministers and Trinity Church listed five. There were eight other Indianapolis C.M.E. congregations named Breeding Tabernacle, Burton Temple, Copeland Chapel, Emmanuel, Gershon, Gethsemane, Stewart Memorial, and Wormack Temple. Statistics for 1980 showed 11,769 C.M.E. adherents in Indiana. Marion County alone accounted for 9,687 of them, ranking the number of C.M.E. adherents eighth among that county's fifty denominations reporting.[11]

Almost continuously after 1906 there was some kind of union discussion among the three major black Methodist denominations. Bishop C. H. Phillips waged an intense personal campaign to defeat one of the most promising union efforts in 1918. Other leaders in the C.M.E., A.M.E., and A.M.E. Zion churches took their turns to delay union or oppose it.[12]

Repeated failure of union was a testimony to the affection with which each of these denominational names and traditions continued to be held. A people formed its identity in these fellowships; essential identities were still involved. Whenever union came to mean yielding the primary place of a cherished name or a territory or a manner of conducting church life, that union was made to wait. The three churches continued as participants with six other denominations in the ongoing Consultation on Church Union. *USA Today* reporter Patrick O'Driscoll was saying at the end of 1987 "the 1.5 million-member African Methodist Episcopal Zion Church and 950,000-member Christian Methodist Episcopal Church aim to unite by the mid-1990s."[13]

NOTES

1. Othal H. Lakey, *The History of the CME Church* (Memphis, Tenn.: CME Publishing House, 1985), 73–116.

2. William B. Gravely, "Christian Methodist Episcopal Church," in *Encyclopedia of Religion in the South*, ed. Samuel S. Hill (Macon, Ga.: Mercer University Press, 1984), 150–53; *History of American Methodism*, 3 vols., ed. Emory Stevens Bucke (New York: Abingdon Press, 1964), 2:283–87; Lakey, *History*, 181.

3. Dennis C. Dickerson, "Black Ecumenism: Efforts to Establish a United Episcopal Church, 1918–1932," *Church History* 52 (December 1983): 479–91; Lakey, *History*, 238–39; Gravely, "Christian Methodist Episcopal Church," 152.

4. C. Eric Lincoln and Lawrence N. Mamiya, *The Black Church in the African American Experience* (Durham, N.C.: Duke University Press, 1990), 60–65; Gravely, "Christian Methodist Episcopal Church," 151–52.

5. *Souvenir, Song Book and Official Programme, Fourth International Convention of the Epworth League Held in Indianapolis, Ind., U.S.A., July 20, 21, 22 and 23, 1899* (Indianapolis, Ind.: Levey Brothers, 1899, 158 p.); C. H. Phillips, *The History of the Colored Methodist Episcopal Church in America*, 3d ed. (Jackson, Tenn.: CME Publishing House, 1925), 301.

6. Phillips, *History*, 300.

7. Lakey, *History*, 525–35.

8. Lakey, *History*, 424, 427.

9. Lakey, *History*, 490, 531–33.

10. Phillips, *History*, 356–57.

11. *1985–86 Directory of Churches and Ministers, Indianapolis and Its Surrounding Counties* (Indianapolis, Ind.: Church Federation of Greater Indianapolis, 1986), 41; Lakey, *History*, 549.

12. Dickerson, "Black Ecumenism," 479–91.

13. *USA Today*, 30 December 1987, 1–2.

METHODIST EPISCOPAL CHURCH (LEXINGTON CONFERENCE)

The predominantly white Methodist Episcopal denomination in the North had only 18,139 black members in 1864. Blacks generally preferred their own denominations. Most of the black Methodist Episcopal churches were in or near Maryland and Delaware. The rest were very thinly scattered across the North. As the Union Army took control in the South the Methodist Episcopal bishops organized new missions and conferences there. Sometimes they took over properties and members of the Methodist Episcopal Church, South. The denomination's Missionary Society sent pastors south. The Board of Church Extension sent assistance for church construction. The Sunday School Union and Tract Society provided printed materials. The Freedmen's Aid Society, Southern Education Society, and Woman's Home Missionary Society sent money and teachers to promote literacy and develop schools. The result was an increased and invigorated minority of black Methodist Episcopal members.[1]

This Northern church elected Francis Burns as its first black bishop in 1852 and John W. Roberts as its second in 1866—both missionary bishops to serve in Africa. By 1864 some black Methodist Episcopal preachers were being fully ordained as traveling elders. That year Delaware Conference and Washington Conference were established, separate and black. By 1868 there were eight black conferences. Besides dozens of elementary and normal schools, the Methodist Episcopal church founded twelve colleges for Southern blacks. These included Ben-nett College (Greensboro, North Carolina), Bethune-Cookman College (Daytona Beach, Florida), Clark University and Gammon Theological Seminary (Atlanta, Georgia), Dillard University (New Orleans, Louisiana), and Meharry Medical School (Nashville, Tennessee).[2]

By the time the Northern and Southern Methodists came to reunion in 1939, the Northern branch had nineteen separate black conferences. These had their own corps of preachers and supervisors, their own *Southwestern Christian Advocate*, and their own sense of black identity. Defining their status in the reunited national denomination had been among the knotty problems during the years of union negotiation. The decision was to create a separate Central Jurisdiction made up of the 315,000 blacks in their nineteen conferences, literally a segregated church within a church. Five jurisdictions in the new Methodist Church would be geographical but Central would be racial, cutting across the others. This black jurisdiction would participate fully in the denomination's operation at the national level. It would continue its own newspaper, renamed the *Central Christian Advocate*. Central Jurisdiction would elect its own bishops, but in normal operations these black bishops would govern only black Methodists.[3]

The result was ambivalence. Blacks were glad to direct their own enterprise and to have generous representation in the councils of the national church. They liked having control of their own turf and the guarantee of a prominent national platform from which to be heard. Yet this plan was a painfully obvious case of segregation by race. It was an arrangement unacceptable to an increasing number of both blacks and whites. One of the black annual conferences resolved in 1955: "We believe that the Central Jurisdiction is a moral sin on the part of the Methodist Church and an insult to its 350,000 Negro members." Effective in 1958 black congregations or whole conferences could elect to transfer to the jurisdiction of their geographical region without regard to race. The General Conference of 1964 determined that the racial Central Jurisdiction should be dissolved by 1968.[4]

The actual dissolution occurred in the midst of yet another union. The Methodists and the Evangelical United Brethren were planning to join to become the United Methodist denomination in 1968. The merging parties agreed that no racially segregated structures would persist in the new church. All would be eliminated by 1972. Black Methodists concerned to see these steps produce true integration formed a caucus named Black Methodists for Church Renewal in 1968. Soon there were chapters of this black caucus in each jurisdiction and in many conferences. They provided a persistent black voice to the whole of Methodism and a connection to national black church consciousness across denominational lines. The integrated United Methodist church continued to give priority to black leadership. In the United States in 1990 about 360,000 United Methodists were black in a denomination of 9.4 million. At the same time there were eleven black United Methodist bishops among the nation's total of forty-six.[5]

Lexington Conference

Indiana's black Methodist Episcopal strength was small after the African Methodist Episcopal congregations had withdrawn. The number of black members among the predominantly white Methodist churches in the state dropped from 442 in 1839 to 138 in 1851. Some black Methodist Episcopal churches in Kentucky asked to become one of those separate black Methodist Episcopal conferences in 1869. Indiana's handful of black Methodist Episcopal congregations were attached to this new Lexington Conference. By 1900 mission work and black immigration had increased Lexington Conference to 12,000 members served by 145 ministers but they were scattered across Kentucky, Indiana, Ohio, and parts of Illinois. Later the conference was further stretched

by adding some churches in Michigan, Wisconsin, and Minnesota. Gradually these churches got black presiding elders (district superintendents), but for a long time white bishops presided.[6]

Lexington Conference often convened at Indianapolis. Many black Methodist Episcopal leaders had associations with the Hoosier capital. Simpson Chapel Church was established there in 1874. Marshall W. Taylor was pastor at Simpson Chapel, presiding elder in Kentucky and Ohio, and editor of the *Southwestern Christian Advocate*. When he preached in Greenfield in 1872 he was considered "perhaps the most eloquent Afro-American in the pulpit of this country."

Edward W. S. Hammond was pastor at Simpson Chapel, presiding elder, editor of the *Southwestern Christian Advocate*, dean of a theological school in Nashville, Tennessee, and author of several books. Hammond's camp meetings in the Greenfield-Indianapolis area from 1881 to 1885 attracted black and white hearers by thousands. When he shared the camp meeting platform in 1885 with Maria Beulah Woodworth-Etter "people began to fall in every direction."

Lewis M. Hagood, a Simpson Chapel pastor and presiding elder, was born of slave parents in Missouri. He eventually graduated from a theological school in Tennessee and from Louisville Medical College. His best known publication was *The Colored Man in the Methodist Episcopal Church*. This was a defense of blacks who preferred to be part of the larger and predominantly white Methodist Episcopal church rather than members of the separate black denominations.[7]

George L. Knox

George L. Knox was a black Indiana layman who chose to stay in the larger Methodist Episcopal church, vocal in his conviction that he could do more for his race there. Knox was a Tennessee slave separated from his family and sold at auction at age three. Twenty years later, during the Civil War, he escaped to Union lines. Indiana troops whom he served brought him north to the Indianapolis area in 1864. Beginning as a porter in a barber shop, he gradually learned the barber trade. From that precarious beginning he began his rise to prominence by opening his own shop in the Greenfield community. James Whitcomb Riley of Greenfield mentioned Knox's barbershop in one of his poems. Living in Indianapolis after 1884, he was able to open the Bates House Barbershop in one of the city's best hotels. The shop was "a thing of beauty" with ten chairs, fifteen ornate baths, and by 1891 a Ladies Hair Dressing Department. In his chain of Indianapolis barbershops, Knox gave employment to forty people. In 1892 Knox purchased the *Indianapolis Freeman*, by the turn of the century boasting the largest circulation of any black journal in America. The illiterate orphaned slave had become Indiana's leading black citizen.[8]

Knox became the most prominent layman in the multi-state black Lexington Conference. At Greenfield he was largely responsible for organizing a Sunday school for blacks in 1870. After a slow start it "flourished like a green bay tree." Knox said "All the colored people of the city, one by one, became members of it—every young and old person and every child." His wife taught Knox the alphabet but many of his earliest exercises in reading and writing came from Superintendent Thomas Snow of the Sunday school. Knox and some white friends pressed for a public school for Greenfield blacks. He was a public school pupil too, reciting his own lessons to its teachers at night.

Two years after the opening of the Sunday school Knox helped form a black Greenfield congregation affiliated with the predominantly white Methodist Episcopal denomination. After black preacher Marshall W. Taylor helped lead the long revival in 1872, Knox was among those baptized at Greenfield when the ground was covered with snow and Brandywine creek was "at high water and ice-cold." Two decades later he commented in his autobiography "There is no doubt that this day marked one of the controlling incidents in my life, as I then considered it and still consider it."[9]

Knox was the prime mover in the series of six Methodist Episcopal camp meetings conducted by black leaders between 1881 and 1886 and attended by thousands. After moving from Greenfield to Indianapolis he became a member of Simpson Chapel and was primarily responsible for construction of its new building. He was a natural candidate for election as delegate to meetings of Lexington Conference. In 1888 Lexington Conference sent him as delegate to the denomination's General Conference in New York and in 1892 in the same capacity to Omaha. Quick to understand ecclesiastical tactics and sure of his oratorical powers, he relished his visibility before thousands on this national stage. He spoke against compulsory and frequent rotation of preachers among the charges. He nominated his friend Edward W. S. Hammond of Lexington Conference to become editor of the *Southwestern Christian Advocate*. He was among those always working to secure election of a black bishop for service among Methodist Episcopal churches in the

United States. Before he died in 1927 he had seen the election of two.[10]

Evansville had two black churches affiliated with the predominantly white Methodist Episcopal Church. There was Fifth Methodist Episcopal Church formed in the 1880s and renting space at the corner of Garfield and Illinois. And there was St. John Methodist Episcopal Church at 33 Bland Avenue organized in the 1890s.[11]

Not much changed for black members in the Midwest when the racially segregated Lexington Conference was included in the new racially segregated Central Jurisdiction in 1939. Election of black bishops to preside over the conferences of Central Jurisdiction did become regular. The congregations were so widely scattered that the average black district superintendent served about half as many churches as his white counterparts.[12]

The segregated Lexington Conference of the Methodist Episcopal church ended in 1964. In the year of its dissolution six of its nineteen Indiana churches (Barnes, Christ, Gorham, St. Paul, Scott, and Simpson) were in Indianapolis. Other Indiana churches or circuits were named Anderson, Connersville, Evansville, Jeffersonville, Madison, Muncie (Trinity), New Castle, Rushville, Shelbyville, Terre Haute, Princeton, North Vernon, and Watson. Total Indiana membership reported for that final year was 3,910.[13]

NOTES

1. Joseph C. Hartzell, "Methodism and the Negro in the United States," *Journal of Negro History* 8 (July 1923): 312–15.

2. *History of American Methodism*, 3 vols., ed. Emory Stevens Bucke (New York: Abingdon Press, 1964), 3:486–95; C. Eric Lincoln and Lawrence H. Mamiya, *The Black Church in the African American Experience* (Durham, N.C.: Duke University Press, 1990), 66.

3. *History of American Methodism*, 3:488, 494; Lincoln and Mamiya, *Black Church*, 67.

4. Frederick A. Norwood, *The Story of American Methodism* (Nashville, Tenn.: Abingdon Press, 1974), 406–13, 433; *History of American Methodism*, 3:491, 494–95.

5. Norwood, *Story*, 429, 433–34; Lincoln and Mamiya, *Black Church*, 67.

6. *Minutes of the Indiana Annual Conference of the Methodist Episcopal Church 1851* (New York: T. Mason and Lane, 1852), 34; George L. Knox, *The Autobiography of George L. Knox*, ed. Willard B. Gatewood, Jr. (Lexington, Ky.: University Press of Kentucky, 1979), 21, 199–200, 217; David E. Skelton, *History of Lexington Conference* (N.p., 1950), 8–11.

7. Lewis M. Hagood, *The Colored Man in the Methodist Episcopal Church* (Cincinnati, Ohio: Cranston and Stowe, 1890, 327 p.); Walter H. Riley, *Forty Years in the Lap of Methodism: History of Lexington Conference of the Methodist Episcopal Church* (Louisville, Ky.:

Mayes Printing Company, 1915), 38, 51–52, 70–95, 102–11, 128–29; Knox, *Autobiography*, 21, 122–27, 217, 224; Skelton, *History*, 30–31, 35–36, 48.

8. Knox, *Autobiography*, [v], 12, 18–19, 22, 25–40, 55–58, 66–74, 141, 200.

9. Knox, *Autobiography*, 12–13, 21, 122–23.

10. Knox, *Autobiography*, 21–22, 140–50, 157–70.

11. Darrel E. Bigham, *We Only Ask a Fair Trial: A History of the Black Community of Evansville, Indiana* (Bloomington, Ind.: Indiana University Press, 1987), 76.

12. *History of American Methodism*, 3:489–92, 515.

13. Letter of Wesley W. Wilson, Coordinator of Archives and Special Collections, DePauw University, Greencastle, Ind. to L. C. Rudolph, 6 July 1992.

BLACK BAPTISTS

Baptists were not prominent in the early Southern colonies. Then Shubal Stearns and Daniel Marshall of New England were converted under the preaching of George Whitefield in the Great Awakening of the middle 1700s. They took their revival energy to North Carolina as "Separate Baptists." These evangelistic "Separates" proceeded to reshape the Baptist enterprise. Baptist churches multiplied in the South.[1]

Blacks brought to America in slavery were not quick to become Christians. Slave owners were slow to evangelize blacks until they were convinced that slaves really had souls and assured that slaves would remain slaves even if converted. By the time the enthusiasm of the Separate Baptists became widespread in the South many blacks were American born. They knew English and understood the preaching. Some masters allowed or even encouraged blacks to join existing Baptist churches. By the end of the 1700s Baptist membership was growing even faster among blacks than among whites. In 1780 blacks made up about 10 percent of America's Baptists. By 1790 they had grown to about 20 percent of the vastly increased Baptist population and 97 percent of black Baptists lived in the South.[2]

Sometimes blacks were seated in a separate section of the church or in a balcony. Sometimes one color held service in the morning and the other in the afternoon. Sometimes a black branch of a congregation would be allowed to have its own deacons and to discipline its own members. Where the number of black members was large, perhaps even a majority, separate preaching places might be arranged. Earnest black converts soon wanted to preach and soon demonstrated how effective their preaching could be. Where there were multiple services, white pastors were often glad to have black preachers share the labor.

Early Black Baptist Churches in the South

There were a few separately organized black Baptist churches in the South before 1800. John Galphin allowed blacks to gather to hear that black Baptist itinerant "Brother Palmer" on his plantation and to form their own congregation there in 1773. That was in Aiken County, South Carolina, just across the river from Savannah, Georgia. The church was called Silver Bluff. During the disruptions of the Revolution much of its membership relocated to become the nucleus for the African Baptist Church of Savannah. A remarkable series of slaves developed into Baptist ministers there.

David George grasped the wartime opportunity to migrate from Savannah to Nova Scotia under British protection and took a contingent of blacks from Nova Scotia to Sierra Leone to form the first Baptist church on the west coast of Africa. George Lisle (sometimes spelled Liele) was freed for ministry by the white Baptist deacon Henry Sharpe who was his master. Lisle was organizer and pastor for the black church in Savannah until it seemed essential that he leave with the British in 1782 to avoid reenslavement. He went on to establish the first Baptist congregation on the island of Jamaica, a church which grew in a few years to a membership of about 1,000.[3]

Black preacher Andrew Bryan dared to remain in Georgia. With the support of his slave congregation and sponsorship of his master along with some other slaveholders, Bryan led the African Baptist Church of Savannah to construct the first permanent church building in America built by blacks for blacks.

> The framing timber was good and solid, hewed out in the forest by its members, and the weatherboarding was all neatly planed smooth. The building was very plain, without any attempt at architectural beauty, almost square and boxlike, high-pitched roof, with small windows; one wide door in the west center of the building and two smaller doors near each end on the south side . . . the pulpit [was] in the east center, built very plain, shaped like an acorn, with a raise from the floor of about three feet, plain board front, a neat cushioned pad for the Bible, and a board seat which would accommodate three. No part of the building inside was ceiled, rafters and studs in their rough state, straight-back pews without doors; and the only pretense to neatness was in the smoothing of the backs and seats and rounding and beading the edges and tops. No part of the building was painted or white-washed, but plain and pure as from the carpenter's hands.[4]

The building was built in 1794. Bryan was allowed to purchase his freedom in 1795. By 1800 the First African Baptist Church of Savannah had 700 members.[5]

There were other black Baptist congregations in the South by the turn of the century—three in Virginia at Petersburg, Richmond, and Williamsburg; one in Kentucky at Lexington; and another in Georgia at Augusta. A Richmond tobacco warehouse slave named Lott Carey repented of his sins, professed his faith, was baptized, and joined the First Baptist Church in 1807. The white pastor's sermon on the third chapter of the Gospel of John inspired Carey to learn to read so he also could do Bible study. He became a licensed preacher in Richmond's First African Church, saved enough money to buy his freedom, and pieced together enough support to sail for Africa as a missionary in January of 1821. When the African state of Liberia was formed that same year, Carey moved to its capital city Monrovia where he established a Baptist church, a school, and a medical practice. He was acting governor of the colony at the time of his accidental death in 1828. "Lott Carey" was to become the name of a continuing black Baptist missionary convention.[6]

All the early black congregations in the South were precarious. They were always subject to abuse by local ruffians. As sensitivity to the slavery issue was intensified by debates with abolitionists, by threats of slave rebellions, and by the mere increasing mass of slave population, southern states passed strenuous laws limiting black assemblies. An 1857 Code of Laws in Mississippi said "Free Negroes or Mulattoes, for exercising the functions of a minister of the gospel, on conviction may be punished by any number of lashes, not exceeding 39, on the bare back, and shall pay the cost."[7]

Early Black Baptist Churches in the North

Up to 1800 the separate Baptist churches were formed in the south where 90 percent of blacks lived. Soon after 1800 some free black Baptists in the North began organizing. Three brothers of the Paul family named Thomas, Benjamin, and Nathaniel were energized by a renewal of revivals in New Hampshire. They preached to scattered black communities throughout New England. Thomas Paul organized the Joy Street Baptist Church in Boston in 1804 and served it as pastor for about twenty-five years. He also served as counselor for some black members in the predominantly white Gold Street Baptist Church in New York.

In 1809 these New Yorkers bought a vacant church building in Harlem and named their newly-separated black congregation the Abyssinian Baptist Church. It was destined to become one of the largest and most influential black churches in America. One of its later pastors, Adam Clayton Powell, Jr., was a champion of civil rights as a member of the United States Congress from 1944 to 1970.[8]

Also in 1809 Henry Cunningham of the Second African Baptist Church in Savannah came north to seek financial aid from Philadelphia Baptists. He organized thirteen black members of the First Baptist Church to form the First African Baptist Church of Philadelphia and became their first pastor. Other black churches soon formed in Northern states.[9]

Though comparatively small in number, this black Baptist membership in the North was very influential. The Northern blacks had often come from the South as escaping slaves or as free black persons fleeing Southern hostility. They kept in communication with blacks in the South. They wanted to use their voices and united efforts against slavery. In the North they were free to begin experimental associations of their independent black Baptist congregations. Association meetings provided a setting for mutual planning and encouragement. The association's common worship could become a revival. The more able preachers in attendance could share resources with colleagues and lift the general ministerial standard by example. Stronger congregations could act to help the weaker ones. There could be deliberate missionary assignments and joint arrangements for support of schools. Those present could unite in a public statement against racial oppression.[10]

The first associations of black Baptist churches were formed in the Midwest. Early missionary activity had established churches at Xenia (1822), Chillicothe (1824), Cincinnati (1831), and Columbus (1835). Six churches totaling fewer than 200 members formed the Providence Association in Ohio in 1836. It was the first association organized by black Baptists in America. Its members promoted formation of additional churches but also shared with enthusiasm in Ohio's welter of antislavery organizations. Black Baptists in Illinois were next to organize with the Wood River Baptist Association in 1838 and the Colored Baptist Association, Friends to Humanity in 1839. These were also stoutly antislavery. The Union Association, formed in 1840, had fifteen churches in Ohio, Indiana, and Illinois by 1845. Before the Civil War two black Baptist associations had been formed in Ohio, two in Illinois, one in Indiana, and one in Canada.[11]

Explosive growth of separate black Baptist churches followed the Civil War. At the beginning of the Civil War there were more black Methodist members in the South than black Baptist members. That soon reversed. Most religious blacks opted for their own Baptist churches. A Baptist church could begin anywhere with a minimum of outside authorization or regulation. Male members could proceed to "be somebody" at once if their leadership was welcomed by their peers. "Mothers" and "Sisters" could also hold honored places. Lack of formal education did not disqualify. The informal services, the heartfelt manner of evangelism, the dramatic baptisms, the democratic decision process in which any member could speak and all members vote, the absence of white domination—all these had great appeal.

The Emancipation Proclamation was issued on 1 January 1863. Within four years the thousands and thousands of Southern blacks who had been members of biracial Baptist congregations had formed their own churches. Black preaching was winning converts steadily. Black congregations and associations multiplied all across the South. Blacks who migrated north took their Baptist preferences with them. They sought Baptist churches or formed them. Sometimes constituents of an established black Methodist church in the North or Midwest would become the nucleus of a new black church—a Baptist church.[12]

Steps toward National Organization

Able black Baptist leaders kept trying to enlist the burgeoning churches and associations into regional or even national conventions. That was a very effervescent enterprise since every congregation and association could affiliate with as many or as few conventions as it chose for whatever period of time and with whatever degree of enthusiasm it chose to continue. Several of these independent conventions of independent churches were tested briefly but faded. Three emerged as worthy survivors. One resulted from a heroic campaign by African missionary W. W. Colley. He was able to gather 151 delegates from eleven states to meet at Montgomery, Alabama, on 24 November 1880. They formed the Baptist Foreign Mission Convention (BFMC). This organization, and especially its African missions, became a focus for black Baptist identity.[13]

Even more important for the future of black Baptists was the vision of William J. Simmons of Louisville. Simmons had been born a slave in Charleston, South Carolina, but as a boy of about ten escaped by sea to Philadelphia as part of his runaway family. After serving as a Civil War soldier, he made his profession of faith and joined the Baptist church attended by his employer in Bordentown, New Jersey. When he inquired about becoming a minister, a series of church sponsors gave him support. He was thirty-one in 1880, already a respected graduate of Howard University, pastor, educator, and politician. That year he accepted the presidency of the Normal and Theological Institute of Louisville. The school had only thirteen pupils and two teachers but he soon led it to prosperity and a reputation for notable alumni. It was later named Simmons University. Simmons was editor of the *American Baptist* and president of the National Negro Press Association. He was district secretary for the Southern states for the American Baptist Home Mission Society. When he spoke black Baptists listened.

Simmons wanted a genuine black Baptist denomination which would direct all of its own missionary and educational enterprises but function in full cooperation with the white Baptist conventions. He used his personal persuasion and his newspaper to rally some 600 black supporters from seventeen states to meet and form the American National Baptist Convention (ANBC) in August of 1886. He preached the chief sermon at the meeting and was elected president. A statistician told that assembly there were already 1,066,131 black Baptists in 9,061 congregations. Simmons said it was "the largest denomination among our race in the United States, and is without doubt larger than all of them put together, but for want of organization has not wielded the power belonging even to its numerical strength." Simmons enlisted women in support of his vision. In his newspaper and in his new national convention, women played a prominent role.[14]

But even four years of the dynamic presidency of Simmons and the zeal of his supporters could not achieve national unity with full cooperation of both black and white Baptists as he envisioned. Simmons himself died in 1890 at the age of forty-two. Foreign missions had remained largely outside the control of his uniting ANBC. A new National Baptist Educational Convention emerged in 1893 to displace the ANBC as guide and fund raiser for the numerous black schools. Fewer black Baptists were interested in white cooperation. Continuing racial oppression by discriminatory laws and jim crow practices eroded their confidence in whites. Sensitive to a host of indignities, black Baptists gravitated to a policy of separation and black power.[15]

The desire to keep their church as a separate focus of black independence and power was heightened by two specific incidents in 1889. Emanuel Love was pastor of the First African Baptist Church of Savannah, editor of the *Weekly Sentinel*, and president of the Baptist Foreign Mission Convention (BFMC). He and his fellow delegates had first-class railroad tickets and assurance of first-class passage to Indianapolis for the week of concurrent annual meetings of the BFMC and the ANBC. When the train turned out to have only one first-class car, they took seats in it. At Baxley, Georgia, a gang of about fifty local men boarded the train and brutally assaulted the black Baptists for daring to share the car with whites. The black church conventions meeting at Indianapolis made stout protests of the incident. These received a perfunctory response from President Benjamin Harrison and scant attention from the secular press.[16]

At the same series of joint meetings at Indianapolis in September of 1889, the black convention members held a celebration of the silver anniversary of work among Afro-Americans by the American Baptist Publication Society (ABPS). Thousands of black churches were regular purchasers of Baptist literature from the ABPS. Such black leaders as William Simmons, Emanuel Love, Walter Henderson Brooks, and Elias Camp Morris were field agents for this white Baptist press. At the 1889 occasion the blacks requested more representation, specifically that some articles by black authors appear in the *Baptist Teacher*. At first the ABPS agreed. The *Teacher* would publish an article by Walter Brooks on "The Doctrine of God," an article by Emanuel Love on "Regeneration," and an article by William Simmons on "The Lord's Supper." But churches of the Southern Baptist Convention were also major customers of the ABPS. Many of them declared they would not buy literature with articles by these black authors. So the names of Brooks, Love, and Simmons were "erased" from the list of contributors. In the exchange of bitter words about all this the black Baptists were wounded still more.[17]

National Baptist Convention of the U.S.A.

Still the drive for unity continued. More and more it became a drive for a separate black Baptist denomination. Such a body would direct a separate black Baptist mission enterprise, foster local black control of the host of black Baptist schools, maintain its own separate publication board, and present a clear black Baptist testimony before the nation. Albert W. Pegues of North Carolina offered a motion to a joint meeting at Montgomery, Alabama, in 1894. Since the purposes of the three continuing national bodies could be as well achieved by one and since the consolidation would save both time and money, he proposed one national organization.

Supporters of unity, not least William Bishop Johnson of Washington, D.C., with his new *National Baptist Magazine*, rallied at least 500 to meet at Atlanta in September of 1895. Booker T. Washington was making that city and time famous with his address to the International Exposition. Black Baptists made the same time and city famous by uniting there under a new constitution.

> Whereas, It is the sense of the Colored Baptists of the United States of America, convened in the city of Atlanta, Ga., Sept. 28, 1895, in the several organizations as "The Baptist Foreign Mission Convention of the United States of America," hitherto engaged in mission work on the West Coast of Africa; and the "National Baptist Convention," which has been engaged in mission work in the United States of America; and the "National Baptist Educational Convention," which has sought to look after the educational interest, that the interest of the way of the Kingdom of God required that the several bodies above named should, and do now, unite in one body.[18]

The new body's name was The National Baptist Convention of the United States of America. Its object was "to do mission work in the United States of America, in Africa, and elsewhere, and to foster the cause of education."[19]

Elias Camp Morris was elected president of the new denomination. He was a slave-born preacher now risen to prominence as pastor of First Baptist Church of Helena, Arkansas, publisher of the weekly *People's Friend*, and founding leader of Arkansas Baptist College. He was president of the National Baptist Convention for the next twenty-eight years. His task was consolidating three independent conventions, now continued within the merger as three largely independent denominational boards.[20]

Lewis G. Jordan was elected corresponding secretary of the Foreign Mission Board. He began with an empty treasury, an office equipped with only three chairs and a record book, and minimal cooperation from the churches. He moved the office of the foreign board to Louisville, established the *Mission Herald*, and used his tenure of twenty-five years to build one of the major foreign mission boards among American denominations.[21] He told black youth gathered in Atlanta in 1902:

> If the Negro of America will but feel his responsibility and under take the evangelization of Africa in God's name, unborn millions of Africa's sons will witness a transformed continent . . . From that great black continent can be carved states or empires, from her cradle will come sons and daughters to rule and reign in the name of Christianity. Negroes of America, God calls you to duty; He calls you to service and He calls you now.[22]

In spite of the initial cost, President E. C. Morris was among the advocates of a separate black Baptist publication program. He said "The sun has forever gone down on any race of people who will not encourage and employ their literary talent." The publication work thrived from its beginning under the wing of the Home Mission Board. In fact, the publication work became a primary enterprise of Richard H. Boyd who was corresponding secretary for home missions.[23]

Boyd was an excellent manager. At its new location in Nashville the National Baptist Publication Board soon became the largest black publishing enterprise in the world. By 1909 it installed a Scott's all-size rotary book printing press, first of its kind south of the Ohio River. From 1 September 1908 to 31 August 1909 it published 11,717,876 copies of Sunday school literature besides songbooks and Bibles. The convention also kept growing. There were about a million members in its affiliated churches when the convention was formed, about two million by 1905, and nearly three million by 1915.[24]

National Baptist Convention of America

In 1915 tensions heightened between convention factions headed by E. C. Morris and R. H. Boyd. President Morris felt it was wise to separate the booming Publication Board from the Home Missions Board. This would also remove it from the personal direction of Boyd and mark it plainly as an enterprise belonging to the whole convention. Boyd resisted. He had taken legal title to the real estate, equipment, and copyrights of the Publication Board in his own name. The smaller portion of the denomination which resisted the consolidation of control by Morris withdrew with Boyd to form a second National Baptist Convention. It was sometimes referred to as the "Boyd Convention," or as the "Unincorporated Convention," or in later years as the National Baptist Convention of America. Members of the Boyd family long remained prominent in its leadership.

E. C. Morris viewed this 1915 separation as a call to consolidate the larger National Baptist Convention with integrated denominational boards and a national convention headquarters. A whole new publishing enterprise was also developed. The convention incorporated for fuller control of its property. Morris was the first of five presidents whose long tenure in office made them powerful symbols of black Baptist leadership. They were E. C. Morris (1894–1922), L. K. Williams (1924–40), D. V. Jemison (1941–52), Joseph H. Jackson (1953–82), and Theodore J. Jemison after 1982. This larger National Baptist Convention was sometimes referred to as the "Incorporated Convention" or by the name of Morris or Jackson or any appropriate one of the long-term presidents. Each of the two conventions developed a full denominational identity and continued to grow apace.[25]

Progressive National Baptist Convention

Another black Baptist division occurred in the course of the civil rights struggles of the 1950s and 1960s. Joseph H. Jackson was rising in power and visibility as president of the larger convention. He and his supporters felt that limitation of presidential tenure or authority would only reduce the denomination's efficiency and prestige. When the United States Supreme Court declared public school segregation unconstitutional in 1954, Jackson favored a cautious and legal "gradualism" in rooting out remainders of racial segregation. In this "gradual" policy he allied with the National Association for the Advancement of Colored People (NAACP).

Some members of Jackson's National Baptist Convention sought more radical change. Their leaders included Gardner C. Taylor, L. Venchael Booth, Martin Luther King, Jr., and Ralph D. Abernathy. They wanted to limit the tenure and authority of the president, specifically the tenure and authority of Jackson. They favored such new civil disobedience tactics as sit-ins, freedom marches, and economic boycotts. They preferred King's confrontational Southern Christian Leadership Conference to the more conservative NAACP. Some of them advocated more opportunity for church leadership by black women. Thwarted in every attempt internally, they elected Taylor as president in a rump convention and tried to seize control of the convention platform. That also failed. In November of 1961 these reformers sent messengers from fourteen states to organize the new Progressive National Baptist Convention to be headquartered in Washington, D.C. Black Baptist leadership loomed large in the civil rights campaigns of the second half of the 1900s.[26]

One more separation occurred in 1988. Following the death of President Carl Sams, a substantial group withdrew from the National Baptist Convention of America (earlier called the "Boyd" or "Unincorporated" convention). They gathered a fourth black Baptist denomination called the National Missionary Baptist Convention. A substantial group of black Baptist churches in Indiana followed the leadership of F. Benjamin Davis into this affiliation.

Interaction with White Baptists

Interaction of black Baptists with white Baptists was always lively and complex. In the nation's early history they were in congregations together. Soon after 1865 most black Baptists formed their own separate churches, but white American Baptists kept sending heavy investments of personnel and money to the South to assist in black education while white Southern Baptists supported black efforts in ministerial training and in evangelism. White donors were generally crucial wherever blacks campaigned to build churches and schools.[27]

A new pattern of interaction emerged in the latter half of the twentieth century as black-white relations matured and as national population movement actually reversed to flow from North to South. Many churches in the black Baptist conventions began making dual affiliations with the major white groups. In 1951 the first black congregation affiliated with the predominantly white Southern Baptist Convention (SBC). By 1984 the SBC included over

800 black churches with some 250,000 members. At least 95 percent of these churches were also affiliated with one of the National Baptist conventions. Perhaps an additional 50,000 blacks held individual membership in some 3,000 predominantly white Southern Baptist congregations.

The new relation was even more striking in the predominantly white American Baptist Church. There the affiliated black congregations were estimated to make up nearly a third of the denomination's membership, a very effective third in the conduct of urban ministry. Black churches of the Progressive National Baptist Convention were particularly likely to become dually aligned with white conventions. All of the national black Baptist denominations also related directly or indirectly to the Baptist World Alliance, the National Council of Churches, and the World Council of Churches.[28]

Scholars considered these complex denominational connections and the fact that many black Baptist churches both inside and outside the denominations had never furnished statistical reports. They admitted, with or without reverence, that only God knew the number of the nation's black Baptists. They generally approached 1990 with an estimate of about seven and one-half million in the National Baptist Convention (Incorporated) and enough in the other three large conventions together to bring the total well over eleven million. Following the 1990 census experts made a new computation. They developed a formula based on a complex sampling technique and applied it to the census statistics. They estimated the number of black Baptist adherents in the United States at 8,737,667, by every count the largest social and religious movement among black Americans.[29]

Black Baptists in Indiana

In Indiana's early years blacks were scarce and scattered. John Morris was prophetic of their eventual affinity with Baptist churches. Maria Creek Church was organized a few miles north of Vincennes in 1809. Morris was one of ten charter members and so the first black person admitted to full Baptist membership in the state.[30]

Most of Indiana's blacks came from the South after the South's huge increase in Baptist affiliation was in process. Many brought with them an affection for Baptist forms and fellowship. In Indiana towns the earliest black church was often Methodist but subsequent and larger black churches were often Baptist. This was the case, for example, at Terre Haute, Bloomington, Rushville, Muncie, South Bend, and Michigan City.[31]

Only a few Hoosier Baptists affirmed that blacks and whites should regularly attend church together. That question was warmly debated among black ministers at an Equal Rights Convention in Indianapolis in 1871. A white Baptist preacher at Bloomfield resigned his pastorate in 1894 because several members of his congregation would not admit black members.[32]

Most adopted the separation logic advanced by President E. C. Morris of the National Baptist Convention in his address to the assembly of the Baptist World Alliance in 1911.

> For a number of years following the close of the Civil War in this country, the great heart of the Christian people North and South went out to the emancipated, and many devout white Christians came to the Negro people to do missionary and educational work among them. Their effort met with signal success. But as the Negro people became educated, it developed that they preferred teachers and preachers from among their own race; hence, the strength of the race was turned towards educating teachers and preachers, so as to supply their schools and churches. The Negroes felt, and rightly so, I think, that their ministers and teachers should associate with them, should eat and drink in their humble homes, and do by contact, by social example much that could not be done by anyone in the schoolroom or pulpit alone. Owing to the wide race distinctions, this could not become a rule with the white ministers and teachers, and the most that they could do without sacrificing their social standing among their own people, was to preach, teach, and baptize the Negroes. The Negroes, as a rule, were opposed to the social intermingling of the races, preferring to maintain their peculiar racial identity. Hence, the demand for Negro churches and Negro preachers became imperative . . . We hope to make it plain that the Negroes of the United States are the logical Christian leaders of the black people of the world . . . I firmly believe that the time will come when there will be "neither Jew nor Greek, bond nor free," white nor black, European nor American, Asiatic or African in the kingdom of God, but all will be one in Christ Jesus. But until that time shall come, we should work along, recognizing the metes and bounds set by an All-Wise Creator, who will, in His own time and way level the hills and mountains: and raise up the valleys, until this division of labor and distribution of tasks shall unite to promote the oneness of Christ and His cause the world over.[33]

This separation was also frequently rationalized by posing some inherent racial difference in worship behavior.[34]

Pioneer Black Baptist Preachers

Indiana received some attention from the generation of black Baptist preachers who had themselves come out of slavery. There was a black Baptist meetinghouse in Ripley Township of Rush County as early as 1831 and a black Regular Union Baptist Church in Nettle Creek Township in Randolph County in 1843.[35]

Zachariah Bassett brought his family to a Quaker settlement in Parke County in 1844 or 1848. Soon he gathered a little Baptist church there among his fellow black immigrants who had come from North Carolina as he did. His sons Miles Bassett and Richard Bassett were admitted to the local Quaker school. Both boys were converted, claimed a call to preach, and invested most of their ministerial lives in Indiana. Zachariah Bassett moved to Howard County in 1856 where a black Baptist church soon appeared in "Bassett Settlement."

Miles Bassett first built up a sizable congregation at Shelbyville. His second congregation at Rising Sun allowed him to supply regularly at Madison as well. Beginning in 1881 he led the congregation of Second Baptist Church at New Albany in their adventure of buying and paying for their second building which was the finest owned by blacks in southern Indiana. Richard Bassett also served at Rising Sun before pastorates of eight years at New Albany and five years at Corinthian Baptist Church of Indianapolis. He was for a time a Sunday school missionary for the state and then pastor at Kokomo from which place he was elected to the state legislature in 1892.[36]

This Bassett family was likely to come to mind when Hoosiers thought of their black Baptist pioneers but the Bassetts were only part of a whole corps of nineteenth century black Baptist preachers. Some were veterans returned from Civil War service.

For example, John R. Miller was a Kentucky slave who enlisted in Company A of the 122nd Regiment of the United States Army. Upon his discharge in 1866 he was too old to feel comfortable in school with the children in his new place of residence at New Albany but he studied hard in a night school. He professed his faith and was baptized at the New Albany Baptist Church in 1867, a member educated enough to serve as clerk of the church for two years. After his licensure in 1870 his Baptist pastorates in Indiana included Second Church in Mitchell, Second Church in Bloomington, Second Church in Lafayette, First Church in Edinburgh, Second Church in Crawfordsville, and Second Church in Columbus. His colleagues often elected him to be presiding officer or corresponding secretary for their church associations.[37]

Paul H. Kennedy of Kentucky enlisted at the age of fifteen in the 109th Regiment of the United States Army. After some schooling and his profession of faith in 1873, he was ordained in 1876 in Tennessee. He was a pastor at Indianapolis in 1888 when he accepted appointment as general missionary for the state of Kentucky.[38]

C. C. Vaughn was the son of slave parents who had been brought to Ohio and set free in 1852. Vaughn had limited access to some of Ohio's black elementary schools before enlisting in the Colored Heavy Artillery of the United States Army where he rose to the rank of sergeant. In 1865–66 this military veteran was the only black student attending Liber College in Indiana. Later he studied at Berea College in Kentucky and became a leading black Baptist teacher and pastor in that state.[39]

James T. White, born and reared at New Providence in Clark County, Indiana, went to Arkansas as an "uppity" black carpetbagger preacher just after the war. By 1868 he was pastor of the First Colored Baptist Church of Helena and a member of the Arkansas State Senate. White wanted black Baptist churches to be separate from white churches but he was always crusading against ignorant preachers. He wanted really good black Baptist missionaries sent to the South to help provide preachers the more educated black Methodists could not ridicule.[40]

Moses Broyles at Indianapolis

Indianapolis quickly became the Indiana city with the largest black population and so the place of greatest opportunity. Black Baptists there met in the home of deacon John Brown. Charles Sachell, an ordained missionary from Cincinnati, visited to organize them as Second Baptist Church in 1846. They called Joshua Thurman from Madison to be pastor and built a tiny church of 20 feet by 30 feet on Missouri Street near the canal. A troubled decade followed, times of congregational tragedy and confusion finally brought to stability in the quarter-century of ministry by Moses Broyles. While Broyles was extraordinary rather than typical, the record of his life and ministry illustrated many concerns and achievements of Indiana's slave-born black Baptist generation.[41]

Broyles never knew the date and place of his birth; it was sometime around 1826 somewhere in Maryland. To settle a master's estate, he and his parents and six siblings were divided among slave traders. Moses went as a four-year-old to a slave trading yard in Fayetteville, Tennessee. There he was bought by John Broyles and reared as a kind of caretaker for the household and the small children of the Broyles family. John Broyles was a fiddler and a gambler and so had announced his intention of teaching Moses how to fiddle and to gamble. However John became concerned about religion, made a profession of faith, and joined the Baptist church in 1838. Moses also "commenced seeking" when about fourteen, intending to keep his religious interest secret. "But when I became earnestly engaged in the work, and entirely gave my heart to the Lord," he said, "I immediately found that peace which none but the true-born Christian knows." He followed a Baptist preacher gone Campbellite into the Christian church in 1844.

John Broyles, now religious, noticed how quickly Moses memorized the hymns and Scriptures and promised to teach him to read and spell so he could become a preacher. However, the time to begin the instruction never seemed to come. Moses learned to read and write by private arrangement with every schoolboy who would teach him. He read the New Testament through five times and the Old Testament twice before moving on to other reading. "For about fifteen years before I commenced going to school I generally gave myself to about two hours study each night," he said, "and I generally made it a point to learn something each day that I had not learned before."

The young white friends of Moses admitted him to their debating society. His church called on him to lead in prayer and in 1848 to begin preaching. As a licensed preacher he could address black Baptists or Methodists occasionally as invited. John Broyles had also told Moses "that if I would continue to be a good boy he would set me free in the fall of 1854, after I should have served him twenty-four years from the time he bought me." In the spring of 1851 Moses proposed to secure this promise by buying his freedom for $300 if John Broyles would allow him to go to the nearby town of Paducah, Kentucky, to earn the money. The agreement was made and recorded in the county court office. Moses nearly exhausted himself at work and study but in three and one half years had purchased his freedom and had saved an additional $300 to use for formal schooling.[42]

It was the schooling which brought him to Indiana in 1854. There were three schools in Indiana which provided expressly for the admission of black students. They were Union Literary Institute in Randolph County under leadership of Quakers, Eleutherian Institute at Lancaster in Jefferson County under leadership of Baptists, and Liber College in Jay County under leadership of Congregationalists and New School Presbyterians. All three had a very precarious existence.[43] Moses Broyles, a freed black bearing his former master's family name, came from western Kentucky to the Eleutherian Institute, ten miles north of Madison.

> I continued in the institution till the spring of 1857, near three years; but as I had given such diligence to the study of the elementary branches, I progressed in those studies so rapidly that I passed from one grade to another and commenced the study of the higher branches the second year. As I could not take a regular college course with the means I had on hand, I studied scientific branches, together with Greek and Latin, the last two years that I attended the Institute. As I found my funds growing short I would work mornings and evenings and Saturdays, chopping cord-wood. In April, 1857, I left the institution and came to Indianapolis to teach school.[44]

At Indianapolis Broyles found the black Baptists in a low state. Six ministers had served the tiny congregation during the eleven years since its founding in 1846 and for extended periods there had been no pastor. Church meetings were divisive and nearly ungovernable. The first church building had been burned "it was thought through incendiary malice"; the second was only partially finished. The latest of the six ministers, a powerful preacher and a charismatic man, left the pastoral office charged with unbecoming conduct toward female members, with pocketing $50 he had inspired the congregation to raise to save a church property in Kalamazoo, and with planning to desert the Baptists for the Methodists taking recent converts with him. At the last minute he had decided not to become a Methodist or to leave the city but to remain and operate free lance among the Indianapolis Baptists.

In the midst of this Broyles had applied to join the church in July of 1857, had been one of the interim preachers for the congregation beginning in August, had been chosen from three candidates to become the new pastor in September, and had been examined and ordained in November. He said:

> The Baptist Church had very little influence in the community. All religious influence was in the A.M.E. Church. As has been seen, the preachers who had led the church had not conducted themselves with that high Christian walk becoming to ministers of the gospel. The common saying therefore was that Baptist ministers were generally bad men. As the business meetings of the church had been held open to the world, and the church meetings were so much characterized with unpleasant disputes, the church was represented to consist of a low, quarrelsome set. I therefore studied and labored, day and night,

endeavoring to improve these sad defects, and to make the reputation of the Second Baptist Church equal to that of any other.[45]

Broyles studied Baptist church government in order to learn his duties and authority and to be prepared to teach the officers and members about theirs. There was no money for salary; for three years all the Second Baptist Church provided him was board. Finishing the church building for worship cost $240, a heavy load of debt to raise. Public schools were not open to blacks until 1869. Black historian Ida Webb Bryant said "The Reverend Broyles conducted a night school in the church in which many of our early Negro citizens, just out of slavery, received all their education." Running an elementary school in a black church was not unusual. Black Methodists of Indianapolis had set a pattern as zealous educators. The people needed basic literacy; many were motivated to learn. Broyles was also principal for a black school in an old building on the west side donated by the Indianapolis city government.[46]

Broyles needed whatever money his subscription schools earned to support his family. "On the 28th day of August, 1862, I married Miss Frances Elizabeth Hill, with whom I have lived a happy, quiet and peaceable life ever since," he said in 1876. "I now give it as my experience, as well as what I have observed, that it is generally much better for a pastor to be married than single." He detailed what he considered six compelling reasons for a minister to have "a steady, high-toned Christian wife, who is affectionate to him and to the members" and concluded: "Ministers should therefore select the most pious, steady and economical women for their wives, and endeavor to live in harmony with them." Frances and Moses Broyles reared six children, all of whom invested their lives in Indianapolis.[47]

Historian Ida Webb Bryant said Broyles was "the first Negro of general recognition over the city." In his own history, prepared in 1876, Broyles was modest. His church seemed to grow slowly at first and he left it twice but "the Lord seemed to chastise me each time, so that I was unhappy all the while I was away." Then came the increased immigration from the South during the Civil War years to provide growth. Many of the new arrivals were Baptists or candidates to become Baptists in the regular revivals at Second Church. Broyles performed seventy-four weddings between 22 May 1865 and 27 August 1867.[48] He had to walk a difficult line between the original members who expected their priority to be respected and the newcomers who were sensitive about receiving their full rights.

There have been baptized into the fellowship of this church since I have had charge of her, five hundred and forty persons. The present membership is six hundred and twenty-six. There are many things to be observed by a pastor in order to be successful in the management of a church. He should always endeavor to harmonize the deacons with himself . . . What is true with regard to deacons is true with regard to all the other officers and leading members of the church . . . I thank the Lord that I have had the harmonious co-operation of the church and all her officers generally.[49]

During the lifetime of Broyles the membership of Second Baptist Church provided nucleus groups for the founding in Indianapolis of White Lick Baptist Church (1866), Olivet Baptist Church (first as Lick Creek 1867), Mount Zion Baptist Church (1869), Georgetown Baptist Church (1872), New Bethel Baptist Church (1875), and a mission at Ray and Morris streets (1875). Thirteen ministers were licensed and thirteen ordained between the beginning of the ministry of Broyles in 1857 and the publication of his book in 1876.[50] Few of them were as well educated as Broyles.

Most of the above named ministers were so limited in education when they commenced preaching that they could not more than read and write, and some of them so limited even that they were not at all efficient. Many of them, by close application in private study and attending school as their opportunities would allow, and being inspired by the Holy Ghost, have become efficient ministers who need not be ashamed."[51]

He was sensitive to criticism about ordaining uneducated clergy but at the same time defensive.

When our people were first liberated, they were almost entirely uneducated, but as there was a deep interest taken in religion, there was a great demand for ministers to preach the gospel. There was, therefore, one of three things that must be done: First, we must supply this demand with white preachers; second, we must wait until colored men are educated; third, we must endeavor to make use of the means already on hand. The course first mentioned has been tried in some places. But as our people have been so much abused by white men, and even by some white preachers, there was not generally enough confidence reposed in them to be effectual in bringing them to Christ, nor to lead and regulate the churches. As our people were generally so limited in education when they were first emancipated, and in some places almost destitute, should the second course mentioned have been adopted, the cause of Christ would have been almost entirely suspended till we could have educated men for the ministry . . . Therefore the course

last mentioned has been pursued. It is plainly seen from this foregoing history that not only has the glorious cause been carried on, but many sinners have been brought to the blessed Savior, and the churches have been and are still nourished and growing.[52]

And he was plain about his own preference for thorough preparation.

I counsel young men who now feel impressed to preach to get as much of an education as you can. No minister can be too well educated to preach the gospel. I want our young ministers to understand that they will be sent to preach to an educated people. Therefore, like Paul, Barnabas and Luke, you will need be educated. I counsel our young unmarried men who are called to the work of the ministry not to marry till you obtain an education. Be saving and economical. Save your means and go to Nashville Institute, where you will not only be taught science and literature, but you will also be taught the true doctrines of the gospel.[53]

Broyles, who had attended an interracial school and had been a member of two predominantly white churches, sided with those who opposed "commingling" of blacks and whites in Indiana congregations. He said black preachers had ample work to do evangelizing the flood of freed blacks. His goal from the beginning of his ministry was to have the black Baptist churches of Indiana united in their own association for fellowship, for statistical reporting, for mutual protection against disorderly members or ministers moving from church to church, for carrying on missionary work, and for sharing in the examination and ordination of ministers. His invitation to the black Baptist churches of Indiana to constitute such an association in 1855 brought delegations from only three churches representing 83 members. Undismayed, they named Moses Broyles moderator and Henry H. White secretary and prepared a constitution.[54]

The association kept increasing in size and in usefulness to the churches. It also provided a platform from which to speak to the larger world. When Indiana finally passed its 1869 law opening the public schools to blacks, the association passed a resolution expressing its pleasure but also a second resolution saying "We . . . demand that common schools be opened in every city and locality in the State, according to law, and if the course of keeping our children out of the common schools is carried out in those cities, we will seek redress in the courts." Both resolutions were reported in the Indianapolis *Journal* of 28 August. Broyles led a committee in 1872 that demanded admission of blacks to white high schools. He reported with pride in 1876 that the single black Baptist association in Indiana had then enrolled fifty churches representing 3,500 members. He had been the association's moderator from 1858 to 1868 and a crucial counselor to his four successors.[55]

Second Baptist Church itself suffered decline after the death of Broyles in 1882. In May of 1887 James W. Carr, sixth son of a free black preacher in Tennessee and graduate of Roger Williams University, answered a desperate call from Indianapolis to become pastor and lead this mother congregation back to health.[56]

Black Baptists at Evansville

Evansville was an early black Baptist center. According to city records, a white man named Woods first gathered Evansville's black Baptists and served as their minister. On 13 May 1865 the congregation elected six trustees and organized as Liberty Baptist Church. Green McFarland was one of the trustees and became the church's pastor in 1866. A. L. Robinson, an antislavery attorney and judge, was appointed clerk. In the bustling city of Evansville black population boomed from 96 in 1860 to 1,408 in 1870 and to 7,405 in 1900. Liberty Church boomed too. City council heard a nuisance complaint in August of 1867 from some white citizens who said the services there ran too late at night and the music was bad. Liberty had a frame building at Seventh and Oak in 1866 and a larger brick building there in 1880.

When Green McFarland died in July of 1882 the membership of Liberty Church was about 500. McFarland had recommended the state's general missionary W. H. Anderson to succeed him as pastor. The congregation preferred and elected J. D. Rouse, an outstanding young man of the congregation educated in Evansville schools and at Roger Williams University. But W. H. Anderson decided to become an Evansville pastor anyway. In 1882 he accepted the call of some seventy-five members who withdrew from Liberty to form a new congregation named McFarland Chapel. Anderson further displayed his displeasure with Liberty and his strength in Indiana by organizing the new Eastern Baptist Association. It enlisted some twenty-three churches across the state and remained a separate body from the Indiana Baptist Association until a merger of all fifty-six member churches in the two was arranged in 1912.[57]

Evansville's black Baptists went on from strength to strength. The largest black enclave in the city was nicknamed "Baptisttown." When a cyclone blew down Liberty's brick building in July of 1886, the congregation rebuilt it bigger and better by December—60 feet by 85 feet with seating for 900. McFarland congregation entered its "elegant new brick chapel" on Christmas day of 1887. Before the turn of the century Liberty claimed about 1,600 members and McFarland 500. Besides these two prominent black congregations, three more were established at Evansville in the 1800s: Independence Missionary Baptist Church at Twelfth and Virginia; Mt. Zion Baptist Church on Louisiana near Heidelbach; Free Will Baptist Church near Nevada and Fulton.[58]

Black Baptist vital signs were good as the twentieth century opened. The national religious census of 1906 reported 18,492 black Baptist churches, 88 of them in Indiana. The National Baptist Convention, formed in 1895, had given the denomination a name and identity. A generation of free born and better educated leaders was rising.

And Indiana was getting a new black population center. At the very time the religious census takers were doing their 1906 tabulation, United States Steel was laying out the townsite for Gary alongside its new plant complex on Lake Michigan. About 200 black construction workers came to help. Samuel J. Duncan was a black millsite cook who stayed on in Gary, helped establish First Baptist Church, and persuaded Charles E. Hawkins of Louisville to come there as its first minister. About 400 blacks lived in Gary in 1910, forerunners of many thousands who were to come in the years following 1914.

Industrial northern Indiana became a black Baptist mission field. Baptists of the black state convention (Boyd Group) and the white state convention (Northern Baptists) agreed in 1917 to share the cost of supporting William Z. Thomas as a black missionary. This union missionary arrangement continued until 1928 by which time the state had 155 black Baptist churches, six of them over 1,000 in membership. William Z. Thomas and Charles E. Hawkins often worked as black missionary colleagues in such places as East Chicago, Hammond, Gary, South Bend, Elkhart, and Fort Wayne. Both were frequently elected as officers of their state convention.[59]

Prominence of Hoosier Black Baptist Leaders

Indiana's early black Baptist leaders were active participants in the national life of their church. Moses Broyles of Second Church in Indianapolis died too soon to take part in the National Baptist Convention but it was a particular satisfaction to him to be in Montgomery, Alabama, in 1880 to take part in the formation of the Baptist Foreign Mission Convention, an essential parent organization of the national convention.

J. D. Rouse of Liberty Church in Evansville was a vice president and board member of the National Baptist Convention, a power in convention assemblies. W. H. Anderson of McFarland Chapel in Evansville was one of a committee named at the 1889 Indianapolis black Baptist sessions to formulate and deliver a protest to the president of the United States concerning the attack on black delegates at Baxley, Georgia. After the National Baptist Convention was formed he was on its executive board. Both Rouse and Anderson held honorary doctorates and were in demand nationally as preachers.[60]

James W. Carr was host pastor to the American National Baptist Convention at Second Baptist in Indianapolis in 1889 and a life member of the Baptist Foreign Mission Convention. After formation of the National Baptist Convention had united these two, he became its vice president for Indiana.[61]

Indiana's black Baptist leaders continued this same pattern of long local service and national visibility into the twentieth century. Pastorates of thirty years were common. Indianapolis ministers such as F. F. Young, J. T. Highbaugh, C. J. Daily, and F. Benjamin Davis became state and national symbols. The pastorates of S. M. Gaines at Madison and L. C. Montgomery at North Vernon exceeded fifty years. From his installation as pastor in 1943, L. C. Jackson made St. Paul Baptist Church the center of an abrasive thirty-year campaign against racial injustice in Gary; Martin Luther King, Sr., once called Jackson "the Daddy of the militant civil rights movement."[62]

The awful weight of debt was removed from many churches during the better economic years following the Second World War. When F. Benjamin Davis compiled his report on "the last 25 years" for the 125th anniversary of the Indiana Missionary Baptist Convention, he listed thirty-five new church buildings completed by this one segment of Indiana's black Baptists (National Baptist Convention of America) between 1957 and 1982, and added a list of twenty-two more church properties substantially renovated or enlarged.[63]

Black Baptist congregations of Indiana made many denominational alignments and realignments, giving each confederation its own name, its own structure of officers, its own pattern of mission work, and its own calendar of meetings. These divisions rarely involved doctrine or worship practice nor were they an actual barrier to fellowship. Certain associations of ministers and officers crossed the denominational lines. Black Baptist individuals from the various denominations were among the thousands attending the annual National

Baptist Congress sponsored by the National Baptist Publishing House at Nashville. For a time Indiana's black Baptists of all denominations held an annual state assembly.

Central Baptist Theological Seminary

There was no single black Baptist institution in the state capable of commanding interdenominational loyalty. In the early years substantial numbers of Indiana's black Baptist youth crossed the Ohio to attend Simmons College in Louisville. Hoosier leaders served on the staff and faculty there. In later years certain strong black Baptist churches in urban centers developed their own institutions to provide day care, schools, housing, and nursing care but these were local congregational endeavors.[64]

The Hoosier institution with the broadest black Baptist support was Central Baptist Theological Seminary. It was the dream of C. J. Dailey, Indianapolis pastor and moderator of a substantial black Baptist federation named Central District Association. Dailey wanted to provide a training school for ministers and church workers. The school opened under his presidency at St. Paul Church in 1943. In 1956 it moved to New Bethel Church in Indianapolis with pastor F. Benjamin Davis as president and dean. Instruction ranged from beginning levels to full degree programs. Central Baptist Seminary was never large but it was consistently ecumenical. Students, faculty, and support were drawn from the broad spectrum of black Baptist associations and beyond. Even the predominantly white Indiana Baptist Convention made some contributions. By the 1990s there were extensions of Central Baptist Seminary operating in black churches at South Bend, Muncie, Fort Wayne, and Terre Haute.[65]

Indiana's black Baptists have never provided comprehensive statistical reports. When the membership study experts did their special computation based on a complex sampling technique applied to the 1990 census data, they estimated Indiana's total number of black Baptist adherents to be 140,166. Black Baptists were certainly not united as this estimate might imply. But counted together and based on this estimate, they would have ranked fifth in number among the state's denominations, after the Catholics, Methodists, Christians, and Lutherans. Counties estimated to have the highest concentration of black Baptist adherents were Marion (56,403), Lake (39,385), Allen (10,273), Saint Joseph (8,001), and Vanderburgh (4,055).

NOTES

1. H. Leon McBeth, *The Baptist Heritage* (Nashville, Tenn.: Broadman Press, 1987), 216, 227–35, 251; William L. Lumpkin, *Baptist Foundations in the South: Tracing through the Separates the Influence of the Great Awakening, 1754–1787* (Nashville, Tenn.: Broadman Press, 1961, 166 p.).

2. McBeth, *Baptist Heritage*, 776–77.

3. Owen D. Pelt and Ralph Lee Smith, *The Story of the National Baptists* (New York: Vantage Press, 1960), 29–32, 35–41; Edward A. Freeman, "Negro Baptist History," *Baptist History and Heritage* 4 (July 1969): 89–99; *Baptist Life and Thought: 1600–1980: A Source Book*, ed. William H. Brackney (Valley Forge, Pa.: Judson Press, 1983), 106–7; Sandy Dwayne Martin, *Black Baptists and African Missions: The Origins of a Movement, 1880–1915* (Macon, Ga.: Mercer University Press, 1989, 242 p.); Bynum Shaw, *Divided We Stand: The Baptists in American Life* (Durham, N.C.: Moore Publishing Company, 1974), 160–61.

4. Shaw, *Divided We Stand*, 163.

5. Leroy Fitts, *A History of Black Baptists* (Nashville, Tenn.: Broadman Press, 1985), 33–46; James Melvin Washington *Frustrated Fellowship: The Black Baptist Quest for Social Power* (Macon, Ga.: Mercer University Press, 1986), 7–22; C. Eric Lincoln and Lawrence H. Mamiya, *The Black Church in the African American Experience* (Durham, N.C.: Duke University Press, 1990), 23–25; Pelt and Smith, *Story*, 28–45; McBeth, *Baptist Heritage*, 776–80; Shaw, *Divided We Stand*, 159–64.

6. Pelt and Smith, *Story*, 53–57; Fitts, *History*, 110–12; McBeth, *Baptist Heritage*, 778, 781–82; Shaw, *Divided We Stand*, 165–66.

7. Pelt and Smith, *Story*, 59–64; Fitts, *History*, 61–63.

8. Fitts, *History*, 46–47, 271–80; Pelt and Smith, *Story*, 48–51; Washington, *Frustrated Fellowship*, 20–21; McBeth, *Baptist Heritage*, 20–21.

9. McBeth, *Baptist Heritage*, 780; Washington, *Frustrated Fellowship*, 21; Pelt and Smith, *Story*, 52; Fitts, *History*, 47–48.

10. Washington, *Frustrated Fellowship*, 25–26.

11. McBeth, *Baptist Heritage*, 781; Fitts, *History*, 51, 61–66; Pelt and Smith, *Story*, 68; Shaw, *Divided We Stand*, 168.

12. David O. Moore, "The Withdrawal of Blacks from Southern Baptist Churches," *Baptist History and Heritage* 16 (July 1981): 12–18; Fitts, *History*, 233–34.

13. Pelt and Smith, *Story*, 85–87; Fitts, *History*, 66–76, 107–57; McBeth, *Baptist Heritage*, 782.

14. Fitts, *History*, 122–23, 167; Washington, *Frustrated Fellowship*, 139, 143.

15. Albert W. Pegues, *Our Baptist Ministers and Schools* (Springfield, Mass.: Wiley and Co., 1892), 439–53; Pelt and Smith, *Story*, 87–91; Washington, *Frustrated Fellowship*, 138–47.

16. Washington, *Frustrated Fellowship*, 147–57.

17. Washington, *Frustrated Fellowship*, 159–70.

18. McBeth, *Baptist Heritage*, 784.

19. Washington, *Frustrated Fellowship*, 159–85; Fitts, *History*, 79–80, 175–218; Pelt and Smith, *Story*, 91–94; McBeth, *Baptist Heritage*, 782–84.

20. Pelt and Smith, *Story*, 95; Fitts, *History*, 81–82.

21. Pelt and Smith, *Story*, 95–96; McBeth, *Baptist Heritage*, 784.

22. Fitts, *History*, 116.

23. McBeth, *Baptist Heritage*, 785.

24. McBeth, *Baptist Heritage*, 785; Fitts, *History*, 82–83; Pelt and Smith, *Story*, 101–5.

25. Pelt and Smith, *Story*, 102–5, 110–26; Fitts, *History*, 82–83, 89–95; McBeth, *Baptist Heritage*, 785–87.

26. Joseph H. Jackson, *The Story of Christian Activism; The History of the National Baptist Convention, U.S.A., Inc.* (Nashville, Tenn.: Townsend Press, 1980), 332–35, 483–95; Fitts, *History*, 98–106, 280–95; Lincoln and Mamiya, *Black Church*, 36–39; McBeth, *Baptist Heritage*, 787–89.

27. John F. Cady, *The Origin and Development of the Missionary Baptist Church in Indiana* (Franklin, Ind.: Franklin College, 1942), 251.

28. Sid Smith, "Growth of Black Southern Baptist Churches in the Inner City," *Baptist History and Heritage* 16 (July 1981): 49–60; Edward L. Wheeler, "An Overview of Black Southern Baptist Involvements," *Baptist History and Heritage* 16 (July 1981): 3–11, 40; McBeth, *Baptist Heritage*, 789–90; Fitts, *History*, 301–9, 314–15; Pelt and Smith, *Story*, 173–75.

29. *Churches and Church Membership in the United States 1990: An Enumeration by Region, State and County Based on Data Reported for 133 Church Groupings* (Atlanta, Ga.: Glenmary Research Center, 1992), 3, 451–53; Lincoln and Mamiya, *Black Church*, 407; Washington, *Frustrated Fellowship*, 200.

30. Israel George Blake, *Finding a Way through the Wilderness: The Indiana Baptist Convention 1833–1983* (Indianapolis, Ind.: Central Publishing Co., 1983), 12.

31. John W. Lyda, "History of Terre Haute, Indiana," *Negro History Society Bulletin* (January 1944): 2–7; Frances V. Halsell Gilliam, *A Time to Speak: A Brief History of the Afro-Americans of Bloomington, Indiana 1865–1965* (Bloomington, Ind.: Pinus Strobus Press, 1985), 32–33; William F. Guide, "Rushville's African-American Community: An Historic Overview," *Black History News and Notes* 44 (May 1991): 5; Hurley Goodall and J. Paul Mitchell, *A History of Negroes in Muncie* (Muncie, Ind.: Ball State University, 1976), 4; Buford Franklin Gordon, *The Negro in South Bend: A Social Study* (South Bend, Ind.: n.p., 1922?), 37–38, 66–67, 70; Gladys Bull Nicewarner, *Michigan City, Indiana: The Life of a Town* (Michigan City, Ind.?: G. B. Nicewarner, 1980), 213–14.

32. Emma Lou Thornbrough, *The Negro in Indiana* (Indianapolis, Ind.: Indiana Historical Bureau, 1957), 368–69; Cady, *Origin and Development*, 251.

33. *Baptist Life and Thought*, 336–37.

34. John Hasse, "The Whites Runnin' because the Blacks Are Movin' in," *Indiana Folklore*, vol. 10, no. 2 (1977): 183–90.

35. Thornbrough, *Negro in Indiana*, 156.

36. William T. Stott, *Indiana Baptist History, 1798–1908* (Franklin, Ind.?: n.p., 1908), 263, 268; Pegues, *Our Baptist Ministers*, 46–53; Fitts, *History*, 60; Thornbrough, *Negro in Indiana*, 157, 308.

37. *125th Celebration of the Indiana Missionary Baptist State Convention, July 3–August 6, 1982*, F. Benjamin Davis, President (Georgetown, Ky.: Kreative Grafiks, 1982?), 16; Pegues, *Our Baptist Ministers*, 342–44.

38. Pegues, *Our Baptist Ministers*, 309–11.

39. Pegues, *Our Baptist Ministers*, 503–8.

40. Washington, *Frustrated Fellowship*, 114, 142.

41. Moses Broyles, *The History of the Second Baptist Church of Indianapolis* (Indianapolis, Ind.: Printing and Publishing House,

1876), 19–26; Jacob Piatt Dunn, *Greater Indianapolis*, 2 vols. (Chicago: Lewis Publishing Company, 1910), 1:573–75; *125th Celebration*, 14.

42. Broyles, *History*, 7–16.

43. Henry Ellis Cheaney, "Attitudes of the Indiana Pulpit and Press toward the Negro, 1860–1880" (Ph.D. diss., University of Chicago, 1961), 254–61; Coy D. Robbins, "The Union Literary Institute," *Black History News and Notes* 7 (November 1981): 8–9; William C. Thompson, "Eleutherian Institute; A Sketch of a Unique Step in the Educational History of Indiana," *Indiana Magazine of History* 19 (June 1923): 109–31; Hugh Smith, "Eleutherian College," *Black History News and Notes* 55 (February 1994): 4–5; Thornbrough, *Negro in Indiana*, 173.

44. Broyles, *History*, 13.

45. Broyles, *History*, 28.

46. Ida Webb Bryant, *Glimpses of the Negro in Indianapolis, 1863–1963* (N.p., 1965?), 3; Joseph J. Russell, "Some Notes on Education in Indiana," *Negro History Bulletin* 39 (January 1976): 512.

47. Broyles, *History*, 32–34.

48. *Ebony Lines* 2 (Fall and Winter 1990): 15–16; Bryant, *Glimpses*, 3; Broyles, *History*, 32.

49. Broyles, *History*, 37.

50. Broyles, *History*, 53–61.

51. Broyles, *History*, 61–62.

52. Broyles, *History*, 63–64.

53. Broyles, *History*, 64.

54. Cheaney, "Attitudes of the Indiana Pulpit and Press," 357–61, 372–73.

55. Thornbrough, *Negro in Indiana*, 324; Stott, *Indiana Baptist History*, 263–68; Cady, *Origin and Development*, 200; *125th Celebration*, 14–15; Cheaney, "Attitudes of the Indiana Pulpit and Press," 246–47.

56. Pegues, *Our Ministers*, 106–13.

57. Darrell E. Bigham, *We Ask Only a Fair Trial* (Bloomington, Ind.: Indiana University Press, 1987), 21–23, 33, 74, 244; *125th Celebration*, 16–18; Pegues, *Our Ministers*, 36–42, 430.

58. Joseph P. Elliott, *A History of Evansville and Vanderburgh County, Indiana* (Evansville, Ind.: Keller Printing Company, 1897), 267–69; *History of Vanderburgh County, Indiana* (Madison, Wis.: Brant and Fuller, 1889), 291–92; Bigham, *We Ask Only a Fair Trial*, 74–76, 181.

59. James B. Lane, *City of the Century: A History of Gary, Indiana* (Bloomington, Ind.: Indiana University Press, 1978), 28, 68–69; *125th Celebration*, 18–21; Cady, *Origin and Development*, 251–52.

60. *125th Celebration*, 15; Washington, *Frustrated Fellowship*, 148–56; Bigham, *We Ask Only a Fair Trial*, 181; Pegues, *Our Ministers*, 40–41.

61. Pegues, *Our Ministers*, 106–13.

62. *125th Celebration*, 19–24; Lane, *City of the Century*, 271–77.

63. *125th Celebration*, 25.

64. *125th Celebration*, 19.

65. *Central Baptist Theological Seminary in Indiana, Indianapolis, Ind., 1983–84* (N.p., 1983?), 70; *Black History News and Notes* 46 (November 1991): 1–2; William Kappen Artis Fox, "The Involvement of Negro Protestants in Cooperative Christianity in a Metropolitan Area" (Master's thesis, Butler University, 1964), 211; *125th Celebration*, 22, 30, 197.

SOUTHERN BAPTISTS

Southern Baptists organized as a separate convention at Augusta, Georgia, in May of 1845. At that time there were 351,951 southern members in 4,126 local Baptist churches.

For thirty years the main body of America's Baptist churches, north and south, had been working together in what they usually called either the Triennial Convention or the General Convention. This was a voluntary society of individuals organized in support of foreign missions in 1814 under leadership of Luther Rice. Many Baptists in the South were zealous supporters of missions. As part of the Triennial Convention and of the parallel American Baptist Home Mission Society formed in 1832, southerners played a major role in missionary affairs both foreign and domestic.

There were some southerners who questioned the efficiency of Baptist missions directed by these two voluntary associations of individuals. They preferred that missions be a denominational activity directly operated and controlled by the regular convention structure made up of loyal Baptist churches. There were also some southerners who said a Home Mission Society headquartered in the Northeast would never send a fair share of mission men and money to the South and Southwest. But when the division came it was really over the issue of slavery.[1]

By the 1830s most white Baptists in southern states viewed slavery as a biblically sanctioned institution. From their church they expected support of their position or at least silence on the subject. They would accept no discrimination against slaveholders as members, officers, or missionaries. What they kept hearing from the North, even from some of their own Baptist missionary society officers in Boston and New York, was high-principled talk of abolition. Baptists in Alabama wrote the Triennial Convention in Boston in November of 1844:

> Our duty at this crisis requires us to demand from the proper authorities in all those bodies to whose funds we have contributed, or with whom we have in any way been connected, the distinct, explicit, avowal that slaveholders are eligible, and entitled, equally with non-slaveholders, to all the privileges and immunities of their several unions; and especially to receive any agency, mission, or other appointment, which may run within the scope of their operation or duties.[2]

The Managers of the Triennial Convention answered: "If any one should offer himself as a missionary, having slaves, and should insist on retaining them as his property, we could not appoint him . . . One thing is certain: we can never be a party to any arrangement which would imply approbation of slavery."[3]

Southern Baptist Convention Established

So 293 delegates met at Augusta to take action the following May. William B. Johnson of South Carolina came prepared to draft a "Constitution" and a "Public Address" which would establish a separate Southern Baptist Convention, a denomination of loyal churches rather than a cluster of voluntary societies of individuals. Its southern identity was heightened through the following years of the secession, the Civil War, and the era of reconstruction.[4]

After 1845 Baptists needed to be designated "Northern" or "Southern." However the geographical separation was never neat. The American Baptist Publication Society in Philadelphia continued to supply the Southern Baptist churches with Bibles, books, tracts, and Sunday school materials through the war years and into the 1890s. Northern Baptists went south to occupy and preserve Baptist buildings in southern areas overrun by Union armies. As many as half of the buildings had been abandoned and were subject to vandalism. In January of 1864 the United States War Department notified its military commanders "You are hereby directed to place at the disposal of the American Baptist Home Mission Society all houses of worship belonging to Baptist Churches South, in which a loyal minister does not now officiate." This extreme grant of authority to the northerners, occasionally abused, saved many Baptist structures but it later polarized Northern and Southern Baptists even further during some painful property disputes.

Northern Baptists also went south in a massive ministry to the thousands and thousands of freed slaves. By 1869 the northern Home Mission Society had a third of its force in the South. By 1894 Northern Baptists were helping to sponsor 32 black colleges in the South with 177 teachers and 5,357 pupils including 432 ministerial students. Morehouse College in Georgia and Bishop College in Texas developed into major black colleges.[5]

In the nineteenth century the Southern Baptist Convention had very limited funds and was inclined to grumble about Northern Baptist "invasion." At the turn of the century Southern Baptists had only sixteen state conventions, all in the old South except for one in Missouri. They spoke often of "territorial limits" and of "boundaries" and of "our Southland." In the twentieth century the roles of North and South reversed. Northern churches began commenting on a Southern Baptist "invasion." Intensely loyal Southern Baptists kept migrating west and north. Many were proud of being southern. Most preferred the evangelistic energy and contagious informality which had marked Baptist churches in the South since the days of Shubal Stearns, Daniel Marshall, and the "Separates" a century before. They liked familiar southern ways of preaching, singing, calling for decision at the altar, and ordering church life.[6]

"Landmark" Doctrines

While "Landmark" doctrines were never official in Baptist churches, they had been widely circulated in the South. Southerners read J. M. Pendleton's tract *An Old Landmark Re-set* (1854) and his *Church Manual* (1867). They read A. C. Dayton's *Theodosia Ernest; or, the Heroine of Faith* (1857). Most of all they read *Old Landmarkism: What Is It?* (1880) by J. R. Graves and the *Tennessee Baptist* which he edited for some forty-seven years. Graves also supplied many Sunday schools with teaching materials.

Baptists convinced of Landmark doctrines could not be expected to join another church. For them Baptist churches were the only true churches; the proper kingdom of God was made up of the sum total of local Baptist churches; the only valid baptism, Lord's Supper, or preaching was that authorized and performed by Baptists so open communion with non-Baptists and "alien immersion" by non-Baptist ministers must be opposed; true and uncorrupted Baptist churches existed in unbroken continuity from the time of Christ. In regions of the South and Southwest outside such older states as Virginia, Georgia, and the Carolinas, the impact of Landmark literature and teachers was immense.[7]

Later generations of Southern Baptists who had never heard of Landmarkism or read a word from or about J. R. Graves preserved some vestige of this tradition of Southern Baptist uniqueness. It was more than affection for a region or for a denomination. For many it was a conviction that Southern Baptists held doctrines set forth in the Scriptures which were not held by members of other denominations, that Southern Baptists were a people embodying a particular sacred history, and that Southern Baptists were bearers of a special and particular commission as evangelists of God. Such a precious heritage was not to be diluted by any mixture with modernism or by ecumenical cooperation in joint ministries with other churches they counted less pure. Such Southern Baptists might go to the North but they were seldom happy in union with Northern Baptists.[8]

Failure of Geographical North-South Divisions

In 1894 a joint committee of Northern and Southern Baptist leaders met at Fort Monroe, Virginia. There was discussion of the overlap of their mission work. The meeting was cordial and recommended careful assignment of territory to avoid "all antagonisms." That was the tenor of comity agreements between the two at

Washington, D.C., in 1909, at Old Point Comfort in Virginia in 1911, and at Hot Springs in Arkansas in 1912.

In fact these comity discussions at the top accomplished little. Southern Baptist members were migrating to new areas. Individual congregations were free to organize anywhere, taking the southern name and affirming southern principles. They could form associations with like-minded congregations. Southern Baptist ministers could hardly resist invitations to visit and assist such spontaneous groups. Nor could established Southern Baptist conventions resist accepting the additional messengers and contributions from new areas.

The Northern Baptist mission society withdrew all work from New Mexico following 1912 rather than continue confrontation with what had become a southern majority. Over the protest of Northern Baptist leaders, the Southern Baptist Convention accepted a breakaway state convention in Arizona in 1928 and made it an evangelism agency for all the Far West. California was the prize. When the Southern Baptist Convention accepted a California state convention in 1942, comity efforts with Northern Baptists were effectively ended.[9]

In 1950 the "Northern" Baptist Convention signified the end of territorial division by becoming the "American" Baptist Convention. Some population from the North was flowing to the southern sun belt; an alternative to Southern Baptists was acceptable and even welcome in southern cities. The Southern Baptist Convention did not change its territorial name. However its national meeting held in San Francisco in 1951 did write the official end to any denominational comity or territorial limitation by approving a resolution that

> Whereas the Southern Baptist Convention has defined its territorial position in reports to the Convention in 1944 and in 1949 by removing territorial limitations, and whereas the Northern Baptist Convention has changed its name so that it is continental in scope, the Home Mission Board and all other Southern Baptist boards and agencies be free to serve as a source of blessing to any community or any people anywhere in the United States.[10]

Impressive Growth

Following this full commitment to territorial expansion, Southern Baptist growth was phenomenal. Southern people had streamed across the nation. Their congregations were generally new ones, always the most attractive and vigorous kind. National interest in religion was high. Six new state conventions affiliated with the Southern

Baptist Convention in the seven years following 1951. On the afternoon of Saturday, 6 July 1963, Southern Baptists formed a church at South Burlington, Vermont, and so were represented with one or more churches in each of the fifty states.[11]

In the course of a "Seventy-Five Million Campaign" in the 1920s, Southern Baptists had come to appreciate and rejoice in their joint power to raise millions of dollars annually for the support of their convention agencies. A favorite cause of church agencies benefiting from this "Cooperative Program" was church extension. Clusters of Southern Baptists in the North could appeal to the Sunday School Board or to the Home Mission Board of the Southern Baptist Convention and expect to get help. Real money was available to survey a prospective field for expansion, to support a pioneer pastor, to purchase a church site, or to erect a building. Convention staff members were experts in growth strategy.

Northern expansion was still such a priority in 1980 that 1,549 home missionaries were assigned to areas entered by Southern Baptists after 1940. By 1980 Southern Baptists reported 13,369,848 members in 35,552 churches. Over 11,500 students were enrolled in their six theological seminaries. They gave $2.3 billion in church offerings that year, $207 million of it for the Cooperative Program. They had become the nation's largest Protestant denomination. There was talk of a Bold Mission Thrust, "the Southern Baptist plan to share the gospel with everyone on this planet by the year 2000."[12]

Development in Indiana

Hoosier Baptists distressed over "looseness in Baptist doctrine and practice" formed the first Southern Baptist Church to be constituted in Indiana. Forty members of First Baptist Church of Hymera in Sullivan County withdrew and organized Second Baptist Church on 17 January 1914. These were days in which Free Will Baptists, General Baptists, and Missionary Baptists of Indiana were cooperating and discussing union. Many Hoosier Baptists were opening their communion services to participation by members of other denominations. Some Baptist churches in northern Indiana were receiving members by transfer who had been immersed by non-Baptists. Some Baptist churches were even granting letters of recommendation and statements of good standing to their members desiring to unite with non-Baptist churches.[13]

Members of the new Second Baptist Church of Hymera wished to define their position against such things. As their rule of doctrine they accepted the New Hampshire Confession of Faith of 1833, beloved of conservatives and southerners. They adopted their church covenant directly from the *Church Manual* of the Landmark pioneer J. M. Pendleton. They affiliated with the Palestine Association of Illinois. The connection of Indiana's conservative Baptists with those of Illinois was a natural one. Baptist immigrants from southern states into Southern Illinois were early in tension with the main body of Illinois Baptists, especially resistant to liberal influences from that "Baptist" institution the University of Chicago. The Illinois conservatives, many of them Landmark in doctrine, formed a separate state convention in 1907. Most of them linked to the Southern Baptist Convention in 1910.[14]

The Second Baptist Church at Hymera, Indiana, did not become a significant source of Southern Baptist growth but the same forces at work eventually made Evansville a Southern Baptist center. Susan Coulter's Bible classes met at First Baptist Church (Northern) and in homes in the Rosedale section of Evansville. These evolved into Rosedale Mission and then, in December of 1920, into the new Rosedale Baptist Church. Dissatisfaction over Baptist union and "alien immersion" was a persistent concern. Soon after its founding Rosedale Church elected to affiliate with the Southern Baptists of Illinois and eventually became First Southern Baptist Church of Evansville. Calvary Baptist Church also changed to the Southern Baptist Convention in 1921. Three new Southern Baptist churches were formed in Evansville before the end of the Great Depression.

The vigor of the Cooperative Program and development of deliberate home missionary strategy brought a burst of Southern Baptist activity in southwestern Indiana after the Second World War. Twelve Southern Baptist churches were organized in the Evansville area in the decade from 1945 to 1955 followed by nine more during 1956 and 1957.[15]

William Helton of Kentucky bought a farm near New Trenton in Franklin County, Indiana, in 1928. He was a Southern Baptist. He and his friends bought a vacant Holiness church building and organized Old Liberty Baptist Church in 1932, beginning point for Southern Baptists in southeastern Indiana. Small sister congregations developed in the vicinity of Old Liberty Church—Smyrna, Philadelphia (later McKendrie), Chapel Church of Laurel, Macedonia. Their affiliations were with Kentucky. Pastor Robert E. Sasser came from Kentucky in fall of 1940 to conduct a revival among them. He acted as moderator to organize some of these very small churches into their own very small association. This first truly indigenous Southern Baptist association in Indiana took the name White Water Association of Southern Baptists.[16]

Here also the big change came during and following the Second World War. Neighboring churches in Ohio joined White Water Association. Van Boone Castleberry became the association's missionary and new affiliated churches appeared at Muncie, Metamora, Richmond, Connersville, and New Castle. In 1951 seven of the Indiana churches reorganized to become the Indiana Association of Missionary Baptists. Sasser was their founding moderator once again. Castleberry stayed on the job as the new association's missionary at $112.50 per month. New churches were added at Blooming Grove, Columbus, Hagerstown, Kokomo, Mount Pleasant, Portland, and Winchester. Castleberry became pastor of First Southern Baptist Church at Connersville in 1955, being succeeded as missionary by Cletus E. Wiley. Within two years there were additional Southern Baptist churches at Batesville, Dublin, Frankfort, Speedway, Richmond, Rushville, and Anderson.

The missionary team of Sasser, Castleberry, and Wiley were able supporters of the denominational policy of establishing Southern Baptist churches in all areas of the state. They surveyed Indianapolis in 1952 and after a tent revival in 1953 installed a mission pastor for First Southern Baptist Church of Indianapolis the following year. The multiplying Indianapolis churches added their strength to a new West Central Association which grew from eight churches in early 1957 to twenty-five churches the next year.[17]

There was Southern Baptist activity in northwestern Indiana. A young Kentuckian named Leonard Cole had gone looking for work in the Chicago area in 1933. He felt the need for the gospel was so great that he must become a pastor there. His group rented an abandoned dance hall in East Chicago where fourteen signed an affirmation in April of 1934: "We, the undersigned, as God's people having at present no place to meet to hear God's word and worship him according to the dictates of our conscience, after earnest prayerful consideration, hereby agree to unite wholeheartedly in the organizing of a New Testament Church." The next month Fred Peek of Alton, Illinois, responded to their invitation to conduct a revival. Under his leadership the fellowship became the First Southern Baptist Church of East Chicago, affiliated with the Southern Baptists of Illinois. Cole was ordained and served as pastor until the end of 1938. In 1939 that church moved to Hammond where its members were able to complete the basement for their new church before being halted in 1941 by the wartime shortage of materials. After the war they erected the building and enlarged it three times to accommodate a membership of 689 by 1957.[18]

Meanwhile Leonard Cole and Durwood Humble conducted a religious census in Black Oak just west of Gary. On 19 March 1939 they organized Black Oak Baptist Church as the second Southern Baptist Church in northwestern Indiana. Cole was its first pastor and Humble was its first Sunday school superintendent. Members tithed their incomes to construct a church building. Out of the work begun in these two churches came the Southern Baptist strength in northwestern Indiana. The Southern Baptists of Illinois sent W. T. Waring as an organizing missionary for the region in 1945. In the postwar decade 1945–1955 the number of Southern Baptist churches in northwestern Indiana increased to eleven. By the end of the next three years there were twenty-four.[19]

Southern Baptist churches also crossed the Ohio River into Indiana from Louisville. Frequently they were sponsored by Louisville churches and affiliated with Long Run Association in Kentucky. Robert Weyler lived in Clarksville, Indiana, but was a deacon in the Southern Baptist Church of Shively in Kentucky. In 1948 he began holding meetings in the basement of his Clarksville home. A decade later, after many revivals and expansions, the membership of Clarksville Southern Baptist Church exceeded 600. Southern Baptist congregations were organized at Corydon (1952), New Salisbury (1952), New Washington (1955), Henryville (1955), Jeffersonville (1956), and New Albany (1956). Southern Baptist Theological Seminary at Louisville made a convenient service point for Baptist leaders in the region. By 1958 there were twenty Indiana churches affiliated with Kentucky's Long Run Association.[20]

State Convention of Baptists in Indiana

Before the end of the 1950s Southern Baptists had considerable strength in Indiana but little unity. The members and churches and associations maintained traditional affiliations with Illinois and Kentucky. They did not know each other well. There were some denominational leaders who took a more comprehensive view: Van Boone Castleberry, Cletus E. Wiley, and Robert E. Sasser of Indiana; Eldred Taylor of the Kentucky state convention; E. Harmon Moore of the Illinois state convention; A. B. Cash of the denomination's Home Mission Board. They kept lifting up the vision of a unified state conven-

tion for Indiana. The Southern Baptist Convention had established substantial requirements for new state conventions in terms of number of churches, number of members, funds to begin operation, and Cooperative Program participation. The growth of Indiana's churches was quickly bringing these standards within reach.

The way had been very carefully prepared at all levels when 250 messengers and 185 visitors met at First Southern Baptist Church of Indianapolis on 3 October 1958 to organize the twenty-eighth state convention in connection with the Southern Baptist Convention. With 111 churches and a membership over 20,000, it was the largest group ever to request admission. Its name would be State Convention of Baptists in Indiana. Its executive would be E. Harmon Moore who was instrumental in its organization and had presented the new constitution and by-laws for approval. Its paper would be the *Indiana Baptist* edited by Moore. There were start-up checks of $3,306.22 from the Illinois convention and $2,864.84 from Kentucky. A projected convention budget of $100,750 was adopted for 1959. The estimate was that Indiana would send $21,250 to the Southern Baptist Convention that first year. In the same year Indiana's work was expected to receive $25,000 from the denomination's Home Mission Board and $9,000 from the Sunday School Board. Convention offices were at Plainfield until relocation in 1964 to the new state headquarters building on Interstate 465 on the west side of Indianapolis.[21]

Indiana's Southern Baptists became consistent supporters of the whole range of the denomination's causes. Congregations built up Sunday schools and Training Unions along with units of the Woman's Missionary Union, the Brotherhood, and the Royal Ambassadors. Mission gifts from the state rose steadily from just over $130,000 in the convention's first year of 1959 to more than $2 million in 1982. Cooperative Program contributions, never more than 75 percent for the work of the local state convention nor less than 25 percent for programs of the Southern Baptist Convention at large, passed the million-dollar level in 1980.

Especially visible in Indiana was the commitment of Southern Baptists to church extension. No town or city should be without a Southern Baptist church; no family should be beyond the reach of such a church's ministry. Local churches were applauded for colonizing new local churches. In 1980 nine home missionaries were at work providing personal evangelistic leadership to every county in the state. Congregations considering building were getting expert technical advice and guaranteed loans. Agencies of the national Southern Baptist

Convention kept allocating portions of their Cooperative Program funds for work in Indiana, $371,487 from the Home Mission Board in 1983, for example, and $39,950 from the Sunday School Board for religious education work.[22]

The result of such united mission effort was impressive growth. Hoosier Southern Baptists whose new state convention began with 20,119 members in 111 churches in 1958 reported 306 churches with 92,174 members (115,560 adherents) in 1990. Their adherents in the state did not equal the 132,970 of the American Baptists but outnumbered the Presbyterians, the Christian Church (Disciples of Christ), or the Missouri Synod Lutherans.

In the early years the Southern Baptists of Indiana made their priority the increase of congregations rather than the increase of convention institutions. A few small institutions did develop in the 1960s. There was the administrative and missionary center of the state office in Indianapolis with its bookstore. By 1969 seven college campuses in Indiana had Baptist Student Union Centers. For urban work there was the Indianapolis Baptist Center. The state convention purchased 396 acres in Morgan County near Monrovia and built the Highland Lakes Baptist Center as a camp and conference site. Income from a bequest helped start the Indiana Boyce Bible School. This program offered periodic training as an extension service from Southern Baptist Theological Seminary in Louisville but maintained no specific campus.[23]

NOTES

1. H. Leon McBeth, *The Baptist Heritage* (Nashville, Tenn.: Broadman Press, 1987), 343–61, 365–70, 381–82; Robert A. Baker, *The Southern Baptist Convention and Its People, 1607–1972* (Nashville, Tenn.: Broadman Press, 1974), 104–17, 171; Walter B. Shurden, "Southern Baptist Convention," in *Encyclopedia of Religion in the South* (Macon, Ga.: Mercer University Press, 1984), 720–24.

2. Shurden, "Southern Baptist Convention," 721.

3. Shurden, "Southern Baptist Convention," 721.

4. McBeth, *Baptist Heritage*, 388–91; Baker, *Southern Baptist Convention*, 164–72.

5. McBeth, *Baptist Heritage*, 398–405.

6. William L. Lumpkin, *Baptist Foundations in the South: Tracing through the Separates the Influence of the Great Awakening 1754–1787* (Nashville, Tenn.: Broadman Press, 1961, 166 p.); G. Thomas Halbrooks, "Growing Pains: The Impact of Expansion on Southern Baptists Since 1942," *Baptist History and Heritage* 17 (July 1982): 51; McBeth, *Baptist Heritage*, 227–35.

7. Hugh Wamble, "Landmarkism: Doctrinaire Ecclesiology among Baptists," *Church History* 33 (December 1964): 429–447; McBeth, *Baptist Heritage*, 58–60, 447–61. A Landmark view of Baptist historical succession was issued in James Milton Carroll, *The Trail of Blood* (Lexington, Ky.: American Baptist Publishing Co., 1931, 66 p.). It was reissued in varying formats with caption titles "Following the Christians down through the Centuries" or "The History of Baptist Churches from the Time of Christ, Their Founder, to the Present Day." It was constantly maintained in print and distributed by multiplied thousands.

8. Karen E. Smith, "Southern Baptist Relationships with Other Baptist Denominations," *Baptist History and Heritage* 25 (July 1990): 14–23; Timothy George, "Southern Baptist Relationships with Other Protestants," *Baptist History and Heritage* 25 (July 1990): 24–34; Halbrooks, "Growing Pains," 50–53.

9. Tom J. Nettles, "Southern Baptists: Regional to National Transition," *Baptist History and Heritage* 16 (January 1981): 13–23; Leon McBeth, "Expansion of the Southern Baptist Convention to 1951," *Baptist History and Heritage* 17 (July 1982): 32–43; Baker, *Southern Baptist Convention*, 355–91.

10. McBeth, "Expansion," 34.

11. Nettles, "Southern Baptists," 15.

12. James L. Austin, "Cooperation: A Southern Baptist Benchmark," *Baptist History and Heritage* 17 (July 1982): 55–56, 61; McBeth, *Baptist Heritage*, 621–32; Baker, *Southern Baptist Convention*, 355–91; Halbrooks, "Growing Pains," 44–54.

13. John F. Cady, *Origin and Development of the Missionary Baptist Church in Indiana* (Franklin, Ind.: Franklin College, 1942), 281–87.

14. A. Ronald Tonks, *Sunrise on the Wabash: A Short History of Indiana Southern Baptists* (Indianapolis, Ind.: State Convention of Baptists in Indiana, 1973), 31–34; A. Ronald Tonks, "State Convention of Baptists in Indiana," in *Encyclopedia of Southern Baptists*, 4 vols. (Nashville, Tenn.: Broadman Press, 1969–82), 3:1776–79; E. Harmon Moore et al., *Hoosier Southern Baptists: Turning Points and Milestones, 1958–1983* (Indianapolis, Ind.: State Convention of Baptists in Indiana, 1983), 21–22, 66–68; McBeth, "Expansion," 35–36; Nettles, "Southern Baptists," 19–20; Baker, *Southern Baptist Convention*, 337.

15. Tonks, *Sunrise on the Wabash*, 34–37; *Hoosier Southern Baptists*, 22.

16. Tonks, *Sunrise on the Wabash*, 47–50; *Hoosier Southern Baptists*, 22–23.

17. Tonks, *Sunrise on the Wabash*, 50–56.

18. Tonks, *Sunrise on the Wabash*, 39–42.

19. Tonks, *Sunrise on the Wabash*, 42–44.

20. Tonks, *Sunrise on the Wabash*, 56–57.

21. *Hoosier Southern Baptists*, 15–20, 25–41, 60–61; Tonks, *Sunrise on the Wabash*, 59–74.

22. *Hoosier Southern Baptists*, 65–93, 128–30, 148, 182, 204; Tonks, *Sunrise on the Wabash*, 76–79, 106; Tonks, "State Convention," 3:1778.

23. Tonks, "State Convention," 3:1777–79; Tonks, *Sunrise on the Wabash*, 88–90, 95, 111–14; *Hoosier Southern Baptists*, 130, 132, 160–64, 167–73.

ETHNIC CATHOLICS

Catholic ministry among the later ethnics was well illustrated among the Italians and the Slovenes of Indianapolis, the Slovaks of the Calumet area, and the Poles of South Bend.[1]

Italians of Indianapolis

Marino Priori led the Italians of Indianapolis to organize Holy Rosary Parish in 1909. They dedicated the grandest Italian church building in the state on 3 May 1925—twin Romanesque campaniles flanking the entrance; nave 62 feet by 65 feet to seat 800; striking main altar lighted by fifteen windows plus two side altars for devotions; ten large stained glass windows; six bells including the 7,000-pound San Salvador, largest in Indianapolis; $8,000 organ in the choir loft; ample statuary; colorful artistic decoration throughout by professor Marco A. Rigucci, graduate of the Academy of Fine Arts in Rome.[2]

Developing such a parish and erecting such a church building was no small achievement. As late as 1920 the whole state of Indiana reported only 6,712 residents actually born in Italy, 754 of them living in Indianapolis. A portion of these Italians were indifferent or hostile toward religion. Back in Europe the head of the Catholic church had long resisted the national unification of Italy. So Italian national patriots, especially the earlier immigrants to America from northern Italy, were often articulate opponents of priests, churches, and church-operated schools.[3]

Nor could one assume that a more "religious" immigrant from southern Italy was much interested in attending church regularly or contributing money toward its support. The calendar of life in southern Italy had been defined by grand celebrations of holy days, especially days devoted to the honor and cultivation of patron saints. These events were combinations of noisy carnival and emotional intercession. They were civic affairs, generally planned and directed for the populace by organizations of prominent laymen rather than clergy. Priests were essential functionaries for such festivals, for Masses, for baptisms, for weddings, and for funeral rites but the maintenance of priests was considered an obligation of large landowners. The clergy were more feared than loved by the people. The church was seen as eternal, wealthy, and itself a source of funding rather than an institution supported by the current stewardship of its members.[4]

So even religious Italians found the Catholic churches of Indiana to be strange. The Irish and German congregations among the Hoosiers expected them to attend church regularly, to make contributions systematically, and to respect the clergy. When the Irish priest of Sacred Heart Church at Clinton said he would have to deny them spiritual services until they attended Mass and contributed regularly, five of the Italian miners used some convenient sticks of dynamite to blast the church building. The Italians so regularly resisted paying to support a church among them that early termination of Italian missions, Catholic and Protestant, was almost routine.[5]

The expressed hope of Indiana's Catholic bishops was that this relatively small minority of Italians would quickly "Americanize" and take their places in the Catholic parishes already established. Italians were not zealous to do this. Nor were the established parishes quick to accommodate them. Most Italians in Indianapolis lived within the parish boundaries of St. Patrick Church. That church had priests who knew Italian but it developed no special ministry for the newcomers. German priest William Heuser at St. Mary Church offered the Italians some pastoral care and studied their language, but Italian children who attended St. Mary School were still expected to learn German.[6]

Protestant churches observed that Italians were essentially unchurched and began establishing missions among them. The First American Catholic Missionary Congress meeting in Chicago in 1908 sounded the alarm against such Protestant invasion. The watchword of that Congress was "Save Our Own; Save the Children of the Immigrants." At Indianapolis the Home Mission Board of the Methodists was the catalyst. In November of 1908 the Methodists appropriated $700 to open an Italian mission in Indianapolis and sent in Nicolo Accomando as missionary.[7]

Catholic bishop Francis Silas Chatard responded very quickly. He called the priest Marino Priori to Indianapolis in order to canvass the Italian community. On 29 January 1909 the bishop bought a lot on Stevens Street near East in the Italian neighborhood. On 2 May the remodeled house on the Stevens Street property was dedicated as a chapel to Our Lady of the Most Holy Rosary. Before the end of the summer Priori could report to Chatard that he had found 165 families and 730 persons in Indianapolis who should belong to an Italian Catholic parish.[8]

Marino Priori was a priest of the Franciscan order with permission to leave Italy for America and to live outside his religious community if an American bishop would provide an assignment. Chatard had invited Priori to Indianapolis Diocese and had first appointed him to serve the Italian stone quarry workers at Bedford and Oolitic. He arrived there just as most of the Italian stone workers were leaving. Resentment against the foreign workers had become so intense that the sheriff of Lawrence County appealed for the National Guard to assure order. So Priori was available for assignment to the new work among Italians at Indianapolis.[9] He was very diligent.

> He scheduled Sunday Low Mass for 7 a.m., High Mass at 10. He taught catechism for children ages 6 to 12 at 3 p.m. and followed with Benediction at 4. You could enroll in the Confraternity of the Holy Rosary each Sunday after Benediction. He invited parishioners to Mass celebrated daily at 6:30 a.m. with Rosary and Bene-

> diction on Tuesdays at 7 a.m. and 4 p.m. Catechism for those preparing for First Communion was taught at 3 p.m. on Wednesdays and Fridays. He heard confessions on Saturdays at 5 p.m. In Holy Rosary's first year, Father Priori baptized 34 babies, officiated at four marriages, and conducted seven funerals. Fifteen boys and 13 girls received First Communion. He established the St. Anthony Society for young men, the Young Ladies' Sodality of the Holy Immaculate Conception, and a parish choir.[10]

A large portion of Marino Priori's energy had to be invested in raising money. Regular giving was not a grace the Italians of Indianapolis were anxious to learn. Being a good Italian did not equate with being a solid supporter of the Italian church. Sunday collections were minuscule. Parishioners told the priest that if he asked for too much money they would join the Methodists. If he persisted, that was counted as proof of clerical hunger for money.[11]

Priori saw the need for a church building. The congregation broke ground for it in spring of 1911 but had to stop with a roofed foundation in spring of 1912 and worship in this "crypt" church for a dozen years. The Sisters of Providence from St. Mary of the Woods agreed to operate a parish school for the Italian children. They did this in a series of crowded, inconvenient, and uncomfortable houses for a dozen years until the new school and convent were finally ready in 1924. During the First World War Priori was asked to help register Italian men for military service and to lead Indianapolis campaigns which collected nearly $10,000 plus clothing for relief of the needy in Italy.

Priori was always soliciting gifts from the wealthier members of Holy Rosary, from Catholics in other congregations, from neighborhood merchants of all faiths, and from friends in other cities. He published a Catholic paper called *Eternal Light*. Income from solicitations in the paper and from its paid advertisements sometimes exceeded Sunday collections. He raised funds through sale of devotional items, raffles, book publication, movies, and radio broadcasts. He leaned on the support of bishops Chatard and Chartrand and on their extension of the credit of the Diocese of Indianapolis. Fruit merchants of the parish promised a donation of 10¢ on every bunch of bananas sold and paid for the church organ.[12]

Bishop Joseph Ritter appointed Ambrose Sullivan to be pastor of Holy Rosary in 1934. The twenty-five years of Priori's ministry had given Indianapolis an Italian parish of about 700 members with an impressive church, school, and convent. However the debt was about $200,000 and the cash on hand was $44.87. Priori's own salary was unpaid. Bishop Ritter said the financial condition of Holy Rosary was "the most difficult problem of the Diocese of Indianapolis." Under leadership of Ambrose Sullivan and his successor William Knapp, Holy Rosary undertook twelve years of fund raising which eclipsed even the campaigns of Marino Priori. They raffled an automobile every month, conducted mammoth bingo games every Friday, operated a gas station alongside the church, and expected a twenty-five-cent contribution toward the debt from attenders at their popular Mass for late sleepers at noon on Sunday. The monthly Holy Rosary spaghetti suppers were legendary. Attendance at the grand annual festival might reach 5,000.

All this activity made Holy Rosary especially visible among the city's parishes. Citizens of the city at large felt involved in the campaign. Parish members took pride in their mutual effort and success. They paid the debt at the end of 1945, built up some savings at the archdiocese office, and redecorated the church. In 1950 parish membership reached a new high of 1,011. The school and eight parish organizations were lively. In 1951 they welcomed Augustine Sansone, a son of their own congregation, as their new pastor.[13]

After more than forty years in central Indianapolis, Holy Rosary parish was already in rapid transition when Sansone was installed. Italians had long found it convenient to locate and live near Holy Rosary, close to the produce terminals, to the city markets, and to a concentration of fellow Italians. But the Indianapolis Produce Terminal relocated on the city's northeast side in 1954. Italian professional persons and skilled workers were no longer dependent on Italian customers. As older parish members died, ownership of their houses often passed to non-Italians. Younger parish members preferred to move to better housing in newer areas of the city. Holy Rosary's school, parish membership, and parish organizations declined. The Archdiocese of Indianapolis became its chief sponsor and policymaker.[14]

The Archbishop kept sending Holy Rosary able priests who had studied at the North American College in Rome, men with facility in Italian. The Archdiocese developed the facilities of Holy Rosary school into an elite high school for boys considering the priesthood. Rectors of this "Latin School" were at the same time Holy Rosary pastors. After community change had brought the parish to its lowest point in the 1970s and decline in priestly vocations had closed the Latin School in 1978, the archdiocesan newspaper and the vocations staff occupied vacated Holy Rosary rooms. Robert W. Sims was primarily assigned to duties on the archdiocesan vocations staff but he also served part-time as priest and administrator for Holy Rosary from 1978 to 1983.

A new identity was taking shape for the church. It became a parish of choice for about 300 members. Some were Italian Catholics remaining in the old neighborhood. Some were non-Italian Catholics now living in the old parish area. Some were outside residents who simply chose to belong to this unique "personal parish without boundaries." In 1983 Holy Rosary became a yoked parish sharing the services of a priest with neighboring St. Patrick Church. Holy Rosary seemed new with its services reflecting the directions of Vatican II, its parish council sharing guidance of parish life with the priest, and its "pastoral minister" for daily parish functions a Sister of Providence from Terre Haute. But the old ethnic heritage was at least occasionally celebrated. The parish motto was Benvenuto (Welcome). Spaghetti suppers and festivals were not unknown. The great San Salvador bell sometimes rang.[15]

Slovenes of Indianapolis

Slovenes became the second largest group of Eastern European immigrants in Indianapolis. Slovenia was part of Austria from 1335 to 1918. After the First World War it was included in the "Kingdom of the Serbs, Croats, and Slovenes," later called Yugoslavia. Some Slovenes were also born on the Italian side of the Italo-Yugoslav boundary of 1918. So Indiana's Slovene immigrants appeared variously in statistical tables as Austrians, Yugoslavians, or Italians. By the outbreak of the First World War about 130,000 Slovenians were living in the United States. Perhaps 1 percent or 1,300 of them lived in Indianapolis.[16]

Jobs in metal working first drew the Slovenes to Indianapolis. In 1880 Benjamin F. Haugh moved his iron foundry from central Indianapolis to the west side of White River. A section of land there was well served by rail lines. It was incorporated as Haughville in 1883 and annexed to Indianapolis in 1897. Cleveland Malleable Iron Company also built a foundry there in 1882 and merged the Cleveland and Indianapolis operations to form National Malleable Castings Company in 1891. Ewart Manufacturing Company (later Link-Belt), a primary user of Malleable products, found Haughville a convenient location. A Slovene named George Lambert (Jurij Lampert) worked for Malleable at Cleveland. As an agent for Malleable, George Lambert crossed the Atlantic seven times after 1895 to enlist Slovene workers. Many of his recruits came to Haughville and packed into boarding houses on the low land around the foundries. Lambert himself moved with his family to a home in Haughville in 1907 and housed fourteen male boarders upstairs.[17]

Slovenians were Catholics. The first three organizations these immigrant laborers formed for mutual support and social activity were named St. Aloysius Lodge, St. Joseph Lodge, and SS. Cyril and Methodius Lodge. It was St. Aloysius Lodge which welcomed visits of Slovene-speaking priests from the Chicago area to Haughville. In 1905 the lodge formed a committee to raise money for a Slovene church. It loaned $600 interest free to purchase church building lots. A delegation of Slovenes took a petition for permission to form their own parish to Denis D. O'Donaghue, auxiliary bishop of Indianapolis. Seeing that there was no hope of integrating these Slavs with the neighboring Irish parish of St. Anthony, O'Donaghue approved the new national parish early in 1906. The Diocese of Indianapolis had no appropriate priest so John Kranjec, a particular friend to the Slovenes of Haughville, wrote to invite a fellow priest he knew in Slovenia to come to Indiana to lead the new congregation.[18]

Joseph Lavric from the Diocese of Ljubljana got things moving quickly at Haughville. He celebrated Sunday Mass for his 720 new parishioners on 29 April 1906. From the beginning the congregation included minorities of Hungarians and Poles plus a scattering of other nationalities. Temporary location was the second floor meeting room and dance hall above the first floor bar at 731 North Warman Avenue. The prospect of their own church was exciting. They bought more suitable lots at the corner of Holmes and Calvelage in September, broke ground in October, and dedicated the completed Holy Trinity Church on 28 April 1907, all within a year of Lavric's arrival. Parishioners labored to excavate the basement with their own hands. Slovene lodge members wearing chest sashes marched in the celebrations. The building was brick and stone, an impressive 110 feet by 40 feet to seat 600. The steeple was 60 feet tall. Anybody who gave $10 toward the cost of the three bells was entitled to have them sounded at the time of his death.[19]

Lavric moved to a Slovene parish in Cleveland in 1909 and his immediate successor stayed only a year. The Diocese of Indianapolis then asked for help from the Franciscans (Friars Minor Conventual) who were able to provide Holy Trinity with a series of five Slovene-speaking priests between 1910 and 1933. It was a demanding time. Between 1906 and 1919 there were 1,019 infants baptized at Holy Trinity. There had to be a school. Sisters of Providence from St. Mary of the Woods taught the school from 1911 to 1915 followed by Sisters of St. Francis from Oldenburg. For the sisters there must be a convent. For the parishioners there must be a social hall. For the priest and the church offices there must be a rectory.

Even with loyal Catholic Slovenes practicing heroic stewardship, money was scarce. Heads of Slovene families were working at Malleable in 1910 for 10¢ to 15¢ per hour. The pay envelope for a week might hold one five-dollar gold piece and one silver dollar. When the Great Depression came, many had no pay at all and the church had additional obligations to aid the unemployed. The Franciscan pastors asked all parishioners who were able to be faithful with regular Sunday collections and pew rents to underwrite parish operating costs. In addition they visited regularly in homes and businesses asking contributions wherever they could toward building projects or toward payment of the parish debt. The joint efforts of these clergy and their members made the bonds of fellowship grow strong but the debt remained large. At the end of 1932 the parish owed $110,000 on buildings plus $5,614.15 for other unpaid bills including salaries of the pastors.[20]

In spring of 1933 Bishop Chartrand of the Diocese of Indianapolis replaced the Franciscans with his own diocesan clergy as pastors. Since the congregation members had learned English it no longer seemed essential to have Slovene-speaking pastors. Guests could be brought in for certain special services for the older parishioners at Christmas and Easter. As the economy improved and full employment returned, the new pastors channeled Slovene thrift and pride into special campaigns against that church debt. There was an annual fund raising festival with booths, rides, and games. Twice during the Second World War the Holy Trinity members organized special drives to purchase U.S. Savings Bonds and sign them over to the parish, thus striking a blow against both the national enemy and the church debt. There was a "May 500 Raffle" in which church donors purchased chances on the drivers in the Indianapolis 500 Auto Race.[21]

Symbol of the new solvency and stability was the pastorate of Edward Bockhold. He came to Holy Trinity in 1938 and stayed for more than thirty years. In May of 1945 the parishioners celebrated both the silver jubilee of Bockhold's ordination and the retirement of all the old indebtedness. Between 1940 and 1955 they renovated and decorated the church including installation of a new organ and eleven new art glass windows. They built a new convent, enlarged the school, and improved the property generally.

Parish life flourished with this beloved priest and Holy Trinity Church at the community's center. During Bockhold's tenure three young men of the parish were ordained priests and twelve young women entered religious orders. During the boom years following the Second World War, Holy Trinity grew to 2,250 parishioners and a school enrollment of 646. Besides multiple Masses on Sunday, three were said each weekday. As Vatican II altered the church landscape, Bockhold took particular pains to involve his people in the changes, even bringing in a Slovene-speaking priest to provide careful explanation of the Council's actions for older parishioners. The ministry of Bockhold along with the special cohesiveness of the Slovene community maintained Holy Trinity as a sturdy ethnic parish well into the 1960s.[22]

Even such a close-knit ethnic community as the Slovenes of Haughville came to feel the force of social change. New immigration from Eastern Europe had nearly ceased. In 1948 Archbishop Schulte no longer saw a need for a "Slovene" parish. A decree from the Sacred Congregation of the Council in Rome made it official on 1 March. Holy Trinity was no longer a national parish. It was now a regular territorial parish for all Catholics living within a particular area between the parishes of St. Anthony Church and St. Michael Church. Those who lived outside its specific boundaries could not be Holy Trinity members without special permission. Slovenes stayed in Haughville and maintained the character of the old neighborhood for a remarkably long time.[23]

But some members did keep moving away, especially the younger ones. Economic opportunities faded in the Haughville area as Malleable, Link-Belt, and Kingan's (later Hygrade) closed. Slovenes who were young parents wanted better housing. College graduates, including those aided by scholarships from the church, were likely to prefer new locations. When vacant Slovene houses passed to newcomers who were blacks or Appalachian whites, the unity and security of the old village atmosphere seemed broken. Public housing moved into former Malleable property. The church building itself became subject to vandalism and even the annual outdoor parish festival was not a safe place. Membership and school enrollment declined.[24]

Pastors after 1970 led the church in ministry to multiple constituencies. It remained home parish for Slovenes still living in the Haughville area. Freed by Vatican II from strict adherence to geographical parish boundaries, Slovene descendants from a wide area continued to return to Holy Trinity for regular worship or for a wide variety of ethnic celebrations. And the church joined several agencies in ministry to all the people of its neighborhood—crisis assistance in many forms, pastoral care, day care, kindergarten, elementary school, recre-

ation. In 1988 the pastor was a black priest. Membership had stabilized at about 900, still substantially Slovene.[25]

Slovaks in the Calumet

Slovaks were not a minority in the Calumet city of Whiting, Indiana, in the 1920s. One observer commented that over 90 percent of Whiting's residents were Slavs and that a large majority of the Slavs were Slovaks.[26]

The northern portions of Lake and Porter counties, somewhat drained by the Grand Calumet and Little Calumet rivers, had been inhospitable to the main stream of American pioneers. Fewer than 100 people lived on these federal lands north of the Little Calumet in 1850. The 111,400 acres in Lake County and 53,305 acres in Porter County ceded to Indiana by Congress as "swamp lands" in 1851 were soon for sale for about $1.25 per acre. There were not many takers. Around the future site of Whiting sand fleas and mosquitoes multiplied, summers were hot, winters were bitter cold, and the sand was knee deep. Good teams of horses or oxen might be able to pull a wagon along the top of a sand ridge but between the ridges lay indeterminate acres and miles of deep sand, streams, lakes, puddles, swamps, sloughs, marsh grass, reeds, and patchy timber. Hunting, fishing, and wild gathering were bountiful beyond description. The scattered residents learned to serve as guides for sportsmen from Chicago and to market at that metropolis whatever natural products they could manage to transport there. One German settler bound cedar fence posts into rafts and towed the rafts by hand along the edge of Lake Michigan to sell in South Chicago.[27]

Chicago was what made the Calumet frontier special. Shortest routes from the East to this western metropolis ran through the Calumet along the southern edge of Lake Michigan. Four rail companies laid their lines across the region between 1852 and 1865. Seven more were added between 1874 and 1903 with the belt lines and network of street railways still to come. In the area which would be the site of Whiting, George M. Roberts donated right-of-way across his land to the Pennsylvania Railroad and was rewarded with a station named Robertsdale sometime before 1872. Nearby the Lake Shore Railway placed one of its stations near the tiny store and post office of Henry Schrage in 1874. A special siding to avoid collisions between trains of the Lake Shore and the Pennsylvania gave its name to the area. Whiting's Siding became Whiting. The population of 115 in the 1880 census was mainly a few families of Germans who earned about $1 a day working on the railroad tracks and rejoiced that Chicago provided some market even for the unspectacular local surpluses of ice and sand.[28]

A new era began for Whiting in 1889. Things moved fast. In early spring Theodore M. Towle arrived and got local merchant Henry Schrage to help him buy up some 235 acres near the lake. All purchases were contracted and paid for by a William P. Cowan. In May Cowan himself was on the scene directing about 1,500 laborers doing major construction. Towle and Cowan concealed their purposes from the scattered Hoosiers and even from the workers. By the end of summer it was plain that Towle and Cowan were really officers of Standard Oil and that the construction was the company's major refinery designed to sell petroleum products to the whole American West. There were tanks, stills, a twenty-inch water line from Lake Michigan, and infrastructure to support it all. The crude to be refined at first was high sulphur or "polecat" oil piped from wells near Lima, Ohio. The stink of the process was too much to locate near all the noses of Chicago. Whiting offered largely unpopulated cheap land, low taxes, and good railroad service. It was convenient both to the lake and to the major market of Chicago.[29]

They fired up the new plant in September of 1890 and on Thanksgiving Day sent off the first shipment of 125 tank cars of kerosene. Soon the nation was being served by products from Whiting in the form of millions of barrels of kerosene, millions of barrels of fuel oil, special oils for signal and mining lights, paraffin for candles, Mica Axle Grease for wagons, coach oil for carriages and buggies, harness oil, and hoof grease. When automobile production boomed after 1903, Standard Oil of Indiana, with its administrative and research center at Whiting, developed the Burton pressure still to crack petroleum in a new way which would convert a much higher percentage of crude oil into gasoline. Twelve of these new stills were operating at Whiting in 1913, 500 in 1917, and 893 in 1922.

The number of refinery employees continued to increase, reaching 4,080 in 1920. Robertsdale citizens sought annexation by Hammond in 1893 in order to receive some protection of their lives and property. Whiting, finally assisted by Standard Oil attorneys in its resistance to annexation by Hammond, incorporated in 1903. Population grew from about 4,000 at the time of incorporation to 6,587 in 1910 and to 10,145 in 1920. At first living conditions at Whiting were dismal. Standard Oil laid out "The Village" in 1889, a few houses for a few selected supervisors who developed a few social clubs among this elite. Ordinary laborers crowded into small dwellings and tar paper shacks on the south side of town. Before 1903 these slums had no pure or running water, no sewers, no sidewalks, no parks, and no city government. Some workers sought release from the sandy barrenness in saloons, dance halls, and whorehouses. They escaped to Chicago as often as they could.[30]

Recent immigrants were the ones most willing to come to Whiting and stay. The refinery wages were above average. Standard Oil paid girls and women 90¢ per day in the candle factory. The lowest paid adult male received $1.50 per day and an expert skilled laborer might make as much as $4.50. The refinery preferred to hire married men with orderly habits. As the foreign born and children of foreign born filled the ranks of company employees, they developed their own network of lodges and social organizations for mutual support. In 1890 there was not so much as a Catholic chapel in the Whiting area. Fifty years later Whiting had six Catholic churches within a radius of seven blocks. Sacred Heart Church was the first of these, a predominantly German and Irish parish which dedicated its new frame building in May of 1891 and mounted a thousand-pound bell in its tower in September of the following year.[31]

A few Slovaks who came as construction workers to build the refinery elected to remain in Whiting. They had come from a native land among the Carpathian Mountains of Central Europe, dominated since the 900s by Hungarians and since 1526 by the ruling Hapsburg powers of Austria-Hungary. Twelve of them organized as Branch 130 of the First Catholic Slovak Union at Whiting on 8 April 1894. All members were practicing Catholics. As the feast day of St. George was 8 April, they placed the branch under his patronage. Every Sunday after dinner they met at the home of John Celovsky to attend to their agenda which included social and insurance decisions.

By 1896 Branch 130 had thirty-two members and a primary concern had become formation of a Slovak Catholic church. Pastor Michael Byrne at Sacred Heart Church in Whiting was hospitable to Slovaks and occasionally arranged visits by a Slovak-speaking priest. However the Slovakians wanted regular confessions and preaching in Slovak. They wanted a priest and parish of their own. They appointed George Berdis and Steve Kubeck a church committee. They sent Kubeck to Joseph Rademacher, bishop of Fort Wayne, with a petition for a Slovak priest. It was signed by ten families. Rademacher said ten was too few. A month later George Berdis, Steve Kubeck, and John Kaminsky came back to the bishop with a list of fifty prospective parishioners—twelve families plus some single persons—along with a sealed letter from Pastor Byrne. Rademacher agreed to write to Austria-Hungary for a Slovak priest.[32]

Benedict Rajcany arrived the day before Easter of 1897. Later legend said Whiting's welcoming committee at the Hammond station was slow to recognize this inconspicuous figure as a priest. "He seemed like some one who had run away from home." The small congregation had no church, no rectory, and no parish organization. Benedict celebrated Easter Mass at Sacred Heart Church after its regular services. He lived in the Sacred Heart rectory all summer, communicating with Pastor Byrne for a time in halting Latin.

The local lodge, Branch No. 130 of the Slovak Catholic Union, owned a tract of five lots in Robertsdale. The small structure built there was a dance pavilion later enclosed and upgraded to a lodge hall. With a minimum of modification, they added a tower and made it a church. "The Church was anything but a Catholic church in its appearance within," reported a parish member. "Candle sticks had large blue and red crepe paper ribbons tied to them . . . The back of the altar was sickly blue and around the border was draped purple crepe paper." It was St. John the Baptist Church the pastor said, because he also came as one "crying in the wilderness." Total cost of lots, hall, and tower was $940. Dedication day was 4 July 1897, complete with visiting delegations from local social lodges of Poles and Greek Catholics and a uniformed band.[33]

The ministry of Benedict Rajcany was not limited because his own parish was small. Because he spoke Slovak, German, and Hungarian he could hear confessions, perform marriages, and administer baptism for a substantial segment of the polyglot population of the area. He organized a Slovak parish in Chicago and one in Joliet, Illinois, serving them until they could call pastors of their own. He visited clusters of Slovaks at East Chicago, South Bend, and more distant places and served them as extensions of his ministry at St. John.

Benedict mastered English quickly. English was the language of the little pioneer school which he and physician William Putnam organized for a handful of Whiting's boys. English quickly became the language of the embryonic St. John parochial school which he and his parish associate, Katherine Wade, operated for boys and girls of St. John from about 1898 to 1900. When the four-room parish school opened in October 1901 with three Sisters of Providence from St. Mary of the Woods as teachers, English was the language. School enrollment reflected the steady increase in Slovak families: 278 pupils in 1908–1909, 516 pupils in 1914, 723 pupils with 15 sisters in 1926.[34]

One block of parish members were critical of Benedict for what they viewed as capitulation to English. This faction of the older generation maintained Slovak in their homes, church services, male and female lodges, Holy Rosary societies, and personal social interchanges. They wanted to require all the church children to learn and use Slovak in the parochial school. The school children generally had no zeal for this. Benedict finally offered to assist a tutor in teaching the Slovak language to special classes held after school and on Saturday. Those classes soon died but the grumbling continued.

Benedict was a true Slovak. He offered Slovakians over a wide area a ministry in their language and suited to their culture. The first English sermon at a Sunday High Mass at St. John was preached by a visiting priest in Benedict's absence in 1921, nearly twenty-five years after the church was established. But Benedict was also an enthusiastic American. In 1902 he was incardinated into the Diocese of Fort Wayne and so enrolled among the permanent priests owing obedience to the American bishop. His parishioners felt his urgency to have them qualified and naturalized as U.S. citizens. Almost all members of St. John had done this well before the First World War era when some enthusiasts counted it patriotic to torment "aliens." As for Benedict, his favorite team was the Chicago White Sox and he rarely missed a weekday home game.[35]

With the enlargement of 1914 the church building would seat 650 but membership was about 2,000 by then so people were still standing in the aisles and outside on the sidewalk on Sundays. The school was expanding and the religious societies were multiplying. Benedict needed help. Particularly reliable weekend helpers were priests from the faculty of St. Joseph's College conducted by the Society of the Precious Blood at Rensselaer, Indiana.[36]

A favorite among the visiting priests was a biology professor named John Kostik. In addition to English and German, he spoke Slovak and Hungarian and was able to hear confessions in Slovene, Croatian, and Polish. Kostik was appointed "permanent assistant" to Benedict in 1925. He undertook a census and pastoral visit to every parish household, asking each to pledge $150 to begin construction of the new church building. Parish membership was about 3,250 which made St. John the earliest and largest Slovak church in the state. In 1927 Benedict resigned and moved to Florida. Church records showed 4,494 baptisms, 1,012 marriages, and 675 deaths during his thirty years as pastor. Sixteen young women of the parish had become Sisters of Providence and three young men had chosen the priesthood.[37]

In an urban pocket without much room for expansion and in a parish now past the peak of its ethnic loyalty, John Kostik and a stream of young assistant clergy from St. Joseph's College and the Society of the Precious Blood led St. John Church into an era of great vitality. The steeple soared 190 feet into the sky above the new church, a kind of symbol of the debt for parish buildings totaling $192,000 in the depression year of 1932. They paid it off in full by 1942. The basement far beneath the steeple, inserted into the new church plan at the last minute at the insistence of a young assistant, was equally important for a parish rich in young people. They made the old church into a combination gymnasium, social hall, and youth center. There was a flowering of societies. One of the assistants said "The assistant's big work at the parish was the organizing of Young People's Sodalities, Junior and Senior Daughters of Mary, Junior and Senior Holy Name Societies, the choir and athletic club." The drama club and orchestra earned wide recognition. For teen dances the St. John gymnasium became the "Crystal Ballroom," attracting hundreds from across the Calumet Region.[38]

They invited Benedict back from Florida to preach in Slovak for the fortieth anniversary of St. John Church in April of 1937. Thirty of the first members of the parish were still living; their grandchildren sang at the Mass. On his way back to Orlando, Benedict died. At the services in Whiting sixteen priests and about 2,000 laypersons were in the procession bearing his body from the rectory to the church. Bishop John F. Noll led the eighty-five priests and prelates in the sanctuary as they chanted the Solemn Office of the Dead. Benedict's body was buried in the shadow of a large cross in the middle of St. John cemetery. Lake County residents seeing the crowds said it was the biggest funeral they had ever seen.

After eighteen years as pastor at St. John Church, John Kostik went to Carthagena, Ohio, to become superior of the motherhouse of the Fathers of the Precious Blood. This was also the order's major seminary at which students for the priesthood were trained in philosophy and theology. His appointment to that position was a recognition that Slovaks had been accorded a place in the main stream of American Catholic life.

Slovaks in Gary

Immigrants from Slovakia kept finding jobs in Indiana's steel mills after Gary was laid out in 1906. They organized Slovak lodges and societies. A group of them with strong religious interest met at the home of John Onder in spring of 1911. They sent a delegation with a petition to Herman J. Alerding, bishop of the Diocese of Fort Wayne. Some had been attending Holy Angels Church with the American parishioners or worshipping with the Poles at St. Hedwig Church but had not found a satisfactory place in either. What they wanted from the bishop was permission to establish a parish for Slovaks in Gary. They wanted a priest who shared their church and national traditions, one who would speak, read, preach, pray, and hear confessions in the familiar tongue.

Alerding promptly gave permission for the parish. Since he had no Slovak priest, he authorized them to search for one he could appoint. They found Desiderius Major who was willing to move from Bridgeport, Connecticut, to Gary. Alerding named him pastor. With about eighty families plus some single persons, they celebrated their first Sunday Mass in a borrowed church building on 29 October 1911. Almost exactly a year later they laid the cornerstone for their church. Pastor Benedict Rajcany of St. John the Baptist Church (Slovak) in Whiting preached the sermon. Immediate debt on the new building, dedicated as Holy Trinity Church, was $16,242. A contribution of $10,000 from United States Steel eased the financial strain.[39]

It proved difficult for Holy Trinity parish to find and keep a pastor. Desiderius Major left after about two years, at least in part due to congregational grumbling. His mother, who came to Gary to be his housekeeper, turned out to be a Hungarian and could not even speak Slovak. Four other pastors came and went within a period of about seven years.

The parish had no shortage of children. The people wanted a parochial school taught by sisters who spoke Slovak. There was no school building but they converted some space under the church. Four teaching Sisters of Saints Cyril and Methodius agreed to come to Gary from Pennsylvania. There were 230 pupils on hand when the basement school opened in September of 1915. When Bishop Alerding made his visit to administer confirmation on 1 October 1917, the confirmation class numbered 189. Even if the money must be borrowed, they simply had to build a school and a convent for their teachers.[40]

A new era began with Ignatius Stepuncik. As a young man of nineteen with some secondary education, Stepuncik made his way to America in 1906 with the current influx of Slovakians. He craved further study and found his opportunity at Indiana's St. Meinrad Seminary. He was ordained a priest in May of 1910 and served parishes in four country towns of Illinois. When he arrived at Holy Trinity in Gary in August of 1921, the balance in the church treasury was $140.85, the church debt was over $31,000, and the economy was in recession. Those members with work in the blast furnaces were likely to be earning 17¢ per hour. Parish stewardship called for contributions of 50¢ per month from each working girl, $1 per month from each single man, and $2 per month from each family.[41]

Stepuncik's ministry combined strenuous thrift with a grand vision. Parish requirements were heavy. In 1927 they scheduled three Masses on Sunday and began the practice of inviting the Benedictine Fathers at Lisle, Illinois, to send a priest to assist. The number of families reported for Holy Trinity was generally between 250 and 300 and the number of persons under the pastor's care about 1,200. In 1936 the five classrooms of the parish school housed the eight grades for 140 boys and 124 girls; salary for all the teaching sisters combined was $1,970. Stepuncik spent very little of the church's income on himself and did much of the repair of church properties with his own hands.

Every year the congregation would chop a block of dollars off the parish debt and add a block of dollars to the treasury being accumulated to build the new church. After years of uneasiness about the stability of banks, the Holy Trinity savings were scattered in 1936.

> $21,818.46 were placed in the American-Russian National Building and Loan Association, from which we withdrew a sum of $1,090.92 on September 25, 1935, leaving a balance of $20,727.54. Mutual Building and Loan Association held $13,724.72, from which we withdrew the sum of $686.25, leaving our balance, $13,038.47. Mid-City Building Savings and Loan Association held $14,951.28. From this we withdrew the sum of $2,990.26 on September 10, 1936. Hence $11,961.02 is still deposited there. At Central Trust and Savings Bank, $135.25 was left on the checking account. At the First National Bank $75.05 was left on checking account together with a $100 "Real Estate Bond." $18,000 were deposited with the bishop at 4% interest.[42]

In one case a failed bank paid off its obligation to the church with half a dozen rundown houses. Stepuncik recouped the investment by maintaining the properties himself and renting them for the church. In appreciation of his diligence the congregation eventually gave him two banquets, a trip to Europe to visit his aged mother, and a Buick.[43]

Stepuncik had built the treasury to $152,771.38 at the end of 1943. In his vision that was money for the new church, but he never saw it built. He died of a brain tumor 9 June 1944. A Catholic colleague commented:

> In the conferral of the order of priesthood the palms of the ordinand are anointed; in the sacrament of the Last Anointing, called Extreme Unction, the sick priest is anointed on the back of the hands. When he lies in church for the last rites the body is turned to face the people. Thus it was with Father Ignatius Stepuncik. In death he faced the parish for the last time. The hands anointed unto death are now no longer raised to bless, to baptize, to pardon. They lie silent awaiting the resurrection.[44]

Bishop John F. Noll sent in Andrew Grutka from Sacred Heart Church of East Chicago as the new pastor. There was a definite change of speed in parish life. Grutka's parish census found 327 Holy Trinity families and over 1,350 persons under pastoral care. A newsletter named *The Trinitarian* reported Sunday Masses at 6:30, 8, 9, 10, and 11. Weekday Masses were at 7 and 8. There were two assistant priests.[45]

Much of Stepuncik's church treasury had to be spent for delayed maintenance. "Buildings of Holy Trinity are very old," said the *Trinitarian*. "They have definitely become very sick. In fact they are almost dead." Convent water lines ruptured within the walls.

> It was hard enough to install the stoker in the school, but when it was connected and a check of all the radiators was made, it was found that every valve and vent was defective and had to be replaced. This fixed up, a check was made on the boiler in the convent and then just as everything appeared all set, it was discovered that the foundation under the boiler was giving way, and a new one had to be placed under it. Digging for a new foundation for the boiler revealed a sewer main and likewise the water supply line.[46]

Before Easter of 1945 the list of projects included: "Three rooms and bath added to convent. Stoker installed. Stoker installed in school. Windows weather stripped . . . Beginning of extensive interior repairs to church including new stoker, complete redecorating, all new statues and stations of the Cross, new sacristy added to church, front entrance rebuilt, asphalt tiling throughout church, new vestments, two new confessionals, sanctuary completely transformed."[47]

The Holy Trinity school had eight sisters teaching eight grades for 119 boys and 120 girls for a combined salary of $3,000. The improvement list for July of 1945 included: "Beginning of extensive repairs to school interior and auditorium: rewiring, fluorescent lights, replastering, refinishing floors, new safety doors at entrances, new stage, new kitchen, storage rooms, partial tuck pointing exterior." Even with the Sisters of Saints Cyril and Methodius in charge of the school, English had largely crowded out the Slovak language. In the first decade of Stepuncik's ministry, preaching and singing in the church were in Slovak but that language was used in the school only on Fridays. By 1932 an Irish priest assisting at Holy Trinity reported that "a large part of the parishioners could not understand Slovak."[48]

An increasing number of the parochial school children did not belong to Holy Trinity parish—130 of 313 in 1949. Grutka sent a note to all the parents:

> Holy Trinity School is a Catholic school, and therefore the study of religion is a requisite for every child. This school was intended primarily for the education of children of Slovak descent. The Slovak language will be taught to all those who desire a knowledge of this language. But it will not be forced upon those who are not interested. The official starting time for classes is 8:40 each morning. Holy Mass begins each morning at 8:00, but attendance is not compulsory. Children should be encouraged to assist at the Holy Sacrifice every morning if possible, because of the tremendous spiritual profit to be derived from it . . . Holy Trinity is not a reform school and teachers cannot take time out to cope with a delinquent child to the detriment of the other pupils. The Sisters have been instructed not to administer any form of corporal punishment whatsoever. If a child should prove troublesome to the extent of disturbing the good order of the classroom, parents will be notified, and should there be no improvement in the child's conduct, he will be dismissed from school.[49]

The number of Holy Trinity parishioners peaked at "over 1400" in the late 1940s and parish societies flourished. The 1950 report of memberships showed: Holy Name Society, 257; Apostleship of Prayer, 108; Apostleship of Prayer, Women, 130; Rosary Society, 337; Christian Mothers, 97; Blessed Virgin Sodality, Seniors, 98; Blessed Virgin Sodality, Juniors, 63; Society for the Propagation of the Faith, 274. Families receiving *Our Sunday Visitor* numbered 425. Members attending Mass said the choir voices were angelic. After years of overcrowding, they celebrated the Midnight Mass on Christmas Eve in Gary's Armory in 1948. There was a plethora of male and female church athletic teams engaged in basketball, softball, and serious horseshoe pitching. The Trinitarian players and the school produced dramas.

By the time work finally began on the new Holy Trinity building the impact of social change had already lowered the membership of this ethnic parish to about 1,200. They let the contracts in summer of 1954 specifying a "contemporary neo-classic" building 104 feet by 91 feet at the corner of Twelfth and Madison. There was seating for 432 persons. A downstairs chapel seating 80 accommodated the smaller congregations desiring non-English services.[50]

Pastor Andrew Grutka was widely recognized beyond the scene of his duties at Holy Trinity parish. During his studies among the Benedictines at St. Procopius College at Lisle, Illinois, and at the North American College at Rome, he had formed an international network of friends. His agenda was full of travel to address such groups as the National Council of Catholic Women, or the Catholic Tri-State Congress in Grand Rapids, or a national workshop for priests held in Detroit. He offered a course in psychology for the nurses at St. Catherine Hospital in East Chicago and chaired the Community Chest drive for Gary. He aired a Catholic news program on Gary radio. Groups in Pennsylvania and West Virginia and Illinois called on him to conduct retreats to encourage spiritual discipline. He was given the honorary rank of monsignor in June of 1956.

When the new Diocese of Gary was formed, Andrew Grutka was the one named to be its first bishop. Gary had never seen so many church dignitaries as gathered for Grutka's consecration on 25 February 1957. Chicago educational television carried the entire program from 9 A.M.. to 1 P.M. The Knights of Columbus and the Steelworkers Union sponsored television reruns. Radio stations across the region reported the ceremony. Grutka was a bishop of Gary with credentials earned in the Calumet. The Sisters of Saints Cyril and Methodius were glad to have such a bishop to celebrate the Roman-Slovanic Pontifical High Mass for their golden jubilee celebration in Pennsylvania in 1959. He could also preach the sermon for them—in Slovak.[51]

Poles at South Bend

Polish Catholics were the ethnic standouts in South Bend. For much of three centuries Poland was dominated by powerful neighbors. Russia, Prussia, and Austria carved and annexed its territories. By 1850 Polish peasants were being divorced wholesale from their ancient land connections and cast onto the labor markets. The Polish population in the United States reached a million in 1890, two million by 1900, and three million by 1910. About 90 percent of these immigrant Poles were Catholics.[52]

Poles came to South Bend in 1867, probably as section hands on the Lake Shore and Michigan Southern Railroad. They saw that this was a place with special potential. Studebaker and Oliver had growing factories in South Bend and Singer opened a cabinet making plant there in 1869. These large industries and the growing labor pool around them generated smaller industries and supporting businesses. South Bend population was nearly doubling every decade: 1,652 in 1850; 3,803 in 1860; 7,206 in 1870; 13,280 in 1880. In the prosperous year of 1870 a railroad hand could earn as much as $1.50 per day and factory workers employed for long hours sometimes made even more. Governor Morton was distributing a pamphlet in Europe inviting immigrants to Indiana. In 1870 Oliver imported Polish laborers directly from Europe. The factories preferred men who would bring their families with them. Many of the early Poles in South Bend came from the districts of Kcynia and Szubin in the province of Poznan.[53]

Life was especially hard for early South Bend Poles. They were late in the stream of immigrant groups and had few special skills to offer. They took the poorest and most dangerous jobs. They had the smallest chance of promotion. The community already had well established economic, social, and political lines. These clannish latecomers were repressed and scorned. Soon they organized in order to support one another. In 1874 came the St. Stanislaus Kostka Society and the St. Casimir Society. Besides providing an agenda of social events, these societies paid sick benefits, assisted with funeral expenses, and rallied support for a Polish Catholic parish.[54]

Poles in South Bend lived on the West Side and in the neighboring farm community, perhaps seventy-five families of them in the early 1870s. St. Patrick was the Catholic church already established on the West Side. Daniel Spillard of the Congregation of Holy Cross was its pastor. Spillard was concerned about ministry to these new immigrants with whom he and his parishioners could barely communicate. He worked with the two Polish societies to schedule separate Masses for their ethnic group, to arrange for one of the laymen to lead devotions in Polish after Mass, and to bring in a Polish-speaking priest like Adolf Banakowski from Chicago to preach and hear confessions occasionally.

All this was a long way from satisfactory to the Poles. Banakowski reported that the Poles of South Bend "do not even want to go to church because they do not have a Polish priest." In 1876 the societies brought Banakowski to South Bend for a special Polish preaching mission. This experience inspired them so much that they moved at once to petition Bishop Joseph Dwenger of Fort Wayne for a Polish parish.[55]

Valentine Czyzewski

All the energies of South Bend's Polonia came to focus on the person of Valentine Czyzewski. He was a native of the Russian-dominated portion of Poland, fluent in both Polish and Lithuanian. He had been a candidate for the priesthood in his homeland but the Russians shut down his seminary in 1863 along with most of the area's churches. He arrived in New York on 6 February 1869 and went directly to northern Indiana. There the Polish farm hands and railroad workers came to know him as a fellow laborer. When Czyzewski attended services at St. Patrick Church in South Bend, Pastor Spillard heard of his interest in the priesthood. The Congregation of Holy Cross, headquartered at Notre Dame, had a special arrangement with the bishop to supply priests to certain parishes in the vicinity of South Bend. Spillard, himself a Holy Cross priest, arranged with Father Sorin at Notre Dame to admit Czyzewski to seminary. On 15 September 1874 Czyzewski professed his own vows in the Congregation of Holy Cross.[56]

When the Poles of South Bend petitioned Bishop Dwenger for a Polish priest in 1876, the bishop knew Czyzewski was in preparation at the seminary at Notre Dame. Czyzewski was ordained 28 December 1876 and two days later sent by his Holy Cross superiors to be pastor to the Poles of South Bend. He was thirty years of age, destined for high visibility in northern Indiana for the next thirty-six years. He represented the faith of the Catholic Church and the authority of its bishop of Fort Wayne. He represented the resources and responsibilities of his connection with the influential Congregation of Holy Cross at Notre Dame. He represented a large, growing, and volatile parish membership. He was a spokesman for Polish national life, language, and culture. At the same time he was an agent of Americanization, determined to provide a host of Polish children with essential skills to be productive citizens.

First they had to build a church. Business was slow and wages low at South Bend in 1877. Polish factory laborers fortunate enough to have work at all received about 15¢ per hour. Czyzewski's priestly stipend was 50¢ for a funeral or $1 for a funeral with sermon. Czyzewski entered at once into his lifetime pattern of developing strong teams of laymen within the Polish societies and sharing parish leadership with them.

With a tremendous joint effort and visits to every Polish family in the county, they raised $3,500. Everybody offered work. Some mortgaged their homes in order to be able to contribute. Bishop Dwenger gave the lot on Monroe Street. The new wooden church building was 83 feet long, 40 feet wide, and 24 feet high. The superior general of the Congregation of Holy Cross and the president of the University of Notre Dame marched in the procession and spoke at the dedication in June of 1877.

There was already a St. Joseph Church in South Bend but this new Polish one on the West Side was popularly known as St. Joseph "across the river." There had to be a school immediately. Polish children were averse to public schools and the feeling was mutual. Peasant immigrant parents, while limited in formal education themselves, would enroll their children if the school was assuredly Polish and assuredly Catholic. Czyzewski and one lay assistant opened such a school in a tiny temporary building in fall of 1877. Within a year there was a school building alongside the new church.[57]

In spring of 1879 a tornado blew down St. Joseph Church and severely damaged the school. The events which followed testified to the power with which industrial employment and this healthy ethnic parish had been drawing Poles to South Bend. The storm was a disaster but morale was high. This time their building campaign raised $33,000. Parishioners volunteered their labor again. St. Stanislaus Kostka Society gave the 3,500-pound bell and St. Casimir Society paid for the organ. They chose a new location at Scott and Napier streets, a new patron saint, and so the new name of St. Hedwig Church. Bishop Dwenger dedicated the Romanesque brick structure in April of 1883. It would seat about 1,000 and raised its steeple 156 feet into the sky.

Teachers from the Holy Cross order came that year to assist Czyzewski in the parish and take charge of the 235 pupils in its parochial school. By 1891 the 800 families in the parish enrolled 676 children in St. Hedwig school. In 1896 this Polish parish spent $28,000 for a three-story brick schoolhouse for its student body exceeding 1,000, the largest parochial grade school in the Diocese of Fort Wayne.[58]

The impact of Valentine Czyzewski was by no means limited to South Bend nor was his pastoral labor confined to the formidable range of functions he fulfilled at St. Hedwig. He became a rural circuit rider, particularly among the Polish farmers at three locations between South Bend and Chicago. These were continuing sources of a stream of Polish youth to the factories of South Bend and to his parish at St. Hedwig.

One such country settlement was near the village of Otis some ten miles west of LaPorte. Jacob Lewandowski and Valentine Kommatka came there about 1860. They were construction men for the railroad. Soon afterward they brought their families and a few other persons from the province of Poznan as permanent settlers. They were day laborers clearing land, ditching, and woodsplitting. The railroad paid part of their wages in land they had cleared. With the few dollars they could save they rented and finally bought additional small tracts which sold for about $20 per acre in 1870. By 1872 there were about sixty Polish families near Otis. Polish priests from Chicago and LaPorte visited them. They dedicated St. Mary Church in 1873 and installed their own Polish-speaking pastor. Otis became the earliest anchor for Polish ministry in northern Indiana. Poles from a wide area would ride the railroad to attend its services. Czyzewski was a highly regarded visiting minister among them.[59]

Another Polish settlement was near the railroad station called Terre Coupe ten miles west of South Bend. A few Poles from Chicago found jobs at a sawmill there about 1870. Fred Miller, operator of a timber and lumber business, then began importing Poles as laborers. He contacted them in the Prussian-ruled area of Poland, had them met in New York, and financed their way to Indiana. They then repaid him with labor in the woods or at the sawmill. The swampy logged-off land was counted of little value. Poles could buy it for about $10 per acre and on generous credit. With this land and whatever else their meager savings purchased, the Terre Coupe Poles became farmers. Polish priests from Chicago and Otis visited them. In 1875 they began renting the township school for Mass and for catechism classes. After Czyzewski was installed as pastor at South Bend in 1877, the Polish farmers of Terre Coupe came to that city with their horse teams and wagons to help build the first Polish church. Czyzewski helped the Terre Coupe community in turn by providing ministry and encouraging their parish leaders. Terre Coupe Poles wanted a church. One settler contributed land. Fred Miller allowed them to cut trees from his forest and saw lumber at his mill without charge. They built St. Stanislaus Kostka Church for $1,800 and dedicated it in 1884.[60]

In a similar way Czyzewski developed a rural mission in 1888 among the colony of Polish farmers near the village of Rolling Prairie. As early as 1871 local landowners there had hired unemployed Poles from Chicago to clear and fence land in winter and to work as farm hands in summer. Their congregation was named in honor of St. John Cantius. Czyzewski and his Holy Cross assistant

Anthony Zubowicz continued to provide oversight to both Terre Coupe and Rolling Prairie for several years until other priests and teachers could be assigned.[61]

Czyzewski also conducted an urban ministry in the city of Chicago. Lithuanians there had organized the St. George Society to preserve their ethnic identity. They were particularly resisting being absorbed by the neighboring St. Stanislaus Church, largest Polish parish in that city. Czyzewski, fluent in both Polish and Lithuanian, was often invited to visit the St. George Society in the years between 1887 and 1892 to preach and to hear confessions. Since Czyzewski knew both languages and knew the people involved, the archbishop of Chicago enlisted him to help resolve the tensions between the Lithuanians and the Poles. At his suggestion and with his help the Lithuanians arranged with Catholic authorities to move their organizational center well away from St. Stanislaus and to develop a new Lithuanian parish of St. George on Thirty-Third Street.[62]

There was another long-standing controversy in Chicago between the giant Polish parish of St. Stanislaus and its mission church named Holy Trinity. They could not agree which religious affiliation of priests should be in charge. The papal delegation sent to Chicago to investigate also visited Notre Dame and conferred with Czyzewski. The decision was to bring in an outside order free of involvement in the old dispute, to request Holy Cross of South Bend to send one of its Polish-speaking priests to Holy Trinity. Czyzewski's young assistant Casimir Sztuczko went to be its pastor. During his fifty-six years there the church grew to include over 25,000 parishioners. Holy Trinity of Chicago became a sister church always closely linked with the Holy Cross priests and with the Polish parishes of South Bend.[63]

Polish parishes did multiply in South Bend. About 75 families had organized the first church in 1877. By 1890 there were about 6,000 Poles in the city and by 1900 that number had doubled to exceed 12,000. St. Hedwig grew crowded; members clamored for their own churches. Czyzewski made an announcement at Sunday Masses on 13 March 1893. "At 3:00 p.m. the Poles who live on the south side of the Grand Trunk railroad tracks, but only those who own their property, will meet to deliberate the choosing of a location to build a church in their area." They favored a location in a neighborhood south of St. Hedwig and full of immigrants from the Warsaw region of Poland. In 1896 Czyzewski formed a lay committee to move ahead on this building project. In March of 1899 the Poles of South Bend dedicated St. Casimir church with a seating capacity of 800 and six classrooms in the basement. The school grew steadily from 250 in 1899 to over 600 in 1910. The nickname of this second parish was Warsawa.[64]

Even as the campaign was on to build St. Casimir for the southwest sector of the city, Poles in the northwest sector were agitating for a parish of their own. The lay committee to accomplish this was at work by the end of 1897. In October of 1898 they broke ground. On 13 May 1900 Czyzewski was celebrant at the splendid dedication ceremony for the church of St. Stanislaus, Bishop and Martyr. It cost $23,900 and had room for 600 people. This third parish was nicknamed Poznan for the European home of many of its members, or Stanislawowo as a village form of the church name, or Zloty Gori (Golden Hills) after the name of a local subdivision of homes built by Studebaker and Oliver for their immigrant workers. Roman Marciniak of Holy Cross, its pastor from 1900 to 1928, led the congregation in building the rectory, the grade school for 500 scholars, and the convent for Sisters of the Holy Family of Nazareth.[65]

Czyzewski had one more church to build. It was for Poles to the west of St. Hedwig, an area called Krakowa because so many of its residents came from the Krakow region of Poland. Czyzewski helped them form the St. Adalbert Fraternal Aid Society in 1905. Then a lay committee began making its solicitation rounds, knocking week after week at the doors of heads of families employed by Oliver Plow Works to work ten hours on weekdays plus nine hours on Saturdays for an average weekly wage of $8.85. There were five years of fund raising picnics, socials, and bazaars. When they got within $8,000 of the goal, Czyzewski himself took a census of the proposed parish and made personal house-to-house collections. They dedicated St. Adalbert Church on 1 September 1911, a building of brick and stone to seat 900. It cost $40,000. St. Adalbert parish extended west to the city limits and into the neighboring swamps and woods. It would become the largest of the four Polish parishes in South Bend.[66]

Within the lifetime of Valentine Czyzewski the Poles had established an impressive presence in South Bend. They constituted a third of the city's population and had come to occupy about a third of its land area. They were thrifty homeowners. At first their children were prone to drop out of school. Within two decades Polish children were flourishing in their own parochial school system. St. Hedwig School was larger than any other parochial school or public school in the city. For the young Polish worker who somehow missed school and was handicapped by ignorance of English and arithmetic,

Czyzewski had arranged night classes at the Laurel Public School near St. Hedwig. The city board of education provided the building and the teachers. Czyzewski's parish house was the center for recruiting and registering Polish students.

The Polish parishes and schools were producing their own leadership for the rising generation. Czyzewski himself enlisted twenty-one priests, thirteen for Holy Cross and eight for dioceses. Five young men from his parish became Brothers of Holy Cross to teach in Polish-American schools. Twenty-seven young women from Polish parishes in South Bend joined the Sisters of the Holy Cross while he lived. There were several seminarians and recruits for other religious communities of women as well.[67]

The St. Hedwig Society of South Bend supported and shared the ethnic pride expressed nationally in the Polish Roman Catholic Congresses of 1896, 1901, and 1904. Some bishops might imagine they could phase out the use of the Polish language in America. The congresses lobbied instead for their right to make Polish the primary language of their churches and schools forever. They also demanded Polish bishops and archbishops to represent and govern the Polish churches of America. A Polish priest named Paul Peter Rhode was finally consecrated auxiliary bishop of Chicago in 1908.[68]

On the afternoon of 30 June 1913 Valentine Czyzewski made his last confession, received the sacrament of extreme unction, turned over the combination to the safe and the keys for the church buildings, and died. The Polish bishop Paul Rhode came to St. Hedwig to celebrate the funeral Mass. Estimates of attendance ranged between 10,000 and 15,000, including a host of dignitaries from across the nation. The mayor of South Bend was among the thousands of mourners walking the six miles from St. Hedwig to the Holy Cross cemetery at Notre Dame. In the procession were four bands and representative delegations from more than fifty parish and ethnic societies. Three newspapers, one Polish and two English, reported the funeral in detail on their front pages. They said it was the biggest funeral South Bend had ever seen.[69]

Polish Church Conflicts at South Bend

Some controversies came to culmination among the Poles of South Bend after Czyzewski died. The issues were the same ones which agitated Polish Catholics wherever they clustered in an American city. Poles who had stretched themselves to pay for parish property were slow to agree to a title making some American bishop the property's sole owner. Poles who believed they had taken over the European role of parish patrons intended to have the traditional patron's voice in selection of pastors.[70]

Czyzewski had carefully explained to the lay committee seeking property and money to build St. Casimir Church in 1898 that whatever they acquired would be legally held by Bishop Rademacher of Fort Wayne. When the Poles bought their own cemetery in 1906 so that Polish Catholics could be buried alongside other Polish Catholics at a location convenient to the West Side, Czyzweski had to break the news to them that the burial ground could not be consecrated until title was delivered to Bishop Alerding as custom required. For two years, until the anger cooled and the issue was resolved, no priest attended a burial there.[71]

The most painful conflicts at South Bend concerned appointment of pastors. The power to appoint belonged to the bishop of Fort Wayne. Most Polish-speaking priests conveniently available belonged to the Congregation of Holy Cross at Notre Dame and owed obedience to the superiors of that order. Assignment of pastors to West Side South Bend was generally done by Holy Cross, the bishop assenting and confirming.[72]

The older Polish community had some ambivalence toward both the bishop and Notre Dame. They were German and Irish instead of Polish. Notre Dame did cater to its small Polish constituency to some extent with an instructor in Polish studies and a Polish literary club. But well before the turn of the century it was becoming a rich, sporty, American-oriented, world class academic and scientific university. Boys from the West Side of South Bend who attended Notre Dame never came out quite as Polish as they were when they went in. Their loyalties had been won to the structure and culture of a wider church.[73]

The first pastoral explosion came at St. Adalbert. When that parish was ready for its first pastor in 1910, Bishop Alerding did not call on Holy Cross but sent John Kubacki who was one of his own diocesan priests. Kubacki was an outsider from Milwaukee and a graduate of Mount St. Mary Seminary in Cincinnati, now in a nest of Holy Cross priests long associated with South Bend. He was a man of immense energy and such zeal for pastoral authority that his parishioners came to call him the "czar of Krakow." Especially irritating on the West Side was Kubacki's affection for some contemporary American reforms. All the later immigrant groups were considered to be imbibers. Poles were generally conceded to be the heaviest drinkers of them all. Valentine Czyzewski had campaigned against excessive drinking among his Polish members and especially against the invasions of liquor into church functions. Now this priest Kubacki not only destroyed the bar they set up at the church picnic, he expected Poles to abstain from alcohol altogether.[74]

Kubacki led the parish members, including women and children, into demonstrations, parades, and rallies designed to close saloons and to abolish the entire liquor trade by 1920. He translated into Polish the classic temperance tract *Ten Nights in a Bar Room* and produced it as a drama at least three times among the immigrants on South Bend's West Side. From South Bend he operated a national crusade against drink among Poles. He became founder and president of the Polish Catholic Total Abstinence Union in 1912; its first convention was held at St. Adalbert. This national group had not only a monthly journal and an officership combining clergy and laity but also a Catholic League of Women, advertised as the first of its kind in the land. Incidentally, he opposed smoking, chewing gum, and the wearing of lipstick. Those who refused to comply were subject to stern pastoral rebuke, even in public or from the pulpit.[75]

Opponents at St. Adalbert were soon asking if God was different in their parish than in the other parishes. They complained to the bishop, to Holy Cross, to the Polish newspaper, and even to a civil court. On Easter Sunday of 1913 nearly a thousand of them protested by attending Mass at other churches rather than with Kubacki at St. Adalbert. It was all to no avail. Kubacki stayed until 1920 when he was finally transferred because of a difference with the bishop about proper routing of the proceeds of a parish collection.

On the very day that Valentine Czyzewski died, the South Bend *News Times* reported that about a hundred families were withdrawing from St. Adalbert to set up an independent church. They would continue to be Polish and religious and Catholic by affiliating with the Polish National Catholic Church presided over by Bishop Francis Hodur, native of Krakow and resident of Scranton, Pennsylvania. After separation from Roman Catholic authority, Hodur had become head of a growing fellowship of independent churches. He was consecrated in Holland in 1907 by three bishops of the Old Catholic Church. The continuing St. Mary of the Rosary Polish National Catholic Church, with its own building on Sample Street near St. Casimir and its own succession of priests, stood as visual testimony to a declaration of independence which divided the Poles of South Bend.[76]

St. Casimir parish had its explosion of independence too. Their pastor was assigned to succeed the deceased Czyzewski at St. Hedwig. They knew they wanted Leon Szybowicz, a popular former assistant recently assigned to a parish in Oregon, as their new pastor. The bishop and the superiors of Holy Cross did not appear to be complying with their wishes. An unofficial group of members held a meeting at Warsaw Hall, the popular dancing place and saloon operated by Democratic ward leader Frank Witucki and often used for parish meetings. They first sent word to Bishop Alerding that they would accept no other pastor but Szybowicz. After a few months without priests or sacraments they offered to accept a diocesan priest rather than a member of Holy Cross. In January of 1914 Bishop Alerding and Holy Cross provincial Andrew Morrisey appointed Holy Cross priest Stanislaus Gruza to be pastor of St. Casimir.[77]

Then the war began. Gruza tried three times in January to move into the St. Casimir rectory but parishioners drove him away. The bishop got a court order to give Gruza possession. The people ripped down the posted copies of the injunction and threatened to kill Gruza if he appeared. When he did appear on 8 February, a large crowd blocked his way. The bishop got a second court order for the sheriff to accompany Gruza and to use whatever force was necessary to guarantee him possession.

While the sheriff was in the church where Gruza was saying the first Mass celebrated there in several months, 1,000 parishioners were milling around the parish grounds. Twenty-three police arrived to quiet them. After a crowd of parish women had stormed and stripped the rectory, a riot broke out in which several people were injured including four policemen. Twenty-three people were arrested on what came to be called "bloody Sunday." The bishop charged George Kajzer and Frank Witucki as leaders of the riot and sued them for $10,000. Gruza reported "peace and tranquility" at St. Casimir by May. Only about 100 families left the parish, a few of them to join the small Polish National Catholic Congregation. The members, the parish, and the image of Polish unity were seriously but only temporarily bruised.[78]

The Polish community of South Bend moved ahead to its grandest period. Enthusiasm for freedom of the Polish homeland inspired participation in the First World War. St. Casimir alone sent 220 members into military service, eleven of them directly to the ranks of the Polish Army. In the community's golden days between the world wars, Poles earned respect by exercising their political strength. St. Hedwig established a Catholic high school open to both boys and girls. Then the four Polish parishes cooperated to make the old Laurel Public School building into their joint high school. Some competent young men went on to college and trained for professions. Such a variety of Polish businesses thrived that all necessities and most luxuries were available in the shops of the West Side. The parishes came to be served by a second generation of priests well attuned to the wants and needs of a second generation of parishioners. They had become Americanized together. After helping each other survive the terrible days of the Great Depression, congregations paid off their church debts and refurbished physical plants.[79]

Decline of Ethnic Urgency

In the very midst of those good days there were signs of dissolution. There was an English sermon at Mass in St. Hedwig in 1938. By 1942 there was at least one Sunday sermon in English at each of the four Polish parishes. An older generation of pastors had insisted that Polish language was the essential bond linking the people with their faith and church. A newer generation of pastors now said that many younger members were unwilling to attend Polish services at all. Sisters of the Holy Cross withdrew from the schools of St. Hedwig in 1937 because competence in Polish among their teachers was fading. Priests preparing for ministry in Polish parishes could take Polish classes at the Holy Cross seminary at Notre Dame, but their command of Polish grammar was often poor. Neither the younger generation of Poles nor the younger generation of priests considered excellence in Polish a high priority.[80]

The end of the Second World War marked the end of an era. Soon the Polish sermon and the Polish hymns were limited to no more than one Mass each Sunday. Parish organizations conducted their meetings in English for the sake of younger members. Statistics still looked respectable in 1957: St. Casimir with 2,237 parishioners and 426 children in school; St. Hedwig with 2,536 parishioners and 254 children in school; St. Stanislaus with 2,200 parishioners and 354 children in school. But Poles of the late 1950s did not want or need the same things as their ancestors did.

Polish Catholics using English began to seem much like other Catholics using English. In fact, the neighboring English-speaking Catholic churches and schools were the ones growing fast because younger Poles with their children were moving from the old West Side. In 1964 South Bend's Polish newspaper *Goniec Polski* ceased publication after sixty-eight years. Hardly anybody needed it any more. That same year the Congregation of Holy Cross, which had sent Valentine Czyzewski to South Bend eighty-seven years before, withdrew from St. Hed-

wig. The order felt it could no longer guarantee a supply of Polish-speaking priests. In 1930 the four Polish parochial grade schools on the West Side had a total enrollment of more than 2,800. In 1980 only the school at St. Adalbert remained and it was reduced to 200.[81]

West Side parishes took steps to adapt. St. Stanislaus tore down its school building and made a parking lot for those who would drive back to church in the old community. St. Hedwig, St. Stanislaus, and St. Casimir modified their church properties to provide "parish centers." These served the needs of the elderly Poles who remained on the West Side and of non-resident Poles who chose to keep coming back. They could also provide meeting rooms and neighborhood services for some of the new West Side constituency. Most of this constituency was no longer Polish but exhibited a wide ethnic variety.[82]

NOTES

1. Indiana's earliest and largest immigrations of Catholics, those of the Irish and Germans, are not under discussion here. In 1882 Indiana's Catholic parishes with predominantly German membership numbered 129, about 60 percent of the state's total. See James J. Divita, *Ethnic Settlement Patterns in Indianapolis* (Indianapolis, Ind.: Marian College, 1988), 16, 21–22, 28–29, 102, 105–6.

2. James J. Divita, *The Italians of Indianapolis: The Story of Holy Rosary Parish, 1909–1984* (Indianapolis, Ind.: Holy Rosary Parish, 1984), 23–24, 33–36; James J. Divita, "Indianapolis' Italian Monument: Holy Rosary Catholic Church," *Marion County/Indianapolis Historical Society Circular* 3 (October–November 1982): 4–7.

3. Special ministries for Italians were formed by Catholics at Bedford, Indianapolis, East Chicago, Gary, Elkhart, and Fort Wayne. Of these Holy Rosary Church at Indianapolis and Immaculate Conception Church at East Chicago persisted as parishes. Between 1908 and 1917 Protestant missions for Italians were established by the Methodists at Indianapolis, by the Presbyterians at Gary and Clinton, and by the Episcopalians at Gary. None of these resulted in a continuing congregation. See James J. Divita, "The Indiana Churches and the Italian Immigrant, 1890–1935," *U.S. Catholic Historian* 6 (Fall 1987): 325–49. See also James J. Divita, "The Italian in Indiana," *Italian Americana* 7 (Spring–Summer 1983): 77–90.

4. Rudolph J. Vecoli, "Prelates and Peasants: Italian Immigrants and the Catholic Church," *Journal of Social History* 2 (Spring 1969): 217–68; Divita, "Indiana Churches," 325–26.

5. Vecoli, "Prelates and Peasants," 236–39; Divita, "Indiana Churches," 333–34.

6. Divita, "Indiana Churches," 329; Divita, *Italians of Indianapolis*, 15.

7. Vecoli, "Prelates and Peasants," 251–53.

8. Divita, "Indiana Churches," 329–30, 332–33; Divita, *Italians of Indianapolis*, 15–21. A register of Holy Rosary families for 1909 is reproduced in Divita, *Italians of Indianapolis*, 17–21.

9. Divita, "Italian in Indiana," 80; Divita, *Italians of Indianapolis*, 14.

10. Divita, *Italians of Indianapolis*, 22–23.

11. Divita, "Indiana Churches," 333.

12. Divita, *Italians of Indianapolis*, 16, 23–26, 28–29, 31–34, 38–41.

13. Divita, "Indiana Churches," 342; Divita, *Italians of Indianapolis*, 41, 44–46, 52–54.

14. The Diocese of Indianapolis was elevated to the status of archdiocese on 19 December 1944 by decree of Pope Pius XII.

15. Divita, *Italians of Indianapolis*, 59–75.

16. James J. Divita, *Slaves to No One: A History of the Holy Trinity Catholic Community in Indianapolis* (Indianapolis, Ind.: Holy Trinity Parish, 1981), 1–6; Elavina S. Stammel and Charles R. Parks, "The Slavic Peoples in Indianapolis" (Master's thesis, Indiana University, 1930), 8–13.

17. Crystal Brenton Fall, "The Foreigner in Indianapolis" (Master's thesis, Indiana University, 1916), 22–27, 37; Divita, *Slaves to No One*, 9–15; Divita, *Ethnic Settlement Patterns*, 39, 43, 49, 51, 62, 64, 65.

18. Divita, *Slaves to No One*, 14–17, 49–55; for description of the Preseren Lodge which was secular and more hospitable to socialism, see p. 53–55.

19. Divita, *Slaves to No One*, 19–22, 37, 39, 59–60; Divita, *Ethnic Settlement Patterns*, 42–43, 68.

20. Divita, *Slaves to No One*, 23–38.

21. Divita, *Slaves to No One*, 39–41, 63–65, 79.

22. Divita, *Slaves to No One*, 63–76, 79.

23. Divita, *Slaves to No One*, 77, 79.

24. Stammel and Parks, "Slavic Peoples," 115–18, 177, 184; Divita, *Ethnic Settlement Patterns*, 110–12; Divita, *Slaves to No One*, 80–86.

25. Divita, *Slaves to No One*, 87–95; Divita, *Ethnic Settlement Patterns*, 97.

26. Edwin G. Kaiser, *History of St. John's Parish, Whiting, Indiana. Fifty Years of Grace, 1897–1947* [Hammond, Ind.: St. John the Baptist Church, 1947], 23.

27. Powell A. Moore, *The Calumet Region: Indiana's Last Frontier* (Indianapolis, Ind.: Indiana Historical Bureau, 1959), 79–81, 93, 178–80, 186; Kaiser, *History*, 13–17.

28. Moore, *Calumet Region*, 83–90, 170–72, 181–88; Kaiser, *History*, 18–19.

29. Moore, *Calumet Region*, 189–94.

30. Moore, *Calumet Region*, 196–211.

31. *Souvenir of the Golden Jubilee, Sacred Heart Church, Whiting, Indiana 1890–1940* [Whiting, Ind.: Sacred Heart Church, 1940], 6, 10; Moore, *Calumet Region*, 198–201.

32. Kaiser, *History*, 23–26.

33. Kaiser, *History*, 25–29, 31–32.

34. Kaiser, *History*, 21, 33–35.

35. Kaiser, *History*, 33, 39–45.

36. William Frederick Howat, *A Standard History of Lake County, Indiana, and the Calumet Region* (Chicago: Lewis Publishing Company, 1915), 445; Kaiser, *History*, 38.

37. *Souvenir. 30-Year Jubilee. Parish of Saint John's Church of Whiting, Indiana. 1897–1927* [Whiting: St. John Church, 1927], 17; Moore, *Calumet Region*, 215; Kaiser, *History*, 161.

38. Edwin G. Kaiser, *Jubilee Year 1897–1972: The Jubilee Story of St. John's, Whiting* (Carthagena, Ohio: Society of the Precious Blood, 1972, 196 p.); Kaiser, *History*, 48–49, 51, 58–60, 74–75; Moore, *Calumet Region*, 203.

39. Edwin G. Kaiser, *50 Golden Years: The Story of Holy Trinity Parish (Slovak), Gary, Indiana* [Gary, Ind.: Holy Trinity Parish, 1961?], 25–35.

40. Kaiser, *50 Golden Years*, 37–43, 183–84.

41. Kaiser, *50 Golden Years*, 41, 47, 49.

42. Kaiser, *50 Golden Years*, 58.

43. Kaiser, *50 Golden Years*, 49, 53–54, 57, 61, 69.

44. Kaiser, *50 Golden Years*, 70.

45. Kaiser, *50 Golden Years*, 69, 70, 75.

46. Kaiser, *50 Golden Years*, 78.

47. Kaiser, *50 Golden Years*, 76.

48. Kaiser, *50 Golden Years*, 54, 57, 76.

49. Kaiser, *50 Golden Years*, 93.

50. Kaiser, *50 Golden Years*, 47–48, 79–81, 88, 107–8, 115.

51. Kaiser, *50 Golden Years*, 85, 90–93, 108, 123, 137–38, 178, 184.

52. M. J. Madaj, "The Polish Immigrant, the American Catholic Hierarchy, and Father Wenceslaus Kruszka," in *The Other Catholics*, selected and introduced by Keith P. Dyrud, Michael Novak, and Rudolph J. Vecoli (New York: Arno Press, 1978), variously paged, this citation 26–28; Frank A. Renkiewicz, "The Polish Settlement of St. Joseph County, Indiana, 1855–1935" (Ph.D. diss., University of Notre Dame, 1967), 1–3.

53. Renkiewicz, "Polish Settlement," 5–6, 29–34.

54. Dean R. Esslinger, *Immigrants and the City: Ethnicity and Mobility in a Nineteenth-Century Midwestern Community* [South Bend] (Port Washington, N.Y.: Kennikat Press, 1975, 156 p.); Daniel S. Buczek, "Polish-Americans and the Roman Catholic Church," in *The Other Catholics*, selected and introduced by Keith P. Dyrud, Michael Novak, and Rudolph J. Vecoli (New York: Arno Press, 1978), variously paged, this citation 40–41; Leo V. Krzywkowski, "The Origin of the Polish National Catholic Church of St. Joseph County, Indiana," (Ph.D. diss., Ball State University, 1972), 57–74; Renkiewicz, "Polish Settlement," 35–38.

55. Donald J. Stabrowski, *Holy Cross and the South Bend Polonia* (Notre Dame, Ind.: Indiana Province Archives Center, 1991), 4–6; Renkiewicz, "Polish Settlement," 39–41.

56. Stabrowski, *Holy Cross*, 2–4; Renkiewicz, "Polish Settlement," 41–42.

57. Stabrowski, *Holy Cross*, 6–9; Renkiewicz, "Polish Settlement," 42–43; Krzywkowski, "Origin," 85, 92.

58. Krzywkowski, "Origin," 90–92; Stabrowski, *Holy Cross*, 9–10.

59. Gladys Bull Nicewarner, *Michigan City, Indiana: The Life of a Town* (Michigan City, Ind.?: G. B. Nicewarner, 1980), 206; Stabrowski, *Holy Cross*, 10; Krzywkowski, "Origin," 88–89; Renkiewicz, "Polish Settlement," 4–9.

60. *Diamond Jubilee. Saint Stanislaus Kostka Parish, Terre Coupe, Indiana, 1884–1959* (N.p., 1959?, 80 p.); Renkiewicz, "Polish Settlement," 5, 9–20; Stabrowski, *Holy Cross*, 10–11.

61. Renkiewicz, "Polish Settlement," 5, 12–20; Stabrowski, *Holy Cross*, 10–11; Krzywkowski, "Origin," 93.

62. Stabrowski, *Holy Cross*, 12–13; Krzywkowski, "Origin," 94.

63. Stabrowski, *Holy Cross*, 13–14.

64. Stabrowski, *Holy Cross*, 15, 17–21; Krzywkowski, "Origin," 94–96.

65. Stabrowski, *Holy Cross*, 21–24; Renkiewicz, "Polish Settlement," 110–13; Krzywkowski, "Origin," 96.

66. Krzywkowski, "Origin," 96–98; Stabrowski, *Holy Cross*, 24.

67. Stabrowski, *Holy Cross*, 15–16, 25; Renkiewicz, "Polish Settlement," 45, 121.

68. Madaj, "Polish Immigrant," 19–25; Buczek, "Polish-Americans," 50–54; Renkiewicz, "Polish Settlement," 182–89; Krzywkowski, "Origin," 138–39.

69. Stabrowski, *Holy Cross*, 31–33; Krzywkowski, "Origin," 108.

70. Jay P. Dolan, *The American Catholic Experience; A History from Colonial Times to the Present* (Garden City, N.Y.: Doubleday and Company, 1985), 181–85.

71. Stabrowski, *Holy Cross*, 25–27; Renkiewicz, "Polish Settlement," 190–93; Krzywkowski, "Origin," 144–45.

72. For rosters of priests trained by Holy Cross at Notre Dame and sent to the Polish parishes of South Bend, see Krzywkowski, "Origin," 136 and Stabrowski, *Holy Cross*, 86–89.

73. Thomas J. Schlereth, *The University of Notre Dame: A Portrait of Its History and Campus* (Notre Dame, Ind.: University of Notre Dame Press, 1976), 37, 58, 78, 104, 109; Krzywkowski, "Origin," 140–44; Renkiewicz, "Polish Settlement," 184–85.

74. Renkiewicz, "Polish Settlement," 21–22, 43–44, 196–99, 225–27; Krzywkowski, "Origin," 106.

75. Stabrowski, *Holy Cross*, 34–35; Renkiewicz, "Polish Settlement," 227–29; Krzywkowski, "Origin," 157–64.

76. Stabrowski, *Holy Cross*, 35–36; Renkiewicz, "Polish Settlement," 198–99; Krzywkowski, "Origin," 164–67. For a brief history and contemporary confession of faith of the Polish National Catholic Church, see *75th Anniversary. St. Michael the Archangel Polish National Catholic Church, East Chicago, Indiana* [East Chicago, Ind.: St. Michael the Archangel Polish National Catholic Church, 1978?, 107 p.].

77. Stabrowski, *Holy Cross*, 36–37; Renkiewicz, "Polish Settlement," 200–202.

78. Stabrowski, *Holy Cross*, 37–40; Renkiewicz, "Polish Settlement," 202–13.

79. Stabrowski, *Holy Cross*, 44–56, 59, 65–66; Renkiewicz, "Polish Settlement," 316–17.

80. Buczek, "Polish-Americans," 58–61; Stabrowski, *Holy Cross*, 44–51, 57–58; Renkiewicz, "Polish Settlement," 215.

81. Stabrowski, *Holy Cross*, 72–73, 76–80.

82. Stabrowski, *Holy Cross*, 75, 82–84.

About Orthodox

No one name or title is quite satisfactory for this family of churches. Some of them are Greek or Russian churches, but millions of Orthodox are neither of these. Sometimes they speak of themselves as the Eastern Orthodox Church or the Orthodox Catholic Church of the East, but Orthodoxy is by no means limited to eastern peoples. There are perhaps five million of the Orthodox in the patriarchates of Constantinople, Alexandria, Antioch, and Jerusalem. These ancient churches are held in special honor and their heads, like the Pope at Rome, bear the title "Patriarch." A hundred million or so of the Orthodox are in "autocephalous" churches (meaning "each with its own head")—in Russia, Romania, Greece, Serbia, Bulgaria, Georgia, Cyprus, Poland, Albania, and Czechoslovakia. Of these Greece and Cyprus are Greek and the rest Slavonic. Heads of these autocephalous churches may be called "Patriarch" or "Archbishop" or "Metropolitan."

Members of these bodies have migrated and multiplied to become an Orthodox diaspora around the world, not least a population of more than three millions among the ethnic richness of North America. So the "eastern" Byzantine Liturgy of St. John Chrysostom may be heard not only in Greek or Russian but also in French, English, German, Dutch, Spanish, or Italian. The Orthodox are generally at pains to distinguish themselves from the doctrines and practices of both Roman Catholics and Protestants, simply stating that they represent the true ancient church from which others have fallen away. St. Stephen Bulgarian Orthodox Church of Indianapolis said in its church consecration program in 1962 "The Eastern Orthodox Church regards herself as the 'Mother Church' of all Christians as she was the first church started by Christ, and over the centuries glories in the fact that she kept the religion pure and unchanged from its inception." Except for the Uniates described below, they grant no special jurisdiction to the Pope at Rome.[1]

The Ecumenical Patriarch at Constantinople is accorded a titular first place as the senior hierarch among the Orthodox heads much as the Archbishop of Canterbury is respected among national Anglican churches. It is an honor without authority, a primacy without power. As symbolized in this loose connection to the Ecumenical Patriarch, most Orthodox bodies are in some loose level of communion with each other. Most Orthodox bishops in the United States cooperate as participants in the Standing Conference of Canonical Orthodox Bishops in the Americas (SCOBA). Most Orthodox persons in America are members of churches represented in this conference.[2]

NOTES

1. Consecration Program, October 14, 1962, St. Stephen's Bulgarian Eastern Orthodox Church, 1435 North Medford Avenue, Indianapolis, Indiana [*Indianapolis, Ind.: the Church, 1962*], [8].

2. Timothy Ware, The Orthodox Church *(New York: Penguin Books, reprinted with revisions, 1983),* 9–16, 192; John Meyendorff, The Orthodox Church: Its Past and Its Role in the World Today *(London: Darton, Longman and Todd, 1962), 183–89; Paul D. Garrett, "Eastern Christianity," in* Encyclopedia of the American Religious Experience: Studies of Traditions and Movements, *ed. Charles H. Lippy and Peter W. Williams, 3 vols. (New York: Charles Scribner's Sons, 1988), 1:341–42; J. Gordon Melton,* Encyclopedia of American Religions, *3d ed. (Detroit: Gale Research, 1989), 9–14, 229–65.*

ORTHODOX

Rome, Constantinople, Alexandria, Antioch, and Jerusalem were five great centers of the early Christian Church. Because of its able leadership and its place at the heart of both church and empire, Rome came to be accorded first place in church councils and its bishop first place among the heads of the five patriarchates. However, all five claimed apostolic foundation and the heritage of the other centers continued.[1]

Constantinople was the glorious new capital of the Roman Empire from the year 330 and of the eastern or Byzantine Empire after 395. In spite of many assaults, this eastern empire was for centuries the center for Greek-speaking Christianity. The Greek missionary monks Cyril and Methodius developed a Slavonic alphabet in order to produce translations of Christian Scriptures and service books in the Slavonic language. These became the tools for the conversion of millions of Slavic peoples including Russians. Constantinople survived the decline of the Roman Empire in the West and was regarded as a kind of "second Rome." After the Ottoman Empire ruled the East and Constantinople fell to the Turks in 1453, Moscow noted its own ecclesiastical prominence and described itself as a kind of "third Rome." In vast regions of the East, Greek and Slavonic had become the tongues of the church.[2]

Meanwhile the Church at Rome had been battered by barbarian incursions but endured and transformed them. Institutions of the church became islands of stability during long periods of disorder and chaos. Its successful missions were among the western tribes, notably the Germanic Franks. Its ablest leaders wrote and taught primarily in Latin. For these western churchmen Greek and Slavonic were hardly basic concerns. So the major churches of East and West lost effective communication. They irritated each other in languages not clearly understood. By the year 1054 the two had nourished enough misunderstandings and exchanged enough insults to produce official schism. Exactly a century and a half later Latin Crusaders out of control violated the Greek world all over again by sacking the city of Constantinople.[3]

Some differences developed. In the eastern churches a parish priest could have a wife if he married before ordination, although bishops and hierarchs were generally chosen from celibates. The seventh ecumenical council (Nicaea 787) defined for both East and West how the honoring of physical religious likenesses was not image worship but an effective and useful practice of pious veneration. However the eastern churches venerated only stylized flat images called "icons" and developed a pattern of worship giving them a place of high honor. Icons were greeted by worshippers at the entrances to the churches. They were especially prominent at the front of the church on the "iconostasis," a screen or partition between altar and congregation behind which the priest conducted substantial parts of the Divine Liturgy. In the West, on the other hand, the religious representations might be flat or in bas-relief but were very often in full round.[4]

In the eastern churches every Mass was a sung high Mass based on the Liturgy of St. John Chrysostom or on the Liturgy of St. Basil the Great. So an eastern service was so long and impressive that any other order seemed anemic by comparison. In the West a shorter low Mass was more common and participation more frequent. The "seven mysteries" of the eastern churches paralleled the "seven sacraments" of the West but each became associated with some differences in practice and emphasis. The eastern schedules of church seasons and feast days varied widely among themselves but even more widely from western calendars.[5]

Heads of the eastern churches were frequently linked to the power and authority of their particular states and dependent on them for their very survival. Many easterners were convinced that only a council representing the whole Christian world could enunciate dogmatic teachings. Such a council was an ecumenical event now made practically impossible by church divisions. In the West, on the other hand, the authority of the Pope at Rome as enunciator and teacher was often asserted and widely accepted, even if that meant conflict with political powers.

Many Christians were uneasy with the divisions, especially in such areas as central Europe where eastern and western constituencies overlapped. Some energetic monastic orders from the West won allegiance of easterners for Rome. Some political rulers compelled submission. Some eastern church scholars who attended the rising universities of the West brought back a respect for the Latin church enterprise. One recognized accommodation was to grant the eastern church communities their married priests, their icons, and their beloved non-Latin liturgy if they would accept the jurisdiction of the Pope at Rome. Those who agreed to do this were called "Uniate" churches, the ones embodying a union of East and West. Hundreds of thousands of Slavs became Uniates, especially Slavs who were called by such names as Rusins (Ruthenians) or Galicians or Ukrainians or Carpatho-Russians, Slavs who lived in lands which lay adjacent to the Carpathian Mountains and came to be controlled by Austria-Hungary.[6]

Russian Orthodox in the Far Northwest

The Russians gave America its first Orthodox churches by way of the North Pacific. They owned Alaska, actively exploiting the fur animals and the natives there after 1743. When Gregory Shelikhov was establishing the town of Kodiak, he convinced the empress and the metropolitan back in St. Petersburg to send missionaries. Ten

monks came in 1794 but found very hard going against harsh frontier conditions as well as the resistance of political and commercial powers.

Nothing seemed to stop the Russian missionary giant John Veniaminov who arrived in 1823. He helped the people build churches. He mastered the language of the Eskaleutians. He translated the Gospel of Matthew, the liturgy, and a catechism into that language. He established a seminary at Sitka to train native clergy. When he was called home to be metropolitan of Moscow in 1868, he continued his support by founding an Orthodox Missionary Society. A century later he was proclaimed a saint in Moscow as "enlightener of the Aleuts and apostle to America."

Although most Eskaleutians and their descendants did remain Orthodox, the impact of this early missionary enterprise in the North was limited. The United States purchased Alaska in 1867. Most Russians left. Americanization of the area meant reducing Russian influence. Russian support faded for missions in America. The seat of the bishop transferred to San Francisco in 1872 and to New York in 1905. So the Russian Orthodox presence was continuous but the focus shifted from converting strangers to caring for the new urban immigrants who were already Orthodox. In such early locations as New Orleans (1864), San Francisco (1868), and New York (1870), the Russian Orthodox church accommodated the Orthodox from all countries for a time.[7]

Attraction of Russian Orthodoxy for a Variety of Slavic Immigrants

The first great wave of eastern Christians came to the United States from those Carpathian Mountains of Austria-Hungary. They were Uniates who used the Byzantine rite but acknowledged the jurisdiction of Rome. In theory there should have been a ready place for them among the Roman Catholics of America. In fact they presented a nasty dilemma to the nation's Irish and German bishops.

On one hand it would be a great risk to ask the diocese to integrate a poor uninvited immigrant priest with a long beard, a strange garb, a strange language, an irregular education, and a completely different pattern for conducting church life. There were troubling reports of failure and even malfeasance among such priests. Worst of all, this immigrant pastor might have been married once or might be married still with an equally strange wife and family gathered round him. On the other hand, refusal of the credentials and application of such a priest was likely to alienate both him and a cluster of immigrants enthusiastic for his ministry. Such immigrant clusters were always ethnically sensitized anyway and likely to want control of their church property in the hands of their own lay trustees.

After the Uniate priest Alexis Toth was denied official status as a priest by Roman Catholic archbishop John Ireland, he took his Minneapolis congregation of 365 Ukrainian immigrants into the Russian Orthodox Church in March of 1891. In spite of some top level Roman Catholic efforts to consolidate, regularize, and accommodate these newcomers, the route from Uniate to Orthodox became a path well trod. By 1916 about 163 such Catholic parishes in America had joined the Orthodox. Thus the American future of the Russian Orthodox church was assured. A majority of its national members were the Slavs who immigrated from the Carpathian regions.[8]

On 28 September 1911 a group of Slavs of Gary, Indiana, met at the home of Kondrat and Anna Krenitsky. Two visiting Russian Orthodox clergy from Chicago met with them. They discussed forming a church and contributed a beginning treasury of $263. The petition for a pastor went to His Eminence Platon, Russian Orthodox archbishop of North America and the Aleutian Islands. The priest Benjamin Kedrovsky arrived in Gary on 22 November. The next year the St. Mary congregation erected a wooden building 32 feet by 72 feet at the corner of 17th Avenue and Fillmore Street. It had a towering cross, onion-shaped cupolas, and pure white paint inside and out. The bell came from a city fire station.

Immigration to the Calumet Region kept increasing the St. Mary constituency. As was customary, Slavic immigrants from many east European areas and of several religious preferences rallied to support this new congregation, to celebrate completion of its building, and to attend the Slavonic language services. Russian Orthodox Day at St. Mary in October of 1928 brought "probably the largest group of dignitaries of the Russian Orthodox Church of North America ever to assemble at one parish." The St. Mary choir took first place in the Gary Music Festival in 1930 and second place that year in the Chicagoland Music Festival. In 1947 the church produced and published its complete Divine Service and Service Book "in the American language," that in step with the inevitable bent of Orthodox ethnics toward bilingual and then predominantly English usage.[9]

Gary was the birthplace of the American Russian Orthodox Youth Association (AROYA) and in 1947 was host city to the convention which expanded AROYA by merger to form a national organization of Russian Orthodox youth. For its fiftieth anniversary the St. Mary congregation was happily at home in its new church building at 45th Avenue and Maryland Street, a stone building complete with bulbous cupolas. There were three Russian Orthodox (now Orthodox Church in America) congregations in Indiana in 1990, two in Lake County and one in Allen.[10]

Uniate Congregations in Northern Indiana

Not nearly all of Indiana's Uniates chose to become Orthodox. St. Mary's Assumption Church in Whiting began and continued as a Byzantine Rite congregation under the jurisdiction of the Pope at Rome. Founded in October of 1899 by immigrants from the Carpathian Mountains region, it was the earliest Byzantine Catholic church in the Calumet Region and indeed in the entire Midwest. Uniate Slavic immigrants living in East Chicago, Indiana Harbor, Hegewisch, and South Chicago attended this church at Whiting. More Uniate immigrants kept coming and Slavs of various traditions were willing to attend because they could all pray together using the Byzantine Slavonic order. St. Mary's became mother to St. Michael Church of Gary and St. Nicholas Church of Hammond (later at Munster).[11]

In East Chicago the Holy Ghost Church on Olcott Avenue laid its cornerstone in 1917 and the Holy Ghost Church in the Indiana Harbor section of the same city opened at Fir Street in 1920. These Uniates were constantly battered by questions from Roman Catholic neighbors: "How can you really be Catholic and have priests who are married?" or "How can you really be Catholic with church services so different from ours?" Roman Catholic authority finally denied the Uniates a married clergy in America.

There were also divisions among the Uniates' own Slavic priests. Pastor Basil Merenkow at Holy Ghost Church on Olcott Avenue in East Chicago was determined that church should be truly Uniate and so united to Rome. A second priest working in the same congregation led a group of members unwilling to be "under the Pope." After a long battle, the civil court judgment in 1922 declared that Holy Ghost Church to be "an independent Greek Catholic Russian Orthodox Church, not under jurisdiction of Rome."

So Basil Merenkow and his followers had to begin again. About 34 of them were listed as Byzantine Ukrainians (Ukrajinyski), about 48 in a broadly mixed category as Byzantine Carpatho-Russians (Potkarpatskih), and a remaining majority as Rusins or Ruthenians. They formed St. Basil Church in East Chicago on 22 April 1923. Their new church building was on Indianapolis Boulevard; its bell cost $341.60 and was warranted "to be of full clear tone and not to crack while being rung in a proper manner for fifteen years."[12] The Uniate character of St. Basil, Byzantine rite plus union with Rome, was clear in its first official resolution on 22 April:

> The Faith of this church and Character of the same, and of each member, at this, the time of its corporate organization is, and shall be forever, Catholic, under the jurisdiction of the Holy Roman See and Its lawful representatives in the United States of America, the Bishop of Ft. Wayne, and the Bishop of the Greek Catholic Diocese of the United States of America. And be it further resolved that this church shall have the right to use the Rusin rites and ceremonies in its worship and ceremonies.[13]

Such devotion persisted among Uniates. These eastern Catholics, though loyal to Rome, would drive for miles past Catholic parish churches to worship with their ethnic colleagues according to a Byzantine rite. There were about a million Uniates in North America in 1990. Byzantine Rite Catholic congregations in Indiana's Lake County included four Ruthenian (Rusin) with 1,686 adherents, one Ukrainian with 64 adherents, and one Romanian with 322 adherents. The only other congregations of Byzantine Rite Catholics reported for the state were the Ruthenian in Marion County with 40 adherents and the Ukrainian in St. Joseph County with 53.[14]

Greek Orthodox at Indianapolis

Greeks were not prominent among the earliest eastern immigrants. In 1900 there were in America an estimated 250,000 Slavic Christians from the Carpathian Mountain region of Central Europe. At the same time there were only about 50,000 Greeks and five Greek parishes in all of North America. But the Greeks had an American archdiocese and about half a million constituents in about 160 churches by 1922. They were destined to become the largest body of Orthodox in the United States.

At first the Greeks were divided between loyalty to the patriarchate at Constantinople and loyalty to the autocephalous church of Greece centered at Athens. During the First World War and the years following they were split more seriously by the conflict in Greece between the Royalists supporting the lineage of King Constantine and the Venizelists supporting the prime minister Eleutherios Venizelos. Lay independence grew strong during the

years in which the leadership of the Orthodox clergy was fragmented by this division. Elected local laymen were often the ones who developed and directed parishes, hiring and ruling priests imported from Athens or Constantinople.[15]

Unity gradually came for the Greeks after Athenagoras Spirou was named archbishop of the Greek Orthodox Church of North and South America in 1930. By the time he was elected ecumenical patriarch in 1949, he and Greek Orthodoxy had become so visible and popular in America that Harry Truman had Athenagoras delivered to his new office in Constantinople (then Istanbul) in the private presidential plane. The Greek Orthodox claimed no continuing connection with Rome except the doctrine shared by East and West in the seven ecumenical councils up to the year 787. They were the proud inheritors of the major eastern rite. For them the natural culture of the church was Greek.[16]

Greek immigration quickened between 1890 and 1920. Most early arrivals were single men or were married men who had left their families behind them. Approximately 95 percent of the Greeks entering the United States between 1899 and 1910 were males. Many planned to live in cheap rented quarters, to save every possible dollar, and to take their accrued capital back to Greece. Michael Kouroubetis, for example, was able to bring his wife and son to join him in Mishawaka in 1921 but kept renting housing because he was committed to a "four-year program" to take the whole family back to Greece. Thirty years after the family's arrival this father finally announced the end of the "program" and the family bought a house in Indiana.[17]

Greeks did many kinds of labor but in American cities they frequently found employment in restaurants, bakeries, sweet shops, and small general stores. A substantial percentage managed to share proprietorship or become owners of pushcarts, shoeshine parlors, confectioneries, and cafes. They were less often employed as laborers in heavy industry and more often engaged in trade.[18]

Indiana had eighty-two Greeks in 1900. Twenty-nine of them lived among the 169,000 residents of Indianapolis. Most of them worked at the New York Central railroad yards at first or were peddlers. Peter Floros had learned the confection trade in Chicago. He opened his confectionery at 45 West Washington in Indianapolis in 1900, the city's first Greek business place. That year Pantelis Cafouros, headwaiter at the Claypool Hotel, joined in a plan with William Laspezes and a Greek priest who was a local railroad worker. They rented a third floor room in a bank building and began conducting religious services. The altar and iconostasis had to be set up prior to every service and removed afterwards. Services ceased when the priest left Indianapolis in 1903.[19]

By 1906 a dozen Greek men were in business in downtown Indianapolis. These leaders organized as a community (*kinotitos*) and elected officers. They established dues for members at $6 per year, about a week's wage for an immigrant. With this more stable base they rented the same room at the bank and hired Nicholas Velonis at $50 per month as pastor. This Holy Trinity was the first Greek Orthodox church in Indiana.

About 180 Greeks were living in Indianapolis by 1908, still the largest Greek community in the state. When Holy Trinity was formally incorporated in 1910, Pantelis Cafouros was president and Peter Floros was treasurer. Board members were Peter Konstandouros, Ernest Koumoundouros, Tomis Sioris, James Christofilakis, John Leckas, John Smyrnis, Paul Costas, James Clones, and George Georgokopoulos. They converted a two-story house into a church on North West Street in 1915. Kyrillios Georgiades, priest for the congregation in 1914 and 1915, moved in upstairs.[20]

Now there was a community of more than 250 Greeks to fast together during Lent or in August for the Falling Asleep of the Mother of God (Assumption). So far as their employment permitted they could celebrate Easter by their own calendar and Greek Independence Day on 25 March. Americans celebrated birthdays on the anniversary of the date they themselves were born but the immigrant Greeks celebrated their birthdays with other Greeks on the church calendar date honoring their particular name saint. They gave presents to each other at parties on St. Basil's Day, that date celebrated eastern fashion on the first day of January. Highlight of a St. Basil's Day party was cutting the *Vasilopita*, a sweet bread with a coin baked in it. Receiver of the piece with the coin was expected to be lucky for the coming year.[21]

At the very time that the Greek parish of Holy Trinity seemed to be coming to a healthy maturity, it was torn in two. On the international scene there were those Greeks who were Royalists and those Greeks who were Venizelists. Both parties became organized in America. At Indianapolis this was reflected in much bitter dialogue and two Greek congregations by 1919. The Royalist party was much larger but after a long and miserable judicial battle the Marion County Superior Court awarded all Holy Trinity property to the Venizelists on 14 December 1923. Over a period of four years the Royalists carried the legal fight for the property to the Indiana Supreme Court, losing all the way. Both parties limped

into the Great Depression impoverished and the Holy Trinity property actually sold for $9,194.98 at a sheriff's auction in November of 1931.[22]

The shock of that sale and the new leadership of John Zazas, wealthiest Greek in Indianapolis and one of the first Greek millionaires in the United States, moved the two groups of Greeks back together. Their new corporation repurchased the Holy Trinity property in 1934. They began meeting together and elected a united slate of officers in 1937. Archbishop Athenagoras Spirou was providing a national symbol of Greek unity, having reclaimed the episcopal function of appointing and discharging priests. The American Hellenic Educational Progressive Association (AHEPA) was a vigorous national promotional agency for Americanizing Greeks with a chapter in Indianapolis since 1929. It estimated the number of Greeks in Indianapolis and neighboring Central Indiana towns to be 1,800 in 1940. They were ready for a new era.[23]

The new era was the Second World War. Greeks were clearly on the "right side" this time and Greek prestige soared. The mother country stood against Nazi invasion. Indianapolis Greeks raised thousands of dollars for Greek War Relief, working alongside such symbolic non-Greek champions as Bishop Richard Kirchhoffer of the Episcopal Diocese of Indianapolis and President Herman Wells of Indiana University. Greek sons entered the United States armed services; four members of Holy Trinity were among those giving their lives.[24]

Chris Hadgigeorge was the first American born and American trained priest to serve the congregation. He joined parish officers Chris Pappas and Louis Andriakos in a door-to-door campaign which quintupled the paid membership of Holy Trinity to 450 in 1950. When they moved from North West Street to the new church at 40th and Pennsylvania in 1960, Archbishop Iakonos Coucouzes came to Indianapolis for the dedication and Pete Chochos was high bidder to cut the ribbon. The prizewinning building was "modern Byzantine" in design with sanctuary seats for 340 and a small chapel among its additional rooms.[25]

Competence in the Greek language declined along with the immigrant generation but did not disappear. Some children in the Sunday school memorized the Lord's Prayer in Greek and a few added the Nicene Creed. Mastery of the formal Greek of an ancient liturgy was even more demanding. Yet a substantial group continued to find it natural, right, and good to combine being American born in citizenship with being Greek Orthodox in faith and to do that as part of Holy Trinity at Indianapolis.[26]

Greek Orthodox at Gary

Soon after the new steel city of Gary was established in 1906, some Greeks settled there. When the first Greek died in 1911 his body had to be taken to Chicago for last rites. That made the Greeks of Gary begin talking about a Greek Orthodox church of their own. In spring of 1912 ten Greek families met for planning. They chose the name St. Constantine; the addition of the name of Constantine's mother Helen came some twelve years later. First services in 1913 were in a rented store building served by visiting priests from Chicago. They requested assignment of a priest from the autocephalous Holy Synod in Greece and received Nicholas Mandilas of Corfu in 1915.[27]

Now they needed a church building. They added their gifts and pledges to donations solicited from Greeks far and wide including Indianapolis, South Bend, and Marion. They broke ground at 13th and Jackson in 1917. When the war delayed construction they worshiped in a tent erected over the finished basement, this in the bitter winter of 1918. Dedication of the new building on 27 September 1919 was described in a Gary paper as "the most pretentious celebration among foreign-born citizens ever held in Gary." Bishop Alexander of Rodostolon officiated at the Divine Liturgy which lasted over four hours. Churchmen wore colorful ecclesiastical garments. The crowd of at least 4,000 contributed about $3,000 to the continuing effort. The Gary paper said, "The new church is one of the most impressive in this section of the country. The fact that the local colony of Greeks has about 300 and is one of the youngest in America makes St. Constantine church stand as a monument of the Gary Greek colony's ideals." The debt endured until 1942.[28]

The church at Gary did not escape the Royalist-Venizelist controversy. Those supporting the crown withdrew from St. Constantine in 1922. In 1926 Crown Prince Paul of Greece came to Gary to share in laying the cornerstone for their new Holy Trinity church at 11th and Jackson. In this case the influence of church authorities and the financial pressures of the Great Depression were enough to bring reunion in 1931.[29]

That very year the priest Irineous Cassimatis interrupted a trip from San Francisco to New York with a stop to visit friends at Gary. He stayed to serve the reunited SS. Constantine and Helen church for the twenty years until his elevation to bishop in 1951. In those years the congregation doubled. Church leaders were planning a new church in a new location in the 1960s. There were about 7,000 Greeks in the Gary area. Suburban acreage at 8000 Madison Street in Merrillville cost $200,000. Archbishop Iakonos dedicated the Hellenic Cultural Center, first unit of the SS. Constantine and Helen complex, on 14 May 1972. On the same visit the archbishop shared in groundbreaking for the addition of the new church. This Merrillville complex became the most prominent center of Greek Orthodoxy in the state.[30]

Greek Orthodox at South Bend

It was the Episcopal bishop Campbell Gray who alerted the Orthodox bishop to the Greeks of South Bend. Campbell Gray suggested that Philaretos Johanides pay a visit from Chicago to South Bend "where a prosperous and progressive group of Greek-Americans are in great need of a Greek Orthodox Church." The two bishops, assisted by clergy of the two faiths, conducted a joint service at South Bend on Sunday, 17 January 1926. There was ecumenical incense and much richness of liturgy and vestment. Philaretos Johanides said in his sermon: "The ties of friendship which exist between the Orthodox and Episcopal churches are gradually becoming stronger and stronger. Today's service in St. James' Episcopal Church is evidence of that friendship and respect."[31]

What Philaretos found at South Bend was a Greek population of about 60 families plus 125 unmarried men. He promptly met with representatives to organize a parish. The Poledor family offered a building lot and those present pledged over $10,000 as the basis of a church building fund. The building committee submitted a petition in proper form to which Philaretos responded:

> In the name of the Father and the Son and the Holy Ghost: know all by this letter: the undersigned Rt. Rev. Philaretos Johanides, Bishop of the Greek Orthodox Diocese of Chicago, Ill., grants permission to the faithful seventeen residents of South Bend, County of St. Joseph, State of Indiana, who signed the petition dated March 4, 1926, and which has been filed in the Archives of the Greek Orthodox Diocese of Chicago, to organize themselves, their families and neighbors and all those Orthodox Christians who will come after them, into a Parish for religious, charitable and educational purposes and which Parish shall be known as Saint Andrews and will be attached hereafter to the Constitution of the Greek Orthodox Diocese of Chicago, the Doctrines, Canons, Discipline, Rites and Usages of the One Holy Apostolic and Catholic Church or shortly and commonly known as the Greek Orthodox Church.[32]

It was understood from the beginning that St. Andrew parish at South Bend would serve the Greeks of Mishawaka, Elkhart, Goshen, and LaPorte as well. They made 1926 a banner year. They bought the property of the St. Paul German Evangelical Lutheran Church at Jefferson Boulevard and William Street and planned to spend $40,000 for its renovation. Philotheos Mazokopakis moved to South Bend from Chicago. He was the priest who led the congregation in the first service in the renovated St. Andrew church on 12 September and addressed the congregation in Greek at a splendid observation of the feast day of St. Andrew there on 5 December.

There were 118 male Greek names on the St. Andrew membership list. In April of 1926 forty-nine male Greeks became charter members of South Bend Chapter No. 100 of the Order of the American Hellenic Educational and Progressive Association (AHEPA); they paid initiation fees of $50 and annual dues of $20. In December of 1926 twenty wives of St. Andrew members formed the Good Samaritan Club; they paid initiation fees of $2 and dues of 50¢ a month besides undertaking a continuous agenda of plays, dances, and bake sales. Both organizations were devoted to St. Andrew Church, chief agencies of its lay support.[33]

St. Andrew Church of South Bend received the attention of some notable Greek Orthodox leaders. Bishop Philaretos of the Diocese of Chicago personally initiated the parish organization. He was back to celebrate the hierarchal Divine Liturgy for the first observance of St. Andrew's feast day in the South Bend church on 5 December 1926. He made the principal address as part of his consecration of the renovated and enlarged St. Andrew complex of church, chapel, and Greek school on 30 November 1930. That was also his farewell address since he had just been named archbishop of the Aegean islands of Syros and Tinos. Philotheos Mazokopakis was the special choice of Phileratos to be ordained and appointed for South Bend, the founding priest under whom the first building complex was completed and the membership doubled to more than 250. In January of 1936 Philotheos announced that he had been elevated to bishop and would return to Greece.[34]

Even the archbishop of the Greek Orthodox Church of North and South America, the great Athenagoras Spirou, chanted the hierarchal Divine Liturgy at South Bend on 17 August 1935. An observer wrote:

The walls of the church echoed with the vibrancy of His Eminence's voice, instilling in the congregation the thrill of a lifetime! With his full gray beard, distinctively ornate and glittering vestments, his pious reverence and king-like bearing, Archbishop Athenagoras was to leave an indelible mark in the minds as well as in the hearts of his listeners on that memorable Saturday morning![35]

On 30 November 1948 Athenagoras returned to celebrate the feast of St. Andrew's Day at South Bend. This time it was the colorful patriarchal Liturgy and St. Andrew was full of church dignitaries. Athenagoras had been elevated to the throne of ecumenical patriarch. He said to the assembly in English: "I have had to make a decision that saddens me beyond words. To ascend the sacred throne as a spiritual leader of the entire Greek Orthodox Church, I must renounce my American citizenship and become a citizen of Turkey, as required by the laws of my church."[36]

In the good years of the early 1950s the congregation of St. Andrew moved to South Michigan Street, into the facilities being offered for sale by Grace Methodist Church. At last they had a sanctuary facing east. It served a congregation of approximately 300 families about evenly divided between the Greeks of South Bend and those of neighboring towns.[37]

Not all the visits by bishops were happy celebrations. There were pastoral problems to be resolved. Nicholas Velis came to South Bend in summer of 1957 with a wife named Presbytera and three children named Demetra, George, and Stanley. The congregation was not ready to tolerate this married priest. He was reassigned to a long pastorate in Spokane. Pastor Dionysios Assimakidis always conducted the entire church service in Greek. He also required the trustees to speak only Greek at their meetings and to follow his precise priestly direction as president. When Iakonos Coucouzes, Greek Orthodox archbishop of North and South America, came to South Bend in October of 1963, Dionysios Assimakidis was replaced. The trustees resigned and were reorganized under archdiocesan uniform by-laws with a lay president. Subsequent visits to South Bend by Iakonos to celebrate St. Andrew's feast day in 1974 and to receive an honorary doctorate at Notre Dame in 1979 found the parish in order.[38]

The eyes of the congregation turned north to the suburbs. On 13 May 1978 a police escort accompanied the procession of members in their cars from the old church on South Michigan to the new location at 52455 North Ironwood Road. There they celebrated the Divine Liturgy to officially open the first building unit called the Good Samaritan Cultural Center; the women's group, the Good Samaritan Club, contributed $100,000 toward development of the new complex. After five more years of pledges, dances, dinners, festivals, bake sales, and bazaars, the South Bend congregation was ready for the highly anticipated 57th observance of the feast day of their patron St. Andrew. On 4 December 1983 they held the "Door Opening" (*Thiranizia*) for the all-new St. Andrew church and were led in the Divine Liturgy by the bishop of Chicago. About 400 attended the opening ceremonies and 330 the grand banquet.[39]

In this fellowship Greek culture was taught and respected. Catechism and liturgical instruction were available for the persistent who would attend Greek school on Thursdays. However, English was printed alongside the Greek in the hymnbooks for the choir and English was the language of church meetings. A parish historian noted: "Many changes have occurred since our parish moved into its new home. One of these changes is the influx of Orthodox from other ethnic backgrounds into our congregation and the fellowship we are sharing. We now have Serbians, Russians, Egyptians, Arabs, Syrians, Armenians, and many converts in our Church body. In reality, our congregation is Pan-Orthodox in nature." St. Andrew in St. Joseph County at South Bend continued as a modest but substantial community holding a respected place among the seven Greek Orthodox churches of the state. Of the others in 1990 three were in Lake County, one in Marion, one in Allen, and one in Porter.[40]

Serbian Orthodox at Gary

There was a larger proportion of eastern Orthodox residents in Gary than in any major city of the United States.[41] Notable among them was a concentration of Serbs. Gary's community of Serbian Orthodox became the nation's largest. They were quick to establish their own ethnic clubs for entertainment and mutual support. Serbs who were religious could worship in various churches in the Calumet Region which offered the Orthodox liturgy in Slavonic. As early as February of 1910 Serb leaders began campaigning for a Serbian Orthodox congregation of their own in Gary. Luka Grkovich, Mato Chuk, Dushan Chelovich, Jovo Marich, Tonasije Nastich, and Steve Orlich advocated a group proclamation the following March saying that life without religion and church was worthless and unthinkable for a Serb. In 1912 Gary's Serbs named a school board. It had few resources besides some generalized good will and a supply of Serbian children to educate. An officer of United States Steel provided a wooden shed at Fourteenth Avenue and Massachusetts Street. The city school system donated some desks. Members of that Serbian school board met Pavle Veljkov at a

Serbian convention in Cleveland and signed him up to come teach at Gary. The school bought a building lot at Twentieth Avenue and Connecticut Street. They could barely meet payments on the land itself but began construction of a building anyway. Serbs competed to see who could contribute the most work days.[42]

There were some apparent miracles. The Serbian benevolent society, named Milos Obilich, came through with a crucial gift of $50. At the time of the consecration of the building, E. G. Buffington of United States Steel donated $500. The simple building was both school and church, named for St. Sava (1176–1235), the greatest of Serbian national saints. The debt was paid in 1916. These were the days when Austria, Bulgaria, and Hungary were aligned against the Serbian nation. Nine brothers in one Gary family, along with 450 other Gary Serbs, volunteered to fight for their homeland on the Salonica front. Many others entered the armed forces of the United States. For a time St. Sava church and school delayed any major expansion. They improved the first building, provided educational and religious services at two outposts, and waited.[43]

The spectacular push for St. Sava came in the midst of the Great Depression. It became a marvel of Serbian solidarity. A separate Serbian church congregation agreed to merge with St. Sava for the sake of a united effort. Each of eight Serbian organizations in Gary agreed to name five of its members to the new church building committee. They were the Serbian Sisters' Circle; the Serbian Singing Society Karageorge; the Serbian Benevolent Society King Peter II; the Serbian Benevolent Society Srbadija; the Serbian National Defense Club; the Serbian Aid and Political Club Lika; the Serbian Benevolent Society Svesni Radnici; and the Serbian Sisters' Circle Queen Mary. United States Steel donated land at the corner of Thirteenth Avenue and Connecticut Street.

Chicago architects designed the new church, parish hall, and parish home. The building committee worked constantly and met every week. All the organizations made initial donations and kept contributing proceeds from their socials and picnics. Teams of solicitors called at the homes of Gary Serbs for donations, pledges, or loans. There were radio announcements asking Serbs to help build a magnificent house of worship. The Gary *Serbian Herald* listed the names of all contributors and the amounts donated.[44]

Almost all of Gary's Serbian people were present on 6 June 1937 to join Bishop Irinej Djordjevich in consecrating the cornerstone. They were still $15,000 short of enough to pay the contractor to get the building roughly finished in time for Christmas services. A gift of $5,000 from Carnegie Illinois Steel came just in time. With a final loan from a Valparaiso bank they finished the church, hall, parish home, school, library, and the fence around it all. Even the gift of three bells from the Serbian Sisters Circle Queen Mary was installed in time for the dedication on 24 November 1938. The Yugoslavian ambassador Konstantin Fotich and Yugoslavian consul Peter Cabrich were among the celebrants. This was the largest Serbian Orthodox congregation in the United States.[45]

Between 1947 and 1953 more than 1,000 Serbian displaced persons fleeing communist Yugoslavia were routed to Gary. Members of St. Sava were chief among those who signed as guarantors. They labored to provide the refugees translation, food, housing, jobs, and continuing counsel on their route to citizenship. The Old Slavonic language of the church liturgy, no longer taught in the schools of Serbia, was difficult even for native Serbs and the latest immigrants. For many Serbs born in America that Slavonic liturgy was incomprehensible. The 9 A.M. service at St. Sava became English in the 1950s; Slavonic service was at 10:30.[46]

Serbian Orthodox churches were thrown into a painful crisis in the early 1960s. Church authorities in Yugoslavia, always under the shadow of the government of the communist marshal Josip Broz Tito, sought to exercise their jurisdiction over their American membership. The congregation of St. Sava in Gary said that the Holy Council of Bishops held at Belgrade in Yugoslavia in 1963 was "enslaved." They said the pronouncements of that council as relayed by the official Commission on Religious Affairs of the state of Yugoslavia were invalid. They aligned themselves instead with a Free Serbian Orthodox Church led by Bishop Dionisije Milivojevich who was at that time in control of the Orthodox headquarters property at St. Sava Monastery at Libertyville, Illinois.[47]

Meanwhile other Serbs asserted their continuing loyalty to the autocephalous "Mother Church" in Belgrade and so with its bishop Firmilian of the Serbian Orthodox Church in the United States of America and Canada. There followed a terrible decade of suits and countersuits in civil courts for control of Serbian church properties. In 1976 the United States Supreme Court decided in favor of the Belgrade "Mother Church" party. Gary Serbs loyal to the Mother Church in Belgrade had already purchased a church building at 4101 Adams Street in spring of 1964 and named it St. Elijah.[48]

East Chicago Serbs loyal to Belgrade withdrew from the St. George church at Indiana Harbor in 1963. After fourteen years of congregational adventures they were ready to build a new Byzantine style St. George church at Schererville. The contract was for $795,000. The Movement of Serbian Chetniks, Ravna Gora, gave $5,000 for one of the three bells at the new St. George in memory of the heroic general Draza Mihailovich and all the Chetniks who had lost their lives in the Second World War.[49]

NOTES

1. Timothy Ware, *The Orthodox Church* (New York: Penguin Books, reprinted with revisions, 1983), 34–36.

2. Kenneth Scott Latourette, *A History of Christianity* (New York: Harper and Brothers, 1953), 306–11, 390–92; Paul D. Garrett, "Eastern Christianity," in *Encyclopedia of the American Religious Experience: Studies of Traditions and Movements*, ed. Charles H. Lippy and Peter W. Williams, 3 vols. (New York: Charles Scribner's Sons, 1988), 1:328; Ware, *Orthodox Church*, 82–85.

3. Raymond Etteldorf, *The Soul of Greece* (Westminster, Md.: Newman Press, 1963), 17–42; John Meyendorff, *The Orthodox Church: Its Past and Its Role in the World Today* (London: Darton, Longman and Todd, 1962), 39–60; Ware, *Orthodox Church*, 61–70.

4. Latourette, *History*, 292–97; Etteldorf, *Soul of Greece*, 148–53, 183–94.

5. Etteldorf, *Soul of Greece*, 77–113; Ware, *Orthodox Church*, 272–75, 286–95, 304–10; Garrett, "Eastern Christianity," 1:328–30.

6. Walter C. Warzeski, *Byzantine Rite Rusins in Carpatho-Ruthenia and America* (Pittsburgh, Pa.: Byzantine Seminary Press, 1971, 332 p.); Keith P. Dyrud, "The Establishment of the Greek Catholic Rite in America as a Competitor to Orthodoxy," in *The Other Catholics* (New York: Arno Press, 1978), 190; Bohdan P. Procko, "Soter Ortynsky: First Ruthenian Bishop in the United States, 1907–1916," *Catholic Historical Review* 58 (January 1973): 513–15; Ware, *Orthodox Church*, 101–11, 178–79; Garrett, "Eastern Christianity," 1:332–35. The term "Uniates" may be used interchangeably with "Eastern Rite Catholics" or "Byzantine Catholics" or "Byzantine Rite Catholics" to refer to those easterners in practice who accept the jurisdiction of Rome; see Garrett, "Eastern Christianity," 1:327.

7. Meyendorff, *Orthodox Church*, 118–19, 185; Ware, *Orthodox Church*, 135, 187–88; Garrett, "Eastern Christianity," 1:330–31.

8. Jay P. Dolan, *The American Catholic Experience: A History from Colonial Times to the Present* (Garden City, N.Y.: Doubleday and Company, 1985), 186–89; Dyrud, "Establishment," 190–226; Garrett, "Eastern Christianity," 1:332, 336–37.

9. Orthodox historian Timothy Ware saw the proper balance of Americanization with loyalty to the old ethnic nationalism as "the chief problem which confronts American Orthodoxy." See Ware, *Orthodox Church*, 189–93.

10. *Golden Jubilee, 1911–1961: St. Mary's Russian Orthodox Church, Gary, Indiana* (Gary, Ind.: the Church, 1961), [11–15].

11. *Anniversary Booklet of the Diamond Jubilee of St. Mary's Assumption Byzantine Catholic Church, 2011 Clark Street, Whiting, Indiana, 1899–1974* [Whiting, Ind.: the Church, 1974], 8; *Anniversary Booklet of the Golden Jubilee of the Church of Saint Basil the*

Great, 4316 Indianapolis Blvd., East Chicago, Indiana, 1923–1973 [East Chicago, Ind.: the Church, 1973], 22.

12. *Anniversary Booklet . . . Saint Basil the Great . . . 1923–1973*, 22, 24, 27.

13. *Anniversary Booklet . . . St. Basil the Great . . . 1923–1973*, 24.

14. Garrett, "Eastern Christianity," 1:342.

15. Demetrios J. Constantelos, *Understanding the Greek Orthodox Church: Its Faith, History, and Practice* (New York: Seabury Press, 1982), 128–47; Carl Christian Cafouros, "The Community of Indianapolis: A Microcosm of the Greek Immigrant Experience" (Master's thesis, University of Illinois at Urbana-Champaign, 1981), 28–30, 35–54; Garrett, "Eastern Christianity," 1:333–35, 340–41.

16. Garrett, "Eastern Christianity," 1:335, 340–41. As ecumenical patriarch, Athenagoras met with Pope Paul VI in Jerusalem in 1964, the first such conference between the Roman Catholic and Greek Orthodox leaders since 1439. The following year they agreed to a revocation of the mutual excommunication decrees of 1054. See *Encyclopedia Britannica*, 15th edition, 1:667.

17. Milton Kouroubetis, *The Greeks of Michiana: A Microcosm of the Greek Experience in America* (South Bend, Ind.: Northern Indiana Historical Society, 1987), 24; Cafouros, "Community of Indianapolis," 7–8.

18. For detailed descriptions of Greek employment patterns at South Bend and Indianapolis, see Kouroubetis, *Greeks of Michiana*, and Cafouros, "Community of Indianapolis."

19. *Seeds of Faith. Holy Trinity Hellenic Orthodox Church, Indianapolis, Indiana* (Speedway, Ind.: Shepard-Poorman, 1980), 12–13; Cafouros, "Community of Indianapolis," 9–11.

20. Cafouros, "Community of Indianapolis," 11–13, 18–20; *Seeds of Faith*, 13–16.

21. Cafouros, "Community of Indianapolis," 20–22, 84; *Seeds of Faith*, 16.

22. James J. Divita, *Ethnic Settlement Patterns in Indianapolis* (Indianapolis, Ind.: Marian College, 1988), 42, 52; Cafouros, "Community of Indianapolis," 35–54.

23. Cafouros, "Community of Indianapolis," 86, 93.

24. Cafouros, "Community of Indianapolis," 103–10; *Seeds of Faith*, 30–31.

25. *Seeds of Faith*, 31–34.

26. Constantelos, *Understanding the Greek Orthodox Church*, 151, 153–54; Garrett, "Eastern Christianity," 1:344; Cafouros, "Community of Indianapolis," 92, 113–14, 120–22.

27. *The First Sixty-Two Years of Saints Constantine and Helen Greek Orthodox Church of Merrillville, Indiana, 1913–1975* (Merrillville, Ind.: the Church, 1975?), 42.

28. *First Sixty-Two Years*, 42–43.

29. Raymond A. Mohl and Neil Betten, "The Immigrant Church in Gary, Indiana: Religious Adjustment and Cultural Defense," *Ethnicity* 8 (March 1981): 6; *First Sixty-Two Years*, 43.

30. *First Sixty-Two Years*, 42–48, 58, 60.

31. Kouroubetis, *Greeks of Michiana*, 131–33.

32. Kouroubetis, *Greeks of Michiana*, 136.

33. Kouroubetis, *Greeks of Michiana*, 126–30, 137–39, 141–50. South Bend Greeks also came to be organized as Daughters of Penelope, Maids of Athena, and Sons of Pericles. While their membership overlapped largely with that of St. Andrew, their association with the church was less overtly stated. See Kouroubetis, *Greeks of Michiana*, 226–36.

34. Kouroubetis, *Greeks of Michiana*, 144–46, 156–70.

35. Kouroubetis, *Greeks of Michiana*, 167.

36. Kouroubetis, *Greeks of Michiana*, 177–80.

37. Kouroubetis, *Greeks of Michiana*, 182–94.

38. Kouroubetis, *Greeks of Michiana*, 200–201, 211–13.

39. Kouroubetis, *Greeks of Michiana*, 219–20.

40. Kouroubetis, *Greeks of Michiana*, 218, 223.

41. Mohl, "Immigrant Church in Gary," 9.

42. *Our Religious Heritage in America. St. Sava Serbian Orthodox Church, Fiftieth Anniversary, 1914–1964. November 14, 15, 1964, Gary Indiana* (Gary, Ind.: the Church, 1964?), 58–59, 196; Mohl, "Immigrant Church in Gary," 9.

43. *Our Religious Heritage*, 79–82.

44. *Our Religious Heritage*, 116–17.

45. Mohl, "Immigrant Church in Gary," 6; *Our Religious Heritage*, 115–19.

46. *Our Religious Heritage*, 142–45, 150.

47. *Our Religious Heritage*, 161–62.

48. J. Gordon Melton, *Encyclopedia of American Religions*, 3d ed. (Detroit: Gale Research, 1989), 254; *St. George Serbian Orthodox Church, Dedication, July 26, 1980* [Griffith, Ind.: the Church, 1980], 20; Garrett, "Eastern Christianity," 1:340.

49. *Fiftieth Anniversary. Serbian Eastern Orthodox Church of Saint George, East Chicago (Indiana Harbor), Indiana. Souvenir Program, Sunday, October 29, 1961* (East Chicago, Ind.: the Church, 1961), [28]; *St. George Serbian Orthodox*, 32.

MUSLIMS

In theory Muslims could have kept their faith anywhere. No clergy, sacraments, or extraordinary facilities were required. There were the five "pillars of Islam." The first was the affirmation "there is no God but Allah and Muhammad is his messenger." The second was prayer facing Mecca with shoes removed and ablutions made, normally at dawn, noon, mid-afternoon, sundown, and late evening. The third was abstaining from sex, food, and drink during the daylight hours of the month of Ramadan. The fourth was paying the prescribed alms to support the needy. And the fifth was making at least one pilgrimage to Mecca if finances allowed. Muslims believed in God, in angels as agents of God, in the Scriptures freed of corruption and perfected in the Quran, in prophets or messengers culminating uniquely in Muhammad, in a coming day of judgment, and in the absolute priority of God's will. All of life was to be shaped by the Quran along with the sayings and example of the Prophet as recalled and interpreted by the Muslim community.

In theory a believer could keep this faith anywhere, but in fact being a solo Muslim was very difficult. A believer longed for the support of fellow believers. Life in a civil state wholly committed to Islamic principles was counted ideal. At the very least there should be a substantial Muslim fellowship united to respect the proper lunar calendar and to establish the regular life of Islamic prayer and practice. Members of such a fellowship could also encourage each other to observe the rules of dress

and diet. For the sake of young people there should be enough of a constituency to provide Muslim schooling and Muslim marriage partners.[1]

Early Muslims in America

America had no such Muslim support community for a long time. Following the migration of the prophet Muhammad from Mecca to Medina in the year 622, Islam had swept over much of the Near East. Its traders had carried the faith deep into Africa and Asia. But the early flow of settlers to America did not come from these places. There were a few Muslims among the early explorers. There were black slaves imported from Africa whose ritual practices and refusal to eat pork have been attributed to Islam. Several Muslims shared in a failed attempt to introduce camels to the American Southwest in the 1850s, a certain Hajj Ali (nicknamed Hi Jolly by Americans) being the one best remembered. Alexander Russell Webb was U.S. consul in the Philippines. He became a student of eastern religions, a convert to Islam in 1888, and author of *Islam in America* in 1893. None of these were the basis for a substantial Muslim establishment.[2]

Muslim strength came to America in the twentieth century. By then its variety was impressive. As the Ottoman Empire deteriorated economic conditions were especially bad in Syria, including the portions later named Lebanon, Jordan, and Palestine. Muslims moved from there to the American Midwest.

A home in Ross, North Dakota, was being used as a mosque in 1900. One of the earliest Muslim communities in America was at Michigan City, Indiana. Industry in the Detroit area attracted Arabs from Syria and Lebanon as well as Muslims who were Turks, Albanians, Yugoslavs, and Indians. The concentration of Muslim mosques, coffee houses, groceries, and restaurants at South Dearborn in Michigan was unique in America. Communities formed around extended Muslim families such as the Ajrams at Cedar Rapids, the Barakats and Alwans at Toledo, the Khans at Sacramento, and the Diabs at Chicago.

There were perhaps 100,000 Muslims in the United States by the early 1960s. They had organized themselves into the Federation of Islamic Associations of the United States and Canada (FIA). About 1,000 gathered at Michigan City, Indiana, for the ninth conference of this FIA in 1959. They elected wealthy sportsman Muhammad Khalil (James Calil) of Detroit as president. Muslims in this small minority seemed to be proceeding on a fairly normal ethnic immigrant track toward "Americanization" and economic success. They were in some danger of losing their Islamic identity.[3]

Increased Muslim Immigration Following the Second World War

There was an important new stream of Muslim immigrants following the Second World War. It was in full flow by the 1960s. National governments of the Near East were undergoing transition. Some of the new political leaders were sending their students to America for university education. At the same time Muslim activists out of governmental favor arrived from such countries as Palestine, Egypt, Iraq, Syria, Yugoslavia, Albania, and the Soviet Union. Estimates of the total number of Muslim students enrolled in American colleges and universities ranged from a high of 750,000 to a low of 100,000.

Muslim merchants and professional persons, especially scientists and engineers, also chose to locate in America. For example, about 6,000 Muslim physicians established practice in the United States. These were no longer simply economic refugees from a few depressed areas overseas. They were by no means limited to the Arabs, who comprised perhaps 20 percent of the world's Muslim population. They were representatives of the most intelligent and best educated from among the Muslims of more than sixty countries. Some were critical of the extent to which those Muslims immigrating earlier had "adjusted" to the American scene. Many newcomers

were moved to formulate and articulate their faith with a new clarity. They became advocates for Islam in the face of an indifferent or even hostile American cultural environment. At Urbana, Illinois, in 1963 they organized the Muslim Student Association (MSA).[4]

By 1971 the secretariat of this lively fellowship was headquartered at the Al-Amin Mosque in Gary, Indiana, and in 1973 a full-time executive director was added. In 1975 they began developing a new headquarters on a tract of 124 acres near Plainfield, Indiana, to serve the United States and Canada. Plainfield was on its way to becoming the nation's most prominent service center for about two million Muslims of "immigrant" origin, constantly generating more organizations and programs to support Muslims and to advance Islam.[5]

Black Muslims

Alongside the two million American Muslims of "immigrant" origin served from Plainfield were another two million "indigenous" Muslims of quite different origin. These were the so-called Black Muslims. A host of African Americans whose forebears had been in America for generations sought and found their identity in Islam. Noble Drew Ali (Timothy Drew) explained that blacks were Asiatics or "Moors." Islam, he said, was the religion of the Moors while Christianity was for whites. He founded the Moorish-American Science Temple in Newark, New Jersey, in 1913. Moorish-American branch locations included Philadelphia and Detroit. About the time Drew Ali died in 1929, W. D. Fard (or Wali Fard, Wallace Fard, W. F. Muhammad) developed the teaching further. Blacks were really Muslims, he said, who should be gathered into "The Lost-Found Nation of Islam in the Wilderness of North America." Fard soon disappeared, assumed by many to have been Allah himself on a mission to designate a new prophet.[6]

Elijah Muhammad was the new prophet who rose to leadership of the Nation of Islam and to the role of "Messenger of God" sent to enlist and separate the blacks into their own Islamic nation. Many identified themselves as Muslim members of the original tribe of Shabazz. The white man was seen as Satan. The message of Elijah Muhammad had great power. His most prominent disciple Malcolm X told the crowd at Manhattan Center on 4 December 1963: "The Honorable Elijah Muhammad is turning hundreds of thousands of American 'Negroes' away from drunkenness, drug addiction, nicotine, stealing, lying, cheating, gambling, profanity, filth, fornication, adultery, and the many other acts of immorality that are almost inseparable from this indecent Western society."[7]

Black Muslims were required to attend at least two meetings per week at the temple. They were urged to hold steady jobs; they were forbidden to gamble, overeat, or buy on credit. One-third of earnings was the suggested contribution to the movement. Both the members and the organization acquired pride and property. The membership was predominantly young, male, lower class, indigenous, American, and ex-Christian. Because their language was violent and their action dramatic, Black Muslims were always in the news. Elijah Muhammad and Malcolm X marshalled the membership with the tabloid *Muhammad Speaks* published weekly from Chicago, with regular radio broadcasts over a national network of stations, and with a militant institutional organization. By 1960 there were sixty-nine temples or missions in twenty-seven states from California to Massachusetts. The membership was variously estimated between 50,000 and 500,000; the constituency was far larger.[8]

The Nation of Islam underwent dramatic changes. Malcolm X, its most effective organizer and evangelist, left the movement in 1964 after a dispute with Elijah Muhammad. He had made a pilgrimage to Mecca that year. As a result of that experience he affirmed racial unity as he had seen it practiced at the center of world Islam. He renounced the Black Muslim gospel of racial separation and took the name el-Hajj Malik el-Shabazz, meaning the Malcolm from the tribe of Shabazz who made the pilgrimage. He was assassinated while lecturing in Harlem on 21 February 1965. Two members of the Nation of Islam were convicted of the murder.[9]

Elijah Muhammad died in February of 1975. One of his six sons, Warith (or Wallace) Deen Muhammad, succeeded him as supreme minister. But Warith was also a scholar, a student of orthodox Sunni Islam on the world scene. Soon after Elijah Muhammad's death, Warith denied that his father had borne any special prophetic role. He declared that whites were no longer to be viewed as devils and could join the movement. He turned from the rigid disciplinary rules of Elijah Muhammad and from the militant organizational control. In fact he declined to be either chief hierarch or economic administrator.

The properties of the Nation of Islam, valued at some $80 million at the death of Elijah Muhammad, were largely dispersed. In 1985 Warith Deen Muhammad actually dissolved the movement's formal organization altogether. Members were simply to be Muslims. He himself chose to continue an informal but highly influential personal ministry as a teacher of Islam. His continuing

means of communication were his weekly *Muslim Journal*, his radio broadcasts, and his wide itineration among a "people" which included multiplied thousands of faithful constituents.[10]

Such radical change was too much for Louis Farrakhan, who gathered a group in 1978 to resurrect the old Nation of Islam. Farrakhan and his followers continued the doctrines and militant practices of Elijah Muhammad. They advocated the earlier goals of racial separation and black nationalism. But they were a distinct minority. The main body of black or indigenous Muslims had become part of the wider Muslim community. They entered into various forms of joint worship and work. Along with their unofficial leader Warith Deen Muhammad, they were in constant dialogue with one another, with the equally large body of immigrant Muslims in America, and with the whole company of world Islam.[11]

Islam in Indiana

Indiana received some early Muslim immigrants. Since they arrived in the twentieth century, the industry of northern Indiana was ready to attract and employ them.[12] Michigan City was a pioneer point for Islam. Hussein Boudeed Mohamed gathered a small group of Syrians and Lebanese to form the Bader Elmoneer Society there in April of 1914. After 15 May 1924 it was known as the Asser El Jadeed Arabian Islamic Society.

The mosque they built at Michigan City in the early 1920s was reported to be the first one separately constructed in the United States. It was a two-and-one-half-story building with minaret. Islamic events for a wide region were hosted there. The congregation members kept "Americanizing" in many respects but continued an Islamic presence at a new location on Brown Road after 1973. In 1976 this immigrant Muslim community at Michigan City had about fifty families from Lebanon and Syria, two from Palestine, and four from India and Pakistan. In September of 1978 about 200 attended the Michigan City celebration (*Eid al-Fitr*) at the close of the fast of Ramadan.[13]

When Elijah Muhammad and Malcolm X raised their voices from Detroit or Chicago for the Black Muslims, they were heard in Indiana. The reader of *Muhammad Speaks* for 22 December 1972 was invited to "visit Muhammad's temples of Islam; hear the life-giving teachings of the Honorable Elijah Muhammad, Messenger of Allah." Meetings listed were on Sunday at 2 P.M. and Friday at 8 P.M. at the temple at 431 South Dundee in South Bend. They were on Wednesday and Friday at

8 P.M. and Sunday at 2 P.M. in the temple at 2246 Broadway in Gary. From stations within the state one could "listen to Mr. Muhammad every week on the radio" at WJOB Gary-Hammond every Sunday at 5:30 P.M.; at WJVA South Bend every Sunday at 4 P.M.; at WTLC Indianapolis every Sunday at 10:30 A.M.; and at WLBC Muncie every Sunday at 10:30 A.M.

Most black or indigenous Muslims in Indiana agreed with Warith Deen Muhammad when he moved to a more moderate and ecumenical position after his father died in 1975. Some, in the manner of Malcolm X, had denied the radical racial separation of Elijah Muhammad's Nation of Islam even earlier. At Gary many African Americans went into Islam soon after Elijah Muhammad died without going through the Black Muslim movement at all.[14]

It was the later immigrants who made Islam stand out in Indiana, especially the foreign university students and the foreign professionals. One of them, Ismail R. Al-Faruqi, was a Palestinian, a trilingual graduate of the American University of Beirut. The new state of Israel displaced him from his position as governor of Galilee. He became a seeker and a scholar of great intensity. In America he earned master's degrees at Indiana and Harvard universities and, in 1952, a doctorate in philosophy at Indiana. Lois Ibsen, holder of the bachelor of music degree from the University of Montana in 1948 and the master of music degree from Indiana University in 1949, became Lois Ibsen Lamya' Al-Faruqi; Lamya' was the Muslim name she chose as a convert.[15]

Ismail Al-Faruqi immersed himself in the study of Islam at the Al-Azhar University in Cairo from 1954 to 1958. Back in North America he taught Islamic studies at McGill University and the University of Chicago and Syracuse University and Temple University. He authored, edited, or translated twenty-five books, published more than 100 articles, was visiting professor in at least twenty-three universities in Africa, Europe, the Middle East, and Asia, and served on the editorial boards of seven major journals. He was founder of a society of American Muslim social scientists. He was founder and first president of the American Islamic College in Chicago. He developed the first program of Islamic studies within a religion department of an American university. Everywhere he was an unabashed representative of Islam, a highly qualified participant in worldwide ecumenical events but a totally reliable Muslim advocate. "There was a time in my life when all I cared about was proving to myself that I could win my physical and intellectual existence from the West, that I could succeed as a man of the West," he said. "But, when I won it, it became meaningless. I asked myself: 'Who am I? an Arab? a Palestinian? a philosopher? a liberal humanist?' My answer was, 'I am a Muslim.'" He dedicated much of his life to correcting misinformation about Islam.[16]

Lois Al-Faruqi earned her doctorate from Syracuse University in 1974 in an interdisciplinary program combining music, art, and religion. She published more than fifty major articles and lectured widely, often on the aesthetics of Islam or on the place of women in Muslim culture. The Faruqis had a particular affection for Muslim youth. When Ismail was introduced to the MSA in 1963, "it was love at first sight." Foreign students were perennial guests among the Faruqi family of seven in their Philadelphia home. Black Muslim children of the neighborhood came there for music lessons. These two Indiana alumni were mentors to scores of young Muslims. At the same time they were builders of an intellectual foundation for a major segment of American Islam. On 27 May 1986 both were murdered by a criminal housebreaker.[17]

It was the MSA which contributed most to Indiana's Islamic character. There were local chapters, grouped into regions and zones. There was an annual general assembly and an executive committee to shape assembly decisions into action plans.[18] In the early years it was economical to hold annual MSA conventions on college campuses. Ezzat Jaradat presided over such a convention in Bloomington, Indiana, beginning 14 May 1976 as did Yaqub Mirza in May of 1977 and Rabie H. Ahmed in May of 1978.[19] Development of the new MSA headquarters near Plainfield planted a substantial Islamic presence right in Indiana's middle.

Many non-student American Muslims were attracted by the vitality of the rising student institution. Graduates who remained in America as professionals or as merchants or as employees in the general economy found it natural to relate to MSA as a center of their continuing Islamic identity. So Plainfield, Indiana, became the mailing address for such organizations as the American Muslim Scientists and Engineers (AMSE), the American Muslim Social Scientists (AMSS), and the Islamic Medical Association (IMA).

By the time of the two annual conventions at Bloomington in May 1981 and May 1982, presided over by Sayyid M. Syeed, it was officially recognized that the breadth of this immigrant Muslim organization had grown far beyond its student membership. The 1981 meeting was still a convention of the MSA. By 1982 the MSA, AMSE, AMSS, and IMA had taken their places as affiliated units within an entity named the Islamic Society of North America (ISNA). This new ISNA came to be headquartered in a new $5 million center and mosque on the acreage near Plainfield.[20]

ISNA sought to enable the immigrant Muslims of America to practice and support their faith within the American religious system of voluntary societies. The United States was not an Islamic nation and its government would not be a primary source of legal or economic support. Contributions from Islamic donors abroad were likely to taper off and end. Muslims needed to develop agencies and disciplines for functioning in a pluralistic culture. They needed to rally that majority of their nominal adherents who did not attend mosque and whose children were more likely to be memorizing American popular music than the Quran. They needed effective ways to commend their faith to non-Muslim Americans, something more creative than recitals of the errors of America.[21]

Success in America would mean faithfulness in Islamic belief and practice. It was also likely to mean volunteering for work, diligence in study, participation in politics, maintaining schools, and providing ministers (imams) whose pastoral duties soon had many similarities to those of the Christian clergy. All this would certainly mean contributing money. Said the advocates of one "action plan": "ISNA has outlined more than 60 projects for the raising of Islam and the Muslim community, and the betterment of life in North America in the coming years. This offers Muslims the world over multiple ways to purify their wealth and to get involved in Islam in America, spiritually, intellectually, and physically."[22]

Many services of ISNA were offered from Plainfield through the pages of *Islamic Horizons*. This monthly went to all major centers of Muslim population in the United States and Canada, estimated a readership of 70,000 in 1986, and claimed to be "read by more Muslims, more frequently, and in more places than any other Muslim journal in this continent." It contained quotations from sacred writings. Islamic leaders contributed expository articles and exhortations. Editors printed their opinions; readers responded to the editors and to each other. Steve Johnson, a Catholic doctoral student at Indiana University who converted to Islam in 1981, frequently gave counsel on effective techniques for Muslim witness in a predominantly Christian culture.[23]

Secretary General Iqbal Unus employed the pages of *Islamic Horizons* to enlist members for ISNA; he also highlighted individual causes of ISNA combined in its annual budget which grew to a million dollars and still cried for expansion.[24] Muslim women dialogued through the paper about their place in Islam.[25] As conferences and

conventions multiplied, *Islamic Horizons* announced their programs and reported on their achievements.

P.O. Box 38 at Plainfield was ready to receive relief contributions for Muslims in distress in such places as Somalia or Bangladesh or Afghanistan. Alms money sent to Plainfield undesignated would be directed to the worthiest of Muslim applicants. Correspondence sent to ISNA at this address could supply a speaker, arrange hospitality for a group at Plainfield's Islamic Center, initiate a correspondence course on Islam, or register an inquirer for intensive study of Arabic.[26]

The North American Islamic Trust (NAIT) at Indianapolis held titles to the MSA properties of the nation including mosques and student houses. It loaned money to purchase sites for new mosques. As the financial agent of ISNA, NAIT supported at Indianapolis the most active Muslim publishing house and the largest Islamic audio-cassette duplication facility in North America.[27] These materials were regularly offered for sale in *Islamic Horizons*. NAIT also advertised its readiness to receive money from clients for investment in a mutual fund which conformed to Islamic principles. Islamic Book Service at 10900 West Washington in Indianapolis used *Islamic Horizons* to advertise its devices programmed to signal prayer times anywhere in the world and point the direction to Mecca.[28] A "matrimonials" page in many issues offered to open communication among persons seeking Muslim marriage partners.

The officers and leading members of ISNA were candid about their goal which was to win North America for Islam. For them association with America was not a taint to be avoided as some Islamic separatists seemed to believe. America was not best viewed as an enemy or a problem. For Muslims sensitive to the activist model of Al-Faruqi, America was Allah's gift of opportunity as a field for mission. ISNA did not wish to become another "Islamic movement" or a captive of any Muslim faction. It sought to be an inclusive service organization for all Muslims, an umbrella for a dozen Muslim organizations and half a hundred nationalities, an enabler for the great joint evangelistic mission, a unifier.[29]

Seeking Islamic Accord

Moderation, unity, and openness as a basis for conducting a mission to America was not an easy stance for American Muslims to maintain. New immigrations kept coming. Old ethnic allegiances were not dead. Professor Akbar Muhammad of the State University of New York observed:

Many so-called Islamic concepts and practices which are apparent in this country are traceable to ethnic origins abroad, or to ethnic circumstances in the United States. Historically, certain Islamic schools of thought become more prevalent than others in particular ethnic groups or nationalities. For example, most Afghans are Hanafis, as are Turks, Indians, Pakistanis and Bangladeshis. Most Egyptians, Indonesians and Malaysians are Shafi'is. Most Sudanese, Libyans, Moroccans, Tunisians, Algerians, Nigerians and Senegambians are Malikis, while the majority of Saudis are Hanbalis. Most Iranians are Shi'is. The Gulf region is heavily populated by Shi'is, Zaydis, Shafi'is and Hanafis. Indeed, different schools and sub-schools exist in individual countries. These differences in some areas of Islamic interpretation are accompanied by non-religious aspects of the ethnic or national culture of Muslim immigrants in America, and perhaps of their offspring . . . The tendency of Muslims in this country is to congregate and socialize with members of their national or cultural group . . . After 'Id prayers and during 'Id celebrations and other Islamic occasions, the worshippers tend to break up into cultural/linguistic groups.[30]

When Iran and Iraq waged war on the Persian Gulf, for example, Iranian and Iraqi minorities in America grew tense. Perennial political and theological differences at home and abroad kept threatening to make American Muslims as sectarian as Protestants.[31]

At the same time non-Muslim Americans would often attribute to Muslims a false and negative unity. Persons fed only on American news media were likely to link all Islam unhappily with oil monopoly or hostage taking. In spite of ISNA's protests that "Islam forbids terrorism" and "there is no compulsion in religion," the adjective "Muslim" was often made to modify the nouns fanatic or fundamentalist or terrorist.[32]

In some notable respects unity did improve. The historian of the Michigan City mosque said: "The congregation, during World War I, was composed primarily of members of the Syrian and Lebanese Moslem community in Michigan City. Since that time, however, and in the same pattern that the United States has developed the present congregation contains a mixture of European, Asian and Latin American descendants."[33]

Even more impressive than this mosque sharing among the immigrants was the erasing of rigid lines between immigrants and the American blacks. Once the immigrant Muslims would have denied that the black separation of the Nation of Islam and their elevation of Elijah Muhammad could be called Islam at all. And the Black Muslims would probably have frisked the immigrants for weapons if they admitted them to their temples

at all. But after Malcolm X and Warith Deen Muhammad adopted orthodox Islam and after Warith Deen Muhammad officially dissolved the separate black Muslim structures, the barriers were down. A community mosque might be known to be predominantly immigrant or predominantly black indigenous but it was no longer exclusively so. At the old Al-Amin mosque on Eleventh Avenue in Gary, the new Al-Fajr mosque on Cold Spring Road in Indianapolis, or the new mosque on Atwater Avenue in Bloomington, all Muslim attenders would be welcome.[34]

Islamic Conventions

Islamic conventions also helped to bridge the old divisions. Annual assemblies of the MSA began modestly at college campuses; five were held at Indiana University in Bloomington between 1976 and 1982. Later, as conventions of ISNA, they became bigger and more inclusive. They moved to larger urban centers. Attendance reached about 4,000 when the Muslims set up their assembly rooms and bazaar booths for the 1986 meeting at the Convention Center in Indianapolis. Senator Richard Lugar was among the fifty speakers invited.[35] Abu Khalil Grant said of the bazaar at the 1987 ISNA convention at Peoria:

> You have to admit, the parade of sales tables is enticing, displaying products for all the senses: over-powering musk oils, books in English, jewelry, Qur'an tapes, books in Arabic, clothing for children and adults, petitions to be signed, magazines, books in Urdu, fancy prayer schedules, protest literature, video tapes of Ahmad Deedat boxing Jimmy Swaggart, "I Love Islam" bumper stickers, "I Love Islam" T-shirts, and relief funds' relief funds.[36]

Jesse Jackson, aspirant to the nation's presidency as candidate of a racially blended constituency that he called a "rainbow coalition," addressed Muslims of the United States and Canada at their 25th Anniversary meeting in the Convention Center at Indianapolis. That was on Labor Day weekend of 1988. Women sat on one side of the auditorium and men on the other with the children gathered at Jackson's feet. He said, "Black and yellow, red and white, they are precious in Allah's sight." A convention goal was registration of Muslim voters before the 1988 election and their full participation in American political processes. After the speech Ahmed Zaki Hammad, president of ISNA, gave Jackson a copy of the Quran, saying: "We believe that your call to take religion seriously will be more complete if you focus more on Islam and the Muslims." Then Hammad asked to have the auditorium lights turned up on that racially varied Muslim audience so Jackson could see "the true hues of a rainbow coalition."[37]

On Labor Day weekend in 1991 there were 140 commercial booths in the bazaar for the ISNA annual convention at Dayton, Ohio, the largest number ever. Attendance was up to 6,064. Jawaad Abdul Rahman of Lawrenceburg, Indiana, said the convention had the three essential components: education, brotherhood and sisterhood, and business.[38]

It had also become the custom of the Muslim constituents of Warith Deen Muhammad (once called Black Muslims or Nation of Islam or Bilalians and still widely known unofficially as the American Muslim Mission) to hold a convention each Labor Day weekend. The one at Atlanta in 1992 had 160 vendors and about 7,000 attending.

The old division between the conventions of the immigrants of ISNA and the conventions of the indigenous with Warith Deen Muhammad began to ease.[39] When Warith Deen Muhammad came to Indianapolis to speak at Indiana's Black Expo on 11 July 1992, Governor Evan Bayh declared it Muslim American Appreciation Day in recognition of Warith's work. The governor's office gave Warith a key to the city. The officers of ISNA invited him to Plainfield where the two groups talked about possible joint projects. They discussed an exchange of convention delegates and agreed to form a committee to consider an occasional joint convention. The very next week the Islamic Circle of North America, an elite Muslim fellowship of Urdu heritage, broke tradition by welcoming Secretary General Ahmed El Hattab of ISNA to address its annual convention.[40]

Christians were paying some attention to these worshipers of Allah also. There were at least tentative openings for Muslim dialogue with Catholics and with major Protestant bodies. The National Council of the Churches of Christ in the U.S.A. established its Office on Christian-Muslim Relations in 1977 and welcomed the attendance of Muslim leaders at governing body meetings as observers.[41]

Statistics on the number of Muslims in the United States remained inexact at best. Nahid Kahn said, "The number of Muslims in North America seems to equal x times the square root of one's mood." There was no clear way to define membership since each mosque was simply a meeting place for an undelineated community rather than an organization to be joined. Nor was there a compilation of reported attendance at the year's greatest

festival (*Eid al-Fitr*) at the end of the fast of Ramadan. Estimates, based on everything from pure conjecture to analysis of the census reports of the nation's ethnic complexion, have ranged from less than one million to at least nine million. Carol Stone's "verifiable and rigorous estimate" published in 1991 placed the number at four million for 1986.[42]

Estimates of the number of Muslims in Indiana have been equally uncertain. Stone concluded that more than one-third of Muslims in the United States were concentrated in New York, California, and Illinois. A compilation published by Yvonne Haddad in 1986 indicated eighty-two mosques or centers in New York, fifty-nine in California, thirty-three in Illinois, and thirty-one in New Jersey. However Indiana was well above the median of states on Haddad's chart with twenty. She reported five of these mosques or centers as Muslim Student Associations on university campuses. The campuses were probably Indiana University at Bloomington; Purdue University at West Lafayette; Indiana University–Purdue University at Indianapolis; Indiana State University at Terre Haute; and Ball State University at Muncie. She reported seven "Masjids of the American Muslim Mission," predominantly black or indigenous congregations likely to be related to the leadership of Warith Deen Muhammad. These probably included Daniel Muhammad Islamic Center in Indianapolis; Gary Masjid; Gary Muslim Center; Masjid Mujahideen in South Bend; Muslim Center in Evansville; and Masjid Muhammad in Michigan City. The remaining eight "Mosques/Centers" on her chart probably included the pioneer Islamic Center at Michigan City; the historic Jamaat Masjid Al-Amin and its school at Gary; Islamic Teaching Center at Plainfield; Masjid Fajr at Indianapolis; and the Angola Islamic Center.[43]

It was the location of the ISNA headquarters at Plainfield which gave Indiana a substantial presence in Muslim history. Concepts of the size and strength of ISNA varied also. In the 1980s there was a small core membership of about 6,500 and a total membership in ISNA and the twelve or so affiliated societies of about 100,000. An issue of *Islamic Horizons* ran about 25,000 copies for an estimated readership of 70,000. An ISNA leaflet for general distribution warranted a printing of about 200,000. In 1987–88 the Islamic Teaching Center, one unit of ISNA based in Plainfield, conducted 165 lectures and 41 interfaith dialogues. That Teaching Center unit received over 4,300 requests for literature. It sent out 8,500 Qurans, 175,000 pamphlets, 27,000 booklets, and 7,000 books. The center reported that it received

1,000 requests for Islamic literature from prison inmates but could fill only half. In spite of these fairly modest figures, the ISNA at Plainfield was in some sense the primary center and service organization for a population of at least two million immigrant Muslims.[44]

NOTES

1. Newell S. Booth, Jr., "Islam in North America," in *Encyclopedia of the American Religious Experience: Studies of Traditions and Movements*, ed. Charles H. Lippy and Peter W. Williams, 3 vols. (New York: Charles Scribner's Sons, 1988), 2:723–25; Yvonne Y. Haddad and Adair T. Lummis, *Islamic Values in the United States: A Comparative Study* (New York: Oxford University Press, 1987), 16–23; Yvonne Y. Haddad, *A Century of Islam in America* (Washington, D.C.: American Institute for Islamic Affairs, 1986), 8; *The Muslim Community in North America*, ed. Earle H. Waugh, Baha Abu-Laban, and Regula B. Qureshi (Edmonton, Alberta: University of Alberta Press, 1983), 99.

2. J. Gordon Melton, *Encyclopedia of American Religions*, 3d ed. (Detroit: Gale Research, 1989), 156; *American Journal of Islamic Studies* 1 (Spring 1984): v–ix; Booth, "Islam in North America," 2:725; *Muslim Community in North America* 94.

3. *The Muslims of America*, ed. Yvonne Y. Haddad (New York: Oxford University Press, 1991), 11–14; Booth, "Islam in North America," 2:725–26; *Muslim Community in North America*, 94–95.

4. *Muslims of America*, 4, 14–18, 126; Haddad, *Century of Islam*, 2, 7, 10–11; *Muslim Community in North America*, 94; *Islamic Horizons* (July 1987): 8.

5. *Muslims of America*, 14–18, 131–32, 240–41; Booth, "Islam in North America," 2:727.

6. C. Eric Lincoln, *The Black Muslims in America* (Boston: Beacon Press, 1973), 17, 18, 23; C. Eric Lincoln, "The American Muslim Mission in the Context of American Social History," in *Muslim Community in North America*, 215–33; Beverly Thomas McCloud, "African-American Muslim Women," in *Muslims of America*, 177–87; Abubaker Y. Al-Shingiety, "The Muslim as the 'Other': Representation and Self-Image of the Muslims in North America," in *Muslims of America*, 53–61; Clifton E. Marsh, *From Black Muslims to Muslims: The Transition from Separatism to Islam, 1930–1980* (Metuchen, N.J.: Scarecrow Press, 1984, 149 p.); C. Eric Lincoln and Lawrence H. Mamiya, *The Black Church in the African American Experience* (Durham, N.C.: Duke University Press, 1990), 388–91; Haddad, *Century of Islam*, 3–5; *Encyclopedia of the American Religious Experience*, 2:765–70; *Muslims of America*, 18–20, 134.

7. *The End of White World Supremacy: Four Speeches by Malcolm X*, edited and with an introduction by Benjamin Goodman (New York: Merlin House, 1971), 123–24. When Black Muslims cast off their slave surnames borrowed from slaveowning masters, they sometimes substituted "X" for their own unknown family name. Thus Malcolm Little became Malcolm X.

8. Lincoln, *Black Muslims*, 4, 20, 24–28; *Muslims of America*, 134; *Encyclopedia of the American Religious Experience*, 2:767.

9. *Encyclopedia of the American Religious Experience*, 2:768; Haddad, *Century of Islam*, 4.

10. Warith Deen Muhammad's paper was first *Muhammad Speaks*, then the *Bilalian News*, then the *American Muslim Journal*, and then the *Muslim Journal*. See Haddad, *Century of Islam*, 4–5.

11. Julia E. Gaber, "Lamb of God or Demagogue? A Burkean Cluster Analysis of the Selected Speeches of Minister Louis Farrakhan" (Ph.D. diss., Bowling Green State University, 1986, 186 p.); Lawrence H. Mamiya, "Minister Louis Farrakhan and the Final Call: Schism in the Muslim Movement," in *Muslim Community in North America*, 234–55.

12. There was one fascinating claim of evidence that the earliest impact of Islam on Indiana came through the nomadic Ben Ishmael Tribe early in the nineteenth century. However, the evidence and the impact appeared scant. See Hugo P. Leaming, "The Ben Ishmael Tribe: A Fugitive Nation of the Old Northwest," in *The Ethnic Frontier*, ed. Melvin G. Holli and Peter d'A. Jones (Grand Rapids, Mich.: William B. Eerdmans, 1977), 97–141.

13. *Islam in Michigan City, Past and Present* (Michigan City, Ind.: Islamic Center, 1976?), 2–3; Gladys Bull Nicewarner, *Michigan City, Indiana: The Life of a Town* (Michigan City, Ind.: the Author, 1980), 212–13.

14. Lincoln, *Black Muslims*, 18; *Muhammad Speaks*, 22 December 1972, 31; and 29 December 1972, 14; Letter of Jim R. Kenward, Community of Al Amin Mosque, Gary, Indiana, to L. C. Rudolph, 14 December 1992.

15. John L. Esposito, "Ismail R. al-Faruqi: Muslim Scholar-Activist," in *Muslims of America*, 65–79; "Tributes to Dr. Ismail al-Faruqi and Dr. Lamya' al Faruqi," *Islamic Horizons* Special Issue (August–September 1986): 84 p.

16. *Islamic Horizons* (August–September 1986): 32.

17. *Islamic Horizons* (August–September 1986): 32–33, 50–51, 78–79; (January–February 1987): 21.

18. The Al-Amin Mosque at Gary was not an early one but its history illustrated some major currents of Islam in Indiana. The building dated from about 1946. It was first a culture center for the Muslim families of Yugoslavs, Bulgarians, and Turks who came in the early twentieth century. Their identity was lost by assimilation; their tombstones remained in Oak Hill Cemetery. In the 1970s Al-Amin provided office space for the national office of the predominantly immigrant MSA. It also served as mosque and center for substantial numbers of blacks who were coming into Sunni or orthodox Islam. Neighborhood youth used it for recreation. After the MSA office moved to Plainfield, the Al-Amin community was predominantly black or indigenous but shared by Muslims of a wide variety. There was a full-time grade school. The mosque treasurer reported in 1992: "Currently at Friday prayers about half of the congregation is African American and one-fourth is from the Indian subcontinent and the rest are Arab. There are two European Americans. We have had a recent influx of Palestinians. They seem to come from the same families and towns. They have a cultural building in Whiting, Indiana. Many of them live in East Chicago. The Indians tend to be professionals (primarily in the medical field) and the Arabs tend to be businessmen with food stores in Gary. Many of them live in Munster and south of Route 30." Information from letter of Jim R. Kenward, Community of Al-Amin Mosque, Gary, Indiana, to L. C. Rudolph, 14 December 1992.

19. *Islamic Horizons* (April 1986): 4.

20. *Islamic Horizons* (January 1984): 2; (July 1984): 4; (March 1985): 2; (June 1985): 2, 8; Meredith B. Herman, "A Phenomenological Study of the Islamic Society of North America" (Th.D. diss., Southern Baptist Theological Seminary, Louisville, Ky., 1989, 305 p.).

21. Contributions to ISNA from Islamic governments overseas ceased by 1988 though individuals abroad continued to support. See *Islamic Horizons* (November 1986): 6; (January–February 1988): 6.

22. Booth, "Islam in North America," 2:727; *Muslim Community in North America*, 22–25; *Islamic Horizons* (March–April 1988): 10.

23. *Islamic Horizons* (November 1984): 3, 8, 10; (January 1985): 8, 10; (March 1985): 4; (September 1985): 8; (October 1985): 3, 5, 6; (December 1985): 8; (January–February 1986): 29; (March 1986): 18; (January–February 1987): 12–13.

24. *Islamic Horizons* (February 1985): 2; (May 1985): 14; (June 1985): 3; (October 1986): 9; John O'Neill, "Runs Big Operation Near Plainfield," Indianapolis *Star*, 14 July 1985.

25. *Islamic Horizons* (April 1986): 8–9; (July 1986): 6; (August 1987): 39.

26. *Islamic Horizons* (April 1984): 7; (September 1984): rear cover; (December 1984): 15; (January 1985): 14; (March 1985): 2; (May 1985): 5; (June 1985): 8; (March 1987): 13; (April 1987): 10; (August 1987): 8–9.

27. *Islamic Horizons* (March–April 1988): 36–41.

28. *Islamic Horizons* (May 1984): 5; (May–June 1986): 6; (July 1986): 12 A–D; (October 1986): rear cover; (July and August 1987): inside front cover.

29. Larry A. Poston, "Da'wa in the West," in *Muslims of America*, 125–35; *Islamic Horizons* (March 1986): 4; (May–June 1989): 6. In an undated leaflet entitled *Lighting the Way to Unity*, ISNA indicated its continuing bridge role with these twelve Muslim societies accessible through Plainfield: Muslim Students Association of US and Canada, Islamic Medical Association of North America, Association of Muslim Scientists and Engineers, Association of Muslim Social Scientists, Muslim Youth of North America, Muslim American Chamber of Commerce and Industry, Council of Islamic Schools of North America, Amana Mutual Fund, American Muslim Council, Fiqh Council of North America, North American Islamic Trust, Muslim Arab Youth Association.

30. Akbar Muhammad, "Some Factors which Promote and Restrict Islamization in America," *American Journal of Islamic Studies* 1 (August 1984): 45.

31. Steve A. Johnson, "Political Activity of Muslims in America," in *Muslims of America*, 111–24; Yvonne Y. Haddad, "American Foreign Policy in the Middle East and Its Impact on the Identity of Arab Muslims in the United States," in *Muslims of America*, 217–35.

32. *Islamic Horizons* (May–June 1987): 15; (March–April 1989): 11, 20, 43, 45.

33. *Islam in Michigan City*, 2.

34. *Muslim Community in North America*, 101–2; Indianapolis *Star*, 3 February 1990; Bloomington *Herald-Times*, 3 January 1994.

35. *Islamic Horizons* (April 1986): 4; (July 1986): 10; (October 1986): 8–13.

36. *Islamic Horizons* (November 1987): 20.

37. *Islamic Horizons* (July–August 1988): 22–23, 58; (September–December 1988): 27–29, 50–56; Indianapolis *Star*, 4 September 1988.

38. *Islamic Horizons* (Winter 1991): 38–42.

39. *Muslim Journal*, 25 September 1992, 1; 16 October 1992, 5.

40. *Islamic Horizons* (Summer 1992): 7–9, 16.

41. *Muslims of America*, 40–43; *Muslim Community in North America*, 275.

42. Nahid Khan, "The Numbers Game," *Islamic Horizons* (September–December 1988): 21–23; Carol L. Stone, "Estimate of Muslims Living in America," in *Muslims of America*, 25–35; Haddad, *Century of Islam*, 1.

43. Stone, "Estimate," 29–30; Haddad, *Century of Islam*, 6.

44. *Islamic Horizons* (March–April 1989): 57; (Winter 1991): 37.

SCIENCE AND RELIGION

Indiana's early citizens engaged day by day in coping with the world of nature. Most of the natural science they learned was of the pragmatic sort valued in country life. Those who were constituents of Christian churches blended their faith nicely with the instruction they received at home or in the rudimentary schools. Leaders of the churches were often the leaders and teachers in these schools. Science had a low profile.

The intellectually privileged few who attended the state's infant academies and colleges during the first half century, at least to 1850, were likely to regard their science and religion as entirely compatible. Strenuous biblical literalism was not a passion among these elite. It was hardly a subject of speculation whether the mountains would literally break forth into singing (Isaiah 55:12) or whether the serpent in the garden walked upright and shared human language (Genesis 3).

Statements by geologists that the earth had been formed over enormous time periods were seldom offered or received as denials of God or challenges to faith. Those concerned to reconcile geology with the Bible learned that the "days" of the first chapter of Genesis had been regarded as ages since the time of such venerable church fathers as Augustine and Albertus Magnus and Thomas Aquinas. For those who found this day-age interpretation awkward, there was the "gap" understanding which provided for an indeterminate period between the events of the first verses of Genesis, sufficient time to accomplish all geologic processes.[1]

If the Hoosier academy or college was engaged in science at all, it was likely to have a professor of natural philosophy or natural history. In such an academic position a professor had ample room to teach and demonstrate all that he knew or could inspire his students to search out about any or all of the natural and physical sciences. A unity of science and religion was assumed. Yankee Presbyterian missionary Benjamin C. Cressy addressed the Zelo-Paideusian Society of the prestigious Washington County Seminary at Salem at its fifth annual exhibition on 14 March 1834. The tenor of his speech was that science and religion together elevate individual as well as national character.

> Let science and religion, then, be encouraged; and ignorance and vice, with all their concomitants of woe, shall recede before the blazing light of that day, when incense and pure offering shall arise from every heart;—when nation after nation shall catch the loud chorus,—peace on earth, good will to men,—and the world, itself, shall be raised to that elevation, to which the human powers seem destined by the great Proprietor of the universe.[2]

Scientific field work concentrated on collection of impressive "cabinets" of natural specimens. Scientific instruction in college was likely to be presented as a disclosure of the "evidences" of God's handiwork everywhere in the universe. In 1853 Professor William C. Larrabee of Indiana Asbury University at Greencastle (DePauw University after 1884) published his *Lectures on the Scientific Evidences of Natural and Revealed Religion.* This course he had offered to thousands of young men in the three schools he served over a period of twenty years. At the end of the marvelously comprehensive compilation of 453 topics he concluded with confidence: "Fear not to bring revelation to the test of science. Be assured, if there seem an inconsistency between any chapter of any department of science and the teachings of revelation, there must be some error in the assumption of fact, or some mistake in interpretation, or some fallacy in your reasoning."[3]

Instruction in natural philosophy was further integrated with basic values and beliefs by a course of lectures in moral philosophy, generally offered by the clergyman who was president of the school. Students who settled for the "scientific" degree might have less of classical languages and increased opportunity to enroll for subjects more natural, pragmatic, or vocational. The scientific course could be as much as a year shorter and seemed to be considered somewhat second class.[4]

It was Richard Owen, the only professing Christian among his generation of that rationalist New Harmony family, who was professor of natural philosophy (zoology, botany, geology, physiology) and chemistry at Indiana University from 1863 to 1879. The famous New Harmony collection of 85,000 scientific specimens came to Bloomington with him. He regarded the days in the first chapters of Genesis as epochs, though as a devout Presbyterian he affirmed that Omnipotence was perfectly competent to create the world in seven days or seven seconds. In his lectures to religious groups Owen testified that his study of science only strengthened his belief in God the creator.[5]

Impact of Darwin

Things were different after Charles Darwin published *On the Origin of Species* in England in 1859.[6] Professor David Worth Dennis of Earlham College described the change for the assembly of the State Science Teachers' Association of Indiana in 1898. "I was a lad of ten in the fall of 1859, when my father and I met a neighbor in the road and my father said to him: 'Darwin says we all came from monkeys.' They straightened themselves in their saddles and laughed until the whole valley resounded: before my boyhood was gone by I saw the community grow first sober, and then the more fiery portion of it angry over this monkey ancestry."[7]

In the *Origin of Species* and succeeding works, Darwin affirmed that natural species were derived from earlier species by transmutation and a selective process of competition. Divine design had previously been the basis of the union of science and religion. Those who began with experience of nature reported compelling evidence of God as creator and sustainer of natural order. Those who began with experience of God affirmed his full involvement in the natural world. Now Darwin was describing a natural world developed and maintained through an impersonal process of elimination or survival. "Descent with modification" he called it. Darwin ended the *Origin of Species* with a halting affirmation of divine design.

> Thus, from the war of nature, from famine and death, the most exalted object which we are capable of conceiving, namely, the production of the higher animals, directly follows. There is grandeur in this view of life, with its several powers, having been originally breathed by the Creator into a few forms or into one; and that, whilst the planet has gone cycling on according to the fixed laws of gravity, from so simple a beginning endless forms most beautiful and most wonderful have been, and are being evolved.[8]

Twenty years later Darwin had retreated even from that cautious position, unable to testify to the participation of God in such merciless natural procedures. He wrote to Thomas Huxley: "I may state that my judgment often fluctuates . . . In my most extreme fluctuations I have never been an atheist in the sense of denying the existence of a God. I think that generally (& more & more as I grow older) but not always, that an agnostic would be the most correct description of my state of mind." A modern biographer called him a "tormented evolutionist." The relation of science to religion was a task he wanted very much to leave to others.[9]

A particularly sensitive point was description of the nature and place of humankind. Most Christians affirmed God's personal involvement with human persons. Following a biblical model Christians affirmed and experienced God as their creator, sustainer, faithful covenant keeper, and gracious redeemer. Darwin, following his model of chance variations and survival of the fittest, published his *Descent of Man* in 1871. In it he described humans as members of an animal species directly derived from previous animal species.

> Man is descended from a hairy quadruped, furnished with a tail and pointed ears, probably arboreal in its habits, and an inhabitant of the Old World. This creature, if its whole structure had been examined by a naturalist, would have been classed among the Quadrumana, as surely as would the common and still more ancient progenitor of the Old and New World monkeys. The

Quadrumana and all the higher mammals are probably derived from an ancient marsupial animal, and this through a long line of diversified forms, either from some reptile-like, or some amphibian-like creature, and this again from some fish-like animal.[10]

Thus the account of the human drama was being read from two widely different scripts. At the same time the biblical documents themselves were undergoing analysis. Scholars were engaged in the "lower criticism" of establishing and comparing the language of the various biblical texts. They were also doing the "higher criticism" of interpreting every portion of the Bible according to the details of its authorship, literary form, and historical context. The members of Indiana's educated public kept shaping their understandings of science and faith. In that enterprise they followed mentors of several kinds.[11]

The neatest way to resolve the tension was to dispense with God and religious faith entirely, or at least to deny them any relevance for the natural world. Secularists were a lively force in the western world by the time Darwin began publishing. They quickly made Darwin's insights into weapons against religion, particularly against ecclesiastical domination of the schools. For them all the natural world had now become a theater of operation for science alone. For them science was the embodiment of all that was vital and exciting, locus of the search for real truth. Notions of God, religion, purpose, or design should be allowed no place in the pure realms of science. Nor should persons advocating such ideas be taken seriously as scientists.[12]

Some of the secularists were especially articulate and aggressive. Thomas H. Huxley, the most raucous example, was nicknamed "Darwin's Bulldog." He was an Englishman but his books and platform appearances made him internationally famous as a crusader. "Warfare has been my business and duty," he declared. To describe himself and those who agreed with him, Huxley coined the term "agnostics." They positioned themselves as champions of truth and light. Persons who resisted their positions on religious grounds were generally regarded as educationally handicapped or as obfuscatory persecutors.[13]

The two basic books of Charles Darwin were available to users of the public library in Indianapolis in the 1870s. So were works of Darwinians more strenuous than Darwin such as Thomas H. Huxley, Herbert Spencer, and Alfred Russel Wallace. The city's substantial rationalist community, mostly German freethinkers, sponsored agnostic lecturers to sharpen the controversial issues for the public mind.[14]

The "Warfare" Theme

Warfare became a compelling military metaphor for the relationship of science and religion. It gripped the imagination of America for more than a century. The warfare motif was given a high profile when John W. Draper of New York published his *History of the Conflict between Religion and Science* in 1874. The preface said, "The history of Science is not a mere record of isolated discoveries; it is a narrative of the conflict of two contending powers, the expansive force of the human intellect on one side, and the compression arising from traditionary faith and human interests on the other."[15]

Draper's book had been solicited as a contribution to the series being published by popular science promoter Edward L. Youmans. It was not so much a history as a controversial tract voiced with a solemn authority. Draper's enemy, and so the enemy of science as he saw it, was the Catholic church. His book caught the public anti-Catholic mood and outsold everything else in the series. It stamped the warfare image on the public mind as it had fifty printings in the United States in about that many years. There were twenty-one editions of it in Great Britain and at least ten translations. The one into Spanish in 1876 earned a place on Rome's list of prohibited books.[16]

Even more important in promoting the warfare image was the work of Andrew Dickson White. Conflict was certainly what White personally experienced when he announced his intention to operate Cornell University as "an asylum for Science—where truth shall be sought for truth's sake, not stretched or cut exactly to fit Revealed Religion." Leaders of church agencies and colleges were not sure of the meaning of White's proposal. To them the whole enterprise smelled of the influence of that prolific evolutionary extremist Herbert Spencer. White was also having his students read works by Henry T. Buckle, W. E. H. Lecky, and John W. Draper. Worst of all, he was spending the federal land grant money which the church schools had hoped to divide among themselves.[17]

After taking many months of pounding from religious opponents, White took the offensive. On 18 December 1869 he lectured in the great hall of the Cooper Institute at New York on "The Battlefields of Science." The whole idea was to point up instances in which religious dogma had interfered with the freedom of science. In the instances he selected dogma was discredited and science, being pure and true, emerged victorious. White said that would always be the case and his collection of instances kept growing.

White repeated the lecture at Boston, New Haven, and Ann Arbor. It was printed in the New York *Daily Tribune* and in expanded form in *Popular Science Monthly*. It became a book entitled *The Warfare of Science* which began:

I purpose to present an outline of the great, sacred struggle for the liberty of science—a struggle which has lasted for so many centuries, and which yet continues. A hard contest it has been; a war waged longer, with battles fiercer, with sieges more persistent, with strategy more shrewd than in any of the comparatively transient warfare of Caesar or Napoleon or Moltke. I shall ask you to go with me through some of the most protracted sieges, and over some of the hardest-fought battle-fields of this war. We will look well at the combatants; we will listen to the battle-cries; we will note the strategy of leaders, the cut and thrust of champions, the weight of missiles, the temper of weapons.[18]

It ran through seven editions in England and America. The warfare became White's obsession culminating in his two-volume *History of the Warfare of Science with Theology in Christendom* published in 1896.[19]

White had great personal prestige as head of one of the four American universities serving as models for modern higher education—Johns Hopkins, University of Michigan, Harvard, and Cornell. He was sure his *History of the Warfare* would serve the best interests of religion as well as science if it induced clergy to stay "in the field left to them." He knew history well enough to avoid the naive anti-Catholicism of Draper. He added weight to his writing by including an impressive scholarly apparatus. With his books and personal crusades he put his mark on the relations of science and religion for generations to come.[20]

In the course of the twentieth century, scholars have invested heavily to counteract and correct the warfare image. They have accused it of taking a dreadful toll on accurate historical interpretation. They have declared it "entirely misleading if not utterly false." One wrote:

There was not a polarisation of "science" and "religion" as the idea of opposed armies implies but a large number of learned men, some scientists, some theologians, some indistinguishable, and almost all of them very religious, who experienced various differences among themselves. There was no organisation apparent on either "side" as the idea of rank and command implies but deep divisions among men of science, the majority of whom were at first hostile to Darwin's theory, and a corresponding and derivative division among Christians who were scientifically untrained, with a large proportion of leading

theologians quite prepared to come to terms peacefully with Darwin. Nor, finally, was there the kind of antagonism pictured in the discharge of weaponry but rather a much more subdued overall reaction to the *Origin of Species* than is generally supposed, and a genuine amiability in the relations of those who are customarily believed to have been at battle. In each of its major implications the military metaphor perverts historical understanding with violence and inhumanity, by teaching one to think of polarity where there was confusing plurality, to see monolithic solidarity where there was division and uncertainty, to expect hostility where there was conciliation and concord.[21]

White and his imitators have been rebutted in detail and charged with "distorting history to serve ideological ends of their own." The warfare metaphor has been labeled "neither useful nor tenable in describing the relationship between science and religion."[22]

After a review of papers presented by eighteen leading historians of science at a three-day conference convened at the University of Wisconsin in April of 1981, the editors concluded:

What view of the encounter between Christianity and science emerges from the essays in this volume? Almost every chapter portrays a complex and diverse interaction that defies reduction to simple "conflict" or "harmony." Although instances of controversy are not hard to find, it cannot be said that scientists and theologians—much less science and Christianity—engaged in protracted warfare . . . The conflicts surrounding Darwin were far more complex than the science-versus-religion formula suggests. They arose between persons who wished to retain an older, theologically grounded view of science and those who advocated a thoroughly positivistic science; scientists as well as clerics could be found on each side, neither of which was motivated solely by scientific considerations.[23]

Nevertheless a host of scientists, religious leaders, writers for the popular media, and members of the general public have been unable to break free from the old imagery of mutual exclusion and war. For more than a century Hoosiers were impacted by that metaphor which has been simple, engaging, triumphal, and nearly irresistible.

A Wide Range of Responses

Hoosier scholars could also be guided by two highly respected teachers who were opponents of Darwinism and refused to accept it to their dying day. Louis Agassiz was a scientist who declined Darwinism for scientific reasons. He busied himself making Harvard into a great center for science after he came there as professor of geology and zoology in 1847. He attracted many gifted students. He believed that the world was constantly or repeatedly willed into being by the mind of the Creator. The rational structures of this creative action could be discerned by the kind of rigorous scientific investigation Agassiz was glad to advocate and practice. Where he saw changes in species he did not regard them as chance events and candidates for preservation in new species by natural selection. He saw both the species and the changes as direct operations of a divinely imprinted plan. In his popular lectures and writings Agassiz championed these views as the most consistent scientific explanation. He was not associated with organized religion. However, many churchgoing people found his conclusions appealing.[24]

Charles Hodge was a theologian who declined Darwinism on theological grounds. Hodge was a professor at Princeton Theological Seminary for half a century, perhaps the most influential Presbyterian teacher of his day. He founded the *Biblical Repertory and Princeton Review* in 1825 and edited it for over forty years. His books included a three-volume *Systematic Theology* published in 1872 and 1873. Three thousand Princeton alumni bore the marks of his instruction. Hodge understood the scientist Agassiz of Harvard and basically agreed with his view of the natural world.

Hodge understood Darwin too. When the international meeting of the Evangelical Alliance was convened in New York in 1873, there arose on the floor an unscheduled discussion of Darwin's work. Hodge responded with an extended impromptu analysis of a recent edition. There were three components to Darwin's theory, Hodge said. They were evolution, natural selection, and natural selection without design. Hodge cited sources to indicate that neither evolution nor natural selection were original with Darwin. What was original was the assertion that the entire sum of all plants and animals with all their characteristics and capabilities could be accounted for without evidence of purpose or design.

Hodge felt no need to counterclaim some or all of the natural world from Darwin in order to have a protected hunting ground for "evidences" to assure himself of God's existence. His premise was that he and God were already well acquainted. The God he knew was the very source and sustainer of the universe, a creation crowned by humankind as the focus of incarnation. When Darwin described a natural world without design he was affirming a universe without God. Simply stated and translated,

offering a universe without God was atheism. So the title at the beginning of Hodge's book in 1874 was the question *What Is Darwinism?* And Hodge's consistent answer at the book's end was, "It is atheism." Many persons who felt that their own knowledge of a creator God was undeniable found Hodge's conclusion compelling. Later interpretation pointed out that Hodge's argument was "from God to design" rather than "from design to God."[25]

A host of academic Americans did not feel the necessity to choose between evolution and divine design. With doctrines of God somewhat more robust than Darwin's, they found the two quite compatible. They said even a prolific and competitive evolutionary theory of origin of species found its best place within a theistic framework. A corps of Christian scholars were prepared to advocate some form of "theistic evolution."[26]

Agassiz was a respected non-Darwinian scientist at Harvard but students increasingly transferred their allegiance from Agassiz to align with Harvard's pioneer botanist Asa Gray. For four years before the publication of *Origin of Species*, Darwin and Gray were in friendly correspondence. They agreed on the principles of natural selection. Darwin said that Gray knew the *Origin of Species* as well as he himself did and that Gray never said a word or used an epithet about the work which did not express the author's meaning. Gray became the foremost defender of Darwinism in America. But Gray always differed from Darwin in theology. He was a Darwinian botanist but he was also a New School Presbyterian whose affirmation of faith and assertion of divine design were as natural to him as his science. In three articles in the *Atlantic Monthly* for 1860 he argued that natural selection was "not inconsistent with natural theology." Darwin himself underwrote the publication of these articles as a pamphlet in 1861.[27]

George Frederick Wright at Andover and at Oberlin became Asa Gray's articulate partner as a champion of Darwinism. Wright was a geologist and a Calvinist. James McCosh intended to give science a new prominence at the College of New Jersey (later Princeton). He became the first American Protestant theologian to publicly express sympathy for Darwinism. From the time of his arrival from Ireland in 1868 to be Princeton's president he was a persistent theistic evolutionist, though insisting that human souls were of some higher and nobler origin. Even the conservative Benjamin B. Warfield of the faculty at Princeton Theological Seminary accepted evolution, seeming to take pleasure in pointing out that Calvin's formulation of the doctrine of creation was "a very evolutionary scheme."[28]

Theistic evolution became a common teaching in Indiana's colleges after some initial reorientation.[29] When the Quakers founded Earlham College at Richmond in 1859, they chose native son Joseph Moore to be professor of natural science. Then they sent him off to Harvard for two years of further preparation. He wrote:

> In my pursuit of science may I be constantly inspired by the highest motive—that of learning more of God as he has displayed himself in all that he has made. God is the author of truth and how can we be better employed than in searching into such things as he has given us the power to investigate. The universe is the work of the divine mind. Since omniscience is one of his attributes, the man who knows the most is in this respect most like his Maker.[30]

At Harvard Moore found the anti-Darwinian Louis Agassiz completing the massive Museum of Comparative Anatomy and arguing vehemently that species were immutable and uniquely created by God. At Harvard at the same time the enthusiastic Darwinian Asa Gray was expanding the herbarium that was the center for plant classification in America. Moore studied with both of these theists but did not agree in detail with either.

Back in Indiana Moore was widely recognized as a scientist both competent to explain his belief in evolution and comfortable in communicating the union of his science and faith. Indiana University and Haverford College awarded him honorary degrees. Science flourished at Earlham College. David Worth Dennis of Wayne County was one of Moore's successors. Dennis was trained at Spiceland Academy, Earlham College, Bonn, and Syracuse. As Earlham's biologist from 1873 to 1916, he succeeded in getting microscopes into the hands of the students. He communicated enthusiasm for scientific field study to a generation of college students and teachers gathered for training institutes.[31]

In 1879 John M. Coulter came to teach the natural sciences at Wabash College. Coulter was a friend and pupil of Asa Gray on his way to international reputation as a botanist and theistic evolutionist.[32]

Professor Richard Owen, surrounded by his great collection of natural specimens at Indiana University, united his theism with evolution. His student Charles Carpenter reported: "Evolution was a new doctrine; Darwin, Huxley, and Tyndall were living then, and he was abreast of their work . . . And we students, surrounded by thousands of forms of life, beheld through his eyes the epic of creation unfolding."[33]

Owen's successor was David Starr Jordan who became professor of natural history in 1879 and the state university's first scientist president in 1885. Jordan's attitude toward organized religion was in the range of lethargy or of benign neglect. His normally inquiring mind resisted any mastery of theology and he remained rather proud of this self limitation. Jordan said his parents left the Baptist church about the time of their marriage. "I was therefore brought up under strong religious influences untouched by conventional orthodoxy . . . I myself early acquired a dislike for theological discussion, believing that it dealt mostly with unrealities negligible in the conduct of life. Consequently I never had to pass through a painful transition while acquiring the broader outlook of science and literature."[34]

A Congregational minister named John L. Jenkins befriended Jordan as a boy, stirring his interest in geology and encouraging him toward a college education. As a young teacher at Butler University, Jordan became a friend of Congregational minister Oscar Carlton McCulloch. "Appreciating his fine work, religious, social, political, and charitable," Jordan said, "I became a member of the Plymouth Congregation—the only religious organization I ever formally joined—and in after years I used occasionally to speak from that pulpit."[35]

In the course of his studies Jordan had become an evolutionist in spite of some personal pain and resistance, "with the grace of a cat the boy 'leads' by its tail across the carpet." He had learned much about science and the teaching of science from his field work with Louis Agassiz who offered him a job at Harvard. He had been impressed even more as a student, friend, and disciple of Andrew Dickson White at Cornell.[36]

Jordan began his study at Cornell the very year President White set off his lecture blast entitled "The Battlefields of Science" and studied there during the years in which White was shaping his influential "warfare" image of the relation of science and religion. In Indiana there were churchmen ready to cast Jordan in the role of enemy and there were, after his election as president, some general grumblings about the university as "that Godless institution." But Jordan, the consistent evolutionist, did not elect to represent science by making war. Instead he went on the road using his great energy and strength of person to win wide respect and friendship for science, for the university, and for himself. He related well with religious colleagues. It was he who twice advocated election of John Merle Coulter, the avowedly religious botanist, to be president of Indiana University.[37]

At Indiana Asbury University at Greencastle (DePauw University after 1884) some work in science was required almost from the time of the school's founding in 1837.

Joseph Tingley was professor of natural science from 1849 to 1879. He had no formal education beyond the four-year college course but was ingenious in improvising and demonstrating scientific equipment. President Matthew Simpson rejoiced that the chair of natural science was no "source of skeptical speculations" while occupied by so devout a Christian as Tingley who was reported in one of his lectures to have "demolished the theory of the evolutionists, Darwin and the rest." Nevertheless Tingley used a botany textbook by the Darwinian Asa Gray.[38]

DePauw's faculty added academic credentials during the administrative years of John Price Durbin John, a native of Brookville. Oliver P. Jenkins was invited to be professor of biology in 1886. He had a Ph.D. from Indiana University, earned chiefly by work with the evolutionist David Starr Jordan. Jenkins and two of his DePauw students joined Jordan in establishing Stanford University and in service on the science faculty there. Contemporary science and religion were compatible at DePauw.[39]

As for John Price Durbin John himself, he left the presidency of DePauw in 1895 to become a popular lecturer with a special goal of integrating science and religion. His most popular speech was entitled "Did Man Make God or Did God Make Man," an answer to agnostic orator Robert G. Ingersoll. In one three-year period he gave this lecture 500 times. It was charged with evolutionary optimism.

> Education everywhere is a process of steps, and not a sudden bridging of extremes. And God himself does not in a single stroke make roses of buds, trees of saplings, or men of babes. If the agnostic is willing to give nature unlimited time in which to develop a savage from a lower animal, he ought not to begrudge the God of nature a few hundred years in accomplishing a mightier task. For I do not hesitate to say that the gulf between an animal and a savage is not so wide or so difficult to bridge as the gulf between the Hebrew freedman as he emerged from centuries of unmitigated slavery and the intelligent, pure and holy man, toward which Christian civilization is now tending, and which is but the continued unfolding of God's ancient plan of education. The agnostic is firing into his own guns when he finds fault with God for following the same plan in revelation that he follows in nature—namely, the plan of evolution—the plan of steps instead of leaps.[40]

Methodist minister John C. Smith included his evolutionary views in the closing sections of his *Reminiscences of Early Methodism in Indiana* published in 1879.

"Whether God created Adam and Eve in a moment, by one grand master-stroke of his all creating power, we are nowhere informed. Reasoning, however, from analogy, we should judge not; but we know that every offspring of this original pair requires twenty years, more or less, to grow and develop into full mental and physical perfection. So of everything else in the animal and vegetable kingdoms. They require time to grow into perfection."[41]

DePauw president George Richmond Grose made reconciliation of learning and religion a chief concern. In a popular book entitled *The Outlook for Religion* published in 1913 he cited testimonies of mutual respect by religious and scientific leaders. "The Bible is a book of religion," he said. "It is not intended to teach science."[42] In a series of articles prepared for the *Adult Bible Class Monthly* and then issued separately as *Religion and the Mind* in 1915, Grose said:

> Unquestionably some education does endanger faith. For example, the first steps in scientific studies are quite likely to unsettle religious beliefs. It is inevitable that the increase of knowledge should modify our childhood conceptions of religion. This process of readjustment of faith and knowledge is always a trying experience. There are two temptations which every earnest student experiences. The first is to dispute the facts of modern learning in the fancied interest of saving one's faith. But this is the way of intellectual dishonesty and moral bankruptcy. The second temptation is hastily to abandon all faith out of a mistaken fidelity to the facts of science. This is alike unsatisfactory, for life must be lived. It has interests which are larger than the laboratory or the market.[43]

Evolution grandly elevated to a doctrine of universal progress could be especially exciting. Henry Ward Beecher, graduated from his Indianapolis pastorate to Plymouth Congregational Church in Brooklyn, was an advocate. As early as 1870 Beecher convened a group of about twenty-five Brooklyn ministers for weekly seminars with the Spencerian evolutionist Edward L. Youmans. Beecher was not so much inspired by Darwin's painful evocation of the lower species and the brutality of natural selection. His hero was Herbert Spencer who projected evolution as a universal principle demonstrated everywhere across a cosmic scale.

By linking Christian doctrine to such an evolutionary conception, Beecher filled the Plymouth Church for his series on evolution in 1885. Hundreds had to be turned away. The sermons were telegraphed to Boston and Chicago and published on the front pages of two newspapers.[44] The book form was entitled *Evolution and Religion: Part I. Eight Sermons Discussing the Bearings of the*

Evolutionary Philosophy on the Fundamental Doctrines of Evangelical Christianity; Part II. Eighteen Sermons Discussing the Application of the Evolutionary Principles and Theories to the Practical Aspects of Religious Life. Beecher said:

> If the whole theory of evolution is but a slow decree of God, and if He is behind it and under it, then the solution not only becomes natural and easy, but it becomes sublime, that in that waiting experiment which was to run through the ages of the world, God had a plan by which the race should steadily ascend, and the weakest become the strongest and the invisible become more and more visible, and the finer and nobler at last transcend and absolutely control its controllers, and the good in men become mightier than the animal in them.[45]

Lyman Abbott, once pastor at Terre Haute and eventually the successor of Beecher at Plymouth Church, was even less inclined to connect religion directly with study of the species in the violent natural world. His *Theology of an Evolutionist* portrayed God as free from any personal involvement in unseemly struggle, much more comfortable as an immanent creative force. Such cool immanentism also found its place among Indiana's educated public, mostly fed from German sources. Religion could be defined with little reference either to the Bible or to the natural world. Religion could be expressed in a vocabulary of reason or feeling or ethical teaching or human social relationships. Science and religion would then have no basis for conflict, in the unlikely case they ever made contact at all. Some later interpreters would declare such liberal accommodation to be in fact an abdication of religious belief altogether, leading to an actual loss of God. Others would note how frequently it was the conservative churches which multiplied and grew while the liberal churches declined.[46]

Early twentieth century Hoosiers might have assumed that science and religion had found a kind of unity in America. Almost all natural scientists had become evolutionists, increasingly "neo-Darwinians" granting less prominence to the process of survival as the source of energy of evolution and more appreciation of the importance of genetic mutations in natural selection. Most theologians were evolutionists too. Theistic evolution was the most common understanding of nature in Indiana's colleges. Hosts of scientists were religious people and hosts of religious people were glad to be students of science. They testified happily to both affiliations, serving as models and mentors. However what appeared to be a considerable consensus lacked a central focus or unified voice.

There were some extreme and noisy evangelists of irreligion claiming a scholarly monopoly for science as they defined it. There were some equally extreme and noisy champions of religious rigidity. Caught between them, fearful of controversy and unprepared to articulate the consensus many of them assumed, the main body of the educated public fell silent on the subject. Public schools, private schools, Sunday schools, textbook publishers, and school teachers generally settled for silence. Instead of harmony between science and religion, the twentieth century brought some especially strange polarizations.

Polarization by Fundamentalists and Secularists

In 1991 historian George Marsden gave a broad definition of evangelicals.

> Roughly speaking, evangelicalism today includes any Christians traditional enough to affirm the basic beliefs of the old nineteenth-century evangelical consensus. The essential evangelical beliefs include (1) the Reformation doctrine of the final authority of the Bible, (2) the real historical character of God's saving work recorded in Scripture, (3) salvation to eternal life based on the redemptive work of Christ, (4) the importance of evangelism and missions, and (5) the importance of a spiritually transformed life.[47]

He thought there were probably 50 million Americans who fit the definition. "A fundamentalist," Marsden said, "is an evangelical who is angry about something"—a conservative "willing to take a stand and fight." In the early 1900s some evangelicals became fundamentalists. They felt that liberals and modernists were selling out the Protestantism which was and ought to be the basis of the nation's greatness. They regarded the Bible as inerrant and resisted much of the scientific or historical analysis being applied to its text.

Between 1878 and 1906 almost every major Protestant denomination experienced at least one heresy trial, usually of a seminary professor. Winona Bible Conference at Winona Lake, Indiana, became a focus for conservative enthusiasm. William Jennings Bryan spoke there in the summer of 1911 on "The Old-Time Religion." Lyman and Milton Stewart put up money to publish a series of twelve paperbacks called *The Fundamentals*. Some 3 million of the individual volumes were issued for free distribution across the English-speaking world between 1910 and 1915. Fundamentalists campaigned to cleanse the new liberalism from all the major Protestant denominations and their schools. Although the books called *The Fundamentals* were moderate and restrained, the evangelical leaders who later took up the fundamentalist mode and name were often extreme. They failed in their efforts to control the major denominations. They then proceeded to establish and maintain their own network of conservative fellowships—denominations, schools, and para-church organizations.[48]

A substantial body of fundamentalists focused their energies on opposing the teaching of biological evolution. The subject was graphic. It could displace dialogue about more traditional religious issues such as the nature and work of God, the nature and authority of the Bible, or the condition and redemption of humankind. Most Christians educated in northern colleges had quietly accepted the insights of Darwinism in the form of theistic evolution. Now a fundamentalist group came projecting Darwinism as the very symbol and embodiment of a dreaded liberalism, modernism, atheism, and German barbarism.[49] After the First World War fundamentalists convinced some southern states to ban the teaching of evolution in public schools.

This partially political cause attracted the famous politician and orator William Jennings Bryan. He offered himself as the champion against Darwinism. Bryan made a colorful speech before the national Presbyterian General Assembly meeting in Indianapolis in 1923 in support of his resolution which would have banned believers in evolution from the office of minister or elder. The resolution was ultimately defeated. Pastor Jean S. Milner of Second Presbyterian Church in Indianapolis moved quickly to present lectures to his congregation affirming that the Bible was not a book of science, that there was no conflict between science and religion, that the theory of evolution was supported by many facts which deserved respect, and that science might provide helpful light on the process of creation.[50]

On the national scene the fundamentalists lost again. They won a sort of victory with William Jennings Bryan prosecuting a 1925 court case in Tennessee against John T. Scopes for allegedly teaching human evolution. But the skeptical defense attorney Clarence Darrow and the huge but hostile media coverage wrote these fundamentalists into American folklore as rubes, hicks, and fools. The relation of science and religion was neither clarified nor improved.[51]

Evolution was receiving scant attention in the public schools by the mid-1920s. Textbook publishers and many school teachers avoided the controversial subject. Scientists, especially some secular ones for whom evolu-

tion was the most crucial organizing principle of reality, were troubled by this omission. Their opportunity came at the end of the 1950s. The Russians launched the satellite Sputnik in 1957, motivating the United States to pour new millions into science. The National Science Foundation granted $7 million to the Biological Sciences Curriculum Study (BSCS) to produce new high school biology texts.[52]

Beginning in 1963 hundreds of thousands of high school students were using the new series of textbooks, regularly instructed in total organic evolution and introduced to their animal ancestry. Public school books were no longer free to speak of theism or of divine purpose and design even if the writers had been so inclined. Yet the entire absence of any such reference left the balance heavily on the secular side.[53]

Once more, it was a group of fundamentalists who led the backlash. In 1964 local book censors in Texas protesting the new BSCS texts solicited the aid of the recently founded Creation Research Society. This society had been developed in the early 1960s by a few likeminded friends in correspondence with William J. Tinkle who taught biology at Taylor University and at Anderson College in Indiana. Members of the Creation Research Society had no patience with people who adapted Genesis to modern science by counting each creation day as an age or by interposing an indeterminate gap of time between the verses or by any means whatever. Most of them, with some hesitation in the case of William Tinkle, simply affirmed verbatim the biblical account in Genesis understood as creation in six twenty-four-hour days followed in due course by an all-encompassing flood.

This creationist position had been explained and defended in *The Genesis Flood* written by John C. Whitcomb of Indiana and Henry M. Morris of Virginia. The Creation Research Society set out to raise $10,000 for textbook production over against the federal grant of $7 million to the BSCS. In 1970 they published *Biology: A Search for Order in Complexity*, an alternative biology text to offer to school textbook selection committees.[54]

With a very modest program of teams, committees, institutes, task forces, and publications these new "creationists" annoyed the secular educational and scientific establishment with an impact far out of proportion to their membership numbers or financial resources. First they got conservative legislators to pass state laws prohibiting the teaching of evolution in the schools. When those laws were invalidated by the courts they campaigned for laws to give "creation science" equal time in the schools with "evolution science."

They took their case to textbook selection committees and to teachers at every level. They discomfited established evolutionists with debates before thousands, even at more than a score of prestigious universities such as Purdue in Indiana. By their calculation the debates, including those in the media, had reached well over 5 million persons by 1984. Their influence seemed to sweep the earth. The books of Morris alone were translated into Chinese, Czech, Dutch, French, German, Japanese, Korean, Portuguese, Russian, and Spanish. A nationwide Gallup poll of Americans in 1982 reported that 44 percent believed in recent special creation, 38 percent in theistic evolution, and 9 percent in nontheistic evolution.[55]

Theistic evolutionists marshalled their replies to these extremists, as in Roland Mushat Frye's book *Is God a Creationist: The Religious Case against Creation-Science*. Some secularists responded emphatically that science simply could not coexist with an all-powerful God who could interfere with natural processes. Said Richard C. Lewentin of Harvard "We cannot live simultaneously in a world of natural causation and of miracles, for if one miracle can occur, there is no limit." Carl Sagan sought to clarify the matter by saying in the opening sentence of his immensely popular *Cosmos,* "The cosmos is all there is, there was, or ever will be." Richard Dawkins gave his book *The Blind Watchmaker* the subtitle "Why the Evidence of Evolution Reveals a Universe without Design." The Opinion Research Corporation conducted a survey of college teachers for the Carnegie Foundation for the Advancement of Teaching in 1984. Thirty percent of faculty members responding to the question "what is your present religion" answered "none."[56]

Silent Majority of Theistic Evolutionists

Spokespersons for the extremes of creationism and secularism were the most vocal. The American Scientific Affiliation (ASA) tried to provide an alternative for less extreme religious conservatives. It was formed in 1941 as an association of evangelical scientists dedicated to correlating science with the Bible. For a time it enjoyed prominence among conservative academics, the 1947 ASA convention at Taylor University and the 1950 convention at Goshen College in Indiana providing examples of its program and leadership. However the ASA preferred to avoid confrontation with creationists or secularists and so lost the visibility such debate would provide. The conflicts which did come were generated by divisions within its own ranks as more zealous conservatives charged its leadership and membership with

capitulation to evolution. Instead of becoming a major provider of bridges across the conflict areas for the general public, the ASA itself became an arena of conflict and found its own base of support eroded. It was not known to the public as a major participant in the nation's discussions and decisions concerning science and religion. So the large bloc of theistic evolutionists between the extremes of creationism and secularism, possibly embarrassed both by the extremists and by their own lack of articulation, remained present but quiet and poorly represented.[57]

That is what Cornelius Troost discovered in his doctoral research project at Indiana University in 1966. Following Andrew D. White's *History of the Warfare of Science with Theology*, Troost wrote an introduction to his dissertation portraying the Christian church as the enemy of science. He asserted that fear of religious opposition kept evolutionary theory out of most high school biology textbooks prior to 1960. "Education in a democracy is intimately related to the values, beliefs, and goals of its people," he said. "Thus the general hostility toward Darwinism in America inevitably contributed to the castration of evolutionary doctrine in secondary education."[58]

The shape of Troost's questionnaire was influenced by faculty members including his especially valued consultant Hermann J. Muller. Responses were to go well beyond ascertaining the extent of the teaching of evolution. Nineteen statements were designed to probe the extent to which biology teachers in Indiana understood evolution; three of the nineteen were "designed to expose teleological thinking." Troost said:

> Most biologists would agree that teleological thinking is fallacious and obfuscatory. Teleological interpretations of evolution are justifiable if they are not metaphysical but oftentimes they are . . . Metaphysical teleology often involves both a creation of the universe by God and His instilling a soul in man at some point in the course of evolution. Thus, either or both of these beliefs could prejudice a respondent when he is confronted with a statement saying that evolution is an autonomous process requiring no supernatural help whatsoever.[59]

Teachers who conceived of evolution as evidencing any design or any supernatural involvement whatsoever were considered confused and their answers "incorrect."[60]

Questionnaires were mailed to 548 tenth grade biology teachers in the state. From the 363 who responded Troost got a lot of "incorrect" answers. He had assumed that teachers who were fundamentalists might not even reply to the questionnaire. Of the teachers who did reply, more than 73 percent accepted purpose as an element in evolution. The religious teachers were not reluctant to teach evolution. The 72 percent who rated themselves "very religious" gave as much emphasis to the subject in their classrooms as their colleagues did. Comments written in on questionnaires frequently supported theistic evolution, e.g., "Evolution seems a natural process carried on by a Power, a Creator, or a God. This need not confuse one's idea of evolution."[61]

Frustrated by the differences between his respondents and his faculty counselors, Troost said, "At least as far as the State of Indiana is concerned, the results of this study indicated that the majority of biology teachers have both inadequate understanding of and attitudes toward evolution which are of an inhibitory nature. This conclusion is based upon the teachers' disagreement with the judgments of the writer's jury and professional biologists." In the last paragraph he mused: "There is a need for a philosophical analysis of the roots of the evolution-religion controversy. Basically, the problem may exist as a difference between two modes of explanation. If there is such a difference, perhaps there are avenues of reconciliation."[62]

Indiana provided major players in America's dramatic encounters between science and religion. Among them were John Zahm, John Merle Coulter, Hermann J. Muller, William Bell Riley, and John C. Whitcomb.

John Zahm

John Augustine Zahm was twelve when his parents moved from Ohio to a two-acre plot near Huntington. John was the oldest son in the family which then had eight children; six more siblings were to come. He continued his schooling at SS. Peter and Paul School. When he was fifteen he wrote to his aunt, a Holy Cross sister at St. Mary's College, to inquire about the religious life and asked that she give his letter to Father Sorin at Notre Dame. After some correspondence, Sorin wrote: "As you seem so anxious to come & try yourself here, I am willing to accept your offer viz.: on your paying $50 to keep you for five months in the College. You may come anytime your parents will deem it expedient."[63]

After fall harvest, Zahm went to Notre Dame with the required clothing and the "1 table-knife, 1 fork, 1 teaspoon, 1 tablespoon" specified in the *Catalogue*. Notre Dame had 39 faculty members and a student body of 448 for that school year of 1867–68. A physical and natural science program had just been added during the Civil War. Back at Notre Dame after his chaplaincy in Sherman's Army was Joseph C. Carrier, trained in science in his native France and now champion of the expansion of Notre Dame's science curriculum. Because of his interest in the priesthood, Zahm was enrolled in the classical course but he participated and excelled in everything, not least in the United Scientific Association directed by Carrier.

In the science lectures Zahm heard Carrier emphasizing that the Book of Genesis did not conflict with historical geology. By 1874 he was a member of the Congregation of Holy Cross, holder of two degrees from Notre Dame, and a recognized campus leader in both teaching and administration. Carrier left Notre Dame to accept the presidency of Saint Mary's College in Texas. Zahm, a subdeacon at age twenty-three, became Notre Dame's professor of chemistry and physics, co-director of the science department, director of the college library, curator of the science museum, and member of the board of trustees. His ability and drive led Notre Dame to national prominence in science and technology. In 1885 he added to his science portfolio the office of vice-president of the University.[64]

As a priest, a scientist, an administrator, a rhetorician, and an enthusiast for Notre Dame, Zahm was a natural participant in the evolution dialogue. Stimuli on the subject were coming from everywhere. International parties were forming: some like scientists Tyndall and Huxley ridiculing religion as a shackler of evolutionary truth; some like Catholic apologists Edward McSweeney and Orestes Brownson striking back at the ridicule rather than precisely addressing evolution as a mechanism of biological change; some like scholars Asa Gray and Saint George Mivart seeking a formulation of evolutionary theory not in conflict with theism.[65]

Zahm's influence may have been showing as the *Scholastic* at Notre Dame came to reflect a moderate position, particularly in the articles by Zahm's assistant Alexander M. Kirsch.

> For our part, we believe strongly in a derivative creation: namely, that God created many species, not in *actu*, but in *potentia*, to be produced by natural powers into their different forms. Some Catholics will be startled probably at this doctrine, but if they consult Suarez and many other theologians they will find that such is really the case, and that therefore we may accept this view since it is reasonable and is not contrary to religious teaching.[66]

When he did get into the controversy personally, Zahm found the experience exhilarating. His first sermon on evolution was preached at Denver in March of 1883, repeated at Notre Dame and Saint Mary's, printed in pamphlet form, and reprinted in the French newspaper

Cosmos: Les Mondes. Already he was on the international stage declaring that there was no conflict between the Church and scientific truth.

Neither the Scriptures nor the Church officially stated an age for the earth, he said, a matter not at all related to faith and morals. Church fathers Augustine, Thomas, and Albertus Magnus had pointed out centuries ago that biblical "days" might be indefinite periods of time. Augustine and Thomas and Suarez had taught derivative creation, that plants and animals were brought into existence by natural causes. The very words of Genesis said "Let the earth bring forth . . . Let the waters bring forth"—derivative creation again.

Zahm said Catholics should beware of the false theories of atheists and agnostics and Protestants offered in the name of science but had nothing to fear from scientific truth itself. There could be no genuine conflict between true science and the Catholic church since both were avenues to God. In the past the universities and the scholars of the Church led the progress of science. In the present Catholics could view evolution calmly, resolving to do scientific work of the best quality.[67]

Zahm received public approval for his stance. He was the first Catholic priest to appear on the Sunday Lecture Program of Indiana University, personally invited by David Starr Jordan. He and his speech "The Catholic Church and Modern Science," were warmly praised by the Bloomington *Progress*. His articles on faith and science in the *American Catholic Quarterly Review*, *Donahoe's Magazine*, and the *North American Review* brought credit to him and to Notre Dame. What had been one facet of his work on the Notre Dame faculty became his primary vocation. He wrote to Sorin in September of 1893: "I . . . am beginning to feel that I have a great mission before me in making known to the Protestant world the true relation of Catholic dogma towards modern science—this is surely a fertile field to labor in, & I trust I may be given the health & strength necessary for the work."[68]

The Catholic summer school movement was national in scope, modeled after the Chautauqua, and promoted by Zahm's faculty colleague Maurice Francis Egan. For four years Zahm was star of that lecture circuit, all the more encouraged to publish by his success. Zahm's biographer wrote:

> During the four years, 1892–1896, Zahm reached the peak of his production as a lecturer and writer on science-religion subjects. He lectured before thousands of Catholic Summer and Winter School students, was publicized in dozens of Catholic and non-Catholic magazines and newspapers while his learned books

touched off a bitter controversy. Even amidst the roar of heated arguments concerning temperance and the American Protective Association and the countless columns in magazines and newspapers covering these controversial topics, he was heard and judged newsworthy. During these years, Zahm became the most widely known American Catholic priest engaged in investigating the theology of evolution. While his popular investigations distressed and alienated many conservative Catholics who accepted only the traditional interpretation of dogma, he won the approval of most liberal students during this nervous age of skepticism.[69]

It was an atmosphere designed to evoke further development of his positions. He claimed the conclusions of his articles and speeches had long been familiar in the Church, but his denial of the universality of the Flood and his view of the antiquity of man seemed novel to many. "Didn't I stir up the bears," he wrote his brother Albert at the end of the first summer lectures in 1893. "Probably the smoke shall have cleared away by the time I return." The next summer he offered an address entitled "The Simian Origin of Man," declaring there was nothing in dogma to preclude the view that man was descended from an anthropoid ape or another animal. He said that more delicate instruments might indeed demonstrate spontaneous generation. Evolution was no new theory but was spoken of in the days of Aristotle and was compatible with the teachings of Thomas Aquinas.

Over 2,000 members attended the International Catholic Scientific Congress in Brussels in September of 1894. Zahm addressed the entire Congress on the fourth and last day. He urged seminaries to instruct their students in the latest methods and findings of science. The bitter warfare between Catholicity and Protestantism was ended, he said, and agnostics were the true foes of the Church. Priests must provide their people with intelligent faith. The address was much praised. At a private audience with Pope Leo XIII six weeks later, Zahm gave the Pope a copy of the address beautifully printed in French and bound in white silk. In February of 1895 the Pope conferred the degree of Doctor of Philosophy on Zahm to "serve as an incentive for him to labor even more wholeheartedly for the development and propagation of Christian science."[70]

Zahm put it all in print. During the four years devoted to the relation of science and religion he wrote five books, four pamphlets, and twenty-one articles. The whole issue of the *American Ecclesiastical Review* for March 1894 was given over to Zahm's articles. The book *Bible, Science and Faith* (1894) expressed his earlier ideas, the sort he presented to the first summer school. In 1896 his *Evolution and Dogma* was ready for publication, a full-orbed summary of his studies on evolution. Its final chapter affirmed that evolution as a theory was in accordance with science and Scripture, and with patristic and scholastic theology. He predicted that it would soon be the generally accepted view. Catholic editor Augustine F. Hewit advised him not to publish the work but Zahm proceeded. Publisher D. H. McBride issued an advertising circular seeking to boost sales by suggesting that the book was highly controversial. It made a large target for all the opposition Zahm had accrued.[71]

Zahm himself was sent to Rome just after *Evolution and Dogma* was published in English, appointed by the general of his order to the office of procurator-general. In spite of a friendly reception and a good beginning in Rome, he became increasingly associated with the "American" group. It was a dangerous association. John Ireland, John J. Keane, and Denis J. O'Connell were regarded as advocates of modernism and progressive church policies. There were many opponents of these positions; their displeasure focused on Zahm and his book.[72]

At the end of a long process came an edict from the Sacred Congregation of the Index dated 10 September 1898: "The work of the Reverend Zahm is prohibited; the decree, however, is not to be published until such a time that the author will be heard out by his Father General whether he is willing to submit to this decree and re-prove his work." Zahm replied on October 3: "I submit unreservedly to the decree and promise to comply at once with all its injunctions. I regret that I have written anything that should be considered deserving of censure & shall be more guarded in the future. In writing the book I had in view only the good of souls & the glory of the Church."[73]

At the time of the condemnation, Zahm was already back at Notre Dame, summoned in January of 1898 to be provincial, top administrator for the United States Province of the Congregation of Holy Cross. In view of his submission, the Index decree condemning his *Evolution and Dogma* was never published. His mission of demonstrating the compatibility of Catholicism and science was exchanged for a sobering load of administration.[74]

In the fifteen years between 1883 and 1898 John Zahm of Indiana had done much to set the tone of American Catholic participation in the dialogue about evolution. Few American Catholic leaders of the period were prepared as he was to respond effectively for the church in reply to a Thomas H. Huxley or an Andrew D. White. Zahm offered a liberal interpretation emphasizing

theistic evolution. More than any other American Catholic he translated Darwin into terms Catholic constituencies could accept and use. Though he himself was silenced, his tradition continued strong.

When Pope John Paul II addressed European academic audiences in 1979 and 1981, he could emphasize that science must be free in the search for truth, he could rehearse "the tragic case of Galileo" as deplored by the Second Vatican Council, and he could quote his predecessor Pope Pius XII about "the work of creative omnipotence, whose strength raised up by the powerful fiat uttered milliards of years ago by the creating mind, has spread through the universe, calling into existence, in a gesture of generous love, matter teaming with energy." Theistic evolution was the theme.[75]

John Merle Coulter

John Merle Coulter was born in China in 1851. About 1844 his father Moses Coulter had come from West Virginia for an inexpensive education at the college at Hanover in Indiana. He had married a daughter of the college founder John Finley Crowe, and had joined her in Presbyterian missionary service in China. In 1852 Moses Coulter died at Ningpo. Caroline Crowe Coulter returned to rear her sons in Indiana. The younger brother Stanley attended Hanover, became a lawyer and a teacher of biology, and was for thirty-nine years a dean at Purdue University. The elder brother John Merle played an even more visible role in the dialogue concerning science and religion.[76]

At age thirteen John Merle Coulter entered the preparatory department of Hanover College. Latin was his principal interest; the Hanover curriculum and Coulter's course of study were heavy with Greek and Latin classics. There had been a professor of natural science at Hanover since 1835, the subject being viewed broadly as was customary. But in 1868, when Coulter was a junior, the board employed Yale graduate Frank Bradley to teach science and approved use of the botany textbook written by Asa Gray of Harvard.

Bradley left Hanover the next year amid reports of some difference of opinion with the board about the age of the earth. His successor was Edward Thomson Nelson, also a Yale postgraduate, who led his students on science field trips in the Hanover hills. One of the students on these excursions was Harvey Young, who was destined to become professor of chemistry and geology at Hanover College from 1879 until his death in 1926. John Merle Coulter became a "botany fiend" too, assembling materials with the others for a report on the flora of Jefferson County.

Coulter still thought of himself as a classicist. When Frank Bradley gave him a summer job on the team doing the United States Geological and Geographical Survey in the Rockies, that was to be a pleasant postgraduate break. In 1873 Hanover College offered him his choice of the faculty chair of natural science or of Latin and he chose the latter. The next year Manuel J. Drennan resigned the chair of natural science and Coulter became at the same time librarian of the college, professor of Latin language and literature, and acting Ayers professor of natural science. At the June meeting of the board in 1876 he asked for transfer to the chair of natural science. He had decided to devote his life to botany.[77]

Coulter was involved in discussion of evolution from the beginning of his academic career, not very hospitable to the theory in the beginning. In an address at Hanover in 1877 he said:

> What is the first tendency of science just springing into birth? Immediately there rush to the foremost rank enthusiasts who are so carried away by their zeal for investigation that they forget the existence of a higher power than themselves and the laws they have discovered—deny, in fact, the existence of everything that they cannot subject to the scrutiny of their microscopes. These leaders have a numerous following, more determined in their erratic notions than they, for with less knowledge comes greater dogmatism. We most heartily regret, then, to be compelled to say that the tendency of science, still in its swaddling clothes, is to materialism.[78]

Coulter wondered if discovery of the new truths may not have been providentially delayed for eighteen centuries so that religious ideas and beliefs were firmly established in the minds and hearts of men, made into a rock-grounded temple of religion into which a maturing science could enter and worship. He poked fun at those who ignored evidences of one Designer of infinite skill and who searched for some inherent power of development.

> But how did that power of development originate: That is the question, and they have searched earth, air and sea in vain for the answer. Not long ago, the scientific world was startled by the statement that at last the origin of life had been discovered in the depths of the Atlantic Ocean, the original protoplasmic cells had been collected, and under the sounding name of *Bathybius princeps* the poor little monad was ushered into the world. A chemist procured a specimen of this mysterious jelly, analyzed it, and lo! our Bathybius was nothing but the sulphate of lime, or gypsum, as dead as the everlasting rocks.[79]

In July of 1879 Coulter told the Hanover College board that he had accepted appointment to a chair at Wabash College. In the summers of 1879 and 1880 he was off from Wabash studying botany at Harvard, studying especially with George Goodale in the botanical laboratory and under the oversight of Asa Gray. Excitement about botany as a pure science, as a useful science, and as a national asset set him off on a remarkable career.[80]

He was president and professor of botany at Indiana University 1891–1893, strongly recommended for that position by David Starr Jordan after Coulter had declined to go to Stanford as part of Jordan's new faculty there.[81] He was president of Lake Forest College in Illinois from 1893 to 1896. When William Rainey Harper secured an endowment of $1 million to build up a botanical department for the University of Chicago, Coulter took charge of its development and of the construction of Hull Botanical Laboratory. More than 175 students earned their doctorates there under his administration, most proceeding to international reputation in their field. He was largely responsible for the foundation of the Boyce Thompson Institute for Plant Research at Yonkers, New York, serving it as scientific adviser and board member until his death in 1928.

Coulter produced eight elementary textbooks for the teaching of plant sciences in secondary schools. He issued two manuals on the botany of the Rocky Mountains and one on the botany of Texas. He founded the *Botanical Gazette* in 1875 and was its editor for fifty years. It became the leading botanical publication in America, recognized in every country as one of the best organs for publication of botanical investigation. Many articles on his own highly technical plant research appeared there. The series of "Contributions from the Hull Botanical Laboratory" in the *Gazette*, reporting the research of Coulter and his students at Chicago, reached 388 numbers by the end of 1928. Professional associations elected him to offices repeatedly. Among many honors was the founding of a John M. Coulter Research Fellowship at the University of Chicago.[82]

Coulter was always concerned to put his science together with his religion and to do it publicly in ways that might help others. His biographer said that the soul of grandfather John Finley Crowe was in Coulter and that Asa Gray was his model as a teacher. Gray was a theistic evolutionist as were Coulter's respected colleagues Liberty

Hyde Bailey at Cornell and Charles Edwin Bessey at the University of Nebraska. Theistic evolution was what Coulter advocated. In Chicago he taught a large Bible class for men in the Sunday school of Hyde Park Presbyterian Church and often occupied the pulpit there. He gave lectures on science and religion at McCormick Theological Seminary and before the Religious Education Association. Some thought he should be matched as a liberal in a debate with William Jennings Bryan but he was not.[83]

Coulter also put it all in print—in *Biblical World* and in *Religious Education* and in *Christian Century* and in *Science Remaking the World* edited by one of his students at Columbia.[84] At the age of seventy-three he joined with his son Merle C. Coulter, a professor of plant genetics at the University of Chicago, to summarize his views in a book of 105 pages called *Where Evolution and Religion Meet*. In its opening pages the book said:

> Why does this prejudice exist? Two reasons seem to be mainly responsible. First, it is felt that evolution contradicts the Bible; and we cannot blame those who are opposed to evolution for this reason, for they have been taught by those whom they have the greatest reason to trust that the Bible is to be relied upon implicitly, and that to question it is sinful. Second, it is the popular impression that evolution requires us to believe that men have descended from monkeys; and this is a shock to one's vanity, for we have a very poor opinion of monkeys. For these two reasons, many people have concluded that the evolution concept is degrading, and hence they will have none of it. We have no desire to criticise those who hold this impression about evolution for the reasons indicated. Their reactions are quite natural, but their information has been incomplete, and those who base their conclusions on incomplete information are quite commonly in error. When one has been completely informed concerning evolution, he realizes that it does not contradict the Bible in any serious way, but really teaches the same fundamental truths from a different point of view. Furthermore, the careful study of evolution is the very thing which shows us that man could not have descended from the monkeys or apes of today. Ages ago the ancestors of man, monkey, and ape sprang from a common source, and the same may be said of all forms of animal life. The account of how man and all other forms of life emerged from such humble beginnings and gradually developed into the more perfect types of today is far from degrading. Instead it presents about the most ennobling and inspiring concept that we have.[85]

Coulter said that the plant and animal kingdoms had plainly developed in a continuous and orderly way. Individual animals and plants came into existence through descent from other animals and plants. Some descendants were modified, changes currently explained by some combination of Lamarck's theory of use and disuse, Darwin's theory of natural selection, and mutation theories of DeVries. Isolation and hybridization played some role after mutation had taken place. Some uninformed persons had equated Darwinism with evolution, assuming both to be enemies of Christianity and assuming scientific criticism of Darwin's explanation to mean an abandonment of the theory of evolution. That, said Coulter, was a foolish oversimplification. He declared himself a Christian who also believed in evolution. "Every proposed explanation may prove inadequate, and yet the facts of evolution remain to be explained."[86]

At the end of *Where Evolution and Religion Meet* Coulter rehearsed his view of the relation of science and religion. Unlike John Zahm, he seemed innocent of the nature, purpose, and historical development of religious dogma. For him "theology," "dogma," and "philosophical speculations" were negative labels. Whatever in religion conflicted with the "discovered facts" of science could be designated dogma, theology, or philosophical speculation and dismissed. Andrew D. White of Cornell issued his *History of the Warfare of Science with Theology* in 1896 but Coulter hardly felt involved so long as it was theology under fire.

Coulter did not much care to talk about science and theology. He wanted to talk about science and religion. His religion affirmed that evolution was "the result of the activities of that all-pervading energy which we have learned to call God." Inorganic evolution was the method by which God moulded matter. Organic evolution was the method by which God developed organisms. Religion was the way God developed human character. True religion was "love stimulating service." Christianity was the exemplary model of love stimulating service and Jesus the one who taught this doctrine with the beautiful clarity one would expect of a good science teacher. In Coulter's view true science and true religion could never conflict. They were complementary.[87]

Hermann J. Muller

Hermann J. Muller, Indiana University faculty member from 1945 to 1967, had no traditional religion to integrate with his convictions about evolution. He had separated from that as a teenager back in New York City. He attended the Sunday school of the 121st Street Unitarian Church from about his ninth to his sixteenth years.

The ideas of evolution and progress taught there fit comfortably with the liberal instruction his family provided.[88]

Preferring a universal rather than a personal God, young Muller considered himself a pantheist. His closest high school friend Edgar Altenburg, of a staunch socialist family and atheist by persuasion, moved him still further from tradition. Altenburg argued: "There are two ways you can describe the universe. You may say 'The Universe is God' and identify yourself as a pantheist; or you may say 'The Universe is' and identify yourself as an atheist. The principle of Occam's Razor states that if two hypotheses both claim to describe a situation, we should choose the hypothesis with the least assumptions. Thus the concept of God is unnecessary and atheism is more rational than pantheism." Muller was an atheist to stay.[89]

Always a brilliant and industrious student, Muller chose to apply his genius to biology. Evolution was the primary stuff of his research. His Nobel Prize in 1946 was for being the first to show that mutations could be induced in living organisms following exposure to X rays. That prize was only one of the scores of honors he received from scientific colleagues around the world. Evolution was a major component of his course work offered for graduate students and advanced undergraduates. Carl Sagan, then an undergraduate at the University of Chicago, worked in Muller's laboratory for a summer.[90]

Evolution was the excitement of Muller's life, the faith he affirmed and championed. Those who wanted to understand the natural world would find the key in evolution. Even altruism had a genetic component and a transmitted value for survival. Evolution was and deserved to be known as the best life-organizing principle. It was the hope of humankind for the future. So it must be made central in education. Its potential for human improvement must be embodied in deliberate eugenic planning including sperm banks.[91] He wrote:

> We should not only bear in mind the urgent need for success, we should also recall that, after all, man has gone from height to height, and that he is now in a position, if only he *will*, to transcend himself intentionally and thereby proceed to elevations yet unimagined. Unintentionally, he no longer can do so. It is up to us to do our bit in this purposive process, and to use what we know constructively, rather than remain in that ivory tower which has the writing on its wall. Our reward will be that of helping man to gain the highest freedom possible—the finding of endless worlds both outside and inside himself, and the privilege of engaging in endless creation.[92]

Muller was a lyric evangelist for evolution. His famous speech in 1959 to celebrate the centennial of Darwin's *Origin of Species*, "One Hundred Years Without Darwinism Are Enough," was an appeal to make evolution the core of life science instruction at all levels of public schools.

> We dare not leave it to the Soviets alone to offer to their rising generation the inspiration that is to be gained from the wonderful world view opened up by Darwin and other Western biologists. This view, founded so solidly upon the discoveries of modern science, is, when fully understood and incorporated into men's personalities, the source of the profoundest idealism and hope. It should lend us support in our struggle for a freer world, for it shows how the most essential properties of living things have led to their perpetual reaching out, self-transformation, and, for some of them, progression, and conquest of the rest of nature, until from a slimy scum they have stood erect, become aware of themselves, evolved social feelings and moral principles, and striven toward the stars.[93]

Muller found no place for God either embodied in nature or beyond it. He thought a people really committed to the exciting possibilities of evolution would find that more than enough. Dedication to the higher ends of human progress would replace "old-style religions." For fellowship with other atheists and rationalists he turned to the American Humanist Association. He was its president from 1955 to 1959 and was chosen its "Humanist of the Year" in 1963.[94] That organization remained well below 50,000 in national membership and limited in public influence. Muller, who had taken a personal leadership role as the BSCS invested the $7 million grant to prepare its new high school biology texts, lived just long enough to experience the conservative "creationist" reaction to those texts. The Arkansas law restricting the teaching of evolution in public schools was on its way to the United States Supreme Court. So in the last year of his life he was rallying scientists to sign a petition justifying evolution as a scientific principle. Evolution was about as firmly established, he said, as the rotundity of the earth.[95]

William Bell Riley

William Bell Riley was born in Greene County, Indiana, in March of 1861. His parents were southern sympathizers. When the war broke out they moved back to Kentucky. From the age of nine young William "made a hand" on the tobacco farm but he had grander ambitions. Whenever he could he watched the proceedings of the local court. He reveled in the legal arguments and intended to become a lawyer.

At the age of eighteen, a few months after he was converted and was baptized in Cephas Van Daren's pond, he arranged to rent the family farm for one year in a heroic effort to earn money for school. Indiana was his destination. From the literature he computed that one could go to school in Valparaiso for $170 per year. By judicious repair of his only suit and by subsisting largely on corn syrup and crackers, he completed one year at Valparaiso Normal School. He said his aim was to use the certificate earned by study at Valparaiso to "teach my way through college" and "adopt the law as my permanent profession."

Because his brother Theophilus got typhoid fever, William had to return to the farm for a time. His goal was the practice of law but there was also a persistent inclination to preach. His conversion had been heartfelt. His father had always harbored a yearning to be a preacher. William resisted any such call. He knew about the pay of Baptist preachers and wanted no more of poverty. Years later he recalled: "My arguments with Him availed me nothing! Days of ill-content about my choice followed each other in what seemed interminable succession; and in spite of the physical weariness with which I fell into my bed night after night, sleep refused to come. The fight was on! After some months of turmoil, at last I reluctantly said, 'I will! I will preach'!"[96]

At the age of twenty he was back in school in Indiana. A generous farm neighbor named James Mason sponsored Riley's enrollment at Hanover College for four "strenuous but delightful years." He brought his own horse and buggy from Kentucky and drove out from Hanover to preach in neighboring country churches. Then he began riding the steamboats from Hanover to Ohio River towns, having contracts to preach for the Baptists two Sundays per month at Carrollton, Kentucky, and two Sundays per month at Warsaw, Kentucky. He had entered Hanover handicapped by a lack of proper secondary schooling but he graduated fourth in the class of 1885. He ranked first in debate. Next came three years at Southern Baptist Theological Seminary in Louisville. As an upper classman there, he was also a Baptist pastor in New Albany, Indiana. Upon graduation in 1888 he took a new pastorate at Lafayette, Indiana, and a new bride named Lillian Howard.[97]

While Riley was at Southern Baptist Seminary, Dwight L. Moody led a five-week revival campaign for Louisville based on the seminary grounds. Moody was a mature evangelist, a national hero, involved that very year of 1887 in forming the Student Volunteer Movement which would enlist thousands of collegians to "evangelize the world in this generation." Riley was one of the seminarians who helped Moody during those weeks. They became friends. Moody conducted revival meetings in Riley's church at Lafayette. When Riley took a church in Chicago, he worked closely with Moody and his school there. Riley liked Moody's plain and direct preaching, powerful in language but free from body antics. He learned Moody's highly personal methods of evangelism. He admired the way Moody built and used institutions to extend his influence. Moody was Riley's most influential model. From Moody and from others around Moody, Riley adopted some doctrines he had not learned at Hanover or at Southern Baptist.[98]

Moody was a premillennialist. A part of his evangelistic urgency was that the whole present order would soon end with the personal return of Christ and the events leading to his earthly reign of a thousand years. "I look upon this world as a wrecked vessel," he liked to say. "God has given me a lifeboat and said to me, 'Moody, save all you can.'" Riley became a premillennialist. "Two years after graduation," he said, "my premillennarianism was adopted as a result of deep and careful Bible study."[99]

In his new place as pastor of First Baptist Church in Minneapolis beginning in 1897, Riley's sermons were pessimistic about any hope based on future human progress. Yet he coupled this pessimism with immense energy for social reform. Until the Lord came, the redeemed should be championing poor laborers and victims of exploitation. They should be waging war on every kind of civic corruption and substance abuse.

Waging war was what Riley did best. Moody avoided controversy lest his evangelism be limited by divisions. Riley, on the other hand, sought controversy and made it a tool of evangelism. Even after the withdrawal of a body of traditional members who opposed Riley, First Baptist Church in Minneapolis grew from 585 members in 1897 to 855 in 1898 and expanded rapidly thereafter.[100]

Another doctrine thriving on the fringes of Moody's evangelistic empire was dispensationalism. John Nelson Darby visited America seven times between 1862 and 1876 to bring dispensationalist teachings from the Plymouth Brethren of England. Cyrus I. Scofield of Dallas, Texas, became an enthusiast and wrote a dispensational system into the Scofield Reference Bible which was published in 1909 and circulated to millions of Americans. The emphasis was on reading the infallible Bible as an instrument of infallible prophecy. Old and New Testaments, especially the books of Daniel and Revelation, revealed a single divine plan. The plan was usually expressed in a series of seven successive ages or covenants. The Jews involved in the earlier covenants were carefully distinguished from Christians who were now under the covenant of grace. The present dispensation, the "church age," was marked by growing apostasy in the denominational churches and by moral decay of the nation.[101]

Moody was a cautious dispensationalist at most, even though his educational colleagues Cyrus I. Scofield of Texas and Emma Dryer of Chicago were among the system's stout advocates. William Bell Riley was never cautious. For him dispensationalism was another tool for warfare and evangelism. He loved the way it fit with his convictions about an inerrant Bible and the early return of Christ. The imagery was unrivaled for evangelism.[102]

Riley's contract with First Baptist Church allowed him to spend four months of each year as a traveling evangelist. Between 1897 and 1910 he conducted revivals throughout the Midwest and Northwest and made an evangelistic tour of England. In 1902 he founded the Northwestern Bible and Missionary Training School at his church. He was increasingly visible in the national network of prophetic Bible conferences sponsored by dispensational premillennialists. Riley helped to organize the prophecy and Bible conference at Moody Bible Institute in 1914. His speech there entitled "The Significant Signs of the Times" marked him as a leader in the movement. His leadership was even more plain in the huge prophecy conferences at New York and Philadelphia in 1918.[103]

So it was the native Hoosier William Bell Riley who was prepared to lead the fundamentalist movement into action. He founded a paper called *Christian Fundamentals in School and Church*. He had enough of just evangelizing, praying, and waiting for the Lord's return. As a leader among the planners, Riley designated the upcoming 1919 prophetic Bible conference at Philadelphia a "world conference on fundamentals." Now the warfare imagery would be a tool of the conservative side. This was to be the first meeting of a new national and interdenominational organization for "the persistent propagation of 'the faith once for all delivered' as the only antidote to that infidelity which is forcing its way beyond the very altars of our churches, and which has already slimed our schools with its deadly saliva."[104]

Over 6,000 came. Speakers included heads of leading premillennial Bible schools. Riley gave the opening address saying this was "an event of more historic moment than the nailing up, at Wittenberg, of Martin Luther's ninety-five theses." They formed the World's Christian Fundamentals Association (WCFA) with a nine-point creed and a dues structure suited to every prospect. President Charles Blanchard of Wheaton College drafted the doctrinal statement. They called on Christian people to avoid "infidel, atheistic education" and promised a list of schools and mission boards uncontaminated by modernism.[105]

William Bell Riley was elected WCFA president. He was also chairman of the Committee on Conferences which immediately arranged a national campaign employing pianists, singers, and fourteen speakers. Riley was one of the speakers, scheduled the conferences into eighteen major cities, and raised most of the money for expenses. The enemy was plain. Riley had drawn the modernist profile in his *Finality of the Higher Criticism* in 1909 and his *Menace of Modernism* in 1917.[106]

> Riley proclaimed that in the past few years colleges, seminaries, and universities across the United States had been infiltrated by numerous Antichrists who taught that the Bible was of human origin and filled with errors, that Jesus was not God in the flesh, and that social reform (man's work) was more important than salvation (God's work). Modernism had even triumphed in a host of once-Christian colleges, where students were now taught Darwinism and the concomitant "sneer at Scripture." As a result of the modernist invasion of higher education, many American youth received a viciously anti-Christian indoctrination that could blight them for life. Such education not only destroyed individuals but, even more important, also threatened the moral underpinnings of American society.[107]

One chapter in Riley's *Menace of Modernism* was entitled "Has the State University Become a Hot-Bed of Heterodoxy?" It reflected his disgust that universities seemed hospitable to secularists and liberal ministers but not to conservatives like him. He wrote: "I have seen a little two by four preacher, who could not get four hundred people to hear him on any occasion and who could not find a publisher in all the land that would take a manuscript from him and risk the expense of printing it, called to a professorship in a great University; and instantly he blossomed into authority on all scientific subjects."[108]

By summer of 1921 Riley reported that he and his colleagues in the WCFA had conducted over 200 conferences, sounding the alarm against modernism in most major cities of the United States and Canada and in many smaller ones besides. The fundamentalist movement had reaped enormous publicity and spun off a host of local Bible conferences. Riley hoped to build a national interdenominational organization so unified and strong it could save the churches and the nation by purging them of modernism.

That hope failed. Fiercely independent fundamentalist leaders were hardly willing to accept direction from Riley or anybody else. Gentler conservatives were wary of the violent language and extremism of the WCFA. Denominational leaders resisted invasion and avoided division. His own Northern Baptist Convention meeting in Indianapolis in June of 1922 decisively voted down Riley's motion to require a conservative creed. Riley's leadership was limited for a time by a serious auto accident in June of 1924. As a national fundamentalist crusade, the WCFA itself gradually waned.[109]

The fading of its first national crusade was by no means the end of the World's Christian Fundamentals Association and certainly not the end of the impact of William Bell Riley. He was highly visible as he led the WCFA and others in a second major effort. This one was particularly directed against the teaching of evolution. Fundamentalists had not been successful in driving modernists out of the major denominations. They would now shift emphasis to driving evolutionists out of the public schools. Enrollment in public high schools nearly doubled between 1920 and 1930. Some teachers in these schools enjoyed shocking the naive students with extreme statements of evolutionary principles. Fundamentalists wanted to exclude the teaching in every form.

Antievolutionism was an old theme for Riley. He had published a sermon entitled "The Theory of Evolution and False Theology" in 1909. He said evolutionists either left God out of creation or accepted only an impersonal force rather than a gracious heavenly Father. He said they counted Jesus no more than a remarkable man and the Bible as a book full of errors. Riley affirmed his support for science in its proper Baconian realm of observable facts and demonstrable laws. Scientists were fine for doing descriptions of specimens and experiments and classification. When they entered the more exciting realm of speculative theories about origins they were no longer scientists but unreliable and dangerous philosophers.[110]

As for Darwinism, Riley counted it deadly to both the doctrines of Christianity and the morals of society. Just such notions of the special rights of the "fittest" had fueled the recent racist outbursts of the Germans. Riley advertised himself as ready to travel any reasonable distance to debate an evolutionist. Opponents must be of high professional standing. Audiences would decide the victor. Debating William Bell Riley was no light matter. He was expert at working crowds, particularly crowds well packed with supporters rallied by fundamentalist ministers in the area. He debated Maynard Shipley, president of the Science League of America; Edward Adams Cantrell, field secretary for the American Civil Liberties Union; Henry Holmes, chair of the philosophy department at Swarthmore College; and Charles Smith, president of the American Association for the Advancement of Atheism. He said he won every encounter.[111]

At the Fourth Annual Convention of the World's Christian Fundamentals Association in 1922 there was less talk of Bible prophecy and more attention to evolution. President Riley said "We increasingly realize that the whole menace in modernism exists in its having accepted Darwinism against Moses, and the evolutionary hypothesis against the inspired Word of God."[112]

The aim now was to get Christian taxpayers and parents organized against the teaching of such poison. The cause was immensely popular and transformed the fundamentalist movement. People with little previous interest in fundamentalism would join a campaign to keep Darwinism out of schools. Riley visited southern states rallying popular support to pressure state legislatures to prohibit the teaching of evolution. Riley and his WCFA helped Tennessee get an antievolutionism law passed in 1925.

When John Thomas Scopes and the American Civil Liberties Union challenged the Tennessee law, it was the 1925 convention of the WCFA which responded "We name as our attorney for this trial William Jennings Bryan and pledge him whatever support is needful to secure equity and justice and to conserve the righteous law of the Commonwealth of Tennessee." Bryan had earlier declined Riley's invitation to become president of the WCFA. However he had been a crusader against evolution since the end of the First World War and now accepted the call to assist in the prosecution of Scopes.[113]

Riley was not present for the famous Scopes trial in which he was invested even more heavily than Bryan. At the time he was occupied in other important controversies at the Northern Baptist Convention at Seattle. After the merciless ridicule of the Scopes trial by the media, it was Riley who claimed victory and honored Bryan in a memorial address. The next year he was feuding with the University of Minnesota and crusading for a state law prohibiting tax supported schools from teaching "that mankind either descended or ascended from a lower order of animals." Plenty of Minnesota Lutherans were antievolutionists but they felt Riley was violating the separation of church and state. The resulting defeat in the 1927 legislature pretty much ended Riley's national antievolution crusade and ended the real glory days of the WCFA as well.[114]

The national fundamentalist crusades faded but Riley's personal influence continued and even expanded. Several southern states went on to pass laws or issue administrative rulings restricting the teaching of evolution. He remained a giant on the lecture and evangelism circuits. Harry Rimmer signed on as field secretary with the WCFA in the late 1920s and proved to be an antievolutionist debater quite as raucous as Riley. By the mid-1930s Rimmer claimed to have addressed 3,876 student audiences in the United States and Canada.

These two crowd pleasers even debated each other at a Bible conference near Minneapolis. Riley held the "day-age" interpretation of the first chapter of Genesis while Rimmer defended the "gap" theory found in his Scofield Bible. Rimmer said:

> The tabernacle wouldn't hold them, and they sat on the platform, stood at the back and down the sides, and outside looking through doors and windows . . . We sure skinned each other without mercy whenever there was a good opening, and had a swell time. When the vote was taken I won by a majority of five to one. Riley conceded defeat and congratulated me, saying it showed what brains could do; make a man able to come into a fellow's own crowd and beat him on the wrong side of the question! I replied: "Nothing of the kind. It showed that truth is mighty and will prevail."[115]

They later repeated the performance at the Bible Institute of Los Angeles.[116]

Most important of all were Riley's church and schools. First Baptist Church of Minneapolis had grown to 3,550 members by the time he retired from its pastorate in 1942. One-tenth of Minnesota's Baptists were in it. To his Northwestern Bible and Missionary Training School founded in 1902 he added Northwestern Evangelical Theological Seminary in 1935 and Northwestern College of Liberal Arts in 1944. In 1946 these schools enrolled 700 students plus an additional 1,000 attending evening classes. As chief administrator of this center, Riley supplied a wide region with pastors, evangelists, youth leaders, teachers, church secretaries, and congregational officers. Of his corps of home missionaries Riley said, "We have made it our business to undertake the hardest and most difficult of fields." These enthusiastic alumni inspired fundamentalist loyalty and provided intensive fellowship for thousands of conservative church members. They were in effect their own denomination.[117]

Riley's dispensationalist premillennialist empire often controlled the Minnesota Baptist Convention and continually harassed the whole national body of Northern Baptists. One section of Riley's fundamentalist followers separated from the Northern Baptists in 1932 and took the denominational name General Association of Regular Baptists. Riley himself finally withdrew from the liberal Northern Baptist Convention in 1947. He said: "I am no longer a young man, having seen my eighty-sixth birthday, and I should be ashamed to die in a fellowship that seemed to me so un-Biblical, and consequently un-Baptist."[118]

That year he died. His biographer called him "the dominant figure in American fundamentalism in the first half of the twentieth century." The native of Greene County, Indiana, had built a conspicuous model. The future of fundamentalism did not depend on success in some great national crusade. It would not be wiped out by the embarrassment of a Scopes trial. It would not only survive but thrive in a network of like-minded churches either within old denominations or in newer fundamentalist denominations or outside denominations altogether. Some churches with major ministries and charismatic leaders would establish independent Bible schools, as many as seventy of them across the nation in the 1930s and 1940s, each with its regional empire.[119]

The end of Riley's united empire was also prophetic in the way it prefigured future divisions of the fundamentalist movement. On his deathbed Riley pointed his finger at young evangelist Billy Graham and said "Billy, you are the one to succeed me. I've known it for a long time. You will be disobeying God if you don't." So Billy became president of the Northwestern empire. He favored emphasis on liberal arts education and wanted to develop a fully accredited college like Wheaton. Only the less separatist and more ecumenical of Riley's followers would accept leadership in that direction, the ones coming increasingly to be known as "evangelicals" or "neo-evangelicals." The more insistent dispensationalists made fast their claim to the continuing name "fundamentalist" by stressing their separation from such world-oriented interests and standards. As militant separatists their zeal was for pure Bible schools to prepare pure leaders to serve pure churches which could snatch souls from the imminent destruction.[120]

Billy Graham resigned the school's presidency in February of 1952. Riley's empire splintered. But the American fundamentalism which Riley embodied and represented continued to flourish. In his native state of Indiana there were fundamentalist megachurches and schools much like his own. Pastor Gregory J. Dickson accepted a call to Indianapolis Baptist Temple in 1955. He led the small congregation to a membership of 8,000 while developing a large church plant on twenty-two acres on the south side of Indianapolis. The Baptist Temple schools ranged from kindergarten to college. Point seven in the "statement of faith" of its Bible Technical College said, "We believe in the Genesis account of creation."[121]

First Baptist Church of Hammond was the particular ministry of pastor Jack Hyles. It was long regarded as the nation's largest congregation, reporting a membership of 67,267 in 1982. The First Baptist sanctuary overflowed twice each Sunday to accommodate 20,000 attenders. The apex of its school system was Hyles Anderson College north of Crown Point. Smaller fundamentalist congregations, often Baptist but including independent churches and those of other denominations as well, were numerous in the state but unreported. Some percentage of almost every mainline Protestant body was likely to be fundamentalist in conviction.[122]

American church history underwent a substantial revision following 1970 as scholars gave fundamentalism more considered attention. It was not really a temporary aberration which ended in the 1920s, they said. It was the continuing reaction of an authentic conservative tradition, a persistent dynamic factor in the nation's religious life.[123]

Creationists

Indiana shared leadership of one more resurgence of strenuous biblical literalism. It was called "creationism."[124] Most earlier fundamentalists had agreed to open the time frame of the Genesis account by considering each creation day to be an indeterminate age (day-age theory) or by inserting indeterminate times between the creation events (gap theory). Creationists would grant their fellow fundamentalists no such equivocation. Nor would they tolerate the large liberal body of theistic evolutionists whom they considered even worse than atheists. At the very time that Darwinists like Hermann J. Muller were celebrating the centennial of *Origin of Species* and demanding unquestioned devotion to the principles of evolution in the public schools, the new creationist bombshell was in preparation. It was *The Genesis Flood* by John C. Whitcomb and Henry M. Morris, finally published in 1961. Its effect was cataclysmic. Whitcomb and Morris were to become regarded by fundamentalists as the Davids who slew the Goliath of evolution.[125]

John C. Whitcomb was an honors graduate of Princeton University and of Grace Theological Seminary at Winona Lake, Indiana. He remained on the faculty at Grace as a teacher of Old Testament. His doctoral dissertation subject was the worldwide flood reported in Genesis and its effects. His contribution became the first 151 pages of *The Genesis Flood* concerning the biblical and historical aspects of the deluge.

Henry M. Morris earned a Ph.D. from the University of Minnesota combining studies in hydraulics and geology. He became a central figure in developing one of the nation's major civil engineering departments at Virginia Polytechnic Institute. His fascination with the Genesis flood was part of a rejuvenation of his evangelical Baptist faith. He became convinced that creation took place in six literal days because the Bible clearly said so and God does not lie. He learned from the adventist George McCready Price, from the fundamentalist William Bell Riley, and from the peripatetic antievolutionist Harry Rimmer. Morris's contribution became the last 349 pages of *The Genesis Flood* concerning the geological effects of the deluge.

The work was complete with notes and scholarly apparatus. Creationists kept stressing a few key points. Because Scripture was inerrant, they could assert with complete confidence that the universe was created in six days of twenty-four hours each. They said creation was recent; the earth was no more than 10,000 years old. In about a year the all-encompassing flood laid down most of the geological strata. Secular evolutionists, theistic evolutionists, and gap theorists were all dangerously at odds with Bible truths and flood geology. They should agree with the Bible and accept correction.[126]

The authors were thrust onto a lecture circuit of campuses, church conventions, and learned society meetings. Whitcomb in Indiana had a speaking schedule filled years in advance. They were besought for articles and syllabi. Whitcomb wrote two more books on the flood and two on creationist astronomy. An army of friends of contemporary science, both inside and outside the churches, were their critics. Such an obvious unbalance of forces proved less a handicap than a guarantee of visibility and sympathy.

Morris channeled his energy into the Creation Research Society formed in 1963. It published a quarterly journal. Society members were Christians who subscribed their belief in the inerrancy of the Bible, special creation of all basic types of living things, and a geologically significant worldwide deluge. Full membership was limited to persons with a graduate degree in a scientific discipline. Within a decade there were about 450 regular members plus 1,600 sustaining members who did not meet the scientific qualification.[127]

They were well timed to focus the dissatisfaction of parents with the way evolution was featured in the new federally funded biology textbooks appearing in the 1960s. To the Creation Research Society Morris and his colleagues added the Creation Science Research Center at San Diego, California, to supply creationist materials suitable for public schools. Morris formed there the Institute for Creation Research with a small staff of scientists and made it a world center for strict creationism. In 1981 the Institute for Creation Research announced its own graduate program in creation sciences.[128]

Legislation to outlaw the teaching of evolution in the public schools did not fare well in the courts. Creationists changed tactics. They campaigned to get creation equal time. In their material for public schools they made few references to the Bible or to the accounts of creation or the flood as presented in Genesis. They knew that inclusion of religious teachings in public school texts would also fare poorly in the courts. Instead they focused on evidences of the flood as a recent worldwide catastrophe and especially on gaps or weaknesses in contemporary "theories" of evolution. Using the vocabulary of science, and according to science as they defined it a nearly idolatrous veneration, the creationists claimed to bring to public education a "creation science" worthy of equal consideration rather than censorship.[129]

Creationists had good grounds to believe that Americans who were given a simplified choice between evolution alone or evolution somehow balanced by a biblical testimony were highly likely to favor the Bible. An Associated Press/NBC poll in 1981 reported that 8 percent of respondents thought only evolution should be taught in public schools, 10 percent thought only creation should be taught, and 76 percent thought both creation and evolution should be taught. There was that 1982 Gallup poll reporting that 9 percent of respondents were atheists, 38 percent were theistic evolutionists and 44 percent were persons who agreed that "God created man pretty much in his present form at one time within the last 10,000 years." Another Gallup poll in 1991 found atheists numbering 9 percent, theistic evolutionists at 40 percent, and persons agreeing with the same strict statement of recent creation totaling 47 percent.[130]

Balance was rarely the mark of the discussion. Polarization and confrontation were the more common modes. Indiana became one of the battlegrounds. There were six textbooks approved by the state for biology classes in grades nine to twelve. On 12 December 1975 the Indiana State Commission on Textbook Adoption approved a seventh textbook. It was the new 1974 version of *Biology: A Search for Order in Complexity* from the Creation Research Society and its teacher's guide entitled

Scientific Creationism. In this edition creationism was to be stripped of its biblical wrappings and presented as flood geology science or creation science, an alternative and essential balance to the teaching of evolution. Within a few months seven Indiana school systems had adopted the new text: West Clark Community Schools, South Ripley Community School Corporation, Bango Community Schools, Union Township Schools, Warsaw Community Schools, East Washington School Corporation, and MSD Martinsville. Of these West Clark and South Ripley made the creation science book their sole textbook for biology.[131]

The choice was soon before the Indiana Civil Liberties Union (ICLU) Screening Committee. The parent American Civil Liberties Union, a famous foe of censorship, was nervous about having its state affiliate fighting to ban a book. However, the ICLU proceeded with a suit against the Textbook Commission on behalf of the Hendren and Marsh families with children in Silver Creek High School. First there was the required formal hearing before the Textbook Commission in Indianapolis in March of 1977. The ICLU presented an impressive parade of expert witnesses ready to object to the book's creation science but even more to the particular fundamentalist religious stance which the creationists had not managed to purge: Mr. William Mosley speaking for regional high school biology teachers; the Rev. Donald Nead as a representative of mainline Protestant groups; Dr. Clark Williamson of the faculty of Christian Theological Seminary; Rabbi Jonathan Stein speaking for Jews; Dr. Robert Risk of ICLU and a national officer of the Humanist Society; Dr. Jon Hendrix of Ball State in addition to Dr. John Bennett and Dr. Jane Kahle of Purdue speaking as professional biologists; Sister Barbara Ann Burman as a Catholic biologist; Dr. David Potter speaking as a professor of neuroscience and zoology at Indiana University.

The only expert witness speaking for the creationist book was Professor Larry G. Butler of Purdue who was a member of the Creation Research Society and had written one of its units. Press and radio gave the Indiana controversy full coverage; there were calls from radio stations in Canada and England. The case was discussed in the *Wall Street Journal*, the New York *Times*, and the *Yale Law Journal*. Walter Cronkite came to interview, and film footage appeared on CBS television.[132]

The Indiana State Commission on Textbook Adoption was not awed by all the witnesses. On 18 March 1977 it declared that the creationist textbook did not violate the law against sectarian materials or the constitutions of the nation or state. The textbook remained on the approved list. Lawyers for the plaintiffs and defendants then filed briefs to accompany the hearing transcript to the court.

William Mundy, deputy attorney general for Indiana, filed for the Textbook Commission. He presented a persistent fundamentalist concern by citing a question earlier raised in an opinion by Justice Black concerning an Arkansas case before the United States Supreme Court. What about infringement of the religious freedom of those who consider evolution an anti-religious doctrine? The state was to be neutral, not favoring one religion or anti-religion over another. "If the theory is considered anti-religious . . . how can the State be bound by the Federal Constitution to permit its teachers to advocate such an 'anti-religious' doctrine to school children?"[133]

The decision rested with Judge Michael T. Dugan of the Marion County Superior Court. Dugan reviewed the case with great care and issued his decision in April with a memorandum of twenty-one pages. He said the findings of the Indiana Textbook Commission were arbitrary, capricious, and an abuse of discretion. He said those findings were inconsistent with the evidence at the hearing. He said that both those findings and the biology textbook were at variance with the law so the findings were reversed and the Textbook Commission bidden to comply.[134]

The Indiana Textbook Commission did not appeal. However, the tension was little eased and the issue far from settled. The families of Silver Creek School who brought the suit suffered local harassment; E. Thomas Marsh was angrily disinherited by his own father. At the very next session of the Indiana legislature, House Bill 1172 was introduced requiring that any public school textbook discussing evolution also offer a balancing treatment of the teaching of special or biblical creation. The bill was favorably reported by the education committee but failed to pass. State Senator James Butler of Kokomo was ready with a creationism bill for the 1981 legislature which lost in committee by one vote.[135]

Persistent Disquiet

Hoosiers kept hearing from some mainline commentators that evolution and religion should not conflict. William R. Eberly made "Creationism and Evolution" the subject of his presidential address to the Indiana Academy of Science in 1982. Said George Plagenz in his syndicated column "Saints and Sinners" in the Bloomington *Herald-Telephone*: "It is not that the monkey story is necessarily untrue. It is just that, if man is a special creation of God, the artist may do a better job than the scientist of getting

us to see this. We may need the artist's conception quite as much as the scientist's. Science, of course, must be true to itself. It must deal only with scientific evidence. But it must not, on that account, rule out all other expressions of truth—those that cannot meet science's own criteria."[136]

At the end of his eleven selections demonstrating that "God is not a creationist," Roland Mushat Frye of the University of Pennsylvania affirmed once more the time-honored "two books" understanding:

> We have available to us not just one book of God, but two: the book of God's Word in Scripture, which concerns the ultimate nature and destiny of humanity, and the book of God's Works in Nature, which contains the created order . . . Science and faith will conflict irreconcilably only if we insist upon confusing and conflating the two books of God. And if we do that, the result will be either bad for science, or bad for religion, or bad for both.[137]

But theistic evolutionists were rarely articulate. A long century after Darwin, evolution remained for many persons, especially for secular enthusiasts and religious enthusiasts, the symbol of a conflict which seemed to permit no compromise. Abrasive encounters between these extremists continued to receive news coverage. It was the creationists who understood especially well how to raise the concerns of the great body of godfearers who felt their convictions were being displaced by an anti-religious orthodoxy in the educational establishment. The language of warfare lived on and no resolution was in view.[138]

NOTES

1. Jon H. Roberts, *Darwinism and the Divine in America: Protestant Intellectuals and Organic Evolution, 1859–1900* (Madison, Wis.: University of Wisconsin Press, 1988), ix, 25–26, 254–55; George M. Marsden, *Understanding Fundamentalism and Evangelicalism* (Grand Rapids, Mich.: William B. Eerdmans, 1991), 136–37. For a chart outlining "day-age," "gap," and "flood geology" interpretations of Genesis, see Ronald L. Numbers, *The Creationists* (New York: Alfred A. Knopf, 1992), xii–xiii.

2. Benjamin C. Cressy, *An Address Delivered before the Zelo-Paideusian Society of Washington County Seminary . . . March 14, 1834* (Salem, Ind.: J. G. and W. H. May, 1834), 17.

3. William C. Larrabee, *Lectures on the Scientific Evidences of Natural and Revealed Religion* (Cincinnati, Ohio: L. Swormstedt and A. Poe, 1853), 395; Roberts, *Darwinism*, 3–31; Marsden, *Understanding Fundamentalism*, 128–34; *God and Nature: Historical Essays on the Encounter between Christianity and Science*, ed. David C. Lindberg and Ronald L. Numbers (Berkeley, Calif.: University of California Press, 1986), 351; Theodore Dwight Bozeman, *Protestants in an Age of Science: The Baconian Ideal and Antebellum*

American Religious Thought (Chapel Hill, N.C.: University of North Carolina Press, 1977, 243 p.).

4. Emma Lou Thornbrough, *Indiana in the Civil War Era, 1850–1880* (Indianapolis, Ind.: Indiana Historical Bureau and Indiana Historical Society, 1965), 520–21; James I. Osborne and Theodore G. Gronert, *Wabash College: The First Hundred Years, 1832–1932* (Crawfordsville, Ind.: R. E. Banta, 1932), 72, 133–37; John F. Cady, *The Centennial History of Franklin College* (Franklin, Ind.: n.p., 1934), 141–42.

5. David Starr Jordan and Amos W. Butler, "New Harmony," *Scientific Monthly* 25 (November 1927): 468–70; Thornbrough, *Indiana in the Civil War Era*, 672.

6. Charles Robert Darwin, *On the Origin of Species by Means of Natural Selection; or, The Preservation of Favoured Races in the Struggle for Life* (London: J. Murray, 1859, 502 p.); James R. Moore, *The Post-Darwinian Controversies: A Study of the Protestant Struggle to Come to Terms with Darwin in Great Britain and America, 1870–1900* (Cambridge, Eng.: Cambridge University Press, 1979), 218–20, 252; Marsden, *Understanding Fundamentalism*, 12–15, 135–41; Roberts, *Darwinism*, ix, 30–31, 233–34; *God and Nature*, 352–55.

7. Frederick Doyle Kershner, Jr., "A Social and Cultural History of Indianapolis, 1860–1914" (Ph.D. diss., University of Wisconsin, 1950), 211.

8. Andrew Denny Rodgers III, *John Merle Coulter: Missionary in Science* (Princeton, N.J.: Princeton University Press, 1944), 294.

9. Adrian Desmond and James Moore, *Darwin: The Life of a Tormented Evolutionist* (London: Michael Joseph, 1991, 808 p.); *God and Nature*, 365.

10. Numbers, *Creationists*, 5.

11. Charles Robert Darwin, *The Descent of Man, and Selection in Relation to Sex*, 2 vols. (London: J. Murray, 1871); Roberts, *Darwinism*, 103–8, 116.

12. Roberts, *Darwinism*, 82–83; Marsden, *Understanding Fundamentalism*, 140–41; *God and Nature*, 362–65.

13. Roberts, *Darwinism*, 52–55, 66–75; Moore, *Post-Darwinian Controversies*, 58–68; Marsden, *Understanding Fundamentalism*, 140; *God and Nature*, 362–65. Prominent among the opponents of a Christian world view, in addition to Huxley, were Herbert Spencer, Edward L. Youmans, John Fiske, and John Tyndall.

14. Thornbrough, *Indiana in the Civil War Era*, 669–70; Kershner, "Social and Cultural History," 212.

15. John W. Draper, *History of the Conflict between Religion and Science* (New York: D. Appleton and Co., 1874, 373 p.); Moore, *Post-Darwinian Controversies*, 24.

16. Moore, *Post-Darwinian Controversies*, 20–29; *God and Nature*, 1–2; Roberts, *Darwinism*, 79.

17. *God and Nature*, 2–3.

18. Andrew D. White, *The Warfare of Science* (London: Henry S. King, 1876), 7–8.

19. Andrew D. White, *A History of the Warfare of Science with Theology in Christendom*, 2 vols. (London: Macmillan, 1896).

20. Moore, *Post-Darwinian Controversies*, 30–49; *God and Nature*, 2–3.

21. Moore, *Post-Darwinian Controversies*, 99–100. See also *God and Nature*, 3–14, 351–68, and Lewis Perry, *Intellectual Life in America: A History* (New York: Franklin Watts, 1984), 291–303.

22. David C. Lindberg and Ronald L. Numbers, "Beyond War and Peace: A Reappraisal of the Encounter between Christianity and Science," *Church History* 55 (September 1986): 338–54.

23. *God and Nature*, 10, 14.

24. Roberts, *Darwinism*, 27–31, 33–38; Moore, *Post-Darwinian Controversies*, 207–11; *God and Nature*, 356–58.

25. Charles Hodge, *What Is Darwinism?* (New York: Scribner, Armstrong, and Company, 1874, 178 p.); Jonathan Wells, *Charles Hodge's Critique of Darwinism: A Historical-Critical Analysis of Concepts Basic to the 19th Century Debate* (Lewiston, N.Y.: Edwin Mellen Press, 1988, 242 p.); Jonathan Wells, "Charles Hodge on the Bible and Science," *American Presbyterians* 66 (Fall 1988): 157–65; Moore, *Post-Darwinian Controversies*, 203–4, 211–12; *God and Nature*, 374–78.

26. David N. Livingstone, *Darwin's Forgotten Defenders; The Encounters between Evangelical Theology and Evolutionary Thought* (Grand Rapids, Mich.: William B. Eerdmans, 1987, 210 p.); Gary S. Smith, "Calvinists and Evolution, 1870–1920," *Journal of Presbyterian History* 61 (Fall 1983): 335–52; Roberts, *Darwinism*, 117–45; *God and Nature*, 378–83.

27. Moore, *Post-Darwinian Controversies*, 269–80; Roberts, *Darwinism*, 18–19, 38–40, 120; *God and Nature*, 358–62.

28. Moore, *Post-Darwinian Controversies*, 71–72, 245–51, 280–98; Marsden, *Understanding Fundamentalism*, 156.

29. For an interesting example of a clergyman college president relating to bumptious scientists with some resentment, see Joseph F. Tuttle, *Physical Science and Christianity: A Baccalaureate Discourse Delivered at Wabash College, Crawfordsville, Indiana . . . June 2, 1873* (Newark, N.J.: Daily Advertiser, 1873, 20 p.).

30. Millard S. Markle, "The Influence of Quakers on Science in Indiana," *Proceedings of the Indiana Academy of Science*, 69 (1959): 245–46.

31. William Cooper, "Joseph Moore: Quaker Evolutionist," *Indiana Magazine of History* 72 (June 1976): 123–37; Opal Thornburg, *Earlham: The Story of the College 1847–1962* (Richmond, Ind.: Earlham College Press, 1963), 94–95, 97–101, 121–25; Markle, "Influence of Quakers on Science," 243–46.

32. Osborne and Gronert, *Wabash College*, 150.

33. Victor L. Albjerg, *Richard Owen, Scotland 1810, Indiana 1890* (Lafayette, Ind.: n.p., 1946), 49.

34. David Starr Jordan, *The Days of a Man: Being Memories of a Naturalist, Teacher and Minor Prophet of Democracy*, 2 vols. (Yonkers-on-Hudson, N.Y.: World Book Company, 1922), 1:46–47.

35. Jordan, *Days of a Man*, 1:36, 48–50, 132.

36. Jordan, *Days of a Man*, 1:114.

37. Thomas D. Clark, *Indiana University: Midwestern Pioneer*, 4 vols. (Bloomington, Ind.: Indiana University Press, 1970–77), 1:202–11; Elizabeth R. O'Lessker, Bruce Harrah-Conforth, and William M. Gering, "David Starr Jordan: His Three Lives," *Indiana Alumni* 48 (October 1985): 8–14; Burton D. Myers, "A Study of Faculty Appointments at Indiana University, 1824–1937," *Indiana Magazine of History* 40 (June 1944): 132.

38. George B. Manhart, *DePauw through the Years*, 2 vols. (Greencastle, Ind.: DePauw University, 1962), 1:36–37.

39. Truman G. Yuncker, "A Century of Botany and Botanists at DePauw University," *Proceedings of the Indiana Academy of Science*, 71 (1961): 242–47; Manhart, *DePauw through the Years*, 1:208–12.

40. John Price Durbin John, *Did Man Make God, or Did God Make Man: A Reply to Robert Ingersoll* (Indianapolis, Ind.: Frank Caldwell, 1898), 41–42.

41. John C. Smith, *Reminiscences of Early Methodism in Indiana* (Indianapolis, Ind.: J. M. Olcott, 1879), 318.

42. George Richmond Grose, *The Outlook for Religion* (Cincinnati, Ohio: Jennings and Graham, 1913), 42.

43. George Richmond Grose, *Religion and the Mind* (New York: Abingdon Press, 1915), 88.

44. George M. Marsden, *Fundamentalism and American Culture: The Shaping of Twentieth-Century Evangelicalism, 1870–1925* (New York: Oxford University Press, 1982), 22–26; Roberts, *Darwinism*, 195–96; Moore, *Post-Darwinian Controversies*, 92–93, 234, 302–3; *God and Nature*, 382–83.

45. Henry Ward Beecher, *Evolution and Religion*, 2 vols. (New York: Fords, Howard, and Hulbert, 1885), 1:429.

46. Lyman Abbott, *The Theology of an Evolutionist* (Boston: Houghton, Mifflin and Co., 1897, 191 p.); James Turner, *Without God, Without Creed; The Origins of Unbelief in America* (Baltimore, Md.: Johns Hopkins University Press, 1985, 316 p.); Dean M. Kelley, *Why Conservative Churches Are Growing: A Study in Sociology of Religion* (San Francisco: Harper and Row, 1977, 184 p.); Roger Finke, *The Churching of America, 1776–1990: Winners and Losers in Our Religious Economy* (New Brunswick, N.J.: Rutgers University Press, 1992, 328 p.); Sydney E. Ahlstrom, *Religious History of the American People* (New Haven, Conn.: Yale University Press, 1972), 763–804; Roberts, *Darwinism*, 126–30, 137–45, 197, 238–41; *God and Nature*, 382–87; Moore, *Post-Darwinian Controversies*, 346–51.

47. Marsden, *Understanding Fundamentalism*, 4–5.

48. William V. Trollinger, *God's Empire: William Bell Riley and Midwestern Fundamentalism* (Madison, Wis.: University of Wisconsin Press, 1990), 4–8; Marsden, *Fundamentalism and American Culture*, 118–23, 132–35; Marsden, *Understanding Fundamentalism*, 38, 41.

49. The case has been repeatedly made that for both secularists and fundamentalists evolution was claiming to be a modern cosmic myth, an all-explanatory metaphor, a world view providing ethical guidelines, and the only permissible account of all phenomena of being or experience. See David N. Livingstone, "Evolution as Myth and Metaphor," *Christian Scholar's Review*, vol. 12, no. 2 (1983): 111–25; Marsden, *Understanding Fundamentalism*, 59–60, 147–49, 179–81.

50. George W. Geib, *Lives Touched by Faith: Second Presbyterian Church, 150 Years* (Indianapolis, Ind.: Second Presbyterian Church, 1988), 102–3.

51. Martin E. Marty, *The Noise of Conflict 1919–1941*, vol. 2 of *Modern American Religion* (Chicago: University of Chicago Press, 1991), 184–93; Ferenc Morton Szasz, *The Divided Mind of Protestant America 1880–1930* (University, Ala.: University of Alabama Press, 1982), 107–35; Edward J. Larson, *Trial and Error: The American Controversy over Creation and Evolution* (New York: Oxford University Press, 1985), 58–75; Marsden, *Understanding Fundamentalism*, 59–60; *God and Nature*, 401–3.

52. Hermann J. Muller, "One Hundred Years Without Darwinism Are Enough," *The Humanist* 19 (June 1959): 139–49.

53. Dorothy Nelkin, *The Creation Controversy: Science or Scripture in the Schools* (New York: W. W. Norton, 1982), 39–53; Henry M. Morris, *A History of Modern Creationism* (San Diego, Calif.: Master Book Publishers, 1984), 69–70, 75–77; Numbers, *Creationists*, 238–40.

54. John C. Whitcomb and Henry M. Morris, *The Genesis Flood* (Philadelphia: Presbyterian and Reformed Publishing Co., 1961, 518 p.); Creation Research Society, *Biology: A Search for Order in Complexity* (Grand Rapids, Mich.: Zondervan Publishing House, 1970, 548 p.); Morris, *History*, 143–203; Numbers, *Creationists*, 184–240.

55. Numbers, *Creationists*, 241–57, 286–87, 319–39, 349; Morris, *History*, 261–66, 308–11; *God and Nature*, 410–15.

56. *Is God a Creationist: The Religious Case against Creation-Science*, ed. Roland Mushat Frye (New York: Charles Scribner's Sons, 1983, 205 p.); *Scientists Confront Creationism*, ed. Laurie R. Godfrey (New York: W. W. Norton, 1983), xxvi; Carl Sagan, *Cosmos* (New York: Random House, 1980), 4; Richard Dawkins, *The Blind Watchmaker: Why the Evidence of Evolution Reveals a Universe without Design* (New York: Norton, 1985, 332 p.); "Public Opinion and Demographic Report," *The Public Perspective: A Roper Center Review of Public Opinion and Polling* 2 (July–August 1991): insert p. 87.

57. Ronald L. Numbers, "Creation, Evolution, and Holy Ghost Religion: Holiness and Pentecostal Responses to Darwinism," *Religion and American Culture* 2 (Summer 1992): 144–45, 155–56; Numbers, *Creationists*, 158–83; Morris, *History of Modern Creationism*, 130–44; Nelkin, *Creation Controversy*, 77–78.

58. Cornelius J. Troost, "An Analysis of Factors Influencing the Teaching of Evolution in the Secondary Schools of Indiana" (Ed.D. diss., Indiana University, 1966), 8.

59. Troost, "Analysis," 92–93.

60. Troost, "Analysis," iii, 58–61.

61. Troost, "Analysis," 93, 95, 102–3, 110, 113.

62. Troost, "Analysis," 98–99, 117.

63. Ralph E. Weber, *Notre Dame's John Zahm, American Catholic Apologist and Educator* (Notre Dame, Ind.: University of Notre Dame Press, 1961), 2; R. Scott Appleby, "Between Americanism and Modernism: John Zahm and Theistic Evolution," *Church History* 56 (December 1987): 474–90.

64. Weber, *Zahm*, 2–8.

65. Weber, *Zahm*, 22–24.

66. Weber, *Zahm*, 25.

67. Weber, *Zahm*, 26–28, 46–47.

68. Weber, *Zahm*, 53.

69. Weber, *Zahm*, 53–54.

70. Weber, *Zahm*, 56–62, 66, 74, 75.

71. John A. Zahm, *Bible, Science, and Faith* (Baltimore, Md.: J. Murphy, 1894, 316 p.); John A. Zahm, *Evolution and Dogma* (Chicago: D. H. McBride, 1896, 461 p.); Weber, *Zahm*, 71, 77–79, 82.

72. Robert T. Handy, *A History of the Churches in the United States and Canada* (New York: Oxford University Press, 1979), 316–26; Ahlstrom, *Religious History*, 825–41.

73. Weber, *Zahm*, 107, 109.

74. Weber, *Zahm*, 99–124; Appleby, "Between Americanism and Modernism," 486–90.

75. *Is God a Creationist*, 154.

76. Andrew Denny Rodgers III, *John Merle Coulter: Missionary in Science* (Princeton, N.J.: Princeton University Press, 1944, 321 p.); John Gaylord Coulter, *The Dean* (Lafayette, Ind.: Haywood Publishing Company, 1940, 272 p.).

77. Rodgers, *John Merle Coulter*, 8, 13–14, 25, 28.

78. Rodgers, *John Merle Coulter*, 39.

79. Rodgers, *John Merle Coulter*, 39–40.

80. Rodgers, *John Merle Coulter*, 47.

81. Clark, *Indiana University*, 1:265–83.

82. George D. Fuller, "John Merle Coulter," *Science*, n.s., 69 (15 February 1929): 177–80.

83. Rodgers, *John Merle Coulter*, 51, 111, 147, 183, 237, 293.

84. Rodgers, *John Merle Coulter*, 237, 296.

85. John M. Coulter and Merle C. Coulter, *Where Evolution and Religion Meet* (New York: Macmillan, 1924), 1–2.

86. Coulter and Coulter, *Where Evolution and Religion Meet*, 7, 23–54, 78–100.

87. Coulter and Coulter, *Where Evolution and Religion Meet*, 98–105; John Merle Coulter, "The Religion of a Scientist," *Biblical World* 41 (February 1913): 82–84; John Merle Coulter, "Science and Religion: The Methods and Results of Science," *Biblical World* 54 (July 1920): 339.

88. Elof Axel Carlson, *Genes, Radiation, and Society: The Life and Work of H. J. Muller* (Ithaca, N.Y.: Cornell University Press, 1981), 11–17, 22.

89. Carlson, *Genes*, 22.

90. For a partial list of honors accorded to Muller, see *Who Was Who in America* 4 (1961–68): 687.

91. Carlson, *Genes*, 380–404, 415.

92. Carlson, *Genes*, 420.

93. Muller, "One Hundred Years," 140.

94. The American Humanist Association was formed in 1941. Accepting the perspective of "A Humanist Manifesto" previously issued in 1933, it regarded the universe as self-existing, not created, and man a part of nature evolved in its processes. It rejected theism and even deism. It advocated several social routes to abundant life understood as complete realization of human personality. See J. Gordon Melton, *The Encyclopedia of American Religions*, 3d ed. (Detroit: Gale Research, 1989), 557–58.

95. Carlson, *Genes*, 415–16, 437; Numbers, *Creationists*, 243; Nelkin, *Creation Controversy*, 34.

96. Marie Acomb Riley, *The Dynamic of a Dream: The Life Story of Dr. William B. Riley* (Grand Rapids, Mich.: William B. Eerdmans, 1938), 19–33; William Vance Trollinger, Jr., *God's Empire: William Bell Riley and Midwestern Fundamentalism* (Madison, Wis.: University of Wisconsin Press, 1990), x, 10–12.

97. Riley, *Dynamic of a Dream*, 29–31, 33–35, 45–48; Trollinger, *God's Empire*, 12–14.

98. Trollinger, *God's Empire*, 13, 24, 27.

99. Trollinger, *God's Empire*, 27; Marsden, *Fundamentalism and American Culture*, 32–39.

100. Trollinger, *God's Empire*, 16–20; Marsden, *Fundamentalism and American Culture*, 127–28.

101. Marsden, *Fundamentalism and American Culture*, 48–55; Ahlstrom, *Religious History*, 808–11; Trollinger, *God's Empire*, 27.

102. Trollinger, *God's Empire*, 27–28; Marsden, *Fundamentalism and American Culture*, 38.

103. Trollinger, *God's Empire*, 23, 29, 37; Marsden, *Fundamentalism and American Culture*, 46, 127, 151–52.

104. Trollinger, *God's Empire*, 37–38.

105. Trollinger, *God's Empire*, 38–39; Marsden, *Fundamentalism and American Culture*, 31, 158, 160.

106. Mark A. Noll, "Christian Colleges, Christian Worldviews, and an Invitation to Research," Introduction to William C. Ringenberg, *The Christian College: A History of Protestant Higher Education in America* (Grand Rapids, Mich.: William B. Eerdmans, 1984), 1–36; George M. Marsden, *The Soul of the American University: From Protestant Establishment to Established Nonbelief* (New York: Oxford University Press, 1994), 267–331; William B. Riley, *The Fi-*

nality of the Higher Criticism: or, The Theory of Evolution and False Theology (N.p. 1909, 223 p.); William B. Riley, *The Menace of Modernism* (New York: Christian Alliance Company, 1917, 181 p.); Trollinger, *God's Empire*, 40.

107. Trollinger, *God's Empire*, 34.

108. Trollinger, *God's Empire*, 35–36.

109. Trollinger, *God's Empire*, 40–44, 54–57.

110. Trollinger, *God's Empire*, 44–46; *God and Nature*, 398–99; Numbers, *Creationists*, 50–53.

111. Trollinger, *God's Empire*, 46–48.

112. Trollinger, *God's Empire*, 48.

113. Trollinger, *God's Empire*, 48–49; Marsden, *Fundamentalism and American Culture*, 169–70.

114. Trollinger, *God's Empire*, 49–52.

115. Numbers, *Creationists*, 66–67.

116. Morris, *History of Modern Creationism*, 88–92; Numbers, *Creationists*, 45–46, 60–71; *God and Nature*, 399–400, 403.

117. Trollinger, *God's Empire*, 8, 22, 110, 156–59. For a twelve-page list of the printed works of William Bell Riley see Trollinger, *God's Empire*, 205–16.

118. Trollinger, *God's Empire*, 57–61, 148; Marsden, *Fundamentalism and American Culture*, 192–93.

119. Trollinger, *God's Empire*, 4, 7–8, 84, 156.

120. George M. Marsden, *Reforming Fundamentalism: Fuller Seminary and the New Evangelicalism* (Grand Rapids, Mich.: W. B. Eerdmans, 1987, 319 p.); Marsden, *Understanding Fundamentalism*, 100–109; Marsden, *Fundamentalism and American Culture*, 193–95; Trollinger, *God's Empire*, 151–59.

121. Richard V. Pierard and James L. Wright, "No Hoosier Hospitality for Humanism: The Moral Majority in Indiana," in *New Christian Politics*, ed. David G. Bromley and Anson Shupe (Macon, Ga.: Mercer University Press, 1984), 195–212; *Bible Technical College: A Ministry of Indianapolis Baptist Temple* (N.p., n.d., 6 p.).

122. Bill J. Leonard, "Independent Baptists: From Sectarian Minority to 'Moral Majority'," *Church History* 56 (December 1987): 504–17; Lee Elder, "Allegations Continue to Hound Fundamentalist Hyles," *Christianity Today* 34 (24 September 1990): 45–46.

123. Trollinger, *God's Empire*, 4–9. See also Marsden, *Fundamentalism and American Culture* and his *Understanding Fundamentalism and Evangelicalism*. The Institute for the Study of American Evangelicals at Wheaton College and the Billy Graham Center Archives at Wheaton College provide extensive bibliographical and archival resources.

124. Ronald L. Numbers, *The Creationists* (New York: Alfred A. Knopf, 1992, 458 p.); Ronald L. Numbers, "The Creationists," in *God and Nature: Historical Essays on the Encounter between Christianity and Science* (Berkeley, Calif.: University of California Press, 1986), 391–423; George M. Marsden, "Why Creation Science?" in his *Understanding Fundamentalism and Evangelicalism* (Grand Rapids, Mich.: William B. Eerdmans, 1991), 153–81; Henry M. Morris, *A History of Modern Creationism* (San Diego, Calif.: Master Book Publishers, 1984, 382 p.); *Scientists Confront Creationism*, ed. Laurie R. Godfrey (New York: W. W. Norton, 1983, 324 p.); Edward O. Dodson and George F. Howe, *Creation or Evolution: Correspondence on the Current Controversy* (Ottawa: University of Ottawa Press, 1990, 175 p.).

125. Numbers, *Creationists*, xii–xiii, 184–213, 338–39; Morris, *History of Modern Creationism*, 58–59, 145–46.

126. Morris, *History of Modern Creationism*, 58–61, 88–92, 146–50; Numbers, *Creationists*, 187–200, 338; *God and Nature*, 407.

127. Morris, *History of Modern Creationism*, 157–67; Numbers, *Creationists*, 214–40; *God and Nature*, 409–10.

128. Morris, *History of Modern Creationism*, 231–72; Numbers, *Creationists*, 239, 283–90; *God and Nature*, 411, 413.

129. Dennis E. Owen, Kenneth D. Wald, and Samuel S. Hill, "Authoritarian or Authority-Minded? The Cognitive Commitments of Fundamentalists and the Christian Right," *Religion and American Culture* 1 (Winter 1991): 77–78, 94–95; *Wall Street Journal*, 9 and 26 December 1986, editorial pages; Numbers, *Creationists*, 319–23.

130. Martin E. Marty, "Scripturality: The Bible as Icon in the Republic," in *Religion and Republic: The American Circumstance* (Boston: Beacon Press, 1987), 140–65; *U.S. News & World Report* 111 (23 December 1991): 56–64; Morris, *History of Modern Creationism*, 310–11; Numbers, *Creationists*, ix, 349.

131. Irving L. Fink, "Bible Biology: Hendren V. Indiana Textbook Commission," in *We the People: Indiana and the United States Constitution. Lectures Given under the Sponsorship of the Indiana Association of Historians* (Indianapolis, Ind.: Indiana Historical Society, 1987), 94–112; Larson, *Trial and Error*, 144–48, 204–5; Numbers, *Creationists*, 238–57.

132. Fink, "Bible Biology," 97–106; Numbers, *Creationists*, 240. For details of Larry Butler's association and dissociation with the Creation Research Society, see Numbers, *Creationists*, 255–57.

133. Fink, "Bible Biology," 106–8.

134. Fink, "Bible Biology," 100, 108–10.

135. Fink, "Bible Biology," 110–11; Bloomington *Herald-Telephone*, 17 December 1981, p. 44.

136. *Proceedings of the Indiana Academy of Science*, 92 (1982): 61–69; George Plagenz, "Saints and Sinners," Bloomington *Herald-Telephone*, 4 August 1984, p. 12.

137. *Is God a Creationist*, 199, 204.

138. Larson, *Trial and Error*, 168–71.

MIDDLETOWN

"Middletown" was a code name for Muncie, Indiana. The names Middletown and Muncie were used interchangeably. Three major sociological research projects have been conducted there. Sociologist David E. Kyvig said "No other American community has been so carefully scrutinized over so long a time as Muncie, and none has contributed more to an understanding of how ordinary people live." American history textbooks regularly supported their accounts and conclusions with specific data gathered at Muncie. After the publication of the first study in 1929, economist Stuart Chase wrote in *The Nation*, "Nothing like it has ever before been attempted; no such knowledge of how the average American community works and plays has ever been packed between the covers of any one book; and I warn you that hereafter nobody has any right to make more than the most casual generalizations about the culture levels of this republic, until he has first read and mastered his *Middletown*."[1]

Middletown I

That first Middletown study was conducted with Rockefeller funding in the 1920s. John D. Rockefeller, Jr., was deeply committed to the support of religion and education. In the years surrounding the First World War he gave enthusiastic leadership to the Interchurch World Movement, to united efforts in world evangelism, and to the international YMCA. He hoped to keep on enlisting the churches to unify in great joint enterprises of practical Christianity and social service which would overcome class divisions. By 1920 Rockefeller's chief agent and adviser for this church and society program was Raymond B. Fosdick, brother of Rockefeller's pastor Harry Emerson Fosdick. Raymond Fosdick had an impressive record of prior service with the League of Nations and with the international YMCA.

Fosdick was not so much interested in unifying the efforts of the churches. His enthusiasm was for unifying the power of the burgeoning social sciences. He thought the best insights of economics, political science, sociology, anthropology, and psychology should be combined to produce a practical "science of society." Such a synthesis would surely make obvious the kind of social policy and social control needed for the survival and advancement of civilization.

The visions of Rockefeller and Fosdick were merged, though not really integrated, in 1923 in the Institute of Social and Religious Research funded by the recently established Laura Spelman Rockefeller Memorial endowment. Rockefeller funds had established a precedent of underwriting expert field studies to determine social and religious needs. High on the list of projects for the new Institute was a professional community survey to disclose the real social dynamics of a typical small industrial city. Muncie was the eventual choice to be "Middletown." It was clearly industrial but not too big. It was "typical," midwestern, and without a large black or foreign-born population to complicate the analysis.[2]

Rockefeller was most interested in the united potential of the churches and Fosdick was most interested in the united potential of the social sciences. Yet the man they commissioned for the first Middletown study was not much interested in either. Robert S. Lynd was a banker's son from New Albany, Indiana. He was a graduate of Princeton University and of Union Theological Seminary in New York and so knew something of organized religion but was hardly friendly to it. He would have preferred that his work be "completely separated from the immediate practical concerns of the churches."

Lynd was not a trained sociologist either. He had done some study of the subject including two social science courses at Columbia while studying in New York, one with the philosopher John Dewey and one with the economist Wesley Mitchell. During the summer of 1921 he did seminary field work at the Standard Oil of Indiana field at Elk Basin in Wyoming. That experience became the basis of his correspondence with Rockefeller about the deplorable state of oil field workers and of his published attacks on company policies to which Rockefeller replied as Standard's chief stockholder. His connections with Rockefeller and the Fosdicks got him the job.[3]

Robert S. Lynd and his recent bride Helen Merrell Lynd arrived in Muncie early in 1924. She was a recent graduate of Wellesley with a lively interest in social science. They hired two statisticians and a stenographer. The five of them invested a total of fifty months searching out and describing all facets of the town's everyday life.

They chose to go about their work like cultural anthropologists studying a primitive tribe. They organized their research and their book in six sections: (1) getting a living; (2) making a home; (3) training the young; (4) using leisure; (5) engaging in religious practices; (6) engaging in community activities. They seemed to attend everything, read everything, and talk to everybody. They produced "an astonishingly informative description of everyday life in a small city." By recording the details of routine behavior and by close rendering of hosts of actual comments and conversations they gave the book an immediate impression of veracity. The authors' persistent strain of satire about small town life only made their well-written account more fun to read.[4] A social historian commented:

> The book is full of the details of everyday life: what time people of different classes got up in the morning, who baked and who bought bread, who owned a car, how the car was used, how many persons went to the movies, how the laundry got done, what was taught in the

schools, who went to church, what the minister said in church, how many women got married, how many couples got divorced, and what values different class members held. All of these became the stock of social history, a veritable treasure trove of data for future generations of scholars to mine.[5]

The Lynd team saw a lot of religion in Middletown during the months of their study. They interviewed ministers and members. They attended hundreds of religious services, YMCA programs, and meetings of church groups. They studied church documents, published and unpublished. They analyzed church items and sermons in the newspapers and took careful notes on sermons they themselves heard. About a fifth of *Middletown* described religion in fascinating detail. The ninety-seven pages in the section "Engaging in Religious Practices" offered four chapters entitled (1) "Dominant Religious Beliefs"; (2) "Where and When Religious Rites Are Carried On"; (3) "Leaders and Participants in Religious Rites"; and (4) "Religious Observances."[6]

The Middletown religious documentation was impressive and useful but interpretation of the data was clearly biased. The Lynds were not Marxists but they were sure that economic forces were determining both human personality and contemporary culture. Capitalistic modernization brought industry and technology which destroyed the stability of old social patterns. The happy skilled workers of 1890 were reduced to anxious twentieth century factory laborers caught in a heartless industrial system. In the process people were socially alienated. There was rigid division between a small ruling business class and a large dispossessed working class. These convictions the Lynds projected everywhere in their interpretation of Middletown data. From this point of view they saw organized religion as an obsolescent survival of a premodern culture.[7] More than fifty years later a professional sociologist analyzed their stance:

> In theory, the sociology of religion stands aloof from the controversies of religion and considers religious phenomena with scientific detachment, measuring them with instruments that are not affected by the preferences of the scientific observer. In practice, it is not easy to maintain this desirable impartiality, and it is even possible to discover antireligion and proreligion factions among the sociologists of religion. The antireligion sociologists of religion (1) do not accept religious experience as intrinsically valid, regarding it either as an illusion or as a sociopsychological device, (2) perceive a contradiction between the rationality of science and the irrationality of religion, and (3) anticipate the decline and ultimate

disappearance of religion. Scholars of the proreligion faction hold nearly opposite views. They (1) interpret religious experience as an interaction between human persons and an external reality, (2) understand science and religion to be dealing quite compatibly with different aspects of experience, and (3) do not regard the decline of religion as inevitable or even probable. Since the appearance of scientific sociology in the 19th century, the antireligion faction has been the more influential . . . As it happened, none of the scholars who had the most influence on the development of modern sociology—Spencer, Marx, Durkheim, Weber, and Simmel—was particularly open to religious experience.[8]

The Lynds were children of their time. They were in the tradition of antireligion sociologists of religion.

Robert Lynd had already turned away from organized religion when he began to observe Muncie's churches in 1924 and had little empathy with the enterprise. Affirmations of faith and of religious experience were no longer meaningful for him. He was sure the role of religion must soon decline. Technology and modernization were the shapers of human behavior and values. If religion did not assert power over technology and modernization it was irrelevant. Attending religious services was reported as "habit," an old pattern persisting longer among the working class and among women. Lynd saw ministers as pathetic symbols of religion's lost relevance.[9]

Secular marriages are increasing, divorce is increasing, wives of both workers and business men would appear to stress loyalty to the church less than did their mothers in training their children, church attendance is apparently less regular than in 1890, Rotary which boasts that it includes all the leaders of the city will admit no minister, social activities are much less centered in the churches, leisure time is increasingly less touched by religious prohibitions in its encroachments upon the Sabbath, more and more community activities are, as the press points out in regard to questions of disease and health, being regarded not as "acts of God" but as subjects for investigation. In theory, religious beliefs dominate all other activities in Middletown; actually, large regions of Middletown's life appear uncontrolled by them.[10]

When the Lynds finished writing the report of their study, their sponsors did not want it published. It satisfied neither the religious interests of Rockefeller nor the social science interests of Raymond Fosdick. Its bias was painfully evident and unwelcome. The Institute for Social and Religious Research made no plan for publication.

Robert Lynd was able to use his part of the work as a dissertation for his doctorate at Columbia. Both Robert and Helen found other employment. Two years later the publisher Alfred Harcourt saw a copy and wired the Lynds for permission to print it. *Middletown* was an instant success in 1929, reviewed on the front pages of the New York *Times* and the *Herald-Tribune*. It quickly went through six printings and took its place on the shelf of classics perennially in stock. Robert Lynd received two offers of tenured professorships and joined the faculty at Columbia in 1931.[11]

Middletown II

Harcourt hoped for another best seller. He convinced Lynd to write a sequel to *Middletown*. That project was to become known as Middletown II. This time there was no Rockefeller funding. Helen Lynd did not return to Muncie. Robert Lynd lived there only during the summer of 1935. The total research time invested by Lynd and his five assistants was about one-tenth that of the original study. There was the same emphasis on social class division, this time focused again and again on the local power of the Ball family. Descriptions of the impact of the Great Depression were especially useful. Published as *Middletown in Transition* in 1937, the second study was received with less enthusiasm than the first. It brought mixed reviews. It also brought Margaret Bourke-White of *Life* magazine to do a photo-essay on Muncie and earned some rejoinders from local citizens.[12]

Religion got less attention in the second Lynd study in the 1930s. This time there was only one brief chapter entitled "Religion." It was more a rehearsal of the author's negative opinions than a report of data from new research. The Lynds were even less patient with traditional Christianity than before. Characteristics of American religion which Alexis de Tocqueville admired in 1835 the Lynds now deplored a century later.[13]

In the 1930s the world was in the grip of the Great Depression so the Lynds felt that any religious program short of strenuous social engineering was inadequate if not culpable. They looked for church leadership in such areas as internationalism, disarmament, pacifism, labor organization, social planning, redistribution of wealth, socialized medicine, and birth control. Instead Muncie's preachers kept talking about supernatural concerns, with occasional celebrations of local loyalties or national patriotism.

The institutions of religion in Muncie had not declined in the way the Lynds had predicted a decade before. The number of congregations had actually grown to sixty-five, representing twenty-two denominations, and there were five new church buildings. The Lynds denied that this was any evidence of vitality. In only one Muncie church did Robert Lynd claim to find "religion awake and on the march." There he heard a sermon entitled "Christianity as the Spiritual Contribution to the Adjustment of Individual and Group Differences" which he could quote with approval. He saw little hope for the rest of Muncie's religious lump. It seemed to him to be a case of the same old irrelevant sermons preached to the same congregations of old gray heads. He suggested that religion, which was ineffectual and should be declining, was hanging on because it was a coping mechanism for citizens undergoing the pain of social displacement.[14]

> One thing everybody in Middletown has in common: insecurity in the face of a complicated world. In this last may lie a clew to the willingness of the dominant portion of the population to accept uncritically as certainties, as fixed points, the fundamental assertions of Christianity as to the existence of God, His being on the side of the "right," the divinity of Jesus, and the promise of a life hereafter. So great is the individual human being's need for security that it may be that most people are incapable of tolerating change and uncertainty in all sectors of life at once; and, if their culture exposes them to stress and uncertainty at many points, they may not only tolerate but welcome the security of extreme fixity and change-lessness elsewhere in their lives. They may even embrace what Vernon Lee has called "vital lies" if they afford this modicum of psychological security.[15]

Middletown III

Fifty years after the first study by the Lynds, a new team of investigators came to Muncie. Theodore Caplow was a sociologist from the University of Virginia; Howard M. Bahr and Bruce A. Chadwick were sociologists from Brigham Young University. Helen Lynd gave them access to the files from Middletown I and Middletown II which had been deposited under seal in the Library of Congress. These three sociologists undertook the new study called Middletown III. They were mature scholars of established reputation. They maintained a field office in Muncie from 1976 to 1978. They took turns living there with portions of their families which included fourteen children.

Supported by major grants from the National Science Foundation, the directors of Middletown III assembled a team of about twenty researchers. Three of their surveys substantially repeated questionnaires used by the Lynds in order to provide exact comparisons. There were ten additional major surveys plus some minor ones. Caplow wrote:

> Like the Lynds and their assistants, we read everything of local interest we could find, attended every public or private occasion to which we could gain access, interviewed the movers and shakers in business and politics and conducted cross-sectional surveys of carefully selected samples of the population: adolescents and adults, individuals and families, employed men, employed women with and without children, people in and out of churches, voluntary associations and government agencies.[16]

They contracted for a retabulation of information about Middletown's population from the original enumerations of the seven decennial censuses from 1910 to 1970. Muncie had never been so analyzed.[17]

The city of Muncie had certainly changed since the studies of the Lynds. The population had doubled from about 40,000 to about 80,000. Some factories had closed and others approached obsolescence. The teachers' college had become a state university and the city's largest employer. The local representatives of federal government had grown from one post office to twenty-nine agencies operating ninety separate programs. Black population had grown to 12 percent and Catholic population to 22 percent. In 1980 twenty-four denominations supported church buildings and salaried ministers. About thirty-five more denominations were represented at various levels and there were also many independent churches.[18]

The viewpoint of the Middletown III researchers was very different from that of the Lynds as well. Senior researcher Theodore Caplow wrote candidly of "the problem of bias." His team was committed to scientific replication of many of the Lynds' studies but would not and could not replicate the Lynds' attitude toward the data concerning religion. The Lynds, in the tradition of "antireligion sociologists of religion," did not consider religious experience as intrinsically valid. Alienated from organized religion, they regarded it as a vestigial institution destined to decline and eventually to disappear. So their account of Middletown's churches was always flavored with condescension and suggestions of exposure. They characterized religion in terms of those elements in it which they considered questionable.

The major researchers for Middletown III, on the other hand, viewed the negative attitude of the Lynds as a vestigial remnant of a more primitive sociology. This was a research team of "proreligion sociologists of religion." They were active in church. They interpreted religious experience as an interaction between human persons and an external reality. They understood science and religion to be dealing quite compatibly with different aspects of experience. They did not regard the decline of religion as inevitable or even probable. Robert Lynd's pessimism about social disintegration in Middletown I and Middletown II was nearly the polar opposite of Caplow's optimism in Middletown III. Just before coming to his research in Muncie, Caplow had published a book entitled *Toward Social Hope*. In it he argued that human society was progressing, that social problems were becoming less serious, and that social science should enunciate these truths.[19]

The Middletown III team did not delay publication for one final volume. As they worked they presented their data and analyses in a flurry of articles published in journals and papers read before professional groups. There were more than fifty of these by 1985. Production of a series of six documentary films on Muncie was funded by the National Endowment for the Humanities; five of these were broadcast on the PBS network. The tenor of the presentations was constant. Modernization at Middletown had continued but values had remained remarkably stable and social change was less than most people suspected.[20]

The first book the project published was *Middletown Families*, issued from the University of Minnesota Press in 1982. The chapter entitled "The Myth of the Declining Family" said:

> The Middletown family is in exceptionally good condition. Tracing the changes from the 1920s to the 1970s, we discovered increased family solidarity, a smaller generation gap, closer marital communication, more religion, and less mobility. With respect to the major features of family life, the trend of the past two generations has run in the opposite direction from the trend that nearly everyone perceives and talks about.[21]

An entire chapter on "Religion and the Family" was at pains to balance some negative impressions of the Lynds on the basis of the Lynds' own data. This chapter by Theodore Caplow and Bruce Chadwick reported that responses to their survey questions indicated no decline of religious faith from 1924 to 1978 and instead some increase. They found no appreciable difference between business-class and working-class responses.[22]

The project's second major book appeared from the same university press in 1983. Its title was *All Faithful People*. It dealt entirely with Middletown's religion.[23] Again it was the continuity of Muncie's religion which most impressed the interpreters.

Mind you, we do not say there have been no changes in organized religion during the past half-century. That would be absurd. Much of this volume is given over to the religious changes that have been occurring in Middletown and in the wider society around it. Liturgies have changed, attitudes have changed, and whole bodies of doctrine have changed radically. The sexual morality preached in Middletown's church in 1980 is quite different from what it was in 1960, let alone 1900. A mass in one of Middletown's Catholic churches nowadays—celebrated in English with the priest facing the congregation and the kiss of peace exchanged afterward—bears little resemblance to the stately Latin ritual of 1960. The same Presbyterians and Lutherans who speak in tongues nowadays would not have spoken to anyone who defended the practice a few years ago. The Episcopal Church has women priests and a new prayer book. The YMCA no longer has any religious importance, but the Jehovah's Witnesses do. Where every church was once explicitly segregated by race, all are now integrated in theory and many are in fact. There are people in Middletown who practice witchcraft seriously and others who shave their heads and meditate on reincarnation. There are enough new things under the sun in Middletown's religion to amaze and delight a curious observer. But we have not been able to find much trace of the great massive trend that was supposed to be carrying us irresistibly out of an age of faith into an age of practical reason. What has happened instead—the persistence and renewal of religion in a changing society—is much more interesting than the secularization that never occurred.[24]

If a substantial movement from religion to secularism had occurred, as the Lynds and many others had expected or announced, the new team of investigators expected to see some of these trends: (1) a decline in the number of churches per capita of the population; (2) a decline in the proportion of the population attending church services; (3) a decline in the number of marriages and funerals held under religious auspices; (4) a decline in religious endogamy; (5) a decline in the proportion of the labor force engaged in religious activity; (6) a decline in the proportion of income devoted to the support of religion; (7) a decline in the attention given to religion in the mass media; (8) a drift toward less emotional forms of participation in religious services; (9) a dwindling of new sects and of new movements in existing churches; (10) increased attention to secular issues in sermons and liturgy. The only one of these trends the researchers found at Muncie was number four, an increase in interdenominational marriage, which looked to them more like the result of a new level of tolerance than a new level of secularism.[25]

Nor did the researchers see evidence that religion was less meaningful to Muncie's residents in the 1970s than it had been in the 1890s or the 1920s or the 1930s. There was hardly an appreciable difference between devotion to religion among men and women or among working-class and business-class persons. One change was evident. There was a remarkable increase in toleration among religious groups and persons, an openness still well short of erasing denominational boundaries.[26]

Disputation over the nature and current status of religion in Muncie, in Indiana, or in the nation, was by no means quieted by the reports from Middletown III. Everybody appreciated the mass of new factual information. However several reviewers of *All Faithful People* expressed their uneasiness with the research team's conclusions. "The authors place too much confidence in some tenuous indicators of religiosity and ignore considerable evidence that indicates secularization," said Norval D. Glenn of the University of Texas.[27] To John R. Earle of Wake Forest University, much of what was reported as "religion" by Middletown III looked like a kind of ineffective religiosity found in conservative and fundamental churches which would always avoid ethical issues and the conflicts necessary to bring about social change.[28] "Welcome to Munciekin Land" was the heading for the review by Gerald Weales in the *New York Review of Books*. Weales said:

> Despite the detailed and potentially useful material gathered by Middletown III, I am made uneasy by *Middletown Families* and *All Faithful People*. The note of complacency in them may be justified by the statistics, but I miss the questioning eye that might have been brought to a description of the society on which that attitude rests. More than that, I wonder about the disquiet beneath the optimism, a disquiet that seems to have escaped the compilers of Middletown III.[29]

Whatever their perspective, those who searched for scientifically gathered information about the nature and development of religion in a specific American community through the twentieth century headed for the Center for Middletown Studies in the Bracken Library of Ball State University in Muncie. It was the nation's best collection of hard data.

NOTES

1. David E. Kyvig, review of *Middletown Families*, by Theodore Caplow et al., *Indiana Magazine of History* 78 (December 1982): 354; Dwight W. Hoover, *Middletown Revisited* (Muncie, Ind.: Ball State University, 1990), 17–23; Stuart Chase, review of *Middletown*, by Robert S. Lynd and Helen Merrell Lynd, *The Nation* 128 (6 February 1929): 164.

2. Charles E. Harvey, "Robert S. Lynd, John D. Rockefeller, Jr., and Middletown," *Indiana Magazine of History* 79 (December 1983): 330–54; Richard Jensen, "The Lynds Revisited," *Indiana Magazine of History* 75 (December 1979): 303–19; Robert S. Lynd and Helen Merrell Lynd, *Middletown: A Study in Contemporary American Culture* (New York: Harcourt, Brace and Company, 1929), 7–9; Hoover, *Middletown Revisited*, 1–2.

3. Harvey, "Robert S. Lynd," 334–36, 348; Hoover, *Middletown Revisited*, 3–4.

4. Jensen, "Lynds Revisited," 303–5; Hoover, *Middletown Revisited*, 5–10.

5. Hoover, *Middletown Revisited*, 7–8.

6. Lynd and Lynd, *Middletown*, 313–409.

7. Hoover, *Middletown Revisited*, 6–9; Jensen, "Lynds Revisited," 305–16.

8. Theodore Caplow et al., *All Faithful People: Change and Continuity in Middletown's Religion* (Minneapolis, Minn.: University of Minnesota Press, 1983), 30–31.

9. Lynd and Lynd, *Middletown*, 322, 329, 343, 346, 359, 400, 405–6.

10. Lynd and Lynd, *Middletown*, 406.

11. Hoover, *Middletown Revisited*, 6–10; Harvey, "Robert S. Lynd," 349–52.

12. Robert S. Lynd and Helen Merrell Lynd, *Middletown in Transition: A Study in Cultural Conflicts* (New York: Harcourt, Brace and Company, 1937, 604 p.); Hillyer H. Straton, "'Middletown Looks at the Lynds': A Contemporary Critique by the Reverend Dr. Hillyer H. Straton of Muncie, Indiana, 1937," ed. Robert S. LaForte and Richard Himmel, *Indiana Magazine of History* 79 (September 1983): 248–64; Hoover, *Middletown Revisited*, 11–16, 46–47; Jensen, "Lynds Revisited," 308; Caplow, *All Faithful People*, 16–17.

13. Lynd and Lynd, *Middletown in Transition*, 295–318; Caplow, *All Faithful People*, 6–9.

14. Lynd and Lynd, *Middletown in Transition*, 248–49, 297–98, 308, 312.

15. Lynd and Lynd, *Middletown in Transition*, 315.

16. Theodore Caplow et al., *Middletown Families: Fifty Years of Change and Continuity* (Minneapolis, Minn.: University of Minnesota Press, 1982), v.

17. Caplow, *Middletown Families*, v–ix; Caplow, *All Faithful People*, vii–x, 17; Hoover, *Middletown Revisited*, 24–27.

18. Caplow, *All Faithful People*, 3–4, 7. Caplow, *Middletown Families* reported on p. 249 that 13 percent of Muncie's residents were Catholics and on p. 251 provided church statistics in a differing format as follows: "In the early 1920s, the Lynds counted 42 church buildings serving a community of 36,000 individuals. There was a church building for every 857 citizens. The 1978 phone directory listed 137 regular churches and a score of other religious groups. Their buildings ranged from majestic structures with stained glass windows to modest one- or two-story chapels, converted office buildings, and storefronts. The 137 churches served a population of 80,000 in 1978. There was a church building for every 584 residents. The ratio of churches to people has increased significantly over the past 50 years."

19. Theodore Caplow, *Toward Social Hope* (New York: Basic Books, 1975, 229 p.); Caplow, *All Faithful People*, 30–33; Hoover, *Middletown Revisited*, 24–25.

20. Hoover, *Middletown Revisited*, 25, 36–40.

21. Caplow, *Middletown Families*, 323.

22. Caplow, *Middletown Families*, 246–68.

23. Caplow, *All Faithful People*, passim.

24. Caplow, *All Faithful People*, 37–38.

25. Hoover, *Middletown Revisited*, 28–29; Caplow, *All Faithful People*, 34–35, 294–98.

26. Caplow, *Middletown Families*, 246–68; Caplow, *All Faithful People*, 87–108, 146–62, 285–87, 305–39.

27. Norval D. Glenn, review of *All Faithful People*, by Theodore Caplow et al., *American Journal of Sociology* 91 (March 1986): 1277–79.

28. John R. Earle, review of *All Faithful People*, by Theodore Caplow et al., *Social Forces* 63 (June 1983): 1110–11.

29. Gerald Weales, review of *All Faithful People*, by Theodore Caplow et al., *New York Review of Books* 31 (26 April 1984): 43–45.

Churches and Church Membership

The census of the United States no longer provides statistics on religious bodies. The Association of Statisticians of American Religious Bodies has prepared a national enumeration for 1990 broken down by region, state, and county.

It is essential to remember that the Association's statistical tables for the nation represent an enumeration only of the 133 religious bodies that provided information. Twenty-one denominations with national memberships of more than 100,000 each, some of them quite large, did not participate. Nor did sixty-six smaller bodies participate who were invited. Hundreds and hundreds of independent congregations did not report.

Eighty-nine religious bodies in Indiana provided 1990 data to the Association of Statisticians of American Religious Bodies for tabulation. The tables for Indiana are reproduced here with permission.

For further particulars, such as methods used to estimate the number of Jewish, black Baptist, and independent adherents, see the basic enumeration publication entitled *Churches and Church Membership in the United States 1990* (Atlanta, Ga.: Glenmary Research Center, 1992), xx, 456 p.

Key to Abbreviations and Church Names in Tables 1 and 2

Lines in *italic* represent a breakdown of Catholic rites or Friends affiliations. They are included in their respective denominational total.

ID No.	Abbrev.	Full Name
001	ADVENT CHR CH	ADVENT CHRISTIAN CHURCH
005	AME ZION	AFRICAN METHODIST EPISCOPAL ZION CHURCH
007	ALBAN ORTH ARC	ALBANIAN ORTHODOX ARCHDIOCESE IN AMERICA
009	ALBAN ORTH DIO	ALBANIAN ORTHODOX DIOCESE OF AMERICA
011	A.W.M.C.	ALLEGHENY WESLEYAN METHODIST CONNECTION
019	AMER BAPT USA	AMERICAN BAPTIST CHURCHES IN THE U.S.A.
022	EASTERN ORTH	AMERICAN CARPATHO-RUSSIAN ORTHODOX GREEK CATHOLIC DIOCESE OF THE U.S.A.
039	AP CHR CH(NAZ)	APOSTOLIC CHRISTIAN CHURCH (NAZARENE)
040	AP CHR CH-AMER	APOSTOLIC CHRISTIAN CHURCHES OF AMERICA
045	APOSTOLIC LUTH	APOSTOLIC LUTHERAN CHURCH OF AMERICA
049	ARMEN AP CH AM	ARMENIAN APOSTOLIC CHURCH OF AMER, EASTERN PRELACY
053	ASSEMB OF GOD	ASSEMBLIES OF GOD
055	AS REF PRES CH	ASSOCIATE REFORMED PRESBYTERIAN CHURCH (GENERAL SYNOD)
057	BAPT GEN CONF	BAPTIST GENERAL CONFERENCE
059	BAPT MISS ASSN	BAPTIST MISSIONARY ASSOCIATION OF AMERICA
060	BRN RVR MB ASC	BARREN RIVER MISSIONARY BAPTISTS ASSOCIATION
061	BEACHY AMISH	BEACHY AMISH MENNONITE CHURCHES
063	BEREAN FUND CH	BEREAN FUNDAMENTAL CHURCH
066	BIBLE CH OF CR	BIBLE CHURCH OF CHRIST, INC., THE
071	BRETHREN (ASH)	BRETHREN CHURCH (ASHLAND, OHIO)
075	BRETHREN IN CR	BRETHREN IN CHRIST CHURCH
080	BYELORSSN ORTH	BYELORUSSIAN COUNCIL OF ORTHODOX CHURCHES IN NORTH AMERICA
081	CATHOLIC	CATHOLIC CHURCH
081a	*ARMENIAN*	*ARMENIAN RITE*
081b	*BYZAN RUTH*	*BYZANTINE RUTHENIAN RITE*
081c	*CHALDEAN*	*CHALDEAN RITE*
081d	*LATIN*	*LATIN RITE*
081e	*MARONITE*	*MARONITE RITE*
081f	*MELKITE-GK*	*MELKITE-GREEK RITE*
081g	*ROMANIAN*	*ROMANIAN BYZANTINE RITE*
081h	*UKRAINIAN*	*UKRANIAN BYZANTINE RITE*
082	CENTRAL BAPT	CENTRAL BAPTISTS
083	CHRIST CATH CH	CHRIST CATHOLIC CHURCH
089	CHR & MISS AL	CHRISTIAN AND MISSIONARY ALLIANCE, THE
093	CHR CH (DISC)	CHRISTIAN CHURCH (DISCIPLES OF CHRIST)
097	CHR CHS&CHS CR	CHRISTIAN CHURCHES AND CHURCHES OF CHRIST
105	CHRISTIAN REF	CHRISTIAN REFORMED CHURCH
111	CH CR,SCIENTST	CHURCH OF CHRIST, SCIENTIST
121	CH GOD (ABR)	CHURCH OF GOD GENERAL CONFERENCE (ABRAHAMIC FAITH)
123	CH GOD (ANDER)	CHURCH OF GOD (ANDERSON, INDIANA)
127	CH GOD (CLEVE)	CHURCH OF GOD (CLEVELAND, TENNESSEE)
133	CH GOD(7TH)DEN	CHURCH OF GOD (SEVENTH DAY), DENVER, COLORADO, THE
143	CG IN CR(MENN)	CHURCH OF GOD IN CHRIST (MENNONITE)
145	CH GOD PROPHCY	CHURCH OF GOD OF PROPHECY
146	CH GOD MTN ASM	CHURCH OF GOD OF THE MOUNTAIN ASSEMBLY, INC.
151	L-D SAINTS	CHURCH OF JESUS CHRIST OF LATTER-DAY SAINTS, THE
157	CH OF BRETHREN	CHURCH OF THE BRETHREN
163	CH OF LUTH BR	CHURCH OF THE LUTHERAN BRETHREN OF AMERICA
164	CH LUTH CONF	CHURCH OF THE LUTHERAN CONFESSION

ID No.	Abbrev.	Full Name
165	CH OF NAZARENE	CHURCH OF THE NAZARENE
167	CHS OF CHRIST	CHURCHES OF CHRIST
171	CH GOD-GEN CON	CHURCHES OF GOD, GENERAL CONFERENCE
175	CONGR CHR CHS	CONGREGATIONAL CHRISTIAN CHURCHES, NATIONAL ASSOCIATION OF
176	CCC, NOT NAT'L	CONGREGATIONAL CHRISTIAN CHURCHES (NOT PART OF ANY NATIONAL CCC BODY)
179	CONSRV BAPT	CONSERVATIVE BAPTIST ASSOCIATION OF AMERICA
181	CONSRV CONGR	CONSERVATIVE CONGREGATIONAL CHRISTIAN CONFERENCE
185	CUMBER PRESB	CUMBERLAND PRESBYTERIAN CHURCH
189	DUCK RIVR BAPT	DUCK RIVER (AND KINDRED) ASSOCIATIONS OF BAPTISTS
191	ENTRPR BPT ASC	ENTERPRISE BAPTISTS ASSOCIATION
193	EPISCOPAL	EPISCOPAL CHURCH, THE
195	ESTONIAN ELC	ESTONIAN EVANGELICAL LUTHERAN CHURCH
199	EVAN CONGR CH	EVANGELICAL CONGREGATIONAL CHURCH
203	EVAN FREE CH	EVANGELICAL FREE CHURCH OF AMERICA, THE
207	E.L.C.A.	EVANGELICAL LUTHERAN CHURCH IN AMERICA
209	EVAN LUTH SYN	EVANGELICAL LUTHERAN SYNOD
211	FEL EVG BIB CH	EVANGELICAL BIBLE CHURCHES, FELLOWSHIP OF (FORMERLY EVANGELICAL MENNONITE BRETHREN)
213	EVAN MENN INC	EVANGELICAL MENNONITE CHURCH INC.
215	EVAN METH CH	EVANGELICAL METHODIST CHURCH
216	EVAN PRESBY CH	EVANGELICAL PRESBYTERIAN CHURCH
217	FIRE BAPTIZED	FIRE BAPTIZED HOLINESS CHURCH, (WESLEYAN), THE
220	FREE LUTHERAN	FREE LUTHERAN CONGREGATIONS, THE ASSOCIATION OF
221	FREE METHODIST	FREE METHODIST CHURCH OF NORTH AMERICA
223	FREE WILL BAPT	FREE WILL BAPTIST, NATIONAL ASSOCIATION OF, INC.
226	FRIENDS-USA	FRIENDS
226a	*CONSERV*	*CONSERVATIVE (WILBURITE) FRIENDS*
226b	*EFI*	*EVANGELICAL FRIENDS INTERNATIONAL (FORMERLY EVANGELICAL FRIENDS ALLIANCE)*
226c	*FGC*	*FRIENDS GENERAL CONFERENCE*
226d	*FGC & FUM*	*FRIENDS GENERAL CONFERENCE & FRIENDS UNITED MEETING (DUALLY AFFILIATED)*
226e	*FUM*	*FRIENDS UNITED MEETING*
226f	*INDEPENDNT*	*FRIENDS INDEPENDENT*
226g	*INDEP EVAN*	*FRIENDS INDEPENDENT EVANGELICAL*
230	FUND METHODIST	FUNDAMENTAL METHODIST CHURCH, INC.
237	GC MENN BR CHS	GENERAL CONFERENCE OF MENNONITE BRETHREN CHURCHES
241	GEN SIX PR BPT	GENERAL SIX PRINCIPLE BAPTISTS
246	GREEK ORTHODOX	GREEK ORTHODOX ARCHDIOCESE OF NORTH AND SOUTH AMERICA
249	AP CATH ASSYR	HOLY APOSTOLIC CATHOLIC ASSYRIAN CHURCH OF THE EAST
257	HUTTERIAN BR	HUTTERIAN BRETHREN
259	IFCA	INDEPENDENT FUNDAMENTAL CHURCHES OF AMERICA
263	INT FOURSQ GOS	INTERNATIONAL CHURCH OF THE FOURSQUARE GOSPEL
265	INT PENT C CHR	INTERNATIONAL PENTECOSTAL CHURCH OF CHRIST
266	INTRSTAT & ASC	INTERSTATE & FOREIGN LANDMARK MISSIONARY BAPTISTS ASSOCIATION
269	JASPER&PVB ASC	JASPER AND PLEASANT VALLEY BAPTISTS ASSOCIATIONS
274	LAT EVAN LUTH	LATVIAN EVANGELICAL LUTHERAN CHURCH IN AMERICA, THE
283	LUTH—MO SYNOD	LUTHERAN CHURCH - MISSOURI SYNOD, THE
284	LUTH CH-AM ASC	LUTHERAN CHURCHES, THE AMERICAN ASSOCIATION OF
285	MENNONITE CH	MENNONITE CHURCH
286	E.PA MENNONITE	EASTERN PENNSYLVANIA MENNONITE CHURCH
287	MENN GEN CONF	MENNONITE CHURCH, THE GENERAL CONFERENCE

ID No.	Abbrev.	Full Name
289	NEW HOPE B ASC	NEW HOPE BAPTIST ASSOCIATION
291	MISSIONARY CH	MISSIONARY CHURCH, THE
292	MORAV CH-AK	MORAVIAN CHURCH IN AMERICA (UNITAS FRATRUM), ALASKA PROVINCE
293	MORAV CH-NORTH	MORAVIAN CHURCH IN AMERICA (UNITAS FRATRUM), NORTHERN PROVINCE
295	MORAV CH-SOUTH	MORAVIAN CHURCH IN AMERICA (UNITAS FRATRUM), SOUTHERN PROVINCE
296	MIDW CONGR FEL	MIDWEST CONGREGATIONAL CHRISTIAN FELLOWSHIP
307	NETH REF CONGR	NETHERLANDS REFORMED CONGREGATIONS
313	N AM BAPT CONF	NORTH AMERICAN BAPTIST CONFERENCE
320	"OLD" MB ASCS	"OLD" MISSIONARY BAPTISTS ASSOCIATIONS
323	OLD ORD AMISH	OLD ORDER AMISH CHURCH
324	OLD ORD RVR BR	OLD ORDER RIVER BRETHREN
325	OLD REG BAPT	OLD REGULAR BAPTISTS
329	OPEN BIBLE STD	OPEN BIBLE STANDARD CHURCHES, INC.
331	ORTH CH IN AM	ORTHODOX CHURCH IN AMERICA
339	PENT CH OF GOD	PENTECOSTAL CHURCH OF GOD
349	PENT HOLINESS	PENTECOSTAL HOLINESS CHURCH, INC.
353	CHR BRETHREN	CHRISTIAN (PLYMOUTH) BRETHREN
355	PRESB CH (USA)	PRESBYTERIAN CHURCH (USA)
356	PRESB CH AMER	PRESBYTERIAN CHURCH IN AMERICA
359	PRIM AD CHR CH	PRIMITIVE ADVENT CHRISTIAN CHURCH
361	PRIM BAPT ASCS	PRIMITIVE BAPTISTS ASSOCIATIONS
363	PRIMITIVE METH	PRIMITIVE METHODIST CHURCH, U.S.A.
367	PROT CONF (LU)	THE PROTES'TANT CONFERENCE (LUTHERAN)
371	REF CH IN AM	REFORMED CHURCH IN AMERICA
373	REF CH IN U.S.	REFORMED CHURCH IN THE UNITED STATES
375	REF EPISCOPAL	REFORMED EPISCOPAL CHURCH
386	REGULAR BAPT	REGULAR BAPTISTS
397	ROMANIAN ORTH	ROMANIAN ORTHODOX EPISCOPATE OF AMERICA
403	SALVATION ARMY	SALVATION ARMY, THE
405	SCHWENKFELDER	SCHWENKFELDER CHURCH, THE
413	S.D.A.	SEVENTH-DAY ADVENTISTS
415	S-D BAPTIST GC	SEVENTH DAY BAPTIST GENERAL CONFERENCE
419	SO BAPT CONV	SOUTHERN BAPTIST CONVENTION
423	SYRIAN ANTIOCH	SYRIAN ORTHODOX CHURCH OF ANTIOCH (ARCHDIOCESE OF THE U.S.A. AND CANADA)
426	2SEED-SPRT BPT	TWO-SEED-IN-THE-SPIRIT PREDESTINARIAN BAPTISTS
430	TRUEVINE B ASC	TRUEVINE BAPTISTS ASSOCIATION
431	UKRANIAN AMER	UKRAINIAN ORTHODOX CHURCH OF AMER (ECUMENICAL PATRIARCHATE)
435	UNITARIAN-UNIV	UNITARIAN UNIVERSALIST ASSOCIATION
436	UNITED BAPT	UNITED BAPTISTS
438	UN BRETH IN CR	UNITED BRETHREN IN CHRIST
441	UN CHRISTIAN	UNITED CHRISTIAN CHURCH
443	UN C OF CHRIST	UNITED CHURCH OF CHRIST
449	UN METHODIST	UNITED METHODIST CHURCH, THE
466	WAYN TR MB ASC	WAYNE TRAIL MISSIONARY BAPTISTS ASSOCIATION
467	WESLEYAN	THE WESLEYAN CHURCH
469	WELS	WISCONSIN EVANGELICAL LUTHERAN SYNOD
496	JEWISH EST	JEWISH ESTIMATE
497	BLACK BAPT EST	BLACK BAPTISTS ESTIMATE
498	INDEP.CHARIS.	INDEPENDENT, CHARISMATIC CHURCHES
499	INDEP.NON-CHAR	INDEPENDENT, NON-CHARISMATIC CHURCHES

Table 1. Indiana Churches and Church Membership by Denomination: 1990

NA-Not applicable. NR-Not reported. *Total adherents estimated from the known number of communicant, confirmed, full members.
- Represents a percent less than 0.1. Percentages may not total due to rounding. Lines in *italic* represent a breakdown of Catholic rites or Friends affiliations. They are included in their respective denominational total.

Denomination	Number of churches	Communicant, confirmed, full members	Total adherents Number	Percent of total population	Percent of total adherents
INDIANA	**7,134**	**1,306,718**	**2,634,841 ***	**47.5**	**100.0**
001 ADVENT CHR CH	2	176	220 *	-	-
005 AME ZION	17	17,757	22,661	.4	.9
011 A.W.M.C.	1	15	19 *	-	-
019 AMER BAPT USA	397	106,106	132,970 *	2.4	5.0
022 EASTERN ORTH	2	286	286	-	-
040 AP CHR CH-AMER	11	2,132	3,777	.1	.1
053 ASSEMB OF GOD	218	27,419	51,907	.9	2.0
057 BAPT GEN CONF	7	647	824 *	-	-
059 BAPT MISS ASSN	3	264	322 *	-	-
061 BEACHY AMISH	10	729	946 *	-	-
071 BRETHREN (ASH)	36	4,168	5,307 *	.1	.2
075 BRETHREN IN CR	4	233	267	-	-
081 CATHOLIC	476	NA	699,188	12.6	26.5
081b *BYZAN RUTH*	*5*	*NA*	*1,726*	-	.1
081d *LATIN*	*466*	*NA*	*696,249*	*12.6*	*26.4*
081f *MELKITE-GK*	*2*	*NA*	*774*	-	-
081g *ROMANIAN*	*1*	*NA*	*322*	-	-
081h *UKRAINIAN*	*2*	*NA*	*117*	-	-
082 CENTRAL BAPT	3	226	291 *	-	-
083 CHRIST CATH CH	1	7	7	-	-
089 CHR & MISS AL	29	1,507	3,085	.1	.1
093 CHR CH (DISC)	221	55,244	89,932	1.6	3.4
097 CHR CHS&CHS CR	482	127,317	160,099 *	2.9	6.1
105 CHRISTIAN REF	14	3,070	5,343	.1	.2
111 CH CR,SCIENTST	48	NR	NR	-	-
121 CH GOD (ABR)	7	308	390 *	-	-
123 CH GOD (ANDER)	159	18,331	22,569	.4	.9
127 CH GOD (CLEVE)	85	8,117	10,212 *	.2	.4
133 CH GOD(7TH)DEN	1	15	20	-	-
145 CH GOD PROPHCY	42	1,403	1,764 *	-	.1
146 CH GOD MTN ASM	12	517	646 *	-	-
151 L-D SAINTS	70	NA	20,901	.4	.8
157 CH OF BRETHREN	105	13,625	17,388 *	.3	.7
165 CH OF NAZARENE	331	36,562	68,131	1.2	2.6
167 CHS OF CHRIST	345	30,366	39,953	.7	1.5
171 CH GOD-GEN CON	22	2,963	3,796 *	.1	.1
175 CONGR CHR CHS	10	1,215	1,524 *	-	.1
176 CCC, NOT NAT'L	13	1,062	1,328 *	-	.1
179 CONSRV BAPT	5	NR	NR	-	-
181 CONSRV CONGR	2	509	644 *	-	-
185 CUMBER PRESB	8	1,391	1,494	-	.1
191 ENTRPR BPT ASC	1	56	71 *	-	-
193 EPISCOPAL	81	14,431	21,102	.4	.8
195 ESTONIAN ELC	1	26	33 *	-	-
199 EVAN CONGR CH	1	31	113	-	-
203 EVAN FREE CH	12	1,984	3,510	.1	.1
207 E.L.C.A.	210	59,222	78,727	1.4	3.0
209 EVAN LUTH SYN	1	46	69	-	-
213 EVAN MENN INC	9	1,109	1,417 *	-	.1
215 EVAN METH CH	6	402	506 *	-	-
216 EVAN PRESBY CH	1	200	207	-	-
220 FREE LUTHERAN	1	158	206	-	-
221 FREE METHODIST	44	4,496	5,450	.1	.2
223 FREE WILL BAPT	27	1,869	2,352 *	-	.1
226 FRIENDS-USA	128	12,915	16,167 *	.3	.6
226c *FGC*	*5*	*116*	*144 **	-	-
226d *FGC & FUM*	*1*	*166*	*203*	-	-
226e *FUM*	*112*	*12,380*	*15,489 **	*.3*	*.6*
226f *INDEPENDNT*	*2*	*10*	*27*	-	-
226g *INDEP EVAN*	*8*	*243*	*304 **	-	-
246 GREEK ORTHODOX	7	NR	NR	-	-
249 AP CATH ASSYR	1	53	329	-	-
259 IFCA	28	NR	NR	-	-
263 INT FOURSQ GOS	20	3,150	3,890 *	.1	.1
265 INT PENT C CHR	1	59	59	-	-
274 LAT EVAN LUTH	1	373	409	-	-
283 LUTH—MO SYNOD	219	82,577	109,895	2.0	4.2
284 LUTH CH-AM ASC	1	263	351	-	-
285 MENNONITE CH	97	12,478	17,976	.3	.7
287 MENN GEN CONF	16	2,526	3,084	.1	.1
291 MISSIONARY CH	69	9,223	14,009	.3	.5
293 MORAV CH-NORTH	4	553	693	-	-
296 MIDW CONGR FEL	20	976	1,206 *	-	-
313 N AM BAPT CONF	1	66	83 *	-	-
323 OLD ORD AMISH	149	NA	22,300	.4	.8
325 OLD REG BAPT	17	384	484 *	-	-
329 OPEN BIBLE STD	2	NR	NR	-	-
331 ORTH CH IN AM	3	NR	NR	-	-
339 PENT CH OF GOD	33	895	2,321	-	.1
349 PENT HOLINESS	2	47	61 *	-	-
353 CHR BRETHREN	10	307	479	-	-
355 PRESB CH (USA)	277	68,579	86,194 *	1.6	3.3
356 PRESB CH AMER	12	1,564	2,001	-	.1
361 PRIM BAPT ASCS	20	381	478 *	-	-
363 PRIMITIVE METH	1	39	69	-	-
371 REF CH IN AM	9	2,094	3,418	.1	.1
397 ROMANIAN ORTH	3	NR	NR	-	-
403 SALVATION ARMY	41	4,043	4,500	.1	.2
413 S.D.A.	87	9,114	11,459 *	.2	.4
419 SO BAPT CONV	306	92,174	115,560 *	2.1	4.4
426 2SEED-SPRT BPT	1	20	24 *	-	-
431 UKRANIAN AMER	1	NR	NR	-	-
435 UNITARIAN-UNIV	17	2,340	3,038	.1	.1
436 UNITED BAPT	20	2,435	3,017 *	.1	.1
438 UN BRETH IN CR	30	3,257	3,433	.1	.1
443 UN C OF CHRIST	173	48,253	60,773 *	1.1	2.3
449 UN METHODIST	1,373	272,999	343,930 *	6.2	13.1
467 WESLEYAN	238	12,483	34,025	.6	1.3
469 WELS	0	1,190	1,660	-	.1
496 JEWISH EST	31	NA	20,314	.4	.8
497 BLACK BAPT EST	NA	111,191	140,166 *	2.5	5.3
498 INDEP.CHARIS.	15	NA	19,855	.4	.8
499 INDEP.NON-CHAR	48	NA	105,157	1.9	4.0

Table 2. Indiana Churches and Church Membership by County and Denomination: 1990

NA-Not applicable. NR-Not reported. *Total adherents estimated from the known number of communicant, confirmed, full members. - Represents a percent less than 0.1. Percentages may not total due to rounding. Lines in *italic* represent a breakdown of Catholic rites or Friends affiliations. They are included in their respective denominational total.

| County and Denomination | Number of churches | Communicant, confirmed, full members | Total adherents | | |
			Number	Percent of total population	Percent of total adherents
INDIANA					
THE STATE.....	7,134	1,306,718	2,634,841 *	47.5	100.0
ADAMS	**76**	**11,068**	**22,283***	**71.7**	**100.0**
019 AMER BAPT USA	2	218	291 *	.9	1.3
053 ASSEMB OF GOD	1	28	46	.1	.2
061 BEACHY AMISH	1	13	17 *	.1	.1
081 CATHOLIC	2	NA	4,394	14.1	19.7
081d LATIN	*2*	*NA*	*4,394*	*14.1*	*19.7*
097 CHR CHS&CHS CR	2	250	334 *	1.1	1.5
123 CH GOD (ANDER)	1	410	466	1.5	2.1
151 L-D SAINTS	1	NA	85	.3	.4
157 CH OF BRETHREN	1	287	383 *	1.2	1.7
165 CH OF NAZARENE	4	390	681	2.2	3.1
193 EPISCOPAL	1	27	27	.1	.1
213 EVAN MENN INC	1	175	234 *	.8	1.1
259 IFCA	2	NR	NR	-	-
283 LUTH—MO SYNOD	7	2,852	3,800	12.2	17.1
287 MENN GEN CONF	1	1,117	1,417	4.6	6.4
291 MISSIONARY CH	4	827	920	3.0	4.1
323 OLD ORD AMISH	22	NA	3,300	10.6	14.8
349 PENT HOLINESS	1	22	29 *	.1	.1
355 PRESB CH (USA)	1	187	250 *	.8	1.1
438 UN BRETH IN CR	4	363	363	1.2	1.6
443 UN C OF CHRIST	4	1,396	1,864 *	6.0	8.4
449 UN METHODIST	12	2,447	3,267 *	10.5	14.7
467 WESLEYAN	1	59	115	.4	.5
ALLEN	**268**	**79,056**	**165,657***	**55.1**	**100.0**
019 AMER BAPT USA	8	2,105	2,698 *	.9	1.6
040 AP CHR CH-AMER	1	109	194	.1	.1
053 ASSEMB OF GOD	4	733	1,158	.4	.7
061 BEACHY AMISH	1	51	65 *	-	-
071 BRETHREN (ASH)	1	37	47 *	-	-
081 CATHOLIC	24	NA	51,000	17.0	30.8
081d LATIN	*24*	*NA*	*51,000*	*17.0*	*30.8*
089 CHR & MISS AL	2	198	336	.1	.2
093 CHR CH (DISC)	3	1,042	1,485	.5	.9
097 CHR CHS&CHS CR	9	3,254	4,171 *	1.4	2.5
105 CHRISTIAN REF	2	433	656	.2	.4
111 CH CR,SCIENTST	1	NR	NR	-	-
123 CH GOD (ANDER)	7	527	727	.2	.4
127 CH GOD (CLEVE)	2	247	317 *	.1	.2
145 CH GOD PROPHCY	1	33	42 *	-	-
151 L-D SAINTS	2	NA	976	.3	.6
157 CH OF BRETHREN	3	752	964 *	.3	.6
165 CH OF NAZARENE	10	1,158	1,667	.6	1.0
167 CHS OF CHRIST	6	720	990	.3	.6
171 CH GOD-GEN CON	4	751	963 *	.3	.6
193 EPISCOPAL	3	1,166	1,657	.6	1.0
207 E.L.C.A.	21	10,274	13,653	4.5	8.2
213 EVAN MENN INC	5	655	840 *	.3	.5

County and Denomination	Number of churches	Communicant, confirmed, full members	Total adherents Number	Percent of total population	Percent of total adherents
221 FREE METHODIST	1	113	149	-	.1
223 FREE WILL BAPT	1	52	67*	-	-
226 FRIENDS-USA	2	44	57*	-	-
226c FGC	*1*	*17*	*22**	*-*	*-*
226e FUM	*1*	*27*	*35**	*-*	*-*
246 GREEK ORTHODOX	1	NR	NR	-	-
263 INT FOURSQ GOS	1	0	0*	-	-
283 LUTH—MO SYNOD	29	18,865	25,455	8.5	15.4
285 MENNONITE CH	9	995	1,482	.5	.9
287 MENN GEN CONF	1	175	220	.1	.1
291 MISSIONARY CH	14	3,005	4,225	1.4	2.6
323 OLD ORD AMISH	11	NA	1,650	.5	1.0
331 ORTH CH IN AM	1	NR	NR	-	-
353 CHR BRETHREN	1	15	30	-	-
355 PRESB CH (USA)	8	3,639	4,664*	1.6	2.8
361 PRIM BAPT ASCS	1	9	12*	-	-
397 ROMANIAN ORTH	1	NR	NR	-	-
403 SALVATION ARMY	2	221	252	.1	.2
413 S.D.A.	2	370	474*	.2	.3
419 SO BAPT CONV	5	1,638	2,099*	.7	1.3
435 UNITARIAN-UNIV	1	205	271	.1	.2
436 UNITED BAPT	1	25	32*	-	-
438 UN BRETH IN CR	4	343	478	.2	.3
443 UN C OF CHRIST	5	2,818	3,612*	1.2	2.2
449 UN METHODIST	37	13,602	17,434*	5.8	10.5
467 WESLEYAN	3	383	715	.2	.4
469 WELS	2	279	390	.1	.2
496 JEWISH EST	2	NA	910	.3	.5
497 BLACK BAPT EST	NA	8,015	10,273*	3.4	6.2
498 INDEP.CHARIS.	2	NA	6,100	2.0	3.7
BARTHOLOMEW	**86**	**22,282**	**34,440***	**54.1**	**100.0**
019 AMER BAPT USA	5	3,292	4,109*	6.5	11.9
053 ASSEMB OF GOD	2	249	544	.9	1.6
081 CATHOLIC	2	NA	3,562	5.6	10.3
081d LATIN	*2*	*NA*	*3,562*	*5.6*	*10.3*
089 CHR & MISS AL	1	34	95	.1	.3
093 CHR CH (DISC)	1	384	721	1.1	2.1
097 CHR CHS&CHS CR	9	4,832	6,031*	9.5	17.5
111 CH CR,SCIENTST	1	NR	NR	-	-
123 CH GOD (ANDER)	1	91	91	.1	.3
127 CH GOD (CLEVE)	1	191	238*	.4	.7
146 CH GOD MTN ASM	1	84	105*	.2	.3
151 L-D SAINTS	2	NA	579	.9	1.7
165 CH OF NAZARENE	4	378	633	1.0	1.8
167 CHS OF CHRIST	4	282	362	.6	1.1
193 EPISCOPAL	1	168	249	.4	.7
207 E.L.C.A.	1	320	368	.6	1.1
215 EVAN METH CH	1	28	35*	.1	.1
221 FREE METHODIST	1	130	163	.3	.5
226 FRIENDS-USA	1	167	208*	.3	.6
226e FUM	*1*	*167*	*208**	*.3*	*.6*
263 INT FOURSQ GOS	1	0	0*	-	-
283 LUTH—MO SYNOD	7	4,081	5,204	8.2	15.1
293 MORAV CH-NORTH	1	346	422	.7	1.2
355 PRESB CH (USA)	3	851	1,062*	1.7	3.1
403 SALVATION ARMY	1	15	18	-	.1
413 S.D.A.	1	96	120*	.2	.3
419 SO BAPT CONV	4	866	1,081*	1.7	3.1
435 UNITARIAN-UNIV	1	44	63	.1	.2
436 UNITED BAPT	1	75	94*	.1	.3
438 UN BRETH IN CR	1	41	41	.1	.1
443 UN C OF CHRIST	1	63	79*	.1	.2
449 UN METHODIST	17	4,592	5,732*	9.0	16.6
467 WESLEYAN	7	367	1,163	1.8	3.4
497 BLACK BAPT EST	NA	215	268*	.4	.8
499 INDEP.NON-CHAR	1	NA	1,000	1.6	2.9
BENTON	**32**	**3,115**	**7,249***	**76.8**	**100.0**
081 CATHOLIC	6	NA	3,124	33.1	43.1
081d LATIN	*6*	*NA*	*3,124*	*33.1*	*43.1*
093 CHR CH (DISC)	1	45	57	.6	.8
097 CHR CHS&CHS CR	6	897	1,150*	12.2	15.9
151 L-D SAINTS	1	NA	69	.7	1.0
165 CH OF NAZARENE	1	20	30	.3	.4
207 E.L.C.A.	1	246	313	3.3	4.3
221 FREE METHODIST	1	7	52	.6	.7
283 LUTH—MO SYNOD	1	28	43	.5	.6
355 PRESB CH (USA)	3	329	422*	4.5	5.8
419 SO BAPT CONV	3	264	338*	3.6	4.7
449 UN METHODIST	7	1,261	1,617*	17.1	22.3
467 WESLEYAN	1	18	34	.4	.5
BLACKFORD	**28**	**2,955**	**5,224***	**37.1**	**100.0**
019 AMER BAPT USA	1	203	252*	1.8	4.8
053 ASSEMB OF GOD	2	64	123	.9	2.4

County and Denomination	Number of churches	Communicant, confirmed, full members	Total adherents Number	Percent of total population	Percent of total adherents
081 CATHOLIC	2	NA	713	5.1	13.6
081d LATIN	*2*	*NA*	*713*	*5.1*	*13.6*
093 CHR CH (DISC)	1	145	382	2.7	7.3
097 CHR CHS&CHS CR	2	175	217*	1.5	4.2
123 CH GOD (ANDER)	1	9	22	.2	.4
157 CH OF BRETHREN	1	48	59*	.4	1.1
165 CH OF NAZARENE	3	330	787	5.6	15.1
207 E.L.C.A.	1	338	419	3.0	8.0
355 PRESB CH (USA)	1	136	169*	1.2	3.2
413 S.D.A.	1	9	11*	.1	.2
438 UN BRETH IN CR	1	45	45	.3	.9
449 UN METHODIST	10	1,352	1,675*	11.9	32.1
467 WESLEYAN	1	101	350	2.5	6.7
BOONE	**56**	**9,153**	**16,596***	**43.5**	**100.0**
019 AMER BAPT USA	2	574	730*	1.9	4.4
053 ASSEMB OF GOD	2	100	151	.4	.9
057 BAPT GEN CONF	1	28	36*	.1	.2
081 CATHOLIC	2	NA	3,206	8.4	19.3
081d LATIN	*2*	*NA*	*3,206*	*8.4*	*19.3*
093 CHR CH (DISC)	3	859	1,501	3.9	9.0
097 CHR CHS&CHS CR	6	1,828	2,326*	6.1	14.0
111 CH CR,SCIENTST	1	NR	NR	-	-
123 CH GOD (ANDER)	1	15	15	-	.1
145 CH GOD PROPHCY	2	67	85*	.2	.5
151 L-D SAINTS	1	NA	373	1.0	2.2
165 CH OF NAZARENE	1	90	250	.7	1.5
167 CHS OF CHRIST	3	195	271	.7	1.6
176 CCC, NOT NAT'L	1	89	113*	.3	.7
193 EPISCOPAL	2	237	385	1.0	2.3
207 E.L.C.A.	3	470	629	1.6	3.8
226 FRIENDS-USA	1	57	73*	.2	.4
226e FUM	*1*	*57*	*73**	*.2*	*.4*
339 PENT CH OF GOD	2	86	180	.5	1.1
355 PRESB CH (USA)	3	1,308	1,664*	4.4	10.0
419 SO BAPT CONV	2	205	261*	.7	1.6
443 UN C OF CHRIST	4	431	548*	1.4	3.3
449 UN METHODIST	11	2,412	3,069*	8.0	18.5
467 WESLEYAN	2	102	425	1.1	2.6
496 JEWISH EST	0	NA	305	.8	1.8
BROWN	**20**	**1,586**	**2,757***	**19.6**	**100.0**
019 AMER BAPT USA	1	223	275*	2.0	10.0
053 ASSEMB OF GOD	1	17	23	.2	.8
081 CATHOLIC	1	NA	709	5.0	25.7
081d LATIN	*1*	*NA*	*709*	*5.0*	*25.7*
097 CHR CHS&CHS CR	1	250	308*	2.2	11.2
111 CH CR,SCIENTST	1	NR	NR	-	-
165 CH OF NAZARENE	1	149	216	1.5	7.8
167 CHS OF CHRIST	2	75	100	.7	3.6
193 EPISCOPAL	1	57	69	.5	2.5
283 LUTH—MO SYNOD	1	174	237	1.7	8.6
285 MENNONITE CH	1	35	60	.4	2.2
419 SO BAPT CONV	1	15	18*	.1	.7
449 UN METHODIST	6	566	697*	5.0	25.3
467 WESLEYAN	2	25	45	.3	1.6
CARROLL	**40**	**5,464**	**7,785***	**41.4**	**100.0**
019 AMER BAPT USA	3	424	532*	2.8	6.8
053 ASSEMB OF GOD	1	41	90	.5	1.2
071 BRETHREN (ASH)	2	271	340*	1.8	4.4
081 CATHOLIC	1	NA	570	3.0	7.3
081d LATIN	*1*	*NA*	*570*	*3.0*	*7.3*
093 CHR CH (DISC)	2	297	546	2.9	7.0
097 CHR CHS&CHS CR	4	887	1,113*	5.9	14.3
127 CH GOD (CLEVE)	1	35	44*	.2	.6
157 CH OF BRETHREN	5	631	792*	4.2	10.2
167 CHS OF CHRIST	1	15	30	.2	.4
207 E.L.C.A.	3	382	570	3.0	7.3
355 PRESB CH (USA)	6	883	1,108*	5.9	14.2
443 UN C OF CHRIST	1	251	315*	1.7	4.0
449 UN METHODIST	8	1,308	1,641*	8.7	21.1
467 WESLEYAN	2	39	94	.5	1.2
CASS	**71**	**11,695**	**19,224***	**50.0**	**100.0**
019 AMER BAPT USA	5	1,587	1,987*	5.2	10.3
053 ASSEMB OF GOD	1	294	435	1.1	2.3
071 BRETHREN (ASH)	1	115	144*	.4	.7
081 CATHOLIC	2	NA	3,324	8.7	17.3
081d LATIN	*2*	*NA*	*3,324*	*8.7*	*17.3*
089 CHR & MISS AL	1	81	170	.4	.9
093 CHR CH (DISC)	2	567	744	1.9	3.9
097 CHR CHS&CHS CR	10	2,461	3,082*	8.0	16.0
111 CH CR,SCIENTST	1	NR	NR	-	-
123 CH GOD (ANDER)	2	141	141	.4	.7
127 CH GOD (CLEVE)	1	198	248*	.6	1.3

County and Denomination	Number of churches	Communicant, confirmed, full members	Total adherents Number	Percent of total population	Percent of total adherents
151 L-D SAINTS	2	NA	787	2.0	4.1
157 CH OF BRETHREN	1	103	129*	.3	.7
165 CH OF NAZARENE	1	181	318	.8	1.7
167 CHS OF CHRIST	3	130	190	.5	1.0
176 CCC, NOT NAT'L	2	179	224*	.6	1.2
193 EPISCOPAL	1	142	220	.6	1.1
207 E.L.C.A.	2	518	715	1.9	3.7
263 INT FOURSQ GOS	1	60	75*	.2	.4
283 LUTH—MO SYNOD	1	338	436	1.1	2.3
353 CHR BRETHREN	1	10	14	-	.1
355 PRESB CH (USA)	5	943	1,181*	3.1	6.1
403 SALVATION ARMY	1	136	175	.5	.9
413 S.D.A.	1	55	69*	.2	.4
443 UN C OF CHRIST	2	321	402*	1.0	2.1
449 UN METHODIST	20	3,074	3,849*	10.0	20.0
467 WESLEYAN	1	61	165	.4	.9
CLARK	**113**	**19,984**	**37,749***	**43.0**	**100.0**
001 ADVENT CHR CH	1	67	83*	.1	.2
019 AMER BAPT USA	5	1,176	1,464*	1.7	3.9
053 ASSEMB OF GOD	2	245	330	.4	.9
081 CATHOLIC	8	NA	10,633	12.1	28.2
081d LATIN	8	NA	10,633	12.1	28.2
093 CHR CH (DISC)	5	892	1,815	2.1	4.8
097 CHR CHS&CHS CR	10	1,201	1,495*	1.7	4.0
123 CH GOD (ANDER)	4	710	710	.8	1.9
127 CH GOD (CLEVE)	1	28	35*	-	.1
145 CH GOD PROPHCY	1	33	41*	-	.1
151 L-D SAINTS	1	NA	417	.5	1.1
165 CH OF NAZARENE	5	251	502	.6	1.3
167 CHS OF CHRIST	12	1,471	1,890	2.2	5.0
193 EPISCOPAL	1	121	171	.2	.5
203 EVAN FREE CH	1	29	71	.1	.2
207 E.L.C.A.	1	264	366	.4	1.0
283 LUTH—MO SYNOD	1	98	123	.1	.3
325 OLD REG BAPT	5	98	122*	.1	.3
355 PRESB CH (USA)	7	855	1,064*	1.2	2.8
413 S.D.A.	2	96	120*	.1	.3
419 SO BAPT CONV	14	6,887	8,574*	9.8	22.7
436 UNITED BAPT	1	92	115*	.1	.3
443 UN C OF CHRIST	2	457	569*	.6	1.5
449 UN METHODIST	23	3,670	4,569*	5.2	12.1
496 JEWISH EST	0	NA	922	1.1	2.4
497 BLACK BAPT EST	NA	1,243	1,548*	1.8	4.1
CLAY	**63**	**8,505**	**12,025***	**48.7**	**100.0**
019 AMER BAPT USA	5	1,223	1,536*	6.2	12.8
053 ASSEMB OF GOD	2	122	318	1.3	2.6
081 CATHOLIC	2	NA	745	3.0	6.2
081d LATIN	2	NA	745	3.0	6.2
093 CHR CH (DISC)	1	66	106	.4	.9
097 CHR CHS&CHS CR	4	2,210	2,776*	11.2	23.1
111 CH CR,SCIENTST	1	NR	NR	-	-
127 CH GOD (CLEVE)	1	23	29*	.1	.2
145 CH GOD PROPHCY	1	33	41*	.2	.3
165 CH OF NAZARENE	4	445	898	3.6	7.5
167 CHS OF CHRIST	6	281	382	1.5	3.2
175 CONGR CHR CHS	1	132	166*	.7	1.4
221 FREE METHODIST	1	31	57	.2	.5
259 IFCA	1	NR	NR	-	-
283 LUTH—MO SYNOD	1	141	162	.7	1.3
355 PRESB CH (USA)	2	352	442*	1.8	3.7
419 SO BAPT CONV	2	199	250*	1.0	2.1
443 UN C OF CHRIST	4	764	960*	3.9	8.0
449 UN METHODIST	23	2,465	3,097*	12.5	25.8
467 WESLEYAN	1	18	60	.2	.5
CLINTON	**61**	**9,038**	**13,384***	**43.2**	**100.0**
019 AMER BAPT USA	5	1,037	1,322*	4.3	9.9
053 ASSEMB OF GOD	2	164	280	.9	2.1
081 CATHOLIC	1	NA	1,052	3.4	7.9
081d LATIN	1	NA	1,052	3.4	7.9
093 CHR CH (DISC)	1	611	776	2.5	5.8
097 CHR CHS&CHS CR	6	1,249	1,592*	5.1	11.9
121 CH GOD (ABR)	1	32	41*	.1	.3
123 CH GOD (ANDER)	2	44	60	.2	.4
151 L-D SAINTS	1	NA	187	.6	1.4
157 CH OF BRETHREN	1	177	226*	.7	1.7
165 CH OF NAZARENE	2	344	538	1.7	4.0
167 CHS OF CHRIST	1	50	100	.3	.7
176 CCC, NOT NAT'L	1	69	88*	.3	.7
181 CONSRV CONGR	1	352	449*	1.4	3.4
207 E.L.C.A.	2	363	445	1.4	3.3
339 PENT CH OF GOD	1	35	77	.2	.6
355 PRESB CH (USA)	5	990	1,262*	4.1	9.4
413 S.D.A.	1	57	73*	.2	.5

County and Denomination	Number of churches	Communicant, confirmed, full members	Total adherents Number	Percent of total population	Percent of total adherents
419 SO BAPT CONV	4	545	695*	2.2	5.2
443 UN C OF CHRIST	2	248	316*	1.0	2.4
449 UN METHODIST	14	2,369	3,021*	9.8	22.6
467 WESLEYAN	7	302	784	2.5	5.9
CRAWFORD	**28**	**2,718**	**4,215***	**42.5**	**100.0**
019 AMER BAPT USA	3	186	234*	2.4	5.6
075 BRETHREN IN CR	1	12	35	.4	.8
081 CATHOLIC	1	NA	204	2.1	4.8
081d LATIN	1	NA	204	2.1	4.8
093 CHR CH (DISC)	1	77	124	1.3	2.9
097 CHR CHS&CHS CR	5	1,345	1,693*	17.1	40.2
151 L-D SAINTS	1	NA	213	2.1	5.1
165 CH OF NAZARENE	2	25	61	.6	1.4
221 FREE METHODIST	1	53	53	.5	1.3
355 PRESB CH (USA)	1	133	167*	1.7	4.0
436 UNITED BAPT	1	28	35*	.4	.8
449 UN METHODIST	8	649	817*	8.2	19.4
467 WESLEYAN	3	210	579	5.8	13.7
DAVIESS	**79**	**8,793**	**17,506***	**63.6**	**100.0**
019 AMER BAPT USA	4	1,162	1,504*	5.5	8.6
053 ASSEMB OF GOD	2	140	195	.7	1.1
061 BEACHY AMISH	1	50	65*	.2	.4
081 CATHOLIC	7	NA	3,703	13.4	21.2
081d LATIN	7	NA	3,703	13.4	21.2
093 CHR CH (DISC)	1	204	498	1.8	2.8
097 CHR CHS&CHS CR	8	2,510	3,249*	11.8	18.6
123 CH GOD (ANDER)	1	49	67	.2	.4
127 CH GOD (CLEVE)	1	46	60*	.2	.3
165 CH OF NAZARENE	2	131	298	1.1	1.7
167 CHS OF CHRIST	4	213	311	1.1	1.8
171 CH GOD-GEN CON	1	59	76*	.3	.4
185 CUMBER PRESB	1	40	50	.2	.3
193 EPISCOPAL	1	34	35	.1	.2
207 E.L.C.A.	1	126	184	.7	1.1
221 FREE METHODIST	1	121	124	.5	.7
285 MENNONITE CH	7	891	1,219	4.4	7.0
323 OLD ORD AMISH	11	NA	1,650	6.0	9.4
355 PRESB CH (USA)	1	169	219*	.8	1.3
413 S.D.A.	2	24	31*	.1	.2
419 SO BAPT CONV	3	420	544*	2.0	3.1
449 UN METHODIST	16	2,303	2,981*	10.8	17.0
467 WESLEYAN	3	101	443	1.6	2.5
DEARBORN	**57**	**9,098**	**18,352***	**47.3**	**100.0**
019 AMER BAPT USA	8	2,338	3,014*	7.8	16.4
081 CATHOLIC	6	NA	5,727	14.7	31.2
081d LATIN	6	NA	5,727	14.7	31.2
089 CHR & MISS AL	1	91	218	.6	1.2
097 CHR CHS&CHS CR	7	1,704	2,197*	5.7	12.0
111 CH CR,SCIENTST	1	NR	NR	-	-
123 CH GOD (ANDER)	1	40	45	.1	.2
165 CH OF NAZARENE	1	37	80	.2	.4
167 CHS OF CHRIST	1	17	30	.1	.2
193 EPISCOPAL	1	45	92	.2	.5
207 E.L.C.A.	4	859	1,079	2.8	5.9
223 FREE WILL BAPT	2	83	107*	.3	.6
283 LUTH—MO SYNOD	4	1,085	1,506	3.9	8.2
355 PRESB CH (USA)	4	377	486*	1.3	2.6
419 SO BAPT CONV	1	42	54*	.1	.3
443 UN C OF CHRIST	3	267	344*	.9	1.9
449 UN METHODIST	10	2,012	2,594*	6.7	14.1
467 WESLEYAN	2	101	151	.4	.8
496 JEWISH EST	0	NA	628	1.6	3.4
DECATUR	**60**	**7,566**	**14,872***	**62.9**	**100.0**
019 AMER BAPT USA	11	3,058	3,931*	16.6	26.4
053 ASSEMB OF GOD	3	124	171	.7	1.1
081 CATHOLIC	5	NA	4,718	20.0	31.7
081d LATIN	5	NA	4,718	20.0	31.7
093 CHR CH (DISC)	2	425	540	2.3	3.6
097 CHR CHS&CHS CR	6	884	1,136*	4.8	7.6
123 CH GOD (ANDER)	1	206	206	.9	1.4
127 CH GOD (CLEVE)	1	45	58*	.2	.4
165 CH OF NAZARENE	1	30	161	.7	1.1
167 CHS OF CHRIST	1	20	20	.1	.1
207 E.L.C.A.	2	173	231	1.0	1.6
221 FREE METHODIST	1	58	71	.3	.5
283 LUTH—MO SYNOD	1	131	194	.8	1.3
355 PRESB CH (USA)	4	475	611*	2.6	4.1
419 SO BAPT CONV	5	417	536*	2.3	3.6
449 UN METHODIST	11	1,420	1,825*	7.7	12.3
467 WESLEYAN	4	100	163	.7	1.1
499 INDEP.NON-CHAR	1	NA	300	1.3	2.0

County and Denomination	Number of churches	Communicant, confirmed, full members	Total adherents Number	Percent of total population	Percent of total adherents
DE KALB	**61**	**8,644**	**15,603***	**44.2**	**100.0**
019 AMER BAPT USA	1	391	506*	1.4	3.2
053 ASSEMB OF GOD	3	178	235	.7	1.5
075 BRETHREN IN CR	1	52	52	.1	.3
081 CATHOLIC	3	NA	3,647	10.3	23.4
081d LATIN	3	NA	3,647	10.3	23.4
089 CHR & MISS AL	1	44	96	.3	.6
093 CHR CH (DISC)	1	285	450	1.3	2.9
097 CHR CHS&CHS CR	6	1,091	1,412*	4.0	9.0
123 CH GOD (ANDER)	3	465	530	1.5	3.4
133 CH GOD(7TH)DEN	1	15	20	.1	.1
157 CH OF BRETHREN	3	318	412*	1.2	2.6
165 CH OF NAZARENE	5	432	827	2.3	5.3
167 CHS OF CHRIST	1	45	62	.2	.4
171 CH GOD-GEN CON	1	169	219*	.6	1.4
207 E.L.C.A.	5	760	1,198	3.4	7.7
265 INT PENT C CHR	1	59	59	.2	.4
283 LUTH—MO SYNOD	3	766	1,068	3.0	6.8
291 MISSIONARY CH	1	163	326	.9	2.1
355 PRESB CH (USA)	2	715	926*	2.6	5.9
419 SO BAPT CONV	1	74	96*	.3	.6
438 UN BRETH IN CR	2	152	152	.4	1.0
449 UN METHODIST	15	2,458	3,182*	9.0	20.4
467 WESLEYAN	1	12	21	.1	.1
496 JEWISH EST	0	NA	107	.3	.7
DELAWARE	**140**	**25,291**	**44,922***	**37.5**	**100.0**
019 AMER BAPT USA	3	1,610	1,940*	1.6	4.3
053 ASSEMB OF GOD	3	435	795	.7	1.8
071 BRETHREN (ASH)	2	236	284*	.2	.6
081 CATHOLIC	2	NA	5,621	4.7	12.5
081d LATIN	2	NA	5,621	4.7	12.5
089 CHR & MISS AL	1	37	109	.1	.2
093 CHR CH (DISC)	5	991	1,766	1.5	3.9
097 CHR CHS&CHS CR	2	636	766*	.6	1.7
111 CH CR,SCIENTST	1	NR	NR	-	-
123 CH GOD (ANDER)	9	731	985	.8	2.2
127 CH GOD (CLEVE)	1	114	137*	.1	.3
145 CH GOD PROPHCY	1	33	40*	-	.1
146 CH GOD MTN ASM	1	64	77*	.1	.2
151 L-D SAINTS	2	NA	672	.6	1.5
157 CH OF BRETHREN	3	156	188*	.2	.4
165 CH OF NAZARENE	16	2,032	3,462	2.9	7.7
167 CHS OF CHRIST	9	1,130	1,472	1.2	3.3
193 EPISCOPAL	1	133	156	.1	.3
207 E.L.C.A.	3	788	1,086	.9	2.4
226 FRIENDS-USA	2	433	522*	.4	1.2
226e FUM	2	433	522*	.4	1.2
263 INT FOURSQ GOS	2	383	462*	.4	1.0
283 LUTH—MO SYNOD	1	373	472	.4	1.1
285 MENNONITE CH	1	3	14	-	-
287 MENN GEN CONF	1	7	12	-	-
296 MIDW CONGR FEL	3	149	180*	.2	.4
353 CHR BRETHREN	1	15	20	-	-
355 PRESB CH (USA)	2	1,097	1,322*	1.1	2.9
356 PRESB CH AMER	1	345	418	.3	.9
403 SALVATION ARMY	1	56	63	.1	.1
413 S.D.A.	2	99	119*	.1	.3
419 SO BAPT CONV	9	1,948	2,348*	2.0	5.2
435 UNITARIAN-UNIV	1	212	304	.3	.7
436 UNITED BAPT	3	930	1,121*	.9	2.5
438 UN BRETH IN CR	2	96	117	.1	.3
443 UN C OF CHRIST	4	910	1,097*	.9	2.4
449 UN METHODIST	32	7,075	8,526*	7.1	19.0
467 WESLEYAN	3	139	355	.3	.8
496 JEWISH EST	1	NA	160	.1	.4
497 BLACK BAPT EST	NA	1,895	2,284*	1.9	5.1
498 INDEP.CHARIS.	1	NA	4,000	3.3	8.9
499 INDEP.NON-CHAR	2	NA	1,450	1.2	3.2
DUBOIS	**45**	**6,321**	**27,710***	**75.7**	**100.0**
053 ASSEMB OF GOD	1	84	240	.7	.9
081 CATHOLIC	11	NA	19,110	52.2	69.0
081d LATIN	11	NA	19,110	52.2	69.0
093 CHR CH (DISC)	1	40	64	.2	.2
097 CHR CHS&CHS CR	4	646	833*	2.3	3.0
151 L-D SAINTS	1	NA	100	.3	.4
165 CH OF NAZARENE	2	130	315	.9	1.1
167 CHS OF CHRIST	2	82	126	.3	.5
207 E.L.C.A.	7	2,196	2,850	7.8	10.3
355 PRESB CH (USA)	1	96	124*	.3	.4
413 S.D.A.	1	21	27*	.1	.1
419 SO BAPT CONV	2	357	460*	1.3	1.7
443 UN C OF CHRIST	6	1,731	2,231*	6.1	8.1
449 UN METHODIST	5	931	1,200*	3.3	4.3
467 WESLEYAN	1	7	30	.1	.1
ELKHART	**227**	**39,868**	**70,640***	**45.2**	**100.0**
005 AME ZION	1	60	72	-	.1
053 ASSEMB OF GOD	6	1,605	2,535	1.6	3.6
061 BEACHY AMISH	4	462	598*	.4	.8
071 BRETHREN (ASH)	6	1,491	1,929*	1.2	2.7
075 BRETHREN IN CR	2	169	180	.1	.3
081 CATHOLIC	5	NA	11,461	7.3	16.2
081d LATIN	5	NA	11,461	7.3	16.2
089 CHR & MISS AL	2	0	52	-	.1
093 CHR CH (DISC)	2	458	568	.4	.8
097 CHR CHS&CHS CR	1	250	323*	.2	.5
105 CHRISTIAN REF	1	168	248	.2	.4
111 CH CR,SCIENTST	2	NR	NR	-	-
123 CH GOD (ANDER)	4	1,126	1,147	.7	1.6
127 CH GOD (CLEVE)	4	312	404*	.3	.6
145 CH GOD PROPHCY	1	33	43*	-	.1
151 L-D SAINTS	2	NA	536	.3	.8
157 CH OF BRETHREN	19	3,310	4,283*	2.7	6.1
165 CH OF NAZARENE	7	949	1,611	1.0	2.3
167 CHS OF CHRIST	3	355	380	.2	.5
171 CH GOD-GEN CON	1	184	238*	.2	.3
193 EPISCOPAL	4	900	1,322	.8	1.9
203 EVAN FREE CH	1	38	130	.1	.2
207 E.L.C.A.	10	2,941	3,811	2.4	5.4
221 FREE METHODIST	2	134	195	.1	.3
223 FREE WILL BAPT	1	60	78*	-	.1
259 IFCA	2	NR	NR	-	-
283 LUTH—MO SYNOD	3	842	1,179	.8	1.7
285 MENNONITE CH	40	6,978	10,157	6.5	14.4
287 MENN GEN CONF	8	959	1,123	.7	1.6
291 MISSIONARY CH	15	2,419	3,584	2.3	5.1
323 OLD ORD AMISH	18	NA	2,700	1.7	3.8
339 PENT CH OF GOD	4	73	227	.1	.3
355 PRESB CH (USA)	3	1,511	1,955*	1.3	2.8
361 PRIM BAPT ASCS	2	18	23*	-	-
403 SALVATION ARMY	2	198	211	.1	.3
413 S.D.A.	2	192	248*	.2	.4
419 SO BAPT CONV	2	202	261*	.2	.4
435 UNITARIAN-UNIV	1	123	178	.1	.3
438 UN BRETH IN CR	1	66	66	-	.1
443 UN C OF CHRIST	6	1,362	1,762*	1.1	2.5
449 UN METHODIST	22	8,019	10,376*	6.6	14.7
467 WESLEYAN	1	22	105	.1	.1
497 BLACK BAPT EST	NA	1,879	2,431*	1.6	3.4
499 INDEP.NON-CHAR	4	NA	1,910	1.2	2.7
FAYETTE	**39**	**5,149**	**10,446***	**40.2**	**100.0**
019 AMER BAPT USA	1	755	938*	3.6	9.0
053 ASSEMB OF GOD	1	90	109	.4	1.0
081 CATHOLIC	1	NA	2,196	8.4	21.0
081d LATIN	1	NA	2,196	8.4	21.0
093 CHR CH (DISC)	3	548	713	2.7	6.8
097 CHR CHS&CHS CR	1	218	271*	1.0	2.6
111 CH CR,SCIENTST	1	NR	NR	-	-
123 CH GOD (ANDER)	1	185	185	.7	1.8
127 CH GOD (CLEVE)	1	101	126*	.5	1.2
145 CH GOD PROPHCY	1	33	41*	.2	.4
151 L-D SAINTS	1	NA	213	.8	2.0
165 CH OF NAZARENE	2	174	348	1.3	3.3
167 CHS OF CHRIST	3	100	127	.5	1.2
193 EPISCOPAL	1	34	57	.2	.5
207 E.L.C.A.	2	228	296	1.1	2.8
283 LUTH—MO SYNOD	1	62	90	.3	.9
355 PRESB CH (USA)	1	291	362*	1.4	3.5
361 PRIM BAPT ASCS	2	48	60*	.2	.6
403 SALVATION ARMY	1	86	86	.3	.8
413 S.D.A.	1	21	26*	.1	.2
419 SO BAPT CONV	1	588	731*	2.8	7.0
449 UN METHODIST	9	1,573	1,955*	7.5	18.7
467 WESLEYAN	1	14	16	.1	.2
499 INDEP.NON-CHAR	2	NA	1,500	5.8	14.4
FLOYD	**67**	**22,186**	**39,998***	**62.1**	**100.0**
001 ADVENT CHR CH	1	109	137*	.2	.3
019 AMER BAPT USA	4	1,407	1,772*	2.8	4.4
053 ASSEMB OF GOD	1	77	101	.2	.3
081 CATHOLIC	5	NA	10,627	16.5	26.6
081d LATIN	5	NA	10,627	16.5	26.6
093 CHR CH (DISC)	5	1,122	1,650	2.6	4.1
097 CHR CHS&CHS CR	4	1,635	2,059*	3.2	5.1
111 CH CR,SCIENTST	1	NR	NR	-	-
123 CH GOD (ANDER)	2	357	357	.6	.9
145 CH GOD PROPHCY	1	33	42*	.1	.1
165 CH OF NAZARENE	3	528	1,020	1.6	2.6
167 CHS OF CHRIST	3	373	465	.7	1.2
193 EPISCOPAL	1	268	389	.6	1.0

County and Denomination		Number of churches	Communicant, confirmed, full members	Total adherents		
				Number	Percent of total population	Percent of total adherents
207	E.L.C.A.	1	192	285	.4	.7
283	LUTH—MO SYNOD	2	842	1,164	1.8	2.9
355	PRESB CH (USA)	2	567	714*	1.1	1.8
403	SALVATION ARMY	1	74	83	.1	.2
413	S.D.A.	1	108	136*	.2	.3
419	SO BAPT CONV	9	7,948	10,009*	15.5	25.0
436	UNITED BAPT	1	66	83*	.1	.2
443	UN C OF CHRIST	1	1,085	1,366*	2.1	3.4
449	UN METHODIST	15	4,665	5,875*	9.1	14.7
467	WESLEYAN	3	31	105	.2	.3
496	JEWISH EST	0	NA	679	1.1	1.7
497	BLACK BAPT EST	NA	699	880*	1.4	2.2
FOUNTAIN		**43**	**4,402**	**6,578***	**36.9**	**100.0**
053	ASSEMB OF GOD	2	176	377	2.1	5.7
081	CATHOLIC	2	NA	753	4.2	11.4
081d	LATIN	2	NA	753	4.2	11.4
093	CHR CH (DISC)	3	256	357	2.0	5.4
097	CHR CHS&CHS CR	8	1,267	1,582*	8.9	24.0
123	CH GOD (ANDER)	1	60	125	.7	1.9
127	CH GOD (CLEVE)	1	21	26*	.1	.4
165	CH OF NAZARENE	4	290	460	2.6	7.0
167	CHS OF CHRIST	1	48	69	.4	1.0
176	CCC, NOT NAT'L	3	313	391*	2.2	5.9
207	E.L.C.A.	2	212	269	1.5	4.1
221	FREE METHODIST	1	107	107	.6	1.6
355	PRESB CH (USA)	2	193	241*	1.4	3.7
419	SO BAPT CONV	1	62	77*	.4	1.2
443	UN C OF CHRIST	2	104	130*	.7	2.0
449	UN METHODIST	10	1,293	1,614*	9.1	24.5
FRANKLIN		**39**	**3,120**	**10,515***	**53.7**	**100.0**
081	CATHOLIC	7	NA	5,261	26.9	50.0
081d	LATIN	7	NA	5,261	26.9	50.0
097	CHR CHS&CHS CR	5	480	620*	3.2	5.9
146	CH GOD MTN ASM	1	49	63*	.3	.6
151	L-D SAINTS	1	NA	259	1.3	2.5
165	CH OF NAZARENE	2	30	122	.6	1.2
207	E.L.C.A.	2	415	519	2.7	4.9
325	OLD REG BAPT	1	14	18*	.1	.2
355	PRESB CH (USA)	1	26	34*	.2	.3
419	SO BAPT CONV	5	759	980*	5.0	9.3
443	UN C OF CHRIST	2	513	662*	3.4	6.3
449	UN METHODIST	10	834	1,077*	5.5	10.2
499	INDEP.NON-CHAR	2	NA	900	4.6	8.6
FULTON		**35**	**3,936**	**5,885***	**31.2**	**100.0**
019	AMER BAPT USA	2	501	632*	3.4	10.7
053	ASSEMB OF GOD	1	47	69	.4	1.2
071	BRETHREN (ASH)	1	67	85*	.5	1.4
081	CATHOLIC	2	NA	746	4.0	12.7
081d	LATIN	2	NA	746	4.0	12.7
093	CHR CH (DISC)	1	342	581	3.1	9.9
097	CHR CHS&CHS CR	1	85	107*	.6	1.8
123	CH GOD (ANDER)	3	431	503	2.7	8.5
127	CH GOD (CLEVE)	1	48	61*	.3	1.0
157	CH OF BRETHREN	1	71	90*	.5	1.5
165	CH OF NAZARENE	1	77	144	.8	2.4
167	CHS OF CHRIST	1	80	85	.5	1.4
259	IFCA	2	NR	NR	-	-
283	LUTH—MO SYNOD	1	261	341	1.8	5.8
355	PRESB CH (USA)	1	162	205*	1.1	3.5
413	S.D.A.	1	9	11*	.1	.2
449	UN METHODIST	14	1,721	2,173*	11.5	36.9
467	WESLEYAN	1	34	52	.3	.9
GIBSON		**67**	**6,634**	**15,186***	**47.6**	**100.0**
053	ASSEMB OF GOD	2	216	319	1.0	2.1
081	CATHOLIC	7	NA	6,367	20.0	41.9
081d	LATIN	7	NA	6,367	20.0	41.9
093	CHR CH (DISC)	2	223	350	1.1	2.3
097	CHR CHS&CHS CR	3	486	608*	1.9	4.0
111	CH CR,SCIENTST	1	NR	NR	-	-
123	CH GOD (ANDER)	2	200	205	.6	1.3
157	CH OF BRETHREN	1	132	165*	.5	1.1
165	CH OF NAZARENE	6	604	1,160	3.6	7.6
167	CHS OF CHRIST	2	48	62	.2	.4
185	CUMBER PRESB	1	26	28	.1	.2
207	E.L.C.A.	1	206	267	.8	1.8
259	IFCA	1	NR	NR	-	-
355	PRESB CH (USA)	7	588	736*	2.3	4.8
403	SALVATION ARMY	1	54	59	.2	.4
419	SO BAPT CONV	5	677	847*	2.7	5.6
443	UN C OF CHRIST	5	529	662*	2.1	4.4
449	UN METHODIST	17	2,433	3,044*	9.5	20.0
467	WESLEYAN	3	84	147	.5	1.0

County and Denomination		Number of churches	Communicant, confirmed, full members	Total adherents		
				Number	Percent of total population	Percent of total adherents
497	BLACK BAPT EST	NA	128	160*	.5	1.1
GRANT		**127**	**19,112**	**31,504***	**42.5**	**100.0**
019	AMER BAPT USA	3	827	1,019*	1.4	3.2
053	ASSEMB OF GOD	5	680	1,256	1.7	4.0
071	BRETHREN (ASH)	1	16	20*	-	.1
081	CATHOLIC	3	NA	3,225	4.3	10.2
081d	LATIN	3	NA	3,225	4.3	10.2
089	CHR & MISS AL	1	92	100	.1	.3
093	CHR CH (DISC)	6	984	2,296	3.1	7.3
097	CHR CHS&CHS CR	4	895	1,103*	1.5	3.5
111	CH CR,SCIENTST	1	NR	NR	-	-
123	CH GOD (ANDER)	4	268	285	.4	.9
127	CH GOD (CLEVE)	1	45	55*	.1	.2
145	CH GOD PROPHCY	1	33	41*	.1	.1
151	L-D SAINTS	1	NA	353	.5	1.1
157	CH OF BRETHREN	1	145	179*	.2	.6
165	CH OF NAZARENE	7	462	836	1.1	2.7
167	CHS OF CHRIST	4	273	331	.4	1.1
176	CCC, NOT NAT'L	1	104	128*	.2	.4
193	EPISCOPAL	2	290	385	.5	1.2
207	E.L.C.A.	2	349	491	.7	1.6
213	EVAN MENN INC	1	228	281*	.4	.9
223	FREE WILL BAPT	2	82	101*	.1	.3
226	FRIENDS-USA	10	1,313	1,618*	2.2	5.1
226e	FUM	10	1,313	1,618*	2.2	5.1
283	LUTH—MO SYNOD	1	326	466	.6	1.5
339	PENT CH OF GOD	1	12	38	.1	.1
355	PRESB CH (USA)	3	624	769*	1.0	2.4
361	PRIM BAPT ASCS	2	62	76*	.1	.2
403	SALVATION ARMY	1	102	115	.2	.4
413	S.D.A.	2	217	267*	.4	.8
419	SO BAPT CONV	4	2,344	2,889*	3.9	9.2
438	UN BRETH IN CR	1	33	35	-	.1
443	UN C OF CHRIST	1	152	187*	.3	.6
449	UN METHODIST	29	4,262	5,254*	7.1	16.7
467	WESLEYAN	20	2,811	5,872	7.9	18.6
496	JEWISH EST	1	NA	100	.1	.3
497	BLACK BAPT EST	NA	1,081	1,333*	1.8	4.2
GREENE		**82**	**9,115**	**13,256***	**43.6**	**100.0**
019	AMER BAPT USA	9	2,843	3,532*	11.6	26.6
053	ASSEMB OF GOD	5	468	846	2.8	6.4
081	CATHOLIC	3	NA	720	2.4	5.4
081d	LATIN	3	NA	720	2.4	5.4
093	CHR CH (DISC)	6	615	1,218	4.0	9.2
097	CHR CHS&CHS CR	6	1,005	1,249*	4.1	9.4
123	CH GOD (ANDER)	1	60	68	.2	.5
127	CH GOD (CLEVE)	4	361	449*	1.5	3.4
151	L-D SAINTS	1	NA	225	.7	1.7
165	CH OF NAZARENE	4	151	324	1.1	2.4
167	CHS OF CHRIST	9	483	624	2.1	4.7
171	CH GOD-GEN CON	3	102	127*	.4	1.0
207	E.L.C.A.	1	148	191	.6	1.4
221	FREE METHODIST	1	19	28	.1	.2
339	PENT CH OF GOD	2	19	54	.2	.4
355	PRESB CH (USA)	2	152	189*	.6	1.4
403	SALVATION ARMY	1	47	56	.2	.4
413	S.D.A.	1	59	73*	.2	.6
443	UN C OF CHRIST	1	299	372*	1.2	2.8
449	UN METHODIST	18	2,242	2,786*	9.2	21.0
467	WESLEYAN	4	42	125	.4	.9
HAMILTON		**98**	**22,606**	**50,239***	**46.1**	**100.0**
019	AMER BAPT USA	2	146	190*	.2	.4
053	ASSEMB OF GOD	3	958	2,788	2.6	5.5
057	BAPT GEN CONF	1	103	134*	.1	.3
071	BRETHREN (ASH)	1	51	66*	.1	.1
081	CATHOLIC	5	NA	16,156	14.8	32.2
081d	LATIN	5	NA	16,156	14.8	32.2
082	CENTRAL BAPT	2	155	201*	.2	.4
093	CHR CH (DISC)	5	1,674	2,910	2.7	5.8
097	CHR CHS&CHS CR	13	3,904	5,073*	4.7	10.1
111	CH CR,SCIENTST	1	NR	NR	-	-
123	CH GOD (ANDER)	3	259	317	.3	.6
127	CH GOD (CLEVE)	1	142	185*	.2	.4
145	CH GOD PROPHCY	1	33	43*	-	.1
151	L-D SAINTS	1	NA	335	.3	.7
157	CH OF BRETHREN	1	94	122*	.1	.2
165	CH OF NAZARENE	2	198	329	.3	.7
167	CHS OF CHRIST	3	262	296	.3	.6
193	EPISCOPAL	2	682	1,082	1.0	2.2
207	E.L.C.A.	3	1,665	2,308	2.1	4.6
221	FREE METHODIST	1	0	54	-	.1
226	FRIENDS-USA	8	1,157	1,503*	1.4	3.0
226e	FUM	7	1,104	1,434*	1.3	2.9

County and Denomination		Number of churches	Communicant, confirmed, full members	Total adherents		
				Number	Percent of total population	Percent of total adherents
226g	INDEP EVAN	1	53	69*	.1	.1
283	LUTH—MO SYNOD	3	1,400	1,922	1.8	3.8
355	PRESB CH (USA)	1	332	431*	.4	.9
356	PRESB CH AMER	1	0	0	-	-
371	REF CH IN AM	1	75	232	.2	.5
413	S.D.A.	3	491	638*	.6	1.3
419	SO BAPT CONV	6	1,011	1,314*	1.2	2.6
443	UN C OF CHRIST	1	353	459*	.4	.9
449	UN METHODIST	16	6,988	9,080*	8.3	18.1
467	WESLEYAN	6	294	641	.6	1.3
496	JEWISH EST	0	NA	872	.8	1.7
497	BLACK BAPT EST	NA	179	233*	.2	.5
499	INDEP.NON-CHAR	1	NA	325	.3	.6
HANCOCK		**61**	**10,019**	**17,794***	**39.1**	**100.0**
053	ASSEMB OF GOD	1	70	94	.2	.5
081	CATHOLIC	2	NA	3,001	6.6	16.9
081d	LATIN	2	NA	3,001	6.6	16.9
093	CHR CH (DISC)	3	587	1,073	2.4	6.0
097	CHR CHS&CHS CR	8	1,918	2,424*	5.3	13.6
123	CH GOD (ANDER)	1	85	157	.3	.9
145	CH GOD PROPHCY	1	33	42*	.1	.2
151	L-D SAINTS	1	NA	353	.8	2.0
165	CH OF NAZARENE	6	581	1,287	2.8	7.2
167	CHS OF CHRIST	2	135	176	.4	1.0
207	E.L.C.A.	1	254	332	.7	1.9
223	FREE WILL BAPT	1	12	15*		.1
226	FRIENDS-USA	2	142	179*	.4	1.0
226e	FUM	2	142	179*	.4	1.0
283	LUTH—MO SYNOD	2	738	1,026	2.3	5.8
325	OLD REG BAPT	1	20	25*	.1	.1
355	PRESB CH (USA)	1	135	171*	.4	1.0
361	PRIM BAPT ASCS	1	19	24*	.1	.1
413	S.D.A.	1	43	54*	.1	.3
419	SO BAPT CONV	2	489	618*	1.4	3.5
443	UN C OF CHRIST	1	147	186*	.4	1.0
449	UN METHODIST	21	4,541	5,740*	12.6	32.3
467	WESLEYAN	2	70	453	1.0	2.5
496	JEWISH EST	0	NA	364	.8	2.0
HARRISON		**78**	**7,965**	**15,816***	**52.9**	**100.0**
019	AMER BAPT USA	1	128	164*	.5	1.0
053	ASSEMB OF GOD	4	456	646	2.2	4.1
081	CATHOLIC	6	NA	4,685	15.7	29.6
081d	LATIN	6	NA	4,685	15.7	29.6
093	CHR CH (DISC)	1	212	554	1.9	3.5
097	CHR CHS&CHS CR	5	480	615*	2.1	3.9
145	CH GOD PROPHCY	2	67	86*	.3	.5
151	L-D SAINTS	1	NA	368	1.2	2.3
165	CH OF NAZARENE	2	185	345	1.2	2.2
167	CHS OF CHRIST	4	330	454	1.5	2.9
207	E.L.C.A.	2	263	368	1.2	2.3
283	LUTH—MO SYNOD	2	684	944	3.2	6.0
355	PRESB CH (USA)	5	406	520*	1.7	3.3
419	SO BAPT CONV	8	1,199	1,536*	5.1	9.7
443	UN C OF CHRIST	1	49	63*	.2	.4
449	UN METHODIST	33	3,488	4,468*	14.9	28.2
467	WESLEYAN	1	18	0	-	-
HENDRICKS		**78**	**13,894**	**27,243***	**36.0**	**100.0**
019	AMER BAPT USA	5	1,234	1,565*	2.1	5.7
053	ASSEMB OF GOD	3	241	490	.6	1.8
081	CATHOLIC	3	NA	6,908	9.1	25.4
081d	LATIN	3	NA	6,908	9.1	25.4
089	CHR & MISS AL	1	29	73	.1	.3
093	CHR CH (DISC)	8	1,134	2,135	2.8	7.8
097	CHR CHS&CHS CR	8	3,135	3,975*	5.2	14.6
123	CH GOD (ANDER)	2	52	55	.1	.2
127	CH GOD (CLEVE)	1	16	20*	-	.1
145	CH GOD PROPHCY	1	33	42*	.1	.2
151	L-D SAINTS	2	NA	755	1.0	2.8
165	CH OF NAZARENE	4	214	494	.7	1.8
167	CHS OF CHRIST	7	610	831	1.1	3.1
193	EPISCOPAL	2	296	463	.6	1.7
207	E.L.C.A.	1	260	376	.5	1.4
209	EVAN LUTH SYN	1	46	69	.1	.3
221	FREE METHODIST	1	104	121	.2	.4
226	FRIENDS-USA	4	750	951*	1.3	3.5
226e	FUM	4	750	951*	1.3	3.5
283	LUTH—MO SYNOD	2	241	340	.4	1.2
355	PRESB CH (USA)	4	404	512*	.7	1.9
361	PRIM BAPT ASCS	1	11	14*	-	.1
413	S.D.A.	1	32	41*	.1	.2
419	SO BAPT CONV	4	1,357	1,721*	2.3	6.3
449	UN METHODIST	12	3,514	4,456*	5.9	16.4
496	JEWISH EST	0	NA	606	.8	2.2
497	BLACK BAPT EST	NA	181	230*	.3	.8
HENRY		**96**	**12,482**	**20,129***	**41.8**	**100.0**
019	AMER BAPT USA	1	705	863*	1.8	4.3
053	ASSEMB OF GOD	1	191	231	.5	1.1
081	CATHOLIC	2	NA	1,105	2.3	5.5
081d	LATIN	2	NA	1,105	2.3	5.5
089	CHR & MISS AL	1	40	72	.1	.4
093	CHR CH (DISC)	4	905	1,835	3.8	9.1
097	CHR CHS&CHS CR	7	645	790*	1.6	3.9
123	CH GOD (ANDER)	2	384	519	1.1	2.6
127	CH GOD (CLEVE)	1	100	122*	.3	.6
146	CH GOD MTN ASM	1	30	37*	.1	.2
151	L-D SAINTS	1	NA	145	.3	.7
157	CH OF BRETHREN	2	90	110*	.2	.5
165	CH OF NAZARENE	9	1,163	2,672	5.6	13.3
167	CHS OF CHRIST	7	337	459	1.0	2.3
193	EPISCOPAL	1	75	131	.3	.7
207	E.L.C.A.	1	291	382	.8	1.9
221	FREE METHODIST	1	98	104	.2	.5
223	FREE WILL BAPT	1	130	159*	.3	.8
226	FRIENDS-USA	10	1,029	1,260*	2.6	6.3
226e	FUM	10	1,029	1,260*	2.6	6.3
263	INT FOURSQ GOS	1	841	1,029*	2.1	5.1
296	MIDW CONGR FEL	1	50	61*	.1	.3
355	PRESB CH (USA)	4	756	925*	1.9	4.6
403	SALVATION ARMY	1	60	69	.1	.3
413	S.D.A.	1	24	29*	.1	.1
419	SO BAPT CONV	9	1,492	1,826*	3.8	9.1
436	UNITED BAPT	2	312	382*	.8	1.9
438	UN BRETH IN CR	1	52	52	.1	.3
443	UN C OF CHRIST	1	221	271*	.6	1.3
449	UN METHODIST	15	2,215	2,711*	5.6	13.5
467	WESLEYAN	5	246	903	1.9	4.5
499	INDEP.NON-CHAR	2	NA	875	1.8	4.3
HOWARD		**109**	**20,819**	**35,924***	**44.4**	**100.0**
005	AME ZION	1	200	275	.3	.8
019	AMER BAPT USA	4	989	1,245*	1.5	3.5
053	ASSEMB OF GOD	4	748	1,461	1.8	4.1
061	BEACHY AMISH	1	68	86*	.1	.2
071	BRETHREN (ASH)	1	24	30*	-	.1
081	CATHOLIC	2	NA	7,320	9.1	20.4
081d	LATIN	2	NA	7,320	9.1	20.4
083	CHRIST CATH CH	1	7	7	-	-
089	CHR & MISS AL	1	42	104	.1	.3
093	CHR CH (DISC)	3	1,046	1,567	1.9	4.4
097	CHR CHS&CHS CR	7	1,851	2,329*	2.9	6.5
111	CH CR,SCIENTST	1	NR	NR	-	-
121	CH GOD (ABR)	1	42	53*	.1	.1
123	CH GOD (ANDER)	1	0	163	.2	.5
127	CH GOD (CLEVE)	3	383	482*	.6	1.3
145	CH GOD PROPHCY	1	33	42*	.1	.1
146	CH GOD MTN ASM	1	87	109*	.1	.3
151	L-D SAINTS	1	NA	426	.5	1.2
157	CH OF BRETHREN	2	264	332*	.4	.9
165	CH OF NAZARENE	4	824	893	1.1	2.5
167	CHS OF CHRIST	2	354	460	.6	1.3
193	EPISCOPAL	1	295	376	.5	1.0
207	E.L.C.A.	2	484	630	.8	1.8
221	FREE METHODIST	1	136	178	.2	.5
226	FRIENDS-USA	13	1,550	1,951*	2.4	5.4
226e	FUM	12	1,531	1,927*	2.4	5.4
226g	INDEP EVAN	1	19	24*	-	.1
259	IFCA	1	NR	NR	-	-
263	INT FOURSQ GOS	2	644	810*	1.0	2.3
283	LUTH—MO SYNOD	3	1,141	1,477	1.8	4.1
285	MENNONITE CH	2	114	164	.2	.5
323	OLD ORD AMISH	2	NA	300	.4	.8
339	PENT CH OF GOD	1	34	76	.1	.2
355	PRESB CH (USA)	2	1,298	1,634*	2.0	4.5
403	SALVATION ARMY	1	223	251	.3	.7
413	S.D.A.	2	140	176*	.2	.5
419	SO BAPT CONV	4	1,290	1,623*	2.0	4.5
435	UNITARIAN-UNIV	1	29	33	-	.1
438	UN BRETH IN CR	1	372	372	.5	1.0
443	UN C OF CHRIST	1	392	493*	.6	1.4
449	UN METHODIST	17	4,094	5,152*	6.4	14.3
467	WESLEYAN	7	389	877	1.1	2.4
469	WELS	1	69	103	.1	.3
496	JEWISH EST	1	NA	0	-	-
497	BLACK BAPT EST	NA	1,163	1,464*	1.8	4.1
499	INDEP.NON-CHAR	1	NA	400	.5	1.1
HUNTINGTON		**74**	**9,962**	**19,621***	**55.4**	**100.0**
019	AMER BAPT USA	3	333	427*	1.2	2.2

County and Denomination		Number of churches	Communicant, confirmed, full members	Total adherents		
				Number	Percent of total population	Percent of total adherents
053	ASSEMB OF GOD	1	123	320	.9	1.6
071	BRETHREN (ASH)	2	149	191*	.5	1.0
081	CATHOLIC	3	NA	5,104	14.4	26.0
081d	LATIN	3	NA	5,104	14.4	26.0
089	CHR & MISS AL	2	51	94	.3	.5
093	CHR CH (DISC)	4	759	1,120	3.2	5.7
097	CHR CHS&CHS CR	2	0	0*	-	-
111	CH CR,SCIENTST	1	NR	NR	-	-
123	CH GOD (ANDER)	1	0	303	.9	1.5
127	CH GOD (CLEVE)	1	17	22*	.1	.1
145	CH GOD PROPHCY	1	33	42*	.1	.2
151	L-D SAINTS	1	NA	400	1.1	2.0
157	CH OF BRETHREN	6	579	742*	2.1	3.8
165	CH OF NAZARENE	4	672	1,438	4.1	7.3
167	CHS OF CHRIST	3	132	210	.6	1.1
193	EPISCOPAL	1	83	114	.3	.6
223	FREE WILL BAPT	3	127	163*	.5	.8
283	LUTH—MO SYNOD	1	772	1,152	3.3	5.9
355	PRESB CH (USA)	1	274	351*	1.0	1.8
403	SALVATION ARMY	1	133	141	.4	.7
419	SO BAPT CONV	1	125	160*	.5	.8
438	UN BRETH IN CR	4	927	927	2.6	4.7
443	UN C OF CHRIST	5	1,298	1,663*	4.7	8.5
449	UN METHODIST	17	3,140	4,022*	11.4	20.5
467	WESLEYAN	5	235	515	1.5	2.6
JACKSON		**78**	**15,972**	**22,081***	**58.5**	**100.0**
019	AMER BAPT USA	7	2,054	2,591*	6.9	11.7
053	ASSEMB OF GOD	1	129	163	.4	.7
081	CATHOLIC	2	NA	1,044	2.8	4.7
081d	LATIN	2	NA	1,044	2.8	4.7
089	CHR & MISS AL	1	26	46	.1	.2
093	CHR CH (DISC)	1	685	798	2.1	3.6
097	CHR CHS&CHS CR	15	2,451	3,091*	8.2	14.0
123	CH GOD (ANDER)	1	62	70	.2	.3
127	CH GOD (CLEVE)	2	190	240*	.6	1.1
157	CH OF BRETHREN	1	25	32*	.1	.1
165	CH OF NAZARENE	6	1,390	2,565	6.8	11.6
167	CHS OF CHRIST	2	119	143	.4	.6
193	EPISCOPAL	1	32	41	.1	.2
207	E.L.C.A.	1	355	468	1.2	2.1
221	FREE METHODIST	1	33	46	.1	.2
263	INT FOURSQ GOS	1	17	21*	.1	.1
283	LUTH—MO SYNOD	9	5,165	6,586	17.5	29.8
325	OLD REG BAPT	1	31	39*	.1	.2
355	PRESB CH (USA)	3	447	564*	1.5	2.6
413	S.D.A.	1	39	49*	.1	.2
419	SO BAPT CONV	2	605	763*	2.0	3.5
443	UN C OF CHRIST	2	156	197*	.5	.9
449	UN METHODIST	15	1,936	2,442*	6.5	11.1
467	WESLEYAN	2	25	82	.2	.4
JASPER		**43**	**6,317**	**12,472***	**50.0**	**100.0**
019	AMER BAPT USA	2	338	434*	1.7	3.5
040	AP CHR CH-AMER	1	92	162	.6	1.3
053	ASSEMB OF GOD	2	204	319	1.3	2.6
081	CATHOLIC	4	NA	3,286	13.2	26.3
081d	LATIN	4	NA	3,286	13.2	26.3
093	CHR CH (DISC)	2	539	797	3.2	6.4
097	CHR CHS&CHS CR	3	440	566*	2.3	4.5
105	CHRISTIAN REF	2	722	1,160	4.6	9.3
123	CH GOD (ANDER)	1	12	17	.1	.1
165	CH OF NAZARENE	2	139	281	1.1	2.3
167	CHS OF CHRIST	2	75	105	.4	.8
193	EPISCOPAL	1	18	30	.1	.2
203	EVAN FREE CH	2	89	128	.5	1.0
283	LUTH—MO SYNOD	4	637	850	3.4	6.8
285	MENNONITE CH	1	70	114	.5	.9
339	PENT CH OF GOD	2	54	239	1.0	1.9
355	PRESB CH (USA)	2	270	347*	1.4	2.8
361	PRIM BAPT ASCS	1	26	33*	.1	.3
371	REF CH IN AM	2	1,018	1,581	6.3	12.7
419	SO BAPT CONV	1	111	143*	.6	1.1
449	UN METHODIST	6	1,463	1,880*	7.5	15.1
JAY		**56**	**4,970**	**8,857***	**41.2**	**100.0**
019	AMER BAPT USA	1	65	82*	.4	.9
053	ASSEMB OF GOD	1	28	82	.4	.9
081	CATHOLIC	3	NA	1,667	7.7	18.8
081d	LATIN	3	NA	1,667	7.7	18.8
089	CHR & MISS AL	1	0	0	-	-
097	CHR CHS&CHS CR	6	824	1,034*	4.8	11.7
123	CH GOD (ANDER)	1	7	7	-	.1
145	CH GOD PROPHCY	1	33	41*	.2	.5
157	CH OF BRETHREN	2	57	72*	.3	.8
165	CH OF NAZARENE	6	552	1,242	5.8	14.0

County and Denomination		Number of churches	Communicant, confirmed, full members	Total adherents		
				Number	Percent of total population	Percent of total adherents
167	CHS OF CHRIST	1	58	61	.3	.7
207	E.L.C.A.	3	504	743	3.5	8.4
215	EVAN METH CH	1	47	59*	.3	.7
226	FRIENDS-USA	3	116	146*	.7	1.6
226e	FUM	3	116	146*	.7	1.6
296	MIDW CONGR FEL	3	91	114*	.5	1.3
355	PRESB CH (USA)	1	285	358*	1.7	4.0
413	S.D.A.	1	13	16*	.1	.2
419	SO BAPT CONV	1	445	559*	2.6	6.3
443	UN C OF CHRIST	2	146	183*	.9	2.1
449	UN METHODIST	17	1,638	2,056*	9.6	23.2
467	WESLEYAN	1	61	335	1.6	3.8
JEFFERSON		**68**	**9,424**	**14,838***	**49.8**	**100.0**
019	AMER BAPT USA	17	4,141	5,132*	17.2	34.6
053	ASSEMB OF GOD	1	349	700	2.3	4.7
081	CATHOLIC	4	NA	2,414	8.1	16.3
081d	LATIN	4	NA	2,414	8.1	16.3
089	CHR & MISS AL	1	58	108	.4	.7
093	CHR CH (DISC)	1	150	204	.7	1.4
097	CHR CHS&CHS CR	7	1,065	1,320*	4.4	8.9
111	CH CR,SCIENTST	1	NR	NR	-	-
123	CH GOD (ANDER)	1	29	31	.1	.2
145	CH GOD PROPHCY	1	33	41*	.1	.3
146	CH GOD MTN ASM	1	20	25*	.1	.2
151	L-D SAINTS	1	NA	233	.8	1.6
165	CH OF NAZARENE	1	58	140	.5	.9
167	CHS OF CHRIST	1	82	107	.4	.7
193	EPISCOPAL	1	127	208	.7	1.4
207	E.L.C.A.	1	136	175	.6	1.2
283	LUTH—MO SYNOD	1	105	156	.5	1.1
285	MENNONITE CH	1	15	21	.1	.1
325	OLD REG BAPT	2	63	78*	.3	.5
355	PRESB CH (USA)	4	514	637*	2.1	4.3
403	SALVATION ARMY	1	81	85	.3	.6
413	S.D.A.	1	44	55*	.2	.4
419	SO BAPT CONV	1	501	621*	2.1	4.2
443	UN C OF CHRIST	1	105	130*	.4	.9
449	UN METHODIST	14	1,648	2,042*	6.9	13.8
467	WESLEYAN	2	100	175	.6	1.2
JENNINGS		**54**	**6,184**	**10,517***	**44.4**	**100.0**
019	AMER BAPT USA	15	3,289	4,137*	17.5	39.3
053	ASSEMB OF GOD	1	34	73	.3	.7
081	CATHOLIC	4	NA	1,844	7.8	17.5
081d	LATIN	4	NA	1,844	7.8	17.5
097	CHR CHS&CHS CR	3	625	786*	3.3	7.5
123	CH GOD (ANDER)	4	124	360	1.5	3.4
127	CH GOD (CLEVE)	1	83	104*	.4	1.0
151	L-D SAINTS	1	NA	180	.8	1.7
165	CH OF NAZARENE	1	210	643	2.7	6.1
167	CHS OF CHRIST	2	80	104	.4	1.0
283	LUTH—MO SYNOD	1	92	134	.6	1.3
285	MENNONITE CH	1	48	74	.3	.7
325	OLD REG BAPT	1	11	14*	.1	.1
355	PRESB CH (USA)	4	205	258*	1.1	2.5
413	S.D.A.	1	46	58*	.2	.6
419	SO BAPT CONV	2	326	410*	1.7	3.9
449	UN METHODIST	11	979	1,231*	5.2	11.7
467	WESLEYAN	1	32	107	.5	1.0
JOHNSON		**83**	**18,693**	**35,622***	**40.4**	**100.0**
019	AMER BAPT USA	5	1,758	2,220*	2.5	6.2
053	ASSEMB OF GOD	5	210	402	.5	1.1
057	BAPT GEN CONF	1	39	49*	.1	.1
081	CATHOLIC	3	NA	6,295	7.1	17.7
081d	LATIN	3	NA	6,295	7.1	17.7
093	CHR CH (DISC)	9	1,544	2,674	3.0	7.5
097	CHR CHS&CHS CR	9	5,234	6,609*	7.5	18.6
123	CH GOD (ANDER)	1	45	80	.1	.2
127	CH GOD (CLEVE)	2	304	384*	.4	1.1
145	CH GOD PROPHCY	1	33	42*	-	.1
151	L-D SAINTS	1	NA	527	.6	1.5
157	CH OF BRETHREN	1	81	102*	.1	.3
165	CH OF NAZARENE	3	292	504	.6	1.4
167	CHS OF CHRIST	3	467	599	.7	1.7
175	CONGR CHR CHS	1	402	508*	.6	1.4
193	EPISCOPAL	1	157	209	.2	.6
207	E.L.C.A.	1	138	170	.2	.5
215	EVAN METH CH	1	67	85*	.1	.2
221	FREE METHODIST	1	13	42	-	.1
283	LUTH—MO SYNOD	2	685	979	1.1	2.7
339	PENT CH OF GOD	1	34	77	.1	.2
355	PRESB CH (USA)	6	1,431	1,807*	2.1	5.1
361	PRIM BAPT ASCS	1	23	29*	-	.1
413	S.D.A.	1	62	78*	.1	.2

County and Denomination		Number of churches	Communicant, confirmed, full members	Total adherents		
				Number	Percent of total population	Percent of total adherents
419	SO BAPT CONV	5	1,766	2,230*	2.5	6.3
443	UN C OF CHRIST	1	95	120*	.1	.3
449	UN METHODIST	10	3,499	4,418*	5.0	12.4
467	WESLEYAN	4	91	296	.3	.8
496	JEWISH EST	0	NA	705	.8	2.0
497	BLACK BAPT EST	NA	223	282*	.3	.8
499	INDEP.NON-CHAR	3	NA	3,100	3.5	8.7
KNOX		**81**	**11,140**	**20,072***	**50.3**	**100.0**
019	AMER BAPT USA	5	1,722	2,105*	5.3	10.5
053	ASSEMB OF GOD	2	72	133	.3	.7
081	CATHOLIC	6	NA	5,380	13.5	26.8
081d	*LATIN*	6	*NA*	*5,380*	*13.5*	*26.8*
093	CHR CH (DISC)	4	739	1,199	3.0	6.0
097	CHR CHS&CHS CR	4	734	897*	2.2	4.5
111	CH CR,SCIENTST	1	NR	NR	-	-
123	CH GOD (ANDER)	2	372	499	1.3	2.5
127	CH GOD (CLEVE)	1	15	18*	-	.1
145	CH GOD PROPHCY	1	33	40*	.1	.2
165	CH OF NAZARENE	3	347	868	2.2	4.3
167	CHS OF CHRIST	4	212	308	.8	1.5
179	CONSRV BAPT	1	NR	NR	-	-
185	CUMBER PRESB	1	91	95	.2	.5
193	EPISCOPAL	1	98	127	.3	.6
207	E.L.C.A.	1	146	235	.6	1.2
221	FREE METHODIST	1	177	212	.5	1.1
263	INT FOURSQ GOS	1	256	313*	.8	1.6
283	LUTH—MO SYNOD	2	669	919	2.3	4.6
355	PRESB CH (USA)	8	542	663*	1.7	3.3
356	PRESB CH AMER	1	34	45	.1	.2
403	SALVATION ARMY	1	59	88	.2	.4
413	S.D.A.	1	45	55*	.1	.3
419	SO BAPT CONV	1	703	859*	2.2	4.3
443	UN C OF CHRIST	3	1,271	1,554*	3.9	7.7
449	UN METHODIST	21	2,736	3,345*	8.4	16.7
467	WESLEYAN	4	67	·115	.3	.6
KOSCIUSKO		**88**	**11,161**	**19,901***	**30.5**	**100.0**
019	AMER BAPT USA	1	133	173*	.3	.9
040	AP CHR CH-AMER	1	109	194	.3	1.0
053	ASSEMB OF GOD	1	78	200	.3	1.0
061	BEACHY AMISH	1	33	43*	.1	.2
071	BRETHREN (ASH)	3	436	567*	.9	2.8
081	CATHOLIC	4	NA	3,010	4.6	15.1
081d	*LATIN*	4	*NA*	*3,010*	*4.6*	*15.1*
097	CHR CHS&CHS CR	1	500	650*	1.0	3.3
111	CH CR,SCIENTST	1	NR	NR	-	-
123	CH GOD (ANDER)	2	606	665*	1.0	3.3
127	CH GOD (CLEVE)	1	12	16*	-	.1
151	L-D SAINTS	1	NA	268	.4	1.3
157	CH OF BRETHREN	8	846	1,099*	1.7	5.5
165	CH OF NAZARENE	2	234	414	.6	2.1
167	CHS OF CHRIST	2	75	112	.2	.6
171	CH GOD-GEN CON	3	270	351*	.5	1.8
193	EPISCOPAL	2	310	464	.7	2.3
207	E.L.C.A.	2	131	182	.3	.9
221	FREE METHODIST	2	367	367	.6	1.8
226	FRIENDS-USA	1	48	62*	.1	.3
226e	*FUM*	1	*48*	*62***	*.1*	*.3*
259	IFCA	1	NR	NR	-	-
263	INT FOURSQ GOS	1	0	0*	-	-
283	LUTH—MO SYNOD	1	295	371	.6	1.9
285	MENNONITE CH	5	375	550	.8	2.8
291	MISSIONARY CH	1	21	54	.1	.3
323	OLD ORD AMISH	4	NA	600	.9	3.0
325	OLD REG BAPT	1	37	48*	.1	.2
339	PENT CH OF GOD	2	48	180	.3	.9
353	CHR BRETHREN	1	77	100	.2	.5
355	PRESB CH (USA)	3	891	1,158*	1.8	5.8
356	PRESB CH AMER	1	40	41	.1	.2
361	PRIM BAPT ASCS	1	11	14*	-	.1
403	SALVATION ARMY	1	137	142	.2	.7
413	S.D.A.	1	32	42*	.1	.2
449	UN METHODIST	23	4,752	6,176*	9.5	31.0
467	WESLEYAN	2	257	1,588	2.4	8.0
LAGRANGE		**101**	**4,869**	**15,605***	**52.9**	**100.0**
019	AMER BAPT USA	1	106	146*	.5	.9
053	ASSEMB OF GOD	1	26	35	.1	.2
061	BEACHY AMISH	1	52	72*	.2	.5
081	CATHOLIC	2	NA	566	1.9	3.6
081d	*LATIN*	2	*NA*	*566*	*1.9*	*3.6*
123	CH GOD (ANDER)	2	250	315	1.1	2.0
146	CH GOD MTN ASM	1	4	6*	-	-
157	CH OF BRETHREN	1	52	72*	.2	.5
165	CH OF NAZARENE	2	152	441	1.5	2.8

County and Denomination		Number of churches	Communicant, confirmed, full members	Total adherents		
				Number	Percent of total population	Percent of total adherents
167	CHS OF CHRIST	1	74	100	.3	.6
193	EPISCOPAL	1	57	64	.2	.4
207	E.L.C.A.	1	449	583	2.0	3.7
283	LUTH—MO SYNOD	2	267	329	1.1	2.1
285	MENNONITE CH	9	1,426	1,767	6.0	11.3
287	MENN GEN CONF	1	124	156	.5	1.0
291	MISSIONARY CH	2	102	175	.6	1.1
323	OLD ORD AMISH	56	NA	8,400	28.5	53.8
355	PRESB CH (USA)	2	197	271*	.9	1.7
419	SO BAPT CONV	1	45	62*	.2	.4
436	UNITED BAPT	1	13	18*	.1	.1
449	UN METHODIST	13	1,473	2,027*	6.9	13.0
LAKE		**349**	**94,785**	**346,097***	**72.8**	**100.0**
005	AME ZION	5	8,150	10,187	2.1	2.9
019	AMER BAPT USA	8	1,996	2,548*	.5	.7
022	EASTERN ORTH	2	286	286	.1	.1
053	ASSEMB OF GOD	20	2,311	3,712	.8	1.1
057	BAPT GEN CONF	1	187	239*	.1	.1
059	BAPT MISS ASSN	1	41	52*	-	-
081	CATHOLIC	64	NA	138,830	29.2	40.1
081b	*BYZAN RUTH*	4	*NA*	*1,686*	*.4*	*.5*
081d	*LATIN*	57	*NA*	*136,236*	*28.6*	*39.4*
081f	*MELKITE-GK*	1	*NA*	*522*	*.1*	*.2*
081g	*ROMANIAN*	1	*NA*	*322*	*.1*	*.1*
081h	*UKRAINIAN*	1	*NA*	*64*	-	-
089	CHR & MISS AL	1	20	35	-	-
093	CHR CH (DISC)	6	530	799	.2	.2
097	CHR CHS&CHS CR	13	3,066	3,914*	.8	1.1
105	CHRISTIAN REF	6	1,370	2,636	.6	.8
111	CH CR,SCIENTST	4	NR	NR	-	-
123	CH GOD (ANDER)	8	956	1,046	.2	.3
127	CH GOD (CLEVE)	6	824	1,052*	.2	.3
145	CH GOD PROPHCY	3	111	142*	-	-
151	L-D SAINTS	1	NA	595	.1	.2
165	CH OF NAZARENE	16	1,977	2,609	.5	.8
167	CHS OF CHRIST	11	948	1,221	.3	.4
175	CONGR CHR CHS	2	125	160*	-	-
179	CONSRV BAPT	1	NR	NR	-	-
191	ENTRPR BPT ASC	1	56	71*	-	-
193	EPISCOPAL	6	833	1,144	.2	.3
203	EVAN FREE CH	2	37	110	-	-
207	E.L.C.A.	15	4,017	5,462	1.1	1.6
221	FREE METHODIST	2	161	161	-	-
246	GREEK ORTHODOX	3	NR	NR	-	-
249	AP CATH ASSYR	1	53	329	.1	.1
259	IFCA	5	NR	NR	-	-
283	LUTH—MO SYNOD	23	8,146	10,674	2.2	3.1
331	ORTH CH IN AM	2	NR	NR	-	-
339	PENT CH OF GOD	3	86	189	-	.1
349	PENT HOLINESS	1	25	32*	-	-
355	PRESB CH (USA)	13	3,814	4,869*	1.0	1.4
356	PRESB CH AMER	2	788	1,019	.2	.3
371	REF CH IN AM	3	571	953	.2	.3
397	ROMANIAN ORTH	1	NR	NR	-	-
403	SALVATION ARMY	3	307	355	.1	.1
413	S.D.A.	6	1,361	1,737*	.4	.5
419	SO BAPT CONV	31	9,950	12,702*	2.7	3.7
435	UNITARIAN-UNIV	2	148	170	-	-
443	UN C OF CHRIST	8	2,142	2,735*	.6	.8
449	UN METHODIST	24	8,376	10,693*	2.2	3.1
467	WESLEYAN	2	54	92	-	-
469	WELS	1	111	168	-	-
496	JEWISH EST	6	NA	1,809	.4	.5
497	BLACK BAPT EST	NA	30,851	39,385*	8.3	11.4
498	INDEP.CHARIS.	2	NA	3,800	.8	1.1
499	INDEP.NON-CHAR	2	NA	77,375	16.3	22.4
LA PORTE		**105**	**20,988**	**47,187***	**44.1**	**100.0**
019	AMER BAPT USA	2	720	896*	.8	1.9
040	AP CHR CH-AMER	1	115	205	.2	.4
053	ASSEMB OF GOD	4	411	727	.7	1.5
057	BAPT GEN CONF	1	155	193*	.2	.4
059	BAPT MISS ASSN	1	123	153*	.1	.3
081	CATHOLIC	13	NA	18,958	17.7	40.2
081d	*LATIN*	13	*NA*	*18,958*	*17.7*	*40.2*
093	CHR CH (DISC)	2	310	815	.8	1.7
097	CHR CHS&CHS CR	6	1,335	1,662*	1.6	3.5
111	CH CR,SCIENTST	2	NR	NR	-	-
123	CH GOD (ANDER)	1	110	133	.1	.3
127	CH GOD (CLEVE)	2	144	179*	.2	.4
145	CH GOD PROPHCY	1	33	41*	-	.1
151	L-D SAINTS	2	NA	361	.3	.8
157	CH OF BRETHREN	2	121	151*	.1	.3
165	CH OF NAZARENE	2	127	277	.3	.6
167	CHS OF CHRIST	3	165	216	.2	.5
175	CONGR CHR CHS	1	53	66*	.1	.1

County and Denomination	Number of churches	Communicant, confirmed, full members	Total adherents Number	Percent of total population	Percent of total adherents
193 EPISCOPAL	3	650	731	.7	1.5
207 E.L.C.A.	5	2,513	3,401	3.2	7.2
221 FREE METHODIST	2	204	204	.2	.4
223 FREE WILL BAPT	2	102	127*	.1	.3
259 IFCA	2	NR	NR	-	-
283 LUTH—MO SYNOD	9	3,060	4,138	3.9	8.8
285 MENNONITE CH	2	133	221	.2	.5
291 MISSIONARY CH	1	72	133	.1	.3
339 PENT CH OF GOD	2	68	154	.1	.3
355 PRESB CH (USA)	3	1,512	1,882*	1.8	4.0
403 SALVATION ARMY	2	243	259	.2	.5
413 S.D.A.	2	183	228*	.2	.5
419 SO BAPT CONV	3	467	581*	.5	1.2
431 UKRANIAN AMER	1	NR	NR	-	-
436 UNITED BAPT	1	61	76*	.1	.2
443 UN C OF CHRIST	3	2,117	2,635*	2.5	5.6
449 UN METHODIST	13	3,511	4,370*	4.1	9.3
467 WESLEYAN	2	118	180	.2	.4
496 JEWISH EST	1	NA	280	.3	.6
497 BLACK BAPT EST	NA	2,052	2,554*	2.4	5.4
LAWRENCE	**86**	**13,445**	**19,881***	**46.4**	**100.0**
019 AMER BAPT USA	16	4,459	5,526*	12.9	27.8
053 ASSEMB OF GOD	1	154	187	.4	.9
081 CATHOLIC	2	NA	1,907	4.5	9.6
081d LATIN	2	NA	1,907	4.5	9.6
093 CHR CH (DISC)	3	607	1,480	3.5	7.4
097 CHR CHS&CHS CR	10	2,687	3,330*	7.8	16.7
123 CH GOD (ANDER)	4	504	593	1.4	3.0
127 CH GOD (CLEVE)	2	246	305*	.7	1.5
145 CH GOD PROPHCY	1	33	41*	.1	.2
151 L-D SAINTS	1	NA	280	.7	1.4
165 CH OF NAZARENE	4	606	1,060	2.5	5.3
167 CHS OF CHRIST	16	1,140	1,453	3.4	7.3
193 EPISCOPAL	1	143	171	.4	.9
221 FREE METHODIST	1	444	444	1.0	2.2
283 LUTH—MO SYNOD	2	299	427	1.0	2.1
339 PENT CH OF GOD	1	57	121	.3	.6
355 PRESB CH (USA)	2	303	375*	.9	1.9
403 SALVATION ARMY	2	144	165	.4	.8
413 S.D.A.	1	111	138*	.3	.7
419 SO BAPT CONV	1	23	29*	.1	.1
449 UN METHODIST	13	1,370	1,698*	4.0	8.5
467 WESLEYAN	2	115	151	.4	.8
MADISON	**150**	**32,192**	**50,726***	**38.8**	**100.0**
005 AME ZION	1	292	438	.3	.9
019 AMER BAPT USA	9	3,440	4,243*	3.2	8.4
053 ASSEMB OF GOD	3	601	1,017	.8	2.0
081 CATHOLIC	4	NA	7,153	5.5	14.1
081d LATIN	4	NA	7,153	5.5	14.1
089 CHR & MISS AL	1	76	185	.1	.4
093 CHR CH (DISC)	10	3,241	4,757	3.6	9.4
097 CHR CHS&CHS CR	7	3,245	4,003*	3.1	7.9
111 CH CR,SCIENTST	1	NR	NR	-	-
123 CH GOD (ANDER)	17	4,160	4,967	3.8	9.8
127 CH GOD (CLEVE)	3	349	430*	.3	.8
145 CH GOD PROPHCY	1	33	41*	-	.1
151 L-D SAINTS	2	NA	562	.4	1.1
157 CH OF BRETHREN	2	320	395*	.3	.8
165 CH OF NAZARENE	10	1,803	2,733	2.1	5.4
167 CHS OF CHRIST	7	983	1,280	1.0	2.5
193 EPISCOPAL	2	362	661	.5	1.3
207 E.L.C.A.	4	792	1,067	.8	2.1
221 FREE METHODIST	2	187	281	.2	.6
223 FREE WILL BAPT	2	137	169*	.1	.3
226 FRIENDS-USA	5	279	344*	.3	.7
226c FGC	1	19	23*		
226e FUM	3	225	278*	.2	.5
226g INDEP EVAN	1	35	43*	-	.1
263 INT FOURSQ GOS	2	68	84*	.1	.2
283 LUTH—MO SYNOD	2	519	629	.5	1.2
296 MIDW CONGR FEL	1	48	59*	-	.1
355 PRESB CH (USA)	2	939	1,158*	.9	2.3
356 PRESB CH AMER	1	0	0	-	-
403 SALVATION ARMY	1	114	118	.1	.2
413 S.D.A.	2	253	312*	.2	.6
419 SO BAPT CONV	3	415	512*	.4	1.0
438 UN BRETH IN CR	1	35	38	-	.1
443 UN C OF CHRIST	1	376	464*	.4	.9
449 UN METHODIST	27	5,756	7,100*	5.4	14.0
467 WESLEYAN	14	759	2,307	1.8	4.5
497 BLACK BAPT EST	NA	2,610	3,219*	2.5	6.3
MARION	**523**	**193,869**	**361,192***	**45.3**	**100.0**
005 AME ZION	6	7,945	10,328	1.3	2.9

County and Denomination	Number of churches	Communicant, confirmed, full members	Total adherents Number	Percent of total population	Percent of total adherents
019 AMER BAPT USA	29	9,132	11,483*	1.4	3.2
040 AP CHR CH-AMER	1	42	72	-	-
053 ASSEMB OF GOD	13	4,384	10,229	1.3	2.8
081 CATHOLIC	43	NA	84,033	10.5	23.3
081b BYZAN RUTH	1	NA	40	-	-
081d LATIN	42	NA	83,993	10.5	23.3
089 CHR & MISS AL	3	294	472	.1	.1
093 CHR CH (DISC)	30	14,071	20,596	2.6	5.7
097 CHR CHS&CHS CR	35	18,160	22,836*	2.9	6.3
105 CHRISTIAN REF	1	67	124	-	-
111 CH CR,SCIENTST	6	NR	NR	-	-
123 CH GOD (ANDER)	14	1,700	2,158	.3	.6
127 CH GOD (CLEVE)	5	1,004	1,263*	.2	.3
145 CH GOD PROPHCY	2	67	84*	-	-
151 L-D SAINTS	6	NA	2,116	.3	.6
157 CH OF BRETHREN	1	150	189*	-	.1
165 CH OF NAZARENE	24	3,687	8,570	1.1	2.4
167 CHS OF CHRIST	36	6,449	8,687	1.1	2.4
179 CONSRV BAPT	2	NR	NR	-	-
185 CUMBER PRESB	1	138	138	-	-
193 EPISCOPAL	10	3,211	4,630	.6	1.3
195 ESTONIAN ELC	1	26	33*	-	-
203 EVAN FREE CH	1	673	1,000	.1	.3
207 E.L.C.A.	19	5,825	7,553	.9	2.1
220 FREE LUTHERAN	1	158	206	-	.1
221 FREE METHODIST	6	1,002	1,230	.2	.3
223 FREE WILL BAPT	1	225	283*	-	.1
226 FRIENDS-USA	8	1,257	1,581*	.2	.4
226c FGC	1	46	58*	-	-
226e FUM	7	1,211	1,523*	.2	.4
246 GREEK ORTHODOX	1	NR	NR	-	-
263 INT FOURSQ GOS	3	297	373*	-	.1
274 LAT EVAN LUTH	1	373	409	.1	.1
283 LUTH—MO SYNOD	15	5,474	7,474	.9	2.1
284 LUTH CH-AM ASC	1	263	351	-	.1
285 MENNONITE CH	1	149	317	-	.1
291 MISSIONARY CH	1	72	32	-	-
293 MORAV CH-NORTH	3	207	271	-	.1
313 N AM BAPT CONF	1	66	83*	-	-
329 OPEN BIBLE STD	1	NR	NR	-	-
339 PENT CH OF GOD	3	103	192	-	.1
353 CHR BRETHREN	1	45	70	-	-
355 PRESB CH (USA)	23	14,306	17,990*	2.3	5.0
356 PRESB CH AMER	2	122	172	-	-
371 REF CH IN AM	1	154	220	-	.1
397 ROMANIAN ORTH	1	NR	NR	-	-
403 SALVATION ARMY	3	305	315	-	.1
413 S.D.A.	9	2,360	2,968*	.4	.8
419 SO BAPT CONV	25	7,438	9,353*	1.2	2.6
435 UNITARIAN-UNIV	4	919	1,151	.1	.3
443 UN C OF CHRIST	15	5,946	7,477*	.9	2.1
449 UN METHODIST	64	29,445	37,027*	4.6	10.3
467 WESLEYAN	14	848	1,951	.2	.5
469 WELS	2	456	638	.1	.2
496 JEWISH EST	5	NA	6,379	.8	1.8
497 BLACK BAPT EST	NA	44,854	56,403*	7.1	15.6
498 INDEP.CHARIS.	6	NA	2,535	.3	.7
499 INDEP.NON-CHAR	12	NA	7,147	.9	2.0
MARSHALL	**71**	**7,618**	**15,642***	**37.1**	**100.0**
053 ASSEMB OF GOD	3	106	160	.4	1.0
081 CATHOLIC	3	NA	2,970	7.0	19.0
081d LATIN	3	NA	2,970	7.0	19.0
097 CHR CHS&CHS CR	1	75	97*	.2	.6
111 CH CR,SCIENTST	1	NR	NR	-	-
121 CH GOD (ABR)	1	29	37*	.1	.2
123 CH GOD (ANDER)	2	118	168	.4	1.1
151 L-D SAINTS	1	NA	161	.4	1.0
157 CH OF BRETHREN	6	835	1,078*	2.6	6.9
165 CH OF NAZARENE	1	82	181	.4	1.2
167 CHS OF CHRIST	2	70	95	.2	.6
193 EPISCOPAL	1	197	265	.6	1.7
207 E.L.C.A.	1	255	328	.8	2.1
283 LUTH—MO SYNOD	3	763	1,062	2.5	6.8
285 MENNONITE CH	2	170	259	.6	1.7
291 MISSIONARY CH	2	132	229	.5	1.5
323 OLD ORD AMISH	16	NA	2,400	5.7	15.3
329 OPEN BIBLE STD	1	NR	NR	-	-
355 PRESB CH (USA)	1	200	258*	.6	1.6
361 PRIM BAPT ASCS	1	47	61*	.1	.4
413 S.D.A.	1	25	32*	.1	.2
419 SO BAPT CONV	1	57	74*	.2	.5
443 UN C OF CHRIST	4	1,210	1,562*	3.7	10.0
449 UN METHODIST	14	2,980	3,846*	9.1	24.6
467 WESLEYAN	2	267	319	.8	2.0

County and Denomination	Number of churches	Communicant, confirmed, full members	Total adherents Number	Percent of total population	Percent of total adherents
MARTIN	**33**	**2,631**	**6,176***	**59.6**	**100.0**
053 ASSEMB OF GOD	1	53	101	1.0	1.6
081 CATHOLIC	5	NA	2,782	26.8	45.0
081d *LATIN*	*5*	*NA*	*2,782*	*26.8*	*45.0*
097 CHR CHS&CHS CR	3	803	1,017*	9.8	16.5
165 CH OF NAZARENE	2	54	109	1.1	1.8
167 CHS OF CHRIST	5	191	255	2.5	4.1
207 E.L.C.A.	1	302	382	3.7	6.2
285 MENNONITE CH	2	61	61	.6	1.0
419 SO BAPT CONV	2	145	184*	1.8	3.0
449 UN METHODIST	10	1,004	1,271*	12.3	20.6
467 WESLEYAN	2	18	14	.1	.2
MIAMI	**60**	**9,850**	**14,819***	**40.2**	**100.0**
019 AMER BAPT USA	7	2,277	2,930*	7.9	19.8
053 ASSEMB OF GOD	1	233	275	.7	1.9
071 BRETHREN (ASH)	5	319	410*	1.1	2.8
081 CATHOLIC	1	NA	1,879	5.1	12.7
081d *LATIN*	*1*	*NA*	*1,879*	*5.1*	*12.7*
089 CHR & MISS AL	1	49	184	.5	1.2
093 CHR CH (DISC)	1	769	1,032	2.8	7.0
097 CHR CHS&CHS CR	2	297	382*	1.0	2.6
111 CH CR,SCIENTST	1	NR	NR	-	-
123 CH GOD (ANDER)	1	61	81	.2	.5
127 CH GOD (CLEVE)	1	46	59*	.2	.4
146 CH GOD MTN ASM	1	10	13*	-	.1
157 CH OF BRETHREN	3	658	847*	2.3	5.7
165 CH OF NAZARENE	1	202	242	.7	1.6
167 CHS OF CHRIST	1	47	61	.2	.4
221 FREE METHODIST	1	47	94	.3	.6
223 FREE WILL BAPT	1	16	21*	.1	.1
226 FRIENDS-USA	1	286	368*	1.0	2.5
226e *FUM*	*1*	*286*	*368*￼*	*1.0*	*2.5*
263 INT FOURSQ GOS	1	179	230*	.6	1.6
283 LUTH—MO SYNOD	1	840	1,164	3.2	7.9
285 MENNONITE CH	2	266	408	1.1	2.8
291 MISSIONARY CH	1	55	39	.1	.3
355 PRESB CH (USA)	1	385	495*	1.3	3.3
403 SALVATION ARMY	1	112	112	.3	.8
419 SO BAPT CONV	1	137	176*	.5	1.2
449 UN METHODIST	21	2,288	2,944*	8.0	19.9
467 WESLEYAN	1	32	65	.2	.4
497 BLACK BAPT EST	NA	239	308*	.8	2.1
MONROE	**103**	**19,338**	**37,345***	**34.3**	**100.0**
019 AMER BAPT USA	8	2,771	3,249*	3.0	8.7
053 ASSEMB OF GOD	7	756	1,237	1.1	3.3
059 BAPT MISS ASSN	1	100	117*	.1	.3
081 CATHOLIC	3	NA	9,294	8.5	24.9
081d *LATIN*	*3*	*NA*	*9,294*	*8.5*	*24.9*
093 CHR CH (DISC)	3	869	1,507	1.4	4.0
097 CHR CHS&CHS CR	11	2,970	3,482*	3.2	9.3
111 CH CR,SCIENTST	1	NR	NR	-	-
121 CH GOD (ABR)	1	9	11*	-	-
123 CH GOD (ANDER)	2	165	172	.2	.5
145 CH GOD PROPHCY	1	33	39*	-	.1
151 L-D SAINTS	3	NA	963	.9	2.6
165 CH OF NAZARENE	5	798	1,387	1.3	3.7
167 CHS OF CHRIST	21	1,658	2,024	1.9	5.4
193 EPISCOPAL	1	358	616	.6	1.6
203 EVAN FREE CH	1	14	35	-	.1
207 E.L.C.A.	1	347	460	.4	1.2
221 FREE METHODIST	1	337	337	.3	.9
223 FREE WILL BAPT	1	17	20*	-	.1
226 FRIENDS-USA	1	94	110*	.1	.3
226e *FUM*	*1*	*94*	*110*￼*	*.1*	*.3*
283 LUTH—MO SYNOD	2	379	488	.4	1.3
355 PRESB CH (USA)	2	590	692*	.6	1.9
356 PRESB CH AMER	1	45	60	.1	.2
361 PRIM BAPT ASCS	1	12	14*	-	-
403 SALVATION ARMY	1	119	132	.1	.4
413 S.D.A.	1	150	176*	.2	.5
419 SO BAPT CONV	3	557	653*	.6	1.7
435 UNITARIAN-UNIV	1	322	402	.4	1.1
443 UN C OF CHRIST	1	817	958*	.9	2.6
449 UN METHODIST	13	4,259	4,993*	4.6	13.4
467 WESLEYAN	2	42	138	.1	.4
496 JEWISH EST	0	NA	1,000	.9	2.7
497 BLACK BAPT EST	NA	750	879*	.8	2.4
499 INDEP.NON-CHAR	2	NA	1,700	1.6	4.6
MONTGOMERY	**62**	**10,668**	**16,059***	**46.6**	**100.0**
019 AMER BAPT USA	5	1,930	2,403*	7.0	15.0
053 ASSEMB OF GOD	1	105	190	.6	1.2
081 CATHOLIC	1	NA	1,836	5.3	11.4
081d *LATIN*	*1*	*NA*	*1,836*	*5.3*	*11.4*
093 CHR CH (DISC)	4	800	1,462	4.2	9.1
097 CHR CHS&CHS CR	12	2,891	3,599*	10.5	22.4
123 CH GOD (ANDER)	1	38	51	.1	.3
127 CH GOD (CLEVE)	1	49	61*	.2	.4
151 L-D SAINTS	1	NA	228	.7	1.4
165 CH OF NAZARENE	2	269	356	1.0	2.2
167 CHS OF CHRIST	4	219	270*	.8	1.7
176 CCC, NOT NAT'L	1	73	91*	.3	.6
181 CONSRV CONGR	1	157	195*	.6	1.2
193 EPISCOPAL	1	102	166	.5	1.0
207 E.L.C.A.	1	289	404	1.2	2.5
226 FRIENDS-USA	1	22	27*	.1	.2
226e *FUM*	*1*	*22*	*27*￼*	*.1*	*.2*
283 LUTH—MO SYNOD	1	166	224	.7	1.4
355 PRESB CH (USA)	4	516	642*	1.9	4.0
413 S.D.A.	1	16	20*	.1	.1
419 SO BAPT CONV	3	338	421*	1.2	2.6
443 UN C OF CHRIST	1	35	44*	.1	.3
449 UN METHODIST	14	2,622	3,264*	9.5	20.3
467 WESLEYAN	1	31	105	.3	.7
MORGAN	**82**	**12,845**	**21,806***	**39.0**	**100.0**
019 AMER BAPT USA	10	1,999	2,543*	4.5	11.7
053 ASSEMB OF GOD	3	237	419	.7	1.9
081 CATHOLIC	2	NA	2,151	3.8	9.9
081d *LATIN*	*2*	*NA*	*2,151*	*3.8*	*9.9*
093 CHR CH (DISC)	4	1,120	1,943	3.5	8.9
097 CHR CHS&CHS CR	13	2,842	3,616*	6.5	16.6
123 CH GOD (ANDER)	3	299	465*	.8	2.1
127 CH GOD (CLEVE)	1	48	61*	.1	.3
151 L-D SAINTS	1	NA	335	.6	1.5
165 CH OF NAZARENE	6	477	1,217	2.2	5.6
167 CHS OF CHRIST	6	469	605	1.1	2.8
193 EPISCOPAL	1	62	75	.1	.3
215 EVAN METH CH	1	21	27*	-	.1
221 FREE METHODIST	1	76	108	.2	.5
226 FRIENDS-USA	3	464	590*	1.1	2.7
226e *FUM*	*3*	*464*	*590*￼*	*1.1*	*2.7*
283 LUTH—MO SYNOD	1	118	154	.3	.7
291 MISSIONARY CH	2	219	377	.7	1.7
355 PRESB CH (USA)	1	337	429*	.8	2.0
413 S.D.A.	1	19	24*	-	.1
419 SO BAPT CONV	7	2,219	2,823*	5.0	12.9
449 UN METHODIST	9	1,749	2,225*	4.0	10.2
467 WESLEYAN	4	70	322	.6	1.5
496 JEWISH EST	0	NA	447	.8	2.0
499 INDEP.NON-CHAR	2	NA	850	1.5	3.9
NEWTON	**26**	**3,268**	**6,179***	**45.6**	**100.0**
019 AMER BAPT USA	2	429	553*	4.1	8.9
053 ASSEMB OF GOD	1	33	50	.4	.8
057 BAPT GEN CONF	1	0	0*	-	-
081 CATHOLIC	3	NA	1,762	13.0	28.5
081d *LATIN*	*3*	*NA*	*1,762*	*13.0*	*28.5*
093 CHR CH (DISC)	2	246	441	3.3	7.1
097 CHR CHS&CHS CR	1	310	400*	3.0	6.5
105 CHRISTIAN REF	1	131	247	1.8	4.0
283 LUTH—MO SYNOD	1	84	111	.8	1.8
287 MENN GEN CONF	1	43	46	.3	.7
355 PRESB CH (USA)	3	363	468*	3.5	7.6
419 SO BAPT CONV	2	387	499*	3.7	8.1
449 UN METHODIST	8	1,242	1,602*	11.8	25.9
NOBLE	**65**	**7,677**	**14,441***	**38.1**	**100.0**
019 AMER BAPT USA	2	132	171*	.5	1.2
053 ASSEMB OF GOD	4	250	412	1.1	2.9
081 CATHOLIC	6	NA	3,092	8.2	21.4
081d *LATIN*	*6*	*NA*	*3,092*	*8.2*	*21.4*
093 CHR CH (DISC)	1	250	405	1.1	2.8
097 CHR CHS&CHS CR	2	160	208*	.5	1.4
111 CH CR,SCIENTST	1	NR	NR	-	-
121 CH GOD (ABR)	1	52	68*	.2	.5
123 CH GOD (ANDER)	1	90	140	.4	1.0
151 L-D SAINTS	1	NA	199	.5	1.4
157 CH OF BRETHREN	1	86	112*	.3	.8
165 CH OF NAZARENE	3	169	466	1.2	3.2
167 CHS OF CHRIST	2	45	51	.1	.4
207 E.L.C.A.	4	536	669	1.8	4.6
283 LUTH—MO SYNOD	3	1,554	2,174	5.7	15.1
291 MISSIONARY CH	2	42	71	.2	.5
325 OLD REG BAPT	1	40	52*	.1	.4
355 PRESB CH (USA)	4	505	656*	1.7	4.5
413 S.D.A.	1	31	40*	.1	.3
436 UNITED BAPT	1	42	55*	.1	.4
443 UN C OF CHRIST	1	90	117*	.3	.8
449 UN METHODIST	20	3,407	4,423*	11.7	30.6

County and Denomination	Number of churches	Communicant, confirmed, full members	Total adherents Number	Percent of total population	Percent of total adherents
467　WESLEYAN	3	196	860	2.3	6.0
OHIO	**13**	**1,811**	**2,288***	**43.0**	**100.0**
019　AMER BAPT USA	3	467	590*	11.1	25.8
097　CHR CHS&CHS CR	1	500	632*	11.9	27.6
165　CH OF NAZARENE	1	74	97	1.8	4.2
207　E.L.C.A.	2	174	217	4.1	9.5
419　SO BAPT CONV	1	112	142*	2.7	6.2
443　UN C OF CHRIST	1	170	215*	4.0	9.4
449　UN METHODIST	3	299	378*	7.1	16.5
467　WESLEYAN	1	15	17	.3	.7
ORANGE	**58**	**6,448**	**9,105***	**49.5**	**100.0**
019　AMER BAPT USA	5	1,369	1,719*	9.3	18.9
053　ASSEMB OF GOD	1	29	25	.1	.3
081　CATHOLIC	2	NA	550	3.0	6.0
081d　　LATIN	2	NA	550	3.0	6.0
093　CHR CH (DISC)	2	160	225	1.2	2.5
097　CHR CHS&CHS CR	9	1,895	2,380*	12.9	26.1
127　CH GOD (CLEVE)	1	87	109*	.6	1.2
165　CH OF NAZARENE	3	211	413	2.2	4.5
167　CHS OF CHRIST	8	330	439	2.4	4.8
226　FRIENDS-USA	4	279	350*	1.9	3.8
226e　　FUM	4	279	350*	1.9	3.8
285　MENNONITE CH	1	75	146	.8	1.6
287　MENN GEN CONF	1	80	80	.4	.9
323　OLD ORD AMISH	1	NA	150	.8	1.6
355　PRESB CH (USA)	1	89	112*	.6	1.2
413　S.D.A.	1	51	64*	.3	.7
419　SO BAPT CONV	1	374	470*	2.6	5.2
449　UN METHODIST	13	1,259	1,581*	8.6	17.4
467　WESLEYAN	4	160	292	1.6	3.2
OWEN	**47**	**4,758**	**6,947***	**40.2**	**100.0**
019　AMER BAPT USA	9	1,699	2,142*	12.4	30.8
053　ASSEMB OF GOD	2	65	106	.6	1.5
081　CATHOLIC	1	NA	210	1.2	3.0
081d　　LATIN	1	NA	210	1.2	3.0
093　CHR CH (DISC)	1	55	89	.5	1.3
097　CHR CHS&CHS CR	4	825	1,040*	6.0	15.0
127　CH GOD (CLEVE)	1	15	19*	.1	.3
145　CH GOD PROPHCY	1	33	42*	.2	.6
165　CH OF NAZARENE	5	337	491	2.8	7.1
167　CHS OF CHRIST	5	459	593	3.4	8.5
207　E.L.C.A.	1	29	31	.2	.4
355　PRESB CH (USA)	2	162	204*	1.2	2.9
361　PRIM BAPT ASCS	1	24	30*	.2	.4
413　S.D.A.	1	66	83*	.5	1.2
443　UN C OF CHRIST	1	48	61*	.4	.9
449　UN METHODIST	10	931	1,174*	6.8	16.9
467　WESLEYAN	1	10	32	.2	.5
499　INDEP.NON-CHAR	1	NA	600	3.5	8.6
PARKE	**44**	**3,979**	**5,443***	**35.3**	**100.0**
019　AMER BAPT USA	5	525	647*	4.2	11.9
053　ASSEMB OF GOD	1	75	100	.6	1.8
081　CATHOLIC	2	NA	476	3.1	8.7
081d　　LATIN	2	NA	476	3.1	8.7
093　CHR CH (DISC)	1	155	197	1.3	3.6
097　CHR CHS&CHS CR	7	966	1,191*	7.7	21.9
111　CH CR,SCIENTST	1	NR	NR	-	-
165　CH OF NAZARENE	3	98	178	1.2	3.3
167　CHS OF CHRIST	3	188	237	1.5	4.4
226　FRIENDS-USA	4	489	603*	3.9	11.1
226e　　FUM	4	489	603*	3.9	11.1
259　IFCA	2	NR	NR	-	-
325　OLD REG BAPT	1	23	28*	.2	.5
339　PENT CH OF GOD	1	12	25	.2	.5
355　PRESB CH (USA)	2	228	281*	1.8	5.2
419　SO BAPT CONV	1	180	222*	1.4	4.1
449　UN METHODIST	8	967	1,193*	7.7	21.9
467　WESLEYAN	2	73	65	.4	1.2
PERRY	**35**	**3,355**	**9,566***	**50.1**	**100.0**
019　AMER BAPT USA	4	751	940*	4.9	9.8
053　ASSEMB OF GOD	1	53	70	.4	.7
081　CATHOLIC	8	NA	5,320	27.8	55.6
081d　　LATIN	8	NA	5,320	27.8	55.6
093　CHR CH (DISC)	1	35	56	.3	.6
097　CHR CHS&CHS CR	1	150	188*	1.0	2.0
127　CH GOD (CLEVE)	1	18	23*	.1	.2
145　CH GOD PROPHCY	1	33	41*	.2	.4
151　L-D SAINTS	1	NA	117	.6	1.2
165　CH OF NAZARENE	1	106	120	.6	1.3
167　CHS OF CHRIST	2	460	495	2.6	5.2

County and Denomination	Number of churches	Communicant, confirmed, full members	Total adherents Number	Percent of total population	Percent of total adherents
193　EPISCOPAL	1	24	29	.2	.3
283　LUTH—MO SYNOD	1	289	363	1.9	3.8
361　PRIM BAPT ASCS	1	9	11*	.1	.1
413　S.D.A.	1	56	70*	.4	.7
443　UN C OF CHRIST	2	756	946*	5.0	9.9
449　UN METHODIST	7	606	758*	4.0	7.9
467　WESLEYAN	1	9	19	.1	.2
PIKE	**36**	**2,612**	**3,848***	**30.8**	**100.0**
019　AMER BAPT USA	1	310	382*	3.1	9.9
053　ASSEMB OF GOD	2	42	109	.9	2.8
081　CATHOLIC	1	NA	400	3.2	10.4
081d　　LATIN	1	NA	400	3.2	10.4
093　CHR CH (DISC)	1	35	56	.4	1.5
097　CHR CHS&CHS CR	3	310	382*	3.1	9.9
123　CH GOD (ANDER)	3	191	246	2.0	6.4
165　CH OF NAZARENE	2	108	251	2.0	6.5
167　CHS OF CHRIST	5	159	206	1.6	5.4
185　CUMBER PRESB	1	102	102	.8	2.7
207　E.L.C.A.	1	175	223	1.8	5.8
221　FREE METHODIST	2	95	114	.9	3.0
355　PRESB CH (USA)	1	146	180*	1.4	4.7
361　PRIM BAPT ASCS	1	10	12*	.1	.3
419　SO BAPT CONV	1	50	62*	.5	1.6
449　UN METHODIST	9	861	1,060*	8.5	27.5
467　WESLEYAN	2	18	63	.5	1.6
PORTER	**95**	**19,747**	**48,205***	**37.4**	**100.0**
040　AP CHR CH-AMER	1	70	125	.1	.3
053　ASSEMB OF GOD	6	474	951	.7	2.0
081　CATHOLIC	8	NA	19,866	15.4	41.2
081d　　LATIN	8	NA	19,866	15.4	41.2
093　CHR CH (DISC)	2	397	908	.7	1.9
097　CHR CHS&CHS CR	3	600	762*	.6	1.6
111　CH CR,SCIENTST	2	NR	NR	-	-
123　CH GOD (ANDER)	1	100	100	.1	.2
127　CH GOD (CLEVE)	2	440	559*	.4	1.2
145　CH GOD PROPHCY	2	67	85*	.1	.2
151　L-D SAINTS	2	NA	740	.6	1.5
165　CH OF NAZARENE	6	1,349	2,093	1.6	4.3
167　CHS OF CHRIST	4	466	604	.5	1.3
193　EPISCOPAL	2	276	406	.3	.8
203　EVAN FREE CH	2	600	1,218	.9	2.5
207　E.L.C.A.	7	2,907	3,903	3.0	8.1
226　FRIENDS-USA	1	9	11*	-	-
226c　　FGC	1	9	11*	-	-
246　GREEK ORTHODOX	1	NR	NR	-	-
259　IFCA	1	NR	NR	-	-
283　LUTH—MO SYNOD	9	4,315	5,410	4.2	11.2
285　MENNONITE CH	3	282	307	.2	.6
325　OLD REG BAPT	1	4	5*	-	-
339　PENT CH OF GOD	1	8	30	-	.1
355　PRESB CH (USA)	6	1,874	2,382*	1.8	4.9
356　PRESB CH AMER	1	61	95	.1	.2
363　PRIMITIVE METH	1	39	69	.1	.1
403　SALVATION ARMY	1	43	44	-	.1
413　S.D.A.	2	63	80*	.1	.2
419　SO BAPT CONV	6	1,850	2,351*	1.8	4.9
443　UN C OF CHRIST	2	201	255*	.2	.5
449　UN METHODIST	7	3,193	4,058*	3.1	8.4
467　WESLEYAN	1	59	297	.2	.6
496　JEWISH EST	1	NA	491	.4	1.0
POSEY	**45**	**6,246**	**13,444***	**51.8**	**100.0**
053　ASSEMB OF GOD	2	273	540	2.1	4.0
081　CATHOLIC	4	NA	4,798	18.5	35.7
081d　　LATIN	4	NA	4,798	18.5	35.7
093　CHR CH (DISC)	2	224	402	1.5	3.0
097　CHR CHS&CHS CR	4	615	790*	3.0	5.9
127　CH GOD (CLEVE)	1	56	72*	.3	.5
151　L-D SAINTS	1	NA	57	.2	.4
165　CH OF NAZARENE	4	270	599	2.3	4.5
167　CHS OF CHRIST	1	28	35	.1	.3
193　EPISCOPAL	2	120	166	.6	1.2
355　PRESB CH (USA)	2	122	157*	.6	1.2
413　S.D.A.	1	5	6*	-	-
419　SO BAPT CONV	2	1,044	1,341*	5.2	10.0
443　UN C OF CHRIST	6	1,601	2,056*	7.9	15.3
449　UN METHODIST	13	1,888	2,425*	9.3	18.0
PULASKI	**31**	**3,128**	**6,681***	**52.8**	**100.0**
019　AMER BAPT USA	1	49	63*	.5	.9
040　AP CHR CH-AMER	1	262	462	3.7	6.9
053　ASSEMB OF GOD	2	29	79	.6	1.2
081　CATHOLIC	5	NA	2,105	16.6	31.5
081d　　LATIN	5	NA	2,105	16.6	31.5

County and Denomination		Number of churches	Communicant, confirmed, full members	Total adherents		
				Number	Percent of total population	Percent of total adherents
093	CHR CH (DISC)	2	180	466	3.7	7.0
097	CHR CHS&CHS CR	2	525	675*	5.3	10.1
145	CH GOD PROPHCY	1	33	42*	.3	.6
165	CH OF NAZARENE	1	265	441	3.5	6.6
167	CHS OF CHRIST	1	15	25	.2	.4
176	CCC, NOT NAT'L	1	46	59*	.5	.9
223	FREE WILL BAPT	1	33	42*	.3	.6
283	LUTH—MO SYNOD	3	418	568	4.5	8.5
353	CHR BRETHREN	1	25	50	.4	.7
355	PRESB CH (USA)	2	185	238*	1.9	3.6
443	UN C OF CHRIST	2	194	249*	2.0	3.7
449	UN METHODIST	5	869	1,117*	8.8	16.7
PUTNAM		**49**	**8,303**	**11,359***	**37.5**	**100.0**
019	AMER BAPT USA	7	1,737	2,116*	7.0	18.6
053	ASSEMB OF GOD	1	184	300	1.0	2.6
081	CATHOLIC	1	NA	626	2.1	5.5
081d	*LATIN*	*1*	*NA*	*626*	*2.1*	*5.5*
093	CHR CH (DISC)	4	1,201	1,626	5.4	14.3
097	CHR CHS&CHS CR	6	1,440	1,754*	5.8	15.4
123	CH GOD (ANDER)	1	15	18	.1	.2
127	CH GOD (CLEVE)	1	114	139*	.5	1.2
151	L-D SAINTS	1	NA	97	.3	.9
165	CH OF NAZARENE	3	218	426	1.4	3.8
167	CHS OF CHRIST	4	313	412	1.4	3.6
175	CONGR CHR CHS	1	40	49*	.2	.4
193	EPISCOPAL	1	111	175	.6	1.5
226	FRIENDS-USA	1	44	54*	.2	.5
226e	*FUM*	*1*	*44*	*54***	*.2*	*.5*
283	LUTH—MO SYNOD	1	141	224	.7	2.0
355	PRESB CH (USA)	3	299	364*	1.2	3.2
413	S.D.A.	0	19	23*	.1	.2
419	SO BAPT CONV	2	448	546*	1.8	4.8
426	2SEED-SPRT BPT	1	20	24*	.1	.2
443	UN C OF CHRIST	1	275	335*	1.1	2.9
449	UN METHODIST	9	1,507	1,835*	6.1	16.2
497	BLACK BAPT EST	NA	177	216*	.7	1.9
RANDOLPH		**74**	**6,666**	**10,311***	**38.0**	**100.0**
053	ASSEMB OF GOD	2	195	518	1.9	5.0
081	CATHOLIC	2	NA	641	2.4	6.2
081d	*LATIN*	*2*	*NA*	*641*	*2.4*	*6.2*
093	CHR CH (DISC)	3	721	1,462	5.4	14.2
097	CHR CHS&CHS CR	3	530	658*	2.4	6.4
123	CH GOD (ANDER)	2	100	104	.4	1.0
165	CH OF NAZARENE	7	798	1,436	5.3	13.9
167	CHS OF CHRIST	2	84	109	.4	1.1
176	CCC, NOT NAT'L	1	11	14*	.1	.1
207	E.L.C.A.	2	340	456	1.7	4.4
226	FRIENDS-USA	13	892	1,107*	4.1	10.7
226e	*FUM*	*11*	*820*	*1,018***	*3.7*	*9.9*
226g	*INDEP EVAN*	*2*	*72*	*89***	*.3*	*.9*
296	MIDW CONGR FEL	12	638	792*	2.9	7.7
355	PRESB CH (USA)	2	175	217*	.8	2.1
419	SO BAPT CONV	2	213	264*	1.0	2.6
449	UN METHODIST	19	1,921	2,385*	8.8	23.1
467	WESLEYAN	2	48	148	.5	1.4
RIPLEY		**55**	**7,367**	**15,870***	**64.5**	**100.0**
019	AMER BAPT USA	12	2,635	3,369*	13.7	21.2
053	ASSEMB OF GOD	2	78	128	.5	.8
081	CATHOLIC	8	NA	6,375	25.9	40.2
081d	*LATIN*	*8*	*NA*	*6,375*	*25.9*	*40.2*
097	CHR CHS&CHS CR	3	430	550*	2.2	3.5
165	CH OF NAZARENE	1	17	50	.2	.3
167	CHS OF CHRIST	1	48	63	.3	.4
207	E.L.C.A.	6	1,734	2,157*	8.8	13.6
283	LUTH—MO SYNOD	1	181	245	1.0	1.5
325	OLD REG BAPT	2	43	55*	.2	.3
419	SO BAPT CONV	3	319	408*	1.7	2.6
443	UN C OF CHRIST	2	280	358*	1.5	2.3
449	UN METHODIST	11	1,539	1,967*	8.0	12.4
467	WESLEYAN	3	63	145	.6	.9
RUSH		**46**	**5,709**	**9,609***	**53.0**	**100.0**
019	AMER BAPT USA	1	500	632*	3.5	6.6
053	ASSEMB OF GOD	1	20	45	.2	.5
081	CATHOLIC	1	NA	1,344	7.4	14.0
081d	*LATIN*	*1*	*NA*	*1,344*	*7.4*	*14.0*
093	CHR CH (DISC)	7	825	1,424	7.9	14.8
097	CHR CHS&CHS CR	9	1,706	2,158*	11.9	22.5
123	CH GOD (ANDER)	1	104	150	.8	1.6
165	CH OF NAZARENE	2	121	235	1.3	2.4
167	CHS OF CHRIST	2	85	105	.6	1.1
193	EPISCOPAL	1	19	26	.1	.3
226	FRIENDS-USA	3	149	188*	1.0	2.0
226e	*FUM*	*3*	*149*	*188***	*1.0*	*2.0*
283	LUTH—MO SYNOD	1	27	31	.2	.3
323	OLD ORD AMISH	2	NA	300	1.7	3.1
355	PRESB CH (USA)	2	317	401*	2.2	4.2
403	SALVATION ARMY	1	59	69	.4	.7
419	SO BAPT CONV	2	556	703*	3.9	7.3
449	UN METHODIST	7	1,145	1,448*	8.0	15.1
467	WESLEYAN	3	76	350	1.9	3.6
SAINT JOSEPH		**198**	**37,494**	**119,120***	**48.2**	**100.0**
005	AME ZION	2	810	972	.4	.8
019	AMER BAPT USA	3	481	602*	.2	.5
040	AP CHR CH-AMER	1	27	47	-	-
053	ASSEMB OF GOD	6	905	1,666	.7	1.4
071	BRETHREN (ASH)	5	415	519*	.2	.4
081	CATHOLIC	30	NA	62,723	25.4	52.7
081d	*LATIN*	*28*	*NA*	*62,418*	*25.3*	*52.4*
081f	*MELKITE-GK*	*1*	*NA*	*252*	*.1*	*.2*
081h	*UKRAINIAN*	*1*	*NA*	*53*	*-*	*-*
093	CHR CH (DISC)	4	1,031	1,386	.6	1.2
097	CHR CHS&CHS CR	5	1,465	1,833*	.7	1.5
105	CHRISTIAN REF	1	179	272	.1	.2
111	CH CR,SCIENTST	2	NR	NR	-	-
121	CH GOD (ABR)	1	108	135*	.1	.1
123	CH GOD (ANDER)	3	311	359	.1	.3
127	CH GOD (CLEVE)	2	218	273*	.1	.2
145	CH GOD PROPHCY	1	33	41*	-	-
151	L-D SAINTS	1	NA	631	.3	.5
157	CH OF BRETHREN	6	691	864*	.3	.7
165	CH OF NAZARENE	3	462	758	.3	.6
167	CHS OF CHRIST	4	340	442	.2	.4
175	CONGR CHR CHS	1	131	164*	.1	.1
193	EPISCOPAL	4	796	1,097	.4	.9
203	EVAN FREE CH	1	298	612	.2	.5
207	E.L.C.A.	9	2,728	3,909	1.6	3.3
226	FRIENDS-USA	1	4	17	-	-
226f	*INDEPENDNT*	*1*	*4*	*17*	*-*	*-*
246	GREEK ORTHODOX	1	NR	NR	-	-
259	IFCA	2	NR	NR	-	-
283	LUTH—MO SYNOD	6	1,922	2,523	1.0	2.1
285	MENNONITE CH	3	190	249	.1	.2
287	MENN GEN CONF	1	8	14	-	-
291	MISSIONARY CH	17	1,485	2,493	1.0	2.1
339	PENT CH OF GOD	1	15	40	-	-
353	CHR BRETHREN	1	15	25	-	-
355	PRESB CH (USA)	8	3,003	3,757*	1.5	3.2
403	SALVATION ARMY	2	203	227	.1	.2
413	S.D.A.	2	722	903*	.4	.8
419	SO BAPT CONV	2	602	753*	.3	.6
435	UNITARIAN-UNIV	1	81	117	-	.1
438	UN BRETH IN CR	1	69	84	-	.1
443	UN C OF CHRIST	7	1,558	1,949*	.8	1.6
449	UN METHODIST	31	9,378	11,731*	4.7	9.8
467	WESLEYAN	6	171	569	.2	.5
469	WELS	1	243	313	.1	.3
496	JEWISH EST	5	NA	1,800	.7	1.5
497	BLACK BAPT EST	NA	6,396	8,001*	3.2	6.7
498	INDEP.CHARIS.	1	NA	2,000	.8	1.7
499	INDEP.NON-CHAR	3	NA	2,250	.9	1.9
SCOTT		**45**	**7,521**	**10,163***	**48.4**	**100.0**
019	AMER BAPT USA	9	2,623	3,323*	15.8	32.7
053	ASSEMB OF GOD	1	25	50	.2	.5
081	CATHOLIC	1	NA	503	2.4	4.9
081d	*LATIN*	*1*	*NA*	*503*	*2.4*	*4.9*
082	CENTRAL BAPT	1	71	90*	.4	.9
097	CHR CHS&CHS CR	7	2,670	3,383*	16.1	33.3
123	CH GOD (ANDER)	1	103	103	.5	1.0
127	CH GOD (CLEVE)	3	369	468*	2.2	4.6
145	CH GOD PROPHCY	1	33	42*	.2	.4
165	CH OF NAZARENE	1	56	154	.7	1.5
167	CHS OF CHRIST	2	134	160	.8	1.6
283	LUTH—MO SYNOD	1	40	49	.2	.5
285	MENNONITE CH	1	15	15	.1	.1
355	PRESB CH (USA)	2	162	205*	1.0	2.0
413	S.D.A.	1	64	81*	.4	.8
419	SO BAPT CONV	2	275	348*	1.7	3.4
436	UNITED BAPT	1	85	108*	.5	1.1
449	UN METHODIST	8	755	957*	4.6	9.4
467	WESLEYAN	2	41	124	6	1.2
SHELBY		**63**	**10,435**	**18,268***	**45.3**	**100.0**
019	AMER BAPT USA	10	2,952	3,742*	9.3	20.5
053	ASSEMB OF GOD	1	89	170	.4	.9
081	CATHOLIC	2	NA	3,056	7.6	16.7
081d	*LATIN*	*2*	*NA*	*3,056*	*7.6*	*16.7*

County and Denomination		Number of churches	Communicant, confirmed, full members	Total adherents		
				Number	Percent of total population	Percent of total adherents
093	CHR CH (DISC)	1	527	841	2.1	4.6
097	CHR CHS&CHS CR	6	1,275	1,616*	4.0	8.8
111	CH CR,SCIENTST	1	NR	NR	-	-
123	CH GOD (ANDER)	1	40	40	.1	.2
151	L-D SAINTS	1	NA	245	.6	1.3
165	CH OF NAZARENE	3	397	875	2.2	4.8
167	CHS OF CHRIST	1	17	22	.1	.1
193	EPISCOPAL	1	51	71	.2	.4
207	E.L.C.A.	2	233	306	.8	1.7
215	EVAN METH CH	1	133	169*	.4	.9
283	LUTH—MO SYNOD	1	95	135	.3	.7
355	PRESB CH (USA)	2	472	598*	1.5	3.3
403	SALVATION ARMY	1	68	70	.2	.4
413	S.D.A.	2	97	123*	.3	.7
419	SO BAPT CONV	3	594	753*	1.9	4.1
443	UN C OF CHRIST	2	466	591*	1.5	3.2
449	UN METHODIST	18	2,818	3,573*	8.9	19.6
467	WESLEYAN	2	111	350	.9	1.9
496	JEWISH EST	0	NA	322	.8	1.8
499	INDEP.NON-CHAR	1	NA	600	1.5	3.3
SPENCER		**48**	**6,702**	**12,255***	**62.9**	**100.0**
019	AMER BAPT USA	5	722	916*	4.7	7.5
081	CATHOLIC	6	NA	3,512	18.0	28.7
081d	LATIN	6	NA	3,512	18.0	28.7
097	CHR CHS&CHS CR	4	2,430	3,084*	15.8	25.2
165	CH OF NAZARENE	3	183	377	1.9	3.1
167	CHS OF CHRIST	1	40	75	.4	.6
207	E.L.C.A.	1	101	138	.7	1.1
283	LUTH—MO SYNOD	1	293	375	1.9	3.1
355	PRESB CH (USA)	1	64	81*	.4	.7
361	PRIM BAPT ASCS	1	8	10*	.1	.1
419	SO BAPT CONV	4	598	759*	3.9	6.2
443	UN C OF CHRIST	4	375	476*	2.4	3.9
449	UN METHODIST	16	1,881	2,387*	12.2	19.5
467	WESLEYAN	1	7	65	.3	.5
STARKE		**31**	**3,258**	**6,848***	**30.1**	**100.0**
053	ASSEMB OF GOD	2	99	218	1.0	3.2
081	CATHOLIC	5	NA	2,050	9.0	29.9
081d	LATIN	5	NA	2,050	9.0	29.9
097	CHR CHS&CHS CR	1	160	204*	.9	3.0
127	CH GOD (CLEVE)	1	17	22*	.1	.3
165	CH OF NAZARENE	1	54	123	.5	1.8
223	FREE WILL BAPT	2	188	240*	1.1	3.5
259	IFCA	1	NR	NR	-	-
283	LUTH—MO SYNOD	3	1,123	1,485	6.5	21.7
285	MENNONITE CH	2	163	338	1.5	4.9
339	PENT CH OF GOD	1	9	20	.1	.3
353	CHR BRETHREN	1	50	70	.3	1.0
413	S.D.A.	1	41	52*	.2	.8
436	UNITED BAPT	4	549	700*	3.1	10.2
443	UN C OF CHRIST	1	148	189*	.8	2.8
449	UN METHODIST	4	657	837*	3.7	12.2
499	INDEP.NON-CHAR	1	NA	300	1.3	4.4
STEUBEN		**48**	**5,553**	**9,905***	**36.1**	**100.0**
019	AMER BAPT USA	2	163	205*	.7	2.1
053	ASSEMB OF GOD	2	201	434	1.6	4.4
081	CATHOLIC	2	NA	1,773	6.5	17.9
081d	LATIN	2	NA	1,773	6.5	17.9
097	CHR CHS&CHS CR	4	777	976*	3.6	9.9
123	CH GOD (ANDER)	1	22	52	.2	.5
151	L-D SAINTS	1	NA	120	.4	1.2
165	CH OF NAZARENE	2	112	246	.9	2.5
167	CHS OF CHRIST	1	45	48	.2	.5
176	CCC, NOT NAT'L	1	78	98*	.4	1.0
193	EPISCOPAL	1	57	88	.3	.9
207	E.L.C.A.	1	512	635	2.3	6.4
283	LUTH—MO SYNOD	3	512	596	2.2	6.0
291	MISSIONARY CH	3	321	716	2.6	7.2
323	OLD ORD AMISH	2	NA	300	1.1	3.0
339	PENT CH OF GOD	1	39	150	.5	1.5
355	PRESB CH (USA)	2	209	263*	1.0	2.7
413	S.D.A.	1	31	39*	.1	.4
419	SO BAPT CONV	1	360	452*	1.6	4.6
438	UN BRETH IN CR	2	90	90	.3	.9
443	UN C OF CHRIST	2	330	415*	1.5	4.2
449	UN METHODIST	12	1,655	2,079*	7.6	21.0
467	WESLEYAN	1	39	130	.5	1.3
SULLIVAN		**65**	**6,520**	**8,829***	**46.5**	**100.0**
019	AMER BAPT USA	6	1,658	2,057*	10.8	23.3
053	ASSEMB OF GOD	4	214	347	1.8	3.9
081	CATHOLIC	1	NA	459	2.4	5.2
081d	LATIN	1	NA	459	2.4	5.2

County and Denomination		Number of churches	Communicant, confirmed, full members	Total adherents		
				Number	Percent of total population	Percent of total adherents
093	CHR CH (DISC)	1	94	116	.6	1.3
097	CHR CHS&CHS CR	4	1,338	1,660*	8.7	18.8
127	CH GOD (CLEVE)	3	170	211*	1.1	2.4
145	CH GOD PROPHCY	1	33	41*	.2	.5
165	CH OF NAZARENE	1	91	189	1.0	2.1
167	CHS OF CHRIST	11	642	894	4.7	10.1
215	EVAN METH CH	1	106	131*	.7	1.5
226	FRIENDS-USA	1	8	10*	.1	.1
226g	INDEP EVAN	1	8	10*	.1	.1
355	PRESB CH (USA)	2	224	278*	1.5	3.1
413	S.D.A.	1	6	7*	-	.1
419	SO BAPT CONV	3	252	313*	1.6	3.5
443	UN C OF CHRIST	1	30	37*	.2	.4
449	UN METHODIST	21	1,612	2,000*	10.5	22.7
467	WESLEYAN	3	42	79	.4	.9
SWITZERLAND		**28**	**2,341**	**3,270***	**42.3**	**100.0**
019	AMER BAPT USA	12	1,765	2,232*	28.8	68.3
081	CATHOLIC	1	NA	229	3.0	7.0
081d	LATIN	1	NA	229	3.0	7.0
123	CH GOD (ANDER)	1	31	31	.4	.9
165	CH OF NAZARENE	2	26	45	.6	1.4
323	OLD ORD AMISH	1	NA	100	1.3	3.1
355	PRESB CH (USA)	1	57	72*	.9	2.2
419	SO BAPT CONV	2	127	161*	2.1	4.9
449	UN METHODIST	7	316	400*	5.2	12.2
467	WESLEYAN	1	19	0	-	-
TIPPECANOE		**102**	**22,665**	**44,629***	**34.2**	**100.0**
019	AMER BAPT USA	3	1,513	1,818*	1.4	4.1
053	ASSEMB OF GOD	3	1,190	3,209	2.5	7.2
081	CATHOLIC	5	NA	11,094	8.5	24.9
081d	LATIN	5	NA	11,094	8.5	24.9
089	CHR & MISS AL	1	32	100	.1	.2
093	CHR CH (DISC)	2	1,128	2,295	1.8	5.1
097	CHR CHS&CHS CR	1	240	288*	.2	.6
111	CH CR,SCIENTST	1	NR	NR	-	-
123	CH GOD (ANDER)	2	125	125	.1	.3
127	CH GOD (CLEVE)	1	9	11*	-	-
151	L-D SAINTS	3	NA	922	.7	2.1
157	CH OF BRETHREN	1	78	94*	.1	.2
165	CH OF NAZARENE	1	228	406	.3	.9
167	CHS OF CHRIST	3	430	720	.6	1.6
193	EPISCOPAL	2	386	737	.6	1.7
199	EVAN CONGR CH	1	31	113	.1	.3
207	E.L.C.A.	3	1,024	1,375	1.1	3.1
213	EVAN MENN INC	1	26	31*	-	.1
221	FREE METHODIST	1	34	51	-	.1
226	FRIENDS-USA	2	39	47*	-	.1
226c	FGC	1	25	30*	-	.1
226e	FUM	1	14	17*	-	-
259	IFCA	2	NR	NR	-	-
263	INT FOURSQ GOS	1	87	105*	.1	.2
283	LUTH—MO SYNOD	4	1,850	2,450*	1.9	5.5
285	MENNONITE CH	1	24	33	-	.1
287	MENN GEN CONF	1	13	16	-	-
339	PENT CH OF GOD	2	71	205	.2	.5
353	CHR BRETHREN	1	30	50	-	.1
355	PRESB CH (USA)	9	3,971	4,772*	3.7	10.7
371	REF CH IN AM	2	276	432	.3	1.0
403	SALVATION ARMY	1	100	112	.1	.3
413	S.D.A.	1	221	266*	.2	.6
419	SO BAPT CONV	8	1,400	1,682*	1.3	3.8
435	UNITARIAN-UNIV	1	102	164	.1	.4
438	UN BRETH IN CR	1	157	157	.1	.4
443	UN C OF CHRIST	2	747	898*	.7	2.0
449	UN METHODIST	21	6,221	7,476*	5.7	16.8
467	WESLEYAN	2	147	657	.5	1.5
469	WELS	1	32	48	-	.1
496	JEWISH EST	3	NA	500	.4	1.1
497	BLACK BAPT EST	NA	703	845*	.6	1.9
499	INDEP.NON-CHAR	1	NA	325	.2	.7
TIPTON		**25**	**3,774**	**6,826***	**42.3**	**100.0**
019	AMER BAPT USA	1	204	255*	1.6	3.7
053	ASSEMB OF GOD	1	16	26	.2	.4
081	CATHOLIC	1	NA	1,243	7.7	18.2
081d	LATIN	1	NA	1,243	7.7	18.2
093	CHR CH (DISC)	2	706	1,429	8.9	20.9
097	CHR CHS&CHS CR	4	865	1,079*	6.7	15.8
127	CH GOD (CLEVE)	1	58	72*	.4	1.1
146	CH GOD MTN ASM	1	68	85*	.5	1.2
165	CH OF NAZARENE	1	85	144	.9	2.1
167	CHS OF CHRIST	1	117	152	.9	2.2
226	FRIENDS-USA	1	10	12*	.1	.2
226e	FUM	1	10	12*	.1	.2

County and Denomination	Number of churches	Communicant, confirmed, full members	Total adherents Number	Percent of total population	Percent of total adherents
283 LUTH—MO SYNOD	1	422	506	3.1	7.4
355 PRESB CH (USA)	1	162	202*	1.3	3.0
419 SO BAPT CONV	1	46	57*	.4	.8
449 UN METHODIST	5	843	1,052*	6.5	15.4
467 WESLEYAN	3	172	512	3.2	7.5
UNION	**11**	**1,167**	**1,823***	**26.1**	**100.0**
081 CATHOLIC	1	NA	360	5.2	19.7
081d LATIN	*1*	*NA*	*360*	*5.2*	*19.7*
165 CH OF NAZARENE	2	137	159	2.3	8.7
226 FRIENDS-USA	1	31	39*	.6	2.1
226e FUM	*1*	*31*	*39**	*.6*	*2.1*
355 PRESB CH (USA)	1	121	153*	2.2	8.4
361 PRIM BAPT ASCS	1	12	15*	.2	.8
419 SO BAPT CONV	1	113	143*	2.0	7.8
449 UN METHODIST	4	753	954*	13.7	52.3
VANDERBURGH	**158**	**49,766**	**95,612***	**57.9**	**100.0**
005 AME ZION	1	300	389	.2	.4
019 AMER BAPT USA	5	1,616	1,997*	1.2	2.1
053 ASSEMB OF GOD	7	1,022	1,474	.9	1.5
071 BRETHREN (ASH)	1	128	158*	.1	.2
081 CATHOLIC	20	NA	29,867	18.1	31.2
081d LATIN	*20*	*NA*	*29,867*	*18.1*	*31.2*
093 CHR CH (DISC)	3	727	1,019	.6	1.1
097 CHR CHS&CHS CR	2	1,545	1,910*	1.2	2.0
111 CH CR,SCIENTST	1	NR	NR	-	-
123 CH GOD (ANDER)	2	118	149	.1	.2
127 CH GOD (CLEVE)	2	108	133*	.1	.1
145 CH GOD PROPHCY	1	33	41*	-	-
151 L-D SAINTS	1	NA	500	.3	.5
165 CH OF NAZARENE	6	517	739	.4	.8
167 CHS OF CHRIST	6	1,090	1,354	.8	1.4
179 CONSRV BAPT	1	NR	NR	-	-
185 CUMBER PRESB	2	698	738	.4	.8
193 EPISCOPAL	1	246	402	.2	.4
203 EVAN FREE CH	1	206	206	.1	.2
207 E.L.C.A.	6	1,422	1,842	1.1	1.9
221 FREE METHODIST	1	90	98	.1	.1
226 FRIENDS-USA	1	10	12*	-	-
226e FUM	*1*	*10*	*12**	-	-
283 LUTH—MO SYNOD	8	2,733	3,543	2.1	3.7
355 PRESB CH (USA)	9	2,005	2,478*	1.5	2.6
403 SALVATION ARMY	2	257	298	.2	.3
413 S.D.A.	2	235	290*	.2	.3
419 SO BAPT CONV	24	16,692	20,630*	12.5	21.6
435 UNITARIAN-UNIV	1	88	103	.1	.1
443 UN C OF CHRIST	14	7,048	8,711*	5.3	9.1
449 UN METHODIST	18	6,955	8,596*	5.2	9.0
467 WESLEYAN	3	596	1,940	1.2	2.0
496 JEWISH EST	3	NA	520	.3	.5
497 BLACK BAPT EST	NA	3,281	4,055*	2.5	4.2
498 INDEP.CHARIS.	2	NA	1,120	.7	1.2
499 INDEP.NON-CHAR	1	NA	300	.2	.3
VERMILLION	**31**	**3,411**	**6,093***	**36.3**	**100.0**
019 AMER BAPT USA	3	733	905*	5.4	14.9
053 ASSEMB OF GOD	3	143	320	1.9	5.3
081 CATHOLIC	2	NA	1,321	7.9	21.7
081d LATIN	*2*	*NA*	*1,321*	*7.9*	*21.7*
093 CHR CH (DISC)	1	218	350	2.1	5.7
097 CHR CHS&CHS CR	2	501	618*	3.7	10.1
127 CH GOD (CLEVE)	1	49	60*	.4	1.0
165 CH OF NAZARENE	4	233	623	3.7	10.2
167 CHS OF CHRIST	1	40	52	.3	.9
226 FRIENDS-USA	2	146	180*	1.1	3.0
226e FUM	*2*	*146*	*180**	*1.1*	*3.0*
355 PRESB CH (USA)	2	237	293*	1.7	4.8
449 UN METHODIST	10	1,111	1,371*	8.2	22.5
VIGO	**119**	**20,267**	**34,817***	**32.8**	**100.0**
019 AMER BAPT USA	7	2,263	2,760*	2.6	7.9
053 ASSEMB OF GOD	5	1,333	2,110	2.0	6.1
081 CATHOLIC	9	NA	6,764	6.4	19.4
081d LATIN	*9*	*NA*	*6,764*	*6.4*	*19.4*
089 CHR & MISS AL	1	29	74	.1	.2
093 CHR CH (DISC)	1	232	412	.4	1.2
097 CHR CHS&CHS CR	9	2,892	3,528*	3.3	10.1
111 CH CR,SCIENTST	1	NR	NR	-	-
123 CH GOD (ANDER)	2	13	68	.1	.2
127 CH GOD (CLEVE)	1	62	76*	.1	.2
145 CH GOD PROPHCY	2	67	82*	.1	.2
151 L-D SAINTS	3	NA	723	.7	2.1
165 CH OF NAZARENE	5	483	725	.7	2.1
167 CHS OF CHRIST	8	901	1,183	1.1	3.4
175 CONGR CHR CHS	2	167	204*	.2	.6
176 CCC, NOT NAT'L	1	100	122*	.1	.4
193 EPISCOPAL	2	473	733	.7	2.1
207 E.L.C.A.	3	600	852	.8	2.4
221 FREE METHODIST	1	44	101	.1	.3
226 FRIENDS-USA	2	33	43*	-	.1
226f INDEPENDNT	*1*	*6*	*10*	-	-
226g INDEP EVAN	*1*	*27*	*33**	-	*.1*
259 IFCA	1	NR	NR	-	-
263 INT FOURSQ GOS	2	318	388*	.4	1.1
283 LUTH—MO SYNOD	1	379	527	.5	1.5
353 CHR BRETHREN	1	25	50	-	.1
355 PRESB CH (USA)	3	808	986*	.9	2.8
403 SALVATION ARMY	1	130	172	.2	.5
413 S.D.A.	3	201	245*	.2	.7
419 SO BAPT CONV	3	904	1,103*	1.0	3.2
435 UNITARIAN-UNIV	1	43	58	.1	.2
443 UN C OF CHRIST	2	639	779*	.7	2.2
449 UN METHODIST	24	5,228	6,377*	6.0	18.3
467 WESLEYAN	10	336	939	.9	2.7
496 JEWISH EST	1	NA	325	.3	.9
497 BLACK BAPT EST	NA	1,564	1,908*	1.8	5.5
499 INDEP.NON-CHAR	1	NA	400	.4	1.1
WABASH	**71**	**9,720**	**14,476***	**41.3**	**100.0**
053 ASSEMB OF GOD	2	145	350	1.0	2.4
071 BRETHREN (ASH)	4	413	517*	1.5	3.6
081 CATHOLIC	3	NA	1,305	3.7	9.0
081d LATIN	*3*	*NA*	*1,305*	*3.7*	*9.0*
089 CHR & MISS AL	1	108	208	.6	1.4
093 CHR CH (DISC)	2	461	716	2.0	4.9
097 CHR CHS&CHS CR	3	455	570*	1.6	3.9
123 CH GOD (ANDER)	1	59	93	.3	.6
127 CH GOD (CLEVE)	1	66	83*	.2	.6
146 CH GOD MTN ASM	1	32	40*	.1	.3
157 CH OF BRETHREN	5	1,338	1,676*	4.8	11.6
165 CH OF NAZARENE	2	152	346	1.0	2.4
167 CHS OF CHRIST	2	130	167	.5	1.2
171 CH GOD-GEN CON	1	214	268*	.8	1.9
175 CONGR CHR CHS	1	165	207*	.6	1.4
207 E.L.C.A.	2	693	871	2.5	6.0
213 EVAN MENN INC	1	25	31*	.1	.2
223 FREE WILL BAPT	4	528	661*	1.9	4.6
226 FRIENDS-USA	1	408	511*	1.5	3.5
226e FUM	*1*	*408*	*511**	*1.5*	*3.5*
259 IFCA	1	NR	NR	-	-
283 LUTH—MO SYNOD	1	92	129	.4	.9
291 MISSIONARY CH	1	103	205	.6	1.4
355 PRESB CH (USA)	2	400	501*	1.4	3.5
413 S.D.A.	1	18	23*	.1	.2
436 UNITED BAPT	1	37	46*	.1	.3
443 UN C OF CHRIST	3	547	685*	2.0	4.7
449 UN METHODIST	20	2,966	3,716*	10.6	25.7
467 WESLEYAN	4	165	551	1.6	3.8
WARREN	**19**	**1,840**	**2,351***	**28.8**	**100.0**
053 ASSEMB OF GOD	1	23	32	.4	1.4
097 CHR CHS&CHS CR	3	685	857*	10.5	36.5
121 CH GOD (ABR)	1	36	45*	.6	1.9
165 CH OF NAZARENE	2	110	181	2.2	7.7
221 FREE METHODIST	1	8	12	.1	.5
355 PRESB CH (USA)	2	174	218*	2.7	9.3
449 UN METHODIST	9	804	1,006*	12.3	42.8
WARRICK	**53**	**7,960**	**19,420***	**43.2**	**100.0**
019 AMER BAPT USA	1	355	453*	1.0	2.3
053 ASSEMB OF GOD	2	97	160	.4	.8
081 CATHOLIC	5	NA	7,269	16.2	37.4
081d LATIN	*5*	*NA*	*7,269*	*16.2*	*37.4*
093 CHR CH (DISC)	1	112	181	.4	.9
097 CHR CHS&CHS CR	1	109	139*	.3	.7
111 CH CR,SCIENTST	1	NR	NR	-	-
151 L-D SAINTS	1	NA	158	.4	.8
165 CH OF NAZARENE	3	209	379	.8	2.0
167 CHS OF CHRIST	1	50	85	.2	.4
185 CUMBER PRESB	1	296	343	.8	1.8
207 E.L.C.A.	2	162	212	.5	1.1
221 FREE METHODIST	1	35	35	.1	.2
223 FREE WILL BAPT	1	36	46*	.1	.2
259 IFCA	1	NR	NR	-	-
283 LUTH—MO SYNOD	1	208	249	.6	1.3
355 PRESB CH (USA)	2	598	764*	1.7	3.9
413 S.D.A.	1	39	50*	.1	.3
419 SO BAPT CONV	4	1,918	2,449*	5.5	12.6
443 UN C OF CHRIST	5	1,313	1,677**	3.7	8.6
449 UN METHODIST	15	2,370	3,026*	6.7	15.6
467 WESLEYAN	1	53	245	.5	1.3

County and Denomination	Number of churches	Communicant, confirmed, full members	Total adherents Number	Percent of total population	Percent of total adherents
498 INDEP.CHARIS.	1	NA	300	.7	1.5
499 INDEP.NON-CHAR	1	NA	1,200	2.7	6.2
WASHINGTON	**68**	**6,733**	**10,442***	**44.0**	**100.0**
019 AMER BAPT USA	9	1,618	2,050*	8.6	19.6
053 ASSEMB OF GOD	1	44	125	.5	1.2
081 CATHOLIC	1	NA	421	1.8	4.0
081d LATIN	*1*	*NA*	*421*	*1.8*	*4.0*
093 CHR CH (DISC)	1	454	969	4.1	9.3
097 CHR CHS&CHS CR	7	875	1,109*	4.7	10.6
123 CH GOD (ANDER)	1	60	80	.3	.8
127 CH GOD (CLEVE)	2	54	68*	.3	.7
145 CH GOD PROPHCY	1	33	42*	.2	.4
146 CH GOD MTN ASM	1	2	3*	-	-
151 L-D SAINTS	1	NA	239	1.0	2.3
165 CH OF NAZARENE	3	175	508	2.1	4.9
167 CHS OF CHRIST	14	1,093	1,438	6.1	13.8
226 FRIENDS-USA	1	85	108*	.5	1.0
226e FUM	*1*	*85*	*108**	*.5*	*1.0*
283 LUTH—MO SYNOD	1	37	67	.3	.6
323 OLD ORD AMISH	2	NA	300	1.3	2.9
355 PRESB CH (USA)	2	213	270*	1.1	2.6
413 S.D.A.	1	13	16*	.1	.2
419 SO BAPT CONV	4	628	796*	3.4	7.6
436 UNITED BAPT	1	120	152*	.6	1.5
449 UN METHODIST	12	1,208	1,530*	6.5	14.7
467 WESLEYAN	2	21	151	.6	1.4
WAYNE	**109**	**17,295**	**27,706***	**38.5**	**100.0**
011 A.W.M.C.	1	15	19*	-	.1
019 AMER BAPT USA	3	1,663	2,060*	2.9	7.4
053 ASSEMB OF GOD	3	249	373	.5	1.3
081 CATHOLIC	4	NA	4,652	6.5	16.8
081d LATIN	*4*	*NA*	*4,652*	*6.5*	*16.8*
089 CHR & MISS AL	2	76	154	.2	.6
093 CHR CH (DISC)	2	599	935	1.3	3.4
097 CHR CHS&CHS CR	7	875	1,084*	1.5	3.9
111 CH CR,SCIENTST	1	NR	NR	-	-
123 CH GOD (ANDER)	2	84	87	.1	.3
127 CH GOD (CLEVE)	1	337	417*	.6	1.5
146 CH GOD MTN ASM	1	67	83*	.1	.3
151 L-D SAINTS	1	NA	518	.7	1.9
157 CH OF BRETHREN	5	339	420*	.6	1.5
165 CH OF NAZARENE	8	852	1,533	2.1	5.5
167 CHS OF CHRIST	5	223	336	.5	1.2
193 EPISCOPAL	1	102	190	.3	.7
207 E.L.C.A.	6	2,027	2,529	3.5	9.1
226 FRIENDS-USA	12	1,065	1,317*	1.8	4.8
226d FGC & FUM	*1*	*166*	*203*	*.3*	*.7*
226e FUM	*10*	*870*	*1,078**	*1.5*	*3.9*
226g INDEP EVAN	*1*	*29*	*36**	*.1*	*.1*
283 LUTH—MO SYNOD	1	40	44	.1	.2
355 PRESB CH (USA)	5	930	1,152*	1.6	4.2
356 PRESB CH AMER	1	129	151	.2	.5
361 PRIM BAPT ASCS	1	32	40*	.1	.1
403 SALVATION ARMY	1	157	158	.2	.6
413 S.D.A.	1	149	185*	.3	.7
419 SO BAPT CONV	10	2,464	3,052*	4.2	11.0
435 UNITARIAN-UNIV	1	24	24	-	.1
443 UN C OF CHRIST	2	167	207*	.3	.7
449 UN METHODIST	18	3,705	4,589*	6.4	16.6
467 WESLEYAN	2	112	390	.5	1.4
496 JEWISH EST	1	NA	0	-	-
497 BLACK BAPT EST	NA	813	1,007*	1.4	3.6
WELLS	**51**	**8,019**	**12,624***	**48.7**	**100.0**
019 AMER BAPT USA	3	559	722*	2.8	5.7
040 AP CHR CH-AMER	2	1,205	2,135	8.2	16.9
081 CATHOLIC	1	NA	750	2.9	5.9
081d LATIN	*1*	*NA*	*750*	*2.9*	*5.9*
123 CH GOD (ANDER)	1	47	58	.2	.5
127 CH GOD (CLEVE)	1	63	81*	.3	.6
157 CH OF BRETHREN	1	54	70*	.3	.6
165 CH OF NAZARENE	2	293	463	1.8	3.7
167 CHS OF CHRIST	1	30	65	.3	.5
171 CH GOD-GEN CON	1	110	142*	.5	1.1
207 E.L.C.A.	3	735	1,032	4.0	8.2
226 FRIENDS-USA	1	6	8*	-	.1
226e FUM	*1*	*6*	*8**	*-*	*.1*
283 LUTH—MO SYNOD	2	565	783	3.0	6.2
291 MISSIONARY CH	2	185	430	1.7	3.4
355 PRESB CH (USA)	2	572	739*	2.8	5.9
413 S.D.A.	1	24	31*	.1	.2
438 UN BRETH IN CR	3	416	416	1.6	3.3
443 UN C OF CHRIST	2	693	895*	3.4	7.1
449 UN METHODIST	19	2,217	2,864*	11.0	22.7

County and Denomination	Number of churches	Communicant, confirmed, full members	Total adherents Number	Percent of total population	Percent of total adherents
467 WESLEYAN	3	245	940	3.6	7.4
WHITE	**40**	**6,152**	**9,441***	**40.6**	**100.0**
019 AMER BAPT USA	7	1,582	2,000*	8.6	21.2
040 AP CHR CH-AMER	1	101	181	.8	1.9
053 ASSEMB OF GOD	1	156	250	1.1	2.6
081 CATHOLIC	2	NA	1,394	6.0	14.8
081d LATIN	*2*	*NA*	*1,394*	*6.0*	*14.8*
093 CHR CH (DISC)	2	542	694	3.0	7.4
097 CHR CHS&CHS CR	3	390	493*	2.1	5.2
157 CH OF BRETHREN	4	289	365*	1.6	3.9
165 CH OF NAZARENE	1	44	64	.3	.7
167 CHS OF CHRIST	2	98	153	.7	1.6
171 CH GOD-GEN CON	1	155	196*	.8	2.1
207 E.L.C.A.	1	133	178	.8	1.9
283 LUTH—MO SYNOD	2	502	665	2.9	7.0
355 PRESB CH (USA)	3	547	691*	3.0	7.3
413 S.D.A.	1	40	51*	.2	.5
449 UN METHODIST	8	1,559	1,971*	8.5	20.9
467 WESLEYAN	1	14	95	.4	1.0
WHITLEY	**52**	**6,491**	**11,405***	**41.2**	**100.0**
019 AMER BAPT USA	1	28	36*	.1	.3
053 ASSEMB OF GOD	1	23	23	.1	.2
057 BAPT GEN CONF	1	135	173*	.6	1.5
081 CATHOLIC	3	NA	2,182	7.9	19.1
081d LATIN	*3*	*NA*	*2,182*	*7.9*	*19.1*
093 CHR CH (DISC)	2	160	267	1.0	2.3
123 CH GOD (ANDER)	2	195	234	.8	2.1
127 CH GOD (CLEVE)	1	20	26*	.1	.2
157 CH OF BRETHREN	4	448	574*	2.1	5.0
165 CH OF NAZARENE	2	411	752	2.7	6.6
167 CHS OF CHRIST	1	39	62	.2	.5
171 CH GOD-GEN CON	6	949	1,216*	4.4	10.7
207 E.L.C.A.	3	773	948	3.4	8.3
216 EVAN PRESBY CH	1	200	207	.7	1.8
221 FREE METHODIST	1	31	57	.2	.5
223 FREE WILL BAPT	1	41	53*	.2	.5
283 LUTH—MO SYNOD	3	835	1,084	3.9	9.5
323 OLD ORD AMISH	1	NA	150	.5	1.3
339 PENT CH OF GOD	1	32	47	.2	.4
355 PRESB CH (USA)	2	247	316*	1.1	2.8
449 UN METHODIST	12	1,881	2,410*	8.7	21.1
467 WESLEYAN	2	43	155	.6	1.4
496 JEWISH EST	0	NA	83	.3	.7
499 INDEP.NON-CHAR	1	NA	350	1.3	3.1

Index

Day-age interpretation of creation, 654, 662
Day Dawn (Adventist periodical), 501–2
Day Star. See Western Midnight Cry
Dayton, A. C., 598
de Ville, John B., 544
Dead: communication with. *See* Spiritualists
Dearborn County: Fourierists, 323; Rationalists, 327; United Brethren, 248
Debates, xi; Brethren, 225–26; Campbellite-Hardshell, 44–46, 49; Campbell's, 69–70, 76–77; Catholic/Klan, 551; creationist, 652; Franklin-Manford, 315; fundamentalist, 661; Mathes-Manford, 80; Owen/Campbell, 281, 282, 291n35; Swedenborgian, 334; Universalist, 312–15
Decatur County: Presbyterians, 115–16
Deism: and Universalists, 311
Deists. *See* Rationalists
Delany Academy, 121
Delaware County: Christians, 64
Delaware Indians, 2, 4, 6; Moravian mission to, 306–7
Democracy: Campbell on, 77; and Jehovah's Witnesses, 529
Dennis, Philip, 195
Denominations, x; Christian withdrawal from, 61–62
DePauw, Washington C., 362
Depew, Mary E., 378
Derrow, Nathan B., 188
Deseille, Louis, 26, 31
Devil, 42
Dickey, John McElroy, 123–24, 131
Dickson, Gregory J., 662–63
Disciples of Christ. *See* Christians
Discipline of members: Amish, 294; Christians, 81–82, 99; Church of God (Cleveland), 452; Evangelical Association, 240; Jehovah's Witness, 533, 537; Presbyterian, 113; Quaker, 201; Shaker, 262
Dispensationalism, 659–60
Divorce: and Robert Dale Owen, 285
Dolan, Jay P., 557n67
Dorland, Anna B., 518
Douglas, John Henry, 211–12, 214–16
Douglass, Frederick, 570
Draper, John W., 645
Dress and decoration: Amish, 294, 295, 296; Assemblies of God, 435; Brethren, 223, 230; Church of God (Anderson), 396; Church of God (Cleveland), 451; Evangelical Association, 236; Holiness, 360, 362; Nazarene, 425; Pentecostal, 373; Quaker, 200, 205; Wesleyan, 378
Dublin: Southern Baptists, 600
Dubois County: Brethren, 223; Presbyterians, 120, 121
Dugan, Michael T., 665
Duncan, James, 319
Dunkers/Dunkards. *See* Brethren
Dunn, Jacob Piatt, 409
Durham, William H., 467

Earlham College, 197, 199, 207, 216, 217; and Holiness, 212–13
Early rain, 433
Earnest Christian (Free Methodist periodical), 386
Eastern Europeans, 543; Catholics, 612–18; Jews, 348–53
Eberly, William R., 665

Ecumenism: Jehovah's Witnesses vs., 533; Muslim/Christian, 639; in Sunday schools, 358–59. *See also* Unions, church
Eddy, Mary Baker, 513–15; development of Christian Science, 515–16; response to critics, 517–18
Edgerton, Walter, 204, 205, 213
Edinburgh: Alexander Campbell in, 102
Edson, Hiram, 502
Education: Adventist, 507–8; African Methodist Episcopal, 565; and creationism, 664–65; fundamentalist, 662–63; Jehovah's Witness, 532; Lutheran, 152; Presbyterian, 134; Quaker, 194, 205–7; Owenite, 282; Rappite, 269. *See also* Colleges and universities; Parochial schools; Sunday schools; Theological education
Eel River Indians, 2
Egbert, Joseph, 484
Eggleston, Edward, 499, 520
Egly, Henry, 295–96
Elders: Brethren, 224; Christian, 77, 105; Evangelical Association, 236; Shaker, 257. *See also* Government, church
Eldredge, Horace S., 485
Eldridge, George N., 414
Eleutherian Institute, 189
Elkhart: Brethren, 224; Congregationalists, 189; Mennonites, 302; Swedenborgians, 334
Elkhart County: Amish, 294–95; Mennonites, 297–300; Salvation Army, 410
Elkhart Institute, 300, 301
Elliott, Josephine, 282
Ellmore, Alfred, 97, 99
Emerson, Ralph Waldo, 517
Emmons, F. W., 72
Entire sanctification: 361–63, 375n32, 383, 385–87; Church of God in Christ, 460; Free Methodist, 386; Quaker, 211–13, 215, 216; Salvation Army, 405. *See also* Holiness
Episcopalians, 159–70, 544; charismatics, 372; and civil rights, 573; Diocese of Indiana, 162–68; high vs. low churches, 168–69; missionaries, 160–63, 169–70; in New Harmony, 289
Epworth League, 359
Errett, Isaac, 104–5
Eternal punishment: Baptist, 39; Universalists vs., 311, 316
Ethnic minorities, 541–44. *See also* Indians
Evangel (Church of God, Cleveland, periodical), 449–50
Evangelical Association (Albrights), 235–43, 243n11; English language in, 242–43; Indiana Conference, 238–40; missionaries, 236–38; organization, 235–36; preachers, 236, 240–42
Evangelical Messenger (Evangelical Association periodical), 242
Evangelical Synod of North America, 179–84
Evangelicals, 178. *See also* Evangelical Association; Evangelical Synod of North America
Evans, Hiram, 548
Evans, Madison, 85
Evans, Mary, 565
Evansville: Black Baptists, 593; Catholics, 29; Christian Scientists, 519; Church of God (Cleveland), 456; Church of God in Christ, 462; Evangelical Synod, 181–82, 184; Free Methodists, 388; freethinkers, 323; Jews,

346, 349; Ku Klux Klan, 547; Methodist Episcopal Church (Lexington Conference), 581; Mormons, 488; Muslims, 639; Presbyterians, 117, 121–22; Southern Baptists, 600; Spiritualists, 342; Unitarians, 310
Evolution, 644–47; fundamentalists vs., 650–52, 658–63; Holiness vs., 362; Quakers vs., 216; theistic, 647–58. *See also* Science
Ewart, Frank J., 366, 439–41
Ewing, Greville, 68
Experience-centered religion. *See* Pentecostals

Fairfield: Adventists, 509
Fairmount: Wesleyans, 379
Family life. *See* Practice
Family Testament (Campbell), 76
Fanning, Tolbert, 95
Farmer, Aaron, 252–53
Farrakhan, Louis, 635
Al-Faruqi, Ismail R., 636
Al-Faruqi, Lois, 636
Fauntleroy, Constance, 287, 289
Fayette County: United Brethren, 250
Feuerlicht, Morris, 348, 350, 550
Field, George, 333–36
Field, Nathaniel, 77–78, 81
Fields of the Wood theme park, 454
Fiery Cross (Klan periodical), 549
Finley, Robert, 21
Finney, Charles, 363
First Church of Christ, Scientist (Boston), 516–18
Fisher, Joseph C., 394
Five Medals (Potawatomi chief), 5, 6, 195
Flaget, Benedict Joseph, 25–26
Flanner House (Indianapolis), 544
Fletcher, John, 361
Flower, Alice Reynolds, 369, 431–32, 435
Flower, J. Roswell, 369, 431–35, 440–41
Flowers, Lindsay and Lovie Mae, 471–72
Floyd County: United Brethren, 248
Flying messengers (Church of God, Anderson), 397
Footwashing: Adventist, 500; Amish, 294; Brethren, 222, 227–29, 233n34; Christian, 65, 81; Church of God (Cleveland), 451; Quaker, 215; United Brethren, 251
Foreign missions: Adventist, 506; Amish, 296; International Church of the Foursquare Gospel, 468; Methodists, 356; Wesleyan, 380
Forster, George, 141
Fort Wayne: Amish, 296; Catholics, 28, 30; Christian Scientists, 519; ethnic congregations, 543; Evangelical Association, 238–40; Free Methodists, 388; freethinkers, 323; German Reformed Church, 175–76; Jews, 346, 348, 349; Johnny Appleseed in, 332–33; Lutherans, 145–47, 150–51; Mormons, 488; Presbyterians, 131; Quakers, 195; Rationalists, 321; Spiritualists, 342; Volunteers of America, 410
Fosdick, Raymond B., 671–73
Fountain County: United Brethren, 253
Fourfold Gospel: Christian and Missionary Alliance, 414–15
Fourier, Charles, 321–23
Fourierists. *See* Rationalists
Foursquare Gospel, 470. *See also* International Church of the Foursquare Gospel

Fox, George, 193–94
Fox, Katherine and Margaret, 338, 340
Frame, Esther, 210–14
Frankfort: Assemblies of God, 436; Southern
　Baptists, 600
Frankfort Pilgrim College, 382
Franklin, Benjamin (1812–1878), 44–45, 49,
　75, 85–96, 97, 109n164; Manford's debate
　with, 315
Franklin College, 56–57
Franklin County: Congregationalists, 188;
　United Brethren, 250
Franz, Frederick, 536
Fraternal Orders: Holiness vs., 360, 362; Jewish,
　346; Wesleyans vs., 378. See also Secret
　societies
Free Labor Advocate (Quaker periodical), 203
Free-love, 320
Free Methodist (periodical), 286
Free Methodists, 363, 365, 383–88
Free Territory Sentinel (Quaker periodical), 207
Free will, 49–51; Hardshells vs., 39, 49
Free Will Baptists, 49, 50–51, 65–66
Freeman, Azel, 121
Freethinkers. See Rationalists
Freie Presse von Indiana (Freethinker
　periodical), 323
French Catholics, 25–27, 30–31
Friends. See Society of Friends
Friends Review (Quaker periodical), 210
Frye, Roland Mushat, 652, 665
Full Gospel Business Men's Fellowship, 372
Fulton, Andrew, 114
Fundamentalists: vs. evolutionary theory,
　650–52, 658–63
Fundraising: Catholic, 604–5, 610–11; Church
　of God (Cleveland), 451, 452–53; Jewish,
　351; Muslim, 637; Salvation Army, 407–8;
　Southern Baptist, 599, 601. See also Tithes
Funk, John F., 298–301

Gamble, Nancy, 462, 463
Garlichs, Hermann, 180
Gary: African-Americans, 545; Black Baptists,
　593; Church of God in Christ, 462; ethnic
　congregations, 543; Greek Orthodox, 628;
　Jews, 349, 350; Muslims, 634, 638, 639,
　640n18; Russian Orthodox, 625; Serbian
　Orthodox, 630–31; Slovaks in, 610–12
Gary-Alerding Settlement House (East Chicago),
　544
Gaston: Nazarenes, 423
Geeting, George Adam, 247
General Association of Regular Baptists,
　55–57, 662
General Baptist Messenger (Baptist periodical), 40
General Baptists, 49–51
General Ministerial Assembly (Church of God,
　Anderson), 397–98
Genesee Conference, 384–85
George, David, 583
German-Americans, 541–42; Anabaptists, 294;
　Catholic, 29–30, 542; Evangelical
　Association, 237, 242; Evangelical Synod,
　180–81, 183–84; freethinkers, 323–24;
　German Reformed, 175, 176; Jews, 345–48;
　Lutheran, 141, 145–47, 152, 154–55;
　Methodist, 542; United Brethren, 246
German language: and Evangelical Association,
　235, 242; and Evangelical Synod, 181,
　183–84; and freethinkers, 323; and the

German Reformed Church, 175; and
　Lutherans, 140; and Mennonites, 294, 295,
　297; and United Brethren, 250
German Reformed Church, 173–76; Evangelical
　Synod, 179–80; and Lutherans, 140, 141,
　149; Western synod, 175
Die Geschäftige Martha (United Brethren
　periodical), 251
Gibeah Bible School, 433
Gibson County: Presbyterians, 121
Gillaspie, S. O., 453, 456
Gimbel, Adam, 346
Gitchell, C. S., 387
Glenwood: Presbyterians, 116
Glossolalia. See Speaking in tongues
Glover, John B., 326
Godecker, Mary Salesia, 28
Goodwin, Elijah, 73–75, 83–85, 94
Goodwin, Marcia Bassett, 106
Goshen: Amish, 295; Mennonites, 300, 303;
　Swedenborgians, 334
Goshen College Biblical Seminary, 300
Gospel Advocate (Christian periodical), 95,
　110n267
Gospel Banner (Mennonite periodical), 298
Gospel Tabernacle, 413–14, 431
Gospel Trumpet (Church of God periodical), 392,
　394–97, 399
Gospel Visitor (Brethren periodical), 230–31
Government, church: Assemblies of God,
　430–31; Brethren, 220–21; Campbell on, 77;
　Catholic, 28–29, 31–32, 553–55; Christian,
　105; Church of God (Cleveland), 451–52;
　Evangelical Association, 235–36; Evangelical
　Synod, 180; Free Methodist, 386–87;
　Jehovah's Witness, 529; Nazarene, 424, 425;
　Shaker, 257; United Brethren, 246–47
Grace, second working of. See Sanctification
Grace Theological Seminary, 229
Graham, Billy, 662
Grant County: Wesleyans, 379
Graves, J. R., 598
Graves, Kersey, 324–25
Gray, Asa, 647, 653
Gray, Campbell, 628
Great Awakening, 39, 62
Great Depression, 544; AME Church during,
　566; Salvation Army during, 407, 409
Great Disappointment, 498–99, 501–4
Great Revival (1800–1805), xi, 62, 117
Great Tent, 493–95
Greek-Americans, 626–30
Greene County: Mormons, 486, 487
Greenwood: Holiness organizations, 362
Griffith, Joshua, 55
Griffith, Walter, 21
Grinnell, Jeremiah A., 208
Grose, George Richmond, 649
Gruber, Jacob, 141–42
Grutka, Andrew, 612
Gruza, Stanislaus, 617
Gurney, Joseph John, 200–203, 205

Hadgigeorge, Chris, 627
Hagerstown: Southern Baptists, 600
Haggard, Rice, 62
Hagood, Lewis M., 580
Hahn, Franklin B., 501–2
Hailandiere, Celestine de la, 27, 31
Haldane, James Alexander, 67, 68
Hall, Lewis J., 463

Hall, Milton L., 463
Hamilton, John, 242
Hamilton County: Adventists, 510; Brethren,
　224; Christians, 64
Hammond, Edward W. S., 580
Hammond: ethnic congregations, 543;
　fundamentalists, 663; Nazarenes, 420;
　Spiritualists, 342
Hanover: Presbyterians, 125
Hanover College, 126, 131, 134
Hardshell Baptists, 39–50, 56n99
Harmony Society, 266–73. See also New
　Harmony; Owenites; Rappites
Harms, Theodor, 152
Harrell, David E., 376n76
Harrison, William Henry, 3–4, 6–7, 248,
　258–59
Harrison County: Brethren, 223; United
　Brethren, 248
Hart, Edward Payson, 387
Hartford City: Assemblies of God, 436
Hartsville College, 253
Harvey, James, 509
Hatfield, John T., 422–23
Haugh, Benjamin F., 605
Haughville (Indianapolis), 605–7
Hauser, Martin, 307–8
Havens, James, 15, 16
Hawkins, Charles E., 593
Hays, John Jacob, 345
Haywood, Garfield T., 439, 441–2
Healing: Assemblies of God, 435; Brethren, 222;
　Christian and Missionary Alliance, 413;
　Christian Science, 514–15; Church of God
　(Anderson), 397; Church of God
　(Cleveland), 451; International Church of
　the Foursquare Gospel, 470; Mormon, 480;
　Pentecostal, 366–71
Heart purity. See Holiness
Hebrew Union College, 348–49
Heidelberg Catechism, 173, 175, 179, 245
Hellums, Thomas, 18
Helton, William, 600
Hendricks County: Christians, 64; Quakers, 197
Henkel family, 141, 142, 145
Henry County: Quakers, 197
Herald of Gospel Liberty (Christian periodical), 61
Herald of Truth (Mennonite periodical), 298–301
Herbruck, Peter, 175–76
Herrick, Horace N., 356–57
Hesburgh, Theodore M., 573
Heyer, John Christian Frederick, 141, 142, 144
Heyer, Philipp, 180
Hicks, Elias, 201–2
Highland Lakes Baptist Center, 602
Himes, Joshua V., 493, 494, 497
Hispanic-Americans, 543
Hobbs, Barnabas C., 197, 199, 204, 207, 213,
　215, 216
Hobbs, William, 196–97, 202, 210
Hodge, Charles, 647
Hodur, Francis, 617
Holidays: Jehovah's Witness vs., 537; Quakers
　vs., 200
Holiness, 361–64; "Nazarite," 384; Quaker,
　207–17; "Regency," 384–85. See also
　Christian and Missionary Alliance; Church of
　God (Anderson); Church of the Nazarene;
　Free Methodists; Pentecostals; Pilgrim
　Holiness; Salvation Army; Sanctification;
　Wesleyans

207, 210, 216; Rationalist, 320, 324, 325, 327; Swedenborgian, 335; Unitarian, 309; United Brethren, 251–53; Universalist, 312, 313; Wesleyan, 380

Pershing: Evangelical Association, 241

Peru: Catholics, 30; Mormons, 488; Spiritualists, 342

Petit, Benjamin, 31

Pfeiffer, Henry H., 161

Pfrimmer, John George, 248–49, 252, 357

Phillips, Charles Henry, 576–77

Piankashaw Indians, 2

Pierce, I. Benjamin, 572

Pietism: and Evangelical Synod, 179, 181; German Reformed, 173

Pike County: Presbyterians, 119, 121

Pilgrim Holiness, 363, 365, 380–82

Pingree, Enoch M., 313

Plagenz, George, 665

Plainfield: Assemblies of God, 433; Muslims, 634, 637–40; Quakers, 214, 218n27

Platz, G. G., 241

Polish-Americans, 543; Catholic, 612–18

Polygamy, 477, 478–79

Portersville: Presbyterians, 120

Portland: Southern Baptists, 600

Posey County: Evangelical Synod, 183; Owenites, 279–90; Rappites, 267–71

Post, Martin M., 132

Potawatomi Indians, 2, 4–6, 8; Catholic, 30–31; and Quakers, 195; and Shakers, 259

Potter, Lemuel, 40, 42, 45–47

Practice (Christian life): Brethren, 220–21, 223; Christian Science, 515, 518, 521n28; Church of God (Cleveland), 450–52; dissent over, 360; Holiness, 362; Jehovah's Witness, 537–38; Jewish, 346, 349, 352; Methodist, 21–22; Mormon, 478, 480; Muslim, 633–35; Nazarene, 425; Orthodox, 623–24; Pentecostal, 373; Quaker, 194–95, 200–201; Rappite, 268–70; Wesleyan, 378–79

Pratt, Orson, 478, 483, 484

Pratt, Parley, 481, 483, 484

Preachers (priests): Baptist, 55; Black Baptist, 589–93; Brethren, 224; Catholic, 29, 616–18; Christian, 83, 90–91; Church of God (Anderson), 397; Church of God (Cleveland), 450–51; Church of God in Christ, 460; Episcopalian, 162–63; Evangelical Association, 236, 240–42; Evangelical Synod, 180–81; Free Methodist, 384–85, 387; German Reformed, 174–75; Methodist, 17, 22–23; Nazarene, 420–24; New Light Christian, 64; Pentecostal, 366–71; Presbyterian, 117–18, 120, 127–35; Quaker, 200, 210; Shamans, 3; Spiritualist, 340–41; Swedenborgian, 335; United Brethren, 253–54. See also Circuit riders; Missions; Payment of preachers; Preaching; Theological education

Preaching: Baptist, 39; Catholic, 27–28; Evangelical Association, 240, 241; Hardshell Baptist, 42–44; Jehovah's Witness, 528–30; Mennonite, 299; Methodist, 16–18; Nazarene, 418, 422; Pentecostal, 367–70; Presbyterian, 116, 127; Quaker, 200; Salvation Army, 404; "Sermon on the Law" (Campbell), 69; Universalist, 313

Predestination: Hardshell Baptist, 39–40, 42, 48, 50; Presbyterian, 129–30

Premillenarianism, 659, 662. See also Second coming of Christ

Prentiss, Henry, 441

Prentiss, W. S., 322

Presbyterians, 40, 113–38, 544; and Congregationalists, 187–88; Cumberland, 117–22; frontier preachers, 127–30; and the German Reformed Church, 176; Old vs. New schools, 123, 125–27, 188; Presbyterian Church in the U.S.A., 122–25; Psalm-singing, 113–17; and sanctification, 363–64; women, 356

Preston, F. J., 410

Priests. See Preachers (priests)

Primitive Baptist (periodical), 48

Primitive Baptists. See Hardshell Baptists

Primitive Christian (Christian periodical), 78

Princeton: Presbyterians, 115, 121, 125

Priori, Marino, 604–5

Prison reform: and Quakers, 199

Progressive Christian (Brethren periodical), 228

Progressive National Baptist Convention, 587–88

The Prophet (Tenskwatawa), 6–8, 195, 307

Protracted meetings: Mennonite, 298; New Light Christian, 64

Psalm-singing Presbyterians, 113–17

Publishing: Jehovah's Witness, 524–25, 527, 529, 532, 537. See also Periodicals

Punishment, eternal: Baptist, 39; Universalists vs., 311, 316

Putnam County: Brethren, 225; Christians, 64; Mormons, 484

Quakers. See Society of Friends

Quimby, Phineas P., 514, 517, 518

Quinn, William Paul, 563

Quinter, James, 225–26, 228, 230–31

Racism. See Abolitionism; Integration

Radio broadcasts: Assemblies of God, 435; Jehovah's Witness, 527–28, 534; Sister Aimee McPherson, 470–71; Oneness Pentecostal, 442–43; Pentecostal, 370–71

Ragatz, John Henry, 241

Railroads, 355

Railton, George, 404–5

Rajcany, Benedict, 609–10

Ramseyer, Joseph E., 296

Randolph County: African Methodist Episcopals, 563; Black Baptists, 589; Quakers, 197; Rationalists, 321

Rapp, Frederick, 266–72; on Robert Owen, 280

Rapp, George, 265–67, 269–72, 273n22; Owen's correspondence to, 279

Rappites, 142, 265–73; doctrine and practice, 268–70; in Indiana, 266–68; return to Pennsylvania, 270–73; and Shakers, 261

Rapture, 371

Rationalists, 179, 180, 319–28; eccentric "scientists," 324–25; Fourierists, 321–23, 327; German freethinkers, 323–24; organizations, 325–26. See also Owen, Robert

Redfield, John Wesley, 383–87

Reed, Isaac, 124, 128, 131, 188, 357

Rees, Seth Cook, 213, 380–81

Reform Judaism, 347–49, 352

Reformer (Christian periodical), 88, 89

Regular Baptists, 38–39, 55–57

Rehmer, Rudolph F., 156n11

Religious Telescope (United Brethren periodical), 251, 252, 253

Restoration movement, 224. See also Campbell, Alexander; Christians

Revels, Hiram R., 565

Revels, Willis R., 565

The Revivalist (Wesleyan periodical), 380

Revivals, xi, 360; Azusa Street revival, 365, 369, 433, 447, 449, 460; Baptist, 55–57; Brethren, 223, 227, 230; Catholic, 27–28; Church of God of Prophecy, 455; Great Revival, xi, 62, 117; Mennonite, 295, 298, 302; Methodist, 20–21; New Light Christian, 64; Pentecostal, 365, 367–70; Presbyterian, 117–18; Quaker, 207–17; Rappite, 266; United Brethren, 247

Rich, Charles C., 484

Richland: Presbyterians, 116

Richland Academy, 116

Richmond: African Methodist Episcopals, 563, 565; Congregationalists, 189; Jews, 348; Lutherans, 155; Mormons, 488; Quakers, 196, 198–99, 202, 207, 209–10, 214, 218n27; Southern Baptists, 600; Swedenborgians, 335–36; Universalists, 312–13

Rigdon, Sidney, 477, 481, 482

Riley, William Bell, 658–63

Rimmer, Harry, 662

Rising Sun: Jews, 346

Ritter, Joseph, 553, 604–5

Roberts, Benjamin T., 383–87

Roberts, Brigham H., 480

Roberts, L. V., 441

Roberts, Oral, 370–72

Roberts, William, 462

Robertson, Pat, 371

Robinson, Elmo, 315, 316

Robson, Walter, 213–14

Rockefeller, John D., Jr., 671–73

Rockville: Christians, 63

Rogers, George, 313, 315

Rohrer, Abraham, 297

Rouse, J. D., 593, 594

Rowe, David L., 493

Rowe, John F., 97

Rudisill, Ephraim, 143

Rudisill, Henry, 146

Rudolf, Francis Joseph, 28

Rush County: African Methodist Episcopals, 563; Black Baptists, 589; Christians, 64; Presbyterians, 116

Rushville: Black Baptists, 588; Alexander Campbell in, 102; Presbyterians, 116; Southern Baptists, 600

Russell, Charles Taze, 523–26, 533

Russell, Elbert, 216, 217

Russell, P. T., 78

Russellites. See Jehovah's Witnesses

Ruter, Calvin W., 15, 16

Ruth, C. W., 418–19

Rutherford, Joseph F., 526–29, 533–34

Sabbath: and Adventists, 504; and Methodists, 22

Sacraments. See Baptism; Communion; Footwashing; Lord's Supper; Love feasts; Ordinances

Sagan, Carl, 652, 658

St. Joseph County: Brethren, 224; Church of God in Christ, 462; Salvation Army, 410

St. Mary's College, 27

L. C. RUDOLPH is an alumnus of Depauw University with graduate degrees from Indiana University and Yale. His thirty-two years as a professor and curator were equally divided between the Presbyterian Theological Seminary at Louisville and the Lilly Library at Indiana University, Bloomington. Among his publications are *Hoosier Zion: The Presbyterians in Early Indiana*, *Story of the Church*, *Francis Asbury*, and *Religion in Indiana*.